LOG ON ▶ **Literature** Online

Textbook Internet resources are just a click away!

STEP 1 ▶   Go to glencoe.com

STEP 2 ▶   Connect to resources by entering *QuickPass* codes.

    GL57805u1   Enter this code with appropriate unit numbers.

STEP 3 ▶   Access your Online Student Edition, games, and more:

Literature and Reading Resources

- Author Search
- Literature Classics
- Big Question Web Quests
- Literary and Text Elements eFlashcards and Games
- InterActive Reading Practice

Selection Resources

- Audio Summaries
- Selection Quizzes
- Selection Vocabulary eFlashcards and Games
- Reading-Writing Connection Activities

Vocabulary and Spelling Resources

- Academic and Selection Vocabulary eFlashcards and Games
- Multi-Language Glossaries

Writing, Grammar, and Research Resources

- Interactive Writing Models
- Writing and Research Handbook
- Graphic Organizers
- Sentence Combining Activities
- Publishing Options

Media Literacy, Speaking, Listening, and Viewing Resources

- Media Analysis Guides
- Project Ideas and Templates
- Presentation Tips and Strategies

Assessment Resources

- TAKS™ Preparation and Practice
- Test-Taking Tips and Strategies

IWB Interactive White Board Ready!

Literature
TEXAS TREASURES

Course 5

Program Consultants

Jeffrey D. Wilhelm, Ph.D.

Douglas Fisher, Ph.D.

Beverly Ann Chin, Ph.D.

Jacqueline Jones Royster, D.A.

Glencoe

Acknowledgments

Grateful acknowledgment is given authors, publishers, photographers, museums, and agents for permission to reprint the following copyrighted material. Every effort has been made to determine copyright owners. In case of any omissions, the Publisher will be pleased to make suitable acknowledgments in future editions.

Acknowledgments continued on p. R118.

The *McGraw-Hill* Companies

 Glencoe

Send all inquiries to:
Glencoe/McGraw-Hill
8787 Orion Place
Columbus, OH 43240-4027

ISBN (student edition): 978-0-07-892780-5
MHID (student edition): 0-07-892780-3
ISBN (teacher edition): 978-0-07-892784-3
MHID (teacher edition): 0-07-892784-6

Printed in the United States of America.

3 4 5 6 7 8 9 10 RJE/LEH 14 13 12 11 10

Consultants

Senior Program Consultants

Jeffrey D. Wilhelm, Ph.D., a former middle and secondary school English and reading teacher, is currently Professor of Education at Boise State University. He is the author or coauthor of numerous articles and several books on the teaching of reading and literacy, including award-winning titles such as *You Gotta BE the Book* and *Reading Don't Fix No Chevys.* He also works with local schools as part of the Adolescent Literacy Project and recently helped establish the National Writing Project site at Boise State University.

Douglas Fisher, Ph.D., is Professor of Language and Literacy Education and Director of Professional Development at San Diego State University, where he teaches English language development and literacy. He also serves as Director of City Heights Educational Pilot, which won the Christa McAuliffe Award from the American Association of State Colleges and Universities. He has published numerous articles on reading and literacy, differentiated instruction, and curriculum design. He is coauthor of the book *Improving Adolescent Literacies: Strategies That Work* and coeditor of the book *Inclusive Urban Schools.*

Program Consultants

Beverly Ann Chin, Ph.D., is Professor of English, Director of the English Teaching Program, former Director of the Montana Writing Project, and former Director of Composition at the University of Montana in Missoula. She currently serves as a Member at Large of the Conference of English Leadership. Dr. Chin is a nationally recognized leader in English language arts standards, curriculum, and assessment. Formerly a high school teacher and an adult education reading teacher, Dr. Chin has taught in English language arts education at several universities and has received awards for her teaching and service.

Jacqueline Jones Royster, D.A., is Professor of English and Senior Vice Provost and Executive Dean of the Colleges of Arts and Sciences at The Ohio State University. She is currently on the Writing Advisory Committee of the National Commission on Writing and serves as chair for both the Columbus Literacy Council and the Ohioana Library Association. In addition to the teaching of writing, Dr. Royster's professional interests include the rhetorical history of African American women and the social and cultural implications of literate practices. She has contributed to and helped to edit numerous books, anthologies, and journals.

Special Consultants

Diane August, Ph.D.
Senior Research Scientist at the Center for Applied Linguistics headquartered in Washington, D.C. President of August & Associates, Independent Consultants.

Donald R. Bear, Ph.D.
Professor, Department of Curriculum and Instruction, and Director, E. L. Cord Foundation Center for Learning and Literacy, University of Nevada, Reno. Coauthor of *Words Their Way* and *Words Their Way with English Learners*.

Randy Bomer, Ph.D.
Associate Professor, Department of Curriculum and Instruction, The University of Texas at Austin. Director, Heart of Texas Writing Project. Former President, National Council of Teachers of English. Author of *Time for Meaning: Crafting Literate Lives in Middle & High School* and coauthor of *For a Better World: Reading and Writing for Social Action*.

Jana Echevarria, Ph.D.
Professor, Educational Psychology, California State University, Long Beach, and Principal Researcher, National Research and Development Center of English Language Learners. Author of *Making Content Comprehensible for English Learners: The SIOP Model*.

David J. Francis, Ph.D.
Department Chair, Psychology, University of Houston. Director, Center for Research on Educational Achievement and Teaching of English Language Learners (CREATE). Director, Texas Institute for Measurement, Evaluation, and Statistics.

FOLDABLES Study Organizer Dinah Zike, M.Ed. Dinah Zike was a classroom teacher and a consultant for many years before she began to develop Foldables®—a variety of easily created graphic organizers. Zike has written and developed more than 150 supplemental books and materials used in classrooms.

Glencoe National Reading and Language Arts Advisory Council

Mary A. Avalos, Ph.D.
Assistant Department Chair,
Department of Teaching
and Learning
Research Assistant
Professor, Department of
Teaching and Learning
University of Miami
Coral Gables, Florida

Wanda J. Blanchett, Ph.D.
Associate Dean for Academic
Affairs and Associate
Professor of Exceptional
Education, School
of Education
University of Wisconsin-
Milwaukee
Milwaukee, Wisconsin

Nancy Drew, Ed.D.
LaPointe Educational
Consultants
Corpus Christi, Texas

Susan Florio-Ruane, Ed.D.
Professor, College of Education
Michigan State University
East Lansing, Michigan

Nancy Frey, Ph.D.
Associate Professor of Literacy
in Teacher Education
School of Teacher Education
San Diego State University
San Diego, California

Victoria Ridgeway Gillis, Ph.D.
Associate Professor
Reading Education
Clemson University
Clemson, South Carolina

Kimberly Lawless, Ph.D.
Associate Professor
Curriculum, Instruction
and Evaluation
College of Education
University of Illinois
at Chicago
Chicago, Illinois

Sharon Fontenot O'Neal, Ph.D.
Associate Professor
Texas State University
San Marcos, Texas

William Ray, M.A.
Lincoln-Sudbury Regional
High School
Sudbury, Massachusetts

Janet Saito-Furukawa, M.Ed.
English Language Arts Specialist
District 4
Los Angeles, California

Bonnie Valdes, M.Ed.
Independent Reading Consultant
CRISS Master Trainer
Largo, Florida

Texas Advisory Board

Mike Eldenburg
Keller High School
Keller ISD
Keller, TX

Laurie Etzel
Bailey Middle School
Austin ISD
Austin, TX

Shakeina Harris
Stevenson Middle School
Houston ISD
Houston, TX

Carol Hopson
Keller Middle School
Keller ISD
Keller, TX

Kris Hoyt
Wayside Middle School
Eagle Mountain-Saginaw ISD
Fort Worth, TX

Debra S. Jones
Bellaire High School
Houston ISD
Bellaire, TX

Debbie Lightfoot
Skyline High School
Dallas ISD
Dallas, TX

Margaret McQuiston
Bowie High School
Austin ISD
Austin, TX

Ama Mpiani
Houston ISD
Houston, TX

Sheila Mulbry
Pond Springs Elementary
Round Rock ISD
Austin, TX

Carolyn Pyles
Mesquite ISD
Mesquite, TX

Donna Sinclair
Creekview Middle School
Eagle Mountain-Saginaw ISD
Fort Worth, TX

Mari Beth Tackett
Bowie Middle School
Irving ISD
Irving, TX

Louis Voelcker
Highlands High School
San Antonio ISD
San Antonio, TX

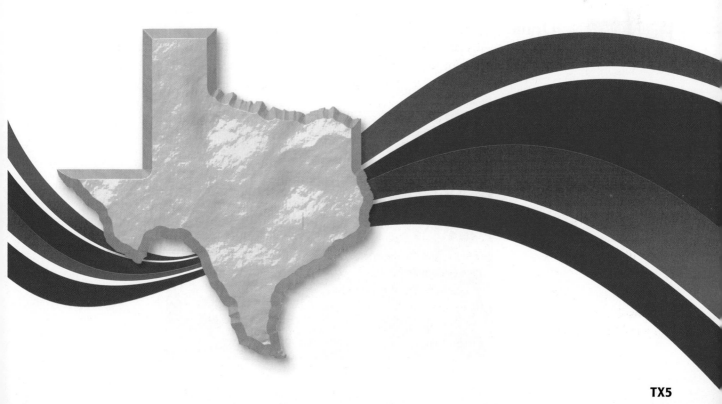

Book Overview

Coming to America,
1985. Malcah Zeldis.

Triumph of the Revolution, Distribution of Food (Trionfo de la revolucion, reparto de los alimentos), 1926–1927. Diego Rivera. Banco de Mexico Trust. Fresco, 3.54 x 3.67 m. Chapel. Universidad Autonoma, Chapingo, Mexico.

The Short Story

TEKS

TEKS

VOCABULARY Academic Vocabulary, **pp. 16, 34, 36–37, 46, 86, 97, 192, 207, 227**; Analogies, **pp. 34, 67, 207**; Antonyms, **p. 175**; Context Clues, **pp. 16, 119**; Denotation and Connotation, **pp. 47, 55, 192**; Dictionary Use, **p. 56**; Synonyms, **p. 135**; Usage, **pp. 86, 141, 161**; Word Origins, **pp. 46, 98, 227**; Word Parts, **p. 97**

GRAMMAR Active and Passive Voice, **p. 35**; Commas, **p. 208**; Quotation Marks, **p. 120**; Reciprocal Pronouns, **p. 68**; Sentence Combining, **pp. 121–122**; Sentence Fragments, **p. 193**; Verbals, **p. 87**; Writing and Punctuating Dialogue, **p. 235**

WRITING Character Sketch, **p. 161**; Dialogue, **p. 135**; Essay, **p. 141**; Expository Essay, **pp. 68, 208**; Letter, **p. 175**; List, **p. 55**; Literary Criticism, **p. 16**; Personal Narrative, **pp. 228–235**; Research Report, **p. 97**; Short Story, **p. 120**; Summary, **p. 35**; Write with Style, **pp. 46, 192**

NONFICTION

TEKS

TEKS

Assessment

When I Get that Feeling, 2000. Colin
Bootman. Oil on board. Private collection.

VOCABULARY Academic Vocabulary, **pp. 272, 289, 297, 320, 351, 359, 388**; Analogies, **pp. 297, 359**; Context Clues, **pp. 289, 344, 420**; Denotation and Connotation, **pp. 309, 411**; Jargon, **p. 310**; Synonyms, **pp. 334, 351, 388**; Usage, **pp. 397, 425**; Word Origins, **p. 320**; Word Parts, **pp. 272, 373**

GRAMMAR Active and Passive Voice, **pp. 321, 374**; Dashes, **p. 360**; Infinitives and Participles, **p. 290**; Restrictive and Nonrestrictive Relative Clauses, **p. 389**; Subject-Verb Agreement, **p. 273**; Subjunctive Mood, **p. 433**; Verb Tense and Mood, **p. 433**

WRITING Analytical Essay, **pp. 426–433**; Editorial, **p. 321**; Essay, **p. 425**; Humorous Anecdote, **p. 334**; Letter, **p. 397**; Literary Criticism, **p. 411**; Personal Narrative, **p. 360**; Persuasive Essay, **p. 374**; Research Report, **pp. 272, 290, 309**; Summary, **p. 389**; Write with Style, **pp. 297, 420**

Poetry

TEKS

TEKS

Personage Lancant Une Pierre a un Oiseau, 1926. Joan Miro. ©ARS, NY.

VOCABULARY Academic Vocabulary, **pp. 468, 480, 493, 498, 502, 508, 517, 524, 530, 539, 558, 571, 577, 582**; Analogies, **p. 486**; Antonyms, **p. 517**; Context Clues, **pp. 457, 530, 548**; Denotation and Connotation, **pp. 524, 535**; Homonyms and Homophones, **p. 458**; Synonyms, **pp. 480, 577**; Usage, **pp. 463, 544, 596**; Word Origins, **pp. 473, 493, 552**; Word Parts, **pp. 468, 508**

GRAMMAR Commas in Contrasting Expressions, **p. 531**; Dashes, **p. 518**; Gerunds, **p. 469**; Pronoun-Antecedent Agreement, **p. 487**; Reciprocal Pronouns, **p. 578**; Run-On Sentences, **p. 613**; Subjunctive Mood, **p. 481**

WRITING Annotation, **p. 596**; Character Sketch, **p. 457**; Description, **pp. 535, 548**; Dialogue, **p. 552**; Essay, **pp. 539, 571**; Expository Essay, **pp. 518, 531, 578**; Free Verse, **p. 582**; Interior Monologue, **p. 463**; Interpretive Response Essay, **pp. 606–613**; Movie Scene, **p. 473**; Poem, **pp. 469, 502**; Prose Poem, **p. 486**; Research Report, **p. 481**; Summary, **p. 544**; Write with Style, **pp. 498, 558**

DRAMA

 TEKS

Protagonist and Antagonist, Interpret Imagery

Tragic Flaw, Recognize Author's Purpose

Blank Verse, Make Inferences About Characters

Monologues, Soliloquies, and Asides, Analyze Theme

Plot, Analyze Figurative Language

Foil, Make and Verify Predictions

Tragic Hero, Evaluate Characters

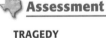
VOCABULARY Academic Vocabulary, **pp. 789, 815**; Analogies, **p. 789**; Context Clues, **pp. 658, 756**; Denotation and Connotation, **pp. 683, 773, 821**; Synonyms, **p. 712**; Usage, **p. 733**; Word Origins, **p. 815**; Word Parts, **pp. 681, 845**

GRAMMAR Commas with Appositives, **p. 790**; Commas with Interjections and Parenthetical Expressions, **p. 816**; Parallel Construction, **p. 861**; Verbals, **p. 682**

WRITING Advice Column, **p. 658**; Editorial, **p. 712**; Interior Monologue, **p. 845**; Journal Entry, **p. 773**; List, **p. 821**; Memo, **p. 756**; Persuasive Essay, **p. 682**; Persuasive Speech, **pp. 854–861**; Script, **p. 790**; Summary, **p. 733**; Write with Style, **p. 815**

Legends and Myths

TEKS

VOCABULARY Academic Vocabulary, **pp. 1011, 1028;** Analogies, **pp. 1011, 1036;** Context Clues, **p. 1054;** Denotation and Connotation, **p. 1064;** Thesaurus Use, **p. 1089;** Usage, **p. 1028;** Word Origins, **p. 1086**

GRAMMAR Dangling Participles, **p. 1029;** Semicolons as Connectors, **p. 1088;** Shifts in Point of View, **p. 1097;** Verbs Used as Nouns, **p. 1087**

WRITING Essay, **p. 1036;** Expository Essay, **p. 1087;** Short Story, **pp. 1064, 1090–1097;** Write with Style, **p. 1011**

CONSUMER AND WORKPLACE
DOCUMENTS

REFERENCE SECTION

Selections by Genre

Fiction

Poetry

Woman Flying a Kite, 1750. Indian. Book illumination painting, miniature painting. Sangaram Singh.

Features

Independent Reading

Assessment

LITERARY FOCUS

Literary History

Language Arts Skills

Writing Workshops

> **Write with Style** 46, 192, 297, 420, 498,
> 815, 903, 1011
>
> **Writing** 55, 135, 141, 161, 175, 334, 397,
> 425, 457, 463, 473, 486, 502, 535, 539,
> 544, 548, 552, 582, 596, 658, 712, 733,
> 756, 773, 821, 845, 963, 1036, 1064

Speaking, Listening, and Viewing Workshops

Speaking and Listening

Grammar Workshops

Vocabulary Workshops

Logic and Persuasion

What makes a message convincing?

Media Workshops

Texas Essential Knowledge and Skills

Introduction

The State of Texas has approved educational standards (TEKS) that should be met or exceeded by every student. In addition, every district must "foster the teaching of United States and Texas history and the free enterprise system . . . .Students will be provided . . . informational texts that can help them to become thoughtful, active citizens who appreciate the basic democratic values of our state and nation."

Reading/Vocabulary Development

10.1 Students understand new vocabulary and use it when reading and writing. Students are expected to:

10.1.A determine the meaning of grade-level technical academic English words in multiple content areas (e.g., science, mathematics, social studies, the arts) derived from Latin, Greek, or other linguistic roots and affixes;

10.1.B Analyze textual context (within a sentence and in larger sections of text) to distinguish between the denotative and connotative meanings of words;

10.1.C infer word meaning through the identification and analysis of analogies and other word relationships;

10.1.D show the relationship between the origins and meaning of foreign words or phrases used frequently in written English and historical events or developments (e.g., *glasnost, avant-garde, coup d'état*); and

10.1.E use a dictionary, a glossary, or a thesaurus (printed or electronic) to determine or confirm the meanings of words and phrases, including their connotations and denotations, and their etymology.

Reading/Comprehension of Literary Text/Theme and Genre

10.2 Students analyze, make inferences and draw conclusions about theme and genre in different cultural, historical, and contemporary contexts and provide evidence from the text to support their understanding. Students are expected to:

10.2.A compare and contrast differences in similar themes expressed in different time periods;

10.2.B analyze archetypes (e.g., journey of a hero, tragic flaw) in mythic, traditional and classical literature; and

10.2.C relate the figurative language of a literary work to its historical and cultural setting.

Reading/Comprehension of Literary Text/Poetry

10.3 Students understand, make inferences and draw conclusions about the structure and elements of poetry and provide evidence from text to support their understanding. Students are expected to analyze the structure or prosody (e.g., meter, rhyme scheme) and graphic elements (e.g., line length, punctuation, word position) in poetry.

Reading/Comprehension of Literary Text/Drama

10.4 Students understand, make inferences and draw conclusions about the structure and elements of drama and provide evidence from text to support their understanding. Students are expected to analyze how archetypes and motifs in drama affect the plot of plays.

Reading/Comprehension of Literary Text/Fiction

10.5 Students understand, make inferences and draw conclusions about the structure and elements of fiction and provide evidence from text to support their understanding. Students are expected to:

10.5.A analyze isolated scenes and their contribution to the success of the plot as a whole in a variety of works of fiction;

10.5.B analyze differences in the characters' moral dilemmas in works of fiction across different countries or cultures;

10.5.C evaluate the connection between forms of narration (e.g., unreliable, omniscient) and tone in works of fiction; and

10.5.D demonstrate familiarity with works by authors from non-English-speaking literary traditions with emphasis on 20th century world literature.

Reading/Comprehension of Literary Text/Literary Nonfiction

10.6 Students understand, make inferences and draw conclusions about the varied structural patterns and features of literary nonfiction and provide evidence from text to support their understanding. Students are expected to evaluate the role of syntax and diction and the effect of voice, tone, and imagery on a speech, literary essay, or other forms of literary nonfiction.

Reading/Comprehension of Literary Text/Sensory Language

10.7 Students understand, make inferences and draw conclusions about how an author's sensory language creates imagery in literary text and provide evidence from text to support their understanding. Students are expected to explain the function of symbolism, allegory, and allusions in literary works.

Reading/Comprehension of Informational Text/Culture and History

10.8 Students analyze, make inferences and draw conclusions about the author's purpose in cultural, historical, and contemporary contexts and provide evidence from the text to support their understanding. Students are expected to analyze the controlling idea and specific purpose of a passage and the textual elements that support and elaborate it, including both the most important details and the less important details.

Reading/Comprehension of Informational Text/Expository Text

10.9 Students analyze, make inferences and draw conclusions about expository text and provide evidence from text to support their understanding. Students are expected to:

10.9.A summarize text and distinguish between a summary and a critique and identify non-essential information in a summary and unsubstantiated opinions in a critique;

10.9.B distinguish among different kinds of evidence used to support conclusions and arguments (e.g., logical, empirical, anecdotal) in texts;

10.9.C make and defend subtle inferences and complex conclusions about the ideas in text and their organizational patterns; and

10.9.D synthesize and make logical connections between ideas and details in several texts selected to reflect a range of viewpoints on the same topic and support those findings with textual evidence.

Reading/Comprehension of Informational Text/Persuasive Text

10.10 Students analyze, make inferences and draw conclusions about persuasive text and provide evidence from text to support their analysis. Students are expected to:

10.10.A explain shifts in perspective in arguments about the same topic and evaluate the accuracy of the evidence used to support the different viewpoints within those arguments; and

10.10.B analyze contemporary political debates for such rhetorical and logical fallacies as appeals to commonly held opinions, false dilemmas, appeals to pity, and personal attacks.

Reading/Comprehension of Informational Text/Procedural Texts

10.11 Students understand how to glean and use information in procedural texts and documents. Students are expected to:

10.11.A evaluate text for the clarity of its graphics and its visual appeal; and

10.11.B synthesize information from multiple graphical sources to draw conclusions about the ideas presented (e.g., maps, charts, schematics).

Reading/Media Literacy

10.12 Students use comprehension skills to analyze how words, images, graphics, and sounds work together in various forms to impact meaning. Students will continue to apply earlier standards with greater depth in increasingly more complex texts. Students are expected to:

10.12.A evaluate how messages presented in media reflect social and cultural views in ways different from traditional texts;

10.12.B analyze how messages in media are conveyed through visual and sound techniques (e.g., editing, reaction shots, sequencing, background music);

10.12.C examine how individual perception or bias in coverage of the same event influences the audience; and

10.12.D evaluate changes in formality and tone within the same medium for specific audiences and purposes.

Writing/Writing Process

10.13 Students use elements of the writing process (planning, drafting, revising, editing, and publishing) to compose text. Students are expected to:

10.13.A plan a first draft by selecting the correct genre for conveying the intended meaning to multiple audiences, determining appropriate topics through a range of strategies (e.g., discussion, background reading, personal interests, interviews), and developing a thesis or controlling idea;

10.13.B structure ideas in a sustained and persuasive way (e.g., using outlines, note taking, graphic organizers, lists) and develop drafts in timed and open-ended situations that include transitions and rhetorical devices used to convey meaning;

10.13.C revise drafts to improve style, word choice, figurative language, sentence variety, and subtlety of meaning after rethinking how well questions of purpose, audience, and genre have been addressed;

10.13.D edit drafts for grammar, mechanics, and spelling; and

10.13.E revise final draft in response to feedback from peers and teacher and publish written work for appropriate audiences.

Writing/Literary Texts

10.14 Students write literary texts to express their ideas and feelings about real or imagined people, events, and ideas. Students are responsible for at least two forms of literary writing. Students are expected to:

10.14.A write an engaging story with a well-developed conflict and resolution, interesting and believable characters, a range of literary strategies (e.g., dialogue, suspense) and devices to enhance the plot, and sensory details that define the mood or tone;

10.14.B write a poem using a variety of poetic techniques (e.g., structural elements, figurative language) and a variety of poetic forms (e.g., sonnets, ballads); and

10.14.C write a script with an explicit or implicit theme and details that contribute to a definite mood or tone.

Writing/Expository and Procedural Texts

10.15 Students write expository and procedural or work-related texts to communicate ideas and information to specific audiences for specific purposes. Students are expected to:

10.15.A write an analytical essay of sufficient length that includes:

10.15.A.i effective introductory and concluding paragraphs and a variety of sentence structures;

10.15.A.ii rhetorical devices, and transitions between paragraphs;

10.15.A.iii a thesis or controlling idea;

10.15.A.iv an organizing structure appropriate to purpose, audience, and context;

10.15.A.v relevant evidence and well-chosen details; and

10.15.A.vi distinctions about the relative value of specific data, facts, and ideas that support the thesis statement;

10.15.B write procedural or work-related documents (e.g., instructions, e-mails, correspondence, memos, project plans) that include:

10.15.B.i organized and accurately conveyed information;

10.15.B.ii reader-friendly formatting techniques; and

10.15.B.iii anticipation of readers' questions;

10.15.C write an interpretative response to an expository or a literary text (e.g., essay or review) that:

10.15.C.i extends beyond a summary and literal analysis;

10.15.C.ii addresses the writing skills for an analytical essay and provides evidence from the text using embedded quotations; and

10.15.C.iii analyzes the aesthetic effects of an author's use of stylistic and rhetorical devices; and

10.15.D produce a multimedia presentation (e.g., documentary, class newspaper, docudrama, infomercial, visual or textual parodies, theatrical production) with graphics, images, and sound that conveys a distinctive point of view and appeals to a specific audience.

Writing/Persuasive Texts

10.16 Students write persuasive texts to influence the attitudes or actions of a specific audience on specific issues. Students are expected to write an argumentative essay to the appropriate audience that includes:

10.16.A a clear thesis or position based on logical reasons supported by precise and relevant evidence;

10.16.B consideration of the whole range of information and views on the topic and accurate and honest representation of these views (i.e., in the author's own words and not out of context);

10.16.C counter-arguments based on evidence to anticipate and address objections;

10.16.D an organizing structure appropriate to the purpose, audience, and context;

10.16.E an analysis of the relative value of specific data, facts, and ideas; and

10.16.F a range of appropriate appeals (e.g., descriptions, anecdotes, case studies, analogies, illustrations).

Oral and Written Conventions/Conventions

10.17 Students understand the function of and use the conventions of academic language when speaking and writing. Students will continue to apply earlier standards with greater complexity. Students are expected to:

10.17.A use and understand the function of the following parts of speech in the context of reading, writing, and speaking:

10.17.A.i more complex active and passive tenses and verbals (gerunds, infinitives, participles);

10.17.A.ii restrictive and nonrestrictive relative clauses; and

10.17.A.iii reciprocal pronouns (e.g., each other, one another);

10.17.B identify and use the subjunctive mood to express doubts, wishes, and possibilities; and

10.17.C use a variety of correctly structured sentences (e.g., compound, complex, compound-complex).

Oral and Written Conventions/Handwriting, Capitalization, and Punctuation

10.18 Students write legibly and use appropriate capitalization and punctuation conventions in their compositions. Students are expected to:

10.18.A use conventions of capitalization; and

10.18.B use correct punctuation marks including:

10.18.B.i comma placement in nonrestrictive phrases, clauses, and contrasting expressions;

10.18.B.ii quotation marks to indicate sarcasm or irony; and

10.18.B.iii dashes to emphasize parenthetical information.

Oral and Written Conventions/Spelling

10.19 Students spell correctly. Students are expected to spell correctly, including using various resources to determine and check correct spellings.

Research/Research Plan

10.20 Students ask open-ended research questions and develop a plan for answering them. Students are expected to:

10.20.A brainstorm, consult with others, decide upon a topic, and formulate a major research question to address the major research topic; and

10.20.B formulate a plan for engaging in research on a complex, multi-faceted topic.

Research/Gathering Sources

10.21 Students determine, locate, and explore the full range of relevant sources addressing a research question and systematically record the information they gather. Students are expected to:

10.21.A follow the research plan to compile data from authoritative sources in a manner that identifies the major issues and debates within the field of inquiry;

10.21.B organize information gathered from multiple sources to create a variety of graphics and forms (e.g., notes, learning logs); and

10.21.C paraphrase, summarize, quote, and accurately cite all researched information according to a standard format (e.g., author, title, page number).

Research/Synthesizing Information

10.22 Students clarify research questions and evaluate and synthesize collected information. Students are expected to:

10.22.A modify the major research question as necessary to refocus the research plan;

10.22.B evaluate the relevance of information to the topic and determine the reliability, validity, and accuracy of sources (including Internet sources) be examining their authority and objectivity; and

10.22.C critique the research process at each step to implement changes as the need occurs and is identified.

Research/Organizing and Presenting Ideas

10.23 Students organize and present their ideas and information according to the purpose of the research and their audience. Students are expected to synthesize the research into a written or an oral presentation that:

10.23.A marshals evidence in support of a clear thesis statement and related claims;

10.23.B provides an analysis for the audience that reflects a logical progression of ideas and a clearly stated point of view;

10.23.C uses graphics and illustrations to help explain concepts where appropriate;

10.23.D uses a variety of evaluative tools (e.g., self-made rubrics, peer reviews, teacher and expert evaluations) to examine the quality of the research; and

10.23.E uses a style manual (e.g.,, *Modern Language Association, Chicago Manual of Style*) to document sources and format written materials.

Listening and Speaking/Listening

10.24 Students will use comprehension skills to listen attentively to others in formal and informal settings. Students will continue to apply earlier standards with greater complexity. Students are expected to:

10.24.A listen responsively to a speaker by taking notes that summarize, synthesize, or highlight the speaker's ideas for critical reflection and by asking questions related to the content for clarification and elaboration;

10.24.B follow and give complex oral instructions to perform specific tasks, answer questions, solve problems, and complete processes; and

10.24.C evaluate how the style and structure of a speech support or undermine its purpose or meaning.

Listening and Speaking/Speaking

10.25 Students speak clearly and to the point, using the conventions of language. Students will continue to apply earlier standards with greater complexity. Students are expected to advance a coherent argument that incorporates a clear thesis and a logical progression of valid evidence from reliable sources and that employs eye contact, speaking rate (e.g., pauses for effect), volume, enunciation, purposeful gestures, and conventions of language to communicate ideas effectively.

Listening and Speaking/Teamwork

10.26 Students work productively with others in teams. Students will continue to apply earlier standards with greater complexity. Students are expected to participate productively in teams, building on the ideas of others, contributing relevant information, developing a plan for consensus-building, and setting ground rules for decision-making.

Reading/Comprehension Skills

RC-10 Students use a flexible range of metacognitive reading skills in both assigned and independent reading to understand an author's message. Students will continue to apply earlier standards with greater depth in increasingly more complex texts as they become self-directed, critical readers. The student is expected to:

RC-10.A reflect on understanding to monitor comprehension (e.g., asking questions, summarizing and synthesizing, making connections, creating sensory images); and

RC-10.B make complex inferences about text and use textual evidence to support understanding.

OER | Open-Ended Response Questions

In the course of literature study, you will read selections and then answer questions about them. This process of answering questions is essential to showing and clarifying your understanding of what you have read and enjoying and appreciating literature. In the subject of literature especially, you will encounter open-ended response questions both in class and on tests. These questions ask you to speak or write fairly detailed answers in response to something you have read. Although they may seem harder than other types of questions, such as multiple-choice questions, you can apply strategies to formulate answers that will help you better understand what you have read and earn a high grade.

Steps for Answering Open-Ended Response Questions

To improve your answers, follow these three steps:

1. Answer the Question

This is the part of the response in black ink in the sample answers that follow. It is the short answer. Even when it is completely right, it does not provide enough information to earn a high score.

2. Cite Evidence from the Text

This is the part of the answer in green ink. Quote from the text if there is a sentence that supports your answer. If not, paraphrase the text that proves your point. You should then explain why the quoted or paraphrased information is important.

3. Extend Your Answer

This is the part of the answer in purple ink. There are several ways to extend your answer. You can connect the text to another text, to yourself, or to the world. Another text is anything you have read that shares a theme or other trait with the work in question. Connecting the text to yourself means supporting your answer with your own personal experience or prior knowledge. Connecting the text to the world means linking it to something you already know about from any field (perhaps history, politics, or psychology). Make sure all your comments are relevant to the question asked.

Sample Questions and Answers

The pages that follow contain questions and answers for several selections in this anthology. The first question asks about an expository text and the second about a literary text. The third, which is called a crossover question, features a question comparing an expository text and a literary text. Each sample answer includes an analysis of what makes the answer worthy of a high score.

Thinking About the Big Picture

Open-ended response questions do not focus on just one particular detail of the text. They are broad questions that require you to consider the selection in its entirety. When you attempt to answer an open-ended response question, you should think about what you have learned from the beginning to the end of the selection. Your answer can be debatable. Another student might answer differently, because open-ended response questions require interpretation. Your task is to make sure that your interpretation is supported by evidence from the text.

A good answer to an open-ended response question demonstrates that you have thought about and formed an opinion about what you have read. Your answer should also show that you have understood the deeper meaning of the selection and can relate that meaning to something else, such as a book you have read, an experience from your life, or a current event.

Expository Text

Read "Cry of the Ancient Mariner" by Carl Safina on pages 142–146. Then think about how you would answer this question:

What is the author trying to persuade readers to think or do?

Sample Answer

The author is trying to persuade readers that we're killing the oceans and enlist help in protecting them. He uses alarming facts to make his point: "Fishing annually extracts more than 80 million tons of sea creatures worldwide." "The biggest sources of coastal pollution are waste from farm animals, fertilizers, and human sewage," which kill sea life. In a photo caption: "Because of humankind's endless trash stream, the seabirds feed plastic to their young." He warns, "The Gulf of Mexico [has] a spreading dead zone—almost empty of marine life—the size of New Jersey." He points out, "The oceans make our planet habitable, and the wealth of oceans spans nutritional, climatological, biological, aesthetic, spiritual, emotional, and ethical areas." He suggests steps we can take, as societies and as individuals: Enforce fishing limits, enforce laws against giant drift nets and whale hunting, prohibit fishing in marine "sanctuaries," require ships to carry modern equipment for handling garbage, and close some areas to fishing. Individuals and families can stop eating fish species that are endangered. I think Safina makes a convincing argument. He provides facts (statistics, quotes from experts, direct personal observation) to back up his opinions. He has impressive credentials himself, as the founder of the National Audubon Society's Living Oceans Program. He gives readers suggestions for how they personally can do something to help, which made me feel both invested and empowered instead of discouraged by how bad things are. His article persuaded me, and I think it's as important as Rachel Carson's *Silent Spring*, which addressed the dangers of pesticides.

Answer the Question This is the short answer.

Cite Evidence from the Text In the answer, the writer quotes the article's most alarming facts and paraphrases the action the author advises.

Extend Your Answer The respondent also connects the text to herself by evaluating how persuasive it is and stating its effect on her. She also connects the text to another text that warns of ecological destruction.

Tip: Quote, Paraphrase, or Summarize?

You can support your ideas about a text in three different ways: summarizing main ideas, paraphrasing key passages, or incorporating direct quotations. When writing short open-ended responses, you want to display your understanding of the text on both a broad and a specific level. Use combinations of these types of support to match the content of the selection and the type of question you are responding to. Summarize when you need to explain main ideas of the essay. Paraphrase when you need to cite longer or more complicated passages. Directly quote any words, phrases, or passages when the author provides a distinct or concise statement of his or her ideas.

Literary Text

Read the story "An Astrologer's Day" by R. K. Narayan on pages 40–44. Then think about how you would answer this question:

What other careers could the astrologer's skills prepare him for?

Sample Answer

Answer the Question
This is the short answer.

Cite Evidence from the Text In the answer, the writer provides quotes to support several different career paths.

Extend Your Answer
The respondent also connects the text to the world by considering what a politician with the astrologer's skills might do.

With training, I think he would make a good psychologist, fiction writer, or actor. He already has "a working analysis of mankind's troubles: marriage, money, and the tangles of human ties." He's good at reading people's inner thoughts and feelings quickly and accurately. His years of experience with hundreds of customers have shown him a wide range of human behavior. "He said things which pleased and astonished everyone: that was more a matter of study, practice, and shrewd guesswork." Since it takes those same skills to create believable characters, he'd also make a good fiction writer or actor. "The power of his eyes was considerably enhanced by their position. . . . To crown the effect he wound a saffron-colored turban around his head. . . . People were attracted to him as bees are attracted to cosmos." I think anyone with the astrologer's skills could do a lot of good in the world—or a lot of harm. He could become a politician with enough power to push programs that would help save the environment and improve people's lives. Or he could seize power and manipulate people for his own selfish purposes.

Tip: Character Traits

If a question asks you to extend your thinking beyond the story, such as imagining a character in a different setting, take notes that will help you understand the character on a deeper level. Find revealing quotations in the selection and consider what is being implied about the character, not only what is directly stated. You will need to use these skills to make inferences that extend beyond the facts of the story.

Quotations	Qualities	Careers
"...inner thoughts..."	insightful	psychologist, writer
"...attracted to him..."	compelling	actor, writer

Crossover Question

Read "What Makes a Hero?" by Amanda Ripley on pages 913–917 and review R. K. Narayan's story "An Astrologer's Day" on pages 40–44. Then think about how you would answer this question:

Is the astrologer in the story a hero, according to any of the definitions in the article?

Sample Answer

The article defines a hero so broadly that I'd have to say yes. "It is in gestures that you know a person's true nature," the article quotes a doctor as saying. The astrologer's gesture of telling Guru Nayak that the man who tried to kill him is dead brings peace. "[Nayak] looked gratified to hear it." Of course, the lie also protects the astrologer from the consequences of his action, which is hardly heroic. The article says, "People still crave heroes . . . to point the way toward a solution." The astrologer points the way to a solution for his customers. "He said things which pleased and astonished everyone." The article says, "Most heroes are walking contradictions." That's certainly true of the astrologer. He is smart and kind enough to predict futures that his customers find reassuring, but he does it for money. He tried to kill a man when he was young and drunk, but he helps that man when he is older and wiser and feels "a great load is gone from me" afterward. I personally don't think the astrologer is a hero because he never sacrifices to help others; it's just a by-product of helping himself. By contrast, my mother is a hero. She works in social services. She makes calls on her day off and has even brought kids home for dinner. The astrologer doesn't measure up. From King Arthur to Superman, heroes make sacrifices to help others.

Answer the Question This is the short answer.

Cite Evidence from the Text The writer cites evidence for her answer by quoting from both texts, from the article to define a hero and from the story to show the astrologer's traits.

Extend Your Answer The writer extends her response by connecting the text to herself and her mother. She also connects the text to other texts about heroes. She could have connected the text to the world by discussing Doctors Without Borders and other real-life present-day heroes.

Tip: Bookmark

When possible, read the open-ended response question before reading the selections. Create a two-sided bookmark for taking crossover notes. At the top of the bookmark on each side, write key words from the question you need to answer. For example, write HERO at the top of the bookmark. Write down the words and phrases in the selection that provide ideas about what it means to be a hero and examples of heroism.

Practice Writing Answers to 🔖 OER Questions

After you read a selection in this anthology, try answering some of the questions in the After You Read section using the strategy described on these pages. You can look for the 🔖 OER label next to questions that have been selected specifically for open-ended response practice.

Spotlight on Texas

Many influential American writers were born in Texas or lived there. Texas writers have excelled in a variety of forms. The following pages describe aspects of Texas literature and film. As you read, take notes about how some Texas writers and filmmakers have approached nonfiction and sports.

Texas Longhorns mascot

Looking Ahead

The following literary works appear in your textbook. These writers are either from Texas or have important ties to the state.

Literary Texas

Cadillac Ranch, Amarillo

Rio Grande

Big Bend National Park

Amarillo

Lubbock

Wichita Falls
Larry McMurtry
born (1936)

Red River

Dallas

Panola County
Walter Prescott Webb
born (1888)

El Paso
Pat Mora born (1942)
Cormac McCarthy settles (1976)

Rio Grande

Indian Creek
Katherine Anne Porter
born (1890)

Davy Crockett dies (1836)
Carmen Tafolla born (1951)
Naomi Shihab Nye resides (1967)
Sandra Cisneros settles (1984)

Mason
Fred Gipson
born (1908)

★ **AUSTIN**
O. Henry settles (1884)

Brazos River

Barbara Jordan
born (1936)

San Marcos

Wharton
Horton Foote
born (1916)

Houston

San Antonio

Galveston Island
Cabeza de Vaca
shipwrecked nearby
(1528)

Crystal City
Tomás Rivera
born (1935)

Live Oak County
J. Frank Dobie
born (1888)

Goliad
John C. Duval escapes
massacre (1836)

Laredo
Roberto Félix Salazar
born (1921)

Brownsville
Américo Paredes born (1915)

Reading Check

Analyze Graphic Information Which of the writers on the map are associated not with a city or town, but with a county?

Big Idea 1: *Historical Nonfiction*

J. Frank Dobie: "Spirit of Freedom"

Because Texas has always been a place of rapid change, nonfiction writers have been essential in helping Texans remember who they were and understand who they are now. One of the most prominent and best-loved Texas nonfiction writers was J. Frank Dobie.

As a young man, James Frank Dobie quit his job as a university professor to manage his uncle's ranch. Though he eventually had a long career as an author and teacher, the year he spent as a ranch manager gave him his focus in life: to capture Texas history and culture for future generations to appreciate.

It was vital to Dobie to preserve stories, customs, memories, and the "spirit of freedom" that he felt were rapidly disappearing from the West. For example, he spoke with Bob Simmons, an 84-year-old ex-slave. Simmons made his living as a mustanger—someone who captured wild horses. "I acted like I was a mustang," Simmons said. "I made the mustangs think I was one of them. Maybe I was in them days." Dobie described how Simmons worked alone to track and trail the mustangs.

"For week following week, across prairies and through thickets, huddled in rain, spread out on the ground in sunshine, listening in starlight to the encircling coyote concerts, lingering for the grazers as unhurried as the shadow of a circling buzzard, this lone man in primeval silence and space lived with the mustangs and, except in not eating grass and in having the long, long thoughts that only a human being can have, lived as one of them."

Big Idea 2: *Sports Literature*

Babe Didrikson Zaharias: "Wonder Girl"

Texas has produced a tremendous number of athletes, including football legend Roger Staubach, tennis ace Zina Garrison, and soccer star Mia Hamm. One of the most gifted Texas athletes was Mildred Ella Didrikson Zaharias, known as "Babe." "Before I was even into my teens, I knew exactly what I wanted to be when I grew up," wrote Zaharias in her memoir, *This Life I've Led.* "My goal was to be the greatest athlete [who] ever lived." Born in Port Arthur, Texas, in 1911, Zaharias grew up at a time when there were few opportunities for female athletes. "I wanted to be an athlete, but I didn't suppose then that I could make a living out of it," she wrote.

"The World-Beating Girl Viking of Texas."

—1932 newspaper headline about Zaharias

In her early twenties, Zaharias became a semiprofessional basketball player for a Texas team called the Golden Cyclones. She led them to a national championship. Amazed by her athleticism, the team owner suggested that she try track and field. "How many events are there?" she asked. When told there were ten, she said she would compete in them all. "Everybody nearly died laughing," she wrote. The team owner paid for her to go to the national championships. She competed in eight track-and-field events, placed first in five, and won the championship—single-handedly, against teams of fifteen to twenty-two women. Sportswriter George Kirksey wrote that it was "the most amazing series of performances ever accomplished by any individual, male or female, in track and field history."

Though Zaharias excelled in many sports, she decided to concentrate on golf because it was one of the only sports that paid female athletes. She won dozens of tournaments and helped to found the Ladies' Professional Golf Association. *Sports Illustrated* and the Associated Press both voted her the greatest female athlete of the twentieth century.

> ### Reading Check
>
> **Evaluate** What makes Bob Simmons and Babe Didrikson Zaharias worth reading about?

Texas on Film: *Six Man, Texas*

E very Friday night in the fall, every small community has a dream," explains director Alan Barber. "Maybe this year there will be enough players with enough talent to take their tiny school to the playoffs—or maybe there will simply be enough players" for a team. Barber's 2007 documentary *Six Man, Texas* examines how six-man football teams reflect the strengths and challenges of small, rural Texas communities.

Meet **Alan Barber**

Texas native Alan Barber produced and directed *Six Man, Texas*. "In the whole of North America, there are about 300 teams playing six-man football," Barber explained. "Almost 200 of them are in Texas." Barber and a group of donors founded a scholarship fund to benefit graduates of small rural schools in Texas.

Percentage of Texas Students Enrolled in Rural Schools

1945
More than 35 percent

2007
Less than 4 percent

Source: *Six Man, Texas*

Fact: Six-Man Football in Rural Texas

Unlike eleven-man football, six-man football has a smaller field—forty by eighty yards—and a fifteen-yard first down. Also, players in six-man games sometimes play both offense and defense for the entire game. In most respects, however, the two types of football are similar. Some fans, players, and coaches prefer six-man because it is higher scoring and faster paced. Coach Bennie Weaver commented that six-man football is "more fun to coach and more fun to watch."

This version of the sport was created in 1934 so that smaller schools would be able to field teams. Some rural towns in Texas are becoming so small that their schools cannot even form six-man teams. However, small-town fans and players are as fiercely loyal to their teams as big-city residents are. Six-man player Colter Snipes of Aquilla, Texas, explained, "We want to put our town on the map."

SIX MAN, TEXAS

"There always has to be a small dog," states retired six-man coach Harvey Wellman in *Six Man, Texas.* "You can't make that an excuse. You have to say 'We're going to compete.'" The documentary focuses on how six-man football teams bring small communities together. If the team loses, "our fans feel like *they* lost the game," says player David Valero. "If we're crying, they're crying." In some towns, stores close before football games because "everyone in town is at that game," explains fan Ken Capps.

The subtitle of the film is "A True Story of Shrinking Texas Towns." Some towns in Texas are withering away because of a changing business climate. "Now, if you don't farm 3,000 acres, you can't make it," explains one farmer. Larger plots of land mean fewer farm families and fewer schools. As schools consolidate, some towns actually disappear because the school is the town's main source of employment. "I would love for my kids to . . . raise a family in Sanderson," says Karen Sanchez, "instead of having to leave [for] Austin, San Antonio, El Paso, Houston. . . . It's tough."

The Patton Springs Rangers kick off to the Guthrie Jaguars

Reading Check
Analyze Cause-and-Effect Relationships How does six-man football affect the community life of small towns?

How to Use *Glencoe Literature*

Why do I need this book?

Glencoe Literature is more than just a collection of stories, poems, nonfiction articles, and other literary works. Every part is built around **Big Ideas,** concepts that you will want to think about, talk about, and maybe even argue about. Big Ideas help you become part of an important conversation. You can join in lively discussions about who we are, where we have been, and where we are going.

Organization

The literature you will read is organized by literary element and genre into six units: The Short Story, Nonfiction, Poetry, Drama, Legends and Myths, and Genre Fiction.

Each unit contains the following:

A **UNIT INTRODUCTION** provides you with the background information to help make your reading experience more meaningful.

- **GENRE FOCUS** defines the literary elements that make up a unit.

- The **LITERARY ANALYSIS MODEL** uses an example to help you identify different literary elements and analyze their use within the text.

- **BIG IDEAS** target concepts that you can trace as you read the literature.

LITERARY SELECTIONS follow each Part Introduction. The selections are organized as follows.

Reading and Thinking

The main literary works in your textbook are arranged in three parts.

- Start with **BEFORE YOU READ**. Learn valuable background information about the literature and preview the skills and strategies that will guide your reading.

    MEET THE AUTHOR presents a detailed biography of the writer whose work you will read and analyze.

    LITERATURE AND READING PREVIEW lists the basic tools you will use to read and analyze the literary work.

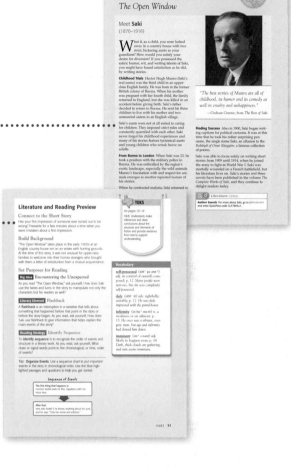

- Next, read the **LITERATURE SELECTION**. As you flip through the selections, you will notice that parts of some texts are highlighted in different colors. At the bottom of the page are color-coded questions that relate to the highlighted text. Yellow represents a *Big Idea*, magenta represents a *Literary Element*, and blue represents a *Reading Strategy*. These questions will help you gain a better understanding of the text.

After You Read

Respond and Think Critically

1. **Connect to Personal Experience** What was your reaction to Vera and Framton Nuttel?

2. **Interpret Characters** Why does Framton Nuttel visit Mrs. Sappleton? What do you think Vera notices about Nuttel as they sit in silence and wait for Mrs. Sappleton?

3. **Interpret Exposition** What makes it possible for Vera to fool Nuttel? Explain your answer and support it with evidence from the story. ◆OER

4. **Make Inferences About Climax** What is Vera's reaction to the appearance of the three men returning from the moor? How do you think this contributes to Nuttel's reaction?

5. **Analyze Motivation** Reread Nuttel and Vera's first conversation on page 12. How might Vera's poise and self-confidence contribute to her believability? In analyzing Vera's behavior, what might you conclude about Vera's motives? Support your response with text evidence.

6. **Analyze Character** The author subtly plays with the idea of hunting in this story. How is Vera like a hunter and Framton Nuttel like her prey?

7. **Big Idea** **Draw Conclusions About Plot** Surprise reversals of events are common in Saki's stories. How does Saki employ this device in "The Open Window"? Identify the passage where the surprise becomes clear to the reader.

Literary Element Flashback

Texas Test Practice (10.5.A)

1. How does Vera's lengthy flashback affect the plot as a whole?
   A. She reveals herself to be untrustworthy and mischievous.
   B. The hunting party is late returning.
   C. Mrs. Sappleton arrives late.
   D. Mr. Nuttel flees and is not able to calm his nerves by visiting his neighbors.

2. How does Vera's fanciful flashback have ironic consequences?
   F. Vera's aunt is puzzled by Mr. Nuttel's abrupt departure.
   G. The hunting party looks exactly the way Vera described it.
   H. Visiting his neighbors does nothing to help Mr. Nuttel's nerves.
   J. Mr. Nuttel believes every word of Vera's tall tale.

Review: Plot

As you learned on page 9, **plot** refers to the sequence of events in a story.

8. **Partner Activity** Meet with a classmate and work together to identify the plot elements of "The Open Window." Create a chart like the one below and fill it in with specific events from the story. Then analyze these isolated scenes and their contribution to the plot as a whole.

Plot Element	Contribution to the Plot
Exposition	Sets up the situation and introduces the characters
Rising Action	
Climax	
Falling Action	
Resolution	

SAKI **15**

Vocabulary

Reading Strategy Connect to Personal Experience

When you **connect** to characters, you focus on their emotions and situations. Review your chart from page 73 to help you answer the following items.

12. Look back at the blue highlighted passages and questions in the story. List feelings, situations, or concepts from this story that are familiar to you from other literary works, films, or television shows.

13. With your classmates, identify entries that appear on a majority of your lists. Discuss why certain concepts or situations are common in literature, film, and television.

Vocabulary Practice

Practice with Usage Respond to these statements to help you explore the meanings of the boldfaced vocabulary words from the story.

1. Tell what a musical **prodigy** might do.

2. Give an example of a **reproach**.

3. Name two words that describe a **reverie**.

4. Give an example of something **discordant**.

5. Describe what happens in a **fiasco**.

Academic Vocabulary

The mother's desire for a prodigy was out of **proportion** with her daughter's average talent.

In the quotation above, *proportion* means "balance." The word *proportion* has additional meanings in specific subject areas, such as mathematics and architecture. Using context clues, try to figure out the meaning of *proportion* in the sentence below. Check a dictionary to confirm your deduction.

The critic praised the columns for their size and proportion.

For more on academic vocabulary, see pages 36–37 and R92–R94.

Enrich and Extend

Speaking and Listening

Literature Groups With a small group, discuss whether it is advantageous to require children to participate in music, sports, academic contests, and similar activities. Try to reach a consensus—a general agreement within a group on an issue.

Teamwork To participate productively in your group, listen to others, build on their ideas, and contribute relevant information. You can avoid conflict by setting up ground rules up front for making decisions and building consensus.

Prepare Before your group meets, look back at "Two Kinds" to review the mother's requirements of Jing-mei and evaluate the advantages and disadvantages of the requirements. Write your evaluations in a chart like the one below. Add details from your own experiences or from the experiences of others you know.

Requirement	Advantage	Disadvantage
take many tests to see if Jing-mei is a genius	raises hopes for mother and Jing-mei	exposes Jing-mei and mother to many failures by Jing-mei

Discuss Participate actively and effectively in your group discussion. Respect others' viewpoints by listening attentively. Deliver your opinions in a normal tone of voice, providing clear, specific examples from your chart to support your judgments.

Report Have one group member orally state your consensus to the class or state that no consensus was reached, being sure to address the class clearly and loudly enough for all to hear.

Evaluate Write a paragraph in which you assess the effectiveness of your discussion. Use the rubric on page 237 to help in your evaluation.

Literature Online

Selection Resources For Selection Quizzes, eFlashcards, and Reading-Writing Connection activities, go to glencoe.com and enter QuickPass code GL57805u1.

86 UNIT 1 THE SHORT STORY

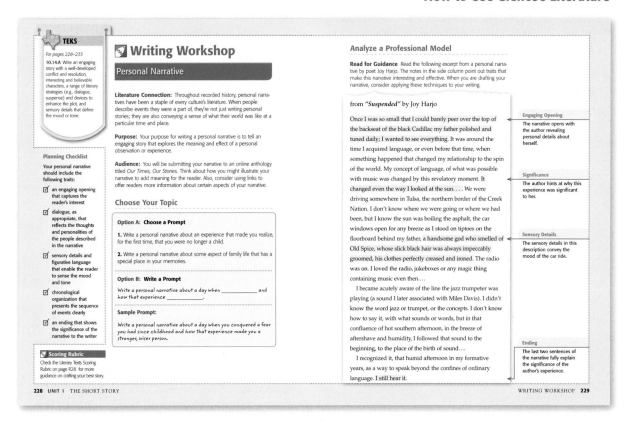

Planning Checklist

Your personal narrative should include the following traits:

☑ an engaging opening that captures the reader's interest

☑ dialogue, as appropriate, that reflects the thoughts and personalities of the people described in the narrative

☑ sensory details and figurative language that enable the reader to sense the mood and tone

☑ chronological organization that presents the sequence of events clearly

☑ an ending that shows the significance of the narrative to the writer

Scoring Rubric
Check the Literary Texts Scoring Rubric on page R28 for more guidance on crafting your best story.

228 UNIT 1 THE SHORT STORY

Writing Workshop
Personal Narrative

Literature Connection: Throughout recorded history, personal narratives have been a staple of every culture's literature. When people describe events they were a part of, they're not just writing personal stories; they are also conveying a sense of what their world was like at a particular time and place.

Purpose: Your purpose for writing a personal narrative is to tell an engaging story that explores the meaning and effect of a personal observation or experience.

Audience: You will be submitting your narrative to an online anthology titled *Our Times, Our Stories.* Think about how you might illustrate your narrative to add meaning for the reader. Also, consider using links to offer readers more information about certain aspects of your narrative.

Choose Your Topic

Option A: Choose a Prompt

1. Write a personal narrative about an experience that made you realize, for the first time, that you were no longer a child.

2. Write a personal narrative about some aspect of family life that has a special place in your memories.

Option B: Write a Prompt

Write a personal narrative about a day when _____ and how that experience _____.

Sample Prompt:

Write a personal narrative about a day when you conquered a fear you had since childhood and how that experience made you a stronger, wiser person.

Analyze a Professional Model

Read for Guidance Read the following excerpt from a personal narrative by poet Joy Harjo. The notes in the side column point out traits that make this narrative interesting and effective. When you are drafting your narrative, consider applying these techniques to your writing.

from *"Suspended"* by Joy Harjo

Once I was so small that I could barely peer over the top of the backseat of the black Cadillac my father polished and tuned daily; I wanted to see everything. It was around the time I acquired language, or even before that time, when something happened that changed my relationship to the spin of the world. My concept of language, of what was possible with music was changed by this revelatory moment. It changed even the way I looked at the sun. . . . We were driving somewhere in Tulsa, the northern border of the Creek Nation. I don't know where we were going or where we had been, but I know the sun was boiling the asphalt, the car windows open for any breeze as I stood on tiptoes on the floorboard behind my father, a handsome god who smelled of Old Spice, whose slick black hair was always impeccably groomed, his clothes perfectly creased and ironed. The radio was on. I loved the radio, jukeboxes or any magic thing containing music even then....

I became acutely aware of the line the jazz trumpeter was playing (a sound I later associated with Miles Davis). I didn't know the word jazz or trumpet, or the concepts. I don't know how to say it, with what sounds or words, but in that confluence of hot southern afternoon, in the breeze of aftershave and humidity, I followed that sound to the beginning, to the place of the birth of sound....

I recognized it, that humid afternoon in my formative years, as a way to speak beyond the confines of ordinary language. I still hear it.

Engaging Opening
The narrative opens with the author revealing personal details about herself.

Significance
The author hints at why this experience was significant to her.

Sensory Details
The sensory details in this description convey the mood of the car ride.

Ending
The last two sentences of the narrative fully explain the significance of the author's experience.

WRITING WORKSHOP **229**

Writing Workshops

Each unit in *Glencoe Literature* includes a Writing Workshop. The workshop walks you through the writing process as you work on an extended piece of writing related to the unit.

- You will create writing goals and apply strategies to meet them.
- You will pick up tips and polish your critical skills as you analyze professional and workshop models.
- You will focus on mastering specific aspects of writing, including organization, grammar, and vocabulary.
- You will use a checklist to evaluate your own writing.

Assessment

English Language Arts

Reading: Fiction

Read the following passages and answer the questions that follow them.

---

from "When the Buffalo Climbed a Tree" by Mark Twain

In this tall tale, a man named Bemis is relating a recent event in which he was up in a tree, trying to remain safe from a dangerous buffalo.

1   I watched the bull, now, with anxiety—anxiety which no one can conceive of who has not been in such a situation and felt that at any moment death might come. Presently a thought came into the bull's eye. I knew it! Said I—if my nerve fails now, I am lost. Sure enough, it was just as I had dreaded, he started in to climb the tree—"

2   "What, the bull?"

3   "Of course—who else?"

4   "But a bull can't climb a tree."

5   "He can't, can't he? Since you know so much about it, did you ever see a bull try?"

6   "No! I never dreamt of such a thing."

7   "Well, then, what is the use of your talking that way, then? Because you never saw a thing done, is that any reason why it can't be done?"

8   "Well, all right—go on. What did you do?"

9   "The bull started up, and got along well for about ten feet, then slipped and slid back. I breathed easier. He tried it again—got up a little higher—slipped again. But he came at it once more, and this time he was careful. He got gradually higher and higher, and my spirits went down more and more. Up he came—an inch at a time—with his eyes hot, and his tongue hanging out. Higher and higher—hitched his foot over the stump of a limb, and looked up, as much as to say, 'You are my meat, friend.' Up again—higher and higher, and getting more excited the closer he got. He was within ten feet of me! I took a long breath,—and then said I, 'It is now or never.' I had the coil of the lariat all ready; I paid it out slowly, till it hung right over his head; all of a sudden I let go of the slack, and the slip-noose fell fairly round his neck! Quicker than lightning I out with the Allen and let him have it in the face. It was an awful roar, and must have scared the bull out of his senses. When the smoke cleared away, there he was dangling in the air, twenty foot from the ground, and going out of one convulsion into another faster than you could count! I didn't stop to count, anyhow I shinned down the tree and shot for home."

10   "Bemis, is all that true, just as you have stated it?"

11   "I wish I may rot in my tracks and die the death of a dog if it isn't."

240   UNIT 1   THE SHORT STORY

Assessment

At the end of each unit, you will be tested on the literature, reading, and vocabulary skills you have just learned. Designed to simulate standardized tests, this test will give you the practice you need to succeed while providing an assessment of how well you have met the unit objectives.

 BOUND BOOK

Try using this organizer to explore your personal responses to the poetry, play and nonfiction.

Organizing Information

Graphic organizers—such as Foldables®, diagrams, and charts—help you keep your information and ideas organized.

Be Cyber Safe and Smart

Cyber Safety

As you explore the *Glencoe Literature* program, you will have many opportunities to go online. When you use the Internet at school or home, you enter a kind of community—the cyber world. In this online world, you need to follow safety rules and protect yourself. Here are some tips to keep in mind:

> ### Words to Know
>
> **cyber world** the world of computers and high-tech communications
> **cyber safety** actions that protect Internet users from harm
> **cyber ethics** responsible code of conduct for using the Internet
> **cyber bully** a person who uses technology to frighten, bother, or harm someone else
> **cyber citizen** a person who uses the Internet to communicate

☑ Be a responsible cyber citizen. Use the Internet to share knowledge that makes people's lives better. Respect other people's feelings and do not break any laws.

☑ Beware of cyber bullying. People can be hurt and embarrassed by comments that have been made public. You should immediately tell your teacher or counselor if you feel threatened by another student's computer postings.

☑ Do not give out personal information, such as your address and telephone number, without your parents' or guardians' permission.

☑ Tell your teacher, parent, or guardian right away if you find or read any information that makes you feel uneasy or afraid.

☑ Do not e-mail your picture to anyone.

☑ Do not open e-mail or text messages from strangers.

☑ Do not tell anyone your Internet password.

☑ Do not make illegal copies of computer games, programs, and software CDs.

Literature Online

For more about Internet safety and responsibility, go to glencoe.com

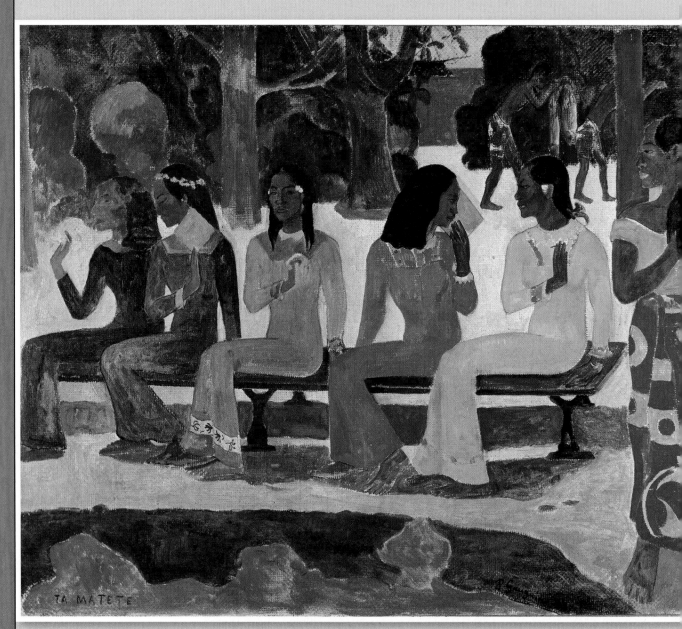

Ta Matete (We Shall Not Go to Market Today), 1892. Paul Gauguin. Gouache on canvas, 73 x 92 cm.
Kunstmuseum, Basel, Switzerland.

View the Art Many of Gauguin's paintings depict the people and lifestyle of the South Pacific. What story-like details can you
infer from this painting?

The Short Story

Looking Ahead

There is no better place to begin a study of literature than with the short story. This concise, imaginative genre allows the reader to focus on a precisely crafted plot, often a single setting, and a limited number of characters. Whether creating a journey that is bizarre, realistic, or insightful, the writer will quickly and artfully make the point, often in a way the reader will never forget.

Each part in Unit One focuses on a Big Idea that can help you connect to the literary works.

PREVIEW	Big Ideas	Literary Focus
PART 1	Encountering the Unexpected	Plot and Setting
PART 2	Making Choices	Theme and Character
PART 3	Life Transitions	Narrator and Voice

TEKS

For pages 2–6

10.5 Understand, make inferences and draw conclusions about the structure and elements of fiction and provide evidence from text to support understanding.

Genre Focus

What are the elements that shape a short story?

Katherine Anne Porter, one of the great American short story writers, said, "Human life itself may be almost pure chaos, but the work of the artist is to take these handfuls of confusion and disparate things, things that seem to be irreconcilable, and put them together in a frame to give them some kind of shape and meaning." Consciously or unconsciously, writers make choices. The writer chooses who will be the star of the story, who will tell the story, where the story will take place, and most importantly—what happens. In short story writing, authors make very precise and focused choices about these elements of fiction.

Plot and Setting

Sequence of Events

Plot is the sequence of events in a story. Most plots begin with the **exposition**, which introduces the characters, setting, and conflicts. **Rising action** develops the conflict with complications and leads to the **climax**, when the story reaches its emotional high point. The **falling action** is the logical result of the climax, and the **resolution** presents the final outcome.

> "You may wonder why we keep that window wide open on an October afternoon," said the niece, indicating a large French window that opened on to a lawn.
>
> —Saki (H. H. Munro), *from* **"The Open Window"**

Time and Place

Setting is the time and place in which a story happens. The setting not only includes physical surroundings but can also include the ideas, customs, values, and beliefs of the period in which the story takes place. Writers use **description** to help readers see, hear, smell, taste, or feel details of the setting. This type of sensory detail—or **imagery**—helps create an emotional response in a reader.

> Now, balanced easily and firmly, he stood on the ledge outside in the slight, chill breeze, eleven stories above the street, staring into his own lighted apartment, odd and different-seeming now.
>
> —Jack Finney, *from* **"Contents of the Dead Man's Pocket"**

Theme and Character

Protagonist and Antagonist

The main character in a story is the **protagonist.** The protagonist faces the main conflict of the story. In many stories, an **antagonist** works against the protagonist in overcoming the conflict. The antagonist is usually a character the reader does not like.

Theme

The central message of a story is its **theme.** For example, a theme might give an insight into human nature or a perception about life. Most often, a theme is implied through elements in the story, such as what happens to the main character or what the character learns.

> Jonathan Iwegbu counted himself extraordinarily lucky. "Happy survival!" meant so much more to him than just a current fashion of greeting old friends in the first hazy days of peace.
>
> —Chinua Achebe, *from* **"Civil Peace"**

> Luis thought that maybe if they ate together once in a while things might get better between them, but he always had something to do around dinnertime and ended up at a hamburger joint.
>
> —Judith Ortiz Cofer, *from* **"Catch the Moon"**

Narrator and Voice

Point of View

The person telling a story is the **narrator.** The perspective from which a story is told is called **point of view.** Stories are usually told from a **first-** or **third-person point of view.** In a story with first-person point of view, the narrator is a character inside the story and uses "I" in telling the story. In a story with third-person point of view, the narrator is outside the story, using "she" or "he" to tell the story.

Voice

Voice is the distinctive use of language that conveys the author's or narrator's personality to the reader. Every narrator, whether speaking from a first-person or third-person point of view, has a **voice.** Authors are careful to make the narrator's vocabulary and syntax consistent.

> The young man was daring and brave, eager to go up to the mountaintop. He had been brought up by good, honest people who were wise in the ancient ways.
>
> —Lame Deer, *from* **"The Vision Quest"**

> No pestilence had ever been so fatal, or so hideous.
>
> —Edgar Allan Poe, *from* **"The Masque of the Red Death"**

 Literature Online

Literature and Reading For more selections in this genre, go to glencoe.com and enter QuickPass code GL57805u1.

Literary Analysis Model

How do literary elements shape a short story?

Ernest Hemingway (1899–1961) influenced the fiction of his time and after. In "Old Man at the Bridge," he succinctly captures the effects of the Spanish Civil War on civilians.

**APPLYING
Literary Elements**

Narrator

The story is told from the first-person point of view.

Setting

The story takes place at a bridge in northeastern Spain during the Spanish Civil War (1936–1939).

Character

As you learn more about the old man, the story's protagonist, you may begin to care about him.

Voice

In the dialogue, the characters' speech is brief. This is characteristic of Hemingway's style.

Old Man at the Bridge

by Ernest Hemingway

An old man with steel rimmed spectacles and very dusty clothes sat by the side of the road. There was a pontoon bridge across the river and carts, trucks, and men, women and children were crossing it. The mule-drawn carts staggered up the steep bank from the
5 bridge with soldiers helping push against the spokes of the wheels. The trucks ground up and away heading out of it all and the peasants plodded along in the ankle deep dust. But the old man sat there without moving. He was too tired to go any further.

It was my business to cross the bridge, explore the bridgehead
10 beyond and find out to what point the enemy had advanced. I did this and returned over the bridge. There were not so many carts now and very few people on foot, but the old man was still there.

"Where do you come from?" I asked him.

"From San Carlos," he said, and smiled.

That was his native town and so it gave him pleasure to
15 mention it and he smiled.

"I was taking care of animals," he explained.

"Oh," I said, not quite understanding.

"Yes," he said, "I stayed, you see, taking care of animals. I was the last one to leave the town of San Carlos."
20 He did not look like a shepherd nor a herdsman and I looked at his black dusty clothes and his gray dusty face and his steel rimmed spectacles and said, "What animals were they?"

"Various animals," he said, and shook his head. "I had to leave them."

I was watching the bridge and the African looking country of
25 the Ebro Delta and wondering how long now it would be before we would see the enemy, and listening all the while for the first noises that would signal that ever mysterious event called contact, and the old man still sat there.

"What animals were they?" I asked.

"There were three animals altogether," he explained. "There were
30 two goats and a cat and then there were four pairs of pigeons."

"And you had to leave them?" I asked.

35　"Yes. Because of the artillery. The captain told me to go because of the artillery."

"And you have no family?" I asked, watching the far end of the bridge where a few last carts were hurrying down the slope of the bank.

40　"No," he said, "only the animals I stated. The cat, of course, will be all right. A cat can look out for itself, but I cannot think what will become of the others."

"What politics have you?" I asked.

"I am without politics," he said. "I am seventy-six years old.
45　I have come twelve kilometers now and I think now I can go no further."

"This is not a good place to stop," I said. "If you can make it, there are trucks up the road where it forks for Tortosa."

"I will wait a while," he said, "and then I will go. Where do the
50　trucks go?"

"Towards Barcelona," I told him.

"I know no one in that direction," he said, "but thank you very much. Thank you again very much."

He looked at me very blankly and tiredly, then said, having
55　to share his worry with some one, "The cat will be all right, I am sure. There is no need to be unquiet about the cat. But the others. Now what do you think about the others?"

"Why they'll probably come through it all right."

"You think so?"

60　"Why not," I said, watching the far bank where now there were no carts.

"But what will they do under the artillery when I was told to leave because of the artillery?"

"Did you leave the dove cage unlocked?" I asked.

65　"Yes."

"Then they'll fly."

"Yes, certainly they'll fly. But the others. It's better not to think about the others," he said.

"If you are rested I would go," I urged. "Get up and try to
70　walk now."

"Thank you," he said and got to his feet, swayed from side to side and then sat down backwards in the dust.

"I was taking care of animals," he said dully, but no longer to me. "I was only taking care of animals."

75　There was nothing to do about him. It was Easter Sunday and the Fascists were advancing toward the Ebro. It was a gray over-cast day with a low ceiling so their planes were not up. That and the fact that cats know how to look after themselves was all the good luck that old man would ever have.

Plot

You may hope that the old man will be able to flee with the others, but, in the climax of the story, he is too tired to stand.

Theme

The implication is that war is unlucky for the civilians whose lives it touches.

Reading Check

Analyze How does the story reach its climax and how is it resolved?

Wrap-Up

Guide to Reading Short Stories

- Short stories often allow readers to focus on one setting and a small number of characters.

- Plot development in short stories tends to be very compact, especially the exposition, falling action, and resolution.

- Reading a short story well involves determining the theme, often by paying attention to what befalls the main character.

- Notice whether the narrator is inside the story (first-person point of view) or outside the story (third-person point of view).

- To help you stay engaged as you read a story, think of your own adjectives to describe the characters and the narrator.

Elements of Short Stories

- **Plot** is what happens in a story.
- **Setting** is where the story takes place.
- **Characters** are the people in a story.
- The **theme** is the story's most meaningful message.
- The **narrator** tells the story.
- **Voice** refers to the kind of language the narrator uses to tell the story.

LOG ON ▶ **Literature** Online

Unit Resources For additional skills practice, go to glencoe.com and enter QuickPass code GL57805u1.

Activities

Use what you have learned about reading and analyzing short stories to complete one of the following activities.

1. Literary Analysis Think about the old man in "Old Man at the Bridge." What is he focused on? Based on this, what guess can you make about his state of mind? Support your inference with details from the story.

2. Speaking and Listening In a small group, discuss the theme of "Old Man at the Bridge." Give each group member a chance to choose a line from the story and explain how it contributes to the theme.

3. Take Notes Try using this study organizer to make inferences and draw conclusions about the literary elements in the stories in Unit 1. Record text evidence to support your inferences and conclusions.

 FOLDABLES STUDY ORGANIZER

Plot
Setting
Theme
Character
Narrator
Voice

See page R20 for folding instructions.

Encountering the Unexpected

Accident in the Hall of Mirrors, 1999. Graeme Wilcox. Acrylic on canvas, 128 x 158 cm.

View the Art Wilcox has painted realistic figures that appear as if they are in a mirror. How are the reflections different from what you would expect? How does the center figure seem to react to his image?

BIG IDEA

People never know exactly what their futures will bring. Many people expect that tomorrow will be much like today. In the short stories in Part 1, you will encounter people and events that are not always what they initially seem to be. As you read these stories, ask yourself, How do people cope when they suddenly encounter the unexpected?

TEKS

For pages 8–9

10.5 Understand, make inferences and draw conclusions about the structure and elements of fiction and provide evidence from text to support understanding.

LITERARY FOCUS

Plot and Setting

How do plot and setting contribute to a story's meaning?

Think of a favorite story. Where does it take place? Can you imagine the same people, events, and themes happening somewhere else? Especially in a short story, where there is often only one setting, the setting can be an essential component of the tale being told. In Edgar Allan Poe's short stories, the macabre settings he so often uses are an integral part of his stories' characteristic twists and turns.

from "The Masque of the Red Death"

by Edgar Allan Poe

The second chamber was purple in its ornaments and tapestries, and here the panes were purple. The third was green throughout, and so were the casements. The fourth was furnished and lighted with orange—the fifth with white—the sixth with violet. The seventh apartment was closely shrouded in black velvet tapestries that hung all over the ceiling and down the walls, falling in heavy folds upon a carpet of the same material and hue. But in this chamber only, the color of the windows failed to correspond with the decorations. The panes here were scarlet—a deep blood color.

Plot

Plot is the sequence of events in a story—a series of related incidents. Plots usually involve a **conflict,** a struggle between opposing forces. An **external conflict** is a struggle between a character and an outside force, such as another character, nature, society, or fate. An **internal conflict** takes place within the mind of a character who struggles with opposing feelings or with indecision.

Most plots develop in five stages. **Exposition** introduces the story's characters, setting, and conflict. **Rising action** occurs as complications, twists, or intensifications of the conflict occur.

The **climax** is the story's most dramatic moment. **Falling action** is the logical result of the climax. The **resolution** presents the final outcome of the story. The events that make up the plot of "Cinderella" are shown in the diagram below.

Order of Events Authors vary the way they present plot events. They use **foreshadowing**—clues or hints to prepare readers for events that will happen later in the story. Authors also use **flashback**—an interruption in the chronological order of a story to tell an event that happened earlier.

CLIMAX

Cinderella dances with the prince, but leaves hurriedly at midnight, losing a slipper.

The stepsisters try to force their feet into the slipper. It fits Cinderella.

A fairy godmother appears and provides Cinderella with clothes, coach, and footman.

FALLING ACTION

Cinderella lives with her stepsisters and their mother. They make her wear rags and do all the hard work.

An invitation to a ball at the palace arrives.

Cinderella goes to the ball.

The prince says he will marry the woman whom the slipper fits.

Cinderella and the prince marry.

The stepsisters prepare for and go to the ball.

They live happily ever after.

EXPOSITION

RISING ACTION

RESOLUTION

Setting

Setting is the time and the place of a story. It also includes the customs, beliefs, and values of that time and place. An author can use the setting to create expectations in a reader. Then, the author can use those expectations to create a mood such as surprise, disappointment, or shock.

LOG ON **Literature** Online

Literature and Reading For more about literary elements, go to glencoe.com and enter QuickPass code GL57805u1.

Quickwrite

Analyze Structure Plot gives a story its structure. In the "Cinderella" example above, the plot progresses in chronological order. In a paragraph, draw a conclusion about how the structure of the story would differ if it began with Cinderella and the prince telling their story to their grandchildren.

Before You Read

The Open Window

Meet **Saki**

(1870–1916)

What if, as a child, you were locked away in a country house with two strict, bickering aunts as your guardians? How would you satisfy your desire for diversion? If you possessed the satiric humor, wit, and writing talents of Saki, you might have found satisfaction as he did, by writing stories.

Childhood Trials Hector Hugh Munro (Saki's real name) was the third child in an upper-class English family. He was born in the former British colony of Burma. When his mother was pregnant with her fourth child, the family returned to England, but she was killed in an accident before giving birth. Saki's father decided to return to Burma. He sent his three children to live with his mother and two unmarried sisters in an English village.

Saki's aunts were not at all suited to caring for children. They imposed strict rules and constantly quarreled with each other. Saki never forgot his childhood experiences and many of his stories feature tyrannical aunts and young children who wreak havoc on adults.

From Burma to London When Saki was 23, he took a position with the military police in Burma. He was enthralled by the region's exotic landscape, especially the wild animals. Munro's fascination with and respect for animals emerges as another repeated feature of his stories.

When he contracted malaria, Saki returned to England. After he was well, he moved to London to pursue his literary career. In 1900 his first work, *The Rise of the Russian Empire,* was published.

> *"The best stories of Munro are all of childhood, its humor and its comedy as well its cruelty and unhappiness."*
>
> —Graham Greene, from *The Best of Saki*

Finding Success Also in 1900, Saki began writing captions for political cartoons. It was at this time that he took his rather surprising pen name, the single name Saki, an allusion to the *Rubáiyát of Omar Khayyám,* a famous collection of poems.

Saki was able to focus solely on writing short stories from 1909 until 1914, when he joined the army to fight in World War I. Saki was mortally wounded on a French battlefield, but his literature lives on. Saki's stories and three novels have been published in the volume *The Complete Works of Saki,* and they continue to delight readers today.

LOG ON ▶ **Literature** Online

Author Search For more about Saki, go to glencoe.com and enter QuickPass code GL57805u1.

Literature and Reading Preview

Connect to the Short Story

Has your first impression of someone ever turned out to be wrong? Freewrite for a few minutes about a time when you were mistaken about a first impression.

Build Background

"The Open Window" takes place in the early 1900s at an English country house set on an estate with hunting grounds. At the time of this story, it was not unusual for upper-class families to welcome into their homes strangers who brought with them a letter of introduction from a mutual acquaintance.

Set Purposes for Reading

Big Idea Encountering the Unexpected

As you read "The Open Window," ask yourself, How does Saki use the twists and turns in the story to manipulate not only the characters but his readers as well?

Literary Element Flashback

A **flashback** is an interruption in a narrative that tells about something that happened before that point in the story or before the story began. As you read, ask yourself, How does Saki use flashback to give information that helps explain the main events of the story?

Reading Strategy Identify Sequence

To **identify sequence** is to recognize the order of events and structure in a literary work. As you read, ask yourself, What clues or signal words point to the chronological, or time, order of events?

....

Tip: Organize Events Use a sequence chart to put important events in the story in chronological order. Use the blue highlighted passages and questions to help you get started.

Sequence of Events

> **The first thing that happens is:**
> Framton Nuttel waits for Mrs. Sappleton with her niece Vera.

⬇

> **After that:**
> Vera asks Nuttel if he knows anything about her aunt, and he says, "Only her name and address."

TEKS

For pages 10–16

10.5 Understand, make inferences and draw conclusions about the structure and elements of fiction and provide evidence from text to support understanding.

Vocabulary

self-possessed (self′ pə zest′) *adj.* in control of oneself; composed; p. 12 *Many people were nervous, but she was completely self-possessed.*

duly (doo′ lē) *adv.* rightfully; suitably; p. 12 *He was duly impressed with the grand house.*

infirmity (in fur′ mə tē) *n.* a weakness or an ailment; p. 13 *He once was a vibrant, energetic man, but age and infirmity had slowed him down.*

imminent (im′ ə nənt) *adj.* likely to happen soon; p. 14 *Dark, thick clouds are gathering, and rain seems imminent.*

The Open Window

Saki

My aunt will be down presently, Mr. Nuttel," said a very **self-possessed** young lady of fifteen; "in the meantime you must try and put up with me."

Framton Nuttel endeavored to say the correct something which should **duly** flatter the niece of the moment without unduly discounting the aunt that was to come. Privately he doubted more than ever whether these formal visits on a succession of total strangers would do much towards helping the nerve cure which he was supposed to be undergoing.

"I know how it will be," his sister had said when he was preparing to migrate to this rural retreat; "you will bury yourself down there and not speak to a living soul, and your nerves will be worse than ever from moping. I shall just give you letters of introduction to all the people I know there. Some of them, as far as I can remember, were quite nice."

Framton wondered whether Mrs. Sappleton, the lady to whom he was presenting one of the letters of introduction, came into the nice division.

"Do you know many of the people round here?" asked the niece, when she judged that they had had sufficient silent communion.

"Hardly a soul," said Framton. "My sister was staying here, at the rectory, you know, some four years ago, and she gave me letters of introduction to some of the people here."

He made the last statement in a tone of distinct regret.

"Then you know practically nothing about my aunt?" pursued the self-possessed young lady.

"Only her name and address," admitted the caller. He was wondering whether Mrs. Sappleton was in the married or widowed

---

Flashback *What information does the flashback in this paragraph provide? How does this contribute to the plot?*

Vocabulary

self-possessed (self´ pə zest´) *adj.* in control of oneself; composed

duly (dōō´ lē) *adv.* rightfully; suitably

Identify Sequence *Is this taking place before or after Framton Nuttel's arrival at the Sappletons' home? Explain how it relates to the flashback that precedes it.*

state. An undefinable something about the room seemed to suggest masculine habitation.

"Her great tragedy happened just three years ago," said the child; "that would be since your sister's time."

"Her tragedy?" asked Framton; somehow in this restful country spot tragedies seemed out of place.

"You may wonder why we keep that window wide open on an October afternoon," said the niece, indicating a large French window[1] that opened on to a lawn.

"It is quite warm for the time of the year," said Framton; "but has that window got anything to do with the tragedy?"

"Out through that window, three years ago to a day, her husband and her two young brothers went off for their day's shooting. They never came back. In crossing the moor to their favorite snipe-shooting ground they were all three engulfed in a treacherous piece of bog.[2] It had been that dreadful wet summer, you know, and places that were safe in other years gave way suddenly without warning. Their bodies were never recovered. That was the dreadful part of it." Here the child's voice lost its self-possessed note and became falteringly human. "Poor aunt always thinks that they will come back some day, they and the little brown spaniel that was lost with them, and walk in at that window just as they used to do. That is why the window is kept open every evening till it is quite dusk. Poor dear aunt, she has often told me how they went out, her husband with his white waterproof coat over his arm, and Ronnie, her youngest brother, singing, 'Bertie, why do you bound?' as he always did to tease her, because she said it got on her nerves. Do you know, sometimes on still, quiet evenings like this, I almost get a creepy feeling that they will all walk in through that window—"

She broke off with a little shudder. It was a relief to Framton when the aunt bustled into the room with a whirl of apologies for being late in making her appearance.

"I hope Vera has been amusing you?" she said.

"She has been very interesting," said Framton.

"I hope you don't mind the open window," said Mrs. Sappleton briskly; "my husband and brothers will be home directly from shooting, and they always come in this way. They've been out for snipe in the marshes today, so they'll make a fine mess over my poor carpets. So like you men-folk, isn't it?"

She rattled on cheerfully about the shooting and the scarcity of birds, and the prospects for duck in the winter. To Framton it was all purely horrible. He made a desperate but only partially successful effort to turn the talk on to a less ghastly topic; he was conscious that his hostess was giving him only a fragment of her attention, and her eyes were constantly straying past him to the open window and the lawn beyond. It was certainly an unfortunate coincidence that he should have paid his visit on this tragic anniversary.

"The doctors agree in ordering me complete rest, an absence of mental excitement, and avoidance of anything in the nature of violent physical exercise," announced Framton, who labored under the tolerably wide-spread delusion that total strangers and chance acquaintances are hungry for the least detail of one's ailments and **infirmities,** their

---

1. A *French window* is a pair of door-like windows hinged at opposite sides and opening in the middle.
2. A *moor* is a tract of open, rolling, wild land, often having marshes. *Snipe* are wetland game birds. A *bog* is a marshy area.

Identify Sequence *What is the sequence of events that leads up to Nuttel wanting to change the topic?*

infirmity (in fur′ mə tē) *n.* a weakness or an ailment

At the Window, 1894. William Merritt Chase. Pastel and paper, 18.5 x 11 in. Brooklyn Museum of Art, NY. Gift of Mrs. Henry Wolf, Austin M. Wolf, and Hamilton A. Wolf.

View the Art What qualities might the girl in this drawing share with the niece in the story?

cause and cure. "On the matter of diet they are not so much in agreement," he continued.

"No?" said Mrs. Sappleton, in a voice which only replaced a yawn at the last moment. Then she suddenly brightened into alert attention—but not to what Framton was saying.

"Here they are at last!" she cried. "Just in time for tea, and don't they look as if they were muddy up to the eyes!"

Framton shivered slightly and turned towards the niece with a look intended to convey sympathetic comprehension. The child was staring out through the open window with dazed horror in her eyes. In a chill shock of nameless fear Framton swung round in his seat and looked in the same direction.

In the deepening twilight three figures were walking across the lawn towards the window; they all carried guns under their arms, and one of them was additionally burdened with a white coat hung over his shoulders. A tired brown spaniel kept close at their heels. Noiselessly they neared the house, and then a hoarse young voice chanted out of the dusk: "I said, Bertie, why do you bound?"

Framton grabbed wildly at his stick and hat; the hall door, the gravel drive, and the front gate were dimly noted stages in his headlong retreat. A cyclist coming along the road had to run into the hedge to avoid **imminent** collision.

"Here we are, my dear," said the bearer of the white mackintosh,[3] coming in through the window; "fairly muddy, but most of it's dry. Who was that who bolted out as we came up?"

"A most extraordinary man, a Mr. Nuttel," said Mrs. Sappleton; "could only talk about his illnesses, and dashed off without a word of good-bye or apology when you arrived. One would think he had seen a ghost."

"I expect it was the spaniel," said the niece calmly; "he told me he had a horror of dogs. He was once hunted into a cemetery somewhere on the banks of the Ganges by a pack of pariah[4] dogs, and had to spend the night in a newly dug grave with the creatures snarling and grinning and foaming just above him. Enough to make any one lose their nerve." Romance[5] at short notice was her specialty. ❧

---

3. A *mackintosh* is a heavy-duty raincoat.
4. The *Ganges* is a river in northern India. A *pariah* is one who is shunned or despised by others. In India, where dogs are not highly regarded, packs of wild dogs are considered pariahs.
5. Here, *romance* means "tales of extraordinary or mysterious events."

Encountering the Unexpected *Why does Saki wait until the last line of the story to tell readers that telling tales was Vera's specialty?*

Vocabulary

imminent (im′ ə nənt) *adj.* likely to happen soon

After You Read

Respond and Think Critically

1. **Connect to Personal Experience** What was your reaction to Vera and Framton Nuttel?

2. **Interpret Characters** Why does Framton Nuttel visit Mrs. Sappleton? What do you think Vera notices about Nuttel as they sit in silence and wait for Mrs. Sappleton?

3. **Interpret Exposition** What makes it possible for Vera to fool Nuttel? Explain your answer and support it with evidence from the story. **OER**

4. **Make Inferences About Climax** What is Vera's reaction to the appearance of the three men returning from the moor? How do you think this contributes to Nuttel's reaction?

5. **Analyze Motivation** Reread Nuttel and Vera's first conversation on page 12. How might Vera's poise and self-confidence contribute to her believability? In analyzing Vera's behavior, what might you conclude about Vera's motives? Support your response with text evidence.

6. **Analyze Character** The author subtly plays with the idea of hunting in this story. How is Vera like a hunter and Framton Nuttel like her prey?

7. **Big Idea** **Draw Conclusions About Plot** Surprise reversals of events are common in Saki's stories. How does Saki employ this device in "The Open Window"? Identify the passage where the surprise becomes clear to the reader.

Literary Element Flashback

 Texas Test Practice (10.5.A)

1. How does Vera's lengthy flashback affect the plot as a whole?

   A. She reveals herself to be untrustworthy and mischievous.

   B. The hunting party is late returning.

   C. Mrs. Sappleton arrives late.

   D. Mr. Nuttel flees and is not able to calm his nerves by visiting his neighbors.

2. How does Vera's fanciful flashback have ironic consequences?

   F. Vera's aunt is puzzled by Mr. Nuttel's abrupt departure.

   G. The hunting party looks exactly the way Vera described it.

   H. Visiting his neighbors does nothing to help Mr. Nuttel's nerves.

   J. Mr. Nuttel believes every word of Vera's tall tale.

Review: Plot

As you learned on page 9, **plot** refers to the sequence of events in a story.

8. **Partner Activity** Meet with a classmate and work together to identify the plot elements of "The Open Window." Create a chart like the one below and fill it in with specific events from the story. Then analyze these isolated scenes and their contribution to the plot as a whole.

Plot Element	Contribution to the Plot
Exposition	Sets up the situation and introduces the characters
Rising Action	
Climax	
Falling Action	
Resolution	

Reading Strategy   Identify Sequence

Within the structure of "The Open Window" is a second narrative. That is the story that Vera tells Nuttel about her uncle's death while hunting on the moors. Review the blue highlighted passages and questions as well as the sequence chart you created on page 11.

9. Use your sequence chart to summarize the story.

10. What does the flashback between Nuttel and his sister contribute to the story? How would the ending of the story be affected if this flashback was not included?

Vocabulary Practice

Practice with Context Clues Identify the context clues in the following sentences that help you determine the meaning of each bold-faced vocabulary word.

1. The older daughter was always confident and **self-possessed,** unlike her nervous younger sister.

2. He was **duly** polite and spoke and acted like a perfect gentleman.

3. Although the long illness had weakened him, the man never complained of his **infirmity.**

4. We knew the arrival of the train was **imminent** when we heard its whistle and then saw light flash on the walls of the tunnel.

Academic Vocabulary

Vera's words and actions allow the reader to **deduce** *that she is creative, spontaneous, and, above all, mischievous.*

Deduce is an academic word. More familiar words and phrases that are similar in meaning are *figure out, infer,* and *conclude.* Show the meaning of **deduce** by completing this sentence starter: I **deduce** that Lauren is not coming to the party _____.

For more on academic vocabulary, see pages 36–37 and R92–R94.

Enrich and Extend

 Research and Report

Literary Criticism Evaluate literary criticism about Saki's work and write a short response in which you explain whether you agree or disagree that the criticism applies to "The Open Window" and to Vera. Present your response to the class.

Prepare Read the following quotation about Saki's work by critic Elizabeth Drew:

> *"The cruelty is certainly there, but it has nothing perverted or pathological about it…It is the genial heartlessness of the normal child, whose fantasies take no account of adult standards of human behavior."*

Determine your position on this quotation or another quotation you find. If you find another quotation, identify any unsubstantiated opinions in the critique. Then summarize the quotation in your own words and note the differences between a summary, which does not include opinions, and a critique, which does. For help with writing a summary, see page 35. Next, craft a thesis stating your position. Use a graphic organizer with story details to support your argument.

Report When you present your response, make eye contact, speak loudly and clearly, and maintain good posture to reflect confidence.

Evaluate Write a paragraph evaluating your report. When your classmates present, offer oral feedback on their performances.

 Literature Online

Selection Resources For Selection Quizzes, eFlash-cards, and Reading-Writing Connection activities, go to glencoe.com and enter QuickPass code GL57805u1.

Before You Read
Contents of the Dead Man's Pocket

Meet **Jack Finney**
(1911–1995)

The author of novels, short stories, and television screenplays, Jack Finney is most famous as a science-fiction writer. Perhaps his best-known work is the novel *The Body Snatchers*, which he published in 1955. Renamed and reissued a year later as *Invasion of the Body Snatchers*, this science-fiction thriller was adapted into a film three times. Each version became a cult classic.

When the novel was first released in the mid-1950s, a time of anti-communist sentiment, critics were quick to interpret it as an allegory based on the real fears of a communist takeover in the United States. Finney scoffed at that interpretation, claiming that his novel was nothing more than popular entertainment. "It was just a story meant to entertain, and with no more meaning than that," Finney once stated, adding that "the idea of writing a whole book in order to say that it's not really a good thing for us all to be alike . . . makes me laugh."

> "One should never use the word 'fun' as an adjective except when referring to the writings of Jack Finney."
>
> —*The San Francisco Examiner*

Born in Milwaukee, Wisconsin, Finney grew up in suburban Chicago. After graduating from Knox College in Galesburg, Illinois, Finney moved to New York City, where he worked as a writer for an advertising agency.

In 1946 he published his first short story, "The Widow's Walk," which won a special prize in an *Ellery Queen's Mystery Magazine* contest. After that breakthrough, he continued to write and publish short stories in many popular magazines, including *The Saturday Evening Post*, *Collier's*, and *McCall's*.

In the early 1950s, Finney, his wife, and their two children moved from New York City to Marin County, California. In 1954, he published his first novel, *5 Against the House*. That novel, *Assault on a Queen* (1959), and *Good Neighbor Sam* (1963) were all adapted into popular films.

After the success of *Invasion of the Body Snatchers*, Finney continued to write science fiction, although he resisted classification as a science-fiction author, considering himself a fantasy writer who was most interested in ordinary people's responses to extraordinary situations. In 1957 he published a short-story collection entitled *The Third Level*, which contains the story you are about to read.

LOG ON **Literature** Online

Author Search For more about Jack Finney, go to glencoe.com and enter QuickPass code GL57805u1.

Literature and Reading Preview

Connect to the Story

What are your priorities in life, and how well do you divide your attention among them? List your priorities. After each one, note whether you are spending the right amount of time on that priority.

Build Background

This story takes place in New York City during a time before personal computers and widespread use of photocopying machines. The main character types documents on a typewriter and uses carbon paper—thin, ink-coated sheets of paper placed between two pieces of writing paper—to make a copy of a document.

Set Purposes for Reading

Big Idea Encountering the Unexpected

As you read "Contents of the Dead Man's Pocket," ask yourself, How does Tom react when he encounters the unexpected?

Literary Element Conflict

Conflict is the struggle between opposing forces. An **external conflict** exists when a character struggles against an outside force, such as another person, nature, or society. An **internal conflict** is a struggle that takes place within the mind of a character who is torn between opposing feelings or goals. A moral dilemma is one kind of internal conflict in which a character struggles to decide what is the right or wrong way to act. As you read, ask yourself, Which type of conflict does Tom experience?

Reading Strategy Respond to Characters

To **respond to characters** in a literary work, ask yourself questions about what you like and dislike, what surprises you, and how you feel about the characters' conflicts and moral dilemmas. As you read the story, ask yourself, How do Tom's dilemmas make me feel? How do they compare with characters' dilemmas in other stories I've read?

....

Tip: Take Notes Note your reactions to characters as you read, especially your reactions to Tom's moral dilemmas.

Character's Action	My Response

TEKS

For pages 17–34

10.5.B Analyze differences in the characters' moral dilemmas in works of fiction across different countries or cultures.

Vocabulary

convoluted (kon′və loo′tid) *adj.* turned in or wound up upon itself; coiled; twisted; p. 21 *Instead of a flat piece of wood, the ornate, antique railing was convoluted.*

improvised (im′prə vīzd′) *adj.* invented, composed, or done without preparation; p. 22 *I was unprepared for John's strange question and had to give an improvised answer.*

taut (tôt) *adj.* tense; tight; p. 23 *The leash grew taut and straight when the dog leaped forward.*

pent-up (pent′ up) *adj.* not expressed or released; held in; p. 26 *I remained calm until I hung up the phone, but then my pent-up feelings made me burst into tears.*

reveling (rev′əl ing) *adj.* taking great pleasure; p. 26 *Reveling in delight, the little boy ran up and down the aisle of toys.*

....

Tip: Analogies To solve an analogy, remember that the relationship might be a synonym, an antonym, a part to whole, or an object and a key quality of the object.

Contents of the Dead Man's Pocket

Jack Finney

Room in New York, 1932. Edward Hopper. Oil on canvas, 29 x 36 in. Sheldon Memorial Art Gallery, University of Nebraska–Lincoln, F. M. Hall Collection. 1936.H-166.

At the little living-room desk Tom Benecke rolled two sheets of flimsy and a heavier top sheet, carbon paper sandwiched between them, into his portable.[1] *Inter-office Memo,* the top sheet was headed, and he typed tomorrow's date just below this; then he glanced at a creased yellow sheet, covered with his own hand-writing, beside the typewriter. "Hot in here," he muttered to himself. Then, from the short hallway at his back, he heard the muffled clang of wire coat hangers in the bedroom closet, and at this reminder of what his wife was doing he thought: Hot, hell—guilty conscience.

He got up, shoving his hands into the back pockets of his gray wash slacks,[2] stepped to the living-room window beside the desk and stood breathing on the glass, watching the expanding circlet of mist, staring down through the autumn night at Lexington Avenue, eleven stories below. He was a tall, lean, dark-haired young man in a pullover sweater, who looked as though he had played not football, probably, but basketball in college. Now he placed the heels of his hands against the top edge of the lower window frame and shoved upward. But as usual the window didn't budge, and he had to lower his hands and then shoot them hard upward to jolt the window open a few inches. He dusted his hands, muttering.

But still he didn't begin his work. He crossed the room to the hallway entrance and, leaning against the doorjamb, hands shoved into his back pockets again, he called, "Clare?" When his wife answered, he said, "Sure you don't mind going alone?"

"No." Her voice was muffled, and he knew her head and shoulders were in the bedroom closet. Then the tap of her high heels sounded on the wood floor and she appeared at the end of the little hallway,

---

Reference, 1991. Jeremy Annett. Oil on canvas. Private collection.

<u>View the Art</u> This painting shows a room filled with papers and books. What do these items tell you about the personality traits of the room's occupant? Are any of these traits shared by Tom?

wearing a slip, both hands raised to one ear, clipping on an earring. She smiled at him—a slender, very pretty girl with light brown, almost blonde, hair—her prettiness emphasized by the pleasant nature that showed in her face. "It's just that I hate you to miss this movie; you wanted to see it too." "Yeah, I know." He ran his fingers through his hair. "Got to get this done though."

She nodded, accepting this. Then, glancing at the desk across the living room, she said, "You work too much, though, Tom—and too hard."

He smiled. "You won't mind though, will you, when the money comes rolling in and I'm known as the Boy Wizard of Wholesale Groceries?"

"I guess not." She smiled and turned back toward the bedroom.

At his desk again, Tom lighted a cigarette; then a few moments later as Clare appeared, dressed and ready to leave, he set it on the rim of the ash tray. "Just after seven," she said. "I can make the beginning of the first feature."

He walked to the front-door closet to help her on with her coat. He kissed her then and, for an instant, holding her close, smelling the perfume she had used, he was tempted to go with her; it was not actually true that he had to work tonight, though he very much wanted to. This was his own project, unannounced as yet in his office, and it could be postponed. But then they won't see it till Monday, he thought once again, and if I give it to the boss tomorrow he might read it over the week-end . . . "Have a good time," he said aloud. He gave his wife a little swat and opened the door for her, feeling the air from the building hallway, smelling faintly of floor wax, stream gently past his face.

He watched her walk down the hall, flicked a hand in response as she waved, and then he started to close the door, but it resisted for a moment. As the door opening narrowed, the current of warm air from the

---

Respond to Characters *How do you feel about Tom's decision to miss the movie? Would you have made the same choice?*

Conflict *What exterior conflict is implied by the dialogue at the top of this column between Tom and his wife, Clare?*

hallway, channeled through this smaller opening now, suddenly rushed past him with accelerated force. Behind him he heard the slap of the window curtains against the wall and the sound of paper fluttering from his desk, and he had to push to close the door.

Turning, he saw a sheet of white paper drifting to the floor in a series of arcs, and another sheet, yellow, moving toward the window, caught in the dying current flowing through the narrow opening. As he watched, the paper struck the bottom edge of the window and hung there for an instant, plastered against the glass and wood. Then as the moving air stilled completely the curtains swinging back from the wall to hang free again, he saw the yellow sheet drop to the window ledge and slide over out of sight.

He ran across the room, grasped the bottom edge of the window and tugged, staring through the glass. He saw the yellow sheet, dimly now in the darkness outside, lying on the ornamental ledge a yard below the window. Even as he watched, it was moving, scraping slowly along the ledge, pushed by the breeze that pressed steadily against the building wall. He heaved on the window with all his strength and it shot open with a bang, the window weight rattling in the casing. But the paper was past his reach and, leaning out into the night, he watched it scud[3] steadily along the ledge to the south, half plastered against the building wall. Above the muffled sound of the street traffic far below, he could hear the dry scrape of its movement, like a leaf on the pavement.

The living room of the next apartment to the south projected a yard or more farther out toward the street than this one; because of this the Beneckes paid seven and a half dollars less rent than their neighbors. And now the yellow sheet, sliding along the stone ledge, nearly invisible in the night,

was stopped by the projecting blank wall of the next apartment. It lay motionless, then, in the corner formed by the two walls—a good five yards away, pressed firmly against the ornate corner ornament of the ledge, by the breeze that moved past Tom Benecke's face.

He knelt at the window and stared at the yellow paper for a full minute or more, waiting for it to move, to slide off the ledge and fall, hoping he could follow its course to the street, and then hurry down in the elevator and retrieve it. But it didn't move, and then he saw that the paper was caught firmly between a projection of the **convoluted** corner ornament and the ledge. He thought about the poker from the fireplace, then the broom, then the mop—discarding each thought as it occurred to him. There was nothing in the apartment long enough to reach that paper.

It was hard for him to understand that he actually had to abandon it—it was ridiculous—and he began to curse. Of all the papers on his desk, why did it have to be this one in particular! On four long Saturday afternoons he had stood in supermarkets counting the people who passed certain displays, and the results were scribbled on that yellow sheet. From stacks of trade publications, gone over page by page in snatched half hours at work and during evenings at home, he had copied facts, quotations and figures onto that sheet. And he had carried it with him to the Public Library on Fifth Avenue, where he'd spent a dozen lunch hours and early evenings adding more. All were needed to support and lend authority to his idea for a new grocery-store display method; without them his idea was a mere opinion. And there they all lay, in his own

---

3. To *scud* is to run or move swiftly.

Vocabulary

convoluted (kon′ və lōō′ tid) *adj.* turned in or wound up upon itself; coiled; twisted improvised shorthand—countless hours of work—out there on the ledge.

For many seconds he believed he was going to abandon the yellow sheet, that there was nothing else to do. The work could be duplicated. But it would take two months, and the time to present this idea, was now, for use in the spring displays. He struck his fist on the window ledge. Then he shrugged. Even though his plan were adopted, he told himself, it wouldn't bring him a raise in pay—not immediately, anyway, or as a direct result. It won't bring me a promotion either, he argued—not of itself.

But just the same, and he couldn't escape the thought, this and other independent projects, some already done and others planned for the future, would gradually mark him out from the score of other young men in his company. They were the way to change from a name on the payroll to a name in the minds of the company officials. They were the beginning of the long, long climb to where he was determined to be, at the very top. And he knew he was going out there in the darkness, after the yellow sheet fifteen feet beyond his reach.

> The mental picture of himself sidling along the ledge outside was absurd—

By a kind of instinct, he instantly began making his intention acceptable to himself by laughing at it. The mental picture of himself sidling along the ledge outside was absurd—it was actually comical—and he smiled. He imagined himself describing it; it would make a good story at the office and, it occurred to him, would add a special interest and importance to his memorandum, which would do it no harm at all.

To simply go out and get his paper was an easy task—he could be back here with it in less than two minutes—and he knew he wasn't deceiving himself. The ledge, he saw, measuring it with his eye, was about as wide as the length of his shoe, and perfectly flat. And every fifth row of brick in the face of the building, he remembered—leaning out, he verified this—was indented half an inch, enough for the tips of his fingers, enough to maintain balance easily. It occurred to him that if this ledge and wall were only a yard aboveground—as he knelt at the window staring out, this thought was the final confirmation of his intention—he could move along the ledge indefinitely.

On a sudden impulse, he got to his feet, walked to the front closet and took out an old tweed jacket, it would be cold outside. He put it on and buttoned it as he crossed the room rapidly toward the open window. In the back of his mind he knew he'd better hurry and get this over with before he thought too much, and at the window he didn't allow himself to hesitate.

Encountering the Unexpected *How has the unexpected experience of losing the yellow paper affected Tom so far?*

Respond to Characters *What is Tom's highest priority? How do you feel about his priorities?*

Vocabulary

improvised (im′ prə vīzd′) *adj.* invented, composed, or done without preparation

Encountering the Unexpected *How does Tom try to combat his fear of falling?*

He swung a leg over the sill, then felt for and found the ledge a yard below the window with his foot. Gripping the bottom of the window frame very tightly and carefully, he slowly ducked his head under it, feeling on his face the sudden change from the warm air of the room to the chill outside. With infinite care he brought out his other leg, his mind concentrating on what he was doing. Then he slowly stood erect. Most of the putty, dried out and brittle, had dropped off the bottom edging of the window frame, he found, and the flat wooden edging provided a good gripping surface, a half inch or more deep, for the tips of his fingers.

Now, balanced easily and firmly, he stood on the ledge outside in the slight, chill breeze, eleven stories above the street, staring into his own lighted apartment, odd and different-seeming now.

First his right hand, then his left, he carefully shifted his finger-tip grip from the puttyless window edging to an indented row of bricks directly to his right. It was hard to take the first shuffling sideways step then—to make himself move—and the fear stirred in his stomach, but he did it, again by not allowing himself time to think. And now—with his chest, stomach, and the left side of his face pressed against the rough cold brick—his lighted apartment was suddenly gone, and it was much darker out here than he had thought.

Without pause he continued—right foot, left foot, right foot, left—his shoe soles shuffling and scraping along the rough stone, never lifting from it, fingers sliding along the exposed edging of brick. He moved on the balls of his feet, heels lifted slightly; the ledge was not quite as wide as he'd expected. But leaning slightly inward toward the face of the building and pressed against it, he could feel his balance firm and secure, and moving along the ledge was quite as easy as he had thought it would be. He could hear the buttons of his jacket scraping steadily along the rough bricks and feel them catch momentarily, tugging a little, at each mortared crack. He simply did not permit himself to look down, though the compulsion to do so never left him; nor did he allow himself actually to think. Mechanically—right foot, left foot, over and again—he shuffled along crabwise, watching the projecting wall ahead loom steadily closer. . . .

Then he reached it and, at the corner—he'd decided how he was going to pick up the paper—he lifted his right foot and placed it carefully on the ledge that ran along the projecting wall at a right angle to the ledge on which his other foot rested. And now, facing the building, he stood in the corner formed by the two walls, one foot on the ledging of each, a hand on the shoulder-high indentation of each wall. His forehead was pressed directly into the corner against the cold bricks, and now he carefully lowered first one hand, then the other, perhaps a foot farther down, to the next indentation in the rows of bricks.

Very slowly, sliding his forehead down the trough of the brick corner and bending his knees, he lowered his body toward the paper lying between his outstretched feet. Again he lowered his fingerholds another foot and bent his knees still more, thigh muscles **taut**, his forehead sliding and bumping down the brick V. Half squatting now, he dropped his left hand to the next indentation and then slowly reached with his right hand toward the paper between his feet.

Respond to Characters *What is your reaction to Tom's situation in the first paragraph in this column?*

Vocabulary

taut (tôt) *adj.* tense; tight

Conflict *What is Tom's internal conflict in the third paragraph in this column?*

Crystallized Abstraction (Day), 2001. Diana Ong. Computer graphics.

__View the Art__ How does Diana Ong's use of color, lines, and shapes reflect the mood of the story and the crisis that Tom is facing?

He couldn't quite touch it, and his knees now were pressed against the wall; he could bend them no farther. But by ducking his head another inch lower, the top of his head now pressed against the bricks, he lowered his right shoulder and his fingers had the paper by a corner, pulling it loose. At the same instant he saw, between his legs and far below, Lexington Avenue stretched out for miles ahead.

He saw, in that instant, the Loew's theater sign, blocks ahead past Fiftieth Street; the miles of traffic signals, all green now; the lights of cars and street lamps; countless neon signs; and the moving black dots of people. And a violent instantaneous explosion of absolute terror roared through him. For a motionless instant he saw himself externally—bent practically double, balanced on this narrow ledge, nearly half his body projecting out above the street far below—and he began to tremble violently, panic flaring through his mind and muscles, and he felt the blood rush from the surface of his skin.

In the fractional moment before horror paralyzed him, as he stared between his legs

Respond to Characters *Why does Tom feel a surge of terror when he actually grasps the yellow paper?*

at that terrible length of street far beneath him, a fragment of his mind raised his body in a spasmodic jerk to an upright position again, but so violently that his head scraped hard against the wall, bouncing off it, and his body swayed outward to the knife edge of balance, and he very nearly plunged backward and fell. Then he was leaning far into the corner again, squeezing and pushing into it, not only his face but his chest and stomach, his back arching; and his fingertips clung with all the pressure of his pulling arms to the shoulder-high half-inch indentation in the bricks.

He was more than trembling now; his whole body was racked with a violent shuddering beyond control, his eyes squeezed so tightly shut it was painful, though he was past awareness of that. His teeth were exposed in a frozen grimace, the strength draining like water from his knees and calves. It was extremely likely, he knew, that he would faint, to slump down along the wall, his face scraping, and then drop backward, a limp weight, out into nothing. And to save his life he concentrated on holding onto consciousness, drawing deliberate deep breaths of cold air into his lungs, fighting to keep his senses aware.

Then he knew that he would not faint, but he could not stop shaking nor open his eyes. He stood where he was, breathing deeply, trying to hold back the terror of the glimpse he had of what lay below him; and he knew he had made a mistake in not making himself stare down at the street, getting used to it and accepting it, when he had first stepped out onto the ledge.

It was impossible to walk back. He simply could not do it. He couldn't bring himself to make the slightest movement. The strength was gone from his legs; his shivering hands—numb, cold and desperately rigid—had lost all deftness; his easy ability to move and balance was gone. Within a step or two, if he tried to move, he knew that he would stumble clumsily and fall.

Seconds passed, with the chill faint wind pressing the side of his face, and he could hear the toned-down volume of the street traffic far beneath him. Again and again he slowed and then stopped, almost to silence; then presently, even this high, he would hear the click of the traffic signals and the subdued roar of the cars starting up again. During a lull in the street sounds, he called out. Then he was shouting *"Help!"* so loudly it rasped his throat. But he felt the steady pressure of the wind, moving between his face and the blank wall, snatch up his cries as he uttered them, and he knew they must sound directionless and distant. And he remembered how habitually, here in New York, he himself heard and ignored shouts in the night. If anyone heard him, there was no sign of it, and presently Tom Benecke knew he had to try moving; there was nothing else he could do.

Eyes squeezed shut, he watched scenes in his mind like scraps of motion-picture film—he could not stop them. He saw himself stumbling suddenly sideways as he crept along the ledge and saw his upper body arc outward, arms flailing. He saw a dangling shoestring caught between the ledge and the sole of his other shoe, saw a foot start to move, to be stopped with a jerk, and felt his balance leaving him. He saw himself falling with a terrible speed as his body revolved in the air, knees clutched tight to his chest, eyes squeezed shut, moaning softly.

Out of utter necessity, knowing that any of these thoughts might be reality in the very next seconds, he was slowly able to shut his mind against every thought but what he now began to do. With fear-soaked slowness, he slid his left foot an inch or two toward his own impossibly

Encountering the Unexpected *What other unexpected experiences does Tom have once he is on the ledge?*

distant window. Then he slid the fingers of his shivering left hand a corresponding distance. For a moment he could not bring himself to lift his right foot from one ledge to the other; then he did it, and became aware of the harsh exhalation of air from his throat and realized that he was panting. As his right hand, then, began to slide along the brick edging, he was astonished to feel the yellow paper pressed to the bricks underneath his stiff fingers, and he uttered a terrible, abrupt bark that might have been a laugh or a moan. He opened his mouth and took the paper in his teeth, pulling it out from under his fingers.

By a kind of trick—by concentrating his entire mind on first his left foot, then his left hand, then the other foot, then the other hand—he was able to move, almost imperceptibly, trembling steadily, very nearly without thought. But he could feel the terrible strength of the **pent-up** horror on just the other side of the flimsy barrier he had erected in his mind; and he knew that if it broke through he would lose this thin artificial control of his body.

During one slow step he tried keeping his eyes closed; it made him feel safer, shutting him off a little from the fearful reality of where he was. Then a sudden rush of giddiness swept over him and he had to open his eyes wide, staring sideways at the cold rough brick and angled lines of mortar, his cheek tight against the building. He kept his eyes open then, knowing that if he once let them flick outward, to stare for an instant at the lighted windows across the street, he would be past help.

He didn't know how many dozens of tiny sidling steps he had taken, his chest, belly and face pressed to the wall; but he knew the slender hold he was keeping on his mind and body was going to break. He had a sudden mental picture of his apartment on just the other side of this wall— warm, cheerful, incredibly spacious. And he saw himself striding through it, lying down on the floor on his back, arms spread wide, **reveling** in its unbelievable security. The impossible remoteness of this utter safety, the contrast between it and where he now stood, was more than he could bear. And the barrier broke then, and the fear of the awful height he stood on coursed through his nerves and muscles.

A fraction of his mind knew he was going to fall, and he began taking rapid blind steps with no feeling of what he was doing, sidling with a clumsy desperate swiftness, fingers scrabbling along the brick, almost hopelessly resigned to the sudden backward pull and swift motion outward and down. Then his moving left hand slid onto not brick but sheer emptiness, an impossible gap in the face of the wall, and he stumbled.

His right foot smashed into his left anklebone; he staggered sideways, began falling, and the claw of his hand cracked against glass and wood, slid down it, and his finger tips were pressed hard on the puttyless edging of his window. His right hand smacked gropingly beside it as he fell to his knees; and, under the full weight and direct downward pull of his sagging body, the open window dropped

---

Respond to Characters *In the first paragraph in this column, how does Tom try to cope with his fear?*

Vocabulary

pent-up (pent´ up) *adj.* not expressed or released; held in

Conflict *What feeling is Tom attempting to overcome in the first paragraph in this column?*

Vocabulary

reveling (rev´əl ing) *adj.* taking great pleasure

shudderingly in its frame till it closed and his wrists struck the sill and were jarred off.

For a single moment he knelt, knee bones against stone on the very edge of the ledge, body swaying and touching nowhere else, fighting for balance. Then he lost it, his shoulders plunging backward, and he flung his arms forward, his hands smashing against the window casing on either side; and—his body moving backward—his fingers clutched the narrow wood stripping of the upper pane.

For an instant he hung suspended between balance and falling, his finger tips pressed onto the quarter-inch wood strips. Then, with utmost delicacy, with a focused concentration of all his senses, he increased even further the strain on his finger tips hooked to these slim edgings of wood. Elbows slowly bending, he began to draw the full weight of his upper body forward, knowing that the instant his fingers slipped off these quarter-inch strips he'd plunge backward and be falling. Elbows imperceptibly bending, body shaking with the strain, the sweat starting from his forehead in great sudden drops, he pulled, his entire being and thought concentrated in his finger tips. Then suddenly, the strain slackened and ended, his chest touching the window sill, and he was kneeling on the ledge, his forehead pressed to the glass of the closed window.

Dropping his palms to the sill, he stared into his living room—at the red-brown davenport across the room, and a magazine he had left there; at the pictures on the walls and the gray rug; the entrance to the hallway; and at his papers, typewriter and desk, not two feet from his nose. A movement from his desk caught his eye and he saw that it was a thin curl of blue smoke; his cigarette, the ash long, was still burning in the ash tray where he'd left it—this was past all belief—only a few minutes before.

His head moved, and in faint reflection from the glass before him he saw the yellow paper clenched in his front teeth. Lifting a hand from the sill he took it from his mouth; the moistened corner parted from the paper, and he spat it out.

> he drew back his right hand, palm facing the glass, and then struck the glass with the heel of his hand.

For a moment, in the light from the living room, he stared wonderingly at the yellow sheet in his hand and then crushed it into the side pocket of his jacket.

He couldn't open the window. It had been pulled not completely closed, but its lower edge was below the level of the outside sill; there was no room to get his fingers underneath it. Between the upper sash and the lower was a gap not wide enough—reaching up, he tried—to get his fingers into; he couldn't push it open. The upper window panel, he knew from long experience, was impossible to move, frozen tight with dried paint.

Very carefully observing his balance, the finger tips of his left hand again hooked to the narrow stripping of the window casing, he drew back his right hand, palm facing the glass, and then struck the glass with the heel of his hand.

His arm rebounded from the pane, his body tottering, and he knew he didn't dare strike a harder blow.

But in the security and relief of his new position, he simply smiled; with only a sheet of glass between him and the room just before him, it was not possible that

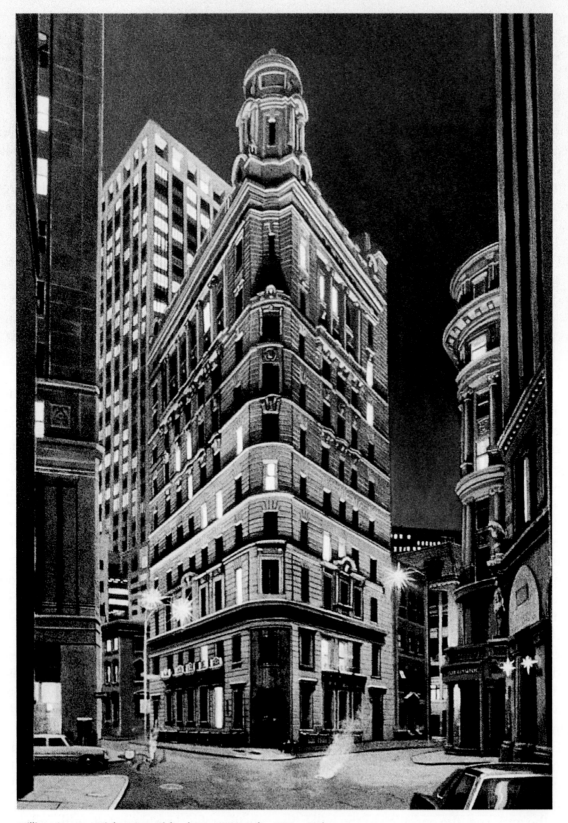

William Street at Night, 1981. Richard Haas. Watercolor, 33¼ x 23 in.

View the Art This painting depicts a grand city building. Is this the sort of building you imagine Tom living in? Why or why not?

there wasn't a way past it. Eyes narrowing, he thought for a few moments about what to do. Then his eyes widened, for nothing occurred to him. But still he felt calm: the trembling, he realized, had stopped. At the back of his mind there still lay the thought that once he was again in his home, he could give release to his feelings. He actually would lie on the floor, rolling, clenching tufts of the rug in his hands. He would literally run across the room, free to move as he liked, jumping on the floor, testing and reveling in its absolute security, letting the relief flood through him, draining the fear from his mind and body. His yearning for this was astonishingly intense, and somehow he understood that he had better keep this feeling at bay.

He took a half dollar from his pocket and struck it against the pane, but without any hope that the glass would break and with very little disappointment when it did not. After a few moments of thought he drew his leg up onto the ledge and picked loose the knot of his shoelace. He slipped off the shoe and, holding it across the instep, drew back his arm as far as he dared and struck the leather heel against the glass. The pane rattled, but he knew he'd been a long way from breaking it. His foot was cold and he slipped the shoe back on. He shouted again, experimentally, and then once more, but there was no answer.

The realization suddenly struck him that he might have to wait here till Clare came home, and for a moment the thought was funny. He could see Clare opening the front door, withdrawing her key from the lock, closing the door behind her and then glancing up to see him crouched on the other side of the window. He could see her rush across the room, face astounded and frightened, and hear himself shouting instructions: "Never mind how I got here! Just open the wind—" She couldn't open it, he remembered, she'd never been able to; she'd always had to call him. She'd have to get the building superintendent or a neighbor, and he pictured himself smiling and answering their questions as he climbed in. "I just wanted to get a breath of fresh air, so—"

He couldn't possibly wait here till Clare came home. It was the second feature she'd wanted to see, and she'd left in time to see the first. She'd be another three hours or—He glanced at his watch; Clare had been gone eight minutes. It wasn't possible, but only eight minutes ago he had kissed his wife good-by. She wasn't even at the theater yet!

It would be four hours before she could possibly be home, and he tried to picture himself kneeling out here, finger tips hooked to these narrow strippings, while first one movie, preceded by a slow listing of credits, began, developed, reached its climax and then finally ended. There'd be a newsreel next, maybe, and then an animated cartoon, and then interminable scenes from coming pictures. And then, once more, the beginning of a full-length picture—while all the time he hung out here in the night.

He might possibly get to his feet, but he was afraid to try. Already his legs were cramped, his thigh muscles tired; his knees hurt, his feet felt numb and his hands were stiff. He couldn't possibly stay out here for four hours, or anywhere near it. Long before that his legs and arms would give out; he would be forced to try changing his position often—stiffly, clumsily, his coordination and strength gone—and he would fall. Quite

Respond to Characters *How have your feelings toward Tom changed? Explain.*

Encountering the Unexpected *What does Tom do on the ledge to try to regain his composure?*

realistically, he knew that he would fall; no one could stay out here on this ledge for four hours.

A dozen windows in the apartment building across the street were lighted. Looking over his shoulder, he could see the top of a man's head behind the newspaper he was reading; in another window he saw the blue-gray flicker of a television screen. No more than twenty-odd yards from his back were scores of people, and if just one of them would walk idly to his window and glance out. . . . For some moments he stared over his shoulder at the lighted rectangles, waiting. But no one appeared. The man reading his paper turned a page and then continued his reading. A figure passed another of the windows and was immediately gone.

In the inside pocket of his jacket he found a little sheaf of papers, and he pulled one out and looked at it in the light from the living room. It was an old letter, an advertisement of some sort; his name and address, in purple ink, were on a label pasted to the envelope. Gripping one end of the envelope in his teeth, he twisted it into a tight curl. From his shirt pocket he brought out a book of matches. He didn't dare let go the casing with both hands but, with the twist of paper in his teeth, he opened the matchbook with his free hand; then he bent one of the matches in two without tearing it from the folder, its red-tipped end now touching the striking surface. With his thumb, he rubbed the red tip across the striking area.

He did it again, then again, and still again, pressing harder each time, and the match suddenly flared, burning his thumb. But he kept it alight, cupping the matchbook in his hand and shielding it with his body. He held the flame to the paper in his mouth till it caught. Then he snuffed out the match flame with his thumb and forefinger, careless of the burn, and replaced the book in his pocket. Taking the paper twist in his hand, he held it flame down, watching the flame crawl up the paper, till it flared bright. Then he held it behind him over the street, moving it from side to side, watching it over his shoulder, the flame flickering and guttering in the wind.

There were three letters in his pocket and he lighted each of them, holding each till the flame touched his hand and then dropping it to the street below. At one point, watching over his shoulder while the last of the letters burned, he saw the man across the street put down his paper and stand—even seeming, to Tom, to glance toward his window. But when he moved, it was only to walk across the room and disappear from sight.

There were a dozen coins in Tom Benecke's pocket and he dropped them, three or four at a time. But if they struck anyone, or if anyone noticed their falling, no one connected them with their source, and no one glanced upward.

His arms had begun to tremble from the steady strain of clinging to this narrow perch, and he did not know what to do now and was terribly frightened. Clinging to the window stripping with one hand, he again searched his pockets. But now—he had left his wallet on his dresser when he'd changed clothes—there was nothing left but the yellow sheet. It occurred to him irrelevantly that his death on the sidewalk below would be an eternal mystery; the window closed—why, how, and from where could he have fallen? No one would be able to identify his body for a time, either—the thought was somehow unbearable and increased his fear. All they'd find

---

Respond to Characters *What does Tom's action with the matches suggest about his state?*

in his pockets would be the yellow sheet. Contents of the dead man's pockets, he thought, *one sheet of paper bearing penciled notations—incomprehensible.*

He understood fully that he might actually be going to die; his arms, maintaining his balance on the ledge, were trembling steadily now. And it occurred to him then with all the force of a revelation that, if he fell, all he was ever going to have out of life he would then, abruptly, have had. Nothing, then, could ever be changed; and nothing more—no least experience or pleasure—could ever be added to his life. He wished, then, that he had not allowed his wife to go off by herself tonight—and on similar nights. He thought of all the evenings he had spent away from her, working; and he regretted them. He thought wonderingly of his fierce ambition and of the direction his life had taken; he thought of the hours he'd spent by himself, filling the yellow sheet that had brought him out here. *Contents of the dead man's pockets,* he thought with sudden fierce anger, *a wasted life.*

He was simply not going to cling here till he slipped and fell; he told himself that now. There was one last thing he could try; he had been aware of it for some moments, refusing to think about it, but now he faced it. Kneeling here on the ledge, the finger tips of one hand pressed to the narrow strip of wood, he could, he knew, draw his other hand back a yard perhaps, fist clenched tight, doing it very slowly till he sensed the outer limit of balance, then, as hard as he was able from the distance, he could drive his fist forward against the glass. If it broke, his fist smashing through, he was safe; he might cut himself badly, and probably would, but with his arm inside the room, he would be secure. But if the glass did not

break, the rebound, flinging his arm back, would topple him off the ledge. He was certain of that.

He tested his plan. The fingers of his left hand clawlike on the little stripping, he drew back his other fist until his body began teetering backward. But he had no leverage now—he could feel that there would be no force to his swing—and he moved his fist slowly forward till he rocked forward on his knees again and could sense that his swing would carry its greatest force. Glancing down, however, measuring the distance from his fist to the glass, he saw that it was less than two feet.

It occurred to him that he could raise his arm over his head, to bring it down against the glass. But, experimenting in slow motion, he knew it would be an awkward girl-like blow without the force of a driving punch, and not nearly enough to break the glass.

Facing the window, he had to drive a blow from the shoulder, he knew now, at a distance of less than two feet; and he did not know whether it would break through the heavy glass. It might; he could picture it happening, he could feel it in the nerves of his arm. And it might not; he could feel that too—feel his fist striking this glass and being instantaneously flung back by the unbreaking pane, feel the fingers of his other hand breaking loose, nails scraping along the casing as he fell.

He waited, arm drawn back, fist balled, but in no hurry to strike; this pause, he knew, might be an extension of his life. And to live even a few seconds longer, he felt, even out here on this ledge in the night, was

---

Encountering the Unexpected *What other unexpected experiences do you think Tom will face in the future?*

Encountering the Unexpected *How might Tom be about to take a leap into the unknown as he attempts to break his window?*

Conflict *How has Tom resolved an internal conflict?*

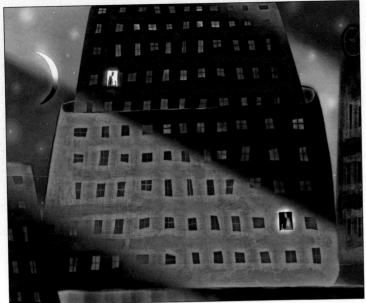

He heard the sound, felt the blow, felt himself falling forward, and his hand closed on the living-room curtains, the shards and fragments of glass showering onto the floor. And then, kneeling there on the ledge, an arm thrust into the room up to the shoulder, he began picking away the protruding slivers and great wedges of glass from the window frame, tossing them in onto the rug. And, as he grasped the edges of the empty window frame and climbed into his home, he was grinning in triumph.

He did not lie down on the floor or run through the apartment, as he had promised himself; even in the first few moments it seemed to him natural and normal that he should be where he was. He simply turned to his desk, pulled the crumpled yellow sheet from his pocket and laid it down where it had been, smoothing it out; then he absently laid a pencil across it to weight it down. He shook his head wonderingly, and turned to walk toward the closet.

There he got out his topcoat and hat and, without waiting to put them on, opened the front door and stepped out, to go find his wife. He turned to pull the door closed and warm air from the hall rushed through the narrow opening again. As he saw the yellow paper, the pencil flying, scooped off the desk and, unimpeded by the glassless window, sail out into the night and out of his life, Tom Benecke burst into laughter and then closed the door behind him. ∾

infinitely better than to die a moment earlier than he had to. His arm grew tired, and he brought it down and rested it.

Then he knew that it was time to make the attempt. He could not kneel here hesitating indefinitely till he lost all courage to act, waiting till he slipped off the ledge. Again he drew back his arm, knowing this time that he would not bring it down till he struck. His elbow protruding over Lexington Avenue far below, the fingers of his other hand pressed down bloodlessly tight against the narrow stripping, he waited, feeling the sick tenseness and terrible excitement building. It grew and swelled toward the moment of action, his nerves tautening. He thought of Clare—just a wordless, yearning thought—and then drew his arm back just a bit more, fist so tight his fingers pained him, and knowing he was going to do it. Then with full power, with every last scrap of strength he could bring to bear, he shot his arm forward toward the glass, and he said, *"Clare!"*

Respond to Characters *What do you think is most important to Tom at this point? How does this affect your opinion of him?*

Conflict *How has Tom resolved both internal and external conflicts?*

After You Read

Respond and Think Critically

1. **Connect to Personal Experience** Which part of the story did you react to most strongly? Explain.

2. **Explain Events** After Tom begins work, what happens to interrupt him, and what does he decide to do? What rules does he make up for himself, and why?

3. **Analyze Symbol** What does the yellow paper represent to Tom? How might his feelings about it have influenced his decision to retrieve it? Why do you think he reacts as he does when he sees the paper at the end of the story?

4. **Analyze Suspense** Tom was on the ledge for eight minutes, yet to the reader it seems much longer. How does Finney build suspense?

5. **Draw Conclusions About Resolution** What does Tom learn from his adventure? Support your answer with evidence from the story. **OER**

6. **Evaluate Plot** Do you think Tom's decision to go after the paper is realistic or does the author create an unbelievable situation? Support your response with evidence from the text.

7. **Big Idea** **Draw Conclusions About Message** What message is the author presenting about the unexpected situation that Tom finds himself in? Do you agree with the message? Explain.

You're the Critic

Allegory or Fantasy?

People often disagree about Finney's purpose for writing. Read this summary of the opposing viewpoints.

> *Many critics of Finney's novel* The Body Snatchers *interpreted the work as an allegory, a symbolic literary work in which the characters, settings, and events stand for things that are larger than themselves. The purpose of such an allegory is to teach a moral lesson. Some critics scoff at the idea of allegorical intent in Finney's work. They say that Finney's stories are just fun reading—suspenseful, thought-provoking fantasies. Finney was modest about his stories, saying that he just wanted to write about ordinary people's responses to extraordinary situations.*

Group Activity Discuss the following questions. Cite evidence from the story and from the critical summary.

1. Do you think Finney's intent was to write allegory or entertainment? Explain.

2. Do you think "Contents of the Dead Man's Pocket" fits the description of Finney's writing as an ordinary person's reaction to an extraordinary situation? Explain.

Literary Element Conflict

Sometimes a conflict can be both **internal** and **external**.

8. Draw Conclusions About Conflict Is Tom's conflict at the company where he works internal, external, or both? Cite evidence from the text to support your answer.

9. Compare and Contrast Moral Dilemmas Think of a story you have read that takes place in a country or culture different from the one in "Contents of the Dead Man's Pocket." How are the internal conflicts of characters in the other story similar to Tom Benecke's moral dilemma? How are they different? Support your response with evidence from the texts.

Review: Resolution

As you learned on page 9, the **resolution** is the part of a plot that reveals the outcome of the conflict. The resolution is sometimes called the *denouement,* a term that comes from a French word meaning "unknotting."

10. Partner Activity During a story's resolution, characters often act on lessons that they learned during the rising action and climax. Work with a classmate to complete a diagram similar to the one below, listing the lessons Tom learns during the course of the plot, and how he acts on them during the resolution.

Lessons Tom Learns → Tom's Action in Resolution

Not worth risking life for career →

Clare is what's most important to him →

LOG ON ▶ **Literature** Online

Selection Resources For Selection Quizzes, eFlashcards, and Reading-Writing Connection activities, go to glencoe.com and enter QuickPass code GL57805u1.

Reading Strategy Respond to Characters

When you **respond to characters** as you read, you are likely to get more from your reading. By paying attention to how characters make you feel, what questions they create for you, and how they might surprise you, you become more engaged in your reading. Refer to the blue highlighted questions and the chart you made on page 18.

11. How did you feel about Tom at the beginning of the story?

12. How did Tom's lying to Clare affect your opinion of him? Explain.

13. How did you feel about Tom at the end of the story? Did his response to his moral dilemma change your opinion of him? Explain.

Vocabulary Practice

Practice with Analogies Choose the word that best completes each analogy.

1. knot : convoluted :: sandpaper :
   a. tight   **b.** rough   **c.** smooth

2. tightrope : taut :: noodle :
   a. safe   **b.** delicate   **c.** slack

3. improvised : rehearsed :: temporary :
   a. voluntary   **b.** permanent   **c.** brief

4. pent-up : held in :: aggressive :
   a. forceful   **b.** relaxed   **c.** excited

5. reveling : pleasure :: weeping :
   a. sadness   **b.** crying   **c.** tears

Academic Vocabulary

*Tom's **document** represented so much effort—and so much expectation—that he risked his life for it.*

Document is a multiple-meaning word. In everyday conversation, someone might refer to any file on a computer as a **document**. Using context clues, figure out the meaning of the word in the sentence above about the story. Check your guess in a dictionary.

For more on academic vocabulary, see pages 36–37 and R92–R94.

Respond Through Writing

Summary

TEKS

10.13.A–E Use elements of the writing process (planning, drafting, editing, and publishing) to compose text.

Report Story Events When you write a summary of a story, you tell a short version of the original and report the main events in sequence. A summary does not include personal opinions. In about one hundred words, write a plot summary of "Contents of the Dead Man's Pocket." Write your plot summary in the present tense.

Purpose and Audience In a **plot summary**, your purpose is to report the main story events and also to explain the main characters' problems and how they are resolved. Your audience is a friend who read the story a long time ago and can't remember the plot.

Plan List the main events. Pare down the story to its key events. For each event, add details about the characters, setting, or conflict that are crucial to understanding what happens. This graphic organizer shows the key events and details needed to summarize "The Open Window."

1. Nuttel visiting Sappletons
   –in country for nerves
   –meets Vera

2. Vera's tale
   –uncle and cousins died hunting
   –aunt went mad; awaits return

3. Uncle and cousins return
   –Nuttel thinks they're ghosts; runs off
   –Vera made up deaths

Draft Write clearly and coherently using standard writing conventions. Use an objective tone throughout your summary. After naming the story and its author, introduce information that is at the core of the story, such as the main character, the conflict, or the setting; then retell the events in order. Use the following sentence frame to get started.

The story begins with _____.

Revise Revision is key to good writing. Ask a peer reader to identify the story, author, main character, conflict or problem, main events, and ending. Add or clarify anything your reader could not identify. Also ask your reader to identify any unnecessary details, and revise accordingly. As you revise, refine key ideas and organize them more logically and fluidly, and use language more precisely and effectively.

Edit Edit your paper, correcting any errors in grammar, spelling, and punctuation and making sure your language conforms to standard English. Use the Grammar Tip in the side column for help with using active and passive voice correctly.

> **Grammar Tip**
>
> **Active and Passive Voice**
>
> When summarizing a story, you should generally use the active voice, in which the subject of the sentence performs the action of the verb:
>
> *Vera **told** Nuttel about her aunt's tragedy.*
>
> A verb is in the passive voice when its action is performed on the subject. Sometimes, the passive voice is preferred or even necessary, such as when it's unclear who or what is performing an action, or if you want to emphasize the action rather than who performed it.
>
> *The window **was thrown** open.* [You don't know who opened it.]
>
> *The hunting party **was lost** on the moor.* [Emphasis on the action, not the subject.]

TEKS

For pages 36–37

10.1.A Determine the meaning of grade-level technical academic English words in multiple content areas (e.g., science, mathematics, social studies) derived from Latin, Greek, or other linguistic roots and affixes.

For a complete list of academic vocabulary words, see pages R92–R94.

Test-Taking Tip

These key academic vocabulary words often appear on standardized tests.

Analyze: to systematically and critically examine all parts of an issue or event

Classify or categorize: to put people, things, or ideas into groups, based on a common set of characteristics

Compare: to show how things are alike

Contrast: to show how things are different

Describe: to present a sketch or an impression

Discuss: to systematically write about all sides of an issue or event

Vocabulary Workshop

Academic Vocabulary

What Is Academic Vocabulary? Words that are commonly used in academic texts, such as textbooks, directions, and tests, are called **academic vocabulary.** Learning academic vocabulary is important because these words will help you read, write, and research in many academic areas. These words will also help you succeed on standardized tests.

Different Kinds of Words Some words are specific to certain disciplines, or areas of study. For example, the words *alliteration, foreshadowing,* and *metaphor* apply to literature. Other words, such as *concept, structure,* and *theory,* are used in many areas of study. The charts below show more examples of both kinds of words. Many academic vocabulary words have Latin or Greek roots and affixes, but some have other linguistic roots. Choose one academic word from each discipline in the first chart below and find its meaning and origin in a dictionary.

Discipline-Specific Words

Discipline	Words
Math	circumference, percentage, rectangle
Science	mitosis, chlorophyll, genus
Social Studies	confederation, federalism, antebellum

General Academic Vocabulary

process	perceive
survey	relevant
research	interpret
indicate	tradition

Academic Words in This Book You will learn about discipline-specific and general academic vocabulary words in this book. Words that are specific to literature and language arts will most often be introduced and explained in Literary Element and Reading Strategy features before and after you read literature texts. You will encounter more general academic vocabulary words in a feature called Academic Vocabulary. This feature appears in the After You Read pages following most literature texts.

Multiple-Meaning Words Many academic vocabulary words, such as *economy,* have more than one meaning. One meaning is the common definition you may be familiar with (*economy* means "the thrifty or efficient use of a material resource, such as money"). Other meanings are more academic and may be unfamiliar to you (*economy* also means "the efficient use of a nonmaterial resource, such as language"). The familiar and unfamiliar definitions are often related. In the case of *economy,* the two definitions are linked by the "efficient use of a resource." The chart below lists additional examples of academic words with more than one meaning.

Word	Definitions	Relationship
select	*v.* to choose *adj.* chosen because of excellence or preference	Both definitions involve choosing
range	*n.* the extent to which something varies *v.* to vary within specified limits	Both definitions involve variation within certain limits
conduct	*n.* a standard of personal behavior *v.* to lead from a position of power	Both definitions involve the correct way to do something

As you encounter academic vocabulary words in this book, you will master the words through various activities. The items below will give you a chance to practice using academic vocabulary.

Practice Complete the following items.

1. respond (ri spond´) *v.* to act in response

In Saki's "The Open Window," when Framton Nuttel sees the men return from hunting, he **responds** *by fleeing from the house.*

Use the word *respond* in a sentence of your own in which you explain how you reacted during a humorous encounter.

2. establish (es tab´lish) *v.* to bring into existence

Jack Finney includes descriptive details about the Beneckes' apartment to help **establish** *the mood in "Contents of the Dead Man's Pocket."*

Use the word *establish* in a sentence of your own in which you describe how your ancestors came to live in your town, state, or country.

3. construct (kən strukt´) *v.* to make or form from disparate parts

Saki uses flashbacks and chronological order to **construct** *the sequence of events in "The Open Window".*

Another meaning of *construct* is "a theoretical entity" as in the sentence "Class is a social construct." This definition of *construct* is pronounced (kon´strukt´). How is this definition related to the one given above?

Test-Taking Tip
These key academic vocabulary words often appear on standardized tests.

Evaluate: to make a judgment and support it with evidence

Explain: to clarify or make plain

Illustrate: to provide examples or to show with a picture or another graphic

Infer: to read between the lines or to use knowledge or experience to draw conclusions, make generalizations, or form predictions

Justify: to prove or to support a position with specific facts and reasons

Predict: to tell what will happen in the future based on an understanding of prior events and behaviors

State: to briefly and concisely present information

Summarize: to give a brief overview of the main points of an event or issue

Trace: to present the steps or stages in a process or an event in sequential or chronological order

Before You Read

An Astrologer's Day

Meet **R. K. Narayan**
(1906–2001)

As a young boy, R. K. Narayan (nä rä´yan) had absolutely no use for school. "Going to school seemed to be a never-ending nuisance each day," he once wrote. Narayan much preferred spending time with his pet monkey, who liked to hang by its tail from the roof, and his pet peacock, who acted as the family watchdog. Despite his aversion to school, Narayan's family placed a high value on education. But Narayan never changed his opinion that school was too serious. Today, Narayan's stories are regularly assigned to students in schools around the world. Considering his unenthusiastic view of formal education, Narayan might have enjoyed this irony.

> "I want a story to be entertaining, enjoyable, and illuminating in some way."
>
> —R. K. Narayan

The Decision to Be a Writer Rasipuram Krishnaswami Narayan was born in Madras, India, and brought up by his grandmother. After graduating from college, he turned to fiction writing as a career. He chose to write in English, a language that he was fond of and knew well. "English is a very adaptable language. And it's so transparent it can take on the tint of any country." Narayan did not find immediate success as a writer and once said that writing "was all frustration and struggle for more than fifteen years." His first novel, *Swami and Friends*, was finally published in 1935 with the help of British writer Graham Greene. Narayan went on to publish numerous other works.

A Literary Voice of India Narayan is probably best known as the creator of Malgudi, a fictional South Indian village that has been called a "zany, eccentric and, at the same time, true to life world." It is the setting for almost all of Narayan's novels and short stories, including "An Astrologer's Day." Of his invented village, Narayan remarked, "Malgudi was an earth-shaking discovery for me, because I had no mind for facts and things like that, which would be necessary in writing about . . . any real place." Narayan's stories about Malgudi are often comic considerations of individuals trying to find peace in a turbulent world.

Critic Judith Freeman writes that Narayan "takes a Western reader into the very heart of an Indian village. . . . The foreignness of the setting, rituals and traditions may seem to us exotic, but the underlying humanity of Narayan's dramas can't fail to strike a familiar chord."

 Literature Online

Author Search For more about R. K. Narayan, go to glencoe.com and enter QuickPass code GL57805u1.

Literature and Reading Preview

Connect to the Story

In your opinion, how much of one's future is decided by the choices one makes, by fate, or by coincidence? Freewrite for a few minutes about this question.

Build Background

Astrology is a form of fortune-telling. Some astrologers claim the ability to foretell an individual's future by drawing and studying a chart called a *horoscope*. A horoscope shows the configuration of the planets and stars at the moment of an individual's birth.

Set Purposes for Reading

Big Idea Encountering the Unexpected

As you read "An Astrologer's Day," ask yourself, What is revealed when a man asks about his future?

Literary Element Mood

The **mood** is the overall emotional quality of a literary work. The writer's choice of language, subject matter, setting, diction, and tone all contribute to the work's mood. **Foreshadowing,** an author's use of hints or clues to prepare readers for events that will happen later, can also contribute to a story's mood. It can add to a sense of mystery or doom, or it can hint at a brighter outcome in the face of difficulty. As you read, ask yourself, How does Narayan create a mood that helps me relate to a different time and culture?

Reading Strategy Analyze Cultural Context

When you **analyze cultural context,** you pay attention to details that reveal the setting, dress, speech, mannerisms, and behaviors characteristic of a particular culture at a particular time in history. These details may also point to a story's **theme**—its message about life—without expressing it directly. As you read, ask yourself, What details does Narayan use to show the customs of 1940s India, and what theme does his particular choice of details suggest?

Tip: Take Notes As you read, take notes about cultural details that relate to the setting, characters, and theme of the story.

Detail	How It Relates to Story

TEKS

For pages 38–46

10.2 Analyze, make inferences and draw conclusions about theme and genre in different cultural, historical, and contemporary contexts and provide evidence from the text to support understanding.

Vocabulary

enhance (en hans′) *v.* to make greater, as in beauty or value; p. 40 *Wearing too much makeup may detract from your beauty, not enhance it.*

impetuous (im pech′ ōō əs) *adj.* rushing headlong into things; rash; p. 41 *It was an impetuous decision, made without any thought.*

paraphernalia (par′ ə fər nāl′ yə) *n.* things used in a particular activity; equipment; p. 42 *The traveling chef carried his own pots, pans, and other cooking paraphernalia.*

piqued (pēkt) *adj.* aroused in anger or resentment; offended; p. 42 *The director was piqued by the play's disastrous reviews.*

incantation (in′kan tā′shən) *n.* words spoken in casting a spell; p. 42 *In Shakespeare's Macbeth, witches utter an eerie incantation.*

Tip: Word Origins You can find a word's origin and history, or etymology, in a dictionary, usually near the beginning or end of an entry.

An Astrologer's Day

R. K. Narayan

Indian Star Chart, ca. 1840. By permission of the British Library.

Punctually at midday he opened his bag and spread out his professional equipment, which consisted of a dozen cowrie[1] shells, a square piece of cloth with obscure mystic charts on it, a notebook and a bundle of palmyra writing. His forehead was resplendent with sacred ash and vermilion,[2] and his eyes sparkled with a sharp abnormal gleam which was really an outcome of a continual searching look for customers, but which his simple clients took to be a prophetic light and felt comforted. The power of his eyes was considerably **enhanced** by their position—placed as they were between the painted forehead and the dark whiskers which streamed down his cheeks: even a half-wit's eyes would sparkle in such a setting. To crown the effect he wound a saffron-colored[3] turban around his head. This color scheme never failed. People were attracted to him as bees are attracted to cosmos or dahlia stalks. He sat under the boughs of a spreading tamarind tree which flanked a path running through the Town Hall Park. It was a remarkable place in many ways: a surging crowd was always moving up and down this narrow road morning till night. A variety of trades and occupations was represented all along its

---

1. A *cowrie* (kour′ē) is a small snail commonly found in warm, shallow waters of the Pacific and Indian Oceans.
2. Here, *obscure* means "difficult to understand" and *mystic* means "having hidden or secret meanings." *Palmyra* (pal mī′rə) refers to paper made from the leaves of the palmyra tree. The man's forehead is full of splendor (*resplendent*) in that it is painted with dark ash and a red pigment called *vermilion*.

Encountering the Unexpected *What do customers misunderstand about the astrologer?*

3. *Saffron* is an orange-yellow color.

Analyze Cultural Context *How does the astrologer's manner of dress suit his character?*

Vocabulary

enhance (en hans′) *v.* to make greater, as in beauty or value way: medicine-sellers, sellers of stolen hardware and junk, magicians and, above all, an auctioneer of cheap cloth, who created enough din all day to attract the whole town. Next to him in vociferousness[4] came a vendor of fried groundnuts,[5] who gave his ware a fancy name each day, calling it Bombay Ice-Cream one day, and on the next Delhi Almond, and on the third Raja's Delicacy, and so on and so forth, and people flocked to him. A considerable portion of this crowd dallied before the astrologer too. The astrologer transacted his business by the light of a flare which crackled and smoked up above the groundnut heap nearby. Half the enchantment of the place was due to the fact that it did not have the benefit of municipal lighting. The place was lit up by shop lights. One or two had hissing gaslights, some had naked flares stuck on poles, some were lit up by old cycle lamps and one or two, like the astrologer's, managed without lights of their own. It was a bewildering criss-cross of light rays and moving shadows. This suited the astrologer very well, for the simple reason that he had not in the least intended to be an astrologer when he began life; and he knew no more of what was going to happen to others than he knew what was going to happen to himself next minute. He was as much a stranger to the stars as were his innocent customers. Yet he said things which pleased and astonished everyone: that was more a matter of study, practice and shrewd guesswork. All the same, it was as much an honest man's labor as any other, and he deserved the wages he carried home at the end of a day.

He had left his village without any previous thought or plan. If he had continued there he would have carried on the work of his forefathers—namely, tilling the land, living, marrying and ripening in his cornfield and ancestral home. But that was not to be. He had to leave home without telling anyone, and he could not rest till he left it behind a couple of hundred miles. To a villager it is a great deal, as if an ocean flowed between.

He had a working analysis of mankind's troubles: marriage, money and the tangles of human ties. Long practice had sharpened his perception. Within five minutes he understood what was wrong. He charged three pice[6] per question and never opened his mouth till the other had spoken for at least ten minutes, which provided him enough stuff for a dozen answers and advices. When he told the person before him, gazing at his palm, "In many ways you are not getting the fullest results for your efforts," nine out of ten were disposed to agree with him. Or he questioned: "Is there any woman in your family, maybe even a distant relative, who is not well disposed[7] towards you?" Or he gave an analysis of character: "Most of your troubles are due to your nature. How can you be otherwise with Saturn where he is? You have an **impetuous** nature and a rough exterior." This endeared him to their hearts immediately, for even the mildest of us loves to think that he has a forbidding exterior.

The nuts-vendor blew out his flare and rose to go home. This was a signal for the astrologer to bundle up too, since it left him in darkness except for a little shaft of

---

4. *Vociferousness* (vō sif′ər əs nəs) means "noisy outcrying."
5. *Groundnuts* are peanuts.

Mood *What does this description of lights add to the mood of the story?*

---

6. A *pice* is a coin of India of very small value.
7. In this paragraph, *disposed* is used twice with slightly different meanings. The first time, you might substitute *likely* or *inclined*. The second time, substitute *favorable* for the phrase "well disposed."

impetuous (im pech′ oo əs) *adj.* rushing headlong into things; rash green light which strayed in from somewhere and touched the ground before him. He picked up his cowrie shells and **paraphernalia** and was putting them back into his bag when the green shaft of light was blotted out; he looked up and saw a man standing before him. He sensed a possible client and said: "You look so careworn. It will do you good to sit down for a while and chat with me." The other grumbled some vague reply. The astrologer pressed his invitation; whereupon the other thrust his palm under his nose, saying: "You call yourself an astrologer?" The astrologer felt challenged and said, tilting the other's palm towards the green shaft of light: "Yours is a nature . . ." "Oh, stop that," the other said. "Tell me something worthwhile. . . ."

Our friend felt **piqued.** "I charge only three pice per question, and what you get ought to be good enough for your money. . . ." At this the other withdrew his arm, took out an anna and flung it out to him, saying, "I have some questions to ask. If I prove you are bluffing, you must return that anna to me with interest."

"If you find my answers satisfactory, will you give me five rupees?"[8]

"No."

"Or will you give me eight annas?"

"All right, provided you give me twice as much if you are wrong," said the stranger. This pact was accepted after a little further argument. The astrologer sent up a prayer to heaven as the other lit a cheroot.[9] The astrologer caught a glimpse of his face by the matchlight. There was a pause as cars hooted on the road, jutka[10] drivers swore at their horses and the babble of the crowd agitated the semi-darkness of the park. The other sat down, sucking his cheroot, puffing out, sat there ruthlessly. The astrologer felt very uncomfortable. "Here, take your anna back. I am not used to such challenges. It is late for me today. . . ." He made preparations to bundle up. The other held his wrist and said, "You can't get out of it now. You dragged me in while I was passing." The astrologer shivered in his grip; and his voice shook and became faint. "Leave me today. I will speak to you tomorrow." The other thrust his palm in his face and said, "Challenge is challenge. Go on." The astrologer proceeded with his throat drying up. "There is a woman . . ."

"Stop," said the other. "I don't want all that. Shall I succeed in my present search or not? Answer this and go. Otherwise I will not let you go till you disgorge[11] all your coins." The astrologer muttered a few **incantations** and replied, "All right. I will speak. But will you give me a rupee if what I say is convincing? Otherwise I will not open my mouth, and you may do what you like." After a good deal of haggling the other agreed. The astrologer said, "You were left for dead. Am I right?"

---

8. The *anna* is a former coin of India that was equal to four pice. The *rupee* is a coin of India (and other countries) equal to sixteen annas.

Mood *How might this scene's abrupt change in mood foreshadow events later in the story?*

---

9. A *cheroot* (shə rōōt´) is a cigar cut square at both ends.
10. A *jutka* (jōōt´ kə) is a two-wheeled, horse-drawn vehicle.
11. Here, *disgorge* means "to give up or hand over."

Untitled, 20th century. Image zoo.

<u>View the Art</u> This abstract painting shows a solitary figure suspended in what could be water or the night sky. How might the figure represent the astrologer? How might it represent his client?

"Ah, tell me more."

"A knife has passed through you once?" said the astrologer.

"Good fellow!" He bared his chest to show the scar. "What else?"

"And then you were pushed into a well nearby in the field. You were left for dead."

"I should have been dead if some passerby had not chanced to peep into the well," exclaimed the other, overwhelmed by enthusiasm. "When shall I get at him?" he asked, clenching his fist.

"In the next world," answered the astrologer. "He died four months ago in a far-off town. You will never see any more of him." The other groaned on hearing it. The astrologer proceeded.

"Guru Nayak—"

"You know my name!" the other said, taken aback.[12]

"As I know all other things. Guru Nayak, listen carefully to what I have to say. Your village is two days' journey due north of this town. Take the next train and be gone. I see once again great danger to your life if you go from home." He took out a pinch of sacred ash and held it out to him. "Rub it on your forehead and go home. Never travel southward again, and you will live to be a hundred."

"Why should I leave home again?" the other said reflectively.[13] "I was only going away now and then to look for him and to choke out his life if I met him." He shook his head regretfully. "He has escaped my hands. I hope at least he died as he deserved." "Yes," said the astrologer. "He

was crushed under a lorry."[14] The other looked gratified to hear it.

The place was deserted by the time the astrologer picked up his articles and put them into his bag. The green shaft was also gone, leaving the place in darkness and silence. The stranger had gone off into the night, after giving the astrologer a handful of coins.

It was nearly midnight when the astrologer reached home. His wife was waiting for him at the door and demanded an explanation. He flung the coins at her and said, "Count them. One man gave all that."

"Twelve and a half annas," she said, counting. She was overjoyed. "I can buy some *jaggery*[15] and coconut tomorrow. The child has been asking for sweets for so many days now. I will prepare some nice stuff for her."

"The swine has cheated me! He promised me a rupee," said the astrologer. She looked up at him. "You look worried. What is wrong?"

"Nothing."

After dinner, sitting on the *pyol*,[16] he told her, "Do you know a great load is gone from me today? I thought I had the blood of a man on my hands all these years. That was the reason why I ran away from home, settled here and married you. He is alive."

She gasped, "You tried to kill!"

"Yes, in our village, when I was a silly youngster. We drank, gambled and quarreled badly one day—why think of it now? Time to sleep," he said, yawning, and stretched himself on the *pyol*. ❧

---

12. The expression *taken aback* means "suddenly surprised or startled."
13. Here, *reflectively* (ri flek′ tiv lē) means "in a way that shows serious and careful consideration."

Encountering the Unexpected *Did it surprise you when the astrologer called his client by the correct name? Explain.*

---

14. Here, a *lorry* is a long, flat, horse-drawn wagon.
15. *Jaggery* is unrefined sugar made from palm tree sap.
16. A *pyol* (pī′ ôl) is a low bench.

Mood *How has the mood of the story changed here?*

After You Read

Respond and Think Critically

1. **Connect to Personal Experience** What was your reaction to the conversation between the astrologer and his wife? Does this new knowledge reinforce or change your opinion of the astrologer? Explain.

2. **Summarize Exposition** Describe the astrologer's current life. How does this differ from the life he expected to live?

3. **Make Inferences About Character** How does the astrologer's appearance help him attract customers? In your opinion, how does the astrologer help the customers and satisfy their needs?

4. **Explain Motivation** What details does the astrologer give the stranger about his past? Why does he advise the stranger to go home immediately?

5. **Analyze Setting** Why is it important that this story takes place in the evening? How would the story have been different if it had taken place earlier in the day?

6. **Make Inferences About Attitude** How would you characterize the astrologer's attitude toward the stranger after their encounter? What attitude did the astrologer seem to have about the incident from his past? Explain.

7. **Compare and Contrast Events** How is the fortune the astrologer provides for Guru Nayak different from the fortunes he usually provides? Explain your answer and support it with evidence from the story. ◁OER

8. **Big Idea** **Draw Conclusions About Suspense** Suspense is the feeling of anticipation you may have as you read. In this story, what details contributed to your feelings of suspense and surprise? Explain.

9. **Analyze Historical Context** How might the astrologer's fate have been different if he had committed his crime in today's technologically advanced world instead of in a rural Indian village many years ago?

Literary Element Mood

Mood helps the reader imagine the feeling of being in the scene and experience the events as the characters do. Writers use diction, descriptive language, and imagery to help create mood.

10. **Describe Mood** In one or two sentences, describe the mood of the scene in which Guru Nayak visits the astrologer. How does Narayan's language contribute to the mood? Support your response with text evidence.

11. **Analyze Mood and Foreshadowing** Look at the passage on page 41 describing the astrologer's departure from his home village. What change in mood is conveyed by the sudden short phrase, "But that was not to be," and the language in the sentences that follow? How does this passage foreshadow events later in the story?

Review: Flashback

As you learned on page 11, a **flashback** is an interruption in the chronological order of a narrative to describe an event that happened earlier.

12. **Partner Activity** Meet with a classmate and imagine that you are the writer and director of a film version of "An Astrologer's Day." Collaborate on a film script for the scene in which the astrologer realizes that Guru Nayak is his former victim but that he must still act as his astrologer. Include a flashback sequence in which the astrologer remembers the attempted murder. Write a description of and dialogue for the flashback sequence and integrate it into your film script. As you write, consider how the flashback affects the scene as a whole.

Reading Strategy Analyze Cultural Context

The cultural details in the story lend it authenticity. Review the blue highlighted passage and question and the chart you made on page 39.

13. The author often ties together the show the astrologer puts on and his success in business. What are some of the cultural details in the story that support this connection?

14. How do the cultural and historical contexts of the story contribute to the theme? Support your response with text evidence.

Vocabulary Practice

Practice with Word Origins Create a word map like the one below for each boldfaced vocabulary word from the story.

enhance	impetuous	paraphernalia
piqued	incantation	

EXAMPLE:

Definition to pretend to be sick or incapable of working

Etymology French *malingre* means "sickly"

malinger

Sample Sentence While others worked, Dan malingered.

Academic Vocabulary

The reader must decide whether the astrologer's youth at the time of his crime against Guru Nayak can, in any way, **negate** *his guilt.*

Negate is an academic word. More familiar words that are similar in meaning are *deny* and *abolish*. Answer this question in one or more complete sentences that use the word *negate*: Who or what could **negate** one of your accomplishments? Explain.

For more on academic vocabulary, see pages 36–37 and R92–R94.

Write with Style

 Apply Description

Assignment Describe a place you know well. Use details to create a recognizable mood.

Get Ideas Think of a place you know well. Then review how details help create mood in "An Astrologer's Day." For example, the green shaft of light and the ensuing darkness not only help to establish a time and place, they also create a mood of mystery.

EXAMPLE

"The nuts-vendor blew out his flare and rose to go home. This was a signal for the astrologer to bundle up too, since it left him in darkness except for a little shaft of green light which strayed in from somewhere and touched the ground before him."

Create a chart like the one below in which you list your place and some of the sensory details that create its mood. Use your chart to help you write your description.

Place	Sensory Details

Give It Structure All the details in your description should come together to create the mood. The details should appear in a logical order. You may choose to organize the details of your description around a central character or event. If you are telling a story, consider using chronological order, problem/solution, or cause-and-effect relationships to organize your writing. If you are simply describing the place, consider moving from general to specific, or vice versa, as you write.

Look at Language Too many adjectives are like too much frosting on a piece of cake. Don't load them on. Focus on fewer, more precise words.

 Literature Online

Selection Resources For Selection Quizzes, eFlashcards, and Reading-Writing Connection activities, go to glencoe.com and enter QuickPass code GL57805u1.

Vocabulary Workshop

Denotation and Connotation

TEKS

10.1.B Analyze textual context (within a sentence and in larger sections of text) to distinguish between the denotative and connotative meanings of words.

Literature Connection Good writers are skilled at suggesting meaning both directly (through **denotation,** the literal meaning of a word) and indirectly (through **connotation,** or the ideas, images, and feelings a word brings with it). In this sentence from "An Astrologer's Day," R. K. Narayan sets the scene of his main character's workplace: "The astrologer *transacted* his business by the light of a flare which crackled and smoked up above the groundnut heap nearby." Notice that in the sentence, Narayan chooses the word *transacted.* He could have chosen *conducted* or *performed*—those words have a meaning similar to *transacted.* But they also have subtle differences that would change the meaning.

A semantic chart like the one below can help you analyze the similarities, differences, and shades of meaning of words such as *transact, conduct,* and *perform.* Follow these instructions to complete the chart.

- In the left-hand column, write the words you will analyze.
- Consult a dictionary to find literal definitions, or denotations, for them. Write the definitions in the second column.
- In the third column, record ideas, images, or feelings that you associate with each word. Such associations are the word's connotations. To figure out a word's connotation, it often helps to study the context of the word—the sentences and larger sections of text that surround the word.

Word	Denotation	Connotation
transact		
conduct		
perform		

Vocabulary Terms
The **denotation** of a word is its literal meaning; the **connotation** of a word is its implied or cultural meaning.

Tip
If, during a test, you are asked about the denotation of a word, think about how you would define the word for someone else. To describe the word's connotation, think about the images and ideas the word brings to mind.

Practice Use what you have learned about denotation and connotation to complete the activities below.

1. Complete this semantic chart on a separate sheet of paper. First, analyze the textual context within the sentence in which *transacted* appears in the story to distinguish between the word's denotation and connotation. Why do you think Narayan chose to use *transacted* instead of *conducted* or *performed?*

2. Find three or four similar words used to describe a setting in another story in this unit. Create a semantic chart for these words. Share your completed charts with your classmates.

LOG ON ▶ **Literature** Online

Vocabulary For more vocabulary practice, go to glencoe.com and enter the QuickPass code GL57805u1.

Before You Read

Civil Peace

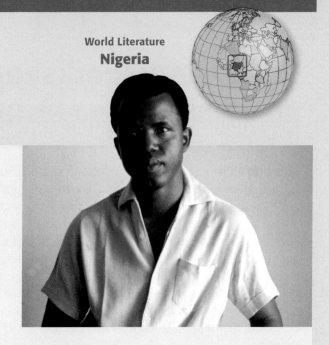

Meet **Chinua Achebe**
(born 1930)

"The story is our escort; without it, we are blind." Chinua Achebe (ə chā´ bā) wrote these words to stress the importance of keeping Africa's precolonial stories and culture alive.

Achebe was born in Ogidi, Nigeria. His family was of Ibo ethnicity and practiced Christianity. While growing up, Achebe experienced traditional village life. After graduating from University College in Ibadan, he worked for more than ten years for the Nigerian Broadcasting Company. Achebe left this job in 1966 partly because of political problems that led to civil war in Nigeria in 1967. The Ibo, one of Nigeria's largest ethnic groups, tried to separate from Nigeria to form the independent Republic of Biafra. Achebe worked for the Ibo cause and represented Biafra as a diplomat.

He has since taught in universities in Nigeria, Massachusetts, and Connecticut. During his career, he has authored five novels, as well as many essays, short stories, poems, and children's stories. He was also the director of Heinemann Education Books Ltd. (now called the Heinemann African Writers Series) and helped foster publication of African and Caribbean writers.

> "It is the story that outlives the sound of war-drums and the exploits of brave fighters."
>
> —Chinua Achebe, from *Anthills of the Savannah*

The African Voice Achebe writes in English so that his stories will have a wider audience. However, his themes revolve around the people of Africa, their struggles under colonial rule, and their fight for independence. Achebe combines the rhythms and speech patterns of the Ibo with the English language to give English-language readers a sense of authentic Nigerian culture. Achebe writes about people honestly, detailing both the good and the bad.

Civil War and Civil Peace Achebe wrote radio programs that supported the Biafrans during the Nigerian civil war, but he could not bring himself to write novels during the war. He did, however, write three short stories about it. "Civil Peace," which provides a true-to-life description of the region after the war, is one of those stories.

The title of Achebe's most popular novel, *Things Fall Apart,* is an allusion to the William Butler Yeats poem "The Second Coming." Achebe's novel, a powerful account of a "strong" man whose life is dominated by fear and anger, is recognized as a masterpiece of modern African literature.

Literature Online

Author Search For more about Chinua Achebe, go to glencoe.com and enter QuickPass code GL57805u1.

Literature and Reading Preview

Connect to the Story

If a disaster occurred today, what would you save to ensure your "happy survival"? Respond to this question in your journal.

Build Background

Nigeria, located on the western coast of Africa, is the most densely populated country on the continent. Once a British colony, it became an independent nation in 1960. A civil war began there in 1967 when the Ibo tried to separate from Nigeria to form the Republic of Biafra. After years of bloody battles, the Ibo were forced to surrender in 1970. This story takes place in Nigeria shortly after the end of the war.

Set Purposes for Reading

Big Idea Encountering the Unexpected

As you read "Civil Peace," ask yourself, How does Jonathan Iwegbu experience both joy and sorrow in encountering the unexpected?

Literary Element Dialect

A **dialect** is a variation of a language spoken within a particular region or by a particular social or ethnic group. Understanding a writer's use of dialect will give you a richer sense of a scene or character. As you read, ask yourself, How does Achebe use dialect to illustrate both British and African elements in Nigeria?

Reading Strategy Analyze Historical Context

When you **analyze historical context,** you think of how the characters, events, and **theme** (a story's message about life) in a story are affected by what is taking place at the time the story is set. As you read, ask yourself, How is the Nigerian civil war related to the theme of the story?

....

Tip: Analyze Theme Use a web diagram like the one below to list the effects of the Nigerian civil war on Jonathan Iwegbu's life. Use this information to help you figure out the story's theme.

TEKS

For pages 48–55

10.2 Analyze, make inferences and draw conclusions about theme and genre in different cultural, historical, and contemporary contexts and provide evidence from the text to support understanding.

Vocabulary

commandeer (kom´ ən dēr´) *v.* to seize for use by the military or government; p. 50 *The general commandeered the commercial airplane for the battle.*

amenable (ə mē´ nə bəl) *adj.* responsive; able to be controlled; p. 50 *After being sedated, the animal was amenable to being treated by the veterinarian.*

retail (re´ tāl) *v.* to sell directly to consumers; p. 51 *The farmer retailed his produce door to door.*

edifice (ed´ ə fis) *n.* a building, especially a large, important-looking one; p. 51 *The castle was an impressive edifice.*

....

Tip: Connotation and Denotation As you read, it often helps to look beyond a word's dictionary meaning, or **denotation,** and consider the emotions and other suggestions, or **connotations,** that the word conveys.

Civil Peace

Chinua Achebe

Jonathan Iwegbu counted himself extraordinarily lucky. "Happy survival!" meant so much more to him than just a current fashion of greeting old friends in the first hazy days of peace. It went deep to his heart. He had come out of the war with five inestimable blessings—his head, his wife Maria's head and the heads of three out of their four children. As a bonus he also had his old bicycle—a miracle too but naturally not to be compared to the safety of five human heads.

The bicycle had a little history of its own. One day at the height of the war it was **commandeered** "for urgent military action." Hard as its loss would have been to him he would still have let it go without a thought had he not had some doubts about the genuineness of the officer. It wasn't his disreputable rags, nor the toes peeping out of one blue and one brown canvas shoes, nor yet the two stars of his rank done obviously in a hurry in biro,[1] that troubled Jonathan; many good and heroic soldiers looked the same or worse. It was rather a certain lack of grip and firmness in his manner. So Jonathan, suspecting he might be **amenable** to influence, rummaged in his raffia bag and produced the two pounds

---

1. The stars signifying the officer's rank had been hand-drawn in ink. *Biro* (bi′ rō) is a British term for a ballpoint pen.

Analyze Historical Context *Why would Jonathan have let his bicycle go "without a thought"? Why did he think of himself as "extraordinarily lucky"?*

Vocabulary

commandeer (kom′ ən dēr′) *v.* to seize for use by the military or government

Vocabulary

amenable (ə mē′ nə bəl) *adj.* responsive; able to be controlled with which he had been going to buy fire-wood which his wife, Maria, **retailed** to camp officials for extra stock-fish and corn meal, and got his bicycle back. That night he buried it in the little clearing in the bush where the dead of the camp, including his own youngest son, were buried. When he dug it up again a year later after the surrender all it needed was a little palm-oil greasing. "Nothing puzzles God," he said in wonder.

He put it to immediate use as a taxi and accumulated a small pile of Biafran money ferrying camp officials and their families across the four-mile stretch to the nearest tarred road. His standard charge per trip was six pounds and those who had the money were only glad to be rid of some of it in this way. At the end of a fortnight[2] he had made a small fortune of one hundred and fifteen pounds.

Then he made the journey to Enugu and found another miracle waiting for him. It was unbelievable. He rubbed his eyes and looked again and it was still standing there before him. But, needless to say, even that monumental blessing must be accounted also totally inferior to the five heads in the family. This newest miracle was his little house in Ogui Overside. Indeed nothing puzzles God! Only two houses away a huge concrete **edifice** some wealthy contractor had put up just before the war was a mountain of rubble. And here was Jonathan's little zinc house of no regrets built with mud

blocks quite intact! Of course the doors and windows were missing and five sheets off the roof. But what was that? And anyhow he had returned to Enugu early enough to pick up bits of old zinc and wood and soggy sheets of cardboard lying around the neighborhood before thousands more came out of their forest holes looking for the same things. He got a destitute carpenter with one old hammer, a blunt plane and a few bent and rusty nails in his tool bag to turn this assortment of wood, paper and metal into door and window shutters for five Nigerian shillings or fifty Biafran pounds. He paid the pounds, and moved in with his overjoyed family carrying five heads on their shoulders.

Visual Vocabulary
A *mango* is a tropical fruit with sweet flesh and a single large seed.

His children picked mangoes near the military cemetery and sold them to soldiers' wives for a few pennies—real pennies this time—and his wife started making breakfast akara balls[3] for neighbors in a hurry to start life again. With his family earnings he took his bicycle to the villages around and bought fresh palm wine which he mixed generously in his rooms with the water which had recently started running again in the public tap down the road, and opened up a bar for soldiers and other lucky people with good money.

At first he went daily, then every other day and finally once a week, to the offices of the Coal Corporation where he used to be

---

2. A *fortnight* is two weeks.

Encountering the Unexpected *Why was Jonathan surprised by the condition of his bicycle?*

---

3. *Akara balls* are ball-shaped bean cakes.

Analyze Historical Context *What do the actions of Jonathan's family members show?*

a miner, to find out what was what. The only thing he did find out in the end was that that little house of his was even a greater blessing than he had thought. Some of his fellow ex-miners who had nowhere to return at the end of the day's waiting just slept outside the doors of the offices and cooked what meal they could scrounge together in Bournvita tins. As the weeks lengthened and still nobody could say what was what Jonathan discontinued his weekly visits altogether and faced his palm wine bar.

Visual Vocabulary
A *queue* (kyū) is a line of people.

But nothing puzzles God. Came the day of the windfall when after five days of endless scuffles in queues and counter queues in the sun outside the Treasury he had twenty pounds counted into his palms as ex gratia[4] award for the rebel money he had turned in. It was like Christmas for him and for many others like him when the payments began. They called it (since few could manage its proper official name) *egg rasher.*

As soon as the pound notes were placed in his palm Jonathan simply closed it tight over them and buried fist and money inside his trouser pocket. He had to be extra careful because he had seen a man a couple of days earlier collapse into near madness in an instant before that oceanic crowd because no sooner had he got his twenty pounds than some heartless ruffian picked it off him. Though it was not right that a man in such an extremity of agony should be blamed yet many in the queues that day were able to remark quietly on the victim's carelessness,

especially after he pulled out the innards of his pocket and revealed a hole in it big enough to pass a thief's head. But of course he had insisted that the money had been in the other pocket, pulling it out too to show its comparative wholeness. So one had to be careful.

Jonathan soon transferred the money to his left hand and pocket so as to leave his right free for shaking hands should the need arise, though by fixing his gaze at such an elevation as to miss all approaching human faces he made sure that the need did not arise, until he got home.

He was normally a heavy sleeper but that night he heard all the neighborhood noises die down one after another. Even the night watchman who knocked the hour on some metal somewhere in the distance had fallen silent after knocking one o'clock. That must have been the last thought in Jonathan's mind before he was finally carried away himself. He couldn't have been gone for long, though, when he was violently awakened again.

"Who is knocking?" whispered his wife lying beside him on the floor.

"I don't know," he whispered back breathlessly.

The second time the knocking came it was so loud and imperious that the rickety old door could have fallen down.

"Who is knocking?" he asked then, his voice parched and trembling.

"Na tief-man and him people," came the cool reply. "Make you hopen de door." This was followed by the heaviest knocking of all.

Maria was the first to raise the alarm, then he followed and all their children.

---

4. Something that is awarded *ex gratia* (eks grāsh´ ē ə) is given as a favor rather than as a legal right. The Latin word *gratia* means "kindness."

Encountering the Unexpected *What visitors might be at the door? Are Jonathan and his wife completely surprised? Explain.*

Children Dancing, c. 1948. Robert Gwathmey. Oil on canvas, 30 x 40 in. The Butler Institute of American Art, Youngstown, OH.

View the Art Inspired by African culture and Pablo Picasso, Gwathmey uses vibrant colors and symbolic abstraction to tell stories about his subjects. How might this painting reflect Jonathan and his family's outlook on life?

"Police-o! Thieves-o! Neighbors-o! Police-o! We are lost! We are dead! Neighbors, are you asleep? Wake up! Police-o!"

This went on for a long time and then stopped suddenly. Perhaps they had scared the thief away. There was total silence. But only for a short while.

"You done finish?" asked the voice outside. "Make we help you small. Oya, everybody!"

"Police-o! Tief-man-o! Neighbors-o! we done loss-o! Police-o! . . ."

There were at least five other voices besides the leader's.

Jonathan and his family were now completely paralyzed by terror. Maria and the children sobbed inaudibly like lost souls. Jonathan groaned continuously.

The silence that followed the thieves' alarm vibrated horribly. Jonathan all but begged their leader to speak again and be done with it.

"My frien," said he at long last, "we don try our best for call dem but I tink say dem all done sleep-o . . . So wetin we go do now? Sometaim you wan call soja? Or you wan make we call dem for you? Soja better pass police. No be so?"

"Na so!" replied his men. Jonathan thought he heard even more voices now

---

Analyze Historical Context *Why does no one in the neighborhood respond when the thieves pound on Jonathan's door? Why do the thieves call for the police?*

Dialect *What does the term "soja" mean? Why are this and other words presented here with unusual spellings?*

than before and groaned heavily. His legs were sagging under him and his throat felt like sandpaper.

"My frien, why you no de talk again. I de ask you say you wan make we call soja?"

"No."

"Awrighto. Now make we talk business. We no be bad tief. We no like for make trouble. Trouble done finish. War done finish and all the katakata[5] wey de for inside. No Civil War again. This time na Civil Peace. No be so?"

"Na so!" answered the horrible chorus.

"What do you want from me? I am a poor man. Everything I had went with this war. Why do you come to me? You know people who have money. We . . ."

"Awright! We know say you no get plenty money. But we sef no get even anini.[6] So derefore make you open dis window and give us one hundred pound and we go commot. Orderwise we de come for inside now to show you guitar-boy like dis . . ."

A volley of automatic fire rang through the sky. Maria and the children began to weep aloud again.

"Ah, missisi de cry again. No need for dat. We done talk say we na good tief. We just take our small money and go nway-orly. No molest. Abi we de molest?"

"At all!" sang the chorus.

"My friends," began Jonathan hoarsely. "I hear what you say and I thank you. If I had one hundred pounds . . ."

"Lookia my frien, no be play we come play for your house. If we make mistake and step for inside you no go like am-o. So derefore . . ."

"To God who made me; if you come inside and find one hundred pounds, take it and shoot me and shoot my wife and children. I swear to God. The only money I have in this life is this twenty-pounds *egg rasher* they gave me today . . ."

"OK. Time de go. Make you open dis window and bring the twenty pound. We go manage am like dat."

There were now loud murmurs of dissent among the chorus: "Na lie de man de lie; e get plenty money . . . Make we go inside and search properly well . . . Wetin be twenty pound? . . ."

"Shurrup!" rang the leader's voice like a lone shot in the sky and silenced the murmuring at once. "Are you dere? Bring the money quick!"

"I am coming," said Jonathan fumbling in the darkness with the key of the small wooden box he kept by his side on the mat.

At the first sign of light as neighbors and others assembled to commiserate with him he was already strapping his five-gallon demijohn to his bicycle carrier and his wife, sweating in the open fire, was turning over akara balls in a wide clay bowl of boiling oil. In the corner his eldest son was rinsing out dregs of yesterday's palm wine from old beer bottles.

Visual Vocabulary
A *demijohn* is a large earthenware or glass bottle, encased in wicker.

"I count it as nothing," he told his sympathizers, his eyes on the rope he was tying. "What is *egg rasher*? Did I depend on it last week? Or is it greater than other things that went with the war? I say, let *egg rasher* perish in the flames! Let it go where everything else has gone. Nothing puzzles God." ❧

---

5. The word *katakata* may be meant to imitate the sound of gunfire. The rest of the phrase is Nigerian dialect for "that went with it."

6. An *anini* (ä nē´ē) is a small Nigerian coin worth less than one cent.

Dialect *What does the author's use of dialect in this column add to the story?*

After You Read

Respond and Think Critically

1. **Connect to Personal Experience** Do you think Jonathan did the right thing by giving the thieves the money? Why or why not?

2. **Explain Attitudes** What is Jonathan Iwegbu's attitude toward life? Explain your answer and support it with evidence from the story. ➦OER

3. **Explain Motivation** Why did Jonathan mistrust the officer who wanted to take his bicycle?

4. **Analyze Character** What does Jonathan mean by his statement, "Nothing puzzles God"? What does this statement reveal about Jonathan's character?

5. **Evaluate Title** Is the title of this story appropriate, or would "Civil War" have been a better title? Explain.

6. **Big Idea** **Draw Conclusions About Theme** What message about life do you think emerges from Jonathan's unexpected, but repeated, good fortune? Support your response with evidence from the story.

7. **Draw Conclusions About the Author** How might Achebe's personal history have influenced his portrayals of Jonathan and the other characters?

Literary Element Dialect

Dialect identifies a group of people and shows their common history.

8. **Analyze Dialect** What words in the text show the British influence in Nigeria?

9. **Make Inferences About Characters** Why do you think the thieves speak with a heavier accent than Jonathan does?

Reading Strategy Analyze Historical Context

Achebe's details about **historical context** clearly illustrate the lawlessness of postwar Nigeria. Review the blue highlighted questions and the web you made on page 49.

10. How would you describe the "civil peace" in Nigeria?

11. How does Jonathan's attitude about the effects of war on him and his family relate to a theme of the story?

LOG ON ▶ **Literature** Online

Selection Resources For Selection Quizzes, eFlashcards, and Reading-Writing Connection activities, go to glencoe.com and enter QuickPass code GL57805u1.

Vocabulary Practice

Practice with Denotation and Connotation

Connotation is the implied, or cultural, meaning of a word. **Denotation** is the literal, or dictionary, meaning of a word. For example, the words *confused* and *flustered* have similar denotations, but *flustered* suggests a nervous, flighty kind of confusion.

Each of these vocabulary words is listed with a word or term that has a similar denotation. Analyze the textual context of each vocabulary word in the story. Then explain the differences between the denotations and connotations below.

1. commandeer   take over
2. amenable   responsive
3. retail   sell
4. edifice   building

Writing

Write a List Imagine that a police officer has come to interview Jonathan about the robbery. List questions that the police officer might ask, and write what you imagine Jonathan's responses might be. Try to mimic Jonathan's dialect in his answers.

TEKS

10.1.E Use a dictionary, a glossary, or a thesaurus (printed or electronic) to determine or confirm the meanings of words and phrases, including their connotations and denotations, and their etymology.

Vocabulary Workshop

Dictionary Use

"There were now loud murmurs of dissent among the chorus: 'Na lie de man de lie; e get plenty money...'"

—Chinua Achebe, from "Civil Peace"

Literature Connection In this scene from "Civil Peace," thieves surround Jonathan's house and demand payment. Their leader agrees to settle for twenty pounds. They are speaking in a Nigerian dialect, but there's a standard English word that is key to this passage. What does *dissent* mean? A printed or electronic dictionary can tell you.

Find a Word The main part of a dictionary consists of word entries and their definitions, or denotations. Look for guide words at the top of each page. These tell you the first and last words listed on the page and can help you locate entries much more quickly than if you simply browse.

The Main Entry A main entry tells you far more about a word than its definition. Here is what one dictionary says about *dissent*:

Entry word is broken into syllables.

The pronunciation is indicated in simplified spelling.

The part or parts of speech of the word are indicated.

dis·sent (di sent′) *v.i.* **1.** to differ in opinion or feeling; withhold approval; disagree (often with *from*): *Many people dissented from the policy of the government. Of the ten board members, only one dissented.* **2.** to refuse to conform to the rules, doctrines, or beliefs of an established church. —*n.* **1.** difference of opinion or feeling; disagreement. **2.** refusal to conform to rules, doctrines, or beliefs of an established church. [Latin *dissentíre* to disagree.] —**Syn.** *v.i.* **1.** see **disagree**

Example sentences show how a word is used.

The etymology explains the history of a word.

Dictionary entries may also provide

- preferred spellings when alternate forms of words are acceptable
- inflected forms of the main entry word, such as plurals, adverbs, or adjectives
- guidelines that show how a word is used in different contexts

---

Practice Use the dictionary entry in this lesson or another dictionary to answer the following questions.

1. What is the etymology, or history, of *dissent*?

2. Why might this dictionary have included two example sentences?

3. What word is given as a synonym for *dissent*? What is the denotation of this synonym? How do the connotations of *dissent* and its synonym differ?

Tip

Words that the dictionary shows as synonyms have about the same meaning, or **denotation**, as the entry word, but they usually have a different **connotation**, or implied meaning or association.

Technology

To use an online dictionary, simply enter a search word to find its definition. Online dictionaries also offer features such as illustrations, word games, language tips, and fun facts.

Vocabulary For more vocabulary practice, go to glencoe.com and enter QuickPass code GL57805u1.

Before You Read

The Masque of the Red Death

Meet **Edgar Allan Poe**
(1809–1849)

With his dark, deep-set eyes and intense gaze, Edgar Allan Poe looked the part of a Romantic poet. The rhythms of his poetry fascinated readers. His mystery and horror stories, with chilling plots and memorable characters, set a standard for subsequent writers.

> *"All that we see or seem*
> *Is but a dream within a dream."*
>
> —Edgar Allan Poe
> from "A Dream Within a Dream"

Early Struggles Poe was born in Boston, Massachusetts, to traveling actors. His father disappeared when Poe was an infant; his mother died when Poe was about two years old. John and Frances Allan of Richmond, Virginia, raised the boy but never legally adopted him. Poe took the Allans' surname as his middle name.

Poe attended the University of Virginia. He was an excellent student but also a gambler, accumulating debts he could not repay. A gifted writer, Poe published his first book of poems at age eighteen. However, he made no money from the book.

Poe served in the army for two years and then entered the military academy at West Point, which dismissed him for skipping classes and drills. Finally, he moved to New York City and turned to writing full-time. His short story "MS. Found in a Bottle" won a writing prize, which led to a job at the *Southern Literary*

Messenger in Richmond. The magazine published many of his reviews, poems, essays, and stories.

Terrifying Tales At 26, Poe married Virginia Clemm, his teenage cousin, and lived with her and her mother. He continued to produce a steady stream of fiction, including the haunting horror tales "The Fall of the House of Usher" and "The Masque of the Red Death." His "Murders in the Rue Morgue" is considered to be the first detective story.

By 1844 Poe's melodic poem "The Raven" had become a great success. However, his life was upended in 1847 when his cherished young wife died of tuberculosis.

In 1849 Poe went to Richmond to give a lecture and was expected later in Philadelphia. But he was found unconscious on a street in Baltimore and died several days later. The cause of his death remains unknown.

LOG ON ▶ **Literature** Online

Author Search For more about Edgar Allan Poe, go to glencoe.com and enter QuickPass code GL57805u1.

Literature and Reading Preview

Connect to the Story

What events do you perceive as beyond your control? Freewrite for a few minutes about these events.

Build Background

Plague is a contagious bacterial disease that spreads rapidly and is usually fatal. Throughout history it has caused major epidemics. The most widespread epidemic began in Constantinople in 1334 and quickly spread throughout Europe, causing an estimated 25 million deaths. The disease came to be known as the Black Death.

Set Purposes for Reading

Big Idea Encountering the Unexpected

As you read "The Masque of the Red Death," ask yourself, How does Poe use setting and plot twists to introduce unexpected events?

Literary Element Allegory

An **allegory** is a narrative work with two levels of meaning—the literal and the symbolic. All or most of the characters, settings, and events in an allegory are **symbols** that stand for ideas beyond themselves. The overall purpose of an allegory is to teach a moral lesson. As you read, ask yourself, What moral lesson does Poe teach the reader through his use of allegorical symbols?

Reading Strategy Interpret Imagery

Writers often use **imagery,** or sensory language that appeals to one or more of the five senses. Imagery utilizes "word pictures" to evoke emotional responses and help readers understand a story's meaning and mood. As you read, ask yourself, Which of Poe's sensory details help generate suspense?

....

Tip: Make Inferences Create a chart that lists images from the story and the inferences you can make based on them.

Imagery	Inference
"Blood was its Avatar and its seal— the redness and the horror of blood."	The Red Death is a horrible disease.

TEKS

For pages 57–67

10.7 Understand, make inferences and draw conclusions about how an author's sensory language creates imagery in literary text and provide evidence from text to support understanding. Explain the function of symbolism, allegory, and allusions in literary works.

Vocabulary

profuse (prə fūs′) *adj.* great in amount; plentiful; p. 59 *A profuse rain often leads to flooding.*

countenance (koun′ tə nəns) *n.* the face; p. 61 *Her smiling countenance revealed her happiness.*

wanton (wont′ ən) *adj.* shamelessly unrestrained; immoral; p. 62 *Sometimes, wild dancing makes dancers seem wanton.*

spectral (spek′ trəl) *adj.* ghostlike; p. 64 *The gleaming snow gave the scene a spectral quality.*

blasphemous (blas′ fə məs) *adj.* showing disrespect or scorn for God or anything sacred; p. 64 *As she grew angrier, her words became increasingly blasphemous.*

....

Tip: Analogies To solve an analogy, determine the relationship between the first pair of words. Then apply that relationship to infer the meaning of the missing word in the second pair.

⊛ The Masque of the Red Death ⊛

Edgar Allan Poe

Bodiam Castle, 1906. Wilfred Ball.

The "Red Death" had long devastated the country. No pestilence had ever been so fatal, or so hideous. Blood was its Avatar[1] and its seal—the redness and the horror of blood. There were sharp pains, and sudden dizziness, and then **profuse** bleeding at the pores, with dissolution.[2] The scarlet stains upon the body and especially upon the face of the victim, were the pest ban[3] which shut him out from the aid and from the sympathy of his fellow-men. And the whole seizure, progress, and termination of the disease, were the incidents of half an hour.

But the Prince Prospero was happy and dauntless[4] and sagacious.[5] When his dominions[6] were half depopulated, he summoned to his presence a thousand hale and light-hearted friends from

---

1. In Hinduism, an *avatar* is a god that takes on human form. Here, the word means a visible form, or embodiment, of the disease.
2. Here, *dissolution* is death.

3. A *pest ban* is an official declaration that a person has been stricken with plague. Here, the blood stains on the victim's body became his or her own pest ban.
4. *Dauntless* means "fearless" or "courageous."
5. *Sagacious* means "wise."
6. The prince's *dominions* are the territories he rules.

Encountering the Unexpected *After the grim description of the Red Death, why do you suppose Prince Prospero and his friends seem so lighthearted?*

among the knights and dames of his court, and with these retired to the deep seclusion of one of his castellated abbeys.[7] This was an extensive and magnificent structure, the creation of the prince's own eccentric yet august taste. A strong and lofty wall girdled it in. This wall had gates of iron. The courtiers, having entered, brought furnaces and massy hammers and welded the bolts. They resolved to leave means neither of ingress nor egress[8] to the sudden impulses of despair or of frenzy from within. The abbey was amply provisioned. With such precautions the courtiers might bid defiance to contagion. The external world could take care of itself. In the meantime it was folly to grieve, or to think. The prince had provided all the appliances of pleasure. There were buffoons, there were improvisatori,[9] there were ballet-dancers, there were musicians, there was Beauty, there was wine. All these and security were within. Without was the "Red Death."

It was toward the close of the fifth or sixth month of his seclusion, and while the pestilence raged most furiously abroad, that the Prince Prospero entertained his thousand friends at a masked ball of the most unusual magnificence.

It was a voluptuous[10] scene, that masquerade. But first let me tell of the rooms in which it was held. There were seven—an imperial suite. In many palaces, however, such suites form a long and straight vista, while the folding doors slide back nearly to the walls on either hand, so that the view of the whole extent is scarcely impeded. Here the case was very different; as might have been expected from the duke's love of the *bizarre*. The apartments were so irregularly disposed[11] that the vision embraced but little more than one at a time. There was a sharp turn at every twenty or thirty yards, and at each turn a novel effect. To the right and left, in the middle of each wall, a tall and narrow Gothic window looked out upon a closed corridor which pursued the windings of the suite. These windows were of stained glass whose color varied in accordance with the prevailing hue of the decorations of the chamber into which it opened.

Visual Vocabulary
Gothic architecture developed in Europe between the twelfth and sixteenth centuries. A Gothic window has a pointed arch and many small panes of stained or clear glass.

That at the eastern extremity was hung, for example, in blue—and vividly blue were its windows. The second chamber was purple in its ornaments and tapestries, and here the panes were purple. The third was green throughout, and so were the casements.[12] The fourth was furnished and lighted with orange—the fifth with

---

7. A *castellated abbey* is a fortified structure originally built as a monastery or intended, as the prince's was, to resemble one.
8. With *means neither of ingress nor egress,* there is no way in and no way out.
9. *Buffoons* are clowns or comedians, and *improvisatori* (im prov′ ə zə tôr′ ē) are poets who improvise, or make up, verses as they perform.
10. Here, *voluptuous* (və lup′ ch‌o͞o əs) means "giving great pleasure to the senses."

Allegory *What does the secluded abbey symbolize?*

11. *Bizarre* means "that which is extremely strange or odd." A bizarre feature of Prospero's abbey is the way the rooms *(apartments)* are arranged *(disposed)* so that only one is visible at a time.
12. *Casements* are windows.

Encountering the Unexpected *How does the description of the layout of the rooms highlight the atmosphere in the story?*

white—the sixth with violet. The seventh apartment was closely shrouded in black velvet tapestries that hung all over the ceiling and down the walls, falling in heavy folds upon a carpet of the same material and hue. But in this chamber only, the color of the windows failed to correspond with the decorations. The panes here were scarlet—a deep blood color. Now in no one of the seven apartments was there any lamp or candelabrum, amid the profusion of golden ornaments that lay scattered to and fro or depended from the roof. There was no light of any kind emanating from lamp or candle within the suite of chambers. But in the corridors that followed the suite, there stood, opposite to each window, a heavy tripod, bearing a brazier of fire, that projected its rays through the tinted glass and so glaringly illumined the room. And thus were produced a multitude of gaudy and fantastic appearances. But in the western or black chamber the effect of the fire-light that streamed upon the dark hangings through the blood-tinted panes was ghastly in the extreme, and produced so wild a look upon the **countenances** of those who entered, that there were few of the company bold enough to set foot within its precincts at all.

It was in this apartment, also, that there stood against the western wall, a gigantic clock of ebony. Its pendulum swung to and fro with a dull, heavy, monotonous clang; and when the minute-hand made the circuit of the face, and the hour was to be stricken,

Visual Vocabulary
A *brazier* is a metal pan used to hold burning coal or charcoal, as a source of heat and light.

Vocabulary

countenance (koun′ tə nəns) n. the face

there came from the brazen[13] lungs of the clock a sound which was clear and loud and deep and exceedingly musical, but of so peculiar a note and emphasis that, at each lapse of an hour, the musicians of the orchestra were constrained to pause, momentarily, in their performance, to hearken to the sound; and thus the waltzers perforce ceased their evolutions; and there was a brief disconcert[14] of the whole gay company; and, while the chimes of the clock yet rang, it was observed that the giddiest grew pale, and the more aged and sedate passed their hands over their brows as if in confused revery or meditation. But when the echoes had fully ceased, a light laughter at once pervaded the assembly; the musicians looked at each other and smiled as if at their own nervousness and folly, and made whispering vows, each to the other, that the next chiming of the clock should produce in them no similar emotion; and then, after the lapse of sixty minutes (which embrace three thousand and six hundred seconds of the Time that flies), there came yet another chiming of the clock, and then were the same disconcert and tremulousness and meditation as before.

But, in spite of these things, it was a gay and magnificent revel. The tastes of the duke were peculiar. He had a fine eye for colors and effects. He disregarded the *decora* of mere fashion. His plans were bold and

---

13. The clock's outer parts are *ebony*, a black wood; its inner workings are brass *(brazen)*.
14. The musicians feel obliged *(constrained)* to stop playing, the waltzers halt their complex patterns of movement *(evolutions)*, and everyone experiences temporary confusion and disorder *(disconcert)*.

Interpret Imagery *How do people react to the sound of the chimes in this paragraph?*

Allegory *What does the chiming of the clock symbolize?*

Costume Ball in the Tuileries: Napoleon III and the Countess Castiglione, 1867. Jean Baptiste Carpeaux. Oil on canvas. Musée d'Orsay, Paris.

View the Art In this painting, Jean Baptiste Carpeaux uses a thick application, visible brushstrokes, and a lack of definition between his subjects to show a party of revelers. How do this painting and Carpeaux's techniques reflect the party in the story?

aders. Be sure they were grotesque. There were much glare and glitter and piquancy and phantasm—much of what has been since seen in "Hernani."[16] There were arabesque figures with unsuited limbs and appointments. There were delirious fancies such as the madman fashions. There were much of the beautiful, much of the **wanton,** much of the *bizarre,* something of the terrible, and not a little of that which might have excited disgust. To and fro in the seven chambers there stalked, in fact, a multitude of dreams. And these—the dreams—writhed in and about, taking hue from the rooms, and causing the wild music of the orchestra to seem as the echo of their steps. And, anon, there strikes the ebony clock which stands in the hall of the velvet. And then, for a moment, all is still, and all is silent save the voice of the clock. The dreams are stiff-frozen as they stand. But the echoes of the chime die away—they have endured but an instant—and a light, half-subdued laughter floats after them as they depart. And now again the music

fiery, and his conceptions glowed with barbaric luster. There are some who would have thought him mad. His followers felt that he was not. It was necessary to hear and see and touch him to be *sure* that he was not.

He had directed, in great part, the movable embellishments of the seven chambers, upon occasion of this great *fête;*[15] and it was his own guiding taste which had given character to the masquer-

---

15. A *fête* (fet) is a large, elaborate party.

---

16. Here, *piquancy* (pē′ kən sē) refers to what is charming, and *phantasm* to what is fantastic and unreal. "*Hernani*," an 1830 drama and, especially, an opera based on the drama, is notable for its use of colorful, imaginative spectacle.

Vocabulary

wanton (wont′ ən) *adj.* shamelessly unrestrained; immoral swells, and the dreams live, and writhe to and fro more merrily than ever, taking hue from the many-tinted windows through which stream the rays from the tripods. But to the chamber which lies most westwardly of the seven there are now none of the maskers who venture; for the night is waning away; and there flows a ruddier light through the blood-colored panes; and the blackness of the sable drapery appals;[17] and to him whose foot falls upon the sable carpet, there comes from the near clock of ebony a muffled peal more solemnly emphatic than any which reaches *their* ears who indulge in the more remote gaieties of the other apartments.

But these other apartments were densely crowded, and in them beat feverishly the heart of life. And the revel went whirlingly on, until at length there commenced the sounding of midnight upon the clock. And then the music ceased, as I have told; and the evolutions of the waltzers were quieted; and there was an uneasy cessation of all things as before. But now there were twelve strokes to be sounded by the bell of the clock; and thus it happened, perhaps that more of thought crept, with more of time, into the meditations of the thoughtful among those who reveled. And thus too, it happened, perhaps, that before the last echoes of the last chime had utterly sunk into silence, there were many individuals in the crowd who had found leisure to become aware of the presence of a masked figure which had arrested the attention of no single individual before. And the rumor of this new presence having spread itself whisperingly around, there arose at length from the whole company a buzz, or murmur, expressive of disapprobation[18] and surprise—then, finally, of terror, of horror, and of disgust.

In an assembly of phantasms such as I have painted, it may well be supposed that no ordinary appearance could have excited such sensation. In truth the masquerade license of the night was nearly unlimited; but the figure in question had out-Heroded Herod,[19] and gone beyond the bounds of even the prince's indefinite decorum. There are chords in the hearts of the most reckless which cannot be touched without emotion. Even with the utterly lost, to whom life and death are equally jests, there are matters of which no jest can be made. The whole company, indeed, seemed now deeply to feel that in the costume and bearing of the stranger neither wit nor propriety existed. The figure was tall and gaunt, and shrouded from head to foot in the habiliments[20] of the grave. The mask which concealed the visage was made so nearly to resemble the countenance of a stiffened corpse that the closest scrutiny must have had difficulty in detecting the cheat. And yet all this might have been endured, if not approved, by the mad revelers around. But the mummer had gone so far as to assume the type of the Red Death. His vesture[21] was dabbled in *blood*—and his broad brow, with all the features of the face, was besprinkled with the scarlet horror.

---

17. To *appal* means "to horrify, dismay, or shock."

18. *Disapprobation* means "disapproval."
19. To have *out-Heroded Herod,* the figure has done something even more outrageous than Herod the Great, the tyrant who, in an effort to kill the baby Jesus, allegedly ordered the murder of all male infants in Bethlehem.
20. *Habiliments* are clothes.
21. A *mummer* is a person dressed in a mask and costume for a party or play, and *vesture* is clothing.

Encountering the Unexpected *What clues does the author give that something is about to happen?*

Interpret Imagery *In a room full of bizarrely costumed people, why does this new figure cause such a stir?*

Eyes in Darkness. Artist unknown.

View the Art In *Eyes in Darkness,* the artist creates a shadowy figure who gazes directly at the viewer in an almost confrontational manner. How does the mystery surrounding this figure compare with what you know about the stranger dressed as the Red Death?

When the eyes of Prince Prospero fell upon this **spectral** image (which, with a slow and solemn movement, as if more fully to sustain its *rôle*, stalked to and fro among the waltzers) he was seen to be convulsed, in the first moment with a strong shudder either of terror or distaste; but, in the next, his brow reddened with rage.

"Who dares"—he demanded hoarsely of the courtiers who stood near him—"who dares insult us with this **blasphemous** mockery? Seize him and unmask him—that we may know whom we have to hang, at sunrise, from the battlements!"

It was in the eastern or blue chamber in which stood the Prince Prospero as he uttered these words. They rang throughout the seven rooms loudly and clearly, for the prince was a bold and robust man, and the music had become hushed at the waving of his hand.

It was in the blue room where stood the prince, with a group of pale courtiers by his side. At first, as he spoke, there was a slight rushing movement of this group in the direction of the intruder, who, at the moment was also near at hand, and now, with deliberate and stately step, made closer approach to the speaker. But from a certain nameless awe with which the mad assumptions of the mummer had inspired the whole party, there were found none who put forth hand to seize him; so that, unimpeded, he passed within a yard of the prince's person; and, while the vast assembly, as if with one impulse, shrank from the centers of the rooms to the walls, he made his way uninterruptedly, but with the same solemn and measured step which had distinguished him from the first, through the blue chamber to the purple—through the purple to the green—through the green to the orange—through this again to the white—and even thence to the violet, ere a decided movement had been made to arrest him. It was then, however, that the Prince Prospero, maddening with rage and the shame of his own momentary cowardice, rushed hurriedly through the six chambers, while none followed him on account of a deadly terror

that had seized upon all. He bore aloft a drawn dagger, and had approached, in rapid impetuosity, to within three or four feet of the retreating figure, when the latter, having attained the extremity of the velvet apartment, turned suddenly and confronted his pursuer. There was a sharp cry—and the dagger dropped gleaming upon the sable carpet, upon which, instantly afterward, fell prostrate in death the Prince Prospero. Then, summoning the wild courage of despair, a throng of the revelers at once threw themselves into the black apartment, and, seizing the mummer, whose tall figure stood erect and motionless within the shadow of the ebony clock, gasped in unutterable horror at finding the grave :cerements: and corpse-like mask, which they handled with so violent a rudeness, untenanted[22] by any tangible form.

Visual Vocabulary
Cerements are strips of cloth used to wrap a dead body.

And now was acknowledged the presence of the Red Death. He had come like a thief in the night. And one by one dropped the revellers in the blood-bedewed halls of their revel, and died each in the despairing posture of his fall. And the life of the ebony clock went out with that of the last of the gay. And the flames of the tripods expired. And Darkness and Decay and the Red Death held illimitable[23] dominion over all. ❧

---

22. *Untenanted* means "unoccupied" or "uninhabited."
23. *Illimitable* means "limitless" or "incapable of being bounded."

Allegory *What is the significance of the dropped dagger?*

Encountering the Unexpected *Why do you think the figure is able to walk from room to room without anyone stopping him?*

After You Read

Respond and Think Critically

1. **Connect to Personal Experience** Describe your feelings about the masked ball at the beginning and as the story progressed.

2. **Explain Description** Why is the Red Death such a feared disease? What aspect of the Red Death is portrayed as sinister? Explain.

3. **Make Inferences About Character** How does Prince Prospero respond to the costume and behavior of the uninvited guest? What does his response reveal about his attitude toward death?

4. **Evaluate Allusion** At the end of the story, Poe alludes to a biblical prophecy that the day of judgment will come "as a thief in the night." Why do you think Poe makes this **allusion,** or indirect reference? Do you think it's an effective allusion? Why or why not? Use evidence from the story to support your answer.

5. **Big Idea** **Draw Conclusions About Foreshadowing** Does Poe prepare you for the ending, or is it unexpected? Explain. What clues in the story might **foreshadow,** or hint at, the ending?

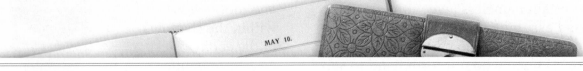

Daily Life & Culture

The Plague

Also called the Black Death, the bubonic plague swept throughout Europe in the mid-1300s. Synthesize the information from both the map and the graph to draw conclusions about the spread of the plague. Then answer the questions that follow.

The second pandemic of the Black Death in Europe, 1347-51

Extent of spread:
1347
Middle of 1348
End of 1348
1349
1350
1351
1353
■ Partially or totally spared
▲ Seriously affected

Encyclopædia Britannica, Inc.

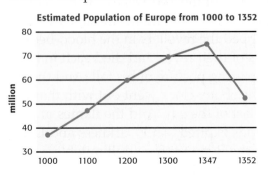

Estimated Population of Europe from 1000 to 1352

million

1000 1100 1200 1300 1347 1352

1. Approximately when did the plague reach Naples? When did the plague reach London? What was the population in Europe at that time?

2. When did the plague reach Kiev and what was the population of Europe then?

3. What conclusions can you draw about the effect of the plague on Europe's population?

Literary Element | Allegory

The underlying meaning of an **allegory** has philosophical, social, religious, or political significance. Characters or material objects **symbolize** something beyond themselves and often stand for abstract ideas, such as justice, evil, or truth.

6. Analyze Moral What is the symbolic significance of Prince Prospero's name? In his representation of Prince Prospero and the revelers, what moral does Poe suggest about class divisions in society?

7. Analyze Symbol How does the abbey's seventh chamber function as a symbol?

8. Draw Conclusions About Allegory What philosophical truth about human life does Poe teach in his allegory? Support your answer with references to the pink highlighted passages and questions in the story.

Review: Setting

As you learned on page 9, **setting** is the time and place in which the events of a story occur. Setting also includes the historical and cultural context of the work—the ideas, customs, values, and beliefs of a particular time and place. In describing the setting, authors may use **figurative language**—expressions, or figures of speech, that may not be literally true, but that still convey some truth.

9. Partner Activity With a partner, create a chart similar to the one below. In the left column, cite examples of figurative language in Poe's description of the abbey and the ball. In the right column, explain how each example is related to the historical and cultural aspects of the setting. Use the example below to get started.

Example	Relation to Setting
p. 61 "there came from the brazen lungs of the clock a sound"	large chiming clocks were probably common in the Middle Ages

Reading Strategy | Interpret Imagery

 Texas Test Practice (10.7)

1. The description of Prince Prospero's seventh room (page 61) is intended to remind the reader of death because

(A) it has two tall gothic windows

(B) all the light originates from two corridors outside the room

(C) alone among the rooms, its window glass is of a different color from the furnishings

(D) an enormous ebony clock stands against its western wall

(E) it is the last in the series of rooms and is furnished entirely in black

Vocabulary Practice

Practice with Analogies Choose the word that best completes each analogy.

1. nose : countenance :: finger :
   a. thumb   **b.** knuckle   **c.** hand

2. generous : stingy :: profuse :
   a. sufficient   **b.** meager   **c.** abundant

3. blasphemous : reverent :: healthy :
   a. robust   **b.** sickly   **c.** hale

4. jealous : possessive :: spectral :
   a. grisly   **b.** gruesome   **c.** ghostly

5. bizarre : ordinary :: wanton :
   a. restrained   **b.** immoral   **c.** cruel

Respond Through Writing

Expository Essay

TEKS

10.15.C.i–iii Write an interpretative response to an expository or a literary text (e.g., essay or review) that extends beyond a summary and literal analysis; addresses the writing skills for an analytical essay and provides evidence from the text using embedded quotations; and analyzes the aesthetic effects of an author's use of stylistic and rhetorical devices.

Analyze Symbolism "The Masque of the Red Death" is an allegory: a story in which the character, setting, and events stand for figures beyond themselves. In an interpretative essay, analyze how Poe uses the clock as a symbol in the allegory. Support your ideas with evidence from the text.

Purpose and Audience When you write an **expository essay** about a literary work, your purpose is to define and explain ideas and relationships in the work. An **interpretative response** is one type of expository essay in which you go beyond a summary and literal analysis of a work to analyze the aesthetic effects of an author's use of stylistic devices. In this assignment, your audience is made up of people who have also read the story.

Plan Find references to the clock in the story and think about how it functions as a symbol by creating a chart like this one.

Question	Answer
What does the clock do?	
How do the chimes affect people?	
What is unique or unusual about the clock?	

Use your ideas and inferences about the clock to come up with the thesis, or controlling idea, for your essay. Plan the organizing structure of your essay and list the main ideas you will use to support your thesis.

Draft As you draft the body of your essay, incorporate evidence from the story. That is, embed quotations about the clock and its effects and then explain them. For example, explain why the size of the clock contributes to its symbolic significance.

Revise Exchange papers with a classmate and evaluate each other's essays. Does each body paragraph contain at least one piece of quoted evidence? Is each piece of quoted evidence followed by an explanation of what it means?

Edit Edit your paper, correcting any errors in grammar, spelling, and punctuation. Use the Grammar Tip in the side column to help you use reciprocal pronouns.

> **Grammar Tip**
>
> **Reciprocal Pronouns**
>
> Use reciprocal pronouns to show that two or more subjects carry out an action at the same time. Reciprocal means "shared by both sides." In modern English, *each other* and *one another* are the reciprocal pronouns you'll commonly encounter.
>
> *The dancers bowed to **each other** before they began the waltz.*
>
> *The musicians looked at **one another** and smiled as if at their own nervousness and folly.*
>
> Traditionally, *each other* is used when only two subjects are carrying out an action, and *one another* is used for groups of more than two. While this is a good rule of thumb, it is not a strict rule of grammar and many good writers use the terms interchangeably.

PART 2

Making Choices

Girl with Red Gloves, 2001. Lizzie Riches. Oil on canvas, 29.92 x 22.83 in. Private collection.

View the Art The artist titled this painting *Girl with Red Gloves,* but the girl also has black gloves before her. What messages about choice does this painting demonstrate?

BIG IDEA

Morning to night, people are faced with choices. Some of those choices have the power to change who we are. In the short stories in Part 2, you will read about difficult choices and surprising consequences. As you read these stories, ask yourself, How do the choices you make affect your life?

TEKS

For pages 70–71

10.5 Understand, make inferences and draw conclusions about the structure and elements of fiction and provide evidence from text to support understanding.

LITERARY FOCUS

Theme and Character

How do short stories develop themes and create characters?

Have you ever been so angry that you said something you later regretted? Perhaps, like many teenagers, you have argued with a parent or guardian and later regretted the fight. How is it sometimes hard for people who are feeling strong emotions to make choices about what they say? How do your feelings affect the choices you make?

Distributed By Universal Press Syndicate. Reprinted with permission. All rights reserved.

"Only two kinds of daughters," she shouted in Chinese. "Those who are obedient and those who follow their own mind! Only one kind of daughter can live in this house. Obedient daughter!"

"Then I wish I weren't your daughter. I wish you weren't my mother," I shouted. As I said these things I got scared. It felt like worms and toads and slimy things crawling out of my chest, but it also felt good, that this awful side of me had surfaced, at last.

"Too late to change this," my mother said shrilly.

And I could sense her anger rising to its breaking point. I wanted to see it spill over.

—Amy Tan, *from* **"Two Kinds"**

Character

A person in a literary work is called a **character.** Main characters are the most important. Secondary characters are less important and are also called minor characters. There are other ways to describe characters. A **round** character reveals more than one personality trait. A **flat character** reveals only one personality trait throughout the story. A **static character** does not change in the course of a story, whereas a **dynamic character** does.

He was as much a stranger to the stars as were his innocent customers. Yet he said things which pleased and astonished everyone: that was more a matter of study, practice and shrewd guesswork.

—R. K. Narayan, *from* **"An Astrologer's Day"**

She was riding with her spinal column braced firmly against the back of the seat, and held a peeling patent-leather handbag in her lap with both hands. She bore the conscious serenity of someone accustomed to poverty.

—Gabriel García Márquez, *from* **"Tuesday Siesta"**

Characterization

Characterization The methods an author uses to develop a character are called **characterization.** Methods of characterization fall into two basic categories: direct and indirect. In **direct characterization,** a writer makes clear and direct statements about a character's personality. For example, in the excerpt above from "Tuesday Siesta," Márquez describes the woman as having "the conscious serenity of someone accustomed to poverty." In **indirect characterization,** the writer uses a character's words and actions as well as other characters' thoughts and statements to reveal a character's personality. In the excerpt from "An Astrologer's Day," Narayan uses the character's thoughts to tell the reader that the man does not see the future but does possess insight into his customers.

Theme

The **theme** of a story is its central message about life. A story's theme is different from its subject. If a story's subject is family, then its theme would be what the author says about family. Sometimes a theme is expressed directly. More commonly, a reader must look closely at the experiences of the main character and the lessons he or she learns to discover the theme. What lessons might the narrator of "Two Kinds" learn? How might those lessons relate to the theme?

Author's Purpose The **author's purpose** will affect the delivery and impact of a story's theme. An author writing to entertain usually communicates the theme through lessons the important characters learn.

He thought of all the evenings he had spent away from her, working; and he regretted them.

—Jack Finney, *from* **"Contents of the Dead Man's Pocket"**

Quickwrite

Make Inferences About Character When reading fiction, you will often need to make inferences about elements based on evidence from the text. Use a graphic organizer like the one below to note details about a character from a story you read in Part 2. In the center oval, write the character's name. In each of the eight ovals, write a word or phrase from the text that describes or relates to the character. Try to identify whether the character is flat or round, as well as static or dynamic, through the details you gather from the story. Finally, write two or three inferences you can make about the character based on the details you have noted.

Character's Name

LOG ON ▶ **Literature** Online

Literature and Reading For more about literary elements, go to glencoe.com and enter QuickPass code GL57805u1.

Before You Read

Two Kinds

Meet **Amy Tan**
(born 1952)

Writing has always been Amy Tan's passion. In fact, she published her first essay, "What the Library Means to Me," when she was just eight years old. Though Tan went on to become an award-winning author, her fame did not come easily.

Troubled Years Amy Tan was born in Oakland, California. Her parents had immigrated to the United States from China. When Tan was a teenager, her father and her older brother both died of brain tumors within the space of a few months. Tan's mother, who began to worry that toxic chemicals in the environment were responsible, moved the family first to Holland, then to Germany, and later to Switzerland. These were difficult years for Tan. She escaped by diving into the world of books. "Reading for me was a refuge," she says.

Tan describes herself at that time as "a horrible child. I was angry. I was numb. Teenagers are already cynical at that age. But I also had this layer of grief that came out in anger." Conflicts arose between mother and daughter, which lasted for years. Some of the issues were cultural, some were generational, and others were purely personal.

Fact and Fiction Later, Tan incorporated this tension into several novels, the first of which was *The Joy Luck Club*, published in 1989. This novel details the many differences between a young Chinese woman and her late mother's Chinese friends. The novel earned a great deal of praise for Tan and has since been turned into a play and a successful film. The story "Two Kinds" comes from that book.

> "*I have a life that inspires me with a lot of stories.*"
>
> —Amy Tan

Tan eventually resolved her differences with her mother, who encouraged her to tell the truth about painful details of their family's past. Many of these details found their way into Tan's next novel, *The Kitchen God's Wife*, as well as later works. Tan has now written five novels, a screenplay of *The Joy Luck Club*, and a book of essays titled *The Opposite of Fate: A Book of Musings*.

In these essays, Tan explores her own cultural heritage. As a young person, Tan has said, she tried to distance herself from her Chinese origins. However, her writing helped her discover how much her Chinese mother had influenced her. "My books have amounted to taking her stories—a gift to me—and giving them back to her."

LOG ON ▶ **Literature** Online

Author Search For more about Amy Tan, go to glencoe.com and enter QuickPass code GL57805u1.

Literature and Reading Preview

Connect to the Story

What experiences truly motivate people to achieve? List several of these experiences and then elaborate on one that motivated you to achieve something significant.

Build Background

This story is set in San Francisco's Chinatown, which is one of the largest Chinese communities outside of Asia. The neighborhood—with its fascinating mix of restaurants, shops, businesses, and religious and cultural institutions—is a crowded and bustling place. The area was settled by Chinese immigrants who arrived during the Gold Rush of 1849.

Big Idea Making Choices

As you read "Two Kinds," ask yourself, How are the narrator's choices different from her mother's?

Literary Element Motivation

Motivation is the reason or cause for a character's actions. Knowing a character's motivation for acting a certain way can help you understand his or her behavior more fully. Sometimes a character is motivated by an **internal conflict,** or a conflict within his or her own mind. A moral dilemma is one type of internal conflict in which a character struggles to decide what is the right or wrong way to act. Often, the options a character faces in a moral dilemma both seem right, though in different ways. As you read "Two Kinds," ask yourself, What motivations drive the characters' behavior?

Reading Strategy Connect to Personal Experience

Connecting is linking what you read to events and situations in your life or in other literary works you have read. When you **connect to personal experience,** you identify more closely with the characters' experiences as well as with the story's central theme. As you read, ask yourself, How can I link the experiences of the characters to my own life?

Tip: Connect Look for connections between story details and your life. Use the blue highlighted passages and questions to help you get started. Complete a simple chart like the one below to note the connections.

Story Detail	Personal Connection
narrator is child of immigrants	my grandparents were immigrants

TEKS

For pages 72–86

10.5.B Analyze differences in the characters' moral dilemmas in works of fiction across different countries or cultures.

Vocabulary

prodigy (prod′ə jē) *n.* an extraordinarily gifted or talented person, especially a child; p. 74 *The child prodigy played the difficult piece well.*

reproach (ri prōch′) *n.* blame; disgrace; discredit; p. 75 *My aunt did not criticize me aloud, but her look was filled with reproach.*

reverie (rev′ər ē) *n.* fanciful thinking; daydream; p. 78 *The teacher's abrupt question snapped me out of my reverie.*

discordant (dis kôrd′ənt) *adj.* not in agreement or harmony; p. 78 *While some violinists make beautiful music, I produce only discordant sounds.*

fiasco (fē as′kō) *n.* a complete or humiliating failure; p. 81 *None of the actors knew their lines, so the play was a fiasco.*

Tip: Word Usage Different contexts call for different levels of formality in word choice. You might use the word *daydream* to tell your thoughts to friends but in a formal composition, you might use the word *reverie* instead.

Two Kinds

Amy Tan

My mother believed you could be anything you wanted to be in America. You could open a restaurant. You could work for the government and get good retirement. You could buy a house with almost no money down. You could become rich. You could become instantly famous.

"Of course, you can be **prodigy**, too," my mother told me when I was nine. "You can be best anything. What does Auntie Lindo know? Her daughter, she is only best tricky."

America was where all my mother's hopes lay. She had come to San Francisco in 1949 after losing everything in China: her mother and father, her family home, her first husband, and two daughters, twin baby girls.

But she never looked back with regret. Things could get better in so many ways.

We didn't immediately pick the right kind of prodigy. At first my mother thought I could be a Chinese Shirley Temple. We'd watch Shirley's old movies on TV as though they were training films. My mother would poke my arm and say, "*Ni kan.* You watch." And I would see Shirley tapping her feet, or singing a sailor song, or pursing her lips into a very round O while saying "Oh, my goodness."

Visual Vocabulary
Shirley Temple was a popular child movie star of the 1930s.

Vocabulary

prodigy (prod′ə jē) *n.* an extraordinarily gifted or talented person, especially a child

---

Motivation *What reasons might the mother have for her optimism about the United States?*

"Ni kan," my mother said, as Shirley's eyes flooded with tears. "You already know how. Don't need talent for crying!"

Soon after my mother got this idea about Shirley Temple, she took me to the beauty training school in the Mission District and put me in the hands of a student who could barely hold the scissors without shaking. Instead of getting big fat curls, I emerged with an uneven mass of crinkly black fuzz. My mother dragged me off to the bathroom and tried to wet down my hair.

"You look like Negro Chinese," she lamented, as if I had done this on purpose.

The instructor of the beauty training school had to lop off these soggy clumps to make my hair even again. "Peter Pan is very popular these days," the instructor assured my mother. I now had hair the length of a boy's, with curly bangs that hung at a slant two inches above my eyebrows. I liked the haircut, and it made me actually look forward to my future fame.

In fact, in the beginning I was just as excited as my mother, maybe even more so. I pictured this prodigy part of me as many different images, and I tried each one on for size. I was a dainty ballerina girl standing by the curtain, waiting to hear the music that would send me floating on my tiptoes. I was like the Christ child lifted out of the straw manger, crying with holy indignity. I was Cinderella stepping from her pumpkin carriage with sparkly cartoon music filling the air.

In all of my imaginings I was filled with a sense that I would soon become perfect. My mother and father would adore me. I would be beyond **reproach.** I would never feel the need to sulk, or to clamor for anything.

But sometimes the prodigy in me became impatient. "If you don't hurry up and get me out of here, I'm disappearing for good," it warned. "And then you'll always be nothing."

Every night after dinner my mother and I would sit at the Formica-topped[1] kitchen table. She would present new tests, taking her examples from stories of amazing children that she had read in *Ripley's Believe It or Not* or *Good Housekeeping, Reader's Digest,* or any of a dozen other magazines she kept in a pile in our bathroom. My mother got these magazines from people whose houses she cleaned. And since she cleaned many houses each week, we had a great assortment. She would look through them all, searching for stories about remarkable children.

The first night she brought out a story about a three-year-old boy who knew the capitals of all the states and even of most of the European countries. A teacher was quoted as saying that the little boy could also pronounce the names of the foreign cities correctly. "What's the capital of Finland?" my mother asked me, looking at the story.

---

1. *Formica* (fôr mī′ kə) is a plastic substance used to cover kitchen and bathroom surfaces because it is resistant to heat and water.

Motivation *What motivates the mother to ask her daughter this question?*

Connect to Personal Experience *What kinds of daydreams about success do you have?*

Vocabulary

reproach (ri prōch′) *n.* blame; disgrace; discredit

All I knew was the capital of California, because Sacramento was the name of the street we lived on in Chinatown. "Nairobi!"[2] I guessed, saying the most foreign word I could think of. She checked to see if that might be one way to pronounce *Helsinki* before showing me the answer.

The tests got harder—multiplying numbers in my head, finding the queen of hearts in a deck of cards, trying to stand on my head without using my hands, predicting the daily temperatures in Los Angeles, New York, and London. One night I had to look at a page from the Bible for three minutes and then report everything I could remember. "Now Jehoshaphat[3] had riches and honor in abundance and . . . that's all I remember, Ma," I said.

And after seeing, once again, my mother's disappointed face, something inside me began to die. I hated the tests, the raised hopes and failed expectations. Before going to bed that night I looked in the mirror above the bathroom sink, and when I saw only my face staring back—and understood that it would always be this ordinary face—I began to cry. Such a sad, ugly girl! I made high-pitched noises like a crazed animal, trying to scratch out the face in the mirror.

And then I saw what seemed to be the prodigy side of me—a face I had never seen before. I looked at my reflection, blinking so that I could see more clearly. The girl staring back at me was angry, powerful. She and I were the same. I had new thoughts, willful thoughts—or, rather, thoughts filled with lots of won'ts. I won't let her change me, I promised myself. I won't be what I'm not. So now when my mother presented her

tests, I performed listlessly, my head propped on one arm. I pretended to be bored. And I was. I got so bored that I started counting the bellows of the foghorns out on the bay while my mother drilled me in other areas. The sound was comforting and reminded me of the cow jumping over the moon. And the next day I played a game with myself, seeing if my mother would give up on me before eight bellows. After a while I usually counted only one bellow, maybe two at most. At last she was beginning to give up hope.

Two or three months went by without any mention of my being a prodigy. And then one day my mother was watching the *Ed Sullivan Show*[4] on TV. The TV was old and the sound kept shorting out. Every time my mother got halfway up from the sofa to adjust the set, the sound would come back on and Sullivan would be talking. As soon as she sat down, Sullivan would go silent again. She got up—the TV broke into loud piano music. She sat down—silence. Up and down, back and forth, quiet and loud. It was like a stiff, embraceless dance between her and the TV set. Finally, she stood by the set with her hand on the sound dial.

She seemed entranced by the music, a frenzied little piano piece with a mesmerizing quality, which alternated between quick, playful passages and teasing, lilting[5] ones.

"*Ni kan*," my mother said, calling me over with hurried hand gestures. "Look here."

I could see why my mother was fascinated by the music. It was being pounded out by a little Chinese girl, about nine years old, with a Peter Pan haircut. The girl had the sauciness[6] of a Shirley Temple. She

---

2. *Nairobi* (nī rō´ bē) is the capital of Kenya in east central Africa.
3. *Jehoshaphat* (ji hosh´ə fat´) was a king of Judah in the ninth century B.C.

4. The *Ed Sullivan Show* was a popular weekly TV variety show that aired from 1955 to 1971.
5. *Lilting* means "light and lively."
6. *Sauciness* means "boldness that is playful and lighthearted."

was proudly modest, like a proper Chinese child. And she also did a fancy sweep of a curtsy, so that the fluffy skirt of her white dress cascaded to the floor like the petals of a large carnation.

In spite of these warning signs, I wasn't worried. Our family had no piano and we couldn't afford to buy one, let alone reams of sheet music and piano lessons. So I could be generous in my comments when my mother bad-mouthed the little girl on TV.

"Play note right, but doesn't sound good!" my mother complained. "No singing sound." "What are you picking on her for?" I said carelessly. "She's pretty good. Maybe she's not the best, but she's trying hard." I knew almost immediately that I would be sorry I had said that.

"Just like you," she said. "Not the best. Because you not trying." She gave a little huff as she let go of the sound dial and sat down on the sofa.

The little Chinese girl sat down also, to play an encore of "Anitra's Tanz," by Grieg. I remember the song, because later on I had to learn how to play it.

Three days after watching the *Ed Sullivan Show* my mother told me what my schedule would be for piano lessons and piano practice. She had talked to Mr. Chong, who lived on the first floor of our apartment building. Mr. Chong was a retired piano teacher, and

Visual Vocabulary
Edvard *Grieg* (grēg), 1843–1907, was a Norwegian composer.

my mother had traded housecleaning services for weekly lessons and a piano for me to practice on every day, two hours a day, from four until six.

When my mother told me this, I felt as though I had been sent to hell. I whined, and then kicked my foot a little when I couldn't stand it anymore.

"Why don't you like me the way I am?" I cried, "I'm *not* a genius! I can't play the piano. And even if I could, I wouldn't go on TV if you paid me a million dollars!"

My mother slapped me. "Who ask you to be genius?" she shouted. "Only ask you be your best. For you sake. You think I want you to be genius! Hnnh! What for! Who ask you!"

"So ungrateful," I heard her mutter in Chinese. "If she had as much talent as she has temper, she'd be famous now."

Mr. Chong, whom I secretly nicknamed Old Chong, was very strange, always tapping his fingers to the silent music of an invisible orchestra. He looked ancient in my eyes. He had lost most of the hair on the top of his head, and he wore thick glasses and had eyes that always looked tired. But he must have been younger than I thought, since he lived with his mother and was not yet married.

I met Old Lady Chong once, and that was enough. She had a peculiar smell, like a baby that had done something in its pants, and her fingers felt like a dead person's, like an old peach I once found in the back of the refrigerator; its skin just slid off the flesh when I picked it up.

I soon found out why Old Chong had retired from teaching piano. He was deaf. "Like Beethoven!" he shouted to me. "We're both listening only in our head!"

Making Choices *What might the narrator's choice to ignore the "warning signs" reveal about her?*

Connect to Personal Experience *Can you recall a situation in which you felt similarly about a decision you did not like? Explain.*

And he would start to conduct his frantic silent sonatas.[7]

Our lessons went like this. He would open the book and point to different things, explaining their purpose: "Key! Treble! Bass! No sharps or flats! So this is C major! Listen now and play after me!"

And then he would play the C scale a few times, a simple chord, and then, as if inspired by an old unreachable itch, he would gradually add more notes and running trills and a pounding bass until the music was really something quite grand.

I would play after him, the simple scale, the simple chord, and then just play some nonsense that sounded like a cat running up and down on top of garbage cans. Old Chong would smile and applaud and say, "Very good! But now you must learn to keep time!"

So that's how I discovered that Old Chong's eyes were too slow to keep up with the wrong notes I was playing. He went through the motions in half time. To help me keep rhythm, he stood behind me and pushed down on my right shoulder for every beat. He balanced pennies on top of my wrists so that I would keep them still as I slowly played scales and arpeggios.[8] He had me curve my hand around an apple and keep that shape when playing chords. He marched stiffly to show me how to make each finger dance up and down, staccato,[9] like an obedient little soldier.

He taught me all these things, and that was how I also learned I could be lazy and get away with mistakes, lots of mistakes. If I hit the wrong notes because I hadn't practiced enough, I never corrected myself. I just kept playing in rhythm. And Old Chong kept conducting his own private **reverie.**

So maybe I never really gave myself a fair chance. I did pick up the basics pretty quickly, and I might have become a good pianist at that young age. But I was so determined not to try, not to be anybody different, that I learned to play only the most ear-splitting preludes, the most **discordant** hymns.

Over the next year I practiced like this, dutifully in my own way. And then one day I heard my mother and her friend Lindo Jong both talking in a loud, bragging tone of voice so that others could hear. It was after church, and I was leaning against a brick wall, wearing a dress with stiff white petticoats. Auntie Lindo's daughter, Waverly, who was my age, was standing farther down the wall, about five feet away. We had grown up together and shared all the closeness of two sisters, squabbling over crayons and dolls. In other words, for the most part, we hated each other. I thought she was snotty. Waverly Jong had gained a certain amount of fame as "Chinatown's Littlest Chinese Chess Champion."

Making Choices *What choice has the narrator made about her piano playing?*

Connect to Personal Experience *When else have you learned about or experienced the type of relationship described here?*

---

7. *Sonatas* are instrumental compositions, commonly written for piano.
8. *Arpeggios* (är pej´ē ōz) are chords in which the notes are played in succession instead of all at the same time.
9. To play music *staccato* (stə kä´tō) is to produce sharp, distinct breaks between successive tones.

Connect to Personal Experience *Have you ever decided not to try your best? If so, how did you feel about your decision later?*

Vocabulary

reverie (rev´ər ē) *n.* fanciful thinking; daydream
discordant (dis kôrd´ənt) *adj.* not in agreement or harmony

"She bring home too many trophy," Auntie Lindo lamented that Sunday. "All day she play chess. All day I have no time do nothing but dust off her winnings." She threw a scolding look at Waverly, who pretended not to see her.

"You lucky you don't have this problem," Auntie Lindo said with a sigh to my mother.

And my mother squared her shoulders and bragged: "Our problem worser than yours. If we ask Jing-mei[10] wash dish, she hear nothing but music. It's like you can't stop this natural talent."

And right then I was determined to put a stop to her foolish pride.

A few weeks later Old Chong and my mother conspired to have me play in a talent show that was to be held in the church hall. By then my parents had saved up enough to buy me a secondhand piano, a black Wurlitzer spinet with a scarred bench. It was the showpiece of our living room.

Visual Vocabulary
A *spinet* (spin′it) is a small, upright piano.

For the talent show I was to play a piece called "Pleading Child," from Schumann's[11] *Scenes from Childhood*. It was a simple, moody piece that sounded more difficult than it was. I was supposed to memorize the whole thing. But I dawdled over it, playing a few bars and then cheating, looking up to see what notes followed. I never really listened to what I was playing. I daydreamed about being somewhere else, about being someone else.

The part I liked to practice best was the fancy curtsy: right foot out, touch the rose on the carpet with a pointed foot, sweep to the side, bend left leg, look up, and smile.

My parents invited all the couples from their social club to witness my debut. Auntie Lindo and Uncle Tin were there. Waverly and her two older brothers had also come. The first two rows were filled with children either younger or older than I was. The littlest ones got to go first. They recited simple nursery rhymes, squawked out tunes on miniature violins, and twirled hula hoops in pink ballet tutus, and when they bowed or curtsied, the audience would sigh in unison, "*Awww*," and then clap enthusiastically.

When my turn came, I was very confident. I remember my childish excitement. It was as if I knew, without a doubt, that the prodigy side of me really did exist. I had no fear whatsoever, no nervousness. I remember thinking, This is it! This is it! I looked out over the audience, at my mother's blank face, my father's yawn, Auntie Lindo's stiff-lipped smile, Waverly's sulky expression. I had on a white dress, layered with sheets of lace, and a pink bow in my Peter Pan haircut. As I sat down, I envisioned people jumping to their feet and Ed Sullivan rushing up to introduce me to everyone on TV.

And I started to play. Everything was so beautiful. I was so caught up in how lovely I looked that I wasn't worried about how I would sound. So I was surprised when I hit the first wrong note. And then I hit another, and another. A chill started at the top of my head and began to trickle down. Yet I couldn't stop playing, as though my hands were bewitched. I kept

10. *Jing-mei* (jing′mā)
11. Robert *Schumann* (shoo′män), 1810–1856, was a German composer.

Motivation *What do you think motivates the narrator's decision here?*

Motivation *What desire motivates the narrator here?*

Little Dancer of Fourteen Years, 1880–1881. Edgar Degas. Philadelphia Museum of Art.

View the Art The model for Degas' sculpture, Marie Van Goethem, was a poor girl from Belgium who dreamed of becoming the most famous dancer in the world. What similarities and differences can you find between Jing-mei and the girl in this sculpture?

thinking my fingers would adjust themselves back, like a train switching to the right track. I played this strange jumble through to the end, the sour notes staying with me all the way.

When I stood up, I discovered my legs were shaking. Maybe I had just been nervous, and the audience, like Old Chong, had seen me go through the right motions and had not heard anything wrong at all. I swept my right foot out, went down on my knee, looked up, and smiled. The room was quiet, except for Old Chong, who was beaming and shouting, "Bravo! Bravo! Well done!" But then I saw my mother's face,

her stricken face. The audience clapped weakly, and as I walked back to my chair, with my whole face quivering as I tried not to cry, I heard a little boy whisper loudly to his mother, "That was awful," and the mother whispered back, "Well, she certainly tried."

And now I realized how many people were in the audience—the whole world, it seemed. I was aware of eyes burning into my back. I felt the shame of my mother and father as they sat stiffly through the rest of the show.

We could have escaped during intermission. Pride and some strange sense of honor must have anchored my parents to their chairs. And so we watched it all: The eighteen-year-old boy with a fake moustache who did a magic show and juggled flaming hoops while riding a unicycle. The breasted girl with white makeup who sang an aria[12] from Madame Butterfly and got an honorable mention. And the eleven-year-old boy who won first prize playing a tricky violin song that sounded like a busy bee.

After the show the Hsus, the Jongs, and the St. Clairs, from the Joy Luck Club, came up to my mother and father.

"Lots of talented kids," Auntie Lindo said vaguely, smiling broadly.

"That was somethin' else," my father said, and I wondered if he was referring to me in a humorous way, or whether he even remembered what I had done.

Visual Vocabulary
Madame Butterfly is a famous opera by Italian composer Giacomo Puccini.

---

12. An *aria* (är′ē ə) is an elaborate composition for solo voice.

Storefront Window, Chinatown, NY, 1993. Don Jacot.

View the Art Look closely—this isn't a photograph, it's a *photorealistic* painting. Artist Don Jacot said he wanted his paintings to "reflect the culture around [him]." What do you think this painting reflects about the culture of Chinatown?

Waverly looked at me and shrugged her shoulders. "You aren't a genius like me," she said matter-of-factly. And if I hadn't felt so bad, I would have pulled her braids and punched her stomach.

But my mother's expression was what devastated me: a quiet, blank look that said she had lost everything. I felt the same way, and everybody seemed now to be coming up, like gawkers at the scene of an accident, to see what parts were actually missing.

When we got on the bus to go home, my father was humming the busy-bee tune and my mother was silent. I kept thinking she wanted to wait until we got home before shouting at me. But when my father unlocked the door to our apartment, my mother walked in and went straight to the back, into the bedroom. No accusations. No blame. And in a way, I felt disappointed. I had been waiting for her to start shouting, so that I could shout back and cry and blame her for all my misery.

I had assumed that my talent-show **fiasco** meant that I would never have to play the

Motivation *Why do you think the mother reacts this way?*

Vocabulary

fiasco (fē as′kō) *n.* a complete or humiliating failure

AMY TAN **81**

piano again. But two days later, after school, my mother came out of the kitchen and saw me watching TV.

"Four clock," she reminded me, as if it were any other day. I was stunned, as though she were asking me to go through the talent-show torture again. I planted myself more squarely in front of the TV.

"Turn off TV," she called from the kitchen five minutes later.

I didn't budge. And then I decided. I didn't have to do what my mother said anymore. I wasn't her slave. This wasn't China. I had listened to her before, and look what happened. She was the stupid one.

She came out from the kitchen and stood in the arched entryway of the living room. "Four clock," she said once again, louder.

"I'm not going to play anymore," I said nonchalantly. "Why should I? I'm not a genius."

She stood in front of the TV. I saw that her chest was heaving up and down in an angry way.

"No!" I said, and I now felt stronger, as if my true self had finally emerged. So this was what had been inside me all along. "No! I won't!" I screamed.

She snapped off the TV, yanked me by the arm and pulled me off the floor. She was frighteningly strong, half pulling, half carrying me toward the piano as I kicked the throw rugs under my feet. She lifted me up and onto the hard bench. I was sobbing by now, looking at her bitterly. Her chest was heaving even more and her mouth was open, smiling crazily as if she were pleased that I was crying.

"You want me to be someone that I'm not!" I sobbed. "I'll never be the kind of daughter you want me to be!"

"Only two kinds of daughters," she shouted in Chinese. "Those who are obedient and those who follow their own mind! Only one kind of daughter can live in this house. Obedient daughter!"

"Then I wish I weren't your daughter. I wish you weren't my mother," I shouted. As I said these things I got scared. It felt like worms and toads and slimy things crawling out of my chest, but it also felt good, that this awful side of me had surfaced, at last.

"Too late change this," my mother said shrilly.

And I could sense her anger rising to its breaking point. I wanted to see it spill over. And that's when I remembered the babies she had lost in China, the ones we never talked about. "Then I wish I'd never been born!" I shouted. "I wish I were dead! Like them."

It was as if I had said magic words. Alakazam!—her face went blank, her mouth closed, her arms went slack, and she backed out of the room, stunned, as if she were blowing away like a small brown leaf, thin, brittle, lifeless.

It was not the only disappointment my mother felt in me. In the years that followed, I failed her many times, each time asserting my will, my right to fall short of expectations. I didn't get straight As. I didn't become class president. I didn't get into Stanford. I dropped out of college.

Unlike my mother, I did not believe I could be anything I wanted to be. I could only be me.

Connect to Personal Experience *Think of a time when you said something you regretted. How did your reaction compare with the narrator's?*

Motivation *Why do you think the narrator has this desire?*

Making Choices *Why is this a significant choice?*

Young Girl at a Grand Piano, 1904. Carl Larsson.

View the Art Carl Larsson was a Swedish Realist painter who often used his own children as models in his art. Compare and contrast the attitude of the girl in this painting with that of Jing-mei.

And for all those years we never talked about the disaster at the recital or my terrible declarations afterward at the piano bench. Neither of us talked about it again, as if it were a betrayal that was now unspeakable. So I never found a way to ask her why she had hoped for something so large that failure was inevitable.

And even worse, I never asked her about what frightened me the most: Why had she given up hope? For after our struggle at the piano, she never mentioned my playing again. The lessons stopped. The lid to the piano was closed, shutting out the dust, my misery, and her dreams.

So she surprised me. A few years ago she offered to give me the piano, for my thirtieth birthday. I had not played in all those years. I saw the offer as a sign of forgiveness, a tremendous burden removed.

"Are you sure?" I asked shyly. "I mean, won't you and Dad miss it?"

"No, this your piano," she said firmly. "Always your piano. You only one can play."

"Well, I probably can't play anymore," I said. "It's been years."

"You pick up fast," my mother said, as if she knew this was certain. "You have natural talent. You could be genius if you want to."

"No, I couldn't."

"You just not trying," my mother said. And she was neither angry nor sad. She said it as if announcing a fact that could never be disproved. "Take it," she said.

But I didn't, at first. It was enough that she had offered it to me. And after that, every time I saw it in my parents' living room, standing in front of the bay window, it made me feel proud, as if it were a shiny trophy that I had won back.

Last week I sent a tuner over to my parents' apartment and had the piano reconditioned, for purely sentimental reasons. My mother had died a few months before, and I had been getting things in order for my father, a little bit at a time. I put the jewelry in special silk pouches. The sweaters she had knitted in yellow, pink, bright orange—all the colors I hated—I put in mothproof boxes. I found some old Chinese silk dresses, the kind with little slits up the sides. I rubbed the old silk against my skin, and then wrapped them in tissue and decided to take them home with me.

After I had the piano tuned, I opened the lid and touched the keys. It sounded even richer than I remembered. Really, it was a very good piano. Inside the bench were the same exercise notes with handwritten scales, the same secondhand music books with their covers held together with yellow tape.

I opened up the Schumann book to the dark little piece I had played at the recital. It was on the left-hand page, "Pleading Child." It looked more difficult than I remembered. I played a few bars, surprised at how easily the notes came back to me. And for the first time, or so it seemed, I noticed the piece on the right-hand side. It was called "Perfectly Contented." I tried to play this one as well. It had a lighter melody but with the same flowing rhythm and turned out to be quite easy. "Pleading Child" was shorter but slower; "Perfectly Contented" was longer but faster. And after I had played them both a few times, I realized they were two halves of the same song. ꙮ

Making Choices *Do you think the mother's choice here is consistent with how she has been portrayed thus far? Why or why not?*

Motivation *Do you think the narrator is correct about the motivation behind her mother's offer? Explain.*

After You Read

Respond and Think Critically

1. **Connect to Personal Experience** What was your reaction to the conflict between Jing-mei and her mother? Do you think that one person was more at fault than the other? Explain.

2. **Explain Events** How does Jing-mei feel when it is her turn to perform at the recital? Why do she and her parents feel so humiliated by her performance?

3. **Interpret Dialogue** What hurtful remark does Jing-mei say to her mother after their big argument? In your opinion, what makes her comments so brutal?

4. **Make Inferences About Character** What reasons does Jing-mei's mother give for offering Jing-mei the piano for her thirtieth birthday? Do you think Jing-mei's mother finally forgives her daughter for her hurtful comment? Explain.

5. **Analyze Events** What do you think is the underlying issue of Jing-mei and her mother's final argument? How does the author illustrate the mounting tension between them?

6. **Analyze Character** How has Jing-mei changed by the end of the story? Explain your answer and suport it with evidence from the text. ◀️ OER

7. **Evaluate Narration** Who narrates this story? How do you think your reaction to the story would be different if another person had narrated it? Explain. Support your answer with evidence from the text.

8. **Big Idea** **Draw Conclusions About Plot** Which choice do you think is most central to the outcome of this story? Support your answer with evidence from the text.

Literary Element Motivation

In literature, a character's **motivation** is not always perfectly clear. At times, a character's motivation may be weak or mixed, making it difficult to discern or understand. Think about the characters in "Two Kinds." Was it easy or difficult to determine the motivation for their actions?

9. **Make Inferences About Character** Although the mother says that she only wants Jing-mei to "be [her] best. For [her] sake," what else might motivate her? Support your answer with details from the text.

10. **Analyze Moral Dilemmas** What moral dilemma does Jing-mei face, and how does this motivate her actions? How does Jing-mei's moral dilemma compare with that of a character from another story in Unit 1? Explain.

Review: Theme

As you learned on page 71, the **theme** is the central message of a literary work that readers can apply to life.

11. **Partner Activity** Meet with another classmate and review the title and main events in the story. Then determine how they contribute to the story's theme. Note the main events and other important details in a web like the one shown here.

Theme:

Reading Strategy — Connect to Personal Experience

When you **connect** to characters, you focus on their emotions and situations. Review your chart from page 73 to help you answer the following items.

12. Look back at the blue highlighted passages and questions in the story. List feelings, situations, or concepts from this story that are familiar to you from other literary works, films, or television shows.

13. With your classmates, identify entries that appear on a majority of your lists. Discuss why certain concepts or situations are common in literature, film, and television.

Vocabulary Practice

Practice with Usage Respond to these statements to help you explore the meanings of the boldfaced vocabulary words from the story.

1. Tell what a musical **prodigy** might do.

2. Give an example of a **reproach**.

3. Name two words that describe a **reverie**.

4. Give an example of something **discordant**.

5. Describe what happens in a **fiasco**.

Academic Vocabulary

The mother's desire for a prodigy was out of **proportion** *with her daughter's average talent.*

In the quotation above, *proportion* means "balance." The word *proportion* has additional meanings in specific subject areas, such as mathematics and architecture. Using context clues, try to figure out the meaning of *proportion* in the sentence below. Check a dictionary to confirm your deduction.

The critic praised the columns for their size and **proportion**.

For more on academic vocabulary, see pages 36–37 and R92–R94.

Enrich and Extend

 Speaking and Listening

Literature Groups With a small group, discuss whether it is advantageous to require children to participate in music, sports, academic contests, and similar activities. Try to reach a consensus—a general agreement within a group on an issue.

Teamwork To participate productively in your group, listen to others, build on their ideas, and contribute relevant information. You can avoid conflict by setting up ground rules up front for making decisions and building consensus.

Prepare Before your group meets, look back at "Two Kinds" to review the mother's requirements of Jing-mei and evaluate the advantages and disadvantages of the requirements. Write your evaluations in a chart like the one below. Add details from your own experiences or from the experiences of others you know.

Requirement	Advantage	Disadvantage
take many tests to see if Jing-mei is a genius	raises hopes for mother and Jing-mei	exposes Jing-mei and mother to many failures by Jing-mei

Discuss Participate actively and effectively in your group discussion. Respect others' viewpoints by listening attentively. Deliver your opinions in a normal tone of voice, providing clear, specific examples from your chart to support your judgments.

Report Have one group member orally state your consensus to the class or state that no consensus was reached, being sure to address the class clearly and loudly enough for all to hear.

Evaluate Write a paragraph in which you assess the effectiveness of your discussion. Use the rubric on page 237 to help in your evaluation.

 Literature Online

Selection Resources For Selection Quizzes, eFlashcards, and Reading-Writing Connection activities, go to glencoe.com and enter QuickPass code GL57805u1.

Grammar Workshop

Verbals

TEKS

10.17.A.i Use and understand the function of the following parts of speech in the context of reading, writing, and speaking: more complex active and passive tenses and verbals (gerunds, infinitives, participles).

Literature Connection A **verbal** is a verb form that functions in a sentence as a noun, an adjective, or an adverb. Learning how to understand and use verbals correctly will help you when you're reading, speaking, or writing. In the passage below from Amy Tan's "Two Kinds," the infinitives *to sulk* and *to clamor* function as direct objects (nouns).

> *"My mother and father would adore me. I would be beyond reproach. I would never feel the need to sulk, or to clamor for anything."*

Examples

A **gerund** is a type of verbal. Gerunds are verb forms that end in *-ing* and are used in the same way a noun is used.

Gerund functioning as subject: Acting would make her a star.

Gerund functioning as direct object: Everybody appreciated her acting.

Infinitives are verb forms that are usually preceded by the word *to* and that are used as nouns, adjectives, or adverbs.

Infinitive as noun: To quit seemed foolish after working so hard.

Infinitive as adjective: She had the urge to quit.

Infinitive as adverb: She could try to quit.

Participles can function as adjectives. Present participles always have an *-ing* ending. Past participles often end in *-ed,* but can take other endings as well.

Present participle as adjective: The smiling girl played the piano with ease.

Past participles as adjectives: Embarrassed, the girl ran away from the shocked audience.

Practice For each of the sentences below, tell which type of verbal is boldfaced. Explain how you know.

1. **Performing** meant everything to her.
2. Though she had already practiced for hours, she decided **to continue.**
3. **Rising** prices affected their choice of piano.
4. She was prepared **to argue.**
5. She did not enjoy **playing.**

Grammar Terms

A **subject** is the "who or what" of a sentence. A **direct object** is a noun naming the "who or what" that receives the action of a **verb.** An **adjective** describes a noun, and an **adverb** describes a verb.

Tip

When a word ends in *-ing,* remember that it is a gerund if it functions as a noun. It is a present participle if it functions as an adjective.

Language Handbook

For more on verbals, see the Language Handbook, pp. R50–R51.

LOG ON ▶ **Literature** Online

Grammar For more grammar practice, go to www.glencoe.com and enter QuickPass code GL57805u1.

Before You Read

Tuesday Siesta

Meet **Gabriel García Márquez**
(born 1928)

Born in Aracataca, Colombia, Gabriel García Márquez lived with his grandparents in "an enormous house, full of ghosts." His grandparents loved telling imaginative folktales, filled with omens, premonitions, and spirits. His grandfather also told stories about his war experiences, the triumphs of the South American revolutionary hero Simón Bolívar, and the plight of impoverished local farmers under an oppressive government. It is only natural then that García Márquez's literature features realistic themes and plots related to the culture and people of his childhood village, fantastic elements from his grandparents' tales, and new magical details from his imagination. He once said that the goal of all his writing is to conjure "the magic in commonplace events." This style of writing has come to be known as magical realism.

> "There's not a single line in all my work that does not have a basis in reality. The problem is that Caribbean reality resembles the wildest imagination."
>
> —Gabriel García Márquez

Education and Early Writing When García Márquez was eight years old, he was sent to a boarding school in the port city of Barranquilla, where his classmates nicknamed him "the Old Man" because he seemed so shy and serious. At twelve, he won a scholarship to a Jesuit school for gifted students, where he became an avid reader and writer. Although he focused on writing nonfiction in college, he wrote fiction as well. In 1946, when he was nineteen, he published his first short story, "The Third Resignation," in the Bogotá newspaper, *El Espectador*.

García Márquez worked for the newspaper for the next ten years. In 1955, after he wrote an exposé on government corruption in Colombia, Gustavo Rojas Pinilla, the Colombian dictator, shut down the newspaper. García Márquez then returned to fiction writing.

International Fame In 1960 García Márquez moved to Mexico City, where he gained fame as a screenwriter, journalist, novelist, and publicist. In 1967 he published his most famous work, the novel *One Hundred Years of Solitude*, which has been translated into many different languages and has sold millions of copies. In 1982 García Márquez received the highest international award for writing—the Nobel Prize in Literature.

Literature and Reading Preview

Connect to the Story

What advice have you gleaned from people or books that has helped you make better choices? Discuss this question with a partner. Consider the best advice you have been given.

Build Background

In tropical climates, many people avoid heatstroke and sunstroke by taking *siestas,* or naps. Siesta time usually begins around noon. Schools, shops, and even post offices often close so that people can go home, have a meal, and then rest for several hours. Later in the day, when the heat of the sun has diminished, activities resume.

Set Purposes for Reading

Big Idea Making Choices

As you read "Tuesday Siesta," ask yourself, What are the circumstances that lead a young man to make a tragic choice?

Literary Element Description

Description is writing that seeks to convey the impression of a setting, a person, an animal, an object, or an event by appealing to the senses. A good writer might use imagery or evocative words to appeal to the reader's senses. Good descriptive writing helps readers imagine a story's characters and setting. As you read, ask yourself, How does García Márquez use details to help you picture the characters and setting?

Reading Strategy Make Inferences About Theme

To **infer** is to make a reasonable guess about the meaning of a literary work based on what the author implies. A story's **theme,** or message, is often related to a work's cultural and historical context. As you read, ask yourself, How do details in the setting, plot, and dialogue give hints about the theme? What can I infer about the theme based on these details?

....

Tip: Take Notes Use a diagram like the one below to record your inferences and draw conclusions about the theme.

Inferences from Setting ex. humid air, stifling smoke — Inferences from Plot — Inferences from Characters — Conclusions About Theme

TEKS

For pages 88–97

10.2 Analyze, make inferences and draw conclusions about theme and genre in different cultural, historical, and contemporary contexts and provide evidence from the text to support understanding.

Vocabulary

interminable (in tur′mi nə bəl) *adj.* lasting, or seeming to last, forever; endless; p. 90 *We tried to be patient, but the rainstorm seemed interminable.*

serenity (sə ren′ə tē) *n.* calmness; peacefulness; p. 91 *The serenity of the deep, silent forest calmed my jittery nerves.*

scrutinize (skrōōt′ən īz′) *v.* to look at closely; to inspect carefully; p. 93 *I'm not sure I will recognize Sally, so I'll scrutinize the face of each woman who gets off the train.*

inscrutable (in skrōō′tə bəl) *adj.* mysterious; p. 94 *His face was inscrutable as he scanned the group—it was impossible to figure out what he was thinking.*

skeptical (skep′ti kəl) *adj.* having or showing doubt or suspicion; questioning; disbelieving; p. 94 *Roger is extremely forgetful, so I'm skeptical that he will remember to call.*

Tuesday Siesta

Gabriel García Márquez
Translated by J. S. Bernstein

The train emerged from the quivering tunnel of sandy rocks, began to cross the symmetrical, **interminable** banana plantations, and the air became humid and they couldn't feel the sea breeze any more. A stifling blast of smoke came in the car window. On the narrow road parallel to the railway there were oxcarts loaded with green bunches of bananas. Beyond the road, in uncultivated spaces set at odd intervals there were offices with electric fans, red-brick buildings, and residences with chairs and little white tables on the terraces among dusty palm trees and rosebushes. It was eleven in the morning, and the heat had not yet begun.

"You'd better close the window," the woman said. "Your hair will get full of soot."

The girl tried to, but the shade wouldn't move because of the rust.

They were the only passengers in the lone third-class car. Since the smoke of the locomotive kept coming through the window, the girl left her seat and put down the only things they had with them: a plastic sack with some things to eat and a bouquet of flowers wrapped in newspaper. She sat on the opposite seat, away from the window, facing her mother. They were both in severe and poor mourning clothes.

Make Inferences About Theme *What inference can you make about the story's theme based on this page? What evidence supports your inference?*

Visual Vocabulary
A *cassock* is a full-length garment worn by the clergy.

The girl was twelve years old, and it was the first time she'd ever been on a train. The woman seemed too old to be her mother, because of the blue veins on her eyelids and her small, soft, and shapeless body, in a dress cut like a cassock. She was riding with her spinal column braced firmly against the back of the seat, and held a peeling patent-leather handbag in her lap with both hands. She bore the conscientious **serenity** of someone accustomed to poverty.

By twelve the heat had begun. The train stopped for ten minutes to take on water at a station where there was no town. Outside, in the mysterious silence of the plantations, the shadows seemed clean. But the still air inside the car smelled like untanned leather. The train did not pick up speed. It stopped at two identical towns with wooden houses painted bright colors. The woman's head nodded and she sank into sleep. The girl took off her shoes. Then she went to the washroom to put the bouquet of flowers in some water.

When she came back to her seat, her mother was waiting to eat. She gave her a piece of cheese, half a corn-meal pancake, and a cookie, and took an equal portion out of the plastic sack for herself. While they ate, the train crossed an iron bridge very slowly and passed a town just like the ones before, except that in this one there was a crowd in the plaza. A band was playing a lively tune

under the oppressive sun. At the other side of town the plantations ended in a plain which was cracked from the drought.

The woman stopped eating.

"Put on your shoes," she said.

The girl looked outside. She saw nothing but the deserted plain, where the train began to pick up speed again, but she put the last piece of cookie into the sack and quickly put on her shoes. The woman gave her a comb.

"Comb your hair," she said.

The train whistle began to blow while the girl was combing her hair. The woman dried the sweat from her neck and wiped the oil from her face with her fingers. When the girl stopped combing, the train was passing the outlying houses of a town larger but sadder than the earlier ones.

"If you feel like doing anything, do it now," said the woman. "Later, don't take a drink anywhere even if you're dying of thirst. Above all, no crying."

The girl nodded her head. A dry, burning wind came in the window, together with the locomotive's whistle and the clatter of the old cars. The woman folded the plastic bag with the rest of the food and put it in the handbag. For a moment a complete picture of the town, on that bright August Tuesday, shone in the window. The girl wrapped the flowers in the soaking-wet newspapers, moved a little farther away from the window, and stared at her mother. She received a pleasant expression in return. The train began to whistle and slowed down. A moment later it stopped.

There was no one at the station. On the other side of the street, on the sidewalk shaded by the almond trees, only the pool hall was open. The town was floating in the heat. The woman and the girl got off the train and

> **"The town was floating in the heat."**

Vocabulary

serenity (sə renˈə tē) *n.* calmness; peacefulness

Description *What does the description in the last five lines of this page tell you about the town? What image does it create?*

Campanario, c. 1947. Joaquín Torres-García. Oil on board laid down on panel, 13¼ x 16½ in. Private collection. ©ARS NY.

View the Art Joaquín Torres-García was a Uruguayan painter who used geometric shapes and symbols to create a uniquely South American style of painting. How does this scene help you envision the town during siesta?

Keeping to the protective shade of the almond trees, the woman and the girl entered the town without disturbing the siesta. They went directly to the parish house.[1] The woman scratched the metal grating on the door with her fingernail, waited a moment, and scratched again. An electric fan was humming inside. They did not hear the steps. They hardly heard the slight creaking of a door, and immediately a cautious voice, right next to the metal grating: "Who is it?" The woman tried to see through the grating.

"I need the priest," she said.

crossed the abandoned station—the tiles split apart by the grass growing up between—and over to the shady side of the street.

It was almost two. At that hour, weighted down by drowsiness, the town was taking a siesta. The stores, the town offices, the public school were closed at eleven, and didn't reopen until a little before four, when the train went back. Only the hotel across from the station, with its bar and pool hall, and the telegraph office at one side of the plaza stayed open. The houses, most of them built on the banana company's model, had their doors locked from inside and their blinds drawn. In some of them it was so hot that the residents ate lunch in the patio. Others leaned a chair against the wall, in the shade of the almond trees, and took their siesta right out in the street.

"He's sleeping now."

"It's an emergency," the woman insisted. Her voice showed a calm determination.

The door was opened a little way, noiselessly, and a plump, older woman appeared, with very pale skin and hair the color of iron. Her eyes seemed too small behind her thick eyeglasses.

"Come in," she said, and opened the door all the way.

They entered a room permeated with an old smell of flowers. The woman of the house

---

1. A *parish house* is the home of the priest of a local church district.

Making Choices *Do you think the mother chooses to arrive when most people are inside? Explain.*

Making Choices *Why does the woman use the tone of voice she uses? Why does she say that it is an emergency?*

led them to a wooden bench and signaled them to sit down. The girl did so, but her mother remained standing, absent-mindedly, with both hands clutching the handbag. No noise could be heard above the electric fan.

The woman of the house reappeared at the door at the far end of the room. "He says you should come back after three," she said in a very low voice. "He just lay down five minutes ago."

"The train leaves at three-thirty," said the woman.

It was a brief and self-assured reply, but her voice remained pleasant, full of undertones.[2] The woman of the house smiled for the first time.

"All right," she said.

When the far door closed again, the woman sat down next to her daughter. The narrow waiting room was poor, neat, and clean. On the other side of the wooden railing which divided the room, there was a worktable, a plain one with an oilcloth cover, and on top of the table a primitive typewriter next to a vase of flowers. The parish records were beyond. You could see that it was an office kept in order by a spinster.[3]

The far door opened and this time the priest appeared, cleaning his glasses with a handkerchief. Only when he put them on was it evident that he was the brother of the woman who had opened the door.

"How can I help you?" he asked.

"The keys to the cemetery," said the woman.

The girl was seated with the flowers in her lap and her feet crossed under the bench. The priest looked at her, then looked at the woman, and then through the wire mesh of the window at the bright, cloudless sky.

"In this heat," he said. "You could have waited until the sun went down."

The woman moved her head silently. The priest crossed to the other side of the railing,

took out of the cabinet a notebook covered in oilcloth, a wooden penholder, and an inkwell, and sat down at the table. There was more than enough hair on his hands to account for what was missing on his head.

"Which grave are you going to visit?" he asked.

"Carlos Centeno's," said the woman.

"Who?"

"Carlos Centeno," the woman repeated.

The priest still did not understand.

"He's the thief who was killed here last week," said the woman in the same tone of voice. "I am his mother."

The priest **scrutinized** her. She stared at him with quiet self-control, and the Father blushed. He lowered his head and began to write. As he filled the page, he asked the woman to identify herself, and she replied unhesitatingly, with precise details, as if she were reading them. The Father began to sweat. The girl unhooked the buckle of her left shoe, slipped her heel out of it, and rested it on the bench rail. She did the same with the right one.

It had all started the Monday of the previous week, at three in the morning, a few blocks from there. Rebecca, a lonely widow who lived in a house full of odds and ends, heard above the sound of the drizzling rain someone trying to force the front door from outside. She got up, rummaged around in her closet for an ancient revolver that no one had fired since the days of Colonel Aureliano Buendía,[4] and went into the living room without turning on the

---

2. *Undertones* are underlying or implied meanings.
3. *Spinster* usually refers to an older woman who has never been married.

4. *Aureliano Buendía* (ou´ rä lyä´ nō bwän dē´ ä) is a character in García Márquez's famous novel, *One Hundred Years of Solitude.*

Make Inferences About Theme *Why does the priest blush? Does this interaction between the priest and the woman change your idea about the story's theme? Explain.*

Vocabulary

scrutinize (skroot´ ən īz´) *v.* to look at closely; to inspect carefully lights. Orienting herself not so much by the noise at the lock as by a terror developed in her by twenty-eight years of loneliness, she fixed in her imagination not only the spot where the door was but also the exact height of the lock. She clutched the weapon with both hands, closed her eyes, and squeezed the trigger. It was the first time in her life that she had fired a gun. Immediately after the explosion, she could hear nothing except the murmur of the drizzle on the galvanized roof. Then she heard a little metallic bump on the cement porch, and a very low voice, pleasant but terribly exhausted: "Ah, Mother." The man they found dead in front of the house in the morning, his nose blown to bits, wore a flannel shirt with colored stripes, everyday pants with a rope for a belt, and was barefoot. No one in town knew him.

"So his name was Carlos Centeno," murmured the Father when he finished writing.

"Centeno Ayala,"[5] said the woman. "He was my only boy."

The priest went back to the cabinet. Two big rusty keys hung on the inside of the door; the girl imagined, as her mother had when she was a girl and as the priest himself must have imagined at some time, that they were Saint Peter's keys.[6] He took them down, put them on the open notebook on the railing, and pointed with his forefinger to a place on the page he had just written, looking at the woman.

"Sign here."

The woman scribbled her name, holding the handbag under her arm. The girl picked up the flowers, came to the railing shuffling her feet, and watched her mother attentively.

The priest sighed.

"Didn't you ever try to get him on the right track?"

The woman answered when she finished signing.

"He was a very good man."

The priest looked first at the woman and then at the girl, and realized with a kind of pious[7] amazement that they were not about to cry. The woman continued in the same tone:

"I told him never to steal anything that anyone needed to eat, and he minded me. On the other hand, before, when he used to box, he used to spend three days in bed, exhausted from being punched."

"All his teeth had to be pulled out," interrupted the girl.

"That's right," the woman agreed. "Every mouthful I ate those days tasted of the beatings my son got on Saturday nights."

"God's will is **inscrutable**," said the Father.

But he said it without much conviction, partly because experience had made him a little **skeptical** and partly because of the heat. He suggested that they cover their heads to guard against sunstroke. Yawning, and now almost completely asleep, he gave them instructions about how to find Carlos Centeno's grave. When they came back, they didn't have to knock. They should put

---

7. The word *pious* (pī′əs) may mean either "having genuine reverence for God" or "having a false or hypocritical religious devotion."

Vocabulary

inscrutable (in skrōō′tə bəl) *adj.* mysterious
skeptical (skep′ti kəl) *adj.* having or showing doubt or suspicion; questioning; disbelieving

---

5. The young man's full name was Carlos *Centeno Ayala* (sen tā′ nō ä yä′ lə). In Spanish-speaking countries, one's first name and surname are, by custom, followed by the mother's maiden name.

6. *Saint Peter's keys* refers to the traditional belief of some Christians that Saint Peter is in charge of the keys to the gates of heaven.

the key under the door; and in the same place, if they could, they should put an offering for the Church. The woman listened to his directions with great attention, but thanked him without smiling.

The Father had noticed that there was someone looking inside, his nose pressed against the metal grating, even before he opened the door to the street. Outside was a group of children. When the door was opened wide, the children scattered. Ordinarily, at that hour there was no one in the street. Now there were not only children. There were groups of people under the almond trees. The Father scanned the street swimming in the heat and then he understood. Softly, he closed the door again.

"Wait a moment," he said without looking at the woman.

His sister appeared at the far door with a black jacket over her nightshirt and her hair down over her shoulders. She looked silently at the Father.

"What was it?" he asked.

"The people have noticed," murmured his sister.

"You'd better go out by the door to the patio," said the Father.

"It's the same there," said his sister. "Everybody is at the windows."

The woman seemed not to have understood until then. She tried to look into the street through the metal grating. Then she took the bouquet of flowers from the girl and began to move toward the door. The girl followed her.

"Wait until the sun goes down," said the Father.

"You'll melt," said his sister, motionless at the back of the room. "Wait and I'll lend you a parasol."

"Thank you," replied the woman. "We're all right this way."

She took the girl by the hand and went into the street. ◥

Making Choices *Why might the mother have chosen not to accept the woman's parasol?*

After You Read

Respond and Think Critically

1. **Connect to Personal Experience** For which character in this story do you feel the most sympathy? Explain.

2. **Interpret Dialogue** Carlos's mother refers to him as a thief but also tells the priest that he was "a very good man." What might she mean by this? Use details from the story to support your answer.

3. **Interpret Events** Why do the townspeople gather around the priest's house? What does the mother's response to their presence tell you about her?

4. **Evaluate Plot** How would you describe the relationship between the mother and the daughter? Do you think the plot would have been more interesting if the daughter had played a larger role? Explain.

5. **Make Inferences About Character** What can you tell about the mother in this story from what she says and does? Support your answer with evidence from the story. **◀︎OER**

6. **Big Idea Draw Conclusions About Events** Carlos, his mother, and the widow who shot him all make choices that contribute to Carlos's death. Whose choices are most responsible for his death? Is one of these characters wholly at fault, is society at fault, or is the blame shared by some combination? Explain.

7. **Analyze Cultural Context** Gabriel García Márquez lived much of his life in Colombia. What challenges does this story present to readers who are not familiar with Colombian culture the way Márquez is, and how can these challenges be addressed? Explain.

Literary Element Description

Writers often use sensory details and colorful words or phrases to describe the people, places, objects, and events in their stories. Descriptions appeal to readers' senses of sight, sound, touch, taste, and smell. Think back to some of the detailed and evocative descriptions in this story.

8. **Analyze Description** Look back at the pink highlighted question on page 91. What picture does this initial description paint of the town? Find other words and phrases García Márquez uses to describe the town. Do they contradict or reinforce this first description? Explain.

9. **Make Inferences About Character** Reread García Márquez's description of the mother in the first paragraph on page 91. Which details are particularly effective in creating a picture of her? What inferences can you make about her character based on this description? Explain.

Review: Character

As you learned on pages 70–71, a **flat** character reveals only one personality trait. By contrast, a **round** character shows varied and sometimes contradictory traits, like the "main characters" in your own life.

10. **Partner Activity** With a partner, use a chart like the one below to classify the characters in this story as flat or round. Then meet with the class to discuss the characters' traits that led to your classifications.

Flat Characters	Round Characters

Reading Strategy — Make Inferences About Theme

 Texas Test Practice (10.2)

1. Which sentence best expresses the theme of "Tuesday Siesta"?

   A. Some crimes are justifiable.

   B. Religious leaders do not always reach out to the poor and oppressed.

   C. Climate affects the way people behave.

   D. Even the relatives of a criminal have the right to mourn their dead with dignity.

Vocabulary Practice

Practice with Word Parts Use a dictionary to find the meaning of each vocabulary word's root, prefix, and suffix. Then find three words that contain the same word parts. Circle the shared word part in each of the related words.

> **interminable   serenity   scrutinize   inscrutable   skeptical**

EXAMPLE:
reflexive

Prefix
re-, "back"

Root
flex, "to bend"

Suffix
-ive, "performing an action"

Related words: (re)tract, in(flec)tion, definit(ive)

Academic Vocabulary

*Gabriel García Márquez **locates** his story in a fantastic version of reality.*

Locate is a multiple-meaning word. In a more casual conversation, someone might ask where a person's home is located. Using context clues, figure out the meaning of the word in the sentence above about García Márquez.

For more on academic vocabulary, see pages 36–37 and R92–R94.

Enrich and Extend

 ### Research and Report

Internet Connection Use the Internet to research a Latin American country and compile information on its culture. Create a travel brochure that includes graphics.

Get Ideas Develop a search plan with research questions, such as questions about religion and customs, and with search terms, such as *Panama culture customs.* Refine your terms and devise a timeline for completing your work.

Research Evaluate a variety of relevant sources for validity, reliability, and objectivity. For each source, including graphical sources, record the following:

✔ author or Web site sponsor, if given

✔ name of Web site and complete URL

✔ the date posted or last updated

✔ the date you viewed the information

✔ complete bibliographic information

Take notes and use source material ethically by using quotation marks for words or phrases that you quote verbatim and attributing ideas and information to their respective sources. Put your notes in a logical order, organized by main idea or topic. Before you draft, develop an outline from your notes.

Report Synthesize information from several sources, including graphics, and draw conclusions about the ideas presented. Create a travel brochure for your country in print, online, or slideshow form. Use formatting and images to make the most important information stand out. Use text to discuss the culture, noting customs or perspectives that vary according to region, class, or other distinctions. Cite your sources at the end, as well as in parenthetical references and image source lines throughout your brochure.

TEKS

10.1.D Show the relationship between the origins and meaning of foreign words or phrases used frequently in written English and historical events or developments (e.g., *glasnost, avant-garde, coup d'état*).

Vocabulary Workshop

Foreign Word Origins

Literature Connection The passage below from Gabriel García Márquez's story "Tuesday Siesta" describes a siesta—the hot, quiet time of the afternoon when shops are closed and townspeople rest in some parts of the world. *Siesta* is a Spanish word that originally comes from the Latin word *sexta,* meaning "noon," or literally, "the sixth hour." *Siesta* now refers to an afternoon nap or rest.

> *"It was almost two. At that hour, weighted down by drowsiness, the town was taking a siesta."*

English includes many words, such as *siesta,* that come from foreign languages. Whether reading literature or having an informal conversation, you are likely to encounter foreign words and phrases that are now commonly used in English. Learning word origins—or the histories of words—from other languages will increase your vocabulary and help you understand new words.

Many foreign words, such as those from French and Spanish, have their origins in Latin. Some words that are now used in English, such as *glasnost,* have origins in historically significant events. The chart below shows several foreign words and phrases commonly used in English.

Etymology

The origin, or **etymology,** of a word is its history. Learn about the etymology of a foreign word or phrase to see how its meaning and use developed over time.

Tip

When you come across an unfamiliar foreign word or phrase, consult a dictionary. Foreign words and phrases commonly used in English have entries in most dictionaries.

Word or Phrase	Origin	Meaning in English
avant-garde	French, "vanguard"	a new or experimental concept in the arts
coup d'état	French, literally "stroke of state"	violent overthrow of a government by another group
faux pas	French, literally "false step"	a social blunder
glasnost	Russian, literally "publicity," from a 1986 Soviet policy instituting open communication	open and frank discussion
incommunicado	Spanish, "to deprive of communication"	without means of communication
zeitgeist	German, "spirit"	the intellectual and cultural spirit of an age

Practice For each word listed, locate its origin in a dictionary. Explain its historical significance as well as its modern meaning in English.

1. armada **3.** blitzkrieg

2. fin de siècle **4.** deus ex machina

LOG ON ▶ **Literature** Online

Vocabulary For more vocabulary practice, go to glencoe.com and enter QuickPass code GL57805u1.

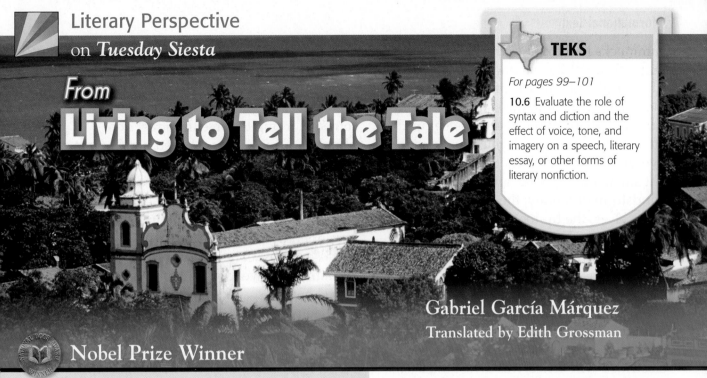

From
Living to Tell the Tale

Gabriel García Márquez
Translated by Edith Grossman

Nobel Prize Winner

TEKS

For pages 99–101

10.6 Evaluate the role of syntax and diction and the effect of voice, tone, and imagery on a speech, literary essay, or other forms of literary nonfiction.

Set a Purpose for Reading

Read to learn about the experience that inspired Gabriel García Márquez's story "Tuesday Siesta."

Build Background

This episode from García Márquez's memoir recounts a 1950 trip he and his mother took to his hometown of Aracataca, near Colombia's Caribbean coast. They made the journey to sell García Márquez's childhood home, which had been recently occupied by his grandparents.

Reading Strategy

Evaluate Imagery

Imagery is descriptive language that appeals to one or more of the five senses: sight, sound, touch, taste, and smell. Imagery helps evoke an emotional response in the reader. When you **evaluate imagery,** you make judgments about the effect of the sensory details in a work. As you read this piece of literary nonfiction, notice sensory details. Ask yourself, What emotions and ideas are suggested by these details? Record your thoughts in a chart like the one below.

Image	Effect
"deserted station whose tiles were beginning to crack under the pressure of grass"	Shows the heat and desolation of the town; suggests decay

While the train stood there I had the sensation that we were not altogether alone. But when it pulled away, with an immediate, heart-wrenching blast of its whistle, my mother and I were left forsaken beneath the infernal sun, and all the heavy grief of the town came down on us. But we did not say anything to each other. The old wooden station with its tin roof and running balcony was like a tropical version of the ones we knew from westerns. We crossed the deserted station whose tiles were beginning to crack under the pressure of grass, and we sank into the torpor[1] of siesta as we sought the protection of the almond trees.

Since I was a boy I had despised those inert siestas because we did not know what to do. "Be quiet, we're sleeping," the sleepers would murmur without waking. Stores, public offices, and schools closed at twelve and did not open again until a little before three. The interiors of the houses floated in a limbo of lethargy. In some it was so unbearable that people would hang their

---

1. *Torpor* means "a lack of physical or mental activity."

hammocks in the courtyard or place chairs in the shade of the almond trees and sleep sitting up in the middle of the street. Only the hotel across from the station, with its bar and billiard room, and the telegraph[2] office behind the church remained open. Everything was identical to my memories, but smaller and poorer, and leveled by a windstorm of fatality: the decaying houses themselves, the tin roofs perforated by rust, the levee[3] with its crumbling granite benches and melancholy almond trees, and all of it transfigured by the invisible burning dust that deceived the eye and calcinated[4] the skin. On the other side of the train tracks the private paradise of the banana company[5], stripped now of its electrified wire fence, was a vast thicket with no palm trees, ruined houses among the poppies, and the rubble of the hospital destroyed by fire. There was not a single door, a crack in a wall, a human trace that did not find a supernatural resonance in me.

My mother held herself very erect as she walked with her light step, almost not perspiring in her funereal dress, and in absolute silence, but her mortal pallor[6] and sharpened profile revealed what was happening to her on the inside.

When we turned the corner, the dust burned my feet through the weave of my sandals. The feeling of being forsaken became unbearable. Then I saw myself and I saw my mother, just as I saw, when I was a boy, the mother and sister of the thief whom María Consuegra had killed with a single shot one week earlier, when he tried to break into her house.

At three in the morning the sound of someone trying to force the street door from the outside had wakened her. She got up without lighting the lamp, felt around in the armoire for an archaic revolver that no one had fired since the War of a Thousand Days[7], and located in the darkness not only the place where the door was but also the exact height of the lock. Then she aimed the weapon with both hands, closed her eyes, and squeezed the trigger. She had never fired a gun before, but the shot hit its target through the door.

He was the first dead person I had seen. When I passed by at seven in the morning on my way to school, the body was still lying on the sidewalk in a patch of dried blood, the face destroyed by the lead that had shattered its nose and come out one ear. He was wearing a sailor's T-shirt with colored stripes and ordinary trousers held up by a rope instead of a belt, and he was barefoot. At his side, on the ground, they found the homemade picklock with which he had tried to jimmy the lock.

The town dignitaries came to María Consuegra's house to offer her their condolences for having killed the thief. I went that night with Papalelo[8], and we found her sitting in an armchair from Manila that looked like an enormous wicker peacock, surrounded by the fervor of her friends who listened to the story she had repeated a thousand times. Everyone agreed with her that she had fired out of sheer fright. It was then that my grandfather asked her if she had heard anything after the shot, and she answered that first she had heard a

---

2. The *telegraph* is a communications system that sends messages with simple electrical signals over wires.
3. In this instance, *levee* refers to an embankment that stops a river from overflowing.
4. *Calcinated* means "heated to a high temperature, then dried."
5. The *banana company* likely refers to a plantation run by United Fruit Company, once a large employer in Central America, Colombia, and the Caribbean islands.
6. *Pallor* means "extreme paleness."

7. The *War of a Thousand Days* refers to the Colombian civil war, fought from 1899 to 1902; it devastated the country's economy and led to more than 60,000 deaths.
8. *Papalelo* is the author's grandfather.

great silence, then the metallic sound of the picklock falling on the cement, and then a faint, anguished voice: "Mother, help me!" María Consuegra, it seemed, had not been conscious of this heart-breaking lament until my grandfather asked her the question. Only then did she burst into tears.

This happened on a Monday. On Tuesday of the following week, during siesta, I was playing tops with Luis Carmelo Correa, my oldest friend in life, when we were surprised by the sleepers waking before it was time and looking out the windows. Then we saw in the deserted street a woman dressed in strict mourning and a girl about twelve years old who was carrying a bouquet of faded flowers wrapped in newspaper. They protected themselves from the burning sun with a black umbrella and were quite oblivious to the effrontery[9] of the people who watched them pass by. They were the mother and younger sister of the dead thief, bringing flowers for his grave.

That vision pursued me for many years, like a single dream that the entire town watched through its windows as it passed, until I managed to exorcise it in a story. But the truth is that I did not become aware of the drama of the woman and the girl, or their imperturbable dignity, until the day I went with my mother to sell the house and surprised myself walking down the same deserted street at the same lethal hour.

"I feel as if I were the thief," I said.

My mother did not understand me. In fact, when we passed the house of María Consuegra she did not even glance at the door where you could still see the patched bullet hole in the wood. Years later, recalling that trip with her, I confirmed that she did remember the tragedy but would have given her soul to forget it. ◦

---

9. *Effrontery* means "boldness or shamelessness."

Respond and Think Critically

1. **Summarize Main Ideas** Write a brief summary of the events in this excerpt before you answer the following questions. For help on writing a summary, see page 35.

2. **Make Inferences About Setting** Review the opening paragraph. What do the details in this paragraph suggest about the condition and **mood,** or feeling, of the town that Márquez and his mother visit? Support your answer with evidence from the text.

3. **Analyze Details** Márquez describes a "feeling of being forsaken." What details throughout the excerpt suggest that this feeling is shared both by Márquez and by the people he describes? Explain.

4. **Make Inferences About Meaning** Márquez tells his mother, "I feel as if I were the thief." Why do you think he identifies with the thief? Provide evidence from the text to support your answer.

5. **Evaluate Imagery** Márquez uses vivid imagery to describe feelings, surroundings, and people. What images help strengthen Márquez's description of the town and of the life-altering incident in his past? Explain, citing at least three images from the excerpt in your answer. Use the graphic organizer on page 99 for help.

6. **Compare and Contrast Texts** What similarities and differences do you see between this excerpt and "Tuesday Siesta"? Support your response with examples from the texts.

Before You Read

When Mr. Pirzada Came to Dine

Meet **Jhumpa Lahiri**
(born 1967)

Jhumpa (joom′ pa) Lahiri began her writing career when she was a child. In elementary school, she and her best friend composed stories during recess, thinking them aloud "sentence by sentence." Many sentences later, in 2000, Lahiri won the Pulitzer Prize for fiction for *Interpreter of Maladies*, her collection of short stories about people in India and Indian immigrants in the United States. "It's been the happiest possible ending," she says.

> *"The question of identity is always a difficult one, but especially so for those who are culturally displaced."*
>
> —Jhumpa Lahiri

The Interpreter of Maladies Jhumpa Lahiri was born in London, but her Bengali parents, a librarian and a teacher, emigrated to Rhode Island, where she grew up. As a child, Lahiri often spent time with her extended family in Calcutta, India, as well. She received her bachelor's degree from Barnard College and then three master's degrees and a doctorate in Renaissance Studies from Boston University. Within a year of completing her dissertation, Lahiri had hired a literary agent, sold a book, and published a story in *The New Yorker*.

Lahiri's work often deals with the difficulties that Indian immigrants face in trying to cope with a new culture. Lahiri notes that her work reflects the sense of displacement she experienced as a child of immigrants. As she says, "For immigrants, the challenges of exile, the loneliness, the constant sense of alienation, the knowledge of and longing for a lost world, are more explicit and distressing than for their children. On the other hand, the problem for the children of immigrants, those with strong ties to their country of origin, is that they feel neither one thing nor the other. The feeling that there was no single place to which I fully belonged bothered me growing up."

Her First Novel In 2003 Lahiri published *The Namesake*. The novel deals with a rebellious son who is learning how to come to terms with Indian and American identities and to understand the significance of his first name, "Gogol." Lahiri says, "I had always been aware of having an unusual name and the difficulties one faces living with a name in a place where it doesn't make sense." The novel allows Lahiri to develop her characters at a slower pace. In her review, Michiko Kakutani called it "a debut novel that is as assured and eloquent as the work of a longtime master of the craft."

Literature Online

Author Search For more about Jhumpa Lahiri, go to glencoe.com and enter QuickPass code GL57805u1.

Literature and Reading Preview

Connect to the Story

How would you interact with friends who know how worried you are about your family's safety? Write a journal entry about how much of your anxiety you would reveal.

Build Background

In 1971, when this story takes place, West Pakistan and East Pakistan were engaged in conflict as a result of East Pakistan's demand for independence from West Pakistan.

Set Purposes for Reading

Big Idea Making Choices

As you read, ask yourself, How do circumstances lead Mr. Pirzada to make the difficult choice to stay in the United States?

Literary Element Theme

A **theme** is a central message of a written work that readers can apply to life. Some works may have more than one theme, and some themes are universal: they span boundaries of time and culture, and they show up in many works of fiction. As you read, ask yourself, What are the major themes in Lahiri's story?

Reading Strategy Compare and Contrast Characters

To **compare and contrast characters** is to determine similarities and differences between them. Comparing and contrasting characters can help you better understand the characters and why they act in certain ways. As you read, ask yourself, How are the characters like and unlike one another?

....

Tip: Take Notes Use a chart like the one below to record similarities and differences between characters.

Mr. Pirzada	from Dacca, is Muslim, speaks Bengali and English
Lilia's father	from Calcutta, is Hindu, speaks Bengali and English
Lilia's mother	
Lilia	

TEKS

For pages 102–119

10.2.A Compare and contrast differences in similar themes expressed in different time periods.

Vocabulary

ascertaining (as′ ər tān′ ing) *v.* finding out definitely; p. 104 *The police were ascertaining who had robbed the bank.*

austere (ôs tēr′) *adj.* without ornament; very simple; p. 106 *Her dress was austere, lacking any embroidery or decoration.*

impeccably (im pek′ə blē) *adv.* without error or flaw; p. 107 *His manners were impeccably polite.*

imperceptible (im′pər sep′tə bəl) *adj.* slight; barely capable of being seen or sensed; p. 108 *The movement in the grass was so imperceptible that we did not see the snake.*

intimidation (in tim′ə dā shən) *n.* act of making one feel afraid or discouraged; p. 113 *The opposing team used intimidation to threaten the soccer players.*

When Mr. Pirzada Came to Dine

Jhumpa Lahiri

Avenue of the Elysian Fields, 1888. Vincent van Gogh. Oil on canvas.

In the autumn of 1971 a man used to come to our house, bearing confections[1] in his pocket and hopes of **ascertaining** the life or death of his family. His name was Mr. Pirzada, and he came from Dacca, now the capital of Bangladesh, but then a part of Pakistan. That year Pakistan was engaged in civil war. The eastern frontier, where Dacca was located, was fighting for autonomy[2] from the ruling regime[3] in the west. In March, Dacca had been invaded, torched, and shelled by the Pakistani army. Teachers were dragged onto streets and shot, women dragged into barracks and raped. By the end of the summer, three hundred thousand people were said to have died. In Dacca Mr. Pirzada had a three-story home, a lectureship in botany at the university, a wife of twenty years, and seven daughters between the ages of six and sixteen whose names all began with the letter A. "Their mother's idea," he explained one day, producing from his wallet a black-and-white picture of seven girls at a picnic, their braids tied with ribbons, sitting cross-legged in a row, eating chicken curry[4] off of banana leaves. "How am I to distinguish? Ayesha, Amira, Amina, Aziza, you see the difficulty."

---

1. *Confections* are sweets, such as candy or preserves.
2. To have *autonomy* is to have the right to self-rule.
3. A *regime* (rə zhēm´) is a government in power.

---

4. *Chicken curry* is chicken cooked with various spices including curry powder, ginger, and turmeric.

Theme *A theme of a story can often develop out of contrasts in setting. How would you describe life in Dacca?*

Each week Mr. Pirzada wrote letters to his wife, and sent comic books to each of his seven daughters, but the postal system, along with most everything else in Dacca, had collapsed, and he had not heard word of them in over six months. Mr. Pirzada, meanwhile, was in America for the year, for he had been awarded a grant from the government of Pakistan to study the foliage[5] of New England. In spring and summer he had gathered data in Vermont and Maine, and in autumn he moved to a university north of Boston, where we lived, to write a short book about his discoveries. The grant was a great honor, but when converted into dollars it was not generous. As a result, Mr. Pirzada lived in a room in a graduate dormitory,[6] and did not own a proper stove or a television set of his own. And so he came to our house to eat dinner and watch the evening news.

At first I knew nothing of the reason for his visits. I was ten years old, and was not surprised that my parents, who were from India, and had a number of Indian acquaintances at the university, should ask Mr. Pirzada to share our meals. It was a small campus, with narrow brick walkways and white pillared buildings, located on the fringes of what seemed to be an even smaller town. The supermarket did not carry mustard oil,[7] doctors did not make house calls, neighbors never dropped by without an invitation, and of these things, every so often, my parents complained. In search of compatriots,[8] they used to trail their fingers, at the start of each new semester, through the columns of the university directory, circling surnames[9] familiar to their part of the world. It was in this manner that they discovered Mr. Pirzada, and phoned him, and invited him to our home.

I have no memory of his first visit, or of his second or his third, but by the end of September I had grown so accustomed to Mr. Pirzada's presence in our living room that one evening, as I was dropping ice cubes into the water pitcher, I asked my mother to hand me a fourth glass from a cupboard still out of my reach. She was busy at the stove, presiding over a skillet of fried spinach with radishes, and could not hear me because of the drone of the exhaust fan and the fierce scrapes of her spatula. I turned to my father, who was leaning against the refrigerator, eating spiced cashews from a cupped fist.

Visual Vocabulary
A *spatula* is a cooking utensil with a broad flexible blade used to spread or mix food.

"What is it, Lilia?"

"A glass for the Indian man."

"Mr. Pirzada won't be coming today. More importantly, Mr. Pirzada is no longer considered Indian," my father announced, brushing salt from the cashews out of his trim black beard. "Not since Partition.[10] Our country was divided. 1947."

When I said I thought that was the date of India's independence from Britain, my father said, "That too. One moment we were free and then we were sliced up," he explained, drawing an X with his finger on

---

5. *Foliage* (fō ′ lē ij) is clusters of leaves or branches.
6. A *dormitory* is a residence building with private rooms, typically for college students.
7. *Mustard oil* is made from mustard seeds and is used in cooking Indian foods.
8. *Compatriots* are people from one's home country.

Making Choices *Why do you think Mr. Pirzada decides to stay in the United States instead of going home?*

9. A *surname* is a person's family name.
10. *Partition* refers to the creation of independent countries out of parts of the British Empire. Partition created India and Pakistan.

the countertop, "like a pie. Hindus here, Muslims there. Dacca no longer belongs to us." He told me that during Partition Hindus and Muslims had set fire to each other's homes. For many, the idea of eating in the other's company was still unthinkable.

It made no sense to me. Mr. Pirzada and my parents spoke the same language, laughed at the same jokes, looked more or less the same. They ate pickled mangoes[11] with their meals, ate rice every night for supper with their hands. Like my parents, Mr. Pirzada took off his shoes before entering a room, chewed fennel[12] seeds after meals as a digestive, drank no alcohol, for dessert dipped **austere** biscuits into successive cups of tea. Nevertheless my father insisted that I understand the difference, and he led me to a map of the world taped to the wall over his desk. He seemed concerned that Mr. Pirzada might take offense if I accidentally referred to him as an Indian, though I could not really imagine Mr. Pirzada being offended by much of anything. "Mr. Pirzada is Bengali, but he is a Muslim," my father informed me. "Therefore

he lives in East Pakistan, not India." His finger trailed across the Atlantic, through Europe, the Mediterranean, the Middle East, and finally to the sprawling orange diamond that my mother once told me resembled a woman wearing a sari.

with her left arm extended. Various cities had been circled with lines drawn between them to indicate my parents' travels, and the place of their birth, Calcutta, was signified by a small silver star. I had been there only once and had no memory of the trip. "As you see, Lilia, it is a different country, a different color," my father said. Pakistan was yellow, not orange. I noticed that there were two distinct parts to it, one much larger than the other, separated by an expanse of Indian territory; it was as if California and Connecticut constituted a nation apart from the U.S.

My father rapped his knuckles on top of my head. "You are, of course, aware of the current situation? Aware of East Pakistan's fight for sovereignty?"

I nodded, unaware of the situation.

We returned to the kitchen, where my mother was draining a pot of boiled rice into a colander. My father opened up the can on the counter and eyed me sharply over the frames of his glasses as he ate some more cashews. "What exactly do they teach you at school? Do you study history? Geography?"

"Lilia has plenty to learn at school," my mother said. "We live here now, she was born here." She seemed genuinely proud of the fact, as if it were a reflection of my character. In her estimation, I knew, I was assured a safe life, an easy life, a fine education, every opportunity. I would never have to eat rationed food, or obey curfews, or watch riots from my rooftop, or hide neighbors in water tanks to prevent them from being shot, as she and my father had. "Imagine having to place her in a

---

11. *Mangoes* are the sweet fruit from the tropical mango tree.
12. *Fennel* is a plant with aromatic seeds used to flavor foods.

Compare and Contrast Characters *Why does Lilia think Mr. Pirzada is Indian?*

Vocabulary

austere (ôs tēr´) *adj.* without ornament; very simple

Compare and Contrast Characters *What differences do you notice between Lilia's father's attitude and her mother's? Explain.*

Making Choices *Why do you think Lilia's mother seems proud of this fact?*

decent school. Imagine her having to read during power failures by the light of kerosene lamps. Imagine the pressures, the tutors, the constant exams." She ran a hand through her hair, bobbed[13] to a suitable length for her part-time job as a bank teller. "How can you possibly expect her to know about Partition? Put those nuts away."

"But what does she learn about the world?" My father rattled the cashew can in his hand. "What is she learning?"

We learned American history, of course, and American geography. That year, and every year, it seemed, we began by studying the Revolutionary War. We were taken in school buses on field trips to visit Plymouth Rock, and to walk the Freedom Trail, and to climb to the top of the Bunker Hill Monument. We made dioramas[14] out of colored construction paper depicting George Washington crossing the choppy waters of the Delaware River, and we made puppets of King George wearing white tights and a black bow in his hair. During tests we were given blank maps of the thirteen colonies, and asked to fill in names, dates, capitals. I could do it with my eyes closed.

The next evening Mr. Pirzada arrived, as usual, at six o'clock. Though they were no longer strangers, upon first greeting each other, he and my father maintained the habit of shaking hands.

"Come in, sir. Lilia, Mr. Pirzada's coat, please."

He stepped into the foyer,[15] **impeccably** suited and scarved, with a silk tie knotted

---

13. *Bobbed* means "cut short."
14. *Dioramas* are three-dimensional miniature scenes.
15. A *foyer* (foi′ ər) is an entrance hall.

Theme *How do you think this detail relates to the story's theme? Explain.*

Vocabulary

impeccably (im pek′ ə blē) *adv.* without error or flaw

Woman's head cover (detail), c. 1860–1870. Gujarat. Silk, printed in imitation of tie-dye. Victoria and Albert Museum, London.

View the Art Some Muslim women in India, Pakistan, and Bangladesh wear head covers, or head scarves, as a sign of modesty. This head scarf comes from the Indian state of Gujarat, which is in the extreme west of the country, adjacent to Pakistan. Do you think Lilia's and Mr. Pirzada's reactions to seeing a woman in a head scarf would differ? Explain.

at his collar. Each evening he appeared in ensembles[16] of plums, olives, and chocolate browns. He was a compact man, and though his feet were perpetually splayed,[17] and his belly slightly wide, he nevertheless maintained an efficient posture, as if balancing in either hand two suitcases of equal weight. His ears were insulated by tufts of graying hair that seemed to block out the unpleasant traffic

---

16. Here, *ensembles* (än säm′ bəls) are clothes of matching colors.
17. *Splayed* feet are spread out awkwardly.

of life. He had thickly lashed eyes shaded with a trace of camphor, a generous mustache that turned up playfully at the ends, and a mole shaped like a flattened raisin in the very center of his left cheek. On his head he wore a black fez made from the wool of Persian lambs, secured by bobby pins, without which I was never to see him. Though my father always offered to fetch him in our car, Mr. Pirzada preferred to walk from his dormitory to our neighborhood, a distance of about twenty minutes

Visual Vocabulary
A *fez* is a tall felt hat, usually red, with a black tassel hanging from the crown.

on foot, studying trees and shrubs on his way, and when he entered our house his knuckles were pink with the effects of crisp autumn air.

"Another refugee, I am afraid, on Indian territory."

"They are estimating nine million at the last count," my father said.

Mr. Pirzada handed me his coat, for it was my job to hang it on the rack at the bottom of the stairs. It was made of finely checkered gray-and-blue wool, with a striped lining and horn buttons, and carried in its weave the faint smell of limes. There were no recognizable tags inside, only a hand-stitched label with the phrase "Z. Sayeed, Suitors" embroidered on it in cursive with glossy black thread. On certain days a birch or maple leaf was tucked into a pocket. He unlaced his shoes and lined them against the baseboard; a golden paste clung to the toes and heels, the result of walking through our damp, unraked lawn. Relieved of his trappings, he grazed

my throat with his short, restless fingers, the way a person feels for solidity behind a wall before driving in a nail. Then he followed my father to the living room, where the television was tuned to the local news. As soon as they were seated my mother appeared from the kitchen with a plate of mincemeat kebabs with coriander chutney.[18] Mr. Pirzada popped one into his mouth.

"One can only hope," he said, reaching for another, "that Dacca's refugees are as heartily fed. Which reminds me." He reached into his suit pocket and gave me a small plastic egg filled with cinnamon hearts. "For the lady of the house," he said with an almost **imperceptible** splay-footed bow.

"Really, Mr. Pirzada," my mother protested. "Night after night. You spoil her."

"I only spoil children who are incapable of spoiling."

It was an awkward moment for me, one which I awaited in part with dread, in part with delight. I was charmed by the presence of Mr. Pirzada's rotund[19] elegance, and flattered by the faint theatricality of his attentions, yet unsettled by the superb ease of his gestures, which made me feel, for an instant, like a stranger in my own home. It had become our ritual, and for several weeks, before we grew more comfortable with one another, it was the only time he spoke to me directly. I had no response, offered no comment, betrayed no visible reaction to the steady stream of honey-filled lozenges, the raspberry truffles, the

---

18. *Mincemeat . . . chutney* is a mixture of chopped apples, raisins, and meat skewered and broiled, served with a relish made with the aromatic herb coriander.
19. *Rotund* means "plump."

Vocabulary

imperceptible (im′pər sep′tə bəl) *adj.* slight; barely capable of being seen or sensed slender rolls of sour pastilles. I could not even thank him, for once, when I did, for an especially spectacular peppermint lollipop wrapped in a spray[20] of purple cellophane, he had demanded, "What is this thank-you? The lady at the bank thanks me, the cashier at the shop thanks me, the librarian thanks me when I return an overdue book, the overseas operator thanks me as she tries to connect me to Dacca and fails. If I am buried in this country I will be thanked, no doubt, at my funeral."

It was inappropriate, in my opinion, to consume the candy Mr. Pirzada gave me in a casual manner. I coveted each evening's treasure as I would a jewel, or a coin from a buried kingdom, and I would place it in a small keepsake box made of carved sandalwood beside my bed, in which, long ago in India, my father's mother used to store the ground areca[21] nuts she ate after her morning bath. It was my only memento of a grandmother I had never known, and until Mr. Pirzada came to our lives I could find nothing to put inside it. Every so often before brushing my teeth and laying out my clothes for school the next day, I opened the lid of the box and ate one of his treats.

That night, like every night, we did not eat at the dining table, because it did not provide an unobstructed view of the television set. Instead we huddled around the coffee table, without conversing, our plates perched on the edges of our knees. From the kitchen my mother brought forth the succession of dishes: lentils with fried onions, green beans with coconut, fish cooked with raisins in a yogurt sauce. I followed with the water glasses, and the plate of lemon wedges, and the chili peppers, purchased on monthly trips to Chinatown and stored by the pound in the freezer, which they liked to snap open and crush into their food.

Before eating Mr. Pirzada always did a curious thing. He took out a plain silver watch without a band, which he kept in his breast pocket, held it briefly to one of his tufted ears, and wound it with three swift flicks of his thumb and forefinger. Unlike the watch on his wrist, the pocket watch, he had explained to me, was set to the local time in Dacca, eleven hours ahead. For the duration of the meal the watch rested on his folded paper napkin on the coffee table. He never seemed to consult it.

Now that I had learned Mr. Pirzada was not an Indian, I began to study him with extra care, to try to figure out what made him different. I decided that the pocket watch was one of those things. When I saw it that night, as he wound it and arranged it on the coffee table, an uneasiness possessed me; life, I realized, was being lived in Dacca first. I imagined Mr. Pirzada's daughters rising from sleep, tying ribbons in their hair, anticipating breakfast, preparing for school. Our meals, our actions, were only a shadow of what had already happened there, a lagging ghost of where Mr. Pirzada really belonged.

At six-thirty, which was when the national news began, my father raised the volume and adjusted the antennas. Usually I occupied myself with a book, but that night my father insisted that I pay attention. On the screen I saw tanks rolling through dusty streets, and fallen buildings, and forests of

---

20. Here, *spray* means that the cellophane has been shaped or twisted to look like a flower.
21. *Areca* nuts come from the betel palm, a type of tall palm tree.

Theme *Why do you think Mr. Pirzada has an outburst when Lilia thanks him for the candy? Do you think this scene reflects one of the story's major themes? Explain.*

Compare and Contrast Characters *How does winding the watch make Mr. Pirzada different from Lilia's family?*

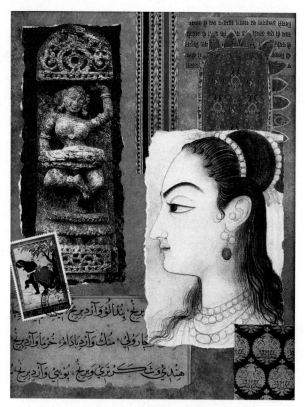

Romantic India I, 2000. Gerry Charm. Collage.

<u>View the Art</u> Gerry Charm is a contemporary American artist who explores the cultures of ancient and modern civilizations through collage. How do you think Lilia would react if an American from her town were to suddenly express an interest in learning about India and Indian culture?

They discussed intrigues I did not know, a catastrophe I could not comprehend. "See, children your age, what they do to survive," my father said as he served me another piece of fish. But I could no longer eat. I could only steal glances at Mr. Pirzada, sitting beside me in his olive green jacket, calmly creating a well in his rice to make room for a second helping of lentils. He was not my notion of a man burdened by such grave concerns. I wondered if the reason he was always so smartly dressed was in preparation to endure with dignity whatever news assailed[23] him, perhaps even to attend a funeral at a moment's notice. I wondered, too, what would happen if suddenly his seven daughters were to appear on television, smiling and waving and blowing kisses to Mr. Pirzada from a balcony. I imagined how relieved he would be. But this never happened.

That night when I placed the plastic egg filled with cinnamon hearts in the box beside my bed, I did not feel the ceremonious satisfaction I normally did. I tried not to think about Mr. Pirzada, in his lime-scented overcoat, connected to the unruly, sweltering world we had viewed a few hours ago in our bright, carpeted living room. And yet for several moments that was all I could think about. My stomach tightened as I worried whether his wife and seven daughters were now members of the drifting, clamoring crowd that had flashed at intervals on the screen. In an effort to banish[24] the image I looked around my room, at the yellow canopied[25] bed with matching flounced[26] curtains, at framed class pictures

unfamiliar trees into which East Pakistani refugees had fled, seeking safety over the Indian border. I saw boats with fan-shaped sails floating on wide coffee-colored rivers, a barricaded university, newspaper offices burnt to the ground. I turned to look at Mr. Pirzada; the images flashed in miniature across his eyes. As he watched he had an immovable expression on his face, composed but alert, as if someone were giving him directions to an unknown destination.

During the commercial my mother went to the kitchen to get more rice, and my father and Mr. Pirzada deplored the policies of a general named Yahyah Khan.[22]

---

22. *Yahyah Khan,* or Agha Mohammad Yahya Khan, was a West Pakistan general who led troops into East Pakistan.

23. *Assailed* means "attacked" or "assaulted."
24. *Banish* means "drive away" or "force to leave."
25. A *canopied* bed has a cloth covering fastened above it.
26. *Flounced* means "gathered" or "pleated."

Compare and Contrast Characters *Why do you think Lilia cannot comprehend the scope and complexities of the war?*

mounted on white and violet papered walls, at the penciled inscriptions by the closet door where my father recorded my height on each of my birthdays. But the more I tried to distract myself, the more I began to convince myself that Mr. Pirzada's family was in all likelihood dead. Eventually I took a square of white chocolate out of the box, and unwrapped it, and then I did something I had never done before. I put the chocolate in my mouth, letting it soften until the last possible moment, and then as I chewed it slowly, I prayed that Mr. Pirzada's family was safe and sound. I had never prayed for anything before, had never been taught or told to, but I decided, given the circumstances, that it was something I should do. That night, when I went to the bathroom I only pretended to brush my teeth, for I feared that I would somehow rinse the prayer out as well. I wet the brush and rearranged the tube of paste to prevent my parents from asking any questions, and fell asleep with sugar on my tongue.

No one at school talked about the war followed so faithfully in my living room. We continued to study the American Revolution, and learned about the injustices of taxation without representation, and memorized passages from the Declaration of Independence. During recess the boys would divide in two groups, chasing each other wildly around the swings and seesaws, Redcoats against the colonies. In the classroom our teacher, Mrs. Kenyon, pointed frequently to a map that emerged like a movie screen from the top of the chalkboard, charting the route of the *Mayflower,* or showing us the location of the Liberty Bell. Each week two members of the class gave a report on a particular aspect of the Revolution, and so one day I was sent to the school library with my friend Dora to learn about the surrender at Yorktown. Mrs. Kenyon handed us a slip of paper with the names of three books to look up in the card catalogue. We found them right away, and sat down at a low round table to read and take notes. But I could not concentrate. I returned to the blond-wood shelves, to a section I had noticed labeled "Asia." I saw books about China, India, Indonesia, Korea. Eventually I found a book titled *Pakistan: A Land and Its People.* I sat on a footstool and opened the book. The laminated jacket crackled in my grip. I began turning the pages, filled with photos of rivers and rice fields and men in military uniforms. There was a chapter about Dacca, and I began to read about its rainfall, and its jute[27] production. I was studying a population chart when Dora appeared in the aisle.

"What are you doing back here? Mrs. Kenyon's in the library. She came to check up on us."

I slammed the book shut, too loudly. Mrs. Kenyon emerged, the aroma of her perfume filling up the tiny aisle, and lifted the book by the tip of its spine as if it were a hair clinging to my sweater. She glanced at the cover, then at me.

"Is this book a part of your report, Lilia?"

"No, Mrs. Kenyon."

"Then I see no reason to consult[28] it," she said, replacing it in the slim gap on the shelf. "Do you?"

As weeks passed it grew more and more rare to see any footage[29] from Dacca on the

---

27. *Jute* is a fiber from the jute plant that is used to make rope, burlap, or sacks.
28. Here, *consult* means "to get information from."
29. *Footage* refers to a segment of newsreel film.

Making Choices *Why do you think Lilia decides to pray for Mr. Pirzada's family?*

Theme *Why do you think Lahiri chose to include this scene? How might it relate to one of the story's themes?*

news. The report came after the first set of commercials, sometimes the second. The press had been censored, removed, restricted, rerouted. Some days, many days, only a death toll was announced, prefaced by a reiteration[30] of the general situation. More poets were executed, more villages set ablaze. In spite of it all, night after night, my parents and Mr. Pirzada enjoyed long, leisurely meals. After the television was shut off, and the dishes washed and dried, they joked, and told stories, and dipped biscuits in their tea. When they tired of discussing political matters they discussed, instead, the progress of Mr. Pirzada's book about the deciduous[31] trees of New England, and my father's nomination for tenure, and the peculiar eating habits of my mother's American coworkers at the bank. Eventually I was sent upstairs to do my homework, but through the carpet I heard them as they drank more tea, and listened to cassettes of Kishore Kumar,[32] and played Scrabble on the coffee table, laughing and arguing long into the night about the spellings of English words. I wanted to join them, wanted, above all, to console Mr. Pirzada somehow. But apart from eating a piece of candy for the sake of his family and praying for their safety, there was nothing I could do. They played Scrabble until the eleven o'clock news, and then, sometime around midnight, Mr. Pirzada walked back to his dormitory. For this reason I never saw him leave, but each night as I drifted off to sleep I would hear them, anticipating the birth of a nation on the other side of the world.

> " . . . each night as I drifted off to sleep I would hear them, anticipating the birth of a nation on the other side of the world."

One day in October Mr. Pirzada asked upon arrival, "What are these large orange vegetables on people's doorsteps? A type of squash?"

"Pumpkins," my mother replied. "Lilia, remind me to pick one up at the supermarket."

"And the purpose? It indicates what?"

"You make a jack-o'-lantern," I said, grinning ferociously. "Like this. To scare people away."

"I see," Mr. Pirzada said, grinning back. "Very useful."

The next day my mother bought a ten-pound pumpkin, fat and round, and placed it on the dining table. Before supper, while my father and Mr. Pirzada were watching the local news, she told me to decorate it with markers, but I wanted to carve it properly like others I had noticed in the neighborhood.

"Yes, let's carve it," Mr. Pirzada agreed, and rose from the sofa. "Hang the news tonight." Asking no questions, he walked into the kitchen, opened a drawer, and returned, bearing a long serrated[33] knife. He glanced at me for approval. "Shall I?"

I nodded. For the first time we all gathered around the dining table, my mother,

---

30. *Reiteration* is repeating or saying over again.
31. *Deciduous* trees lose their leaves each year.
32. *Kishore Kumar* was a famous actor and singer in Indian films.

33. A *serrated* knife has a sawlike edge.

Compare and Contrast Characters *What draws Mr. Pirzada and Lilia's parents together?*

Theme *Why does Mr. Pirzada decide not to watch the news? Does this change your ideas about the theme? Explain.*

my father, Mr. Pirzada, and I. While the television aired unattended we covered the tabletop with newspapers. Mr. Pirzada draped his jacket over the chair behind him, removed a pair of opal[34] cuff links, and rolled up the starched sleeves of his shirt.

"First go around the top, like this," I instructed, demonstrating with my index finger.

He made an initial incision[35] and drew the knife around. When he had come full circle he lifted the cap by the stem; it loosened effortlessly, and Mr. Pirzada leaned over the pumpkin for a moment to inspect and inhale its contents. My mother gave him a long metal spoon with which he gutted the interior until the last bits of string and seeds were gone. My father, meanwhile, separated the seeds from the pulp and set them out to dry on a cookie sheet, so that we could roast them later on. I drew two triangles against the ridged surface for the eyes, which Mr. Pirzada dutifully carved, and crescents for eyebrows, and another triangle for the nose. The mouth was all that remained, and the teeth posed a challenge. I hesitated.

"Smile or frown?" I asked.

"You choose," Mr. Pirzada said.

As a compromise I drew a kind of grimace,[36] straight across, neither mournful nor friendly. Mr. Pirzada began carving, without the least bit of **intimidation,** as if he had been carving jack-o'-lanterns his whole life. He had nearly finished when the national news began. The reporter

Home Coming—After a Long Absence, 1998.
Shanti Panchal. Watercolor on paper,
98 x 79 cm. Private collection.

View the Art In explaining his creative process, artist Shanti Panchal said that "escape and shifting of focus is the essence of survival." How might this statement apply to the situation that Mr. Pirzada finds himself in?

mentioned Dacca, and we all turned to listen: An Indian official announced that unless the world helped to relieve the burden of East Pakistani refugees, India would have to go to war against Pakistan. The reporter's face dripped with sweat as he relayed the information. He did not wear a tie or a jacket, dressed instead as if he himself were about to take part in the battle. He shielded his scorched face as he hollered things to the cameraman. The knife slipped from Mr. Pirzada's hand and made a gash dipping toward the base of the pumpkin.

---

34. *Opal* is a type of mineral used as a gemstone.
35. *Initial incision* means the "first cut."
36. A *grimace* (grim' is) is a twisting of the face into an ugly or painful smile.

Vocabulary

intimidation (in tim' ə dā shən) *n.* act of making one feel afraid or discouraged

"Please forgive me." He raised a hand to one side of his face, as if someone had slapped him there. "I am—it is terrible. I will buy another. We will try again."

"Not at all, not at all," my father said. He took the knife from Mr. Pirzada, and carved around the gash, evening it out, dispensing altogether with[37] the teeth I had drawn. What resulted was a disproportionately large hole the size of a lemon, so that our jack-o'-lantern wore an expression of placid[38] astonishment, the eyebrows no longer fierce, floating in frozen surprise above a vacant, geometric gaze.

For Halloween I was a witch. Dora, my trick-or-treating partner, was a witch too. We wore black capes fashioned from dyed pillowcases and conical hats with wide cardboard brims. We shaded our faces green with a broken eye shadow that belonged to Dora's mother, and my mother gave us two burlap sacks that had once contained basmati rice,[39] for collecting candy. That year our parents decided that we were old enough to roam the neighborhood unattended. Our plan was to walk from my house to Dora's, from where I was to call to say I had arrived safely, and then Dora's mother would drive me home. My father equipped us with flashlights, and I had to wear my watch and synchronize it with his. We were to return no later than nine o'clock.

When Mr. Pirzada arrived that evening he presented me with a box of chocolate-covered mints.

"In here," I told him, and opened up the burlap sack. "Trick or treat!"

"I understand that you don't really need my contribution this evening," he said, depositing the box. He gazed at my green face, and the hat secured by a string under my chin. Gingerly he lifted the hem of the cape, under which I was wearing a sweater and a zipped fleece jacket. "Will you be warm enough?"

I nodded, causing the hat to tip to one side.

He set it right. "Perhaps it is best to stand still."

The bottom of our staircase was lined with baskets of miniature candy, and when Mr. Pirzada removed his shoes he did not place them there as he normally did, but inside the closet instead. He began to unbutton his coat, and I waited to take it from him, but Dora called me from the bathroom to say that she needed my help drawing a mole on her chin. When we were finally ready my mother took a picture of us in front of the fireplace, and then I opened the front door to leave. Mr. Pirzada and my father, who had not gone into the living room yet, hovered in the foyer. Outside it was already dark. The air smelled of wet leaves, and our carved jack-o'-lantern flickered impressively against the shrubbery by the door. In the distance came the sounds of scampering feet, and the howls of the older boys who wore no costume at all other than a rubber mask, and the rustling apparel of the youngest children, some so young that they were carried from door to door in the arms of their parents.

"Don't go into any of the houses you don't know," my father warned.

---

37. *Dispensing . . . with* means "getting rid of."
38. *Placid* means "calm; undisturbed."
39. *Basmati rice* is a kind of long-grain rice grown in India.

Theme *Is there more than one reason for which Mr. Pirzada feels he needs to be forgiven? Explain. How does this relate to a theme of the story?*

Compare and Contrast Characters *How does this detail emphasize the differences between children's lives in Boston and in East Pakistan?*

Making Choices *How does Mr. Pirzada's comment reflect his own actions?*

Mr. Pirzada knit his brows together. "Is there any danger?'

"No, no," my mother assured him. "All the children will be out. It's a tradition."

"Perhaps I should accompany them?" Mr. Pirzada suggested. He looked suddenly tired and small, standing there in his splayed, stockinged feet, and his eyes contained a panic I had never seen before. In spite of the cold I began to sweat inside my pillowcase.

"Really, Mr. Pirzada," my mother said, "Lilia will be perfectly safe with her friend."

"But if it rains? If they lose their way?"

"Don't worry," I said. It was the first time I had uttered those words to Mr. Pirzada, two simple words I had tried but failed to tell him for weeks, had said only in my prayers. It shamed me now that I had said them for my own sake.

He placed one of his stocky fingers on my cheek, then pressed it to the back of his own hand, leaving a faint green smear. "If the lady insists," he conceded, and offered a small bow.

We left, stumbling slightly in our black pointy thrift-store shoes, and when we turned at the end of the driveway to wave good-bye, Mr. Pirzada was standing in the frame of the doorway, a short figure between my parents, waving back.

"Why did that man want to come with us?" Dora asked.

"His daughters are missing." As soon as I said it, I wished I had not. I felt that my saying it made it true, that Mr. Pirzada's daughters really were missing, and that he would never see them again.

"You mean they were kidnapped?" Dora continued. "From a park or something?"

"I didn't mean they were missing. I meant, he misses them. They live in a different country, and he hasn't seen them in a while, that's all."

We went from house to house, walking along pathways and pressing doorbells. Some people had switched off all their lights for effect, or strung rubber bats in their windows. At the McIntyres' a coffin was placed in front of the door, and Mr. McIntyre rose from it in silence, his face covered with chalk, and deposited a fistful of candy corns into our sacks. Several people told me that they had never seen an Indian witch before. Others performed the transaction without comment. As we paved our way with the parallel beams of our flashlights we saw eggs cracked in the middle of the road, and cars covered with shaving cream, and toilet paper garlanding[40] the branches of trees. By the time we reached Dora's house our hands were chapped from carrying our bulging burlap bags, and our feet were sore and swollen. Her mother gave us bandages for our blisters and served us warm cider and caramel popcorn. She reminded me to call my parents to tell them I had arrived safely, and when I did I could hear the television in the background. My mother did not seem particularly relieved to hear from me. When I replaced the phone on the receiver it occurred to me that the television wasn't on at Dora's house at all. Her father was lying on the couch, reading a magazine, with a glass of wine on the coffee

---

Compare and Contrast Characters *Why is Mr. Pirzada so worried about the girls, while Lilia's mother does not seem concerned about their safety?*

Making Choices *Why does Lilia choose to tell Mr. Pirzada not to worry at this point, instead of earlier in the story?*

40. A *garland* is a wreath, usually of flowers or leaves. Here, the garland is toilet paper strewn through the branches.

Compare and Contrast Characters *Why are Dora's parents not watching the news?*

JHUMPA LAHIRI **115**

table, and there was saxophone music playing on the stereo.

After Dora and I had sorted through our plunder, and counted and sampled and traded until we were satisfied, her mother drove me back to my house. I thanked her for the ride, and she waited in the driveway until I made it to the door. In the glare of her headlights I saw that our pumpkin had been shattered, its thick shell strewn in chunks across the grass. I felt the sting of tears in my eyes, and a sudden pain in my throat, as if it had been stuffed with the sharp tiny pebbles that crunched with each step under my aching feet. I opened the door, expecting the three of them to be standing in the foyer, waiting to receive me, and to grieve for our ruined pumpkin, but there was no one. In the living room Mr. Pirzada, my father, and mother were sitting side by side on the sofa. The television was turned off, and Mr. Pirzada had his head in his hands.

What they heard that evening, and for many evenings after that, was that India and Pakistan were drawing closer and closer to war. Troops from both sides lined the border, and Dacca was insisting on nothing short of independence. The war was to be waged on East Pakistani soil. The United States was siding with West Pakistan, the Soviet Union with India and what was soon to be Bangladesh. War was declared officially on December 4, and twelve days later, the Pakistani army, weakened by having to fight three thousand miles from their source of supplies, surrendered in Dacca. All of these facts I know only now, for they are available to me in any history book, in any library. But then it

Girls in a Wood. Indian Art.

View the Art In this painting, three Indian girls spend their leisure time in a beautiful wood. How does this scene compare with the situation of Mr. Pirzada's daughters in East Pakistan?

remained, for the most part, a remote mystery with haphazard[41] clues. What I remember during those twelve days of the war was that my father no longer asked me to watch the news with them, and that Mr. Pirzada stopped bringing me candy, and that my mother refused to serve anything other than boiled eggs with rice for dinner. I remember some nights helping my mother spread a sheet and blankets on the couch so that Mr.

---

41. *Haphazard* means "random; occurring by chance."

Pirzada could sleep there, and high-pitched voices hollering in the middle of the night when my parents called our relatives in Calcutta to learn more details about the situation. Most of all I remember the three of them operating during that time as if they were a single person, sharing a single meal, a single body, a single silence, and a single fear.

In January, Mr. Pirzada flew back to his three-story home in Dacca, to discover what was left of it. We did not see much of him in those final weeks of the year; he was busy finishing his manuscript, and we went to Philadelphia to spend Christmas with friends of my parents. Just as I have no memory of his first visit, I have no memory of his last. My father drove him to the airport one afternoon while I was at school. For a long time we did not hear from him. Our evenings went on as usual, with dinners in front of the news. The only difference was that Mr. Pirzada and his extra watch were not there to accompany us. According to reports Dacca was repairing itself slowly, with a newly formed parliamentary government. The new leader, Sheikh Mujib Rahman, recently released from prison, asked countries for building materials to replace more than one million houses that had been destroyed in the war. Countless refugees returned from India, greeted, we learned, by unemployment and the threat of famine.[42] Every now and then I studied the map above my father's desk and pictured Mr. Pirzada on that small patch of yellow, perspiring heavily, I imagined, in one of his suits, searching for his family. Of course, the map was outdated by then.

Finally, several months later, we received a card from Mr. Pirzada commemorating[43] the Muslim New Year, along with a short letter. He was reunited, he wrote, with his wife and children. All were well, having survived the events of the past year at an estate belonging to his wife's grandparents in the mountains of Shillong.[44] His seven daughters were a bit taller, he wrote, but otherwise they were the same, and he still could not keep their names in order. At the end of the letter he thanked us for our hospitality, adding that although he now understood the meaning of the words "thank you" they still were not adequate to express his gratitude. To celebrate the good news my mother prepared a special dinner that evening, and when we sat down to eat at the coffee table we toasted our water glasses, but I did not feel like celebrating. Though I had not seen him for months, it was only then that I felt Mr. Pirzada's absence. It was only then, raising my water glass in his name, that I knew what it meant to miss someone who was so many miles and hours away, just as he had missed his wife and daughters for so many months. He had no reason to return to us, and my parents predicted, correctly, that we would never see him again. Since January, each night before bed, I had continued to eat, for the sake of Mr. Pirzada's family, a piece of candy I had saved from Halloween. That night there was no need to. Eventually, I threw them away. ∾

---

42. *Famine* is an extreme lack of food, leading to starvation.

43. *Commemorating* means "honoring the memory of."
44. *Shillong* is a part of India north of East Pakistan.

Compare and Contrast Characters *What has finally given all the adults the same single-minded sense of fear?*

Theme *Why do you think that this is the first time Lilia feels Mr. Pirzada's absence? How does this connect to the theme?*

Making Choices *Why has Lilia decided to throw the candy away?*

After You Read

Respond and Think Critically

1. **Connect to Personal Experience** What was your reaction when you realized that Mr. Pirzada decided to stay in the United States instead of returning to Dacca and to his family? Explain.

2. **Explain Events** Why does Mr. Pirzada come to dinner at Lilia's house? Why does he give Lilia candy?

3. **Make Inferences About Character** What does Mr. Pirzada discover about his family when he gets back to Dacca? Why do you think Lilia's family never sees him again? Explain.

4. **Analyze Symbolism** Analyze Lahiri's use of food in the story, such as the food Lilia's mother serves and the candy Mr. Pirzada brings Lilia. What does the food represent? Use evidence from the story to support your answer.

5. **Evaluate Genre** Lahiri vividly describes the war and political situation in East Pakistan. How accurate do you think a writer should be in a fictional story? Explain.

6. **Draw Conclusions About Character** What is one way that Lilia is affected by Mr. Pirzada's visits? Explain your answer and support it with evidence from the story. **OER**

7. **Big Idea** **Draw Conclusions About Moral Dilemmas** Who do you think has made the most difficult choice in the story? Explain.

Daily Life & Culture

The Aftermath of Partition

In 1947, the partition of British India along religious lines created two independent nations, Muslim-dominated East and West Pakistan and Hindu India. On the Indian sub-continent, culture and regional differences are stronger identification markers than religion. This became clear when, in 1971, the largely Muslim West Pakistan army waged war on the inhabitants of East Pakistan, most of whom were Muslims themselves.

1. Find East and West Pakistan and Calcutta on the map shown here. What might have been the consequences of East Pakistan's separation from Calcutta, its economic hub?

2. What can you infer about the reasons the people of East Pakistan wanted self-rule?

Literary Element Theme

To discover a story's **theme,** you might look at the experiences of the main characters and ask what message about life the story communicates. Some themes are universal and are expressed in many works from different times and places.

8. Draw Conclusions About Theme Review the pink highlighted passages and questions throughout the story. What theme does Lahiri express through the experiences of Lilia and Mr. Pirzada? Explain.

9. Compare and Contrast Themes Read the play *The Ring of General Macías* beginning on page 828. How does it express a theme similar to that of Lahiri's story? Compare and contrast the two works' themes.

Review: Motivation

As you learned on page 73, **motivation** is the stated or implied reason that a character acts, thinks, or feels a certain way. Motivation may be an external circumstance, an internal value, or an emotional impulse.

10. Partner Activity Meet with a classmate and discuss the different motivations that the two main characters, Lilia and Mr. Pirzada, experience during the story. Create a two-column chart like the one below in which you list the character's name in the left column and his or her motivations in the right column. Remember that characters can have several motivations.

Character	Motivation
Mr. Pirzada	misses his wife and daughters
	has no proper stove or television

LOG ON ▶ **Literature** Online

Selection Resources For Selection Quizzes, eFlashcards, and Reading-Writing Connection activities, go to glencoe.com and enter QuickPass code GL57805u1.

Reading Strategy Compare and Contrast Characters

 Texas Test Practice (10.5)

1. Which detail about Mrs. Kenyon best underscores the contrast between her cultural background and that of Lilia's family?

A. She teaches elementary school.

B. She assigns Lilia and Dora a report on the surrender of Yorktown.

C. She frequently uses a map to show her students geography of colonial America.

D. She takes *Pakistan: A Land and Its People* away from Lilia.

Vocabulary Practice

Practice with Context Clues You can often determine the meaning of an unfamiliar word by looking at the **context,** or other words and sentences that surround the unfamiliar word. Identify the context clues below that help you determine the meaning of each boldfaced vocabulary word.

1. Maria consulted several sources when **ascertaining** the value of the used car.

2. The princess, who was used to elaborate meals, did not enjoy the **austere** meal of bread and carrots.

3. The runner navigated the obstacle course **impeccably,** never even touching, let alone knocking over, a single pin.

4. Some could not see the nearly **imperceptible** shift from green to bluish-green.

5. The bully rarely lifted a hand, relying instead on **intimidation.**

Respond Through Writing

Short Story

Apply Characterization Lahiri creates complex, nuanced characters by providing sensory details about how they look, speak, think, and act. That is, she *shows,* rather than *tells,* what her characters are like. Write a short story in which you use sensory details to *show* characters.

Purpose and Audience Your purpose is to write a short story using **characterization**. To use **direct characterization,** make explicit statements about a character. To employ **indirect characterization,** reveal a character's personality through the individual's words, thoughts, and actions and through what other characters say and think about the character. Your audience is made up of other readers your age.

Plan First, make a story map to be sure you have a setting, characters, and a conflict or problem, as well as a series of events that leads to a resolution of that conflict. Next, make two-column character charts to help you create interesting and believable characters. Model them on the following chart, which Lahiri might have made for Mr. Pirzada.

Trait	Details That Show Trait
family-oriented	winds his watch to time in Dacca, where family is
private	never talks about this ritual

Draft As you draft, provide sensory details (sights, sounds, smells, tastes, and textures) to *show* (not tell) characters and reveal the significance of their actions, gestures, movements, dialogue, appearances, and feelings. In addition, make sure your story has a clear plot, including a well-developed conflict and resolution. You should use suspense and other plot devices to hold readers' interest, and be sure that the mood and tone of your story are appropriate to the subject.

Revise Exchange your story with a classmate's. Make and incorporate suggestions for additional ways to use sensory details to improve characterization and have a consistent mood and tone.

Edit Edit your story, correcting any errors in grammar, spelling, and punctuation. Use the Grammar Tip in the side column to help you use quotation marks.

TEKS

10.14.A Write an engaging story with a well-developed conflict and resolution, interesting and believable characters, a range of literary strategies (e.g., dialogue, suspense) and devices to enhance the plot, and sensory details that define the mood or tone.

> **Grammar Tip**

Quotation Marks

When you write dialogue, place commas and periods inside the quotation marks.

"Really, Mr. Pirzada," my mother protested. *"Night after night. You spoil her."*

You can also use double quotation marks to show irony or sarcasm in a narrator's thoughts. Use single quotation marks to show irony or sarcasm inside characters' dialogue.

Her father's "small" snack consisted of almost a whole can of salted cashews.

"Mrs. Kenyon told me to focus on the more 'immediate' topic of the American Revolution," Lilia complained.

Grammar Workshop

Sentence Combining

TEKS

For pages 121–122

10.17.C Use a variety of correctly structured sentences (e.g., compound, complex, compound-complex).

Literature Connection At the beginning of "When Mr. Pirzada Came to Dine," Jhumpa Lahiri combines several ideas into one sentence.

> *"In the autumn of 1971 a man used to come to our house, bearing confections in his pocket and hopes of ascertaining the life or death of his family"*

Lahiri might have chosen to open her story by not combining ideas and by using short sentences like these: *This happened in the autumn of 1971. A man used to come to our house. He had confections in his pocket. He also had hopes of ascertaining the life or death of his family.*

To write effectively, you must make similar choices about sentence length and structure. Combining short sentences into longer ones helps you develop your own writing style.

Examples

Solution 1 Use a prepositional phrase, a group of words that begins with a preposition and ends with a noun or a pronoun.

> **Original:** Mr. Pirzada arrived every evening. He always brought a bag of sweets.

> **Combined:** Mr. Pirzada arrived every evening with a bag of sweets.

Solution 2 Use an appositive, a noun or pronoun placed next to another noun or pronoun to give additional information about it. An **appositive phrase** is an appositive plus any words that modify it.

> **Original:** East Pakistan was Mr. Pirzada's home. It is now Bangladesh.

> **Combined:** East Pakistan, now Bangladesh, was Mr. Pirzada's home.

Solution 3 Use a participial phrase. A **participle** is a verb form, often ending in *–ing* or *–ed,* that functions as an adjective. A participial phrase—which includes a participle and other words that add to it—also functions as an adjective. In the sentence *Worried about his family, Mr. Pirzada buried his face in his hands,* for example, *worried* is the participle and *worried about his family* is the phrase. They both describe Mr. Pirzada.

Drafting Tip

Vary the length and structure of your sentences. Work for a rhythmic, interesting balance of long and short sentences, remembering that brevity often has dramatic force. Balance these out with longer compound, complex, and compound-complex sentences for variety. By using different kinds of sentence openers—and by sometimes placing information in the middle of a sentence—you can create stylistic interest.

Revising Tip

As you revise an essay, read your draft aloud, stopping now and then to experiment with clusters of sentences. This process is faster than rewriting and helps you decide on a "best sentence" to write down.

Separate: *The reporter described the war. He was dripping with sweat.*

Combined: *Dripping with sweat, the reporter described the war.*

Solution 4 Use a subordinating conjunction to join two clauses, or ideas, into a complex sentence in which one clause is dependent upon the other. Subordinating conjunctions include words such as *after, although, as, because, if, since,* and *when.*

Separate: *Mr. Pirzada couldn't use the knife. His hands were shaking.*

Combined: *Mr. Pirzada couldn't use the knife because his hands were shaking.*

Solution 5 Use a coordinating conjunction to join words or groups of words with equal grammatical weight into a compound sentence. Coordinating conjunctions include words such as *and, but, or, so, nor, for,* and *yet.* Use both a coordinating and a subordinating conjunction to join three or more clauses into a compound-complex sentence.

Separate: *Mr. Pirzada returned home. He wrote to say his family was safe. Lilia did not feel like celebrating.*

Combined: *Mr. Pirzada returned home and wrote to say his family was safe, but Lilia did not feel like celebrating.*

Solution 6 Use an adjective clause (also called a relative clause), a group of words with a subject and a predicate that modify a noun or a pronoun. Adjective clauses often begin with *who, whom, whose, that,* and *which.*

Separate: *Mr. Pirzada visited most nights. He worked at the university.*

Combined: *Mr. Pirzada, who worked at the university, visited most nights.*

Test-Taking Tip

Remember that there are many ways of combining sentences. When deciding which solution works best, ask yourself the following questions:

☑ Is my solution free of excess words?

☑ Does my solution emphasize the important idea of the sentence?

☑ Does my solution flow naturally when I read it aloud?

☑ Is my solution a complete sentence with a subject and predicate and not just a long fragment?

Literature Online

Grammar For more grammar practice, go to glencoe.com and enter QuickPass code GL57805u1.

Revise

1. Use a prepositional phrase to combine the following sentences: *Mr. Pirzada was a short, dapper man. He had a curly moustache.*

2. Use a subordinating conjunction and an appositive phrase or an adjective clause to combine these sentences: *The adults finished eating. They discussed Kishore Kumar. Kishore Kumar was a famous Indian actor.*

3. Use a participial phrase and a coordinating conjunction to combine the following sentences: *Lilia prayed for peace. She was worried about Mr. Pirzada's family. The war dragged on for months.*

Before You Read

To Da-duh, in Memoriam

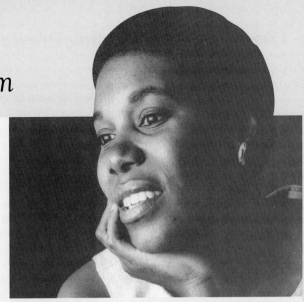

Meet **Paule Marshall**
(born 1929)

A basement kitchen may sound like an unlikely place for a writer to find her inspiration, but that is where the award-winning African American writer Paule Marshall found hers.

Homegrown Inspiration "I grew up among poets," Marshall wrote in her autobiographical essay, "From the Poets in the Kitchen." Each afternoon, these "poets," who, in reality, were ordinary housewives, gathered around the kitchen table of the brownstone home in the close-knit, West-Indian community of 1930s Brooklyn, New York, where Marshall was born and raised. Marshall sat in the corner and listened as the women, including her mother, talked "endlessly, passionately, poetically, and with impressive range."

The Rhythm of Language During these late afternoon conversations, Marshall learned about the "old country," the small Caribbean island of Barbados, the homeland of Marshall's parents. Her ear became attuned to their idiomatic, rhythmic language that was a combination of English words, Barbadian syntax, and African sounds. These women were to become Marshall's primary writing teachers. "They taught me my first lessons in the narrative art. They trained my ear. They set a standard of excellence." While Marshall also credits both white and African American "literary giants" with helping her find her literary voice, she attributes the best of her work to these women. It is a "testimony to the rich legacy of language and culture they so freely passed on to me in the wordshop of the kitchen."

> "My work asks that you become involved, that you think."
>
> —Paule Marshall

Finding the Writer's Path Marshall was around eight or nine years old when she "graduated" from the corner of her kitchen to the neighborhood library. She was a voracious reader, consuming volumes by Austen, Thackeray, Fielding, and Dickens. One day she picked up a book by Paul Laurence Dunbar. Until then, she had been unaware that there was an African American voice in literature.

In 1953 Marshall graduated with honors from Brooklyn College with a degree in English Literature. In 1954 she published her first short story, "The Valley Between." Today, Marshall is widely read and recognized as, according to critic Carol Field, a "highly gifted writer." Her first book, *Brown Girl, Brownstones*, is now considered a classic coming-of-age novel.

Literature Online

Author Search For more about Paule Marshall, go to glencoe.com and enter QuickPass code GL57805u1.

Literature and Reading Preview

Connect to the Story

Is it ever acceptable to argue with a grandparent or another older person? Discuss this question with a partner. Talk about whether such an argument would ever be acceptable.

Build Background

"To Da-duh, in Memoriam" takes place in Barbados in the 1930s. Barbados is a tiny Caribbean island with mostly flat terrain. The stalks of sugar cane referred to in the story can grow from seven to thirty feet high. Although the people of Barbados speak English, the folk culture is of African origin.

Set Purposes for Reading

Big Idea Making Choices

As you read "To Da-duh, in Memoriam," ask yourself, How does the narrator's relationship with her grandmother affect her later in life?

Literary Element Characterization

Characterization is the methods a writer uses to develop a character. A writer may use direct statements, or **direct characterization,** to describe a character. The writer may also reveal the character's attributes through **indirect characterization,** or through his or her words, thoughts, and actions or through what other characters think and say about the character. As you read the story, ask yourself, How does Marshall use characterization to reveal the characters of the narrator and her grandmother?

Reading Strategy Make Inferences About Characters

To **infer** is to make a reasonable guess about some element of a story based on textual evidence the writer supplies. As you read "To Da-duh, in Memoriam," ask yourself, How can I observe details to make complex inferences about the characters?

....

Tip: Take Notes Use a chart like the one below to record the inferences you draw about the narrator and Da-duh.

Detail	Inference
"intense, unrelenting struggle between her back . . . and the rest of her"	Da-duh is proud, strong, and determined.

TEKS

For pages 123–135

RC-10.B Make complex inferences about text and use textual evidence to support understanding.

Vocabulary

formidable (fôr′ mi də bəl) *adj.* causing fear, dread, or awe by reason of size, strength, or power; p. 127 *Defeat was almost guaranteed against such a formidable opponent.*

decrepit (di krep′ it) *adj.* broken down by long use or old age; p. 128 *A strong wind would surely blow down the decrepit wooden shack.*

hurtle (hurt′ əl) *v.* to move rapidly, especially with much force or noise; p. 129 *They hurtle toward the finish line on their homemade scooters.*

arrogant (ar′ ə gənt) *adj.* full of self-importance; haughty; p. 129 *She spoke in an arrogant tone, as if the rest of us were inferior to her.*

malicious (mə lish′ əs) *adj.* having or showing a desire to harm another; p. 133 *His malicious actions resulted in injuries to several bystanders.*

To Da-duh, in Memoriam

Paule Marshall

Wash Day. Victor Collector. Oil on canvas. Private collection.

"...Oh Nana! all of you
is not involved in this
evil business Death,
Nor all of us in life."
—*from "At My
Grandmother's Grave,"*
by Lebert Bethune

I did not see her at first I remember. For not only was it dark inside the crowded disembarkation[1] shed in spite of the daylight flooding in from outside, but standing there waiting for her with my mother and sister I was still somewhat blinded from the sheen of tropical sunlight on the water of the bay which we had just crossed in the landing boat, leaving behind us the ship that had brought us from New York lying in the offing.[2] Besides, being only nine years of age at the time and knowing nothing of islands I was busy attending to the alien sights and sounds of Barbados, the unfamiliar smells.

I did not see her, but I was alerted to her approach by my mother's hand which suddenly tightened around mine, and looking up I traced her gaze through the gloom in the shed until I finally made out the small, purposeful, painfully erect figure of the old woman headed our way.

Her face was drowned in the shadow of an ugly rolled-brim brown felt hat, but the details of her slight body and of the struggle taking place within it were clear enough—an intense, unrelenting[3] struggle between her back which was beginning to bend ever so slightly under the weight of her eighty-odd years and the rest of her which sought to deny those years and hold that back straight, keep it in line. Moving swiftly toward us (so swiftly it seemed she did not intend stopping when she reached us but would sweep past us out the doorway which opened onto the sea and like Christ walk upon the water!), she was caught between the sunlight at

her end of the building and the darkness inside—and for a moment she appeared to contain them both: the light in the long severe old-fashioned white dress she wore which brought the sense of a past that was still alive into our bustling present and in the snatch of white at her eye; the darkness in her black high-top shoes and in her face which was visible now that she was closer.

It was as stark and fleshless as a death mask, that face. The maggots might have already done their work, leaving only the framework of bone beneath the ruined skin and deep wells at the temple and jaw. But her eyes were alive, unnervingly so for one so old, with a sharp light that flicked out of the dim clouded depths like a lizard's tongue to snap up all in her view. Those eyes betrayed a child's curiosity about the world, and I wondered vaguely seeing them, and seeing the way the bodice of her ancient dress had collapsed in on her flat chest (what had happened to her breasts?), whether she might not be some kind of child at the same time that she was a woman, with fourteen children, my mother included, to prove it. Perhaps she was both, both child and woman, darkness and light, past and present, life and death—all the opposites contained and reconciled in her.

"My Da-duh," my mother said formally and stepped forward. The name sounded like thunder fading softly in the distance.

"Child," Da-duh said, and her tone, her quick scrutiny of my mother, the brief embrace in which they appeared to shy from each other rather than touch, wiped out the fifteen years my mother had been away and restored the old relationship.

---

1. To *disembark* is to get off a ship or plane.
2. In this context, *in the offing* means "just in view from the shore."
3. An *unrelenting* (un'ri len'ting) struggle is one that does not ease or lessen in intensity.

Characterization *What does the description in the second paragraph reveal about the old woman?*

Make Inferences About Characters *What can you infer about the woman from how she is dressed?*

Tropical Scene. Albert Bierstadt (1830–1902). Oil on paper laid on board. Private collection.

View the Art Bierstadt was an American painter whose vibrant landscapes were intended to awe and impress the viewer. What qualities do you think the tropical scene in this painting shares with the settings described in the story?

My mother, who was such a **formidable** figure in my eyes, had suddenly with a word been reduced to my status.

"Yes, God is good," Da-duh said with a nod that was like a tic.[4] "He has spared me to see my child again."

We were led forward then, apologetically because not only did Da-duh prefer boys but she also liked her grandchildren to be "white," that is, fair-skinned; and we had, I was to discover, a number of cousins, the outside children of white estate managers and the like, who qualified. We, though, were as black as she.

---

4. Here, a *tic* is an involuntary twitch.

My sister being the oldest was presented first. "This one takes after the father," my mother said and waited to be reproved.

Frowning, Da-duh tilted my sister's face toward the light. But her frown soon gave way to a grudging smile, for my sister with her large mild eyes and little broad winged nose, with our father's high-cheeked Barbadian cast to her face, was pretty.

"She's goin' be lucky," Da-duh said and patted her once on the cheek. "Any girl child that takes after the father does be lucky."

She turned then to me. But oddly enough she did not touch me. Instead leaning close, she peered hard at me, and then quickly drew back. I thought I saw her hand start up as though to shield her eyes. It was almost as if she saw not only me, a thin truculent[5] child who it was said took after no one but myself, but something in me which for some reason she found disturbing, even threatening. We looked silently at each other for a long time there in the noisy shed, our gaze locked. She was the first to look away.

"But Adry," she said to my mother and her laugh was cracked, thin, apprehensive. "Where did you get this one here with this fierce look?"

"We don't know where she came out of, my Da-duh," my mother said, laughing also. Even I smiled to myself. After all I had won the encounter. Da-duh had recognized my small strength—and this was all I ever asked of the adults in my life then.

"Come, soul," Da-duh said and took my hand. "You must be one of those New York terrors you hear so much about."

Visual Vocabulary
Lorry is what the British call a truck.

She led us, me at her side and my sister and mother behind, out of the shed into the sunlight that was like a bright driving summer rain and over to a group of people clustered beside a **decrepit** lorry. They were our relatives, most of them from St. Andrews although Da-duh herself lived in St. Thomas, the women wearing bright print dresses, the colors vivid against their darkness, the men rusty black suits that encased them like strait-jackets.

---

5. To be *truculent* is to be fierce and ready to fight.

Characterization *Why do you think Marshall has the narrator describe herself as a "truculent child"?*

Vocabulary

decrepit (di krep′ it) *adj.* broken down by long use or old age

---

Da-duh, holding fast to my hand, became my anchor as they circled round us like a nervous sea, exclaiming, touching us with their calloused hands, embracing us shyly. They laughed in awed bursts: "But look Adry got big-big children!" / "And see the nice things they wearing, wristwatch and all!" / "I tell you, Adry has done all right for sheself in New York. . . ."

Da-duh, ashamed at their wonder, embarrassed for them, admonished them the while. . . . "Why you all got to get on like you never saw people from 'Away' before? You would think New York is the only place in the world to hear wunna.[6] That's why I don't like to go anyplace with you St. Andrews people, you know. You all ain't been colonized."

We were in the back of the lorry finally, packed in among the barrels of ham, flour, cornmeal and rice and the trunks of clothes that my mother had brought as gifts. We made our way slowly through Bridgetown's clogged streets, part of a funereal[7] procession of cars and open-sided buses, bicycles and donkey carts. The dim little limestone shops and offices along the way marched with us, at the same mournful pace, toward the same grave ceremony—as did the people, the women balancing huge baskets on top their heads as if they were no more than hats they wore to shade them from the sun. Looking over the edge of the lorry I watched as their feet slurred the dust. I listened, and their voices, raw and loud and dissonant in the heat, seemed to be grappling with each other high overhead.

Da-duh sat on a trunk in our midst, a monarch amid her court. She still held

---

6. *To hear wunna* may be Da-duh's way of saying "to have wonders."
7. *Funereal* means "like, or suitable to, a funeral."

Characterization *What does the detail at the top of this column about Da-duh holding the narrator's hand tell you about Da-duh?*

my hand, but it was different now. I had suddenly become her anchor, for I felt her fear of the lorry with its asthmatic motor (a fear and distrust, I later learned, she held of all machines) beating like a pulse in her rough palm.

As soon as we left Bridgetown behind though, she relaxed, and while the others around us talked she gazed at the canes standing tall on either side of the winding marl[8] road. "C'dear," she said softly to herself after a time. "The canes this side are pretty enough."

They were too much for me. I thought of them as giant weeds that had overrun the island, leaving scarcely any room for the small tottering houses of sunbleached pine we passed or the people, dark streaks as our lorry **hurtled** by. I suddenly feared that we were journeying, unaware that we were, toward some dangerous place where the canes, grown as high and thick as a forest, would close in on us and run us through with their stiletto blades. I longed then for the familiar: for the street in Brooklyn[9] where I lived, for my father who had refused to accompany us ("Blowing out good money on foolishness," he had said of the trip), for a game of tag with my friends under the chestnut tree outside our aging brownstone house.

"Yes, but wait till you see St. Thomas canes," Da-duh was saying to me. "They's canes father, bo," she gave a proud

---

8. A *marl* road is paved with crumbly clay of the sort used to make cement.
9. *Brooklyn* is one of New York City's five boroughs, or districts.

Make Inferences About Characters *What kind of inference can you make about the narrator from her attitude toward the cane?*

Vocabulary

hurtle (hurt′ əl) *v.* to move rapidly, especially with much force or noise

arrogant nod. "Tomorrow, God willing, I goin' take you out in the ground and show them to you."

True to her word Da-duh took me with her the following day out into the ground. It was a fairly large plot adjoining her weathered board and shingle house and consisting of a small orchard, a good-sized canepiece and behind the canes, where the land sloped abruptly down, a gully. She had purchased it with Panama money sent her by her eldest son, my uncle Joseph, who had died working on the canal. We entered the ground along a trail no wider than her body and as devious and complex as her reasons for showing me her land. Da-duh strode briskly ahead, her slight form filled out this morning by the layers of sacking petticoats she wore under her working dress to protect her against the damp. A fresh white cloth, elaborately arranged around her head, added to her height, and lent her a vain, almost roguish air.

Her pace slowed once we reached the orchard, and glancing back at me occasionally over her shoulder, she pointed out the various trees.

"This here is a breadfruit," she said. "That one yonder is a papaw. Here's a guava. This is a mango. I know you don't have anything like these in New York. Here's a sugar apple." (The fruit looked more like artichokes than apples to me.) "This one bears limes. . . ." She went on for some time, intoning the names of the trees as though they were those of her gods. Finally, turning to me, she said, "I know

---

Making Choices *Based on what you already know about Da-duh, why do you think she wants to show her land to her granddaughter?*

Vocabulary

arrogant (ar′ə gənt) *adj.* full of self-importance; haughty you don't have anything this nice where you come from." Then, as I hesitated: "I said I know you don't have anything this nice where you come from. . . ."

"No," I said and my world did seem suddenly lacking.

Da-duh nodded and passed on. The orchard ended and we were on the narrow cart road that led through the canepiece, the canes clashing like swords above my cowering head. Again she turned and her thin muscular arms spread wide, her dim gaze embracing the small field of canes, she said—and her voice almost broke under the weight of her pride, "Tell me, have you got anything like these in that place where you were born?"

"No."

"I din' think so. I bet you don't even know that these canes here and the sugar you eat is one and the same thing. That they does throw the canes into some damn machine at the factory and squeeze out all the little life in them to make sugar for you all so in New York to eat. I bet you don't know that."

"I've got two cavities and I'm not allowed to eat a lot of sugar."

But Da-duh didn't hear me. She had turned with an inexplicably angry motion and was making her way rapidly out of the canes and down the slope at the edge of the field which led to the gully below. Following her apprehensively down the incline amid a stand of banana plants whose leaves flapped like elephants' ears

in the wind, I found myself in the middle of a small tropical wood—a place dense and damp and gloomy and tremulous with the fitful play of light and shadow as the leaves high above moved against the sun that was almost hidden from view. It was a violent place, the tangled foliage fighting each other for a chance at the sunlight, the branches of the trees locked in what seemed an immemorial[10] struggle, one both necessary and inevitable. But despite the violence, it was pleasant, almost peaceful in the gully, and beneath the thick undergrowth the earth smelled like spring.

> *"It was a violent place, the tangled foliage fighting each other for a chance at the sunlight . . ."*

This time Da-duh didn't even bother to ask her usual question, but simply turned and waited for me to speak.

"No," I said, my head bowed. "We don't have anything like this in New York."

"Ah," she cried, her triumph complete. "I din' think so. Why, I've heard that's a place where you can walk till you near drop and never see a tree."

"We've got a chestnut tree in front of our house," I said.

"Does it bear?" She waited. "I ask you, does it bear?"

"Not anymore," I muttered. "It used to, but not anymore."

She gave the nod that was like a nervous twitch. "You see," she said. "Nothing can bear there." Then, secure behind her scorn,

---

10. An *immemorial* struggle would be one that extended back beyond memory or record.

Make Inferences About Characters *Why does the narrator make a negative comment about sugar?*

Make Inferences About Characters *Why does Da-duh show the narrator all of these wonderful places?*

she added, "But tell me, what's this snow like that you hear so much about?"

Looking up, I studied her closely, sensing my chance, and then I told her, describing at length and with as much drama as I could summon not only what snow in the city was like, but what it would be like here, in her perennial summer kingdom.

". . . And you see all these trees you got here," I said. "Well, they'd be bare. No leaves, no fruit, nothing. They'd be covered in snow. You see your canes. They'd be buried under tons of snow. The snow would be higher than your head, higher than your house, and you wouldn't be able to come down into this here gully because it would be snowed under. . . ."

She searched my face for the lie, still scornful but intrigued. "What a thing, huh?" she said finally, whispering it softly to herself.

"And when it snows you couldn't dress like you are now," I said. "Oh no, you'd freeze to death. You'd have to wear a hat and gloves and galoshes and ear muffs so your ears wouldn't freeze and drop off, and a heavy coat. I've got a Shirley Temple[11] coat with fur on the collar. I can dance. You wanna see?"

Before she could answer I began, with a dance called the Truck which was popular back then in the 1930s. My right forefinger waving, I trucked around the nearby trees and around Da-duh's awed and rigid form. After the Truck I did the Suzy-Q, my lean hips swishing, my sneakers sidling zigzag over the ground. "I can sing," I said and did so, starting with "I'm Gonna Sit Right Down and Write Myself a Letter," then without pausing, "Tea For Two," and ending with "I Found a Million Dollar Baby in a Five and Ten Cent Store."

For long moments afterwards Da-duh stared at me as if I were a creature from Mars, an emissary from some world she did not know but which intrigued her and whose power she both felt and feared. Yet something about my performance must have pleased her, because bending down she slowly lifted her long skirt and then, one by one, the layers of petticoats until she came to a drawstring purse dangling at the end of a long strip of cloth tied round her waist. Opening the purse she handed me a penny. "Here," she said half-smiling against her will. "Take this to buy yourself a sweet at the shop up the road. There's nothing to be done with you, soul."

From then on, whenever I wasn't taken to visit relatives, I accompanied Da-duh out into the ground, and alone with her amid the canes or down in the gully I told her about New York. It always began with some slighting remark on her part: "I know they don't have anything this nice where you come from," or "Tell me, I hear those foolish people in New York does do such and such. . . ." But as I answered, recreating my towering world of steel and concrete and machines for her, building the city out of words, I would feel her give way. I came to know the signs of her surrender: the total stillness that would come over the little hard dry form, the probing gaze that like a surgeon's knife sought to cut through my skull to get at the images there, to see if I were lying; above all, her fear, a fear nameless and profound, the same one I had felt beating in the palm of her hand that day in the lorry.

---

11. *Shirley Temple* was a popular child movie star of the 1930s.

Making Choices *In the first full paragraph in this column, why does the narrator choose to respond to her grandmother's question in the way she does?*

Making Choices *Why do you think Da-duh chooses to take the child with her, instead of someone else?*

Make Inferences About Characters *Why does Da-duh react as she does when the child talks about New York City?*

Over the weeks I told her about refrigerators, radios, gas stoves, elevators, trolley cars, wringer washing machines, movies, airplanes, the cyclone at Coney Island, subways, toasters, electric lights: "At night, see, all you have to do is flip this little switch on the wall and all the lights in the house go on. Just like that. Like magic. It's like turning on the sun at night."

Visual Vocabulary
Coney Island is an area in Brooklyn with an amusement park. The *Cyclone* was a popular ride there.

"But tell me," she said to me once with a faint mocking smile, "do the white people have all these things too or it's only the people looking like us?"

I laughed. "What d'ya mean," I said. "The white people have even better." Then: "I beat up a white girl in my class last term."

"Beating up white people!" Her tone was incredulous.

"How you mean!" I said, using an expression of hers. "She called me a name."

For some reason Da-duh could not quite get over this and repeated in the same hushed, shocked voice, "Beating up white people now! Oh, the lord, the world's changing up so I can scarce recognize it anymore."

One morning toward the end of our stay, Da-duh led me into a part of the gully that we had never visited before, an area darker and more thickly overgrown than the rest, almost impenetrable. There in a small clearing amid the dense bush, she stopped before an incredibly tall royal palm which rose cleanly out of the ground, and drawing the eye up with it, soared high above the trees around it into the sky. It appeared to be touching the blue dome of sky, to be flaunting its dark crown of fronds right in the blinding white face of the late morning sun.

Da-duh watched me a long time before she spoke, and then she said, very quietly, "All right, now, tell me if you've got anything this tall in that place you're from."

I almost wished, seeing her face, that I could have said no. "Yes," I said. "We've got buildings hundreds of times this tall in New York. There's one called the Empire State Building that's the tallest in the world. My class visited it last year and I went all the way to the top. It's got over a hundred floors. I can't describe how tall it is. Wait a minute. What's the name of that hill I went to visit the other day, where they have the police station?"

"You mean Bissex?"

"Yes, Bissex. Well, the Empire State Building is way taller than that."

"You're lying now!" she shouted, trembling with rage. Her hand lifted to strike me.

"No, I'm not," I said. "It really is, if you don't believe me I'll send you a picture postcard of it soon as I get back home so you can see for yourself. But it's way taller than Bissex."

All the fight went out of her at that. The hand poised to strike me fell limp to her side, and as she stared at me, seeing not me but the building that was taller than the highest hill she knew, the small stubborn light in her eyes (it was the same amber as the flame in the kerosene lamp she lit at dusk) began to fail. Finally, with a vague gesture that even in the midst of her defeat still tried

Make Inferences About Characters *What does the narrator's wish that she could say "no" tell you about the relationship between the narrator and Da-duh?*

Making Choices *Why does the narrator make a point of saying the Empire State Building is taller?*

Characterization *How does the light in Da-duh's eyes help characterize her in the scene at the end of this page?*

to dismiss me and my world, she turned and started back through the gully, walking slowly, her steps groping and uncertain, as if she were suddenly no longer sure of the way, while I followed triumphant yet strangely saddened behind.

The next morning I found her dressed for our morning walk but stretched out on the Berbice chair in the tiny drawing room where she sometimes napped during the afternoon heat, her face turned to the window beside her. She appeared thinner and suddenly indescribably old.

"My Da-duh," I said.

"Yes, nuh," she said. Her voice was listless and the face she slowly turned my way was, now that I think back on it, like a Benin mask, the features drawn and almost distorted by an ancient abstract sorrow.

"Don't you feel well?" I asked.

"Girl, I don't know."

"My Da-duh, I goin' boil you some bush tea," my aunt, Da-duh's youngest child, who lived with her, called from the shed roof kitchen.

"Who tell you I need bush tea?" she cried, her voice assuming for a moment its old authority. "You can't even rest nowadays without some **malicious** person looking for you to be dead. Come girl," she motioned me to a place beside her on the old-fashioned lounge chair, "give us a tune."

I sang for her until breakfast at eleven, all my brash irreverent Tin Pan Alley[12] songs, and then just before noon we went out into the ground. But it was a short,

dispirited walk. Da-duh didn't even notice that the mangoes were beginning to ripen and would have to be picked before the village boys got to them. And when she paused occasionally and looked out across the canes or up at her trees it wasn't as if she were seeing them but something else. Some huge, monolithic[13] shape had imposed itself, it seemed, between her and the land, obstructing her vision. Returning to the house she slept the entire afternoon on the Berbice chair.

She remained like this until we left, languishing away the mornings on the chair at the window gazing out at the land as if it were already doomed; then, at noon, taking the brief stroll with me through the ground during which she seldom spoke, and afterwards returning home to sleep till almost dusk sometimes.

On the day of our departure she put on the austere, ankle length white dress, the black shoes and brown felt hat (her town clothes she called them), but she did not go with us to town. She saw us off on the road outside her house and in the midst of my mother's tearful protracted[14] farewell, she leaned down and whispered in my ear, "Girl, you're not to forget now to send me the picture of that building, you hear."

By the time I mailed her the large colored picture postcard of the Empire State Building she was dead. She died during the famous '37 strike which began shortly after we left. On the day of her death England sent planes flying low over the island in a show of force—so low, according to my aunt's letter, that the downdraft from them shook the ripened mangoes

---

12. *Tin Pan Alley* was a district in New York City associated with composers and publishers of popular music. These pop songs were bright and lively, often treating their subjects with rude and disrespectful *(brash, irreverent)* mockery.

13. A *monolithic* shape would resemble a monument or another structure formed from a single, giant block of stone.

14. A *protracted* (prō trak′ təd) farewell would be one that takes a lot of time.

Central Park Skyline, 1999. Mary Iverson.

<u>View the Art</u> In this painting, a towering cityscape is juxtaposed against the dense green foliage of Central Park. How does this image reflect the conflict between the narrator and Da-duh?

from the trees in Da-duh's orchard. Frightened, everyone in the village fled into the canes. Except Da-duh. She remained in the house at the window so my aunt said, watching as the planes came swooping and screaming like monstrous birds down over the village, over her house, rattling her trees and flattening the young canes in her field. It must have seemed to her lying there that they did not intend pulling out of their dive, but like the hardback beetles which hurled themselves with suicidal force against the walls of the house at night, those menacing silver shapes would hurl themselves in an ecstasy of self-immolation[15] onto the land, destroying it utterly.

When the planes finally left and the villagers returned they found her dead on the Berbice chair at the window.

She died and I lived, but always, to this day even, within the shadow of her death. For a brief period after I was grown I went to live alone, like one doing penance,[16] in a loft above a noisy factory in downtown New York and there painted seas of sugarcane and huge swirling Van Gogh suns and palm trees striding like brightly-plumed Tutsi[17] warriors across a tropical landscape, while the thunderous tread of the machines downstairs jarred the floor beneath my easel, mocking my efforts. ∿

---

15. *Self-immolation* is the act of setting oneself on fire.

16. *Penance* (pen′ əns) is a punishment one undergoes, usually voluntarily, to show sorrow for having committed a sin or offense.
17. The *Tutsi* are a people in central Africa.

Make Inferences About Characters *What does the narrator mean when she says she lives within the shadow of her grandmother's death?*

Characterization *How does the author reveal that the narrator remains troubled by the conflict with her grandmother?*

After You Read

Respond and Think Critically

1. **Connect to Personal Experience** Do you think that either Da-duh or the narrator "won" their battle of wills? Explain.

2. **Explain Conflict** Describe the narrator's first impression of Da-duh. Why do you think the narrator tries to "win" in her initial encounter with Da-duh?

3. **Analyze Character** How does the narrator's attitude toward her grandmother change from the beginning to the end of the story? Explain your answer and support it with evidence from the story. ✎OER

4. **Make Inferences About Events** At what point in the story do Da-duh's appearance and behavior abruptly change? Describe this change. What do you think causes this change, and what does it signify?

5. **Draw Conclusions About Theme** Which of these aphorisms best describes one theme of this story: "Birds of a feather flock together" or "Opposites attract"? Explain.

6. **Big Idea** **Draw Conclusions About Character** How did the narrator choose to treat Da-duh? Is her decision understandable? Support your answer with text evidence.

Literary Element Characterization

Marshall uses both **direct characterization** and **indirect characterization** in her story.

7. **Describe Characterization** Give an example from the story of each characterization type.

8. **Draw Conclusions About Character** What can you conclude about the narrator's feelings toward Da-duh based on both direct and indirect characterizations? Provide evidence from the story to support your answer.

Reading Strategy Make Inferences About Characters

Review the blue highlighted questions in the story to help you answer these questions.

9. How are the narrator and Da-duh alike? How are they different?

10. List at least two important details that helped you form each opinion.

LOG ON ▶ **Literature** Online

Selection Resources For Selection Quizzes, eFlash-cards, and Reading-Writing Connection activities, go to glencoe.com and enter QuickPass code GL57805u1.

Vocabulary Practice

Practice with Synonyms A synonym is a word that has the same or nearly the same meaning as another word. With a partner, match each boldfaced vocabulary word below with its synonym. You will not use all the answer choices. Use a thesaurus or dictionary to check your answers.

1. formidable
2. decrepit
3. hurtle
4. arrogant
5. malicious

a. fearsome
b. evil
c. rampant
d. haughty
e. dilapidated
f. resonant
g. propel

Writing

Write a Story In this story, the narrator tells her grandmother about "refrigerators, radios, gas stoves, elevators," and other technology. Write a brief story about the narrator and Da-duh set in the present day and comprised mostly of dialogue. In it, the girl should explain, and Da-duh should comment on, computers, the Internet, and other technological breakthroughs.

Before You Read

The Censors

Meet **Luisa Valenzuela**
(born 1938)

As the political situation in her homeland grew increasingly violent, Luisa Valenzuela turned to writing to cope. One of the most recognized Latin American writers in the United States, Valenzuela writes novels and short stories that expose the injustices of society through satire and wit.

> "[Luisa Valenzuela] wears an opulent, baroque crown, but her feet are naked."
>
> —Carlos Fuentes

Luisa Valenzuela was born in Argentina to a well-respected physician and a writer. She began her career as a journalist working for magazines and newspapers in Buenos Aires. When she was just seventeen, Valenzuela wrote and published her first story. In 1966 her first novel, *Hay que sonreír* (translated as *Clara*), was published. During the 1970s, Argentina's economy deteriorated and the political situation in the country became very volatile. According to Valenzuela, the political atmosphere in Argentina pushed her to leave her home: "I decided to leave in order not to fall into self-censorship. Exile may be devastating, but perspective and separation sharpen the aim."

A Unique Style Known for her experimental style, Valenzuela blends the ordinary with the fantastical. Critics often note her ability to play with words and language. Many critics also classify her work as magical realism, a type of fiction that inserts fantastic events

into a believable, ordinary reality. However, Valenzuela seeks to push the boundaries of the genre. She says that "Magical realism was a beautiful resting place, but the thing is to go forward."

Politics and Society Valenzuela's most popular novel, *The Lizard's Tail*, details a sorcerer's rise, fall, and return to power. The book gives voice to the political upheaval and social change that took place in Argentina during the 1970s. Using dark humor, Valenzuela offers a powerful satire of government censorship and the difficult circumstances of war. Her stories identify the absurdities of society and expose the shameful operations of totalitarian regimes. As she says, "If the country is to heal, each and every shadow of the dark times has to come out into the open."

Achievements and Endeavors Valenzuela has published numerous novels and collections of short stories, and many of her works have been translated into other languages. Currently, she teaches creative writing in New York. She frequently returns home to Buenos Aires.

 Literature Online

Author Search For more about Luisa Valenzuela, go to glencoe.com and enter QuickPass code GL57805u1.

Literature and Reading Preview

Connect to the Story

How might your life change if you lost your freedom of speech? Discuss this question with a small group.

Build Background

"The Censors" was first published in 1976, the year that a military faction overthrew Argentina's government. The new government severely restricted constitutional liberties and systematically began to eliminate any opposition to their regime. Innocent citizens as well as dissidents were tortured and killed. Thirteen to fifteen thousand citizens were killed in the *Guerra Sucia*—the "Dirty War," as it came to be called.

Set Purposes for Reading

Big Idea Making Choices

As you read "The Censors," ask yourself, What choices does Juan make to "protect" himself and Mariana from the censors?

Literary Element Irony

Irony is a contrast between what is expected and what actually happens. In **situational irony,** the outcome of a situation is the opposite of a character's expectations. In **dramatic irony,** the reader knows information that the characters do not. As you read, ask yourself, How and why does Valenzuela use irony in this story?

Reading Strategy Analyze Cause-and-Effect Relationships

One event often impacts another event, but this impact may not be explicit. When you **analyze cause-and-effect relationships,** you analyze the effects of characters' ideas and actions on a story's overarching structure, or plot. As you read, ask yourself, How is each event influenced by the events that preceded it?

....

Tip: Chart Causes and Effects Using a graphic organizer like the one below, make inferences about the cause-and-effect relationships that drive the plot of this story.

TEKS

For pages 136–141

10.5 Understand, make inferences and draw conclusions about the structure and elements of fiction and provide evidence from text to support understanding.

Vocabulary

irreproachable (ir´ i prō´ chə bəl) *adj.* free from blame or criticism; faultless; p. 138 *The boy's kind behavior was irreproachable.*

albeit (ôl bē´ it) *conj.* although; even if; p. 139 *I like the fall, albeit I am always eager for spring.*

ulterior (ul tēr´ē ər) *adj.* intentionally withheld or concealed; p. 139 *Sam had an ulterior motive for not wanting to tell the truth.*

subversive (səb vur´ siv) *adj.* seeking to weaken, destroy, or overthrow; p. 140 *Subversive people wished to overthrow the government.*

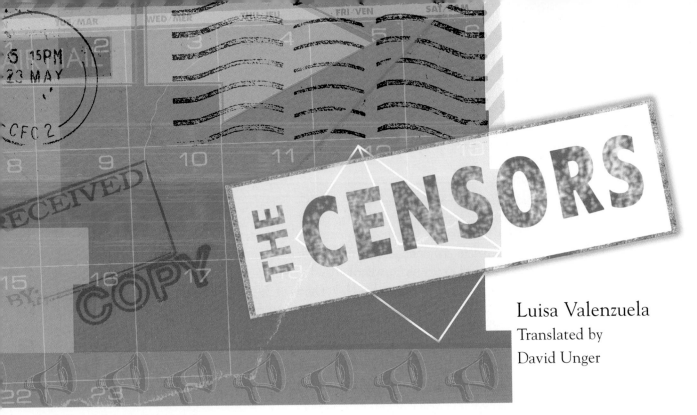

THE CENSORS

Luisa Valenzuela

Translated by
David Unger

Postal Montage. Natalie Racioppa.

Poor Juan! One day they caught him with his guard down before he could even realize that what he had taken as a stroke of luck was really one of fate's dirty tricks. These things happen the minute you're careless, as one often is. Juancito[1] let happiness—a feeling you can't trust—get the better of him when he received from a confidential source Mariana's new address in Paris and knew that she hadn't forgotten him. Without thinking twice, he sat down at his table and wrote her a letter. *The* letter that now keeps his mind off his job during the day and won't let him sleep at night (what had he scrawled, what had he put on that sheet of paper he sent to Mariana?).

Juan knows there won't be a problem with the letter's contents, that it's **irreproachable**, harmless. But what about the rest? He knows that they examine, sniff, feel, and read between the lines of each and every letter, and check its tiniest comma and most accidental stain. He knows that all letters pass from hand to hand and go through all sorts of tests in the huge censorship offices and that, in the end, very few continue on their way. Usually it takes months, even years, if there aren't any snags; all this time the freedom, maybe even the life, of both sender and receiver is in jeopardy. And that's why Juan's so troubled: thinking that something might happen to Mariana because of his letters. Of all people, Mariana, who must finally feel safe there where she always dreamt she'd live. But he knows that the *Censor's Secret Command*

---

1. *Juancito* (wan sē′ tō)

Businessmen Reading the Fine Print.
Bruno Budrovic.

View the Art How does this image complement the tone of the story?

operates all over the world and cashes in on the discount in air fares; there's nothing to stop them from going as far as that hidden Paris neighborhood, kidnapping Mariana, and returning to their cozy homes, certain of having fulfilled their noble mission.

Well, you've got to beat them to the punch, do what everyone tries to do: sabotage the machinery, throw sand in its gears, get to the bottom of the problem so as to stop it.

This was Juan's sound plan when he, like many others, applied for a censor's job—not because he had a calling or needed a job: no, he applied simply to intercept his own letter, a consoling **albeit** unoriginal idea. He was hired immediately, for each day more and more censors are

needed and no one would bother to check on his references.

Ulterior motives couldn't be overlooked by the *Censorship Division*, but they needn't be too strict with those who applied. They knew how hard it would be for the poor guys to find the letter they wanted and even if they did, what's a letter or two when the new censor would snap up so many others? That's how Juan managed to join the *Post Office's Censorship Division*, with a certain goal in mind.

The building had a festive air on the outside that contrasted with its inner staidness.[2] Little by little, Juan was absorbed by his job, and he felt at peace since he was doing everything he could to get his letter for Mariana. He didn't even worry when, in his first month, he was sent to *Section K*

Making Choices *What do you think the outcome of Juan's choice to become a censor might be?*

---

2. *Staidness* (stād´ nəs) is the state or quality of being serious, steady, or conservative in character.

LUISA VALENZUELA **139**

where envelopes are very carefully screened for explosives.

It's true that on the third day, a fellow worker had his right hand blown off by a letter, but the division chief claimed it was sheer negligence on the victim's part. Juan and the other employees were allowed to go back to their work, though feeling less secure. After work, one of them tried to organize a strike to demand higher wages for unhealthy work, but Juan didn't join in; after thinking it over, he reported the man to his superiors and thus got promoted.

You don't form a habit by doing something once, he told himself as he left his boss's office. And when he was transferred to *Section J*, where letters are carefully checked for poison dust, he felt he had climbed a rung in the ladder.

By working hard, he quickly reached *Section E* where the job became more interesting, for he could now read and analyze the letters' contents. Here he could even hope to get hold of his letter, which, judging by the time that had elapsed, had gone through the other sections and was probably floating around in this one.

Soon his work became so absorbing that his noble mission blurred in his mind. Day after day he crossed out whole paragraphs in red ink, pitilessly chucking many letters into the censored basket. These were horrible days when he was shocked by the subtle and conniving ways employed by people to pass on **subversive** messages; his instincts were so sharp that he found behind a simple "the weather's unsettled" or "prices continue to soar" the wavering hand of someone secretly scheming to overthrow the Government.

His zeal brought him swift promotion. We don't know if this made him happy. Very few letters reached him in *Section B*—only a handful passed the other hurdles—so he read them over and over again, passed them under a magnifying glass, searched for microprint with an electronic microscope, and tuned his sense of smell so that he was beat by the time he made it home. He'd barely manage to warm up his soup, eat some fruit, and fall into bed, satisfied with having done his duty. Only his darling mother worried, but she couldn't get him back on the right track. She'd say, though it wasn't always true: Lola called, she's at the bar with the girls, they miss you, they're waiting for you. Or else she'd leave a bottle of red wine on the table. But Juan wouldn't overdo it: any distraction could make him lose his edge and the perfect censor had to be alert, keen, attentive, and sharp to nab cheats. He had a truly patriotic task, both self-denying and uplifting.

His basket for censored letters became the best fed as well as the most cunning basket in the whole *Censorship Division*. He was about to congratulate himself for having finally discovered his true mission, when his letter to Mariana reached his hands. Naturally, he censored it without regret. And just as naturally, he couldn't stop them from executing him the following morning, another victim of his devotion to his work. ❧

Making Choices *What choice has Juan made by reporting his coworker? Do you think his opinion here is right? Explain.*

Vocabulary

subversive (səb vur′ siv) *adj.* seeking to weaken, destroy, or overthrow

---

Analyze Cause-and-Effect Relationships *What do the cause and effect in the first sentence in this column reveal about Juan's superiors?*

Irony *Explain the irony in the last paragraph.*

After You Read

Respond and Think Critically

1. **Connect to Personal Experience** Did your feelings about Juan change during the course of the story? Explain.

2. **Explain Events** Why are "more and more censors" needed, making it easy for Juan to get hired?

3. **Make Inferences About Setting** What does Juan fear will happen to Mariana as a result of his letter? What does this tell you about the kind of government Juan lives under?

4. **Examine Subject** What do you think is being criticized in this story? Explain your answer and support it with evidence from the text. **OER**

5. **Evaluate Plot** What parts of this story seem logical and believable to you? Are there any parts that are unbelievable? Use details from the story to support your answer.

6. **Big Idea** **Draw Conclusions About Plot** Do you think Juan's choices or the government's have a greater impact on the outcome of the story? Explain.

Literary Element Irony

Writers sometimes use irony to express an idea without having to spell it out for readers.

7. **Draw Conclusions About Character** What conclusion can you draw about Juan based on his decision to join the Censorship Division and on the ironic outcome of his decision? Provide evidence from the story to support your answer.

8. **Evaluate Irony** Look back at the pink high-lighted question on page 140. Do you think Valenzuela's use of irony is effective in this story? Explain.

Reading Strategy Analyze Cause-and-Effect Relationships

One cause may have multiple effects, and one effect may have multiple causes. Review the graphic organizer you made on page 137.

9. Do any events in the story have more than one cause? Explain.

10. Choose one cause-and-effect relationship from the story. How would changing the cause affect the story's structure? Provide evidence from the text to support your inference.

Vocabulary Practice

Practice with Usage Respond to these statements to help you explore the meanings of the boldfaced vocabulary words from the story.

1. Explain how a person with **irreproachable** manners behaves.
2. Describe a situation in which you might say that you are "happy, **albeit** exhausted."
3. Name a character from a book or movie known for having an **ulterior** motive.
4. Tell why some ideas are considered **subversive**.

Writing

Write an Essay Think about other twentieth-century authors you are familiar with who are from non–English speaking literary traditions. Choose one of those authors' works to compare with "The Censors." Write an essay exploring ways in which the two works are similar. Support your assertions with text evidence.

LOG ON **Literature** Online

Selection Resources For Selection Quizzes, eFlash-cards, and Reading-Writing Connection activities, go to glencoe.com and enter QuickPass code GL57805u1.

TEKS

For pages 142–146

10.8 Analyze the controlling idea and specific purpose of a passage and the textual elements that support and elaborate it, including both the most important details and the less important details.

Set a Purpose for Reading

As you read, ask yourself, What environmental concern does the writer raise and what choices does he advocate?

Preview the Article

1. From the title, how would you describe what the tone of the article might be?

2. Skim the article. What do you think it will be about?

Reading Strategy

Determine the Main Idea and Supporting Details

In order to determine the **main idea**, ask yourself, What is this article's controlling idea? What is its specific purpose? The main idea is not always obvious, so use the **supporting details** in the text to guide you. As you read, complete a graphic organizer like the one shown below to show the main idea and the less and more important supporting details.

Main Idea:

Supporting Detail 1: Fishing destroys over eighty million sea creatures each year.

Supporting Detail 2:

TIME

Cry of the Ancient Mariner

"Even in the middle of the deep blue sea, the albatross feels the hard hand of humanity"

By CARL SAFINA

AT THE LONELY CENTER OF THE NORTH PACIFIC Ocean, farther from just about everything than just about anywhere, lies Midway Atoll, a coral reef enclosed by a lagoon. I've come with Canadian writer and zoologist Nancy Baron to the world's largest Laysan albatross colony—400,000 exquisite masters of the air—a feathered nation gathered to breed, cramming an isle a mile by two.

Ravenous, goose-size chicks so jam the landscape that it resembles a poultry farm. Many have waited more than a week for a meal, while both parents forage the ocean's vast expanse. An adult glides in on 7-ft. wings. After flying perhaps 2,000 miles nonstop to return here, in 10 minutes she will be gone again, searching for more food. She surveys the scene through lovely dark pastel-shadowed eyes, then calls, "Eh-eh-eh." Every nearby chick answers, but she recognizes her own chick's voice and weaves toward it.

Aggressive with hunger, the whining chick bites its parent's bill to stimulate her into throwing up her payload. The adult hunches, vomiting, pumping out fish eggs and several squid. The chick swallows in seconds what its parent logged 4,000 miles to get. The chick begs for more. The adult arches her neck and vomits again. Nothing comes. We whisper, "What's wrong?"

Slowly comes the surreal sight of a green plastic toothbrush emerging from the bird's gullet. With her neck arched, the mother cannot fully pass the straight brush. She tries several times to disgorge it, but can't. Nancy and I can hardly bear this. The albatross reswallows and, with the brush stuck inside, wanders away.

Message from the Albatross

In the world in which albatrosses came from, the birds swallowed pieces of floating pumice, or lightweight, volcanic glass, for the fish eggs stuck to them. Albatrosses transferred this survival strategy to toothbrushes, bottle caps, nylon netting, toys, and other floating junk. Where chicks die, a pile of colorful plastic particles that used to be in their stomachs often marks their graves.

Through the intimate bond between parent and offspring flows the continuity of life itself. That our human trash stream crosses even this sacred bond is evidence of a wounded world, its relationships disfigured. The albatross's message: Consumer culture has reached every watery point on the compass. From sun-bleached coral reefs to icy polar waters, no place, no creature, remains apart.

Set the Record Straight

If albatrosses' eating plastic seems surprising, so do many of the oceans' problems. The facts often defy common perceptions. Examples:

• Most people think oil spills cause the most harm to ocean life. They don't. Fishing does. When a tanker wrecks, news crews flock to film gooey beaches and dying animals. Journalists rush right past the picturesque fishing boats whose huge nets and 1,000-hook longlines cause far more havoc on the marine world than spilled oil.

Fishing annually extracts more than 80 million tons of sea creatures worldwide. An additional 20 million tons of unwanted fish, seabirds, marine mammals, and turtles get thrown overboard, dead. Overfishing has seriously reduced major populations of cod, swordfish, tuna, snapper, grouper, and sharks. Instead of sensibly living off nature's interest, many fisheries have mined the wild capital, and famous fishing banks lie bankrupt, including the revered cod grounds of New England and Atlantic Canada.

Enforcing fishing limits—to give the most devastated fish populations a chance to rebuild—could ultimately enable us to catch at least 10 million more tons of sea life than we do now. Government-subsidized shipbuilders and fleets drive much of the overfishing. Ending those subsidies—as New Zealand has already done—would mean paying less to get more in the long run.

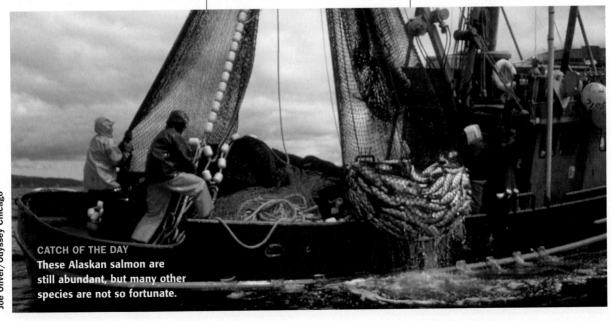

Joe Oliver/Odyssey Chicago

CATCH OF THE DAY
These Alaskan salmon are still abundant, but many other species are not so fortunate.

• Most ocean pollution doesn't come from ships. It comes from land. Gravity is the sea's enemy. Silt running off dirt roads and clear-cut forest land ruins coral reefs and U.S. salmon rivers. Pesticides and other poisons sprayed into the air and washed into rivers find the ocean. (Midway's albatrosses have in their tissues as much of the industrial chemicals called PCBs as do Great Lakes bald eagles.) The biggest sources of coastal pollution are waste from farm animals, fertilizers, and human sewage. They can spawn red tides and other harmful algae blooms that rob oxygen from the water, killing sea life. The Mississippi River, whose fine heartland silt once built fertile delta wetlands, now builds in the Gulf of Mexico a spreading dead zone—almost empty of marine life—the size of New Jersey. Improving sewage treatment and cleaning up the runoff from farms will be increasingly vital to preserving coastal water quality.

• Fish farming—aquaculture—doesn't take pressure off wild fish. Many farms use large numbers of cheap, wild-caught fish as feed to raise fewer shrimp and fish of more profitable varieties. And industrial-scale fish- and shrimp-aquaculture operations sometimes damage the

VIOLATING A SACRED BOND
Because of humankind's endless trash stream, the seabirds feed plastic to their young.

coastlines where the facilities are located. The farms can foul the water, destroy mangroves and marshes, drive local fishers out of business, and serve as breeding grounds for fish diseases. In places such as Bangladesh, Thailand, and India, which grow shrimp mainly for export to richer countries, diseases and pollution usually limit a farm's life to 10 years. The companies then move and start again.

To avoid becoming just another environmental headache, aquaculture needs standards. Raising fish species foreign to the local habitat should be discouraged, since escapees can drive out native fish or infect them with disease. Penning fish in open waterways is also problematic. Even when the impact on the environment is minimized— as it is with well-run Maine salmon farms—rows of large fish corrals in natural waterways can be eyesores. Fish farming is best done in indoor, onshore facilities. The

❝The Mississippi River . . . now builds in the Gulf of Mexico a spreading dead zone . . .❞

fish rarely escape, and the wastewater can be treated before being released. Growing vegetarian species such as tilapia is ideal, since they don't have to be fed wild fish.

• The biologically richest stretches of ocean are more disrupted than the richest places on land. Continents still have roadless wilderness areas where motorized vehicles have never gone. But on the world's continental shelves, it is hard to find places where boats dragging nets haven't etched tracks into sea-floor habitats. In Europe's North Sea and along New England's Georges Bank and Australia's Queensland coast, trawlers, boats used for catching fish in large nets, may scour the bottom four to eight times every year. And the U.S. National Marine Sanctuaries hardly deserve the name. Commercial and recreational fishing with lines, traps, or nets is allowed almost everywhere in these "sanctuaries."

New Zealand and the Philippines are among the countries that have set up reserves in which fish are actually left alone. Marine life tends to recover in these areas, then spread beyond them, providing cheap insurance against overfishing outside the reserves.

Though the oceans' problems can seem overwhelming, solutions are emerging and attitudes are changing. Most people have shed the fantasy that the sea can provide

WHAT YOU CAN DO

AVOID EATING SEAFOOD FROM ENDANGERED POPULATIONS

Like fish but don't want to help wipe out a species? The Monterey Bay Aquarium in California has published a menu of dos and don'ts. Some excerpts:

BEST CHOICES

Dungeness crab
Halibut (Alaska)
Mahi-mahi
Salmon (Alaska, wild caught)
Tilapia
Striped bass

BAD CHOICES

Atlantic cod
Orange roughy
Chilean sea bass
Shark
Shrimp
Swordfish

food forever, lessen endless pollution, and accept unlimited trash. In 1996, the U.S. passed the Sustainable Fisheries Act, which set up rules against overfishing—a recognition that protecting sea life is good business. Some fish, such as striped bass and redfish, are recovering because of catch limits. Alaskan,

Falkland, Australian, and New Zealand longline boats are taking care not to kill albatrosses. Turtles are being saved by trapdoors in shrimp nets so they can escape.

Joining Together to Help the Seas

The oceans' future depends most of all on international cooperation. Working through the U.N., the world's nations have outlawed giant drift nets. Other treaties to protect the seas and the fish in them are in the works, though not all nations are enthusiastic about signing them. Among top fishing nations, Japan relies heavily on seafood and yet is exceptionally disrespectful toward the ocean. It has disagreed with international limits on catches of southern bluefin tuna and used "scientific research" as a phony justification for hunting whales in the International Whaling Commission's Antarctic Sanctuary. A world leader in so many ways, Japan would greatly improve its moral position by helping to heal the seas.

A good place to start that healing would be to give albatrosses a future with more food and less plastic trash to swallow. A U.N. marine-pollution treaty makes dumping plastics illegal, but policing at sea is impractical. Nonetheless, ships could be required to carry up-to-date equipment for handling garbage and storing liquid waste that might otherwise be dumped into the water.

Routine discharges put more oil into the sea than major spills.

We should expand our idea of zoning from land to sea. Instead of an ocean free-for-all, we should mark some areas for fishing only with traps and hooks and lines, and others as wildlife sanctuaries. As we've seen with once rich cod grounds, if we don't declare some areas closed by foresight, they will declare themselves closed by collapse. The map of the land has many colors, while in most minds the sea is still the blank space between continents. Let's start coloring in that blue expanse and map a more sensible future for the sea.

Four centuries ago, poet John Donne wrote that no man is an island entire to himself. On Midway an albatross gagging on a toothbrush taught me that no island is an island. In the oceans, less is truly more: less trash, less habitat destruction, and catching fewer fish now will mean more food later on for both people and wildlife. The oceans make our planet habitable, and the wealth of oceans spans nutritional, climatological, biological, aesthetic, spiritual, emotional, and ethical areas. Like the albatross, we need the seas more than the seas need us. Will we understand this well enough to reap all the riches that a little restraint, cooperation, and compassion could bring?

— Updated 2005,
from TIME, Special Earth Day
Issue, Spring 2000

Carl Safina, founder of the National Audubon Society's Living Oceans Program, is the author of Song for the Blue Ocean.

Respond and Think Critically

1. **Summarize Main Ideas** Write a brief summary of the main ideas in this article before you answer the following questions. For help on writing a summary, see page 389.

2. **Connect to Personal Experience** How did you feel about the importance of preventing the destruction of marine life before and after you read the article?

3. **Analyze Details** What is one solution to the problem of overfishing that the writer provides? What details does he provide to support this solution? Explain.

4. **Analyze Evidence** On what, in the writer's opinion, does the ocean's future depend? How does the writer support his opinion on this concern?

5. **Analyze Controlling Idea** What is the main idea of this article? How does it relate to the writer's purpose? Identify details Safina uses to support and elaborate on his main idea.

6. **Evaluate Evidence** How can you tell which of the writer's claims are facts and which are opinions? How do you think this affects the validity of his claims?

7. **Draw Conclusions About the Writer** The writer is the founder of the National Audubon Society's Living Oceans Program. The National Audubon Society is a network of community-based centers as well as scientific and educational programs geared toward sustaining the life of birds and promoting conservation. How do you think the writer's background influenced his opinions and writing style?

8. **Evaluate Ideas** Review the choices that the writer presents for cleaning up the ocean. Which of these options do you think would be the easiest to implement and why?

PART 3

Life Transitions

All the Days of My Life No. 2, 1999. Evelyn Williams. Oil on canvas, 48.03 x 59.84 in. Private collection.

View the Art The figures in this painting appear to be sharing a moment in daily life. Describe the mood of this painting. What can you infer from the figures and their expressions and gestures?

BIG IDEA

Life transitions are universal, common in all cultures. Some cultures mark transitions with ceremony, while others simply observe a gradual shift in perspective and worldview. In the short stories in Part 3, you will encounter various rites of passage. As you read these stories, ask yourself, How do you, your family, and your friends mark transitions in your lives?

TEKS

For pages 148–149

10.5 Understand, make inferences and draw conclusions about the structure and elements of fiction and provide evidence from text to support understanding.

LITERARY FOCUS

Narrator and Voice

How are stories told?

Who will tell the story? This is an important question for anyone who is writing a short story. Choosing a narrator is a decision that shapes the style of a story. A narrator can speak from within the story, providing first-person narration, or from outside the story. Based on who is telling it, a story can be told in vastly different ways.

from *"Everyday Use"*

by Alice Walker

Sometimes Maggie reads to me. She stumbles along good-naturedly but can't see well. She knows she is not bright. Like good looks and money, quickness passed her by. She will marry John Thomas (who has mossy teeth in an earnest face) and then I'll be free to sit here and I guess just sing church songs to myself. Although I never was a good singer. Never could carry a tune. I was always better at a man's job. I used to love to milk till I was hooked in the side in '49. Cows are soothing and slow and don't bother you, unless you try to milk them the wrong way.

Cows, 1890. Vincent van Gogh. Oil on canvas. Musee des Beaux-Arts, Lille, France.

Point of View

A story with a **first-person point of view** is told by a character in the story, referred to as "I." The reader sees people and events through the eyes of one character, and the reader cannot know more than this character knows. For example, the reader cannot know what another character thinks. **Limited third-person point of view** is similar. The narrator is outside the story, but only reveals the thoughts of one character, referred to as "he" or "she." A **third-person omniscient point of view** differs greatly from the first two: The narrator is outside the story but knows everything about the characters and events.

Voice

Voice is the distinctive use of language that conveys the author's or narrator's personality to the reader. Sentence structure, word choice, and tone are elements that contribute to voice. Often, when reading multiple works by the same author, a reader can recognize the author's voice by his or her unique use of language.

A narrator has a voice too, because the author gives the narrator a particular way of speaking and using language, which contributes to the overall emotional quality of the story. The narrator's voice also contributes to the setting, plot, and theme.

> When at last he started on his quest, it was a beautiful morning in late spring. The grass was up, the leaves were out, nature was at its best. Two medicine men accompanied him.
>
> —Lame Deer, *from "The Vision Quest"*

Diction Good writers choose their words carefully. This choice of words is called **diction.** Authors use diction to give the reader a specific feeling or to convey a particular meaning. Consider the difference in diction between these two examples:

> Constance hates lap swimming.
> Constance loathes repetitive lap swimming.

Tone Diction also helps communicate the **tone** of a story, or the author's attitude toward his or her subject. An author's tone might be sympathetic, objective, serious, ironic, sad, bitter, or humorous.

For example, when we look at the title of Isabel Allende's story, "And of Clay Are We Created," we get a sense of the story's tone. If she had called her story "We Are Created of Clay," it would have a playful tone. Instead, the title she wrote immediately communicates the story's solemn tone through its long length and formal structure.

Style

Style is the different language choices an author makes. How sophisticated is the narrator's vocabulary? Does he or she speak in long, flowing sentences or short, choppy ones? Is the language formal or informal? It makes a difference whether the author writes about an *automobile* or a *car*. Like tone, style can tell a reader about the author's purpose in writing and his or her attitude toward the subject and audience.

> Luis heard a car drive up and someone honk their horn. His father emerged from inside a new red Mustang that had been totaled. He usually dismantled every small feature by hand before sending the vehicle into the *cementerio*, as he called the lot. Luis watched as the most beautiful girl he had ever seen climbed out of a vintage white Volkswagen Bug.
>
> —Judith Ortiz Cofer, *from "Catch the Moon"*

Quickwrite

Analyze Style Write a few sentences describing your classroom, or some other room, in your own style. Do not worry about trying to sound like a writer; write the way you talk. After you write your sentences, use the checklist below to analyze your style. Based on the language choices you made, what can you infer about your style? Think about your choices, then rewrite your description for a different purpose. Write as if you were trying to sell the room. Then analyze your style in the second description.

- ☐ Words: long or short?
- ☐ Sentences: long or short?
- ☐ Language: formal or informal?
- ☐ How would you describe the tone?
- ☐ How would you describe the voice?

Before You Read

Everyday Use

Meet **Alice Walker**
(born 1944)

If Alice Walker's brother had not accidentally shot her in the eye with a BB gun when she was eight, she might not have become a writer. After children at school made fun of her, she "retreated into solitude, and read stories and began to write poems." Her great love for the written word had begun.

Early Years Walker grew up in Eatonton, Georgia, a small town where her parents farmed. They were sharecroppers—people who rented other people's land to grow crops. Sharecroppers made just enough money to survive and viewed education as the means to a better life for their children. Walker received a scholarship to Spelman College in Atlanta, the nation's oldest college for African American women. At Spelman during some of the most important years of the Civil Rights Movement, Walker became a political activist.

> "We will be ourselves and free, or die in the attempt. Harriet Tubman was not our great-grandmother for nothing."
>
> —Alice Walker

A Child of the Civil Rights Movement Walker was ten years old when the Supreme Court ruled that "separate but equal" was unconstitutional in schools. Her parents in the rural South knew only the days of segregation and racism, but Walker came to know a different way of life. Walker saw people beaten and battered for protesting for their rights, yet she also experienced what it was like to live in a world that was not completely segregated. Walker knew that the changes she went through were difficult for the previous generation. She wrote, "In the Sixties many of us scared our parents profoundly when we showed up dressed in our 'African' . . . clothes. We shocked them. . . ." In "Everyday Use," Walker portrays the clash between generations that sometimes resulted from this rapid change.

An African American Woman's Voice Walker has published many volumes of fiction, nonfiction, and poetry. Her most famous book, *The Color Purple*, won the Pulitzer Prize and the American Book Award. Steven Spielberg's movie version garnered numerous Academy Award nominations.

One of Walker's greatest influences was Zora Neale Hurston, whom Walker praised for portraying African American people as "complete, complex, *undiminished* human beings." Walker's own work reflects a similar commitment to portraying the beauty and complexity of the African American experience.

 Literature Online

Author Search For more about Alice Walker, go to glencoe.com and enter QuickPass code GL57805u1.

Literature and Reading Preview

Connect to the Story

Why might adult family members disapprove of how other members of their family live? Write a journal entry about a time when you saw this happen in real life or in movies or television, and explain how the family members dealt with the situation.

Build Background

"Everyday Use" takes place in the rural South in the 1970s. At that time, there was often a great contrast between African Americans living in cities, especially in the North, and African Americans living in the rural South.

Set Purposes for Reading

Big Idea Life Transitions

As you read "Everyday Use," ask yourself, How does the story address change: who changes, who does not change, and why?

Literary Element Tone

Tone is the writer's attitude toward his or her subject. A writer can convey tone through a variety of literary techniques, such as word choice, punctuation, sentence structure, or figures of speech. "Everyday Use" is told from the **first-person point of view,** which means the reader only has insight into the narrator's thoughts and feelings. As you read the story, ask yourself, How does the author's tone convey the narrator's attitude toward her daughters?

Reading Strategy Question

When you **question,** you monitor your comprehension by asking yourself whether specific information in a literary work is important, as well as whether you understand what you have read. As you read, ask yourself, What do the details in this story say about Mama and her daughters?

Tip: Make a Chart Use a chart like the one below to ask questions and monitor your comprehension. Use the blue highlighted text and questions to help you get started.

My Question	What I Understand
Why will Maggie be nervous?	Maggie is embarassed by her scars

TEKS

For pages 150–161

RC-10.A Reflect on understanding to monitor comprehension (e.g., asking questions).

Vocabulary

sidle (sīd′ əl) *v.* to move sideways; p. 153 *The shy child quietly sidled up to me.*

furtive (fur′ tiv) *adj.* secret; shifty; sly; p. 154 *The guilty man wore a furtive smile while maintaining his innocence.*

oppress (ə pres′) *v.* to control or govern by the cruel or unjust use of force or authority; p. 156 *Some governments further oppress people living in poverty.*

doctrine (dok′ trin) *n.* particular principle or position that is taught or supported, as of a religion; p. 157 *They believe in the doctrine of original sin.*

Tip: Word Usage When speaking or writing, select words not only for their meaning but for the context in which you will place them. For example, you might use *sneaky* when talking with your friends about an action but *furtive* when writing an analysis of a character.

ALICE WALKER **151**

◆ EVERYDAY USE ◆

Fog over Rural Road in Great Smoky Mountains.
William Manning.

Alice Walker

I will wait for her in the yard that Maggie and I made so clean and wavy yesterday afternoon. A yard like this is more comfortable than most people know. It is not just a yard. It is like an extended living room. When the hard clay is swept clean as a floor and the fine sand around the edges lined with tiny, irregular grooves, anyone can come and sit and look up into the elm tree and wait for the breezes that never come inside the house.

Maggie will be nervous until after her sister goes: she will stand hopelessly in corners, homely and ashamed of the burn scars down her arms and legs, eying her sister with a mixture of envy and awe. She thinks her sister has held life always in the palm of one hand, that "no" is a word the world never learned to say to her.

You've no doubt seen those TV shows where the child who has "made it" is confronted, as a surprise, by her own mother and father, tottering in weakly from backstage. (A pleasant surprise, of course: What would they do if parent and child came on the show only to curse out and insult each other?) On TV mother and child embrace and smile into each other's faces. Sometimes the mother and father weep, the child wraps them in her arms

Question *What have you learned about Maggie so far?*

and leans across the table to tell how she would not have made it without their help. I have seen these programs.

Sometimes I dream a dream in which Dee and I are suddenly brought together on a TV program of this sort. Out of a dark and soft-seated limousine I am ushered into a bright room filled with many people. There I meet a smiling, gray, sporty man like Johnny Carson who shakes my hand and tells me what a fine girl I have. Then we are on the stage and Dee is embracing me with tears in her eyes. She pins on my dress a large orchid, even though she has told me once that she thinks orchids are tacky flowers.

Visual Vocabulary
Johnny Carson hosted *The Tonight Show,* the popular late-night TV talk show, from 1962 to 1992.

In real life I am a large, big-boned woman with rough, man-working hands. In the winter I wear flannel nightgowns to bed and overalls during the day. I can kill and clean a hog as mercilessly as a man. My fat keeps me hot in zero weather. I can work outside all day, breaking ice to get water for washing; I can eat pork liver cooked over the open fire minutes after it comes steaming from the hog. One winter I knocked a bull calf straight in the brain between the eyes with a sledge hammer and had the meat hung up to chill before nightfall. But of course all this does not show on television. I am the way my daughter would want me to be: a hundred pounds lighter, my skin like an uncooked barley pancake. My hair glistens in the hot bright lights. Johnny Carson has much to do to keep up with my quick and witty tongue.

But that is a mistake. I know even before I wake up. Who ever knew a Johnson with a quick tongue? Who can even imagine me looking a strange white man in the eye? It seems to me I have talked to them always with one foot raised in flight, with my head turned in whichever way is farthest from them. Dee, though. She would always look anyone in the eye. Hesitation was no part of her nature.

"How do I look, Mama?" Maggie says, showing just enough of her thin body enveloped in pink skirt and red blouse for me to know she's there, almost hidden by the door.

"Come out into the yard," I say.

Have you ever seen a lame animal, perhaps a dog run over by some careless person rich enough to own a car, **sidle** up to someone who is ignorant enough to be kind to him? That is the way my Maggie walks. She has been like this, chin on chest, eyes on ground, feet in shuffle, ever since the fire that burned the other house to the ground.

Dee is lighter than Maggie, with nicer hair and a fuller figure. She's a woman now, though sometimes I forget. How long ago was it that the other house burned? Ten, twelve years? Sometimes I can still hear the flames and feel Maggie's arms sticking to me, her hair smoking and her dress falling off her in little black papery flakes. Her eyes seemed stretched open, blazed open by the flames reflected in them. And Dee. I see her standing off under the sweet gum tree she used to dig gum out of; a look of concentration on her face as she watched the last dingy gray

Question *Why might the narrator have this dream?*

Tone *What tone does the author create through her choice of words in this paragraph? Explain.*

Vocabulary

sidle (sīd′ əl) *v.* to move sideways

board of the house fall in toward the red-hot brick chimney. Why don't you do a dance around the ashes? I'd wanted to ask her. She had hated the house that much.

I used to think she hated Maggie, too. But that was before we raised the money, the church and me, to send her to Augusta[1] to school. She used to read to us without pity; forcing words, lies, other folks' habits, whole lives upon us two, sitting trapped and ignorant underneath her voice. She washed us in a river of make-believe, burned us with a lot of knowledge we didn't necessarily need to know. Pressed us to her with the serious way she read, to shove us away at just the moment, like dimwits, we seemed about to understand.

Dee wanted nice things. A yellow organdy[2] dress to wear to her graduation from high school; black pumps to match a green suit she'd made from an old suit somebody gave me. She was determined to stare down any disaster in her efforts. Her eyelids would not flicker for minutes at a time. Often I fought off the temptation to shake her. At sixteen she had a style of her own: and knew what style was.

I never had an education myself. After second grade the school was closed down. Don't ask me why: in 1927 colored asked fewer questions than they do now. Sometimes Maggie reads to me. She stumbles along good-naturedly but can't see well. She knows she is not bright. Like good looks and money, quickness passed her by. She will marry John Thomas (who has mossy teeth in an earnest face) and then I'll be free to sit here and I guess just sing church songs to myself. Although I never was a good singer. Never could carry a tune. I was always better at a man's job. I used to love to milk till I was hooked in the side in '49. Cows are soothing and slow and don't bother you, unless you try to milk them the wrong way.

I have deliberately turned my back on the house. It is three rooms, just like the one that burned, except the roof is tin; they don't make shingle roofs any more. There are no real windows, just some holes cut in the sides, like the portholes in a ship, but not round and not square, with rawhide holding the shutters up on the outside. This house is in a pasture, too, like the other one. No doubt when Dee sees it she will want to tear it down. She wrote me once that no matter where we "choose" to live, she will manage to come see us. But she will never bring her friends. Maggie and I thought about this and Maggie asked me, "Mama, when did Dee ever *have* any friends?"

She had a few. **Furtive** boys in pink shirts hanging about on washday after school. Nervous girls who never laughed. Impressed with her they worshiped the well-turned phrase, the cute shape, the scalding humor that erupted like bubbles in lye. She read to them.

When she was courting Jimmy T she didn't have much time to pay to us, but turned all her faultfinding power

---

1. *Augusta* is a city in Georgia.
2. *Organdy* is a lightweight fabric, usually made of cotton.

Question *What questions do you have about the fire or about Dee's relationship to it?*

Life Transitions *How have things changed since Mama was young?*

Tone *Based on the tone here, what can you infer about the relationship between Mama and Dee?*

Vocabulary

furtive (fur' tiv) *adj.* secret; shifty; sly

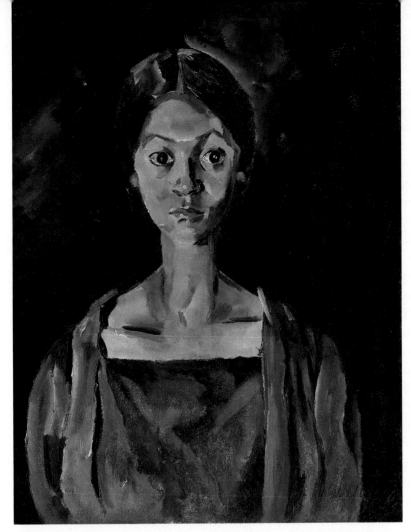

Girl in a Green Dress, 1930. William H. Johnson. Oil on canvas, 24¼ x 19 ½ in. National Museum of American Art, Washington, DC.

__View the Art__ William H. Johnson's art focuses on the African American experience. His earlier works—like this one—are influenced by the Expressionist style, a form that emphasizes intense emotions. Which of the two sisters in the story might be more like the girl in this portrait? Explain.

It is hard to see them clearly through the strong sun. But even the first glimpse of leg out of the car tells me it is Dee. Her feet were always neat-looking, as if God himself had shaped them with a certain style. From the other side of the car comes a short, stocky man. Hair is all over his head a foot long and hanging from his chin like a kinky mule tail. I hear Maggie suck in her breath. "Uhnnnh," is what it sounds like. Like when you see the wriggling end of a snake just in front of your foot on the road. "Uhnnnh."

Dee next. A dress down to the ground, in this hot weather. A dress so loud it hurts my eyes. There are yellows and oranges enough to throw back the light of the sun. I feel my whole face warming from the heat waves it throws out. Earrings gold, too, and hanging down to her shoulders. Bracelets dangling and making noises when she moves her arm up to shake the folds of the dress out of her armpits. The dress is loose and flows, and as she walks closer, I like it. I hear Maggie go "Uhnnnh" again. It is her sister's hair. It stands straight up like the wool on a sheep. It is black as night and around the edges are two long pigtails

on him. He *flew* to marry a cheap city girl from a family of ignorant flashy people. She hardly had time to recompose herself.

When she comes I will meet—but there they are!

Maggie attempts to make a dash for the house, in her shuffling way, but I stay her with my hand. "Come back here," I say. And she stops and tries to dig a well in the sand with her toe.

Life Transitions *Why do the man's hair and beard signify change to Mama?*

that rope about like small lizards disappearing behind her ears.

"Wa-su-zo-Tean-o!"[3] she says, coming on in that gliding way the dress makes her move. The short stocky fellow with the hair to his navel is all grinning and follows up with "Asalamalakim,[3] my mother and sister!" He moves to hug Maggie but she falls back, right up against the back of my chair. I feel her trembling there and when I look up I see the perspiration falling off her chin.

"Don't get up," says Dee. Since I am stout it takes something of a push. You can see me trying to move a second or two before I make it. She turns, showing white heels through her sandals, and goes back to the car. Out she peeks next with a Polaroid. She stoops down quickly and lines up picture after picture of me sitting there in front of the house with Maggie cowering behind me. She never takes a shot without making sure the house is included. When a cow comes nibbling around the edge of the yard she snaps it and me and Maggie *and* the house. Then she puts the Polaroid in the back seat of the car, and comes up and kisses me on the forehead.

Meanwhile Asalamalakim is going through motions with Maggie's hand. Maggie's hand is as limp as a fish, and probably as cold, despite the sweat, and she keeps trying to pull it back. It looks like Asalamalakim wants to shake hands but wants to do it fancy. Or maybe he don't know how people shake hands. Anyhow, he soon gives up on Maggie.

"Well," I say. "Dee."

"No, Mama," she says. "Not 'Dee,' Wangero Leewanika Kemanjo!"[4]

"What happened to 'Dee'?" I wanted to know.

"She's dead," Wangero said. "I couldn't bear it any longer, being named after the people who **oppress** me."

"You know as well as me you was named after your aunt Dicie," I said. Dicie is my sister. She named Dee. We called her "Big Dee" after Dee was born.

"But who was *she* named after?" asked Wangero.

"I guess after Grandma Dee," I said.

"And who was she named after?" asked Wangero.

"Her mother," I said, and saw Wangero was getting tired. "That's about as far back as I can trace it," I said. Though, in fact, I probably could have carried it back beyond the Civil War through the branches.

"Well," said Asalamalakim, "there you are."

"Uhnnnh," I heard Maggie say.

"There I was not," I said, "before 'Dicie' cropped up in our family, so why should I try to trace it that far back?"

He just stood there grinning, looking down on me like somebody inspecting a Model A car. Every once in a while he and Wangero sent eye signals over my head.

Visual Vocabulary
The *Model A* was manufactured by the Ford Motor Company from 1927 to 1931.

Tone *Based on Dee's statement, how do you think the tone of the story might change?*

Question *How do you think Asalamalakim's comment makes Mama feel?*

Vocabulary

oppress (ə pres′) *v.* to control or govern by the cruel or unjust use of force or authority

---

3. *Wa-su-zo-Tean-o!* (wä sōō′ zō tēn′o) and *Asalamalakim* (ä säl ä mä′ lä kēm) are greetings.
4. *Wangero Leewanika Kemanjo* (wän gär′ō lē wä′ nē kə ke män′jō)

Giving Thanks, 1942. Horace Pippin.
The Barnes Foundation, Merion Station, PA.

View the Art Horace Pippin uses a primitive style with bold colors and flat forms to depict the everyday lives of African Americans, their history, and their struggle for equality. What elements from the story are reflected in this image?

"How do you pronounce this name?" I asked.

"You don't have to call me by it if you don't want to," said Wangero.

"Why shouldn't I?" I asked. "If that's what you want us to call you, we'll call you."

"I know it might sound awkward at first," said Wangero.

"I'll get used to it," I said. "Ream it out again."

Well, soon we got the name out of the way. Asalamalakim had a name twice as long and three times as hard. After I tripped over it two or three times he told me to just call him Hakim-a-barber.[5] I wanted to ask him was he a barber, but I didn't really think he was, so I didn't ask.

"You must belong to those beef cattle peoples down the road," I said. They said "Asalamalakim" when they met you, too, but they didn't shake hands. Always too

busy: feeding the cattle, fixing the fences, putting up salt-lick shelters, throwing down hay. When the white folks poisoned some of the herd the men stayed up all night with rifles in their hands. I walked a mile and a half just to see the sight.

Hakim-a-barber said, "I accept some of their **doctrines,** but farming and raising cattle is not my style." (They didn't tell me, and I didn't ask, whether Wangero (Dee) had really gone and married him.)

We sat down to eat and right away he said he didn't eat collards and pork was unclean. Wangero, though, went on through the chitlins and corn bread, the greens and everything else. She talked a blue streak over the sweet potatoes. Everything delighted her. Even the fact

---

Tone *Why do you think the writer uses a wry, humorous tone here? Explain.*

---

5. *Hakim-a-barber* (hä kēm' ä bär' bər)

Question *Do you think Mama knew all along that Asalamalakim was a greeting, not a name? Explain.*

Vocabulary

doctrine (dok' trin) n. a particular principle or position that is taught or supported, as of a religion

ALICE WALKER **157**

that we still used the benches her daddy made for the table when we couldn't afford to buy chairs.

"Oh, Mama!" she cried. Then turned to Hakim-a-barber. "I never knew how lovely these benches are. You can feel the rump prints," she said, running her hands underneath her and along the bench. Then she gave a sigh and her hand closed over Grandma Dee's butter dish. "That's it!" she said. "I knew there was something I wanted to ask you if I could have." She jumped up from the table and went over in the corner where the churn stood, the milk in it clabber[6] by now. She looked at the churn and looked at it.

Visual Vocabulary
A *dasher* is part of a churn, an old-fashioned device for making butter.

"This churn top is what I need," she said. "Didn't Uncle Buddy whittle it out of a tree you all used to have?"

"Yes," I said.

"Uh huh," she said happily. "And I want the dasher, too."

"Uncle Buddy whittle that, too?" asked the barber.

Dee (Wangero) looked up at me.

"Aunt Dee's first husband whittled the dash," said Maggie so low you almost couldn't hear her. "His name was Henry, but they called him Stash."

"Maggie's brain is like an elephant's," Wangero said, laughing. "I can use the churn top as a centerpiece for the alcove[7] table," she said, sliding a plate over the churn, "and I'll think of something artistic to do with the dasher."

When she finished wrapping the dasher the handle stuck out. I took it for a moment in my hands. You didn't even have to look close to see where hands pushing the dasher up and down to make butter had left a kind of sink in the wood. In fact, there were a lot of small sinks; you could see where thumbs and fingers had sunk into the wood. It was beautiful light yellow wood, from a tree that grew in the yard where Big Dee and Stash had lived.

After dinner Dee (Wangero) went to the trunk at the foot of my bed and started rifling through it. Maggie hung back in the kitchen over the dishpan. Out came Wangero with two quilts. They had been pieced by Grandma Dee and then Big Dee and me had hung them on the quilt frames on the front porch and quilted them. One was in the Lone Star pattern. The other was Walk Around the Mountain. In both of them were scraps of dresses Grandma Dee had worn fifty and more years ago. Bits and pieces of Grandpa Jarrell's Paisley shirts. And one teeny faded blue piece, about the size of a penny matchbox, that was from Great Grandpa Ezra's uniform that he wore in the Civil War.

"Mama," Wangero said sweet as a bird. "Can I have these old quilts?"

I heard something fall in the kitchen, and a minute later the kitchen door slammed.

---

6. *Clabber* is the thick, clotted part of sour milk.

Life Transitions *Why is Dee so interested in these every-day objects?*

Tone *What does the tone here reveal about the narrator's attitude toward Hakim-a-barber?*

---

7. An *alcove* (al´ kōv) is a small room or recessed opening off of a larger room.

Question *Who might have slammed the kitchen door? Why?*

Quilts on the Line, 1994. Anna Belle Lee Washington. Oil on canvas, 20 x 30 in. National Museum of American Art, Washington, DC.

View the Art A former social worker, Anna Belle Lee Washington paints images that focus on connections between people. Quilts are a prominent feature in many of her paintings. Compare and contrast the family and the setting of this painting with those in the story. What are the most striking similarities and differences?

"Why don't you take one or two of the others?" I asked. "These old things was just done by me and Big Dee from some tops your grandma pieced before she died."

"No," said Wangero. "I don't want those. They are stitched around the borders by machine."

"That'll make them last better," I said.

"That's not the point," said Wangero. "These are all pieces of dresses Grandma used to wear. She did all this stitching by hand. Imagine!" She held the quilts securely in her arms, stroking them.

"Some of the pieces, like those lavender ones, come from old clothes her mother handed down to her," I said, moving up to touch the quilts. Dee (Wangero) moved back just enough so that I couldn't reach the quilts. They already belonged to her.

"Imagine!" she breathed again, clutching them closely to her bosom.

"The truth is," I said, "I promised to give them quilts to Maggie, for when she marries John Thomas."

She gasped like a bee had stung her.

"Maggie can't appreciate these quilts!" she said. "She'd probably be backward enough to put them to everyday use."

Tone *Has the tone changed from the beginning of the story? Explain.*

Life Transitions *How does this passage suggest a fundamental difference in values between Dee, Mama, and Maggie?*

"I reckon she would," I said. "God knows I been saving 'em for long enough with nobody using 'em. I hope she will!" I didn't want to bring up how I had offered Dee (Wangero) a quilt when she went away to college. Then she had told me they were old-fashioned, out of style.

"But they're *priceless!*" she was saying now, furiously; for she has a temper. "Maggie would put them on the bed and in five years they'd be in rags. Less than that!"

"She can always make some more," I said. "Maggie knows how to quilt."

Dee (Wangero) looked at me with hatred. "You just will not understand. The point is these quilts, *these* quilts!"

"Well," I said, stumped. "What would *you* do with them?"

"Hang them," she said. As if that was the only thing you *could* do with quilts.

Maggie by now was standing in the door. I could almost hear the sound her feet made as they scraped over each other.

"She can have them, Mama," she said, like somebody used to never winning anything, or having anything reserved for her. "I can 'member Grandma Dee without the quilts."

I looked at her hard. She had filled her bottom lip with checkerberry snuff[8] and it gave her face a kind of dopey, hangdog look. It was Grandma Dee and Big Dee who taught her how to quilt herself. She stood there with her scarred hands hidden in the folds of her skirt. She looked at her sister with something like fear but she wasn't

mad at her. This was Maggie's portion. This was the way she knew God to work.

When I looked at her like that something hit me in the top of my head and ran down to the soles of my feet. Just like when I'm in church and the spirit of God touches me and I get happy and shout. I did something I never had done before: hugged Maggie to me, then dragged her on into the room, snatched the quilts out of Miss Wangero's hands and dumped them into Maggie's lap. Maggie just sat there on my bed with her mouth open.

"Take one or two of the others," I said to Dee.

But she turned without a word and went out to Hakim-a-barber.

"You just don't understand," she said, as Maggie and I came out to the car.

"What don't I understand?" I wanted to know.

"Your heritage," she said. And then she turned to Maggie, kissed her, and said, "You ought to try to make something of yourself, too, Maggie. It's really a new day for us. But from the way you and Mama still live you'd never know it."

She put on some sunglasses that hid everything above the tip of her nose and her chin.

Maggie smiled; maybe at the sunglasses. But a real smile, not scared. After we watched the car dust settle I asked Maggie to bring me a dip of snuff. And then the two of us sat there just enjoying, until it was time to go in the house and go to bed. ∾

---

8. *Snuff* (snəf) is finely ground tobacco that can be sniffed, snorted, placed against the gums or chewed. *Checkerberry* (che kər ber ē) is the fruit of the wintergreen plant.

Question *Why does Dee want the quilts now, when she did not want to take one to college?*

Tone *How does the tone convey how Mama feels about the way Dee's visit ended? How does the author create that tone?*

After You Read

Respond and Think Critically

1. **Connect to Personal Experience** To whom would you have given the quilts? Explain.

2. **Make Inferences About Attitudes** How does Mama describe each daughter before Dee's arrival? How do you think Mama feels about her daughters based on her descriptions?

3. **Make Inferences About Motivation** Why do you think Mama decided that Maggie, and not Dee, should get the quilts? Support your answer with evidence from the text. 🔲OER

4. **Analyze Setting** How do you think the story would be different if the characters lived in another time and place? Why do you think the writer chose the setting she did?

5. **Evaluate Character** Do you think the character of Hakim-a-barber makes the story richer and more interesting? Why or why not? Support your answer with text evidence.

6. **Big Idea Draw Conclusions About Character** Why is Mama unhappy with how Dee has changed since leaving home? What is your opinion of the changes that Dee has undergone? Support your response with evidence from the story.

Literary Element | Tone

The tone in "Everyday Use" conveys a great deal about the various dynamics in Mama's family.

7. **Draw Conclusions About Tone** What tone does the author establish as Mama begins narrating the story? How does the tone change as events unfold? Support your answer with evidence from the text.

8. **Evaluate Tone** What literary devices does the author use to create the tone? Are they effective? Reread the pink highlighted passages and questions to help you.

Reading Strategy | Question

Review the chart you made on page 151.

9. What are Walker's ideas about change and the clash between old and new ways?

10. Do you think Walker's goal was to write a story with clear-cut answers? Explain.

LOG ON ▶ **Literature** Online

Selection Resources For Selection Quizzes, eFlashcards, and Reading-Writing Connection activities, go to glencoe.com and enter QuickPass code GL57805u1.

Vocabulary Practice

Practice with Usage Respond to these statements to help you explore the meanings of the boldfaced vocabulary words from the story.

1. Describe what people do when they **sidle**.

2. Describe how a **furtive** person might act.

3. Name two ways in which a government might **oppress** its citizens.

4. Identify a **doctrine** in which you believe.

⚡ Writing

Write a Character Sketch Write a description of Maggie's personality, using details from the story to support the points you make. Keep in mind that you need not accept Mama's interpretations of Maggie's actions.

Comparing Literature

Across Genres

TEKS

For pages 162–181

10.5.C Evaluate the connection between forms of narration (e.g., omniscient) and tone in works of fiction.

Compare Literature About Life's Lessons

How do writers and storytellers pass along lessons they have learned about life? The three literary works compared here—a short story, a legend, and a letter—each share wisdom.

COMPARE THE **Big Idea** Life Transitions

Young people setting off on their own, even for a short time, face challenges. The three literary works you are about to read treat the idea of life transitions in different ways. As you read, ask yourself, How do the young people in these works find strength in their families, their cultures, and their own inner resources?

COMPARE Narrators

The perspective from which a literary work is told is called the **point of view.** Letters and personal essays are always told in the first-person point of view because the narrator is the writer. In fiction, the narrator can be inside or outside the story. A **first-person narrator** is a character who has access only to his or her own thoughts and feelings. A **third-person narrator** speaks to the reader from outside the story. As you read, ask yourself, How is the point of view of each literary work suited to the author's purpose?

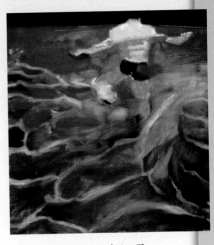

Figure In Water. Kari Van Tine.

COMPARE Author's Culture

The writers featured here address rites of passage within their cultures—rituals associated with a change in status for an individual. The rite of passage takes different forms in each of these literary works: Lessing's story involves an individual, internal conflict; Lame Deer's legend involves the relationship between an individual and his community; and Fitzgerald's letter involves fatherly advice to his daughter. As you read, ask yourself, What do these rites of passage have in common, and how are they different?

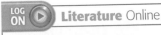

LOG ON ▶ **Literature** Online

Author Search For more about the authors, go to glencoe.com and enter QuickPass code GL57805u1.

Before You Read

Through the Tunnel

Meet **Doris Lessing**
(born 1919)

Doris Lessing's life has been marked by numerous fresh starts, beginning in childhood. At the age of four, Lessing traveled with her parents on a transcontinental journey by train, leaving their home in Persia (now Iran) and traversing Russia, Europe, and England. From there, her family began their quest for a new life in Southern Rhodesia (now Zimbabwe).

Adjusting to Africa Lessing's world as an energetic child was the African bush. She reveled in the land's wildlife, spaciousness, and smells. As was customary at the time for expatriates, Lessing was sent to boarding schools—first a convent and then to a British girls' school. There, the young teenager developed pinkeye. Even after she had fully recovered, Lessing insisted that her eyesight was ruined: her mother came and got her, and "that was the end of [her] life at school." Educating herself at home, Lessing developed her writing skills. Her first novel, *The Grass Is Singing,* was published in 1950. Her early work draws heavily on her years in Africa.

Unaffected by Criticism Lessing's books have received mixed reviews. Critics have characterized her style as being "blunt," having "analytical purity," and possessing "frankness and clarity." The range of literary forms Lessing has tackled is impressive: short stories, fiction, nonfiction, "space fiction," essays, and plays. In 1962 Lessing published the controversial feminist novel *The Golden Notebook.* It quickly became a best seller. Her nonfiction books include *The Wind Blows away Our Words,* concerning the wars in Afghanistan during the 1980s, and *African Laughter: Four Visits to Zimbabwe,* an account of the new nation. Lessing was awarded the Nobel Prize in Literature in 2007.

> *"That is what learning is. You suddenly understand something you've understood all your life, but in a new way."*
>
> —Doris Lessing

Critic William Peden summed up Lessing's strengths: "She tells a story which can be read with delight and wonder . . . a meaningful commentary on one or another phase of the endlessly varied human experience."

LOG ON ▶ **Literature** Online

Author Search For more about Doris Lessing, go to glencoe.com and enter QuickPass code GL57805u1.

Literature and Reading Preview

Connect to the Story

Why do you think people challenge themselves to accomplish dangerous goals? Discuss this question with a partner.

Build Background

This story takes place on the Mediterranean coast during the 1940s or 1950s. Here, boys dove off rocks and practiced breath-hold diving. This type of diving uses no equipment other than goggles or a facemask.

Set Purposes for Reading

Big Idea Life Transitions

As you read, ask yourself, What is Jerry's personal challenge and why is this transition so important to him at this time in his life?

Literary Element Point of View

A story's **point of view** is the perspective from which it is told. In the **third-person omniscient point of view,** the narrator is not a character in the story, but someone who comments on the action from outside the story and knows everything about all the characters. A story's point of view can influence the narrator's attitude. As you read, ask yourself, What does the point of view in this story reveal about the characters and events?

Reading Strategy Visualize

When you **visualize,** you form a mental image of events and places in a story through the descriptive words that the writer uses to appeal to the reader's senses of sight, sound, touch, taste, and smell. As you read, ask yourself, How is visualizing a scene an effective way to remember and understand what I read?

Tip: Create Sensory Images Use a chart like the one below to record Jerry's description of his tunnel experience and the corresponding senses. In the far right column, take notes on how the sensory images help you understand the story. Refer to the blue highlighted question on page 172 to help you.

Descriptive Phrases	Sense	Helps Me Understand
"fanged and angry boulders"	sight	the situation is dangerous

Vocabulary

conscientiously (kon′shē en′ shəs lē) *adv.* thoughtfully and carefully; p. 165 *Slowly and conscientiously,* the jury examined the evidence.

contrition (kən trish′ən) *n.* sorrow for one's sin or wrongdoing; repentance; p. 165 *A thief who shows contrition is on his way to being reformed.*

supplication (sup′lə kā′shən) *n.* an earnest and humble request; p. 167 *After numerous supplications,* the downtrodden man was finally given a job.

beseeching (bi sēch′ing) *adj.* begging; asking earnestly; p. 170 *The homeless woman raised beseeching hands to all who passed by.*

incredulous (in krej′ə ləs) *adj.* unwilling or unable to believe; p. 172 *We were incredulous at the child's story of the candy-stealing ghost.*

Tip: Antonyms You can find Internet sites that list antonyms by entering *antonyms* and other search terms such as *reference* and *thesaurus* into a search field.

Through the Tunnel

Doris Lessing

Beach. Bobbi Tull.

$\mathcal{G}$oing to the shore on the first morning of the vacation, the young English boy stopped at a turning of the path and looked down at a wild and rocky bay, and then over to the crowded beach he knew so well from other years. His mother walked on in front of him, carrying a bright striped bag in one hand. Her other arm, swinging loose, was very white in the sun. The boy watched that white, naked arm, and turned his eyes, which had a frown behind them, toward the bay and back again to his mother. When she felt he was not with her, she swung around. "Oh, there you are, Jerry!" she said. She looked impatient, then smiled. "Why, darling, would you rather not come with me? Would you rather—"

She frowned, **conscientiously** worrying over what amusements he might secretly be longing for, which she had been too busy or too careless to imagine. He was very familiar with that anxious, apologetic smile. **Contrition** sent him running after her. And yet, as he ran, he looked back over his shoulder at the wild bay; and all

---

Point of View *By expressing Jerry's and his mother's perspectives, how does the narrator help you understand the mother's character?*

Vocabulary

conscientiously (kon′ shē en′shəs lē) *adv.* thoughtfully and carefully

contrition (kən trish′ən) *n.* sorrow for one's sin or wrongdoing; repentance

DORIS LESSING   **165**

morning, as he played on the safe beach, he was thinking of it.

Next morning, when it was time for the routine of swimming and sunbathing, his mother said, "Are you tired of the usual beach, Jerry? Would you like to go somewhere else?"

"Oh, no!" he said quickly, smiling at her out of that unfailing impulse of contrition—a sort of chivalry.[1] Yet, walking down the path with her, he blurted out, "I'd like to go and have a look at those rocks down there."

She gave the idea her attention. It was a wild looking place, and there was no one there; but she said, "Of course, Jerry. When you've had enough, come to the big beach. Or just go straight back to the villa,[2] if you like." She walked away, that bare arm, now slightly reddened from yesterday's sun, swinging. And he almost ran after her again, feeling it unbearable that she should go by herself, but he did not.

She was thinking, Of course he's old enough to be safe without me. Have I been keeping him too close? He mustn't feel he ought to be with me. I must be careful.

He was an only child, eleven years old. She was a widow. She was determined to be neither possessive nor lacking in devotion. She went worrying off to her beach.

As for Jerry, once he saw that his mother had gained her beach, he began the steep descent to the bay. From where he was, high up among red-brown rocks, it was a scoop of moving bluish green fringed with white. As he went lower, he saw that it spread among small :promontories: and inlets of rough, sharp rock, and the crisping, lapping surface showed stains of

Visual Vocabulary
Promontories are high points of land or rock overlooking water.

purple and darker blue. Finally, as he ran sliding and scraping down the last few yards, he saw an edge of white surf and the shallow, luminous movement of water over white sand, and, beyond that, a solid, heavy blue.

He ran straight into the water and began swimming. He was a good swimmer. He went out fast over the gleaming sand, over a middle region where rocks lay like discolored monsters under the surface, and then he was in the real sea—a warm sea where irregular cold currents from the deep water shocked his limbs.

When he was so far out that he could look back not only on the little bay but past the promontory that was between it and the big beach, he floated on the buoyant surface and looked for his mother. There she was, a speck of yellow under an umbrella that looked like a slice of orange peel. He swam back to shore, relieved at being sure she was there, but all at once very lonely.

On the edge of a small cape that marked the side of the bay away from the promontory was a loose scatter of rocks. Above them, some boys were stripping off their clothes. They came running, naked, down to the rocks. The English boy swam

---

1. Here, *chivalry* (shiv′ əl rē) means "an act of courtesy or politeness."
2. *Villa,* an Italian word, means "house," usually one in the country or at the seashore.

Visualize *What mental picture does the word "wild" in the third paragraph provoke? How does it contrast with the beach where the characters swim and sunbathe?*

Point of View *The omniscient narrator reveals the mother's concerns in this column. What internal conflict might she be experiencing?*

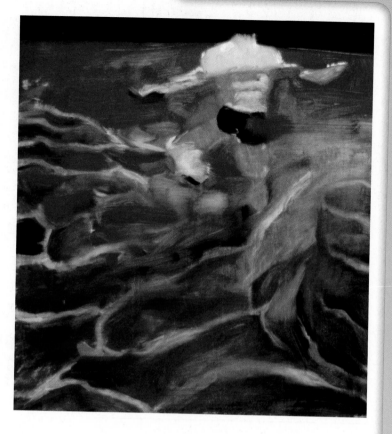

Figure In Water. Kari Van Tine.

<u>View the Art</u> The dark atmosphere of this painting contrasts with the sunny days when Jerry attempts his feat. How might this dark mood relate to Jerry's obsessive and potentially self-destructive desire to mimic the older boys?

toward them, but kept his distance at a stone's throw. They were of that coast; all of them were burned smooth dark brown and speaking a language he did not understand. To be with them, of them, was a craving that filled his whole body. He swam a little closer; they turned and watched him with narrowed, alert dark eyes. Then one smiled and waved. It was enough. In a minute, he had swum in and was on the rocks beside them, smiling with a desperate, nervous **supplication**. They shouted cheerful greetings at him; and then, as he preserved his nervous, uncomprehending smile, they understood that he was a foreigner strayed from his own beach, and they proceeded to

forget him. But he was happy. He was with them.

They began diving again and again from a high point into a well of blue sea between rough, pointed rocks. After they had dived and come up, they swam around, hauled themselves up, and waited their turn to dive again. They were big boys—men, to Jerry. He dived, and they watched him; and when he swam around to take his place, they made way for him. He felt he was accepted, and he dived again, carefully, proud of himself.

Soon the biggest of the boys poised himself, shot down into the water, and did not come up. The others stood about, watching. Jerry, after waiting for the sleek brown head to appear, let out a yell of warning;

Vocabulary

supplication (sup′lə kā′shən) *n.* an earnest and humble request

Life Transitions *Why might Jerry value the boys' acceptance so much?*

School of Fish, 1991. John Bunker. Mixed media.

they looked at him idly and turned their eyes back toward the water. After a long time, the boy came up on the other side of a big dark rock, letting the air out of his lungs in a sputtering gasp and a shout of triumph. Immediately the rest of them dived in. One moment, the morning seemed full of chattering boys; the next, the air and the surface of the water were empty. But through the heavy blue, dark shapes could be seen moving and groping.

Jerry dived, shot past the school of underwater swimmers, saw a black wall of rock looming at him, touched it, and bobbed up at once to the surface, where the wall was a low barrier he could see across. There was no one visible; under him, in the water, the dim shapes of the swimmers had disappeared. Then one, and then another of the boys came up on the far side of the barrier of rock, and he understood that they had swum through

some gap or hole in it. He plunged down again. He could see nothing through the stinging salt water but the blank rock. When he came up the boys were all on the diving rock, preparing to attempt the feat again. And now, in a panic of failure, he yelled up, in English, "Look at me! Look!" and he began splashing and kicking in the water like a foolish dog.

They looked down gravely, frowning. He knew the frown. At moments of failure, when he clowned to claim his mother's attention, it was with just this grave, embarrassed inspection that she rewarded him. Through his hot shame, feeling the pleading grin on his face like a scar that he could never remove, he looked up at the group of big brown boys on the rock and

Point of View *The narrator explains Jerry's response to failure with a simile at the end of this column. What does this figure of speech imply about Jerry?*

shouted, *"Bonjour! Merci! Au revoir! Monsieur, monsieur!"*[3] while he hooked his fingers round his ears and waggled them.

Water surged into his mouth; he choked, sank, came up. The rock, lately weighted with boys, seemed to rear up out of the water as their weight was removed. They were flying down past him, now, into the water; the air was full of falling bodies. Then the rock was empty in the hot sunlight. He counted one, two, three. . . .

At fifty, he was terrified. They must all be drowning beneath him, in the watery caves of the rock! At a hundred, he stared around him at the empty hillside, wondering if he should yell for help. He counted faster, faster, to hurry them up, to bring them to the surface quickly, to drown them quickly—anything rather than the terror of counting on and on into the blue emptiness of the morning. And then, at a hundred and sixty, the water beyond the rock was full of boys blowing like brown whales. They swam back to the shore without a look at him.

He climbed back to the diving rock and sat down, feeling the hot roughness of it under his thighs. The boys were gathering up their bits of clothing and running off along the shore to another promontory. They were leaving to get away from him. He cried openly, fists in his eyes. There was no one to see him, and he cried himself out.

It seemed to him that a long time had passed, and he swam out to where he could see his mother. Yes, she was still

---

3. *"Bonjour! . . . monsieur!"* These words are French for "Hello! Thanks! Good-bye! Sir, sir!"

Visualize *What mental image do you have as you read "boys blowing like brown whales"?*

there, a yellow spot under an orange umbrella. He swam back to the big rock, climbed up, and dived into the blue pool among the fanged and angry boulders. Down he went, until he touched the wall of rock again. But the salt was so painful in his eyes that he could not see.

He came to the surface, swam to shore, and went back to the villa to wait for his mother. Soon she walked slowly up the path, swinging her striped bag, the flushed, naked arm dangling beside her. "I want some swimming goggles," he panted, defiant and **beseeching**.

She gave him a patient, inquisitive look as she said casually, "Well, of course, darling."

But now, now, now! He must have them this minute, and no other time. He nagged and pestered until she went with him to a shop. As soon as she had bought the goggles, he grabbed them from her hand as if she were going to claim them for herself, and was off, running down the steep path to the bay.

Jerry swam out to the big barrier rock, adjusted the goggles, and dived. The impact of the water broke the rubber-enclosed vacuum, and the goggles came loose. He understood that he must swim down to the base of the rock from the surface of the water. He fixed the goggles tight and firm, filled his lungs, and floated, face down, on the water. Now, he could see. It was as if he had eyes of a different kind—fish eyes that showed

everything clear and delicate and wavering in the bright water.

Under him, six or seven feet down, was a floor of perfectly clean, shining white sand, rippled firm and hard by the tides. Two grayish shapes steered there, like long, rounded pieces of wood or slate. They were fish. He saw them nose toward each other, poise motionless, make a dart forward, swerve off, and come around again. It was like a water dance. A few inches above them the water sparkled as if sequins were dropping through it. Fish again—myriads of minute fish, the length of his fingernail, were drifting through the water, and in a moment he could feel the innumerable tiny touches of them against his limbs. It was like swimming in flaked silver. The great rock the big boys had swum through rose sheer out of the white sand—black, tufted lightly with greenish weed. He could see no gap in it. He swam down to its base.

Again and again he rose, took a big chestful of air, and went down. Again and again he groped over the surface of the rock, feeling it, almost hugging it in the desperate need to find the entrance. And then, once, while he was clinging to the black wall, his knees came up, and he shot his feet out forward and they met no obstacle. He had found the hole.

He gained the surface, clambered about the stones that littered the barrier rock until he found a big one, and, with this in his arms, let himself down over the side of the rock. He dropped, with the weight, straight to the sandy floor.

Clinging tight to the anchor of stone, he lay on his side and looked in under the dark shelf at the place where his feet had gone. He could see the hole. It was an irregular, dark gap; but he could not see deep into it. He let go of his anchor, clung

---

Visualize *What mental image does "fanged and angry boulders" help you create?*

Vocabulary

beseeching (bi sēch′ ing) *adj.* begging; asking earnestly with his hands to the edges of the hole, and tried to push himself in.

He got his head in, found his shoulders jammed, moved them in sidewise, and was inside as far as his waist. He could see nothing ahead. Something soft and clammy touched his mouth; he saw a dark frond[4] moving against the grayish rock, and panic filled him. He thought of octopuses, of clinging weed. He pushed himself out backward and caught a glimpse, as he retreated, of a harmless tentacle of seaweed drifting in the mouth of the tunnel. But it was enough. He reached the sunlight, swam to shore, and lay on the diving rock. He looked down into the blue well of water. He knew he must find his way through that cave, or hole, or tunnel, and out the other side.

First, he thought, he must learn to control his breathing. He let himself down into the water with another big stone in his arms, so that he could lie effortlessly on the bottom of the sea. He counted. One, two, three. He counted steadily. He could hear the movement of blood in his chest. Fifty-one, fifty-two. . . . His chest was hurting. He let go of the rock and went up into the air. He saw that the sun was low. He

Visual Vocabulary
A *tentacle* is a long, flexible limb that could belong to a plant or to a creature such as an octopus.

rushed to the villa and found his mother at her supper. She said only, "Did you enjoy yourself?" and he said, "Yes."

All night the boy dreamed of the water-filled cave in the rock, and as soon as breakfast was over he went to the bay.

That night, his nose bled badly. For hours he had been underwater, learning to hold his breath, and now he felt weak and dizzy. His mother said, "I shouldn't overdo things, darling, if I were you."

That day and the next, Jerry exercised his lungs as if everything, the whole of his life, all that he would become, depended upon it. Again his nose bled at night, and his mother insisted on his coming with her the next day. It was a torment to him to waste a day of his careful self training, but he stayed with her on that other beach, which now seemed a place for small children, a place where his mother might lie safe in the sun. It was not his beach.

He did not ask for permission, on the following day, to go to his beach. He went, before his mother could consider the complicated rights and wrongs of the matter. A day's rest, he discovered, had improved his count by ten. The big boys had made the passage while he counted a hundred and sixty. He had been counting fast, in his fright. Probably now, if he tried, he could get through that long tunnel, but he was not going to try yet. A curious, most unchildlike persistence, a controlled impatience, made him wait. In the meantime, he lay underwater on the white sand, littered now by stones he had brought down from the upper air, and studied the entrance to the tunnel. He knew every jut and corner of it, as far as it was possible to see. It was as if he already felt its sharpness about his shoulders.

He sat by the clock in the villa, when his mother was not near, and checked his time.

---

4. A *frond* is a large leaf with many divisions, or a leaf-like part of a plant such as seaweed.

Life Transitions *How might swimming through the tunnel be a transition for Jerry?*

Point of View *What sort of change in Jerry's character is the narrator describing when Jerry resolves to control his breathing?*

He was **incredulous** and then proud to find he could hold his breath without strain for two minutes. The words "two minutes," authorized by the clock, brought close the adventure that was so necessary to him.

In another four days, his mother said casually one morning, they must go home. On the day before they left, he would do it. He would do it if it killed him, he said defiantly to himself. But two days before they were to leave—a day of triumph when he increased his count by fifteen—his nose bled so badly that he turned dizzy and had to lie limply over the big rock like a bit of seaweed, watching the thick red blood flow on to the rock and trickle slowly down to the sea. He was frightened. Supposing he turned dizzy in the tunnel? Supposing he died there, trapped? Supposing—his head went around, in the hot sun, and he almost gave up. He thought he would return to the house and lie down, and next summer, perhaps, when he had another year's growth in him—*then* he would go through the hole.

But even after he had made the decision, or thought he had, he found himself sitting up on the rock and looking down into the water; and he knew that now, this moment, when his nose had only just stopped bleeding, when his head was still sore and throbbing—this was the moment when he would try. If he did not do it now, he never would. He was trembling with fear that he would not go; and he was trembling with horror at that long, long tunnel under the rock, under the sea. Even in the open sunlight, the barrier rock seemed very wide and very heavy; tons of rock pressed down on where he would go. If he died there, he would lie until one day—perhaps not before next year—those big boys would swim into it and find it blocked.

He put on his goggles, fitted them tight, tested the vacuum. His hands were shaking. Then he chose the biggest stone he could carry and slipped over the edge of the rock until half of him was in the cool, enclosing water and half in the hot sun. He looked up once at the empty sky, filled his lungs once, twice, and then sank fast to the bottom with the stone. He let it go and began to count. He took the edges of the hole in his hands and drew himself into it, wriggling his shoulders in sidewise as he remembered he must, kicking himself along with his feet.

Soon he was clear inside. He was in a small rock-bound hole filled with yellowish-gray water. The water was pushing him up against the roof. The roof was sharp and pained his back. He pulled himself along with his hands—fast, fast—and used his legs as levers. His head knocked against something; a sharp pain dizzied him. Fifty, fifty-one, fifty-two. . . . He was without light, and the water seemed to press upon him with the weight of rock. Seventy-one, seventy-two. . . . There was no strain on his lungs. He felt like an inflated balloon, his lungs were so light and easy, but his head was pulsing.

He was being continually pressed against the sharp roof, which felt slimy as well as sharp. Again he thought of octopuses, and wondered if the tunnel might be filled with weed that could tangle him. He gave himself a panicky, convulsive kick forward, ducked his head, and swam.

Point of View *Based on the narrator's description, how realistic and convincing is Jerry's internal conflict? Explain.*

Vocabulary

incredulous (in krej′ə ləs) *adj.* unwilling or unable to believe

---

Visualize *To what senses do the words and images in the first full paragraph in this column appeal?*

Rocky Sea Shore, 1916–1919. Edward Hopper. Oil on canvas panel, 9½ x 12¹⁵/₁₆ in. Collection of Whitney Museum of American Art, New York. Josephine N. Hopper Bequest. 70.166.

View the Art Edward Hopper is known for his simple, clear style. How does the setting of this painting compare with the setting in the story?

His feet and hands moved freely, as if in open water. The hole must have widened out. He thought he must be swimming fast, and he was frightened of banging his head if the tunnel narrowed.

A hundred, a hundred and one. . . . The water paled. Victory filled him. His lungs were beginning to hurt. A few more strokes and he would be out. He was counting wildly; he said a hundred and fifteen, and then, a long time later, a hundred and fifteen again. The water was a clear jewel-green all around him. Then he saw, above his head, a crack running up through the rock. Sunlight was falling through it, showing the clean, dark rock of the tunnel, a single mussel shell, and darkness ahead.

He was at the end of what he could do. He looked up at the crack as if it were filled with air and not water, as if he could put his mouth to it to draw in air. A hundred and fifteen, he

Visual Vocabulary
A *mussel* is a kind of shellfish. Mussels are in the same scientific classification as clams, oysters, and scallops.

heard himself say inside his head—but he had said that long ago. He must go on into the blackness ahead, or he would drown. His head was swelling, his lungs cracking. A hundred and fifteen, a hundred and fifteen pounded through his head, and he feebly clutched at rocks in the dark, pulling himself forward, leaving the brief space of sunlit water behind. He felt he was dying. He was no longer quite conscious. He struggled on in the darkness between lapses into unconsciousness. An immense, swelling pain filled his head, and then the darkness cracked with an explosion of green light. His hands, groping forward, met nothing; and his feet, kicking back, propelled him out into the open sea.

He drifted to the surface, his face turned up to the air. He was gasping like a fish. He felt he would sink now and drown; he could not swim the few feet back to the rock. Then he was clutching it and pulling himself up on to it. He lay face down, gasping. He could see nothing but a red-veined, clotted dark. His eyes must have burst, he thought; they were full of blood. He tore off his goggles[5] and a gout[5] of blood went into the sea. His nose was bleeding, and the blood had filled the goggles.

He scooped up handfuls of water from the cool, salty sea, to splash on his face, and did not know whether it was blood or salt water he tasted. After a time, his heart quieted, his eyes cleared, and he sat up. He could see the local boys diving and playing half a mile away. He did not want them. He wanted nothing but to get back home and lie down.

In a short while, Jerry swam to shore and climbed slowly up the path to the villa. He flung himself on his bed and slept, waking at the sound of feet on the path outside. His mother was coming back. He rushed to the bathroom, thinking she must not see his face with bloodstains, or tearstains, on it. He came out of the bathroom and met her as she walked into the villa, smiling, her eyes lighting up.

"Have a nice morning?" she asked, laying her hand on his warm brown shoulder a moment.

"Oh, yes, thank you," he said.

"You look a bit pale." And then, sharp and anxious, "How did you bang your head?"

"Oh, just banged it," he told her.

She looked at him closely. He was strained; his eyes were glazed-looking. She was worried. And then she said to herself, Oh, don't fuss! Nothing can happen. He can swim like a fish.

They sat down to lunch together.

"Mummy," he said, "I can stay under water for two minutes—three minutes, at least." It came bursting out of him.

"Can you, darling?" she said. "Well, I shouldn't overdo it. I don't think you ought to swim any more today."

She was ready for a battle of wills, but he gave in at once. It was no longer of the least importance to go to the bay. ᘯ

---

5. Here, *gout* refers to a mass of fluid that gushes or bursts forth.

Life Transitions *Why is Jerry no longer interested in the local boys?*

Life Transitions *Why do you think Jerry kept his triumph of swimming through the tunnel to himself?*

After You Read

Respond and Think Critically

1. **Connect to Personal Experience** Would you have challenged yourself as Jerry does if you had been in his place? Explain.

2. **Summarize Events** Summarize what Jerry does when he goes to the beach the second time. Why do you think Jerry decides he must go through the tunnel?

3. **Interpret Plot** How is Jerry's preparation unlike the real test? In your opinion, what is the most dramatic moment of Jerry's actual test? Explain.

4. **Evaluate Characterization** How would you describe the mother's feelings toward Jerry? Do you think the mother is a realistic character? Support your answer with text evidence.

5. **Evaluate Author's Craft** How has Lessing made Jerry's decision to go through the tunnel seem credible or genuine? Does it seem believable that Jerry does not tell his mother what he has accomplished? Support your response with text evidence.

6. **Big Idea** **Draw Conclusions About Characters** Both Jerry and his mother go through a major transition in this story. How is each character's response to the other helpful to these transitions?

Literary Element Point of View

A **third-person omniscient narrator** can give insight into all characters.

7. **Analyze Point of View** How would the story be different if it were told in the first-person point of view by Jerry?

8. **Analyze Tone** How does Lessing's use of the third-person omniscient point of view help establish Jerry's feelings toward his mother? How does this help set the tone of the story?

Reading Strategy Visualize

Review the chart you made on page 164.

9. What does Jerry experience as he swims through the tunnel? What images help you feel what Jerry feels in this scene?

10. How do Lessing's sensory images help you understand the text? Pick an example from the story and explain.

LOG ON ▶ **Literature** Online

Selection Resources For Selection Quizzes, eFlashcards, and Reading-Writing Connection activities, go to glencoe.com and enter QuickPass code GL57805u1.

Vocabulary

Practice with Antonyms An antonym is a word that has a meaning opposite to that of another word. With a partner, match each bold-faced vocabulary word below with its antonym. You will not use all the answer choices. Then use a thesaurus or dictionary to check your answers.

1. conscientiously
2. contrition
3. supplication
4. beseeching
5. incredulous

a. demanding
b. consistency
c. revelation
d. certain
e. edict
f. remorselessness
g. carelessly

Writing

Write a Letter Was Jerry brave or foolish to swim through the tunnel? Write a letter to Jerry in which you express your opinion of his adventure.

Build Background

Lame Deer is a spiritual name that has been handed down from father to son in one Sioux family. Richard Erdoes met John Fire Lame Deer in 1967 and recorded this story.

THE VISION QUEST

Told by Lame Deer

Recorded by Richard Erdoes

Mountain Spirit. Stephan Daigle.

A young man wanted to go on a *han-bleceya,* or vision seeking, to try for a dream that would give him the power to be a great medicine man. Having a high opinion of himself, he felt sure that he had been created to become great among his people and that the only thing lacking was a vision.

The young man was daring and brave, eager to go up to the mountaintop. He had been brought up by good, honest people who were wise in the ancient ways and who prayed for him. All through the winter they were busy getting him ready, feeding him wasna,[1] corn, and plenty of good meat to make him strong. At every

---

1. *Wasna* is a high-energy food made of meat, fat, and berries pounded together.

Visual Vocabulary

A *travois* (trə voi′) is a V-shaped sled made of hide or netting supported by two long poles that are harnessed to a horse or dog.

Visual Vocabulary

A *sweat lodge* is a hut in which steam is produced by pouring or sprinkling water over red-hot rocks contained in a central pit.

meal they set aside something for the spirits so that they would help him to get a great vision. His relatives thought he had the power even before he went up, but that was putting the cart before the horse, or rather the travois before the horse, as this is an Indian legend.

When at last he started on his quest, it was a beautiful morning in late spring. The grass was up, the leaves were out, nature was at its best. Two medicine men accompanied him.

They put up a sweat lodge to purify him in the hot, white breath of the sacred steam. They sanctified him with the incense of sweet grass, rubbing his body with sage, fanning it with an eagle's wing. They went to the hilltop with him to prepare the vision pit and make an offering of tobacco bundles. Then they told the young man to cry, to humble himself, to ask for holiness, to cry for power, for a sign from the Great Spirit, for a gift which would make him into a medicine man. After they had done all they could, they left him there.

He spent the first night in the hole the medicine men had dug for him, trembling and crying out loudly. Fear kept him awake, yet he was cocky, ready to wrestle with the spirits for the vision, the power he wanted. But no dreams came to ease his mind. Toward morning before the sun came up, he heard a voice in the swirling white mists of dawn. Speaking from no particular direction, as if it came from different places, it said: "See here, young man, there are other spots you could have picked; there are other hills around here. Why don't you go there to cry for a dream? You disturbed us all night, all us creatures and birds; you even kept the trees awake. We couldn't sleep. Why should you cry here? You're a brash young man, not yet ready or worthy to receive a vision."

But the young man clenched his teeth, determined to stick it out, resolved to force that vision to come. He spent another day in the pit, begging for enlightenment which would not come, and then another night of fear and cold and hunger.

When dawn arrived once more, he heard the voice again: "Stop disturbing us; go away!" The same thing happened the third morning. By this time he was faint with hunger, thirst, and anxiety. Even the air seemed to oppress him, to fight him. He was panting. His stomach felt shriveled up, shrunk tight against his backbone. But he was determined to endure one more night, the fourth and last. Surely the vision would come. But again he cried for it out of the dark and loneliness until he was hoarse, and still he had no dream.

Just before daybreak he heard the same voice again, very angry: "Why are you still here?" He knew then that he had suffered in vain; now he would have to go back to his people and confess that he had gained no knowledge and no power. The only thing he could tell them was that he got bawled out every morning. Sad and cross, he replied, "I can't help myself; this is my last day, and

I'm crying my eyes out. I know you told me to go home, but who are you to give me orders? I don't know you. I'm going to stay until my uncles come to fetch me, whether you like it or not."

All at once there was a rumble from a larger mountain that stood behind the hill. It became a mighty roar, and the whole hill trembled. The wind started to blow. The young man looked up and saw a boulder poised on the mountain's summit. He saw lightning hit it, saw it sway. Slowly the boulder moved. Slowly at first, then faster and faster, it came tumbling down the mountainside, churning up earth, snapping huge trees as if they were little twigs. And the boulder was coming right down on him!

The young man cried out in terror. He was paralyzed with fear, unable to move. The boulder dwarfed everything in view; it towered over the vision pit. But just as it was an arm's length away and about to crush him, it stopped. Then, as the young man stared open-mouthed, his hair standing up, his eyes starting out of his head, the boulder *rolled up the mountain,* all the way to the top. He could hardly believe what he saw. He was still cowering motionless when he heard the roar and rumble again and saw that immense boulder coming down at him once more. This time he managed to jump out of his vision pit at the last moment. The boulder crushed it, obliterated it, grinding the young man's pipe and gourd rattle into dust.

Again the boulder rolled up the mountain, and again it came down. "I'm leaving, I'm leaving!" hollered the young man. Regaining his power of motion, he scrambled down the hill as fast as he could. This time the boulder actually leap-frogged over him, bouncing down the slope, crushing and pulverizing everything in its way. He ran unseeingly, stumbling, falling, getting up again. He did not even notice the boulder rolling up once more and coming down for the fourth time. On this last and most fearful descent, it flew through the air in a giant leap, landing right in front of him and embedding itself so deeply in the earth that only its top was visible. The ground shook itself like a wet dog coming out of a stream and flung the young man this way and that.

Gaunt, bruised, and shaken, he stumbled back to his village. To the medicine men he said: "I have received no vision and gained no knowledge. I have made the spirits angry. It was all for nothing."

"Well, you did find out one thing," said the older of the two, who was his uncle. "You went after your vision like a hunter after buffalo, or a warrior after scalps. You were fighting the spirits. You thought they owed you a vision. Suffering alone brings no vision nor does courage, nor does sheer will power. A vision comes as a gift born of humility, of wisdom, and of patience. If from your vision quest you have learned nothing but this, then you have already learned much. Think about it." ∾

Discussion Starter

Can an experience be useful even if you fail to reach your goal? Discuss this question in a small group. List some benefits a person might get from an experience even if the original goal is not reached. Use specific details from the legend to support your opinions. Then share your conclusions with the rest of the class.

Build Background

In the summer of 1933, F. Scott Fitzgerald was in Maryland working on his novel *Tender Is the Night*. His wife was being treated for the mental illness that would last the rest of her life. During that time he wrote the following letter to their beloved daughter, Scottie, who was twelve years old and away at summer camp.

Dear Pie

F. Scott Fitzgerald to
Frances Scott "Scottie" Fitzgerald

La Paix, Rodgers' Forge,
Towson, Maryland,
August 8, 1933.

Dear Pie:

I feel very strongly about you doing duty. Would you give me a little more documentation about your reading in French? I am glad you are happy—but I never believe much in happiness. I never believe in misery either. Those are things you see on the stage or the screen or the printed page, they never really happen to you in life.

All I believe in in life is the rewards for virtue (according to your talents) and the *punishments* for not fulfilling your duties, which are doubly costly. If there is such a volume in the camp library, will you ask Mrs. Tyson to let you look up a sonnet of Shakespeare's in which the line occurs *"Lilies that fester smell far worse than weeds."*

Have had no thoughts today, life seems composed of getting up a *Saturday Evening Post* story. I think of you, and always pleasantly; but if you call me "Pappy" again I am going to take the

American novelist F. Scott Fitzgerald, his wife Zelda, and daughter, Scottie, go for a motor jaunt in Italy.

White Cat out and beat his bottom *hard, six times for every time you are impertinent.* Do you react to that?

I will arrange the camp bill.
Halfwit, I will conclude.

Things to worry about:

Worry about courage
Worry about cleanliness
Worry about efficiency
Worry about horsemanship
Worry about . . .

Things not to worry about:

Don't worry about popular opinion
Don't worry about dolls
Don't worry about the past
Don't worry about the future
Don't worry about growing up
Don't worry about anybody getting ahead of you
Don't worry about triumph
Don't worry about failures unless it comes through your own fault
Don't worry about mosquitoes
Don't worry about flies
Don't worry about insects in general
Don't worry about parents

Don't worry about boys
Don't worry about disappointments
Don't worry about pleasures
Don't worry about satisfactions

Things to think about:

What am I really aiming at?
How good am I really in comparison to my contemporaries in regard to:
(a) Scholarship
(b) Do I really understand about people and am I able to get along with them?
(c) Am I trying to make my body a useful instrument or am I neglecting it?

With dearest love,

P.S. My come-back to your calling me Pappy is christening you by the word Egg, which implies that you belong to a very rudimentary state of life and that I could break you up and crack you open at my will and I think it would be a word that would hang on if I ever told it to your contemporaries. "Egg Fitzgerald." How would you like that to go through life with "Eggie Fitzgerald" or "Bad Egg Fitzgerald" or any form that might occur to fertile minds? Try it once more and I swear to God I will hang it on you and it will be up to you to shake it off. Why borrow trouble?

Love anyhow.

Quickwrite

Fitzgerald writes that he does not believe much in happiness or misery, only in rewards and punishments. Do you agree or disagree with his opinion? Reread the first two paragraphs of the letter and write a paragraph explaining your views.

Wrap-Up: Comparing Literature

Across Genres

- ***Through the Tunnel*** by Doris Lessing

- ***The Vision Quest*** by Lame Deer

- ***Dear Pie*** by F. Scott Fitzgerald

COMPARE THE `Big Idea` Life Transitions

Writing Make two three-column charts with the following headings: Things to Worry About, Things Not to Worry About, Things to Think About. Then fill in one chart to give to Jerry in "Through the Tunnel" and the other to give to the young man in "The Vision Quest." What wisdom can you share with each to help them through their life transitions?

COMPARE Narrator

Group Activity "Through the Tunnel" is told from a **third-person omniscient**, or all-knowing, **point of view**. "The Vision Quest," in which the narrator reveals the thoughts and feelings of only one character, has a **third-person limited point of view**. "Dear Pie," a letter, has a **first-person point of view**. In a group, discuss the following questions.

1. How would "Through the Tunnel" be different if it were told from the first-person point of view by Jerry's mother?

2. Suppose that someone else had accompanied the young man on his vision quest and had written about it. From what point of view would the account be written? How might the tone of the story be different?

3. What do you learn about F. Scott Fitzgerald from "Dear Pie"? Do you think he is a good parent? Explain.

COMPARE Author's Culture

Speaking and Listening The characters in "Through the Tunnel" and "The Vision Quest" experience rites of passage. Investigate initiation customs of a society or a group. Present an oral report comparing the customs you studied with those in one of the stories. Compile your main points in a chart.

Initiation Customs of (society or group)	Initiation Customs in (story or legend)	Comparison of Initiation Customs

Before You Read

Catch the Moon

Meet **Judith Ortiz Cofer**
(born 1952)

"Latina wherever I am," is the way Judith Ortiz Cofer sees herself. When she was a child, her family moved from her birthplace of Puerto Rico to Paterson, New Jersey. However, they made frequent trips back to Puerto Rico, so she always felt close to her cultural roots. She has a childhood memory of sitting in her grandmother's living room, which was furnished with mahogany rocking chairs. "It was on these rockers that my mother, her sisters and my grandmother sat on these afternoons of my childhood to tell their stories, teaching each other and my cousin and me what it was like to be a woman, more specifically, a Puerto Rican woman."

> "I write in English, yet I write obsessively about my Puerto Rican experience."
>
> —Judith Ortiz Cofer

Bilingual Advantage Early on, Cofer experienced a disadvantage of the family's frequent moving. Cofer was teased for having "a Spanish accent when [she] spoke English; and, when [she] spoke Spanish, [she] was told that [she] sounded like a 'Gringa.' " Cofer transformed this into an advantage when she began writing fiction and poetry. Writer Marian C. Gonsior says that Cofer deals with "the effect on Puerto Rican Americans of living in a world split between the island culture of their homeland and the teeming tenement life of the United States." After receiving her bachelor's degree from Augusta College in Georgia, Cofer began her long teaching career, first as a bilingual teacher in Florida public schools and then as an English and Spanish teacher at colleges and universities. She is currently the Regents' and Franklin Professor of English and Creative Writing at the University of Georgia, Athens.

Writer of Poetry and Fiction In graduate school Cofer began writing poetry in order to express the concerns of Latina women. Cofer believes that "poetry has made me more disciplined. . . . Poetry taught me about economizing in language and about the power of language." Ten years later, Cofer began writing fiction, and her first novel, *The Line of the Sun*, was nominated for a Pulitzer Prize in 1989. Cofer has also written *An Island Like You: Stories of the Barrio*, a book of short stories for young adults. The stories are set in Paterson, New Jersey, and deal with the problems facing Puerto Rican teenagers. Mexican American author Sandra Cisneros says, "In these stories, both hilarious and tragic, [Cofer] has captured the isolated lives of those wobbling between two clashing cultures—childhood and adulthood." "Catch the Moon" is one of the stories in *An Island Like You*.

Literature and Reading Preview

Connect to the Story

Why does it feel good to give someone a gift? Freewrite for a few minutes about a gift you have given someone and how it made you feel to give it.

Build Background

A *barrio* is an urban neighborhood where most of the people are of Hispanic heritage. People in a *barrio* may have been born in the United States or have come from Spanish-speaking countries.

Set Purposes for Reading

Big Idea **Life Transitions**

As you read "Catch the Moon," ask yourself, How does a self-centered young man learn the value of giving selflessly?

Literary Element **Point of View**

Point of view is the standpoint from which a story is told. In the **third-person limited point of view**, the narrator describes events as one character perceives them. This enables readers to focus on this particular character's thoughts and feelings, though the information about other characters is much more limited. As you read, ask yourself, Why did Cofer choose to tell the story from the third-person limited point of view?

Reading Strategy **Interpret Imagery**

Writers use **imagery,** or sensory language, to appeal to the senses. Imagery helps readers see, hear, smell, taste, or feel what the writer is describing. As you read, ask yourself, What are examples of imagery in this story? What do they signify?

....

Tip: Take Notes Use a chart like the one below to record instances of imagery, or sensory language, and your interpretation of them.

Imagery	Interpretation
p. 184 "steel jungle of his car junkyard"	Here "steel jungle" is used figuratively to suggest a place that is hard and dense with debris.

TEKS

For pages 182–192

10.7 Understand, make inferences and draw conclusions about how an author's sensory language creates imagery in literary text and provide evidence from text to support understanding.

Vocabulary

harass (hə ras′) *v.* to bother or annoy repeatedly; p. 185 *Several times a day the bully would harass the children.*

makeshift (māk′shift′) *adj.* suitable as a temporary substitute for the proper or desired thing; p. 186 *He used a tent as his makeshift home.*

vintage (vin′tij) *adj.* characterized by enduring appeal; classic; p. 186 *He drove a vintage Model T car.*

relic (rel′ik) *n.* that which is cherished for its age or sentimental associations; memento; keepsake; p. 189 *Our photo albums have been passed down as relics from one generation to the next.*

Catch the Moon

Judith Ortiz Cofer

Luis Cintrón sits on top of a six-foot pile of hubcaps and watches his father walk away into the steel jungle of his car junkyard. Released into his old man's custody after six months in juvenile hall—for breaking and entering—and he didn't even take anything. He did it on a dare.

But the old lady with the million cats was a light sleeper, and good with her aluminum cane. He has a scar on his head to prove it.

Now Luis is wondering whether he should have stayed in and done his full time. Jorge Cintrón of Jorge Cintrón & Son, Auto Parts and Salvage, has decided that Luis should wash and polish every hubcap in the yard. The hill he is sitting on is only the latest couple of hundred wheel covers

that have come in. Luis grunts and stands up on top of his silver mountain. He yells at no one, "Someday, son, all this will be yours," and sweeps his arms like the Pope blessing a crowd over the piles of car sandwiches and mounds of metal parts that cover this acre of land outside the city. He is the "Son" of Jorge Cintrón & Son, and so far his father has had more than one reason to wish it was plain Jorge Cintrón on the sign.

Luis has been getting in trouble since he started high school two years ago,

---

Interpret Imagery *What does the image of Luis standing on the "silver mountain" tell you about him?*

mainly because of the "social group" he organized—a bunch of guys who were into **harassing** the local authorities. Their thing was taking something to the limit on a dare or, better still, doing something dangerous, like breaking into a house, not to steal, just to prove that they could do it. That was Luis's specialty, coming up with very complicated plans, like military strategies, and assigning the "jobs" to guys who wanted to join the Tiburones.[1]

Tiburón means "shark," and Luis had gotten the name from watching an old movie[2] about a Puerto Rican gang called the Sharks with his father. Luis thought it was one of the dumbest films he had ever seen. Everybody sang their lines, and the guys all pointed their toes and leaped in the air when they were supposed to be slaughtering each other. But he liked their name, the Sharks, so he made it Spanish and had it air-painted on his black T-shirt with a killer shark under it, jaws opened wide and dripping with blood. It didn't take long for other guys in the barrio to ask about it.

Man, had they had a good time. The girls were interested too. Luis outsmarted everybody by calling his organization a social club and registering it at Central High. That meant they were legal, even let out of last-period class on Fridays for their "club" meetings. It was just this year, after a couple of botched[3] jobs, that the teachers had started getting suspicious. The first

one to go wrong was when he sent Kenny Matoa to *borrow* some "souvenirs" out of Anita Robles's locker. He got caught. It seems that Matoa had been reading Anita's diary and didn't hear her coming down the hall. Anita was supposed to be in the gym at that time but had copped out with the usual female excuse of cramps. You could hear her screams all the way to Market Street.

She told the principal all she knew about the Tiburones, and Luis had to talk fast to convince old Mr. Williams that the club did put on cultural activities such as the Save the Animals talent show. What Mr. Williams didn't know was that the animal that was being "saved" with the ticket sales was Luis's pet boa, which needed quite a few live mice to stay healthy and happy. They kept E.S. (which stood for "Endangered Species") in Luis's room, but she belonged to the club and it was the members' responsibility to raise the money to feed their mascot. So last year they had sponsored their first annual Save the Animals talent show, and it had been a great success. The Tiburones had come dressed as Latino Elvises and did a grand finale to "All Shook Up" that made the audience go wild. Mr. Williams had smiled while Luis talked, maybe remembering how the math teacher, Mrs. Laguna, had dragged him out in the aisle to rock-and-roll with her. Luis had gotten out of that one, but barely.

His father was a problem too. He objected to the T-shirt logo, calling it disgusting and vulgar. Mr. Cintrón prided himself on his own neat, elegant style of dressing after work, and on his manners and large vocabulary, which he picked up by taking correspondence courses in just about everything.

---

1. *Tiburones* (tē´ boo rō´ nās)
2. *[old movie...]* The narrator is describing the feature film *West Side Story*, a 1961 musical based on Shakespeare's play *Romeo and Juliet*, set in the youth gang atmosphere of New York City in the late 1950s.
3. *Botched* means "badly or clumsily done."

Vocabulary

harass (hə ras´) *v.* to bother or annoy repeatedly

Life Transitions *Do you think Luis feels any remorse for the actions of the Tiburones? Explain.*

Luis thought that it was just his way of staying busy since Luis's mother had died, almost three years ago, of cancer. He had never gotten over it.

All this was going through Luis's head as he slid down the hill of hubcaps. The tub full of soapy water, the can of polish, and the bag of rags had been neatly placed in front of a **makeshift** table made from two car seats and a piece of plywood. Luis heard a car drive up and someone honk their horn. His father emerged from inside a new red Mustang that had been totaled. He usually dismantled every small feature by hand before sending the vehicle into the *cementerio*,[4] as he called the lot. Luis watched as the most beautiful girl he had ever seen climbed out of a **vintage** white Volkswagen Bug. She stood in the sunlight in her white sundress waiting for his father, while Luis stared. She was like a smooth wood carving. Her skin was mahogany, almost black, and her arms and legs were long and thin, but curved in places so that she did not look bony and hard—more like a ballerina. And her ebony hair was braided close to her head. Luis let his breath out, feeling a little dizzy. He had forgotten to breathe. Both the girl and his father heard him. Mr. Cintrón waved him over.

"Luis, the señorita here has lost a wheel cover. Her car is twenty-five years old, so

it will not be an easy match. Come look on this side."

Luis tossed a wrench he'd been holding into a toolbox like he was annoyed, just to make a point about slave labor. Then he followed his father, who knelt on the gravel and began to point out every detail of the hubcap. Luis was hardly listening. He watched the girl take a piece of paper from her handbag.

"Señor Cintrón, I have drawn the hubcap for you, since I will have to leave soon. My home address and telephone number are here, and also my parents' office number." She handed the paper to Mr. Cintrón, who nodded.

"Sí, señorita, very good. This will help my son look for it. Perhaps there is one in that stack there." He pointed to the pile of caps that Luis was supposed to wash and polish. "Yes, I'm almost certain that there is a match there. Of course, I do not know if it's near the top or the bottom. You will give us a few days, yes?"

Luis just stared at his father like he was crazy. But he didn't say anything because the girl was smiling at him with a funny expression on her face. Maybe she thought he had X-ray eyes like Superman, or maybe she was mocking him.

"Please call me Naomi, Señor Cintrón. You know my mother. She is the director of the funeral home. . . ." Mr. Cintrón seemed surprised at first; he prided himself on having a great memory. Then his friendly expression changed to one of sadness as he recalled the day of his wife's burial. Naomi did not finish her sentence. She reached over and placed her hand on Mr. Cintrón's arm for a moment. Then she said "Adiós" softly, and got in her shiny white car. She waved to them as she left, and her gold bracelets flashing in the sun nearly blinded Luis.

---

4. *Cementerio* (se men tā′ rē ō) is Spanish for "cemetery."

Point of View *What does the first sentence in this column tell you about Luis?*

Interpret Imagery *How would you interpret the description of the beautiful girl in the midst of the junkyard?*

Point of View *Why do you think Luis stares at his father?*

September 16, c. 1955. René Magritte. Oil on canvas, 14 x 10⅞ in. The Minneapolis Institute of Arts. ©ARS, NY.

<u>View the Art</u> René Magritte, a Belgian Surrealist painter, often included elements of mystery, comedy, and danger in his art. How does this painting express the title and mood of the story?

Mr. Cintrón shook his head. "How about that," he said as if to himself. "They are the Dominican owners of Ramirez Funeral Home." And, with a sigh, "She seems like such a nice young woman. Reminds me of your mother when she was her age."

Hearing the funeral parlor's name, Luis remembered too. The day his mother died, he had been in her room at the hospital while his father had gone for coffee. The alarm had gone off on her monitor and nurses had come running in, pushing him outside. After that, all he recalled was the anger that had made him punch a hole in his bedroom wall. And afterward he had refused to talk to anyone at the funeral. Strange, he did see a black girl there who didn't try like the others to talk to him, but actually ignored him as

she escorted family members to the viewing room and brought flowers in. Could it be that the skinny girl in a frilly white dress had been Naomi? She didn't act like she had recognized him today, though. Or maybe she thought that he was a jerk.

Luis grabbed the drawing from his father. The old man looked like he wanted to walk down memory lane. But Luis was in no mood to listen to the old stories about his falling in love on a tropical island. The world they'd lived in before he was born wasn't his world. No beaches and palm trees here. Only junk as far as he could see. He climbed back up his hill and studied Naomi's sketch. It had obviously been done very carefully. It was signed "Naomi Ramirez" in the lower right-hand corner. He memorized the telephone number.

Luis washed hubcaps all day until his hands were red and raw, but he did not come across the small silver bowl that would fit the VW. After work he took a few practice Frisbee shots across the yard before showing his rows and rows of shiny rings drying in the sun. His father nodded and showed him the bump on his temple where one of Luis's flying saucers had gotten him. "Practice makes perfect, you know. Next time you'll probably decapitate[5] me." Luis heard him struggle with the word *decapitate*, which Mr. Cintrón pronounced in syllables. Showing off his big vocabulary again, Luis thought. He looked closely at the bump, though. He felt bad about it.

"They look good, hijo."[6] Mr. Cintrón made a sweeping gesture with his arms over the yard. "You know, all this will have to be

5. To *decapitate* is to cut the head off of something.
6. *Hijo* (ēʹhō) is Spanish for "son."

Life Transitions *Does the second full paragraph in this column show a change in Luis's attitude? Explain.*

Scrap Merchant, 1983. Reg Cartwright. Oil on canvas, 91.4 x 76.2 cm. Private collection.

View the Art Reg Cartwright is a British painter and illustrator whose work is influenced by Cubism. What might this painting suggest about how Luis feels while working in his father's junkyard?

classified. My dream is to have all the parts divided by year, make of car, and condition. Maybe now that you are here to help me, this will happen."

"Pop . . ." Luis put his hand on his father's shoulder. They were the same height and build, about five foot six and muscular. "The judge said six months of free labor for you, not life, okay?" Mr. Cintrón nodded, looking distracted. It was then that Luis suddenly noticed how gray his hair had turned—it used to be shiny black like his own—and that there were deep lines in his face. His father had turned into an old man and he hadn't even noticed.

"Son, you must follow the judge's instructions. Like she said, next time you get in trouble, she's going to treat you like an adult, and I think you know what that means. Hard time, no breaks."

"Yeah, yeah. That's what I'm doing, right? Working my hands to the bone instead of enjoying my summer. But listen, she didn't put me under house arrest, right? I'm going out tonight."

"Home by ten. She did say something about a curfew, Luis." Mr. Cintrón had stopped smiling and was looking upset. It had always been hard for them to talk more than a minute or two before his father got offended at something Luis said, or at his sarcastic tone. He was always doing something wrong.

Luis threw the rag down on the table and went to sit in his father's ancient Buick, which was in mint condition. They drove home in silence.

After sitting down at the kitchen table with his father to eat a pizza they had picked up on the way home, Luis asked to borrow the car. He didn't get an answer then, just a look that meant "Don't bother me right now."

Before bringing up the subject again, Luis put some ice cubes in a Baggie and handed it to Mr. Cintrón, who had made the little bump on his head worse by rubbing it. It had GUILTY written on it, Luis thought.

"Gracias, hijo." His father placed the bag on the bump and made a face as the ice touched his skin.

They ate in silence for a few minutes more; then Luis decided to ask about the car again.

"I really need some fresh air, Pop. Can I borrow the car for a couple of hours?"

"You don't get enough fresh air at the yard? We're lucky that we don't have to sit in a smelly old factory all day. You know that?"

"Yeah, Pop. We're real lucky." Luis always felt irritated that his father was so grateful to own a junkyard, but he held his anger back and just waited to see if he'd get the keys without having to get in an argument.

"Where are you going?"

"For a ride. Not going anywhere. Just out for a while. Is that okay?"

Point of View *Do you think Mr. Cintrón would agree with Luis's perception that Luis is "always doing something wrong"? Explain.*

His father didn't answer, just handed him a set of keys, as shiny as the day they were manufactured. His father polished everything that could be polished: door-knobs, coins, keys, spoons, knives, and forks, like he was King Midas counting his silver and gold. Luis thought his father must be really lonely to polish utensils only he used anymore. They had been picked out by his wife, though, so they were like **relics.** Nothing she had ever owned could be thrown away. Only now the dishes, forks, and spoons were not used to eat the yellow rice and red beans, the fried chicken, or the mouth-watering sweet plantains that his mother had cooked for them. They were just kept in the cabinets that his father had turned into a museum for her. Mr. Cintrón could cook as well as his wife, but he didn't have the heart to do it anymore. Luis thought that maybe if they ate together once in a while things might get better between them, but he always had something to do around dinnertime and ended up at a hamburger joint. Tonight was the first time in months they had sat down at the table together.

Visual Vocabulary
A *plantain* (plant′ən) is a tropical fruit similar to a banana that must be cooked before eating.

Luis took the keys. "Thanks," he said, walking out to take his shower. His father kept looking at him with those sad, patient eyes. "Okay. I'll be back by ten, and keep the ice on that egg," Luis said without looking back.

Interpret Imagery *What does the image of the cabinets being used as a museum suggest about Mr. Cintrón's feelings toward his wife?*

Vocabulary

relic (rel′ik) *n.* that which is cherished for its age or sentimental associations; memento; keepsake

---

He had just meant to ride around his old barrio, see if any of the Tiburones were hanging out at El Building, where most of them lived. It wasn't far from the single-family home his father had bought when the business started paying off: a house that his mother lived in for three months before she took up residence at St. Joseph's Hospital. She never came home again. These days Luis wished he still lived in that tiny apartment where there was always something to do, some-body to talk to.

Instead Luis found himself parked in front of the last place his mother had gone to: Ramirez Funeral Home. In the front yard was a huge oak tree that Luis remembered having climbed during the funeral to get away from people. The tree looked different now, not like a skeleton, as it had then, but green with leaves. The branches reached to the second floor of the house, where the family lived.

For a while Luis sat in the car allowing the memories to flood back into his brain. He remembered his mother before the illness changed her. She had not been beautiful, as his father told everyone; she had been a sweet lady, not pretty but not ugly. To him, she had been the person who always told him that she was proud of him and loved him. She did that every night when she came to his bedroom door to say good-night. As a joke he would sometimes ask her, "Proud of what? I haven't done anything." And she'd always say, "I'm just proud that you are my son." She wasn't perfect or anything. She had bad days when nothing he did could make her smile, especially after she got sick. But he never heard her say anything negative about anyone. She always blamed *el destino*, fate, for what went wrong. He missed her. He missed her so much.

Suddenly a flood of tears that had been building up for almost three years started pouring from his eyes. Luis sat in his father's car, with his head on the steering wheel, and cried, "Mami, I miss you."

When he finally looked up, he saw that he was being watched. Sitting at a large window with a pad and a pencil on her lap was Naomi. At first Luis felt angry and embarrassed, but she wasn't laughing at him. Then she told him with her dark eyes that it was okay to come closer. He walked to the window, and she held up the sketch pad on which she had drawn him, not crying like a baby, but sitting on top of a mountain of silver disks, holding one up over his head. He had to smile.

The plate-glass window was locked. It had a security bolt on it. An alarm system, he figured, so nobody would steal the princess. He asked her if he could come in. It was soundproof too. He mouthed the words slowly for her to read his lips. She wrote on the pad, "I can't let you in. My mother is not home tonight." So they looked at each other and talked through the window for a little while. Then Luis got an idea. He signed to her that he'd be back, and drove to the junkyard.

Luis climbed up on his mountain of hubcaps. For hours he sorted the wheel covers by make, size, and condition, stopping only to call his father and tell him where he was and what he was doing. The old man did not ask him for explanations, and Luis was grateful for that. By lamppost light, Luis worked and worked, beginning to understand a little why his father kept busy all the time. Doing something that had a beginning, a middle, and an end did something to your head. It was like the satisfaction Luis got out of planning "adventures" for his Tiburones, but there was another element involved here that had nothing to do with showing off for others. This was a treasure hunt. And he knew what he was looking for.

Finally, when it seemed that it was a hopeless search, when it was almost midnight and Luis's hands were cut and bruised from his work, he found it. It was the perfect match for Naomi's drawing, the moon-shaped wheel cover for her car, Cinderella's shoe. Luis jumped off the small mound of disks left under him and shouted, "Yes!" He looked around and saw neat stacks of hubcaps that he would wash the next day. He would build a display wall for his father. People would be able to come into the yard and point to whatever they wanted.

Luis washed the VW hubcap and polished it until he could see himself in it. He used it as a mirror as he washed his face and combed his hair. Then he drove to the Ramirez Funeral Home. It was almost pitch-black, since it was a moonless night. As quietly as possible, Luis put some gravel in his pocket and climbed the oak tree to the second floor. He knew he was in front of Naomi's window—he could see her shadow through the curtains. She was at a table, apparently writing or drawing, maybe waiting for him. Luis hung the silver disk carefully on a branch near the window, then threw the gravel at the glass. Naomi ran to the window and drew the curtains aside while Luis held on to the thick branch and waited to give her the first good thing he had given anyone in a long time. ∾

Interpret Imagery *What sensory language does the author use in the first sentence in this column? What does this imagery suggest about Luis's emotional response?*

Point of View *How does the second full paragraph in this column show the third-person limited point of view?*

Life Transitions *What do you think the last sentence of the story means?*

After You Read

Respond and Think Critically

1. **Connect to Personal Experience** Were you surprised by Luis's actions at the end of the story? Explain. How did your feelings about Luis change as you read the story?

2. **Analyze Character** Describe the relationship between Luis and his father. Do you think there is a chance for them to build a better relationship? Use details from the story to support your answer.

3. **Make Inferences About Character** What does Luis leave in the tree for Naomi? What do you think Luis discovers about himself as he searches for his gift to Naomi?

4. **Make Inferences About Motivation** What do you think Luis's reasons are for giving the gift to Naomi?

5. **Evaluate Title** What does the title suggest about the overall mood of the story? Do you think it's a good title? Why or why not?

6. **Big Idea** **Draw Conclusions About Character** What kind of character transition has Luis made by the end of the story? Support your response with text evidence.

7. **Draw Conclusions About Author's Beliefs** As a child, Cofer spoke both English and Spanish but struggled with each. In the story, Luis's father is enrolled in a correspondence class to improve his vocabulary. Why is it important to him to have a good vocabulary? Do you think the author has the same beliefs? Explain.

Literary Element Point of View

The third-person limited narrator of "Catch the Moon" describes events as only Luis perceives them. Readers hear Luis's thoughts as he describes his gang activities and comments on his father and Naomi. Readers have to judge whether Luis's comments are fair and infer what his thoughts reveal about his character. Readers also should be alert to **dramatic irony** in the story: a contrast between what Luis thinks and what the reader knows is true. Refer to the pink highlighted questions to help you answer the questions below.

8. **Evaluate Character** The narrator does not reveal Naomi's opinion of Luis. After she leaves the junkyard, Luis worries that "maybe she thought that he was a jerk." How accurate is Luis's concern? Explain.

9. **Analyze Irony** The narrator reveals Luis's pride in his gang activities. Contrast Luis's feelings about his gang activities with your own perspective on gangs. What dramatic irony do you notice?

Review: Plot and Setting

Plot is the series of events that make up a story's structure. **Setting** is the time and place in which the story takes place. As you learned on page 9, a key feature of the plot is **exposition**, which introduces the story's characters, setting, and situation.

10. **Partner Activity** Meet with a classmate to discuss and make inferences about what the structure and exposition of the story reveal about Luis, specifically regarding the setting he is in and why he is there. Working with your partner, create a graphic organizer similar to the one below and fill it with details about Luis, the setting, and his situation.

Details About Structure	Details About Setting	Inference
Flashback on page 185	Luis now works in junkyard	Luis was released into father's custody

👉 **Texas Test Practice** (10.7)

1. The contrasting images of the meals the father and son currently eat and the food that Mrs. Cintrón used to cook highlight

   (A) Luis's anger with his father

   (B) a loss of intimacy in the family

   (C) that neither man can cook

   (D) Luis's love for his mother

   (E) that the junkyard is making a profit

Vocabulary Practice

Practice with Denotation and Connotation

Denotation is the literal, or dictionary, meaning of a word. **Connotation** is the implied, or cultural, meaning of a word. For example, the words *fib* and *lie* have a similar denotation, a "mistruth," but *lie* has a stronger connotation.

Each of the vocabulary words is listed below with a word that has a similar denotation. Choose the word that has a stronger connotation.

1. **harass**   bother

2. **makeshift**   temporary

3. **vintage**   classic

4. **relic**   artifact

Academic Vocabulary

Naomi helps Luis realize that there is an **alternative** *to the life he is living.*

Alternative is an academic word. In casual conversation, someone might refer to an alternative school or alternative medicine. These adjectives suggest the meaning of the noun *alternative*. What alternative might you consider to the way you usually spend your after-school time? Why?

For more on academic vocabulary, see pages 36–37 and R92–R94.

 Apply Point of View

Assignment Use the first-person point of view to retell the last two paragraphs of the story from Luis's point of view.

Get Ideas Make a sequence chain to list the events that take place in the last two paragraphs, and for each event, write a comment that Luis himself might make. Base your word choices on the words and phrasing that Luis uses elsewhere in the story.

Event	Luis's comment
Luis finally finds the matching hubcap.	Just when I figured I was never gonna find it, I saw this hubcap shaped like the moon and I knew it was the matching one. It was perfect.
Luis washes and polishes the hubcap.	
Luis drives to the funeral home.	

Give It Structure Narrate the events in the order in which they occur. Use transition words that signal chronological order where they are needed.

Look at Language Remember to use the pronoun *I* only as a subject and the pronoun *me* only as an object. For example, Luis might say, "I am into cars" or "My friends and I are into cars." He could also say "Cars are cool to me" or "Cars are cool to me and my friends." In the first pair of sentences, *I* is the subject. In the second pair of sentences, *Cars* is the subject and *me* is the object. Be sure each word that Luis speaks in the narrative reflects not only his perspective but also his characteristic speech patterns.

 Literature Online

Selection Resources For Selection Quizzes, eFlashcards, and Reading-Writing Connection activities, go to glencoe.com and enter QuickPass code GL57805u1.

Grammar Workshop

Sentence Fragments

TEKS

10.17.C Use a variety of correctly structured sentences (e.g., compound, complex, compound-complex).

Literature Connection A **sentence fragment** is a word or group of words that make up only part of a sentence. People often use fragments in casual conversation, as in this quotation from Judith Ortiz Cofer's story "Catch the Moon":

> "'Home by ten. She did say something about a curfew, Luis.'
> Mr. Cintrón had stopped smiling and was looking upset."

It is often acceptable to use sentence fragments in creative writing and casual dialogue. For formal writing and speaking in academic and business contexts, however, you should avoid fragments and use Standard American English instead.

Problem The passage below contains several sentence fragments.

> Luis just stared at his father. Like he was crazy. But he didn't say anything. Because the girl was smiling at him with a funny expression on her face.

Solution 1 Form a **compound sentence.** Compound sentences have two or more main clauses and can be joined by a comma, coordinating conjunction, or semicolon.

> Luis just stared at his father like he was crazy, but he didn't say anything.

Solution 2 Form a **complex sentence.** Complex sentences have one main clause and one or more subordinate clauses.

> He didn't say anything because the girl was smiling at him.

Solution 3 Form a **compound-complex sentence.** Compound-complex sentences have two or more main clauses and at least one subordinate clause.

> Luis just stared at his father like he was crazy, but he didn't say anything because the girl was smiling at him.

Revise Use the strategies shown above to correct the sentence fragments in this paragraph.

> Luis and his father had not gotten along. Since his mother's death. Often got into trouble and was punished. Luis saw Naomi at the junkyard. The most beautiful girl in the world. Worked hard to find a match for her missing hubcap. He memorized her telephone number. Had written on the paper with her drawing of the hubcap.

Vocabulary Terms

A sentence is a group of words that expresses a complete thought. A **sentence fragment** does not express a complete thought and often lacks a subject, a verb, or both.

Tip

When writing for a test, check carefully to make sure each sentence has a subject and a verb and conveys a complete thought.

Language Handbook

For more on sentence fragments, see the Language Handbook page R55.

Sentence Fragments for Effect

At times a sentence fragment can be used to create a dramatic effect. In such an instance, what is left unsaid can be as effective as what is said—in a wry observation, for example, or an exclamation. Consider the following: *An impossible situation.* or *Under no circumstances!*

LOG ON ▶ **Literature** Online

Grammar For more grammar practice, go to glencoe.com and enter QuickPass code GL57805u1.

Before You Read

And of Clay Are We Created

Meet **Isabel Allende**
(born 1942)

For most of her life, Isabel Allende (ēs′äbel ä yen′dä) has felt like a wanderer. Although she is Chilean, she was born in Lima, Peru, where her father held a diplomatic post. Her parents divorced when she was young, and she lived with her grandparents for several years in Santiago, Chile. When her mother remarried, Allende moved with her mother and stepfather, also a diplomat, to La Paz, Bolivia.

Life in Chile From Bolivia, the family was next stationed in Beirut, Lebanon, and then moved on to Europe. The threat of war in the Middle East returned Allende back to her grandfather's house in Chile. She was fifteen years old and wanted to put down roots. Her grandfather provided Allende with an intensive education in Chilean history and geography, which deepened her love for her country. Trips that she and her grandfather took to different parts of Chile fueled this love, as did her reading of great Chilean poets, including Pablo Neruda and Gabriela Mistral.

> "*I write to preserve memory. I write what should not be forgotten.*"
>
> —Isabel Allende

Allende's grandfather also gave her gifts that she would later call upon as a writer. He entertained her with folktales and admonished her with proverbs. He told her fascinating accounts of strange characters in their family and recited lengthy poems from memory.

In 1959 Allende started working for the United Nations Food and Agricultural Organization in Santiago, first as a secretary, then as an editor and a press officer. She later became a broadcast journalist and wrote for and edited a feminist magazine.

Exile Isabel Allende's life changed forever on September 11, 1973, when the president of Chile, Salvador Allende, was killed and a brutal military dictatorship took over. The murdered president had been Isabel's beloved uncle. Within a few years, it was no longer safe for Allende and her family to stay in Chile, so they went into exile in Venezuela.

Allende could not find a job in journalism in Venezuela and worked as a teacher for several years. In 1981 she began writing a letter to her grandfather, who was almost 100 years old and in poor health, and continued working on it for an entire year. The letter became the manuscript for her first novel, *The House of the Spirits*.

Since 1982 Allende has written nearly a dozen books, most of them novels.

Literature and Reading Preview

Connect to the Story

What are some different factors that might influence how you would respond during a natural disaster? Discuss this question with a partner.

Build Background

This story is based on an event that occurred in the South American country of Colombia. In November 1985, an active, snow-covered volcano erupted. Heat from the eruption melted snow and ice and sent a monstrous mudslide crashing into the valley; 25,000 people and 15,000 animals perished in the disaster, and thousands of people were injured or left homeless.

Set Purposes for Reading

Big Idea Life Transitions

As you read, ask yourself, How does Allende use the mud as a device to hold the lives of the characters in suspension?

Literary Element Persona

A **persona** is the person created by the author to tell a story. Even if the story is told from a first-person point of view, as is "And of Clay Are We Created," the narrator is not the author. As you read, ask yourself, What are the characteristics of the first-person narrator in the story?

Reading Strategy Interpret Imagery

Imagery is descriptive words and phrases that appeal to one or more of the senses: sight, sound, smell, taste, and touch. Authors use imagery, or sensory details, to create images that evoke emotional responses in readers and help them understand the story's meaning and mood. As you read, ask yourself, How does Allende use sensory details to create powerful images?

....

Tip: Take Notes Use a chart to record sensory details in this story. Use the blue highlighted questions to help you get started. As you complete the chart, make inferences about how Allende uses sensory language to evoke emotion.

Detail	Sense	Inference
p. 203 "her silk hair against his cheek"	touch	Rolf misses his sister

TEKS

For pages 194–207

10.7 Understand, make inferences and draw conclusions about how an author's sensory language creates imagery in literary text and provide evidence from text to support understanding.

Vocabulary

presentiment (pri zen′ tə mənt) *n.* a feeling that something is about to happen; p. 197 *Although the scientists had no monitoring equipment, they had a presentiment that the volcano would soon erupt.*

equanimity (ēk′ wə nim′ ə tē) *n.* the ability to remain calm and assured; p. 197 *The equanimity of the mayor helped calm the hurricane survivors.*

fortitude (fôr′ tə tōod′) *n.* firm courage or strength of mind in the face of pain or danger; p. 197 *Relief workers often show fortitude when they aid people during a disaster.*

pandemonium (pan′ də mō′ nē əm) *n.* wild disorder and uproar; p. 199 *Pandemonium broke out as looters smashed store windows.*

tribulation (trib′ yə lā′ shən) *n.* great misery or distress; suffering; p. 203 *A natural disaster nearly always brings tribulation, but it sometimes brings people together as well.*

And of Clay Are We Created

Isabel Allende

Translated by
Margaret Sayers Peden

Volcano, 1999. Sally Elliott. Watercolor on paper, 27.9 x 38.1 cm. Private collection.

They discovered the girl's head protruding from the mudpit, eyes wide open, calling soundlessly. She had a First Communion name, Azucena.[1] Lily. In that vast cemetery where the odor of death was already attracting vultures from far away, and where the weeping of orphans and wails of the injured filled the air, the little girl obstinately clinging to life became the symbol of the tragedy.

The television cameras transmitted so often the unbearable image of the head budding like a black squash from the clay that there was no one who did not recognize her and know her name. And every time we saw her on the screen, right behind her was Rolf Carlé,[2] who had gone there on assignment, never suspecting that he would find a fragment of his past, lost thirty years before.

---

1. *Azucena* (ä zōō sē´nä)

Interpret Imagery *What mood does Allende create with the imagery in the first paragraph? Explain.*

---

2. *Rolf Carlé* (rälf cär lä´)

Life Transitions *What questions does the last sentence in this paragraph prompt for you?*

First a subterranean[3] sob rocked the cotton fields, curling them like waves of foam. Geologists had set up their seismographs[4] weeks before and knew that the mountain had awakened again. For some time they had predicted that the heat of the eruption could detach the eternal ice from the slopes of the volcano, but no one heeded their warnings; they sounded like the tales of frightened old women. The towns in the valley went about their daily life, deaf to the moaning of the earth, until that fateful Wednesday night in November when a prolonged roar announced the end of the world, and walls of snow broke loose, rolling in an avalanche of clay, stones, and water that descended on the villages and buried them beneath unfathomable[5] meters of telluric[6] vomit. As soon as the survivors emerged from the paralysis of that first awful terror, they could see that houses, plazas, churches, white cotton plantations, dark coffee forests, cattle pastures—all had disappeared. Much later, after soldiers and volunteers had arrived to rescue the living and try to assess the magnitude of the cataclysm, it was calculated that beneath the mud lay more than twenty thousand human beings and an indefinite number of animals putrefying in a viscous soup. Forests and rivers had also been swept away, and there was nothing to be seen but an immense desert of mire.[7]

When the station called before dawn, Rolf Carlé and I were together. I crawled out of bed, dazed with sleep, and went to prepare coffee while he hurriedly dressed. He stuffed his gear in the green canvas backpack he always carried, and we said goodbye, as we had so many times before. I had no **presentiments.** I sat in the kitchen, sipping my coffee and planning the long hours without him, sure that he would be back the next day.

He was one of the first to reach the scene, because while other reporters were fighting their way to the edges of that morass[8] in jeeps, bicycles, or on foot, each getting there however he could, Rolf Carlé had the advantage of the television helicopter, which flew him over the avalanche. We watched on our screens the footage captured by his assistant's camera, in which he was up to his knees in muck, a microphone in his hand, in the midst of a bedlam[9] of lost children, wounded survivors, corpses, and devastation. The story came to us in his calm voice. For years he had been a familiar figure in newscasts, reporting live at the scene of battles and catastrophes with awesome tenacity. Nothing could stop him, and I was always amazed at his **equanimity** in the face of danger and suffering; it seemed as if nothing could shake his **fortitude** or deter his curiosity. Fear

---

8. A *morass* (mə ras´) is any difficult, confused, or entangling condition or situation.
9. Here, *bedlam* refers to the noisy uproar and confusion of the situation.

Persona *Summarize what you learn about the narrator from the first sentence in this column.*

Vocabulary

presentiment (pri zen´ tə mənt) *n.* a feeling that something is about to happen

equanimity (ēk´wə nim´ ə tē) *n.* the ability to remain calm and assured

fortitude (fôr´ tə tōōd´) *n.* firm courage or strength of mind in the face of pain or danger

---

3. Something *subterranean* is beneath the earth's surface.
4. *Seismographs* are scientific instruments that record the intensity and duration of earthquakes.
5. Here, *unfathomable* (un fath´ əm ə bəl) means "immeasurable."
6. *Telluric* (te loor´ik) means "coming or rising from the earth."
7. The decaying *(putrefying)* corpses are buried in the muddy slime, a thick and syrupy *(viscous)* soup; the landscape has become a wasteland of mud *(mire)*.

Landscape (Camaldoli), 1928. Arthur Bowen Davies. Albright-Knox Art Gallery, Buffalo, NY.

__View the Art__ In this painting, the sleepy countryside of Camaldoli, Italy, sits in the shadow of an active volcano. How must the people in the story, such as Azucena, have felt the moment they realized the slumbering volcano nearby had suddenly erupted? Explain.

seemed never to touch him, although he had confessed to me that he was not a courageous man, far from it. I believe that the lens of the camera had a strange effect on him; it was as if it transported him to a different time from which he could watch events without actually participating in them. When I knew him better, I came to realize that this fictive distance seemed to protect him from his own emotions.

Rolf Carlé was in on the story of Azucena from the beginning. He filmed the volunteers who discovered her, and the first persons who tried to reach her; his camera zoomed in on the girl, her dark face, her large desolate eyes, the plastered-down tangle of her hair. The mud was like quicksand around her, and anyone attempting to reach her was in danger of sinking. They threw a rope to her that she made no effort to grasp until they shouted to her to catch it; then she pulled a hand from the mire and tried to move, but immediately sank a little deeper. Rolf threw down his knapsack and the rest of his equipment and waded into the quagmire, commenting for his assistant's microphone that it was cold and that one could begin to smell the stench of corpses.

"What's your name?" he asked the girl, and she told him her flower name. "Don't move, Azucena," Rolf Carlé directed, and kept talking to her, without a thought for what he was saying, just to distract her, while slowly he worked his way forward in mud up to his waist. The air around him seemed as murky as the mud.

It was impossible to reach her from the approach he was attempting, so he retreated and circled around where there seemed to be firmer footing. When finally he was close enough, he took the rope and tied it beneath her arms, so they could pull her out. He smiled at her with that smile that crinkles his eyes and makes him look like a little boy; he told her that everything was fine, that he was here with her now, that soon they would have her out. He signaled the others to pull, but as soon as the cord tensed, the girl screamed. They tried again, and her shoulders and arms appeared, but they could move her no farther; she was trapped. Someone suggested that her legs might be caught in the collapsed walls of her house, but she said it was not just rubble, that she was also held by the bodies of her brothers and sisters clinging to her legs.

"Don't worry, we'll get you out of here," Rolf promised. Despite the quality of the transmission, I could hear his voice break, and I loved him more than ever. Azucena looked at him, but said nothing.

> *The girl could not move, she barely could breathe, but she did not seem desperate . . .*

During those first hours Rolf Carlé exhausted all the resources of his ingenuity to rescue her. He struggled with poles and ropes, but every tug was an intolerable torture for the imprisoned girl. It occurred to him to use one of the poles as a lever but got no result and had to abandon the idea. He talked a couple of soldiers into working with him for a while, but they had to leave because so many other victims were calling for help. The girl could not move, she barely could breathe, but she did not seem desperate, as if an ancestral resignation allowed her to accept her fate. The reporter, on the other hand, was determined to snatch her from death. Someone brought him a tire, which he placed beneath her arms like a life buoy, and then laid a plank near the hole to hold his weight and allow him to stay closer to her. As it was impossible to remove the rubble blindly, he tried once or twice to dive toward her feet, but emerged frustrated, covered with mud, and spitting gravel. He concluded that he would have to have a pump to drain the water, and radioed a request for one, but received in return a message that there was no available transport and it could not be sent until the next morning.

"We can't wait that long!" Rolf Carlé shouted, but in the **pandemonium** no one stopped to commiserate.[10] Many more

---

Life Transitions *What does Azucena's idea about why she cannot move tell you about her feelings concerning the situation?*

10. No one stopped to show or express sympathy—to *commiserate* (kə miz′ ə rāt′).

Vocabulary

pandemonium (pan′ də mō′ nē əm) *n.* wild disorder and uproar hours would go by before he accepted that time had stagnated and reality had been irreparably distorted.

A military doctor came to examine the girl, and observed that her heart was functioning well and that if she did not get too cold she could survive the night.

"Hang on, Azucena, we'll have the pump tomorrow," Rolf Carlé tried to console her.

"Don't leave me alone," she begged.

"No, of course I won't leave you."

Someone brought him coffee, and he helped the girl drink it, sip by sip. The warm liquid revived her and she began telling him about her small life, about her family and her school, about how things were in that little bit of world before the volcano had erupted. She was thirteen, and she had never been outside her village. Rolf Carlé, buoyed by a premature optimism, was convinced that everything would end well: the pump would arrive, they would drain the water, move the rubble, and Azucena would be transported by helicopter to a hospital where she would recover rapidly and where he could visit her and bring her gifts. He thought, She's already too old for dolls, and I don't know what would please her; maybe a dress. I don't know much about women, he concluded, amused, reflecting that although he had known many women in his lifetime, none had taught him these details. To pass the hours he began to tell Azucena about his travels and adventures as a newshound, and when he exhausted his memory, he called upon imagination, inventing things he thought might entertain her. From time to time she dozed, but he kept talking in the darkness, to assure her that he was still there and to overcome the menace of uncertainty.

That was a long night.

Life Transitions *What is the mood at this point in the story? What hint does the author give that things are likely to change?*

Many miles away, I watched Rolf Carlé and the girl on a television screen. I could not bear the wait at home, so I went to National Television, where I often spent entire nights with Rolf editing programs. There, I was near his world, and I could at least get a feeling of what he lived through during those three decisive days. I called all the important people in the city, senators, commanders of the armed forces, the North American ambassador, and the president of National Petroleum, begging them for a pump to remove the silt, but obtained only vague promises. I began to ask for urgent help on radio and television, to see if there wasn't *someone* who could help us. Between calls I would run to the newsroom to monitor the satellite transmissions that periodically brought new details of the catastrophe. While reporters selected scenes with most impact for the news report, I searched for footage that featured Azucena's mudpit. The screen reduced the disaster to a single plane and accentuated the tremendous distance that separated me from Rolf Carlé; nonetheless, I was there with him. The child's every suffering hurt me as it did him; I felt his frustration, his impotence. Faced with the impossibility of communicating with him, the fantastic idea came to me that if I tried, I could reach him by force of mind and in that way give him encouragement. I concentrated until I was dizzy—a frenzied and futile activity. At times I would be overcome with compassion and burst out crying; at other times, I was so drained I felt as if I were staring through a telescope at the light of a star dead for a million years.

I watched that hell on the first morning broadcast, cadavers of people and animals awash in the current of new rivers formed overnight from the melted snow. Above the mud rose the tops of trees and the bell towers of a church where several people had taken refuge and were patiently awaiting rescue teams. Hundreds of soldiers and volunteers from the Civil Defense were clawing through rubble searching for survivors, while long rows of ragged specters awaited their turn for a cup of hot broth. Radio networks announced that their phones were jammed with calls from families offering shelter to orphaned children. Drinking water was in scarce supply, along with gasoline and food. Doctors, resigned to amputating arms and legs without anesthesia, pled that at least they be sent serum and painkillers and antibiotics; most of the roads, however, were impassable, and worse were the bureaucratic obstacles that stood in the way. To top it all, the clay contaminated by decomposing bodies threatened the living with an outbreak of epidemics.

"The sky is weeping," Azucena murmured . . .

Azucena was shivering inside the tire that held her above the surface. Immobility and tension had greatly weakened her, but she was conscious and could still be heard when a microphone was held out to her. Her tone was humble, as if apologizing for all the fuss. Rolf Carlé had a growth of beard, and dark circles beneath his eyes; he looked near exhaustion. Even from that enormous distance I could sense the quality of his weariness, so different from the fatigue of other adventures. He had completely forgotten the camera; he could not look at the girl through a lens any longer. The pictures we were receiving were not his assistant's but those of other reporters who had appropriated Azucena, bestowing on her the pathetic responsibility of embodying the horror[11] of what had happened in that place. With the first light Rolf tried again to dislodge the obstacles that held the girl in her tomb, but he had only his hands to work with; he did not dare use a tool for fear of injuring her. He fed Azucena a cup of the cornmeal mush and bananas the Army was distributing, but she immediately vomited it up. A doctor stated that she had a fever, but added that there was little he could do: antibiotics were being reserved for cases of gangrene. A priest also passed by and blessed her, hanging a medal of the Virgin around her neck. By evening a gentle, persistent drizzle began to fall.

"The sky is weeping," Azucena murmured, and she, too, began to cry.

"Don't be afraid," Rolf begged. "You have to keep your strength up and be calm. Everything will be fine. I'm with you, and I'll get you out somehow."

Reporters returned to photograph Azucena and ask her the same questions, which she no longer tried to answer. In the meanwhile, more television and movie teams arrived with spools of cable, tapes, film, videos, precision lenses, recorders, sound consoles, lights, reflecting screens, auxiliary motors, cartons of supplies, electricians, sound technicians, and cameramen: Azucena's face was beamed to millions of screens around the world. And all the while Rolf Carlé kept pleading for a pump.

11. *[appropriated . . . horror]* In other words, the reporters are using televised images of Azucena's situation, making her a living symbol of the tragedy.

Interpret Imagery *What do the sensory details in the first five lines of this column tell you about the scene?*

Persona *From the last paragraph on this page, how does the narrator feel about the media swarm around Azucena?*

The improved technical facilities bore results, and National Television began receiving sharper pictures and clearer sound; the distance seemed suddenly compressed, and I had the horrible sensation that Azucena and Rolf were by my side, separated from me by impenetrable glass. I was able to follow events hour by hour; I knew everything my love did to wrest the girl from her prison and help her endure her suffering; I overheard fragments of what they said to one another and could guess the rest; I was present when she taught Rolf to pray, and when he distracted her with the stories I had told him in a thousand and one nights beneath the white mosquito netting of our bed.

When darkness came on the second day, Rolf tried to sing Azucena to sleep with old Austrian folk songs he had learned from his mother, but she was far beyond sleep. They spent most of the night talking, each in a stupor of exhaustion and hunger, and shaking with cold. That night, imperceptibly, the unyielding floodgates that had contained Rolf Carlé's past for so many years began to open, and the torrent of all that had lain hidden in the deepest and most secret layers of memory poured out, leveling before it the obstacles that had blocked his consciousness for so long. He could not tell it all to Azucena; she perhaps did not know there was a world beyond the sea or time previous to her own; she was not capable of imagining Europe in the years of the war. So he could not tell her of defeat, nor of the afternoon the Russians had led them to the concentration camp to bury prisoners dead from starvation. Why should he describe to her how the naked bodies piled like a mountain of firewood resembled fragile

china? How could he tell this dying child about ovens and gallows? Nor did he mention the night that he had seen his mother naked, shod in stiletto-heeled red boots, sobbing with humiliation. There was much he did not tell, but in those hours he relived for the first time all the things his mind had tried to erase. Azucena had surrendered her fear to him and so, without wishing it, had obliged Rolf to confront his own. There, beside that hellhole of mud, it was impossible for Rolf to flee from himself any longer, and the visceral[12] terror he had lived as a boy suddenly invaded him. He reverted to the years when he was the age of Azucena, and younger, and, like her, found himself trapped in a pit without escape, buried in life, his head barely above ground; he saw before his eyes the boots and legs of his father, who had removed his belt and was whipping it in the air with the never-forgotten hiss of a viper coiled to strike. Sorrow flooded through him, intact and precise, as if it had lain always in his mind, waiting. He was once again in the armoire where his father locked him to punish him for imagined misbehavior, there where for eternal hours he had crouched with his eyes closed, not to see the darkness, with his hands over his ears, to shut out the beating of his heart, trembling, huddled like a cornered animal. Wandering in the mist of his memories he found his sister Katherina, a sweet, retarded child who spent her life hiding, with the hope that her father would forget the disgrace of her having been born. With Katherina, Rolf crawled beneath the dining room table, and with her hid there under the long

---

12. Here, *visceral* means "emotional or instinctive rather than intellectual."

Persona *What can you infer about the narrator's feelings as she witnesses the interactions between Rolf and the girl? Explain.*

Life Transitions *How are Rolf and Azucena both facing a great life transition?*

white tablecloth, two children forever embraced, alert to footsteps and voices. Katherina's scent melded with his own sweat, with aromas of cooking, garlic, soup, freshly baked bread, and the unexpected odor of putrescent clay. His sister's hand in his, her frightened breathing, her silk hair against his cheek, the candid gaze of her eyes. Katherina . . . Katherina materialized before him, floating on the air like a flag, clothed in the white tablecloth, now a winding sheet, and at last he could weep for her death and for the guilt of having abandoned her. He understood then that all his exploits as a reporter, the feats that had won him such recognition and fame, were merely an attempt to keep his most ancient fears at bay, a stratagem[13] for taking refuge behind a lens to test whether reality was more tolerable from that perspective. He took excessive risks as an exercise of courage, training by day to conquer the monsters that tormented him by night. But he had come face to face with the moment of truth; he could not continue to escape his past. He was Azucena; he was buried in the clayey mud; his terror was not the distant emotion of an almost forgotten childhood, it was a claw sunk in his throat. In the flush of his tears he saw his mother, dressed in black and clutching her imitation-crocodile pocketbook to her bosom, just as he had last seen her on the dock when she had come to put him on the boat to South America. She had not come to dry his tears, but to tell him to pick up a shovel: the war was over and now they must bury the dead.

"Don't cry. I don't hurt anymore. I'm fine," Azucena said when dawn came.

"I'm not crying for you," Rolf Carlé smiled. "I'm crying for myself. I hurt all over."

The third day in the valley of the cataclysm began with a pale light filtering through storm clouds. The President of the Republic visited the area in his tailored safari jacket to confirm that this was the worst catastrophe of the century; the country was in mourning; sister nations had offered aid; he had ordered a state of siege; the Armed Forces would be merciless, anyone caught stealing or committing other offenses would be shot on sight. He added that it was impossible to remove all the corpses or count the thousands who had disappeared; the entire valley would be declared holy ground, and bishops would come to celebrate a solemn mass for the souls of the victims. He went to the Army field tents to offer relief in the form of vague promises to crowds of the rescued, then to the improvised hospital to offer a word of encouragement to doctors and nurses worn down from so many hours of **tribulations.** Then he asked to be taken to see Azucena, the little girl the whole world had seen. He waved to her with a limp statesman's hand, and microphones recorded his emotional voice and paternal[14] tone as he told her that her courage had served as an example to the nation. Rolf Carlé interrupted to ask for a pump, and the President assured him that he personally would attend to the matter. I caught a glimpse of Rolf for a few seconds kneeling beside the mudpit. On the evening news broadcast, he was still in the same position;

---

14. Here, *paternal* means "fatherly."

Interpret Imagery *What point is the writer making by including the detail about how the president was dressed?*

Vocabulary

tribulation (trib′yə lā′shən) *n.* great misery or distress; suffering

---

13. A *stratagem* is a trick or scheme for achieving some purpose.

Country Road, 1813. Alexei Savrasov.
The State Tretyakov Gallery, Moscow, Russia.

View the Art Alexei Savrasov's landscapes, like this one that shows the aftermath of a storm, have been praised for their lyrical yet realistic depiction of the awakening of the natural world. Do you think the natural disaster in Allende's story represents total destruction, a new beginning, or some combination of the two? Explain.

and I, glued to the screen like a fortune-teller to her crystal ball, could tell that something fundamental had changed in him. I knew somehow that during the night his defenses had crumbled and he had given in to grief; finally he was vulnerable. The girl had touched a part of him that he himself had no access to, a part he had never shared with me. Rolf had wanted to console her, but it was Azucena who had given him consolation.

I recognized the precise moment at which Rolf gave up the fight and surrendered to the torture of watching the girl die. I was with them, three days and two nights, spying on them from the other side of life. I was there when she told him that in all her thirteen years no boy had ever loved her and that it was a pity to leave this world without knowing love. Rolf assured her that he loved her more than he could ever love anyone, more than he loved his mother, more than his sister, more than all the women who had slept in his arms, more than he loved me, his life companion, who would have given anything to be trapped in that well in her place, who would have exchanged her life for Azucena's, and I watched as he leaned down to kiss her poor forehead, consumed by a sweet, sad emotion he could not name. I felt how in that instant both were

saved from despair, how they were freed from the clay, how they rose above the vultures and helicopters, how together they flew above the vast swamp of corruption and laments. How, finally, they were able to accept death. Rolf Carlé prayed in silence that she would die quickly, because such pain cannot be borne.

By then I had obtained a pump and was in touch with a general who had agreed to ship it the next morning on a military cargo plane. But on the night of that third day, beneath the unblinking focus of quartz lamps and the lens of a hundred cameras, Azucena gave up, her eyes locked with those of the friend who had sustained her to the end. Rolf Carlé removed the life buoy, closed her eyelids, held her to his chest for a few moments, and then let her go. She sank slowly, a flower in the mud.

You are back with me, but you are not the same man. I often accompany you to the station and we watch the videos of Azucena again; you study them intently, looking for something you could have done to save her, something you did not think of in time. Or maybe you study them to see yourself as if in a mirror, naked. Your cameras lie forgotten in a closet; you do not write or sing; you sit long hours before the window, staring at the mountains. Beside you, I wait for you to complete the voyage into yourself, for the old wounds to heal. I know that when you return from your nightmares, we shall again walk hand in hand, as before. ∽

Life Transitions *From what you have learned about Azucena, how might she have helped Rolf make the transition to an attitude of surrender?*

Persona *What do you learn about the narrator's relationship with Rolf? Does this detail surprise you? Explain.*

Interpret Imagery *What image does Allende create at the top of this column? What does it mean?*

After You Read

Respond and Think Critically

1. **Connect to Personal Experience** Which character in the story do you admire most? Why?

2. **Explain Symbolism** What are Azucena's circumstances at the beginning of the story? What did she come to symbolize as the story progressed? ⬅️ OER

3. **Analyze Irony** Irony is a contrast between appearance and reality. What ironic situations did you notice in this story? How do you think these ironies furthered the main message of the story? Explain.

4. **Evaluate Title** What do you think the title of this story means? In your opinion, is it an appropriate title? Why or why not?

5. **Analyze Genre** One critic wrote that Allende sometimes blurs the lines between genres. She is capable of moving "between the personal and the political, between reality and fantasy." Do these observations apply to this story? Why or why not? Include evidence from the story in your answer.

6. **Big Idea** **Draw Conclusions About Characters** Rolf and Azucena experience a transition together. How do they exchange roles toward the end of the stroy? Include evidence from the story in your answer.

7. **Evaluate Cultural Context** Allende is a twentieth-century author from a non–English speaking literary tradition. Do you think that reading works by authors from this tradition expands your understanding of the world? Why or why not? Include evidence from the story in your response.

Visual Literacy

Put Events in Time Order

Make a timeline like the one below. Reread "And of Clay Are We Created," filling in the timeline as you read. Above the timeline, include external events relating to the mudslide and the rescue operation. Below the timeline, include what is happening to Rolf Carlé internally as he participates in the disaster.

External
Events

Day 1   Day 2   Day 3

Internal
Events
(for Rolf)

Group Activity Share your timeline with your classmates. Then discuss the following questions, referring to your timelines. Look back at the story to resolve any disagreements about the sequence of events.

1. Summarize the different efforts Rolf makes to save Azucena.

2. How does Rolf's attitude toward Azucena change as the story progresses? Find specific evidence from the story to support your answer.

3. Why do you think Rolf tries so hard to save Azucena? Support your answer with two or more reasons.

Literary Element — Persona

A **persona** is the person created by the author to tell a story. Adopting a persona allows an author to distance himself or herself from the reader. The attitudes and beliefs expressed by the narrator may not be the same as those of the author.

8. **Interpret Narrator** Even though Allende distances herself from the reader through a persona, her narrator is nevertheless affected by the action of the story. What consequences does the narrator face as a result of Rolf's attempt to save Azucena?

9. **Draw Conclusions About the Author** Reread the information about Isabel Allende on page 194. What do the unnamed narrator and Allende have in common? How might Allende have drawn on her own life to create both the narrator and Rolf?

10. **Evaluate Narrator** Why do you think Allende chose the persona of someone not at the scene of the action? How would the story be different if Rolf Carlé had been the narrator?

Review: Voice

As you learned on page 149, **voice** is the distinctive use of language that conveys the author's or the narrator's personality.

11. **Partner Activity** The first-person narrator of this story may be considered an unreliable—rather than objective—narrator because her feelings for Rolf affect the way she presents information. Work with a classmate to analyze her voice. Create a web diagram like the one below in which you list examples that exemplify her voice as she describes Rolf and his actions. Use the examples to describe the narrator's voice overall.

Reading Strategy — Interpret Imagery

Refer to the chart that you began on page 195 and answer the following questions.

12. Skim the story to find more sensory details to add to your chart. Make an inference about how Allende uses this sensory language to evoke emotion. Provide evidence from the story to support your answer.

13. Which image in this story provoked the strongest emotional reaction from you? What was the image's meaning? Why was it effective?

Vocabulary Practice

Practice with Analogies Choose the word that best completes each analogy.

1. ecstasy : celebrant :: tribulation :
   a. surveyor **b.** victim **c.** participant

2. hostility : unfriendliness :: pandemonium :
   a. simplicity **b.** insecurity **c.** confusion

3. fortitude : weakness :: bedlam :
   a. peace **b.** cruelty **c.** uproar

4. chance : fate :: presentiment :
   a. premonition **b.** nightmare **c.** change

5. equanimity : serenity :: obscurity :
   a. insensitivity **b.** uneasiness **c.** vagueness

Academic Vocabulary

*Allende makes a **link** between the mud or clay in which Azucena is mired and a metaphorical mud or clay out of which life is created.*

Link is an academic word. More familiar words with similar meanings are *connection*, *bond*, and *relationship*. To study this word further, fill out a graphic organizer like the one below.

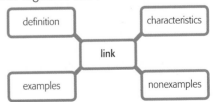

For more on academic vocabulary, see pages 36–37 and R92–R94.

Respond Through Writing

Expository Essay

TEKS

10.15.C.i–iii Write an interpretative response to an expository or a literary text that extends beyond summary and literal analysis; addresses the writing skills for an analytical essay and provides evidence from the text using embedded quotations; and analyzes the aesthetic effects of an author's use of stylistic and rhetorical devices.

Interpret Imagery "And of Clay Are We Created" relies heavily on sensory details to create aesthetic effects. In an essay, analyze how Allende uses sensory details to create powerful images in this story and interpret the nuances or ambiguity in those images. Support your ideas with evidence from the story.

Purpose and Audience Your purpose is to write an essay in which you **interpret** Allende's use of imagery—that is, use your own knowledge of the world and understanding of the text to create meaning. You will address **nuances,** or subtle distinctions and shades of meaning, and **ambiguities,** or lack of certainty that results from details that suggest unclear or contradictory interpretations. Your audience is other readers who may not agree with your interpretation.

Plan As you read, look back at the chart you made on page 195 in which you recorded sensory details. Expand or alter the chart as needed to help you interpret imagery.

Sense	Story Detail	Effect of the Image	Nuances/ Ambiguity
touch	"her silk hair against his cheek"	creates feelings of softness, closeness, intimacy	Two strangers become like father and daughter

Draft Demonstrate a clear focus by stating your thesis in the opening paragraph. Create well-organized body paragraphs by beginning each one with a topic sentence that relates to, supports, or explains your thesis. Follow the topic sentence with quoted evidence from the story. Make sure you use language that advances your purpose.

Go beyond a summary and literal analysis by following each example with your interpretation of the shades of meaning, multiple meanings, or contradictions that the quoted evidence suggests. Conclude your essay by restating your thesis in a fresh way.

Revise Exchange essays with a classmate. Identify each other's thesis statement and supporting ideas. Offer suggestions for increased, more detailed, or more specific references to the text.

Edit Edit your essay, correcting any errors in grammar, spelling, and punctuation. Use the Grammar Tip in the side column to help you use commas with relative clauses.

> **Grammar Tip**
>
> ### Commas with Adjective Clauses
>
> An **adjective clause,** also called a relative clause, is a group of words with a subject and a predicate that modifies a noun or pronoun.
>
> A nonrestrictive adjective clause is not essential to the meaning of the sentence. Nonrestrictive adjective clauses are set off with commas.
>
> *Allende's imagery, which is peppered throughout the story, is open to interpretation.*
>
> A restrictive adjective clause is essential to the meaning of the sentence. Restrictive adjective clauses are not set off with commas.
>
> *The image that gives us our first glimpse of Azucena is powerful and distressing.*

Media Workshop

Evaluate Media Messages

TEKS

For pages 209–214

10.12.A,D Evaluate how messages presented in media reflect social and cultural views in ways different from traditional texts. Evaluate changes in formality and tone within the same medium for specific audiences and purposes.

Literature Connection On November 13, 1985, the South American country of Colombia was devastated by the eruption of a long dormant volcano called Nevado del Ruiz, in the Andes Mountains. The lava from the volcano melted the mountain area's packed snow and created fast moving, fatal landslides that wiped out the small mountain town of Armero. An estimated 23,000 people were killed. Chilean-born writer Isabel Allende based her story "And of Clay Are We Created" on an actual event that occurred in the aftermath of the volcano. Because Allende's work fictionalizes a true event, she is able to fill in the emotions and thoughts of her characters without being bound by the facts of the event. Media coverage, however, is limited by the images it captures and the quotes from people involved in the event.

Media Messages

Both electronic and print media are able to present information and ideas in ways that are different from traditional texts such as books or short stories. Radio, television, CDs, DVDs, movies, documentary films, and the Internet are all **electronic media** that use sound and moving images to reach its audience. **Print media,** such as newspapers, magazines, and billboards, rely on images and text to communicate its message.

Whether print or electronic, media conveys messages about social and cultural views. When you watch a media report about an event that occurred halfway around the globe, you are being presented with a message about that culture and society. The same thing happens when you encounter a media message about people or places here in the United States—you are learning about your national culture and society.

Strategies for Evaluating Media Messages

The information you see or read in a media message is the result of someone creating that message. The media creator's viewpoints, beliefs, and sometimes biases determine what you see or hear. The message can also reflect social and cultural views beyond the creator. By examining the media images and messages you encounter, you can learn about the cultural views of a society. Refer to the chart on the next page to help you evaluate media messages.

LOG ON ▶ **Literature** Online

Media Literacy For project ideas, templates, and media analysis guides, go to glencoe.com and enter QuickPass code GL57805u1.

Strategy		Questions to Ask Yourself
cultural elements	☑	What cultural values or assumptions are being conveyed? Do we learn anything about people's beliefs? Are they stated outright in the message? Or are they evident in the images being used in the message?
social elements	☑	What do we learn about the behavior or interactions of the society? Is there information about demographics, social organization, or social movements? How are these messages transmitted in the media piece?
purpose	☑	Why was this message created? To entertain? To persuade? To inform? Are the creators focusing on any cultural elements? Are they telling us anything about the society in general?
target audience	☑	Who is this message intended to affect? How has the content been shaped to appeal to the intended audience?
message	☑	What is the primary message being communicated?
source	☑	Who created the media message? Do the creators' viewpoints or biases interfere in any way with the message? What cultural information is the source providing?
language	☑	How do the creators use language in the message? Is the language formal or informal? Does the language create a specific tone in the media piece?

Activity
Create a Chart

Use the chart on this page as a guide to evaluate how the messages in a print or online news story reflect social and cultural views in ways different from traditional texts. Create a chart with a third column in which you answer the questions in the second column.

> **Focus Lesson**

Formality and Tone

The way media messages are presented can often provide you with information about the message or the creators of the message.

Formality refers to the style of language and presentation used in a media message. In a newspaper article about a natural disaster, you will find formal, or serious, language. The same report on a TV newscast will share this style and presentation. **Informal** language and presentation is often used on late night TV talk shows as well as in lifestyle or entertainment coverage in newspapers or magazines.

Tone is the attitude the media creator has toward his or her subject. You can sometimes get a sense of the attitude behind the media message simply through the words the creators use or the way in which they speak about the subject. For example, a TV sportscaster might describe a tough home team loss as "another highlight in a season of lowlights." Depending on how the sportscaster delivers that line, it can either mean the team played a good game despite a bad season (a hopeful tone), or the team had yet another lousy performance (a sarcastic tone).

Media Impact: **Documentary Transcript**

Build Background The long-running PBS documentary program *Nova* explores social, cultural, political, and scientific subjects. The episode from which the following transcript is taken investigates the elusive science of predicting when volcanoes will erupt and examines the innovative work of a number of geologists and seismologists. Many of these scientists knew that the Nevado del Ruiz volcano was going to erupt at some point in the future, and they warned the Colombian authorities. Because the science was imprecise, however, nobody could pinpoint when the eruption would occur. The show originally aired in 2002.

Fumes continue to rise from the Nevada del Ruiz volcano nearly two weeks after it erupted.

Tone

This image creates a sense of foreboding by showing unscathed buildings in front of the still rumbling volcano.

Volcano's Deadly Warning

The greatest volcanic disaster in recent history began quietly in the winter of 1984. High in the Colombian Andes, a monstrous volcano called Nevado del Ruiz awoke, smoking and rumbling. It alarmed the local people who lived on the flanks of the mountain. They sensed danger, but no one anticipated the volcano's destructive potential.

A small team of scientists ventured to the top of the volcano to investigate. Near the summit, they encountered thick clouds of sulfurous gas. Nevado del Ruiz had come alive for the first time in over 100 years.

But would it erupt? And what would be the consequences?

At the National Library, a young scientist named Marta Calvache made a frightening discovery. She tracked down

Formality

The language the narrator uses is very precise and formal.

Activity
Listening and Speaking

Meet in small groups to discuss the following questions.

1. What is the intended purpose of this documentary?

2. What effect does switching between the narrator's formal language and the scientists' less formal language have on the viewer? What effect does the narrator's formal style have on the documentary? Support your response with text evidence.

3. What message do we get about Colombian society from this documentary and the accompanying images? Explain your answer.

Cultural Elements

Calvache provides information about the massive devastation from the volcano over 100 years ago. She also provides insight into the townspeople's attitudes toward the possible dangers.

Purpose

This aerial view is intended to give the viewer a better sense of the volcano's devastation and the amount of land that was destroyed.

manuscripts that described Ruiz's fury in the past. Centuries ago, volcanic blasts had melted the mountain's ice cap, sending torrents of mud down the valleys obliterating everything in their path.

MARTA CALVACHE (Colombian Institute of Geoscience): A lot of people died, and they describe how they died. Some of them they were in the mud. And people were not able to help them for several days, and they died there because of the lack of water and food. The details of the description were very frightening.

NARRATOR: Calvache's team drew up a hazard map showing the path of an eruption and where the melted ice and debris would surge down the mountain. The gravest threat was to the volcano's eastern flank. There, a single valley was fed by two rivers. Each of the rivers would pick up mud and rocks. Then they would meet, becoming one overwhelming deluge.

Calvache traced the path of the raging waters to a town of 28,000 people, Armero. Armero was a generally peaceful town, unaffected by the guerrilla warfare that disrupted much of Colombia. Now its townspeople were told that they risked annihilation from a volcano 40 miles away.

MARTA CALVACHE: They were saying, "That is not going to happen. It, it doesn't happen for more than 100 years. Why is it going to happen now?"

NARRATOR: It was easy to deny the mountain's violent potential. On the surface Ruiz seemed relatively calm. Only the scientists had seen, up close, the brewing inferno. And volcanoes can steam and rumble for years without exploding.

Two days after the volcano erupted, an entire town is buried under mud.

The authorities would agree to evacuate Armero only if they were told exactly when Ruiz would erupt and how serious the eruption would be. But the scientists couldn't answer either of those questions.

FERNANDO GIL (Colombian Institute of Geoscience): The volcano is incredibly complicated, and we were unable to give them a prediction. That is, we couldn't tell them how big the eruption would be, and we couldn't tell them when it would happen.

NARRATOR: The scientists feared that an evacuation, if it came at all, would come too late.

FERNANDO GIL: There was undoubtedly a great sense of doubt, a fear of not knowing what was going to happen at all. So yes, we felt impotent.

NARRATOR: In imminent danger, the town of thousands could only watch and wait. On November 13, 1985, the waiting ended.

MARTA CALVACHE: It was very, very dark. It was raining, raining very strongly. It was really especially bad weather.

NARRATOR: The storm concealed a greater threat. Forty miles away, Ruiz had erupted.

FERNANDO GIL: Around nine o'clock, when we were about to go to sleep, we began to hear sounds coming from the volcano. We went to the main door and looked towards the mountain. It was overcast, but explosions like flashes of lightning could be seen. The sound got louder, but all the time there was these muffled sounds.

NARRATOR: Hot volcanic gas was melting the ice cap, sending a torrential flood on its way down the valley. The next morning, the town of Armero was buried under six feet of mud and water, and many of its 28,000 inhabitants were missing.

MARTA CALVACHE: It was really shocking to see that. It's like, you don't realize it the first time, well, those are bodies. And then you see one and you start to distinguish, but many, many, many, many, many bodies there. I think it was—it was difficult.

NARRATOR: More than 25,000 people died. For the scientists who had foreseen the disaster, the reality was unbearable.

Language

Even though this is a news-based documentary, the creators add some drama to the story with these two lines. Notice how the short sentences add tension to the narration.

Message

By describing the scientists' reaction to the eruption, the message seems to be that the townspeople should have heeded the scientists' warnings and the scientists should have been more forceful about their warning.

Media Impact: **Newspaper Article**

Build Background Seven months after Nevado del Ruiz erupted, *The Christian Science Monitor* ran a follow-up story on what happened to the victims of the volcano and how the recovery efforts had progressed. The news story describes uneven progress. Government officials had not responded as efficiently as they could, and some Colombians not affected by the volcano were taking advantage of relief programs and resources. Citizens most affected by the disaster formed their own organizations to help speed up the recovery efforts.

from Colombia Volcano Survivors' Plight

By Clara Germani, *The Christian Science Monitor,* June 6, 1986

Though their community leaders and the Colombian government have struggled through six months of controversy over how to accommodate their needs, most of the survivors still sit dazed and displaced:

- Nearly all of them have lost part or all of their families. One man here lost 26 relatives; another has heard a brother-in-law survived, but is unsure how to find him.

- They are mostly idle, because the local agricultural economy was totally disrupted by the disaster. Those who have gone to urban areas such as Bogota, Medellin, or Cali have found their prospects dimmed by high urban unemployment.

- They've been violently separated from their past—a fact that seems amplified by their current condition. One Armero survivor offers without prompting to describe his six-mile tumble on a wave of mud and his return to find a mud flat where once thrived a town that was home to several generations of his family.

The goal of both the Colombian government and the survivor organizations established after the disaster is to channel $30 million of international aid sent here into rebuilding the region. In the meantime, they try to meet the refugees' immediate needs of food and shelter.

Resurgir, the government's relief and reconstruction agency for volcano survivors, is building 5,000 new homes on high ground in the region surrounding Armero. Half of those new homes are planned to be built here in Lerida, where 3,000 survivors are living temporarily in several camps. Rebuilding efforts are focused in this region, which has the biggest concentration of survivors.

Before You Read

Lullaby

Meet **Leslie Marmon Silko**
(born 1948)

Isuppose at the core of my writing is the attempt to identify what it is . . . to grow up neither white nor fully traditional Indian," Leslie Marmon Silko has written. Silko, who is of Laguna Pueblo, Mexican, and white descent, grew up on the Laguna Pueblo Reservation. Although her writing often focuses on Native American identity, Silko does not claim to represent Native Americans in general. Silko has written, "I am only one human being, one Laguna woman."

"I was never afraid or lonely though I was high in the hills, many miles from home—because I carried with me the feeling I'd acquired from listening to the old stories."

—Leslie Marmon Silko

Steeped in Tradition Leslie Marmon Silko was born in Albuquerque, New Mexico. Her father was a professional photographer and manager of the Marmon Trading Post in Old Laguna, the small village where Silko and her two sisters grew up. Silko's extended family contributed to the rich culture and historical legacy of Old Laguna. Silko credits her family's love of books and storytelling as being instrumental in the development of her own creativity and interest in literature. She also notes that the physical and social landscape surrounding her hometown provide the setting and background for much of her writing.

Silko attended the University of New Mexico, where she studied English and creative writing. While there, she published her first short story, "The Man to Send Rain Clouds." In 1974 she went on to publish several additional short stories in a Native American anthology, as well as *Laguna Woman*, a collection of poetry. After moving to Ketchikan, Alaska, Silko began writing the novel *Ceremony*, which was published in 1977. She later returned to the Southwest and has since published novels, poetry, and short stories.

Other Artistic Pursuits Silko has also been involved in the visual arts of filmmaking and photography and has published photographs in acclaimed arts magazines as well as in her own literary works. Her fiction and poetry collection *Storyteller*, published in 1981, features photos of her family and childhood environment. Silko founded the Laguna Film Project and filmed *Arrowboy and the Witches*, an hour-long version of her story "Estoy-eh-moot and the Kunideeyahs."

Author Search For more about Leslie Marmon Silko, go to glencoe.com and enter QuickPass code GL57805u1.

Literature and Reading Preview

Connect to the Story

Why do you think memories are so powerful? Freewrite for a few minutes about one of your fondest or strongest memories.

Build Background

"Lullaby" takes place in west central New Mexico, near the Cañoncito (Navajo) Reservation. In the 1950s, U.S. government health agencies began testing Navajos for pulmonary tuberculosis, also known as TB. Infected people were sent away—sometimes against their will—to special hospitals, called sanatoriums, for long-term care.

Set Purposes for Reading

Big Idea Life Transitions

As you read, ask yourself, How does Silko use the experiences of death, loss, and change to portray life in transition?

Literary Element Style

An author's word choice, sentence structure, and use of figurative language make up the **style** of a literary work. Style can reveal the author's purpose and attitude toward his or her subject, characters, and audience. As you read, ask yourself, How does Silko's choice and arrangement of words help her to create her particular style?

Reading Strategy Evaluate Characters

Characters are the people portrayed in a literary work. When you **evaluate characters**, you make judgments or form opinions about them. Such evaluations help the reader develop a framework for explaining a character's actions, statements, thoughts, and feelings. As you read, ask yourself, Where does Silko provide opportunities for the reader to evaluate different characters?

....

Tip: Ask Questions Fill in a chart like the one shown with details from the story that help you form opinions about Ayah. Use the blue highlighted passages and questions to help you get started.

Detail	Opinion About Ayah
"She smiled at the snow which was trying to cover her little by little."	She is at home in nature.

TEKS

For pages 215–227

10.5 Understand, make inferences and draw conclusions about the structure and elements of fiction and provide evidence from text to support understanding.

Vocabulary

arroyo (ə roi′ ō) *n.* a dry gully or stream bed; p. 218 *The thirsty horse did not find water as it cantered along the arroyo.*

crevice (krev′ is) *n.* a narrow crack into or through something; p. 221 *Mark watched his father fill in the crevice in the wall.*

sparse (spärs) *adj.* thinly spread or distributed; p. 224 *The berries were so sparse that we could not gather enough to make a pie.*

distortion (dis tôr′ shən) *n.* an appearance of being twisted or bent out of shape; p. 225 *The crack in the mirror caused a distortion in my reflection.*

Lullaby

Leslie Marmon Silko

Owl Watching Over Wildlife. Stephan Daigle.

The sun had gone down but the snow in the wind gave off its own light. It came in thick tufts like new wool—washed before the weaver spins it. Ayah[1] reached out for it like her own babies had, and she smiled when she remembered how she had laughed at them. She was an old woman now, and her life had become memories. She sat down with her back against the wide cottonwood tree, feeling the rough bark on her back bones; she faced east and listened to the wind and snow sing a high-pitched Yeibechei[2] song. Out of the wind she felt warmer, and she could watch the wide fluffy snow fill in her tracks, steadily, until the direction she had come from was gone. By the light of the snow she could see the dark outline of the big **arroyo** a few feet away. She was sitting on the edge of Cebolleta[3] Creek, where in the springtime the thin cows would graze on grass already chewed flat to the ground. In the wide deep creek bed where only a trickle of water flowed in the summer, the skinny cows would wander, looking for new grass along winding paths splashed with manure.

Ayah pulled the old Army blanket over her head like a shawl. Jimmie's blanket—the one he had sent to her. That was a long time ago and the green wool was faded, and it was unraveling on the edges. She did not want to think about Jimmie. So she thought about the weaving and the way her mother had done it. On the tall wooden loom set into the sand under a tamarack[4] tree for shade. She could see it clearly. She had been only a little girl when her grandma gave her the wooden combs to pull the twigs and burrs from the raw, freshly washed wool. And while she combed the wool, her grandma sat beside her, spinning a silvery strand of yarn around the smooth cedar spindle. Her mother worked at the loom with yarns dyed bright yellow and red and gold. She watched them dye the yarn in boiling black pots full of beeweed petals, juniper berries, and sage. The blankets her mother made were soft and woven so tight that rain rolled off them like birds' feathers. Ayah remembered sleeping warm on cold windy nights, wrapped in her mother's blankets on the hogan's[5] sandy floor.

The snow drifted now, with the northwest wind hurling it in gusts. It drifted up around her black overshoes—old ones with little metal buckles. She smiled at the snow which was trying to cover her little by little. She could remember when they had no black rubber overshoes; only the high buckskin leggings that they wrapped over their elkhide moccasins. If the snow was dry or frozen, a person could walk all day and not get wet; and in the evenings the beams of the ceiling would hang with lengths of pale buckskin leggings, drying out slowly.

Visual Vocabulary
In yarn-making, the *spindle* is a round, tapered stick that is turned by hand to twist wool fibers into a thread of yarn.

---

1. *Ayah* (ä´yə)
2. The *Yeibechei* (yä´bə chā) are masked Navajo dancers who sing in high-pitched voices.
3. *Cebolleta* (se´bō yā´tä) is also the name of a town in the story.

Evaluate Characters *What does this sentence reveal about Ayah?*

Vocabulary

arroyo (ə roi´ ō) *n.* a dry gully or stream bed

---

4. *Tamarack* is another name for larch, a tree in the pine family.
5. A *hogan* is a traditional Navajo dwelling made of wood and covered with earth.

She felt peaceful remembering. She didn't feel cold any more. Jimmie's blanket seemed warmer than it had ever been. And she could remember the morning he was born. She could remember whispering to her mother, who was sleeping on the other side of the hogan, to tell her it was time now. She did not want to wake the others. The second time she called to her, her mother stood up and pulled on her shoes; she knew. They walked to the old stone hogan together, Ayah walking a step behind her mother. She waited alone, learning the rhythms of the pains while her mother went to call the old woman to help them. The morning was already warm even before dawn and Ayah smelled the bee flowers blooming and the young willow growing at the springs. She could remember that so clearly, but his birth merged into the births of the other children and to her it became all the same birth. They named him for the summer morning and in English they called him Jimmie.

It wasn't like Jimmie died. He just never came back, and one day a dark blue sedan with white writing on its doors pulled up in front of the boxcar shack where the rancher let the Indians live. A man in a khaki uniform trimmed in gold gave them a yellow piece of paper and told them that Jimmie was dead. He said the Army would try to get the body back and then it would be shipped to them; but it wasn't likely because the helicopter had burned after it crashed. All of this was told to Chato[6] because he could understand English. She stood inside the doorway holding the baby while Chato listened. Chato spoke English like a white man and he spoke Spanish too. He was taller than the white man and he stood straighter too. Chato didn't explain why; he just told the military man they could keep the body if they found it. The white man looked bewildered; he nodded his head and he left. Then Chato looked at her and shook his head, and then he told her, "Jimmie isn't coming home anymore," and when he spoke, he used the words to speak of the dead. She didn't cry then, but she hurt inside with anger. And she mourned him as the years passed, when a horse fell with Chato and broke his leg, and the white rancher told them he wouldn't pay Chato until he could work again. She mourned Jimmie because he would have worked for his father then; he would have saddled the big bay[7] horse and ridden the fence lines each day, with wire cutters and heavy gloves, fixing the breaks in the barbed wire and putting the stray cattle back inside again.

She mourned him after the white doctors came to take Danny and Ella away. She was at the shack alone that day they came. It was back in the days before they hired Navajo women to go with them as interpreters. She recognized one of the doctors. She had seen him at the children's clinic at Cañoncito[8] about a month ago. They were wearing khaki uniforms and they waved papers at her and a black ball-point pen, trying to make her understand their English words. She was frightened by the way they looked at the children, like the lizard watches the fly. Danny was swinging on the tire swing on the elm tree behind the rancher's house, and Ella was toddling around the front door, dragging the broomstick horse Chato made for her. Ayah could see they wanted her to sign the papers, and Chato had taught her to sign her name. It

---

6. *Chato* (chä ′ tō)

Evaluate Characters *What does this detail tell you about Chato?*

---

7. Here, *bay* is the horse's color—a reddish brown.
8. *Cañoncito* (kän′ yōn sē′ tō) is the name of the Navajo reservation located in west central New Mexico.

Style *What does this simile mean?*

LESLIE MARMON SILKO **219**

was something she was proud of. She only wanted them to go, and to take their eyes away from her children.

She took the pen from the man without looking at his face and she signed the papers in three different places he pointed to. She stared at the ground by their feet and waited for them to leave. But they stood there and began to point and gesture at the children. Danny stopped swinging. Ayah could see his fear. She moved suddenly and grabbed Ella into her arms; the child squirmed, trying to get back to her toys. Ayah ran with the baby toward Danny; she screamed for him to run and then she grabbed him around his chest and carried him too. She ran south into the foothills of juniper trees and black lava rock. Behind her she heard the doctors running,

Visual Vocabulary
A *cholla* (choi′ ə) is a spiny, shrubby, or treelike cactus.

but they had been taken by surprise, and as the hills became steeper and the cholla cactus were thicker, they stopped. When she reached the top of the hill, she stopped to listen in case they were circling around her. But in a few minutes she heard a car engine start and they drove away. The children had been too surprised to cry while she ran with them. Danny was shaking and Ella's little fingers were gripping Ayah's blouse.

She stayed up in the hills for the rest of the day, sitting on a black lava boulder in the sunshine where she could see for miles all around her. The sky was light blue and cloudless, and it was warm for late April. The sun warmth relaxed her and took the fear and anger away. She lay back on the rock and watched the sky. It seemed to her that she could walk into the sky, stepping through clouds endlessly. Danny played

with little pebbles and stones, pretending they were birds' eggs and then little rabbits. Ella sat at her feet and dropped fistfuls of dirt into the breeze, watching the dust and particles of sand intently. Ayah watched a hawk soar high above them, dark wings gliding; hunting or only watching, she did not know. The hawk was patient and he circled all afternoon before he disappeared around the high volcanic peak the Mexicans called Guadalupe.[9]

Late in the afternoon, Ayah looked down at the gray boxcar shack with the paint all peeled from the wood; the stove pipe on the roof was rusted and crooked. The fire she had built that morning in the oil drum stove had burned out. Ella was asleep in her lap now and Danny sat close to her, complaining that he was hungry; he asked when they would go to the house. "We will stay up here until your father comes," she told him, "because those white men were chasing us." The boy remembered then and he nodded at her silently.

If Jimmie had been there he could have read those papers and explained to her what they said. Ayah would have known then, never to sign them. The doctors came back the next day and they brought a BIA[10] policeman with them. They told Chato they had her signature and that was all they needed. Except for the kids. She listened to Chato sullenly; she hated him when he told her it was the old woman who died in the winter, spitting blood; it was her old grandma who had given the children this disease. "They don't spit blood," she said coldly. "The whites lie."

---

9. *Guadalupe* (gwä′ dä loo′ pä)
10. The Bureau of Indian Affairs, or *BIA*, is the federal agency in charge of administering government policies toward Native Americans.

Life Transitions *Why do you think Ayah remembers even the smallest details of this day?*

Monument Valley at Sunset. Robert McIntosh.

View the Art Monument Valley is located on the Navajo reservation on the border of southern Utah and northern Arizona. Where in the story does Silko describe a setting or time that corresponds with the image in the painting?

She held Ella and Danny close to her, ready to run to the hills again. "I want a medicine man first," she said to Chato, not looking at him. He shook his head. "It's too late now. The policeman is with them. You signed the paper." His voice was gentle.

It was worse than if they had died: to lose the children and to know that somewhere, in a place called Colorado, in a place full of sick and dying strangers, her children were without her. There had been babies that died soon after they were born, and one that died before he could walk. She had carried them herself, up to the boulders and great pieces of the cliff that long ago crashed down from Long Mesa; she laid them in the **crevices** of sandstone and buried them in fine brown sand with round quartz pebbles that washed down the hills in the rain. She had endured it because they had been with her. But she could not bear this pain. She did not sleep for a long time after they took her children. She stayed on the hill where they had fled the first time, and she slept rolled up in the blanket Jimmie had sent her. She carried the pain in her belly and it was fed by everything she saw: the blue sky of their last day together and the dust and pebbles they played with; the swing in the elm tree and broomstick horse choked life from her. The pain filled her stomach and there was no room for food or for her lungs to fill with air. The air and the food would have been theirs.

Evaluate Characters *What is your opinion of Chato based on his reaction?*

Vocabulary

crevice (krev′ is) *n.* a narrow crack into or through something

Life Transitions *Why is the absence of Danny and Ella more upsetting to Ayah than the deaths of her other children?*

Style *How does the author describe Ayah's feelings after losing her children?*

She hated Chato, not because he let the policeman and doctors put the screaming children in the government car, but because he had taught her to sign her name. Because it was like the old ones always told her about learning their language or any of their ways: it endangered you. She slept alone on the hill until the middle of November when the first snows came. Then she made a bed for herself where the children had slept. She did not lie down beside Chato again until many years later, when he was sick and shivering and only her body could keep him warm. The illness came after the white rancher told Chato he was too old to work for him anymore, and Chato and his old woman should be out of the shack by the next afternoon because the rancher had hired new people to work there. That had satisfied her. To see how the white man repaid Chato's years of loyalty and work. All of Chato's fine-sounding English talk didn't change things.

It snowed steadily and the luminous light from the snow gradually diminished into the darkness. Somewhere in Cebolleta a dog barked and other village dogs joined with it. Ayah looked in the direction she had come, from the bar where Chato was buying the wine. Sometimes he told her to go on ahead and wait; and then he never came. And when she finally went back looking for him, she would find him passed out at the bottom of the wooden steps to Azzie's Bar. All the wine would be gone and most of the money too, from the pale blue check that came to them once a month in a government envelope. It was then that she would look at his face and his hands, scarred by ropes and the barbed wire of all those years, and she would think, this man is a stranger; for forty years she had smiled at him and cooked his food, but he remained a stranger. She stood

up again, with the snow almost to her knees, and she walked back to find Chato.

It was hard to walk in the deep snow and she felt the air burn in her lungs. She stopped a short distance from the bar to rest and readjust the blanket. But this time he wasn't waiting for her on the bottom step with his old Stetson hat pulled down and his shoulders hunched up in his long wool overcoat.

She was careful not to slip on the wooden steps. When she pushed the door open, warm air and cigarette smoke hit her face. She looked around slowly and deliberately, in every corner, in every dark place that the old man might find to sleep. The bar owner didn't like Indians in there, especially Navajos, but he let Chato come in because he could talk Spanish like he was one of them. The men at the bar stared at her, and the bartender saw that she left the door open wide. Snowflakes were flying inside like moths and melting into a puddle on the oiled wood floor. He motioned to her to close the door, but she did not see him. She held herself straight and walked across the room slowly, searching the room with every step. The snow in her hair melted and she could feel it on her forehead. At the far corner of the room, she saw red flames at the :mica: window of the old stove door; she looked behind the stove just to make sure. The bar got quiet except for the Spanish polka music playing on the jukebox. She stood by the stove and shook the snow from her blanket and held it near the stove to dry. The wet wool smell reminded her of newborn goats in early March, brought inside to warm near the fire. She felt calm.

Visual Vocabulary
Mica is a mineral (abundant in New Mexico) that can be split into thin, strong, flexible sheets. A sheet of colorless mica makes a decent, inexpensive substitute for glass.

Vision Quest, 1999. John Newcomb.
Acrylic on canvas. Private collection.

View the Art A vision quest is a Native American ritual in which the participant, usually an adolescent boy, seeks spiritual power and knowledge by communing with a guardian spirit animal through prayer, fasting, isolation, or other means. How might Ayah's story be a sort of vision quest?

In past years they would have told her to get out. But her hair was white now and her face was wrinkled. They looked at her like she was a spider crawling slowly across the room. They were afraid; she could feel the fear. She looked at their faces steadily. They reminded her of the first time the white people brought her children back to her that winter. Danny had been shy and hid behind the thin white woman who brought them. And the baby had not known her until Ayah took her into her arms, and then Ella had nuzzled close to her as she had when she was nursing. The blonde woman was nervous and kept looking at a dainty gold watch on her wrist. She sat on the bench near the small window and watched the dark snow clouds gather around the mountains; she was worrying about the unpaved road. She was frightened by what she saw inside too: the strips of venison drying on a rope across the ceiling and the children jabbering excitedly in a language she did not know. So they stayed for only a few hours. Ayah watched the government car disappear down the road and she knew they were already being weaned from these lava hills and from this sky. The last time they came was in early June, and Ella stared at her the way the men in the bar were now staring. Ayah did not try to pick her up; she smiled at her instead and spoke cheer-

Life Transitions *What does the author mean by this statement?*

fully to Danny. When he tried to answer her, he could not seem to remember and he spoke English words with the Navajo. But he gave her a scrap of paper that he had found somewhere and carried in his pocket; it was folded in half, and he shyly looked up at her and said it was a bird. She asked Chato if they were home for good this time. He spoke to the white woman and she shook her head. "How much longer?" he asked, and she said she didn't know; but Chato saw how she stared at the boxcar shack. Ayah turned away then. She did not say good-bye.

She felt satisfied that the men in the bar feared her. Maybe it was her face and the way she held her mouth with teeth clenched tight, like there was nothing any-one could do to her now. She walked north down the road, searching for the old man. She did this because she had the blanket, and there would be no place for him except with her and the blanket in the old adobe barn near the arroyo. They always slept there when they came to Cebolleta. If the money and the wine were gone, she would be relieved because then they could go home again: back to the old hogan with a dirt roof and rock walls where she herself had been born. And the next day the old man could go back to the few sheep they still had, to follow along behind them, guiding them, into dry sandy arroyos where **sparse** grass grew. She knew he did not like walking behind old ewes when for so many years he rode big quarter horses and worked with cattle. But she wasn't sorry for him; he should have known all along what would happen.

There had not been enough rain for their garden in five years; and that was when Chato finally hitched a ride into the town and brought back brown boxes of rice and sugar and big tin cans of wel-fare[11] peaches. After that, at the first of the month they went to Cebolleta to ask the postmaster for the check; and then Chato would go to the bar and cash it. They did this as they planted the garden every May, not because anything would survive the summer dust, but because it was time to do this. The journey passed the days that smelled silent and dry like the caves above the canyon with yellow painted buffaloes on their walls.

He was walking along the pavement when she found him. He did not stop or turn around when he heard her behind him. She walked beside him and she noticed how slowly he moved now. He smelled strong of woodsmoke and urine. Lately he had been forgetting. Sometimes he called her by his sister's name and she had been gone for a long time. Once she had found him wandering on the road to the white man's ranch, and she asked him why he was going that way; he laughed at her and said, "You know they can't run that ranch without me," and he walked on deter-mined, limping on the leg that had been crushed many years before. Now he looked at her curiously, as if for the first time, but he kept shuffling along, moving slowly along the side of the highway. His gray hair had grown long and spread out on the shoulders of the long overcoat. He wore the old felt hat pulled down over his ears. His boots were worn out at the toes and he had stuffed pieces of an old red shirt in the holes. The rags made his feet

---

11. The canned peaches came from a government *welfare* program to help needy people.

Style *What does this description say about Ayah's and Chato's lives?*

Vocabulary

sparse (spärs) *adj.* thinly spread or distributed

look like little animals up to their ears in snow. She laughed at his feet; the snow muffled the sound of her laugh. He stopped and looked at her again. The wind had quit blowing and the snow was falling straight down; the southeast sky was beginning to clear and Ayah could see a star.

"Let's rest awhile," she said to him. They walked away from the road and up the slope to the giant boulders that had tumbled down from the red sandrock mesa throughout the centuries of rainstorms and earth tremors. In a place where the boulders shut out the wind, they sat down with their backs against the rock. She offered half of the blanket to him and they sat wrapped together.

The storm passed swiftly. The clouds moved east. They were massive and full, crowding together across the sky. She watched them with the feeling of horses— steely blue-gray horses startled across the sky. The powerful haunches pushed into the distances and the tail hairs streamed white mist behind them. The sky cleared. Ayah saw that there was nothing between her and the stars. The light was crystalline.[12] There was no shimmer, no **distortion** through earth haze. She breathed the clarity of the night sky; she smelled the purity of the half moon and the stars. He was lying on his side with his knees pulled up near his belly for warmth. His eyes were closed now, and in the light from the stars and the moon, he looked young again.

She could see it descend out of the night sky: an icy stillness from the edge of the thin moon. She recognized the freezing. It came gradually, sinking snowflake by snowflake until the crust was heavy and deep. It had the strength of the stars in Orion, and its journey was endless. Ayah knew that with the wine he would sleep. He would not feel it. She tucked the blanket around him, remembering how it was when Ella had been with her; and she felt the rush so big inside her heart for the babies. And she sang the only song she knew to sing for babies. She could not remember if she had ever sung it to her children, but she knew that her grandmother had sung it and her mother had sung it:

Visual Vocabulary
The constellation *Orion* contains two of the brightest stars in the sky. In Greek mythology, Orion is traditionally depicted as a hunter wearing a belt with a sword at his side.

> The earth is your mother,
>   she holds you.
> The sky is your father,
>   he protects you.
> Sleep,
> sleep.
> Rainbow is your sister,
>   she loves you.
> The winds are your brothers,
>   they sing to you.
> Sleep,
> sleep.
> We are together always
> We are together always
> There never was a time
> when this
> was not so. ❧

---

12. Here, *crystalline* means "clear and pure as a crystal."

Evaluate Characters *Do Ayah's actions indicate that she has forgiven Chato? Explain.*

Life Transitions *Why do you think Ayah finds the lullaby comforting?*

After You Read

Respond and Think Critically

1. **Connect to Personal Experience** For which character did you have more sympathy, Ayah or Chato? Explain.

2. **Interpret Flashback** In the first three paragraphs of the story, what reminds Ayah of events in the past? Why might Ayah's thoughts turn so often to the past?

3. **Interpret Events** Why does Chato react as he does when the white doctors come to take Danny and Ella? Could Chato and Ayah have done anything to prevent the doctors from taking their children? Explain.

4. **Make Inferences About Attitudes** In your opinion, how does Ayah feel about her husband? Support your response with evidence from the story.

5. **Analyze Character** When Ayah finally finds Chato near the end of the story, how does he look and act? What do Chato's appearance and actions reveal about him?

6. **Make Inferences About Events** What do you think happens to Chato at the end of the story? Support your response with text evidence.

7. **Make Inferences About Title** Why do you think the author chose to title this story "Lullaby"?

8. **Big Idea** **Draw Conclusions About Characters** Think about the many obstacles and tragedies that have shaped Ayah's and Chato's transitions in life. Have they triumphed over adversity, or has it defeated them? Explain.

Literary Element | Style

 Texas Test Practice (10.5)

1. What idea does Silko introduce in the opening three sentences (page 218) that she continues to use as a motif throughout the story?

   (A) sunlight and darkness
   (B) laughter and play
   (C) snow and rain
   (D) sheep and wool
   (E) weaving and blankets

2. In the last prose paragraph of the story (page 225) Silko speaks of "the freezing," by which she means

   (A) extreme cold
   (B) the past
   (C) a deep sleep
   (D) death
   (E) Ayah's lost children

Review: Narrator

As you learned on pages 148–149, the narrator is the person who tells a story.

9. **Partner Activity** With a classmate, discuss the narrator's role in this story. Create a graphic organizer like the one below to help you think about the narrator's relationship to the main characters. Then answer the questions.

- What is the narrator's relationship to the characters in the story? Give reasons for your answer.

- How would the story be different if Ayah were the narrator? If Chato were the narrator? Do you think Silko made the best choice of narrator for this story? Explain.

Reading Strategy — Evaluate Characters

When you **evaluate characters,** you form opinions and make judgments about them. Review the blue highlighted passages and questions and your chart from page 216 to help you answer the following questions.

10. What is your opinion of Ayah? Give three details from the story to provide support for your answer.

11. How does your opinion of Ayah affect your enjoyment of the story? Explain.

Vocabulary Practice

Practice with Word Origins Studying the etymology, or origin and history, of a word can help you better understand and explore its meaning. Create a word map like the one below for each of these vocabulary words from the story.

arroyo   crevice   sparse   distortion

EXAMPLE

Definition
moving from place to place

Etymology
Latin *migrare* means "to move"

migratory

Sample sentence
Each year, flocks of migratory birds pass over our home on their way to their winter home.

Academic Vocabulary

*The Bureau of Indian Affairs is an agency of the **federal** government.*

Federal is an academic word. It applies specifically to a government in which states have individual powers but are governed collectively by a central authority. *Federal* is also often used to refer to anything related to or organized by the national, rather than state, government. Complete this sentence starter: Mr. Michaelson voted for **federal** _____ because _____.

For more on academic vocabulary, see pages 36–37 and R92–R94.

Enrich and Extend

 Speaking and Listening

Performance With a partner, write a dialogue that might take place between Ayah and a dear friend. Perform it for the class.

Prepare Write a dialogue that reflects one or more parts of Ayah's life and involves a sympathetic listener. Rehearse it until you are sure your dialogue and performance accurately and sympathetically convey Ayah's personality and perspective.

Perform As you perform, strive to re-create the tone you hear as you read. Vary your volume and pitch according to the meaning you want to convey, use gestures and body language that complement your dialogue, and adopt the postures of two friends who are earnestly engaged in each other's thoughts. Monitor the effect of your dialogue on your audience, and adjust as needed:

If the audience is—	then—
looking away	make eye contact with them
doodling or fidgeting	bring up the volume, or make a dramatic change in posture or gestures
straining to follow or understand	slow down the pace, or speak more clearly

Evaluate After the performance, decide with your partner how successful your performance was and how it might have been better. In your evaluation, consider how style and content of spoken language varies in different contexts and influences the listener's understanding.

TEKS

For pages 228–235

10.14.A Write an engaging story with a well-developed conflict and resolution, interesting and believable characters, a range of literary strategies (e.g., dialogue, suspense) and devices to enhance the plot, and sensory details that define the mood or tone.

Planning Checklist

Your personal narrative should include the following traits:

☑ an engaging opening that captures the reader's interest

☑ dialogue, as appropriate, that reflects the thoughts and personalities of the people described in the narrative

☑ sensory details and figurative language that enable the reader to sense the mood and tone

☑ chronological organization that presents the sequence of events clearly

☑ an ending that shows the significance of the narrative to the writer

Scoring Rubric

Check the Literary Texts Scoring Rubric on page R28 for more guidance on crafting your best story.

Writing Workshop

Personal Narrative

Literature Connection: Throughout recorded history, personal narratives have been a staple of every culture's literature. When people describe events they were a part of, they're not just writing personal stories; they are also conveying a sense of what their world was like at a particular time and place.

Purpose: Your purpose for writing a personal narrative is to tell an engaging story that explores the meaning and effect of a personal observation or experience.

Audience: You will be submitting your narrative to an online anthology titled *Our Times, Our Stories.* Think about how you might illustrate your narrative to add meaning for the reader. Also, consider using links to offer readers more information about certain aspects of your narrative.

Choose Your Topic

Option A: Choose a Prompt

1. Write a personal narrative about an experience that made you realize, for the first time, that you were no longer a child.

2. Write a personal narrative about some aspect of family life that has a special place in your memories.

Option B: Write a Prompt

Write a personal narrative about a day when _____ and how that experience _____.

Sample Prompt:

Write a personal narrative about a day when you conquered a fear you had since childhood and how that experience made you a stronger, wiser person.

Analyze a Professional Model

Read for Guidance Read the following excerpt from a personal narrative by poet Joy Harjo. The notes in the side column point out traits that make this narrative interesting and effective. When you are drafting your narrative, consider applying these techniques to your writing.

from *"Suspended"* by Joy Harjo

Once I was so small that I could barely peer over the top of the backseat of the black Cadillac my father polished and tuned daily; I wanted to see everything. It was around the time I acquired language, or even before that time, when something happened that changed my relationship to the spin of the world. My concept of language, of what was possible with music was changed by this revelatory moment. It changed even the way I looked at the sun. . . . We were driving somewhere in Tulsa, the northern border of the Creek Nation. I don't know where we were going or where we had been, but I know the sun was boiling the asphalt, the car windows open for any breeze as I stood on tiptoes on the floorboard behind my father, a handsome god who smelled of Old Spice, whose slick black hair was always impeccably groomed, his clothes perfectly creased and ironed. The radio was on. I loved the radio, jukeboxes or any magic thing containing music even then….

I became acutely aware of the line the jazz trumpeter was playing (a sound I later associated with Miles Davis). I didn't know the word jazz or trumpet, or the concepts. I don't know how to say it, with what sounds or words, but in that confluence of hot southern afternoon, in the breeze of aftershave and humidity, I followed that sound to the beginning, to the place of the birth of sound….

I recognized it, that humid afternoon in my formative years, as a way to speak beyond the confines of ordinary language. I still hear it.

Engaging Opening
The narrative opens with the author revealing personal details about herself.

Significance
The author hints at why this experience was significant to her.

Sensory Details
The sensory details in this description convey the mood of the car ride.

Ending
The last two sentences of the narrative fully explain the significance of the author's experience.

PLAN Your Narrative

Key Trait Ideas Writing a personal narrative allows you to explore an idea or an event in your past and analyze how it has contributed to who you are today. To plan your narrative, look for depth in your experiences that you may not have noticed while the events were taking place.

▶ Step 1: Make a Time Frame

A time frame can help you explore experiences from different times of your life and come up with a topic for your narrative.

0 to 5 years old	my first day in preschool
5 to 10 years old	the day my grandma died
10 to 15 years old	a school trip to the Center for Great Apes
Present	trying out for the soccer team

▶ Step 2: Gather Details

Use a cluster diagram to help you recall all of the essential details of the experience you'll be writing about.

▶ Step 3: Freewrite to Explore Meaning

Freewriting can help you to express the significance of your experience more clearly.

I liked going to zoos when I was a kid. Seeing all the different animals. The trip to the Center was different. These apes had been used by people for their own purposes. Some had been harmed. I remember one of the chimps made a mask out of a paper bag and passed it to a visitor. Then she made a second mask so she and the visitor could look at each other through their masks. My eyes teared up. The chimp was playing a game with the visitor!

Conduct an Interview

If you're having trouble developing your topic, you may want to find a new one. The planning stage is not a time for just developing ideas. It is also a time for finding out whether ideas for writing will actually work. For new material, try interviewing family members about stories that come to mind when they think about you as a child.

Writing and Research For planning, drafting, and revising tools, go to glencoe.com and enter QuickPass code GL57805u1.

DRAFT Your Narrative

Key Traits Organization and Word Choice Typically, narratives with more details are more interesting because the reader can easily imagine things as they happened to you. Organize your events and details so they have the greatest impact on your reader.

▶ Step 1: Focus on Sensory Details

Sensory details appeal to the five senses: sight, sound, smell, taste, and touch. Such details help you to re-create an experience for your readers.

Sight:

> The thirty-foot-high domed enclosures surrounded by guava, banana, and other tropical trees . . . .

Sound:

> The guide began to drone . . . .

▶ Step 2: Make a Plan

Group the events that will make up your narrative so that it has a clear beginning, middle, and end.

Beginning	Middle	End
trip announcement	We arrive.	Mrs. Dagostino reads my report to the class.
I couldn't care less.	I'm bored.	
	We start observing the chimps.	I join a summer program on great apes.
	I see the game the chimp is playing with the visitor.	I hope to study primates in college.
	I'm moved to tears.	

▶ Step 3: Include Strong Dialogue

Dialogue can reveal characters' personalities, move the plot along, and help you to re-create events.

> "Tomorrow," Mrs. Dagostino announced enthusiastically, "we'll be visiting the Center for Great Apes." She continued brightly, "This is a very special opportunity for us. Not many people are allowed to visit, you know! I've waited two years to take a class there!"

Drafting Checklist

Your narrative should include the following traits:

- ☑ a clear beginning, middle, and ending
- ☑ chronological organization
- ☑ effective sensory details
- ☑ a statement of the significance of the experience

Changed by a Chimp

"Tomorrow," Mrs. Dagostino announced enthusiastically, "we'll be visiting the Center for Great Apes." She continued brightly, "This is a very special opportunity for us. Not many people are allowed to visit, you know! I've waited two years to take a class there!"

"Who cares?" I thought. I wasn't the least bit interested in looking at a bunch of old chimps. Mrs. Dagostino then explained that this was a place for "retired" chimps—chimps that had been used in entertainment and research and were now no longer useful. "A retirement home for chimps," I groaned. "How ridiculous!"

When we arrived, the guide began to drone about "special enriching environments" and "complex primates." With glazed eyes, I shifted from foot to foot and daydreamed. The thirty-foot-high domed enclosures surrounded by guava, banana, and other tropical trees were about as interesting to me as twelve extra pages of math homework.

When we were finally allowed to walk around the perimeter of the chimps' enclosure, some students stopped to do what we had been instructed to do: observe the chimps' behaviors, take notes, and discuss what we saw. I noticed a chimp that seemed to be communicating with two adult visitors. The chimp picked up a brown bag that had been left in its enclosure and tore the bag into a piece of paper about six inches by eight inches long. Then he tore an opening in one end. When he held the paper up to his face, I realized that he had created a mask. One of the visitors brought her hand to her mouth and closed her eyes. I knew that she had experienced what I had at that moment: the animal behind the fence was, in some way, speaking to us.

The chimp handed the mask through the fence to the visitors and then made a second mask. In a few minutes, the visitors and the chimp were looking at each other through these torn bags. They were also, I understood, silently communicating. I just stood there thinking what it must be like for this "complex primate" to be used for research purposes or to live its life in any enclosure—even one as nice as the one provided by the Center for Great Apes. It was a moving realization.

Three days later, Mrs. Dagostino read my report on the Center for Great Apes aloud to the class. The following summer, I enrolled in a summer program that focused on chimpanzees and orangutans. And next year, when I apply to college, I will look for a school where I can study primates. Whatever chimps may have to tell us, I plan on finding out.

Chronological Organization

The sequence of events in this paragraph allows the reader to see the action just as it unfolded that day.

Transitions

Transitional words and phrases, such as "Three days later . . . ," reinforce the organizational structure.

Significance

The writer's reflections reveal the significance of the event in his life.

Your Turn

Using your organizational plan and the details of your experience, write the first draft of your personal narrative.

REVISE Your Narrative

Key Traits Voice and Word Choice Consider whether you are addressing your purpose and audience in your narrative. Are you providing your readers with the experience you want them to have? Experiment with your word choice and sentence structure to keep your writing lively and engaging.

Revising Checklist

Before you start your revision, ask yourself these questions:

- ☑ Does my narrative have a clear beginning, middle, and end?

- ☑ Have I organized my narrative chronologically so that the sequence of events is clear?

- ☑ Have I included sensory details to bring the narrative to life for my readers?

- ☑ Have I included the traits in the planning and drafting checklists (pages 228 and 231)?

- ☑ Have I clearly stated the significance of the experience to me?

▶ Step 1: Focus on the Details

Do your details create a mood for your story? Vibrant details enhance the reading experience, enabling your audience to see what you saw, hear what you heard, and sense the overall mood of the setting.

Original:

> The enclosures, surrounded by trees, were about as interesting to me as twelve extra pages of math homework.

Revision:

> The thirty-foot-high domed enclosures surrounded by guava, banana, and other tropical trees were about as interesting to me as twelve extra pages of math homework.

▶ Step 2: Strengthen Your Transitions

Do you use transitions to guide the reader through your experience? Add transitional words and phrases, such as *next, later that day,* and *in the morning,* to signal the sequence of events in your narrative.

Original:

> The Chimp handed the mask through the fence to the visitors and made a second mask. The visitors and the chimp were looking at each other through these torn bags.

Revision:

> The Chimp handed the mask through the fence to the visitors and then made a second mask. In a few minutes, the visitors and the chimp were looking at each other through these torn bags.

▶ Step 3: Don't Just Tell, Show

Do your characters speak for themselves? Let the characters in your narrative be active participants in the story.

Telling:

> Mrs. Dagostino announced that we would be visiting the Center for Great Apes.

Showing:

> "Tomorrow," Mrs. Dagostino said enthusiastically, "we'll be visiting the Center for Great Apes."

EDIT Your Narrative

Key Trait Conventions Edit by correcting any errors in spelling, grammar, and mechanics. In addition to completing the exercise below, review the grammar tips and workshops in the unit to identify areas in your writing that you would like to strengthen.

> ## Grammar Tip
>
> **Writing and Punctuating Dialogue** Follow these simple rules for writing and punctuating dialogue correctly.
>
> **1.** The exact words spoken by a character should be in quotation marks.
>
> *"This is a very special opportunity for us."*
>
> **2.** When the speaker's words are interrupted by a reference to the speaker, set off the interrupting words with commas.
>
> *"Tomorrow," Mrs. Dagostino announced enthusiastically, "we'll be visiting the Center for Great Apes."*
>
> **3.** Introductory words should also be set off with a comma as should words following the quotation.
>
> *She continued brightly, "This is a very special opportunity for us."*
>
> *"This is a very special opportunity for us," she continued brightly.*
>
> One exception to this rule occurs when the quoted words end with a question mark or an exclamation mark.
>
> *"This is a very special opportunity for us!" she continued brightly.*
>
> **4.** Begin a new paragraph each time the speaker changes.
>
> *"You'll spend time observing the behavior of these fascinating and intelligent animals," she said.*
>
> *"Will we be able to touch the chimps?" David asked.*

PUBLISH Your Narrative

Key Trait Presentation An anthology is a collection of literary works—poems, essays, stories, plays, and so on. As a class, you will create an online anthology so that you can share your work with a wider audience.

Build a Web site that is easy to navigate. Include a table of contents that links to individual narratives. Consider including illustrations, such as photographs and drawings, to enhance the presentation of each narrative. Wherever possible, add a link to something mentioned in a narrative that has its own Web site. Announce the Web site launch to students in your school so they can enjoy your work.

Editing Checklist

For your final revision, check the following:

- ☑ Have I misspelled any words? If you are unsure of the spelling of a word, check an online or print dictionary or use your word processor's spell checker.

- ☑ Have I made any errors in mechanics or grammar? Have I followed the rules of Standard American English? Use the Language Handbook on pages R48–R71 to correct common grammar and mechanical errors.

- ☑ Is my writing legible? Be sure your handwriting is neat or that you have followed your teacher's guidelines for word-processing.

LOG ON ▶ **Literature** Online

Writing and Research For editing and publishing tools, go to glencoe.com and enter QuickPass code GL57805u1.

TEKS

For pages 236–237

10.24.C Evaluate how the style and structure of a speech support or undermine its purpose or meaning.

Choosing a Tone

If you are reflecting on a serious or sad experience, you will probably choose a formal tone. For less somber personal narratives, however, consider a conversational tone. You can include everyday expressions with a relaxed, person-to-person tone to draw your listeners in.

Speaking, Listening, and Viewing Workshop

Personal Narrative Presentation

Literature Connection Personal narratives can often be enhanced by adding visual aids to help readers and listeners visualize your subject matter. Any written work can be delivered, changed, or enhanced with the addition of visual aids and music. In this workshop, you will present a personal narrative that uses visuals to help express the events and their significance.

> **Assignment** | **Create an oral presentation of your personal narrative and deliver it to an audience.**

Plan Your Presentation

Presenting an essay orally is not the same thing as simply reading it aloud. It is a chance to use your voice, body language, and visual aids to communicate meaning to an audience.

- Read your essay aloud to yourself and think about your audience. Ask yourself which parts of your essay will be most interesting, which will be hardest to understand, and which could be interpreted visually.
- Next, make notes. For example, circle or highlight the most important details, dialogue, and description. Underline anything that can be cut or better explained. Jot down ideas for visuals in the margins.
- Revise your essay to make it a spoken script. In the script, retain all of your best details, dialogue, and descriptions. Expand and enliven them. Omit details that contribute little to an overall impression or theme. Add brief, interesting bits of explanation wherever needed.
- Finally, make note cards. After you rehearse and learn your presentation, these cards will serve as reminders or cues during your delivery.

—write your most important points on note cards
—be sure to add any new bits of information to your note cards

Create Your Visual Media

As you create your script and note cards, concentrate on the images you want to display or project. There are many options for visual aids—drawings, collages, photographs, and video. Be sure to credit anything that is not your own work. You can also incorporate colors, shapes, and designs into your project to represent a feeling or mood. Because you are telling a story, one way to plan your visuals is by sequencing images along a plot diagram.

Once you have a plan, assemble your images in order and write brief prompts on your note cards that cue you to display each one at the right time.

Rehearse

▶You can rehearse your presentation the first few times by yourself. Get used to using your note cards as prompts and learn your presentation thoroughly. Be sure to practice the actual gestures you will use.

▶Next, practice in front of a classmate or a family member. Ask your listener to comment on how effectively you used each of the verbal and nonverbal techniques listed in the chart below. If possible, rehearse once more in front of the same person, incorporating his or her suggestions.

Verbal Techniques	Nonverbal Techniques
☑ **Rate** Speak at a normal pace, using pauses for effect.	☑ **Visibility** Be sure that everyone can see your presentation.
☑ **Language** Use the conventions of language to communicate ideas effectively.	☑ **Eye Contact** Make eye contact with your audience.
☑ **Enunciation** Speak clearly and to the point.	☑ **Posture** Avoid leaning or slouching.
☑ **Volume** Be sure to speak loudly enough that everyone can hear you.	☑ **Gestures** Use purposeful gestures to emphasize important points.

Independent Reading

Short Stories and Novels

IN ONLY A FEW PAGES, SHORT STORIES DO IT ALL: THEY INTRODUCE CHARACTERS, setting, and the first events of the plot; they build up tension or suspense and rise to a climax; they develop characters; they present a theme; and they deliver a satisfying ending. For more short stories with a variety of themes, try the two suggestions below. For novels that incorporate the Big Ideas of Encountering the Unexpected, Making Choices, and Life Transitions, try the titles from the Glencoe Literature Library on the next page.

Texas Author

The House on Mango Street

Sandra Cisneros

This collection of related short stories details the life of Esperanza, a Mexican American girl. Like the young Sandra Cisneros, who often uses her life experiences as subjects in both her fiction and nonfiction, Esperanza Cordero lives in a Latino community in Chicago. Esperanza's hopes, joys, and fears are explored in a series of short vignettes, each of which focuses on a seemingly minor incident, such as an interaction with a mean boy or a troubling episode at school. The stories in *The House on Mango Street* can stand individually, or the book can be read as a novel.

Calling the Wind: Twentieth Century African-American Short Stories

edited by Clarence Major

This collection of 59 short stories begins with a tale written by Charles Chestnutt in 1899 and ends with Terry McMillan's short story "Quilting on the Rebound," written in 1991. In between are stories by some of the greatest authors of the twentieth century, including Richard Wright, Ralph Ellison, Langston Hughes, James Baldwin, Ernest Gaines, Toni Morrison, and Jamaica Kincaid. In his introduction, Major explains that the collection sets out, among other things, to deny readers the chance for racial stereotyping.

The Friends

Rosa Guy

Encountering the unexpected, the main character tries to understand the problems that develop between her and her best friend.

Nectar in a Sieve

Kamala Markandaya

The process of making choices to adapt to life's ordeals is recorded through the eyes of a woman from a small village in India.

My Ántonia

Willa Cather

This novel is about the struggles and rewards and life transitions of pioneer life on the Great Plains in the nineteenth century.

CRITICS' CORNER

"Poe assumed in his tales one crucial condition: every mind is either half-mad or capable of slipping easily into madness. He was not so much concerned with precisely what madness was but with the conditions and stages whereby madness came to exist and evidenced itself in otherwise average, commonplace human beings."

—Edward H. Davidson, *Selected Writings of Edgar Allan Poe*

Complete Stories and Poems of Edgar Allan Poe

Edgar Allan Poe

For more thrilling tales from one of the earliest and greatest masters of horror and suspense, try this collection of his complete works. Popular tales include "The Tell-Tale Heart," the story of a heart that goes on beating after death, as well as "The Murders in the Rue Morgue," a forerunner of the detective story genre.

 Write a Response

Read one of the books shown and write a response to it for your classmates. Select a genre for your response that will best express what you want your audience to know about the book. For example, you can write a personal narrative that describes the effect the book had on you, a persuasive essay to convince others to read it, or a script to act out an exciting part from the story.

Assessment

English Language Arts

Reading: Fiction

Read the following passages and answer the questions that follow them.

from *"When the Buffalo Climbed a Tree"* by Mark Twain

In this tall tale, a man named Bemis is relating a recent event in which he was up in a tree, trying to remain safe from a dangerous buffalo.

1   I watched the bull, now, with anxiety—anxiety which no one can conceive of who has not been in such a situation and felt that at any moment death might come. Presently a thought came into the bull's eye. I knew it! Said I—if my nerve fails now, I am lost. Sure enough, it was just as I had dreaded, he started in to climb the tree—"

2   "What, the bull?"

3   "Of course—who else?"

4   "But a bull can't climb a tree."

5   "He can't, can't he? Since you know so much about it, did you ever see a bull try?"

6   "No! I never dreamt of such a thing."

7   "Well, then, what is the use of your talking that way, then? Because you never saw a thing done, is that any reason why it can't be done?"

8   "Well, all right—go on. What did you do?"

9   "The bull started up, and got along well for about ten feet, then slipped and slid back. I breathed easier. He tried it again—got up a little higher—slipped again. But he came at it once more, and this time he was careful. He got gradually higher and higher, and my spirits went down more and more. Up he came—an inch at a time—with his eyes hot, and his tongue hanging out. Higher and higher—hitched his foot over the stump of a limb, and looked up, as much as to say, 'You are my meat, friend.' Up again— higher and higher, and getting more excited the closer he got. He was within ten feet of me! I took a long breath,—and then said I, 'It is now or never.' I had the coil of the lariat all ready; I paid it out slowly, till it hung right over his head; all of a sudden I let go of the slack, and the slip-noose fell fairly round his neck! Quicker than lightning I out with the Allen and let him have it in the face. It was an awful roar, and must have scared the bull out of his senses. When the smoke cleared away, there he was dangling in the air, twenty foot from the ground, and going out of one convulsion into another faster than you could count! I didn't stop to count, anyhow I shinned down the tree and shot for home."

10   "Bemis, is all that true, just as you have stated it?"

11   "I wish I may rot in my tracks and die the death of a dog if it isn't."

"The Unicorn in the Garden" by James Thurber

1   Once upon a sunny morning a man who sat in a breakfast nook looked up from his scrambled eggs to see a white unicorn with a golden horn quietly cropping the roses in the garden. The man went up to the bedroom where his wife was still asleep and woke her. "There's a unicorn in the garden," he said. "Eating roses." She opened one unfriendly eye and looked at him. "The unicorn is a mythical beast," she said, and turned her back on him. The man walked slowly downstairs and out into the garden. The unicorn was still there; he was now browsing among the tulips. "Here, unicorn," said the man, and pulled up a lily and gave it to him. The unicorn ate it gravely. With a high heart, because there was a unicorn in his garden, the man went upstairs and roused his wife again. "The unicorn," he said, "ate a lily." His wife sat up in bed and looked at him, coldly. "You are a booby," she said, "and I am going to have you put in the booby-hatch." The man, who had never liked the words "booby" and "booby-hatch," and who liked them even less on a shining morning when there was a unicorn in the garden, thought for a moment. "We'll see about that," he said. He walked over to the door. "He has a golden horn in the middle of his forehead," he told her. Then he went back to the garden to watch the unicorn; but the unicorn had gone away. The man sat among the roses and went to sleep.

2   And as soon as the husband had gone out of the house, the wife got up and dressed as fast as she could. She was very excited and there was a gloat in her eye. She telephoned the police and she telephoned the psychiatrist; she told them to hurry to her house and bring a strait-jacket. When the police and the psychiatrist arrived, they sat down in chairs and looked at her, with great interest. "My husband," she said, "saw a unicorn this morning." The police looked at the psychiatrist and the psychiatrist looked at the police. "He told me it ate a lily," she said. The psychiatrist looked at the police and the police looked at the psychiatrist. "He told me it had a golden horn in the middle of its forehead," she said. At a solemn signal from the psychiatrist, the police leaped from their chairs and seized the wife. They had a hard time subduing her, for she put up a terrific struggle, but they finally subdued her. Just as they got her into the strait-jacket, the husband came into the house.

3   "Did you tell your wife you saw a unicorn?" asked the police. "Of course not," said the husband. "The unicorn is a mythical beast." "That's all I wanted to know," said the psychiatrist. "Take her away. I'm sorry sir, but your wife is as crazy as a jay bird." So they took her away, cursing and screaming, and shut her up in an institution. The husband lived happily ever after.

4   Moral: don't count your boobies until they are hatched.

Use "When the Buffalo Climbed a Tree" to answer questions 1–3.

1 In what manner does Bemis tell his story?
   A With humor
   B With sincerity
   C With disbelief
   D With hesitancy

2 Bemis's listener reacts to the story with —
   F doubt
   G relief
   H ridicule
   J excitement

3 Which event from the story occurs during rising action in the plot?
  A The buffalo slips and slides back.
  B Bemis fires his Allen at the buffalo.
  C The buffalo dangles above the ground.
  D The listener asks if the story is really true.

Use "The Unicorn in the Garden" to answer questions 4–14.

4 The man's reaction to having a unicorn in the garden is one of —
  F shock
  G excitement
  H disbelief
  J quiet delight

5 Which word best describes the tone of the story?
  A Solemn
  B Amazed
  C Sympathetic
  D Humorous

6 Read the following dictionary entry.

  grave \'grāv\ *adj* **1.** important; meriting careful attention **2.** likely to produce serious harm **3.** extremely serious; great **4.** having a serious and dignified quality — **gravely** *adv.*

  Which definition best matches the meaning of the word *gravely* as it is used in the middle of paragraph 1?
  F Definition 1
  G Definition 2
  H Definition 3
  J Definition 4

7 The main conflict in this story is between —
  A the husband and wife
  B the wife and the unicorn
  C the police and the psychiatrist
  D the husband's experiences and his beliefs

8 The wife reacts to her husband's news about the unicorn with an attitude of —
  F fury
  G ridicule
  H amazement
  J mild surprise

9 The author develops the character of the husband mainly through —
  A the husband's actions
  B the husband's thoughts
  C the wife's actions towards him
  D the narrator's descriptions of him

10 Which of the following best describes the character of the wife in this story?
  F Flat and static
  G Flat and dynamic
  H Round and static
  J Round and dynamic

11 The story suggests that the husband says he hadn't told his wife he saw a unicorn because —
  A he has already forgotten about it
  B he is glad to have his wife taken away
  C he wants to protect the unicorn from the public
  D he assumes he imagined the unicorn and is embarrassed

12 Which of the following quotations from the story is an example of foreshadowing?
  F *"The unicorn," he said, "ate a lily."*
  G *His wife sat up in bed and looked at him, coldly.*
  H *"We'll see about that," he said.*
  J *The man sat among the roses and went to sleep.*

13 The climax of the story occurs when —
  A the man sees the unicorn
  B the wife threatens her husband
  C the police and psychiatrist arrive
  D the wife is taken away

14 **Open-Ended Item** What is ironic about what happens in Thurber's story?

Vocabulary Skills: Sentence Completion

For each item, choose the word that best completes the sentence.

1   The courtroom anxiously awaited the jury's ____ verdict after hours of deliberation.
   A imminent
   B austere
   C impetuous
   D self-possessed

2   The mayor was ____ elected by the town's citizens.
   F tautly
   G duly
   H arrogantly
   J humorously

3   Rosa Parks, a famous civil rights figure, carried herself with strength and determination; her ____ served as a model for others.
   A infirmity
   B contrition
   C reverie
   D fortitude

4   I was afraid the stranger who seemed so friendly might have some ____ motive for offering to help me.
   F skeptical
   G ulterior
   H profuse
   J irreproachable

5   Bullies often successfully use ____ to get what they want.
   A reveling
   B serenity
   C intimidation
   D supplication

6   The steep mountains presented a truly ____ barrier to the hikers.
   F convoluted
   G decrepit
   H imperceptible
   J formidable

7   The couple believed that long talks could only ____ their already-close relationship.
   A enhance
   B reproach
   C scrutinize
   D commandeer

8   I used my necktie as a ____ leash for the lost dog in order to return him to the address on his tags.
   F vintage
   G amenable
   H discordant
   J makeshift

9   I know my English teacher will be ____ when I tell her that my dog ate my homework, but he actually did!
   A inscrutable
   B subversive
   C incredulous
   D improvised

10 Investors who fear that their investments will not do well tend to watch the stock market with ____ .
   F equanimity
   G presentiments
   H pandemonium
   J paraphernalia

LOG ON ▶ **Literature** Online

Standards Practice For more standards practice, go to glencoe.com and enter QuickPass code GL57805u1.

Revising and Editing

Read the following draft of part of a student's report about Mark Twain and answer the questions that follow it.

(1) Mark Twain who was a nineteenth-century humorist is known as one of the greatest writers who ever lived. (2) Many of the stories that he wrote are humorous but have a serious side, which makes them more interesting. (3) Twain's most famous novel, *The Adventures of Huckleberry Finn,* is both humorous and serious, as is much of his work. (4) He sometimes relied on satire and irony. (5) He used these methods to point out things he wanted to criticize in human nature.

(6) Twain tried to make people examine their own behavior. (7) He noticed problems in society. (8) And in human interactions. (9) When he wrote his stories. (10) He often commented on what he had noticed. (11) He is known for stating such observations in interesting ways. (12) For example, he said, "One of the most striking differences between a cat and a lie is that a cat has only nine lives."

1 What revision, if any, is needed in sentence 1?
- **A** Mark Twain, who was a nineteenth-century humorist, is known as one of the greatest writers, who ever lived.
- **B** Mark Twain who was a nineteenth-century humorist is known as one of the greatest writers, who ever lived.
- **C** Mark Twain, who was a nineteenth-century humorist, is known as one of the greatest writers who ever lived.
- **D** No revision is needed.

2 What revision, if any, is needed in sentence 2?
- **F** Many of the stories, that he wrote, are humorous but have a serious side which makes them more interesting.
- **G** Many of the stories, that he wrote, are humorous but have a serious side, which makes them more interesting.
- **H** Many of the stories that he wrote are humorous but have a serious side which makes them more interesting.
- **J** No revision is needed.

3 What is the most effective way to combine sentences 4 and 5?

A He sometimes relied on satire and irony to make points that were critical of human nature.

B Sometimes, he relied on satire and irony, and these methods were useful to him for making points about human nature.

C He relied on satire and irony to make points that were critical of human nature, but only sometimes.

D He sometimes relied on satire and irony, and he was sometimes critical of human nature by using those methods.

4 What makes sentence 8 a sentence fragment?

F It lacks only a subject.
G It lacks only a verb.
H It lacks both a subject and a verb.
J It is a subordinate clause.

5 What makes sentence 9 a sentence fragment?

A It lacks only a subject.
B It lacks only a verb.
C It lacks both a subject and a verb.
D It is a subordinate clause.

Written Composition

Read the information and instructions below in order to write a short narrative.

It is sometimes hard to convince a listener that what you are saying is true. Write a personal narrative about a time when you told someone something that was true but was hard for the person to believe.

REMEMBER—YOU SHOULD

❑ begin with an opening that captures the reader's attention

❑ use first-person narration

❑ organize your writing so that it has a beginning, middle, and end

❑ include dialogue if and where it is appropriate

❑ correct errors in spelling, capitalization, punctuation, grammar, and sentence structure

Coming to America, 1985. Malcah Zeldis.

View the Art Malcah Zeldis's painting shows the epic scale of the journey from the old world to the new. If you were to write nonfiction about the journey to America, what would you focus on?

NONFICTION

Looking Ahead

Nonfiction—writing about real people, events, and ideas—includes autobiographies, memoirs, biographies, diaries, letters, essays, news articles, and speeches. Through reading nonfiction, we find others who share our experiences, feelings, passions, and values. Our ideas, ideals, and causes are articulated and defended by the nonfiction writer.

Each part in Unit Two focuses on a Big Idea that can help you connect to the literary works.

PREVIEW	Big Ideas	Literary Focus
PART 1	The Power of Memory	Autobiography and Biography
PART 2	Quests and Encounters	Expository and Personal Essay
PART 3	Keeping Freedom Alive	Logic and Persuasion

TEKS

For pages 248–252

10.6 Understand, make inferences and draw conclusions about the varied structural patterns and features of literary nonfiction and provide evidence from text to support understanding.

GENRE FOCUS

What are the different types of nonfiction?

The motivations for writing and reading nonfiction are as diverse as writers and readers. Some writers seek to share the lives of others with readers to provide insight. Others share their own experiences.

Autobiography and Biography

Writing About Oneself

A literary work that tells the story of an author's own experiences can be an autobiography or a memoir. **Autobiography** usually refers to a work that attempts to tell a person's entire life. **Memoir** usually refers to a work that focuses on the author's personal experiences during a particular event or period.

> Our father kept in his breast pocket a little black notebook. There he noted jokes he wanted to remember. Remembering jokes was a moral obligation. People who said, "I can never remember jokes," were like people who said, obliviously, "I can never remember names," or "I don't bathe."
>
> —Annie Dillard, *from* **"An American Childhood"**

Writing About Another

Whether it is long or short, an account of another person's life is called a **biography.** Biographies typically satisfy readers' curiosity about the lives of famous, successful, or inspiring people, such as artists, royalty, or media stars.

> De Kooning brought over a portfolio of drawings and began leafing through them. At last, he seemed to settle on one. He looked at it. But then he slipped the drawing back into the portfolio. "No," he said, "I want to give one that I'll miss."
>
> —Mark Stevens and Annalyn Swan,
> **from *De Kooning: An American Master***

Expository and Personal Essay

Essays are short works of nonfiction that focus on a single topic. Essays communicate ideas or opinions. **Expository essays** explain or inform, usually in an objective way. Expository essays may be formal, or they may be personal, or informal.

Formal and Informal Essays

Formal essays are serious and impersonal in tone, meaning the author expresses a serious attitude toward his or her subject matter. A formal essay typically develops a controlling idea, or thesis, in a logical and highly organized way. Many persuasive essays are formal in style. For example, newspaper editorials—jointly authored, persuasive articles that give the opinion of the editors or publishers on a topic—are often formal in style.

Personal essays, also called **informal essays,** entertain while they inform. They are usually written in a light, conversational style, often in the first person. They can be written on any topic that the writer wishes to share with the reader. Informal essays often relate to an experience in the writer's life. Many magazines and blogs include informal essays.

Logic and Persuasion

Writing to Persuade

Persuasive essays and articles promote an opinion. They try to change the way readers think about subjects ranging from letter writing to space travel. **Speeches** are often persuasive, given to encourage a certain behavior or to win the listener over to a cause.

One type of persuasion is **argument,** which relies on logic, reason, and evidence to convince the reader of the truth of a claim. The evidence may consist of examples, facts, and opinions; it may also consist of various kinds of appeals. This excerpt from King's speech contains sarcasm, which is a type of emotional appeal.

Secondly, let us keep the issues where they are. The issue is injustice. The issue is the refusal of Memphis to be fair and honest in its dealings with its public servants, who happen to be sanitation workers. Now, we've got to keep attention on that. That's always the problem with a little violence. You know what happened the other day, and the press dealt only with the window-breaking. I read the articles. They very seldom got around to mentioning the fact that one thousand, three hundred sanitation workers were on strike, and that Memphis is not being fair to them, and that Mayor Loeb is in dire need of a doctor. They didn't get around to that.

—Martin Luther King Jr., *from* **"I've Been to the Mountaintop"**

LITERARY ANALYSIS MODEL

How do literary elements create meaning in nonfiction?

Robert E. Hemenway (born 1941) has been a professor of English and American Studies and a University Dean and Chancellor. His literary biography *Zora Neale Hurston* was a "Best Books" pick by the *New York Times* in 1978.

APPLY
Literary Elements

Nonfiction

Nonfiction is writing about real people and events.

Nonfiction

In trying to determine which category of non-fiction the excerpt belongs to, you can rule out the **essay** because the author is narrating events in the life of a person, not expressing ideas and opinions. You can also rule out **speech**.

from *Zora Neale Hurston*
by Robert E. Hemenway

In the first week of January, 1925, Zora Neale Hurston arrived in New York City with one dollar and fifty cents in her purse, no job, no friends, but filled with "a lot of hope." She came from Washington, leaving a steady job as a manicurist in a
5 Seventh Avenue barbershop to explore the opportunities for a career as a writer. As a part-time student at Howard University for the previous five years, she had been an aspiring English major, much praised for her short stories and poems, and she had a vague idea of studying writing in one of Manhattan's
10 many colleges. She carried most of her belongings in her bag, including a number of manuscripts that she hoped would impress. Even if they did not, she was confident of her ability to survive in the big city; she had been on her own since the age of fourteen. Brown skinned, big boned, with freckles and
15 high cheekbones, she was a striking woman; her dark brown eyes were both impish and intelligent, her voice was rich and black—with the map of Florida on her tongue.
    She went first to the offices of the National Urban League on East Twenty-third Street, where she asked to be introduced to
20 Charles S. Johnson, editor of the Urban League's magazine, *Opportunity: A Journal of Negro Life.* A month earlier he had pub-lished one of her short stories, and since September he had been encouraging her to submit material to the literary contest his magazine currently sponsored. Johnson, director of research
25 for the league, had single-handedly turned *Opportunity* into an expression of "New Negro" thought. "New Negroes" were black people who made clear that they would not accept a sub-ordinate role in American society, and Johnson believed that young writers like Zora Neale Hurston would help prove the

30 cultural parity of the races. He urged her to stay in New York, and as she settled in, he helped her find a series of odd jobs. Mrs. Johnson often gave Zora carfare to make sure she could accept the frequent dinner invitations at the Johnson house.

35 For a young girl from rural Florida and provincial Washington who had been working for ten years to secure an education, this interest and help must have made all the sacrifice seem worthwhile. She had arrived at a hard-won sense of self built around the knowledge that because she was black her life had been graced in unusual ways, and she had confidence that she could express that

40 grace in fiction. The story Johnson had printed a month earlier, "Drenched in Light," embodied this personal vision she brought to New York; it was her initial contribution to the cultural uprising that Johnson and others were calling a "Harlem Renaissance."

"Drenched in Light" was Hurston's calling card on literary

45 New York, the tangible evidence she could point to that she was indeed a serious writer. It is also a statement of personal identity. It tells of a day in the life of Isie Watts, a "little brown figure perched upon the gate-post" in front of her Eatonville, Florida, home. Isie likes to race up and down the road to Orlando, "hailing gleefully

50 all travelers." As a result, "everybody in the country" knows "Isie Watts, the joyful," and how she likes to laugh and play, beg rides in cars, and live to the fullest every minute of her young life. Isie gets into various scrapes, including an impish attempt to shave her sleeping grand-

55 mother, and eventually is given a ride by a passing white motorist, despite her grandmother's disapproval. There is no building toward a dramatic climax, and very little plot. The structure of the story is thematic. The point is that Isie, poor and black, is far from tragic; rather, she is "drenched

60 in light," a condition which endears her to everyone, although it presents her grandmother with a discipline problem. Isie is persistently happy, and the implication is that whites suffer from an absence of such joy. Isie's white benefactor ends the story, "I want a little of her sunshine to

65 soak into my soul. I need it."

Hurston may have been manipulating white stereotypes of black people here, but it is not a matter of satire. She remembered Eatonville as a place of great peace and happiness, identifying that happiness as a function

70 of her family and communal existence.

Writer Zora Neale Hurston

Biography

Hurston is referred to as "she" rather than "I," so you can rule out **autobiography** and **memoir** and determine that the kind of nonfiction you are reading is **biography.**

Biography

Biographies can be short or long. This excerpt is from a book-length biography.

Reading Check

Interpret What would you expect the rest of this book to be about?

WRAP-UP

Guide to Reading Nonfiction

- When reading nonfiction, first determine what type of work you are reading.

- Try to identify the author's purpose. Is he or she writing to explain, to inform, to entertain, or to persuade?

- If the author's purpose is to inform or explain, look for a thesis statement and support for the thesis.

- If the author's purpose is to entertain, look for literary elements, such as figurative language, dialogue, and suspense.

- If the author's purpose is to persuade, determine whether the author is presenting an argument, emotional appeals, or a combination of both.

 Literature Online

Unit Resources For additional skills practice, go to glencoe.com and enter QuickPass code GL57805u2.

Types of Nonfiction

- **Literary nonfiction** includes writing about literature and about real people and events.

- An **autobiography** tells the story of the writer's life.

- A **memoir** tells about an event or period in the writer's life.

- A **biography** tells the story of another person's life.

- An **essay** is a short work of nonfiction on a single topic. An essay can be **formal** or **informal.**

- Informal, or **personal,** essays are meant primarily to entertain. Formal essays may be intended to explain or persuade.

- **Persuasive** essays and speeches are intended to change the way people act and think. Argument persuades through logic, reason, and evidence.

Activities

Use what you have learned about reading and analyzing nonfiction to complete one of these activities.

1. Generate Questions In small groups, discuss the excerpt from *Zora Neale Hurston* and list three questions you could research that are suggested by the text.

2. Research/Inquire Analyze the author's motivation for writing about Hurston. Use your analysis as the first entry in a chart that shows your ideas about the kinds of motivations writers might have for writing different kinds of literary nonfiction.

3. Take Notes Try using this study organizer to make inferences about the features of literary nonfiction. For each text in this unit, take notes on what the features tell you about the text.

 THREE-TAB BOOK

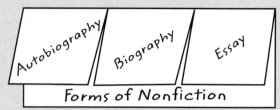

See page R20 for folding instructions

THE POWER OF MEMORY

Souvenir, 1891. Émile Friant. Oil on canvas. Musée de la Ville de Paris, Musée du Petit-Palais, France.

View the Art This painting depicts an elderly woman lost in thought as children play by the waterside. How might memories and the power of memory become more important as one grows older?

BIG IDEA

Shared personal memories have the power to create a bond between the writer and reader. Historical memories have the power to shape national identities. In the nonfiction works in Part 1, you will read excerpts from life stories that could change the way you view the world. As you read these texts, ask yourself, When someone shares a personal memory with me, do I feel closer to them or understand them better? Why or why not?

TEKS

For pages 254–255

10.6 Understand, make inferences and draw conclusions about the varied structural patterns and features of literary nonfiction and provide evidence from text to support understanding.

LITERARY FOCUS

AUTOBIOGRAPHY AND BIOGRAPHY

How do nonfiction writers choose which details to include?

Nonfiction writing should be factual, and an autobiography or biography should tell the facts of the life of its subject. But which facts should be told? To write down all the facts of any life, or even of one day, is inconceivable. The art of autobiography and biography is in choosing interesting and telling facts and in explaining them in an engaging way.

from *De Kooning: An American Master*

by Mark Stevens and Annalyn Swan

De Kooning could get by without much English, though it was not always easy. In the beginning, he knew how to order only one thing in restaurants—a hamburger. (When he finally tried to order something else at the local restaurant, the waiter said, "Hamburger, right?" de Kooning meekly nodded.) On the job, he found he had much to learn about the way his new country operated, which often differed from the careful, artisanal manners of Holland. "I was impressed by the workers' efficiency and their tools," he said. "We worked without stopping for eight hours and used much larger and better brushes than those we had in Holland. I learned a great deal on how to mix pigment with water and oil."

Pirate (Untitled II), 1981. Willem De Kooning. Oil on canvas, 88 x 76 3/4 in. Sidney and Harriet Janis Collection Fund. The Museum of Modern Art, NY. © ARS, NY.

Autobiography

When a person writes about his or her own life, it is called **autobiography.** *Auto-* is from the Greek word meaning "self." In an autobiography, the subject of the work is also the author. Authors have many purposes for sharing the stories of their lives. Some, such as Martin Luther King Jr., write to help others live satisfying and meaningful lives. Others, such as Mark Mathabane, write to explain the significance of their own lives.

> All of the confusion I had about school seemed to leave my mind, like darkness giving way to light.
>
> —Mark Mathabane, **from** *Kaffir Boy*

Memoir A **memoir** is autobiographical writing that focuses on a specific period or event in the writer's life. Memoirs are usually written from the first-person point of view. They often emphasize the writer's thoughts and feelings, his or her relationship with others, or the personal impact of historical events. Annie Dillard's memoir captures her mother's unusual personality.

> "Spell 'poinsettia,'" Mother would throw out at me, smiling with pleasure. "Spell 'sherbet.'" The idea was not to make us whizzes, but, quite the contrary, to remind us—and I, especially, needed reminding—that we didn't know it all just yet.
>
> —Annie Dillard, *from* "Terwilliger Bunts One"

LOG ON ▶ **Literature** Online

Literature and Reading For more about literary elements, go to glencoe.com and enter QuickPass code GL57805u2.

Biography

The word *biography* comes from the Greek *bio-,* meaning "life," and *-graphy,* meaning "writing." In **biography** the author gives the reader an account of another person's life. The author uses the pronouns "he" or "she" to refer to the subject. Biographies can be book-length, but they can also be short pieces.

Woman in Calico, 1944. William H. Johnson. Oil on paperboard, 67.4 x 52.0 cm. Smithsonian American Art Museum, Washington, DC.

Quickwrite

Make Inferences Choose one of the literary works in Part 1 of this unit. Write a paragraph indentifying the features of autobiography or biography in the work you choose. Make inferences about how these features function in the text.

Before You Read

from *Farewell to Manzanar*

Meet **Jeanne Wakatsuki Houston** (born 1934)
Meet **James D. Houston** (1933–2009)

Jeanne Wakatsuki Houston was only seven years old when her family, along with other Japanese Americans, was relocated to an internment camp. It took her nearly 25 years to talk about her life in the Manzanar internment camp, but when she did, she broached the subject in the form of an award-winning book, *Farewell to Manzanar*, co-authored by her husband, James D. Houston.

> "[Writing was] a way of coming to terms with the impact these years have had on my life."
>
> —Jeanne Wakatsuki Houston

The United States at War When Japan attacked a United States fleet at Pearl Harbor in 1941, the U.S. was drawn into World War II. Many people unfairly blamed Japanese Americans. Despite the fact that many of them had U.S. citizenship, they were distrusted and systematically discriminated against. For example, Japanese American people in the fishing industry were seen as threats to national security because in theory, they could smuggle oil to the Japanese navy. Wakatsuki Houston's father was arrested because he was a fisherman.

Memories of Internment Wakatsuki Houston was born in Inglewood, California. When the war began, Wakatsuki Houston's family was sent to the Manzanar internment camp, where the conditions were harsh. Manzanar was built very quickly, so no modern conveniences existed. Approximately 11,000 people of Japanese ancestry lived there in a one-square-mile block of wooden barracks, surrounded by barbed wire and posted guards. The people in the camp worked hard to build a community by planting gardens, painting, and forming schools and churches. Many were full-fledged U.S. citizens and many did not even speak Japanese. Despite their loyalty to the United States, however, they were treated as if they were the enemy. For Wakatsuki Houston, the experience of Manzanar changed her life.

After her family's release in 1945, Wakatsuki Houston continued to struggle to overcome prejudice and the shame of being punished simply for being Japanese. During her college years, she met and married James D. Houston. She went back to visit Manzanar in 1972, a visit that she says helped her come to terms with the experience. According to Wakatsuki Houston, "Papa's life ended at Manzanar, though he lived for twelve more years after getting out. Until this trip I had not been able to admit that my own life really began there."

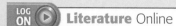

Literature and Reading Preview

Connect to the Historical Narrative

How would you feel if you were given 48 hours to pack a few of your belongings and leave your home? Freewrite for a few minutes about what you might take with you, and why.

Build Background

In February 1942, President Franklin D. Roosevelt issued Executive Order 9066, which gave the U.S. War Department the authority to confine Japanese Americans to special camps for the duration of World War II. Some 110,000 Japanese Americans, two-thirds of them U.S. citizens, were relocated to ten remote, prison-like camps.

Set Purposes for Reading

Big Idea The Power of Memory

As you read, ask yourself, How does sharing memories help people make connections to other people?

Literary Element Historical Narrative

A **historical narrative** is a nonfiction account that tells about important historical events. As you read, ask yourself, What details does the author use to tell the story of Japanese Americans in an internment camp?

Reading Strategy Summarize

When you **summarize,** you determine the most important ideas in a text and then restate them concisely in your own words. A summary should not include nonessential information and it should not include opinions as a critique would. As you read, ask yourself, Do I remember and understand the text better when I summarize?

....

Tip: Summarize Details As you read, use a graphic organizer and the blue highlighted passages and questions to help you list details. Then write a brief summary of the most important ideas.

Detail	Detail	Detail
When I was born [Papa] was farming near Inglewood.	We moved to Ocean Park; he was picked up there.	Papa was gone; mother moved us to Terminal Island.

After Papa was arrested near our home in Ocean Park, mother moved us to Terminal Island to be near other Japanese.

Summary

TEKS

For pages 256–272

RC-10.A Reflect on understanding to monitor comprehension (e.g., summarizing).

Vocabulary

patriarch (pā′trē ärk′) *n.* the male head of a family or group; p. 261 *My brother became the patriarch of our family after my father died.*

designation (dez′ig nā′shən) *n.* a distinguishing name or mark; p. 262 *The scientist gave the seeds that were not watered the designation "test group."*

alleviate (ə lē′vē āt′) *v.* to make easier to bear; relieve; lessen; p. 264 *The medicine promised to alleviate his suffering.*

subordinate (sə bôr′də nāt′) *v.* to cause to be, or treat as, secondary, inferior, or less important; p. 270 *A mother subordinates her own needs to care for the needs of her children.*

....

Tip: Word Parts You can find the meanings of common prefixes, such as *a-, ad-, ante-, bi-, de-, per-, pre-, pro-,* and *sub-,* by looking them up in a dictionary.

JEANNE WAKATSUKI HOUSTON AND JAMES D. HOUSTON   **257**

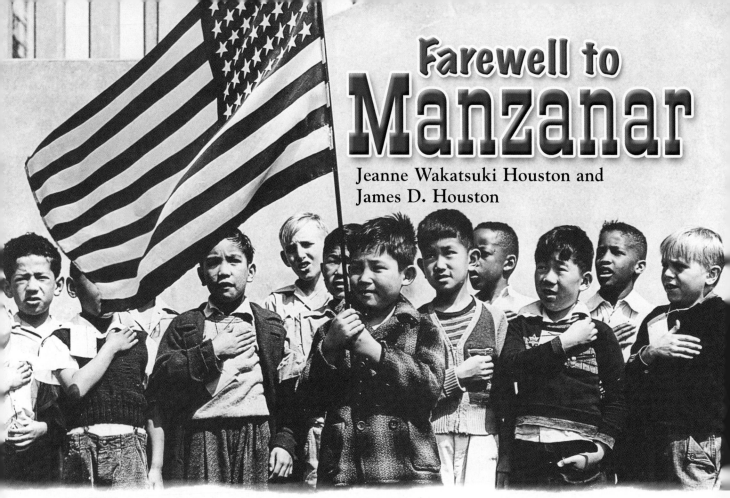

Farewell to Manzanar

Jeanne Wakatsuki Houston and
James D. Houston

School Children Say Pledge of Allegiance in San Francisco, April 16, 1942. Dorothea Lange. Silver Gelatin Photograph.

In December of 1941 Papa's disappearance didn't bother me nearly so much as the world I soon found myself in.

He had been a jack-of-all-trades. When I was born he was farming near Inglewood. Later, when he started fishing, we moved to Ocean Park, near Santa Monica, and until they picked him up, that's where we lived, in a big frame house with a brick fireplace, a block back from the beach. We were the only Japanese family in the neighborhood. Papa liked it that way. He didn't want to be labeled or grouped by anyone. But with him gone and no way of knowing what to expect, my mother moved all of us down to Terminal Island.[1]

Woody[2] already lived there, and one of my older sisters had married a Terminal Island boy. Mama's first concern now was to keep the family together; and once the war began, she felt safer there than isolated racially in Ocean Park. But for me, at age seven, the island was a country as foreign as India or Arabia would have been. It was the first time I had lived among other Japanese, or gone to school with them, and I was terrified all the time.

---

1. *Terminal Island,* part of the Port of Los Angeles, is at the city's southern tip.

2. *Woody* is one of the narrator's brothers.

Historical Narrative *Why does Mama feel safer in Terminal Island?*

This was partly Papa's fault. One of his threats to keep us younger kids in line was "I'm going to sell you to the Chinaman." When I had entered kindergarten two years earlier, I was the only Oriental in the class. They sat me next to a Caucasian girl who happened to have very slanted eyes. I looked at her and began to scream, certain Papa had sold me out at last. My fear of her ran so deep I could not speak of it, even to Mama, couldn't explain why I was screaming. For two weeks I had nightmares about this girl, until the teachers finally moved me to the other side of the room. And it was still with me, this fear of Oriental faces, when we moved to Terminal Island.

In those days it was a company town, a ghetto owned and controlled by the canneries. The men went after fish, and whenever the boats came back—day or night—the women would be called to process the catch while it was fresh. One in the afternoon or four in the morning, it made no difference. My mother had to go to work right after we moved there. I can still hear the whistle—two toots for French's, three for Van Camp's—and she and Chizu would be out of bed in the middle of the night, heading for the cannery.

The house we lived in was nothing more than a shack, a barracks with single plank walls and rough wooden floors, like the cheapest kind of migrant workers' housing. The people around us were hardworking, boisterous, a little proud of their nickname, *yo-go-re*, which meant literally *uncouth one*, or roughneck, or dead-end kid. They not only spoke Japanese exclusively, they spoke a dialect peculiar to Kyushu,[3] where their families had come from in Japan, a rough,

fisherman's language, full of oaths and insults. Instead of saying *ba-ka-ta-re*, a common insult meaning *stupid*, Terminal Islanders would say *ba-ka-ya-ro*, a coarser and exclusively masculine use of the word, which implies gross stupidity. They would swagger and pick on outsiders and persecute anyone who didn't speak as they did. That was what made my own time there so hateful. I had never spoken anything but English, and the other kids in the second grade despised me for it. They were tough and mean, like ghetto kids anywhere. Each day after school I dreaded their ambush. My brother Kiyo, three years older, would wait for me at the door, where we would decide whether to run straight home together, or split up, or try a new and unexpected route.

None of these kids ever actually attacked. It was the threat that frightened us, their fearful looks, and the noises they would make, like miniature Samurai, in a language we couldn't understand.

At the time it seemed we had been living under this reign of fear for years. In fact, we lived there about two months. Late in February the navy decided to clear Terminal Island completely. Even though most of us were American-born, it was dangerous having that many Orientals so close to the Long Beach Naval Station, on the opposite end of

Visual Vocabulary
For centuries, the *Samurai* (sam′ oo rī′) were a class of fearsome warriors. Japan abolished its class system in the 1860s.

---

3. *Kyushu* is the southernmost of Japan's four main islands.

Summarize *Read to the end of this paragraph. How does Wakatsuki Houston describe the other Japanese at Terminal Island?*

Historical Narrative *Why did the navy think it was dangerous to have Asian Americans close to the Long Beach Naval Station?*

the island. We had known something like this was coming. But, like Papa's arrest, not much could be done ahead of time. There were four of us kids still young enough to be living with Mama, plus Granny, her mother, sixty-five then, speaking no English, and nearly blind. Mama didn't know where else she could get work, and we had nowhere else to move *to*. On February 25 the choice was made for us. We were given forty-eight hours to clear out.

The secondhand dealers had been prowling around for weeks, like wolves, offering humiliating prices for goods and furniture they knew many of us would have to sell sooner or later. Mama had left all but her most valuable possessions in Ocean Park, simply because she had nowhere to put them. She had brought along her pottery, her silver, heirlooms like the kimonos Granny had brought from Japan, tea sets, lacquered tables, and one fine old set of china, blue and white porcelain, almost translucent. On the day we were leaving, Woody's car was so crammed with boxes and luggage and kids we had just run out of room. Mama had to sell this china.

Visual Vocabulary
A *kimono* (ki mō´nō) is a loose robe or gown tied with a sash, traditionally worn as an outer garment by Japanese men and women.

One of the dealers offered her fifteen dollars for it. She said it was a full setting for twelve and worth at least two hundred. He said fifteen was his top price. Mama started to quiver. Her eyes blazed up at him. She had been packing all night and trying to calm down Granny, who didn't understand why we were moving again and what all the rush was about. Mama's nerves were shot, and now navy jeeps were patrolling the streets. She didn't say another word. She just glared at this man, all the rage and frustration channeled at him through her eyes.

He watched her for a moment and said he was sure he couldn't pay more than seventeen fifty for that china. She reached into the red velvet case, took out a dinner plate and hurled it at the floor right in front of his feet.

The man leaped back shouting, "Hey! Hey, don't do that! Those are valuable dishes!"

Mama took out another dinner plate and hurled it at the floor, then another and another, never moving, never opening her mouth, just quivering and glaring at the retreating dealer, with tears streaming down her cheeks. He finally turned and scuttled out the door, heading for the next house. When he was gone she stood there smashing cups and bowls and platters until the whole set lay in scattered blue and white fragments across the wooden floor.

The American Friends Service[4] helped us find a small house in Boyle Heights, another minority ghetto, in downtown Los Angeles, now inhabited briefly by a few hundred Terminal Island refugees. Executive Order 9066 had been signed by President Roosevelt, giving the War Department authority to define military areas in the western states and to exclude from them anyone who might threaten the war effort. There was a lot of talk about internment, or moving inland, or something like that in store for all Japanese Americans. I remember my brothers sitting around the table talking very intently about what we were

---

4. The *American Friends Service* is a Quaker charity that provides assistance to political and religious refugees and other displaced persons.

Summarize *Summarize the information Wakatsuki Houston provides in this paragraph about the factors that affected Japanese Americans as the war progressed.*

Dust Storm at Manzanar (California), July 3, 1942. Dorothea Lange. Silver Gelatin Photograph.

View the Art Manzanar, located in Owens Valley in California, is a high altitude desert with brutally hot summers, freezing cold winters, and constant dust storms. How might the harsh climate have impacted the lives of the prisoners at Manzanar?

going to do, how we would keep the family together. They had seen how quickly Papa was removed, and they knew now that he would not be back for quite a while. Just before leaving Terminal Island Mama had received her first letter, from Bismarck, North Dakota. He had been imprisoned at Fort Lincoln, in an all-male camp for enemy aliens.

Papa had been the **patriarch**. He had always decided everything in the family. With him gone, my brothers, like councilors in the absence of a chief, worried about what should be done. The ironic thing is, there wasn't much left to decide. These were mainly days of quiet, desperate waiting for what seemed at the time to be inevitable. There is a phrase the Japanese use in such situations, when something difficult must be endured. You would hear the older heads, the Issei,[5] telling others very quietly, "Shikata ga nai" (It cannot be helped). "Shikata ga nai" (It must be done).

Mama and Woody went to work packing celery for a Japanese produce dealer. Kiyo and my sister May and I enrolled in the local school, and what sticks in my

5. *Issei* (ēs′sā′) literally means "first generation" and refers to Japanese natives who immigrated to the United States.

memory from those few weeks is the teacher—not her looks, her remoteness. In Ocean Park my teacher had been a kind, grandmotherly woman who used to sail with us in Papa's boat from time to time and who wept the day we had to leave. In Boyle Heights the teacher felt cold and distant. I was confused by all the moving and was having trouble with the class-work, but she would never help me out. She would have nothing to do with me.

This was the first time I had felt outright hostility from a Caucasian. Looking back, it is easy enough to explain. Public attitudes toward the Japanese in California were shifting rapidly. In the first few months of the Pacific war, America was on the run. Tolerance had turned to distrust and irrational fear. The hundred-year-old tradition of anti-Orientalism on the west coast soon resurfaced, more vicious than ever. Its result became clear about a month later, when we were told to make our third and final move.

The name Manzanar meant nothing to us when we left Boyle Heights. We didn't know where it was or what it was. We went because the government ordered us to. And, in the case of my older brothers and sisters, we went with a certain amount of relief. They had all heard stories of Japanese homes being attacked, of beatings in the streets of California towns. They were as frightened of the Caucasians as Caucasians were of us. Moving, under what appeared to be government protection, to an area less directly threatened by the war seemed not such a bad idea at all. For some it actually sounded like a fine adventure.

Our pickup point was a Buddhist church in Los Angeles. It was very early, and misty, when we got there with our luggage. Mama had bought heavy coats for all of us. She grew up in eastern Washington and knew that anywhere inland in early April would be cold. I was proud of my new coat, and I remember sitting on a duffel bag trying to be friendly with the Greyhound driver. I smiled at him. He didn't smile back. He was befriending no one. Someone tied a numbered tag to my collar and to the duf-fel bag (each family was given a number, and that became our official **designation** until the camps were closed), someone else passed out box lunches for the trip, and we climbed aboard.

I had never been outside Los Angeles County, never traveled more than ten miles from the coast, had never even ridden on a bus. I was full of excitement, the way any kid would be, and wanted to look out the win-dow. But for the first few hours the shades were drawn. Around me other people played cards, read magazines, dozed, waiting. I set-tled back, waiting too, and finally fell asleep. The bus felt very secure to me. Almost half its passengers were immediate relatives. Mama and my older brothers had succeeded in keeping most of us together, on the same bus, headed for the same camp. I didn't real-ize until much later what a job that was. The strategy had been, first, to have everyone liv-ing in the same district when the evacuation began, and then to get all of us included under the same family number, even though names had been changed by marriage. Many families weren't as lucky as ours and suf-fered months of anguish while trying to arrange transfers from one camp to another.

Summarize *How does the author summarize the prejudice against the Japanese in America at this time?*

Historical Narrative *What do these details suggest about the dangers of scapegoating a group of people?*

Vocabulary

designation (dez´ ig nā´shən) *n.* a distinguishing name or mark

We rode all day. By the time we reached our destination, the shades were up. It was late afternoon. The first thing I saw was a yellow swirl across a blurred, reddish setting sun. The bus was being pelted by what sounded like splattering rain. It wasn't rain. This was my first look at something I would soon know very well, a billowing flurry of dust and sand churned up by the wind through Owens Valley.[6]

We drove past a barbed-wire fence, through a gate, and into an open space where trunks and sacks and packages had been dumped from the baggage trucks that drove out ahead of us. I could see a few tents set up, the first rows of black barracks, and beyond them, blurred by sand, rows of barracks that seemed to spread for miles across this plain. People were sitting on cartons or milling around, with their backs to the wind, waiting to see which friends or relatives might be on this bus. As we approached, they turned or stood up, and some moved toward us expectantly. But inside the bus no one stirred. No one waved or spoke. They just stared out the windows, ominously silent. I didn't understand this. Hadn't we finally arrived, our whole family intact? I opened a window, leaned out, and yelled happily. "Hey! This whole bus is full of Wakatsukis!"

Outside, the greeters smiled. Inside there was an explosion of laughter, hysterical, tension-breaking laughter that left my brothers choking and whacking each other across the shoulders.

We had pulled up just in time for dinner. The mess halls[7] weren't completed yet. An outdoor chow line snaked around a half-finished building that broke a good part of the wind. They issued us army mess kits, the round metal kind that fold over, and plopped in scoops of canned Vienna sausage, canned string beans, steamed rice that had been cooked-too long, and on top of the rice a serving of canned apricots. The Caucasian servers were thinking that the fruit poured over rice would make a good dessert. Among the Japanese, of course, rice is never eaten with sweet foods, only with salty or savory foods. Few of us could eat such a mixture. But at this point no one dared protest. It would have been impolite. I was horrified when I saw the apricot syrup seeping through my little mound of rice. I opened my mouth to complain. My mother jabbed me in the back to keep quiet. We moved on through the line and joined the others squatting in the lee[8] of half-raised walls, dabbing courteously at what was, for almost everyone there, an inedible concoction.

After dinner we were taken to Block 16, a cluster of fifteen barracks that had just been finished a day or so earlier—although finished was hardly the word for it. The shacks were built of one thickness of pine planking covered with tarpaper. They sat on concrete footings, with about two feet of open space between the floor-

Visual Vocabulary
A soldier in the field eats from a *mess kit*, which is a metal container that holds eating utensils and opens into a plate with two compartments.

---

6. Manzanar was built in *Owens Valley*, near Death Valley, about 200 miles north of Los Angeles.
7. A *mess hall* is a place where meals are eaten.

The Power of Memory *Why does the author remember the people in the bus and the greeters laughing?*

8. *Lee* is shelter or protection, especially on the side of something facing away from the wind.

Summarize *Summarize the information given in this paragraph about the food at Manzanar. What point is the author making here?*

boards and the ground. Gaps showed between the planks, and as the weeks passed and the green wood dried out, the gaps widened. Knotholes gaped in the uncovered floor.

Each barracks was divided into six units, sixteen by twenty feet, about the size of a living room, with one bare bulb hanging from the ceiling and an oil stove for heat. We were assigned two of these for the twelve people in our family group; and our official family "number" was enlarged by three digits—16 plus the number of this barracks. We were issued steel army cots, two brown army blankets each, and some mattress covers, which my brothers stuffed with straw.

The first task was to divide up what space we had for sleeping. Bill and Woody contributed a blanket each and partitioned off the first room: one side for Bill and Tomi, one side for Woody and Chizu and their baby girl. Woody also got the stove, for heating formulas.

The people who had it hardest during the first few months were young couples like these, many of whom had married just before the evacuation began, in order not to be separated and sent to different camps. Our two rooms were crowded, but at least it was all in the family. My oldest sister and her husband were shoved into one of those sixteen-by-twenty-foot compartments with six people they had never seen before—two other couples, one recently married like themselves, the other with two teenage boys. Partitioning off a room like that wasn't easy. It was bitter cold when we arrived, and the wind did not abate.[9] All they had to use for room dividers were those army blankets, two of which were barely enough to keep one person warm. They argued over whose blanket should be

sacrificed and later argued about noise at night—the parents wanted their boys asleep by 9:00 P.M.—and they continued arguing over matters like that for six months, until my sister and her husband left to harvest sugar beets in Idaho. It was grueling[10] work up there, and wages were pitiful, but when the call came through camp for workers to **alleviate** the wartime labor shortage, it sounded better than their life at Manzanar. They knew they'd have, if nothing else, a room, perhaps a cabin of their own.

That first night in Block 16, the rest of us squeezed into the second room—Granny, Lillian, age fourteen, Ray, thirteen, May, eleven, Kiyo, ten, Mama, and me. I didn't mind this at all at the time. Being youngest meant I got to sleep with Mama. And before we went to bed I had a great time jumping up and down on the mattress. The boys had stuffed so much straw into hers, we had to flatten it some so we wouldn't slide off. I slept with her every night after that until Papa came back.

We woke early, shivering and coated with dust that had blown up through the knot-holes and in through the slits around the doorway. During the night Mama had unpacked all our clothes and heaped them on our beds for warmth. Now our cubicle looked as if a great laundry bag had exploded and then been sprayed with fine dust. A skin of sand covered the floor. I looked over Mama's shoulder at Kiyo, on top of his fat mattress, buried under jeans and overcoats and sweaters. His eyebrows were gray, and he was starting to giggle.

---

10. *Grueling* work is very difficult, exhausting work.

Summarize *Summarize what happened to the author's sister and brother-in-law.*

Vocabulary

alleviate (ə lē′ vē āt′) *v.* to make easier to bear; relieve; lessen

---

9. The fact that the wind did not *abate* means that it did not lessen in force or intensity.

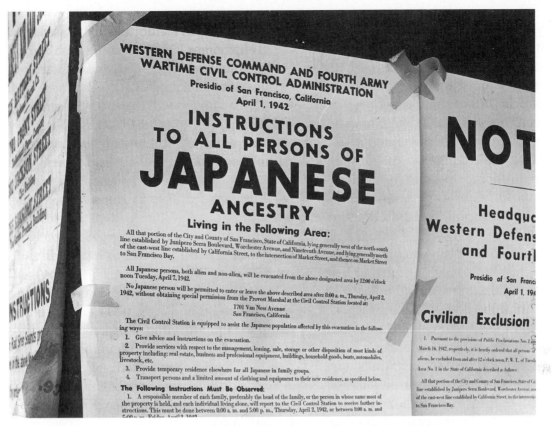

Posted notice informing people of Japanese ancestry of imminent relocation rules due to fears of treason and spying during early years of WWII, April 1, 1942. Dorothea Lange. Silver Gelatin Photograph.

View the Art If you saw a sign like this posted today, how would it make you feel? Explain.

He was looking at me, at my gray eyebrows and coated hair, and pretty soon we were both giggling. I looked at Mama's face to see if she thought Kiyo was funny. She lay very still next to me on our mattress, her eyes scanning everything—bare rafters, walls, dusty kids—scanning slowly, and I think the mask of her face would have cracked had not Woody's voice just then come at us through the wall. He was rapping on the planks as if testing to see if they were hollow.

"Hey!" he yelled. "You guys fall into the same flour barrel as us?"

"No," Kiyo yelled back. "Ours is full of Japs."

The Power of Memory *Why does the author remember moments of humor during her stay at Manzanar?*

All of us laughed at this.

"Well, tell 'em it's time to get up," Woody said. "If we're gonna live in this place, we better get to work."

He gave us ten minutes to dress, then he came in carrying a broom, a hammer, and a sack full of tin can lids he had scrounged somewhere. Woody would be our leader for a while now, short, stocky, grinning behind his mustache. He had just turned twenty-four. In later years he would tour the country with Mr. Moto, the Japanese tag-team wrestler, as his sinister assistant Suki—karate chops through the ropes from outside the ring, a chunky leg reaching from under his kimono to trip up Mr. Moto's foe. In the ring Woody's smile looked sly and crafty; he hammed it up. Offstage it was whimsical, as if some joke were bursting to be told.

"Hey, brother Ray, Kiyo," he said. "You see these tin can lids?"

"Yeah, yeah," the boys said drowsily, as if going back to sleep. They were both young versions of Woody.

"You see all them knotholes in the floor and in the walls?"

They looked around. You could see about a dozen.

Woody said, "You get those covered up before breakfast time. Any more sand comes in here through one of them knotholes, you have to eat it off the floor with ketchup."

"What about sand that comes in through the cracks?" Kiyo said.

Woody stood up very straight, which in itself was funny, since he was only about five-foot-six.

"Don't worry about the cracks," he said. "Different kind of sand comes in through the cracks."

He put his hands on his hips and gave Kiyo a sternly comic look, squinting at him through one eye the way Papa would when he was asserting his authority. Woody mimicked Papa's voice: "And I can tell the difference. So be careful."

The boys laughed and went to work nailing down lids. May started sweeping out the sand. I was helping Mama fold the clothes we'd used for cover, when Woody came over and put his arm around her shoulder. He was short; she was even shorter, under five feet.

He said softly, "You okay, Mama?"

She didn't look at him, she just kept folding clothes and said, "Can we get the cracks covered too, Woody?"

Outside the sky was clear, but icy gusts of wind were buffeting our barracks every few minutes, sending fresh dust puffs up through the floorboards. May's broom could barely keep up with it, and our oil heater could scarcely hold its own against the drafts.

"We'll get this whole place as tight as a barrel, Mama. I already met a guy who told me where they pile all the scrap lumber."

"Scrap?"

"That's all they got. I mean, they're still building the camp, you know. Sixteen blocks left to go. After that, they say maybe we'll get some stuff to fix the insides a little bit."

Her eyes blazed then, her voice quietly furious. "Woody, we can't live like this. Animals live like this."

It was hard to get Woody down. He'd keep smiling when everybody else was ready to explode. Grief flickered in his eyes. He blinked it away and hugged her tighter. "We'll make it better, Mama. You watch."

We could hear voices in other cubicles now. Beyond the wall Woody's baby girl started to cry.

"I have to go over to the kitchen," he said, "see if those guys got a pot for heating bottles. That oil stove takes too long—something wrong with the fuel line. I'll find out what they're giving us for breakfast."

"Probably hotcakes with soy sauce," Kiyo said, on his hands and knees between the bunks.

"No." Woody grinned, heading out the door. "Rice. With Log Cabin Syrup and melted butter."

I don't remember what we ate that first morning. I know we stood for half an hour in cutting wind waiting to get our food. Then we took it back to the cubicle and ate huddled around the stove. Inside, it was warmer than when we left, because Woody was already making good his promise to

---

Historical Narrative *How does Kiyo's comment reflect the misperceptions many people in the United States had about Japanese Americans?*

Children Awaiting Relocation (Assembly Center, Turlock, California), May 2, 1942. Dorothea Lange. Silver Gelatin Photograph.

<u>View the Art</u> Acclaimed photographer Dorothea Lange was hired by the War Relocation Authority (WRA) to document the evacuation and internment of thousands of Californians of Japanese ancestry. What does this photograph suggest about life in the internment camp?

Mama, tacking up some ends of lath[11] he'd found, stuffing rolled paper around the door frame.

Trouble was, he had almost nothing to work with. Beyond this temporary weather stripping, there was little else he could do. Months went by, in fact, before our "home" changed much at all from what it was the day we moved in—bare floors, blanket partitions, one bulb in each compartment dangling from a roof beam, and open ceilings overhead so that mischievous boys like Ray and Kiyo could climb up into the rafters and peek into anyone's life.

The simple truth is the camp was no more ready for us when we got there than we were ready for it. We had only the dimmest ideas of what to expect. Most of the families, like us, had moved out from southern California with as much luggage as each person could carry. Some old men left Los Angeles wearing Hawaiian shirts and Panama hats and stepped off the bus at an altitude of 4000 feet, with nothing available but sagebrush and tarpaper to stop the April winds pouring down off the back side of the Sierras.[12]

---

11. In construction, *lath* is any of the thin, narrow strips of wood used as a foundation for plaster or tiles.

12. The *Sierras,* or Sierra Nevada Mountains, run through eastern California. Manzanar was between these mountains and Death Valley.

Group of evacuees of Japanese ancestry lined up outside train after arriving at Santa Anita Assembly Center from San Pedro as row of US soldiers face them, March 31, 1942. Dorothea Lange. Silver Gelatin Photograph.

<u>View the Art</u> What is the mood of this photograph? What are some of the thoughts or feelings that the people in the evacuee line might be experiencing in this scene?

The War Department was in charge of all the camps at this point. They began to issue military surplus from the First World War—olive-drab knit caps, earmuffs, peacoats, canvas leggings. Later on, sewing machines were shipped in, and one barracks was turned into a clothing factory. An old seamstress took a peacoat of mine, tore the lining out, opened and flattened the sleeves, added a collar, put arm holes in and handed me back a beautiful cape.

By fall dozens of seamstresses were working full-time transforming thousands of these old army clothes into capes, slacks and stylish coats. But until that factory got going and packages from friends outside began to fill out our wardrobes, warmth was more important than style. I couldn't help laughing at Mama walking around in army earmuffs and a pair of wide-cuffed, khaki-colored wool trousers several sizes

The Power of Memory *What is significant about the author's memory of the seamstresses?*

too big for her. Japanese are generally smaller than Caucasians, and almost all these clothes were oversize. They flopped, they dangled, they hung.

It seems comical, looking back; we were a band of Charlie Chaplins marooned in the California desert. But at the time, it was pure chaos. That's the only way to describe it. The evacuation had been so hurriedly planned, the camps so hastily thrown together, nothing was completed when we got there, and almost nothing worked.

I was sick continually, with stomach cramps and diarrhea. At first it was from the shots they gave us for typhoid, in very heavy doses and in assembly-line fashion: swab, jab, swab, *Move along now,* swab, jab, swab, *Keep it moving.* That knocked all of us younger kids down at once, with fevers and vomiting. Later, it was the food that made us sick, young and old alike. The kitchens were too small and badly ventilated. Food would spoil from being left out too long. That summer, when the heat got fierce, it would spoil faster. The refrigeration kept breaking down. The cooks, in many cases, had never cooked before. Each block had to provide its own volunteers. Some were lucky and had a professional or two in their midst. But the first chef in our block had been a gardener all his life and suddenly found himself preparing three meals a day for 250 people.

Historical Narrative *What does this information tell you about living conditions at Manzanar?*

"The Manzanar runs" became a condition of life, and you only hoped that when you rushed to the latrine, one would be in working order.

That first morning, on our way to the chow line, Mama and I tried to use the women's latrine in our block. The smell of it spoiled what little appetite we had. Outside, men were working in an open trench, up to their knees in muck—a common sight in the months to come. Inside, the floor was covered with excrement, and all twelve bowls were erupting like a row of tiny volcanoes.

Mama stopped a kimono-wrapped woman stepping past us with her sleeve pushed up against her nose and asked, "What do you do?"

"Try Block Twelve," the woman said, grimacing. "They have just finished repairing the pipes."

It was about two city blocks away. We followed her over there and found a line of women waiting in the wind outside the latrine. We had no choice but to join the line and wait with them.

Inside it was like all the other latrines. Each block was built to the same design, just as each of the ten camps, from California to Arkansas, was built to a common master plan. It was an open room, over a concrete slab. The sink was a long metal trough against one wall, with a row of spigots for hot and cold water. Down the center of the room twelve toilet bowls were arranged in six pairs, back to back, with no partitions. My mother was a very modest person, and this was going to be agony for her, sitting down in public, among strangers.

One old woman had already solved the problem for herself by dragging in a large cardboard carton. She set it up around one of the bowls, like a three-sided screen. OXYDOL was printed in large black letters down the front. I remember this well, because that was the soap we were issued for laundry; later on, the smell of it would permeate these rooms. The upended carton was about four feet high. The old woman behind it wasn't much taller. When she stood, only her head showed over the top.

She was about Granny's age. With great effort she was trying to fold the sides of the screen together. Mama happened to be at the head of the line now. As she approached the vacant bowl, she and the old woman bowed to each other from the waist. Mama then moved to help her with the carton, and the old woman said very graciously, in Japanese, "Would you like to use it?"

Happily, gratefully, Mama bowed again and said, *"Arigato"* (Thank you). *"Arigato gozaimas"* (Thank you very much). "I will return it to your barracks."

"Oh, no. It is not necessary. I will be glad to wait."

The old woman unfolded one side of the cardboard, while Mama opened the other; then she bowed again and scurried out the door.

Those big cartons were a common sight in the spring of 1942. Eventually sturdier partitions appeared, one or two at a time. The first were built of scrap lumber. Word would get around that Block such and such had partitions now, and Mama and my older sisters would walk halfway across the camp to use them. Even after every latrine in camp was screened, this quest for privacy continued. Many would wait until late at night. Ironically, because of this, midnight was often the most crowded time of all. Like so many of the women there, Mama never did get used to the latrines. It was a humiliation she just learned to endure: *shikata ga nai,* this cannot be helped. She would quickly **subordinate** her own desires to those of the family or the community, because she knew cooperation was the only way to survive. At the same time she placed a high premium on personal privacy, respected it in others and insisted upon it for herself. Almost everyone at Manzanar had inherited this pair of traits from the generations before them who had learned to live in a small, crowded country like Japan. Because of the first they were able to take a desolate stretch of wasteland and gradually make it livable. But the entire situation there, especially in the beginning—the packed sleeping quarters, the communal mess halls, the open toilets—all this was an open insult to that other, private self, a slap in the face you were powerless to challenge. ✑

shikata ga nai, this cannot be helped

The Power of Memory *How would it affect you to see friends or family members endure humiliations such as the ones Mama endured?*

Summarize *What does this summary of conditions at Manzanar show the reader? What might have been the author's purpose in including it here?*

Vocabulary

subordinate (sə bôr′də nāt′) *v.* to cause to be, or treat as, secondary, inferior, or less important

After You Read

Respond and Think Critically

1. **Connect to Personal Experience** What detail about Manzanar affected you most? Explain.

2. **Make Inferences About the Author** How did the author feel about moving to Terminal Island? Why do you think the author felt this way?

3. **Explain Events** What did Mama do when the secondhand dealer offered her a low price for her valuable dishes? Why did she do this?

4. **Compare and Contrast Behavior** How did the teacher at Boyle Heights treat the author? Compare and contrast that teacher with the teacher from Ocean Park.

5. **Evaluate Narrative Details** Why does the author mention various events in U.S. history throughout the text? Do you think this makes her story more effective? Explain.

6. **Evaluate Description** Why does the author offer descriptions of her houses throughout this time period? Do the comparisons of the houses achieve an important purpose within the text? Use evidence from the text to support your responses.

7. **Big Idea** **Draw Conclusions About Historical Events** The author said that going back to visit Manzanar made her realize that her life began there. What lessons did you learn about U.S. internment of Japanese Americans from reading about Wakatsuki Houston's memories? Support your answer with details from her story.

8. **Draw Conclusions About Cultural Context** Executive Order 9066 came as a shock to Japanese Americans. Do you think an event like the Japanese internment could happen in the United States today? Why or why not?

Literary Element Historical Narrative

A **historical narrative** can blend elements of objectivity and subjectivity. For instance, some facts that Wakatsuki Houston mentions are verifiable and are recounted in numerous other sources. Other details she describes are anecdotal, deal with feelings and perceptions, and come from her personal memories.

9. **Draw Conclusions About Historical Narrative** How would this narrative be different if it had been written by someone who had no personal experience of Manzanar? Would it be as effective? Explain.

10. **Evaluate Historical Context** Does Wakatsuki Houston give enough objective details about the historical period to help the reader understand the context of the narrative? Explain.

Review: Autobiography

As you learned on page 255, an **autobiography** is a person's account of his or her own life. In most autobiographies, the writer tells the story from the first-person point of view, using the pronoun *I*. The use of this point of view makes most autobiographies very personal and subjective.

11. **Partner Activity** Meet with another student and list some details from the text that you would not find in a more objective source, such as an encyclopedia. Then draw conclusions about how these details help you better understand this episode in U.S. history.

Details	Conclusion
Mama breaks her valuable china.	gives a personal account; offers a perspective that a strictly factual account wouldn't

Texas Test Practice (RC-10.A)

1. Which sentence best summarizes the main idea of this excerpt from *Manzanar*?

A. For the families involved, internment was bewildering, unjust, and humiliating.

B. Japanese Americans had done nothing to threaten national security.

C. Many families of Japanese origin were not involved in mainstream American culture.

D. Internment camps for Japanese Americans were poorly planned and constructed.

E. The old and the young adapted differently to the restrictions of internment camps.

Vocabulary Practice

Practice with Word Parts Use a dictionary to find the meaning of each vocabulary word's root. Organize the meanings in a diagram as shown. Then use the word correctly in a sentence.

patriarch designation alleviate subordinate

EXAMPLE:

Root:	→	bene, "good, well"
Root:	→	dict, "say"
Suffix:	→	-ion "act of"

The holy man said a **benediction***.*

Academic Vocabulary

The people at Manzanar lived in square, **geometric** *shacks.*

Geometric is a discipline-specific word that derives from Greek. The prefix *geo-* means "earth; ground." Using your knowledge and context clues, determine the meaning of *geometric* in the model sentence above. Check your response by consulting a dictionary. Finally, demonstrate your understanding by using each of these related words in a sentence.

a. geology   **b.** geomorphic   **c.** geometry

Enrich and Extend

Research and Report

Internet Connection Use the Internet to research the internment of Japanese Americans during World War II. Write an informational report.

Get Ideas Brainstorm or consult with others to help narrow your topic. Formulate a major research question to address the topic. Then list five questions to focus and clarify your research. Develop a timeline for completing your work and a search plan that includes primary sources. Look for sources that reflect a wide range of viewpoints and that identify the major issues about Japanese internment.

Research Take notes, creating separate electronic files or notecards for each bit of information you record. Modify your research question as needed to refocus your plan. Evaluate the reliability and objectivity of each source. Paraphrase and summarize most information; directly quote only memorable or incisive ideas. For all information you record—quoted, paraphrased, or summarized—integrate citations. Organize your notes by main ideas.

Information from Site	Example of Parenthetical Citation
Author given;	(Hashimori)
if no author, cite sponsor;	(University of Utah Historic Collections)
if no author or sponsor, cite Web site title	("Children of the Camps")

Report As you evaluate the relevance of information and synthesize ideas and details from at least three sources, use topic sentences for main ideas and supporting sentences for specific data, facts, and ideas. Include graphics such as charts. Use all source material ethically by citing your sources at the end, as well as in parenthetical references. Present your report to the class.

Grammar Workshop

Subject-Verb Agreement

TEKS

10.17.B Identify and use the subjunctive mood to express doubts, wishes, and possibilities.

Literature Connection In a sentence, the **verb** (or action word) must agree with the **subject** (or actor) in both person and number. In the sentence below from *Farewell to Manzanar,* although the subject, *barracks,* looks plural, it functions as a unit and takes the singular auxiliary verb *was.*

> "Each barracks was divided into six units, sixteen by twenty feet, about the size of a living room. . . ."

A verb may express the indicative or the subjunctive mood. The **indicative** makes a statement ("She takes the bus home") or asks a question. The **subjunctive** expresses doubts, wishes, and possibilities. In the subjunctive, the *-s* gets dropped from the third-person singular ("We suggest that she **take** the bus home"). To state a condition contrary to fact, the subjunctive uses the past tense, and *were,* not *was* ("If she **were** late, she would have taken the bus home").

More examples of subject-verb agreement:

With a compound subject that is joined by *and* . . .

Use a singular verb if the parts of the subject make up a single unit. **Use a plural verb** if the parts of the subject are not considered a unit.

Rice and fruit is an unheard-of combination to the Japanese. The neighborhood bully and his friend were frightening.

With a compound subject that is joined by *or* or *nor* . . .

Use a verb that agrees with the subject closest to it.

Either their homework or their chores keep the children inside.

With a subject that is a collective noun . . .

Use a singular verb if the noun refers to a group as a whole.

The committee has to come to a decision by noon.

Practice Write out the correct form of the verb in each sentence below.

1. The family (tries, try) to stick together and support each other.
2. Neither Mother nor the other parents (stops, stop) worrying.
3. Manzanar and another camp (is, are) located on the west coast.
4. The family members wish that they (was, were) free to leave.

Subjects and Verbs

A **verb** is the action word in a sentence, and the **subject** is who or what performs the action. **Subject-verb agreement** occurs when the subject and verb match in person and number.

Tip

To help ensure subject-verb agreement, identify each subject as singular or plural and use an appropriate verb.

Language Handbook

For more on subject-verb agreement, see the Language Handbook, pp. R56–R57.

LOG ON **Literature** Online

Grammar For more grammar practice, go to glencoe.com and enter QuickPass code GL57805u2.

Before You Read

from *Kaffir Boy*

Meet **Mark Mathabane**
(born 1960)

What was it like to grow up in South Africa under the system of apartheid? For Mark Mathabane (mä tä bä′ne) "it meant hate, bitterness, hunger, pain, terror, violence, fear, dashed hopes and dreams."

Dark Childhood Mathabane spent his early years living in poverty and fear under the apartheid government, which relegated black South Africans to ghettos and treated them as inferior people. Constant police raids and relocation to worthless parcels of land where work and education were scarce made life unbearable for black South Africans.

Mathabane's family lived in Alexandra township, in a square-mile ghetto packed with 200,000 black South Africans. Barely subsisting on the ten dollars that Mathabane's father made each week, the family already found life in the Alexandra township to be brutal and harsh. But when Mathabane's father was arrested for being unemployed, the family fell into even deeper poverty.

> "*Books aren't written with the comfort of readers in mind. I know I didn't write* Kaffir Boy *that way.*"
>
> —Mark Mathabane

Escape from Oppression Although illiterate, Mathabane's mother understood the importance of education and insisted that her son attend school. Mathabane decided to master English, which black South Africans were forbidden to learn. At the age of thirteen, he took up tennis and five years later won a tennis scholarship to an American college; he called the scholarship "my passport to freedom."

In 1986 Mathabane published his first book, *Kaffir Boy*, an honest portrayal of the horrors of growing up under apartheid. Despite being banned by the South African government for its powerful anti-apartheid sentiment, this autobiography was hugely successful.

A New Life *Kaffir Boy in America*, an account of Mathabane's arrival and first years in the United States, followed in 1989. This sequel relates Mathabane's difficulties in adapting to a new culture and lifestyle in a land that was wonderfully different from, but possessed unfortunate similarities to, the apartheid system. One of his most recent books is the memoir *Miriam's Song* (2001), about his sister's experience of the last days of apartheid.

LOG ON ▶ **Literature** Online

Author Search For more about Mark Mathabane, go to glencoe.com and enter QuickPass code GL57805u2.

Literature and Reading Preview

Connect to the Autobiography

How does education change the way you see the world? Freewrite for a few minutes about the ways your education has affected your perception of the world.

Build Background

Under apartheid, black South Africans, who made up more than 75 percent of the population, and other nonwhite people were forced to live and work under a system of strict racial segregation. Apartheid sparked strong opposition and came to a definitive end in 1994 with the electoral victory of Nelson Mandela's African National Congress.

Set Purposes for Reading

Big Idea The Power of Memory

As you read this excerpt from *Kaffir Boy*, ask yourself, How does Mathabane show the power of memory to change one's life for the better?

Literary Element Theme

Theme is the central message of a work of literature that readers can apply to life. Finding the theme of a story helps you connect with the author's purpose in writing. As you read, ask yourself, What is the central theme of this literary text?

Reading Strategy Analyze Cause-and-Effect Relationships

A **cause-and-effect relationship** is a connection between the reason for an occurrence and the occurrence itself. Analyzing these relationships helps to explain why things happen and why a character or person makes the decisions he or she makes. As you read, ask yourself, What influences the people in *Kaffir Boy* to make the decisions they do?

....

Tip: Make Inferences Use the blue highlighted questions and a chart like the one below to identify causes and effects in the text and make inferences about their meaning.

Cause	Effect	Inference
His gang refuses to go to school.	Narrator decides not to go to school.	The gang strongly influences the narrator.

TEKS

For pages 274–289

10.6 Understand, make inferences and draw conclusions about the varied structural patterns and features of literary nonfiction and provide evidence from text to support understanding.

Vocabulary

coterie (kō′tə rē) *n.* a small group of people who share a particular interest and often meet socially; p. 279 *Janelle and her airplane-loving coterie crafted model airplanes.*

admonish (ad mon′ish) *v.* to warn, as against a specific action; p. 279 *José's parents admonished him to stay out of the canyon.*

peruse (pə rōōz′) *v.* to read through or examine carefully; p. 281 *The doctor perused the medical journals for detailed information.*

credence (krēd′əns) *n.* trustworthiness, especially in the reports or statements of others; p. 283 *The lawyer's argument had more credence than the accounts of bystanders.*

vehemently (vē′ə mənt lē) *adv.* strongly; intensely; passionately; p. 285 *The peace activists argued vehemently against the war.*

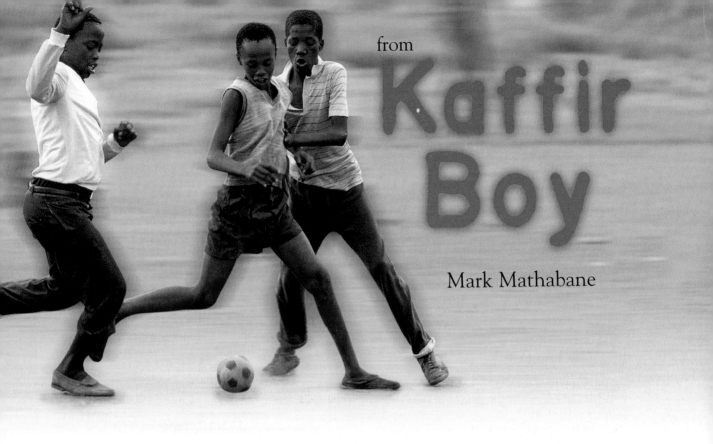

from

Kaffir Boy

Mark Mathabane

"Education will open doors where none seem to exist."

When my mother began dropping hints that I would soon be going to school, I vowed never to go because school was a waste of time. She laughed and said, "We'll see. You don't know what you're talking about." My philosophy on school was that of a gang of ten-, eleven-, and twelve-year-olds whom I so revered that their every word seemed that of an oracle.[1]

These boys had long left their homes and were now living in various neighborhood junkyards, making it on their own. They slept in abandoned cars, smoked glue and benzene,[2] ate pilchards[3] and brown bread, sneaked into the white world to caddy and, if unsuccessful, came back to the township to steal beer and soda bottles from shebeens,[4] or goods from the Indian traders on First Avenue. Their life style was exciting, adventurous, and full of surprises; and I was attracted to it. My mother told me that they were no-gooders, that they would amount to nothing, that I should not associate with them, but I paid no heed. What does she know? I used to tell myself. One thing she did not know was that the gang's way of life had captivated me wholly, particularly their philosophy on school: they hated it and considered an education a waste of time.

They, like myself, had grown up in an environment where the value of an education

---

1. In Greek mythology, the gods sometimes spoke through an *oracle*, or a person such as a priestess.
2. The boys are taking a risk with *benzene*, a poisonous liquid obtained from coal.
3. *Pilchard*s are small fish of the herring family.

4. *Shebeens* are taverns operating without government license or approval.

Analyze Cause-and-Effect Relationships *What was the cause of Mathabane's aversion to school?*

was never emphasized, where the first thing a child learned was not how to read and write and spell, but how to fight and steal and rebel; where the money to send children to school was grossly[5] lacking, for survival was first priority. I kept my membership in the gang, knowing that for as long as I was under its influence, I would never go to school.

One day my mother woke me up at four in the morning.

"Are they here? I didn't hear any noises," I asked in the usual way.

"No," my mother said. "I want you to get into that washtub over there."

"What!" I balked, upon hearing the word washtub. I feared taking baths like one feared the plague. Throughout seven years of hectic living the number of baths I had taken could be counted on one hand with several fingers missing. I simply had no natural inclination for water; cleanliness was a trait I still had to acquire. Besides, we had only one bathtub in the house, and it constantly sprung a leak.

"I said get into that tub!" My mother shook a finger in my face.

Reluctantly, I obeyed, yet wondered why all of a sudden I had to take a bath. My mother, armed with a scrobbrush and a piece of Lifebuoy soap, purged[6] me of years and years of grime till I ached and bled. As I howled, feeling pain shoot through my limbs as the thistles of the brush encountered stubborn calluses, there was a loud knock at the door.

Instantly my mother leaped away from the tub and headed, on tiptoe, toward the bedroom. Fear seized me as I, too, thought of the police. I sat frozen in the bathtub, not knowing what to do.

"Open up, Mujaji [my mother's maiden name]," Granny's voice came shrilling through the door. "It's me."

My mother heaved a sigh of relief; her tense limbs relaxed. She turned and headed to the kitchen door, unlatched it, and in came Granny and Aunt Bushy.

"You scared me half to death," my mother said to Granny. "I had forgotten all about your coming."

"Are you ready?" Granny asked my mother.

"Yes—just about," my mother said, beckoning me to get out of the washtub.

She handed me a piece of cloth to dry myself. As I dried myself, questions raced through my mind: What's going on? What's Granny doing at our house this ungodly[7] hour of the morning? And why did she ask my mother, "Are you ready?" While I stood debating, my mother went into the bedroom and came out with a stained white shirt and a pair of faded black shorts.

"Here," she said, handing me the togs, "put these on."

"Why?" I asked.

"Put them on I said!"

I put the shirt on; it was grossly loose-fitting. It reached all the way down to my ankles. Then I saw the reason why: it was my father's shirt!

"But this is Papa's shirt," I complained. "It don't fit me."

"Put it on," my mother insisted. "I'll make it fit."

"The pants don't fit me either," I said. "Whose are they anyway?"

---

5. Here, *grossly* means "totally; entirely."
6. To *purge* is to cleanse or get rid of whatever is unclean or undesirable.

Theme *Do you think the author has strong convictions of his own at this point? Explain.*

Theme *What does the bathing scene suggest about the author's attachment to his old way of life?*

---

7. In this context, *ungodly* means "outrageous; shocking."

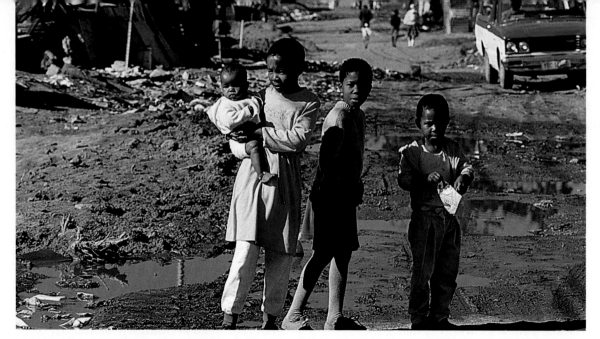

Children in Alexandra Township. Louise Gubb.

View the Art Alexandra continues to be one of the poorest areas in the Gauteng region of South Africa, suffering from overcrowding, crime, and a lack of infrastructure. Half of all young people in the area do not receive education. What does the background in this photograph tell you about daily life for these children? How might the older three react to being enrolled in school like the author was?

"Put them on," my mother said. "I'll make them fit."

Moments later I had the garments on; I looked ridiculous. My mother started working on the pants and shirt to make them fit. She folded the shirt in so many intricate ways and stashed it inside the pants, they too having been folded several times at the waist. She then choked the pants at the waist with a piece of sisal rope to hold them up. She then lavishly smeared my face, arms, and legs with a mixture of pig's fat and vaseline. "This will insulate you from the cold," she said. My skin gleamed like the morning star, and I felt as hot as the center of the sun, and I smelled God knows like what. After embalming me, she headed to the bedroom.

Visual Vocabulary
Sisal is a coarse, strong fiber obtained from the leaves of a tropical plant.

"Where are we going, Gran'ma?" I said, hoping that she would tell me what my mother refused to tell me. I still had no idea I was about to be taken to school.

"Didn't your mother tell you?" Granny said with a smile. "You're going to start school."

"What!" I gasped, leaping from the chair where I was sitting as if it were made of hot lead. "I am not going to school!" I blurted out and raced toward the kitchen door.

My mother had just reappeared from the bedroom and guessing what I was up to, she yelled, "Someone get the door!"

Aunt Bushy immediately barred the door. I turned and headed for the window. As I leaped for the windowsill, my mother lunged at me and brought me down. I tussled, "Let go of me! I don't want to go to school! Let me go!" but my mother held fast onto me.

"It's no use now," she said, grinning triumphantly as she pinned me down.

Turning her head in Granny's direction, she shouted, "Granny! Get a rope quickly!"

Granny grabbed a piece of rope nearby and came to my mother's aid. I bit and clawed every hand that grabbed me, and howled protestations against going to school; however, I was no match for the two determined matriarchs.[8] In a jiffy they had me bound, hands and feet.

"What's the matter with him?" Granny, bewildered, asked my mother. "Why did he suddenly turn into an imp[9] when I told him you're taking him to school?"

"You shouldn't have told him that he's being taken to school," my mother said. "He doesn't want to go there. That's why I requested you come today, to help me take him there. Those boys in the streets have been a bad influence on him."

As the two matriarchs hauled me through the door, they told Aunt Bushy not to go to school but stay behind and mind the house and the children.

The sun was beginning to rise from beyond the veld[10] when Granny and my mother dragged me to school. The streets were beginning to fill with their everyday traffic: old men and women, wizened,[11] bent, and ragged, were beginning their rambling; workless men and women were beginning to assemble in their usual **coteries** and head for shebeens in the back-yards where they discussed how they escaped the morning pass raids[12] and contemplated the conditions of life amidst intense beer drinking and vacant, uneasy laughter; young boys and girls, some as young as myself, were beginning their aimless wanderings along the narrow, dusty streets in search of food, carrying bawling infants piggyback.

As we went along some of the streets, boys and girls who shared the same fears about school as I were making their feelings known in a variety of ways. They were howling their protests and trying to escape. A few managed to break loose and make a mad dash for freedom, only to be recaptured in no time, **admonished** or whipped, or both, and ordered to march again.

As we made a turn into Sixteenth Avenue, the street leading to the tribal school I was being taken to, a short, chubby black woman came along from the opposite direction. She had a scuttle[13] overflowing with coal on her *doek*-covered (cloth-covered) head. An infant, bawling deafeningly, was loosely swathed with a piece of sheepskin onto her back. Following closely behind the woman, and picking up pieces of coal as they fell from the scuttle and placing them in a small plastic bag, was a half-naked, potbellied, and thumb-sucking boy of about four. The woman stopped abreast.[14] For some reason we stopped too.

"I wish I had done the same to my oldest son," the strange woman said in a regretful

---

8. *Matriarchs* (mā′trē ärks′) are women who head families or who have great authority in other groups.
9. Here, *imp* means "a mischievous child."
10. In South Africa, the *veld* (velt) is a rolling grassland with scattered trees or bushes.
11. When the elderly become *wizened* (wiz′ ənd), they are shriveled or withered due to age.

The Power of Memory *Why might Mathabane remember so vividly the details of that day later in life?*

Vocabulary

coterie (kō′tə rē) *n.* a small group of people who share a particular interest and often meet socially

12. *Pass raids* refers to the practice whereby police periodically stopped black South Africans to see that they had the proper papers authorizing them to be in specific areas.
13. Here, a *scuttle* is a coal container.
14. *Abreast* means "alongside others."

Vocabulary

admonish (ad mon′ish) *v.* to warn, as against a specific action

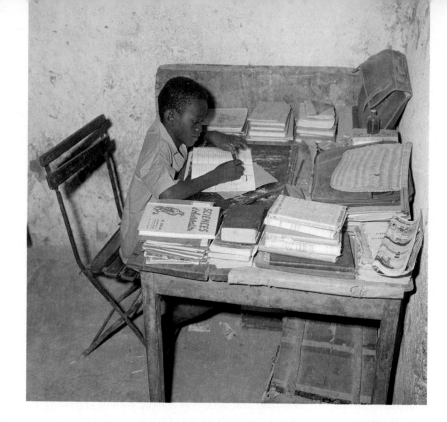

A schoolboy does homework at his desk, Mali. 1960, Paul Almasy Mali.

View the Art Resources for education are scarce throughout Africa, but many organizations have targeted education as a key component for fighting poverty and hunger. How do this child's attitude and activities reflect the theme of Mathabane's tale?

voice, gazing at me. I was confounded[15] by her stopping and offering her unsolicited opinion.

"I wish I had done that to my oldest son," she repeated, and suddenly burst into tears; amidst sobs, she continued, "before . . . the street claimed him . . . and . . . turned him into a tsotsi."[16]

Granny and my mother offered consolatory remarks to the strange woman.

"But it's too late now," the strange woman continued, tears now streaming freely down her puffy cheeks. She made no attempt to dry them. "It's too late now," she said for the second time, "he's beyond any help. I can't help him even if I wanted to. *Uswile*[17] [He is dead]."

"How did he die?" my mother asked in a sympathetic voice.

"He shunned school and, instead, grew up to live by the knife. And the same knife he lived by ended his life. That's why whenever I see a boy-child refuse to go to school, I stop and tell the story of my dear little *mbitsini*[18] [heartbreak]."

Having said that, the strange woman left as mysteriously as she had arrived.

"Did you hear what that woman said!" my mother screamed into my ears. "Do you want the same to happen to you?"

I dropped my eyes. I was confused.

"Poor woman," Granny said ruefully. "She must have truly loved her son."

Finally, we reached the school and I was ushered into the principal's office, a tiny cubicle facing a row of privies[19] and a patch of yellowed grass.

"So this is the rascal we'd been talking about," the principal, a tall, wiry man,

---

15. To be *confounded* is to be confused or bewildered.
16. A *tsotsi* (tsot´ sē) is an armed street hoodlum or gangster.
17. *Uswile* (o͞o swēl´ ā)

18. *mbitsini* (əm bit sē´ nē)
19. *Privies* (priv´ ēz) are outhouses, or toilets.

Analyze Cause-and-Effect Relationships *What does the woman think caused her son to become a* tsotsi?

Theme *Why is it significant that Mathabane encounters this woman?*

foppishly[20] dressed in a black pin-striped suit, said to my mother as we entered. His austere,[21] shiny face, inscrutable and imposing, reminded me of my father. He was sitting behind a brown table upon which stood piles of dust and cobweb-covered books and papers. In one upper pocket of his jacket was arrayed a variety of pens and pencils; in the other nestled a lily-white handkerchief whose presence was more decorative than utilitarian.[22] Alongside him stood a disproportion-ately portly[23] black woman, fashionably dressed in a black skirt and a white blouse. She had but one pen, and this she held in her hand. The room was hot and stuffy and buzzing with flies.

"Yes, Principal," my mother answered, "this is he."

"I see he's living up to his notoriety," re-marked the principal, noticing that I had been bound. "Did he give you too much trouble?"

"Principal," my mother sighed. "He was like an imp."

"He's just like the rest of them, Principal," Granny sighed. "Once they get out into the streets, they become wild. They take to the many vices of the streets like an infant takes to its mother's milk. They begin to think that there's no other life but the one shown them by the *tsotsis*. They come to hate school and forget about the future."

"Well," the principal said. "We'll soon remedy all that. Untie him."

"He'll run away," my mother cried.

"I don't think he's that foolish to attempt that with all of us here."

"He *is* that foolish, Principal," my mother said as she and Granny began untying me. "He's tried it before. Getting him here was an ordeal in itself."

The principal rose from his seat, took two steps to the door and closed it. As the door swung closed, I spotted a row of canes of different lengths and thicknesses hanging behind it. The principal, seeing me staring at the canes, grinned and said, in a manner suggesting that he had wanted me to see them, "As long as you behave, I won't have to use any of those on you."

Use those canes on me? I gasped. I stared at my mother—she smiled; at Granny—she smiled too. That made me abandon any inkling of escaping.

"So they finally gave you the birth certificate and the papers," the principal addressed my mother as he returned to his chair.

"Yes, Principal," my mother said, "they finally did. But what a battle it was. It took me nearly a year to get all them papers together." She took out of her handbag a neatly wrapped package and handed it to the principal. "They've been running us around for so long that there were times when I thought he would never attend school, Principal," she said.

"That's pretty much standard proce-dure, Mrs. Mathabane," the principal said, unwrapping the package. "But you now have the papers and that's what's important.

"As long as we have the papers," he continued, minutely **perusing** the contents

---

20. Someone dressed *foppishly* is dressed in the style of one who pays too much attention to his or her clothes.
21. *Austere* means "serious, strict, or severe."
22. Something that is *utilitarian* is functional or practical.
23. A *portly* person has a heavy or stout but dignified appearance.

Analyze Cause-and-Effect Relationships *What effect do you think the principal's remark about the canes will have on Mathabane's commitment to attending school?*

peruse (pə rōōz′) *v.* to read through or examine carefully of the package, "we won't be breaking the law in admitting your son to this school, for we'll be in full compliance with the requirements set by the authorities in Pretoria."[24]

"Sometimes I don't understand the laws from Pitori,"[25] Granny said. "They did the same to me with my Piet and Bushy. Why, Principal, should our children not be allowed to learn because of some piece of paper?"

"The piece of paper you're referring to, Mrs. Mabaso [Granny's maiden name]," the principal said to Granny, "is as important to our children as a pass is to us adults. We all hate passes; therefore, it's only natural we should hate the regulations our children are subjected to. But as we have to live with passes, so our children have to live with the regulations, Mrs. Mabaso. I hope you understand, that is the law of the country. We would have admitted your grandson a long time ago, as you well know, had it not been for the papers. I hope you understand."

"I understand, Principal," Granny said, "but I don't understand," she added paradoxically.

One of the papers caught the principal's eye and he turned to my mother and asked, "Is your husband a Shangaan, Mrs. Mathabane?"

"No, he's not Principal," my mother said. "Is there anything wrong? He's Venda and I'm Shangaan."[26]

The principal reflected for a moment or so and then said, concernedly, "No, there's nothing seriously wrong. Nothing that we can't take care of. You see, Mrs. Mathabane, technically, the fact that your child's father is a Venda makes him ineligible to attend this tribal school because it is only for children whose parents are of the Shangaan tribe. May I ask what language the children speak at home?"

"Both languages," my mother said worriedly, "Venda and Shangaan. Is there anything wrong?"

The principal coughed, clearing his throat, then said, "I mean which language do they speak more?"

"It depends, Principal," my mother said, swallowing hard. "When their father is around, he wants them to speak only Venda. And when he's not, they speak Shangaan. And when they are out at play, they speak Zulu and Sisotho."[27]

"Well," the principal said, heaving a sigh of relief. "In that case, I think an exception can be made. The reason for such an exception is that there's currently no school for Vendas in Alexandra. And should the authorities come asking why we took in your son, we can tell them that. Anyway, your child is half-half."

Everyone broke into a nervous laugh, except me. I was bewildered by the whole thing. I looked at my mother, and she seemed greatly relieved as she watched the principal register me; a broad smile broke across her face. It was as if some enormously heavy burden had finally been lifted from her shoulders and her conscience.

"Bring him back two weeks from today," the principal said as he saw us to the door. "There're so many children registering today that classes won't begin until two weeks hence. Also, the school needs repair

27. *Zulu* and *Sisotho* are ethnic groups as well as languages.

Theme *How do the first four lines in this column contribute to a recurring theme in the story?*

The Power of Memory *Considering her own life, why might it be so important to Mathabane's mother that he be admitted to the school?*

24. The rules come from South Africa's capital, *Pretoria.*
25. *Pitori* is Granny's pronunciation of "Pretoria."
26. The people of South Africa belong to many different ethnic groups, including *Venda* and *Shangaan,* each with its own language.

and cleaning up after the holidays. If he refuses to come, simply notify us, and we'll send a couple of big boys to come fetch him, and he'll be very sorry if it ever comes to that."

As we left the principal's office and headed home, my mind was still against going to school. I was thinking of running away from home and joining my friends in the junkyard.

I didn't want to go to school for three reasons: I was reluctant to surrender my freedom and independence over to what I heard every school-going child call "tyrannous discipline." I had heard many bad things about life in tribal school—from daily beatings by teachers and mistresses who worked you like a mule to long school hours—and the sight of those canes in the principal's office gave ample **credence** to rumors that school was nothing but a torture chamber. And there was my allegiance to the gang.

But the thought of the strange woman's lamentations over her dead son presented a somewhat strong case for going to school: I didn't want to end up dead in the streets. A more compelling argument for going to school, however, was the vivid recollection of all that humiliation and pain my mother had gone through to get me the papers and the birth certificate so I could enroll in school. What should I do? I was torn between two worlds.

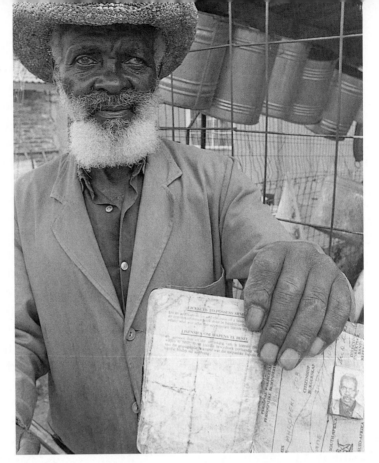

South African man with passbook. Juda Ngwenya.

View the Art During apartheid, black South Africans were required to carry a passbook with them that stated where they were allowed to work and live. If their passbooks were not in order, they could be arrested and jailed. As the principal in _Kaffir Boy_ explains it, how are the student regulations similar to the passbooks?

But later that evening something happened to force me to go to school.

I was returning home from playing soccer when a neighbor accosted[28] me by the gate and told me that there had been a bloody fight at my home.

"Your mother and father have been at it again," the neighbor, a woman, said.

"And your mother left."

I was stunned.

"Was she hurt badly?"

---

28. In this case, to _accost_ is to approach and speak to, often in a pushy way.

Theme _What does the contrast between the two different worlds have to do with the themes of the story?_

MARK MATHABANE **283**

"A little bit," the woman said. "But she'll be all right. We took her to your grandma's place."

I became hot with anger.

"Is anyone in the house?" I stammered, trying to control my rage.

"Yes, your father is. But I don't think you should go near the house. He's raving mad. He's armed with a meat cleaver. He's chased out your brother and sisters, also. And some of the neighbors who tried to intervene he's threatened to carve them to pieces. I have never seen him this mad before."

I brushed aside the woman's warnings and went. Shattered windows convinced me that there had indeed been a skirmish of some sort. Several pieces of broken bricks, evidently broken after being thrown at the door, were lying about the door. I tried opening the door; it was locked from the inside. I knocked. No one answered. I knocked again. Still no one answered, until, as I turned to leave:

"Who's out there?" my father's voice came growling from inside.

"It's me, Johannes,"[29] I said.

"Go away, . . . !" he bellowed. "I don't want you or that . . . mother of yours setting foot in this house. Go away before I come out there and kill you!"

"Let me in!" I cried. "Dammit, let me in! I want my things!"

"What things? Go away, you black swine!"

I went to the broken window and screamed obscenities at my father, daring him to come out, hoping that if he as much as ever stuck his black face out, I would pelt him with the half-a-loaf brick in my hand. He didn't come out. He continued launching a tirade[30] of obscenities at my mother and her mother. . . . He was drunk, but I wondered where he had gotten the money

to buy beer because it was still the middle of the week and he was dead broke. He had lost his entire wage for the past week in dice and had had to borrow bus fare.

"I'll kill you someday for all you're doing to my mother," I threatened him, overwhelmed with rage. Several nosey neighbors were beginning to congregate by open windows and doors. Not wanting to make a spectacle of myself, which was something many of our neighbors seemed to always expect from our family, I backtracked away from the door and vanished into the dark street. I ran, without stopping, all the way to the other end of the township where Granny lived. There I found my mother, her face swollen and bruised and her eyes puffed up to the point where she could scarcely see.

"What happened, Mama?" I asked, fighting to hold back the tears at the sight of her disfigured face.

"Nothing, child, nothing," she mumbled, almost apologetically, between swollen lips. "Your papa simply lost his temper, that's all."

"But why did he beat you up like this, Mama?" Tears came down my face. "He's never beaten you like this before."

My mother appeared reluctant to answer me. She looked searchingly at Granny, who was pounding millet with pestle and mortar and mixing it with sorghum[31] and

Visual Vocabulary
A *pestle* is a blunt tool used to pound or grind substances in a *mortar*, a thick, hard bowl, often made of wood or stone.

31. *Millet* is a grain similar to wheat, and *sorghum* is a syrup made from a tropical grass.

Analyze Cause-and-Effect Relationships *What effect is Mathabane's visit to the school having on his family?*

29. The author's name was *Johannes* (yō hä′nis) before he changed it to Mark.
30. A *tirade* (tī rād′) is a long, angry, or scolding speech.

nuts for an African delicacy. Granny said, "Tell him, child, tell him. He's got a right to know. Anyway, he's the cause of it all."

"Your father and I fought because I took you to school this morning," my mother began. "He had told me not to, and when I told him that I had, he became very upset. He was drunk. We started arguing, and one thing led to another."

"Why doesn't he want me to go to school?"

"He says he doesn't have money to waste paying for you to get what he calls a useless white man's education," my mother replied. "But I told him that if he won't pay for your schooling, I would try and look for a job and pay, but he didn't want to hear that, also. 'There are better things for you to work for,' he said. 'Besides, I don't want you to work. How would I look to other men if you, a woman I owned, were to start working?' When I asked him why shouldn't I take you to school, seeing that you were now of age, he replied that he doesn't believe in schools. I told him that school would keep you off the streets and out of trouble, but still he was belligerent."

"Is that why he beat you up?"

"Yes, he said I disobeyed his orders."

"He's right, child," Granny interjected. "He paid *lobola* [bride price] for you. And your father ate it all up before he left me."

To which my mother replied, "But I desperately want to leave this beast of a man. But with his *lobola* gone I can't do it. That worthless thing you call your husband shouldn't have sold Jackson's scrawny cattle and left you penniless."

"Don't talk like that about your father, child," Granny said. "Despite all, he's still your father, you know. Anyway, he

asked for *lobola* only because he had to get back what he spent raising you. And you know it would have been taboo for him to let you or any of your sisters go without asking for *lobola*."

"You and Papa seemed to forget that my sisters and I have minds of our own," my mother said. "We didn't need you to tell us whom to marry, and why, and how. If it hadn't been for your interference, I could have married that schoolteacher."

Granny did not reply; she knew well not to. When it came to the act of "selling" women as marriage partners, my mother was **vehemently** opposed to it. Not only was she opposed to this one aspect of tribal culture, but to others as well, particularly those involving relations between men and women and the upbringing of children. But my mother's sharply differing opinion was an exception rather than the rule among tribal women. Most times, many tribal women questioned her sanity in daring to question well-established mores.[32] But my mother did not seem to care; she would always scoff at her opponents and call them fools in letting their husbands enslave them completely.

Though I disliked school, largely because I knew nothing about what actually went on there, and the little I knew had painted a dreadful picture, the fact that a father would not want his son to go to school, especially a father who didn't go to school, seemed hard to understand.

"Why do you want me to go to school, Mama?" I asked, hoping that she might,

---

32. The customs and moral standards followed by most people in a given society are called *mores* (môr´āz).

The Power of Memory *How is Mathabane's mother trying to pass along her strong convictions to her son?*

Vocabulary

vehemently (ve´ə mənt lē) *adv.* strongly; intensely; passionately

The Power of Memory *What aspects of the life of Mathabane's father might explain his attitudes toward education and a working wife?*

Alexandra Township, South Africa. Louise Gubb.

View the Art A recent estimate suggests that more than half of Alexandra's population lives in shacks and informal dwellings like these. What does this photograph tell you about life under apartheid?

somehow, clear up some of the confusion that was building in my mind.

"I want you to have a future, child," my mother said. "And, contrary to what your father says, school is the only means to a future. I don't want you growing up to be like your father."

The latter statement hit me like a bolt of lightning. It just about shattered every defense mechanism and every pretext [33] I had against going to school.

"Your father didn't go to school," she continued, dabbing her puffed eyes to reduce the swelling with a piece of cloth dipped in warm water, "that's why he's

doing some of the bad things he's doing. Things like drinking, gambling, and neglecting his family. He didn't learn how to read and write; therefore, he can't find a decent job. Lack of any education has narrowly focused his life. He sees nothing beyond himself. He still thinks in the old, tribal way, and still believes that things should be as they were back in the old days when he was growing up as a tribal boy in Louis Trichardt. Though he's my husband, and your father, he doesn't see any of that."

"Why didn't he go to school, Mama?"

"He refused to go to school because his father led him to believe that an education was a tool through which white people were going to take things away from him, like they did black people in the old days. And that a white man's education was worthless insofar as black people were concerned because it prepared them for

---

33. A *pretext* is a false reason or excuse one gives to hide a true reason or motive.

Analyze Cause-and-Effect Relationships *Why do you think his mother's statement had such a strong effect on Mathabane?*

jobs they can't have. But I know it isn't totally so, child, because times have changed somewhat. Though our lot isn't any better today, an education will get you a decent job. If you can read or write you'll be better off than those of us who can't. Take my situation: I can't find a job because I don't have papers, and I can't get papers because white people mainly want to register people who can read and write. But I want things to be different for you, child. For you and your brother and sisters. I want you to go to school, because I believe that an education is the key you need to open up a new world and a new life for yourself, a world and life different from that of either your father's or mine. It is the only key that can do that, and only those who seek it earnestly and perseveringly will get anywhere in the white man's world. Education will open doors where none seem to exist. It'll make people talk to you, listen to you, and help you; people who otherwise wouldn't bother. It will make you soar, like a bird lifting up into the endless blue sky, and leave poverty, hunger, and suffering behind. It'll teach you to learn to embrace what's good and shun what's bad and evil. Above all, it'll make you a somebody in this world. It'll make you grow up to be a good and proud person. That's why I want you to go to school, child, so that education can do all that, and more, for you."

A long, awkward silence followed, during which I reflected upon the significance of my mother's lengthy speech. I looked at my mother; she looked at me.

Finally, I asked, "How come you know so much about school, Mama? You didn't go to school, did you?"

"No, child," my mother replied. "Just like your father, I never went to school." For the second time that evening, a mere statement of fact had a thunderous impact on me. All the confusion I had about school seemed to leave my mind, like darkness giving way to light. And what had previously been a dark, yawning void in my mind was suddenly transformed into a beacon of light that began to grow larger and larger, until it had swallowed up, blotted out, all the blackness. That beacon of light seemed to reveal things and facts, which, though they must have always existed in me, I hadn't been aware of up until now.

"But unlike your father," my mother went on, "I've always wanted to go to school, but couldn't because my father, under the sway of tribal traditions, thought it unnecessary to educate females. That's why I so much want you to go, child, for if you do, I know that someday I too would come to go, old as I would be then. Promise me, therefore, that no matter what, you'll go back to school. And I, in turn, promise that I'll do everything in my power to keep you there."

With tears streaming down my cheeks and falling upon my mother's bosom, I promised her that I would go to school "forever." That night, at seven and a half years of my life, the battlelines in the family were drawn. My mother on the one side, illiterate but determined to have me drink, for better or for worse, from the well of knowledge. On the other side, my father, he too illiterate, yet determined to have me drink from the well of ignorance. Scarcely aware of the magnitude of the decision I was making or, rather, the decision which was being emotionally thrust upon me, I chose to fight on my mother's side, and thus my destiny was forever altered. ❧

The Power of Memory *How do you think his mother's statements might affect Mathabane's feelings now and later in his life?*

After You Read

Respond and Think Critically

1. **Connect to Personal Experience** What scene from this excerpt lingers in your mind? What about the scene is memorable?

2. **Summarize Background** Summarize Mathabane's attitude toward school as the excerpt begins. Explain where this attitude came from.

3. **Explain Behavior** How does Mathabane's mother show how much she cares for her son? Support your answer with evidence from the text. OER

4. **Analyze Conflict** How does Mathabane's father react to the day's events? How does the conflict between Mathabane's parents reflect their different outlooks on their son's life? Support your answer with text evidence.

5. **Evaulate Setting** How important is the setting—the time and place—of this autobiographical story? How does it influence the events that occur? Explain.

6. **Analzye Cultural Context** Consider Mathabane's use of cultural details such as the treatment of women. What do these details help to communicate about South Africa during that time? Explain.

7. **Big Idea Draw Conclusions About Author's Perspective** What point is Mathabane making about the effect of his mother's stories? What does this suggest about the power of memories? Cite details from the text in your answer.

8. **Draw Conclusions About the Author** Mathabane writes that he chose "to fight on [his] mother's side." What might his life have been like if he had chosen to fight on his father's side instead? Explain.

Daily Life & Culture

A Life Apart

Apartheid classified South Africans into one of three categories: the Bantu, or black citizens, the "Coloured," or biracial citizens, and white citizens. The Bantu group was separated and divided into powerless tribal "homelands" called Bantustans. These areas had few jobs and limited opportunities for education. Once they had been ousted from urban areas, Bantu access to cities was strictly regulated. Nonwhite South Africans were required to carry a "pass," or documents that allowed their presence in otherwise restricted areas. Social interaction between the races was also strictly limited.

Group Activity Discuss the following questions with your classmates.

1. What are some ways that people can try to change oppressive policies like apartheid?

2. What similarities and differences do you see between apartheid and the slavery and segregation laws that once existed in the United States? Explain.

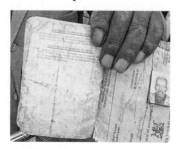

Literary Element | Theme

Some works of literature have a **stated theme,** which is expressed directly. Most works have an **implied theme,** which is revealed gradually through events, dialogue, or description.

9. Draw Conclusions About Theme What is the central theme in this excerpt from *Kaffir Boy*? Is this theme stated or implied? Explain.

10. Analyze Theme and Setting How does the historical and cultural setting described by Mathabane affect the theme? Support your answer with evidence from the text.

Review: Voice

As you learned on page 149, **voice** is the distinctive use of language that conveys the author's or narrator's personality to the reader. Voice is determined by elements of style such as word choice and tone.

11. Partner Activity With a classmate, offer three examples of writing from *Kaffir Boy* that demonstrate Mathabane's voice. For each example, explain how the language strengthens the effect of Mathabane's story. Make a chart like the one below.

Example	Why Voice Is Distinctive
"The streets were beginning to fill with their everyday traffic: old men and women, wizened, bent, and ragged, were beginning their rambling..."	The author uses vivid, creative language to make the scene come alive for the reader.

Reading Strategy | Analyze Cause-and-Effect Relationships

 Texas Test Practice (10.6)

1. The main reason the narrator agrees to go to school is:

A. a chance encounter with a stranger who tells of her dead son.

B. his mother's determination that he not end up like his father.

C. the sight of the canes hanging on the principal's door.

D. the thought of his mother's humiliating efforts to get the correct papers.

Vocabulary Practice

Practice with Context Clues Identify the context clues that help you determine the meaning of each boldfaced vocabulary word.

1. The **coterie** of Go players met every week at the Yakamuras' house.

2. My parents **admonish** me often on the subject of not falling behind in my studies.

3. We will **peruse** the information for several hours before we make a decision.

4. Lily did not know whether to distrust the story or to give it **credence.**

5. Will **vehemently** urged his listeners to support plans for the new park.

Academic Vocabulary

*Apartheid is a system that the **officialdom** of South Africa now rejects.*

Officialdom is a discipline-specific word that derives from Anglo-Saxon. The suffix *–dom* means "dignity; office; realm." Using your knowledge and context clues, determine the meaning of *officialdom* in the model sentence above. Check your response by consulting a dictionary. Finally, demonstrate your understanding by using each of these related words in a sentence.

a. kingdom   **b.** stardom   **c.** serfdom

Respond Through Writing

Research Report

Investigate Apartheid Research the apartheid system in South Africa during the 1900s. Using reliable and accurate primary and secondary sources, prepare a research report of 1,500 words or more on some aspect of South African apartheid policy. Incorporate information and examples from Mathabane's memoir into your report.

Purpose and Audience Your purpose is to write a research report in support of a thesis about an aspect of the policy that denied rights to the Bantu and other groups. Use **primary sources** (firsthand accounts of an event written or recorded at the time an event took place) and **secondary sources** (sources written by people who did not experience or observe the event). Your audience for this report is your class and teacher.

Plan Write four or five questions to guide your research and help you formulate and modify a major question to focus on. Use a variety of reliable, valid, accurate, and objective sources to find the answers, and take notes. Develop a thesis that reveals your focus, such as the specific rights that were denied. Then evaluate the information you have gathered and outline or paraphrase the main ideas you will use to develop and support your thesis. Address any major debates related to your focus.

Draft Use your introduction to define and summarize *apartheid* and to present your thesis. Use your body paragraphs to synthesize information and present evidence in a logical progression, choosing only those details that strengthen your thesis. As you weave in sources, make sure you cite them correctly and ethically using a standard style manual format. Add a chart, a graph, or an illustration to convey information.

Revise Ask yourself:

☑ What information does my reader still need to understand my thesis?

☑ Where do I need to give more background information?

☑ Where should I add an introduction or an explanation to make the meaning of a quotation clearer or more relevant to my thesis?

Revise for clarity by rewriting any potentially misleading information.

Edit Edit your paper, correcting any errors in spelling, grammar, and punctuation. Use the Grammar Tip in the side column to help you use infinitives and participles correctly. Use a style manual to help you format your paper.

 ## TEKS

10.23.A–E Organize and present ideas and information according to the purpose of the research and audience. Synthesize the research into a written or oral presentation that marshals evidence in support of a clear thesis; provides an analysis for the audience; uses graphics and illustrations; uses a variety of evaluative tools; and uses a style manual to document sources.

Grammar Tip

Infinitives and Participles

An **infinitive** is a verb form that is preceded by the word *to* and is used as a noun, an adjective, or an adverb.

To study every day is productive. [infinitive as subject]

She felt a need *to reply.* [infinitive as adjective]

The mothers were prepared *to sacrifice.* [infinitive as adverb]

A **participle** is a verb form that can function as an adjective. Present participles always have an -ing ending. Past participles often end in -ed, but they can take other endings as well.

Rising demands for education caused overcrowding.

Before You Read

Living Well. Living Good.

Meet **Maya Angelou**
(born 1928)

Maya Angelou had a difficult early life, but she overcame her obstacles to become a successful performer and writer. She is considered one of the most influential African American women of her time.

Angelou was born Marguerite Johnson in St. Louis, Missouri. She spent most of her childhood in Stamps, Arkansas, with her paternal grandmother. As a young girl, she spent a lot of time reading books and developed a love of literature, in particular of the works of Langston Hughes and William Shakespeare.

> *"In all my work, what I try to say is that as human beings we are more alike than we are unalike."*
>
> —Maya Angelou

In 1940 Angelou and her brother were taken to San Francisco, California. Five years later, at the age of seventeen, Angelou graduated from high school and gave birth to a son. To support herself and her son, she held odd jobs, working as a waitress, cook, and dancer. During the 1950s, she performed professionally using the stage name of Maya Angelou.

Literary Career Begins After touring 22 countries performing in a production of *Porgy and Bess*, Angelou left the United States. For a few years she lived in Cairo, Egypt, where she worked as an associate editor for the *Arab Observer*. In 1962 she moved to Ghana. There she wrote for the *African Review* and worked

at the University of Ghana's School of Music and Drama.

When Angelou returned to the United States, James Baldwin, whom she had met through the Harlem Writers Guild several years earlier, encouraged her to write an autobiography. At first she rejected the idea, but later she reconsidered and decided to write *I Know Why the Caged Bird Sings*. This autobiography details her life from her childhood in Stamps to the birth of her son.

Continued Success After the success of her first autobiography, Angelou published four more. In addition to her autobiographies, Angelou wrote several collections of poetry, including *Just Give Me a Cool Drink of Water 'fore I Diiie*, which was nominated for a Pulitzer Prize in 1972. Angelou also wrote and presented a poem called "On the Pulse of Morning" for the 1993 inauguration of President Bill Clinton.

LOG ON ▶ **Literature** Online

Author Search For more about Maya Angelou, go to glencoe.com and enter QuickPass code GL57805u2.

Literature and Reading Preview

Connect to the Essay

If you had all the money you wanted, what would you still need to live a good life? Discuss this question with a partner.

Build Background

This essay includes a reference to meals consisting of pigs' feet, greens, and fried chicken. These and similar foods are sometimes called "soul food." This culinary tradition began when Africans became enslaved people in the American South. They combined African and European cooking methods into a new American style of cooking.

Set Purposes for Reading

Big Idea The Power of Memory

As you read, ask yourself, Why has Angelou's memory of this anecdote stayed with her?

Literary Element Anecdote

An **anecdote** is a brief account of an interesting occurrence. Anecdotes add depth and variety to a text and help the reader visualize the characters and events. As you read the essay, ask yourself, How does Angelou use anecdotes to deepen our understanding of her approach to life?

Reading Strategy Draw Conclusions About Author's Beliefs

The purpose of an essay may be to convey the beliefs of the author. By looking for cultural and historical clues, you can **draw conclusions about the author's beliefs** and gain a deeper appreciation for the work itself. As you read, ask yourself, What does this essay say about Angelou's beliefs?

....

Tip: Look at Details Look at the details the author has included in the essay to get the information you need to draw your conclusions. Use a chart like the one below.

Details	Conclusion
Angelou notes that sofas and chairs were tautly upholstered.	Angelou respects Aunt Tee's neatness.

TEKS

For pages 291–297

10.8 Analyze, make inferences and draw conclusions about the author's purpose in cultural, historical, and contemporary contexts and provide evidence from the text to support understanding.

Vocabulary

meticulous (mi tik′yə ləs) *adj.* characterized by great or excessive concern about details; p. 291 *Editors have to be meticulous when they are proofreading.*

commodious (kə mō′dē əs) *adj.* having or containing ample room; spacious; p. 292 *The house was commodious for a family of four.*

convivial (kən viv′ē əl) *adj.* fond of merriment and parties with good company; sociable; p. 293 *Everyone agreed she was a convivial person.*

scenario (si nār′ē ō′) *n.* an outline or model of an expected or imagined series of events; p. 293 *The worst-case scenario is that it will rain.*

inhibit (in hib′it) *v.* to hold back one's natural impulses; to restrain; p. 293 *A lack of encouragement can inhibit a child's talents.*

Living Well. Living Good.

Maya Angelou

Interior at Ciboure, 1912. Henri Matisse. Canvas. Musee Toulouse-Lautrec, Albi, France.

Aunt Tee was a Los Angeles member of our extended family.[1] She was seventy-nine when I met her, sinewy,[2] strong, and the color of old lemons. She wore her coarse, straight hair, which was slightly streaked with gray, in a long braided rope across the top of her head. With her high cheekbones, old gold skin, and almond eyes, she looked more like an Indian chief than an old black woman. (Aunt Tee described herself and any favored member of her race as Negroes. *Black* was saved for those who had incurred her disapproval.)

She had retired and lived alone in a dead, neat ground-floor apartment. Wax flowers and china figurines sat on elaborately embroidered and heavily starched doilies. Sofas and chairs were tautly upholstered. The only thing at ease in Aunt Tee's apartment was Aunt Tee.

I used to visit her often and perch on her uncomfortable sofa just to hear her stories. She was proud that after working thirty years as a maid, she spent the next thirty years as a live-in housekeeper, carrying the keys to rich houses and keeping **meticulous** accounts.

"Living in lets the white folks know Negroes are as neat and clean as they are, sometimes more so. And it gives the Negro maid a chance to see white folks ain't no

---

1. Parents and their children make up what is called the nuclear family. One's *extended family* includes other relatives who are related by blood or marriage.
2. Here, *sinewy* (sin′ ū ē) could mean "physically powerful" or "vigorously healthy."

smarter than Negroes. Just luckier. Sometimes."

Aunt Tee told me that once she was housekeeper for a couple in Bel Air,[3] California, lived with them in a fourteen-room ranch house. There was a day maid who cleaned, and a gardener who daily tended the lush gardens. Aunt Tee oversaw the workers. When she had begun the job, she had cooked and served a light breakfast, a good lunch, and a full three- or four-course dinner to her employers and their guests. Aunt Tee said she watched them grow older and leaner. After a few years they stopped entertaining and ate dinner hardly seeing each other at the table. Finally, they sat in a dry silence as they ate evening meals of soft scrambled eggs, melba toast, and weak tea. Aunt Tee said she saw them growing old but didn't see herself aging at all.

She became the social maven.[4] She started "keeping company" (her phrase) with a chauffeur down the street. Her best friend and her friend's husband worked in service[5] only a few blocks away.

On Saturdays Aunt Tee would cook a pot of pigs' feet, a pot of greens, fry chicken, make potato salad, and bake a banana pudding. Then, that evening, her friends—the chauffeur, the other housekeeper, and her husband—would come to Aunt Tee's **commodious** live-in quarters. There the four would eat and drink, play records and dance. As the evening wore on, they would settle down to a serious game of bid whist.[6]

Naturally, during this revelry jokes were told, fingers snapped, feet were patted, and there was a great deal of laughter.

Aunt Tee said that what occurred during every Saturday party startled her and her friends the first time it happened. They had been playing cards, and Aunt Tee, who had just won the bid, held a handful of trumps. She felt a cool breeze on her back and sat upright and turned around. Her employers had cracked her door open and beckoned to her. Aunt Tee, a little peeved, laid down her cards and went to the door. The couple backed away and asked her to come into the hall, and there they both spoke and won Aunt Tee's sympathy forever.

"Theresa, we don't mean to disturb you . . ." the man whispered, "but you all seem to be having such a good time . . ."

The woman added, "We hear you and your friends laughing every Saturday night, and we'd just like to watch you. We don't want to bother you. We'll be quiet and just watch."

The man said, "If you'll just leave your door ajar, your friends don't need to know. We'll never make a sound." Aunt Tee said she saw no harm in agreeing, and she talked it over with her company. They said it was OK with them, but it was sad that the employers owned the gracious house, the swimming pool, three cars, and numberless palm trees, but had no joy. Aunt Tee told me that laughter and relaxation had left the house; she agreed it was sad.

---

3. *Bel Air* is one of the wealthiest areas in Los Angeles.
4. A *maven* is one who has special knowledge or experience and is an expert in a given field.
5. The two friends *in service* are servants in another house.
6. *Bid whist* is a card game, somewhat like bridge, for two players or two teams of two players.

Anecdote *How can you tell that Angelou is recounting an anecdote?*

The Power of Memory *Why would Aunt Tee feel that it was especially meaningful to share this memory with Angelou?*

When I Get that Feeling, 2000. Colin Bootman.
Oil on board. Private collection.

That story has stayed with me for nearly thirty years, and when a tale remains fresh in my mind, it almost always contains a lesson which will benefit me.

My dears, I draw the picture of the wealthy couple standing in a darkened hallway, peering into a lighted room where black servants were lifting their voices in merriment and comradery, and I realize that living well is an art which can be developed. Of course, you will need the basic talents to build upon: They are a love of life and ability to take great pleasure from small offerings, an assurance that the world owes you nothing and that every gift is exactly that, a gift. That people who may differ from you in political stance, sexual persuasion, and racial inheritance can be founts of fun, and if you are lucky, they can become even **convivial** comrades.

Living life as art requires a readiness to forgive. I do not mean that you should suffer fools gladly, but rather remember your own shortcomings, and when you encounter another with flaws, don't be eager to righteously seal yourself away from the offender forever. Take a few breaths and imagine yourself having just committed the action which has set you at odds.

Because of the routines we follow, we often forget that life is an ongoing adventure. We leave our homes for work, acting and even believing that we will reach our destinations with no unusual event startling us out of our set expectations. The truth is we know nothing, not where our cars will fail or when our buses will stall, whether our places of employment will be there when we arrive, or whether, in fact, we ourselves will arrive whole and alive at the end of our journeys. Life is pure adventure, and the sooner we realize that, the quicker we will be able to treat life as art: to bring all our energies to each encounter, to remain flexible enough to notice and admit when what we expected to happen did not happen. We need to remember that we are created creative and can invent new **scenarios** as frequently as they are needed.

Life seems to love the liver of it. Money and power can liberate only if they are used to do so. They can imprison and **inhibit** more finally than barred windows and iron chains. ∾

Draw Conclusions About Author's Beliefs *What does Angelou's statement about life reveal about her beliefs?*

Vocabulary

convivial (kən viv′ē əl) *adj.* fond of merriment and parties with good company; sociable

scenario (si när′ē ō′) *n.* an outline or model of an expected or imagined series of events

inhibit (in hib′it) *v.* to hold back one's natural impulses; to restrain

---

The Power of Memory *What is Angelou implying about the power of memories in the first paragraph on this page?*

After You Read

Respond and Think Critically

1. **Connect to Personal Experience** What was your impression of Aunt Tee's attitude toward her employers? Explain.

2. **Describe Personality Traits** How would you describe Aunt Tee's personality traits? How do these traits relate to the life she has lived? Explain.

3. **Make Inferences About Attitudes** Describe Aunt Tee's parties and her employers' routines. How happy are Aunt Tee and her employers? Support your answer with text evidence.

4. **Draw Conclusions About Meaning** To Angelou, what does "living well, living good" mean? Support your answer with evidence from the text. ✎OER

5. **Big Idea** **Draw Conclusions About the Author** Memory can influence our lives in many ways. Did memories influence Aunt Tee? Explain. How might the memory of Aunt Tee have influenced Angelou's life? Explain.

6. **Evaluate Evidence** Angelou says that people are "more alike than we are unalike." How well does she illustrate this idea in her essay? Support your answer with text evidence.

7. **Evaluate Ideas** Evaluate Angelou's suggestions about "living well." Is it possible to live the way she suggests? Why or why not?

Literary Element Anecdote

An **anecdote** is a short account from someone's life. Essay writers often use anecdotes to support their opinions, clarify their ideas, grab the reader's attention, or entertain. Anecdotes can also be used to reveal aspects of a person's character.

8. **Analyze Author's Craft** Why do you think Angelou structures "Living Well. Living Good." around her aunt's anecdote?

9. **Analyze Structure** How would the essay be different if Angelou had not included her aunt's anecdote?

10. **Analyze Anecdote** In the final paragraph, Angelou writes: "Life seems to love the liver of it." How might Aunt Tee's story be used to illustrate this statement?

Review: Theme

As you learned on page 275, **theme** is the central idea about life in a piece of literature. Most themes are not stated directly; they are implied, meaning that the reader must infer the central idea.

11. **Partner Activity** Discuss the theme of "Living Well. Living Good." with a classmate. First, determine the theme based on clues in the text. Then, support your theme statement by listing specific examples from the essay. Use a web diagram like the one below to organize your ideas.

Draw Conclusions About Author's Beliefs

 Texas Test Practice (10.8)

1. The description of the evening meal that Aunt Tee's employers eat (page 294) serves to

  (A) emphasize their disinterest in wealth

  (B) point out their dull, colorless lives

  (C) suggest that they are in failing health

  (D) underscore the idea that the poor can enjoy life more than the rich

  (E) reveal that Aunt Tee disliked her job

Vocabulary Practice

Practice with Analogies Choose the word pair that best completes each analogy.

1. meticulous : perfectionist ::
  a. tiny : housekeeper   **b.** irritable : grouch

2. commodious : space ::
  a. large : gigantic   **b.** luxurious : comfort

3. convivial : socialite ::
  a. victorious : winner   **b.** careless : child

4. outline : scenario ::
  a. diagram : sentence   **b.** deceive : truth

5. inhibit : restrain ::
  a. argue : agree   **b.** imagine : visualize

Academic Vocabulary

The author combines details in this essay to ***promote*** *the idea that life should be lived well every day.*

Promote is a multiple-meaning word. A teacher might **promote** a student to the next grade, while an ad campaign might **promote** a product. Using context clues, try to figure out the meaning of *promote* in the sentence above.

For more on academic vocabulary, see pages 36–37 and R92–R94.

Write with Style

 Apply Tone

Assignment Write a character sketch focused on someone who reflects your own beliefs about how to live life. Use a tone that is consistent with your feelings about the person and with your beliefs.

Get Ideas Tone is an author's attitude toward his or her subject matter. A tone can be inspirational or critical, happy or sad, humorous or serious. Look back at the chart you made about Angelou's beliefs on page 292. List details you could use to show your own beliefs and attitude toward your subject.

> Tone: Respect/Admiration
>
> _Steven Gomez_
> • president of conservation committee; library volunteer; scout leader
> • says more with the light in his eyes than some people say with a hundred words

Give It Structure Do not state your beliefs or attitude directly. Instead, let the details of your character sketch convey your attitude. Then decide on a logical order for your details.

Look at Language Word choice contributes to your style. As you write, pay close attention to your choice of words and their connotation. "Light in one's eye" is not the same as a *twinkle; volunteer* does not carry the same connotations as *helper*.

Proofread Each draft should refine key ideas and organize them more logically and fluidly, use language more precisely and effectively, and clarify your purpose. Make sure your final draft is free of spelling and grammatical errors.

Before You Read

First Impressions from *De Kooning: An American Master*

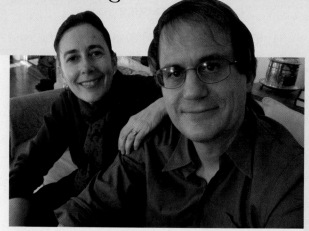

Meet **Mark Stevens and Annalyn Swan**

Mark Stevens, an art critic for *New York* magazine, has written about a wide variety of artists. His subjects range from masters such as Vincent van Gogh and Willem de Kooning to folk and outsider artists. Stevens's wife and coauthor, Annalyn Swan, is an award-winning music critic who has written for magazines including *Time*, *The New Republic*, *The Atlantic Monthly*, and *New York*. She has also been a senior arts editor at *Newsweek*.

A Long Time Coming Swan and Stevens dedicated ten years of their lives to researching and writing their biography of Willem de Kooning. While one conducted research and interviews exploring the first half of de Kooning's life, the other did research about the second half. Then the couple worked together to shape their material into a coherent whole.

> "We were lucky. We had a subject that never bored us. . . . we really liked de Kooning."
>
> —Annalyn Swan

Writing About a Life The art of biography writing has developed as times and literary traditions have changed. Many authors today see biography as the artful retelling of fact; to be successful, a biographer should fail neither art nor truth.

Over the many years of their research and writing, Stevens and Swan found that their respect and admiration for de Kooning deepened. They were keen to do justice to this original and complex man. Swan said, "That de Kooning was an immigrant colored everything in his life. He was forever caught between Europe and the New World, suffused with private longings, regret, loneliness and joy. . . . For a biographer, exploring such a complicated subject is fascinating."

Stevens and Swan's years of labor were validated when they were awarded a Pulitzer Prize in 2005. One reviewer had this to say about their work: "When we get the chance to look at the whole life and work of Willem de Kooning, the upheaval in American art in the middle of the 20th century comes into clearer focus. That alone makes *De Kooning: An American Master* . . . an important book."

LOG ON ▶ **Literature** Online

Author Search For more about Mark Stevens and Annalyn Swan, go to glencoe.com and enter QuickPass code GL57805u2.

Literature and Reading Preview

Connect to the Biography

How would you handle the challenges of everyday life if no one around you spoke your language? Write a journal entry that explores this question.

Build Background

Willem de Kooning was born in the Netherlands in 1904. He eventually became a leader in an artistic movement called Abstract Expressionism. Abstract artists make no attempt to re-create the world as it really exists.

Set Purposes for Reading

Big Idea | The Power of Memory

As you read, ask yourself, How do Stevens and Swan re-create de Kooning's experience of his arrival in the United States?

Literary Element | Author's Purpose

The **author's purpose** is the author's intent in writing a literary work. Understanding the author's purpose enables you to grasp why the author presents certain events and people as he or she does. It's often helpful to consider the cultural and historical context of a work. As you read, ask yourself, What do Stevens and Swan hope to accomplish by sharing de Kooning's first impressions of America with the reader?

Reading Strategy | Make Generalizations About Events

When you **make generalizations,** you apply a collection of facts or details from specific situations to more general circumstances. Generalizations may relate universal themes and ideas to a text. As you read, ask yourself, Why are these events occurring?

....

Tip: Take Notes As you read, record specific examples in the text and then generalize. Use the blue highlighted passages and questions for help.

Passage	Generalization
De Kooning first lived with other Dutch immigrants.	This made him feel comfortable, since his surroundings were new.

TEKS

For pages 298–309

10.8 Analyze, make inferences and draw conclusions about the author's purpose in cultural, historical, and contemporary contexts and provide evidence from the text to support understanding.

Vocabulary

obligatory (ə blig′ə tôr′ē) *adj.* required or necessary; p. 301 *The student went to class regularly because the teacher said attendance was obligatory.*

belie (bi lī′) *v.* to misrepresent; to give a false impression of; p. 304 *The warm loving light in the small child's eyes belied her refusal to hug her mother.*

torrential (tô ren′chəl) *adj.* flowing rapidly and abundantly; p. 304 *Walking in the torrential rain left us completely soaked.*

....

Tip: Denotation and Connotation Remember that words often suggest positive or negative feelings or ideas. Reacting to these connotations is part of active reading.

The Statue of Liberty. Francis Hopkinson Smith (1851–1915).

First Impressions

from *De Kooning: An American Master*

Mark Stevens and Annalyn Swan

"I didn't think there were any artists in America."

"Look Bill, America!" With that shout from the sailors, de Kooning looked out over the water—and looked again. He saw "a sort of Holland, lowlands, just like back home," as he remembered it. No skyscrapers with glittering lights. No beckoning Statue of Liberty. Not only was he disappointed at his first glimpse of America, he was also apprehen-

sive as the ship steamed into the Virginia port of Newport News on July 30. The voyage itself had been stressful. He found the English ship filthy and, for much of the trip, was forced to hide in the hot, dark engine room where the sailors—while never officially acknowledging his presence—gave him lots of work. . . .

What sort of country, de Kooning wondered, was this America? He felt particularly uneasy because he knew no English, which forced him to rely completely upon friends. Cohan, as cheerful and optimistic as ever, proved a resourceful companion who helped

---

The Power of Memory *Why was de Kooning disappointed when he first saw America?*

steer de Kooning to New York without passing through the usual entry point for immigrants on Ellis Island—the **obligatory** first step for legal entrance into the United States by way of Manhattan. The passage of the Immigration Act of 1924 had sharply curtailed the flow of immigrants into America, and, while the new quotas were less restrictive for northern Europeans than for others, illegal immigrants like Cohan and de Kooning faced certain deportation from Ellis Island. Calling upon his network of Dutch friends, Cohan arranged to board a coast vessel carrying goods from Newport News to Boston.

Throughout the next week, as they steamed up the eastern seaboard, de Kooning and Cohan stoked the engines and worked as firemen. Disembarking in Boston, they proceeded by train to Rhode Island, where, with a group of Dutch sailors, they boarded another coast vessel bound for the old South Street port at the tip of Manhattan. Although South Street had been the center of the city's harbor life from the colonial era through the nineteenth century, the shipping business had mostly moved by the 1920s to docks along the Hudson River on the West Side of Manhattan. South Street was a quiet back door into the city for those who wanted to avoid scrutiny.

"We had enough money to buy a ticket on a passenger boat," de Kooning remembered of the trip from Rhode Island, "with music and dancing, and early one morning I just walked off the ship and I couldn't believe it—I was free on the streets of New York." As at Newport News, he was not overwhelmed by his first impressions. De Kooning, who always relished the debunking[1] observation, said about his first view of New York: "This I remember: no skyscrapers. They had disappeared in the fog." Their few possessions in hand, the group of Dutchmen headed purposefully uptown to Barclay Street, where they boarded one of the ferries connecting Manhattan to Hoboken, New Jersey, the town across the river where they planned to stay. This is probably when de Kooning saw the counterman recklessly pouring coffee into the row of cups and was suddenly seized by the difference between Holland and America—the first slow and deliberate, the other driven, haphazard, profligate.[2]

Like most immigrants, de Kooning spent his early months in America swaddled among his own countrymen. Hoboken was the logical place for a Dutch stowaway to live during the first unsettling days, as Cohan, the impresario of their emigration, recognized. Once a sleepy river town and leafy retreat for New Yorkers eager to escape the summer heat, Hoboken had become by the 1920s an important shipping town with a population of about seventy thousand. Four ferries connected it with its huge neighbor. The ships of nine big oceangoing lines docked at its piers, including the Netherlands-American Steam Navigation Company, which attracted a number of Dutch settlers. By the time de Kooning arrived, the traditionally German flavor of Hoboken had almost disappeared, owing in part to a huge wave of Italian immigrants around the turn of the century. There remained a northern European overlay to

Make Generalizations About Events *Reread this paragraph. What generalizations can you make about the obstacles faced by immigrants and their approach to these obstacles?*

Vocabulary

obligatory (ə blig′ə tôr′ē) *adj.* required or necessary

1. *Debunking* means "exposing a myth."
2. *Profligate* means "reckless or extravagant."

Author's Purpose *What contrast do the authors describe? What does the contrast suggest about the purpose of this section of the biography?*

the city, however, along with a liberal sprinkling of Dutch inhabitants. The first Dutch Reformed Church had been founded in 1850 and maintained a high profile in the local community, and the Holland Seaman's Home provided a welcoming refuge for Dutch, German, and Scandinavian sailors and immigrants. "My sailor friends knew the Dutch settlement there, and they brought me to the Dutch Seaman's Home, a sort of boarding house," de Kooning said. "Thanks to them the landlady gave me three weeks' credit. It was a nice, very clean little house. I liked it quite well."

Located at 332 River Street, the Holland Seaman's Home was across the road from the docks lining the river and near the Lutheran Seaman's Mission. Just down River Street were the Holland bakery, the Holland Hotel, and a restaurant called Holland. Despite his desire to leave the Old World, de Kooning—who instantly dropped his Dutch name, Willem, in favor of the all-American "Bill"— found the traces of home comforting. Plenty of work was available. More than thirty painters and decorators worked in Hoboken in 1926, a number of them either German or Dutch immigrants. Their establishments bore such names as Braue and Schermerhorn, Otto Burckhardt and Son, and Fred Schlegel. "Three days later I was a housepainter," de Kooning said, "and got nine dollars a day, a nice salary for that time."

For someone who with a few notable exceptions paid little attention to how he dressed, de Kooning showed a particular preoccupation with clothes during his early days in America: they represented both a badge of success and a symbol of a new identity. After only one week of work, de Kooning proudly remembered, "I could buy a new suit, black for Sundays, low-belt trousers, nice workmen's clothes, for I didn't want to be different. . . . I do like a fine suit and a nice tie." If in one week he could afford a suit, "In three weeks I could pay off my rent and had new underwear and socks." Like many immigrants, de Kooning also wanted to demonstrate his success to his family and maintain the legend of a land of riches. A photograph taken in 1926, and no doubt sent home to Holland, shows de Kooning and a Dutch friend on the ferry between New York and Hoboken. De Kooning is lolling back against the railing, clearly at ease with the camera, the world, and his relative prosperity. In contrast to his Dutch companion, who is dressed in a poorly fitting jacket and workingman's cap, de Kooning is handsomely turned out. His three-piece suit is elegant, his shirt collar starchily correct. On his head is a fedora, raked jauntily over his forehead and all but hiding his eyes.

De Kooning could get by without much English, though it was not always easy. In the beginning, he knew how to order only one thing in restaurants—a hamburger. (When he finally tried to order something else at the local restaurant, the waiter said, "Hamburger, right?" de Kooning meekly nodded.) On the job, he found he had much to learn about the way his new country operated, which often differed from the careful, artisanal[3] manners of Holland. "I was impressed by the workers' efficiency and their tools," he said. "We worked without stopping for eight hours and used much larger and better brushes than those we had in Holland. I learned a great deal on how to

3. *Artisanal* describes the skilled work that artisans, or craftspeople, do.

The Power of Memory *What significance did clothing have for de Kooning as he began his life in America?*

Author's Purpose *Why do the authors describe the cultural and historical context for de Kooning's early years in the United States in such detail?*

mix pigment with water and oil." He was struck by the American willingness simply to slap new paint over old; in Holland, housepainters would strip a window down to the wood before repainting. He also tried his hand at sign painting, and came away with a high regard for the veterans with whom he worked. "Sign painting was difficult for me because they used other letters here," he said. "How those old guys smoking their pipes did it, I don't know."

De Kooning soon found helpful and congenial Dutch friends. Leo Cohan, who worked as a cook in a restaurant in Hoboken, sometimes arranged for de Kooning to get free meals; between lodgings, de Kooning occasionally stayed in Cohan's rented room. A man named Wimpy Deruyter—a ship's mechanic who befriended de Kooning on the voyage to America—visited whenever he was back in town. De Kooning's keenest friendship, however, was with a Dutch singer named Bart van der Schelling. Well known for never keeping a job or having any money, Bart was big, charming, and exceedingly attractive. (He would later fight in the Spanish Civil War and eventually became a naïve,[4] or "primitive," painter.) Like Leo Cohan, he remained close to de Kooning for years: in the early thirties Bill and Bart spent so much time together they seemed like brothers.

On Sundays, de Kooning would go sightseeing with friends. Little remained of

Willem de Kooning, 1953. Tony Vaccaro.

the rustic charm that had once brought New Yorkers across the river to Hoboken. Its main allure in the Prohibition[5] era was its great number of speakeasies;[6] a local poll taken in 1930 named Hoboken the "wettest"[7] city in New Jersey. But there was some greenery in the area. Only steps

---

4. *Naïve painters* usually have no formal artistic training and are known for painting directly on a canvas without preliminary drawings.

5. The *Prohibition era* officially began in 1919 with the 18th Amendment to the Constitution, which prohibited the sale or consumption of alcoholic beverages anywhere in the U.S. The 18th Amendment was repealed in 1933 with the 21st Amendment.

6. *Speakeasies* were places that existed during the Prohibition era where people could go to purchase illegal alcohol.

7. *Wet* means that alcohol was available for purchase, so the reference to Hoboken being the *"wettest" city in New Jersey* means that one could find a lot of places to obtain alcohol.

Make Generalizations About Events *What general insights into Holland and America did de Kooning gain from working as a house painter in Hoboken?*

from the Holland Seaman's Home was Hudson Square, which looked over the river. Just beyond lay the Stevens Institute of Technology, which was housed in a mansion on a promontory known as Castle Point. De Kooning went there often to look across the water at the city. With friends like Bart, Wimpy, and Leo—who sounded like a troupe of comics—de Kooning also began to explore New York. He felt comfortable with its kaleidoscopic jumble of ethnic groups, which recalled the mixing of Dutch and foreigners around the Rotterdam[8] docks. He saw the poverty, too, which **belied** the myth of easy riches: the slums on the Lower East Side;[9] the tenements with windowless inner rooms and public toilets on every other floor; the two-bit flophouses on the Bowery.[10] (One day, he would come to love the photographs of Weegee—the great chronicler of the city's meaner streets.[11]) But that was not the New York that caught his eye. The Roaring Twenties were one of the city's great decades. It thrived on too much money, not enough sleep, and worried cries from the rest of the country about "decadence."[12] The WPA[13] guide to the city, compiled as part of the 1930s Federal Writers' Project, perfectly captured the proudly self-conscious, rhetorical flair of the period:

> All through the 1920s New York had been not only the symbol of America but the symbol of the modern—the fortunate giant in his youth, the world city whose past weighed least heavily upon its future. . . . It was a city infallible in finance, **torrential** in pace, unlimited in resource, hard as infrangible diamonds, forever leaping upon the moment beyond. "You can get away with anything," said Ellen Thatcher in John Dos Passos' *Manhattan Transfer*, "if you do it quick enough." Speed—with its dividend, sensation—became the master formula in every human activity and technique: Wall Street, dancing, crime, the theater, construction, even death.

What de Kooning thrilled to was the pop energy of the city, which was exotic to a Dutchman who grew up in the subdued culture of northern Europe. Here was freedom from the constraints of class, taste, and disapproving looks; here was a new kind of openness, an invitation to wonder. One of the first places he visited was Coney Island, a masterpiece of rhinestone splendor that provided entertainment for New York's lower and middle classes. Cecil Beaton described it this way during the 1930s:

---

8. *Rotterdam* is a city in the southwestern portion of the Netherlands.
9. The *Lower East Side* of New York City's Manhattan borough attracted many immigrants because of the availability of cheap housing.
10. *Flophouses* were cheap hotels or rooming houses that could be found in a section of Manhattan called *the Bowery.*
11. *Weegee* is the professional name of photographer Arthur Fellig, who became famous for his crime-scene photos.
12. *Decadence* is the process of falling into decay or decline.
13. The *WPA* is the Works Progress Administration Federal Arts Project. The program started in the 1930s and was known for hiring a wide range of artists.

Vocabulary

belie (bi līʹ) *v.* to misrepresent; to give a false impression of

Author's Purpose *De Kooning became an innovative, groundbreaking artist. In this passage, what do the authors suggest about his influences?*

Vocabulary

torrential (tô renʹchəl) *adj.* flowing rapidly and abundantly

Coney Island, 1931. John Wenger. Watercolor and tempera over pencil on paperboard, 55.1 x 71.1 cm. Brooklyn Museum of Art, New York.

View the Art Coney Island has featured amusement parks, thrill rides, and a colorful boardwalk of attractions since the 1800s. How does this painting help viewers understand Coney Island's appeal?

Every Saturday and Sunday a million people go to bathe at Coney Island, reached by subway in half an hour. They stay until the electric bulbs silhouette the minarets, domes and turrets, illumine the skeletons of roller-coasters and the magnificent pleasure-palace of George C. Tilyou (the Barnum of Coney Island), which with its many columns and electrical splendour, resembles something from the Pan-American exposition of 1900. The passengers on the Cyclone rend the air with their concerted screams.

"I liked the sentimental side of the people," de Kooning said, "the girls, the houses on the avenues, and the skyscrapers." Not surprisingly, he relished Times Square. Perhaps it reminded him of the square at the foot of the Coolsingel[14] in Rotterdam, where he had whiled away time with the Randolfis. Except it was bigger, more extravagant, crazier. Like the harbor of Rotterdam, Times Square was a crossroads populated by . . . just about everyone. Times Square in 1926 was lined with movie houses, shooting galleries, and amusement arcades. At night, it shimmered with thousands of brightly colored

---

14. *Coolsingel* is a main street in the old part of Rotterdam.

electric lights. De Kooning had himself photographed amid the bustle of Times Square. He looked like a man at home. Once de Kooning found his footing in America, Hoboken seemed too much like North Rotterdam. Crowded tenements, cold-water walk-ups, and communal backyard toilets or privies were the realities of working-class life in Hoboken; he had not left Rotterdam to move to a similarly depressed city across the ocean. More important, he missed living in a bohemian milieu. It was one thing to be a workingman living among artists or people like the Randolfis who flourished on the margins of society. It was quite another to be a workingman among workers. On Sundays, a friend with an old car sometimes drove him to Storm King, a high promontory of land up the Hudson with sweeping views down the river. "We would stand by the parapet and look at the view of the city," de Kooning said. "It used to scare me to death. I would say to myself, 'There's no art here. You came to the wrong place.'" Although he visited the galleries on Fifty-seventh Street, they mostly showed plummy European paintings intended for conservative apartments on the Upper East Side. He saw nothing like Mondrian.[15]

Leo Cohan urged de Kooning to move across the river. "I said to him, 'Bill, you mustn't hang around in Hoboken. You must go to Manhattan. There you'll find other artists.'" In Hoboken, de Kooning began to hear about a community in the

Door to the River, 1960. Willem de Kooning. The Willem de Kooning Foundation.

View the Art De Kooning is associated with a form known as *action painting*, characterized by rapid, forceful brushstrokes, abstraction, and emotional expression. How does this painting reflect the characteristics of action painting?

city called Greenwich Village, where poets and painters were said to live. He determined its location—south of Fourteenth Street and north of Canal Street—and one day found himself amid the oddly angled streets and old brownstones. But he could not find "the Village" he had heard about. "There were just lots of Italians standing around on corners. Inside, you know, the Village was nice, but from the outside, you couldn't tell it was there—it was so quiet." Then, while still living in Hoboken, de Kooning met a Sicilian artist named Mirabaggo, who lived in the Village. When a barber

---

15. Piet *Mondrian* was a Dutch abstract painter.

whom Mirabaggo knew retired, he bought the empty barbershop and opened a coffeehouse decorated with plaster copies of Greek and Roman sculpture. De Kooning began to spend time there on weekends. Soon he was also going to Café Rienzi, another coffeehouse that opened shortly after Mirabaggo's. He began to discover old Village hangouts, such as the Pepper Pot, the MacDougal Tavern, and the Jumble Shop. All of them had been in varying degrees haunts of writers and artists since the 1890s. Of greatest importance to de Kooning, however, was the living presence of painters. "Here in Greenwich Village there was a strong tradition of painting and poetry," he said. "I had not known this, and it brought back memories of my interests when I was 14, 15 or 16 years old."

Now that he had located an American art world, de Kooning naturally wanted to join it. He made some drawings and illustrations to replace the portfolio that he had left behind in Belgium, and began to read the Help Wanted ads for commercial artists in the Manhattan newspapers, just as he had in Brussels. When one ran in the *New York World* he dropped off his portfolio at the stated address. To his dismay, the place was mobbed with applicants for the job. He had all but given up hope when a man appeared holding aloft a portfolio and shouting, "Where's de Kooning?" The American's pronunciation was jarring. In Dutch, de Kooning was pronounced with a hard "o"—as in Koning. In American, he was de Kooning.

The job was his. De Kooning was so pleased—his first triumph in America!— that he signed up immediately, no questions asked. "I didn't even ask them the salary because I thought if I made twelve dollars a day as a house painter [de Kooning variously described his Hoboken wages as nine or twelve dollars a day] I would make at least twenty dollars a day being an artist." The elation abruptly ended after a week when he was handed twenty-five dollars. "I was so astonished I asked him if that was a day's pay," said de Kooning. "He said, 'No, that's for the whole week.'" De Kooning had learned the hard way that less skilled labor could pay more than an arts-related job and that life in America was not going to be easy. "It turned out to be quite different from what I thought," de Kooning said of America. "Nowhere near as luxurious as I imagined it."

Disgruntled, de Kooning spent the weekend wondering whether or not to return to housepainting in Hoboken. Cohan and other Dutch friends urged him to keep the new job. As Cohan sensed, art and the company of artists would finally prove far more important to his friend than a fatter paycheck. Although de Kooning by no means considered himself a serious painter—that would only come years later—he made an essential decision that weekend: he must at least live in the neighborhood of art. His hopes of making a fortune waned, but his interest in an American art world strengthened. A little more than a year after his arrival in Hoboken, de Kooning packed his few possessions, said good-bye to his sailor friends, and took the ferry into Manhattan. ↶

Make Generalizations About Events *What does this anecdote illustrate about the experiences of many immigrants to America?*

The Power of Memory *Why do you think this recollection is significant for de Kooning?*

The Power of Memory *What influenced de Kooning's decision to stay in Greenwich Village?*

After You Read

Respond and Think Critically

1. **Connect to Personal Experience** What did you consider most interesting or surprising about de Kooning's experiences? Explain.

2. **Describe Impressions** What was surprising about de Kooning's first glimpse of the United States? How did his first impressions affect him?

3. **Analyze Cultural Context** What reasons do Stevens and Swan cite for de Kooning's departure from Hoboken? Why might the move have helped his career as an artist? Explain.

4. **Make Inferences About Motivation** At first, de Kooning viewed success in the United States in terms of income. Later, his views of success shifted. What do you think motivated the change in his attitude? Explain.

5. **Analyze Biography** To be successful, a biographer must provide facts about a person's life and must also capture the person's personality. How do Stevens and Swan accomplish this goal? Support your answer with evidence from the text.

6. **Evaluate Description** De Kooning eventually became an influential and innovative abstract painter. Does the biographers' description of de Kooning's arrival in the United States help you understand what contributed to his success? Explain.

7. **Big Idea** **Draw Conclusions About Historical Context** Based on de Kooning's memories of his early years in the United States, what can you conclude about the lives of immigrants at that time? Explain.

Literary Element Author's Purpose

Authors often write to achieve one or more of the following **purposes:** to persuade, to inform, to explain, to entertain, or to describe. One might attribute several of these purposes to Stevens and Swan's biography of Willem de Kooning.

8. **Draw Conclusions About Authors' Purpose** Which purpose do you think most applies to this biography? Cite several passages that support your claim.

9. **Analyze Cultural and Historical Context** How do details of the cultural and historical context help serve the author's purpose? Explain.

Review: Biography

As you learned on page 255, a **biography** is an account of someone's life written by someone else. In addition to describing a person's life, a biographer's purpose is also to provide insight into the time and place in which the person lived.

10. **Partner Activity** Pair up with a classmate and examine the biography excerpt you just read. Determine how the authors' use of quotations helps provide a historical and cultural context. Working with your partner, create a two-column chart similar to the one below.

Examples of Quotations from Other Sources	Explanation of Historical or Cultural Context
p. 305 "Every Saturday and Sunday a million people go to bathe at Coney Island,..."	Visiting Coney Island was an inexpensive form of entertainment, so it attracted people from the lower and middle classes.

Making generalizations helps readers understand the main points and implications of a work. For example, considering de Kooning's experiences enables you to generalize about other immigrants' lives at the time.

11. What generalizations can you make about de Kooning's reasons for coming to the United States? What did de Kooning find disappointing about his new country, and what did he find exciting? To answer, refer to the blue highlighted passages and questions and your graphic organizer from page 299.

12. What generalizations can you make about the lives of working-class people at the time of de Kooning's arrival? Explain.

Vocabulary

Practice with Denotation and Connotation

Denotation is the literal, or dictionary, meaning of a word. **Connotation** is the implied, or cultural, meaning of a word. For example, the words *embarrassing* and *humiliating* have a similar denotation, but *humiliating* suggests a more profound embarrassment and has a more negative connotation.

Each boldfaced vocabulary word is listed below with a word that has a similar denotation. Decide whether the second word is more negative, more positive, or about the same, as the vocabulary word, and explain why.

1. obligatory   required

2. belie   misrepresent

3. torrential   heavy

Enrich and Extend

 Connect to Art

Research Report Research de Kooning and his fellow New York "rebel artists" who helped create Abstract Expressionism. Create a multimedia presentation about the artists and their art that will appeal to your classmates.

Investigate Generate four or five research questions about who the artists were, how they became friends, and what made their art groundbreaking,. Answer your questions by determining, locating, and exploring relevant primary and secondary sources. Systematically record the information you gather, compiling notes with art terms and their definitions. Use a table to organize your research.

Source	Assessment
Sylvester, David. <u>Modern Art.</u> NY: Franklin Watts, 1965. Primary source.	author—respected British art critic and curator; book—documented primary source

Create Use appropriate software to create a multimedia slideshow or other multimedia presentation of your findings. Include reproductions or videos of the work of the Abstract Expressionists, and integrate music of the time period. Include a final slide that documents your sources. See pages R41–R43 for help with bibliographic style.

Report As you compile information in your report, use your visuals to help explain art terms. Make links between the artists, the movement, and what the artwork shows, being sure to convey a distinct point of view. Focus on what defines Abstract Expressionism, explaining varying perspectives on the era while maintaining a focus on the central concerns and accomplishments of the artists.

 Literature Online

Selection Resources For Selection Quizzes, eFlashcards, and Reading-Writing Connection, go to glencoe.com and enter QuickPass code GL57805u2.

Vocabulary Workshop

Jargon

Literature Connection You may not be familiar with the word *artisanal* in the quotation below from "First Impressions" from *De Kooning: An American Master.*

> "On the job, he found he had much to learn about the way his new country operated, which often differed from the careful, artisanal manners of Holland."

You may, however, have read or heard the word *artisan*, meaning "a skilled worker," and know many words with the suffix *–al*, which means "like" or "characterized by." The context, or setting in which the word appears, also gives you a clue that *artisanal* means "skillfully crafted."

Words like *artisanal*, which are related to a specific field or occupation, are called **jargon**. Certain content areas, such as science, math, social studies and the arts, also have jargon. This specialized language can include specific meanings for common words. For example, in "First Impressions," a painter is described as *naïve*, which generally means "lacking experience and understanding." As jargon related to art, though, it refers to a painting style characterized by a lack of formal training. The chart below shows several examples of jargon.

Vocabulary Terms

Jargon is the specialized or technical language of a trade, a profession such as law or medicine, art, and sports.

Test-Taking Tip

When you encounter unfamiliar jargon in a text, look for Latin, Greek, and other roots and affixes you already know. Then consider the subject of the text and the context of the sentence to determine the meaning of the word.

Jargon	Content Area	Meaning When Used as Jargon	Root or Affix
neonatal	science	adjective referring to newborn babies	from the Greek *neo-*, meaning "new"
circumference	mathematics	the distance around a circle	from the Latin *circa-*, meaning "around"
czar	social studies	person who is in charge of a policy or an agenda	derived from the Latin title "Caesar"

Practice Identify the jargon in each of the following sentences related to "First Impressions." Then use the context and your knowledge of Latin, Greek, and other roots and affixes to help you write a definition for the jargon. Check your answers using a dictionary.

1. De Kooning learned how to mix pigments with oil and water while painting houses.

2. In Holland, housepainters always stripped windows down to the wood before repainting them.

3. De Kooning often painted in a style that featured forceful brushstrokes.

Literature Online

Vocabulary For more vocabulary practice, go to glencoe.com and enter the QuickPass code GL57805u2.

Before You Read

Typhoid Fever
from *Angela's Ashes*

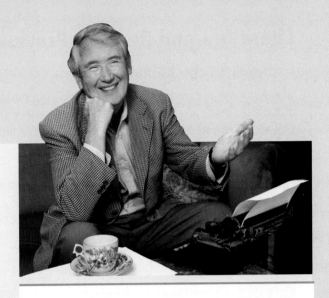

Meet **Frank McCourt**

(1930–2009)

"*I learned the significance of my own insignificant life.*"

—Frank McCourt

"When I look back on my childhood I wonder how I survived at all. It was, of course, a miserable childhood: the happy childhood is hardly worth your while." Thus begins Frank McCourt's powerful memoir, *Angela's Ashes.*

Frank McCourt was born in Brooklyn, New York, to recently immigrated Irish parents. His father, Malachy McCourt, struggled with alcoholism and unemployment. His mother, Angela Sheehan, bore the grim task of raising young children in the face of unrelenting poverty. In the mid-1930s, the McCourts moved back to Limerick, Ireland, to better their lives.

An Irish Childhood In Ireland, however, the McCourts fared no better, given the country's economic depression, unstable employment, and wretched living conditions. Angela tried to sustain the family by scrimping and saving and by soliciting help from Catholic charities and the government. She also endured the deaths of three of her children.

Breaking Free When he was nineteen, McCourt decided to return to the United States to begin a new life. After working a series of jobs, McCourt served in the Korean War, which entitled him to benefits under the GI Bill and funded his education at New York University. He became a teacher and taught in New York City public schools for 27 years.

A Story to Tell McCourt knew he had a story to tell and struggled for years trying to tell it. "All along I wanted to do this book badly. I would have to do it or I would have died

howling." In 1996, at the age of 66, he finally published *Angela's Ashes.*

McCourt's gritty story gripped readers almost immediately. When he wrote *Angela's Ashes*, McCourt did not want to write something "charming or lyrical." Instead, he wanted to offer a description of his poverty-stricken Irish childhood that was real and honest. He won several prestigious awards for the book, including the Pulitzer Prize.

Two years later, McCourt followed *Angela's Ashes* with *'Tis*, the second work in his memoir series. *'Tis* chronicles his adventures in the United States, including his first job, his time in the military, his college education, and his profession as a teacher. McCourt published another book, in 2005, *Teacher Man*. It is based on his own unique experience of teaching in the U.S. public school system.

Literature Online

Author Search For more about Frank McCourt, go to glencoe.com and enter QuickPass code GL57805u2.

Literature and Reading Preview

Connect to the Memoir

When you are sick, what do you do to keep your mind occupied? Write a journal entry about the last time you were sick and what you did or thought about to pass the time.

Build Background

Typhoid fever is an infection spread via food, water, and milk contaminated with the *Salmonella typhi* bacteria. Diphtheria is a disease caused by bacteria that have been infected by certain viruses. If left untreated, both diseases can be fatal.

Set Purposes for Reading

Big Idea The Power of Memory

As you read, ask yourself, How does McCourt portray his childhood decades after he lived it?

Literary Element Voice

Voice is the distinctive use of language that conveys the author's personality or opinions to the reader. Voice is determined by elements of style such as word choice and tone. As you read, ask yourself, What does the author's voice reveal about his personality and credibility?

Reading Strategy Analyze Style

When you **analzye style**, you examine the expressive qualities that distinguish an author's work, including word choice and the length and arrangement of sentences, as well as the use of figurative language and **imagery**, or descriptive language that appeals to the senses. As you read, ask yourself, How can style reveal an author's attitude and purpose?

....

Tip: Ask Questions Ask yourself questions about the effect imagery has on style as you read. Record your ideas in a chart like the one shown below.

Question	Example	Effect
What kinds of imagery does McCourt use?	"an owl and a pussycat that went to sea in a green boat with honey and money"	He uses fantastical and nonsensical imagery to create an air of innocence.

TEKS

For pages 311–320

10.6 Evaluate the role of syntax and diction and the effect of voice, tone, and imagery on a speech, literary essay, or other forms of literary nonfiction.

Vocabulary

induce (in dōōs′) *v.* to lead or move by persuasion; to bring about; p. 315 *The physicians decided to induce labor.*

potent (pōt′ənt) *adj.* having strength or authority; powerful; p. 315 *The black widow spider injects a potent venom into its victims.*

....

Tip: Word Origins Remember that knowledge of a word's origins supplies you with clues to, rather than a full account of, a word's current meaning.

A Sick Ward at the Salpetriere. Mabel Henrietta May. Oil on canvas. Musée de l'Assistance Publique, Hopitaux de Paris, France.

Typhoid Fever

from Angela's Ashes   Frank McCourt

The other two beds in my room are empty. The nurse says I'm the only typhoid patient and I'm a miracle for getting over the crisis.

The room next to me is empty till one morning a girl's voice says, Yoo hoo, who's there?

I'm not sure if she's talking to me or someone in the room beyond.

Yoo hoo, boy with the typhoid, are you awake?

I am.

Are you better?

I am.

Well, why are you here?

I don't know. I'm still in the bed. They stick needles in me and give me medicine.

What do you look like?

I wonder. What kind of a question is that? I don't know what to tell her.

Yoo hoo, are you there, typhoid boy?

I am.

What's your name?

Frank.

That's a good name. My name is Patricia Madigan. How old are you?

Ten.

Oh. She sounds disappointed.

But I'll be eleven in August, next month.

Well, that's better than ten. I'll be fourteen in September. Do you want to know why I'm in the Fever Hospital?

I do.

Analyze Style *McCourt does not use quotation marks to set off dialogue. What effect does this style have?*

I have diphtheria and something else.

What's something else?

They don't know. They think I have a disease from foreign parts because my father used to be in Africa. I nearly died. Are you going to tell me what you look like?

I have black hair.

You and millions.

I have brown eyes with bits of green that's called hazel.

You and thousands.

I have stitches on the back of my right hand and my two feet where they put in the soldier's blood.

Oh, God, did they?

They did.

You won't be able to stop marching and saluting.

There's a swish of habit and click of beads and then Sister Rita's voice. Now, now, what's this? There's to be no talking between two rooms especially when it's a boy and a girl. Do you hear me, Patricia?

I do, Sister.

Do you hear me, Francis?

I do, Sister.

You could be giving thanks for your two remarkable recoveries. You could be saying the rosary. You could be reading *The Little Messenger of the Sacred Heart* that's beside your beds. Don't let me come back and find you talking.

She comes into my room and wags her finger at me. Especially you, Francis, after thousands of boys prayed for you at the Confraternity.[1] Give thanks, Francis, give thanks.

She leaves and there's silence for awhile. Then Patricia whispers, Give thanks, Francis, give thanks, and say your rosary, Francis, and I laugh so hard a nurse runs in to see if I'm all right. She's a very stern nurse from the County Kerry and she frightens me. What's this, Francis? Laughing? What is there to laugh about? Are you and that Madigan girl talking? I'll report you to Sister Rita. There's to be no laughing for you could be doing serious damage to your internal apparatus.

She plods out and Patricia whispers again in a heavy Kerry accent, No laughing, Francis, you could be doin' serious damage to your internal apparatus. Say your rosary, Francis, and pray for your internal apparatus.

Mam visits me on Thursdays. I'd like to see my father, too, but I'm out of danger, crisis time is over, and I'm allowed only one visitor. Besides, she says, he's back at work at Rank's Flour Mills and please God this job will last a while with the war on and the English desperate for flour. She brings me a chocolate bar and that proves Dad is working. She could never afford it on the dole. He sends me notes. He tells me my brothers are all praying for me, that I should be a good boy, obey the doctors, the nuns, the nurses, and don't forget to say my prayers. He's sure St. Jude pulled me through the crisis because he's the patron saint[2] of desperate cases and I was indeed a desperate case.

Patricia says she has two books by her bed. One is a poetry book and that's the one she loves. The other is a short history of England and do I want it? She gives it to Seamus,[3] the man who mops the floors every day, and he brings it to me. He says, I'm not supposed to be bringing anything from a dipteria room to a typhoid room

---

1. A *confraternity* is a group of people dedicated to a religious cause.

2. A *patron saint* is a saint to whom a craft, an activity, or the protection of a person or place is dedicated.

3. *Seamus* (shā′mus)

with all the germs flying around and hiding between the pages and if you ever catch dipteria on top of the typhoid they'll know and I'll lose my good job and be out on the street singing patriotic songs with a tin cup in my hand, which I could easily do because there isn't a song ever written about Ireland's sufferings I don't know.

Oh, yes, he knows Roddy McCorley. He'll sing it for me right enough but he's barely into the first verse when the Kerry nurse rushes in. What's this, Seamus? Singing? Of all the people in this hospital you should know the rules against singing. I have a good mind to report you to Sister Rita.

Ah, God, don't do that, nurse.

Very well, Seamus. I'll let it go this one time. You know the singing could lead to a relapse in these patients.

When she leaves he whispers he'll teach me a few songs because singing is good for passing the time when you're by yourself in a typhoid room. He says Patricia is a lovely girl the way she often gives him sweets from the parcel her mother sends every fortnight. He stops mopping the floor and calls to Patricia in the next room, I was telling Frankie you're a lovely girl, Patricia, and she says, You're a lovely man, Seamus. He smiles because he's an old man of forty and he never had children but the ones he can talk to here in the Fever Hospital. He says, Here's the book, Frankie. Isn't it a great pity you have to be reading all about England after all they did to us, that there isn't a history of Ireland to be had in this hospital.

The book tells me all about King Alfred and William the Conqueror and all the kings and queens down to Edward, who had to wait forever for his mother, Victoria, to die before he could be king. The book has the first bit of Shakespeare I ever read.

Bernadette Soubirous, Visionary of Lourdes, 1844–1879. Artist unknown.

<u>View the Art</u> Notice how the artist uses light and shades of color to highlight elements in the painting. Do you think the image captures the personality of Sister Rita? Support your opinion.

*I do believe, **induced** by **potent** circumstances*
That thou art mine enemy.

The history writer says this is what Catherine, who is a wife of Henry the Eighth, says to Cardinal Wolsey, who is trying to have her head cut off. I don't know what it means and I don't care

The Power of Memory *Why might McCourt remember reading Shakespeare so many years later?*

Stained glass window of Saint Elizabeth Healing the Sick, 13th century. Gothic. St. Elizabeth, Marburg, Germany.

View the Art Thirteenth-century Germanic stained glass features detailed backgrounds, figures with expressive faces, and ornate geometric frames around the scenes depicted. Do the figures in this scene reflect the people in "Typhoid Fever"? Why or why not?

makes no sense and when I say that Patricia gets huffy and says that's the last poem she'll ever read to me. She says I'm always reciting the lines from Shakespeare and they make no sense either. Seamus stops mopping again and tells us we shouldn't be fighting over poetry because we'll have enough to fight about when we grow up and get married. Patricia says she's sorry and I'm sorry too so she reads me part of another poem which I have to remember so I can say it back to her early in the morning or late at night when there are no nuns or nurses about,

because it's Shakespeare and it's like having jewels in my mouth when I say the words. If I had a whole book of Shakespeare they could keep me in the hospital for a year.

Patricia says she doesn't know what induced means or potent circumstances and she doesn't care about Shakespeare, she has her poetry book and she reads to me from beyond the wall a poem about an owl and a pussycat that went to sea in a green boat with honey and money and it

The wind was a torrent of darkness among the gusty trees,
The moon was a ghostly galleon tossed upon cloudy seas,
The road was a ribbon of moonlight over the purple moor,[4]
And the highwayman came riding
Riding riding
The highwayman came riding, up to the old inn-door.
He'd a French cocked-hat[5] *on his forehead, a bunch of lace at his chin,*

Voice *What does McCourt's use of figurative language at the top of this column tell you about his personality as a child?*

4. A *moor* is a wide, boggy expanse of land.
5. A *French cocked-hat* is a triangular hat with its brim turned upward in three places.

A coat of the claret[6] velvet, and breeches[7]
  of brown doe-skin,
They fitted with never a wrinkle, his boots
  were up to the thigh.
And he rode with a
  jewelled twinkle,
His pistol butts a-twinkle,
His rapier[8] hilt a-twinkle, under the jewelled
  sky.[9]

Every day I can't wait for the doctors and nurses to leave me alone so I can learn a new verse from Patricia and find out what's happening to the highwayman and the landlord's red-lipped daughter. I love the poem because it's exciting and almost as good as my two lines of Shakespeare. The redcoats are after the highwayman because they know he told her, I'll come to thee by moonlight, though hell should bar the way.

I'd love to do that myself, come by moonlight for Patricia in the next room, though hell should bar the way. She's ready to read the last few verses when in comes the nurse from Kerry shouting at her, shouting at me, I told ye there was to be no talking between rooms. Diptheria is never allowed to talk to typhoid and visa versa. I warned ye. And she calls out, Seamus, take this one. Take the by. Sister Rita said one more word out of him and upstairs with him. We gave ye a warning to stop the blathering but ye wouldn't. Take the by, Seamus, take him.

Ah, now, nurse, sure isn't he harmless. 'Tis only a bit o' poetry.

Take that by, Seamus, take him at once.

He bends over me and whispers, Ah, God, I'm sorry, Frankie. Here's your English history book. He slips the book under my shirt and lifts me from the bed. He whispers that I'm a feather. I try to see Patricia when we pass through her room but all I can make out is a blur of dark head on a pillow.

Sister Rita stops us in the hall to tell me I'm a great disappointment to her, that she expected me to be a good boy after what God had done for me, after all the prayers said by hundreds of boys at the Confraternity, after all the care from the nuns and nurses of the Fever Hospital, after the way they let my mother and father in to see me, a thing rarely allowed, and this is how I repaid them lying in the bed reciting silly poetry back and forth with Patricia Madigan knowing very well there was a ban on all talk between typhoid and diphtheria. She says I'll have plenty of time to reflect on my sins in the big ward upstairs and I should beg God's forgiveness for my disobedience reciting a pagan English poem about a thief on a horse and a maiden with red lips who commits a terrible sin when I could have been praying or reading the life of a saint. She made it her business to read that poem so she did and I'd be well advised to tell the priest in confession.

The Kerry nurse follows us upstairs gasping and holding on to the banister. She tells me I better not get the notion she'll be

---

6. *Claret,* also the name of a red wine, is a dark, purplish red color.
7. *Breeches* is another term for pants.
8. A *rapier* is a narrow, long-bladed, two-edged sword.
9. This poem excerpt is from "The Highwayman," a famous narrative poem by Alfred Noyes, a popular British poet in the early twentieth century.

Voice *What does McCourt's use of imagery in the first sentence of the second paragraph in this column tell you about his personality?*

The Power of Memory *Why do you think McCourt remembers and is able to re-create details like "a blur of dark head on a pillow"?*

Analyze Style *What elements of humor do you see in McCourt's writing? Explain.*

running up to this part of the world every time I have a little pain or a twinge.

There are twenty beds in the ward, all white, all empty. The nurse tells Seamus put me at the far end of the ward against the wall to make sure I don't talk to anyone who might be passing the door, which is very unlikely since there isn't another soul on this whole floor. She tells Seamus this was the fever ward during the Great Famine[10] long ago and only God knows how many died here brought in too late for anything but a wash before they were buried and there are stories of cries and moans in the far reaches of the night. She says 'twould break your heart to think of what the English did to us, that if they didn't put the blight on the potato they didn't do much to take it off. No pity. No feeling at all for the people that died in this very ward, children suffering and dying here while the English feasted on roast beef and guzzled the best of wine in their big houses, little children with their mouths all green from trying to eat the grass in the fields beyond, God bless us and save us and guard us from future famines.

Seamus says 'twas a terrible thing indeed and he wouldn't want to be walking these halls in the dark with all the little green mouths gaping at him. The nurse takes my temperature, 'Tis up a bit, have a good sleep for yourself now that you're away from the chatter with Patricia Madigan below who will never know a gray hair.

She shakes her head at Seamus and he gives her a sad shake back.

Nurses and nuns never think you know what they're talking about. If you're ten going on eleven you're supposed to be simple like my uncle Pat Sheehan who was dropped on his head. You can't ask ques-

tions. You can't show you understand what the nurse said about Patricia Madigan, that she's going to die, and you can't show you want to cry over this girl who taught you a lovely poem which the nun says is bad.

The nurse tells Seamus she has to go and he's to sweep the lint from under my bed and mop up a bit around the ward. Seamus tells me she's a right oul' witch for running to Sister Rita and complaining about the poem going between the two rooms, that you can't catch a disease from a poem . . . . He never heard the likes of it, a little fella shifted upstairs for saying a poem and he has a good mind to go to the *Limerick Leader*[11] and tell them print the whole thing except he has this job and he'd lose it if ever Sister Rita found out. Anyway, Frankie, you'll be outa here one of these fine days and you can read all the poetry you want though I don't know about Patricia below, I don't know about Patricia, God help us.

He knows about Patricia in two days because she got out of the bed to go to the lavatory when she was supposed to use a bedpan and collapsed and died in the lavatory. Seamus is mopping the floor and there are tears on his cheeks and he's saying, 'Tis a dirty rotten thing to die in a lavatory when you're lovely in yourself. She told me she was sorry she had you reciting that poem and getting you shifted from the room, Frankie. She said 'twas all her fault.

It wasn't, Seamus.

I know and didn't I tell her that. ❧

---

10. The *Great Famine* refers to the Irish potato famine of the 1840s, during which over one million Irish citizens died from starvation and disease.

11. *Limerick* is the town in Ireland in which the story takes place. The *Limerick Leader* is a local newspaper.

Voice *What does the narrator's resolution not to cry tell you about his level of maturity?*

The Power of Memory *How do you think Patricia's death and her sorrow over McCourt's departure affected McCourt?*

After You Read

Respond and Think Critically

1. **Connect to Personal Experience** How did you feel after reading the excerpt? What specifically about the text made you feel this way?

2. **Clarify Setting** What is the first reason Sister Rita gives for telling Frank and Patricia not to talk to each other? What does this tell you about the time and place in which this excerpt takes place?

3. **Analyze Attitudes** What are the subjects of Frank's and Patricia's poetry? What does their love for these written passages tell you about their different tastes in literature?

4. **Analyze Theme** How is the idea of friendship important in this excerpt? Support your answer with evidence from the text. [OER]

5. **Analyze Dialogue** Does Frank and Patricia's dialogue sound like the dialogue of a ten-year-old and a fourteen-year-old, respectively? Support your answer with examples from the text.

6. **Evaluate Characterization** How does McCourt portray adults in the excerpt? Is his portrayal of them effective? Why or why not?

7. **Big Idea** **Draw Conclusions About Structure** In memoirs, authors have the chance to present their past using a narrative style and structure. Do you think this excerpt reads more like fiction or nonfiction? Support your response with text evidence.

Daily Life and Culture

Diphtheria

Diphtheria is an infectious bacterial disease that usually affects the respiratory system but can affect the skin as well. After the development of the first diphtheria vaccine, the incidence of the disease dropped dramatically. Synthesize the information in the two graphical sources and answer the questions.

1. Approximately how many cases of diphtheria occurred in 1980? Approximately how many more cases occurred in 1980 than occurred in 1990? What was the percent of immunization coverage during each of these years?

2. What was the approximate number of diphtheria cases in 1995? What was the percent of immunization coverage at that time?

3. Synthesize the information from both graphs. What conclusions can you draw about the impact of immunization coverage on the incidence of disease of diphtheria?

Diphtheria Global Annual Reported Incidence, 1980-2005

Diphtheria Immunization Coverage, 1980-2005

Literary Element Voice

An author uses **voice** to communicate his or her personality or opinions to the reader. When analyzing a writer's voice, look at how the writer uses elements such as sentence structure, word choice, and tone.

8. **Evaluate Voice** Is the voice in this excerpt credible as that of a young boy or that of an adult? Support your response with text evidence.

9. **Analyze Voice** What effect does McCourt's use of voice have on the text? What stylistic devices does McCourt use to create his voice? Reread the highlighted text on page 316 to help you get started.

Review: Memoir

As you learned on page 255, **memoir** is a type of narrative nonfiction that presents the story of a period in the writer's life. It is usually written from the first-person point of view and emphasizes the narrator's own experience of this period. It may also reveal the impact of significant historical events on his or her life.

10. **Partner Activity** With a classmate, discuss "Typhoid Fever" as a memoir. Working with your partner, create a two-column chart similar to the one below. Fill in the left-hand column with a feature of the memoir and one example from the text. In the right-hand column, draw a conclusion about how this feature functions in the text.

Feature and Example	Conclusion
First-person Narrative; "I'm a miracle..."	Audience feels like author is talking to them

Reading Strategy Analyze Style

 Texas Test Practice (10.6)

1. The opening dialogue between the narrator and Patricia (page 313) serves to

   (A) inform the reader about health care in Ireland

   (B) prepare the reader for tragedy

   (C) reveal the average child's thinking skills

   (D) show children to be open and honest

   (E) point out differences in the way boys and girls view the same situation

Vocabulary Practice

Practice with Word Origins Studying the etymology, or origin and history, of a word can help you understand and explore its meaning. Create a word map like the one below for each of these vocabulary words from the text.

induce   potent

EXAMPLE:

Definition a historical account told in time order

Etymology Greek *chronos* means "time"

chronicle

Sample Sentence The novel was a chronicle of three generations.

Foreign Words in English

*Young Frank's ability to quote passages from Shakespeare shows that he is an **aficionado** of the author.*

Aficionado is a foreign word that is commonly used in English. Using an online or a print dictionary, determine the relationship between the original source language and original meaning of this word. Then write the modern definition of *aficionado*. Finally, demonstrate your knowledge of the word by using it in a sentence of your own creation.

Respond Through Writing

Editorial

Offer a Solution McCourt's essay reflects the biases of a certain place, time, and group of people regarding the behavior of children in a hospital. Imagine you are a reporter for the *Limerick Leader.* Write an editorial suggesting a more or less strict approach to the behavior of Patricia and Francis. Explain why your solution is reasonable, and refute the counterarguments and biases that you see as part of the problem.

Purpose and Audience Your purpose is to write an **editorial,** or short article written to express an opinion. You will refute **counterarguments,** or opposing arguments, and **biases,** or values or ways of thinking that prevent people from considering facts in an objective way. Your audience is readers of the newspaper.

Plan Begin by identifying your audience, purpose, and controlling idea or thesis, which is your opinion. Then list points you will make to support your thesis, or the reasons for your opinion. Consider a range of information and views and also list counterarguments and biases you will address, such as the Sisters' belief that reciting or listening to poetry will harm the children.

Draft As you draft, put your arguments in a logical order. For example, you could begin with your least important idea and build to your most important or convincing one. For each reason you discuss, present evidence, such as commonly accepted beliefs, facts, expert opinions, or logical reasoning. Incorporate persuasive techniques and rhetorical devices by using these frames or others like them:
Appeal to Ethical Belief It is only right that ____ .
Appeal to Logic The most logical thing to do is ____ .
Rhetorical Question What good would it do to ____ ?

Revise Exchange papers with a partner. Be sure you can identify each other's thesis or opinion and at least two logical, well-supported reasons that directly support the thesis. Also, identify at least one counterargument and one bias that your partner has addressed. Revise your essay to improve your thesis, reasons, evidence, or responses to possible arguments or ways of thinking that oppose your own.

Edit Edit your paper, correcting any errors in spelling, grammar, and punctuation. Use the Grammar Tip in the side column to help you use active and passive voice.

TEKS

10.16.A–F Write persuasive texts to influence the attitudes or actions of a specific audience on specific issues. Write an argumentative essay that includes a clear thesis or position; consideration of the whole range of information and views on a topic; counter-arguments; an organizing structure; an analysis of the relative value of specific data, facts, and ideas; and a range of appropriate appeals.

Grammar Tip

Active and Passive Voice

When reading, writing, or speaking, you should almost always use the active voice.

In active voice, the subject of the sentence performs an action. For example, *"Sister Rita stops us in the hall . . ."* Active voice is powerful and direct. In passive voice, an action is done to a subject. For example, *The ward was used by famine victims.* Passive voice often sounds weak and uncertain.

There are times, however, when passive voice is preferred. It is typically used when the doer of an action is unknown or unimportant. *They were told to be quiet,* is a good example of passive voice. Here, the doer of the action is unknown.

Literary Perspective
on *Angela's Ashes*

from

Looking Forward to the Past

A Profile of Frank McCourt

Carolyn T. Hughes

Frank McCourt, 1998, New York.

TEKS

For pages 322–325

10.8 Analyze, make inferences and draw conclusions about the author's purpose in cultural, historical, and contemporary contexts and provide evidence from the text to support understanding.

 National Book Award Winner

Set a Purpose for Reading
Read to learn about McCourt's personal journey in writing *Angela's Ashes.*

Build Background
Author Frank McCourt, who spent his childhood in Limerick, Ireland, revisits his early years in *Angela's Ashes.* In this profile, Hughes discusses why McCourt was inspired to write a memoir of his childhood in Limerick.

Reading Strategy

Analyze Author's Purpose
Authors may write to persuade, inform, explain, entertain, or describe. When you **analyze the author's purpose** in a cultural, historical, or contemporary context, you examine how these outside factors impact the author's purpose. As you read, use a diagram like the one below to take notes on the details of the profile.

Angela's Ashes is McCourt's attempt to come to terms with his childhood— one so beset by tragedy and misfortune that he has called his work simply an "epic of woe." In 1930 McCourt was born in Brooklyn, to Irish immigrants Malachy and Angela. His parents, crushed by the recent death of their daughter and by the alcoholic Malachy's inability to hold a job, moved the family back to Ireland—but bad luck followed them. McCourt's twin brothers died shortly after the family returned to Limerick, and he himself almost perished from typhoid fever. But the greatest challenge for McCourt to contend with was his father's continued drinking and eventual abandonment of the family. In 1941 Malachy McCourt, Sr., left for England, ostensibly to get a factory job. He was supposed to send home money. It never happened. He disappeared, leaving his family to fend for themselves.

At times, the landscape of *Angela's Ashes* is so bleak it's downright depressing. But McCourt's use of a child narrator (an idea that came to him "in a dream") works to soften the tragedy of the story. Instead of being delivered through an adult's jaded vision, the events are relayed from an innocent, even lighthearted perspective, without judgment, which makes room for the poignancy and humor so celebrated by readers and critics.

Much of *Angela's Ashes* is devoted to the depiction of McCourt's educational experience at Leamy National School in Limerick, where, he says, his teachers had about as light a touch as the Marquis de Sade.[1] When McCourt became a teacher himself, he was determined to provide a creative, productive environment for his students. He began his career in 1959 at McKee Vocational and Technical High School on Staten Island, and after 13 years went on to Stuyvesant High, where he became the kind of teacher students dream of. Claire Costello, a Stuyvesant alumna who now works as a Manhattan attorney, says that McCourt was so popular that students who were not assigned to his classes would audit them (now not many teachers can claim *that* kind of approbation).[2] In class McCourt was known to play Irish records, and even to break out his harmonica and play a tune or two himself. While his approachability endeared him to his students, McCourt insists he learned more from his students than they did from him.

"I found that in the beginning of my teaching career, just like everybody else, I would put on an act and try to be what I wasn't: the teacher who knows *everything*. Sometimes I felt I was saying things that I really didn't mean. 'Oh, yeah, I understand *The Waste Land*,[3] I understand Shakespeare,' when I might not. But one of the things I discovered in the classroom was honesty. I don't mean it from any moral or ethical sense. It's a powerful tool to tell the truth."

The practice of telling the truth was an exercise that would prove important for McCourt. And in having to articulate to his students lessons on how to write, he was formulating the strategies that he would eventually put to use himself. "I told them, 'If you write, it's like having a Geiger counter[4] you can run over your life. There will be hot spots—when you had your first fight with your brother, when you fell in love, your first kiss, and all that—then you look for conflict.' The ol' conflict dilemma. I also told them to get the stories of their fathers and mothers and grandparents. There are grandparents sitting at home now who are mines of information and stories. They want to tell them, but most people cast them aside. I told my students, 'There's your material; get out the tape recorder, take notes.'"

McCourt acknowledges being an avid note taker himself and says it helped him with the writing of his book. "I've been keeping journals for forty years, and there were things I discovered in my notebooks that I had forgotten about—like how my mother was attracted to my father and his hangdog look. Well, one of the reasons why he had a hangdog look then was because he had just been released from three months in prison for hijacking a truck. He thought it was full of cans of pork and beans, but it turned out to be buttons." McCourt laughs. "I had forgotten about that completely."

Although McCourt has spent much of his life teaching writing, he admits he's suspicious of today's writing programs. "It depends on the person, but I think you'd be better off falling in love, you'd be better off getting rejected by someone. These are valuable experiences!" McCourt says. "My point is, anything is worth writing about. I gave my students an assignment. I said, 'Look, pick somebody in this class, don't look at

---

1. The *Marquis de Sade* (1740–1814) was a French nobleman and writer condemned for his abusive behavior.
2. *Approbation* means "praise."
3. *The Waste Land* is a famous poem by American writer T. S. Eliot.

---

4. A *Geiger counter*, an instrument with a tube and electronic equipment, is used to detect particles of radiation.

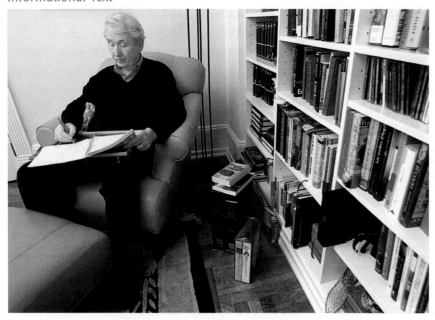

Frank McCourt in New York. January 4, 2000. Tore Bergsake.

them right now, but you are going to write about this person. You are going to observe them for a month and then write.' It forced them, encouraged them, to observe another human being and perhaps realize the significance of insignificance."

One of the major reasons it took McCourt so long to write *Angela's Ashes* was that he didn't understand the truth of his own lesson. He marginalized the significance of his early life, believing that his family's crushing poverty rendered their story inconsequential. His background, in fact, was a source of embarrassment: "In my twenties and thirties, I didn't want to write about being poor. I had to overcome a lot of fear—overcome the shame. I guess you could say I was suffering from low self-esteem."

In 1969, McCourt did attempt to write a book about his life. "I think I called it *If You Were in the Lane*. It was completely derivative. I was imitating everybody, even Evelyn Waugh.[5] Imagine me writing like Evelyn Waugh!"

Although he didn't give up writing completely, it was 25 years before McCourt would try to tackle his own story again. In the meantime he wrote the occasional article—he published a piece about a Jewish cemetery in Limerick in the *Village Voice* and a series of articles about New York for the *Manhattan Spirit*. McCourt even tried his hand as an entertainer. In 1984, he starred with brother Malachy, an actor, Manhattan bar owner, and renowned bon vivant,[6] in a cabaret show called *A Couple of Blaguards*. The show premiered in New York and went on to Chicago, San Francisco, and Ireland. The brothers McCourt sang Irish songs and told stories about their family. (The play, directed by Howard Platt, is now enjoying a successful run at New York's Triad Theater.)

When McCourt retired from teaching and finally turned to the writing of *Angela's Ashes*, it didn't take long for him to finish it. He wrote most of the book at his home in Pennsylvania. "I started it in October 1994. The actual writing took a year—actually, less than a year because I was distracted by various events and people visiting, so maybe it took ten months of straight writing. I just got up every morning and I wrote. What was it Red Smith[7] said? 'You sit at the desk and you open a vein.' That was my routine. I wrote on the right-hand page of my notebook, and on the left-hand

---

5. *Evelyn Waugh* (1903–1966) was a British writer, known for his satiric portrayals of the British upper classes.

6. *Bon vivant* means "a person with sophisticated tastes, especially of food and drink."

7. *Red Smith* (1905–1982) was an American sports columnist.

side I jotted down notes about what I needed to dig deeper into." McCourt didn't have any set schedule for how many hours a day he would work: "I didn't push. . . . When it came, it came." Having his wife as a sounding board helped. "I would read passages to Ellen—and she thought it was fine."

McCourt showed the first 159 pages to Molly Friedrich, a New York City neighbor who also happens to be a literary agent. She agreed to work with McCourt, and passed the manuscript on to Nan Graham, editor in chief at Scribner. Graham, no easy sell, loved it: "I edited *The Liar's Club*,"[8] Graham says. "I've seen a lot of memoirs, but from the beginning I thought the work and voice in *Angela's Ashes* was extraordinary. I bought the book within a week. There really was so little to do as far as editing. This man is a stunning writer."

McCourt handed in his final draft to Graham on November 30, 1995, the 328th anniversary of the birth of Jonathan Swift,[9] one of McCourt's favorite writers (he has a thing for significant dates). Although working on the book was emotionally draining, McCourt felt an overwhelming sense of accomplishment when he finished it. "I would have been very unhappy if I had died without writing it. I would have begged for another year. 'Jesus, give me another year!' I would have died howling. So I did it, and I'm glad it's out of the way. You see, it's a great thing to know why you were put on this earth. I was a teacher, but teaching was my second occupation. All the time I was a writer not writing, just jotting things down in notebooks and so on. But all the time the book was developing in my head as I taught the kids at Stuyvesant. It was forming and waiting to be born." ∾

---

8. *The Liar's Club* was author Mary Karr's popular 1995 memoir.

9. *Jonathan Swift* (1667–1745) was an Irish author celebrated for his satiric prose in such works as *Gulliver's Travels*.

Respond and Think Critically

1. **Summarize Main Ideas** Write a brief summary of the main ideas in this article before you answer the following questions. For help on writing a summary, see page 389.

2. **Analyze Perspective** Why did McCourt decide to use a child's point of view to narrate *Angela's Ashes*? What might this say about his perspective on childhood?

3. **Make Inferences About Author's Purpose** Hughes delves into McCourt's upbringing, his offbeat methods of teaching, and his brief stint as an actor. Why do you think she includes these cultural and historical details of McCourt's life? Do these details support McCourt's message about writing? Why or why not?

4. **Draw Conclusions About Author's Purpose** Hughes says that "one of the major reasons it took McCourt so long to write *Angela's Ashes* was that he didn't understand the truth of his own lesson." Think about the cultural and historical context of McCourt's life. What do you think Hughes means by this comment? What do you think Hughes believes the act of writing can teach a person?

5. **Evaluate Ideas** What is your opinion of McCourt's claim that "anything is worth writing about"? Explain.

6. **Draw Conclusions About Memoir** McCourt attempted to write a book about his life in 1969. It took another 25 years before he wrote *Angela's Ashes*. Do you think the passing of time distanced him from or made him more aware of his memories of the past? Support your answer with text evidence.

Before You Read

Terwilliger Bunts One
from *An American Childhood*

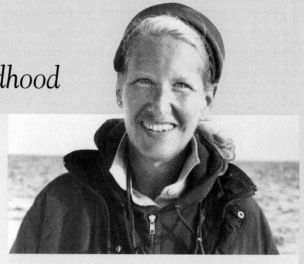

Meet **Annie Dillard**
(born 1945)

As a child, Annie Dillard was encouraged by her parents to investigate the world around her. That keen attention to detail and fascination for living things is reflected in Dillard's writing, whether she is describing a grasshopper on her window or discussing her family's idiosyncrasies.

> *"The dedicated life is worth living. You must give with your whole heart."*
>
> —Annie Dillard

An American Childhood Annie Dillard, the oldest of three daughters, had an unusual childhood. Her parents, the Doaks, were creative thinkers who encouraged and inspired creativity in Dillard and her sisters. The world was open to the Doak sisters to explore, question, and discover. During adolescence, Dillard began experimenting with writing poetry. She read poets of all kinds and particularly admired the works of Ralph Waldo Emerson. Dillard wrote poetry in her own style as well as in the style of her favorite poets. She was also a voracious reader; she notes that, at the age of thirteen, "I was reading books on drawing, painting, rocks, criminology, birds, moths, beetles, stamps, ponds and streams, medicine." In fact, Dillard reread her favorite book—*The Field Book of Ponds and Streams*—every year.

Tinker Creek and Beyond In college Dillard wrote a forty-page paper about Henry David Thoreau, and her book *Pilgrim at Tinker Creek* is often compared to Thoreau's *Walden; or Life in the Woods*. Dillard spent time living in nature next to Tinker Creek in Virginia's Roanoke Valley. In *Pilgrim at Tinker Creek*, Dillard examines the beautiful and sometimes brutal natural world. *Pilgrim at Tinker Creek* won the Pulitzer Prize for Nonfiction in 1975, when Dillard was only thirty years old.

Dillard was inspired by the birth of her first daughter to complete a memoir, entitled *An American Childhood*. Dillard describes growing up with eccentric parents: a father who quit his lucrative job to mimic Mark Twain's journey down the Mississippi River and a mother who encouraged her daughters to explore the world outside the family home as soon as they could remember their phone number. According to Michael J. Farrell, "Dillard urges us not to turn away, coaxes us instead to look Life in the eye." Whether writing about the natural world or the human one, Dillard observes with an unflinching gaze.

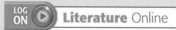
LOG ON ▶ **Literature** Online

Author Search For more about Annie Dillard, go to glencoe.com and enter QuickPass code GL57805u2.

Literature and Reading Preview

Connect to the Memoir

How do you use humor in your daily life? List moments throughout your day that you lighten with humor.

Build Background

An American Childhood is set in Pittsburgh, Pennsylvania, in the 1950s. At that time, most middle-class married women did not work outside the home or pursue their own careers. In this essay, Dillard suggests that women in the 1950s were as capable, and even as brilliant as anyone else, despite their lack of opportunity.

Set Purposes for Reading

Big Idea The Power of Memory

As you read, ask yourself, How does Dillard link her humorous memories of her mother to her development as a writer?

Literary Element Humor

Humor is the quality of a text that makes the people and situations described seem funny, amusing, or ludicrous. To create a humorous effect, authors may incorporate sarcasm, exaggeration, or irony. As you read this memoir, ask yourself, In what ways is Dillard's mother surprising and original? How does the mother use humor to make a point?

Reading Strategy Connect to Personal Experience

Authors often write about situations, settings, or characters that the reader can relate to. **Connecting to personal experience** can help you better understand the author's message. As you read, ask yourself, What situations in the text remind me of instances in my own life?

....

Tip: Make a Chart Notice events, characters, or situations from the excerpt that seem familiar to you. Record your thoughts in a chart like the one below. Use the blue highlighted questions for help.

Situations in the text	Reminds me of . . .
Out of the blue, Mother suddenly rolled down the beach.	I have an aunt who is also spontaneous and fun.

TEKS

For pages 326–334

10.6 Understand, make inferences and draw conclusions about the varied structural patterns and features of literary nonfiction and provide evidence from the text to support understanding.

Vocabulary

tremulously (trem′yə ləs lē) *adv.* in a trembling or vibrating way; p. 329 *After he heard the knock at the door, he tremulously asked, "Who's there?"*

eschew (es chōō′) *v.* to keep apart from something disliked or harmful; avoid; p. 329 *Because loud music hurts my ears, I eschew it.*

advocate (ad′və kāt′) *v.* to publicly support; p. 330 *I advocate the passing of that law, and I will be sure to vote for it.*

stolid (stol′id) *adj.* showing little or no emotion; p. 331 *Her face was stolid after hearing the bad news; we never knew how sad she was.*

....

Tip: Synonyms A **synonym** is a word that has the same, or nearly the same, meaning as another word.

Terwilliger Bunts One

from An American Childhood

S&H Green Stamps, 1965. Andy Warhol.
The Andy Warhol Foundation for the Visual Arts.

Annie Dillard

One Sunday afternoon Mother wandered through our kitchen, where Father was making a sandwich and listening to the ball game. The Pirates were playing the New York Giants at Forbes Field. In those days, the Giants had a utility infielder[1] named Wayne Terwilliger. Just as Mother passed through, the radio announcer cried—with undue drama—"Terwilliger bunts one!"

"Terwilliger bunts one?" Mother cried back, stopped short. She turned. "Is that English?"

"The player's name is Terwilliger," Father said. "He bunted."

"That's marvelous," Mother said. "'Terwilliger bunts one.' No wonder you listen to baseball. 'Terwilliger bunts one.'"

For the next seven or eight years, Mother made this surprising string of syllables her own. Testing a microphone, she repeated, "Terwilliger bunts one"; testing a pen or a typewriter, she wrote it. If, as happened surprisingly often in the course of various improvised gags, she pretended to whisper something else in my ear, she actually whispered, "Terwilliger bunts one." Whenever someone used a French phrase, or a Latin one, she answered solemnly, "Terwilliger bunts one." If Mother had had, like Andrew Carnegie,[2] the opportunity to cook up a motto for a coat of arms,[3] hers would have read simply and tellingly, "Terwilliger bunts one." (Carnegie's was "Death to Privilege.")

She served us with other words and phrases. On a Florida trip, she repeated

---

1. In this context, *utility* means "useful generally rather than in a specialized function." So, a *utility infielder* is capable of playing shortstop or first, second, or third base.

   Humor *What does Dillard's mother find amusing about "Terwilliger bunts one"?*

2. Based in Pittsburgh, *Andrew Carnegie* (1835–1919) made a fortune in the steel industry and donated $350 million to social and educational institutions.

3. A *coat of arms* is an arrangement of symbols on a shield that, along with a motto, represents one's ancestry.

tremulously, "That . . . is a royal poinciana." I don't remember the tree; I remember the thrill in her voice. She pronounced it carefully, and spelled it. She also liked to say "portulaca."[4]

The drama of the words "Tamiami Trail" stirred her, we learned on the same Florida trip. People built Tampa on one coast, and they built Miami on another. Then—the height of visionary[5] ambition and folly—they piled a slow, tremendous road through the terrible Everglades to connect them. To build the road, men stood sunk in muck to their armpits. They fought off cottonmouth moccasins and six-foot alligators. They slept in boats, wet. They blasted muck with dynamite, cut jungle with machetes; they laid logs, dragged drilling machines, hauled dredges, heaped limestone. The road took fourteen years to build up by the shovelful, a Panama Canal in reverse, and cost hundreds of lives from tropical, mosquito-carried diseases. Then, capping it all, some genius thought of the word Tamiami: they called the road from Tampa to Miami, this very road under our spinning wheels, the Tamiami Trail. Some called it Alligator Alley. Anyone could drive over this road without a thought.

Hearing this, moved, I thought all the suffering of road building was worth it (it wasn't my suffering), now that we had this new thing to hang these new words on—Alligator Alley for those who like things cute, and, for connoisseurs like Mother, for lovers of the human drama in all its boldness and terror, the Tamiami Trail.

Back home, Mother cut clips from reels of talk, as it were, and played them back at leisure. She noticed that many Pittsburghers confuse "leave" and "let." One kind relative brightened our morning by mentioning why she'd brought her son to visit: "He wanted to come with me, so I left him." Mother filled in Amy and me on locutions we missed. "I can't do it on Friday," her pretty sister told a crowded dinner party, "because Friday's the day I lay in the stores."[6]

(All unconsciously, though, we ourselves used some pure Pittsburghisms. We said "tele pole," pronounced "telly pole," for that splintery sidewalk post I loved to climb. We said "slippy"—the sidewalks are "slippy." We said, "That's all the farther I could go." And we said, as Pittsburghers do say, "This glass needs washed," or "The dog needs walked"—a usage our father **eschewed;** he knew it was not standard English, nor even comprehensible English, but he never let on.)

"Spell 'poinsettia,'" Mother would throw out at me, smiling with pleasure. "Spell 'sherbet.'" The idea was not to make us whizzes, but, quite the contrary, to remind us—and I, especially, needed reminding—

---

4. The *royal poinciana* and the *portulaca* (pôr′ chə lakə) are native to the tropics and bear bright flowers.

5. Here, *visionary* refers to imagining something in perfect but unrealistic form. People had foreseen the benefits of connecting the two cities but overlooked practical considerations involved in constructing the road.

Humor *What does the author reveal here about her mother's personality?*

Humor *What element of humor does Dillard use in this passage? Explain.*

Vocabulary

tremulously (trem′ yə ləs lē) *adv.* in a trembling or vibrating way

---

6. *Locutions* are forms or styles of verbal expression. Where this woman said she had to *lay in the stores,* Mother might have said she had to go grocery shopping.

The Power of Memory *What do Dillard's memories of Pittsburgh add to the essay?*

Vocabulary

eschew (es chōō′) *v.* to keep apart from something disliked or harmful; avoid that we didn't know it all just yet. "There's a deer standing in the front hall," she told me one quiet evening in the country.

"Really?"

"No. I just wanted to tell you something once without your saying, 'I know.'"

Supermarkets in the middle 1950s began luring, or bothering, customers by giving out Top Value Stamps or Green Stamps.[7] When, shopping with Mother, we got to the head of the checkout line, the checker, always a young man, asked, "Save stamps?"

"No," Mother replied genially, week after week, "I build model airplanes." I believe she originated this line. It took me years to determine where the joke lay.

Anyone who met her verbal challenges she adored. She had surgery on one of her eyes. On the operating table, just before she conked out, she appealed feelingly to the surgeon, saying, as she had been planning to say for weeks, "Will I be able to play the piano?" "Not on me," the surgeon said. "You won't pull that old one on me."

It was, indeed, an old one. The surgeon was supposed to answer, "Yes, my dear, brave woman, you will be able to play the piano after this operation," to which Mother intended to reply, "Oh, good, I've always wanted to play the piano." This pat scenario bored her; she loved having it interrupted. It must have galled[8] her that usually her acquaintances were so predictably unalert; it must have galled her that, for the length of her life, she could surprise everyone so continually, so easily, when she had been the same all along. At any rate, she loved anyone who, as she put it, saw it coming, and called her on it.

She regarded the instructions on bureaucratic forms as straight lines.[9] "Do you **advocate** the overthrow of the United States government by force or violence?" After some thought she wrote, "Force." She regarded children, even babies, as straight men.[10] When Molly learned to crawl, Mother delighted in buying her gowns with drawstrings at the bottom, like Swee'pea's, because, as she explained energetically, you could easily step on the drawstring without the baby's noticing, so that she crawled and crawled and crawled and never got anywhere except into a small ball at the gown's top.

Visual Vocabulary
Swee'pea is the baby in "Popeye" cartoons.

When we children were young, she mothered us tenderly and dependably; as we got older, she resumed her career of anarchism.[11] She collared us into her gags. If she answered the phone on a wrong number, she told the caller, "Just a minute," and dragged the receiver to Amy or me, saying, "Here, take this, your name is Cecile," or, worse, just, "It's for you." You had to think on your feet. But did you want to perform well as Cecile, or did

---

7. *[Top Value . . . Stamps]* Stores gave customers a certain number of stamps per dollar spent. These stamps were saved up and later exchanged for merchandise.

8. Here, *galled* means "irritated."

Humor *What does the exchange with the surgeon reveal about what Dillard's mother values in life?*

---

9. *Bureaucratic* refers to the rigidly formal paperwork and procedures involved in dealing with government officials and agencies. For Mother, these things were setups for jokes—the *straight lines* that led to punch lines.

10. *Straight men* are people who assist comedians by feeding them straight lines or serving as objects of fun.

11. Here, *anarchism* refers to active resistance against what is oppressive and undesirable.

Connect to Personal Experience *What would you do in this situation? Why?*

Vocabulary

advocate (ad′və kāt′) *v.* to publicly support

you want to take pity on the wretched caller?

During a family trip to the Highland Park Zoo, Mother and I were alone for a minute. She approached a young couple holding hands on a bench by the seals, and addressed the young man in dripping[12] tones: "Where have you been? Still got those baby-blue eyes; always did slay me. And this"—a swift nod at the dumbstruck young woman, who had removed her hand from the man's—"must be the one you were telling me about. She's not so bad, really, as you used to make out. But listen, you know how I miss you, you know where to reach me, same old place. And there's Ann over there—see how she's grown? See the blue eyes?"

And off she sashayed,[13] taking me firmly by the hand, and leading us around briskly past the monkey house and away. She cocked an ear back, and both of us heard the desperate man begin, in a high-pitched wail, "I swear, I never saw her before in my life. . . ."

On a long, sloping beach by the ocean, she lay stretched out sunning with Father and friends, until the conversation gradually grew tedious, when without forethought she gave a little push with her heel and rolled away. People were stunned. She rolled deadpan and apparently effortlessly, arms and legs extended and tidy, down the beach to the distant water's edge, where she lay at ease just as she had been, but half in the surf, and well out of earshot.

She dearly loved to fluster people by throwing out a game's rules at whim—[14] when she was getting bored, losing in a dull sort of way, and when everybody else was taking it too seriously. If you turned your back, she moved the checkers around on the board. When you got them all straightened out, she denied she'd touched them; the next time you turned your back, she lined them up on the rug or hid them under your chair. In a betting rummy game called *Michigan,* she routinely played out of turn, or called out a card she didn't hold, or counted backward, simply to amuse herself by causing an uproar and watching the rest of us do double takes and have fits. (Much later, when serious suitors came to call, Mother subjected them to this fast card game as a trial by ordeal; she used it as an intelligence test and a measure of spirit. If the poor man could stay a round without breaking down or running out, he got to marry one of us, if he still wanted to.)

She excelled at bridge, playing fast and boldly, but when the stakes were low and the hands dull, she bid slams[15] for the devilment of it, or raised her opponents' suit to bug them, or showed her hand, or tossed her cards in a handful behind her back in a characteristic swift motion accompanied by a vibrantly innocent look. It drove our **stolid** father crazy. The hand was over before it began, and the guests were appalled. How do you score it, who deals now, what do you do with a crazy person who is having so much fun? Or they were down seven, and the guests were appalled. "Pam!" "Dammit, Pam!" He groaned. What ails such people? What on earth possesses them? He rubbed his face.

She was an unstoppable force; she never let go. When we moved across town, she persuaded the U.S. Post Office to let her keep her old address—forever—because

---

12. *Dripping* here refers to using excessive charm or appeal.
13. She *sashayed* or walked in a way that showed a seeming lack of interest.
14. The phrase *at whim* means "suddenly and unexpectedly."

15. When she *bid slams,* Mother "went for broke," betting that she would win every or all but one of the tricks in a round of play.

Vocabulary

stolid (stol´id) *adj.* showing little or no emotion

ANNIE DILLARD **331**

Ringling Brothers and Barnum & Bailey—Trains. Artist unknown.

View the Art Traveling circuses used posters that featured exaggeration and excitement to attract audiences. What idea in the essay does this advertisement help illustrate?

she'd had stationery printed. I don't know how she did it. Every new post office worker, over decades, needed to learn that although the Doaks' mail is addressed to here, it is delivered to there.

Mother's energy and intelligence suited her for a greater role in a larger arena— mayor of New York, say—than the one she had. She followed American politics closely; she had been known to vote for Democrats. She saw how things should be run, but she had nothing to run but our household. Even there, small minds bugged her; she was smarter than the people who designed the things she had to use all day for the length of her life.

"Look," she said. "Whoever designed this corkscrew never used one. Why would anyone sell it without trying it out?" So she invented a better one. She showed me a drawing of it. The spirit of American enterprise never faded in Mother. If capitalizing and tooling up[16] had been as interesting as theorizing and thinking up, she would have fired up a new factory every week, and chaired several hundred corporations.

"It grieves me," she would say, "it grieves my heart," that the company that

16. *Capitalizing* and *tooling up* has to do with providing the finances and equipment necessary to start up a new business or factory.

Humor *Reread this paragraph. What effect did the mother's humor seem to have on people around her?*

Connect to Personal Experience *What were the best qualities possessed by Dillard's mother? Who do you know with similar qualities?*

made one superior product packaged it poorly, or took the wrong tack[17] in its advertising. She knew, as she held the thing mournfully in her two hands, that she'd never find another. She was right. We children wholly sympathized, and so did Father; what could she do, what could anyone do, about it? She was Samson[18] in chains. She paced.

She didn't like the taste of stamps so she didn't lick stamps; she licked the corner of the envelope instead. She glued sandpaper to the sides of kitchen drawers, and under kitchen cabinets, so she always had a handy place to strike a match. She designed, and hounded workmen to build against all norms,[19] doubly wide kitchen counters and elevated bathroom sinks. . . . She drew plans for an over-the-finger toothbrush for babies, an oven rack that slid up and down, and— the family favorite—Lendalarm. Lendalarm was a beeper you attached to books (or tools) you loaned friends. After ten days, the beeper sounded. Only the rightful owner could silence it.

She repeatedly reminded us of P. T. Barnum's dictum:[20] You could sell anything to anybody if you marketed it right. The adman who thought of making Americans believe they needed underarm deodorant was a visionary. So, too, was the hero who made a success of a new product, Ivory soap. The executives were horrified, Mother told me, that a cake of this stuff floated. Soap wasn't supposed to float. Anyone would be able to tell it was mostly whipped-up air. Then some inspired adman made a leap: Advertise that it floats. Flaunt it. The rest is history.

She respected the rare few who broke through to new ways. "Look," she'd say, "here's an intelligent apron." She called upon us to admire intelligent control knobs and intelligent pan handles, intelligent andirons and picture frames and knife sharpeners. She questioned everything, every pair of scissors, every knitting needle, gardening glove, tape dispenser. Hers was a restless mental vigor that just about ignited the dumb household objects with its force.

Torpid[21] conformity was a kind of sin; it was stupidity itself, the mighty stream against which Mother would never cease to struggle. If you held no minority opinions, or if you failed to risk total ostracism for them daily, the world would be a better place without you. . . .

She simply tried to keep us all awake. And in fact it was always clear to Amy and me, and to Molly when she grew old enough to listen, that if our classmates came to cruelty, just as much as if the neighborhood or the nation came to madness, we were expected to take, and would be each separately capable of taking, a stand. ✎

---

17. The company took the wrong course of action or *tack*.
18. In the Bible, *Samson* is powerful and mighty until an enemy tricks him. Soon Samson is chained up in prison.
19. Here, the *norms* are rules, standards, and accepted practices.
20. In the 1800s, *Barnum* presented many popular entertainments, including what is now the Ringling Brothers and Barnum & Bailey Circus. The actual words of his famous saying (*dictum*) were "There's a sucker born every minute."

---

21. Something that's *torpid* is dull and lifeless.

The Power of Memory *What qualities did Dillard's mother encourage in her daughters?*

After You Read

Respond and Think Critically

1. **Connect to Personal Experience** What makes Dillard's mother original and surprising? Explain.

2. **Interpret Behavior** What words and phrases does Dillard's mother enjoy repeating? What does her habit of repeating these phrases reveal about her? Support your answer.

3. **Analyze Description** Dillard describes several incidents that demonstrate how her mother behaved around others. List important details from three of these incidents. Explain what these details add to your understanding of the mother's personality. Support your answer with evidence from the text.

4. **Make Inferences About Details** What does Dillard mean when she says the "spirit of American enterprise never faded in Mother"?

5. **Evaluate Characterization** "My mother was always completely irrepressible," Dillard has been quoted as saying. How well does Dillard illustrate her mother's "irrepressible" quality? Support your evaluation with details from the essay.

6. **Big Idea** **Draw Conclusions About Theme** What regrets does Dillard have about her mother's life? How do memories of her mother help reinforce life lessons for Dillard?

Literary Element Humor

Essayists often use humorous **anecdotes,** or brief accounts of interesting occurances.

7. **Make Inferences About Humor** Why do you think Dillard chose to use funny anecdotes to convey a portrait of her mother? Support your answer with details from the text.

8. **Evaluate Humor** Dillard's mother used sarcasm and exaggeration to amuse herself and others. Which examples of her humor did you find most entertaining? Explain your answer.

Reading Strategy Connect to Personal Experience

Use your chart from page 327 to answer the following questions.

9. Which of your personal experiences most helped you relate to Dillard's stories about her mother?

10. Do you think most readers would be able to connect to these stories? Why or why not?

LOG ON ▶ **Literature** Online

Selection Resources For Selection Quizzes, eFlash-cards, and Reading-Writing Connection activities, go to glencoe.com and enter QuickPass code GL57805u2.

Vocabulary Practice

Practice with Synonyms With a partner, match each boldfaced vocabulary word below with its synonym. Use a dictionary or the glossary on pages R76–R91 to check your answers. You will not use all the answer choices.

1. tremulously   **a.** avoid

2. eschew   **b.** tremblingly

3. advocate   **c.** listlessly

4. stolid   **d.** haughty

        e. unemotional

        f. recommend

Writing

Write a Humorous Anecdote In one or two paragraphs, write an anecdote about a person you know, in which the person reveals an amusing quirk or stong sense of humor. Include concrete details to help your audience understand what you find amusing about the person.

PART 2

QUESTS AND ENCOUNTERS

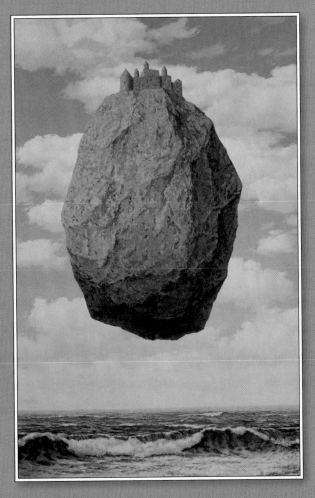

Le Château des Pyrénées, 1959. René Magritte. Oil on canvas, 100 x 140 cm. Israel Museum, Jerusalem.

View the Art René Magritte, a Belgian Surrealist painter, used symbols to express the mystery and absurdity of perception and reality. How might this image represent a quest to be undertaken or a thought-provoking encounter?

BIG IDEA

Sometimes what seems like an ordinary day is transformed into something extraordinary. Unexpectedly, your routine is turned into a quest or a meeting is elevated to an encounter. In the nonfiction works in Part 2, you will read essays about ordinary and extraordinary quests and encounters. As you read these texts, ask yourself, When in my life have ordinary events become extraordinary?

TEKS

For pages 336–337

10.6 Understand, make inferences and draw conclusions about the varied structural patterns and features of literary nonfiction and provide evidence from text to support understanding.

LITERARY FOCUS

EXPOSITORY AND PERSONAL ESSAY

What is an essay?

Essayists write for many reasons. They may wish to share an experience with their readers, or make them think about a new idea. Others are motivated by a political purpose or a passion for truth. In "The Tucson Zoo," Lewis Thomas seeks to share an experience with his readers.

from "The Tucson Zoo"

by Lewis Thomas

I was transfixed. As I now recall it, there was only one sensation in my head: pure elation mixed with amazement at such perfection. Swept off my feet, I floated from one side to the other, swiveling my brain, staring astounded at the beavers, then at the otters. I could hear shouts across my corpus callosum, from one hemisphere to the other. I remember thinking, with what was left in charge of my consciousness, that I wanted no part of the science of beavers and otters; I wanted never to know how they performed their marvels; I wished for no news about the physiology of their breathing, the coordination of their muscles, their vision, their endocrine systems, their digestive tracts. I hoped never to have to think of them as collections of cells. All I asked for was the full hairy complexity, then in front of my eyes, of whole, intact beavers and otters in motion.

The Essay

An **essay** is a short work of nonfiction that focuses on a single topic and that communicates an idea or opinion. The essays in this part were written to inform or to share experiences with the reader. Essays are generally categorized as **expository, personal,** and **persuasive.**

The Expository Essay

The word *expository* is derived from the verb *expose,* which means "to make known or to explain." Whenever you write to inform, to give directions, to explain an idea, or to make something clear, you are writing **exposition.** Writers of expository works sometimes weave narrative stories into their writing.

Many expository essays follow a general structure of introduction, body, and conclusion.

- The **introduction** serves to pique the reader's interest. It also often includes the **thesis,** or main idea, of the essay. Sometimes, though, a writer saves the thesis statement for the end of the work.

- The **body** develops the thesis with supporting details, such as facts, examples, sensory details, observations, or personal experiences.

- The **conclusion** typically restates the thesis and provides the reader with a final thought.

The Personal Essay

Personal essays are usually informal in their language and tone, and they often contain passages of expository writing. A personal essay often reflects on an incident in the writer's life. The writer may share a life lesson with the reader or perhaps shed light on a time or place long gone. Other personal essays can be written to please oneself or an audience of like-minded readers.

A personal essay can also be a kind of writing that is common on applications, such as those for college admissions. These essays should be more formal in language and tone. When you write a personal essay for a college application, your audience will be a selection committee.

None of the social issues of 1957 had a chance of catching my attention that year. All that existed for me was my grandmother, rising from the surf like a Dahomean queen, shaking her head free of her torturous rubber cap, beaming down at me when I finally took the first strokes on my own.

—Jewelle L. Gomez, *from "A Swimming Lesson"*

Mother Giving Swimming Lessons (detail), 1999. Riva Brown.

Quickwrite

Make Inferences Reread the excerpt from "The Tuscon Zoo" on page 336. How does Thomas describe his encounter with the animals? In a paragraph, explain how you know the excerpt is from an essay and explain how the excerpt uses typical features of an essay.

Before You Read

A Swimming Lesson

Meet **Jewelle L. Gomez**
(born 1948)

What do I hope to achieve by writing? Changing the world!" Award-winning writer and social activist Jewelle L. Gomez attributes much of her success to her great-grandmother. "My great-grandmother . . . was born on an Indian reservation in Iowa and had been a widow for fifty years. She maintained an intellectual curiosity and graciousness that no amount of education could have created. She formed the basis of much of my intellectual yearnings."

"My writing flows directly out of the great storytelling that runs in my family."

—Jewelle L. Gomez

In Her Blood Gomez was born in Boston to parents of African American, Native American, and Portuguese ancestry. She lived with her great-grandmother until she was 22 years old. Although she lived in poverty as a child and young adult, Gomez was able to attend college. She earned a bachelor's degree from Northeastern University and a master's degree from Columbia University School of Journalism. Before becoming a published writer, Gomez worked as a television production assistant in Boston and as a stage manager for plays in New York City.

Growing up in a family of storytellers, Gomez always knew she wanted to be a writer. But she struggled for many years before discovering a subject that inspired her. A play written by African American poet Ntozake Shange changed her life. The play celebrated ordinary African American women, portraying them as strong and beautiful. Until that point, Gomez had never seen or read anything that described African American women as heroes. Watching Shange's play, she found herself thinking of her grandmother and great-grandmother. What if she wrote about them and other women like them? At that moment, she discovered a subject she wanted to write about for the rest of her life.

Fact and Imagination Growing up during the Civil Rights Movement and the Black Power Movement of the 1960s taught Gomez about social activism. It seemed everyone she knew was trying to make U.S. society a better place for people of color. Since then, Gomez's strong belief in equality—for minorities, women, and other groups—has been the guiding force in her writing and her life. "All oppressions are interconnected," she once said. Themes having to do with equality, power, and responsibility are evident in her essays, plays, poetry, novels, and short stories.

LOG ON **Literature** Online

Author Search For more about Jewelle L. Gomez, go to glencoe.com and enter QuickPass code GL57805u2.

Literature and Reading Preview

Connect to the Essay

What skill do you possess that you learned from a family member or another adult? Discuss this question with a partner. Consider the methods that person used to teach you the skill.

Build Background

This essay is set in the summer of 1957 at Revere Beach in Revere, Massachusetts, five miles north of Boston. People from the entire Boston metropolitan area were able to reach Revere Beach by public transportation. At that time, Boston itself was heavily segregated. Roxbury, the neighborhood where the author lived, was mostly African American.

Set Purposes for Reading

Big Idea Quests and Encounters

As you read, ask yourself, How does Gomez's encounter with the beach teach her more than just how to swim?

Literary Element Narrative Essay

The structural pattern of a **narrative essay** is similar to that of a short nonfiction story. Written in the first person, narrative essays usually relate events drawn from the author's own life, allowing the reader to directly experience the author's perspective. Compared with a formal essay, a narrative essay differs in its use of a conversational tone. As you read, ask yourself, Why did Gomez choose the narrative essay form for this essay?

Reading Strategy Activate Prior Knowledge

When you **activate prior knowledge,** you use what you already know to deepen your understanding of a literary work. As you read, think about what you already know about the people and places described in "A Swimming Lesson." Ask yourself, how can I use my prior knowledge of the 1950s in Boston to help me understand this essay?

....

Tip: Make a Chart As you read, record details about which you have prior knowledge. Use the blue highlighted passage and question for help.

Detail	Prior Knowledge
The grandmother and Gomez ride the train from Roxbury to Revere Beach.	Boston is segregated, but Revere Beach was a destination for everyone. The trip to the beach has special import.

TEKS

For pages 338–344

10.6 Understand, make inferences and draw conclusions about the varied structural patterns and features of literary nonfiction and provide evidence from text to support understanding.

Vocabulary

benevolence (bə nev′ə ləns) *n.* kindness; generosity; p. 341 *Gabriel's benevolence was apparent in his tireless work for the poor.*

vulnerable (vul′nər ə bəl) *adj.* easily damaged or hurt; p. 341 *Children are vulnerable to injuries.*

mainstream (mān′strēm′) *adj.* representing the most widespread attitudes and values of a society or group; p. 341 *The play was very popular because it appealed to mainstream audiences.*

superfluous (soo pur′floo əs) *adj.* not needed; unnecessary; p. 341 *The student's research paper contained a great deal of superfluous information.*

invaluable (in val′ū ə bəl) *adj.* very great in value; p. 341 *I probably would not have found the building without my father's invaluable directions.*

....

Tip: Context Clues Use context clues to infer the meaning, or part of the meaning, of an unfamiliar word. Context clues can be found in the words and phrases that surround the word.

A Swimming Lesson

Jewelle L. Gomez

At nine years old I didn't realize my grandmother, Lydia, and I were doing an extraordinary thing by packing a picnic lunch and riding the elevated train from Roxbury[1] to Revere Beach. It seemed part of the natural rhythm of summer to me. I didn't notice how the subway cars slowly emptied of most of their Black passengers as the train left Boston's urban center and made its way into the Italian and Irish suburban neighborhoods to the north. It didn't seem odd that all of the Black families stayed in one section of the beach and never ventured onto the boardwalk to the concession stands or the rides except in groups.

I do remember Black women perched cautiously on their blankets, tugging desperately at bathing suits rising too high in the rear and complaining about their hair "going back." Not my grandmother, though. She glowed with unashamed athleticism as she waded out, just inside the reach of the waves, and moved along the riptide[2] parallel to the shore. Once submerged, she would load me onto her back and begin her long, tireless strokes. With the waves partially covering us, I followed her rhythm with my short, chubby arms, taking my cues from the powerful movement of her back muscles. We did this again and again until I'd fall off, and she'd catch me and set me upright in the strong New England surf. I was thrilled by the wildness of the ocean and my grandmother's fearless relationship to it. I loved the way she never consulted her mirror after her swim, but always looked as if she had been born to the sea, a kind of aquatic heiress.

---

1. Boston's *Roxbury* neighborhood is southwest of downtown.

Narrative Essay *From this sentence, what do you learn about the relationship between white and African American people at Revere Beach?*

2. The *riptide* is the strong surface current that flows rapidly away from shore, returning to sea the water carried landward by waves.

Quests and Encounters *How does the author's grandmother seem to feel about her encounters with the ocean?*

None of the social issues of 1957 had a chance of catching my attention that year. All that existed for me was my grandmother, rising from the surf like a Dahomean[3] queen, shaking her head free of her torturous rubber cap, beaming down at me when I finally took the first strokes on my own. She towered above me in the sun with a **benevolence** that made simply dwelling in her presence a reward in itself. Under her gaze I felt part of a long line of royalty. I was certain that everyone around us—Black and white—saw and respected her magnificence.

Although I sensed her power, I didn't know the real significance of our summers together as Black females in a white part of town. Unlike winter, when we were protected by the cover of coats, boots and hats, summer left us **vulnerable** and at odds with the expectations for women's bodies—the narrow hips, straight hair, flat stomachs, small feet—handed down from the **mainstream** culture and media. But Lydia never noticed. Her long chorus-girl legs ended in size-nine shoes, and she dared to make herself even bigger as she stretched her broad back and became a woman with a purpose: teaching her granddaughter to swim.

My swimming may have seemed a **superfluous** skill to those who watched our lessons. After all, it was obvious that I wouldn't be doing the backstroke on the Riviera[4] or in the pool of a penthouse spa. Certainly nothing in the popular media at that time made the "great outdoors" seem a hospitable place for Black people. It was a place in which we were meant to feel comfortable at best and hunted at worst. But my prospects for utilizing my skill were irrelevant to me, and when I finally got it right I felt as if I had learned some **invaluable** life secret.

When I reached college and learned the specifics of slavery and the Middle Passage,[5] the magnitude of that "peculiar institution"[6] was almost beyond my comprehension; it was like nothing I'd learned before about the history of my people. It was difficult making a connection with those Africans who had been set adrift from their own land. My initial reaction was "Why didn't the slaves simply jump from the ships while they were still close to shore, and swim home?" The child in me who had learned to survive in water was crushed to find that my ancestors had not necessarily shared this skill. Years later when I visited West Africa and learned of the poisonous, spiny fish that inhabit most of the coastal waters, I understood why

---

3. *Dahomean* (də hō′mā ən) refers to Dahomey, a country in western Africa now called Benin (ben in′). Several kingdoms flourished in this region from the 1300s to the 1600s.

Activate Prior Knowledge *Consider what you know about relations between African Americans and whites at this time. Why was it important for Gomez to feel pride in herself and her family?*

Vocabulary

benevolence (bə nev′ə ləns) *n.* kindness; generosity

vulnerable (vul′nər ə bəl) *adj.* easily damaged or hurt

mainstream (mān′strēm′) *adj.* representing the most widespread attitudes and values of a society or group

---

4. A popular resort area, the *Riviera* lies along the Mediterranean coasts of Italy and France.
5. The *Middle Passage* was the route followed by slave traders from Africa to the Americas. Through the months-long voyage, slaves suffered filth, disease, abuse, and death.
6. Prior to the Civil War, Southerners referred to slavery as their *peculiar institution*, meaning that they considered it to be vital to their economy and way of life.

Vocabulary

superfluous (soo pur′floo əs) *adj.* not needed; unnecessary

invaluable (in val′ū ə bəl) *adj.* very great in value

swimming was not the local sport there that it was in New England. And now when I take to the surf, I think of those ancestors and of Lydia.

The sea has been a fearful place for us. It swallowed us whole when there was no escape from the holds of slave ships. For me, to whom the dark fathoms of a tenement hallway were the most unknowable thing so far encountered in my nine years, the ocean was a mystery of terrifying proportions. In teaching me to swim, my grandmother took away my fear. I began to understand something outside myself—the sea—and consequently something about myself as well. I was no longer simply a fat little girl: My body had become a sea vessel—sturdy, enduring, graceful. I had the means to be safe.

Before she died last summer I learned that Lydia herself couldn't really swim that well. As I was splashing, desperately trying to learn the right rhythm—face down, eyes closed, air out, reach, face up, eyes open, air in, reach—Lydia was brushing the ocean's floor with her feet, keeping us both afloat. When she told me, I was stunned. I reached into my memory trying to combine this new information with the Olympic vision I'd always kept of her. At first I'd felt disappointed, tricked, the way I used to feel when I'd learn that a favorite movie star was only five feet tall. But then I quickly realized what an incredible act of bravery it was for her to pass on to me a skill she herself had not quite mastered—a skill that she knew would always bring me a sense of accomplishment. And it was more than just the swimming. It was the ability to stand on any beach anywhere and be proud of my large body, my African hair. It was not fearing the strong muscles in my own back; it was gaining control over my own life. ༄

After You Read

Respond and Think Critically

1. **Connect to Personal Experience** What is your reaction to Lydia's deception? Explain.

2. **Explain Personality Traits** As a child, what did Gomez find admirable about her grandmother? Explain your answer and support it with evidence from the essay. **OER**

3. **Make Inferences About Attitudes** According to Gomez, why might observers have considered her swimming lessons a waste of time? Why do you think Gomez views the lessons differently? Support your answer.

4. **Compare and Contrast Attitudes** What historical information has helped Gomez understand her ancestors' attitude toward the sea? Explain how Gomez's attitude compares with that of her ancestors.

5. **Analyze Author's Beliefs** What are the "social attitudes of 1957" to which Gomez refers in this essay? How does her adult view of these issues relate to her childhood view of them?

6. **Evaluate Description** How well did Gomez describe her childhood days at the beach? Did you come away with a vivid picture of those days? Cite details from the essay in your answer.

7. **Big Idea** **Draw Conclusions About Personal Experience** How strong an influence was Gomez's grandmother on Gomez's journey toward success? After reading this essay, what can you conclude about the positive effects a role model can have on a person's life? Support your answer with evidence from the text.

Literary Element Narrative Essay

A good narrative essay, or nonfiction story, contains the structural patterns and elements of any good narrative: characters, setting, and plot. Like short stories, most narrative essays include a central conflict or problem and have a climax and resolution. Many narrative essays are autobiographical, and the author's purpose is to tell about life experiences and life lessons.

8. **Compare and Contrast Genres** Compare and contrast the structure of Gomez's essay with the structure of a short story. Use details from the essay to support your answer.

9. **Make Inferences About Structure** Narratives usually contain a resolution—a tying up of any loose ends in the story. What is the resolution of "A Swimming Lesson"? Support your answer.

Review: Author's Purpose

As you learned on page 299, the **author's purpose** is the author's reason for writing a literary work. Authors typically write for one or more of the following purposes: to inform, to persuade, to describe, to explain, or to entertain. To determine an author's purpose, it may help to consider the historical or cultural context in which he or she wrote.

10. **Group Activity** With two other students, review the essay to locate evidence that will help you determine the author's purpose. List the evidence in a chart like the one shown. Together, discuss and record your inferences about the author's purpose.

Evidence	Inference
Despite mainstream images, the grandmother is comfortable with herself.	The essay's purpose may be to describe how Gomez learned self-acceptance and pride.

Reading Strategy Activate Prior Knowledge

Using your prior knowledge about people, places and events can help you better understand a story. Refer to the chart you made on page 339.

11. Review the first paragraph in the second column on page 341. What does your prior knowledge of the 1950s help you to understand about Gomez's points? Explain.

12. What does your knowledge of the era help you to understand about the grandmother's actions? Support your answer with evidence from the text.

Vocabulary Practice

Practice with Context Clues In the following sentences, identify the context clues that help you determine the meanings of the boldfaced vocabulary words.

1. One theme of the book was the **benevolence** of the generous king.

2. Homes built on the seashore or on cliffs are **vulnerable** to damage during storms.

3. The teacher made a list of **mainstream** newspapers that included the widely read *Los Angeles Times* and *New York Times.*

4. The director decided to do away with the **superfluous** fourth camera and used three cameras instead.

5. We could not tell the difference between the **invaluable** statue and the trinket from the souvenir stand.

Enrich and Extend

 Speaking and Listening

Literature Groups With a small group, discuss whether children can ever become productive members of society without good role models and mentors. Set a discussion goal, and, when you have met it, present your ideas to the class.

Teamwork To participate productively in your group, listen to others, build on their ideas, and contribute relevant information. You can avoid conflict by setting up ground rules up front for making decisions and building consensus.

Prepare Set a purpose. If your purpose is to explore different points of view fully, set criteria for meeting that goal.

- compile and consider each group member's personal experience
- compile and consider evidence from "A Swimming Lesson"
- compile and consider evidence from public and historical experience, such as the lives of famous people who were orphans

Discuss Use comprehension skills to listen attentively, and ask questions when you do not understand a point or the support for it. Actively evaluate as you listen to each group member's ideas, deciding how well each person's ideas answer questions about the need for role models or mentors. Support your judgment of ideas with specific examples.

Report Have one group member present the consensus, or have several group members explain varying points of view. Each speaker should make eye contact, use gestures effectively, and employ language that will engage the audience.

Evaluate Evaluate your work for clarity of content; use of evidence; verbal skills, including word choice and syntax; and nonverbal skills, including gestures.

Before You Read

The Tucson Zoo

Meet **Lewis Thomas**
(1913–1993)

Award-winning author Lewis Thomas was a renowned physician and research biologist. He taught at some of the top medical schools in the United States. As a writer, he established a reputation as a master of the short essay. In his inquisitive musings on nature, science, technology, and other subjects, he celebrated the mystery and marvel of life.

> "We are built to make mistakes, coded for error."
>
> —Lewis Thomas

Medical Background The son of a doctor and a nurse, Thomas had an early interest in the medical profession. He enrolled at Princeton University at fifteen and graduated when he was only nineteen years old. He entered Harvard Medical School at an exciting and dynamic time for the field of medicine—clinical science and antibiotics were both in the early stages of development. He graduated from medical school at the age of 23.

During the course of his medical career, he worked at many U.S. universities, including New York University, Yale, Johns Hopkins, Tulane, and the University of Minnesota. His roles at these institutions varied. Over the years, he worked as a researcher, a teacher, an administrator, and a pediatrician, among other specialties. He also served in the U.S. Navy Medical Corps.

Writer and Researcher Thomas's interest in writing began almost as early as his interest in science and medicine. He developed an interest in poetry while at Princeton, and after medical school, during his internship at Boston City Hospital, he supported himself in part by publishing poems in various magazines, including *Harper's Bazaar* and the *Saturday Evening Post*. Before becoming a respected prose writer, he began writing his essays simply "for fun."

Popular Appeal The interest and wonder that Thomas brought to both science and life was at the heart of his appeal to a wide audience. He combined common sense, daily observations, and detailed scientific knowledge in his writing. Thomas's philosophy of life and science could be symbolized by the concept of symbiosis, a relationship between organisms that benefits both. As one writer explained, "Thomas's scientific training enabled him to show how human biology is . . . linked to the biology of the planet as a whole."

Thomas's first book, *The Lives of a Cell: Notes of a Biology Watcher,* is a collection of essays originally published in his column in the *New England Journal of Medicine*. In 1975 *The Lives of a Cell: Notes of a Biology Watcher* won a National Book Award. Thomas's other works include *The Medusa and the Snail* (1979), *The Youngest Science* (1983), *Late Night Thoughts on Listening to Mahler's Ninth Symphony* (1983), and *The Fragile Species* (1992).

LOG ON **Literature** Online

Author Search For more about Lewis Thomas, go to glencoe.com and enter QuickPass code GL57805u2.

Literature and Reading Preview

Connect to the Essay

Do you act on instinct, or do you analyze your reactions and emotions? Discuss this question with a partner.

Build Background

The cortex of the brain has two hemispheres, or sides. The left side is analytical while the right hemisphere is creative. The *corpus callosum,* which Thomas refers to in his essay, is an arch of nervous tissue that bridges the two hemispheres and allows them to communicate with each other.

Set Purposes for Reading

Big Idea **Quests and Encounters**

As you read, ask yourself, How does Thomas explore his encounter and interpret it as a journey of human discovery?

Literary Element **Structure**

Structure refers to the particular order or pattern a writer uses to present ideas. Narratives commonly follow a chronological order, while the structure of persuasive or expository writing may vary. As you read, ask yourself, How does Thomas structure his essay?

Reading Strategy **Draw Conclusions About Meaning**

When readers **draw conclusions about meaning,** they actively think about and interpret content and structure while reading. As you read, ask yourself, What conclusions can I draw from this essay?

....

Tip: Ask and Answer Questions Asking and then answering questions about the essay's structure and content while you read can help you draw conclusions.

Question	Answer
Why does Thomas begin writing about animals but end up writing about DNA?	Starting off with something people connect to helps them understand the rest of the essay.

TEKS

For pages 345–351

10.8 Analyze the controlling idea and specific purpose of a passage and the textual elements that support and elaborate it, including both the most important details and the less important details.

Vocabulary

elation (i lā′shən) *n.* a feeling of great joy; ecstasy; p. 347 *The whole team experienced elation when Mara scored the winning goal.*

intact (in takt′) *adj.* entire; untouched, uninjured, and having all parts; p. 348 *She dropped the egg, but somehow it remained intact.*

exultation (eg′zul tā′shən) *n.* joy; jubilation; p. 348 *The woman experienced exultation when her lost child was found.*

debasement (di bās′mənt) *n.* the state of being lowered in quality, value, or character; degradation; p. 349 *Those collectibles have suffered a debasement in their value recently.*

attribute (at′rə būt′) *n.* a quality or characteristic of a person or thing; p. 349 *Honesty is a good attribute to possess.*

The Tucson Zoo

Lewis Thomas

Science gets most of its information by the process of reductionism,[1] exploring the details, then the details of the details, until all the smallest bits of the structure, or the smallest parts of the mechanism, are laid out for counting and scrutiny. Only when this is done can the investigation be extended to encompass the whole organism or the entire system. So we say.

Sometimes it seems that we take a loss, working this way. Much of today's public anxiety about science is the apprehension that we may forever be overlooking the whole by an endless, obsessive preoccupation with the parts. I had a brief, personal experience of this misgiving one afternoon in Tucson, where I had time on my hands and visited the zoo, just outside the city. The designers there

have cut a deep pathway between two small artificial ponds, walled by clear glass, so when you stand in the center of the path you can look into the depths of each pool, and at the same time you can regard the surface. In one pool, on the right side of the path, is a family of otters; on the other side, a family of beavers. Within just a few feet from your face, on either side, beavers and otters are at play, underwater and on the surface, swimming toward your face and then away, more filled with life than any creatures I have ever seen before, in all my days. Except for the glass, you could reach across and touch them.

I was transfixed. As I now recall it, there was only one sensation in my head: pure **elation** mixed with amazement at such perfection. Swept off my feet, I floated from one side to the other, swiveling my brain, staring astounded at the beavers, then at the otters. I could hear shouts across my corpus

---

1. *Reductionism* is a method of explaining complex processes or structures by reducing them to more basic principles or units.

Structure How does the last full sentence in this column change the essay's structure?

callosum, from one hemisphere to the other. I remember thinking, with what was left in charge of my consciousness, that I wanted no part of the science of beavers and otters; I wanted never to know how they performed their marvels; I wished for no news about the physiology[2] of their breathing, the coordination of their muscles, their vision, their endocrine systems,[3] their digestive tracts. I hoped never to have to think of them as collections of cells. All I asked for was the full hairy complexity, then in front of my eyes, of whole, **intact** beavers and otters in motion.

It lasted, I regret to say, for only a few minutes, and then I was back in the late twentieth century, reductionist as ever, wondering about the details by force of habit, but not, this time, the details of otters and beavers. Instead, me. Something worth remembering had happened in my mind, I was certain of

that; I would have put it somewhere in the brain stem; maybe this was my limbic system[4] at work. I became a behavioral scientist, an experimental psychologist, an ethologist,[5] and in the instant I lost all the wonder and the sense of being overwhelmed. I was flattened.

But I came away from the zoo with something, a piece of news about myself: I am coded, somehow, for otters and beavers. I exhibit instinctive behavior in their presence, when they are displayed close at hand behind glass, simultaneously below water and at the surface. I have receptors[6] for this display. Beavers and otters possess a "releaser" for me, in the terminology of ethology, and the releasing was my experience. What was released? Behavior. What behavior? Standing, swiveling flabbergasted, feeling **exultation** and a rush of friendship. I could not, as the result of the transaction, tell you anything more about beavers and otters than you already know. I learned nothing new about them. Only about me, and I suspect also about you, maybe about human beings at large: we are endowed with genes which code out our reaction to beavers and otters, maybe our reaction to each other as well. We are stamped with stereotyped, unalterable patterns of response, ready to be released. And the behavior released in us, by such

---

2. *Physiology* is the branch of biology that studies the functions of living organisms and their parts.
3. The *endocrine system* consists of glands that secrete hormones into the bloodstream, affecting such bodily processes as growth and sexual development.

Draw Conclusions About Meaning *What does Thomas come to realize in the second paragraph in this column?*

Vocabulary ....

intact (in takt´) *adj.* entire; untouched, uninjured, and having all parts

---

4. The *limbic system* is a region of the brain involved in the control of emotions and some types of behavior.
5. *Ethology* (eth ol´ə jē) is the study of animal behavior, including instinctive, or inherited, behavior.
6. *Receptor* refers to a sensory nerve cell that responds to a stimulus in the environment and sends a message to the brain.

Draw Conclusions About Meaning *Why does Thomas feel flattened by the events he's experienced?*

Vocabulary ....

exultation (eg´zul tā´shən) *n.* joy; jubilation

confrontations, is, essentially, a surprised affection. It is compulsory behavior and we can avoid it only by straining with the full power of our conscious minds, making up conscious excuses all the way. Left to ourselves, mechanistic and autonomic,[7] we hanker for friends.

Everyone says, stay away from ants. They have no lessons for us; they are crazy little instruments, inhuman, incapable of controlling themselves, lacking manners, lacking souls. When they are massed together, all touching, exchanging bits of information held in their jaws like memoranda, they become a single animal. Look out for that. It is a **debasement,** a loss of individuality, a violation of human nature, an unnatural act.

Sometimes people argue this point of view seriously and with deep thought. Be individuals, solitary and selfish, is the message. Altruism,[8] a jargon word for what used to be called love, is worse than weakness, it is sin, a violation of nature. Be separate. Do not be a social animal. But this is a hard argument to make convincingly when you have to depend on language to make it. You have to print up leaflets or publish books and get them bought and sent around, you have to turn up on television and catch the attention of millions of other human beings all at once, and then you have to say to all of them, all at once, all collected and paying attention: be solitary; do not depend on each other. You can't do this and keep a straight face.

Maybe altruism is our most primitive **attribute,** out of reach, beyond our control. Or perhaps it is immediately at hand, waiting to be released, disguised now, in our kind of civilization, as affection or friendship or attachment. I don't see why it should be unreasonable for all human beings to have strands of DNA coiled up in chromosomes, coding out instincts for usefulness and helpfulness. Usefulness may turn out to be the hardest test of fitness for survival, more important than aggression, more effective, in the long run, than grabbiness. If this is the sort of information biological science holds for the future, applying to us as well as to ants, then I am all for science.

Visual Vocabulary
Chromosomes are strands of DNA and proteins in the nucleus of cells. DNA carries the genes that pass on hereditary information from parent to child.

One thing I'd like to know most of all: when those ants have made the Hill, and are all there, touching and exchanging, and the whole mass begins to behave like a single huge creature, and *thinks,* what on earth is that thought? And while you're at it, I'd like to know a second thing: when it happens, does any single ant know about it? Does his hair stand on end? ∾

---

7. In psychology, *compulsory* means "arising from an irresistible, illogical urge." Here, *mechanistic* means "physically or biologically determined," and *autonomic* means "involuntary and spontaneous."

8. In ethology, *altruism* is an animal's self-sacrificing behavior that benefits another animal or group of animals. Similarly, for humans, the term means "unselfish concern for others."

Quests and Encounters *How does the encounter with beavers and otters lead Thomas to the conclusion that if "left to ourselves . . . we hanker for friends"?*

Draw Conclusions About Meaning *Explain what you think the author means in the sentence beginning "Usefulness may turn out to be . . .".*

Vocabulary

debasement (di bās′mənt) n. the state of being lowered in quality, value, or character; degradation

Vocabulary

attribute (at′rə būt′) n. a quality or characteristic of a person or thing

After You Read

Respond and Think Critically

1. **Connect to Personal Experience** Were you surprised by Thomas's conclusions about people? Why or why not?

2. **Draw Conclusions About the Author** What does Thomas learn about himself by watching the beavers and otters? Explain your answer and support it with evidence from the essay. **OER**

3. **Clarify Details** According to Thomas, why does everyone say to "stay away from ants"? What message do some people learn from ants?

4. **Make Inferences About Ideas** What ideas does Thomas present about altruism? What do you think Thomas means in his final reference to ants?

5. **Draw Conclusions About Author's Purpose** In your opinion, what was Thomas's purpose in writing this essay? Support your response.

6. **Evaluate Ideas** Do you agree with the conclusions that Thomas draws about instinctive behavior in people? Why or why not? Support your response with text evidence.

7. **Evaluate Analogy** Thomas uses the analogy of ants' behavior to argue that people are social by nature. Is his analogy effective? Explain.

8. **Big Idea** **Draw Conclusions About the Author** What does this essay suggest that new encounters can do for a person? Would you say that Thomas is on a quest? If so, what is his quest? Support your response.

Literary Element Structure

All expository texts have a **structure**, or organizational pattern. Writers can organize or order their ideas in expository writing in a variety of ways. For example, a writer can use a structure following a pattern of **cause and effect** to present an event or occurrence and explain why it happened. Writers can also use a **problem/solution** structure to describe a problem and offer a solution.

9. **Draw Conclusions About Structure** How would you describe the essay's structure? Support your answer with examples from the text. Refer to the highlighted question on page 347 to help you.

10. **Evaluate Structure** Can you think of an alternative structure for this essay? Do you think your proposed alternative would be more or less effective? Explain.

Review: Voice

As you learned on page 312, **voice** in a literary work is the distinctive use of language that conveys the personality of the writer or narrator to the reader. Voice is determined by elements of style, such as word choice and tone. A unique aspect of Thomas's voice is that he writes as both a learned scientist and an animal lover.

11. **Partner Activity** With a classmate, evaluate the effect of Thomas's voice by focusing on his word choice. Use a two-column chart like the one below. In the first column, list a word or phrase that conveys Thomas's voice. In the next column, evaluate how his voice affects the essay.

Word Choice	Effect
p. 347 elation	tells the reader he is an animal lover
p. 348 full hairy complexity	
p. 348 I was flattened.	

Reading Strategy Draw Conclusions About Meaning

Texas Test Practice (10.9)

1. In the paragraph beginning "Everyone says, stay away from ants" (page 349) Thomas is

   (A) making the point that humans are not comparable to ants

   (B) summarizing an argument that he will later refute

   (C) pointing out the importance of social activity in all creatures

   (D) establishing the similarity between ants and otters

   (E) arguing that ants are superior to people

Vocabulary Practice

Practice with Synonyms A synonym is a word that has the same, or nearly the same, meaning as another word. With a partner, brainstorm three synonyms for each boldfaced vocabulary word below. Explain why you chose your words.

elation   intact   exultation
debasement   attribute

EXAMPLE:
ambiguous
Synonyms: *vague, confusing, murky*
Sample explanation: Something that is ambiguous is hard to understand.

Academic Vocabulary

Beavers and otters live in specific **bioregions***; they cannot survive in all climates.*

Bioregion is a discipline-specific word that derives from Greek. The prefix *bio-* means "life." Using your knowledge and context clues, determine the meaning of *bioregion* in the model sentence above. Check your response by consulting a dictionary. Finally, demonstrate your understanding by using each of these related words in a sentence.

a. biomedical   **b.** biophysics   **c.** biosphere

Enrich and Extend

 Speaking and Listening

Debate Thomas argues against reductionism in our responses to life. Instead, he favors "big picture" thinking. With a partner, debate which represents a preferable way to learn—an emphasis on the whole or an emphasis on parts.

Prepare Each person should begin by taking a side, formulating a thesis or position, and marshaling evidence to support that position. Support might consist of examples, statistics, testimony, or other facts. All support should be credible and relevant.

Debate A debate requires you to inform and persuade at the same time. You may need to use technical language to inform; you should also incorporate informal language to be persuasive. Present your thesis first; then support each reason with ample facts that inform and persuade. Consider saving your most persuasive reason or clincher evidence for last. Include the following appeals:

Appeal	Example in Support of My Thesis
Logical—uses facts, statistics, and other solid evidence to make or support claims	
Emotional—presents information and ideas that target emotions	
Ethical—addresses the listener's values and morals	

Evaluate Write one paragraph evaluating your participation and the effectiveness of your speaking style in the debate.

Before You Read

Straw into Gold: The Metamorphosis of the Everyday

Meet **Sandra Cisneros**

(born 1954)

S andra Cisneros is one of the most distinctive voices in American literature today. Born in Chicago to a Mexican American mother and a Mexican father, Cisneros spent her childhood living uncomfortably between two worlds. The family frequently traveled to Mexico for extended periods of time. Each time they returned to the United States, the family would settle in a new location in Chicago's *barrios.* The frequent moves made it difficult for Cisneros to make friends. Being the only girl in a family of brothers did not help either, as she often felt left out.

> *"You can't erase what you know. You can't forget who you are."*
>
> —Sandra Cisneros

Because she was shy, she was often lonely. But, Cisneros writes, "that loneliness . . . was good for a would-be writer—it allowed me time to think and think, to imagine, to read and prepare myself." In high school, a teacher helped Cisneros nurture her love of writing. After high school, Cisneros received a scholarship to Loyola University in Chicago. She graduated in 1976 with a bachelor's degree in English and went on to the prestigious University of Iowa Writers' Workshop.

Finding Her Voice At the Iowa Writers' Workshop, Cisneros felt keenly aware of her status as an outsider. Yet, it was at the Workshop that Cisneros found her voice. She realized that the very thing she had tried to

escape—the shame and separation of being different—made her unique. She knew then that her role as a writer was to depict the loneliness, isolation, tragedies, and triumphs of the outsider.

Mango Street In 1982 Cisneros received her first National Endowment for the Arts grant, which allowed her to write full-time. Two years later, she published her breakthrough work, *The House on Mango Street,* a series of vignettes about a young girl, Esperanza, growing up in a Chicago *barrio.* The stories, a blend of fiction and poetry, echo Cisneros's own youth and her yearning to make sense of her life in relation to her surroundings.

Cisneros is a long-time resident of San Antonio, Texas. She is the founder of a San Antonio writers' workshop that emphasizes community services.

In 1995 Cisneros received a MacArthur Fellowship—a prestigious monetary award known as the "genius grant." The award is indicative of her high status in the American literary world.

LOG ON **Literature** Online

Author Search For more about Sandra Cisneros, go to glencoe.com and enter QuickPass code GL57805u2.

Literature and Reading Preview

Connect to the Essay

How can thinking about the past help you understand the person you are today? Freewrite for a few minutes about an event from the past that has shaped you as a person.

Build Background

The National Endowment for the Arts (NEA) was created by Congress in 1965 and is an independent agency of the federal government. Artists of every medium, from dance to literature, apply to the NEA for grant money they can use to support themselves while pursuing artistic endeavors.

Set Purposes for Reading

Big Idea Quests and Encounters

As you read this essay, ask yourself, How does Cisneros connect everyday life to the idea of the heroic quest?

Literary Element Thesis

The **thesis** is the main idea in a work of nonfiction. The thesis may be stated directly or implied by the details and examples in the work. Analyzing these details and examples can help clarify the author's purpose. As you read, ask yourself, What is Cisneros's main idea, or thesis, in this essay and what details support it?

Reading Strategy Analyze Text Structure

Text structure is the particular order or pattern a writer uses to present ideas. Cisneros's essay is a reflective essay, which is a type of personal essay. Reflective essays are structured as narratives. Cisneros's narrative contains **flashbacks,** or interruptions in the chronological order of the narrative to show events that happened earlier. As you read, ask yourself, What important information about Cisneros do I learn from the flashbacks?

....

Tip: Ask Questions As you read, record events in Cisneros's life and what you learn about her based on the events. Note the time and place of each event. Use the blue highlighted passages and questions for help.

Event	Conclusion
As an adult studying in France, Cisneros prepares tortillas for the first time.	Cisneros learns that she is capable of facing challenges and succeeding.

TEKS

For pages 352–359

10.8 Analyze the controlling idea and specific purpose of a passage and the textual elements that support and elaborate it, including both the most important details and the less important details.

Vocabulary

intuitively (in tōō′ə tiv lē) *adv.* knowing, sensing, or understanding instinctively; p. 355 *The stand-up comedian intuitively knew what not to joke about.*

taboo (ta bōō′) *n.* a cultural or social rule forbidding something; p. 355 *Speaking disrespectfully to one's elders is a social taboo.*

....

Tip: Analogies Paying attention to analogies can help you infer a word's meaning. Check your answer to an analogy by reading it backward: start with your answer, and find its relationship to the last term in the item. Then see whether that is the same relationship that the first two terms have.

STRAW INTO GOLD

The Metamorphosis of the Everyday

Sandra Cisneros

Women Making Tortilla Dough. Diego Rivera. Fresco. The Art Archive/Ministry of Public Information Mexico/Dagli Orti. ©2009 Banco de México Diego Rivera Frida Kahlo Museums Trust, Mexico, D.F./Artists Rights Society (ARS), NY.

When I was living in an artists' colony in the south of France, some fellow Latin-Americans who taught at the university in Aix-en-Provence invited me to share a home-cooked meal with them. I had been living abroad almost a year then on an NEA grant, subsisting mainly on French bread and lentils so that my money could last longer. So when the invitation to dinner arrived, I accepted without hesitation. Especially since they had promised Mexican food.

What I didn't realize when they made this invitation was that I was supposed to be involved in preparing the meal. I guess they assumed I knew how to cook Mexican food because I am Mexican. They wanted specifically tortillas, though I'd never made a tortilla in my life.

It's true I had witnessed my mother rolling the little armies of dough into perfect circles, but my mother's family is from Guanajuato; they are *provincianos*, country folk. They only know how to make flour tortillas. My father's family, on the other hand, is *chilango*[1] from Mexico City. We ate corn tortillas but we didn't make them. Someone was sent to the corner tortilleria to buy some. I'd never seen anybody make corn tortillas. Ever.

---

1. *Chilango* (chē län´gō) is a Mexican slang term that means "native to Mexico City."

Somehow my Latino hosts had gotten a hold of a packet of corn flour, and this is what they tossed my way with orders to produce tortillas. *Así como sea.* Any ol' way, they said and went back to their cooking.

Why did I feel like the woman in the fairy tale who was locked in a room and ordered to spin straw into gold? I had the same sick feeling when I was required to write my critical essay for the MFA[2] exam—the only piece of noncreative writing necessary in order to get my graduate degree. How was I to start? There were rules involved here, unlike writing a poem or story, which I did **intuitively**. There was a step by step process needed and I had better know it. I felt as if making tortillas—or writing a critical paper, for that matter—were tasks so impossible I wanted to break down into tears.

Somehow though, I managed to make tortillas—crooked and burnt, but edible nonetheless. My hosts were absolutely ignorant when it came to Mexican food; they thought my tortillas were delicious. (I'm glad my mama wasn't there.) Thinking back and looking at an old photograph documenting the three of us consuming those lopsided circles I am amazed. Just as I am amazed I could finish my MFA exam.

I've managed to do a lot of things in my life I didn't think I was capable of and which many others didn't think I was capable of either. Especially because I am a woman, a Latina, an only daughter in a family of six men. My father would've liked to have seen me married long ago. In our culture men and women don't leave their father's house except by way of marriage. I crossed my father's threshold with nothing carrying me but my own two feet. A woman whom no one came for and no one chased away.

To make matters worse, I left before any of my six brothers had ventured away from home. I broke a terrible **taboo**. Somehow, looking back at photos of myself as a child, I wonder if I was aware of having begun already my own quiet war.

I like to think that somehow my family, my Mexicanness, my poverty, all had something to do with shaping me into a writer. I like to think my parents were preparing me all along for my life as an artist even though they didn't know it. From my father I inherited a love of wandering. He was born in Mexico City but as a young man he traveled into the U.S. vagabonding. He eventually was drafted and thus became a citizen. Some of the stories he has told about his first months in the U.S. with little or no English surface in my stories in *The House on Mango Street* as well as others I have in mind to write in the future. From him I inherited a sappy heart. (He still cries when he watches Mexican soaps—especially if they deal with children who have forsaken their parents.)

---

2. *MFA* stands for Master of Fine Arts—an academic degree.

Quests and Encounters *Why does Cisneros use this particular analogy?*

Analyze Text Structure *What two events in her life does Cisneros compare in this paragraph? What did she learn from these events?*

Vocabulary

intuitively (in tōō′ə tiv lē) *adv.* knowing, sensing, or understanding instinctively

---

Thesis *Reread this paragraph. What clues does it provide about the essay's main idea?*

Vocabulary

taboo (ta bōō′) *n.* a cultural or social rule forbidding something

South Side Street, Chicago. Franklin McMahon.

View the Art McMahon depicts a streetscape with vacant buildings on Chicago's South Side. How does the economic situation in the painting relate to Cisneros's situation in this essay?

My mother was born like me—in Chicago but of Mexican descent. It would be her tough streetwise voice that would haunt all my stories and poems. An amazing woman who loves to draw and read books and can sing an opera. A smart cookie.

When I was a little girl we traveled to Mexico City so much I thought my grandparents' house on La Fortuna, number 12, was home. It was the only constant in our nomadic ramblings from one Chicago flat to another. The house on Destiny Street, number 12, in the colonia Tepeyac would be perhaps the only home I knew, and that nostalgia for a home would be a theme that would obsess me.

My brothers also figured greatly in my art. Especially the older two; I grew up in their shadows. Henry, the second oldest and my favorite, appears often in poems I have written and in stories which at times only borrow his nickname, Kiki. He played a major role in my childhood. We were bunk-bed mates. We were co-conspirators. We were pals. Until my oldest brother came back from studying in Mexico and left me odd woman out for always.

What would my teachers say if they knew I was a writer now? Who would've guessed it? I wasn't a very bright student. I didn't much like school because we moved so much and I was always new and funny looking. In my fifth-grade report card I have nothing but an avalanche of C's and D's, but I don't remember being that stupid. I was good at art and I read plenty of library books and Kiki laughed at all my jokes. At home I was fine, but at school I never opened my mouth except when the teacher called on me.

When I think of how I see myself it would have to be at age eleven. I know I'm thirty-two on the outside, but inside I'm eleven. I'm the girl in the picture with skinny arms and a crumpled skirt and crooked hair. I didn't like school because all they saw was the outside me. School was lots of rules and sitting with your hands folded and being very afraid all the time. I liked looking out the window and thinking. I liked staring at the girl across the way writing her name over and over again in red ink. I wondered why the boy with the dirty collar in front of me didn't have a mama who took better care of him.

Analyze Text Structure *Reread this paragraph. What time in her life does Cisneros look back to?*

I think my mama and papa did the best they could to keep us warm and clean and never hungry. We had birthday and graduation parties and things like that, but there was another hunger that had to be fed. There was a hunger I didn't even have a name for. Was this when I began writing?

In 1966 we moved into a house, a real one, our first real home. This meant we didn't have to change schools and be the new kids on the block every couple of years. We could make friends and not be afraid we'd have to say goodbye to them and start all over. My brothers and the flock of boys they brought home would become important characters eventually for my stories—Louie and his cousins, Meme Ortiz and his dog with two names, one in English and one in Spanish.

My mother flourished in her own home. She took books out of the library and taught herself to garden—to grow flowers so envied we had to put a lock on the gate to keep out the midnight flower thieves. My mother has never quit gardening.

This was the period in my life, that slippery age when you are both child and woman and neither, I was to record in *The House on Mango Street*. I was still shy. I was a girl who couldn't come out of her shell.

How was I to know I would be recording and documenting the women who sat their sadness on an elbow and stared out a window? It would be the city streets of Chicago I would later record, as seen through a child's eyes.

I've done all kinds of things I didn't think I could do since then. I've gone to a prestigious university, studied with famous writers, and taken an MFA degree. I've taught poetry in schools in Illinois and Texas. I've gotten an NEA grant and run away with it as far as my courage would take me. I've seen the bleached and bitter mountains of the Peloponnesus.[3] I've lived on an island. I've been to Venice twice. I've lived in Yugoslavia. I've been to the famous Nice[4] flower market behind the opera house. I've lived in a village in the pre-Alps and witnessed the daily parade of promenaders.

I've moved since Europe to the strange and wonderful country of Texas, land of Polaroid-blue skies and big bugs. I met a mayor with my last name. I met famous Chicana and Chicano artists and writers and *políticos*.[5]

Texas is another chapter in my life. It brought with it the Dobie-Paisano Fellowship, a six-month residency on a 265-acre ranch. But most important, Texas brought Mexico back to me.

In the days when I would sit at my favorite people-watching spot, the snakey Woolworth's counter across the street from the Alamo[6] (the Woolworth's which has since been torn down to make way for progress), I couldn't think of anything else I'd rather be than a writer. I've traveled and lectured from Cape Cod to San Francisco, to Spain, Yugoslavia, Greece, Mexico, France, Italy, and now today to Texas. Along the way there has been straw for the taking. With a little imagination, it can be spun into gold. ∿

---

3. *Peloponnesus* (pĕl´ə pə nē´səs) is the peninsula forming the southern part of mainland Greece.
4. *Nice* (nēs) is a port city in southern France.
5. *Políticos* (pô lē´ tē kôs) means "politicians."
6. The *Alamo* is a mission chapel in San Antonio, Texas. It was the site of a famous battle in Texas's war for independence from Mexico.

Quests and Encounters *In what ways do you think Texas brings back Mexico for Cisneros?*

Thesis *What do straw and gold represent for Cisneros?*

After You Read

Respond and Think Critically

1. **Connect to Personal Experience** What things in Cisneros's experience of life are similar to your own? Explain.

2. **Interpret Symbol** What do the tortillas that Cisneros makes **symbolize**, or represent, in this essay? Explain your answer and support it with evidence from the text. **OER**

3. **Make Inferences About the Author** Why did Cisneros not enjoy school? What do her memories of school reveal about the kind of child Cisneros was? Support your answer with text evidence.

4. **Summarize Events** Review the essay and list at least three challenges Cisneros has faced. Then summarize Cisneros's response to each challenge.

5. **Make Inferences About Details** What details in the essay suggest that Cisneros's life has been atypical or unusual, given her background? Support your answer with text evidence.

6. **Evaluate Diction** How would you describe Cisneros's **diction**, or choice of words, in this essay? Do you think her diction is effective? Explain, using text evidence to support your response.

7. **Big Idea** **Draw Conclusions About the Author** Cisneros goes on a quest to trace her origins as a writer. How does the essay help her succeed in this quest? Support your response with text evidence.

You're the Critic

Style and Craft

Critics and fellow writers have praised Sandra Cisneros for her evocative and detailed language. In her fiction, Cisneros weaves Spanish phrases, poetry, interior monologue, images, and engaging sensory details into the story to enliven her narrative structure. Read the two excerpts of literary criticism about Cisneros's writing style below.

> *"Cisneros' finest skill is her descriptive language. It conjures up gorgeous visions of colors and forms."*
> —Carol Memmott, USA Today

> *"Sandra Cisneros is one of the most brilliant of today's young writers. Her work is sensitive, alert, nuanceful...rich with music and picture."*
> —Gwendolyn Brooks

Partner Activity Discuss and answer the following questions with a partner.

1. How do these excerpts apply to "Straw Into Gold: The Metamorphosis of the Everyday"? Explain.

2. Describe Cisneros's writing style, considering elements such as voice, tone, and word choice. How well does Cisneros's style in this essay help to serve her purpose? Explain your answer. Use the excerpts above as models.

Literary Element Thesis

 Texas Test Practice (10.6)

1. Which statement best expresses the thesis of Cisneros's essay?

   (A) Lonely people often have a special insight into the lives of others.

   (B) Latina women are as capable of succeeding as the men in their families.

   (C) Difficult lives produce great writing.

   (D) Obstacles can be surmounted through hard work and determination.

   (E) Strong families help create strong individuals.

2. How does the essay's title relate to the author's anecdote of how she made tortillas?

   (A) Life is like a fairy tale.

   (B) We are sometimes asked to accomplish impossible tasks.

   (C) To the hungry, food is like gold.

   (D) Foolish people cannot tell straw from gold or a good tortilla from a bad one.

   (E) We can often achieve what at first seems impossible.

Review: Author's Purpose

As you learned on page 299, the **author's purpose** is the author's reason for writing a literary work.

8. Group Activity With a small group of classmates, discuss this essay, focusing on Cisneros's purpose or purposes for writing. Considering the cultural, historical, and contemporary details in the essay, how would you describe her purpose for writing? Be sure to cite examples from the text to support your ideas.

Reading Strategy Analyze Text Structure

Text structure is a crucial component of a piece of writing because it helps the author guide readers through a literary work. In this essay, Cisneros describes incidents that happened at various points throughout her life. She writes from the point of view of the present day, but uses flashbacks to provide information about earlier experiences.

9. At what point in the essay does Cisneros introduce an extended flashback? At what point does the flashback end? Support your answer with text evidence.

10. What information does Cisneros provide about her adult life? What does this additional information help you to conclude about the person Cisneros has become? Explain.

Vocabulary Practice

Practice with Analogies Choose the word that best completes each analogy.

1. exit : departure :: intuitively :
   a. instinctively **b.** intelligently **c.** inaccurately

2. requirement : demands :: taboo :
   a. describes **b.** recommends **c.** forbids

*Cisneros was faced with seemingly impossible tasks; **nevertheless,** she executed them.*

Academic Vocabulary

*Cisneros was able to **withstand** many difficulties in the course of becoming a successful writer.*

Withstand is an academic word that derives from Middle and Old English. The root word *stand* has several meanings, including "to support oneself on the feet," "to rise in a straight manner," "to maintain one's position," and "to be in a particular state." Using your knowledge and context clues, determine the meaning of *withstand* in the model sentence. Check your response by consulting a dictionary. Finally, demonstrate your understanding of the root word *stand* by using each of these related words in a sentence.

   a. understand **b.** standard **c.** handstand

Respond Through Writing

Personal Narrative

TEKS

10.13 Use elements of the writing process (planning, drafting, revising, editing, and publishing) to compose text.

Develop a Theme In this essay, Cisneros reflects on how her past has shaped who she is today. She discovers a pattern of "turning straw into gold" and explores the subject of overcoming obstacles. Write a personal narrative in which you explore your own past and how it has made you who you are today. Like Cisneros, use your essay to present a theme about the lessons you have learned in your life.

Purpose and Audience Your purpose is to write a personal narrative that includes a **theme,** or central message about life. In your essay, include details that will help readers understand your theme. Your audience is your teacher and your classmates.

Plan First, list people, events, and personal experiences that have helped shape you. Next, write down ideas about how each has helped to make you who you are today. Then look for themes in your notes. Do you see a pattern of beating the odds, fighting back, letting things go, or taking chances? That pattern may be the theme of your life story.

Draft As you describe your past, connect your experiences to an abstract idea, or an analogy, such as spinning straw into gold. You might also, like Cisneros, compare your story with a fairy tale, myth, or fable. Structure each paragraph to reveal the theme of your life through an analogy. You might use this order of information or Cisneros's example to guide you:

Elements of a Personal Narrative Paragraph
> **Event/Experience:** I was called upon to make tortillas.
> **Details:** Impossible task; I had never done it before, but I made the tortillas.
> **Reflections/Connections/Analogy:** It was like being asked to spin straw into gold.
> **Theme, stated or implied by details:** I overcame the obstacle; I did it somehow.

Revise Exchange essays with a partner. Determine whether your partner's essay clearly shows how the past has influenced his or her life. Also, identify the essay's theme. As you revise your essay, refine key ideas and organize them more logically and fluidly, use language more precisely and effectively, and clarify your purpose.

Edit Edit your essay, correcting any errors in grammar, spelling, and punctuation. Use the Grammar Tip in the side column to help you use dashes.

> **Grammar Tip**
>
> **Dashes**
>
> Dashes are often used in personal or informal writing. They can set off and emphasize parenthetical, or extra, information.
>
> *My mother was born like me—in Chicago but of Mexican descent.*
>
> Dashes can also be used like parentheses to add comments.
>
> *I felt as if making tortillas—or writing a critical paper, for that matter—were tasks so impossible I wanted to break down into tears.*
>
> Note that dashes can be used in pairs or singly. In both cases, there are no spaces on either side of a dash.

PART 3

KEEPING FREEDOM ALIVE

Lift Up Thy Voice and Sing, ca. 1942–1944. William H. Johnson, Oil on paperboard, 25.55 x 21.26 in. Smithsonian American Art Museum, Washington, DC.

View the Art William H. Johnson's bright colors and flattened perspective were inspired by art he saw in North Africa. How do these artistic choices help convey a message of hope in this painting?

BIG IDEA

Freedom can mean many things. There is freedom to express yourself. There is also the freedom to pursue your dreams, even if that means making sacrifices along the way. In the nonfiction works in Part 3, you will read speeches, articles, and essays from people who have reached for freedom. As you read these works, ask yourself, What does freedom mean to me, and what would I give up to keep it?

TEKS

For pages 362–367

10.10.B Analyze contemporary political debates for such rhetorical and logical fallacies as appeals to commonly held opinions, false dilemmas, appeals to pity, and personal attacks.

LITERARY FOCUS

LOGIC AND PERSUASION

What makes a message convincing?

Authors use logic and persuasive techniques to convince an audience to think, act, or exercise their freedom in a particular way. In the quotation below from "On Women's Right to Vote," note how Susan B. Anthony makes her point about giving women the right to vote.

It was we, the people; not we, the white male citizens, nor yet we, the male citizens, but we, the whole people who formed the Union. And we formed it, not to give the blessings of liberty, but to secure them; not to the half of ourselves and the half of our posterity, but to the whole people— women as well as men. And it is downright mockery to talk to women of their enjoyment of the blessings of liberty while they are denied the use of the only means of securing them provided by this democratic republican goverment—the ballot.

—Susan B. Anthony, **"On Women's Right to Vote"**

Persuasion

Persuasion is a type of speech or writing, usually nonfiction, that attempts to convince an audience to think or act in a particular way. Creators of persuasive works use various techniques to sway readers, but all persuasion shares one element: the argument.

Argument In persuasion, an **argument** is a statement of opinion about a problem or an issue and the support for the statement. The statement is called the **proposition**. The propo-

sition is usually is usually in the form of a declarative sentence. Anthony's proposition begins "And it is downright . . . ." You might have phrased it like this: *Women cannot truly enjoy their rights if they are denied the only way to secure them: by voting.* A good proposition should be debatable. In other words, it must be possible to present support for or against it.

Support The **support** for an argument includes reasons and evidence. **Reasons** explain why someone should accept the proposition. **Evidence** consists of examples, facts, and expert opinions. Strong arguments often include a **counterargument**, a brief argument that attempts to disprove opposing opinions about the problem or issue.

ARGUMENT

Proposition
(debatable statement)

Reasons
(explanations)

Evidence
(examples, facts,
expert opinions)

Logic

Logic is a method used to structure clear and effective arguments. The strongest arguments are based on sound reasoning, or logical thinking. An argument may be structured logically by using either inductive or deductive reasoning.

Inductive reasoning involves drawing a general conclusion from specific facts: *All people, white and non-white, male and female, built the Union. It was formed to secure rights for all people, not half of them. So, all people in the Union should have the same rights.*

Deductive reasoning involves drawing a specific conclusion from general and specific facts: *"The people" includes women and men, white and non-white, citizen and non-citizen. The Union was built by those people to secure their rights, which include voting rights. So, all people in the Union should be granted the right to vote.*

Persuasive Techniques

Most arguments make use of persuasive techniques known as appeals, including appeals to logic, emotion, ethics, and authority. Examine the appeals in these examples from the rest of Anthony's speech.

An **appeal to logic** presents facts and logical thinking, or reasoning, in support of a proposition.

For any state to make sex a qualification that must ever result in the disfranchisement of one entire half of the people is to pass a bill of attainder, or an *ex post facto* law, and is therefore a violation of the supreme law of the land.

An **appeal to emotion** attempts to stir up positive or negative feelings in the audience.

It is an odious aristocracy: a hateful oligarchy of sex; the most hateful aristocracy ever established on the face of the globe; . . . .

An **appeal to ethics** draws upon shared values and beliefs within the intended audience.

. . . this oligarchy of sex, . . . which ordains all men sovereigns, all women subjects, carries dissension, discord, and rebellion into every home of the nation.

An **appeal to authority** is based on the testimony of a source widely regarded as expert or reliable.

Webster, Worchester, and Bouvier all define a citizen to be a person in the United States, entitled to vote and hold office.

Rhetorical Devices

Persuasive techniques may also include **rhetorical devices,** which use language to enhance persuasion. One of the most common rhetorical devices is parallelism. **Parallelism** is the repetition of words, phrases, or sentences that have the same grammatical form. Anthony uses this device, as seen in the example from her essay below.

To them this government has no just powers derived from the consent of the governed. To them this government is not a democracy.

Quickwrite

Analyze Persuasion What types of persuasive techniques does Anthony use in the excerpt on the previous page? In your opinion, is Anthony's argument based on sound reasoning? Write two or three paragraphs explaining your answers and support them with textual evidence.

Logical and Rhetorical Fallacies

As you have learned, a strong argument is a logical one. However, even if an argument uses a logical structure, it may be illogical, or invalid. An invalid argument often includes logical and rhetorical fallacies, which are errors in reasoning. By examining the excerpts from a politial debate that follow, you can learn how fallacies can affect an argument.

Human Spaceflight Is a Necessity

The following excerpt is taken from an article in support of human spaceflight.

The number of truly remarkable and important human achievements is small. The next opportunity for groundbreaking advances will come in the form of human spaceflight and exploration of distant planets—experiences that will infinitely enrich our lives. Spaceflight will provide us with an opportunity to expand beyond Earth—a growing necessity as our planet becomes increasingly vulnerable to a variety of dangers. Not only could we fall victim to a devastating natural disaster, but we also face threats from man-made devastations such as terrorism, nuclear war, and biological warfare. Because Earth is becoming more and more uninhabitable, it is imperative that we look to space and other planets for a viable alternative. Human spaceflight is not merely a choice—it is a necessity.

Robert Park: Human Spaceflight Is an Outdated Idea

Robert L. Park is a professor of physics at the University of Maryland. This excerpt is from his book Voodoo Science.

The space station cannot be justified on scientific grounds. The science planned for the space station . . . is not so much wrong as simply unimportant. The story of the space station is a story of misplaced dreams and unwarranted hype . . . .

In the early days of the space program, a permanently manned space station had seemed like an inevitable step in the conquest of space. From such a platform it would be possible to make astronomical observations free of distortion by Earth's atmosphere, monitor weather systems, relay communications around the globe, provide navigational assistance to ships and aircraft, and detect clandestine military operations. By 1984, however, these functions were all being performed by unmanned satellites. What's more, the robots were doing them far better and more cheaply than would ever have been possible with humans.

Logical Fallacies

A **logical fallacy** is an error in reasoning in which the speaker or writer tries to make an appeal to logic, but the logic is faulty. Logical fallacies include false dilemmas.

A **false dilemma** presents two choices as the only ones available, when there are actually other options.

If we don't build expand our space program immediately, our freedom to explore human potential is at an end.

Rhetorical Fallacies

Rhetorical fallacies are errors in reasoning that occur when the speaker or writer uses misleading appeals to emotion, ethics, or authority. Rhetorical fallacies include appeals to pity, personal attacks, and appeals to commonly held opinions.

An **appeal to pity** is a persuasive technique that attempts to stir up compassion. If an appeal to pity is relevant to the argument for which it is offered as evidence, it may not be a fallacy.

Look into the scared eyes of a child who has been told Earth is dying. After that, you'll support research into space colonization. (fallacy)

Young children depend on adults to ensure a safe planet. Increasing funding for research into space colonization would mean the potential for living in space if anything happened to Earth. (not a fallacy)

A **personal attack** used in an argument focuses on the opponent's personality, character, or other qualities instead of on the opponent's supporting evidence.

Only a short-sighted moron would deny the potential for life in space.

An **appeal to commonly held opinion** is a persuasive technique in which evidence is based almost entirely on a widely held belief.

Scientific study advances humankind, so anyone who opposes study in space is against human progress.

Use this checklist to detect logical and rhetorical fallacies.

Checklist for Detecting Logical and Rhetorical Fallacies	
✓	Does the speaker or writer present only two choices when more are available? **(false dilemma)**
✓	Does the speaker or writer attempt to stir up compassion to persuade you? **(appeal to pity)** Is the appeal relevant to the argument?
✓	Does the speaker or writer focus on the opponent's personality, character, or other qualities instead of on the opponent's supporting evidence? **(personal attack)**
✓	Is the evidence based almost entirely on a widely held belief instead of facts? **(appeal to commonly held opinion)**

Reading Check

Analyze Rhetorical and Logical Fallacies

1. Review both excerpts, looking for logical and rhetorical fallacies. Are the last two sentences of the article on human spaceflight an example of a false dilemma? Why or why not?

2. What appeal to a commonly held opinion does the article on human spaceflight include?

3. Does the Park excerpt include a personal attack? Explain your answer.

4. Which argument do you find most convincing, and why?

Keeping alive the freedom to explore and to improve the human condition applies to exploring space for the purposes of scientific discovery and human colonization. Who should fund space exploration and how much should be spent on it has long been under debate. In recent years companies and governments have spent large sums on satellites, spacewalks, rockets, and other projects. The following sample editorials from a student newspaper address this issue. As you read, pay attention to how the students support their arguments and the types of persuasive techniques they use.

U.S. Government Funding Is Crucial

by Jose Martinez

Everyone knows that it is a matter of national pride for the United States to be number one in the space race. Space exploration must be government-funded because it is too important to be left to private industry. The news media reported the successful launch of Falcon 1 by the private company SpaceX. What many sources did not mention was that SpaceX's first three tries to launch rockets failed. Faced with technical problems, many private companies will go out of business or shift focus, especially if the economy weakens. In contrast, the U.S. government is stable and can stay focused on a task for years, even decades. How many private companies can make that claim?

Many children want to be astronauts. Would you crush their dreams by leaving space exploration up to unreliable companies? Our space program should not depend on money-hungry businesspeople who chase after the dollars of super-rich "space tourists." Either the U.S. government funds space exploration or our dreams of space will dissolve into chaos.

Appeal to Commonly Held Opinion

The writer assumes that every American believes that space exploration is essential. However, some may believe that their tax dollars could be better spent elsewhere.

Personal Attack

Instead of presenting additional supporting evidence, the writer insults the people who support privately funded space travel.

Private Funding Is the Way of the Future

by Giang Nguyen

Government is always wasteful, so the idea that the U.S. government will do a better job at space exploration than private companies is ridiculous. We face a choice between efficient private enterprise and slow-to-change U.S. government bureaucracy. The National Aeronautics and Space Administration (NASA) has announced that, because of spending freezes, it will have no way of transporting astronauts to the space station between 2010 and at least 2015. NASA officials expect to buy flight space for American astronauts on Russian space vehicles—but what if the United States and Russia experience political tensions? Do we really want do-little, know-nothing politicians in charge of funding space missions?

Orbital Sciences Corporation, SpaceX, and other private companies are designing efficient, reusable rockets that will make space travel less expensive and more practical than it is now. Why not shift the burden to private investors instead of taxing citizens so heavily that they can hardly afford to buy bread for their children?

False Dilemma

Many outcomes are possible. Private companies, the U.S. government, and other countries' governments could fund space travel.

Appeal to Pity

The writer fails to explain how much the average U.S. taxpayer actually pays to fund NASA.

Reading Check

Analyze Rhetorical and Logical Fallacies

1. Which of these arguments do you believe is more persuasive? As a class, evaluate the support that each side presents.

2. Find the appeal to pity and the false dilemma in the first editorial. Work with a partner to copy down each fallacy and write a brief explanation of why it is a fallacy.

3. Find the appeal to commonly held opinion and the personal attack in the second editorial. Work with a partner to copy down each fallacy and write a brief explanation of why it is a fallacy.

Before You Read

On Women's Right to Vote

Meet **Susan B. Anthony**
(1820–1906)

It seems unbelievable today, but picture an adult woman (and U.S. citizen) going to a local polling place to vote—and getting arrested. That is what happened to Susan B. Anthony when she attempted to cast her ballot for a presidential candidate in 1872. Unjustly convicted of the "crime" (the judge had decided that she was guilty before the trial began) and fined $100, she refused to pay the fee. Anthony's choice to act on her belief that women should have the same voting rights as men was a risky one at that time. Yet Anthony was a bold and determined woman, and such brave actions characterized her life, work, and writing.

An Early Achiever Anthony was born into a Massachusetts Quaker family whose religious values encouraged her independent spirit and ensured that she could express herself freely. Anthony was three when she began to read and write, and she received an excellent education, unlike many women of her time. She began teaching in 1840 and eventually became the respected headmistress at a school in upstate New York.

A Lasting Partnership A decisive career and life change for Anthony came in 1851 when she met Elizabeth Cady Stanton. Stanton was already active in the women's rights movement when Anthony joined the cause. The two women became lifelong friends and colleagues. Although Stanton was the principal speechwriter, both women lectured and published articles and books, including the first volumes of *History of Woman Suffrage*. Many recognized Anthony's determined spirit and organizational skills as the human engine that propelled the women's rights movement forward.

> *"The fight must not cease; you must see that it does not stop. . . . Failure is impossible."*
>
> —Susan B. Anthony

Women's Rights Leader Anthony had always been involved in social causes. She had begun her activist career as a temperance reformer, helping those who suffered from the effects of alcoholism. Later she joined leading abolitionists in the struggle to end slavery. However, she spent the majority of her time advocating the passage of the Nineteenth Amendment—the addition to the Constitution that gave women the right to vote. Unfortunately, Anthony did not live to see this crucial legal victory, one that suffragists worked for five decades to enact. In 1979 Anthony's contributions were recognized when she became the first female historical figure to be put on a U.S. coin—the Susan B. Anthony dollar. It is a fitting tribute to a woman who devoted much of her life to protecting the rights of all women in the United States.

LOG ON ▶ **Literature** Online

Author Search For more about Susan B. Anthony, go to glencoe.com and enter QuickPass code GL57805u2.

Literature and Reading Preview

Connect to the Speech

What actions would you take if you felt that your rights were being violated? Freewrite for a few minutes about what you would do in order to protect and secure your rights.

Build Background

In 1873, when Anthony delivered this speech, many people in the United States were fighting for woman suffrage. *Suffrage* means "the right to vote." In 1920, the Nineteenth Amendment was added to the Constitution, and all American women were finally able to vote.

Set Purposes for Reading

Big Idea Keeping Freedom Alive

As you read Anthony's speech, ask yourself, How does she define freedom?

Literary Element Rhetorical Devices

Rhetorical devices are tools of persuasion, such as appeals to logic, emotion, ethics, or authority, used by an author or a speaker. Noting an author's rhetorical devices can help you become a discriminating reader of persuasive texts. As you read, ask yourself, What rhetorical devices does Anthony use?

Reading Strategy Evaluate Evidence

When you **evaluate evidence,** you judge the effectiveness of an author's support for his or her argument. As you read this speech, distinguish among the different kinds of evidence Anthony uses to support her arguments and conclusions: logical, empirical (factual), and anecdotal (brief stories). Ask yourself, How effective is Anthony's evidence?

Tip: Evaluate Evidence As you read, record examples of evidence provided by Anthony. Then note what type of evidence each example is and evaluate its effectiveness. Use a chart like the one below.

Evidence	Type and Effectiveness
The Constitution says "We the people" not "We the male citizens"	This evidence is logical and effective. Anthony reasons that both women and men formed the Union, so all deserve equal rights.

TEKS

For pages 368–373

10.9.B Distinguish among different kinds of evidence used to support conclusions and arguments (e.g., logical, empirical, anecdotal) in texts.

Vocabulary

domestic (də mes′tik) *adj.* relating to one's own country; p. 370 *We must mind our domestic policy, while not ignoring global strategy.*

ordain (ôr dān′) *v.* to order or establish; to appoint; p. 370 *The king ordained that food would not be taxed.*

odious (ō′dē əs) *adj.* disgusting or offensive; p. 371 *An odious smell was coming from the garbage.*

aristocracy (ar′is tok′rə sē) *n.* a type of government in which a minority of upper-class individuals rule; p. 371 *The country was governed by a wealthy aristocracy.*

dissension (di sen′shən) *n.* disagreement within a group; p. 371 *Decisions were hindered by the dissension in the group.*

On Women's Right to Vote

Susan B. Anthony

Friends and fellow citizens: I stand before you tonight under indictment[1] for the alleged crime of having voted at the last presidential election, without having a lawful right to vote. It shall be my work this evening to prove to you that in thus voting, I not only committed no crime, but, instead, simply exercised[2] my citizen's rights, guaranteed to me and all United States citizens by the National Constitution, beyond the power of any state to deny.

The preamble of the Federal Constitution says: "We, the people of the United States, in order to form a more perfect union, establish justice, insure **domestic** tranquility, provide for the common defense, promote the general welfare,[3] and secure the blessings of liberty to ourselves and our posterity,[4] do **ordain** and establish this Constitution for the United States of America."

It was we, the people; not we, the white male citizens; nor yet we, the male citizens; but we, the whole people, who formed the Union. And we formed it, not to give the blessings of liberty, but to secure them; not to the half of ourselves and the half of our posterity, but to the whole people—women as well as men. And it is a downright mockery to talk to women of their enjoyment of the blessings of liberty while they are denied the use of the only means of securing them provided by this democratic republican government—the ballot.

For any state to make sex a qualification that must ever result in the disfranchise-

---

1. An *indictment* is a statement that charges someone with committing a crime.
2. Here, *exercised* means "used or practiced."
3. Here, *welfare* refers to well-being.
4. *Posterity* means "future generations."

Rhetorical Devices *Reread the first two sentences of this paragraph. How does this ethical appeal appeal to listeners' sense of fairness?*

Keeping Freedom Alive *Why does Anthony believe that women need the right to vote?*

ment[5] of one entire half of the people is to pass a bill of attainder,[6] or an *ex post facto* law,[7] and is therefore a violation of the supreme law of the land. By it the blessings of liberty are forever withheld from women and their female posterity.

To them this government has no just powers derived from the consent of the governed. To them this government is not a democracy. It is not a republic. It is an **odious aristocracy**; a hateful oligarchy[8] of sex; the most hateful aristocracy ever established on the face of the globe; an oligarchy of wealth, where the rich govern the poor. An oligarchy of learning, where the educated govern the ignorant, or even an oligarchy of race, where the Saxon rules the African, might be endured; but this oligarchy of sex, which makes father, brother, husband, sons, the oligarchs over the mother and sisters, the wife and daughters, of every household—which ordains all men sovereigns,[9] all women subjects, carries **dissension**, discord, and rebellion into every home of the nation.

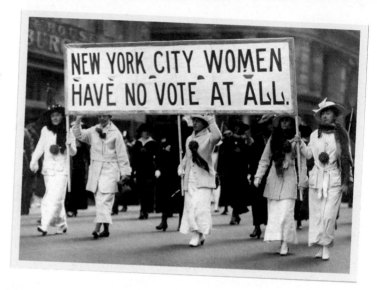

Women marching for woman suffrage in New York City. c. 1910.

View the Art Women across the country used various tactics to draw attention and build support for the suffrage movement, from lobbying and petitions to marches and protests. How does the sign in this photograph echo the argument of Anthony's speech?

---

5. *Disfranchisement* means "the taking away of someone's rights as a citizen."
6. A *bill of attainder* is an act of the legislature in which someone is declared guilty of a serious crime without a trial.
7. An *ex post facto law* is a law that punishes an individual for committing a crime even though the act was not considered criminal when the person committed it.
8. An *oligarchy* is a government in which a small group has authority.
9. *Sovereigns* are individuals invested with supreme authority.

Evaluate Evidence *How well do Anthony's assertions in this paragraph support her argument?*

Webster, Worcester, and Bouvier[10] all define a citizen to be a person in the United States, entitled to vote and hold office. The only question left to be settled now is: Are women persons? And I hardly believe any of our opponents will have the hardihood to say they are not. Being persons, then, women are citizens; and no state has a right to make any law, or to enforce any old law, that shall abridge their privileges or immunities.[11] Hence, every discrimination against women in the constitutions and laws of the several states is today null and void, precisely as is every one against Negroes.

---

10. *Webster, Worcester, and Bouvier* refers to Noah Webster, Joseph Emerson Worcester, and John Bouvier, all of whom published dictionaries.
11. Here, *immunities* means "protection from penalties or prosecution."

Rhetorical Devices *What is the effect of Anthony's appeals to logic and to authority?*

After You Read

Respond and Think Critically

1. **Connect to Personal Experience** Do you agree with Anthony's argument? Explain.

2. **Summarize Supporting Details** What are two reasons Anthony gives for why women should be allowed to vote? Support your answer with details from the speech.

3. **Make Inferences About Tone** How would you characterize Anthony's tone in this speech? Why might she have used this tone? Explain.

4. **Make Inferences About Historical Context** Why does Anthony close her speech with a reference to "Negroes"? Explain.

5. **Evaluate Comparisons** To what does Anthony compare laws forbidding women to vote? Is her comparison a valid one? Explain.

6. **Big Idea** **Draw Conclusions About the Author** What do you conclude about Anthony's motivations for giving the speech? Why does Anthony believe that freedom requires giving all citizens the right to vote? Explain.

7. **Analyze Author's Perspective** Do you think Anthony would be satisfied with the social status of American women today? Defend your answer.

Primary Visual Artifact

Propaganda Postcard

This propaganda poster is meant to sway people to think that the suffrage movement would destroy traditional gender roles and family structure. These views were sometimes expressed through images such as this postcard from 1910.

Group Activity Discuss the following questions with your classmates.

1. How does the postcard convey its message about suffrage differently from Anthony's more traditional speech? What is unfair or untruthful about the cultural and social bias conveyed in this postcard?

2. Compare this image with the one on page 371. How might these images influence an audience? How do their techniques differ? Explain.

My wife's joined the Suffrage Movement, (I've suffered ever since!)

Literary Element Rhetorical Devices

 Texas Test Practice (10.9)

1. In the paragraph beginning "For any state to make sex a qualification . . ." (page 370) Anthony

   (A) uses analogy

   (B) appeals to logic

   (C) uses repetition

   (D) appeals to ethics

   (E) appeals to emotion

2. What does Anthony compare to a "hateful oligarchy of sex" (page 371)?

   (A) the English aristocracy

   (B) an oligarchy

   (C) Saxon rule over the African

   (D) the Constitution of the United States

   (E) the United States government

Review: Argument

As you learned on page 362, **argument** refers to a statement of opinion about a problem or an issue and the support for the statement. Many persuasive techniques can be used to bolster an argument.

8. Partner Activity With a classmate, discuss Anthony's argument for allowing women to vote. Draw conclusions about her argument, using evidence from the text to support your conclusions. Why does she include the points she does? Create a two-column chart similar to the one below. In the first column, list one of the logical points Anthony makes to support her argument. In the second column, list conclusions about her argument, basing them on her points.

Anthony's Argument	Conclusions
Women played a role in establishing the United States.	Anthony hopes to show that women deserve a role in government.

Reading Strategy Evaluate Evidence

Anecdotal evidence relies on stories or assertions that appeal to a listener's common sense. Anecdotal evidence is by its nature not verifiable, so it may be weak—although it may also exert a strong pull on an audience. **Empirical evidence** includes facts and data. **Logical evidence** appeals to reason and can be evaluated on the strength of its parts. To answer the following questions, refer to the graphic organizer on page 369 and the blue highlighted passages and questions.

9. What is one example of anecdotal evidence in the speech? Explain what makes it anecdotal.

10. In your opinion, did bias in Anthony's speech affect her credibility? Explain.

Vocabulary Practice

Practice with Word Parts Use a printed or online dictionary to find the meaning of each vocabulary word's root and any prefixes or suffixes in the word. Then use a dictionary to help you find words that contain the same prefix, suffix, or root as the vocabulary word. Circle the word part that could help a person guess each word's meaning.

domestic   ordain   odious

aristocracy   dissension

EXAMPLE:
archaic

Root
archaeo, "early; old"

Suffix
-ic, "having, being, or related to"

Related words: archaeology, energetic

Respond Through Writing

Persuasive Essay

Argue a Position Susan B. Anthony argued for women's right to vote. Find out your school's policy on freedom of speech for students. Write an essay in which you argue for or against this policy, making use of appeals to logic, emotion, and authority.

Purpose and Audience Your purpose is to write a persuasive essay in which you use **appeals to logic** (references to reason, facts, or statistics to support a claim or an opinion), **appeals to emotion** (use of words or information to arouse the reader's emotions in order to persuade), or **appeals to authority** (references to any learned or respected figure or institution to support a claim or an opinion). Your audience consists of teachers and classmates throughout your school.

Plan Brainstorm ways in which free speech could be used and abused by students. Then enter terms such as "free speech" and "high school" into an Internet search engine to discover issues that might help you arrive at your own opinion. Create an outline stating your thesis or opinion and list, in order, the logical reasons you will use to support it.

Draft As you draft, strengthen your arguments by considering a whole range of views on the topic. Consider quoting reliable, credible sources you found on the Internet or school authorities. Analyze the relative value of the facts and ideas you come across. Include appropriate appeals to bolster your argument. Use frames like these for introducing and countering arguments:

Some might object that _____, but my answer to that is _____.
While it is true that _____, that does not necessarily mean that _____.

Decide whether the most effective placement for your opinion statement or claim is at the beginning or end of your essay.

Revise Exchange papers with a partner. Identify and evaluate each other's appeals to logic, emotion, and authority. Identify at least one way in which your partner refuted a counterargument or opposing view. Use feedback to revise your work.

Edit Edit your essay, correcting any errors in spelling, grammar, and punctuation. Use the Grammar Tip in the side column to help you use active and passive voice.

 TEKS

10.16.A–F Write persuasive texts to influence the attitudes or actions of a specific audience on specific issues. Write an argumentative essay to the appropriate audience that includes a clear thesis or position; consideration of the whole range of information and views on the topic; counter-arguments; an organizing structure; an analysis of the relative value of specific data, facts, and ideas; and a range of appropriate appeals.

> **Grammar Tip**

Active and Passive Voice

Use the active voice when the doer of the action is known.

Susan B. Anthony ensured progress toward equal rights for women.

Use the passive voice when the doer of the action is unknown.

Political pamphlets were left on the sidewalk to spread the idea of woman suffrage.

Use the passive voice when the doer of the action is not important—or not as important as the action, or when the passive voice shifts emphasis to a more worthy subject.

Freedom of speech was added to the Constitution with the Bill of Rights.

Before You Read

I've Been to the Mountaintop

Meet **Martin Luther King Jr.**
(1929–1968)

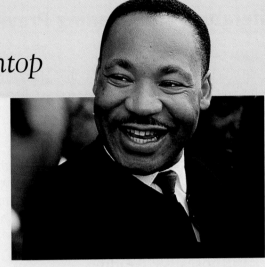

During the historic March on Washington in 1963, Martin Luther King Jr. set the moral tone for the Civil Rights Movement with his famous "I Have a Dream" speech. In 1964 he was awarded the Nobel Peace Prize for leading nonviolent demonstrations to help African Americans gain civil rights. With great courage and insight, King inspired Americans of all backgrounds to come together to work for a more just and compassionate society.

> *"I have a dream my four little children will one day live in a nation where they will not be judged by the color of their skin but by the content of their character."*
>
> —Martin Luther King Jr.

Launching the Civil Rights Movement Born the son of a minister in Atlanta, Georgia, King began his rise to leadership by entering Morehouse College at the age of fifteen. After receiving a PhD in theology from Boston University, King became a minister in a Montgomery, Alabama, church. Shortly after moving there, King became a leader of the first major nonviolent protest of the Civil Rights Movement. Inspired by the life and teachings of Mohandas Gandhi, whose doctrine of passive resistance was to become his own guiding principle, King began the Montgomery bus boycott. The African American citizens of Montgomery, who had been required to give up their seats for whites, stayed off the buses for more than a year to force an end to segregation. Their peaceful protest was successful, and King's leadership skills drew national attention.

Expanding the Struggle After the boycott, King served as president of the Southern Christian Leadership Conference and helped spread the civil rights struggle throughout the South and the nation. In 1963, when the center of the struggle shifted to Birmingham, Alabama, King and other demonstrators were jailed, and violence exploded in the streets. However, King's stance on nonviolent resistance remained firm. While behind bars, King wrote his famous document *Letter from a Birmingham Jail,* in which he answered his critics and galvanized support for his program of civil disobedience.

In the mid to late 1960s, King expanded his agenda to include protests against the rapidly escalating war in Vietnam. In 1968, at the age of 39, King fell victim to an assassin's bullet. At his funeral, over a thousand people, including political leaders and foreign dignitaries, crowded into King's church, Ebenezer Baptist Church in Atlanta, Georgia. Outside, almost 100,000 more paid tribute. King's message of respect, for democracy and for the dignity of all people, still lives.

 Literature Online

Author Search For more about Martin Luther King Jr., go to glencoe.com and enter QuickPass code GL57805u2.

Literature and Reading Preview

Connect to the Speech

Would you be willing to stand up for the rights of other people even if you might be harmed in the process? Discuss this question with a partner.

Build Background

In April 1968, Martin Luther King Jr. traveled to Memphis, Tennessee, to support African American sanitation workers who were on strike against the city. Memphis Mayor Henry Loeb had refused to recognize and negotiate with the nearly all-African American union organization that had called the strike.

Set Purposes for Reading

Big Idea | Keeping Freedom Alive

In this speech, King argues that freedom and equality belong to everyone. As you read, ask yourself, What arguments does King include to support his ideas?

Literary Element | Allusion

An **allusion** is an indirect reference to a well-known person, character, place, event, concept, or literary work. An allusion is different from a quotation because it does not give the source of the reference; the reader is expected to know it. As you read, ask yourself, Where and why does King include allusions?

Reading Strategy | Evaluate Diction and Syntax

Diction is the writer's choice of words. **Syntax** is the way the writer organizes words to form sentences. As you read, ask yourself, What effect do King's diction and syntax have on his message?

....

Tip: Ask Questions Ask yourself questions as you read, such as: What strong examples of diction and syntax can I find? How do these words help convey King's message? How do King's sentences strengthen his message? As you read, fill in a chart like the one shown below with examples from the speech, and evaluate their effect.

Words/Sentences	Effect
"But I wouldn't stop there." (pages 377–378, repeated 6 times)	Creates repetition and makes his ideas more memorable

TEKS

For pages 375–388

10.6 Evaluate the role of syntax and diction and the effect of voice, tone, and imagery on a speech, literary essay, or other forms of literary nonfiction.

Vocabulary

grapple (grap′əl) *v.* to struggle, as though wrestling; to come to terms with; p. 378 *The city council is meeting tonight to discuss how best to grapple with town budget issues.*

relevant (rel′ə vənt) *adj.* related to the issue at hand; p. 381 *Though pollution is an important issue, it is not relevant to our discussion of the need for a new library.*

agenda (ə jen′də) *n.* an outline of tasks to be accomplished; p. 382 *The agenda lists what we need to discuss during this meeting.*

compassionate (kəm pash′ə nit) *adj.* having or showing sympathy for another's misfortune, combined with a desire to help; p. 383 *A variety of compassionate organizations work to help victims of disasters.*

I've Been to the Mountaintop

Martin Luther King Jr.

Segregation Protest March. Birmingham, AL.

Thank you very kindly, my friends. As I listened to Ralph Abernathy[1] in his eloquent and generous introduction and then thought about myself, I wondered who he was talking about. It's always good to have your closest friend and associate say something good about you. And Ralph is the best friend that I have in the world.

I'm delighted to see each of you here tonight in spite of a storm warning. You reveal that you are determined to go on anyhow. Something is happening in Memphis, something is happening in our world.

As you know, if I were standing at the beginning of time, with the possibility of general and panoramic view of the whole human history up to now, and the Almighty said to me, "Martin Luther King, which age would you like to live in?"—I would take my mental flight by Egypt through, or rather across the Red Sea, through the wilderness on toward the promised land. And in spite of its magnificence, I wouldn't stop there. I would move on by Greece, and take my mind to Mount Olympus. And I would see Plato, Aristotle, Socrates, Euripides and Aristophanes[2] assembled around the Parthenon[3] as they

---

1. With King and other African American ministers, *Ralph Abernathy* founded the Southern Christian Leadership Conference (SCLC), an organization devoted to the nonviolent struggle against racism and discrimination.

2. The lives of these five Greek teachers and writers spanned a 160-year period ending with Aristotle's death in 322 B.C. Their ideas greatly influenced modern Western civilization.

3. The *Parthenon,* a temple built in the fifth century B.C., still stands in Athens, Greece.

discussed the great and eternal issues of reality.

But I wouldn't stop there. I would go on, even to the great heyday of the Roman Empire. And I would see developments around there, through various emperors and leaders. But I wouldn't stop there. I would even come up to the day of the Renaissance, and get a quick picture of all that the Renaissance did for the cultural and esthetic life of man. But I wouldn't stop there. I would even go by the way that the man for whom I'm named had his habitat. And I would watch Martin Luther as he tacked his ninety-five theses[4] on the door at the church in Wittenberg.

But I wouldn't stop there. I would come on up even to 1863, and watch a vacillating president by the name of Abraham Lincoln finally come to the conclusion that he had to sign the Emancipation Proclamation. But I wouldn't stop there. I would even come up to the early thirties, and see a man grappling with the problems of the bankruptcy of his nation. And come with an eloquent cry that we have nothing to fear but fear itself.[5]

But I wouldn't stop there. Strangely enough, I would turn to the Almighty, and say, "If you allow me to live just a few years in the second half of the twentieth century, I will be happy." Now that's a strange statement to make, because the world is all messed up. The nation is sick. Trouble is in the land. Confusion all around. That's a strange statement. But I know, somehow, that only when it is dark enough, can you see the stars. And I see God working in this period of the twentieth century in a way that men, in some strange way, are responding—something is happening in our world. The masses of people are rising up. And wherever they are assembled today, whether they are in Johannesburg, South Africa; Nairobi, Kenya; Accra, Ghana; New York City; Atlanta, Georgia; Jackson, Mississippi; or Memphis, Tennessee—the cry is always the same—"We want to be free."

And another reason that I'm happy to live in this period is that we have been forced to a point where we're going to have to **grapple** with the problems that men have been trying to grapple with through history, but the demands didn't force them to do it. Survival demands that we grapple with them. Men, for years now, have been talking about war and peace. But now, no longer can they just talk about it. It is no longer a choice between violence and nonviolence in this world; it's nonviolence or nonexistence.

That is where we are today. And also in the human rights revolution, if something isn't done, and in a hurry, to bring the colored peoples of the world out of their long years of poverty, their long years of

Visual Vocabulary
Martin Luther (1483–1546) was a German theologian whose arguments challenging certain teachings of the Roman Catholic Church led to the Protestant Reformation.

---

4. Here, *theses* means "arguments."
5. In these two sentences, King is referring to President Franklin D. Roosevelt, who led the United States during the Great Depression of the 1930s.

Allusion *How would you characterize the kinds of people and events that King is alluding to?*

Keeping Freedom Alive *What issues do you think the people in these places have in common?*

Vocabulary

grapple (grap´əl) *v.* to struggle, as though wrestling; to come to terms with

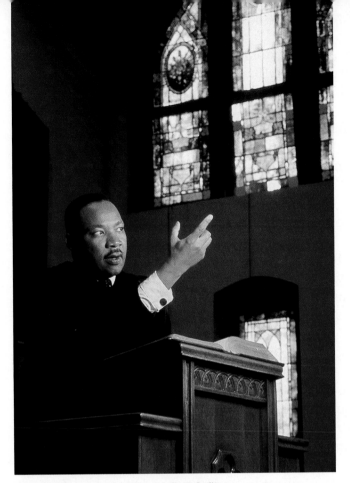

Portrait of Martin Luther King Jr. Flip Schulke.

View the Art Schulke traveled with and documented Martin Luther King Jr. and other civil rights leaders during the 1960s. What do you think King's body language here reveals about his speaking style?

hurt and neglect, the whole world is doomed. Now, I'm just happy that God has allowed me to live in this period, to see what is unfolding. And I'm happy that he's allowed me to be in Memphis.

I can remember, I can remember when Negroes were just going around as Ralph has said, so often, scratching where they didn't itch, and laughing when they were not tickled. But that day is all over. We mean business now, and we are determined to gain our rightful place in God's world. And that's all this whole thing is about. We aren't engaged in any negative protest and in any negative arguments with anybody. We are saying that we are determined to be men. We are determined to be people. We are saying that we are God's children. And that we don't have to live like we are forced to live.

Now, what does all of this mean in this great period of history? It means that we've got to stay together. We've got to stay together and maintain unity. You know, whenever Pharaoh[6] wanted to prolong the period of slavery in Egypt, he had a favorite, favorite formula for doing it. What was that? He kept the slaves fighting among themselves. But whenever the slaves get together, something happens in Pharaoh's court, and he cannot hold the slaves in slavery. When the slaves get together, that's the beginning of getting out of slavery. Now let us maintain unity.

Secondly, let us keep the issues where they are. The issue is injustice. The issue is the refusal of Memphis to be fair and honest in its dealings with its public servants, who happen to be sanitation workers. Now, we've got to keep attention on that. That's always the problem with a little violence. You know what happened the other day, and the press dealt only with the window-breaking. I read the articles. They very seldom got around to mentioning the fact that one thousand, three hundred sanitation workers were on strike, and that Memphis is not being fair to them, and that Mayor Loeb is in dire[7] need of a doctor. They didn't get around to that.

---

6. In the Bible, the *Pharaoh* (ruler) of ancient Egypt enslaved the Israelites until Moses led them out of Egypt and into Canaan, which they called the "promised land."

7. *Dire* means "dreadful" or "terrible."

Evaluate Diction and Syntax *Reread from the beginning of the paragraph to this point. What words does King use to create strong emphasis?*

Allusion *What point does the allusion to Pharaoh's court help bring home to King's listeners?*

Now we're going to march again, and we've got to march again, in order to put the issue where it is supposed to be. And force everybody to see that there are thirteen hundred of God's children here suffering, sometimes going hungry, going through dark and dreary nights wondering how this thing is going to come out. That's the issue. And we've got to say to the nation: we know it's coming out. For when people get caught up with that which is right and they are willing to sacrifice for it, there is no stopping point short of victory.

We aren't going to let any mace stop us. We are masters in our nonviolent movement in disarming police forces; they don't know what to do. I've seen them so often. I remember in Birmingham, Alabama, when we were in that majestic struggle there we would move out of the 16th Street Baptist Church day after day; by the hundreds we would move out. And Bull Connor[8] would tell them to send the dogs forth and they did come; but we just went before the dogs singing, "Ain't gonna let nobody turn me round." Bull Connor next would say, "Turn the fire hoses on." And as I said to you the other night, Bull Connor didn't know history. He knew a kind of physics that somehow didn't relate to the transphysics[9] that we knew about. And that was the fact that there was a certain kind of fire that no water could put out. And we went before the fire hoses; we had known water. If we were Baptist or some other denomination, we had been immersed. If we were Methodist, and some others, we had been sprinkled, but we knew water.[10]

That couldn't stop us. And we just went on before the dogs and we would look at them; and we'd go on before the water hoses and we would look at it, and we'd just go on singing "Over my head I see freedom in the air." And then we would be thrown in the paddy wagons, and sometimes we were stacked in there like sardines in a can. And they would throw us in, and old Bull would say, "Take them off," and they did; and we would just go in the paddy wagon singing, "We Shall Overcome." And every now and then we'd get in the jail, and we'd see the jailers looking through the windows being moved by our prayers, and being moved by our words and our songs. And there was a power there which Bull Connor couldn't adjust to; and so we ended up transforming Bull into a steer, and we won our struggle in Birmingham.

Now we've got to go on to Memphis just like that. I call upon you to be with us Monday. Now about injunctions: We have an injunction[11] and we're going into court tomorrow morning to fight this illegal, unconstitutional injunction. All we say to America is, "Be true to what you said on paper." If I lived in China or even Russia, or any totalitarian country, maybe I could understand the denial of certain basic First Amendment privileges, because they hadn't

---

8. *Bull Connor,* whose given name was Eugene, was Birmingham's Commissioner of Public Safety and a candidate for mayor in the 1964 election.
9. *Physics* is the study of the physical properties of light, heat, electricity, magnetism, and so on. With the invented word *transphysics,* King refers to things that transcend, or go beyond, the physical, such as morality and philosophy.

Evaluate Diction and Syntax *Review King's choice of words in this paragraph. What effect does his word choice have on his message?*

---

10. King is referring to the Christian ritual of baptism, which may involve immersion in water or the sprinkling or pouring of water over a person's head.
11. An *injunction* is a court order barring a specific action, such as a march, demonstration, or strike.

Allusion *Why does King make these allusions in these two sentences?*

committed themselves to that over there. But somewhere I read of the freedom of assembly. Somewhere I read of the freedom of speech. Somewhere I read of the freedom of the press. Somewhere I read that the greatness of America is the right to protest for right. And so just as I say, we aren't going to let any injunction turn us around. We are going on.

We need all of you. And you know what's beautiful to me, is to see all of these ministers of the Gospel. It's a marvelous picture. Who is it that is supposed to artic-ulate the longings and aspirations of the people more than the preacher? Somehow the preacher must be an Amos,[12] and say, "Let justice roll down like waters and righteousness like a mighty stream." Somehow, the preacher must say with Jesus, "The spirit of the Lord is upon me, because he hath anointed me to deal with the problems of the poor."[13]

And I want to commend the preachers, under the leadership of these noble men: James Lawson, one who has been in this struggle for many years; he's been to jail for struggling; but he's still going on, fighting for the rights of his people. Rev. Ralph Jackson, Billy Kiles; I could just go right on down the list, but time will not permit. But I want to thank them all. And I want you to thank them, because so often, preachers aren't con-cerned about anything but themselves. And I'm always happy to see a **relevant** ministry.

It's alright to talk about "long white robes over yonder," in all of its symbolism. But ultimately people want some suits and dresses and shoes to wear down here. It's alright to talk about "streets flowing with milk and honey," but God has commanded us to be concerned about the slums down here, and his children who can't eat three square meals a day. It's alright to talk about the new Jerusalem, but one day, God's preacher must talk about the New York, the new Atlanta, the new Philadelphia, the new Los Angeles, the new Memphis, Tennessee. This is what we have to do.

Now the other thing we'll have to do is this: Always anchor our external direct action with the power of economic withdrawal. Now, we are poor people, individually, we are poor when you compare us with white society in America. We are poor. Never stop and forget that collectively, that means all of us together, collectively we are richer than all the nations in the world, with the exception of nine. Did you ever think about that? After you leave[14] the United States, Soviet Russia, Great Britain, West Germany, France, and I could name the others, the Negro collectively is richer than most nations of the world. We have an annual income of more than thirty billion dollars a year, which is more than all of the exports of the United States, and more than the national budget of Canada. Did you know that? That's power right there, if we know how to pool it.

We don't have to argue with anybody. We don't have to curse and go around acting bad with our words. We don't need any bricks and bottles, we don't need any Molotov cocktails, we just need to go around to these stores, and to these massive indus-tries in our country, and say, "God sent us by

---

12. The Hebrew prophet *Amos* lived in the eighth century B.C.
13. Here, King has freely paraphrased the words that Jesus was reading from the prophet Isaiah.

Keeping Freedom Alive *What arguments does King make against the court injunction?*

14. Here, the expression *after you leave* means "not counting" or "apart from."

Allusion *In this paragraph, King alludes to common ideas of heaven and the afterlife. What point does he make about these ideas?*

here, to say to you that you're not treating his children right. And we've come by here to ask you to make the first item on your **agenda**—fair treatment, where God's children are concerned. Now, if you are not prepared to do that, we do have an agenda that we must follow. And our agenda calls for withdrawing economic support from you . . ."

But not only that, we've got to strengthen black institutions. I call upon you to take your money out of the banks downtown and deposit your money in Tri-State Bank—we want a "bank-in" movement in Memphis. So go by the savings and loan association. I'm not asking you something that we don't do ourselves at SCLC. Judge Hooks and others will tell you that we have an account here in the savings and loan association from the Southern Christian Leadership Conference. We're just telling you to follow what we're doing. Put your money there. You have six or seven black insurance companies in Memphis. Take out your insurance there. We want to have an "insurance-in."

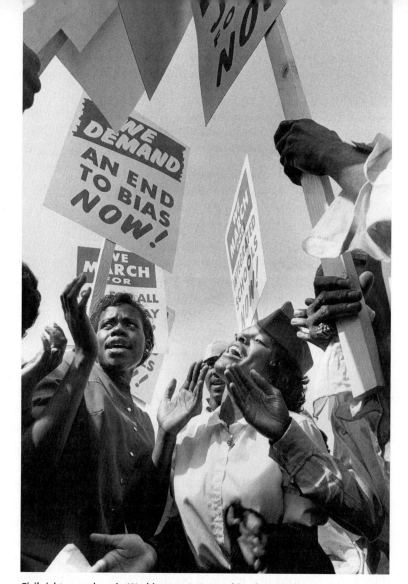

Civil rights marchers in Washington, D.C. Marching for equality.

View the Art This photograph of a civil rights demonstration focuses on two exuberant women in a crowd of marchers. What does the photograph convey about the feelings of the marchers?

Now these are some practical things we can do. We begin the process of building a greater economic base. And at the same time, we are putting pressure where it really hurts. I ask you to follow through here.

Now, let me say as I move to my conclusion that we've got to give ourselves to this struggle until the end. Nothing would be more tragic than to stop at this point, in Memphis. We've got to see it through. And when we have our march, you need to be

---

Evaluate Diction and Syntax *What words and phrases strike you as especially effective in conveying King's message about the boycott?*

Vocabulary

agenda (ə jen′də) *n.* an outline of tasks to be accomplished there. Be concerned about your brother. You may not be on strike. But either we go up together, or we go down together.

Let us develop a kind of dangerous unselfishness. One day a man came to Jesus; and he wanted to raise some questions about some vital matters in life. At points, he wanted to trick Jesus, and show him that he knew a little more than Jesus knew, and through this, throw him off base. Now that question could have easily ended up in a philosophical and theological debate. But Jesus immediately pulled that question from mid-air, and placed it on a dangerous curve between Jerusalem and Jericho. And he talked about a certain man, who fell among thieves. You remember that a Levite and a priest passed by on the other side. They didn't stop to help him. And finally a man of another race came by. He got down from his beast, decided not to be **compassionate** by proxy.[15] But with him, administered first aid, and helped the man in need. Jesus ended up saying, this was the good man, this was the great man, because he had the capacity to project the "I" into the "thou," and to be concerned about his brother. Now you know, we use our imagination a great deal to try to determine why the priest and

> "Let us develop a kind of dangerous unselfishness."

the Levite didn't stop. At times we say they were busy going to church meetings—an ecclesiastical gathering—and they had to get on down to Jerusalem so they wouldn't be late for their meeting. At other times we would speculate that there was a religious law that "One who was engaged in religious ceremonials was not to touch a human body twenty-four hours before the ceremony." And every now and then we begin to wonder whether maybe they were not going down to Jerusalem, or down to Jericho, rather to organize a "Jericho Road Improvement Association." That's a possibility. Maybe they felt that it was better to deal with the problem from the causal root, rather than to get bogged down with an individual effort.

But I'm going to tell you what my imagination tells me. It's possible that these men were afraid. You see, the Jericho road is a dangerous road. I remember when Mrs. King and I were first in Jerusalem. We rented a car and drove from Jerusalem down to Jericho. And as soon as we got on that road, I said to my wife, "I can see why Jesus used this as a setting for his parable."[16] It's a winding, meandering road. It's really conducive for ambushing. You start out in Jerusalem, which is about 1200 miles, or rather 1200 feet above sea level. And by the time you get down to Jericho, fifteen or twenty minutes later, you're about 2200 feet below sea level. That's a dangerous road. In the days of Jesus it came to be known as the "Bloody Pass."

---

15. In ancient Israel, men of the *Levite* tribe were temple priests or assistants. One might expect the two religious men to help, especially since the victim is also Jewish. Instead, it is *a man of another race* who decides not to leave it to someone else—a *proxy*, or substitute—to help.

Evaluate Diction and Syntax *Reread this sentence. How does King combine words to create rhythm and make his speech memorable?*

Vocabulary

compassionate (kəm pash′ə nit) *adj.* having or showing sympathy for another's misfortune, combined with a desire to help

16. A *parable* is a brief story intended to illustrate some truth or moral lesson.

Allusion *According to King, what kinds of excuses do people make for not stopping to help one another?*

And you know, it's possible that the priest and the Levite looked over that man on the ground and wondered if the robbers were still around. Or it's possible that they felt that the man on the ground was merely faking. And he was acting like he had been robbed and hurt, in order to seize them over there, lure them there for quick and easy seizure. And so the first question that the Levite asked was, "If I stop to help this man, what will happen to me?" But then the Good Samaritan came by. And he reversed the question: "If I do not stop to help this man, what will happen to him?"

That's the question before you tonight. Not, "If I stop to help the sanitation workers, what will happen to all of the hours that I usually spend in my office every day and every week as a pastor?" The question is not, "If I stop to help this man in need, what will happen to me?" "If I do not stop to help the sanitation workers, what will happen to them?" That's the question.

Let us rise up tonight with a greater readiness. Let us stand with a greater determination. And let us move on in these powerful days, these days of challenge to make America what it ought to be. We have an opportunity to make America a better nation. And I want to thank God, once more, for allowing me to be here with you.

You know, several years ago, I was in New York City autographing the first book that I had written. And while sitting there autographing books, a demented[17] black woman came up. The only question I heard from her was, "Are you Martin Luther King?"

And I was looking down writing, and I said yes. And the next minute I felt something beating on my chest. Before I knew it I had been stabbed by this demented woman. I was rushed to Harlem Hospital. It was a dark Saturday afternoon. And that blade had gone through, and the X rays revealed that the tip of the blade was on the edge of my aorta, the main artery. And once that's punctured, you drown in your own blood—that's the end of you.

It came out in the *New York Times* the next morning, that if I had sneezed, I would have died. Well, about four days later, they allowed me, after the operation, after my chest had been opened, and the blade had been taken out, to move around in the wheel chair in the hospital. They allowed me to read some of the mail that came in, and from all over the states, and the world, kind letters came in. I read a few, but one of them I will never forget. I had received one from the President and the Vice-President. I've forgotten what those telegrams said. I'd received a visit and a letter from the Governor of New York, but I've forgotten what the letter said. But there was another letter that came from a little girl, a young girl who was a student at the White Plains High School. And I looked at that letter, and I'll never forget it. It said simply, "Dear Dr. King: I am a ninth-grade student at the White Plains High School." She said, "While it should not matter, I would like to mention that I am a white girl. I read in the paper of your misfortune, and of your suffering. And I read that if you had sneezed, you would have died. And I'm simply writing you to say that I'm so happy that you didn't sneeze."

And I want to say tonight, I want to say that I am happy that I didn't sneeze. Because if I had sneezed, I wouldn't have been around here in 1960, when students all over the South started sitting in at lunch counters. And I knew that as they were sitting in, they were really standing up for the best in the American dream. And taking the whole nation back to those great

---

17. *Demented* means "insane."

Keeping Freedom Alive *What attitude or spirit does King encourage his listeners to adopt?*

Civil rights leader Dr. Martin Luther King Jr. and wife, Coretta Scott King (with bonnet and sunglasses) looking energized as they lead demonstrators on the fourth day of their march from Selma to Montgomery, AL.

walls of democracy which were dug deep by the Founding Fathers in the Declaration of Independence and the Constitution. If I had sneezed, I wouldn't have been around in 1962, when Negroes in Albany, Georgia,[18] decided to straighten their backs up. And whenever men and women straighten their backs up, they are going somewhere, because a man can't ride your back unless it is bent. If I had sneezed, I wouldn't have been here in 1963, when the black people of Birmingham, Alabama, aroused the conscience of this nation, and brought into being the Civil Rights Bill. If I had sneezed, I wouldn't have had a chance later that year, in August, to try to tell America about a dream that I had had. If I had sneezed, I wouldn't have been down in Selma, Alabama,[19] to see the great movement there. If I had sneezed, I wouldn't have been in Memphis to see a community rally around those brothers and sisters who are suffering. I'm so happy that I didn't sneeze.

And they were telling me, now it doesn't matter now. It really doesn't matter what happens now. I left Atlanta this morning, and as we got started on the plane, there were six of us, the pilot said over the public address system, "We are sorry for the delay, but we have Dr. Martin Luther King on the plane. And to be sure that all of the bags were checked, and to be sure that nothing would be wrong with the plane, we had to check out everything carefully. And we've had the plane protected and guarded all night."

19. In *Selma, Alabama,* in 1965, King led a march to protest restrictions on African American voting rights. Soon afterward, the Voting Rights Act of 1965 was passed.

18. In 1962 King took part in demonstrations in *Albany, Georgia,* protesting the segregation of public facilities.

Keeping Freedom Alive *What does King hope to illustrate by mentioning these events?*

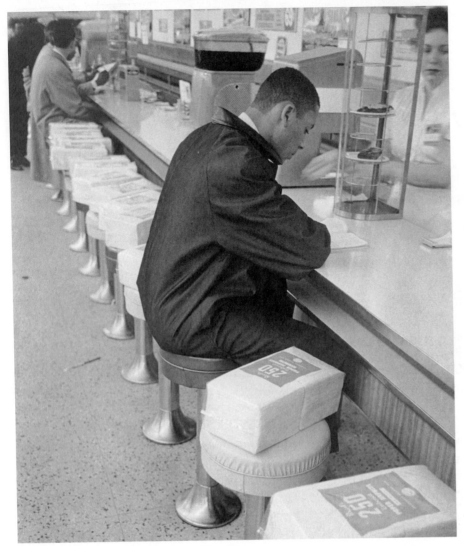

An African American student sits at a lunch counter reserved for white customers during a sit-in to protest segregation. Packages of napkins have been placed on nearby stools to discourage other protesters from joining the sit-in.

And then I got into Memphis. And some began to say the threats, or talk about the threats that were out. What would happen to me from some of our sick white brothers?

Well, I don't know what will happen now. We've got some difficult days ahead. But it doesn't matter with me now. Because I've been to the mountaintop. And I don't mind. Like anybody, I would like to live a long life. Longevity has its place. But I'm not concerned about that now. I just want to do God's will. And He's allowed me to go up to the mountain. And I've looked over. And

I've seen the promised land. I may not get there with you. But I want you to know tonight, that we, as a people will get to the promised land. And I'm happy, tonight. I'm not worried about anything. I'm not fearing any man. Mine eyes have seen the glory of the coming of the Lord. ∾

Allusion *In this final passage, King alludes to the "promised land" and ends by quoting the patriotic American song "The Battle Hymn of the Republic." What is the meaning of the passage?*

After You Read

Respond and Think Critically

1. **Connect to Personal Experience** Which sentence or passage made the greatest impression on you? Why?

2. **Make Inferences About the Author** Summarize King's mental journey through history. In which age does he want to live? What might you infer about King's character and beliefs on the basis of the age he chooses? Explain.

3. **Analyze Details** What plan of action does King outline for African American people in Memphis? What is the purpose of King's plan of action? Support your answer with details.

4. **Evaluate Ideas** King seems to foresee his own death. How did the prophetic aspects of this speech affect your reaction to it?

5. **Analyze Argument** What is the moral, or ethical, argument for King's nonviolent approach to change? What is the practical argument? Support your response with evidence from the speech.

6. **Big Idea** **Draw Conclusions About the Author** If King were alive today what issues pertaining to freedom would he be addressing? Explain your answer.

7. **Draw Conclusions About Historical Events** After reading this speech, what can you conclude about King and his influence on the Civil Rights Movement? How would you characterize the movement? Support your answer.

Visual Literacy

Image of a Leader

In this photograph, Reverend Martin Luther King Jr. leads a march from Selma to Montgomery, Alabama, to protest the lack of suffrage for African Americans. The date is March 1965. The photographer chooses not to show those who were opposed to racial desegregation. Instead, he focuses on the pride and promise of those leading the march.

Group Activity Discuss the following questions in a small group. Refer to the photograph and cite specific details to support your responses.

1. What visual techniques help this photograph convey a message about the pride and promise of the Civil Rights Movement? How does the photograph reflect social and cultural views in ways different from King's more traditional speech? Support your answer with concrete details.

2. Compare this photograph with the one on page 385. Different photographers may cover the same or similar events, yet convey different messages. How do the individual perceptions of the two different photographers influence the message conveyed to their audiences? Explain.

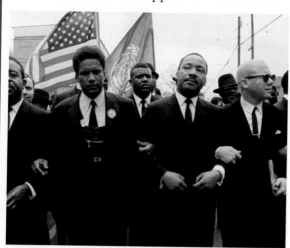

Literary Element | Allusion

In this speech, King uses both historical and biblical **allusions**. For example, King says, "I would take my mental flight by Egypt through, or rather across the Red Sea, through the wilderness toward the promised land." He is alluding to the biblical story in which Moses leads the Israelites out of slavery in Egypt to the promised land of Canaan.

8. Explain Function of Allusions What function do King's many biblical and historical allusions serve in his speech? Before answering, review the pink highlighted passages and questions.

9. Evaluate Author's Rhetorical Strategy In your opinion, do King's allusions effectively support his purpose? Explain.

Review: Tone

As you learned on page 151, **tone** is the writer's attitude toward his or her subject. Tone is conveyed through elements such as word choice, sentence structure, and figurative language. In this speech, King's tone conveys a variety of attitudes, such as seriousness, sadness, sarcasm, optimism, humor, and sympathy.

10. Partner Activity With a classmate, analyze King's tone and its effect on this speech. Create and complete a graphic organizer similar to the one below. Provide textual evidence, identify the tone, and evaluate the effect that the tone in each example has on the speech.

Tone: confidence
Evidence: "...We are determined to be men. We are determined to be people.... We don't have to live like we are forced to live."

Effect:
Conveys a strong positive message to audience and motivates them to look to the future and take action.

Selection Resources For Selection Quizzes, eFlashcards, and Reading-Writing Connection activities, go to glencoe.com and enter QuickPass code GL57805u2.

Reading Strategy | Evaluate Diction and Syntax

 Texas Test Practice (10.6)

1. King's listing of cities on page 378 serves primarily to

(A) introduce contrast.

(B) draw attention to a commonly accepted hypothesis.

(C) underscore the point that strikes are effective.

(D) underscore the point that people around the world want freedom.

(E) indicate places where change is not needed.

Vocabulary Practice

Practice with Synonyms A synonym is a word that has the same or a similar meaning as another word. Match each boldfaced vocabulary word below with its synonym. You will not use all the answer choices.

1. compassionate   **a.** plan
2. grapple   **b.** applicable
3. relevant   **c.** decline
4. agenda   **d.** struggle
         e. kindhearted

Foreign Words in English

Martin Luther King Jr. had a **rapport** *with many other civil rights leaders.*

Rapport is a foreign word that is commonly used in English. Using an online or a print dictionary, determine the relationship between the original source language and original meaning of this word. Then write the modern definition of *rapport*. Finally, demonstrate your knowledge of the word by using it in a sentence of your own creation.

Respond Through Writing

Summary

TEKS

10.9.A Summarize text and distinguish between a summary and a critique and identify non-essential information in a summary and unsubstantiated opinions in a critique.

Report Main Ideas or Events When you write a summary of nonfiction, you restate the main ideas or events in a short version of the original. A summary does not include personal opinions or nonessential information. Also note the difference between a summary and a **critique** which gives a critical analysis or thoughtful evaluation of a literary work. In about 100 words, summarize Martin Luther King Jr.'s speech.

Purpose and Audience Your purpose is to write a summary in which you **restate,** or retell written or spoken text in your own words. Your audience for this summary is your teacher.

Plan Skim the text to find the main ideas or events. Look for answers to the following six questions: *who? what? when? where? why?* and *how?* You may find it helpful to make notes in a chart like the one below, which was created for "On Women's Right to Vote" on page 370.

Who	Susan B. Anthony
What	the speech "On Women's Right to Vote"
When	1873
Where	the United States
Why	to argue for woman suffrage
How	by citing passages from the U.S. Constitution

Draft Draw on the answers to the six questions as you draft your summary. Follow a logical order.

Revise Have a partner read your summary and ask him or her to circle the answers to the six questions listed above. If your partner cannot find the answers to all the questions, you may have to revise your summary. Have your partner identify any nonessential information in your summary. Nonessential information is extra information that the reader does not need in order to understand what the nonfiction piece is about. Nonessential information should be cut.

Edit Edit your paper, correcting any errors in grammar, spelling, and punctuation. Use the Grammar Tip in the side column for help with restrictive and nonrestrictive clauses.

Grammar Tip

Restrictive and Nonrestrictive Relative Clauses

When you are reading, writing and speaking, you may notice that an adjective clause is sometimes needed to make the meaning of a sentence clear. Such a clause is called a **restrictive clause.**

*Nonviolent protest was the form of protest **that King preferred.***

When an adjective clause is not absolutely needed in order to express the complete meaning of a sentence, it is called a **nonrestrictive clause.** A nonrestrictive clause must always be set off with commas.

*King, **who won a Nobel Peace Prize**, supported a movement to help striking janitors.*

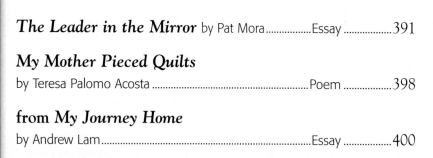

Comparing Literature

Across Genres

TEKS

For pages 390–403

10.10 Analyze, make inferences and draw conclusions about persuasive text and provide evidence from the text to support analysis.

Compare Literature About Heritage

A mix of familial and cultural traditions and experiences help to form an individual's heritage. How do you envision your own heritage? In the following essays and poem, authors Pat Mora, Teresa Palomo Acosta, and Andrew Lam evoke heritage and the richness of the immigrant experience.

COMPARE THE `Big Idea` **Keeping Freedom Alive**

These literary works suggest that a sense of heritage shapes the way we exercise our personal freedom. As you read, ask yourself, How do these writers celebrate the freedom to be found in the United States? How do they show the importance of balancing personal freedom with an appreciation for one's heritage and background?

COMPARE Author's Culture

Mora and Acosta, who are both Mexican American, have spent much of their lives in Texas. Lam was eleven years old when his family moved to California from Vietnam. Each author describes values held by immigrant parents. The works also suggest the experience of a new generation—one that is making a new culture, in part through assimilation. As you read each text, ask yourself, What is distinctive about each author's background and culture?

COMPARE Author's Perspective

An author's **perspective** is the combination of experiences, values, and ideas that shape an author's viewpoint about something. Authors frequently write from their own experiences. Their personal values may shape the way they choose to write about a topic. As you read each of these texts, ask yourself, What perspective does each author write from? How does each author's perspective influence the way he or she addresses issues related to heritage?

LOG ON ▶ **Literature** Online

Author Search For more about Pat Mora, Teresa Palomo Acosta, and Andrew Lam go to glencoe. com and enter QuickPass code GL57805u2.

Before You Read

The Leader in the Mirror

Meet **Pat Mora**
(born 1942)

El Paso, Texas, native Pat Mora writes poems, children's books, adult novels, and memoirs, partly because she noticed a voice like hers was missing from the books she read in school. "There were times when I wished that my Mexican heritage were a part of my school day," she has said. "I wished that I had seen things about Mexican culture on the bulletin boards and in the library. One of the reasons that I write children's books is because I want Mexican culture and Mexican-American culture to be a part of our schools and libraries."

Life on the Border All four of Pat Mora's grandparents emigrated from Mexico and settled in El Paso during the Mexican Revolution. They spoke only Spanish. Mora's mother was one of many children in her generation who translated between her Spanish-speaking parents and the English-speaking community. Mora's parents valued education. She has praised them for letting her set her own course and never trying to influence her choices. After college, Mora taught school and earned a master's degree from the University of Texas El Paso. She also began writing.

Mora's youth in El Paso, where the city of Juárez, Mexico, sprawls on the other side of the Rio Grande, instilled in her a love for the "border experience." Many interviewers have asked her to explain why borders figure prominently in her work (one of her books of poetry is even titled *Borders*). Mora calls her hometown a place with a "friction of languages, histories, values, economic disparity, attraction and revulsion. That constant tension is the geographic/emotional place from which I come."

> "I write because I believe that Hispanics need to take their rightful place in American literature."
>
> —Pat Mora

Working for Families In addition to writing and speaking, Pat Mora has long worked with teachers and public institutions to promote reading and literacy for children and families. She is the founder of El Día de los niños/El Día de los libros (Children's Day/Book Day). This program links children and parents to books, languages, and cultures though year-round library programs.

Mora strongly advocates cooperative programs to improve literacy. She points out that people of diverse backgrounds and opinions unite when they work for children. "Often people are a bit nervous about working with those who are different from themselves. We can more easily set aside this reluctance when we share a clear, common goal. Surely, in a democracy, we can understand how key family literacy is."

LOG ON ▶ **Literature** Online

Author Search For more about Pat Mora, go to glencoe.com and enter QuickPass code GL57805u2.

Literature and Reading Preview

Connect to the Essay

What is important for you to accomplish in order to be true to yourself? Freewrite for a few minutes about this question.

Build Background

Pat Mora received her inspiration for El Día de los niños/El Día de los libros from a Mexican tradition, Dia del niño. Among the goals of the day are to honor home languages and cultures and highlight the importance of linking all children to different cultures.

Set Purposes for Reading

Big Idea Keeping Freedom Alive

As you read, ask yourself, What skills does Pat Mora value? How does she think these skills can benefit the country?

Literary Element Tone

Tone is a writer's attitude toward his or her subject matter. Tone is conveyed through elements of style, such as **diction,** or word choice. A writer's tone may reveal such attitudes as sympathy, objectivity, or pride. As you read, ask yourself, What does Mora's choice of words suggest about her attitudes toward young people, education, and family?

Reading Strategy Analyze Argument

An **argument** is a type of persuasive writing in which logic and reason is used to influence a reader's actions. An argument is made up of a proposition, or claim, and evidence that supports the proposition. Evidence consists of examples, facts, and opinions, and often includes appeals to logic (facts and reason), emotion (shared feelings), ethics (shared values or beliefs), and authority (reliable sources). As you read, ask yourself, What does Mora want me to think or do? How is she trying to persuade me?

Tip: Make Inferences As you read, notice evidence that Mora includes to forward her argument. Use a chart like the one below to record details of the text. What persuasive argument is Mora making through these details? Record your inferences.

Detail	Inference
Mora thanks relatives and teachers for helping students succeed.	Mora thinks education is highly important.

aspiration (as′pə rā′ shən) *n.* a desire to achieve something or the object of such a desire; p. 393 *Kelly's highest aspiration was to sing with the Metropolitan Opera.*

catalyst (kat′ əl ist) *n.* a force that facilitates action or change; p. 395 *The deadline for the award competition was Catherine's catalyst for finally finishing the poem.*

squander (skwon′ dər) *v.* to waste through irresponsible behavior; p. 396 *We were asked not to squander hot water since the campsite had a limited supply.*

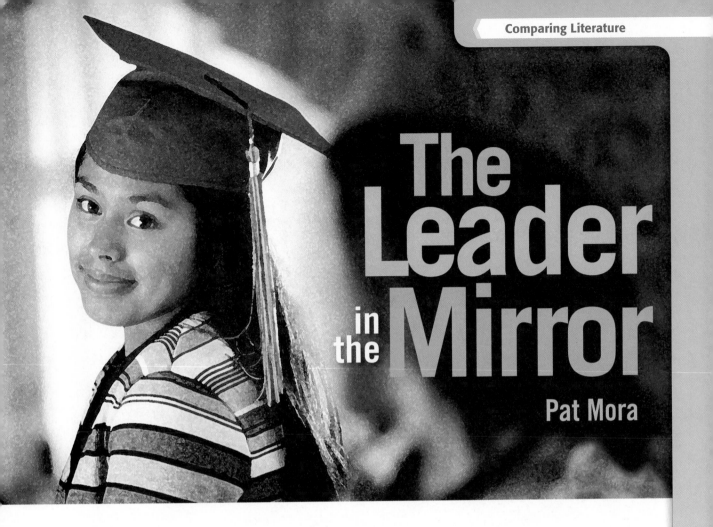

The Leader in the Mirror

Pat Mora

Each year, the newspaper in my hometown of El Paso, Texas, honors the top five academic achievers from the local high schools at an annual banquet. Last year when I addressed the group, the room at the fancy hotel was full of proud students and their relatives. The **aspirations** of the students were like a dose of powerful vitamins, filling parents, educators and guests with energy.

I began by congratulating the family members and teachers for being steady beacons for those young people. In a society that undervalues families and educators, they had truly lived their commitments.

As I was planning the talk I would give to this group, I wondered how best to create an occasion for reflection. What could I say to the audience about the daily struggle to create a meaningful life?

I remembered planning parties for my children when they were young: the careful selection of party favors, the mementos[1] for the guests to carry away. Since this banquet was to be a party of sorts, an academic

---

1. A *memento* is an object that serves as a reminder.

Tone *Reread this column. How would you describe Mora's attitude toward the task of giving the speech to students, relatives, and teachers?*

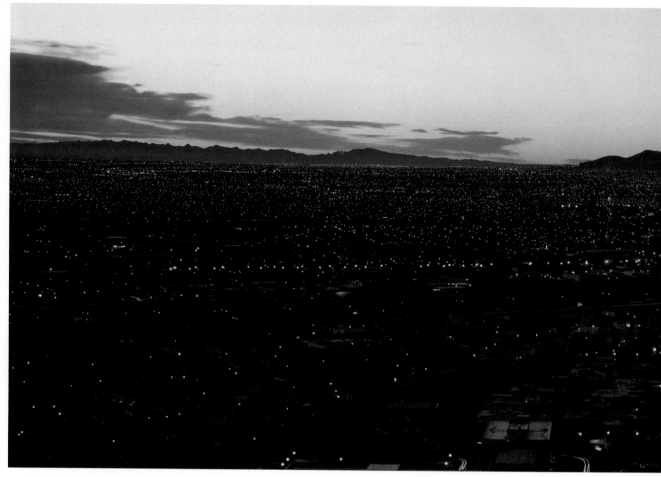

Border Between El Paso and Juarez

celebration, I asked myself what favors I would choose for each place at the table.

I knew I would be very popular with the students if I could give them keys to a new red car or tickets to an island vacation. But I am a writer, not a millionaire. So I decided to give them imaginary gifts: Each student would receive confetti, a tape recorder, a photograph and a mirror—symbols and metaphors to take with them through life.

I hoped that most of the students were going to enroll in college. The confetti would be for their private celebrations, those solitary moments when they had passed a test that worried them, finished a difficult paper at 2 A.M., found a summer internship. Sometimes, even when no one else is around, it's important to celebrate when we have struggled and succeeded—to sprinkle a little confetti on our own heads.

Why a tape recorder? I read them my poem "Immigrants."

Keeping Freedom Alive *What qualities and actions do you think Mora is trying to foster in the students?*

Immigrants
wrap their babies in the American flag,
feed them mashed hot dogs and apple pie,
name them Bill and Daisy,
buy them blonde dolls that blink blue
eyes or a football and tiny cleats
before the baby can even walk,
speak to them in thick English,
hallo, babee, hallo,
whisper in Spanish or Polish
when the baby sleeps, whisper
in a dark parent bed, that dark
parent fear, "Will they like
our boy, our girl, our fine american
boy, our fine american girl?"

As a writer, I understand the value and necessity of knowing my past, of keeping that door open. My family stories are my **catalyst** for creativity. All of us have people in our lives whose voices merit saving if we'll only take the time.

Analyze Argument *How does Mora appeal to emotion and to authority in this paragraph?*

Vocabulary

catalyst (kat´ əl ist) n. a force that facilitates action or change

My own father was once a paper boy for the newspaper hosting the banquet. I might not have known that fact, nor his long history of hard work, had I not been listening to him with my tape recorder a few years ago. I did not want the students to wait as long as I had to begin preserving the rich inheritance of their family voices. The strength of their heritage would give them the courage to face the future.

My third gift was a photograph of the El Paso/Juárez border: the Chihuahua Desert, the Rio Grande, a stern mountain, two sprawling border cities. Like our families, our geography is part of who we are.

When I was growing up on the U.S. side of that border, the society around me tried in subtle and not-so-subtle ways to convince me that my Mexican heritage was inferior to that of Anglo-Americans. I hope that today's educators on the border and throughout this nation are now committed to multiculturalism, to motivating the next generation to draw on their heritage as a resource for learning. The U.S. has been described as the first international country: Our varied cultures are our common wealth.

Borders—and if we're attentive, we realize we all live on borders, whether they are national or not—are sites of tension and sites for learning. Borders invite us to confront differences, inequities[2] and stereotypes. They invite us to work for multicultural cooperation and to celebrate multilingual richness.

The final gift of the evening, a mirror, was for serious gazing. I asked the students if they saw a leader when they looked into their mirrors. My guess is that too many of our young people do not see themselves as leaders because they don't look, dress or sound like the images of leaders presented to us. But leaders come in all colors, shapes and sizes. Some are talkative while others are quiet, but they all share a determination to contribute to the society of the future.

I urged the students to look often in their mirrors and to ask themselves these questions: "Am I satisfied with this world? If not, what will I do to improve it?" For if we are shaped by our surroundings, we in turn shape them. We deceive ourselves if we believe that we can live neutral lives.

One-third of this nation now traces its heritage to regions other than Western Europe. We will continue to **squander** our talent if our leaders—in politics, science, business, education and the arts—do not reflect our grand variety. I urged the students (and all of us) to ponder the strength of the mountains around us, to rise to the challenges. ✎

---

2. *Inequities* are instances of injustice or unfairness.

Keeping Freedom Alive *Why does Mora think that multiculturalism enhances personal and societal freedom?*

Analyze Argument *Reread the last paragraph. What does Mora want her readers to accomplish? What persuasive details does she use to support her position?*

Vocabulary

squander (skwon′ dər) *v.* to waste through irresponsible behavior

After You Read

Respond and Think Critically

1. **Connect to Personal Experience** What was your reaction to the gifts Mora gave the students? Explain.

2. **Summarize Main Ideas and Supporting Details** Summarize the main ideas of this essay in your own words. What details does Mora include to support these ideas?

3. **Analyze Details** Mora says that society "undervalues families and educators." Why does she think this is a dangerous mistake? To answer, consider the poem Mora reads, her stories about her family, and her ideas about geography and leadership.

4. **Make Inferences About Claims** What do you think Mora means when she says that heritage can give students "the courage to face the future"? Explain.

5. **Evaluate Claims** In your opinion, does Mora adequately support her statement that "We will continue to squander our talent if our leaders . . . do not reflect our grand variety"? Explain.

6. **Big Idea** **Draw Conclusions About Main Idea** What main idea does the essay convey about personal freedom and how that freedom should be exercised in society? Support your response with text evidence.

Literary Element Tone

Diction and sentence structure help to create tone.

7. **Draw Conclusions About Tone** What is the overall tone of Mora's essay? Support your answer with at least three examples of diction or structure that help create the tone.

8. **Evaluate Tone** How does Mora's tone help strengthen the impact of the speech? Explain, citing details from the text in your answer.

Reading Strategy Analyze Argument

Refer to the chart on page 392 and the blue highlighted questions as you answer these questions.

9. Mora says that "borders . . . are sites of tension and sites for learning." What details in the essay help illustrate this point?

10. What kinds of evidence does Mora use to advance her arguments? Give three examples of evidence in the essay. For each example, explain what type of evidence it is.

LOG ON ▶ **Literature** Online

Selection Resources For Selection Quizzes, eFlashcards, and Reading-Writing Connection activities, go to glencoe.com and enter QuickPass code GL57805u2.

Vocabulary Practice

Practice with Usage Respond to these statements to help you explore the meanings of the boldfaced vocabulary words from the essay.

1. Name one **aspiration** a student beginning high school might have.

2. Explain why a major exam might be the **catalyst** for a student's decision to form a study group.

3. Briefly summarize a story or movie in which a character **squanders** a great opportunity.

⚡ Writing

Write a Letter Reflect for a moment on the role heritage plays in your own life. Then write a friend or a relative a letter about the importance of valuing one's heritage. Make sure to organize your points logically and to anticipate any questions your reader might have. Use reader-friendly formatting techniques such as proper margins and spacing.

Build Background

Austin writer Teresa Palomo Acosta grew up in McGregor, Texas, where her Mexican parents settled during the Great Depression. Her most famous poem, "My Mother Pieced Quilts," reflects her personal history.

For generations, women have "pieced" quilts out of fabrics from old garments and household linens. The odds and ends of material tell stories of their own.

MY MOTHER PIECED QUILTS

Teresa Palomo Acosta

they were just meant as covers
in winters
as weapons
against pounding january winds

5   but it was just that every morning I awoke to these
october ripened canvases
passed my hand across their cloth faces
and began to wonder how you pieced
all these together
10 these strips of gentle communion cotton and flannel nightgowns
wedding organdies
dime store velvets

how you shaped patterns square and oblong and round
positioned
15 balanced
then cemented them
with your thread
a steel needle
a thimble

20   how the thread darted in and out
       galloping along the frayed edges, tucking them in
       as you did us at night
       oh how you stretched and turned and re-arranged
       your michigan spring faded curtain pieces
25   my father's santa fe work shirt[1]
       the summer denims, the tweeds of fall

       in the evening you sat at your canvas
       —our cracked linoleum floor the drawing board
       me lounging on your arm
30   and you staking out the plan:
       whether to put the lilac purple of easter against the red plaid of
          winter-going-
       into-spring
       whether to mix a yellow with blue and white and paint the
       corpus christi[2] noon when my father held your hand
35   whether to shape a five-point star from the
       somber black silk you wore to grandmother's funeral

       you were the river current
       carrying the roaring notes
       forming them into pictures of a little boy reclining
40   a swallow flying
       you were the caravan master at the reins
       driving your threaded needle artillery across the mosaic cloth
          bridges
       delivering yourself in separate testimonies.

       oh mother you plunged me sobbing and laughing
45   into our past
       into the river crossing at five
       into the spinach fields
       into the plainview[3] cotton rows
       into tuberculosis wards
50   into braids and muslin dresses
       sewn hard and taut to withstand the thrashings of twenty-five years

       stretched out they lay
       armed/ready/shouting/celebrating

       knotted with love
55   the quilts sing on

---

1. *Santa Fe work shirts* were named for the Santa Fe Railroad.
2. *Corpus Christi,* Texas, is a port city on the Gulf of Mexico.
3. *Plainview,* Texas, is the county seat of the top cotton-growing county in Texas.

> **Quickwrite**
>
> In two or three paragraphs, discuss the following questions: What does the quilt symbolize to the speaker of the poem? How does the description of the quilt help to convey a message about the value of heritage?

TERESA PALOMO ACOSTA   **399**

Build Background

Andrew Lam is a San Francisco-based writer who was eleven years old when his family left Vietnam in 1975. When the government of South Vietnam collapsed that same year, two million Vietnamese people dispersed around the globe. At that time, Vietnam was an agrarian country where most people tended crops and livestock. The traditional religions included Confucianism, in which a key element is ancestor worship.

FROM My Journey Home

ANDREW LAM

In her suburban home with a pool shimmering in the back yard at the edge of Silicon Valley, my mother prays. Every morning she climbs a chair and piously lights a few joss sticks for the ancestral altar on top of the living room's bookcase and mumbles her solemn prayers. On the shelves below, however, stand my father's MBA diploma, his real estate broker's license, my older siblings' engineering and business degrees, my own degree in biochemistry, our combined sports trophies, and, last but not least, the latest installments of my own unending quest for self-reinvention—plaques and obelisk-shaped crystals and framed certificates—my journalism awards.

What mother's altar and the shelves carrying their various knick-knacks underneath seek to tell is the typical Vietnamese-American tragicomedy, one where Old World Fatalism[1] meets the American Dream. Almost half of Vietnamese living abroad ended up living in North America, and the largest of this population resettled in California.

It is no mistake that the second largest Vietnamese population outside of Vietnam is centered around Silicon Valley. Nor is it mere luck that Vietnamese, drawing from our Confucian traditions which strongly emphasize discipline, respect and education, chose the sciences as a way to enter the American middle class. Here, within two decades or so, we have moved from living at the receiving end of the industrial revolution, have gone from being citizens of a poor agrarian based society, to becoming important players in the Information Age.

---

1. *Fatalism* is a belief that events are predetermined in such a way that human beings can have no effect on them.

None of this means much to my mother. The most resistant to change in my family, she watches the incense smoke undulate before her eyes and sighs. She came from a small village in the Thai Binh province, the kind that was suspicious of outsiders. Then history swept her away and she became uprooted herself. So far from home and hearth she prays but she also wonders: Do ghosts cross the ocean? Do they hear her solemn prayers amidst this world of lilting computers, soaring planes and satellite dishes and modems? The world has moved on too fast, gone too high tech, too frantic, too bright, so it seems, to accommodate ghosts.

Perhaps it could not be helped. For the Vietnamese living abroad has begun to dream his Golden Dream. It seeped in his psyche one night and he woke in the morning to find, to his own amazement, that he can readily pronounce words like mortgage, escrow,[2] aerobic, tax shelter, overtime, MBA, BMW, stock options.

Gone is the cyclical nature of his provincial thinking, and lost is his land-bound mentality. He finds that he can see the future. That he is upwardly mobile. He imagines owning his own home, his own business, the kids in college, the kids as becoming important Americans. Indeed, his American optimism has chased away his Vietnamese nightmare. Compared to the bloody battle fields, the malaria-infested New Economic Zone,[3] a vindictive communist regime that monitored everyone's movement, the squalid refugee camps scattered across Southeast Asia, the murders and rapes and starving and drowning on the high seas, California is still, indeed, paradise.

And so a community that previously saw itself as exiles, as survivors of some historical tragedy, as a people who were prepared to return to their homeland to tend their abandoned ancestral graves and to face their oppressors, slowly changes its mind. Soon enough houses are bought, jobs are had, children are born, old folks are buried, and businesses and malls are opened. That is to say our roots sink, slowly but deeply, into the American loam.[4] Soon enough Little Saigons,[5] up and down the Californian coast as well as elsewhere began to blossom and sprout. And the stories of the horrible war and terrifying escape over the high seas slowly gave way to gossips of new found successes in the Golden Land. . . .

I came here when I was 11. In my teen years I had stopped speaking Vietnamese altogether. Nor do I pray to the spirits of my ancestors any longer. As an adult and a writer, however, I have grown intrigued about my own inheritance. . . .

I am not, of course, unaware that my innocence was gone the moment I crossed the Pacific Ocean to the American shore. Nor am I so sentimental as to suggest, in this age of mobility and information flow, of global economy and hybrid identities, that the return from city to land is possible, especially when the contrary has become de facto[6] world wide. What intrigues me simply is this: what story could I possibly tell that would convey the

---

2. *Escrow* is a document, money, or other property deposited with a third party to be returned upon fulfillment of certain conditions.
3. Unemployed people who crowded Vietnam's cities were once relocated to *New Economic Zones,* theoretically to increase "agricultural output." In fact, most New Economic Zones were patches of jungle in which people felt exiled.

---

4. *Loam* is a type of soil.
5. *Little Saigons* are Vietnamese neighborhoods in cities around the globe. Saigon, the former capital of South Vietnam, is now called Ho Chi Minh City.
6. *De facto* means "existing in reality; actual."

ANDREW LAM **401**

he wants to do when he grows up and he shrugs. "Astronaut," he answers matter-of-factly, as if it's the simplest thing in the world. Yet going back three generations and he stands knee deep in mud in his rice fields gawking at the stars. But no more. The stars may very well be possible. His energy is free from the arduous grip of land-bound imagination, and it is growing and reconstituting in new and marvelous ways.

And recently I read about a farmer who escaped Vietnam to become a well-known, successful businessman in the high-tech industry. He has returned to open shops in Vietnam. I could almost see the farmer turned high-tech entrepreneur as a character in some epic global novel. In his high-rise, he sits staring down into the microchip on his finger and smiles: from certain angles at least, the tiny thing with its grids and lines that combines his ambition and memories, appears like the green rich rice field writ very small. ⌘

transformational experience of a people who were once land bound but have become instead mobile?

For it seems to me that if ritual and storytelling is a way for a people to partake in a shared vision of themselves, then the Vietnamese abroad must find new ways to reconcile between his agrarian past and his cosmopolitan future, between, that is, his laptop and his memories of ghosts.

The new Vietnamese?

I've seen him. He's my little cousin surfing the web and watching Chinese martial art videos dubbed in Vietnamese while talking to his friends on his cell phone in English. Above him the ancestral altar still wafts incense. On the computer screen, images shift and flow, and this too is his new home. He seems to be at ease with all these conflicting ideas, dissimilar languages. He seems both grounded and mobile, and his imagination, his sense of himself is trans-geographical.[7] Ask what

---

7. The prefix *trans-* means "across," "beyond," or "through." A *trans-geographical* sense of one's self could refer to a sense of self derived from experience with multiple locations.

> **💬 Discussion Starter**
>
> Meet with a small group to discuss the ways in which immigrants to the United States balance tradition with the need to assimilate in a new country. As a group, discuss why both assimilation and preservation of tradition are important. Also discuss the difficulties immigrants face as they strive to find a balance between the two.

Wrap-Up: Comparing Literature

Across Genres

- *The Leader in the Mirror* by Pat Mora

- *My Mother Pieced Quilts* by Teresa Palomo Acosta

- from *My Journey Home* by Andrew Lam

COMPARE THE Big Idea Keeping Freedom Alive

Writing In her essay, Mora suggests that by valuing heritage, people can help strengthen the country and promote freedom. Review the essays and the poem. For each text, locate details that suggest that individuals can embody their heritage while moving forward fully as Americans. Then write an essay about this issue using details from these texts.

COMPARE Author's Culture

Group Activity A *culture* can be defined as a set of shared attitudes, beliefs, customs, and practices. How would you compare the cultures described in the essays and poem? With a small group, discuss the following questions.

1. How do you think Mora, Lam, and the speaker of Acosta's poem would summarize their families' immigrant experiences? What do the authors and the speaker remember about their families, and how did their families influence them? Support your response with text evidence.

2. From reading these works, what similarities do you see between the experiences, traditions, and values of immigrants from different countries? What differences stand out?

COMPARE Author's Perspective

Speaking and Listening To discover an author's perspective, notice the ideas they express or imply in a text. What beliefs, attitudes, or experiences may be influencing the author's opinions and ideas? With a partner, review all three texts. Use charts like the one below to list details from the texts and your inferences about the perspectives these details suggest. Then, in an oral report, present your insights to your class.

Details	Inferences
Mora writes, "My own father was once a paper boy for the newspaper hosting the banquet." (page 396)	Mora's family experienced poverty and struggle. Mora's background helps her to value immigrants and their stories.

Literature Online

Selection Resources For Selection Quizzes, eFlashcards, and Reading-Writing Connection activities, go to glencoe.com and enter QuickPass code GL57805u2.

Before You Read

Address on the Anniversary of Lincoln's Birth

Meet **Carl Sandburg**
(1878–1967)

Few people would have predicted that Carl Sandburg would grow up and become a noteworthy writer of his generation. The son of working-class Swedish immigrants, Sandburg was born in Galesburg, Illinois. He left school after eighth grade in order to work at a variety of jobs that included washing dishes, shining shoes, selling newspapers, and driving a milk truck.

Early Books Sandburg enlisted in the army during the Spanish-American war and later returned to Galesburg, where he enrolled at Lombard College. Sandburg worked for a while as a journalist in Milwaukee and Chicago but then began writing poetry and published *Chicago Poems*. This work was controversial because Sandburg wrote about the working class and used colloquial, as opposed to literary, language. To some critics, using "the language of factory and sidewalk" was almost an insult; to others, it was a bold and distinguishing characteristic.

> "Slang is a language that rolls up its sleeves, spits on its hands and goes to work."
>
> —Carl Sandburg

Sandburg began to travel around the country, collecting poems, folk stories, and songs. He made a series of public appearances, at which he recited his own poems and sang some of the folk songs that he had collected. Later, Sandburg published a book of several hundred songs that he had collected over time, called *American Songbag*.

The Lincoln Books From an early age, Sandburg had an interest in Abraham Lincoln. In the mid-1920s, Sandburg began collecting information about Lincoln for a biography. Originally, he envisioned it as a children's book, but it gradually grew into a large, two-volume work called *Abraham Lincoln: The Prairie Years*. The book covered the period between Lincoln's birth and his move to Washington, D.C., when he became president.

The book was a popular success that presented a portrait of Lincoln that few had seen before; Sandburg's Lincoln was a complex individual, not a legend. Sandburg later produced a four-volume biography about Lincoln's later life called *Abraham Lincoln: The War Years*. This book earned him a Pulitzer Prize in 1939.

LOG ON ▶ **Literature** Online

Author Search For more about Carl Sandburg, go to glencoe.com and enter QuickPass code GL57805u2.

Literature and Reading Preview

Connect to the Speech

What would cause you to admire a national leader? List several qualities that you would expect to find in a leader you admire. Why are those qualities important?

Build Background

Abraham Lincoln was elected president in 1861. That same year the south seceded from the United States to form the Confederate States of America—an event that preceded the Civil War. Lincoln accepted the fact that only a vigorous war effort would restore the Union.

Set Purposes for Reading

Big Idea Keeping Freedom Alive

As you read "Address on the Anniversary of Lincoln's Birth," ask yourself, How does Sandburg relate his impressions of Lincoln to the preservation of freedom and national unity?

Literary Element Quotation

A **quotation** is a passage taken from another author's text and inserted word for word into a speech or work of literature. The use of quotations can provide insights about a writer's character or message. As you read, ask yourself, How does Sandburg incorporate Lincoln's words into his own, original text?

Reading Strategy Distinguish Fact and Opinion

A **fact** is a statement that can be proven beyond a reasonable doubt. An **opinion** is a personal interpretation or belief. As you read, ask yourself, Is what I am reading fact or opinion? How can this help me evaluate the author's message and purpose?

....

Tip: Identify Facts and Opinions Use a chart like the one below to list facts and opinions as you read.

Fact	Opinion
"He enforced conscription of soldiers for the first time in American history." p. 407	Lincoln is described as a man "who is both steel and velvet." p. 406

TEKS

For pages 404–411

10.6 Understand, make inferences and draw conclusions about the varied structural patterns and features of literary nonfiction and provide evidence from text to support understanding.

Vocabulary

paradox (par´ə doks´) *n.* a statement that seems contradictory and yet may be true; p. 406 *They were puzzled by the paradox in the song lyrics.*

imperative (im per´ə tiv) *adj.* expressing a command or an order; p. 407 *Their mother said it was imperative that they come straight home after school.*

turbulent (tur´byə lənt) *adj.* causing unrest, violent action, or disturbance; p. 407 *Turbulent seas caused the captain to seek calmer waters.*

emancipation (i man´sə pā´ shən) *n.* the process of becoming free from control or the power of another; p. 407 *After their emancipation, the former slaves were no longer considered property.*

valor (val´ər) *n.* courageous spirit; personal bravery; p. 408 *The soldiers showed valor when they did not flee from the enemy's gunfire.*

Address on the Anniversary of Lincoln's Birth

CARL SANDBURG

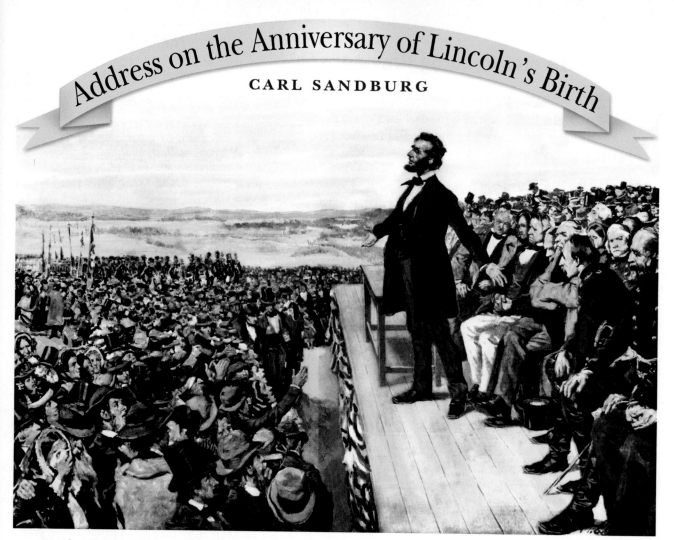

President Lincoln's Address at Gettysburg.
Artist unknown. Hand colored halftone.

Not often in the story of mankind does a man arrive on earth who is both steel and velvet, who is as hard as rock and soft as drifting fog, who holds in his heart and mind the **paradox** of terrible storm and peace unspeakable and perfect. Here and there across centuries come reports of men alleged to have these contrasts. And the incomparable Abraham Lincoln, born

150 years ago this day, is an approach if not a perfect realization of this character.

In the time of the April lilacs in the year 1865, on his death, the casket with his body was carried north and west a thousand miles, and the American people wept as never before. Bells sobbed, cities wore crepe, people stood in tears and with hats off as the railroad burial car paused in the leading cities of seven states, ending its journey at Springfield, Illinois, the home town.

During the four years he was president, he at times, especially in the first three

Vocabulary

paradox (par´ə doks´) *n.* a statement that seems contradictory and yet may be true months, took to himself the powers of a dictator. He commanded the most powerful armies till then assembled in modern warfare. He enforced conscription of soldiers for the first time in American history. Under **imperative** necessity he abolished the right of habeas corpus. He directed politically and spiritually the wild, massive, **turbulent** forces let loose in civil war.

He argued and pleaded for compensated **emancipation** of the slaves. The slaves were property, they were on the tax books along with horses and cattle, the valuation of each slave next to his name on the tax assessor's books. Failing to get action on compensated emancipation, as a chief executive having war powers, he issued the paper by which he declared the slaves to be free under "military necessity." In the end nearly $4 million worth of property was taken away from those who were legal owners of it, property confiscated, wiped out as by fire and turned to ashes, at his instigation and executive direction. Chattel[1] property recognized and lawful for 300 years was expropriated, seized without payment.

In the month the war began he told his secretary, John Hay,[2] "My policy is to have no policy." Three years later in a letter to a Kentucky friend made public, he confessed plainly, "I have been controlled by events." His words at Gettysburg were sacred, yet strange with a color of the familiar: "We cannot consecrate—we cannot hallow—this ground. The brave men, living and dead, who struggled here, have consecrated it, far beyond our poor power to add or detract."

He could have said "the brave Union men." Did he have a purpose in omitting the word *Union?* Was he keeping himself and his utterance clear of the passion that would not be good to look at when the time came for peace and reconciliation? Did he mean to leave an implication that there were brave Union men, and brave Confederate men, living and dead, who had struggled there? We do not know of a certainty. Was he thinking of the Kentucky father whose two sons died in battle, one in Union blue, the other in Confederate gray, the father inscribing on the stone over their double grave, "God knows which was right"? We do not know. . . .

While the war winds howled, he insisted that the Mississippi was one river meant to belong to one country, that railroad connection from coast to coast must be pushed through and the Union Pacific Railroad[3] made a reality. While the luck of war wavered and broke and came again, as generals failed and campaigns were lost, he held enough forces of the North together to raise new armies and supply them, until generals were found who made war as victorious war has always been

---

1. *Chattel*, in this context, means "slave."
2. *John Milton Hay*, President Lincoln's secretary, became Secretary of State in 1898.

Keeping Freedom Alive *What does Lincoln's statement about chattel property reveal about his attitude toward freedom?*

Vocabulary

imperative (im per′ə tiv) *adj.* expressing a command or an order

turbulent (tur′byə lənt) *adj.* causing unrest, violent action, or disturbance

emancipation (i man′sə pā′shən) *n.* the process of becoming free from control or the power of another

---

3. The *Union Pacific Railroad* came into being when President Lincoln signed the Pacific Railway Act, which directed the Union Pacific and the Central Pacific companies to construct a transcontinental railroad.

Quotation *How do the quotations in the paragraph at the top of this column help the reader understand Lincoln?*

The Death of Lincoln. Alonzo Chappel. Oil on canvas. Chicago Historical Society.

View the Art In 1865, Abraham Lincoln was assassinated. What might this painting suggest about the way Lincoln was regarded by his peers? How does it reflect Sandburg's thoughts on Lincoln?

made—with terror, frightfulness, destruction, and on both sides, North and South, **valor** and sacrifice past words of man to tell.

In the mixed shame and blame of the immense wrongs of two crashing civilizations, often with nothing to say, he said nothing, slept not at all, and on occasions he was seen to weep in a way that made weeping appropriate, decent, majestic. . . .

The people of many other countries take Lincoln now for their own. He belongs to them. He stands for decency, honest dealing, plain talk, and funny stories. "Look where he came from. Don't he know all us strugglers, and wasn't he a kind of tough struggler all his life right up to the finish?" Something like that you can hear in any nearby neighborhood and across the seas.

Millions there are who take him as a personal treasure. He had something they would like to see spread everywhere over the world. Democracy? We can't find words to say exactly what it is, but he had it. In his blood and bones he carried it. In the breath of his speeches and writings it is there. Popular government? Republican institution? Government where the people have the say-so, one way or another telling their elected leaders what they want? He had the idea. It's there in the lights and shadows of his personality, a mystery that can be lived but never fully spoken in words.

Distinguish Fact and Opinion *What in the statement about weeping is factual? What cannot be proved?*

Vocabulary

valor (val'ər) *n.* courageous spirit; personal bravery

Funeral of Abraham Lincoln, at Springfield, Illinois, 1868. S.M. Fassett.

Our good friend the poet and playwright Mark Van Doren[4] tells us, "To me, Lincoln seems, in some ways, the most interesting man who ever lived. He was gentle, but his gentleness was combined with a terrific toughness, an iron strength."

How did Lincoln say he would like to be remembered? His beloved friend, Representative Owen Lovejoy[5] of Illinois, had died in May of 1864 and friends wrote to Lincoln and he replied that the pressure of duties kept him from joining them in efforts for a marble monument to Lovejoy, the last sentence of his letter saying, "Let him have the marble monument along with the well-assured and more enduring one in the hearts of those who love liberty, unselfishly, for all men."

So perhaps we may say that the well-assured and most enduring memorial to Lincoln is invisibly there, today, tomorrow, and for a long time yet to come in the hearts of lovers of liberty, men and women who understand that wherever there is freedom there have been those who fought, toiled, and sacrificed for it. ∾

---

4. *Mark Van Doren* (1894–1973) was an American poet and teacher who is known for his verse *The Last Days of Lincoln* (1959).
5. *Owen Lovejoy* was elected to the House of Representatives from the state of Illinois in 1856 and served five terms.

Quotation *What does Sandburg hope to accomplish by quoting Mark Van Doren here?*

After You Read

Respond and Think Critically

1. **Connect to Personal Experience** How did you react to Sandburg's claim that the "most enduring memorial to Lincoln is invisibly there, today, tomorrow, and for a long time yet to come in the hearts of lovers of liberty"? Explain.

2. **Interpret Author's Views** According to Sandburg, what makes people everywhere feel that Lincoln is "their own"? What does this comment suggest about how Sandburg viewed the lives of people everywhere?

3. **Analyze Attitudes** From the quotations, what was Lincoln's opinion about the way in which he conducted the Civil War? What might these comments reveal about his state of mind and his personal ability?

4. **Evaluate Structure** In the first paragraph, Sandburg portrays Lincoln in terms of metaphorical contrasts, such as "steel and velvet." Is this an effective introduction? Explain.

5. **Analyze Structure** The speech ends with the phrase "wherever there is freedom there have been those who fought, toiled, and sacrificed for it." How does this conclusion fit into Sandburg's discussion of Lincoln?

6. **Evaluate Rhetorical Technique** Sandburg twice claims that "we do not know" when he speculates about Lincoln's thoughts. By doing this, does he help or hinder the reader's understanding of Lincoln? Explain.

7. **Big Idea** **Draw Conclusions About Viewpoints** Lincoln is often referred to as "the great emancipator." How does this speech support this view? Support your response with text evidence. ☞OER

Literary Element Quotation

Authors sometimes use **quotations** to provide the reader with greater insight into an author's or another person's life or philosophy.

8. **Make Inferences About Quotations** Why does Sandburg include quotations in his speech? Reread the pink highlighted question on page 407 to help you get started.

9. **Analyze Quotations** Explain how the following Lincoln quotation contributes to Sandburg's purpose: "Let him have the marble monument along with the well-assured and more enduring one in the hearts of those who love liberty, unselfishly, for all men." Support your answer with evidence from the text.

Review: Persuasion

As you learned on pages 362–367, **persuasion** is writing that attempts to convince readers to think or act in a particular way. Writers of persuasive works often appeal to reason or emotion.

10. **Partner Activity** With a classmate, discuss Sandburg's use of persuasion in his speech. Create a chart similar to the one below to help you identify examples of persuasive writing and the inferences you can make about them.

Examples of Persuasive Writing	Inferences
emotional appeal: "Bells sobbed, cities wore crepe, people stood in tears."	Sandburg uses an emotional appeal to show the reader how beloved Lincoln was.

Reading Strategy · Distinguish Fact and Opinion

 Texas Test Practice (10.6)

1. In the second paragraph of the address, Sandburg is making an unprovable assertion when he states that

(A) Lincoln died in April
(B) the casket was carried 1,000 miles
(C) Americans wept as never before
(D) bells rang and people removed their hats as the train paused in major cities
(E) the journey ended in Springfield

Vocabulary Practice

Practice with Denotation and Connotation

Denotation is the literal, or dictionary, meaning of a word. **Connotation** is the implied, or cultural, meaning of a word. For example, the words *awful* and *unspeakable* have a similar denotation, but they have different connotations:

Weaker: *awful*   **Stronger:** *unspeakable*

Work with a partner to complete a graphic organizer like the one below for each bold-faced vocabulary word.

paradox   imperative
turbulent   emancipation   valor

EXAMPLE:

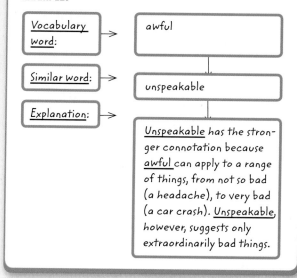

| Vocabulary word: | → | awful |

| Similar word: | → | unspeakable |

| Explanation: | → | Unspeakable has the stronger connotation because awful can apply to a range of things, from not so bad (a headache), to very bad (a car crash). Unspeakable, however, suggests only extraordinarily bad things. |

Extend and Enrich

 Research and Report

Literary Criticism Write five blurbs, or excerpts from complete reviews, that might appear on the cover of a magazine containing Sandburg's speech about Lincoln.

Prepare Read the following quotation from the *New York Times* about Sandburg's biography of Lincoln:

"A new experience awaits the reader of Carl Sandburg's book on Lincoln. There has never been a biography quite like this before . . . . There is no question here of a new school of biographical writing. The thing Mr. Sandburg has done cannot well be repeated; his achievement is an intensely individual one, suffused by the qualities which are peculiarly his own as a poet. As those who have read him know, they are not qualities of conventional poetry, nor is this new book of his merely an emotional rendering of the Lincoln story. It is as full of facts as Jack Horner's pie was full of plums."

Just as this reviewer praised, and, perhaps, sold the book, decide how you want to praise or sell Sandburg's speech to your audience. Then find brief bits of evidence from the speech, such as poetic phrases, clever puns, or insightful facts, to support your praise.

Meet with classmates to collaborate on writing the blurbs. Use the quotation from the *New York Times* as a model. Remember that your blurbs should be more than summaries and should include information and opinions that you would find in a critique. For more about the differences between a summary and a critique, see page 389.

Report Read each blurb aloud to the class. Make eye contact, speak clearly, and show enthusiasm and conviction through your gestures and stance. Use an enthusiastic tone of voice to engage your audience.

Evaluate Decide how effective each of the following was in praising or "selling" the speech: your tone, clarity, and body language, as well as the main idea of and support for each blurb. Write a suggestion for self-improvement in one or more areas.

TEKS

For pages 412–414

10.10 Analyze, make inferences and draw conclusions about persuasive text and provide evidence from the text to support analysis.

Set a Purpose for Reading

Read to discover why some contemporaries of Abraham Lincoln did not appreciate his now legendary speaking and writing skills.

Preview the Article

1. Whom do you think "they" refers to in the title of the article?
2. From the title, what kind of tone do you expect this article to have?

Reading Strategy Analyze Persuasive Techniques

Persuasion is a type of writing that attempts to convince readers to think or act in a particular way. Writers of persuasive works use appeals to sway their readers. When you think about how a writer tries to persuade you, you are **analyzing persuasive techniques.** As you read, ask yourself, What persuasive techniques does Wilson use to make his point? Compile your notes in a chart like the one below.

Technique & Example	Effect
Appeal to a commonly held opinion: Wilson takes for granted that no writer's words are more admired than Lincoln's.	Convinces the reader to believe the statement without supporting evidence

TIME

They Said He Was a Lousy Speaker

By **DOUGLAS L. WILSON**

NO AMERICAN WRITER'S WORDS ARE MORE admired than those of Abraham Lincoln. By the time of his assassination in 1865, he had written passages by which everything that followed would be measured. But such an ability was the last thing the American public expected from the obscure prairie lawyer who took office just four years earlier. "We have a President without brains," wrote the country's leading historian, George Bancroft. Bancroft was, admittedly, a Democrat, but many self-respecting Republicans were also concerned about the implications of having an untried self-educated "rail splitter"[1] as a leader in time of grave national crisis. Charles Francis Adams, a leading Republican and the son and grandson of Presidents, wrote of the new President-elect in his diary: "Good natured, kindly, honest, but frivolous and uncertain." The doubts and fears of many Americans were expressed by a newspaper editor who asked, "Who will write this ignorant man's state papers?"

The Northern intelligentsia[2] was initially blind to Lincoln's writing ability for at least two reasons. First, there was the strong impression, reinforced by his unkempt appearance and awkward demeanor, that he was a rube.[3] His obvious discomfort in formal clothes on ceremonial occasions and his

---

1. A *rail-splitter* is someone who splits logs to make a wooden fence.
2. The *intelligentsia* are a group of people thought to have superior intelligence.
3. A *rube* is an unsophisticated rural person.

constant fidgeting with his ill-fitting kid gloves did little to dispel those misgivings. Moreover, he insisted on entertaining sophisticated visitors by telling country stories in a broad hoosier accent. Wall Street lawyer George Templeton Strong wrote in his diary after their first meeting that the President was a "barbarian," a "ya-hoo." And Strong liked him.

Another reason Lincoln's writing ability was underrated was that his typically plain diction and straightforward expression were at odds with the public's expectations. The recognized standard for a statesmanlike address in mid-19th century America called for considerably more formality and pretension. The prose of acknowledged masters of that kind of writing—such as Lincoln's fellow orator at Gettysburg, Edward Everett, or Massachusetts Senator Charles Sumner—generally featured elevated diction, self-consciously artful expression and a certain moral unction.[4] Lincoln's insistence on direct and forthright language, by contrast, seemed "odd" or "peculiar," as in this passage from a public letter he sent to Horace Greeley, founder and editor of the *New York Tribune,* an antislavery paper:

"My paramount object in this struggle is to save the Union, and is not either to save or to destroy slavery. If I could save

Abraham Lincoln, April 10, 1865

the Union without freeing any slave I would do it, and if I could save it by freeing all the slaves I would do it; and if I could save it by freeing some and leaving others alone I would also do that."

When discerning observers noticed that his words had power, they often assumed that someone else must have written them. His Secretary of State, William H. Seward, was a noted orator and wordsmith who was thought to have had a hand in Lincoln's first Inaugural. That was in fact true, but few of Seward's suggested changes were stylistic improvements, and we know from the manuscript that his chief contribution—a more concilia-tory[5] ending—was brilliantly rewritten by Lincoln. The Secretary of the Treasury, Salmon P. Chase, was sometimes

---

4. *Unction* means "exaggerated, excessive, or affected emotion."

5. If something is *conciliatory,* it has the ability to soothe or to gain good will.

thought to be responsible for Lincoln's best work, and occasionally it was credited to the Secretary of War, Edwin M. Stanton. But when approached with such a suggestion by a friend, Stanton told him bluntly, "Lincoln wrote it—every word of it. And he is capable of more than that."

In the hindsight of history, we can see that Stanton knew what he was talking about. But how was it that Lincoln turned out to be so exceptional a writer and that it was so little apparent to his contemporaries? Studying Lincoln's writing over the years has convinced me that most of the factors that contributed to Lincoln's extraordinary literary achievement were invisible to his public and were even contrary to its general sense of who he was. As a child, he was fascinated with words and meanings and obsessed with clarity, both in understanding and in being understood. He wrote all his life for local newspapers, although mostly anonymously, and harbored a lifelong tendency to meet provocation with a written response. By the 1850s, when he came to political prominence, he had already formed the habit of making notes on scraps of paper of ideas and phrases as they occurred to him, which he then used in composing speeches. And perhaps his most valuable and most unsuspected trait as a writer was his devotion to revision.

We know, of course, how it all turned out. Nowhere is that more evident than in the contrast between two speeches given on November 19, 1863. Everett, who had been a president of Harvard, a Congressman, a Senator and a Governor of Massachusetts as well as a Secretary of State and a minister to England, was chosen to deliver the principal address at the dedication of the new national cemetery on the battlefield at Gettysburg. Lincoln was invited almost as an afterthought. One man spoke for two hours, the other for two minutes. One speech was printed and distributed in advance and has rarely been read since. The other is one of the most famous compositions in the American language.

—from TIME June 26, 2005

Respond and Think Critically

1. **Summarize Main Ideas** Write a brief summary of the main ideas in this article before you answer the following questions. For help on writing a summary, see page 389.

2. **Identify Tone** Tone is the author's attitude toward his or her subject. What is the tone of this article? What details contribute to this tone?

3. **Analyze Primary Sources** Look back at the public letter Lincoln sent to Horace Greeley. How does the letter exemplify Lincoln's skill as a writer and a public speaker? Support your response with text evidence.

4. **Analyze Persuasive Techniques** What persuasive techniques did you identify in Wilson's writing and in the quotations he uses? Cite four examples and explain their effects.

5. **Analyze Rhetorical and Logical Fallacies** List three words or phrases that Lincoln's critics used to describe the president. What rhetorical and logical fallacies are evident in these words and phrases? What effect do these fallacies have on the reader's opinion of Lincoln? See pages 362–367 for more on fallacies.

6. **Compare and Contrast Viewpoints** What similarities and differences are there between the comments of Lincoln's supporters and those of his critics? Support your response with text evidence.

7. **Draw Conclusions About Controlling Ideas** Look back at Carl Sandburg's "Address on the Anniversary of Lincoln's Birth." What contrasting qualities within Lincoln's character do Sandburg and Wilson describe? Explain how these contrasting characteristics contributed to Lincoln's ability as a public speaker.

Before You Read

The American Cause

Meet **John Dos Passos**
(1896–1970)

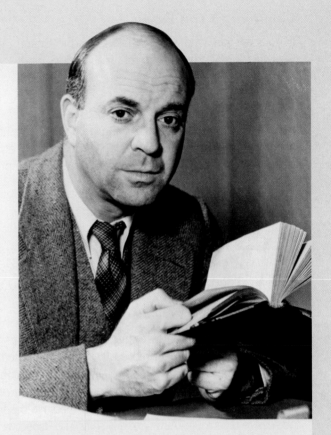

John Dos Passos's childhood encouraged him to study his country from an outsider's point of view. In his lifetime of writing, Dos Passos explored and reported changes in U.S. society, politics, and history.

John Roderigo Dos Passos was born in Chicago. His father worked as a prominent corporate lawyer. His mother traveled extensively, taking her son with her to Mexico and Europe. Dos Passos later claimed he had a "hotel childhood" because he traveled so much. In those years, he developed a love of Europe, especially France. He also developed a passion for reading, writing, and studying languages.

In 1912, at the age of fifteen, Dos Passos entered Harvard University. There he established a close friendship with the poet E. E. Cummings. In 1917 the writings of both appeared in the collection *Eight Harvard Poets*.

> "I was thoroughly embarked on an effort to keep up a contemporary commentary on history's changes."
> —John Dos Passos

Social and Political Interests During World War I, Dos Passos served as an ambulance driver in France and Italy. He based his first novel, *One Man's Initiation—1917*, which appeared in 1920, on his wartime experiences. A second book, *Three Soldiers*, published in 1921, explored the bitterness men felt while serving in the armed forces. It gained attention as a significant war novel.

Literary Career In 1925 Dos Passos established his literary reputation with his novel *Manhattan Transfer*. In the novel, he experimented with new writing techniques and created characters that reflected U.S. social orders. In the 1930s, Dos Passos published the trilogy *U.S.A.*, which critics praised as a landmark work of literature. For Dos Passos, the trilogy was a tool for encouraging political action.

In life, Dos Passos grew more conservative in his outlook and turned to writing about history. However, the politics and culture of the United States continued to be a major focus in his writing. He published books about Thomas Jefferson and other historical figures, as well as another trilogy, *District of Columbia*.

Author Search For more about John Dos Passos, go to glencoe.com and enter QuickPass code GL57805u2.

Literature and Reading Preview

Connect to the Essay

In your opinion, what is admirable about the United States? Freewrite for five minutes about this question.

Build Background

Dos Passos wrote "The American Cause" in 1955. He was well aware of the challenges faced by the young Germans he addressed. At the time, Germany lacked political and economic stability. By contrast, the United States was enjoying a postwar boom in its economy and population.

Set Purposes for Reading

Big Idea Keeping Freedom Alive

As you read this essay, ask yourself, What does Dos Passos value about the United States?

Literary Element Persuasive Essay

A **persuasive essay** is an essay that employs techniques designed to convince an audience to think or act in a certain way. These techniques might include appeals to logic, emotion, ethics, or authority as well as shifts in perspective on the topic. As you read, note conclusions about Dos Passos's message based on his persuasive techniques. Also note any shifts in perspective and the accuracy of the evidence Dos Passos uses to support his views.

Reading Strategy Distinguish Fact and Opinion

A **fact** is information that can be proven. An **opinion** is a personal interpretation. When you **distinguish fact and opinion,** you determine if the author's statements are facts or opinions. As you read, ask yourself, Does Dos Passos support his points with facts, opinions, or both?

....

Tip: Make a Chart As you read, use a chart like the one below to record examples of facts and opinions.

Detail	Fact or Opinion	Possible Effect
I didn't tell them they should admire the U.S. for its victories	Opinion: He suggests that war victories are not the most admirable thing.	Encourages reader to consider effects of war.

Vocabulary

negation (ni gā´ shən) *n.* act of denying; negative statement or denial; p. 417 *The governor gave a carefully worded negation when asked about her decision to cut funding.*

inherent (in her´ ənt) *adj.* existing naturally in someone or something; p. 418 *All human beings have an inherent right to be treated with respect.*

unstratified (un strat´ ə fīd) *adj.* not structured into different social classes; p. 418 *An unstratified society treats all people as equals.*

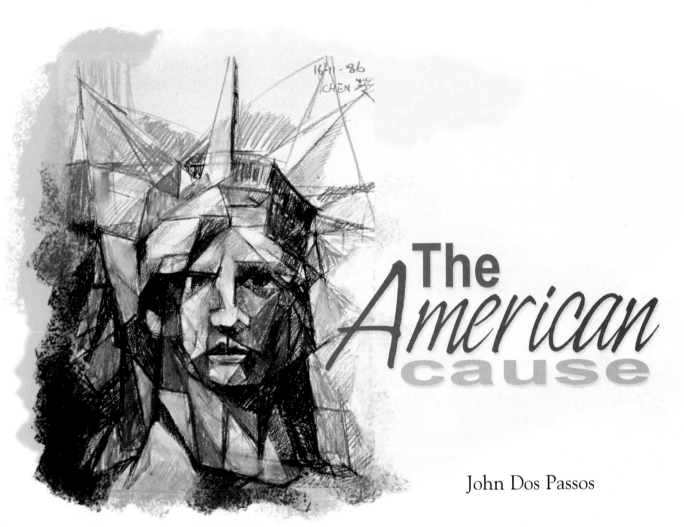

The American cause

John Dos Passos

Liberty in Cubism (III). Tsing-Fang Cheu. Mixed media on paper.

Not long ago I received a letter from some German students asking me to explain to them in three hundred words why they should admire the United States. "Young people in Germany," they wrote, "as in other places in the world are disillusioned, weary of pronouncements on the slogan level. They are not satisfied with **negations**, they have been told over and over again what to hate and what to fight. . . . They want to know what to be and what to do."

This is what I didn't tell them: I didn't tell them that they should admire the United States for the victories of our armed forces or because we had first developed the atomic bomb or the hydrogen bomb, or because we had shinier automobiles or more washing machines and deep freeze[1] or more televisions or ran up more passenger miles of airplane travel a year than any other people in the world. I didn't tell them to admire us for

1. A *deep freeze* is a very large, stand-alone freezer.

Distinguish Fact and Opinion *Does this passage include statements of fact or opinion? How can you tell?*

Vocabulary

negation (ni gā′ shən) *n.* act of denying; negative statement or denial getting more productive work done with less back breaking than any other people in the world or for our high wages, or our social security system. I didn't tell them to admire us because our popular leaders had the sweetest smiles before the television cameras or because we lived on a magnificent continent that offered an unbelievable variety of climates, mountains, plains, rivers, estuaries, seashores. Some of these are very good things but they are not things that would help them "to know what to be and what to do."

This is what I told them: I told them they should admire the United States not for what we were but for what we might become. Self-governing democracy was not an established creed, but a program for growth. I reminded them that industrial society was a new thing in the world and that although we Americans had gone further than any people in spreading out its material benefits we were just beginning, amid crimes, illusions, mistakes, and false starts, to get to work on how to spread out what people needed much more: the sense of belonging, the faith in human dignity, the confidence of each man in the greatness of his own soul without which life is a meaningless servitude.[2]

I told them to admire our failures because they might contain the seeds of great victories to come, not of the victories that come through massacring men, women, and children, but of the victories that come through overcoming the evil **inherent** in mankind through urgent and warmhearted use of our best brains. I told them to admire us for our foolish trust in other peoples, for our failure to create an empire when empire building was easy. I told them to admire us for our still **unstratified** society, where every man has the chance, if he has the will and the wit, to invent his own thoughts and to make his own way. I told them to admire us for the hope we still have that there is enough goodness in man to use the omnipotence[3] science has given him to ennoble[4] his life on earth instead of degrading it. Self-government, through dangers and distortions and failures, is the American cause. Faith in self-government, when all is said and done, is faith in the eventual goodness of man. ✑

---

2. *Servitude* is submission to another person's will; a person in servitude has little or no independence.

> Persuasive Essay *Explain the shift in perspective that Dos Passos begins here. What can you conclude about his reasons for making this shift? Is the evidence he uses accurate? Explain.*

---

3. *Omnipotence* means "state of being all powerful."
4. *Ennoble* means "to make noble" or "to elevate."

Keeping Freedom Alive *What connection between freedom and self-government does Dos Passos imply? Explain.*

Vocabulary

inherent (in her′ ənt) *adj.* existing naturally in someone or something

unstratified (un strat′ ə fīd) *adj.* not structured into different social classes

After You Read

Respond and Think Critically

1. **Connect to Personal Experience** Do you think Dos Passos's essay is still relevant today? Explain.

2. **Summarize Ideas** In your own words, summarize what Dos Passos says people need more than material benefits. How easy is it to obtain these things?

3. **Make Inferences About Author's Perspective** List three "very good" things Dos Passos says he excludes from his list of things to admire. What do these exclusions suggest about his political and social views?

4. **Analyze Ideas** According to Dos Passos, what is the basic American cause? How does this cause relate to his point that the United States should be admired for "what we might become"?

5. **Evaluate Argument** Dos Passos argues that American society is "unsatisfied." Is this argument valid? Why or why not? Support your response with evidence from the text.

6. **Evaluate Evidence** Evidence consists of examples, facts, and opinions, and often includes appeals to logic (based on reason), to ethics (based on shared values), to authority, or to emotion (based on shared feelings). What kinds of evidence does Dos Passos use to support his argument and conclusions? Is this evidence effective? Explain.

7. **Big Idea** **Draw Conclusions About Author's Beliefs** Based on his essay, what can you conclude about how Dos Passos viewed freedom and democracy? Support your answer with evidence from the text.

Literary Element Persuasive Essay

The author of a **persuasive essay** relies on appeals to both logic and emotion. A good persuasive writer anticipates the possible concerns and objections of the audience. The writer then uses this insight to directly address possible arguments.

8. **Evaluate Shifts in Perspective** Review the pink highlighted passage and question on page 418. Are Dos Passos's shift in perspective and his supporting evidence effective? Explain and support your conclusions with details from the text.

9. **Draw Conclusions About Persuasive Text** What assumption lies beneath Dos Passos's belief in "the evil inherent in mankind"? How does this evil relate to what Dos Passos sees as the common human goal? Support your response with text evidence.

Review: Rhetorical Devices

As you learned on page 369, **rhetorical devices** are the language of persuasion, such as parallelism, repetition, use of anecdote, and logic. Effective rhetorical devices often appeal to logic, ethics, emotion, or authority.

10. **Partner Activity** With a classmate, review the text to locate the rhetorical devices Dos Passos uses. Consider how these devices enhance the persuasiveness of his argument. Make a chart like the one below to record your findings.

Rhetorical Device	Example	Effect
repetition	"I didn't tell them"	Repetition enhances the force of Dos Passos's argument.

Reading Strategy — Distinguish Fact and Opinion

In order to **distinguish fact and opinion,** review the chart you made on page 416. Decide which details relate to the past, which focus on the future, and which are easiest to disprove.

11. Dos Passos argues that the best days for the United States lie in the future. Is this a fact or an opinion? Support your response with text evidence.

12. Identify three details from the essay that are based on facts. How can you tell?

Vocabulary Practice

Practice with Antonyms An **antonym** is a word that has a meaning opposite to that of another word. Match each boldfaced vocabulary word below with its antonym. Use a dictionary or the glossary on pages R68–R83 to check your answers. You will not use all the answer choices.

1. negation

2. inherent

3. unstratified

a. learned

b. approval

c. intrinsic

d. separated

Academic Vocabulary

*A person who studies multiple languages, as did John Dos Passos, may eventually become a **polyglot**.*

Polyglot is an academic word that derives from Greek. The prefix *poly-* means "more than one; many; much." Using your knowledge and context clues, determine the meaning of *polyglot* in the model sentence above. Check your response by consulting a dictionary. Finally, demonstrate your understanding by using each of these related words in a sentence.

a. polygraph   **b.** polymer   **c.** polyphony

Write with Style

Apply Persuasion

Assignment Write a persuasive essay directed to an audience of teenagers from another country. In your essay, support the position that the United States is a good place to live and explain why.

Get Ideas Start by taking notes to help you plan. Create a clear thesis statement, and list the logical reasons you'll use to support your thesis. Brainstorm to find appeals, such as descriptions, anecdotes, case studies, analogies, and illustrations, to bolster your argument. Locate and list facts and statistics that will strengthen your case. On a separate sheet of paper, list information and views on the topic that might possibly be presented to refute your own information and views. Then, list the evidence that will help you address any such counterarguments.

Give It Structure Create an organizing structure for your essay appropriate to your purpose and audience. For help, create an outline like the one below. State your thesis and supporting logical reasons. Incorporate the evidence from your notes.

```
I. Thesis statement
   A. Logical reason
      1. supporting evidence
      2. supporting evidence
   B. Logical reason
      1. supporting evidence
      2. supporting evidence
II. Counterargument
   A. Logical refutation
      1. supporting evidence
      2. supporting evidence
```

Look at Language Adjust your language as needed to help you connect to your audience. In making your argument, analyze the value of specific data, facts, and ideas.

Before You Read

from *Nobel Prize Speech*

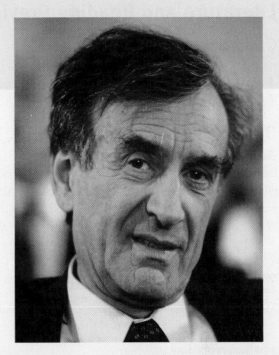

Meet **Elie Wiesel**

(born 1928)

Surviving a life-threatening event can be both an incredible relief and an unrelenting burden. Elie Wiesel survived the Holocaust, one of history's most horrific atrocities. After Allied forces liberated concentration camps, Wiesel, along with millions of displaced Jews and other persecuted groups, began piecing their lives together.

Hasidic Roots Wiesel was born in 1928 in the Jewish community of Sighet in Transylvania, Romania. His childhood was shaped by his deep religious devotion. Wiesel was greatly influenced by his grandfather and mother who introduced him into the Hasidic community, and his life revolved around religious studies.

> *It is still the child in me that I am trying to entertain or to reach with my stories, which are his stories.*
> —Elie Wiesel

Holocaust Survivor Wiesel was a teenager during World War II. When he was fifteen in 1944, Nazis stormed Sighet and forced his family into Jewish ghettos, neighborhoods where Jews were required to live before deportation to concentration camps in Poland.

At Auschwitz, Wiesel was separated from his mother and his youngest sister, both of whom he would never see again. For the next year, Wiesel and his father were forced to work under extreme conditions. Wiesel's father died from exposure to the elements, starvation, and dysentery after a death march to another concentration camp. After American troops liberated the camp in 1945, Wiesel was hospitalized for intestinal problems. During this time, Wiesel outlined a book that described his experiences, but pledged to wait ten years before fleshing it out.

Broken Silence Orphaned and alone, Wiesel was taken to France. After studying at Sorbonne University, he became a journalist. An interview with French writer Francois Mauriac caused Wiesel to break his silence; Mauriac encouraged Wiesel to commit his experiences to paper.

Wiesel's first written account of his experiences became the unforgettable *La Nuit* (Night). Since then, the memoir has been translated into thirty different languages. Today, Wiesel is a prominent speaker, professor, and writer and is the head of the United States Holocaust Memorial Council. He also won a Nobel Peace Prize for his humanitarian work.

Author Search For more about Elie Wiesel, go to glencoe.com and enter QuickPass code GL57805u2.

Literature and Reading Preview

Connect to the Speech

Why is it important to honor the memory of those who have died in an atrocity such as the Holocaust? Freewrite for a few minutes about why you think this is important.

Build Background

Elie Wiesel won the Nobel Peace Prize in 1986 for his humanitarian efforts as a lead spokesman on the Holocaust and for his efforts to garner support for persecuted people around the world. After being presented with the Nobel Diploma and Medal, Wiesel gave the speech from which this excerpt is taken.

Set Purposes for Reading

Big Idea Keeping Freedom Alive

As you read, think about why remembering past injustices is necessary to maintain freedom in the present.

Literary Element Speech

A **speech** is a public address or talk. In most speeches, the speaker tries to influence the audience's behavior, beliefs, and attitudes. Although the main purpose of a speech is to persuade, it can also inform and entertain.

Reading Strategy Analyze Rhetorical Devices

Rhetorical devices are techniques used in persuasive writing and speeches to elicit a response from the reader or audience. These devices include repetition, parallelism, analogy, logic, rhetorical questions, and the skillful use of connotation and anecdote. As you read, ask yourself, What effect do Wiesel's rhetorical devices have on me?

....

Tip: Note Examples To analyze how rhetorical devices are used in this speech, identify examples and determine what response Wiesel is trying to evoke with each one. Compile your notes in a chart like the one below. Use the blue highlighted question to help you get started.

Example	Device	Response
"How could the world remain silent?"	rhetorical question	It makes one wonder how the Holocaust could happen.

TEKS

For pages 421–425

10.10 Analyze, make inferences and draw conclusions about persuasive text and provide evidence from the text to support analysis.

Vocabulary

transcend (tran send´) *v.* to rise above or go beyond limits; p. 424 *The movie's superior special effects transcended our imagination.*

bewilderment (bi wil´ dər mənt) *n.* confusion; p. 424 *Due to the security guard's bewilderment, the jewel thief easily slipped away unnoticed.*

neutrality (noo tral´ ə tē) *n.* avoidance of choosing a side; p. 424 *Switzerland always exercises its neutrality during wars.*

....

Tip: Usage When you encounter new words, it might help you to answer a specific question about the word. For example, When would you use the word **bewilderment**?

NOBEL PRIZE SPEECH

Elie Wiesel

It is with a profound sense of humility that I accept the honor—the highest there is—that you have chosen to bestow upon me. I know your choice **transcends** my person. Do I have the right to represent the multitudes who have perished? Do I have the right to accept this great honor on their behalf? I do not. No one may speak for the dead, no one may interpret their mutilated dreams and visions. And yet, I sense their presence. I always do—and at this moment more than ever. The presence of my parents, that of my little sister. The presence of my teachers, my friends, my companions . . .

This honor belongs to all the survivors and their children and, through us to the Jewish people with whose destiny I have always identified.

I remember: it happened yesterday, or eternities ago. A young Jewish boy discovered the Kingdom of Night.[1] I remember his **bewilderment,** I remember his anguish. It all happened so fast. The ghetto. The deportation. The sealed cattle car. The fiery altar upon which the history of our people and the future of mankind were meant to be sacrificed.

I remember he asked his father: "Can this be true? This is the twentieth century, not the Middle Ages. Who would allow such crimes to be committed? How could the world remain silent?" And now the boy is turning to me. "Tell me," he asks, "what have you done with my future, what have you done with your life?" And I tell him that I have tried. That I have tried to keep memory alive, that I have tried to fight those who would forget. Because if we forget, we are guilty, we are accomplices.

And then I explain to him how naïve we were, that the world did know and remained silent. And that is why I swore never to be silent whenever wherever human beings endure suffering and humiliation. We must take sides. **Neutrality** helps the oppressor, never the victim. Silence encourages the tormentor, never the tormented.

---

1. *The Kingdom of Night* is a phrase used to describe the Holocaust, also known as the Shoah.

Analyze Rhetorical Devices *What type of rhetorical devices does Wiesel use in the first paragraph? What responses do these devices evoke in you? Explain.*

Vocabulary

transcend (tran send′) *v.* to rise above or go beyond limits

bewilderment (bi wil′ dər mənt) *n.* confusion

Speech *What emotions does Wiesel's anecdote about deportation to the concentration camp evoke?*

Keeping Freedom Alive *Reread the last paragraph. What does Wiesel believe happens when nations keep silent when humans are being persecuted?*

Vocabulary

neutrality (nōō tral′ ə tē) *n.* avoidance of choosing a side

After You Read

Respond and Think Critically

1. **Connect to Personal Experience** Which passage in the speech evoked the strongest emotion in you? Explain.

2. **Identify Main Idea** What is the main idea of the speech? What specific details does Wiesel use to support this main idea? 🔎OER

3. **Describe Tone** How would you describe Wiesel's tone in this speech? Consider his word choice and style. Support your response with evidence from the text.

4. **Analyze Author's Purpose** Authors typically write to inform, to entertain, to describe, to explain, or to persuade. What is Wiesel's main purpose in giving this speech? How can you tell? Support your response with details from the speech.

5. **Evaluate Details** What details does Wiesel use to evoke the horrors of the Holocaust? Are these details effective? Why or why not? Support your response with text evidence.

6. **Big Idea** **Draw Conclusions About Author's Beliefs** Based on this speech, what can you conclude about Wiesel's attitude toward freedom? Support your response with text evidence.

Literary Element | Speech

Persuasive speeches often include appeals to logic, emotion, ethics, and authority to sway the audience.

7. **Analyze Persuasive Techniques** Identify at least two appeals in Wiesel's speech. How does each one help persuade the audience? Support your response with text evidence.

8. **Make Inferences About Structure** Why does Wiesel focus on the past before talking about what must be done in the present?

Reading Strategy | Analyze Rhetorical Devices

Wiesel uses rhetorical devices to appeal to the emotions of his audience. Review your chart on page 422 and answer these questions.

9. Identify at least two rhetorical devices in the speech. How does Wiesel use these devices to strengthen his message?

10. In your opinion, what was the most effective rhetorical device in Wiesel's speech? Explain.

Vocabulary Practice

Practice with Usage Respond to these statements to help you explore the meanings of the boldfaced vocabulary words from the speech.

1. Explain how you might **transcend** a difficult situation.

2. Name something that would cause a sense of **bewilderment**.

3. Identify an incident that might require **neutrality**.

Writing

Write an Essay How does memory help us learn from history and avoid repeating mistakes? How can memory serve as a tool to fight injustice? How does its value compare with diplomacy, military power, and other political tools? Write an essay answering these questions, and cite evidence from Wiesel's speech to support your ideas.

LOG ON ▶ **Literature** Online

Selection Resources For Selection Quizzes, eFlashcards, and Reading-Writing Connection activities, go to glencoe.com and enter QuickPass code GL57805u2.

TEKS

For pages 426–433

10.15.A.i-vi Write an analytical essay of sufficient length that includes effective introductory and concluding paragraphs and a variety of sentence structures; rhetorical devices, and transitions between paragraphs; a thesis or controlling idea; an organizing structure appropriate to purpose, audience, and context; relevant evidence and well-chosen details; and distinctions about the relative value of specific data, facts, and ideas that support the thesis statement.

Writing Workshop

Analytical Essay

Literature Connection: In her essay, "Living Well. Living Good." Maya Angelou introduces readers to her Aunt Tee. Through Aunt Tee's words, Angelou explores the distinguishing characteristics of a life well-lived. She compares her Aunt's life to the lives of the people Aunt Tee has worked for to illustrate the qualities required to live "life as art."

Purpose: Your purpose for writing this compare-contrast essay is to analyze how looking at similarities and differences helps you understand and explain complex ideas.

Audience: You will be submitting your essay to a community newspaper, so be sure to select a topic that will appeal to its readers.

Choose Your Topic

Planning Checklist

Your analytical essay should include the following traits:

- ☑ an engaging introduction of the subjects to be compared and a clear thesis statement
- ☑ a variety of sentence structures
- ☑ transitional words and phrases between sentences and paragraphs
- ☑ a solid organizing structure to guide the reader

Option A: Choose a Prompt

1. Analyze the best way to inspire a change in your community by comparing and contrasting the success of people you know or have read about and the changes they have made in their own communities.

2. Analyze an event or time period that you read about in this unit by comparing and contrasting two related photographs or paintings. You can choose art that appears in this book, or find your own pieces to study. Explain what each piece says about the event or time period.

Option B: Write a Prompt

Analyze how _____ is similar to and different from _____.

Sample Prompt:

Analyze how year-round schools are similar to and different from traditional schools.

Scoring Rubric

Check the **Scoring Rubric** for Expository Texts on page R29 for more guidance on crafting your best essay.

Analyze a Professional Model

Read for Guidance In this essay, Anne Morrow Lindbergh expresses her appreciation for the word *sayonara*. When she was boarding a train in Japan in the 1930s, Lindbergh heard *sayonara* spoken repeatedly. To explain why she prefers it to other statements of parting, she compares its literal meaning to the literal and implied meanings of *good-bye* in other languages.

from *"Sayonara"* by Anne Morrow Lindbergh

For *Sayonara*, literally translated, "Since it must be so," of all the good-byes I have heard is the most beautiful. Unlike the *Auf Wiedersehens* and *Au revoirs*, it does not try to cheat itself by any bravado "Till we meet again," any sedative to postpone the pain of separation. It does not evade the issue like the sturdy blinking *Farewell*. *Farewell* is a father's *good-bye*. It is—"Go out in the world and do well, my son." It is encouragement and admonition. It is hope and faith. But it passes over the significance of the moment; of parting it says nothing. It hides its emotion. It says too little. While *Good-bye* ("God be with you") and *Adios* say too much. They try to bridge the distance, almost to deny it. *Good-bye* is a prayer, a ringing cry. "You must not go—I cannot bear to have you go! But you shall not go alone unwatched. God will be with you. God's hand will be over you" and even—underneath, hidden, but it is there, incorrigible—"I will always be with you; I will watch you—always." It is a mother's *good-bye*. But *Sayonara* says neither too much nor too little. It is a simple acceptance of fact. All understanding of life lies in its limits. All emotion, smoldering, is banked up behind it. But it says nothing. It is really the unspoken good-bye, the pressure of a hand, "Sayonara."

Topic Sentence

This topic sentence introduces the subject by defining the key term.

Transitions

The author uses "unlike" to show the contrast with other examples.

Rhetorical Devices

The writer repeats "It is" at the beginning of each sentence to let the reader know she hasn't changed examples.

Conclusion

This transitional phrase signals the reader that the author is returning to her main idea.

PLAN Your Essay

Key Trait Ideas As you think about a possible topic for your essay, remember that the best subjects are not complete opposites but rather persons, places, and things that share some similarities.

▶ Step 1: Brainstorming and Researching

In small groups, brainstorm with your classmates. One member of the group might throw out a subject and another might suggest a contrasting subject.

> road bikes vs. mountain bikes
>
> state universities vs. private universities
>
> reggae music vs. ska
>
> traditional schooling vs. year-round schooling

Once you've settled on a topic, do some research to explore your topic and discover the details that will guide your comparison.

▶ Step 2: Create a Venn Diagram

A Venn diagram has three parts: the left side describes the attributes of one subject, the right side the attributes of a second subject, and the middle the attributes they both share.

Schools

traditional — year-round

August thru June, 8 a.m. to 3 p.m., spring break, summer vacation, schools closed during breaks

180 class days, holidays off

school begins in July, length of day varies, students not all in school at same time, extended breaks, schools open year-round

▶ Step 3: Develop a Controlling Idea

All the details in your essay should relate to the controlling idea.

Controlling Idea:

> The year-round school calendar is quite different from the traditional school calendar and offers students and schools flexibility.

Planning Tip

The Internet offers a wealth of research possibilities—but, beware! There is as much disinformation on the Internet as there is solid and accurate information. Stick with resources you know are reliable, such as well-known encyclopedias, journals, and authors.

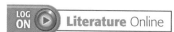 **Literature** Online

Writing and Research For planning, drafting, and revising tools, go to glencoe.com and enter QuickPass code GL57805u2.

DRAFT Your Essay

Key Trait Organization Expository and analytical essays are most effective when they have a strong organizational structure. The structure should vary based on your purpose and audience.

▶ Step 1: Make a Plan

Generally speaking, essays that compare and contrast are organized in one of two ways. The first is called subject-by-subject; you discuss all the characteristics of one subject and then compare them with all the attributes of the second subject. The second organizational structure is feature-by-feature; you discuss one feature of Subject A and then compare it with that feature in Subject B. Then you discuss a second feature, and so on. Here's an example of subject-by-subject organization.

> I. introduction and controlling idea
>   A. traditional
>   1. August through June
>   2. 8 a.m. to 3 p.m.
>   3. spring break, summer vacation
>   4. schools closed during breaks
>   B. year-round
>   1. starts in July
>   2. hours vary
>   3. students not all in school at same time
>   4. extended breaks
>   5. schools open year-round

▶ Step 2: Develop Your Comparison

Clearly state the subjects being compared.

> Next week the Mayfair School Board is going to begin debating a proposal that could effectively bring an end to the traditional summer break: year-round schooling. The adoption of year-round schooling would dramatically reshape the school calendar . . . .

Use transitional words to signal comparisons and contrasts.

> In contrast, year-round school calendars take different forms.

▶ Step 3: Draw a Conclusion

Conclude your essay with a restatement of, or a rationale for, the comparison.

> The more Mayfair residents know about year-round schooling, the better able they will be to make the right decision for Mayfair's students.

Rhetorical Devices

Rhetorical devices include repetition and parallelism, which are helpful tools when writing compare-contrast essays. Keep your sentences parallel when making direct comparisons or contrasts to emphasize the relationship between the ideas.

Drafting Checklist

Your essay should include the following traits:

- ☑ **Controlling Idea**—a clear statement of the comparison you're going to make

- ☑ **Organizational Structure**—subject-by-subject or feature-by-feature

- ☑ **Transitional Words and Phrases**—to signal comparisons and contrasts between sentences and paragraphs

School Days

Most adults have fond memories of summer vacations: lazy days filled with baseball games, trips to the beach, hanging out with friends, reading a good book on the front porch, and, best of all, no school. Next week the Mayfair School Board is going to begin debating a proposal that could effectively bring an end to the traditional summer break: year-round schooling. The adoption of year-round schooling would dramatically reshape the school calendar, so it's critical for all Mayfair residents to understand exactly how year-round schooling differs from the way our schools operate today.

Here's how the traditional school year works nearly everywhere in the U.S. The school year typically begins in August and ends the following June. Students are in class for about 180 days during that time. The class day usually begins at 8 a.m. and ends at 3 p.m. Throughout the school year, students get time off for holidays, and most schools have a spring break lasting a week or so. Students may attend summer school for remedial or extra-credit classes.

In contrast, year-round school calendars take different forms. A single-track calendar has all the students in school at the same time. The school year typically starts in late July and runs for 180 days. Students get an extended break during the fall, another during the winter or spring, and a

---

Thesis

The thesis statement clearly introduces the subject of the essay.

Organization

This sentence makes the writer's organizational structure clear—she has chosen subject-by-subject organization.

Transition

This transitional phrase signals that the writer will now discuss the differences between the two calendars.

third during the summer. The school shuts down during these extended breaks.

Another year-round option is the multi-track calendar. Students are assigned to different schedules known as tracks. All students are not in school at the same time. Some students will be on vacation while others are in class. One advantage of the multi-track calendar is increased student capacity. Because all students are not in school at the same time, there is room for additional students.

Like the single-track calendar, the school year starts in late July. Some multi-track schools use the "Concept 6" calendar. This calendar divides the school year into six eight-week blocs. Students might be in class for two months, then take two months off, back for two months, then off for another two, and so on. Another option is four months in class, two months off, another four months of class, and then another two months off. Schools using multi-track calendars are open year-round.

Whether Mayfair will adopt year-round schooling will depend on careful consideration of the issues and, most importantly, informed input from the citizens of our city. The more Mayfair residents know about year-round schooling, the better able they will be to make the right decision for Mayfair's students.

Transition

This transitional phrase signals a similarity between single- and multi-track calendars.

Conclusion

The concluding sentence reinforces the need for the comparisons made in the essay.

Your Turn

Using your plan, write the first draft of your essay. Be sure that your organizational structure is consistent and that your details make clear the differences between your two subjects.

REVISE Your Essay

Key Traits Ideas and Voice As you consider ways to improve your essay, look back at your planning and drafting checklists. Does your draft include all of the important traits?

▶ Step 1: Elaborate

Are your comparisons detailed? Elaboration is the use of facts, details, anecdotes, or examples to develop an idea or support a statement. Different types of elaboration will have different effects on your essay.

Original:

> Most adults have fond memories of summer vacations.

Revision:

> Most adults have fond memories of summer vacations: lazy days filled with baseball games, trips to the beach, hanging out with friends, reading a good book on the front porch, and, best of all, no school.

Elaborating with examples creates a more personal appeal and can provide opportunities to add variety in your sentence styles.

▶ Step 2: Use Modifiers for Emphasis

Is your writing descriptive? Well-chosen adjectives and adverbs can add punch to your writing and help you craft your writing style and voice.

Original:

> Whether Mayfair will adopt year-round schooling will depend on consideration of the issues and, most importantly, input from the citizens of our city.

Revision:

> Whether Mayfair will adopt year-round schooling will depend on careful consideration of the issues and, most importantly, informed input from the citizens of our city.

▶ Step 3: Achieve Coherence

Do the ideas fit together properly? Use transitions to ensure that all of your sentences are clearly and logically connected.

> Throughout the school year, students get time off . . . .
>
> In contrast, year-round school calendars . . . .

Revising Checklist

Before you start your revision, ask yourself these questions:

- ☑ Will my audience understand why I am comparing and contrasting these two ideas?

- ☑ Are all the paragraphs developing the comparisons and contrasts I identified in my thesis?

- ☑ Does my word choice and sentence structure seem appropriate for my audience? Have I incorporated new vocabulary?

- ☑ Do I include the traits in the Planning Checklist (page 426) and the Drafting Checklist (page 429)?

EDIT Your Essay

Key Trait **Conventions** Edit by correcting any errors in spelling, grammar, and mechanics. Review the grammar tips and workshops in the unit to identify areas in your writing that you would like to strengthen and to help you use the conventions of academic language.

▶ Grammar Tip

Verb Tense and Mood A verb must agree with its subject in number and person.

Number

A singular subject takes a singular verb; a plural subject takes a plural verb.

> *Another* option is . . . .
>
> *Other* options are . . . .

Person

When the subject is third-person singular, an *–s* or an *–es* is added to the base form of the verb.

> *They speak. . . .*
>
> *He speaks . . . .*

Subjunctive Mood An exception to the number rule occurs when a verb is in the subjunctive mood. A verb is in the subjunctive mood when it expresses a condition that is doubtful or just not factual, or when it expresses a doubt, a wish, a regret, a request, or a demand. The subjunctive mood is often found in introductory clauses beginning with *if*. In these cases, a singular subject takes a plural verb.

Incorrect

> *If I was you, I would choose year-round schooling.*

Correct

> *If I were you, I would choose year-round schooling.*

Editing Checklist

For your final revision, check the following:

- ☑ Have I misspelled any words? If you are unsure of the spelling of a word, check an online or print dictionary or use your word processor's spell checker.

- ☑ Have I made any errors in mechanics or grammar? Have I followed the rules of Standard American English? Use the Language Handbook on pages R48–R71 to correct common grammar and mechanical errors.

- ☑ Is my writing legible? Be sure your handwriting is neat or that you have followed your teacher's guidelines for word-processing.

PUBLISH Your Essay

Key Trait **Presentation** Submit your essay to your community newspaper. An essay like "School Days" would be both timely and informative for a city considering a major change in the lives of its citizens. What's more, the writer's voice would stand out because she's a student—one of the people who will be most affected by such a change.

Before you submit your essay, ask a family member or friend to read it through to check for any errors you might have missed.

 Literature Online

Writing and Research For editing and publishing tools, go to glencoe.com and enter QuickPass code GL57805u2.

TEKS

For pages 434–435

10.25 Advance a coherent argument that incorporates a clear thesis and a logical progression of valid evidence from reliable sources and that employs eye contact, speaking rate (e.g., pauses for effect), volume, enunciation, purposeful gestures, and conventions of language to communicate ideas effectively.

Speaking, Listening, and Viewing Workshop

Illustrated Presentation

Literature Connection The excerpt from the Houstons' memoir *Farewell to Manzanar* is illustrated with photographs taken by American photojournalist Dorothea Lange. The photos complement the story by showing the reality of the Japanese-American internment. In this workshop, you will deliver an illustrated oral version of your compare-contrast essay.

> **Assignment** **Prepare and deliver an illustrated oral presentation of your compare-contrast essay.**

Plan Your Presentation

- -

Your compare-contrast essay can be illustrated with a variety of media, such as photos, graphic organizers, and drawings. To get started, read over your essay and note passages that lend themselves to visuals. Think of your audience. What would help them better understand and appreciate your presentation? The writer of the student essay on page 430 might choose these illustrations:

- photographs of schools in Mayfair
- a graphic organizer, such as a Venn diagram, that illustrates the comparison being made
- a chart showing how single- and multi-track calendars differ

Remember, your visuals must be large enough to be seen by everyone in class. You can have them enlarged at an office supply store, or you can project them from a computer.

—write your most important points on note cards
—be sure to add any new bits of information to your note cards

Prepare a Script

Like any performance, an illustrated oral presentation needs a well-developed script. Your script should include the following:

- the text of your essay, including a clear thesis and evidence
- prompts for when to direct the audience's attention to your visuals
- what to say about each visual
- prompts for physical movements, such as gestures

As you're scripting, you'll have to add additional text to explain your visuals. You may also want to rewrite some parts of your essay so that they work better in an oral format.

Rehearse Your Presentation

Rehearsals are key to a good performance—you do not need to memorize your presentation, but you should familiarize yourself with what you intend to say and coordinate your narrative with your images. Practice in front of family or friends. Ask for feedback on ways to make your performance more effective.

Techniques for Delivering an Illustrated Presentation

Verbal Techniques	Nonverbal Techniques
☑ **Pace** Vary your speaking rate, never rushing, and use pauses for effect.	☑ **Facial Expression** Convey interest in your subject through your facial expressions.
☑ **Enunciation** Speak clearly and to the point, enunciating your words.	☑ **Focus** When talking about your images, point them out. Otherwise, make eye contact with your audience.
☑ **Volume** Speak so that everyone can hear you.	☑ **Posture** Stand up straight and hold your head up.
☑ **Language** Use the conventions of language, including correct grammar, to communicate ideas effectively.	☑ **Gestures** Use purposeful gestures to emphasize ideas.

Presentation Tips

Use the following checklist to evaluate your illustrated oral presentation:

☑ Were your thesis and main ideas clear?

☑ Did your visuals add effective support to the thesis and main ideas?

☑ Did you present a coherent argument using valid evidence from reliable sources?

☑ Did you use nonverbal techniques such as gestures and eye contact to connect effectively with your audience?

Listen Responsively

When you are listening to the presentation,

☑ use comprehension skills to listen attentively

☑ take notes that summarize, synthesize, or highlight the speaker's ideas

☑ ask questions related to the content for clarification and elaboration

Remember to wait until the speaker has finished presenting before asking any questions.

LOG ON ▶ **Literature** Online

Speaking, Listening, and Viewing For project ideas, templates, and presentation tips, go to glencoe.com and enter QuickPass code GL57805u2.

Independent Reading

Nonfiction and Novels

PEOPLE HAVE BEEN WRITING NONFICTION EVER SINCE THEY SCRATCHED into stone the first records of loans and trades, births and deaths, and suns and moons. Nonfiction writing encompasses everything from history to data analyses. For more nonfiction with a variety of themes, try the first two suggestions below. For novels that incorporate the Big Ideas of *The Power of Memory, Quests and Encounters,* and *Keeping Freedom Alive,* try the titles from the Glencoe Literature Library on the next page.

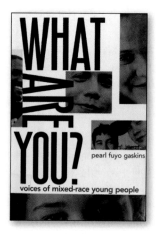

What Are You? Voices of Mixed-Race Young People

Pearl Fuyo Gaskins

Gaskins, whose mother was Japanese and whose father was American, spent years gathering reflections from mixed-race students. They reflect on the issues of appearing not to belong to any one group, of being categorized inaccurately, and of never being able to check the correct "box" about race because more than one box applies. Many affirm their own identities with statements such as "I know who I am," while some focus on the assumptions others make about them.

The Edge of the Sea

Rachel Carson

How do small sea creatures hold on to rocks while strong waves wash over them? How does the arctic jellyfish survive "being solidly frozen for hours"? Carson, a keen observer of nature and an early environmentalist, reveals the dramatic and varied communities of plant and animal life along the rocky shores, sandy beaches, and coral reefs of the Atlantic Ocean. Delicate drawings depict the rich variety of life forms.

Isaac's Storm

Erik Larson

On September 8, 1900, one of the worst storms in U.S. history hit Galveston, Texas. This account captures the aftermath of the storm.

GLENCOE LITERATURE LIBRARY

Night

Elie Wiesel

This autobiographical novel shows the power of memory and brings the brutal reality of the Holocaust to life.

The Autobiography of Miss Jane Pittman

Ernest J. Gaines

The strength and courage of Jane Pittman, a formerly enslaved woman, are an inspiration and a testament to the concept of keeping freedom alive.

CRITICS' CORNER

"Mountains Beyond Mountains *is inspiring, disturbing, and completely absorbing. It will rattle our complacency; it will prick our conscience. One senses that Farmer's life and work has affected Kidder, and it is a measure of Kidder's honesty that he is willing to reveal this to the reader. . . . I had the . . . feeling after reading* Mountains Beyond Mountains *that . . . something had changed in me and it was impossible not to become involved.*"

—Abraham Verghese, the *New York Times Book Review*

Mountains Beyond Mountains

Tracy Kidder

This Pulitzer-Prize-winning biography chronicles the career of Dr. Paul Farmer, an American doctor who has spent much of his life solving health care problems for the people of Haiti and other nations. Committed to the ideal of equality in health care, Farmer and many other dedicated volunteers devote their considerable talents and energy to controlling diseases and saving lives by taking measures that others have found too difficult or expensive.

 Write a Journal

Keep a reader-response journal in which you record your thoughts as you read one of the books listed on these pages. Include your feelings about the characters and events, or connect this book to other works you have read. Publish your journal for your class.

Assessment

English Language Arts

Reading: Nonfiction

Read the following passage and answer the questions that follow it.

from *Wouldn't Take Nothing for My Journey Now* by Maya Angelou

1   When my son was six and I twenty-two, he told me quite solemnly that he had to talk to me. We both sat down at the kitchen table, and he asked with an old man's eyes and a young boy's voice, "Mother, do you have any sweaters that match?" I was puzzled at first. I said, "No," and then I understood he was talking about the pullover and cardigan sets which were popular with white women. And I said, "No, I don't," maybe a little huffily. And he said, "Oh, I wish you did. So that you could wear them to school when you come to see me."

2   I was tickled but I am glad I didn't laugh because he continued, "Mother, could you please only come to school when they call you?" Then I realized that my attire, which delighted my heart and certainly activated my creativity, was an embarrassment to him.

3   When people are young, they desperately need to conform, and no one can embarrass a young person in public so much as an adult to whom he or she is related. Any outré action or wearing of "getups" can make a young person burn with self-consciousness.

4   I learned to be a little more discreet to avoid causing him displeasure. As he grew older and more confident, I gradually returned to what friends thought of as my eccentric way of dressing. I was happier when I chose and created my own fashion.

5   I have lived in this body all my life and know it much better than any fashion designer. I think I know what looks good on me, and I certainly know what feels good on me.

6   I appreciate the creativity which is employed in the design of fabric and the design of clothes, and when something does fit my body and personality, I rush to it, buy it quickly, and wear it frequently. But I must not lie to myself for fashion's sake. I am only willing to purchase the item which becomes me and to wear that which enhances my image of myself to myself.

7   If I am comfortable inside my skin, I have the ability to make other people comfortable inside their skins although their feelings are not my primary reason for making my fashion choice. If I feel good inside my skin and clothes, I am thus free to allow my body its sway, its natural grace, its natural gesture. Then I am so comfortable that whatever I wear looks good on me even to the external fashion arbiters.

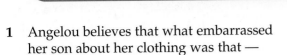

1 Angelou believes that what embarrassed her son about her clothing was that —
   A it didn't fit properly
   B it was too ordinary
   C it wasn't sufficiently fancy
   D it wasn't like what other mothers' wore

2 Angelou suggests that the reason young people are easily embarrassed is that they are —
   F clumsy
   G insecure
   H ignorant
   J not yet creative

3 When Angelou says, in paragraph 3, that young people "desperately need to conform," she means that they need to —
   A become independent
   B look and act like others
   C express their individuality
   D find fault with their parents

4 The way the word *outré* is used in paragraph 3 suggests that it means —
   F feverish
   G shameful
   H immodest
   J unconventional

5 What does the use of the phrase "burn with self-consciousness" in paragraph 3 suggest about the feeling the author is describing?
   A It is warm.
   B It is bright.
   C It is intense.
   D It lasts only a short time.

6 The author's attitude toward her son, as revealed in this selection, can best be described as —
   F angry
   G critical
   H admiring
   J understanding

7 What is the most likely meaning of the word *eccentric* in paragraph 4?
   A Casual
   B Unusual
   C Confusing
   D Ridiculous

8 Angelou suggests that her favorite clothing is that which allows her to —
   F be herself
   G impress others
   H blend into the background
   J be the center of attention

9 Read this dictionary entry.

   primary \\'prī mer ē\ *adj* **1.** first in time; earliest **2.** highest in importance **3.** belonging to the first stage in a process **4.** having to do with the simpler parts that make up something complex

   Which definition best matches the meaning of the word *primary* as it is used in the first sentence of paragraph 7?
   A Definition 1
   B Definition 2
   C Definition 3
   D Definition 4

10 What is the overall tone of the reading selection?

   F Sarcastic

   G Humorous

   H Regretful

   J Reflective

11 What does this excerpt reveal about Angelou's personality?

   A She is a very private person.

   B She tends to ignore other people.

   C She has confidence in who she is.

   D She worries about what others think of her.

12 **Open-Ended Item** What do you think the main idea of this excerpt is? Support your answer with evidence from the selection.

Vocabulary Skills: Sentence Completion

For each item, choose the word that best completes the sentence.

1 The student set an hour aside to _____ his notes before the next day's test.
   A peruse
   B ordain
   C induce
   D advocate

2 An ice pack can help to _____ the pain and swelling of a twisted ankle.
   F inhibit
   G squander
   H alleviate
   J transcend

3 The unexpected good news filled them with _____.
   A valor
   B elation
   C credence
   D neutrality

4 Before the championship game, the coach tried to imagine all possible _____ in which his team could win.
   F advocates
   G agenda
   H scenarios
   J catalysts

5 Her unwillingness to help _____ her expressions of concern.
   A belied
   B eschewed
   C admonished
   D eschewed

6 The old man's _____ expression revealed no emotion.
   F stolid
   G potent
   H imperative
   J vulnerable

7 Bring only what is absolutely necessary, nothing _____.
   A relevant
   B obligatory
   C tremulous
   D superfluous

8 The carefully drawn map was _____ in helping us find our way.
   F intact
   G invaluable
   H turbulent
   J commodious

9 The most _____ people are usually good listeners.
   A superfluous
   B meticulous
   C mainstream
   D compassionate

10 If your _____ is to become an astronaut, you should take every science course that is offered.
   F attribute
   G paradox
   H dissension
   J aspiration

Revising and Editing

Read the following first draft of a student's essay and answer the questions that follow it.

(1) My family knows that macaroni and cheese were my favorite dinner when I was a child, and either cookies or ice cream was my favorite dessert. (2) I'll admit that I used to be a picky (and boring) eater. (3) If I was still six, I'd like the food the school serves in the cafeteria and wouldn't like the meals that are served at fancy restaurants. (4) However, I've grown up, and my tastes have changed. (5) Neither my parents nor my sister seems to understand this when they pack my lunch which I find annoying, because peanut butter and jelly is starting to get boring.

(6) I've noticed that other families have more interesting food than we do at home. (7) They also try different restaurants when they eat out. (8) At a friend's house, I was served stuffed eggplant and snapper with red pepper sauce. (9) The food delighted me, and I wished it were a regular meal at our house. (10) Then, as I sat there moping, I realized something. (11) Why sit around and wish that other people would change? (12) I could, myself, learn to cook! (13) Then I could try new things and serve them to my family. (14) Maybe they would enjoy them as much as I think I would.

1   What change, if any, should be made in sentence 1?
    A   Change *family knows* to **family know**
    B   Change *macaroni and cheese were* to **macaroni and cheese was**
    C   Change *cookies or ice cream was* to **cookies and ice cream were**
    D   Make no change

2   What change, if any, should be made in sentence 3?
    F   Change *I was* to **I were**
    G   Change *school serves* to **school serve**
    H   Insert a comma after *meals*
    J   Make no change

3   What change, if any, should be made in sentence 5?
    A   Change *seems* to **seem**
    B   Insert a comma after *lunch*
    C   Change *peanut butter and jelly is* to **peanut butter and jelly are**
    D   Make no change

4   Which word in sentence 8 or 9 is a participle?
    F   *served*
    G   *stuffed*
    H   *delighted*
    J   *wished*

5 Which sentence is written in the passive voice?

   A Sentence 2

   B Sentence 4

   C Sentence 6

   D Sentence 8

6 Which sentence contains a verb that expresses the subjunctive mood?

   F Sentence 7

   G Sentence 9

   H Sentence 11

   J Sentence 12

Written Composition

Read the information and instructions below in order to write a short essay.

Everyone changes as he or she grows up. Most people become more self-confident, as Maya Angelou mentions happened with her son. However, there are some interests, personality traits, and even behaviors that change very little, if at all.

Write a short essay that analyzes how you are similar to and different from what you were like as a young child.

REMEMBER—YOU SHOULD

❏ brainstorm by using a Venn diagram or other method

❏ decide on either a "subject-by-subject" or "feature-by-feature" organizational method

❏ use transitions to signal comparisons and contrasts and maintain coherence

❏ use vivid, clear language to communicate your ideas

❏ correct errors in spelling, capitalization, punctuation, grammar, and sentence structure

---

Orpheus, 1969. Marc Chagall. Oil on canvas, 97 x 130 cm. Private collection.

View the Art Marc Chagall's paintings and other works have been called musical, poetic, and dream-like. Do you think *Orpheus* fits this description? Why or why not?

Poetry

Looking Ahead

Like other forms of literature, poetry concerns real life, but it distills that life to its essence. Poetry is the most concentrated form of literature: it makes every word and even every syllable count. All good poems allow the reader to experience the power and magic of words in a way that no other form of literature can.

Each part in Unit Three focuses on a Big Idea that can help you connect to the literary works.

PREVIEW	Big Ideas	Literary Focus
PART 1	The Energy of the Everyday	Form and Structure
PART 2	Loves and Losses	Language
PART 3	Issues of Identity	Sound Devices

TEKS

For pages 446–450

10.3 Understand, make inferences and draw conclusions about the structure and elements of poetry and provide evidence from text to support understanding.

Genre Focus

What distinguishes poetry from prose?

How does poetry give a sense of the mystery and marvel of life? It uses what African American poet Quincy Troupe calls "the music of language." Says Troupe, "I want the words to sing." The elements of poetry, while they may be found in other genres, are essential to the art of poetry.

The Form and Structure of Poetry

Lines and Stanzas

Poetry is arranged in lines and stanzas. A **line** is a horizontal row of words, which may or may not form a complete sentence. A **stanza** is a group of lines forming a unit.

> The mother smiled to know her child
> was in a sacred place,
> but that smile was the last smile
> to come upon her face.
>
> —Dudley Randall, *from "Ballad of Birmingham"*

Rhythm and Meter

A poet chooses words and arranges them to create **rhythm,** the pattern of beats created by the arrangement of stressed and unstressed syllables in a line. **Meter** is a regular rhythm. The basic unit in measuring rhythm is the **foot,** which usually contains one stressed syllable marked with (´) and one or more unstressed syllables marked with (˘).

> Hăd I´ / thĕ heávens' / ĕmbrói / dĕred clóths
> Ĕnwróught / wĭth góld / ănd síl / vĕr líght
> —William Butler Yeats, *from "He Wishes for the Cloths of Heaven"*

Rhyme

Rhyme is the repetition of similar or identical sounds at the ends of words that appear close to each other. **Internal rhyme** occurs within lines of poetry. **End rhyme** occurs at the ends of lines. **Rhyme scheme,** the pattern formed by end rhymes, is shown by a row of letters (*aabb*) in which a different letter of the alphabet signals each new rhyme.

> Black reapers with the sound of steel on stones a
> Are sharpening scythes. I see them place the hones   a
> In their hip-pockets as a thing that's done,   b
> And start their silent swinging, one by one. b
> —Jean Toomer, *from "Reapers"*

The Language of Poetry

Imagery

Imagery is descriptive language that appeals to one or more of the five senses: sight, sound, touch, taste, and smell. This use of sensory detail helps create an emotional response in the reader.

In a shoe box stuffed in an old nylon stocking
Sleeps the baby mouse I found in the
    meadow,
Where he trembled and shook beneath a stick
—Theodore Roethke, *from* **"The Meadow Mouse"**

Figurative Language

Figurative language is language used for descriptive effect. Expressions of figurative language are not literally true but express some truth beyond the literal level.

- A **simile** uses the word *like* or *as* to compare two seemingly unlike things.

- A **metaphor** compares two or more things by implying that one thing *is* another.

- **Personification** involves giving human characteristics to an animal, object, or idea.

simile
She laughs like wild water, shaking
—Chitra Banerjee Divakaruni, *from* **"Woman with Kite"**

personification
Sometime too hot the eye of heaven shines,
—William Shakespeare, *from* **"Shall I Compare Thee to a Summer's Day?"**

metaphor
the spring rain
    is a
    thread of pearls
—Lady Ise, *from* **a tanka**

The Sound of Poetry

Sound Devices

Alliteration is the repetition of consonant sounds at the beginnings of nonrhyming words or syllables in neighboring words. **Consonance** is the repetition of consonant sounds at the ends of nonrhyming words or syllables. **Assonance** is the repetition of vowel sounds in neighboring nonrhyming words. **Onomatopoeia** is the use of a word or phrase, such as *swoosh* or *clank,* that imitates or suggests the sound of what it describes.

alliteration
past the puff-cheeked clouds, she
follows it, her eyes slit-smiling at the sun.
—Chitra Banerjee Divakaruni, *from* **"Woman with Kite"**

consonance
and kisses are a better fate
—E. E. Cummings, *from* **"since feeling is first"**

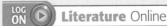

Literature Online

Literature and Reading For more selections in this genre, go to glencoe.com and enter QuickPass code GL57805u3.

Literary Analysis Model
How do literary elements create meaning in a poem?

Abraham Lincoln is the subject of "O Captain! My Captain!" In the poem, Walt Whitman captures his emotions after the assassination of President Lincoln. Walt Whitman (1819–1892) is one of the pioneers of modern poetry.

APPLYING
Literary Elements

Stanza (lines 1–4)

The first half of each stanza, or major division, focuses on the crowd.

Speaker (lines 5–8)

The second half of each stanza focuses on the speaker's sadness.

Imagery (lines 3 and 6)

The sound of bells and the sight of blood are vivid sensory details.

Repetition (lines 1 and 9; 8, 16, and 24)

The repeated use of words such as *Captain* and phrases such as "fallen cold and dead" helps create a musical and emotional effect.

Alliteration (lines 10–11)

The repeated initial consonant sounds in phrases such as "*F*lag is *F*lung" and "*r*ibbon'd *wr*eaths" produce musical effects as well.

O Captain! My Captain!
by Walt Whitman

O Captain! my Captain! our fearful trip is done;
The ship has weather'd every rack, the prize we sought is won;
The port is near, the bells I hear, the people all exulting,
While follow eyes the steady keel, the vessel grim and daring:
5   But O heart! heart! heart!
        O the bleeding drops of red,
            Where on the deck my Captain lies,
                Fallen cold and dead.

O Captain! my Captain! rise up and hear the bells;
10 Rise up—for you the flag is flung—for you the bugle trills,
For you bouquets and ribbon'd wreaths—for you the shores
    a-crowding,
For you they call, the swaying mass, their eager faces turning;
    Here Captain! dear father!
        This arm beneath your head;
15   It is some dream that on the deck,
             You've fallen cold and dead.

My Captain does not answer, his lips are pale and still;
My father does not feel my arm, he has no pulse nor will;
The ship is anchor'd safe and sound, its voyage closed and
    done;
20 From fearful trip, the victor ship, comes in with object won;
    Exult, O shores, and ring, O bells!
      But I, with mournful tread,
          Walk the deck my Captain lies,
             Fallen cold and dead.

Figurative Language (lines 17–18)

The speaker uses metaphor in comparing Lincoln to a captain and a father.

Rhythm (lines 21–24)

The pattern of stressed and unstressed syllables produces a regular rhythm.

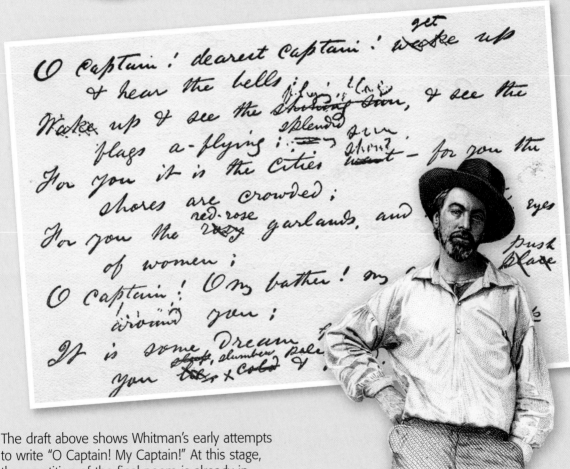

The draft above shows Whitman's early attempts to write "O Captain! My Captain!" At this stage, the repetition of the final poem is already in place, as well as the metaphor of Lincoln as the captain and father to the country. Whitman uses specific words to create imagery that is powerful and packed with meaning. What emotions do these stanzas capture?

Reading Check

Evaluate In your opinion, which of the literary elements did Whitman use most successfully in "O Captain! My Captain!"? Explain your choice.

Wrap-Up

Guide to Reading Poetry

- Poets use words differently than do writers of prose.

- Reading poetry well involves using your emotions, experiences, and imagination as well as your intelligence.

- Read a poem from beginning to end several times.

- Focus on what the words of the poem are actually saying.

- Respond to the poem as a whole before analyzing it.

Elements of Poetry

- A **line** is a row of words; a **stanza** is a group of lines that form a unit.

- The pattern of stressed and unstressed syllables in a line of poetry creates **rhythm.**

- **Rhyme** and other sound devices repeat certain sounds to create musical effects.

- **Imagery** is descriptive language that appeals to the five senses.

- **Figurative language** compares unlike things in imaginative ways.

 LOG ON ▶ **Literature** Online

Unit Resources For additional skills practice, go to glencoe.com and enter QuickPass code GL57805u3.

Activities

Use what you have learned about reading and analyzing poetry to do one of these actvities.

1. Speaking and Listening How would you present the poem "O Captain! My Captain!" to convey the speaker's intense emotions? Record a dramatic reading of Whitman's poem to play for the class.

2. Visual Literacy Create a concept web illustrating the elements that work together to create meaning in a poem.

3. Take Notes You might try using this graphic organizer to help you make inferences about the elements of poetry in this unit. Provide evidence from the poems you read to support your understanding.

 FOLDABLES Study Organizer **THREE-POCKET BOOK**

Form and Structure   Language   Sound Devices

PART 1

The Energy of the Everyday

The Girl with Paddleboat, 1865. Gustave Courbet.

View the Art Gustave Courbet, a French painter whose work shunned Romanticism and embraced Realism, often portrayed average citizens at everyday tasks. Does this painting capture the energy of the everyday? Why or why not?

BIG IDEA

We sometimes hear people say, "If I had it to do over again, I would take time to stop and smell the roses." We are constantly surrounded with opportunities to take in the wonder of life. The poems in Part 1 find wonder in everyday experiences. As you read the poems, ask yourself, What are some of my favorite memories of everyday experiences? What made those times special?

TEKS

For pages 452–453

10.3 Understand, make inferences and draw conclusions about the structure and elements of poetry and provide evidence from text to support understanding.

LITERARY FOCUS

Form and Structure

How do form and structure affect meaning in a poem?

What is a poem? What are its parts? While many poems at first appear to be simple collections of rhymed lines, their structure can be far more complex. The structure of prose is a relatively simple matter of proper sentences grouped into paragraphs. The structure of poetry offers many more possibilities to explore. In the following cartoon, Calvin presents his father with an ode.

Line and Stanza

Line A **line** of poetry is a row consisting of a word or words that may or may not form a complete sentence. **Poetic structure** refers to the organization of words, lines, and images, as well as of ideas. Poets often organize their poems into **stanzas**—the "paragraphs" of poetry. Poems can have stanzas of varying lengths or have no stanza divisions at all. **Form** refers to the organizing principle that shapes a work of literature. It may refer to aspects beyond external structure, such as established criteria related to genre.

Stanza A **stanza** is a group of lines followed by a line of space. A stanza of two lines that rhyme is a **couplet.** The rhyme scheme is *aa.* Stanzas of four, six, and eight lines are respectively called **quatrains, sestets,** and **octaves.**

Rhythm

Stressed and unstressed syllables create a pattern in poetry, called **rhythm.** When the pattern is predictable it is called **meter,** but it does not have to be predictable. Rhythm can create a musical quality, but it can also draw attention to certain words or ideas.

Rhyme

The term **rhyme scheme** refers to the rhyming pattern of a poem. **Internal rhyme** occurs within lines of poetry. **End rhyme** occurs at the ends of lines. **Slant rhyme** occurs when words include sounds that are similar but not identical. Lowercase letters are used to show rhyme schemes. Each end sound is assigned its own letter. Study the rhyme scheme that follows.

Heart! We will forget him!⠀⠀⠀⠀⠀⠀⠀a
You and I—tonight!⠀⠀⠀⠀⠀⠀⠀⠀⠀⠀b
You may forget the warmth he gave—⠀⠀c
I will forget the light!⠀⠀⠀⠀⠀⠀⠀⠀⠀b

—Emily Dickinson, *from* **"Heart! We Will Forget Him"**

Foot The **foot** is the basic unit of stressed and unstressed syllables used to describe rhythm in poetry. A foot usually has two or three syllables.

Meter Predictable rhythms are called **meter.** Different meters are named for how many feet are in each line. **Trimeter** has three feet, **tetrameter** has four feet, **pentameter** has five feet, and **hexameter** has six feet. Iambic pentameter appears in many English poems. An **iamb** is a foot that has an unstressed syllable followed by a stressed syllable, and pentameter means there are five of them in a line.

Shall I / compare / thee to / a sum / mer's day?

Thou art / more lov / ely and / more tem / perate.

—William Shakespeare, *from* **"Shall I Compare Thee to a Summer's Day?"**

Scansion **Scansion** is the analysis of lines of verse to show their meter. When you scan a poem, mark stressed syllables with (´) and mark unstressed syllables with (˘).

Rough winds do shake the darling buds of May,

And summer's lease hath all too short a date.

—William Shakespeare, *from* **"Shall I Compare Thee to a Summer's Day?"**

Poetic Forms

Lyric Poem Lyric poems are short poems by one speaker who expresses thoughts and feelings to create a single, unified impression. Jimmy Santiago Baca's poem "I Am Offering This Poem" is an example of a lyric poem.

It's all I have to give,
and all anyone needs to live,
and to go on living inside,
when the world outside
no longer cares if you live or die;
remember,
⠀⠀⠀⠀⠀⠀⠀⠀⠀I love you

—Jimmy Santiago Baca, *from* **"I Am Offering This Poem"**

Free Verse Poetry without a fixed pattern of meter and rhyme is called **free verse.** Some free verse uses sound devices and a rhythm similar to speaking patterns.

Speaking indifferently to him,
who had driven out the cold
and polished my good shoes as well.
What did I know, what did I know
of love's austere and lonely offices?

—Robert Hayden, *from* **"Those Winter Sundays"**

Quickwrite

Make Inferences Based on what you have learned about the form and structure of poetry, write a paragraph about how structure affects one of the poems in Part 1. Support your response with text evidence.

LOG ON ▶ **Literature** Online

Literature and Reading For more about literary elements, go to glencoe.com and enter QuickPass code GL57805u3.

Before You Read

Those Winter Sundays

Meet **Robert Hayden**
(1913–1980)

Ever wonder what will happen to your classmates, those burrowing book-worms, who enjoy reading for reading's sake? Well, they just might grow up to be famous authors and poets. Robert Hayden was one of those bookish students, and he went on to become a poet and professor, earning a living through the written word.

> *"I loved those books, partly because they took me completely out of the environment I lived in, and they appealed to my imagination. . . ."*
>
> —Robert Hayden

A Life with Books Hayden was born in Detroit, Michigan. Growing up, he was too nearsighted to play sports with his friends, so he found companionship in books. After high school, he read many contemporary poets including those of the Harlem Renaissance—which he discovered by accident, stumbling upon the famous anthology *The New Negro* at a time when he could not afford to go to college. Later he won a scholarship to Detroit City College (now called Wayne State University), where he majored in foreign languages and minored in English.

After receiving a master's degree in 1944, Hayden began his academic career. He spent 23 years at Fisk University, where he eventually became a professor of English. He ended his academic career at the University of Michigan, teaching there for eleven years. Hayden once said that he considered himself to be "a poet who teaches in order to earn a living so that he can write a poem or two now and then."

Politics, Poetry, and Faith Hayden's poetry was deeply influenced by the poetry of his mentor and graduate school professor, W. H. Auden. Hayden created stanza structures that are creative and original, even when they appear in traditional forms. In this way, his poetry balances free verse and traditional forms. Hayden's poetry is usually arranged into even stanzas with lines in regular patterns. Another main feature of Hayden's verse is that he avoids full rhyme; in some cases, he substitutes assonance or consonance.

The subject matter of Hayden's poetry tends to focus on historical themes and events, and he was influenced by the politics of the times. He experienced discrimination and segregation while he lived in Nashville. However, he refrained from writing aggressively about the injustices he witnessed. Instead, he strove to approach subjects such as civil rights as "an artist and not a propagandist."

LOG ON ▶ **Literature** Online

Author Search For more about Robert Hayden, go to glencoe.com and enter QuickPass code GL57805u3.

Literature and Reading Preview

Connect to the Poem

How often do you reflect on what the people closest to you do to show their love for you? Freewrite for a few minutes about their love for you and how you have responded.

Build Background

Hayden's poems often balance painful experiences with hope, possibility, and a celebration of humanity. Hayden said, "I believe in the essential oneness of all people." His poems often portray the universal human concerns of loss and love.

Set Purposes for Reading

Big Idea The Energy of the Everyday

As you read, ask yourself, How does Hayden capture the different moods and actions of his characters through vivid imagery?

Literary Element Line and Stanza

A **line** in a poem can consist of a single word or row of words. A **stanza** is a group of lines forming a unit in a poem and is similar to a paragraph in prose. Typically, stanzas are separated by a line of space. As you read, ask yourself, What is the author's focus and thematic intent for each stanza?

Reading Strategy Analyze Tone

Tone refers to an author's attitude toward his or her subject matter. A writer's tone might project a variety of attitudes such as sympathy or humor. As you read, ask yourself, What is the tone, and what does it suggest about the author's message?

....

Tip: Ask Questions Use a diagram like the one below to identify the tone of the poem. Fill in the circles with descriptions from the poem and note the tone conveyed. Use the highlighted passage and question to help you.

TEKS

For pages 454–457

10.3 Analyze the structure or prosody and graphic elements (e.g., line length) in poetry.

Vocabulary

chronic (kron´ik) *adj.* persistent; ongoing, especially of sickness or pain; p. 456 *Chronic backaches made it difficult for my mom to garden.*

indifferently (in dif´ər ənt lē) *adv.* not concerned about someone or something; without a preference; p. 456 *When Mr. Tate spoke, his children listened indifferently, as they were not interested.*

austere (ôs tēr´) *adj.* stern; severe in appearance; p. 456 *Micky's austere expression let us know that he was disappointed.*

descriptions of the cold
blueblack, splintering, breaking

descriptions of the house

Tone

descriptions of his father

descriptions of love

Those Winter Sundays

Robert Hayden

Sundays too my father got up early
and put his clothes on in the blueblack cold,
then with cracked hands that ached
from labor in the weekday weather made
5 banked fires[1] blaze. No one ever thanked him.

I'd wake and hear the cold splintering, breaking.
When the rooms were warm, he'd call,
and slowly I would rise and dress,
fearing the **chronic** angers of that house,

10 Speaking **indifferently** to him,
who had driven out the cold
and polished my good shoes as well.
What did I know, what did I know
of love's **austere** and lonely offices?[2]

Lynford, 1969. Karen Armitage. Oil on canvas. Private collection.

View the Art Armitage often paints solitary figures who appear deep in thought. How would you describe this man's expression and mood? Compare and contrast them with the mood conveyed by the speaker of the poem.

---

1. *Banked fires* are ones that have been covered with ashes to keep them burning at a very low level.
2. *Offices* can mean both "duties and responsibilities" or "favors and kindness."

Analyze Tone *How do these five words contribute to the tone of the poem?*

Vocabulary

chronic (kron´ik) *adj.* persistent; ongoing, especially of sickness or pain

indifferently (in dif´ ər ənt lē) *adv.* not concerned about someone or something; without a preference

austere (ôs tēr´) *adj.* stern; severe in appearance

After You Read

Respond and Think Critically

1. **Connect to Personal Experience** Which one line or image from "Those Winter Sundays" resonated most with you? Explain.

2. **Make Inferences About Speaker** Why do you think the speaker spoke indifferently to his father? In the third stanza, how has the father "driven out the cold"?

3. **Interpret Speaker** What does the speaker now understand that he did not understand before? Support your response. **OER**

4. **Analyze Figurative Language** How does the speaker personify the cold? How does this reflect his feelings? Support your answer.

5. **Big Idea** **Draw Conclusions About Descriptions** How do Hayden's descriptions bring greater significance to the daily responsibilities of a parent? Support your response with text evidence.

6. **Draw Conclusions About Author's Purpose** What was Hayden's purpose in writing this poem?

Literary Element Line and Stanza

Examining the contribution each **line** and **stanza** makes to the overall movement and thematic development of the poem can help you better understand the poet's purpose and intention.

7. **Identify Structure** What is the specific focus of each stanza?

8. **Analyze Line Length** Reread the highlighted text on page 456. How does the length of this line impact the meaning of the poem?

Reading Strategy Analyze Tone

 Texas Test Practice (10.3)

1. The description of the cold house

  (A) creates an affectionate, nostalgic tone

  (B) contrasts with the warmth of feeling the speaker had for his father

  (C) mirrors the lack of sympathy the speaker felt for his father

  (D) reveals that the speaker's feelings toward his father remain unchanged

  (E) suggests that the speaker is incapable of expressing love

Vocabulary Practice

Practice with Context Clues Identify the context clues in the following sentences that help you determine the meaning of each bold-faced vocabulary word.

1. Every time Jane fidgeted, Grandmother gave her an **austere**, disapproving look.

2. Over the years, Duncan suffered from **chronic** allergies and could not find relief no matter what he did.

3. Shipra did not care which movie we saw, so she reacted **indifferently** when I chose one.

Writing

Write a Character Sketch Use the information presented in "Those Winter Sundays" to write a character sketch of the speaker's father—a description of his personality and character traits. As you write, be sure to consider not only what the speaker directly states but also what you can infer based on the tone.

 Literature Online

Selection Resources For Selection Quizzes, eFlashcards, and Reading-Writing Connection activities, go to glencoe.com and enter QuickPass code GL57805u3.

TEKS

10.1.E Use a dictionary, a glossary, or a thesaurus (printed or electronic) to determine or confirm the meanings of words and phrases, including their connotations and denotations, and their etymology.

Vocabulary Workshop

Homonyms and Homophones

Literature Connection In this excerpt from his poem "Those Winter Sundays," Robert Hayden uses the word *banked,* meaning not "stored for safekeeping" or "steeply inclined," but rather "covered with ashes to burn slowly."

> "... *with cracked hands that ached | from labor in the weekday weather made | banked fires blaze.*"

Words like *banked* that sound and are spelled alike but have different meanings are called **homonyms.** Words such as *there* and *their,* which sound alike but are spelled differently, are called **homophones.** Homonyms and homophones can be confusing, but the context, or setting, in which a word appears usually provides clues to the word's meaning. From Hayden's use of *banked* to describe fires and our own knowledge of them, we can determine the appropriate definition. You can also use a dictionary, glossary, or thesaurus to determine or confirm the meaning of the word.

Part of the reason why English is difficult for many non-native speakers to learn is its many homophones.

Examples

ate/eight	none/nun	some/sum
for/fore/four	one/won	their/there/they're
here/hear	right/rite/write	to/too/two
higher/hire	row/roe	wholly/holy/holey
its/it's	scent/sent/cent	
morning/mourning	site/sight/cite	

Homonyms and Homophones

Homonyms are words that sound alike and are spelled alike but have different meanings. **Homophones** are words that sound alike but are spelled differently and have different meanings.

Tip

Homographs are words that look alike in writing but have different word origins and sometimes different pronunciations. Context clues help distinguish homographs from homonyms.

Practice Decide which homonym or homophone belongs in each sentence below. Use a dictionary, glossary, or thesaurus to determine or confirm your response.

1. Father (passed/past) him a pair of freshly shined shoes.
2. The boy was the sole (heir/air) to the family fortune.
3. The warmth helped (heel/heal) their chilled bodies.
4. The stars counteracted the loneliness of the (night/knight).
5. He did not (know, no) how to express his feelings to his father.

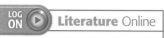 **Literature** Online

Vocabulary For more vocabulary practice, go to glencoe.com and enter the QuickPass code GL57805u3.

Before You Read

Creatures

Meet Billy Collins
(born 1941)

Billy Collins has managed a most unusual feat for a contemporary poet: popular and critical acclaim. Whether musing about the three blind mice or a museum painting, Collins writes with a wry humor that gently ushers the reader into his poem and reveals truths about the human experience using twists of language and thought. Collins says that he envisions the beginning of a poem as "a kind of welcome mat where I invite the reader inside."

Beginnings Collins is a native of New York City, the son of a nurse and an electrician. After high school, he attended the College of the Holy Cross in Worchester, Massachusetts. Collins then earned a doctorate in Romantic Poetry from the University of California at Riverside in 1971. He returned to New York to teach at the City University of New York.

> "I believe poetry belongs in unexpected places—in elevators and on buses and subways."
>
> —Billy Collins

During the 1970s, Collins's poetry began to appear in many literary publications, including the *American Poetry Review,* the *Paris Review,* and the *New Yorker.* In 1977 Collins published his first book of poetry, *Pokerface,* followed by his second collection, *Video Poems,* in 1980. Eight years later, Collins published *The Apple that Astonished Paris.* His next book, *Questions About Angels,* was included in the 1990 National Poetry Series.

A National Reputation With the publication of *Questions About Angels,* Collins's popularity reached the national level. The New York Public Library named him a "Literary Lion" in 1992, and the following year he was awarded the Bess Hokin Prize by the prestigious *Poetry* magazine. His poems appeared in the *Best American Poetry* anthologies in 1992, 1993, and 1997. He continued to publish and also edited two anthologies of poetry and released a CD of Collins reading 33 of his poems. His other accolades include various literary prizes and fellowships from the Guggenheim Foundation and the National Endowment for the Arts.

Collins was named Poet Laureate of the United States in 2001, a position he held for two years. During that time, he developed *Poetry 180: A Poem a Day for High Schools.* Collins selected 180 poems, one to be read aloud each morning along with the school announcements. He described the project as a "jukebox of poems" and emphasized that the students were not to analyze the poetry—they were to simply experience the language.

LOG ON ▶ **Literature** Online

Author Search For more about Billy Collins, go to glencoe.com and enter QuickPass code GL57805u3.

Literature and Reading Preview

Connect to the Poem

Do you ever see creatures in clouds or ordinary objects? Discuss this question with a partner. Consider whether these observations change based on a person's age or experience.

Build Background

Appearances sometimes defy reality, and it is possible for people to view the same object or occurrence in different ways. When something can be perceived or interpreted differently, each person brings his or her own background knowledge and imagination into the process.

Set Purposes for Reading

Big Idea The Energy of the Everyday

As you read this poem, ask yourself, What creatures are seen in everyday objects and how does the speaker react to them?

Literary Element Enjambment

Enjambment is the continuation of the sense of a sentence or phrase from one line of a poem to the next without a pause:

> *Many times I would be daydreaming*
> *on the carpet and one would appear next to me,*

As you read, ask yourself, Where does enjambment occur?

Reading Strategy Analyze Poetic Structure

When you **analyze poetic structure**, you analyze the organization of words, lines, and images, and ideas in a poem. As you read, ask yourself, How does Collins structure "Creatures"?

Tip: Make Inferences About Structure As you read, use a chart like the one below to make inferences about how the structure of the poem affects the meaning. Use the blue highlighted question to help you.

Stanza	Structure	Inference
1	comparison/ contrast	comparison shows that speaker is even more imaginative than Hamlet

TEKS

For pages 459–463

10.3 Understand, make inferences, and draw conclusions about the structure of poetry and provide evidence from text to support understanding. Analyze the structure or prosody and graphic elements (e.g., punctuation, word position) in poetry.

Vocabulary

submerged (səb murjd´) *adj.* hard to see; sunken; p. 461 *The real plan was submerged in a mass of detail.*

bureau (byoor´ō) *n.* a chest of drawers for the bedroom; p. 461 *Please put the clothes back in the bureau.*

melancholy (mel´ən kol´ ē) *adj.* depressed; dejected; p. 462 *The dark and rainy day created a melancholy mood in the school.*

grimace (grim´ is) *v.* to make a face expressing disgust, disapproval, or pain; p. 462 *The boy grimaced at his mother when she scolded him.*

fissure (fish´ər) *n.* a narrow crack; p. 462 *The earthquake caused a fissure in the earth.*

Tip: Word Usage A dictionary definition provides limited guidance when it comes to using words. You can gather additional clues from reading and listening to words used in context.

Invisible Afghan with Apparition on Beach of Face of Garcia in Form of Fruit Dish with 3 Figs, 1938. Salvador Dali. Private collection.

Creatures

Billy Collins

Hamlet° noticed them in the shapes of clouds,
but I saw them in the furniture of childhood,
creatures trapped under surfaces of wood,

one **submerged** in a polished sideboard,
5 one frowning from a chair-back,
another howling from my mother's silent **bureau**,
locked in the grain of maple, frozen in oak.

1 **Hamlet:** In Shakespeare's *Hamlet,* Act III, Scene II, Hamlet compares the shape of a cloud to a camel, a weasel, and a whale.

Vocabulary

submerged (səb murjd′) *adj.* hard to see; sunken
bureau (byoor′ō) *n.* a chest of drawers for the bedroom

I would see these presences, too,
in a swirling pattern of wallpaper
10   or in the various greens of a porcelain lamp,
each looking so **melancholy**, so damned,
some peering out at me as if they knew
all the secrets of a secretive boy.

Many times I would be daydreaming
15   on the carpet and one would appear next to me,
the oversize nose, the hollow look.

So you will understand my reaction
this morning at the beach
when you opened your hand to show me
20   a stone you had picked up from the shoreline.

"Do you see the face?" you asked
as the cold surf circled our bare ankles.
"There's the eye and the line of the mouth,
like it's **grimacing**, like it's in pain."

25   "Well, maybe that's because it has a **fissure**
running down the length of its forehead
not to mention a kind of twisted beak," I said,

taking the thing from you and flinging it out
over the sparkle of blue waves
30   so it could live out its freakish existence
on the dark bottom of the sea

and stop bothering innocent beachgoers like us,
stop ruining everyone's summer.

Analyze Poetic Structure *What is the function of lines 17–18 in the poem's structure?*

Enjambment *How do lines 19–20 exemplify enjambment?*

Vocabulary

melancholy (mel´ən kol´ē) *adj.* depressed; dejected
grimace (grim´ is) *v.* to make a face expressing disgust, disapproval, or pain
fissure (fish´ər) *n.* a narrow crack

After You Read

Respond and Think Critically

1. **Connect to Personal Experience** How do you feel about the creature after reading the poem? Why?

2. **Summarize Description** In your own words, summarize how the speaker describes the "creatures" in the furniture.

3. **Make Inferences About Speaker** How does the speaker react to the stone his companion finds on the beach? Why do you think the speaker reacts this way?

4. **Evaluate Speaker** Does the speaker's reaction to the stone seem rational? Why or why not? Support your answer with evidence from the text.

5. **Evaluate Author's Craft** Why do you think Collins makes the speaker directly address his companion in the fifth stanza? Is this technique effective? Explain.

6. **Big Idea** **Draw Conclusions About Description** The everyday is usually considered non-threatening. How has Collins used description to make the everyday seem threatening? Support your response with text evidence.

7. **Analyze Style** Collins's poems are known for their playful, conversational style. Where can you identify that style in "Creatures"?

Literary Element Enjambment

Poets use **enjambment** to create a conversational tone and flow in their poems.

8. **Analyze Punctuation** Where does the poet use enjambment in the poem? What effect does this lack of punctuation at the ends of lines have?

9. **Evaluate Word Position** How effective is the author's use of enjambment? Support your response with evidence from the text.

Reading Strategy Analyze Structure

Poets may structure a poem by cause and effect, chronological order, and problem and solution. Refer to the chart you made on page 460.

10. How do the adjectives the speaker uses support his reaction in the final two lines?

11. What structure does Collins use to organize the ideas in the poem? Support your response.

Vocabulary Practice

Practice with Usage Respond to these statements to help you explore the meanings of the boldfaced vocabulary words from the poem.

1. Name something that is likely to be **submerged.**

2. Tell what a **bureau** is likely to contain.

3. Describe your face, posture, or body language when you are **melancholy**.

4. Identify two things that might make you **grimace.**

5. Explain what you would do if you came across a **fissure** while hiking.

Writing

Write an Interior Monologue What might the speaker's companion be thinking during the events described in the last five stanzas of "Creatures"? Write an interior monologue (a verbalization of the thoughts running through someone's mind) that expresses the companion's reactions.

Before You Read

Shall I Compare Thee to a Summer's Day?

Meet **William Shakespeare**
(1564–1616)

O ver the years he has had many names. Some have called him "Gentle Will." Many are familiar with his most common nickname, "The Bard." And though the name Shakespeare brings to mind images of great onstage romance, horrific tragedy, and uproarious comedy, he was, before all else, "The Poet."

The Early Years Born to Mary Arden and John Shakespeare, William lived his early years in Stratford-upon-Avon, England, where he most likely received an extensive education in Latin literature and grammar, history, and mythology. This immersion in the classics fuels much of the imagery in Shakespeare's works.

Little else is known about his early life, but literary historians do know that in 1582 he married Anne Hathaway, with whom he had three children, Susanna, Hamnet, and Judith. By 1592, Shakespeare began showing up in the world of London theater, though there are conflicting stories as to how he arrived there.

> "[Shakespeare] was not of an age, but for all time!"
>
> —Ben Jonson

The Poet Shakespeare's first poems, *Venus and Adonis* and *The Rape of Lucrece*, were published in 1593 and 1594. Both were narrative works that demonstrated Shakespeare's education in ancient Roman history and mythology, specif- ically the mythical romance of the goddess Aphrodite and the mortal Adonis and the tale of the rape of Lucrece—the daughter of an important ancient Roman family that supposedly incited a rebellion in Rome.

Shakespeare the Poet is best known and regarded for his sonnets. Although probably written in the 1590s, Shakespeare's 154 sonnets were not published until 1609. These poems express a universal theme of the power of love and beauty over nature and time.

Ghosts of Rhyme and Rhythm Several mysteries surround this collection of sonnets. Someone dedicated the first 126 of the sonnets to a set of initials, a person who has been known to history only as W. H. Anothor oddity is that sonnets 127–152 are dedicated to a mysterious "dark lady." Theories abound as to whom this person might be and to whom those initials might belong, but the world may never know the true answer.

Shakespeare lived to the age of 52, not an unusual age for the seventeenth century. Both his poetic drama and dramatic poetry live on today as some of the most quoted and esteemed literature of all time.

Literature Online

Author Search For more about William Shakespeare, go to glencoe.com and enter QuickPass code GL57805u3.

Literature and Reading Preview

Connect to the Sonnet

To what would you compare someone you love or the emotion of love itself? Respond to this question in your journal.

Build Background

Throughout history, people in love have expressed their feelings by giving tokens of their affection, such as flowers, poems, jewelry, and locks of hair. In this sonnet, the speaker expresses his love by making his beloved the subject of the poem.

Set Purposes for Reading

Big Idea The Energy of the Everyday

As you read this poem, ask yourself, How does Shakespeare use everyday occurrences?

Literary Element Meter and Rhythm

Meter is the regular pattern of stressed and unstressed syllables that give a line of poetry a predictable rhythm, or pattern of beats. **Rhythm** gives poetry a musical quality, adds emphasis to certain words, and helps reinforce meaning. The basic unit of meter is the **foot**, consisting of one or two stressed syllables (marked ´) and/or one or more unstressed syllables (marked ˘). As you read, ask yourself, What is the pattern of stressed and unstressed syllables in each line?

Reading Strategy Analyze Form

Form is the organizing principle that shapes a work of literature. A poem's form is determined by several factors: the number and length of lines, the number of stanzas, the rhyme scheme, and the meter. This is a Shakespearean sonnet. As you read, ask yourself, What are the elements of this form?

....

Tip: Draw Conclusions About Structure Choose two lines from the poem and mark the meter with the appropriate stress symbols. Use the chart below as a guide. In the third row, draw a conclusion about how the structure of the poem affects its meaning. Use the blue highlighted question to help you.

Scansion	˘ / ˘ / ˘ / ˘ / ˘ /
Line	And often is his gold complexion dimmed
Conclusion	the author wants to emphasize the word "gold"

TEKS

For pages 464–468

10.3 Understand, make inferences and draw conclusions about the structure and elements of poetry and provide evidence from text to support understanding. Analyze the structure or prosody and graphic elements in poetry.

Vocabulary

temperate (tem´pər it) *adj.* calm and free from extremes of temperature; p. 466 *Most areas in the state of Virginia, which experiences few extreme temperatures, are considered temperate in climate.*

complexion (kəm plek´shən) *n.* general appearance, especially of the face; p. 466 *The young man's complexion had become sunburned after working outside all day.*

....

Tip: Analogies To complete an analogy, decide on the relationship represented by the first pair of words. Then apply that relationship to the second pair of words. For example, consider the following analogy:

temperate : extreme :: quiet : loud

The words *temperate* and *extreme* are antonyms as are the words *quiet* and *loud*.

Shall I Compare Thee to a Summer's Day?

William Shakespeare

The Great Oak, Moat Lawn with Rhododendrons & Azaleas—Morning, June, 2004. Charles Neal. Oil on canvas.

Shall I compare thee to a summer's day?
Thou art more lovely and more **temperate**.
Rough winds do shake the darling buds of May,
And summer's lease hath all too short a date.
5   Sometime too hot the eye of heaven shines,
And often is his gold **complexion** dimmed;
And every fair[1] from fair sometime declines,
By chance, or nature's changing course untrimmed:[2]
But thy eternal summer shall not fade
10   Nor lose possession of that fair thou ow'st,[3]
Nor shall Death brag thou wand'rest in his shade,
When in eternal lines to time thou grow'st.
    So long as men can breathe or eyes can see,
    So long lives this, and this gives life to thee.

---

1. *Fair,* in this context, is a synonym for *beauty.*
2. Here, *untrimmed* means "stripped of beauty."
3. *[thou ow'st]* Read this poetic phrase as "you own" or "you possess."

Meter and Rhythm *How would you describe the meter in the first four lines of the poem?*

Vocabulary

temperate (tem´pər it) *adj.* calm and free from extremes of temperature
complexion (kəm plek´ shən) *n.* general appearance, especially of the face

After You Read

Respond and Think Critically

1. **Connect to Personal Experience** Does this poem reflect your personal views on love? Explain.

2. **Interpret Speaker** Who might the speaker of this poem be? In your opinion, who is the speaker addressing? Use details from the poem to support your answers.

3. **Explain Comparisons** What two things is the speaker comparing? Which one does the speaker consider to be superior? How do you know this?

4. **Make Inferences About Author's Perspective** According to the speaker, why will the subject of the poem have a summer that is eternal? What might this tell you about the poet's reason for writing the poem?

5. **Draw Conclusions About Speaker** In your opinion, will the speaker's love ever fade? If the speaker's love fades, will the subject's beauty fade along with the speaker's love? Use details from the poem to support your answer.

6. **Evaluate Speaker** Critic Helen Vendler has said that Shakespeare's speakers have "a 'real voice' coming from a 'real mind' like our own." Do you agree with Vendler about the speaker in this sonnet? Why or why not?

7. **Big Idea** **Draw Conclusions About Meaning** This poem is generally considered a powerful and fervently romantic love poem. How does this poem also connect to nature and everyday occurrences?

Primary Visual Artifact

The Betrothed Couple

Lucas van Leyden (1494–1533) was a sixteenth century Dutch engraver and painter known for his ability to capture narrative in his painting. A precocious student, he completed many works while still in his teens. In his early paintings, he often did not fully articulate, or give clear definition to, all shapes and objects, in the composition. As he matured, Leyden began to merge narrative and composition, as in his masterpiece, the triptych *The Last Judgment*. Here, in *The Betrothed Couple*, Leyden shows a simpler scene, that of a man offering his beloved a ring as a symbol of his love.

Group Activity Discuss the following questions with your classmates.

The Betrothed Couple, 16th century AD. Lucas van Leyden. Musee des Beaux-Arts, Palais Rohan.

1. How realistic is the scene? Cite details that show whether the composition is fully articulated.

2. How does this expression of love compare with the speaker's expression of love in "Shall I Compare Thee to a Summer's Day?"?

Literary Element | Meter and Rhythm

The basic unit of **meter** is the foot. The length of a metrical line can be expressed in terms of the number of feet it contains. The meter in "Shall I Compare Thee to a Summer's Day?" is **iambic pentameter**, the most common meter in English poetry. In iambic pentameter, the predominant foot, or unit of rhythm, is the iamb. An iamb consists of an unstressed syllable followed by a stressed one. There are five feet in each line of iambic pentameter. Sometimes poets vary the rhythm to create certain effects.

8. Interpret Meter What is unusual about the meter in line 11? Explain.

9. Analyze Meter What effect does Shakespeare create by varying the meter and rhythm of this line? Support your answer with evidence from the poem.

Review: Personification

Personification is a figure of speech in which an animal, an object, a force of nature, or an idea is given human characteristics.

10. Partner Activity With a classmate, discuss the use of personification in "Shall I Compare Thee to a Summer's Day?" Work together to find three examples of personification. Why might Shakespeare have chosen to use personification? Use a chart like the one below to organize your ideas.

Example of Personification	Possible Reason
"Nor shall Death brag thou wand'rest in his shade"	Giving death human characteristics is a common, traditional device

LOG ON ▶ **Literature** Online

Selection Resources For Selection Quizzes, eFlashcards, and Reading-Writing Connection activities, go to glencoe.com and enter QuickPass code GL57805u3.

Reading Strategy | Analyze Form

A Shakespearean sonnet is a lyric poem of fourteen lines, following strict patterns of meter and rhyme. Review the chart you made on page 465 to draw conclusions about the structure of the poem.

11. How might the meter and rhythm be important to the meaning of the poem?

12. What is the rhyme scheme of this sonnet? How is this sonnet structured?

13. The last two lines of a sonnet often present a conclusion to the issues or questions discussed in the stanzas preceding them. What is the effect of the last two lines in the Shakespearean sonnet you have just read?

Vocabulary Practice

Practice with Analogies Choose the word that best completes each analogy. Use a dictionary if you need help.

1. temperate : moderate :: loyal :

   a. faithful   **b.** treacherous   **c.** respectful

2. complexion : appearance :: attitude :

   a. composition   **b.** behavior   **c.** visage

Academic Vocabulary

*In writing sonnets, poets can't make **arbitrary** decisions; they must follow rules of the form.*

Arbitrary is an academic word. More familiar words that are similar in meaning include *chance, inconsistent*, and *random*. To study this word further, answer these questions: What **arbitrary** choices have you made lately? What made your choices arbitrary?

For more on academic vocabulary, see pages 36–37 and R92–R94.

Respond Through Writing

Sonnet

TEKS

10.14.B Write a poem using a variety of poetic techniques (e.g., structural elements, figurative language) and a variety of poetic forms (e.g., sonnets).

Develop a Comparison Write a sonnet about a beloved friend or family member in which you create a metaphor to compare him or her to an object, a place, or an idea. Use Shakespeare's sonnet "Shall I Compare Thee to a Summer's Day?" as a model for writing. To develop the comparison, relate distinct characteristics of the subject to specific details found in the object or idea of comparison.

Purpose and Audience The purpose is to express your feelings about a particular person. The audience is the subject of the poem and others who may also appreciate the subject.

Plan Create a chart like the one below showing all the traits you admire in your subject. Then add anything else that might share or resemble those traits. To make your sonnet more interesting, find something unexpected as the source for your comparison. Finally, narrow the list to three specific shared traits that you will use to develop your metaphor.

Traits I Admire About Dad	Things That Share Traits
always gives good advice	advice columnist

Draft Sonnets have specific structural elements: they must have fourteen lines, and they require a specific rhyme scheme and meter. As you develop your traits and details, keep in mind the rhyme scheme you will use for your sonnet: *abab cdcd efef gg.* One way to draft the sonnet is to focus each quatrain on one specific comparison. In the final couplet, present a conclusion you can draw based on the metaphor you have developed. If you wish, write your sonnet using iambic pentameter.

Revise Exchange your sonnet with a partner. Read each other's sonnet to check the rhyme schemes and the clarity of the comparison. You should be able to describe the subject and explain the metaphor after reading the poem.

Edit Edit your poem, correcting any errors in grammar, spelling, and punctuation. Use the Grammar Tip in the side column to help you use gerunds.

Grammar Tip

Gerunds

A **gerund** is a verb form that ends in *-ing* and is used as a noun. A gerund may function as a subject, the object of a verb, or the object of a preposition.

Using gerunds in your sonnet can help address problems with your rhyme scheme and meter.

Original:
She walked in with the grace of a gazelle

And made all smile it was easy to tell

Revised using a gerund:
Walking with the grace of a gazelle was her style

None who saw her could help but smile

Before You Read

Reapers

Meet **Jean Toomer**
(1894–1967)

Jean Toomer envisioned a new American identity, forged from many races. "Here in America we are in the process of forming a new race," Toomer once said. "I had seen the divisions, the separatisms and antagonisms . . . [yet] a new type of man was arising in this country—not European, not African, not Asiatic—but American. And in this American I saw the divisions mended, the differences reconciled."

A Divided Identity Born in Washington, D.C., Toomer spent most of his childhood living in white neighborhoods while attending African American schools. As a child, he lived with his mother and his grandfather, who was the first governor of African American descent in U.S. history. Even as a child, Toomer was deeply aware of racial divisions in his society. Toomer had both European and African ancestry, and strangers often misidentified him as belonging to one race or another. By the time he graduated from high school, Toomer began to deny any racial identity, instead preferring to classify himself as an American.

> "We learn the rope of life by untying its knots."
>
> —Jean Toomer

After high school, Toomer completed courses in a variety of subjects at several universities, but he never received a degree. Instead, he pursued his literary studies on his own. He attended lectures and read the works of William Shakespeare and Leo Tolstoy. Between 1918 and 1923, Toomer wrote a number of short stories, poems, and plays. He drew his inspiration from the poetry of Walt Whitman and Charles Baudelaire.

Finding His Heritage In 1921 Toomer took a teaching job in Georgia, which turned out to be a life-changing experience. Toomer viewed his time in Georgia as a return to his African American roots. As a result, Toomer wrote *Cane,* an experimental novel combining short stories, poems, and a play. The book, published in 1923, inspired authors of the Harlem Renaissance, a great flourishing of African American arts from the 1920s through the 1940s.

Toomer's Legacy Despite his early literary success, Toomer's writing was nearly forgotten after his death. Gradually, the significance of his work gained recognition. In 1969 critic Robert Bone wrote: "It was Jean Toomer's genius to discover and to celebrate the qualities of 'soul,' and thereby to inaugurate the Negro Renaissance. For this alone he will be enshrined as a major figure in the canon of American Negro letters."

LOG ON ▶ **Literature** Online

Author Search For more about Jean Toomer, go to glencoe.com and enter QuickPass code GL57805u3.

Literature and Reading Preview

Connect to the Poem

Do you think machines and technology have diminished the need for human contact? In a journal entry, write your views.

Build Background

Reaping by hand is exhausting work: the same motion is repeated hundreds and thousands of times, and the work is performed in a stooped-over position.

Set Purposes for Reading

Big Idea **The Energy of the Everyday**

As you read "Reapers," ask yourself, How does Toomer endow a seemingly ordinary event with new energy and emotion?

Literary Element **Rhyme and Rhyme Scheme**

Rhyme is the repetition of similar or identical sounds at the ends of words that appear close to each other. **Rhyme scheme** is the pattern that end rhymes form in a stanza or in a poem. As you read, ask yourself, What is the effect of the rhyme and the rhyme scheme in Toomer's poem?

Reading Strategy **Analyze Rhythm and Meter**

Rhythm is the pattern of beats created by the arrangement of stressed and unstressed syllables. **Meter** is a regular pattern of those syllables. When you **analyze rhythm and meter,** you study how poets use them to enhance the meaning of their work or to give it a musical quality. As you read, ask yourself, How does Toomer's use of rhythm and meter create meaning?

....

Tip: Analyze Meter Listen to the "beat" of the poem and analyze how the rhythm and meter enhance the images of the reapers. Use a graphic organizer like the one below to list images you visualize and how they affect your understanding.

> Line: "And start their silent swinging, one by one."

⬇

> Images from meter and rhyme: regular motion of people working in the fields; people working in a synchronized way

⬇

> Effect on mood: somber, tedious, repetitive—makes me think of tiring and dull work

TEKS

For pages 470–473

10.3 Analyze the structure or prosody (e.g. meter, rhyme scheme) and graphic elements in poetry.

Vocabulary

reaper (rē′pər) *n.* machine or person that cuts grain for harvesting; p. 472 *The reaper worked in the field all day.*

scythe (sīth) *n.* cutting implement made of a long, curved single-edged blade; p. 472 *The man used a scythe to cut through the long wheat in the field.*

hone (hōn) *n.* whetstone or similar tool used to sharpen knives and other types of blades; p. 472 *He used a hone to make the knives razor-sharp.*

Harvesting, 19th century. Adolphe Joseph Thomas Monticelli. Oil on canvas, 121 x 92.5 cm. Ciurlionis State Art Museum. Kaunas, Lithuania.

Reapers

Jean Toomer

Black **reapers** with the sound of steel on stones
Are sharpening **scythes**. I see them place the **hones**
In their hip-pockets as a thing that's done,
And start their silent swinging, one by one.
5 Black horses drive a mower through the weeds,
And there, a field rat, startled, squealing bleeds.
His belly close to ground. I see the blade,
Blood-stained, continue cutting weeds and shade.

The Energy of the Everyday *How do lines 7–8 add meaning to an otherwise ordinary object?*

Vocabulary

reaper (rē´pər) *n.* machine or person that cuts grain for harvesting
scythe (sīth) *n.* cutting implement made of a long, curved single-edged blade
hone (hōn) *n.* whetstone or similar tool used to sharpen knives and other types of blades

After You Read

Respond and Think Critically

1. **Connect to Personal Experience** What image or description in the poem did you find most striking? Explain.

2. **Summarize Attitudes** Describe in your own words what the reapers do. What attitude do the reapers seem to have toward their work? [OER]

3. **Make Inferences About Events** What happens to the field rat in the poem? Why does Toomer include this incident?

4. **Make Inferences About Details** What connections do you see between the reapers and the horses? Why do you think Toomer links the reapers and the horses?

5. **Analyze Alliteration** Alliteration is the repetition of consonant sounds at the beginnings of nonrhyming words. Find at least two examples of alliteration in the poem. How do these examples affect your reading of the poem?

6. **Big Idea** **Draw Conclusions About Imagery** How does the imagery in "Reapers" add to the reader's sensory experience of "the everyday"? Support your response.

Literary Element · Rhyme and Rhyme Scheme

Toomer uses a particular **rhyme** and **rhyme scheme** to create a certain effect in "Reapers."

7. **Identify Rhyme** What kind of rhyme does "Reapers" have? Explain.

8. **Analyze Rhyme Scheme** What is the rhyme scheme of "Reapers"? How does it impact the meaning of the poem? Support your answer.

Reading Strategy · Analyze Meter and Rhythm

Refer to the graphic organizer you made on page 471 to help you answer the following questions.

9. How are the rhythm and meter important to the meaning of the poem? Support your answer with text evidence.

10. How does the rhythm of this poem reflect its content? If the poem did not have this kind of rhythm, would it have the same impact? Explain.

LOG ON ▶ **Literature** Online

Selection Resources For Selection Quizzes, eFlashcards, and Reading-Writing Connection activities, go to glencoe.com and enter QuickPass code GL57805u3.

Vocabulary Practice

Practice with Word Origins Studying the etymology, or origin and history, of a word can help you better understand and explore its meaning. Create a word map like the one below for each of these vocabulary words from the poem.

reaper   scythe   hone

EXAMPLE:
dictum

Definition an important statement, announcement, or judgment
Etymology Latin *dicere* means "say"
Sample sentence The king issued a dictum that applied to all his subjects.

Writing

Write a Movie Scene Write directions for filming the events presented in "Reapers." First, decide how to divide the events into a series of individual camera shots. You may choose to divide the events by line or by couplet. Then, for each shot, describe what the camera should show, how close the camera should be to the activity, how the camera should move, and what sounds viewers should hear.

Ode to My Socks

Meet **Pablo Neruda**
(1904–1973)

Equally enchanted with a pair of socks, an artichoke, or olive oil, the poet Pablo Neruda (pä´blō nā roo´dä) could transform an ordinary object into a rich treasure. He was a master of the ode, a poem that praises its subject matter, and collected these poems in a book called *Elemental Odes.* These odes are full of celebration for the objects and circumstances of everyday life, a reflection of Neruda's desire to write for the common person rather than for an elite audience.

Neruda was born Neftalí Ricardo Reyes Basoalto in rural Chile. His father was a railway worker, and his mother was a teacher. Neruda began writing poetry at the age of ten and published his first book of poems at age nineteen, under the pen name Pablo Neruda. He later legally changed his name.

> "*I could not live separated from nature.*"
>
> —Pablo Neruda

A Life of Poetry and Passion His second book, *Twenty Love Poems and a Song of Despair,* was an instant success, and Neruda was well on his way to becoming a world-renowned poet. However, despite his early success with poetry, he did not neglect his other passions, namely his interest in politics and social causes. Shortly after the publication of his first two books, he went to Asia as Chile's honorary consul. This was the first of many positions in his consular career, which would take him to Spain, France, and Mexico.

Love, Nature, and Social Concerns Neruda is widely known for his passionate and poignant expressions of love. However, his works cover a broad range of subjects. Neruda wanted his poetry to be accessible; he did not believe in poetry as an elitist art form. His major work, *Canto General,* was a book of 340 poems that celebrated the history of Latin America from ancient times. He was equally passionate about social justice for the people of his native Chile and was involved in political causes there throughout his life.

Chile awarded Neruda the National Literature Prize in 1945. In 1971 he received the Nobel Prize in Literature "for poetry that with the action of an elemental force brings alive a continent's destiny and dreams."

 Literature Online

Author Search For more about Pablo Neruda, go to glencoe.com and enter QuickPass code GL57805u3.

Literature and Reading Preview

Connect to the Poem

Of your prized possessions, which is most valuable to you? Why? Freewrite for a few minutes about this question.

Build Background

An **ode** is a long, serious lyric poem that is elevated in tone and style. Neruda's odes celebrate their subjects, but they do not use the lofty style characterized by traditional odes. Rather, they sing the praises of the ordinary and the essential.

Set Purposes for Reading

Big Idea The Energy of the Everyday

As you read, ask yourself, How does Neruda's reverence for his socks capture the magic and energy of the everyday?

Literary Element Free Verse

Free verse is poetry without a fixed pattern of rhyme, meter, line length, or stanza arrangement. As you read, ask yourself, How does the unrestrained feel of the free verse form affect the way in which Neruda communicates his ideas?

Reading Strategy Monitor Comprehension

Monitoring comprehension by paraphrasing and questioning can help you better understand a poem's figurative language, symbolism, and overall meaning. As you read, ask yourself, Am I doing all I can to understand the poem?

....

Tip: Track Your Understanding After reading the poem once, revisit each stanza individually. As you complete a stanza, paraphrase it and ask yourself questions about its meaning. Use a chart like the one below to monitor your comprehension.

Stanza	Maru Mori brought me / a pair / of socks / which she knitted herself / with her sheepherder's hands, / two socks as soft / as rabbits.
Paraphrase	A loved one or friend knitted, with her own hands, a delicate pair of socks.
Question	Why has the author described Maru Mori's hands as "sheepherder's hands"?
Answer	Sheepherders, by trade, protect and care for flocks of sheep. This image is a metaphor for his friend's loving ways.

TEKS

For pages 474–480

RC-10.A Reflect on understanding to monitor comprehension (e.g., asking questions).

Vocabulary

immense (i mens´) *adj.* immeasurable; vast; huge; p. 477 *I felt immense pleasure in presenting the student with the scholarship.*

sacred (sā´krid) *adj.* worthy of reverence; p. 478 *The archaeologist eagerly uncovered the sacred texts.*

remorse (ri môrs´) *n.* distress stemming from the guilt of past wrongs; p. 478 *The sobbing prisoner showed remorse in court.*

....

Tip: Synonyms Even though synonyms may have similar denotations, they may still have slightly different meanings and connotations.

Personage Lancant Une Pierre a un Oiseau, 1926. Joan Miró. © ARS, NY.

Ode to My Socks

Pablo Neruda

Translated by Robert Bly

Maru Mori brought me
a pair
of socks
which she knitted herself
5   with her sheepherder's hands,
two socks as soft
as rabbits.
I slipped my feet
into them

10   as though into
two
cases
knitted
with threads of
15   twilight
and sheepskin.

Violent socks,
my feet were
two fish made
20   of wool,
two long sharks
sea-blue, shot
through
by one golden thread,
25   two **immense** blackbirds,
two cannons:
my feet
were honored
in this way
30   by
these
heavenly
socks.
They were
35   so handsome
for the first time
my feet seemed to me
unacceptable
like two decrepit
40   firemen, firemen
unworthy
of that woven
fire,
of those glowing
45   socks.

Nevertheless
I resisted
the sharp temptation
to save them somewhere

Monitor Comprehension *How might you paraphrase this line?*

Vocabulary

immense (i mens´) *adj.* immeasurable; vast; huge

50   as schoolboys
    keep
    fireflies,
    as learned men
    collect
55   **sacred** texts,
    I resisted
    the mad impulse
    to put them
    into a golden
60   cage
    and each day give them
    birdseed
    and pieces of pink melon.
    Like explorers
65   in the jungle who hand
    over the very rare
    green deer
    to the spit[1]
    and eat it
70   with **remorse**,
    I stretched out
    my feet
    and pulled on
    the magnificent
75   socks
    and then my shoes.

    The moral
    of my ode is this:
    beauty is twice
80   beauty
    and what is good is doubly
    good
    when it is a matter of two socks
    made of wool
85   in winter.

---

1. A *spit* is a rod on which meat is roasted.

The Energy of the Everyday *What kind of impulse is the author trying to convey here?*

Free Verse *What elements of free verse does the writer use here?*

Vocabulary

sacred (sā′krid) *adj.* worthy of reverence
remorse (ri môrs′) *n.* distress stemming from the guilt of past wrongs

After You Read

Respond and Think Critically

1. **Connect to Personal Experience** How has Neruda's tribute to socks affected your feelings about material possessions?

2. **Interpret Imagery** What does the speaker call his feet? Why might the speaker choose to represent feet in so many ways?

3. **Analyze Poetic Techniques** How does Neruda express the meaningfulness of the socks? Support your response with evidence from the poem.

4. **Analyze Poetic Form** Explain how Neruda has veered from the traditional form of an ode. Why do you think Neruda chose to break with tradition in writing this ode?

5. **Make Inferences About Structure** How might Neruda's decision to summarize his ode in the last stanza affect the reader's interpretation of its ideas? Explain.

6. **Big Idea** **Draw Conclusions About Subject Matter** Neruda is known for his praise of the ordinary. What examples best illustrate this characteristic in "Ode to My Socks"? Explain.

7. **Evaluate Figurative Language** Many of Neruda's odes focus on simple subjects found in nature. Although socks are not "found in nature," how does Neruda use figurative language to connect them to the natural world in the poem? Is this technique effective? Explain.

You're the Critic

Ode to the Elementary

Pablo Neruda's odes differ greatly from the traditional form. Although some traditionalists might prefer the conventional form, most readers and critics respond favorably to Neruda's innovative approach. Read the excerpt of literary criticism below and answer the questions that follow.

> "The 'Elemental Odes'. . . were like nothing else people had seen. With them, Neruda hoped to reach a wider audience than he already had, and his hope was realized. The 'Odes' gained immediate and universal praise. They are about the things of everyday life: a lemon, a dead carob tree, a boy with a hare, a stamp album. And they were read by people who had never before paid attention to poetry. Written in very short lines, some as short as a single word, the 'Odes' tumble *effortlessly down the page in chainlike sentences. Everything is seen in its best light, everything has value, everything deserves to be the subject of a poem."*
>
> —Mark Strand, the *New Yorker*

1. How do you think someone who prefers traditional odes, which have an elevated style, would respond to Strand's comments?

2. Which opinion do you agree with more: that Neruda created a valuable and accessible new kind of ode, or that his modifications degraded the form? Support your opinion.

The Magician, 1992. Maria Angelica Ruiz-Tagle. Oil on canvas, 130 x 97 cm.

Literary Element | Free Verse

Free verse allows the poet to arrange lines and stanzas according to sound, importance of ideas, appearances, or any other criteria. Neruda's free verse has been compared to "a river of print flowing down the page."

8. Draw Conclusions About Form Which lines in "Ode to My Socks" would you say are the most unconventional? Explain.

9. Analyze Line Length How do the varied line lengths affect the recitation of the poem? Review the pink highlighted text and question on page 478 to help you.

Review: Structure

As you learned on page 452, **structure** is the distinct order or arrangement writers use to present ideas. Ideas may be presented in chronological order, according to relevancy, in order of importance, or in some other manner.

10. Group Activity With a group of two or three classmates, draw conclusions about the structure of "Ode to My Socks." Each student should analyze one stanza. Once all have examined a stanza, record your group's findings in a chart like the one below. Use the left column to indicate the stanza number. Use the center column to describe the stanza's structure. Use the right column to draw a conclusion.

Stanza	Structure	Conclusion
Stanza 1	This stanza is ordered sequentially. First Maru Mori brings the socks, then the speaker puts them on.	the speaker explains how he got the socks.

LOG ON ▶ **Literature** Online

Selection Resources For Selection Quizzes, eFlashcards, and Reading-Writing Connection activities, go to glencoe.com and enter QuickPass code GL57805u3.

Reading Strategy | Monitor Comprehension

Refer to the chart you made on page 475 as you answer the following questions.

11. Write a paraphrase of "Ode to My Socks." What does writing a paraphrase help you understand about the poem?

12. What do you think is the most important aspect of the poem—its subject matter, tone, style, or something else? Explain.

Vocabulary Practice

Practice with Synonyms A **synonym** is a word that has the same or nearly the same meaning as another word. With a partner, match each bold-faced vocabulary word below with its synonym. Use a thesaurus or dictionary to check your answers. You will not use all the answer choices.

1. immense
2. sacred
3. remorse

a. dismayed
b. holy
c. regret
d. despair
e. vast

Academic Vocabulary

*An everyday object like a sock is not **compatible** with some people's idea of beauty.*

Compatible is an academic word. In more casual conversation, a person might say that a certain couple is **compatible**. To study this word further, fill out the graphic organizer below.

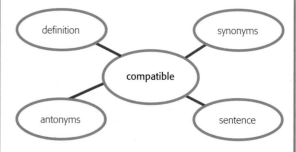

For more on academic vocabulary, see pages 36–37 and R92–R94.

Respond Through Writing

Research Report

Investigate Poetry Poetry is a form of personal expression, but it can also express social, political, and cultural ideas. This type of commentary is achieved through the poem's content and its tone. Research how tone in poetry can express social, political, or cultural attitudes or dissent and present your findings in a research report of at least 1,500 words.

Purpose and Audience Your purpose is to synthesize research into a written report. Your audience is made up of your teacher and classmates.

Plan Reread Neruda's biography on page 474. Consider what you learn about his political attitudes. Think about who and what is honored in "Ode to My Socks." Then find additional poems by Neruda and other poets whose tone expresses social, political, or cultural attitudes or dissent. Synthesize your research and develop a thesis based on the tone you hear in Neruda's work as well as the work of two other poets. Plan paragraphs supporting your thesis.

Draft As you draft, include evidence from the poems to support your thesis. Explain how quotations from the poems express cultural, social, or political attitudes or dissent. Provide an analysis for your audience that reflects a logical progression of ideas and a clearly stated point of view. Integrate and comment on literary criticism from other writers. Add graphics or illustrations to help explain concepts where appropriate.

Revise Use the rubric below to evaluate the quality of your research report. Then revise to improve your essay.

Sources: Uses a variety of reliable sources; uses a style manual to document sources	Evidence: Body paragraphs accurately convey and evaluate information from a variety of sources
Thesis/Controlling Idea: Thesis makes a clear, interesting, focused claim about tone in specified poems	Audience: Anticipates and addresses any potential misunderstandings; provides all necessary background

Revise for clarity by rewriting any potentially misleading information.

Edit Edit your paper, correcting any errors in spelling, grammar, and punctuation. Use the Grammar Tip in the side column to help you use the subjunctive mood correctly. Use a style manual to format your paper.

 TEKS

10.23.A–E Organize and present ideas and information according to the purpose of the research and audience. Synthesize the research into a written or an oral presentation that marshals evidence; provides an analysis for the audience; uses graphics and illustrations; uses a variety of evaluative tools; and uses a style manual.

> **Grammar Tip**

Subjunctive Mood

You can use the subjunctive mood to express doubts, wishes, and possibilities. To form the subjunctive mood, verbs such as *prefer, wish,* or *recommend* are often followed by the verb "to be" in the subjunctive mood—*be* in the present tense.

He prefers that the socks be soft.

It is important to remember that in the subjunctive mood, the past tense of the verb "to be" is *were.*

I wish that pair of socks were mine.

The subjunctive mood is also commonly used after "if" clauses.

If Maru Mori were making me socks, I would thank her.

Before You Read

A Storm in the Mountains

Meet **Aleksandr Solzhenitsyn**
(1918–2008)

I n a life rendered chaotic—personally, professionally, and politically—Aleksandr Isayevich Solzhenitsyn created order through his writing.

Solzhenitsyn served in the Russian army during World War II. However, in 1945 he was arrested and charged with treason for writing a personal letter in which he criticized Soviet ruler Joseph Stalin. The government sentenced Solzhenitsyn, without a fair trial, to eight years in a camp for political prisoners.

> "Own only what you can carry with you; know language, know countries, know people. Let your memory be your travel bag."
>
> —Aleksandr Solzhenitsyn

During his imprisonment, Solzhenitsyn worked as a mathematician and physicist. He was later transferred to a forced-labor camp, where he was diagnosed with intestinal cancer. It was not treated until he was near death. Eventually, he was sent to Khazakhstan for treatment and survived. Finally, in 1956, he was freed from exile.

Memory as Inspiration Throughout his entire ordeal, Solzhenitsyn wrote in secret. The experiences of his forced imprisonment and illness served as the basis for his writing. Eventually, Solzhenitsyn decided to take his secret writing public. He published his first work, *One Day in the Life of Ivan Denisovich*, a widely read tale of

an "everyman" dealing with the horrors of a single day in a forced labor camp. The book sparked political attention and activity in both the Soviet Union and abroad.

The Line That Shifts Awarded the Nobel Prize for Literature in 1970, Solzhenitsyn did not accept his prize in person, fearing that the Soviet government would not allow him to reenter the country.

The Gulag Archipelago (1973)—a catalogue of Soviet abuses detailing the harsh labor camps called the "Gulag"—established Solzhenitsyn as a chronicler of modern Russian history. The controversial publication led to another exile in 1974. Solzhenitsyn lived in the United States until *glasnost*—a political openness that allowed for criticism of the government—brought Russians wider accessibility to his writing, prompting a return to his homeland. He died near Moscow in 2008.

Literature and Reading Preview

Connect to the Poem

Recall a time when you witnessed severe weather. How did it make you feel? Describe the experience to a partner.

Build Background

The former Soviet Union, also known as the Union of Soviet Socialist Republics, or U.S.S.R., was vast in size, and its climate varied greatly. Extreme weather was common; only winter and summer existed as distinct seasons. The milder temperatures of spring and fall were typically short-lived points during periods of rapid weather change.

Set Purposes for Reading

Big Idea The Energy of the Everyday

As you read, ask yourself, What descriptive language does Solzhenitsyn use to describe an event as common as a storm?

Literary Element Prose Poetry

An alternative to verse form, **prose poetry** avoids line breaks and uses sentence and paragraph form instead. Even though prose poetry is printed as a short prose compostition, it uses elements of poetry, such as rhythm, internal rhyme, figures of speech, assonance and consonance, symbolism, and imagery. As you read, ask yourself, How does this prose poem use imagery to convey ideas and emotions?

Reading Strategy Visualize

When you **visualize,** you use words and sensory images to create a mental picture. Authors often use imagery to help readers experience the environment or mood of a poem or story. Visualizing is not limited to visual images; it encompasses perceptions from all five senses. As you read the poem, ask yourself, How can I create a mental representation of the sensations described?

·······

Tip: Create a List Use a chart like the one below to list words or phrases from the poem that appeal to your senses. You may want to draw a quick sketch of visual images that appeal to you.

Words/Expressions	Sense
"Everything was black—no peaks, no valleys, no horizon to be seen."	Sight

TEKS

For pages 482–486

RC-10.A Reflect on understanding to monitor comprehension (e.g., creating sensory images).

Vocabulary

searing (sēr′ing) *adj.* extremely hot or bright; p. 485 *The searing sunlight woke me up before my alarm clock went off.*

chaos (kā′os) *n.* a state of disorder and confusion; p. 485 *After the tornado hit, the town was filled with chaos.*

gorge (gôrj) *n.* the passageway between two higher land areas, such as a narrow valley; p. 485 *The Grand Canyon is one of the United States' most famous gorges.*

serpentine (sur′pən tēn′) *adj.* snake-like; twisting; winding; p. 485 *He had to pay attention as he drove on the serpentine mountain road.*

primal (prī′məl) *adj.* a basic, original state of being; p. 485 *One primal instinct is survival.*

·······

Tip: Analogies Comparing two analogies can help you infer word meaning. Determine the relationship of the first pair of words. Apply that relationship when selecting a word for the second pair.

Before the Separation, 1999. Brenda Chrystie.

A Storm in the Mountains

Aleksandr Solzhenitsyn
Translated by Michael Glenny

It caught us one pitch-black night at the foot of the pass. We crawled out of our tents and ran for shelter as it came towards us over the ridge.

Everything was black—no peaks, no valleys, no horizon to be seen, only the **searing** flashes of lightning separating darkness from light, and the gigantic peaks of Belaya-Kaya and Djuguturlyuchat[1] looming up out of the night. The huge black pine trees around us seemed as high as the mountains themselves. For a split second we felt ourselves on terra firma;[2] then once more everything would be plunged into darkness and **chaos**.

The lightning moved on, brilliant light alternating with pitch blackness, flashing white, then pink, then violet, the mountains and pines always springing back in the same place, the hugeness filling us with awe;[3] yet when they disappeared, we could not believe that they had ever existed.

The voice of the thunder filled the **gorge**, drowning the ceaseless roar of the rivers. Like the arrows of Sabaoth,[4] the lightning flashes rained down on the peaks, then split up into **serpentine** streams as though bursting into spray against the rock face, or striking and then shattering like a living thing.

As for us, we forgot to be afraid of the lightning, the thunder, and the downpour, just as a droplet in the ocean has no fear of a hurricane. Insignificant yet grateful, we became part of this world—a **primal** world in creation before our eyes.

---

1. *Belaya-Kaya* and *Djuguturlyuchat* are mountains in the western Caucasus mountain range in Russia.
2. *Terra firma* means "solid ground."
3. *Awe* is a feeling of wonderment or amazement.
4. *Sabaoth*, a biblical reference, means "armies."

Visualize *How does Solzhenitsyn's imagery help you visualize, or see in your mind's eye, the setting of the poem?*

Vocabulary

searing (sēr´ing) *adj.* extremely hot or bright
chaos (kā´os) *n.* a state of disorder and confusion
gorge (gôrj) *n.* the passageway between two higher land areas, such as a narrow valley
serpentine (sur´pən tēn´) *adj.* snake-like; twisting; winding
primal (prī´məl) *adj.* a basic, original state of being

After You Read

Respond and Think Critically

1. **Connect to Personal Experience** What example of imagery in the poem did you find most striking? Explain.

2. **Describe Setting** Where is the speaker? Describe the setting of the poem. Cite details from the poem in your answer.

3. **Describe Events** How would you describe the main event of the poem? What do you learn about this event? Cite details from the poem in your answer.

4. **Analyze Diction** How does the speaker describe the lightning in the fourth paragraph? What is the effect of the author's choice of words here? Explain.

5. **Analyze Speaker** How do the speaker's feelings about the storm shift over the course of the poem? Support your response.

6. **Big Idea** **Draw Conclusions About the Author** How does the speaker feel about nature and about everyday occurences such as storms? What does the poem reveal about the author's powers of observations? Explain.

7. **Make Inferences About Cultural Context** Solzhenitsyn suffered great injustice under a repressive Russian dictatorship, yet he always felt deeply connected to his country. How might this poem reflect Solzhenitsyn's feelings for Russia? Explain.

Literary Element Prose Poetry

Unlike poetry that uses stanzas, **prose poetry** follows a prose style, but maintains rhythm.

8. **Analyze Style** Choose a sentence from the poem and explain how it blends poetic elements with a prose format.

9. **Analyze Prose Poetry** Where in the prose poem does the writing most resemble poetry? Support your answer with text evidence.

Reading Strategy Visualize

Visualizing allows the reader to connect to the poem and understand its tone and meaning.

10. Which images help you understand the poem? Use the chart on page 483 and the blue high-lighted question to help you.

11. Which details do you think best create sensory images in the poem? Explain.

LOG ON ▶ **Literature** Online

Selection Resources For Selection Quizzes, eFlashcards, and Reading-Writing Connection activities, go to glencoe.com and enter QuickPass code GL57805u3.

Vocabulary Practice

Practice with Analogies Choose the word that best completes each analogy.

1. searing : hot :: freezing :
   a. cold   **b.** temperature   **c.** desert

2. chaotic : disorder :: boisterous :
   a. male   **b.** silence   **c.** party

3. gorge : land :: channel :
   a. television   **b.** sea   **c.** forest

4. serpentine : twisting :: circuitous :
   a. circus-like   **b.** circular   **c.** capable

5. primal : original :: confident :
   a. selfish   **b.** adult   **c.** self-assured

Writing

Write a Prose Poem Think about encounters you have had with the natural world. Choose one and write a prose poem about it, using "A Storm in the Mountains" as a model. Be sure to include sensory details to convey the mood of the experience and help readers clearly visualize the images you create.

Grammar Workshop

Pronoun-Antecedent Agreement

TEKS

10.17.A.iii Use and understand the function of the following parts of speech in the context of reading, writing, and speaking: reciprocal pronouns (e.g., each other).

Literature Connection In this line from "A Storm in the Mountains," Aleksandr Solzhenitsyn describes the speaker's experience in the first person plural.

> *"We crawled out of our tents and ran for shelter as it came towards us over the ridge."*

The quotation is an example of correct **pronoun reference** because the pronouns *our* and *us* are the same person (first, second, and third), number, and gender (masculine, feminine, neuter) as the subject of the sentence, *we*. **Reciprocal pronouns** can be used to simplify sentences. For example, instead of writing "I said hello to Kate and she said hello to me," one can write "Kate and I said hello to **each other**" (reciprocal pronoun). Incorrect pronoun reference is the use of a pronoun that has an unclear antecedent or does not agree with its antecedent.

Examples

Problem A pronoun has an unclear antecedent in a sentence.

The prisoner gave his cellmate his book.
They sent Solzhenitsyn to a prison camp.

Solution Replace the pronoun with an appropriate noun.

The prisoner gave his cellmate the cellmate's book.
The government sent Solzhenitsyn to a prison camp.

Problem A pronoun does not agree with its antecedent.

A writer must choose what they include in their work.

Solution Replace the pronoun with one that agrees with its antecedent or reword the sentence.

A writer must choose what to include in his or her work.
Writers must choose what they include in their work.

Pronoun Reference

Correct **pronoun reference** is agreement of a pronoun with its antecedent in person, number, and gender.

Tip

To identify incorrect pronoun references on a test, find the antecedent for each pronoun. If there is not one, replace the pronoun with an appropriate noun. If the antecedent differs in person, gender, and/or number from the pronoun, change the pronoun to agree with the antecedent.

Language Handbook

For more on pronoun reference, see the Language Handbook, pp. R57–R58.

Practice Rewrite the following sentences to correct any incorrect pronoun references.

1. Aleksandr Solzhenitsyn had to work as a mathematician because one had little money.

2. Solzhenitsyn was born in Russia during a time when you had to censor their ideas.

3. Solzhenitsyn and his public had a regard for itself.

LOG ON ▶ **Literature** Online

Grammar For more grammar practice, go to glencoe.com and enter QuickPass code GL57805u3.

The Print of the Paw, To An Aged Bear

Meet **N. Scott Momaday**

(born 1934)

Poet and novelist Navarre Scott Momaday absorbed the storytelling culture of American Indians throughout his youth. His father, a Kiowa, was a talented painter. His mother, of mixed English and Cherokee heritage, wrote children's books. Both of his parents taught literature and art on reservations throughout the southwestern United States.

A Teaching Heritage As they moved among the Apache, the Navajo, and the Pueblo, Momaday developed his creative writing skills. His parents encouraged his love of classic literature as much as they cultivated his love of traditional Native American storytelling. After earning a degree from the University of New Mexico, Momaday followed in his parents' footsteps by teaching on the Jicarilla Apache Reservation in New Mexico.

> *"If you are really compelled to write, that's where happiness is."*
> —*N. Scott Momaday*

Stanford University later offered Momaday a poetry fellowship to its creative writing program. He spent the next five years studying under poet and critic Yvor Winters. In 1963, Momaday left Stanford with a PhD in English literature.

Next, he moved to Santa Barbara to take a teaching position at the University of California. Over the next five years, he channeled his ideas of conflict between nature and the modern world into his first novel, *House Made of Dawn.*

Lifestyles in Conflict Still his best-known work, *House Made of Dawn* tells the story of a conflicted Army veteran, Abel, who returns to his Kiowa pueblo. Having seen the world and all of its technological wonders, Abel struggles with his people's traditions and lifestyle.

House Made of Dawn earned Momaday a Pulitzer Prize in Fiction in 1969. Few authors have earned this major recognition; fewer still have earned it for their debut work. The book revitalized interest in the plight and the heritage of Native Americans. Soon after, Momaday moved to Berkeley, California. He used the prestige of his award to help launch courses in Native American oral tradition.

Rekindling Tradition Momaday spent the next three decades of his career teaching that course at several prestigious universities. Meanwhile, he published books that showcase the American Indian style of storytelling.

LOG ON ▶ **Literature** Online

Author Search For more about N. Scott Momaday, go to glencoe.com and enter QuickPass code GL57805u3.

Literature and Reading Preview

Connect to the Poems

How would you react if you came across the paw print of a bear? Freewrite for a few minutes about this question.

Build Background

Native American culture holds bears and other animals in high regard. Many Native American tribes honor animals through various rituals. Kinship between animals and people is acknowledged.

Set Purposes for Reading

Big Idea The Energy of the Everyday

As you read these poems, ask yourself, How does the poet link animals, humans, and the natural world?

Literary Element Speaker

The **speaker** is the voice speaking in a poem, much like the narrator in a work of prose. The speaker may be the poet or a character created to represent a specific point of view. As you read, ask yourself, Who is the speaker in each of the poems?

Reading Strategy Apply Background Knowledge

When you **apply background knowledge,** you use what you already know to help you make sense of a text and appreciate the perspective, or attitude, communicated by the text. By using what you already know about the author, the subject matter, and life, you deepen your understanding of opinions or viewpoints expressed. As you read, ask yourself, Considering what I already know, what ideas about life are suggested by these poems?

Tip: Understand Perspective As you read, notice words and phrases used to describe bears and bear prints. Record them in a chart like the one below. Also record your inferences about the perspective suggested by the words and phrases.

Descriptive Details	Perspective Suggested by Details
"the great beast moved with meticulous grace"	The author comes from a culture that sees a kinship between people and animals. This detail suggests admiration for the bear.

TEKS

For pages 488–493

10.3 Understand, make inferences and draw conclusions about the structure and elements of poetry and provide evidence from text to support understanding.

Vocabulary

cipher (sī´fər) *n.* a signifying figure; a number or symbol; p. 490 *A zero is a cipher representing a numberless quantity.*

glyph (glif) *n.* an engraved, symbolic figure; p. 490 *Scientists study ancient glyphs to learn secrets from, and clues about, the past.*

conflagration (kon´flə grā´shən) *n.* a huge fire; p. 491 *Even veteran firefighters rarely witnessed this kind of conflagration.*

The Print of the Paw

N. Scott Momaday

It lies among leaves. Indeed, a leaf,
fast and broken, is impressed in the
heel's deep hollow. The leaf is yellow and brown, and brittle at the
edges. The edges have been crushed;
there is a fine dust of color, like
pollen, in the mold. Deeper than the
heel's hollow are the claw's piercings.
They are precisely placed in the earth
as if the great beast moved with
meticulous grace. The toes turn
inward, perhaps to describe like a
keel[1] the center of gravity upon which
a great weight is balanced. Were I to
construct a model of this bear, based
upon this single print, it would turn
out to be a mythic and wondrous
thing. It would be a **cipher**, a **glyph**, a
huge shape emergent on the wall of a
cave, a full figure in polychrome—[2]
splotches of red and yellow in
black outline. And I would be an
artist of the first rank on this
occasion, if on no other, for I should
proceed directly, in the disinterested
manner of a child, from
this nearly perfect print of the paw.
And all who should lay eyes upon
my work would know, beyond any
shadow of a doubt, how much I love
the bear whose print this is.

Jemez Springs, 1997

2. *Polychrome* means "decorated in many colors."

The Energy of the Everyday *What effect does the
"nearly perfect" paw print have on the speaker?*

Vocabulary

cipher (sī′fər) *n.* a signifying figure; a number or symbol
glyph (glif) *n.* an engraved, symbolic figure

1. A *keel* is the long piece of wood or steel along the bottom
of a boat or ship that helps keep it stable.

Weapons and Physiognomy of the Grizzly Bear, 1846. George Catlin. Oil on canvas. Smithsonian American Art Museum, Washington, DC.

To An Aged Bear

N. Scott Momaday

Hold hard this infirmity.
It defines you. You are old.

Now fix yourself in summer,
In thickets of ripe berries,

5   And venture toward the ridge
Where you were born. Await there

The setting sun. Be alive
To that old **conflagration**

One more time. Mortality
10 Is your shadow and your shade.

Translate yourself to spirit;
Be present on your journey.

Keep to the trees and waters.
Be the singing of the soil.

Santa Fe, 1995

Speaker *What are your impressions of this poem's speaker?*

Vocabulary

conflagration (kon´flə grā´shən) *n.* a huge fire

After You Read

Respond and Think Critically

1. **Connect to Personal Experience** Did these poems alter the way you feel or think about bears in the wild? Explain your answer.

2. **Interpret Analogies** To what type of vessel does the speaker compare the bear's claws in "The Print of the Paw"? What impression does this analogy evoke? Support your answer. ▷OER

3. **Analyze Mood** Review "The Print of the Paw." How would you describe its mood, or emotional quality? What words and phrases in lines 1–16 help to create the mood? What words and phrases in lines 16–31 help to heighten the mood? Explain.

4. **Make Inferences About Diction** In "To An Aged Bear," what does the speaker tell the bear to "await"? In the context of the poem, to what else might this phrase refer? Explain.

5. **Analyze Metaphors** In "To An Aged Bear," what two words does the speaker use to describe mortality? By using these words, what is the speaker saying about mortality and the bear's relationship to it? Support your answer with evidence from the poem.

6. **Evaluate Imagery** What images of nature do you find in "To An Aged Bear"? Are these images effective in creating a setting for the poem? Why or why not?

7. **Big Idea** **Draw Conclusions About Meaning** "Death is part of everyday." Does "To An Aged Bear" support this statement? Explain and cite details from the poem in your answer.

Literary Element Speaker

Each **speaker** in Momaday's poems expresses his or her feelings and ideas in a different style and form. Review the poems, paying attention to each speaker.

8. **Make Inferences About Speaker** What can you infer about the speaker's interests in "The Print of the Paw"? Who might the speaker be? Support your response with text evidence.

9. **Evaluate Speakers** Is it your impression that you are hearing from the same speaker in both poems? Why or why not? Support your answer with details from the texts. Use the pink highlighted passage and question to help you.

Review: Prose Poetry

As you learned on page 483, prose poetry avoids line breaks and uses sentence and paragraph form instead. Nevertheless, it contains many of the same elements as verse poetry, including rhythm, symbolism, and imagery.

10. **Partner Activity** With a classmate, discuss "The Print of the Paw." Where in the poem does the writing most resemble prose? What conventional poetic elements do you see in the poem? Working with your partner, create a two-column chart like the one below. Fill in the left-hand column with details that reflect the prose aspects of the poem. Fill in the right-hand column with examples of more conventional poetic devices.

Details that reflect prose characteristics	Details in common with verse poetry
full sentences	figurative language, such as "precisely placed in the earth as if the great beast moved with meticulous grace"

Reading Strategy — Apply Background Knowledge

When you **apply background knowledge** to your reading of the poems, you can better understand their context. To answer the following questions, review the chart on page 489.

11. Do you think that the speaker in each poem represents Momaday's own point of view? Explain.

12. How does knowing about the author's American Indian heritage help you understand the poems?

Vocabulary Practice

Practice with Word Origins Studying the etymology, or origin and history, of a word can help you understand its meaning. Create a word map, like the one below, for each of these vocabulary words from the poems.

cipher   glyph   conflagration

EXAMPLE:

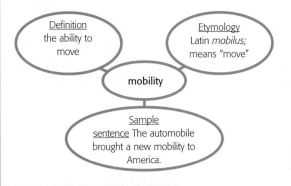

Definition — the ability to move

Etymology — Latin *mobilus;* means "move"

mobility

Sample sentence — The automobile brought a new mobility to America.

Academic Vocabulary

The speaker **inspects** a leaf that the bear crushed underfoot.

Inspect is an academic word. A detective might **inspect** a crime scene for clues. A mechanic might **inspect** a car to be sure it is in safe working order. What object or place might you inspect? Why?

For more on academic vocabulary, see pages 36–37 and R92–R94.

Enrich and Extend

 Speaking and Listening

Oral Interpretation Recite and present to your class oral interpretations of "The Print of the Paw" and "To An Aged Bear."

Prepare Decide whether, and how well, the prose poetry format of "The Print of the Paw" and the traditional poetic form of "To an Aged Bear" influence and fit each poem's meaning. As you rehearse your recital of each poem—first by yourself, and then for a partner—consider how the style and content of your delivery should vary for each poem and how they will influence listeners' understanding.

Perform Make notes in a chart like this one to show how you will demonstrate understanding of the poems and engage your audience.

	Verbal Techniques	Nonverbal Techniques
"The Print of the Paw"	Pace—faster than "Aged Bear," like reading a paragraph Tone—admiration, wonder	Body language— relaxed stance Gestures—mime picking up and examining a leaf
"To An Aged Bear"	Pace— Tone—	Body language— Gestures—

As you recite each poem, use techniques that suit your audience and the poems. Make choices about tone of voice, appropriate body language and gestures, and the best times for direct eye contact.

Evaluate Decide how clearly and effectively you recited the poems. Then write a paragraph rating the delivery and content of your recitations and interpretations. Listen critically and respond appropriately to your classmates' recitations.

Literature Online

Selection Resources For Selection Quizzes, eFlashcards, and Reading-Writing Connection activities, go to glencoe.com and enter QuickPass code GL57805u3.

Before You Read

Three Haiku

Meet **Matsuo Bashō**

(1644–1694)

Japanese poet Matsuo Bashō devoted his life to perfecting the haiku. The shortest poetic form in the world, the haiku contains just seventeen syllables, in three lines of five, seven, and five syllables. Inspired by the teachings of Zen Buddhism, which emphasize surpassing logical, everyday thought, seventeenth-century Japanese poets turned their attention to capturing the small details of life, particularly focusing on nature.

Bashō and his contemporaries thought of themselves as guides. The early writers of haiku strove to place the reader within an experience in nature—such as observing a misty rain or listening closely to a bird's call. Writing as specifically and simply as they could about the details of such an experience, they hoped the poem might lead their reader to enlightenment. "What is important," Bashō wrote, "is . . . returning to daily experience, seek therein the true and the beautiful."

> "Every day is a journey, and the journey itself is home."
> —Matsuo Bashō

From Samurai Son to Master Poet Born in 1644 to a family of samurai warriors in the province of Iga, Bashō spent most of his youth in service to a feudal lord. During the first half of his life, a new era of Japanese culture unfolded, when a drastic policy caused the country to close itself to foreigners. This resulted in a new interest in Japanese art,

ethics, history, and poetry. Bashō and the young lord he served, Todo Yoshitada, became close companions, sharing a passion for poetry. When Yoshitada died in his early twenties, it is believed Bashō's grief inspired him to leave Iga and set out for a life committed to poetry, traveling, and Zen ideology.

Travel The details of Bashō's life after his departure from Iga are obscure, though it is certain that he became a master of haiku by his early thirties and gained many disciples. One such disciple built him a cottage near Edo (now Tokyo).

During the remainder of his life, Bashō continued to produce elegant haiku that explored beauty, loneliness, and suffering. He eventually became a Zen priest, giving up all possessions and wandering on pilgrimages with fellow priests and poets. He spent the last ten years of his life traveling through Japan; one such journey to the northern interior of Japan is captured in his most famous work, *Narrow Road to the Deep North*, a kind of travel diary in *haiban* form, or prose alternating with haiku.

LOG ON ▶ **Literature** Online

Author Search For more about Matsuo Bashō, go to glencoe.com and enter QuickPass code GL57805u3.

Literature and Reading Preview

Connect to the Haiku

For many people, the seasons call to mind beginnings and endings in their own lives. Freewrite for a few minutes about why this might be.

Build Background

Matsuo Bashō once said, "Don't follow in the footsteps of the old poets, seek what they sought." He also said that a good poem should "seem light as a shallow river flowing over its sandy bed."

Set Purposes for Reading

Big Idea The Energy of the Everyday

As you read the three haiku, ask yourself, How do these poems reflect attentiveness to the details of changing seasons?

Literary Element Haiku

Haiku is an unrhymed Japanese verse form consisting of seventeen syllables that are arranged in three lines. The first and third lines have five syllables each; the second line has seven syllables. While some English translations of haiku lose the poet's original syllable count, the traditional goal of haiku—to suggest large ideas using simple, few words—remains. As you read, ask yourself, How closely do these translations conform to haiku line and stanza requirements?

Reading Strategy Interpret Imagery

Imagery refers to sensory language that appeals to one or more of the five senses and evokes emotional responses in the reader. When you **interpret imagery,** you use your own knowledge of the world and your understanding of the text to create meaning from the images. As you read, ask yourself, What do the images signify?

··

Tip: Visualize As you read, picture the author's accounts of nature. Record your visualizations in a chart and make an inference about the meaning of each image. Use the blue highlighted question for help.

TEKS

For pages 494–498

10.7 Understand, make inferences and draw conclusions about how an author's sensory language creates imagery in literary text and provide evidence from text to support understanding.

Pine and Bamboo and Cranes, 17th century. Japanese school. Watercolour on panel. American Museum of Natural History, NY.

Line	Visualization	Inference
"It would melt / in my hand."	A hand cupped and holding a lump of frost.	This image is poignant and suggests that life is always changing.

Autumn Tree.
Japanese School
17th century. Silk
painting. Private
collection.

Three Haiku

Matsuo Bashō
Translated by Robert Hass

It would melt
in my hand—
the autumn frost.

First day of spring—
I keep thinking about
the end of autumn.

Spring!
a nameless hill
in the haze.

Interpret Imagery *To which sense does the image in the last poem appeal? What do you think is the significance of this image?*

After You Read

Respond and Think Critically

1. **Connect to Personal Experience** Are the images in the three haiku familiar to you? Explain. Describe your feelings about the changing seasons.

2. **Make Inferences About Author's Craft** In the first haiku, what substance melts in the speaker's hand? Why might the author have chosen to include this kind of sensory detail here? Explain.

3. **Make Inferences About the Speaker** What is the speaker in the second haiku reminded of on spring's first day? What inference can you make about the speaker's life from his feelings about the end of autumn?

4. **Analyze Description** How does the speaker describe spring in the third haiku? What is the effect of the author's decision to describe spring using this image? Explain.

5. **Evaluate Author's Craft** How well has Bashō evoked the wonder of changing seasons in these short poems? Could he have done a better job with longer poems? Support your answer.

6. **Analyze Details** Nature is often described as both a powerful and gentle force. What powerful elements of nature do these haiku suggest? What gentle elements do they suggest? Explain, using text evidence to support your response.

7. **Big Idea** **Draw Conclusions About Meaning** Through his writing, Bashō sought to connect readers to the truth and beauty of everyday life. What does Bashō's journey have to teach you about the journey you are taking in your own life? Explain.

Literary Element Haiku

Haiku generally address some subject in nature and simultaneously deal with grand ideas in a very limited amount of space. The strict format makes haiku a challenge to create, but Bashō's work is a demonstration of how beauty can be both encompassing and concise.

8. **Analyze Haiku** What conflicting elements are present in the haiku? How do these elements help the author communicate stirring messages in the space of three lines?

9. **Draw Conclusions About Theme** What striking ideas about the relationship between birth and death in nature are suggested by the author? Explain.

Review: Line and Stanza

As you learned on page 452, a **line** in a poem usually consists of a single word or a row of words. A **stanza** is a group of lines forming a unit in a poem or song, similar to the paragraph in prose. The lines in haiku consist of only one word or very few words because the goal of the haiku poet is to convey an idea or impression within a strict poetic form using as few words as possible. The one-stanza, seventeen-syllable form demands that the poet express his or her ideas concisely, without unnecessary elaboration.

10. **Partner Activity** With a partner, discuss the following questions.

- Could any words be deleted from these three haiku without detracting from their meaning? Explain.

- Why might the brevity of these three haiku make a strong impression on the reader? Support your answer with details from the poems.

Texas Test Practice (10.7)

1. The first haiku includes

   A. an auditory image of autumn's beauty

   B. no specific appeal to the senses

   C. an olefactory image conjuring up the musty odors of autumn

   D. a tactile detail suggesting the chill delicacy of autumn

2. The image in the third haiku appeals mainly to the sense of

   F. sight

   G. sound

   H. touch

   J. taste

Academic Vocabulary

*Haiku, which relies on a **minimal** number of words, can express volumes of meaning and sentiment.*

Minimal is an academic word. In more casual conversation, a person might refer to the **minimal** effort someone made to be helpful or friendly. To study this word further, fill out a graphic organizer like the one below.

For more on academic vocabulary, see pages 36–37 and R92–R94.

 # Write with Style

 ## Apply Imagery

Assignment Choose one image from Bashō's haiku. Describe a scene in nature based on that image.

Get Ideas Look at the chart you made on page 495 to help you visualize and make inferences about imagery. Choose one image to expand on. Create a cluster diagram around the image to generate more details that appeal to the senses.

Give It Structure Use spatial order to structure your writing. For example, you may begin with observations from afar and then zoom in; describe from top to bottom or left to right; or start in the center and move toward the perimeter. Unify your writing by creating a controlling impression and editing out any details that do not support that impression.

Look at Language All the details you select should come together to create a mood, such as loss, peacefulness, or mystery. Carefully choose words to best evoke that mood.

LOG ON ▶ **Literature** Online

Selection Resources For Selection Quizzes, eFlashcards, and Reading-Writing Connection activities, go to glencoe.com and enter QuickPass code GL57805u3.

Before You Read

Two Tanka

Meet **Lady Ise**
(c. 875–c. 938)

Considered one of the Thirty-six Poetic Geniuses of Japan, Lady Ise enjoyed the celebrity status and fame that accompanied literary accomplishment in ancient Japan. Her achievement is especially impressive considering that official poetry during that era was written primarily by men.

A Woman of the Court Lady Ise served in Emperor Uda's Kyoto court and was known there for her literary works. Ise was part of a court "salon," a place where women developed and enjoyed their own culture. In addition to her writing, Ise was also a talented musician.

Murasaki Shikibu, c. 978–1014. Japanese court lady and author, who wrote Genji Monogatari *(Tale of the* Genji*).*

> ". . . Why then do rumors /
> Like swirling pillars of dust /
> Rise as high as the heavens?"
>
> —Lady Ise

Ise's poetry is formal in style, the rigidity of its structure reflecting the formality of the court. It subtly critiques the political scene and the role of women. Much of her work is found in a collection of Japanese poetry known as the *Kokin Wakashū*, or *Kokinshū*, published around the year 905. The first in a series of imperially commissioned collections of Japanese poetry, the *Kokinshū* is also the first major work in *kana*, a Japanese writing system using syllable-based characters. In addition, Ise assembled the *Ise Shū*, a separate collection of her own work. The first 32 or 33 poems of this collection, usually referred to as her "diary," and their prose introductions are assumed to be autobiographical, but scholars question how much fiction they contain.

Ise was well represented in official Japanese collections. She also participated in poetry contests, in which she often triumphed over leading male poets.

Lady Ise's Life Many of the facts of Lady Ise's life are uncertain. Scholars believe that she was the daughter of Fujiwara no Tsugukage, a provincial governor of Ise. Ise entered the service of the consort of Emperor Uda at about the age of fifteen. After the emperor's death, Ise continued in service to the household until her death. Evidence suggests that her two children were of royal heritage. Her son died in infancy; however, her daughter, Nakatsukasa, lived to become an accomplished poet.

 LOG ON **Literature** Online

Author Search For more about Lady Ise, go to glencoe.com and enter QuickPass code GL57805u3.

Literature and Reading Preview

Connect to the Tanka

What types of moments are worth capturing? List several of these moments and explain why they should be remembered.

Build Background

Rhyme is typically not a feature of Japanese poetry because all Japanese words end in one of five vowels. Japanese words do not have stressed syllables, so rhythm is not a device used in Japanese poetry. Japanese poetry can be distinguished from Japanese prose by its traditional syllabic pattern.

Set Purposes for Reading

Big Idea **The Energy of the Everyday**

As you read, ask yourself, How does Ise paint a picture of the everyday using words that appeal to readers' emotions?

Literary Element Tanka

Tanka is an unrhymed Japanese verse form. Most tanka focus on a single thought or idea related to love or to an appreciation of nature, common topics in Japanese poetry. Tanka adhere to a strict form that consists of five lines. The first and third lines have five syllables each; the other lines have seven syllables each. Keep in mind that the two tanka presented here are translated from Japanese to English. Therefore, the syllables per line may not always fit the prescribed structure. As you read, ask yourself, How does the tanka form contribute to the meaning of the poems?

Reading Strategy Compare and Contrast Imagery

When reading poetry, it helps to **compare and contrast images,** sensory language, and descriptions that appeal to the five senses. As you read, ask yourself, How does the speaker portray images from nature?

....

Tip: Draw Conclusions About Images Use a Venn diagram like the one below to record similarities and differences between the images in the two tanka. Then draw a conclusion about what these similarities and differences mean.

TEKS

For pages 499–502

10.7 Understand, make inferences and draw conclusions about how an author's sensory language creates imagery in literary text and provide evidence from text to support understanding.

Deer Under a Maple Tree. Mori Sushin Tessan. Hand painted, ink and colour on paper. British Library, London.

First Tanka	Both	Second Tanka
There are bright shiny droplets of water.	These images suggest spring.	The geese spread wings as they prepare to take flight.

Print of a River Under Cherry Blossoms, 1833–1834.
Ando Hiroshige.

Two Tanka

Lady Ise

Hanging from the branches of a green
willow tree,
the spring rain
is a
thread of pearls.

—Translated by Willis Barnstone

Lightly forsaking[1]
the Spring mist as it rises,
the wild geese are setting off.
Have they learned to live
in a flowerless country?

—Translated by Etsuko Terasaki
with Irma Brandeis

---

1 *Forsaking* means "turning away from" or
   "abandoning."

The Energy of the Everyday *How does line 3
of the second tanka evoke the energy of the
everyday?*

After You Read

Respond and Think Critically

1. **Connect to Personal Experience** What about these images seems familiar to you? Describe the images in your own words.

2. **Interpret Comparisons** What two things are compared in the first tanka? What insights about these things does the comparison bring to mind? Explain.

3. **Make Inferences About Details** What question does the speaker ask in the second tanka? What might be its meaning? Explain.

4. **Evaluate Imagery** Do the images of spring in these poems reflect common conceptions of the season? Do they provide new ways to think about the season? Explain.

5. **Analyze Mood** How would you describe the **mood,** or emotional quality, of these poems? Which details in each poem help to create a mood? Explain.

6. **Make Inferences About Theme** What larger ideas about life might these poems be pointing to? Support your response with text evidence.

7. **Big Idea** **Draw Conclusions About Historical Context** Lady Ise's poetry is now over a thousand years old. Does her subject matter (nature and other aspects of the everyday) still appeal to readers in the present day? Explain, supporting your answer with evidence from the poems.

Literary Element Tanka

Because **tanka** are so short and simple, the tanka writer must rely on precise words to suggest ideas.

8. **Analyze Tanka** How does the length of each poem affect the impression it leaves upon the reader? Explain.

9. **Make Inferences About Author's Craft** Lady Ise could have selected other details to evoke spring. Why do you think she selected the details she did? Explain.

Reading Strategy Compare and Contrast Imagery

Comparing and contrasting imagery in poems helps readers draw conclusions about themes.

10. What example of figurative language does the author use to create imagery in the first tanka? Explain.

11. Compare and contrast the images in the two tanka. Based on the images the author chose, what can you conclude about the differences in the themes of the poems? Use the Venn diagram you created on page 500 to help you.

Academic Vocabulary

Many tanka poets wrote about nature, including such things as geese, saplings, and rain.

Sapling is a discipline-specific word that derives from Anglo-Saxon. The suffix *-ling* means "little." Using your knowledge and context clues, determine the meaning of *sapling* in the model sentence above. Check your response by consulting a dictionary. Finally, demonstrate your understanding by using each of these related words in a sentence.

a. yearling   **b.** duckling   **c.** sibling

Writing

Write a Poem Write a tanka of your own, using the structural elements and techniques described on page 500. Include figurative language in your tanka. Remember, a tanka is usually, but not necessarily, related to love or the appreciation of nature.

LOG ON ▶ **Literature** Online

Selection Resources For Selection Quizzes, eFlashcards, and Reading-Writing Connection activities, go to glencoe.com and enter QuickPass code GL57805u3.

Before You Read

Woman with Kite

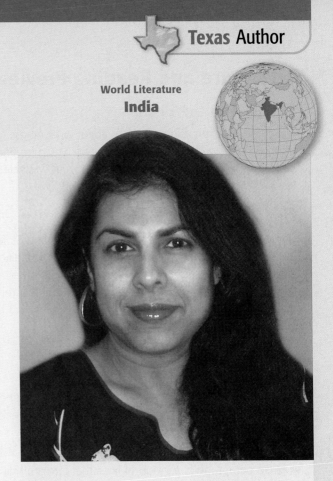

Meet **Chitra Banerjee Divakaruni** (born 1956)

When Chitra Divakaruni arrived in the United States from India in 1976, the nineteen-year-old from Calcutta received a shock. As she walked with her family in Chicago, she was taunted by white teens who shouted racial slurs. At first, she kept quiet about the episode. Later she wrote, "I never talked to anyone about it; I felt ashamed. Writing was a way to go beyond the silence." When Divakaruni found her voice, she used it to speak for the marginalized and the silenced, namely women and immigrants.

> "Women in particular respond to my work because I'm writing about them."
>
> —Chitra Banerjee Divakaruni

A New Awareness In the United States, Divakaruni found many new opportunities. She earned a PhD from the University of California at Berkeley. She also began to reevaluate the circumstances of women in India. She saw how women's options were limited by lack of education and oppressive marriages, and that these experiences continued even after they came to the United States. "At Berkeley, I volunteered at the women's center," she says. "As I got more involved, I became interested in helping battered women." In 1991 she and her friends created Maitri, an organization that provides services to Indian American women. "I saw that a lot of problems stemmed from issues of domestic violence," Divakaruni said.

Speaking for Women Divakaruni began writing poems about immigrant women forging a new identity while retaining ties to tradition. She also wrote short stories about these women, which she collected in *Arranged Marriages*. Divakaruni's poetry, short stories, and novels have won many awards, including two Pushcart Prizes and the American Book Award. She was nominated for the Texas Bluebonnet Award in 2005.

From her home near Houston, Divakaruni still pursues her goal of speaking for women. In addition to teaching at the University of Houston, she serves on the board of Maitri and the advisory board of Daya, a Houston-based organization that helps women dealing with domestic violence in Texas and beyond.

LOG ON ▶ **Literature** Online

Author Search For more about Chitra Banerjee Divakaruni, go to glencoe.com and enter QuickPass code GL57805u3.

Literature and Reading Preview

Connect to the Poem

Have you ever put aside concerns about what others might think in order to do something you knew would be good for you? Write a journal entry about a time when you acted fearlessly on your own behalf.

Build Background

Many authors who have immigrated to the United States from elsewhere write about the conflict of their social traditions with those of Western society. Immigrants often face broad challenges involving not only language barriers, but also religious concerns and marked differences in gender roles.

Set Purposes for Reading

Big Idea **The Energy of the Everyday**

As you read this poem, ask yourself, How does the poet infuse everyday objects and experiences with passion and energy?

Literary Element **Verse Paragraph**

A **verse paragraph** is a group of lines that forms a unit in a poem. A verse paragraph may have any number of lines. Verse paragraphs help to distinguish topics within a poem. As you read, ask yourself, How does Divakaruni use verse paragraphs to emphasize key thoughts?

Reading Strategy **Make Inferences About Theme**

The **theme** of a literary work is the overall message it expresses about people, the world, or life. When you **make inferences about theme,** you look at details of the work, such as cultural or historical context, to make an educated guess about its message. As you read, ask yourself, What message about life is the poem communicating?

·····································

Tip: Make a Chart Record striking details from the poem. Considering what you know about the world and human nature, what theme do these details suggest? Record your inferences.

Details	Inferences About Theme
"... feels the kite,/ translucent purple square, rise in a resistant arc ..."	The theme may have something to do with the importance of finding success despite obstacles.

TEKS

For pages 503–508

10.2 Analyze, make inferences and draw conclusions about theme and genre in different cultural, historical, and contemporary contexts and provide evidence from the text to support understanding.

Vocabulary

querulous (kwer′ə ləs) *adj.* argumentative; uncooperative; p. 505 *Because of the actor's querulous nature, he is very difficult to work with.*

disgruntled (dis grun′tld) *adj.* in a state of sulky dissatisfaction; p. 505 *The disgruntled children spent the rainy day complaining about being stuck in the house.*

translucent (trans lōō′sənt) *adj.* allowing light to pass through; almost clear; see-through; p. 506 *She could make out the shapes of the performers through the translucent curtain.*

fleck (flek′) *v.* to leave spots or streaks; p. 506 *Mud from the road flecked the windshield, making it difficult for the driver to see.*

·····································

Tip: Word Parts Some suffixes tell you a word's part of speech. For example, -*ous* and -*ent*/-*ant* are suffixes that indicate adjectives.

Woman Flying a Kite, 1750. Rajupt. Indian miniature. Collection Sangaram Singh, Jaipur.

Woman with Kite

Chitra Banerjee Divakaruni

Meadow of crabgrass, faded dandelions,
querulous child-voices. She takes
from her son's **disgruntled** hands the spool
of a kite that will not fly.

Vocabulary

querulous (kwer´ə ləs) *adj.* argumentative; uncooperative
disgruntled (dis grun´tld) *adj.* in a state of sulky
dissatisfaction

---

5   Pulls on the heavy string, ground-glass rough
     between her thumb and finger. Feels the kite,
     translucent purple square, rise in a resistant arc,
     flapping against the wind. Kicks off her *chappals*,°
     tucks up her *kurta*° so she can run with it,
10   light **flecking** off her hair as when she was
     sexless-young. Up, up

     past the puff-cheeked clouds, she
     follows it, her eyes slit-smiling at the sun.
     She has forgotten her tugging children, their
15   *give me, give me* wails. She sprints
     backwards, sure-footed, she cannot
     fall, connected to the air, she
     is flying, the wind blows through her, takes
     her red *dupatta*,° mark of marriage.
20   And she laughs like a woman should never laugh

     so the two widows on the park bench
     stare and huddle their white-veiled heads
     to gossip-whisper. The children have fallen,
     breathless, in the grass behind.
25   She laughs like wild water, shaking
     her braids loose, she laughs
     like a fire, the spool a blur
     between her hands,
     the string unraveling all the way
30   to release it into space, her life,
     into its bright, weightless orbit.

8 **chappals:** traditional Indian sandals resembling flip-flops.
9 **kurta:** loose shirt, often worn by both men and women in India and Pakistan.

19 **dupatta:** long scarf traditionally worn by Indian women across both shoulders and sometimes used to cover the head. A *dupatta* has long been regarded as a symbol of modesty.

Verse Paragraph *What effect does the poet create by breaking after line 11?*

The Energy of the Everyday *What do the similes, or comparisons, in lines 25–27 tell you about the woman?*

Vocabulary

translucent (trans lōō′ sənt) *adj.* allowing light to pass through; almost clear; see-through
fleck (flek′) *v.* to leave spots or streaks

After You Read

Respond and Think Critically

1. **Connect to Personal Experience** What is your opinion of the woman's behavior? Explain.

2. **Interpret Imagery** What images are included in the first two lines of the poem? What **mood,** or emotional feeling, do these images contribute to the opening? Explain.

3. **Make Inferences About Cultural Context** What three items of traditional Indian clothing does the poet mention? Why do you think she includes these items? Explain.

4. **Analyze Meaning** What garment does the wind blow away? What significance might this incident have? Consider what you learn about the woman in lines 1–20.

5. **Make Inferences About Symbol** What happens to the kite? What might the kite symbolize? Support your answer with evidence from the poem. <mark>OER</mark>

6. **Analyze Imagery** What images in the poem suggest obstacles and difficulties in the woman's life? What images suggest success or breaking free from constriction? Explain. In your answer, refer to both auditory and visual images.

7. **Big Idea** **Draw Conclusions About Behavior** What pressures might the woman face in her everyday life? How does she transform or transcend these pressures? Support your answer with evidence from the poem.

8. **Analyze Cultural Influences** Divakaruni created an organization that provides services to Indian American women. How does her portrayal of the woman in the poem suggest a sensitivity toward women's issues? Explain your answer.

Literary Element Verse Paragraph

Contemporary poets often use **verse paragraphs** to organize their ideas. In "Woman with Kite," Divakaruni uses three verse paragraphs to distinguish topics within the poem.

9. **Analyze Poetic Form** How many lines are in each verse paragraph in "Woman with Kite"? Is the pattern of the verses regular or irregular? Explain what effect you think the pattern has on the poem.

10. **Draw Conclusions About Style** Divakaruni could have chosen to structure her poem without verses. Why do you think she chose to break the poem into three verses? Support your answer with evidence from the poem. Use the pink highlighted question for help.

Review: Enjambment

As you learned on page 460, **enjambment,** also known as a run-on line, is the continuation of a sentence or phrase from one line of a poem to the

next without a pause between the lines. Enjambment offers poets the opportunity to underscore the dramatic elements of their work.

11. **Partner Activity** With a classmate, look for six examples of enjambment in "Woman with Kite." Working with your partner, create a two-column chart similar to the one below. Fill in the left column with examples of enjambment. In the right column, describe how this device gives the words at the beginning or at the end of the line a deeper meaning or more dramatic effect.

Key words	Deeper meaning
"Kicks off her chappals, / tucks up her kurta"	Emphasizes abandoning traditional behavior

Reading Strategy · Make Inferences About Theme

The genre and cultural, historical, and contemporary context of a work can affect its theme.

12. What do you think is the overall theme of "Woman with Kite"? How important is the main character's cultural background to the theme of the poem? Support your answer.

13. How does the genre Divakaruni chose—poetry—help to strongly communicate the theme? Consider her use of poetic devices.

Vocabulary Practice

Practice with Word Parts For each boldfaced vocabulary word, find the meaning of the word's root and the meanings of any prefixes or suffixes in the word. Use a printed or online dictionary to help you. List the meanings in a diagram like the one shown. Then find two or three words that contain the same prefix, suffix, or root as the vocabulary word. Circle the word part that could help a person guess each word's meaning.

querulous   disgruntled   translucent   fleck

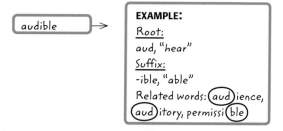

audible →

EXAMPLE:
Root:
aud, "hear"
Suffix:
-ible, "able"
Related words: (aud)ience, (aud)itory, permissi(ble)

Academic Vocabulary

*The woman in the poem breaks stereotypes about how a **mature** person should act.*

Mature is an academic word. A parent might suggest that a child will have certain privileges when he or she is more **mature**. Use context clues to figure out the meaning of **mature** in the sentence above.

For more on academic vocabulary, see pages 36–37 and R92–R94.

Enrich and Extend

Connect to Social Studies

Research a Hobby or Sport Research a popular hobby, sport, or game in India. Create a report with a bibliography, and present your report orally to your classmates.

Investigate Follow these steps:

- ☑ Ask research questions and establish a timeline for completing your work.
- ☑ Locate multiple primary and secondary sources.
- ☑ Assess sources, ruling out those whose authorship or authority is unknown or questionable.
- ☑ Focus your topic; avoid topics that are too broad or too narrow.
- ☑ Use notecards, a table, or e-files to take and organize notes on your specific focus.
- ☑ As you take notes, look up any unfamiliar terms.
- ☑ Note discrepancies and different perspectives among sources.
- ☑ Paraphrase or summarize most information, but quote when the words are just right and will create interest in your oral report.

Create Draft your report, making sure it has an introduction, a body, and a conclusion. Follow the guidelines on pages R40–R43 to create your bibliography, entitled "Works Cited," on a separate page.

Report Be sure your report correctly integrates and cites information from your sources. Refer to information about parenthetical documentation on page R39. Maintain the flow of ideas by introducing your sources and linking them with transitional words and phrases that help to show where sources agree, disagree, or leave questions unanswered. Share your oral presentation with your classmates.

 Literature Online

Selection Resources For Selection Quizzes, eFlashcards, and Reading-Writing Connection activities, go to glencoe.com and enter QuickPass code GL57805u3.

PART 2

Loves and Losses

River Diego, 1996, Daniel Nevins, Oil, acrylic, and collage on wood.
Private collection.

View the Art Nevins is known for his narrative paintings. How might
this painting tell a narrative about Loves and Losses?

BIG IDEA

The poems in Part 2 express the joys and insights love can bring as well as the
emptiness and ache of its loss. As you read the following poems, ask yourself,
What elements of poetry work to express love and loss? What is each author's
purpose in using these elements?

LITERARY FOCUS

The Language of Poetry

In what distinctive ways does poetry use language?

In his autobiography, William Carlos Williams described writing "The Great Figure": "I heard a great clatter of bells and the roar of a fire engine passing the end of the street down Ninth Avenue. I turned just in time to see the golden figure 5 on a red background flash by. The impression was so sudden and forceful that I took a piece of paper out of my pocket and wrote a short poem." That poem inspired Williams's friend Charles Demuth to paint *The Figure 5 in Gold*. The artist used colors to create visual images; the poet used words to create images that appeal to a variety of senses.

Among the rain
and lights
I saw the figure 5
in gold
on a red
fire truck
moving
tense
unheeded
to gong clangs
siren howls
and wheels rumbling
through the dark city

—William Carlos Williams, **"The Great Figure"**

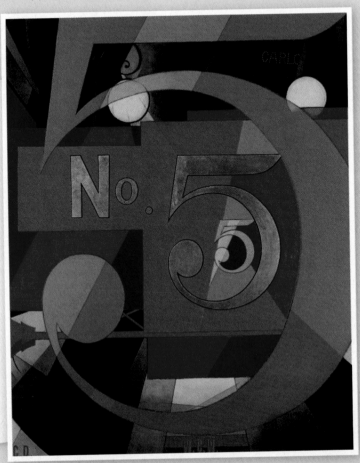

The Figure 5 in Gold, 1928. Charles Demuth. Oil on composition board, 91.4 x 75.6 cm. Metropolitan Museum of Art, New York.

Imagery

Imagery refers to descriptive language that appeals to one or more of the five senses: sight, sound, touch, taste, and smell. This use of sensory detail can trigger a memory or an idea, or evoke a sensory experience in the reader. Consider some of the images in "The Great Figure":

Images	Sensory Appeal
"Among the rain"	sight and touch
"the figure 5 / in gold"	sight
"gong clangs"	sound

Figurative Language

Figurative language is language used for descriptive effect, often to imply ideas indirectly. Expressions of figurative language are not literally true but express some truth beyond the literal level. Poets often use figurative language to convey fresh and original comparisons. Figures of speech are types of figurative language. Among the most common are simile, metaphor, personification, and hyperbole.

Simile Poets often make imaginative comparisons to convey ideas, feelings, and insights. One kind of comparison is called a **simile.** In this figure of speech, the writer uses words such as *like* or *as* or the phrase "as if" to make the comparison. For example, in "The Meadow Mouse," Theodore Roethke writes, "His absurd whiskers sticking out like a cartoon mouse." This comparison suggests that the mouse's whiskers look silly and exaggerated, like a cartoon.

Metaphor In contrast to a simile, a **metaphor** implies a comparison instead of stating it directly. Metaphors do not use *like* or *as*.

> No one lived there
> but silence, a pale china gleam
>
> —Rita Dove, *from "Parlor"*

In this metaphor, the speaker is comparing silence to a soft glimmer of light. An **extended metaphor** continues the comparison throughout a paragraph, a stanza, or an entire work.

Personification This figure of speech gives human characteristics to nonhuman things. Emily Dickinson uses personification in her poem "Heart! We Will Forget Him!"

> Heart! We will forget him!
> You and I — tonight!
> You may forget the warmth he gave —
> I will forget the light!

Dickinson personifies the heart by addressing it directly and giving it the human ability to forget.

Hyperbole This figure of speech uses an obvious overstatement or exaggeration for either serious or comic effect. For example, when the speaker in William Butler Yeats's poem, "He Wishes for the Cloths of Heaven," says, "I have spread my dreams under your feet," the exaggeration conveys the passion and the love the speaker has for his subject.

Quickwrite

Make Inferences About Sensory Language
Find three or four more examples of imagery in William Carlos Williams's poem on the previous page. Then write a paragraph in which you explain how Williams's sensory language helps you understand the meaning of the poem. Support your response with evidence from the text.

 Literature Online

Literature and Reading For more about literary elements, go to glencoe.com and enter QuickPass code GL57805u3.

Before You Read

After Great Pain, A Formal Feeling Comes
and Heart! We Will Forget Him!

Meet **Emily Dickinson**

(1830–1886)

Now considered one of the most important poets in American literature, Emily Dickinson saw her name in print only once: as second-place finisher for her entry in a bread contest. In fact, during her lifetime, her work remained largely private.

Emily Dickinson was born in Amherst, Massachusetts, to a prominent New England family. Her education included one year at Mount Holyoke Female Seminary, where she was greatly influenced by the Puritan religious tradition. Dickinson never married, and for nearly her entire life, she lived with her parents and her younger sister, Lavinia.

> *"The brain is wider than the sky."*
>
> —Emily Dickinson

A Private Life Dickinson began writing poems early in her life. However, of the nearly 1,800 poems she penned, Dickinson published only ten during her lifetime, and even then, she published them anonymously.

After Dickinson's death in 1886, her sister Lavinia discovered Dickinson's work in her bedroom. Lavinia decided to reveal her sister's talent to the world. In 1890 and 1891, two collections of Dickinson's poetry were published, followed in later years by subsequent editions.

Throughout her life, Dickinson preferred solitude over socializing—a fact that has led to much speculation about her personal life. Despite many popular theories of loneliness or lovesickness, her self-imposed isolation may be viewed in another way. In the mid-nineteenth century, after completing their education, young women of Dickinson's social and economic standing were expected to marry and have children. Perhaps Dickinson desired something different for herself.

A Room of Her Own By not marrying, Dickinson carved out a space for herself to be able to write her poetry. She did, however, have family around her. Dickinson cared for her ailing mother and was much involved in the lives of her brother's children. The domestic sphere is one of Dickinson's major topics.

A Daring New Voice Dickinson's poetic style was daring and unique. In her choice of topics, she departed from her female contemporaries by veering away from sentimentality and toward questioning life, death, and nature.

LOG ON **Literature** Online

Author Search For more about Emily Dickinson, go to glencoe.com and enter QuickPass code GL57805u3.

Literature and Reading Preview

Connect to the Poems

How do people typically respond to emotionally painful events? Discuss this question with a small group.

Build Background

Dickinson wrote "Heart! We Will Forget Him!" in the late 1850s. Her letters from the time describe the joy and frustration she experienced as a result of her love for an unnamed man. She wrote "After Great Pain, A Formal Feeling Comes" in 1862, a year when the danger of the Civil War threatened many of Dickinson's friends.

Set Purposes for Reading

Big Idea Loves and Losses

As you read the poems, ask yourself, How does Dickinson describe love and loss?

Literary Element Personification

Personification is a figure of speech in which an animal, an object, a force of nature, or an idea is given human characteristics. Recognizing personification can help you understand the poet's intentions. As you read, ask yourself, Which objects does Dickinson personify? Why?

Reading Strategy Compare and Contrast Tone

Tone is a poet's attitude toward his or her subject matter. Tone, whether it be playful, serious, or sad, can give you clues about how the poet feels about his or her subject. As you read, ask yourself, How do the poems' tones contribute to their meanings?

....

Tip: Ask Questions Use a chart like the one below to help you draw conclusions about Dickinson's tone in the poems.

Questions	"After Great Pain, A Formal Feeling Comes"	"Heart! We Will Forget Him!"
Who is the speaker?	Someone who has suffered a painful loss	
Who does the speaker address?		The speaker's heart

TEKS

For pages 512–517

10.3 Understand, make inferences and draw conclusions about the structure and elements of poetry and provide evidence from text to support understanding.

Vocabulary

ceremonious (ser´ə mō´nē əs) *adj.* carefully observant of the formal acts required by ritual, custom, or etiquette; p. 514 *Sam's graduation was a ceremonious occasion.*

recollect (rek´ə lekt´) *v.* to remember; p. 514 *We used pictures to help Grandma recollect her childhood.*

stupor (stoo´pər) *n.* a state of extreme lethargy; p. 514 *After twenty hours of traveling, Dan arrived in a stupor.*

lag (lag) *v.* to fall behind; p. 515 *If you continue to lag, we will be late for practice.*

Cotswold Park, Winter Woodland (Morning, December). Charles Neal. Oil on canvas.

After Great Pain, A Formal Feeling Comes

Emily Dickinson

After great pain, a formal feeling comes —
The Nerves sit **ceremonious**, like Tombs —
The stiff Heart questions was it He, that bore,
And Yesterday, or Centuries before?

5   The Feet, mechanical, go round —
Of Ground, or Air, or Ought[1]—
A Wooden way
Regardless grown,
A Quartz contentment, like a stone —

10   This is the Hour of Lead —
Remembered, if outlived,
As Freezing persons, **recollect** the Snow —
First — Chill — then **Stupor** — then the letting go —

---

1. Here, *Ought* means "anything" and is an archaic variant of *aught.*

Compare and Contrast Tone *How does this stanza's extra line help convey the tone of the poem?*

Vocabulary

ceremonious (ser´ə mō´ nē əs) *adj.* carefully observant of the formal acts required by ritual, custom, or etiquette

recollect (rek´ə lekt´) *v.* to remember

stupor (sto͞o´ pər) *n.* a state of extreme lethargy

Heart! We Will Forget Him!

Emily Dickinson

Ricordo di un dolore o Ritratto di Santina Negri (Memory of a Sorrow/Portrait of Santina Negri), 1889. Giuseppe Pellizza da Volpedo. Oil on canvas, 107 x 79 cm. Bergamo, Italy.

Heart! We will forget him!
You and I — tonight!
You may forget the warmth he gave —
I will forget the light!

When you have done, pray tell me
That I may straight begin!
Haste! lest[1] while you're **lagging**
I remember him!

---

1. Here, *lest* means "in order to prevent any possibility that."

Loves and Losses *Why do you think the speaker directly addresses the Heart?*

Vocabulary

lag (lag) *v.* to fall behind

After You Read

Respond and Think Critically

1. **Connect to Personal Experience** Do you think "After Great Pain, A Formal Feeling Comes" and "Heart! We Will Forget Him!" express positive ideas about love and loss? Explain.

2. **Make Inferences About Speaker** A simile is a figure of speech, using *like* or *as,* that is used to compare two things. In "After Great Pain, A Formal Feeling Comes," to what are nerves compared? What does this simile suggest about the speaker's physical feelings?

3. **Analyze Simile** Identify two similes in "After Great Pain, A Formal Feeling Comes." Discuss how Dickinson uses them to convey her grief in the poem. Support your response with text evidence.

4. **Interpret Meaning** What does the speaker in "Heart! We Will Forget Him!" want to be told? Why does the speaker need this information?

5. **Evaluate Punctuation** Analyze Dickinson's use of exclamation marks in "Heart! We Will Forget Him!" Do you find them effective? Explain.

6. **Big Idea** **Draw Conclusions About the Author** Dickinson is praised for the conciseness and intensity of her poems. How do these qualities serve her ideas of love and loss? Support your response with text evidence.

7. **Evaluate Theme** Are Dickinson's themes still relevant to readers today? Explain. Support your response with text evidence.

Daily Life & Culture

Living Single

Before 1800, it was extremely uncommon and difficult to live as a single woman. This idea began to change during the nineteenth century, when the proportion of never-married women rose steadily. Emily Dickinson lived as a single, middle-class woman during a period marked by the emergence of the women's rights movement and vigorous debate over the proper roles for women.

Women in general did not have many options or much real power. Single women, however, did retain certain civil rights that women who married did not have. Single women could, for example, make contracts and open bank accounts, and they often served as treasurers for the increasing number of women's organizations that developed during the pre-

war era. Many feminists debated the opportunities available to women and pushed for women's rights.

1. How do the lives of single, middle-class women of the 1800s compare to the lives of single, middle-class women of today?

2. Why do you think Emily Dickinson chose to live in relative seclusion? Explain.

Elizabeth Cady Stanton and Women's Rights

Personification

Writers use **personification** to give human qualities, such as emotions, physical gestures, and powers of speech, to nonhuman things.

8. Analyze Personification Pick one example of personification from "After Great Pain, A Formal Feeling Comes" or "Heart! We Will Forget Him!" Explain how the use of personification affects the meaning of the poem.

9. Draw Conclusions About Personification How would the absence of personification affect Dickinson's poems? Support your answer with evidence from the texts.

Review: Rhythm and Rhyme

As you learned on pages 452–453, **rhythm** is the pattern of beats created by the order of stressed and unstressed syllables and **rhyme** is the repetition of similar or identical sounds at the ends of words that appear close to each other.

10. Partner Activity With a classmate, analyze the rhythm and rhyme of Dickinson's two poems. In some of her poems, Dickinson follows a traditional *abab* or *abac* rhyme scheme. In many of her poems, however, Dickinson deviates from this pattern. With your partner, analyze the rhyme scheme in "After Great Pain, A Formal Feeling Comes" or "Heart! We Will Forget Him!" Explain the effect the rhyme scheme has on meaning. Use a chart like the one below to record your answers.

"Heart! We Will Forget Him!"		
Stanza	Rhyme Scheme	Effect
Stanza 1	abcb	gives the poem an upbeat feel; seems like speaker is hopeful
Stanza 2		

LOG ON ▶ **Literature** Online

Selection Resources For Selection Quizzes, eFlashcards, and Reading-Writing Connection activities, go to glencoe.com and enter QuickPass code GL57805u3.

Compare and Contrast Tone

 Texas Test Practice (10.3)

1. By personifying parts of her own body in both poems, the speaker creates:

A. a relieved tone, permitting her to overcome her sadness.

B. a solemn tone, distancing her from pain.

C. an angry tone, giving her something to rage at.

D. an objective tone, allowing her to forget her grief.

Vocabulary Practice

Practice with Antonyms An **antonym** is a word that has a meaning opposite to that of another word. Match each boldfaced vocabulary word below with its antonym. Use a thesaurus or dictionary to check your answers. You will not use all the answer choices.

1. ceremonious   **a.** informal
2. recollect   **b.** consistency
3. stupor   **c.** forget
4. lag   **d.** keep up
            e. awareness

Academic Vocabulary

Do the dashes in this poem **restrain** *the emotion, or do they help to emphasize it?*

Restrain is an academic word. A person might **restrain** a dog or an impulse. To study this word further, fill out the graphic organizer below.

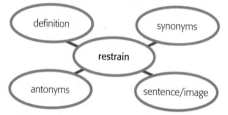

For more on academic vocabulary, see pages 36–37 and R92–R94.

Respond Through Writing

Expository Essay

 TEKS

10.13.C Revise drafts to improve style, word choice, figurative language, sentence variety, and subtlety of meaning after rethinking how well questions of purpose, audience, and genre have been addressed.

Analyze Style Dickinson uses dashes, capitalization, diction, other punctuation, personification, and rhyme scheme in unique ways. Choose two or three of these aspects of her style and analyze how they create or reinforce meaning in the poems.

Purpose and Audience Style is the particular way an author writes. **Diction** is a writer's choice of words. In this case, your purpose is to explain Dickinson's style and diction to an audience of other students.

Plan To help you organize your essay, make a three-column chart like the one shown below.

Aspect of Style	Example from Poem	Contribution to Meaning
dashes		
unexpected capitalization		
slant (almost) rhymes		

List examples and explain how they contribute to the meaning of the poem. Use your chart to determine the aspects of style you will include in your thesis. Then outline your introduction, body, and conclusion. Include the quotations from the poems that you will use as examples.

Draft As you draft, remember to discuss style and to demonstrate your understanding of both works. State your thesis clearly in your introductory paragraph. Then structure your body paragraphs by beginning with a topic sentence that supports your thesis, providing one or more examples, and fully explaining how the examples support your thesis. Make sure each paragraph includes relevant information and valid inferences.

Revise Exchange essays with a classmate. Evaluate how well the essay has addressed the purpose, audience, and genre in the essay. Then revise drafts to improve style, word choice, sentence variety, and subtlety of meaning. Be sure to write clearly and coherently using standard writing conventions.

Edit Edit your paper, correcting any errors in grammar, spelling, and punctuation. Use the Grammar Tip in the side column to help you use dashes for parenthetical information.

> **Grammar Tip**
>
> **Dashes**
>
> Dashes are often used in personal, informal, and analytical writing to emphasize certain ideas or create a certain style. They can also be used like parentheses to add additional information.
>
> For example, if you wanted to add information about Dickinson's birth to a sentence, you could write
>
> *Dickinson (who was born in 1830) lived a reclusive life.*
>
> You could also add this parenthetical information using dashes
>
> *Dickinson—who was born in 1830—lived a reclusive life.*
>
> Note that dashes can be used in pairs, as in the example above, or alone.
>
> *Dickinson wrote over 1,800 poems—only ten were published in her lifetime.*
>
> In both cases there should be no space on either side of the dash.

Before You Read

The Meadow Mouse

Meet Theodore Roethke
(1908–1963)

In his book *Teacher Man*, author Frank McCourt recounts searching for poems that his restless high school students would enjoy. No other poem touched his students as deeply as "My Papa's Waltz" by Theodore Roethke. Students from a variety of backgrounds saw their lives and complicated feelings about their families captured perfectly by Roethke's words.

Roethke was a much loved and honored poet during his lifetime, winning the Pulitzer Prize and the National Book Award. His poems are closely observed lyrics that detail the processes of the natural world.

> "Any serious writer uses the imagery he saw and heard and felt about him as a youth. This is the imagery most vivid to him. It becomes symbolic."
>
> —Theodore Roethke

Memory and Poetry Roethke fashioned many of his poems from strong memories about his childhood in Saginaw, Michigan. Roethke's father and grandfather were florists, and Roethke grew up in a world of flowers, plants, and large commercial greenhouses. Like Emerson and Whitman, Roethke almost mystically identified with nature: "In my veins, in my bones I feel it."

During Roethke's sophomore year of high school, his father died from lung cancer. Roethke was devastated by the loss. At seventeen, he entered the University of Michigan, the first in his family to attend college. Later, in graduate school at Harvard University, he gave three of his poems to poet and professor Robert Hillyer. Hillyer said, "Any editor who wouldn't buy these is a fool!" Encouraged, Roethke turned to poetry as a career.

Teacher and Writer Roethke also began to teach, eventually serving as professor at Michigan State College, Pennsylvania State University, Bennington College, and the University of Washington. Over the years, Roethke mentored many important poets, including Richard Hugo, James Wright, and David Wagoner. According to Hugo, Roethke was "an outrageous man who would take outrageous stances and create something beautiful out of them. . . . That gave me a faith that you could be a pretty ridiculous person and still do something worthwhile or beautiful."

Roethke died of a heart attack when he was only 55. He left behind grateful students and many classic poems.

Literature and Reading Preview

Connect to the Poem

How does your impression of wild animals differ from your impression of domestic ones? Respond in a journal entry.

Build Background

The most common rodents in North America are meadow voles, also called meadow mice. Similar to mice, they have short tails, blunt snouts, small eyes and ears, and short limbs. They are somewhat larger than house mice, and they have shaggier fur. Because voles have enormous appetites, they sometimes cause great damage to crops and trees. Their natural predators include cats, foxes, coyotes, weasels, hawks, owls, snakes, and skunks.

Set Purposes for Reading

Big Idea Loves and Losses

As you read the poem, ask yourself, How does Roethke convey the ideas of love and loss?

Literary Element Mood

The **mood** is the emotional quality of a literary work. A writer's diction, subject matter, setting, and tone—as well as sound devices such as rhyme and rhythm—contribute to creating mood. As you read, ask yourself, How would I describe the mood of each section of this poem?

Reading Strategy Analyze Diction

Diction is a writer's choice of words and is an important element in the writer's voice or style. Skilled writers choose their words carefully to convey a particular tone and meaning. As you read, ask yourself, What words and phrases in the poem seem particularly effective?

Tip: Note Words In a chart like the one below, list words and phrases that you find interesting or intriguing. In the right-hand column, make an inference about how this diction hints at the writer's meaning.

Words and Phrases	Inference About Diction
Trembling (line 6)	the mouse is frightened and very vulnerable

TEKS

For pages 519–524

10.3 Understand, make inferences and draw conclusions about the structure and elements of poetry and provide evidence from text to support understanding.

Vocabulary

minuscule (min′əs kūl′) *adj.* very, very small; p. 521 *Sarah's miniscule cookie was one tenth the size of Lisa's.*

hapless (hap′ lis) *adj.* unlucky or unfortunate; p. 522 *The hapless student had to walk ten miles after missing the last bus.*

Tip: Denotation and Connotation
A word's **denotation** is its dictionary meaning; its **connotations** are the emotional associations it evokes. To identify a word's connotations, think about the images and ideas the word brings to mind. For example, in the sentence *The hapless student had to walk ten miles after missing the last bus,* the word *hapless* has negative connotations, suggesting great misfortune.

The Meadow Mouse

Theodore Roethke

1

In a shoe box stuffed in an old nylon stocking
Sleeps the baby mouse I found in the meadow,
Where he trembled and shook beneath a stick
Till I caught him up by the tail and brought him in,
5   Cradled in my hand
A little quaker, the whole body of him trembling,
His absurd whiskers sticking out like a cartoon-
        mouse,
His feet like small leaves,
Little lizard-feet,
10   Whitish and spread wide when he tried to
        struggle away,
Wriggling like a **minuscule** puppy

Now he's eaten his three kinds of cheese and
        drunk from his bottle-cap watering-trough—
So much he just lies in one corner,
His tail curled under him, his belly big
15   As his head; his bat-like ears
Twitching, tilting toward the least sound.

Do I imagine he no longer trembles
When I come close to him?
He seems no longer to tremble.

The Raspberry-Mouse. Ditz. Private collection.

View the Art Does this mouse capture your sympathies the way the meadow mouse captured the sympathies of the speaker? Explain why or why not.

Analyze Diction *Why do you think the poet chose the word* cradled *rather than* carried?

Vocabulary

minuscule (min´əs kūl´) *adj.* very, very small

2

20 But this morning the shoe-box house on the back porch
   is empty.
Where has he gone, my meadow mouse,
My thumb of a child that nuzzled in my palm?—
To run under the hawk's wing,
Under the eye of the great owl watching from the elm-tree,
25 To live by courtesy of the shrike,[1] the snake, the tom-cat.

I think of the nestling[2] fallen into the deep grass,
The turtle gasping in the dusty rubble of the highway,
The paralytic stunned in the tub, and the water rising,—
All things innocent, **hapless**, forsaken.

---

1. A *shrike* is a bird that feeds on small animals. It is sometimes called a butcherbird.
2. A *nestling* is a young bird that has not yet left the nest.

Mood *What emotions do these lines convey?*

Vocabulary

hapless (hap′ lis) *adj.* unlucky or unfortunate

After You Read

Respond and Think Critically

1. **Connect to Personal Experience** What went through your mind as you finished reading this poem?

2. **Make Inferences About Speaker** What does the speaker do after finding the meadow mouse? What does the speaker's action suggest about his personality and values? ◀ᴅOER

3. **Interpret Behavior** How does the mouse behave at the beginning of the poem? How does the speaker interpret the mouse's behavior after it has been fed?

4. **Analyze Speaker's Beliefs** In lines 21–22, the speaker calls the mouse "my meadow mouse, / My thumb of a child." Is the speaker reasonable or misguided to think of the mouse as his own? Explain.

5. **Analyze Theme** What is the **theme**, or idea about life or human nature, of this poem? Consider what happens in section 2 and what this event causes the speaker to think about.

6. **Analyze Simile** A **simile** is a figure of speech using a word such as *like* or *as* to compare seemingly unlike things. What effect do the similes in lines 7 and 8 create? Support your answer with evidence from the text.

7. **Big Idea** **Draw Conclusions About Imagery** Which images in section 1 convey the endearing qualities of the mouse? Which images in section 2 convey the speaker's sense of loss?

Literary Element Mood

 Texas Test Practice (10.3)

1. How do lines 5–6 help establish a tender mood?

   A. The imagery suggests the vulnerability of the mouse.

   B. The speaker uses contradictions.

   C. The speaker describes his love of nature.

   D. The speaker laments his loss of the mouse.

2. The mood of section 2 can best be described as—

   F. bitter and cynical

   G. playful and lighthearted

   H. calm and accepting

   J. threatening and fearful

Review: Verse Paragraph

As you learned on page 504, a **verse paragraph** is a group of lines that forms a unit. Unlike a stanza, a verse paragraph may vary widely in number of lines. Contemporary poets often use verse paragraphs in free verse to organize their ideas.

8. **Partner Activity** With a partner, examine the five verse paragraphs in "The Meadow Mouse" and identify the ideas that each one conveys. Complete a chart like the one below.

Verse paragraph	Idea
Lines 1–11	delight in observing the mouse's features and actions

Roethke carefully chooses words and phrases to convey his feelings. Review the chart you made on page 520 and then answer these questions.

9. Roethke describes the mouse as "cradled in my hand." What images does this phrase bring to mind? Reread the highlighted text and question on page 521 to help you answer the question.

10. What effect do the three adjectives in the last line create? Explain.

Vocabulary Practice

Practice with Denotation and Connotation

Although the words *politician* and *legislator* have similar denotations, the word *politician* can have negative connotations, while *legislator* generally does not. To distinguish between the denotative and connotative meanings of words, be sure to analyze the word's textual context, or the sentence in which the word appears.

Read the sentences below, and use the textual context of the sentences to distinguish between the denotation and connotation of the boldfaced words. Note each word's denotation and connotation on a separate sheet of paper.

1. The huge bass gobbled up the **minuscule** minnow.

2. Tripping over his shoelaces, the **hapless** boy toppled headlong down the stairs.

Enrich and Extend

 Speaking and Listening

Oral Interpretation Organize and present an oral interpretation of Roethke's poem "The Meadow Mouse" to convey its literal and implied meanings.

Prepare Rehearse the poem several times, and, if possible, memorize it. Refer to the chart you made on page 520 to identify words and phrases to emphasize in your presentation. As you rehearse, choose and practice techniques that support meaning and mood. Rehearse the poem until you can perform it smoothly, focusing on volume, pacing, enunciation, eye contact, and gestures. Consider using props, visual aids, and music to enhance your performance.

Use a chart like the one below to identify key lines in the poem and your techniques for conveying mood.

Key Lines	Mood	Tone of Voice and/or Gestures
"Cradled in my hand" (line 5)	tenderness	warm and gentle tone

Perform Present your dramatic reading to the class. Read slowly and clearly, pausing briefly from time to time to reinforce meaning. Convey the changes in mood as the poem moves from the speaker's affection for the mouse to his sense of bewilderment and loss and finally to his feelings of compassion for other endangered living things.

Evaluate Decide how clearly and effectively you interpreted the poem. Consider asking members of your audience to identify what went well in your performance and what needed improvement. Then write a paragraph to critique and evaluate your skills in oral interpretation. When your classmates present their interpretations, listen critically and respond appropriately.

 Literature Online

Selection Resources For Selection Quizzes, eFlashcards, and Reading-Writing Connection activities, go to glencoe.com and enter QuickPass code GL57805u3.

Down by the Salley Gardens and He Wishes for the Cloths of Heaven

Meet **William Butler Yeats**
(1865–1939)

When William Butler Yeats was fourteen years old, he could not spell and struggled with grammar. Today, however, Yeats is considered one of the most influential poets of the twentieth century.

A Voice of Ireland The oldest child of John Butler Yeats, a lawyer who later became a portrait painter, Yeats was born in Dublin, Ireland. His family moved to London when he was two, but he returned to Ireland often, spending holidays with his grandparents in the Irish countryside. He did not receive any formal schooling until he was twelve. A few years later, in 1880, his family returned to Dublin.

Yeats's mother helped him develop a love of Ireland and an interest in Irish folklore and legend that remained with him all his life. When he was in his early twenties, Yeats began to write poetry. Soon afterward, he met the Irish nationalist John O'Leary, who helped channel the young man's love of Irish literature and myths into the cause of preserving Irish identity. At the time, the British were trying to eliminate Gaelic, the traditional language of Ireland. Yeats and others feared that Ireland's cultural heritage—especially its literature and folklore—would vanish with the outlawed language.

One way Yeats worked to preserve Irish literature and culture was through drama. In the late 1880s, he began writing plays, which were often based on Irish legends. In 1896 he met Lady Gregory, an aristocrat and fellow playwright. Yeats, Lady Gregory, and others helped found the Irish Literary Theatre in 1899, which in time grew into the renowned Abbey Theatre.

Love and Loss Yeats met Maud Gonne, an actress and a fiery political activist, when he was a young man in Dublin. They shared an interest in freeing Ireland from English domination. Yeats fell in love, but Gonne refused two of his marriage proposals. When Yeats wrote about love and loss, he seared the pain of his own unrequited love onto the page.

> "*Think like a wise man but express yourself like the common people.*"
>
> —William Butler Yeats

Ironically, when Yeats won the Nobel Prize in Literature in 1923, it was awarded for his drama, which has not endured to the extent of his poetry.

LOG ON ▶ **Literature** Online

Author Search For more about William Butler Yeats, go to glencoe.com and enter QuickPass code GL57805u3.

Literature and Reading Preview

Connect to the Poems

How does love feel when it is not returned? Respond to this question in your journal.

Build Background

Both "Down by the Salley Gardens" and "He Wishes for the Cloths of Heaven" deal with love. In the first poem, the speaker berates himself for getting love wrong. The second poem is a tribute to someone the speaker loves deeply.

Set Purposes for Reading

Big Idea Loves and Losses

As you read these poems, ask yourself, How does Yeats express feelings of love, longing, and loss?

Literary Element Lyric Poetry

Lyric poetry expresses strong personal thoughts and feelings and is typically short and musical. The subject of a lyric poem can be an object, a person, or an event, but the emphasis of the poem is an emotional experience. As you read, ask yourself, What elements of lyric poetry do these poems reflect?

Reading Strategy Analyze Repetition and Rhyme

Repetition is the recurrence of sounds, words, phrases, lines, or stanzas in a poem. The pattern that end rhymes form in a stanza or poem is called the **rhyme scheme.** Poets use repetition and rhyme to enhance a poem's rhythm or to emphasize particular sounds. As you read, ask yourself, What examples of repetition and rhyme can I identify in these poems?

....

Tip: Take Notes Use a chart like the one below to analyze rhyme scheme. As you read each poem, record the rhyme scheme in the center column. In the right column, analyze how the rhyme scheme impacts the poem.

	Rhyme Scheme	Analysis
Down by the Salley Gardens		
He Wishes for the Cloths of Heaven		

TEKS

For pages 525–530

10.3 Analyze the structure or prosody (e.g., rhyme scheme) and graphic elements in poetry.

Vocabulary

embroidered (em broi′dərd) *adj.* decorated with needlework; p. 528 *The Guatemalan women wore colorful, intricately embroidered dresses to the fiesta.*

tread (tred) *v.* to step or walk on; p. 528 *We encourage our guests to tread lightly on the antique carpet.*

....

Tip: Context Clues When you come across an unfamiliar term, pay close attention to the surrounding words and try to determine a possible meaning. For example, in the sentence *The Guatemalan women wore colorful, intricately embroidered dresses to the fiesta,* the words *colorful, intricately,* and *dresses* provide clues that suggest that *embroidered* means "sewn with decorative designs."

The Artist's Garden at Giverny, 1900. Claude Monet. Oil on canvas. Musée d'Orsay, Paris.

Down by the Salley Gardens

William Butler Yeats

Down by the salley[1] gardens my love and I did meet;
She passed the salley gardens with little snow-white feet.
She bid me take love easy, as the leaves grow on the tree;
But I, being young and foolish, with her would not agree.
In a field by the river my love and I did stand,
And on my leaning shoulder she laid her snow-white hand.
She bid me take life easy, as the grass grows on the weirs;[2]
But I was young and foolish, and now am full of tears.

---

1. *Salley* is a variation of *sallow,* which is a type of willow tree.
2. Here, *weirs* are dams.

Analyze Repetition and Rhyme *What does the repetition of the word "grow(s)" in lines 3 and 7 suggest about the meaning of the poem?*

Loves and Losses *What cause and effect are suggested in the last line?*

Lotto Tapestry from Ushak, Anatolia. Turkish.
Museo Nazionale del Bargello, Florence.

He Wishes for the Cloths of Heaven

William Butler Yeats

Had I the heavens' **embroidered** cloths,
Enwrought[1] with golden and silver light,
The blue and the dim and the dark cloths
Of night and light and the half light,
I would spread the cloths under your
    feet:
But I, being poor, have only my dreams;
I have spread my dreams under your
    feet;
Tread softly because you tread on my
    dreams.

---

1. *Enwrought* means "made with"; here, it means
   "embroidered with."

Lyric Poetry *How do the repeated words at the
ends of the lines tie in with the definition of lyric
poetry?*

Vocabulary

embroidered (em broi′dərd) *adj.* decorated with
needlework
tread (tred) *v.* to step or walk on

After You Read

Respond and Think Critically

1. **Connect to Personal Experience** With which of the emotions in these poems do you identify most or least? Explain.

2. **Interpret Imagery** What advice did the speaker's love give him in "Down by the Salley Gardens"? Why do you think she referred to the leaves and grass as examples?

3. **Clarify Meaning** Why didn't the speaker agree with his love? At the end of the poem, why is the speaker "full of tears"?

4. **Analyze Mood** How does the mood in the first seven lines of "Down by the Salley Gardens" differ from the mood at the end? Explain.

5. **Make Inferences About Speaker** What does the speaker in "He Wishes for the Cloths of Heaven" say he has spread under his love's feet? What can you infer about the treatment he hopes to receive from his love?

6. **Evaluate Diction** How well does Yeats's **diction,** or word choice, convey intense emotion in "He Wishes for the Cloths of Heaven"? Cite words and phrases from the poem to support your answer.

7. **Big Idea** **Draw Conclusions About the Author** What might you conclude about Yeats's own experiences with love and loss based on these poems? Use evidence from the poems and the author biography on page 525 to support your response.

You're the Critic

Beautifully Simple or Simply Silly?

Read the two excerpts of literary criticism below. Both critics agree that Yeats was a man of genius. As you read the excerpts, notice the difference in tone between the two critics.

"[Yeats] has made for himself a poetical style which is much more simple, as it is much more concise, than any prose style; and, in the final perfecting of his form, he has made for himself a rhythm which is more natural, more precise in its slow and wandering cadence, than any prose rhythm. . . . Poetry, if it is to be of the finest quality, is bound to be simple, a mere breathing, in which individual words almost disappear into music."

—Arthur Symons

"[Yeats] hangs in the balance between genius and (to speak rudely) fool."

—Edward Dowden

Group Activity Discuss the following questions with your classmates.

1. Do you think Yeats's poetry style is simpler than "any prose style"? Explain.

2. What do you think Edward Dowden means by his statement?

Literary Element Lyric Poetry

Often short and highly musical, **lyric poetry** expresses personal thoughts and emotions, rather than telling a story as narrative poetry does.

8. **Analyze Elements of Poetry** What elements of "Down by the Salley Gardens" make it possible to imagine the poem set to music?

9. **Analyze Lyric Poetry** What qualities in "He Wishes for the Cloths of Heaven" identify it as a lyric poem? Cite evidence from the poem.

Review: Speaker

As you learned on page 489, the speaker is the voice speaking in a poem and is similar to a narrator in a work of prose.

10. **Partner Activity** Meet with a classmate and discuss the speakers' circumstances in each poem. Create a chart like the one below to contrast how the speaker feels in each poem with how the speaker might feel if his situation changed. What if the speaker in "Down by the Salley Gardens" had written the poem when he and his love were still together? What if the speaker in "He Wishes for the Cloths of Heaven" broke up with his love? How would the speakers' feelings change?

	"Down by the Salley Gardens"	"He Wishes for the Cloths of Heaven"
How the speaker feels now	remorseful	
How the speaker might feel if circumstances changed		

LOG ON ▶ **Literature** Online

Selection Resources For Selection Quizzes, eFlashcards, and Reading-Writing Connection activities, go to glencoe.com and enter QuickPass code GL57805u3.

Reading Strategy Analyze Repetition and Rhyme

Writers use **repetition** and **rhyme** to emphasize important ideas, to create rhythm, and to increase a feeling of unity in a work. Review the blue highlighted question on page 527 and your chart on page 526 and answer the following questions.

11. Choose one of the poems and list three examples of repetition within it. How do these examples help to strengthen the work?

12. Analyze one example of rhyme in the poems that struck you as particularly effective. What did the rhyme accomplish in the poem? Support your answer with evidence from the text.

Vocabulary Practice

Practice with Context Clues Identify the context clues in the following sentences that help you determine the meaning of each bold-faced vocabulary word.

1. Colorful threads form a complex pattern on the **embroidered** blouse.

2. The stairs are worn from the footsteps of many people who **tread** on them each day.

Academic Vocabulary

In "Down by the Salley Gardens," the speaker *reverses* his youthful ideas about love.

Reverse is a word that has many different meanings. Using context clues, figure out the meaning of *reverse* in each sentence below and then explain the difference between the two meanings.

1. She signed her name on the **reverse** side of the contract.

2. If you will **reverse** the image, you'll see what I mean.

For more on academic vocabulary, see pages 36–37 and R92–R94.

Respond Through Writing

Expository Essay

TEKS

10.15.A.i–v Write an analytical essay of sufficient length that includes effective introductory and concluding paragraphs and a variety of sentence structures; rhetorical devices, and transitions betweeen paragraphs; a thesis; an organizing structure; and relevant evidence.

Analyze Theme Both poems by Yeats deal with the topics of love and loss. What does each poem say specifically about these topics? In an essay, analyze the theme of each poem. Build your essay around a thesis that contrasts the themes. Support your ideas with examples from the text.

Purpose and Audience Your purpose is to analyze and contrast the **themes,** or messages about life, of the two poems. Your audience is other students learning about Yeats.

Plan For each poem, list specific words and phrases that help you infer the theme. Complete the following to formulate a thesis statement:

Both (Poem 1) and (Poem 2) are about _____,
but (Poem 1) says _____, while (Poem 2) says _____.

Draft After you have formulated a clear thesis, provide credible, valid, and relevant evidence to support it. Consider this organizing structure:

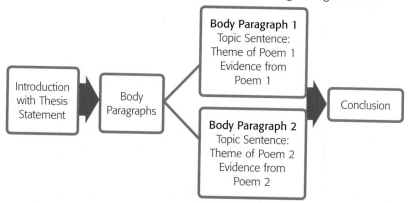

Develop an introduction, a body, and a conclusion. Use transitional words and phrases to achieve coherence, and vary your sentence structure appropriately. As you draft, support your ideas with detailed references to the text. Remember to include valid inferences based on your analysis.

Revise Exchange essays with a classmate and evaluate each other's essays. Provide comments for your classmate and revise your own paper according to the comments you receive.

Edit Edit your paper. Correct errors in grammar, spelling, and punctuation. Use the Grammar Tip for help using commas in contrasting expressions.

> **Grammar Tip**
>
> **Commas in Contrasting Expressions**
>
> Use commas to set off various types of contrasting expressions.
>
> An **antithetical phrase** uses words such as *not* or *unlike* to qualify what precedes it. Use commas to set off antithetical phrases.
>
> *Yeats's poems, unlike his plays, have stood the test of time.*
>
> Some parenthetical expressions, such as *on the contrary* and *on the other hand,* also show contrast. Set these off with commas.
>
> *Yeats, on the other hand, did not attend school until he was twelve.*

Before You Read

I Am Offering This Poem

Meet **Jimmy Santiago Baca**
(born 1952)

Jimmy Santiago Baca, a self-descibed "child of the earth" and "Chicano," is today a famous poet. Yet his path to literary success was neither conventional nor easy. Formerly illiterate, Baca did not learn to read and write until he reached adulthood. Baca was 21 and serving a prison term before he struggled to pull some meaning from a bilingual book given to him as a gift. Eventually, the words before him ceased to resemble a confusing mix of letters and transformed into decipherable, meaningful syllables and sentences. Asked to describe this experience of self-teaching, Baca explained the process as revolutionary.

> "I came upon poetry in much the same way that an infant first gasps for breath."
>
> —Jimmy Santiago Baca

A Deserted Poet Born in Santa Fe, New Mexico, Jimmy Santiago Baca has both Apache and Chicano heritage. He was deserted by his parents when he was only two years old; he then spent several years with his grandmother before being sent to an orphanage. Baca lived on the streets until he was faced with incarceration. He spent six years in prison, including four years in isolation, during which he taught himself to read and write.

Captive and nearly hopeless, Baca found a passion for poetry—"I was writing things that I remember doing as a kid and as an adult and so forth. And what happened was that, in a

place like prison where all sensory enjoyment was deprived, language became more real, more tangible than bars or concrete, than the structure of buildings in the landscape." Encouraged by a fellow prisoner, Baca submitted some of his poetry to *Mother Jones* magazine. Editor Denise Levertov printed Baca's poems and ultimately published his first major collection: *Immigrants in Our Own Land.*

Poet of the People Since the publication of his first book, Baca has produced many compositions, including novels and screenplays. In 2001, he published an award-winning memoir titled *A Place To Stand*, and in 2004 a collection of short stories, *The Importance of a Piece of Paper*, was released. Currently, he continues to write in several genres and travels across the United States facilitating writing workshops for adults and children. Wherever he goes, he carries a powerful message: "Poetry is what we speak to each other."

Baca is a recipient of the National Poetry Award, the American Book Award, the International Hispanic Heritage Award, and the Pushcart Prize.

 Literature Online

Author Search For more about Jimmy Santiago Baca, go to glencoe.com and enter QuickPass code GL57805u3.

Literature and Reading Preview

Connect to the Poem

The speaker in this poem compensates for a lack of material wealth with love. What value do you place on love? Write a journal entry in which you respond to this question.

Build Background

The traditional homes of Navajo Indians, called hogans, are most often built from logs and mud. Occasionally constructed from stone, the humble dwellings have no windows and frame a single entrance facing east.

Set Purposes for Reading

Big Idea Loves and Losses

As you read "I Am Offering This Poem," ask yourself, How does the speaker show love?

Literary Element Metaphor and Simile

A **simile** is a figure of speech that makes a direct comparison between two seemingly dissimilar objects or ideas by connecting them with the words *like* or *as.* **Metaphors** also compare two seemingly unlike things, but metaphors imply the comparison rather than stating it directly and do not use the connectives *like* or *as.* As you read, ask yourself, How does the speaker use simile and metaphor?

Reading Strategy Preview and Review

When you **preview,** you look over a text before you read it to get a sense of the information you will learn and the information you will need to know. When you **review,** you go back over what you have read in order to remember the most important points and to organize your ideas. As you read, ask yourself, How did previewing help me understand the text? What information might I want to review?

....

Tip: Scan Use a chart like the one below to jot down lines from the poem that interest you. List why they interest you. Then note the stylistic patterns of the author.

Line of Interest	Why I Like It	Author's Stylistic Choice
to warm your belly in winter	This is an interesting way to describe a full belly. Usually, fullness is illustrated through a sense of heaviness and not temperature.	The author's descriptions are unusual without using unfamiliar words.

TEKS

For pages 532–535

10.3 Understand, make inferences, and draw conclusions about the structure and elements of poetry and provide evidence from text to support understanding.

Vocabulary

mature (mə choor´) *adj.* having reached a desired state; p. 534
The seed has grown into a vast and mature tree.

dense (dens) *adj.* thick; p. 534
The girl's hair was dense with waves and curls.

....

Tip: Connotation and Denotation
As you read, think about which words have emotional impact, which words don't, and why.

I am offering this poem to you,
since I have nothing else to give.
Keep it like a warm coat
when winter comes to cover you,
5   or like a pair of thick socks
the cold cannot bite through,

             I love you,

I have nothing else to give you,
so it is a pot full of yellow corn
10 to warm your belly in winter,
it is a scarf for your head, to wear
over your hair, to tie up around your face,

             I love you,

Keep it, treasure this as you would
15 if you were lost, needing direction,
in the wilderness life becomes when
   mature;
and in the corner of your drawer,
tucked away like a cabin or hogan
in **dense** trees, come knocking,
20 and I will answer, give you directions,
and let you warm yourself by this fire,
rest by this fire, and make you feel safe,

             I love you,

It's all I have to give,
25 and all anyone needs to live,
and to go on living inside,
when the world outside
no longer cares if you live or die;
remember,

30   I love you.

I Am Offering This Poem

Jimmy Santiago Baca

Angola's Dreams Grasp Finger Tips, 1973. Emilio Cruz.
Smithsonian American Art Museum, Washington, DC.

Metaphor and Simile *What literary device is the poet employing in line 11? Explain.*

Preview and Review *Besides expressing feelings for one person, what else is the speaker expressing in this poem?*

Vocabulary

mature (mə choor´) *adj.* having reached a desired state
dense (dens) *adj.* thick

After You Read

Respond and Think Critically

1. **Connect to Personal Experience** Whom do you think this poem is intended for? Explain. How would you expect the recipient to feel after reading the poem?

2. **Make Inferences About Speaker** What reason does the speaker give for offering this poem? What does this suggest about the speaker? **OER**

3. **Analyze Structure** How does Baca divide the poem's stanzas? How does the first stanza compare with the second? With the third and fourth stanzas? Support your answer with text evidence.

4. **Evaluate Structure** Is the poem's structure effective in conveying its message? How else might the poem be structured and still communicate this message? Explain.

5. **Draw Conclusions About Style** Baca has had little formal training in poetry. How do you think this has affected his writing style? Support your answer with text evidence.

6. **Big Idea** **Draw Conclusions About Author's Perspective** Baca has experienced great loss in his life, including the loss of loved ones and his own freedom. How might these losses have inspired "I Am Offering This Poem"?

Literary Element Metaphor and Simile

In order for a metaphor or a simile to be effective, the comparison must be convincing.

7. **Make Inferences About Metaphor and Simile** Identify two or three metaphors or similes in the poem. What can you infer about each one's meaning? Support your response with text evidence.

8. **Analyze Metaphor and Simile** Change one of the poem's metaphors to a simile and change one of its similes to a metaphor. How does the switch affect the descriptions?

Reading Strategy Preview and Review

By **previewing**, you can find clues about the content of a text before you begin reading. **Reviewing** the material will help you to remember important details. Refer to the chart you made on page 533.

9. The speaker compares his or her love to things that provide warmth. What does this tell you about the speaker?

10. Restate the speaker's message in your own words. Reread the blue highlighted question on page 534 to help you.

Vocabulary Practice

Practice with Denotation and Connotation
Denotation is the literal, or dictionary, meaning of a word. **Connotation** is the implied, or cultural, meaning of a word. Each vocabulary word below is listed alongside a word that has a similar denotation. Choose the word that has a more powerful connotation and explain why.

1. mature   aged

2. dense   impenetrable

⚡ Writing

Write a Description Think of meaningful scenes from your life to help you write comparisons of your own. Write one or two sentences that each contain a simile. Then rewrite each sentence so that it uses a metaphor instead of a simile. When you rewrite your simile as a metaphor, do not simply remove the word *like* or *as*. Instead, restructure and extend the idea.

Before You Read

since feeling is first

Meet **E. E. Cummings**
(1894–1962)

In his later poetry, E. E. Cummings experimented with poetic form and language to create a distinctive style. He also wrote essays, short stories, a novel, plays, children's fiction, and a travel diary. But Cummings was not only a writer. He was a painter, who had many solo exhibitions, and a professor of poetry at Harvard University.

Starting Out Edward Estlin Cummings was born in Cambridge, Massachusetts, home of Harvard University. His father was a professor at the school, which Cummings later attended. While at Harvard, Cummings was influenced by the works of experimental writers such as Gertrude Stein and Ezra Pound. He graduated with a master's degree in English and Classical Studies in 1916.

> "It takes courage to grow up and become who you really are."
>
> —E. E. Cummings

By April of 1917, World War I was raging in Europe, but the United States had not yet entered the war. Cummings volunteered to serve as an ambulance driver in France. Due to a misunderstanding, he was imprisoned on suspicion of treason for three months in a French detention camp.

A Champion of the Individual After the war, Cummings returned to Paris to study art. He turned his experiences in the French detention camp into his first book, *The Enormous Room*, published in 1922. This fictionalized account

of his captivity depicted it as a time of personal growth. In 1923 he published a book of poetry, *Tulips and Chimneys*. While many of the poems are conventional in style, some show the playful form and punctuation that are hallmarks of Cummings's later work.

Cummings moved to New York City in 1924 and found himself regarded as a celebrity. *Vanity Fair* magazine gave him a long-term assignment as an essayist and a portrait artist. This allowed him to set up his lifelong routine of painting after lunch and writing after dinner. Over the ensuing years, Cummings wrote twelve volumes of poems and won numerous awards.

Cummings wrote some of his poems in free verse, with no fixed meter or rhyme, but many have a rhyming sonnet structure. Despite the unusual form of many of Cummings's poems, his topics are often traditional: love, nature, childhood. Yet he was critical of conventional thinking and of society's restrictions on freedom of expression. In one of his lectures at Harvard, Cummings said, "So far as I am concerned, poetry and every other art was, is, and forever will be strictly and distinctly a question of individuality."

LOG ON ▶ **Literature** Online

Author Search For more about E. E. Cummings, go to glencoe.com and enter QuickPass code GL57805u3.

Literature and Reading Preview

Connect to the Poem

Do you ever make a decision based on the way you feel? Freewrite for a few minutes about times when you have let your feelings dictate your decisions.

Build Background

E. E. Cummings is known for manipulating **syntax,** or word order, in his poetry. Cummings uses familiar words in unexpected places to surprise his readers and call their attention to the flexibility of language.

Set Purposes for Reading

Big Idea Loves and Losses

As you read "since feeling is first," ask yourself, What does Cummings consider to be of lesser value than feeling?

Literary Element Juxtaposition

Juxtaposition is placing two or more distinct items, ideas, or sets of words side by side in order to compare or contrast them. As you read the poem, ask yourself, How does Cummings use juxtaposition and word position to increase his readers' understanding of the power of feeling?

Reading Strategy Paraphrase

Paraphrasing is taking the author's exact words and rephrasing them in your own words. Paraphrasing a poem can help you understand unusual phrasing and punctuation. As you read, ask yourself, How can I paraphrase Cummings's ideas?

....

Tip: List Important Words Use a chart like the one below to list important words as you read. Note which part of speech each word is—noun, verb, adjective, or adverb. Be sure you understand the meaning of each word. Make the chart any length you need. Then try rewriting lines of the poem in your own words.

Word	Part of Speech	Meaning
feeling	noun	emotion

TEKS

For pages 536–539

10.3 Analyze the structure or prosody and graphic elements (e.g., word position) in poetry.

since feeling is first

E. E. Cummings

Composition, 1933. Joan Miró. Oil on canvas,
1.66 x 1.33 m. Prague, Czech Republic. © ARS, NY.

since feeling is first
who pays any attention[1]
to the syntax of things
will never wholly kiss you;
5   wholly to be a fool
while Spring is in the world

my blood approves,
and kisses are a better fate
than wisdom
10   lady i swear by all flowers. Don't cry
—the best gesture of my brain is less than
your eyelids' flutter which says

we are for each other: then
laugh, leaning back in my arms
15   for life's not a paragraph

And death i think is no parenthesis[2]

---

1. Here, *who pays any attention* is the subject of the statement
   rather than a question.
2. In this context, a *parenthesis* is a digression or afterthought.

Juxtaposition *Why does Cummings choose to compare kisses
and wisdom?*

After You Read

Respond and Think Critically

1. **Connect to Personal Experience** What does the poem suggest to you about where feelings should rank in your own life?

2. **Clarify Meaning** What kind of person does the poem's speaker say "will never wholly kiss you"? What do you think Cummings means by this?

3. **Make Inferences About Meaning** In the poem, when is it acceptable to be a fool? Why do you think the speaker limits being foolish to a particular time period?

4. **Analyze Enjambment** Enjambment is a type of graphic element in which the sense of a sentence or phrase continues from one line to the next without a pause. Find at least two instances of enjambment in Cummings's poem. What effect do they have on the poem's overall meaning?

5. **Analyze Metaphors** Identify what is being compared in the two metaphors at the end of the poem. What point is Cummings making through the use of these metaphors? Support your response with text evidence.

6. **Evaluate Style** Does Cummings's disregard for rules of capitalization strengthen or weaken the poem? Support your answer with evidence from the text.

7. **Big Idea** **Draw Conclusions About Genre** When you read "since feeling is first," did it seem like a love poem? Explain why or why not.

Literary Element Juxtaposition

In "since feeling is first," Cummings juxtaposes intellectual activity with emotional response.

8. **Analyze Word Position** Identify at least two examples of juxtaposition in the poem. In each case, how does the word position affect the meaning of the juxtaposed ideas? Reread the pink highlighted question on page 538 to help you.

9. **Evaluate Juxtaposition** How effective are these juxtapositions in conveying the speaker's meaning? Explain.

Reading Strategy Paraphrase

When you **paraphrase**, you completely restate the original text in your own words. Refer to the chart you made on page 537 and answer these questions.

10. What message does Cummings try to communicate in "since feeling is first"?

11. Support your opinion by paraphrasing at least two quotations from the poem.

Academic Vocabulary

*E. E. Cummings uses the **element** of juxtaposition in his poem to show the relationships between certain ideas.*

Element is an academic word. In a more casual conversation, someone might describe a suspense movie as having the **element** of surprise. Using context clues, figure out the meaning of the word *element* in the sentence above about the poem.

For more on academic vocabulary, see pages 36–37 and R92–R94.

Writing

Write an Essay Write a short essay in which you identify and explain the juxtapositions and metaphors for emotion and reason that Cummings uses in "since feeling is first."

LOG ON **Literature** Online

Selection Resources For Selection Quizzes, eFlashcards, and Reading-Writing Connection activities, go to glencoe.com and enter QuickPass code GL57805u3.

Before You Read

Horses Graze

Meet **Gwendolyn Brooks**
(1917–2000)

"I want to write poems," said Gwendolyn Brooks, "that I could take . . . into the street, into the halls of a housing project." Witty, original, and sometimes outspoken, Brooks is one of the most respected American poets of the twentieth century. Brooks captured the hopes of urban African Americans, as well as their feelings of rage and despair in the face of racism and poverty.

An Early Love of Poetry Many characters in Brooks's poems are based on people who lived in her neighborhood on Chicago's South Side. Brooks knew the South Side intimately, having spent most of her life there. She was born to parents who had little money but who did have a deep love of literature and high expectations for their children. When Brooks, at age seven, brought her mother her first poems, her mother said, "You are going to be the lady Paul Laurence Dunbar," referring to a prominent African American poet.

> "*If you love songs and rap, you love poetry.*"
>
> —Gwendolyn Brooks

By the time she was sixteen, Brooks had written more than 75 poems, and she had met two of the leading African American writers of her day, Langston Hughes and James Weldon Johnson. Both writers encouraged her to continue writing. Hughes became her friend and mentor. With the publication of her second book, *Annie Allen*, Brooks became the first

African American writer to win the Pulitzer Prize for poetry. Brooks later became Poet Laureate of Illinois, poetry consultant to the Library of Congress, and a member of the National Women's Hall of Fame.

Change of Course In her early books, Brooks chronicled the dreams and disappointments of everyday African Americans using traditional verse forms such as the ballad and the sonnet. In the 1960s, Brooks's poetry underwent an immense change in tone and content. Inspired by African American activism, Brooks began to write more overtly political poems. "This is not time for sonnets," she once said, "but a time for raw, ragged free verse."

As Blyden Jackson notes, Brooks's poems brim with "insights and revelations of universal application." They speak to the human condition and to all citizens of the world.

Literature Online

Author Search For more about Gwendolyn Brooks, go to glencoe.com and enter QuickPass code GL57805u3.

Literature and Reading Preview

Connect to the Poem

How do the concerns of animals compare with those of humans? Make lists of concerns for animals and for humans.

Build Background

Horses have wide, flat teeth for grinding plants and long foot bones that enable swift running. For centuries, horses were used extensively in warfare, agriculture, and transportation.

Set Purposes for Reading

Big Idea Loves and Losses

As you read, ask yourself, What might the poem be saying about human flaws and weaknesses?

Literary Element Repetition

Repetition is a literary device in which sounds, words, phrases, lines, or stanzas are repeated for emphasis. Writers use repetition to emphasize an important point, to expand an idea, or to help create rhythm. Repetition also increases the unity of a work. As you read the poem, ask yourself, What are examples of repetition and what ideas do they reinforce?

Reading Strategy Draw Conclusions About Meaning

When you draw conclusions, you use pieces of information to make a general statement about people, places, events, and ideas. When you **draw conclusions about** a poem's **meaning,** you look at details throughout the poem and decide what the author wanted to say through these details.

Tip: Record Details As you read, examine the elements of the poem and record details. Use these details to draw conclusions about the poem's meaning. Use a diagram like the one below. Refer to the blue highlighted question to help you.

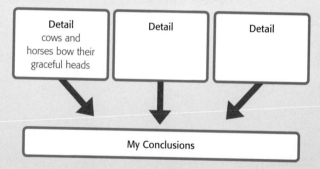

Detail	Detail	Detail
cows and horses bow their graceful heads		

My Conclusions

TEKS

For pages 540–544

10.3 Understand, make inferences and draw conclusions about the structure and elements of poetry and provide evidence from text to support understanding.

Vocabulary

oblivion (ə blivʹē ən) *n.* a lack of awareness or memory; p. 542 *After the song's popularity passed, the band fell into oblivion.*

crest (krest) *n.* a peak, high point, or climax; p. 543 *Leah's joy was at its crest; she had never been happier.*

affirmation (afʹər māʹshən) *n.* positive agreement or judgment; p. 543 *As she bent down toward the child, the mother's face shone with affirmation.*

Tip: Word Usage Select words carefully, always keeping their specific usage in mind. For example, even though *grazing* means "eating" you would not thank your hosts for grazing at their dinner table.

Horses Graze

Gwendolyn Brooks

Indo-Aryan Pottery Horses, ca. 2000 BC.

Cows graze.
Horses graze.
They
eat
5   eat
  eat.
Their graceful heads
are bowed
bowed
10   bowed
in majestic° **oblivion**.
They are nobly oblivious
to your follies,
your inflation,°

11 **majestic:** a quality of dignified greatness.
14 **Inflation:** an economic condition that occurs when consumer prices continuously rise or the purchasing power of money continuously declines; it can also mean "pomposity" or "empty pretentiousness."

Repetition *What does the repetition of* eat *and* bowed *help the author to stress?*

Draw Conclusions About Meaning *What does the detail in lines 12–14 contribute to the meaning of the poem?*

Vocabulary

oblivion (ə bliv′ē ən) *n.* a lack of awareness or memory

15   the knocks and nettles° of administration.
        They
          eat
          eat
          eat.
20   And at the **crest** of their brute satisfaction,
        with wonderful gentleness, in **affirmation**,
        they lift their clean calm eyes and they lie down
        and love the world.
        They speak with their companions.
25   They do not wish that they were
            otherwhere.
        Perhaps they know that creature
            feet may press
        only a few earth inches at a time,
        that earth is anywhere earth,
        that an eye may see,
30   wherever it may be,
        the Immediate arc, alone, of life,
            of love.
        In Sweden,
        China,
        Afrika,
35   in India or Maine
        the animals are sane;
        they know and know and know
        there's ground below
        and sky
40   up high.

15 knock: a sharp blow or hit.
nettle: a weedy plant that releases a
substance that is irritating to the
skin; metaphorically, nettle can be
anything that irritates.

Landscape with Horses, 18th–19th century.
Yi Myong-Gi. Ink and coloured paper. Musée
Guimet Paris.

> **Vocabulary**
>
> **crest** (krest) *n.* a peak, high point, or climax
> **affirmation** (af′ər mā′shən) *n.* positive agreement or
> judgment

After You Read

Respond and Think Critically

1. **Connect to Personal Experience** What image or description in the poem did you find most striking? Explain.

2. **Clarify Meaning** How does the speaker describe the animals in lines 7–11? Explain what you think "bowed / in majestic oblivion" means.

3. **Make Inferences About Meaning** According to the speaker, what do the animals "know," and in what way are they "sane"? What might the poet be implying here?

4. **Analyze Diction** *Inflation* is one of the few words used to describe humans in the poem. Why might Brooks have chosen it? Explain.

5. **Evaluate Argument** What does the speaker think people could learn from animals? Is the speaker's argument effective? Support your answer with evidence from the text.

6. **Big Idea** **Draw Conclusions About Meaning** What does this poem suggest to you about what is truly important in life? What does it suggest about the things that all people, and all creatures, have in common? Support your answer with text evidence.

7. **Draw Conclusions About Author's Perspective** How does this poem reveal Brooks's commitment to social activism?

Literary Element Repetition

In poetry, **repetition** emphasizes words or ideas and adds a musical quality to the work.

8. **Identify Repetition** Identify three examples of repetition in the poem. How is it distributed throughout the poem?

9. **Analyze Repetition** What rhythmic or musical quality does the repetition have? What ideas or meanings are reinforced? Explain, supporting your answer with evidence from the text.

Reading Strategy Draw Conclusions About Meaning

Refer to the diagram you made on page 541 to help you answer the following questions.

10. What conclusion can you draw about the differences between animals and humans from the details in lines 24–31? Explain.

11. What elements of poetry are used in lines 32–40? Pick one example and draw a conclusion about how it creates meaning in the poem. Support your answer with evidence from the text.

Vocabulary Practice

Practice with Usage Respond to these statements to help you explore the meanings of the boldfaced vocabulary words from the poem.

1. Name two characteristics of a state of **oblivion.**

2. Describe what you might feel at the **crest** of a successful endeavor.

3. Identify two things you might say in **affirmation** of someone or something.

Writing

Write a Summary In your own words, write a summary of "Horses Graze," making sure that you convey the poem's essential meaning. For help with summarizing, see page 35.

LOG ON **Literature** Online

Selection Resources For Selection Quizzes, eFlashcards, and Reading-Writing Connection activities, go to glencoe.com and enter QuickPass code GL57805u3.

Before You Read

Parlor

Meet **Rita Dove**
(born 1952)

"O ne can be a poet, but you have to have a life," poet Rita Dove says. "If you don't have a life, then I don't see where you're going to write your poems from." In order to inspire her own poetry, Dove devotes her time to many pursuits, including music, singing, and dancing.

> "All the moments that make up a human being have to be written about, talked about, painted, danced, in order to really talk about life."
>
> —Rita Dove

Finding Her Voice Dove was born in the industrial city of Akron, Ohio, to a middle-class family. Her father was the first African American research chemist at a nationally prominent tire manufacturer. Dove's parents encouraged her to read, and as she says, "Going to the library was the one place we got to go without asking really for permission." Dove began writing at an early age, but she did not think she could have a career writing poetry. As she explains, "I didn't know writers could be real live people, because I never knew any writers." Fortunately, Dove had a high school English teacher who noticed her talent and invited her to a writer's conference. There her deep interest in literary endeavors took hold, and Dove went on to study poetry in college and in Germany on a prestigious Fulbright scholarship. She also attended the highly esteemed University of Iowa Writers' Workshop.

A Champion for Poetry Many of Dove's poems deal with topics related to history and family and trying to achieve a sense of one's place. Her most famous work, *Thomas and Beulah*, is a re-creation of her grandparents' lives from the 1920s to the 1960s. The book earned Dove a Pulitzer Prize.

Dove has enjoyed much success as a poet. She served as Poet Laureate of the United States from 1993 to 1995, the youngest person and the first African American to do so. For Dove, the position "offers someone as a spokesperson for literature and poetry in this country. It means that one becomes an automatic role model." Dove's works have proven to appeal to a wide audience. She has read her poetry at a White House State dinner and also on the popular children's television show *Sesame Street*. In 2004 she published the poetry collection *American Smooth*. She currently works as the Commonwealth Professor of English at the University of Virginia in Charlottesville.

LOG ON ▶ **Literature** Online

Author Search For more about Rita Dove, go to glencoe.com and enter QuickPass code GL57805u3.

Literature and Reading Preview

Connect to the Poem

Have you ever disagreed with someone about an important topic? Freewrite for a few minutes about your experience.

Build Background

Transistor radios were popular in the 1950s and 1960s. These lightweight radios ran on batteries and were small enough to hold in the hand or fit in a pocket.

Set Purposes for Reading

Big Idea Loves and Losses

As you read, ask yourself, What lessons does the speaker learn from his or her grandmother's life and death?

Literary Element Imagery

Imagery is sensory language that appeals to one or more of the five senses and creates an emotional response in the reader. For example, a writer might describe a sunset as a "symphony of color," appealing to the senses of sight and sound and creating a sense of uplift. As you read "Parlor," ask yourself, What details appeal to the five senses? What is the emotional effect of these details?

Reading Strategy Draw Conclusions About Meaning

When you **draw conclusions about meaning,** you use a number of pieces of information to make a general statement about the meaning of details in a work. As you read the poem, notice details about people and the setting. Ask yourself, What important information do I learn from these details?

....

Tip: Make a Chart As you read the poem, use a chart like the one below to record details about the speaker, the grandmother, and places and events mentioned in the poem. Write down the conclusions you form about the meaning of these details.

Detail from Poem	Meaning
"We passed through on the way to anywhere else."	The family needed to walk through the grandmother's parlor in order to reach other rooms in the house. The parlor and the grandmother had great significance to the speaker.

TEKS

For pages 545–548

10.7 Understand, make inferences and draw conclusions about how an author's sensory language creates imagery in literary text and provide evidence from text to support understanding.

Vocabulary

china (chī′nə) *n.* fine, glossy pottery used for tableware; p. 547 *I washed and dried the china after we ate dinner.*

aglow (ə glō′) *adj.* glowing; p. 547 *The house was so aglow with lights, she could see into every room.*

....

Tip: Context Clues When you come across an unfamiliar word, use context clues—the words and phrases surrounding the word—to help you figure out the word's meaning.

Two Tea Cups. Kari Van Tine.

Parlor

Rita Dove

We passed through
on the way to anywhere else.
No one lived there
but silence, a pale **china** gleam,

5   and the tired eyes of saints
aglow on velvet.

Mom says things are made
to be used. But Grandma insisted
peace was in what wasn't there,
10 strength in what was unsaid.

It would be nice to have a room
you couldn't enter, except in your mind.
I like to sit on my bed
plugged into my transistor radio,
15 "Moon River" pouring through my
     head.

How do you *use* life?
How do you *feel* it? Mom says

things harden with age; she says
Grandma is happier now. After the
     funeral,
20 I slipped off while they stood around
remembering—away from all
the talking and eating and weeping

to sneak a peek. She wasn't there.
Then I understood why
25 she had kept them just so:

so quiet and distant,
the things that she loved.

Vocabulary

china (chī′ nə) *n.* fine, glossy pottery used for tableware
aglow (ə glō′) *adj.* glowing

Imagery *What does the image in line 22 tell you about the speaker's family? What is its emotional effect?*

RITA DOVE **547**

After You Read

Respond and Think Critically

1. **Connect to Personal Experience** What was your reaction to the poem's ending? Explain your answer.

2. **Make Inferences About Attitudes** What impression of the grandmother's parlor do you receive from lines 1–6? From lines 7–10, what can you infer about the rest of the family's attitude toward the parlor? Explain.

3. **Interpret Meaning** The grandmother insists that "peace was in what wasn't there." What do you think she means by this? Support your answer with evidence from the poem. **OER**

4. **Compare and Contrast Attitudes** Reread lines 11–15. How is the speaker's attitude toward privacy similar to the grandmother's? How is it different? Explain.

5. **Analyze Mood** Review lines 16–17. How would you characterize the **mood,** or emotional quality, of the poem up to this point? How does the mood shift after line 17? Support your answer with evidence from the poem.

6. **Big Idea** **Draw Conclusions About Theme** What lesson does the speaker learn about the grandmother and about love and loss? Support your answer with evidence.

Literary Element Imagery

To help you answer the following questions, refer to the pink highlighted question on page 547.

7. **Analyze Imagery** List four images from the poem: two that appeal to the sense of sight and two that appeal to the sense of sound. What effect do these images have on the mood of the poem? Support your answer with evidence from the poem.

8. **Draw Conclusions About Imagery** What do the images you listed help you to understand about the speaker and the grandmother? Explain.

Reading Strategy Draw Conclusions About Meaning

Drawing conclusions about meaning can deepen your understanding of a work.

9. What is the meaning of the mother's remark that "things harden with age"? Support your answer with evidence from the poem.

10. Review lines 23–27 and the chart you made on page 546. In line 25, what does "them" refer to? What is the significance of the final lines? Explain.

Vocabulary Practice

Practice with Context Clues Identify the context clues in the following sentences that help you determine the meaning of each bold-faced vocabulary word.

1. They received a set of **china** for their wedding, and they used it every night at dinner.

2. The lights on the computer were **aglow,** so she knew it was on.

Writing

Write a Description Do you, or does someone you know, have a room filled with beloved things? Write a description of the room and its contents. Use imagery to create an emotional response in the reader. Order your description spatially, describing the objects in the order one would encounter them while walking through the room.

LOG ON ▶ **Literature** Online

Selection Resources For Selection Quizzes, eFlash-cards, and Reading-Writing Connection activities, go to glencoe.com and enter QuickPass code GL57805u3.

Before You Read

Secondhand Grief

Meet Sherman Alexie
(born 1966)

Sherman Alexie has overcome medical issues and the poverty of a reservation to become one of the preeminent Native American authors of our time.

An Early Love of Literature Alexie learned to read by the age of three. When he was five years old, he was reading books such as John Steinbeck's *The Grapes of Wrath*. Alexie's love of literature isolated him from other children on the Spokane, Washington, reservation where his family lived.

Alexie decided to attend high school away from the reservation, where he hoped to obtain a better education than his parents had received. While at Reardan High, he excelled in academics and became a basketball star. Additionally, he was the only Native American to attend the school during his time there.

> "If I were a doctor, nobody would be inviting me to talk to reservations. . . Writers can influence more people."
>
> —Sherman Alexie

Alexie attended Gonzaga University in Spokane on a scholarship. In his junior year, he transferred to Washington State University in Pullman. Alexie planned to become a doctor, but decided to switch majors after fainting several times in anatomy class. Alexie enrolled in a poetry workshop and discovered he excelled at writing. With his teacher's encouragement, he decided to make a career of it.

Same Passion, Different Forms Alexie has published twenty books, including the recent collection of poems *Dangerous Astronomy*. Alexie draws on his experience and perspective to tell stories about modern Native American life. He addresses the ideas of displacement, loss, and love, while challenging audiences to look past clichéd portrayals of Native Americans in mass media. His characters strive for meaningful lives in the face of racism and economic disadvantage.

Alexie reaches out to audiences through a variety of media. He co-authored a screenplay based on one of his short stories, which became the award-winning, independent motion picture *Smoke Signals*. The film is the first feature film entirely written, directed, produced, and acted by Native Americans. Alexie also mentors young film writers through the Sundance Institute and judges a variety of writing contests.

LOG ON **Literature** Online

Author Search For more about Sherman Alexie, go to glencoe.com and enter QuickPass code GL57805u3.

Literature and Reading Preview

Connect to the Poem

How connected do you feel to other people in your community? Write a journal entry about friendships or connections you have with people in your community.

Build Background

Alexie frequently writes about the conflicting desires and emotions felt by characters who leave their homes or societies to live elsewhere. In these new places, they may feel alienated and alone, yet may also have opportunities.

Set Purposes for Reading

Big Idea Loves and Losses

As you read, ask yourself, How does Alexie highlight the son's loneliness among a sea of people?

Literary Element Diction

Diction is a writer's choice of words. Diction is an important element in a writer's voice or style. Understanding why authors choose some words over others will help you understand the tone and meaning of a poem. As you read, ask yourself, How does Alexie's careful choice of words influence my experience of the poem?

Reading Strategy Visualize

When you **visualize**, you picture a text's events and descriptions in your mind's eye. Visualizing can help you reflect on your understanding of a text, bettering your comprehension.

···

Tip: Create a Chart Use a chart like the one below to record images and events in the poem. Visualize these images and events and take notes about what the details in the poem help you to picture.

Detail	What I Visualize
"both of them wearing / identical suits and ties"	I see a little boy with his father. Their similar appearance reflects the closeness they feel.

TEKS

For pages 549–552

RC-10.A Reflect on understanding to monitor comprehension (i.e., creating sensory images).

Vocabulary

nostalgic (nos tal′jik) *adj.* longing for persons, things, or situations from the past; p. 551 *The old man was nostalgic for the music of his youth.*

marvel (mär′vəl) *v.* to become filled with wonder or astonishment; p. 551 *The young girl marveled at the dolls in the toy store.*

·····································

Tip: Word Origins In a dictionary, a word's origins usually appear in square brackets. Root words appear in italics.

Décalcomanie, 1966. René Magritte. Oil on canvas, 81 x 100 cm. Private collection. © ARS, NY

Secondhand Grief

Sherman Alexie

After his father dies
The son wears his clothes.

First, the black shoes
then the wool pants

5 and finally the blazer
with **nostalgic** lapels.

When he was a child
walking with his father

both of them wearing
10 identical suits and ties

the neighbors **marveled**
at how much they looked alike.

A thousand miles away
from his father's grave

15 He steps into his favorite overcoat
and then steps outside

to walk among fathers
and sons, strangers

strangers, strangers
20 strangers, strangers

strangers, strangers
strangers, all of them.

Diction *Reread lines 2–6. Which highly specific words does Alexie use to describe the father's clothes?*

Loves and Losses *What losses does the son experience?*

Vocabulary

nostalgic (nos tal′jik) *adj.* longing for persons, things, or situations from the past

marvel (mär′vəl) *v.* to become filled with wonder or astonishment

After You Read

Respond and Think Critically

1. **Connect to Personal Experience** Is it important to you to follow in the footsteps of someone you admire? Why or why not?

2. **Interpret Symbols** What might the father's clothes represent for the son? Support your answer with text evidence. OER

3. **Interpret Title** Why do you think Alexie calls the son's grief "secondhand"? What feeling or idea might the title suggest? Explain.

4. **Make Inferences About Background** What does the son remember about his childhood? Based on the son's memories, what can you infer about his relationship with his father? Explain.

5. **Analyze Repetition** Why is the word *strangers* repeated? What does the repetition suggest about the son's new location and about his emotional state? Explain.

6. **Analyze Theme** What does this poem suggest about how a person constructs a personality or identity? What details of the poem help to make the point? Explain.

7. **Big Idea** **Draw Conclusions About Meaning** What does the poem suggest that the son has lost in addition to his father? Support your response with text evidence.

Literary Element Diction

An author's choice of words, or **diction**, is an important element of an author's style.

8. **Analyze Diction** List three examples of words and phrases from the poem, and explain how they help to create a mood. Use the pink highlighted question for help.

9. **Evaluate Diction** Would you characterize Alexie's diction as direct and everyday, or more formal? Support your answer with details from the poem.

Reading Strategy Visualize

Review the chart you made on page 550 and answer the following questions.

10. What kind of scene did you visualize when you read the last eight lines of the poem?

11. What does the repetition of *strangers* help you to visualize? How does visualizing help you to monitor your comprehension? Explain.

LOG ON ▶ **Literature** Online

Selection Resources For Selection Quizzes, eFlashcards, and Reading-Writing Connection activities, go to glencoe.com and enter QuickPass code GL57805u3.

Vocabulary Practice

Practice with Word Origins Studying the etymology, or origin and history, of a word can help you better understand and explore its meaning. Create a word map, like the one below, for each of these vocabulary words from the poem.

nostalgic   marvel

EXAMPLE:

Definition
Present but not obvious or active

latent

Etymology
Latin *latens* means "to lie hidden"

Sample Sentence
Sam has a latent tendency to be lazy; he tends to avoid chores.

Writing

Write a Dialogue Write a dialogue between the child and his father as they are out walking, "both of them wearing / identical suits and ties." Make use of differences in diction to show the distinctive personalities of the two speakers.

Before You Read

Ballad of Birmingham

Meet **Dudley Randall**
(1914–2000)

A man whose first poem was published when he was only thirteen, Dudley Randall later started a publishing company with just twelve dollars. His tireless work and dedication brought recognition to a generation of African American writers.

Before Birmingham Born in Washington, D.C., Randall grew up in Detroit after a series of family migrations. Over the years, he was a foundry worker, a soldier, a postal worker, and a librarian.

The Broadside Dudley Randall is renowned for founding Broadside Press in 1965. This successful firm got its name from Randall's printing of his poem "Ballad of Birmingham" on a single sheet of paper, known in publishing lingo as a "broadside." Randall followed up that poem with another of his, "Dressed All in Pink," then continued the series with broadside printings of previously published work by Margaret Walker and Robert Hayden.

> *"A poet writes about what he feels, what agitates his heart and sets his pen in motion."*
>
> —Dudley Randall

Broadside Press then began to publish poetry collections, such as Randall's *Poem Counterpoem* (co-written with Margaret Esse Danner), *Cities Burning, Love You,* and *More to Remember.* By bringing into the literary spotlight such prominent writers as Alice Walker, Amiri Baraka, and Sonia Sanchez, Broadside Press proved itself to be an important and valuable resource for a number of minority writers.

The Mind of a Poet "The Ballad of Birmingham" is the most famous of Randall's poems, many of which were written during the tumultuous period of the Civil Rights Movement. The collection *Cities Burning* is a response to the Detroit race riot of 1967. Brought about in part by police brutality toward African Americans, the chaos lasted for five days. Forty-three people died and more than seven thousand people were arrested.

His Legacy Randall's success as a poet grew while he was a poet in residence at the University of Detroit and during his later appointment as poet laureate of Detroit in 1981. The National Endowment for the Arts awarded Randall a Lifetime Achievement Award in 1996.

Literature and Reading Preview

Connect to the Poem

Think of a time you read or heard about a tragic event. Write a list of ways you could respond creatively to a tragic event.

Build Background

Birmingham was the site of much racial turbulence during the Civil Rights Movement. "Ballad of Birmingham" is a response to the September 15, 1963, bombing of the Sixteenth Street Baptist Church. The bombing killed four young African American girls.

Set Purposes for Reading

Big Idea Loves and Losses

As you read, ask yourself, How does Randall put a human face on historical facts? How does he evoke the pain and poignance of a mother's loss?

Literary Element Narrative Poetry

Narrative poetry is verse that tells a story. A literary ballad, such as "Ballad of Birmingham," usually recounts an exciting or a dramatic episode. As you read, ask yourself, How does Randall's choice of the ballad form help him effectively tell this story?

Reading Strategy Apply Background Knowledge

What you learn when you read is connected in part to what you already know. **Applying background knowledge** to your reading of a text can help you better understand and interpret the text. As you read "Ballad of Birmingham," ask yourself, What do I already know about the event this poem describes?

....

Tip: Take Notes Create a chart like the one below to keep track of what you know about the subject.

Detail	Background Knowledge
Birmingham	a city in Alabama; the site of activity during the Civil Rights Movement

TEKS

For pages 553–558

10.3 Understand, make inferences and draw conclusions about the structure and elements of poetry and provide evidence from text to support understanding.

Landscape, 2006. Julian Cifuentes. Oil on canvas.

Ballad of Birmingham

Dudley Randall

"Mother dear, may I go downtown
instead of out to play,
and march the streets of Birmingham
in a freedom march today?"

5   "No, baby, no, you may not go,
for the dogs are fierce and wild,
and clubs and hoses, guns° and jails
ain't good for a little child."

"But, mother, I won't be alone.
10 Other children will go with me,
and march the streets of Birmingham
to make our country free."

"No, baby, no, you may not go,
for I fear those guns will fire.
15 But you may go to church instead,
and sing in the children's choir."

7 **clubs, and hoses, guns:** common weapons used by police and military troops to frighten and suppress demonstrators during peace and civil rights marches.

Apply Background Knowledge *What information do you know about a church in Birmingham?*

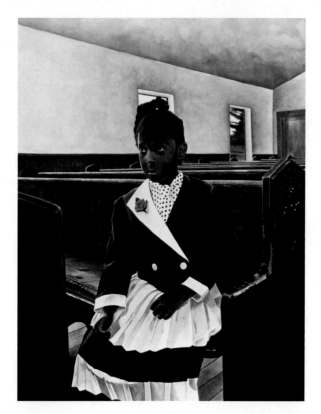

Sunday Best, 20th century. Ben Watson III. Watercolor. Private collection.

She has combed and brushed her nightdark hair,
and bathed rose petal sweet,
and drawn white gloves on her small brown hands,
20 and white shoes on her feet.

The mother smiled to know her child
was in the sacred place,
but that smile was the last smile
to come upon her face.

25 For when she heard the explosion,
her eyes grew wet and wild.
She raced through the streets of Birmingham
calling for her child.

She clawed through bits of glass and brick,
30 then lifted out a shoe.
"O, here's the shoe my baby wore,
but, baby, where are you?"

Narrative Poetry *What do lines 17–20 contribute to the story the poem is telling?*

After You Read

Respond and Think Critically

1. **Connect to Personal Experience** How did you feel at the end of the poem? Explain.

2. **Summarize Details** Reread the first four stanzas. What do the images and details reveal about Birmingham in the 1960s? Support your answer with evidence from the poem.

3. **Make Inferences About Irony** Irony is a contrast or discrepancy between what is expected and what actually happens. What is an example of irony in the poem? What can you infer about the atmosphere in Birmingham at this time from this example? Explain.

4. **Analyze Suspense** What details in the poem create dramatic tension? What details suggest a sense of calm? Explain how these details combine to create suspense. Support your answer with evidence from the poem.

5. **Evaluate Imagery** Which images in the poem were most effective at conveying sadness or tragedy? Explain.

6. **Draw Conclusions About Ideas** What point is the poem making about the importance of protesting injustice? In what sense could the poem be said to support the Civil Rights Movement? Support your answer with text evidence.

7. **Big Idea** **Draw Conclusions About Author's Craft** When the Birmingham bombing occurred, people throughout the United States were horrified. Why did the author choose to focus his retelling of the event on a mother? What is the effect of this choice? Explain.

Literary Element Narrative Poetry

Narrative poetry comes in many forms. **Ballads** are poems or songs that tell a story. They generally fall into two types: folk ballads, where the author is unknown, and literary ballads—such as "Ballad of Birmingham"—where the author is known.

8. **Make Inferences About Elements of Poetry** What is the main event in this ballad? How does the event help to define it as a ballad? Explain.

9. **Evaluate Ballad** Why do you think Randall selected the ballad form for his poem? In your opinion, does the form of this poem increase its appeal or help to enhance its message? Support your answer with evidence from the poem.

Review: Rhyme and Rhyme Scheme

As you learned on page 471, **rhyme** is the repetition of similar or identical sounds at the ends of words that appear close to each other. **End rhyme** occurs at the ends of lines of poetry. **Rhyme scheme** is the pattern that end rhymes form in a stanza or poem. You can determine the rhyme scheme of a poem by designating a different letter of the alphabet for each new rhyme. In a ballad stanza, only the second and fourth lines rhyme.

10. **Partner Activity** With a partner, take turns reading Randall's poem aloud. Listen for the rhyme scheme. Then determine the rhyme scheme by assigning letters to the end of each line. Does the rhyme scheme follow the pattern of the ballad stanza throughout the poem? Create a chart like the one shown below. Use it to help you and your partner as you discuss the question and determine the rhyme scheme of the poem stanza by stanza.

Stanza	End Words	Rhyme Pattern
1	downtown	a
	play	b
	Birmingham	c
	today	b

"Ballad of Birmingham" blends historical fact and fictionalized retelling. To understand the full meaning of the poem, it is essential to **apply background knowledge.** Refer to the chart you made on page 553 and the blue highlighted question to answer the following questions.

11. If you did not already know about the Birmingham church bombing, would you have interpreted the poem differently? Explain.

12. How did your background knowledge of the church bombing and the Civil Rights Movement affect your response to this poem?

Academic Vocabulary

A literary critic might say Randall's poem is meant to **convince** *the reader that there was no safe place for the child to be.*

Convince is an academic word. Familiar words and phrases that are similar in meaning are *persuade* and *prove to.* To study this word further, fill out a graphic organizer like the one below.

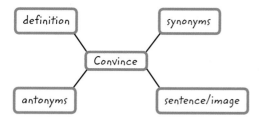

For more on academic vocabulary, see pages 36–37 and R92–R94.

Write with Style

 Apply Form

Assignment Like many ballads, "Ballad of Birmingham" recounts actual events. Ballads typically deal with tragic disasters or heroic quests and deeds. These incidents might make headlines today. Write your own ballad dealing with a striking incident or heroic quest of the present day.

Get Ideas Look through newspapers, magazines, or books for accounts of dramatic events that might lend themselves to the ballad form. In choosing a subject, make sure you pick a dramatic incident that can be recounted through dialogue or questions and answers that further the story.

Give It Structure Freewrite for a few minutes to come up with the basic outline of your ballad. Then think about how to structure your ballad by dividing your story up into stanzas similar to the ones used by Randall. Remember that the poetic techniques used in ballads are strong, simple beats and uncomplicated rhyme schemes. Adopt a rhyme scheme for your ballad similar to the one used by Randall. Use a graphic organizer like the one below to determine how you will develop your story in each stanza.

As you write, focus each stanza on dialogue that tells the story. Remember that ballads have a tendency to suggest rather than directly state.

Look at Language To make your ballad come alive, include vivid **figurative language.** Figurative language uses figures of speech, or expressions that are not literally true but express some truth beyond the literal level. For example, you might include vivid metaphors, similes, or personification.

Media Workshop

Compare Media Coverage

TEKS

For pages 559–564

10.12.A–D Evaluate how messages presented in media reflect social and cultural views in ways different from traditional texts; analyze how messages in media are conveyed through visual and sound techniques; examine how individual perception or bias in coverage of the same event influences the audience; and evaluate changes in formality and tone within the same medium for specific audiences or purposes.

Literature Connection A 1963 news event—the bombing of the 16th Street Baptist Church in Birmingham, Alabama—inspired Dudley Randall to write the poem "Ballad of Birmingham." News photographs captured the story in vivid images. Three decades later, a reporter from National Public Radio broadcast a new perspective. These forms of media coverage—the poem, the news photographs, and the radio broadcast—pay tribute to a historic moment in the Civil Rights Movement of the 1960s.

Forms of Media

Every day you are exposed to different kinds of media messages in a variety of **genres,** or forms. **Print media** convey messages through images and texts, such as newspapers, magazines, books, and billboards. **Electronic media** use sound and moving images to reach audiences. Radio, television, CDs, DVDs, movies, videotapes, documentary films, and the Internet are all forms of electronic media.

Each media genre has its own unique characteristics that determine the message and the way it influences you as a reader, listener, or viewer. Consider the difference between watching a short news report about a scientific discovery and reading a lengthy magazine article about the same discovery. Which kind of media coverage teaches you more? All media genres have strengths and weaknesses, and all are intended to stir a wide range of reactions among their audiences.

Strategies for Comparing Media Coverage

All media messages are intended to shape the audience's attitudes. How the information is presented reflects the viewpoints, perceptions, or even biases of people who create the messages. The limitations of the media genre determine which of the many techniques can be used to craft a powerful and effective message. When comparing how different media genres cover or present information on the same topic or news event, look at what elements the genres have in common. Sources, language, images—these are elements you'll find in most print and electronic media. Also consider the genres' strengths: TV is a visual medium, radio is all about sounds, and newspapers are primarily text-based. Refer to the chart on the next page to help you analyze, or deconstruct, and compare media strategies and genres.

 Literature Online

Media Literacy For project ideas, templates, and media analysis guides, go to glencoe.com and enter QuickPass code GL57805u3.

Strategy		Questions to Ask Yourself
source	☑	Who created this media message? Do the creators' viewpoints, perceptions, or biases affect the message or the audience? How believable is the evidence that the source presents to support the message?
purpose	☑	Why was this message created? To persuade? To entertain? To inform? Does the media genre help or hinder the purpose of the message?
language	☑	How is language used to deliver the message? What is the tone? Does it shift? Is the language formal? Informal? Technical? Does the language convey political or cultural ideas, trends, or beliefs? What connotations does the language have?
target audience	☑	Is the message designed for a specific audience? Are stereotypes of people—such as children or teenagers—used to sway the reader, listener, or viewer? Does the media genre exclude certain audiences?
visual techniques	☑	How is the message or information visually composed? Are visual elements used to represent ideas or to evoke a certain emotional response? Have visual shots been presented in a particular way to produce a desired effect?
sound techniques	☑	How is sound used to convey information? Does the piece include sound effects or background music to create a mood or to reinforce the message?

Activity

Create a Comparison Chart

Use the chart on this page as a guide to examine the coverage of a news story from two different media genres. Create an expanded version of the chart in which you add additional columns, one for each media genre you examine. Use the new columns to analyze the questions in the second column. Analyze how words, images, graphics, and sounds work together to impact meaning in the media you choose.

> ### Focus Lesson

Persuasive Techniques: Logical Fallacies

The messages in many media genres are intended to get the viewer, listener, or reader to agree with a viewpoint or take a specific action. Some creators of messages use the persuasive technique of logical fallacy, or purposeful error in reasoning, to try to sway the audience. Try to spot the following types of logical fallacies in all media genres:

- **overgeneralization** using sweeping statements with no reasonable supporting evidence as proof
- **either-or fallacy** presenting only two possible sides or solutions to an issue when there are more options
- **bandwagon** urging people to do something because everyone else is doing it
- **false cause** drawing a cause-and-effect relationship between two events that follow one after another but are completely unrelated
- *ad hominem* attacking someone personally to shift attention away from the person's views or ideas
- **red herring** purposely changing the subject in order to avoid the issue at hand

Media Coverage: **News Photographs**

Build Background For over one hundred years, news photographers from the Associated Press (AP) have taken pictures that help viewers see history as it happened. The AP news photos shown here provide unique perceptions of the 1963 church bombing in Birmingham, Alabama.

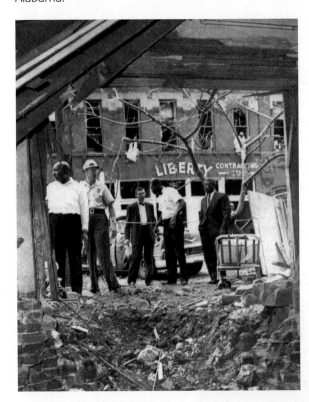

Composition

Notice how the wooden doorframe serves as a kind of frame within the photo: the rubble and damage are inside the church, but outside life continues on.

The destruction of the 16th Street Baptist Church was caused by a bomb that exploded in a basement room.

Cultural Symbol

By September 1963, Dr. Martin Luther King Jr. had become the face of the Civil Rights Movement. Notice how almost everyone in the crowd is watching him.

Dr. Martin Luther King Jr. spoke at the 1963 funeral service for the four girls killed in the Birmingham church bombing.

This photo is taken from a low angle, meaning the photographer was filming from below the subjects. This effect makes the subjects look bigger or more impressive. Notice the effect this angle has on the way you view the men holding hands and the large columns behind them.

Civil rights leaders clasp hands and sing at the 1963 memorial service held in New York City for the victims of the Birmingham bombing.

Visual Technique

The photographer has taken this picture as if he is standing in line with the churchgoers. From this perspective, you see the rebuilt church from the point of view of the people returning to it. Notice what the people are wearing and how they are walking in an orderly line into the church.

Activity

Listening and Speaking

Meet in small groups to discuss the following questions:

1. What was your reaction to each of these news photographs?

2. Do you think visual images can tell a story about a news event better than a spoken or written version? Explain.

3. Imagine you are a documentary maker and are ready to add audio to the images shown here. What sound techniques would you use to help convey the message of these photographs? Consider the sound of the narrator's voice, sound effects, and background music.

In June 1964, members of the 16th Street Baptist Church return to the newly rebuilt church for the first time.

Media Coverage: **Radio Transcript**

Build Background Since 1963, news coverage of the search for suspects involved in the bombing of the Sixteenth Street Baptist Church continued for decades. Over the years, radio, television, newsmagazines, and other media have all tracked the progress of this criminal investigation. The National Public Radio (NPR) transcript below from 2003 reflects on the impact of the bombing and reports on the men who were finally brought to justice.

16th Street Baptist Church Bombing

Forty Years Later, Birmingham Still Struggles with Violent Past

The bells of the 16th Street Baptist Church in Birmingham, Alabama, tolled Monday in remembrance of the four girls who were killed when a bomb exploded at the church on this day 40 years ago.

The church is still grappling with its place in history, Melanie Peeples reports. Just last year, the last living man believed responsible for the attack, Bobby Frank Cherry, was convicted of the crime.

The bomb exploded mid-morning, during Sunday services. Carolyn McKinstry, who was 14 years old at the time, was secretary of her Sunday school class. She was taking attendance records into the sanctuary when the bomb went off.

"I heard something that sounded, at first, a little like thunder and then just this terrific noise and the windows came crashing in," McKinstry told NPR in 2001. "And then a lot of screaming, just a lot of screaming and I heard someone say, 'Hit the floor.' And I remember being on the floor . . . and it was real quiet."

The bomber had hidden under a set of cinder block steps on the side of the church, tunneled under the basement and placed a bundle of dynamite under what turned out to be the girls' rest room. The blast killed four girls: Cynthia Wesler, Carole Robertson and Addie Mae Collins—all 14—and 11-year-old Denise McNair. More than 20 others were injured, including Addie Mae's sister Sarah, who lost an eye in the attack.

McKinstry says it was no accident that the Ku Klux Klan targeted the 16th Street Baptist Church. "It was the largest black church in Birmingham, but because of its central location it was used for a lot of other things, all kinds of meetings, national, local and so forth," she recalls.

Sound Techniques

As you read this transcript, imagine how sound techniques could be used to convey information. Consider the sound of the narrator's voice, sound effects, and background music.

Source

The reporter uses an eyewitness as a source for the story. Notice that the reporter allows the source to describe what happened in her own words.

Source

The reporter provides the key facts about the victims of the bombing.

Opinion

McKinstry uses reasons to support her opinion about why the bombers chose the 16th Street Baptist Church.

Description

The reporter's vivid words help radio listeners visualize the church and its location.

Language

Notice the difference in word choices in this paragraph. The first two sentences are the reporter's retelling of the facts of the FBI investigation. The third sentence expresses McKinstry's personal reaction.

Objective Account

The reporter closes the news story with facts that inform listeners about the outcome of the criminal investigation.

Activity

Answer the following questions with a partner.

1. What was your reaction to this news report? How did it differ from your reaction to the news photographs? Which format did you prefer and why?

2. How do the photos and report present a different social and cultural view of the bombing from Dudley Randall's "Ballad of Birmingham" (page 555)? What are the strengths and weaknesses of each format?

3. Imagine altering this report for a different audience (such as an activism group) and purpose. How would the tone and the formality of the language change?

The Byzantine-style structure, with two domed towers and a roomy basement auditorium, served as the hub for the mass meetings of the civil rights movement, drawing leaders like Martin Luther King Jr. Marchers would assemble at the church and then cross the street to demonstrate at Kelly Ingram Park, the site of violent clashes between Birmingham police and civil rights activists.

The brutal attack and the death of four girls rocked the nation and drew international attention to the violent struggle for civil rights in Birmingham. But despite the outrage and an intense FBI investigation, no one was charged in the crime. That was the real horror of it, according to McKinstry.

"These are friends of mine," she said. "And we come to Sunday school one day and they're gone. They're dead. They're just blown away and Birmingham goes on with business as usual."

It was more than a decade before state authorities took action. Then Attorney General Bill Baxley charged Klan leader Robert "Dynamite Bob" Chambliss with murder. In 1977, he was convicted.

Chambliss died in jail, never publicly admitting to the bombing. Baxley left office before he could pursue charges against Chambliss' suspected accomplices. One of them has since died.

Thirty-eight years after the bombing, Thomas Blanton Jr. was finally convicted of murder and sentenced to life in prison. A year later, in May 2002, Bobby Frank Cherry was also found guilty for the deaths of the four girls, and given a mandatory sentence of life in prison.

The 16th Street Baptist Church in Birmingham

PART 3

Issues of Identity

Real Truth. Jerzy Kolacz.

View the Art Jerzy Kolacz believes that art plays a key role in self discovery. Consider the title and multiple images in this painting. How does this painting relate to the ideas of identity and change?

BIG IDEA

Your identity is more than the clothes you wear, your interests, or your thoughts and emotions. Through all the changes of life, part of you does not change—that something by which you recognize yourself, no matter what. The poems in Part 3 deal with changing identity. As you read them, ask yourself, How have I changed in the last several years? What about me has not changed?

TEKS

For pages 566–567

10.3 Understand, make inferences and draw conclusions about the structure and elements of poetry and provide evidence from text to support understanding.

LITERARY FOCUS

Sound Devices

What makes poetry musical?

Most poems are written to be heard, like music, or to be imagined aloud in the reader's mind. The actor Ossie Davis said of Langston Hughes's work, "Langston Hughes belongs to whoever is listening. A possession in common, like the sights and sounds of a street corner hangout, or the barbershop debate over pretty girls, and baseball players: Open your ears and your heart if you've got one; Langston will walk right in and do the rest." As you read poetry, can you hear music in the words?

Alliteration

Alliteration refers to the repetition of consonant sounds at the beginnings of nonrhyming words or syllables in neighboring words. Notice the use of alliteration, the repetition of *w, s,* and *p* sounds, in these lines:

when i watch you
wrapped up like garbage
sitting, surrounded by the smell
of too old potato peels

—Lucille Clifton, *from* **"miss rosie"**

Assonance

When the repeated sound is a vowel sound in stressed syllables of neighboring nonrhyming words, the sound device is called **assonance**. Listen for the *ē* sounds in this line:

She bid *me* take love *easy,* as the *leaves* grow on the *tree;*

—W. B. Yeats, *from* **"Down by the Salley Gardens"**

Consonance

Alliteration, described above, is actually a special kind of **consonance,** the repetition of consonant sounds at the ends of nonrhyming words or stressed syllables. Note the repetition of the *s* and *l* sounds in the following line:

She passed the salley gardens with little
    snow-white feet.

—W. B. Yeats, *from* **"Down by the Salley Gardens"**

In the following two lines, note the repetition of *r* sounds:

You may forget the warmth he gave—
I will forget the light!

—Emily Dickinson, *from* **"Heart! We Will Forget Him!"**

Onomatopoeia

Onomatopoeia is the use of a word or phrase that imitates or suggests the sound of what it describes, like the words *buzz* and *thump.*

Rhyme

Rhyme is the repetition of similar or identical sounds at the ends of words that appear close to each other. For example, *cat* and *hat* rhyme, as do *willowier* and *billowier.* Rhymes at the ends of lines of poetry are called **end rhymes.**

Apples I didn't pick upon some bough.
But I am done with apple-picking now.

—Robert Frost, *from* **"After Apple-Picking"**

Rhyming words within one line are called **internal rhyme:**

The mother *smiled* to know her *child*

—Dudley Randall, *from* **"Ballad of Birmingham"**

Both end and internal rhymes can be **slant rhymes,** or rhymes that are close, but not exact.

His feet like small leaves,
Little lizard-feet,

—Theodore Roethke, *from* **"The Meadow Mouse"**

Quickwrite

Make Inferences About the Elements of Poetry In a chart like the one below, record the examples of alliteration, assonance, and consonance you notice as you read the poems in Part 3. Then record your inferences about the effect these devices have in terms of emphasis, musicality, or emotional impact.

Element	Effect
Assonance in "Down by the Salley Gardens": "She bid me take love easy, as the leaves grow on the tree"	creates unity within the poem; adds musicality

Literature Online

Literature and Reading For more about literary elements, go to glencoe.com and enter QuickPass code GL57805u3.

Before You Read

miss rosie

Meet **Lucille Clifton**
(born 1936)

Lucille Clifton has been compared with great poets such as Walt Whitman and Emily Dickinson. Her poems celebrate the everyday and the ordinary while revealing the complexities of life.

In her poems, Clifton often focuses on the struggles of people in the inner city. Despite gritty portrayals, Clifton's poems maintain a sense of hope and spiritual strength. Clifton's family history plays a large part in her ability to write about the pain of living while also offering a message about the ability to overcome: one of her female ancestors was kidnapped and brought to the United States against her will and another was the first African American woman to be lynched in Virginia.

> "All of our stories become The Story. If mine is left out, something's missing."
>
> —Lucille Clifton

Humble Beginnings Clifton was born in New York during the Great Depression. Her father was a steel mill worker, and her mother worked as a laundress and homemaker. Clifton's mother also enjoyed writing poetry. Even though neither of her parents had been formally educated, they passed on an appreciation for learning. Clifton was prepared to enter college at the age of sixteen. She studied drama at Howard University and became an actor before seriously cultivating her interest in poetry.

Clifton's first book, a poetry collection titled *Good Times*, was published in 1969. It was

hailed by the *New York Times* as one of the year's ten best books. Since then, Clifton has published several volumes of poetry. She has also written more than twenty children's books, including an award-winning fiction series about the life of a young African American boy named Everett Anderson.

Taking Her Place Clifton's many poems and stories have garnered her a rightful place among America's best writers. She has won many honors, including an Emmy Award, for her work. She was nominated for a Pulitzer Prize in 1988, becoming the first author to have two poetry books, *Next* and *Good Woman*, selected as finalists in the same year.

Some of Clifton's major works of poetry include *Good News About the Earth*, *An Ordinary Woman*, *Quilting: Poems 1987–1990*, and *The Terrible Stories*. She also penned *Generations: A Memoir*, a work of prose focusing on her family's origins.

Literature and Reading Preview

Connect to the Poem

What makes you like or dislike a person when you first meet him or her? With a partner, discuss how someone's first impression can affect you.

Build Background

People's identities are often tied to their roles in life. Roles change over time. For example, your role now might be a student, friend, or sibling; later your role could be a teacher or parent. Many of Lucille Clifton's poems examine the roles and identities of women in society.

Set Purposes for Reading

Big Idea Issues of Identity

As you read, ask yourself, How has the identity of Miss Rosie changed over time?

Literary Element Alliteration

Alliteration is the repetition of consonant sounds at the beginnings of nonrhyming words or syllables in neighboring words. Alliteration can help you picture what an author is trying to portray. As you read, ask yourself, How does Clifton's use of alliteration affect the text?

Reading Strategy Interpret Imagery

Imagery, or sensory language, is language that appeals to one or more of the five senses. Writers use imagery to create an emotional response in the reader. When you **interpret imagery,** you look closely at sensory language to determine its meaning and how it impacts the text. As you read, ask yourself, What sensory language does Clifton use? What meaning is she trying to relay?

....

Tip: Make Inferences About Sensory Language Use a chart like the one below to record the sensory language Clifton uses and how it creates meaning in the poem.

Sensory Language	Meaning
"wrapped up like garbage"	the speaker is trying to say that Miss Rosie is physically unappealing
"you wet brown bag of a woman"	the speaker feels pity for Miss Rosie

TEKS

For pages 568–571

10.7 Understand, make inferences, and draw conclusions about how an author's sensory language creates imagery in literary text and provide evidence from text to support understanding.

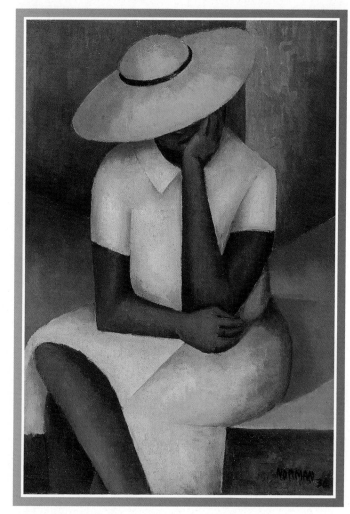

Yellow Hat, 1936. Norman Lewis. Oil on burlap, 36½ x 26 in.
Collection of Loide Lewis and the late Reginald Lewis.

View the Art How does the woman in the painting compare
with your image of the speaker in the poem or with the
young Miss Rosie?

miss rosie

Lucille Clifton

when i watch you
wrapped up like garbage
sitting, surrounded by the smell
of too old potato peels
5   or
when i watch you
in your old man's shoes
with the little toe cut out
sitting, waiting for your mind
10   like next week's grocery
i say
when i watch you
you wet brown bag of a woman
who used to be the best looking
    gal in georgia
15   used to be called the Georgia Rose
i stand up
through your destruction
i stand up

Alliteration *How is this line a good example of
alliteration?*

Issues of Identity *How does this description of
Miss Rosie change her identity?*

After You Read

Respond and Think Critically

1. **Connect to Personal Experience** How do you feel about Miss Rosie? Did you feel differently about her at the end of the poem than you did at the beginning? Explain.

2. **Interpret Description** How does Clifton describe Miss Rosie in lines 9–10? What does this description imply about Miss Rosie?

3. **Make Inferences About Speaker** How does the speaker respond to Miss Rosie by the end of the poem? In your opinion, what does the speaker think about Miss Rosie?

4. **Analyze Metaphor** What metaphor does Clifton use to describe Miss Rosie? How does this comparison illustrate Miss Rosie's transformation?

5. **Analyze Diction** Because this poem is so short, Clifton's **diction,** or word choice, is very deliberate. Why do you think she chooses the word *destruction* in line 17? How would the meaning of the line change if Clifton had used a word with a similar meaning, such as *ruin* or *annihilation*? Consider the connotation of each word.

6. **Big Idea** **Draw Conclusions About Theme** How does this poem relate to issues of identity? Explain and support your answer with evidence from the poem.

Literary Element Alliteration

Alliteration is often used by poets who like working with the sounds of words.

7. **Identify Alliteration** Where does Clifton use alliteration in this poem? Give two examples.

8. **Analyze Alliteration** What effect does Clifton's use of alliteration have on the poem? Explain your response. Reread the pink highlighted text and question on page 570 to help you get started.

Reading Strategy Interpret Imagery

Refer to the chart you made on page 569 as you answer the questions.

9. List three examples of imagery from the poem. What emotions do these images evoke?

10. What do you think Clifton's purpose is when she juxtaposes certain images such as "wet brown bag" and "Georgia Rose"? Explain.

Academic Vocabulary

*Rosie's current condition arouses **intense** feelings in the speaker, which are conveyed most forcefully in the poem's final lines.*

Intense is an academic word. In a more casual conversation, a speaker might describe a situation as **intense,** suggesting that it was filled with tension or that it was extreme in some way. Using context clues, try to figure out the meaning of the word *intense* in the sentence above. Check your guess in a dictionary.

For more on academic vocabulary, see pages 36–37 and R92–R94.

Writing

Write an Essay Author Ronald Baugham writes that "the poem . . . functions both as a lament for the woman destroyed and as a tribute to the new black woman who rises from the ashes of her predecessor's destruction." How does the poem function as both a tribute and a lament? In an essay, formulate a response to this question and Baugham's claim. Identify words in the poem to support your view.

Before You Read

After Apple-Picking

Meet **Robert Frost**
(1874–1963)

Robert Frost won the highest admiration and respect throughout the twentieth century and was asked by President John F. Kennedy to read a poem, "The Gift Outright," at his inauguration.

Frost wanted his poetry to appeal to the general book-buying public rather than to find favor in literary circles. He wanted readers to look beyond the realism of the natural environment, seeking deeper meaning and significance in his poems.

Frost's life was based in skepticism and deep thought driven by a desire to achieve success as a poet. He was born in San Francisco but moved to New England at the age of eleven. While still in high school he developed a love of poetry, a passion he shared with his future wife and fellow student, Elinor White. Frost published his first poem, "My Butterfly: An Elegy," at twenty. The next year, he and Elinor were married.

> "Poetry is a process
> Poetry is the renewal of words
> Poetry is the dawning of an idea"
>
> —Robert Frost

His Own Man True to his unconventional path to acclaim as a writer, Frost abandoned his college studies. He once explained that organized education was "never [his] taste." Instead he worked on a farm and at a variety of blue-collar jobs. Nonetheless, he continued to pursue his literary goals and eventually returned to college, this time as a teacher. His tenacity and ambition, motivation, and hardiness provided the essential characteristics underlying his many literary accomplishments.

Cultural Connections Frost spent much of his life in New England and used its natural environment and culture as the basis for his poetry. In his poetry, Frost used ordinary language that revealed complex feelings and undercurrents of doubt and uncertainty. Although Frost used traditional rhyme schemes, meter, and verse forms, his poems contain emotions and ideas linked typically to Modernist poets.

Frost was awarded Pulitzer Prizes for four books, including his *Collected Poems*. He was poet-in-residence for Harvard University, Amherst College, and Dartmouth University. Finally, he was the poetry consultant (now referred to as "poet laureate") to the Library of Congress from 1958 to 1959.

LOG ON ▶ **Literature** Online

Author Search For more about Robert Frost, go to glencoe.com and enter QuickPass code GL57805u3.

Literature and Reading Preview

Connect to the Poem

How have your thoughts shaped who you are? Write a journal entry about where you fit in the world.

Build Background

Much of Robert Frost's work focuses on the lifestyle and landscape of rural New England, where he spent many years working on farms, teaching, and writing. His poems also explore such universal issues as war, love, death, and desire, often through the use of metaphors and symbols.

Set Purposes for Reading

Big Idea Issues of Identity

As you read the poem, ask yourself, What facets of the speaker's identity do I see in the poem?

Literary Element Assonance and Consonance

Assonance is the repetition of the same or similar vowel sounds in the stressed syllables of neighboring nonrhyming words. **Consonance** is the repetition of consonant sounds at the ends of nonrhyming words or stressed syllables. As you read, ask yourself, Where does Frost use assonance and consonance and what effect do they create?

Reading Strategy Clarify Meaning

An author's meaning is not always obvious in a literary work. When you **clarify meaning**, it can help you to better understand what you are reading. Reread any confusing or challenging lines or examine how end punctuation signals a complete thought. As you read, ask yourself, What other meanings might a phrase contain?

Tip: Make Inferences Create a chart like the following, writing a line or phrase from the poem in the first column. Consider how Frost uses various poetic elements. Then, in the second column, make inferences about the meaning of the phrases.

Complete Phrase	Inference
"Toward heaven still"	trying unsuccessfully to climb to heaven

TEKS

For pages 572–577

10.3 Understand, make inferences and draw conclusions about the structure and elements of poetry and provide evidence from text to support understanding.

Vocabulary

bough (bou) *n.* a tree branch; p. 574 *Akim broke off a bough to chop for firewood, while Roman gathered smaller twigs for kindling.*

essence (es′əns) *n.* perfume; p. 574 *Her soap contains the essence of lilac.*

hoary (hôr′ē) *adj.* white or gray with age; covered with frost; p. 574 *The old, dusty photographs had a hoary sheen.*

russet (rus′it) *adj.* a deep reddish-brown; p. 575 *The tree's russet-colored leaves were a definite sign that fall was approaching.*

Tip: Synonyms Synonyms are always the same part of speech.

Scrumping Apples. Caroline Paterson.
Watercolor on paper. Private collection.

After Apple-Picking

Robert Frost

My long two-pointed ladder's sticking through a tree
Toward heaven still,
And there's a barrel that I didn't fill
Beside it, and there may be two or three
5   Apples I didn't pick upon some **bough**.
But I am done with apple-picking now.
Essence of winter sleep is on the night,
The scent of apples: I am drowsing off.
I cannot rub the strangeness from my sight
10   I got from looking through a pane of glass
I skimmed this morning from the drinking trough
And held against the world of **hoary** grass.

Vocabulary

bough (bou) *n.* a tree branch
essence (es´əns) *n.* perfume
hoary (hôr´ē) *adj.* white or gray with age; covered with frost

It melted, and I let it fall and break.
But I was well
15 Upon my way to sleep before it fell,
And I could tell
What form my dreaming was about to take.
Magnified apples appear and disappear,
Stem end and blossom end,
20 And every fleck of **russet** showing clear.
My instep arch not only keeps the ache,
It keeps the pressure of a ladder-round.
I feel the ladder sway as the boughs bend.
And I keep hearing from the cellar bin
25 The rumbling sound
Of load on load of apples coming in.
For I have had too much
Of apple-picking: I am overtired
Of the great harvest I myself desired.
30 There were ten thousand thousand fruit to touch,
Cherish in hand, lift down, and not let fall.
For all
That struck the earth,
No matter if not bruised or spiked with stubble,
35 Went surely to the cider-apple heap
As of no worth.
One can see what will trouble
This sleep of mine, whatever sleep it is.
Were he not gone,
40 The woodchuck could say whether it's like his
Long sleep, as I describe its coming on,
Or just some human sleep.

Assonance and Consonance *What effect does the assonance in this line create? The consonance? Explain.*

Issues of Identity *How might these lines help you identify the speaker's state of mind?*

Clarify Meaning *How does this phrase evoke a darker, hidden meaning in Frost's poem?*

Vocabulary

russet (rus´it) *adj.* a deep reddish-brown

After You Read

Respond and Think Critically

1. **Connect to Personal Experience** What emotions did the poem stir in you? Explain.

2. **Summarize Events** Though the poem is about one topic, several events are described. Summarize what happens in the poem.

3. **Make Inferences About Meaning** What is the "pane of glass" in line 10? What deeper meaning do you think Frost tries to convey with this image? **OER**

4. **Make Inferences About Imagery** What images does the speaker use in the first five lines of the poem? How do these images convey what the speaker thinks about apple picking? Explain.

5. **Analyze Metaphor** For what is apple picking a metaphor? What does this metaphor tell you about the overall meaning of the poem? Support your answer with evidence from the text.

6. **Analyze Rhyme** What type of rhyme does Frost use in this poem? What effect do the rhymes have on the tone of the poem? Support your response with evidence from the poem.

7. **Big Idea** **Draw Conclusions About Speaker** What is the identity of the speaker in "After Apple-Picking"? Support your response with text evidence.

Primary Source Quotation

The Meaning of Poetry

Robert Frost wrote many times about what poetry meant to him and how he personally interpreted it. Read the following quotations about poetry from Robert Frost, then answer the questions that follow.

"A poem begins in delight and ends in wisdom."

"A poem begins as a lump in the throat, a sense of wrong, a homesickness, a lovesickness."

"Poetry has got me indirectly or directly practically all the living I have had."

1. What might Frost mean when he says that a poem begins with "delight and ends in wisdom"? Have you had any personal experiences with delight or wisdom as a result of reading poetry? Explain.

2. What might a "lump in the throat," homesickness, lovesickness, and feelings that something is wrong have in common? Why might these things motivate someone to write?

3. How can poetry "get" you life experiences? Do you agree with this statement? Explain.

4. Of these three quotations, which do you respond to most? Explain your choice.

Literary Element | Assonance and Consonance

Assonance and **consonance** are sound devices that are generally more apparent when you hear a poem read aloud than when you read a poem silently. Poets use assonance and consonance to enhance both the rhythm and imagery in a poem.

8. Identify Assonance Identify an example of assonance in "After Apple-Picking." What vowel sound is repeated?

9. Analyze Consonance Identify an example of consonance in the poem. What effect does it have? Explain. Reread the pink highlighted text on page 575 to help you answer the question.

Review: Alliteration

As you learned on page 569, **alliteration** is the repetition of consonant sounds at the beginnings of nonrhyming words or syllables in neighboring words. Writers use alliteration to emphasize words, reinforce meaning, or create a musical effect. An example of alliteration is the phrase "Later we located the laughing loons of Laredo."

10. Partner Activity Discuss alliteration in "After Apple-Picking" with a classmate. Create a chart like the one below and fill it in with examples from the poem that demonstrate alliteration.

Line	Alliteration
1	"My long two-pointed ladder's"

After you have identified examples of alliteration in the poem, discuss with your partner the possible significance of each example.

LOG ON ▶ **Literature** Online

Selection Resources For Selection Quizzes, eFlashcards, and Reading-Writing Connection activities, go to glencoe.com and enter QuickPass code GL57805u3.

Reading Strategy | Clarify Meaning

An important element of poetry is punctuation—or the lack of it. Poets sometimes might not include punctuation or might use it inconsistently. Review the chart you made on page 573 and answer the following questions to make inferences about Frost's use of punctuation.

11. How might Frost's meaning in "After Apple-Picking" be clarified by finding the punctuation stops?

12. How do you think your understanding of the poem would change if Frost had not used punctuation? Support your answer with text evidence.

Vocabulary Practice

Practice with Synonyms A synonym is a word that has the same or nearly the same meaning as another word. With a partner, match each boldfaced vocabulary word below with its synonym. Use a thesaurus or dictionary to check your answers. You will not use all the answer choices.

1. bough	**a.** reddish
2. essence	**b.** frosty
3. hoary	**c.** essential
4. russet	**d.** perfume
	e. branch

Academic Vocabulary

A *potential* interpretation for the sleep at the end of "After Apple-Picking" is eternal rest.

Potential is a multiple-meaning word. Using context clues, try to figure out the meaning of *potential* in each sentence below.

1. Before it falls over the dam, the water has **potential** energy.

2. Alphonso considered the career because of the **potential** earning power he associated with it.

For more on academic vocabulary, see pages 36–37 and R92–R94.

Respond Through Writing

Expository Essay

Evaluate Sound Devices "After Apple-Picking" is full of sound devices. Write an interpretative essay of 1,500 words in which you evaluate how well the sound devices support the meaning of the poem.

Purpose and Audience Your purpose is to write an interpretative response that extends beyond a summary and literal analysis and evaluates the aesthetic effects of the sound devices Frost uses in "After Apple-Picking." You should explain how well the sound devices support the meaning of the poem. Your audience is your classmates.

Plan List sound devices from the poem that seem especially interesting or effective. Make a two-column chart in which you list an example of a sound device and the function or purpose of the device. Use the ideas in column two of your chart to formulate your essay's thesis or controlling idea. Then outline your body paragraphs. Make sure your handwriting is legible so you can understand your notes.

Draft Each of your paragraphs should contain a topic sentence that makes an evaluative statement, evidence and quotations from the poem that support the statement, and an explanation of how the evidence relates to your judgment. Follow this model:

Evaluative Paragraph Structure

Topic Sentence: Frost uses [sound device] such as ___ to ___.

Sentence 2: For example, in line ___, Frost uses [alliteration, assonance, consonance, repetition, or onomatopoeia] to show/emphasize/suggest ___.

Other Sentences: Explanation, relationship to thesis.

Revise As you revise, be sure that you have correctly used terms that name sound devices. Identify objections that the reader may present and add details and explanations to clarify and strengthen your argument. Make sure your introduction and conclusion are effective and that you use a variety of sentence structures and transitions between paragraphs. If you write your essay by hand, make sure it is legible.

Edit Edit your paper, correcting any errors in spelling, grammar, and punctuation. Use the Grammar Tip in the side column to help you use reciprocal pronouns correctly.

> ### Grammar Tip

> #### Reciprocal Pronouns
> Reciprocal pronouns are used to express the same feelings or actions among multiple subjects.
>
> *Each other* is used to express similarities between two people. For example, you could rewrite the sentence "Robert Frost supported his wife and his wife supported him" as:
>
> *Robert Frost and his wife supported **each other.***
>
> *One another* is used to express similarities between more than two people. For example, the sentence "Robert and Elinor helped their children through harsh New England winters, and their children also helped them," could be simplified:
>
> *The members of the Frost family helped **one another** through harsh New England winters.*

Before You Read

Arabic Coffee

Meet **Naomi Shihab Nye**
(born 1952)

Naomi Shihab Nye published her first poem at the age of seven, in *Wee Wisdom*, a children's magazine. Nye loved reading and writing from a very young age. She writes, "I liked the portable, comfortable shape of poems. . . . And especially the way they took you to a deeper, quieter place."

Quiet Observer Indeed, Nye has been called a "quiet observer of the human condition." Of her own work, Nye writes, "I have always loved the gaps, the spaces between things, as much as the things. I love staring, pondering, mulling, puttering. I love the times when someone or something is late—there's that rich possibility of noticing more, in the meantime."

Born to an American mother and a Palestinian father in St. Louis, Missouri, Nye was a perceptive child. In the introduction to her collection of poems *19 Varieties of Gazelle*, she writes, "I got into the habit of writing little things down from the very beginning—not because they were more interesting than anyone else's 'little things,' but just so I could think about them."

Professional Poet Nye attended high school in a variety of exotic locales: Ramallah, Jordan; Old City, Jerusalem; and San Antonio, Texas. She earned a bachelor's degree from Trinity University in San Antonio in 1974 and began working as a writer-in-residence at various universities around the country, eventually settling in San Antonio. She has authored or edited over twenty volumes of poetry, essays, and fiction, and served as poetry editor for *The Texas Observer.*

Nye has won several prestigious awards and fellowships, including four Pushcart Prizes, two Texas Institute of Letters awards, and, in 1997, a Guggenheim Fellowship. She was also a finalist in 2002 for a National Book Award in young people's literature.

> *"We have no borders when we read."*
>
> —Naomi Shihab Nye

No Borders In her writing, Nye explores shared experiences and differences between cultures, as well as perspectives of people from countries around the world. Whether she is writing about her home life in Texas, the tragedy of cultural and political conflicts (such as the Palestinian-Israeli conflict), or the power of strength in the face of adversity, one consistent topic in her poetry is how people are connected.

 Literature Online

Author Search For more about Naomi Shihab Nye, go to glencoe.com and enter QuickPass code GL57805u3.

Literature and Reading Preview

Connect to the Poem

When you spend time with loved ones, what do you do to show that you care for them? List several of these actions.

Build Background

Arabic coffee, sometimes called Turkish coffee, is prepared differently than most coffee in the United States. To prepare Arabic coffee, one boils water and coffee grounds together in the same pot until the coffee grounds rise to the top and sink back down again. The coffee is then poured into cups, with the grounds at the bottom. The result is a strong, thick, and flavorful beverage. In many Arabic cultures, the preparation of coffee is an important social custom.

Set Purposes for Reading

Big Idea Issues of Identity

As you read, ask yourself, How might the speaker's family and social customs have formed her identity?

Literary Element Symbol

A **symbol** is any person, place, object, or experience that exists on a literal level within a work but also represents something on a figurative level. As you read the poem, ask yourself, How does Nye use the preparation and serving of coffee as a symbol?

Reading Strategy Analyze Rhythm

Rhythm is the pattern of beats created by the arrangement of stressed and unstressed syllables in a line. When you **analyze rhythm** in an unrhymed poem, you pay attention to how structure, diction, and sound devices work together to create rhythm. As you read this poem, ask yourself, How does Nye create a flow and pace events and emotions?

....

Tip: Note Rhythm Note how the author creates rhythm using the elements listed above. In a chart like the one below, list passages from the poem and explain how they convey rhythm.

Passage from Poem	Rhythm style
"small white cups"	Succession of using one-syllable words

TEKS

For pages 579–582

10.7 Explain the function of symbolism, allegory, and allusions in literary works.

Arabic Coffee

Naomi Shihab Nye

Creamers, 2001. Pam Ingalls.

It was never too strong for us:
make it blacker, Papa, thick in the bottom,
tell again how years will gather
in small white cups,
5   how luck lives in a spot of grounds.°

Leaning over the stove, he let it
boil to the top, and down again.
Two times. No sugar in his pot.
And the place where men and women
10 break off from one another°
was not present in that room.
The hundred disappointments,
fire swallowing olive-wood beads°
at the warehouse, and the dreams
15 tucked like pocket handkerchiefs
into each day, took their places
on the table, near the half-empty
dish of corn. And none was
more important than the others,
20 and all were guests. When
he carried the tray into the room,
high and balanced in his hands,
it was an offering to all of them,
stay, be seated, follow the talk
25 wherever it goes. The coffee was
the center of the flower.
Like clothes on a line saying
You will live long enough to wear me,
a motion of faith. There is this,
30 and there is more.

5 Here, the speaker describes tasseography, fortune-telling with tea leaves or coffee grounds that began centuries ago in China. One interprets the pattern of tea leaves or coffee grounds left in a cup after drinking the beverage. The reader uses certain symbols to "read" a deeper meaning.

10 Lines 9–10 refer to a practice that exists in many cultures, in which men and women stay separated from one another during public and social functions.

13 Olive-wood beads: wooden beads made from olive trees, often used for religious or ornamental jewelry.

Issues of Identity *What does the speaker mean by the statement in lines 18–20?*

After You Read

Respond and Think Critically

1. **Connect to Personal Experience** Do you identify with the experience described in the poem? Explain why or why not.

2. **Make Inferences About Speaker** How does the speaker like coffee prepared? Why do you think the speaker first tells us her personal preference before explaining how Papa prepares it for others?

3. **Interpret Imagery** What things are said to take their place at the table? Why do you think Nye chooses these images?

4. **Interpret Meaning** How do you interpret the following line: *"You will live long enough to wear me"*? Why do you think Nye chose to italicize this line? Explain.

5. **Analyze Metaphor** What metaphor does Nye use in lines 25–26? What does this suggest about the importance of the coffee for this gathering?

6. **Evaluate Imagery** Why might the speaker compare dark coffee grounds in the bottom of small white cups to luck and people gathering together? Is this an effective image? Explain.

7. **Big Idea** **Draw Conclusions About Meaning** In what ways is this poem about identity? Support your response.

8. **Analyze Author's Perspective** How does this poem express Nye's interest in cross-cultural exploration and connections between people?

Literary Element   Symbol

Nye uses symbols throughout "Arabic Coffee" to help the reader understand the meaning of the poem.

9. **Interpret Symbols** How do "clothes on a line" symbolize hope and faith? Explain.

10. **Analyze Symbolism** When the speaker explains how her father prepares coffee for the guests, what do you think this act symbolizes? How is the symbolism important to the poem? Support your answer with evidence from the text.

Reading Strategy   Analyze Rhythm

"Arabic Coffee" has a **rhythm** that is established by the author's choice of words, diction, and where she chooses to start and end lines. Review the chart you made on page 580.

11. What effect does the author create by making the first stanza one long sentence? Explain.

12. How does Nye's diction help create rhythm? Support your answer with examples from the text.

Academic Vocabulary

*The speaker's father enjoys the **convention** of preparing Arabic coffee for guests.*

Convention is an academic word that derives from Latin. The prefix *con-* means "together; with." Using your knowledge and context clues, determine the meaning of *convention* in the model sentence above. Check your response by consulting a dictionary. Finally, demonstrate your understanding by using each of these related words in a sentence.

a. conspire   **b.** congregate   **c.** converge

For more on academic vocabulary, see pages 36–37 and R92–R94.

Writing

Write Free Verse Write several lines of free verse in which an object, animal, or event symbolizes an abstract concept. Write about the symbol but be sure the underlying abstraction is clear.

 Literature Online

Selection Resources For Selection Quizzes, eFlashcards, and Reading-Writing Connection activities, go to glencoe.com and enter QuickPass code GL57805u3.

from *Interview with*

Naomi Shihab Nye

from *The Language of Life*

Emmy Award Winner

TEKS

For pages 583–585

RC-10.A Reflect on understanding to monitor comprehension (e.g., synthesizing).

Texas Author | Bill Moyers

Set a Purpose for Reading

Read to discover how Naomi Shihab Nye's approach to writing relates to the art of everyday conversation and the themes in "Arabic Coffee."

Build Background

Raised in Texas, Bill Moyers is a distinguished journalist, author, and frequent host of television documentaries. His diverse experience includes being deputy director of the Peace Corps and press secretary under President Lyndon Johnson. This excerpt comes from his book *The Language of Life*, a collection of interviews with poets. Moyers conducted this interview with Nye during the biennial Dodge Poetry Festival in New Jersey.

Reading Strategy Synthesize

When you **synthesize,** you combine ideas and details from several texts to reach a new understanding. As you read, record details from the interview that enrich your understanding of Nye's poem "Arabic Coffee."

Detail from Interview		**Detail from "Arabic Coffee"**		**Synthesis**
One theme in Nye's poetry is how people are connected.	**+**	The serving of coffee symbolizes community.	**=**	Nye values community.

MOYERS: When you sit down to write, do you know why you're doing it?

NYE: I know why I'm *hungry* to do it. My first hunger of every day is to let words come through me in some way, and I don't always feel that I succeed in doing it— sometimes I feel that I am just an audience for words floating by and through. But the possibilities seem inexhaustible:[1] I don't know what story will rise up out of that deep well of experience, and I'm always fascinated by how there's something there to work with every morning.

MOYERS: Do you wait, or is it work to bring that story up from its source?

NYE: Sometimes you wait, but the more receptive[2] you are on a regular basis, the more easily things are given to you; so it's not as if you wait for hours with nothing going on. You may not get anything that goes anywhere, but many possibilities are always generated. There is great energy released just by the act of being receptive

---

1. *Inexhaustible* means "not capable of being used up."
2. To be *receptive* is to be open to new ideas.

Naomi Shihab Nye.

nations happen. The unpredictable quality of writing always fascinates me. An image comes to you and you think you might know what it's about or where it wants to take you, and invariably[3] the poems which matter to you turn out to be those poems which took you somewhere other than where you thought you needed to go.

MOYERS: Poetry is a form of conversation for you, isn't it?

NYE: Absolutely. Poetry is a conversation with the world; poetry is a conversation with the words on the page in which you allow those words to speak back to you; and poetry is a conversation with yourself. Many times I meet students and see a little look of wariness in their faces—"I'm not sure I *want* to do this or I'm not sure I *can* do this"—I like to say, "Wait a minute. How nervous are you about the conversation you're going to have at lunch today with your friends?" And they say, "Oh, we're not nervous at all about *that*. We do *that* every day." Then I tell them they can come to feel the same way about writing. Writing doesn't have to be an exotic or stressful experience. You can just sit down with a piece of paper and begin talking and see what speaks back.

to words. The poet David Ignatow has talked about keeping the door open—it could be a door in a relationship or a door between the poet and words so that words can come through—and I believe that when you regularly sit down to write, when you regularly make yourself available to words, they come through more readily for you.

MOYERS: But you're not being passive.

NYE: Not at all. As you rub these words together they spark and whole new combi-

---

3. *Invariably* means "always."

MOYERS: Talking out loud? When you're alone?

NYE: Well, sometimes. I often begin talking out loud, whether I'm alone or not. My son will say, "You were talking to yourself right now." And I say. "That's what I was doing; but I was so comfortable with you that I didn't notice it." I often just repeat a phrase I've heard or some words I want to write down so I won't forget them. In our culture especially I think we need to talk to ourselves more, and we also need to *listen* to ourselves more.

MOYERS: Some people think there's so much talk in America—the talk shows, call-in shows, interviews, C-Span, CNN,[4] press conferences, TV commercials—that it's all just a babble.

---

4. *C-Span* is a non-profit cable television network that broadcasts Congressional sessions, book events, and other public-interest programming. *CNN* is a cable news network.

NYE: Maybe what I mean is a different kind of talk, because the kind I'm thinking about is a very slow and deliberate, delighted kind of talk. My favorite quote comes from Thailand, "Life is so short we must move very slowly." I think that poems help us to do that by allowing us to savor a single image, a single phrase. Think about haiku—those little seventeen syllable poems—how many people have savored a single haiku poem over hundreds of years? Reading a poem slows you down, and when you slow down you are likely to read it more than one time. You read it more slowly than you would speak to somebody in a store, and we *need* that slow experience with words, as well as those quick and jazzy ones. ❧

Respond and Think Critically

1. **Summarize Main Ideas** Write a brief summary of the main ideas in this interview before you answer the following questions. For help on writing a summary, see page 389.

2. **Describe Ideas** How would you describe Nye's views on how one should approach writing? Support your response with evidence from the interview.

3. **Analyze Symbol** Nye talks about the idea of "keeping a door open." What does the door represent? Why is the door important to Nye?

4. **Make Inferences About Meaning** What does Nye mean when she says we need to have a "slow experience with words, as well as those quick and jazzy ones?" Support your answer with details from the text.

5. **Evaluate Style** How would you describe Moyers's interview style? Is he conversational, direct, confrontational, or something else? Do you think his style is effective? Explain, using evidence from the text to support your responses.

6. **Synthesize Ideas** Look back at your diagram on page 583. Based on your reading of Nye's biography (page 579), "Arabic Coffee" (page 581), and this interview, how would you describe Nye's attitude toward everyday experiences and objects? Use evidence from the texts to support your response.

TEKS

For pages 586–590

10.8 Analyze, make inferences and draw conclusions about the author's purpose in cultural, historical, and contemporary contexts and provide evidence from the text to support understanding.

Set a Purpose for Reading

Read to explore Chang-rae Lee's identification with his culture.

Preview the Article

Writer Chang-rae Lee comments on the unshakable bond between his relatives in Korea and himself.

1. From the title, what do you think the writer values?

2. What purpose do text features such as subheads and pull quotes serve in this article? How are they similar to or different from text features you've seen in other articles?

Reading Strategy Analyze Cultural Context

When you **analyze cultural context,** you consider the customs, beliefs, values, and arts of a group of people and use this knowledge to better understand the main idea and purpose of a text. To understand the cultural context of this article, record the writer's experiences with each culture in a chart.

Korea	United States
close family	language

TIME

We Are Family

The author with his parents in 1967, before they emigrated from South Korea to the United States.

During a visit to his native South Korea, novelist Chang-rae Lee learns that living abroad and losing his language are no barriers to belonging.

By **CHANG-RAE LEE**

THE LAST TIME I STOOD BEFORE MY GRANDFATHER'S grave, in the spring of 1989, it had been newly dug. My uncle had driven my father and me to Yong-In City, one hour south of Seoul, so that we could pay our respects. I remember the fog burning off to reveal the new season bursting forth in blooms of wild cherry and persimmon all around us on the hillside. And yet, there was a worn-out quality at the site. The burial ground was a three-meter-wide amphitheater carved out of the steep face of the hillside. The fresh earth was laid bare, roughly cut roots jutting out from the sheer wall of dirt. In the center of the dugout, the mound beneath which my grandfather was buried showed the first wispy strands of baby grass. There was no headstone as yet.

My father was on the verge of tears, finally seeing where his father lay. I wanted to feel the same pinch of loss, the same onrush of sadness. But I couldn't. Our family left Korea for America when I wasn't yet three, and since then I'd spent perhaps five hours total in my grandfather's presence. All I knew of him was that he'd lost his hardware business in Pyongyang to the communists on the eve of the Korean War. And when my father knelt low and bowed respectfully, the image I saw of my grandfather's face was drawn not from any memory of life but from the black-and-white picture of him that hung prominently in my childhood home.

I pictured that image once more when I visited his grave in May 2003. I was in Korea to visit my family, particularly to see my ailing maternal grandmother, and to do some research for my next novel. I had come once again with my uncle, a professor of business, but this time with his two sons as well, one of whom was just back from a year of language study in San Diego. Our mood as we climbed up the hill was expansive and lighthearted, and it seemed we were more on a picnicking hike than a dutiful visit to our ancestral dead. But as we ascended the path to the grave, the talk quieted.

Finally, at the end of a narrow deer path, there came an opening, and we emerged onto the same burial landing I had visited 14 years ago. To my surprise, there were two mounds instead of one and now a black granite headstone centered between, carved on the faces and sides with Chinese characters. I asked about the second mound and my uncle said that my grandmother and stepgrandmother had been unearthed from their resting places in Seoul and moved here some years before to join my grandfather.

"What is all the writing?" I asked. We were crouched by the black slab of rock.

"It's your grandfather's name. Your grandmothers' names are here," he said, pointing them out.

"And what about all these other characters?"

> **"IN THEIR FIRST YEARS IN AMERICA, . . . THEY DIDN'T ALWAYS ALLOW THEMSELVES TO EXPERIENCE MANY EMOTIONS"**

"These are his children. Here's your father. Here are your other uncles, then me, and your aunt. And here are the names of our spouses. This one is your mother's."

"My mother's?"

I touched the unfamiliar language sharply carved into the stone, almost saying her name aloud. She died a few years after my grandfather did, of stomach cancer.

"I didn't know it was done this way."

"Oh yes," my uncle said. "Everyone is here."

Learning to Belong

I kept thinking back on that phrase during the rest of my stay in Seoul: Everyone is here. As uttered by my uncle, it was a simple answer to a simple question, a matter of fact and a literal record. And so it was. And yet, as I thought about the notion, it became more than just a straightforward record of my ancestors. For I realized how differently than I my uncle and his sons viewed that dark stone, how the names to them were just an ordinary fact of their lives, like the ancient arrangement of the planets. To me, raised away in the States, the listing seemed more remarkable than that, a kind of supernatural alliance, extraordinary and wonderful.

For in our immigrant family of four, we were all we ever had. In the town where we lived (a small northern suburb of New York City), we were one of a handful of nonwhite families. Every great once in a while, there would be an uncle or aunt passing through New York, and they'd stay with us a few days or a week. In the evenings, my parents would chatter at the dinner table with special enthusiasm about all the reports from Seoul. My parents were generally happy, easygoing people, but in their first years in America, I would say they didn't always allow themselves to experience many emotions, perhaps because they felt outside of and flustered by all

BLOOD TIES
Lee's ailing grandmother gave him a reason to journey home and reconnect with his mother's extended family.

the strangeness of their new world. And it was only when "home" made its return that they seemed to truly liven up.

In later years, my parents considered America to be their only home, and although they possessed the means to do so by the time my mother died in 1991, our family had made only four visits to Korea in 23 years. Even as a serious teen, I didn't mind the summer trips we took as a family. Korea was a lot better than, say, a car trip to family friends, not so much because of any reconnecting with the family but for the food.

Best of all, were the grand meals we'd have at our relatives' cramped apartments or houses, the dozens of dishes completely covering the low tables they'd set out for us—the men sitting at the main table, the women lodged at one nearer the kitchen. In the fog of my jet-lagged mind, the only things that made sense to me amid the superfast talk, which I mostly couldn't understand, were all the bracing flavors, the radish kimchi and marinated raw crab and sesame-leaf pancakes. Even my father seemed somewhat overwhelmed by the rush of native language, occasionally asking people to repeat what they'd said.

And this is how I found myself on my recent trip, out with my father's side of the family at a popular barbecue restaurant, straining to understand everyone's questions about my family and work. I could say only a few words in response, my speaking ability in Korean not as developed as my aural comprehension. After the initial assurances that I could tolerate spicy food and a recounting of the names and ages of my daughters, I naturally retreated into the customary table rituals of the barbecue. I attended to grilling the meat and whole cloves of garlic, readying the bean paste and the fragrant shoots of chrysanthemum, cupping the fresh lettuce leaf to wrap all of it in. While the others ate heartily and engaged in their lively conversations, I was happy for their company and just as pleased simply to sit there and eat, gleaning what talk I could.

There was no awkwardness due to the differences of our language or the brief time we'd spent together during our lives. Somehow all was fine. They were family. There was a certain ease in the gathering that I have rarely felt in my life. There was

"SHE WAS STARING RIGHT INTO MY EYES, GAZING, I'M SURE, AT THE REMNANTS OF HER FIRST CHILD, MY MOTHER"

GENERATIONS **Author Lee with daughters Annika (left) and Eva, at their Princeton, New Jersey, home.**

a level of comfort drawn, I think, from not having to explain myself in the customary ways. I wasn't defined by the cultural and personal stereotypes that are part of my "regular" existence as a teacher and writer and maybe (if there really is such a person) as an Asian American.

I kept thinking how plainly, deeply satisfying it was to be back among my cousins and aunts and uncles. With them, at least, I was not a provisional "I," not an ethnic, or outsider, or an artist or intellectual, but simply someone whose connections to others were clear and traceable and real.

Keep the Family Together

The next night, I went to my maternal aunt's house south of the Han River, where my grandmother Halmoni was staying. She was my only living grandparent, in her late 80s, and from recent reports, not doing terribly well. Her back was finally giving way, and she wasn't very mobile; my cousin told me she sometimes crawled to the bathroom rather than ask anyone for help.

I was nervous about seeing Halmoni in a bad state, not only for the sadness of such a sight but for the sake of her own pride. I almost wished I could have simply telephoned her my wishes of good health and love. When I rang the bell of my aunt's house, a young cousin greeted me and led me inside. My two aunts were busy back in the kitchen making final preparations for dinner. My cousin and I sat down in the living room. Before I could say anything, my aunts came out, both wiping their hands on their aprons. We all hugged each other, then my younger aunt asked her son where Halmoni was.

My cousin said he'd go look for our grandmother upstairs, but then Halmoni cleared her throat in the next room, effectively announcing herself. She came in, not crawling at all but walking with slowed, careful steps, her hunched back bent down almost to 90 degrees. She wrapped her arms around me, her face pressed into my chest, hardly taller now with her fallen posture than my six-year-old daughter. I could smell the faint almondy oiliness of her hair. And as much as I didn't want to think of her as frail, she most clearly was, her hold of me like the cling of someone straining to grab on more than to hug. Soon enough, we were sitting together on the sofa, her hands cupping mine, gently kneading them just as she had often done to my sister and me as children.

"It's too far for you to come," she said. "It's good you didn't try to bring your family. You yourself shouldn't have bothered."

"It's no bother."

My cousin piped in, "Halmoni, he came over to see you, you know."

"Even more reason," she said, though half-smiling. She asked earnestly, "Are you tired?"

"I'm fine."

"You must be hungry."

"Not so much."

She called out to the kitchen, telling her daughters that I needed to eat right away. My younger aunt came out and said she could set the table, that we didn't have to wait for the men to arrive (which was of course possible, though an impossibility).

"Really," I told her. "I want to wait."

She nodded and went back to the kitchen. Halmoni made a raspy sound in her throat at me, a distinctive Korean mother-style scold, the sound of which contains just the pitch to make one feel at once guilty and beloved.

"Are you feeling well these days?" I asked, having practiced the phrase (in Korean) on the subway ride.

"Sometimes I have a little trouble with my back. But not today. Your father is in good health?"

"Yes."

"You visit him regularly?"

"I try to."

"You must do so always," she said, tapping my hand for emphasis. "Keep the family together." She paused. "And your stepmother, she is well, too?"

"Yes."

Halmoni nodded.

"That's good," she said. "It's how it should be."

She was staring right into my eyes, gazing, I'm sure, at the remnants of her first child, my mother, the only one, with any mercy, who would precede her to the grave. I pictured my mother's black granite headstone back in New York, and then, too, my paternal grandfather's stone, and then Halmoni's and my father's and even my own, all the written names, cast wide.

—Updated 2005, from TIME Asia, August 18/25, 2003

Respond and Think Critically

1. **Summarize Main Ideas** Write a brief summary of the main ideas in this article before you answer the following questions. For help on writing a summary, see page 389.

2. **Interpret Structure** Why do you think Lee opens his article with a description of his grandfather's gravesite?

3. **Interpret Behavior** How did Lee react to the names of his late family members on the black granite headstone? Why do you think this reaction is significant?

4. **Analyze Cultural Context** What were Lee's ties to his Korean heritage? How did his cultural ties impact his purpose in writing the article? Support your answer with evidence from the text.

5. **Analyze Meaning** How does Lee approach the subject of loss in the article? What does he learn or gain from his losses? Support your answer with evidence from the text.

6. **Evaluate Structure** Lee does not follow a traditional structure in his writing. It is not chronological or sequential. What techniques does he use to organize the article? Is his structure an effective way to relay meaning? Explain.

7. **Draw Conclusions About Meaning** Lee comments that he did not have to explain himself to his relatives "as a teacher and writer and maybe (if there really is such a person) as an Asian American." What is he saying about Asian American identity?

Comparing Literature

Across Genres

TEKS

For pages 591–605

10.2.A Compare and contrast differences in similar themes expressed in different time periods.

Compare Literature About Jazz

Jazz music is an essential part of American culture. The texts compared here highlight the contributions of African Americans to literature and music.

COMPARE THE ⬛ Big Idea Issues of Identity

Identity may be defined as individuality or character. It is both who we are and what we are. Identity relates to our family histories, where we come from, and where we are now. As you read, ask yourself, How is jazz an important part of each author's identity?

Jazz Singer, 1997. Gil Mayers.

COMPARE Theme

Theme is the central message of a literary work, often expressed as a general statement about life. Some themes are **universal,** meaning that they are widely held ideas about life that recur in different cultural and historical contexts and across time. As you read, ask yourself, What are the themes of the different texts? How are they similar? How are they different?

COMPARE Author's Perspective

An **author's perspective** is the combination of experiences, values, and ideas that shape the way an author looks at the world or at a particular subject. These three authors share a love of jazz but each writes from a different perspective—Langston Hughes from that of a poet, Studs Terkel from that of a biographer and critic, and Wynton Marsalis from that of a musician and teacher. As you read, ask yourself, How does the perspective of each writer determine the content and style of each text?

LOG ON ▶ **Literature** Online

Author Search For more about Langston Hughes, Studs Terkel, and Wynton Marsalis, go to glencoe.com and enter QuickPass code GL57805u3.

Before You Read

Dream Boogie and *Motto*

Meet **Langston Hughes**
(1902–1967)

African American writer Langston Hughes dedicated his life to improving race relations. His works linked prejudice and poverty to feelings of heartbreak and hopelessness among African Americans.

> "I have discovered in life that there are ways of getting almost anywhere you want to go, if you really want to go."
>
> —Langston Hughes

Early Wanderings Hughes was born in Joplin, Missouri, to parents who soon separated. His childhood consisted of living with either one parent or the other, or with a relative. Hughes turned to books for companionship. His love of reading led Hughes to write. The poetry of Walt Whitman and Carl Sandburg inspired him to use free verse and common speech patterns.

During the 1920s, Hughes held a variety of odd jobs in Harlem in New York City and then became a steward on a ship bound for West Africa. While abroad, Hughes learned about other cultures by traveling to Europe, Africa, Mexico, Russia, and Japan.

Speaking His Mind In 1921 Hughes published his first poem, "The Negro Speaks of Rivers," in the journal *Crisis*, edited by the noted African American author and civil rights leader W. E. B. Du Bois. Like Du Bois, Hughes believed that

African Americans could find renewal by understanding and taking pride in their cultural roots.

In 1926 Hughes published his first book of verses, *The Weary Blues*. He blended African American and white rhythms and poetic forms. He became a major force in a growing African American cultural movement called the Harlem Renaissance. When Hughes graduated from Lincoln University in 1929, he became one of the first African Americans to earn a living solely through writing. Hughes became a leader in integrating major forms of African American music—jazz, blues, and gospel—with his poetic lyrics.

Awards Hughes grew more prosperous through his hard work. He became involved in such literary pursuits as prose writing, playwriting, journalism, and film projects. In later life, Hughes received the Spingarn Medal from the NAACP for his many contributions to the betterment of African Americans. He was invited to join the National Institute of Arts and Letters in 1961.

LOG ON ▶ **Literature** Online

Author Search For more about Langston Hughes, go to glencoe.com and enter QuickPass code GL57805u3.

Literature and Reading Preview

Connect to the Poems

How much power do published words have to bring about change in people's lives? Freewrite for a few minutes about a book or story that affected you in a profound way.

Build Background

Hughes portrayed the African American experience in the mid-1900s. During this time, many African Americans had dreams that went unrealized because of racism.

Set Purposes for Reading

Big Idea Issues of Identity

As you read, ask yourself, How does Hughes express his thoughts in a style that displays a distinctive musical quality reminiscent of jazz music?

Literary Element Rhyme and Rhyme Scheme

Rhyme is the repetition of similar or identical sounds at the ends of words that appear close to each other. **Rhyme scheme** is the pattern that **end rhymes** (rhymes occurring at the ends of lines of poetry) form in a stanza or poem. As you read the poems, ask yourself, How does Hughes use rhyme and rhyme scheme to help convey his message?

Reading Strategy Make Inferences About Theme

To **make inferences about theme** is to make an educated guess about the meaning of a literary work based on textual evidence, cultural and historical context, and your background knowledge. As you read, consider Hughes's choice of genre and ask yourself, Which details help me find each poem's theme?

Tip: Question Create a chart like the one below to organize your ideas and make inferences about the poems' themes. Use the blue highlighted question to help you get started.

Poem	Cultural/Historical Context	Inference About Theme or Genre
"Motto"	African American culture 1930s	African American poets favored nontraditional forms

Vocabulary

deferred (di furd´) *adj.* put off; postponed; p. 594 *Joan's deferred loans would not have to be paid until after graduation.*

motto (mot´ ō) *n.* maxim or proverb that expresses a principle; p. 595 *One popular motto is "seize the day."*

Dream Boogie

Langston Hughes

Good morning, daddy!
Ain't you heard
The boogie-woogie rumble
Of a dream **deferred**?

5 Listen closely:
You'll hear their feet
Beating out and beating out a—

       You think
       It's a happy beat?

10 Listen to it closely:
Ain't you heard
something underneath
like a

       What did I say?

15 Sure,
I'm happy!
Take it away!

       Hey, pop!
       Re-bop![1]
20   *Mop!*

       Y-e-a-h!

Show Time (of the Blues), 20th century. Romare Bearden.

---

1. *Re-bop* is another term for "bebop," a style of jazz characterized by a staccato two-note phrase that was the music's trademark.

Make Inferences About Theme *Why does the speaker ask if it's "a happy beat" and if "something underneath" is heard?*

Issues of Identity *What do you think Hughes suggests about the speaker's relationship to the music in the concluding lines beginning with "I'm happy"?*

Vocabulary

deferred (di furd´) *adj.* put off; postponed

Bopping at Birdland (Stomp Time), 1979. Romare Bearden. Color lithograph on paper, 24 x 33¼ in. Smithsonian American Art Museum, Washington, DC.

MOTTO

Langston Hughes

I play it cool
And dig[1] all jive[2]
That's the reason
I stay alive.

5   My **motto**,
As I live and learn,
                    is:

*Dig And Be Dug
In Return.*

---

1. *Dig* is slang for "to like."
2. *Jive* may refer to swing music and the dancing performed to it or to the glib jargon of hipsters.

Rhyme and Rhyme Scheme *What is the rhyme scheme in the first stanza?*

Vocabulary

motto (mot´ō) *n.* maxim or proverb that expresses a principle

After You Read

Respond and Think Critically

1. **Connect to Personal Experience** If you could ask Langston Hughes one question about his poetry, what would it be?

2. **Make Inferences About Meaning** In "Dream Boogie," what questions does the speaker ask the audience? What do these questions suggest about the nature of the music? Explain.

3. **Evaluate Poetic Technique** In "Dream Boogie," how does Hughes convey the speaker's energy? Is his technique effective? Support your answer with evidence from the text.

4. **Paraphrase Ideas** In "Motto," what are the speaker's actual words for the motto? Rephrase the motto in your own words.

5. **Make Inferences About the Speaker** In "Motto," how does the speaker say that he stays alive? What does this suggest to you about his situation in life?

6. **Analyze Mood** Where in these poems does Hughes reflect the mood of desperation that many African Americans felt at this time? Explain.

7. **Big Idea** **Draw Conclusions About Meaning** What does Hughes mean when he refers to a deferred dream? Explain.

Literary Element Rhyme and Rhyme Scheme

Established poets such as Hughes often adapt rhyme scheme for added meaning and innovation.

8. **Explain Rhyme Scheme** How do the italicized words in "Dream Boogie" contribute to the poem's rhyme scheme?

9. **Analyze Rhyme Scheme** How do you think the rhyme schemes affect the meanings of Hughes's poems? Support your answer with evidence from the text.

Reading Strategy Make Inferences About Theme

Use your chart from page 593 to help you answer the following questions.

10. What theme is conveyed in these two poems?

11. How does the genre of these texts enhance their theme within their specific cultural and historical context? Explain.

Vocabulary Practice

Practice with Usage Respond to the statements below to help you explore the meanings of the boldfaced vocabulary words.

1. Identify a time when you have **deferred** something. Tell why it was deferred.

2. Explain what your personal **motto** might be.

Writing

Write an Annotation Write a footnote explaining the use of the term *boogie-woogie* in line 3 of "Dream Boogie." Use a dictionary to find the basic definition of the term, but do additional research on the Internet or in a library to help you explain the significance of Hughes's use of the term.

LOG ON ▶ **Literature** Online

Selection Resources For Selection Quizzes, eFlashcards, and Reading-Writing Connection activities, go to glencoe.com and enter QuickPass code GL57805u3.

Build Background

Giants of Jazz, from which this Dizzy Gillespie chapter is taken, was Studs Terkel's first book. It contains biographies of thirteen jazz greats. *Giants of Jazz* was reprinted in 2002 and still sells well fifty years after its initial publication.

Dizzy Gillespie

Explorer of New Sounds

from *Giants of Jazz*   Studs Terkel

John Birks Gillespie was a lively, impish little boy.

"John Birks! John Birks!" his harried mother called out. "Where in the world is that child?" Of her nine children, this youngest one was the most irrepressible.

From the parlor came the sound of a pounding piano. She peered into the room, chuckled softly to herself, and shook her head. The four-year-old had clambered up on the high stool and was furiously stabbing at the keyboard with his pudgy little fingers. He gloried in the making of loud sounds.

All kinds of instruments were strewn about the Gillespie household, in Cheraw, South Carolina. The father was a bricklayer by day and an amateur musician by night. As leader of the local band, he was the guardian of the other members' instruments.

The small boy quickly tired of the piano and scurried toward a clarinet that lay upon the table. He tooted into it a few times. His large, luminous eyes wandered to the nearby mandolin. Curious, he plucked at the strings. Now a huge instrument loomed up before him. It rested in a corner, against the wall. It was a bass viol.[1] He approached it cautiously. With all his might, he plucked at a thick, taut string. The vibrating sound startled him. He jumped back. Soon he was at the piano again, blithely pounding away. Here he could make the most noise with the least effort. John Birks Gillespie was acquainting himself with musical instruments. All kinds. . . .

[At the age of fourteen, John's] idol was a trumpet player. There was a radio at the Harringtons. Each week it was a ritual to listen to the broadcast from New York's Savoy Ball Room.[2] Roy Eldridge's trumpet was featured with the band of Teddy Hill. Young Gillespie listened intently to the solos of Eldridge. This man had his own

---

1. A *viol* is one of a family of stringed instruments with a flat back that is played with a curved bow.
2. The *Savoy Ball Room,* in the Harlem neighborhood of New York City, was where many big bands played.

special style; his horn had an amazingly wide range, rich colors, and a sharp bite.

"Little Jazz," as Eldridge was called, had gone beyond the New Orleans trumpet style as perfected by Louis Armstrong. He had discovered in the trumpet its own special quality. He added a new dimension to its playing. Young Gillespie sensed this and determined to simulate the style of Eldridge as closely as possible. He began to teach himself the technique of this horn with thoroughness and persistence. At times it was an ordeal for his mother in her search for peace and quiet. She was not the only one who moaned, "That noise is driving me crazy."

The members of the school band practiced wherever they could. As soon as they were kicked out of one home, they paraded into another. When the last weary mother cried, "Out, children. I can't hear myself think," they played in the open field. They blew loudly, joyously, and often off-key.

John Gillespie had a good ear. Soon he was considered the best trumpet player around. But he had one trouble. He could play in only one key: B-flat. It was his best-kept secret. That is, till the day Sonny Matthews returned to town. Sonny was Cheraw's best piano player. During his absence, Gillespie had gained his fine reputation as a trumpeter.

"Where's this John Birks I been hearin' about?" Sonny asked on his first day back. He invited Gillespie to his house for a two-man jam session.

"What do you wanna play, man?" asked the host.

"Anything. I don't care," replied the cocky young trumpeter.

"Okay, let's make it 'Nagasaki.'"

Sonny struck up a few chords on the piano. No sound came from the horn. John

Birks Gillespie was mortified. Matthews was playing in the key of C!

From that moment on, an embarrassed young man with a horn vowed to learn every key. . . .

Lottie Gillespie moved her family to Philadelphia in 1935. Though it was a new world for John, he wasn't one bit afraid. He was confident and saucy. Hat cocked to one side, eyes twinkling mischievously, he was ready for any kind of prank. Here his fun-loving ways earned him the nickname of Dizzy. It stuck. . . .

In his constant quest for a new style on the trumpet, he heard a sound that intrigued him. It was 1939. He was working for Edgar Hayes at the World's Fair in New York. Hayes's clarinet player, Rudy Powell, was playing a riff, a repeated phrase, of changing chords. Dizzy rushed to the piano.

"I always go to the piano when I want to try out something new. You see, you can skip around on the piano so easily. You can pick out chords, skip notes, jump intervals. Then you transpose it for the trumpet."

He played the arrangement over and over. He was excited. An idea was taking form in his mind. "I realized there could be so much more in music than what everybody else was playing." Gillespie knew now there must be some new way of playing the trumpet.

Late in 1939, he joined the orchestra of Cab Calloway. There were some excellent musicians in the band. Among them were Chu Berry at the tenor sax, Hilton Jefferson at the alto, Cozy Cole at the drums, and Milt Hinton at the bass. During his two years with Calloway, Dizzy recorded more than fifty sides. More important, it was his period of groping for new ways to express himself. There were difficulties. Some of the band's veterans were irritated by Gillespie's unorthodoxies.

A portrait of trumpeter Dizzy Gillespie (1917–1993) in performance. He was known for his co-creation of the popular jazz bebop style.

"What's he trying to do anyway?"

"Why doesn't he stick to the arrangements?"

"The guy's a 'character.'"

Calloway himself was not too happy with Dizzy's didoes.[3] Occasionally during his musical explorations Dizzy would get lost. When he'd miss the final high note, after a long-range progression, the leader angrily muttered, "All right now! Enough of that! No more of that Chinese music!"

There were others in the band who sensed the pioneer in young Gillespie. Gently they encouraged him.

"Come here, kid," said Milt Hinton, the bass player, during an intermission. "Let's go on the roof and practice."

During the Calloway engagement at New York's Cotton Club, the two men were often on the roof, quietly working together. Hinton walked the bass, while Gillespie tried different chords and melodic patterns on his trumpet.

"I like what you're trying to do," said Hinton. "Keep it up, kid."

Dizzy did keep it up, thanks to the opening of a little nightclub in Harlem. It was called Minton's Play House. Teddy Hill managed it. He encouraged young musicians to gather here after hours, to play exactly as they felt.

Gillespie became a regular habitué, together with Thelonious Monk, a pianist, and Kenny Clarke, a drummer. Clarke was experimenting as a drummer as Dizzy was as a trumpeter. His rhythm was implied rather than emphasized. He varied his punctuation, instead of steadily pounding away at the drum at four-to-the-bar. Here, too, Charlie Christian often came, after his regular stint with Goodman.

Another young musician seeking a new avenue in jazz frequented Minton's. He was an alto-sax player in the swing band of Jay McShann, recently arrived from Kansas City. His name was Charlie Parker. Later, Dizzy and he were to really cross paths and become the two major figures in the development of the jazz known as "bop."

At Minton's, Dizzy's closest associate was Thelonious Monk.

"Monk and I would work on an idea," remembers Dizzy. "Then I'd try it out the next night with Calloway. Cab didn't like it. It was too strange for him."

The word spread quickly among musicians. Minton's was the place to visit for exciting jam sessions and new approaches. Soon the place was packed with players, many of whom had limited talents. The regulars had to find some way to keep the mediocre ones off the bandstand.

"What're we going to do about those cats who can't blow at all, but it takes

---

3. A *dido* is a mischievous prank.

them seven choruses to prove it?" asked the perplexed Gillespie. "By the time they get off, the night's shot."

"Let's practice in the afternoon," suggested Monk. "We'll work out variations so complex it'll scare 'em away."

That's how it began. Bewildered musicians of lesser talents shook their heads and walked off the stand. Gradually Dizzy and his colleagues became more and more interested in what they were doing. They explored more deeply. And a new jazz style was evolving. . . .

When Dizzy and Parker played, the music had drive and humor and warmth. Many of their imitators lacked this, because they lacked musicianship. These two artists were not seeking mimics, but colleagues. In the years that followed, numerous young musicians came into prominence. They were happily equipped with the attributes Gillespie and Bird sought—good craftsmanship, imagination, and daring. Hundreds of records were cut, originals as well as standards. Young musicians were developing new melodic lines based on chord sequences of popular jazz numbers. New recording companies came into being, scores of them.

Modern jazz was here to stay.

In Europe as in America the impact was felt. Though Gillespie's 1948 tour through Scandinavia was a financial flop, it was not due to the music. The band was mismanaged. Dizzy's later appearances in Europe were enthusiastically received.

Perhaps the highlight of Dizzy Gillespie's career was his tour of the Middle East in 1956. Under the auspices of the U.S. State Department, he led a big band into such lands as India, Iraq, Turkey, and Lebanon. These were places where most people had never heard live jazz, let alone American artists. These concerts were divided into two parts. The first half dealt with origins, ranging from the African drums and spirituals to big band classics. The second half consisted of modern jazz.

Dizzy Gillespie was a wonderful ambassador of goodwill. He and his music won over these people immediately.

"I have never seen these people let themselves go like this," observed an American official at Damascus.[4] He himself had been suspicious of jazz.

In Ankara, Dizzy refused to play at an important gathering until the little ragamuffins outside the wall were let in.

"Man, we're here to play for the people."

Dizzy called a young native trumpeter to the stage. The boy was so moved he could hardly speak. Gillespie handed him his cigarette case. Engraved on it were the words: "In token of the brotherhood of jazz."

Does it matter what label is given to jazz? Be it traditional or be it modern, if a talented man plays it with joy and love, that's all that matters.

Says Dizzy Gillespie: "I'm playing the same notes, but it comes out different. You can't teach the soul. You got to bring out your soul on those valves." ∾

---

4. *Damascus* is the capital of Syria.

Quickwrite

Terkel chose "Explorer of New Sounds" for the title of his chapter on Dizzy Gillespie. Is this the best title for the chapter? Write a paragraph about the effectiveness of the title and whether you think, from the information in this excerpt, that Gillespie was an "explorer of new sounds."

Build Background

Wynton Marsalis, who is known for his jazz artistry, continues to inspire budding musicians today.

This letter is from his book, *To a Young Musician*, a collection of letters written to a young musician who admired Marsalis's talent.

Expression of Jazz, 1993. Maurice Faulk. Acrylic on canvas board.

Playing Jazz

Wynton Marsalis

July 18, 2003

Dear Anthony,

How are you, man? Glad to hear you got something from my last letter. Don't just read that stuff and lock it away in your head. Figure out how to apply it.

Tours go on and on. We just out here, from one city to the next. I just head where they tell me. So excuse the distance between these notes. I try to write when I can.

Man, last night we played a small, intimate club inside a Boston hotel. Can't complain at all; gig just felt good. Small places, man. The people all around you, making all kind of noise and grooving. It just inspires the band. Folks in the audience let the sound wash all over them, especially when our drummer, Herlin,[1] gets sanctified on the tambourine in 5/4.

After the gig, someone brought us a full-course meal—black-eyed peas, corn bread, barbecued ribs, mashed potatoes,

---

1. *Herlin* is Wynton Marsalis's longtime drummer Herlin Riley.

WYNTON MARSALIS **601**

even had the nerve to have some corn pudding. People cook for you when you sound good and have good manners. In all seriousness, though, no matter how often something like that happens, and it happens a lot, the love and generosity of spirit that we feel out here is always humbling. And it makes missing your family a bit more tolerable. But boy, if you don't like people, you'll have a lonely time out here.

I wanted to rap with you about playing. Yes, that simply, that essentially—what it takes to play jazz music. Playing covers four essential bases: the expansion of your musical vocabulary, employing charisma in your sound, locating your personal objective, and embracing swing. Let's spend some time chopping all four up.

First, the more vocabulary you know, the more you can play. It's just like talking. A person can know twenty words very well and communicate successfully. But there's gonna be a whole pile of things that he or she never talks about. You need to have vocabulary on all aspects of jazz—melodies, harmonies, rhythms, and personal effects. It's always best to start with what you should know—things from your region, then national things. In other words, if you're from Kansas City, you need to know what the Kansas City blues sounds like. Then you need to know American themes and tunes. And today you need to know more music, especially in the global sense. All over the world, styles of music have specific objectives. Learning those objectives will serve you well, allowing you to incorporate a greater breadth of material into your own vocabulary. Musicians in the Latin tradition always complain that the jazz musicians don't know any of their music. Study and learn whatever music catches your fancy from around the world with people who

know it and can play it. The enhancement to your own music will be invaluable. Studying the vocabulary of music is like etymology.[2] If they're interested in romance languages, people will study Latin, from which all those languages descend. In the same manner, most groove music comes from the African 6/8 rhythm—the claves[3] in Cuban music to the shuffle of the Mississippi blues. But if you don't know your own language, your own vocabulary, forget about learning someone else's.

Second, always bring charisma to your sound. People want to *hear* some music. They don't come out to see robots toot horns. They want to be uplifted, amazed, and enlightened. Infuse your sound with charisma. What you do when playing for the public isn't much different from any stage-based performance. Imagine the actor who trots out onstage only to deliver lines in bland fashion with no regard to distinguishing his or her craft. Would that make you enthusiastic? You have to understand and locate your distinct approach to the music, and then infuse your playing with that sentiment. Whatever your approach turns out to be, deliver it with force, power, and conviction. With *fun*, man. This is *playing*.

But while you're up on that bandstand blowing with force and power, keep in mind that playing jazz is like anything else in life: When you start a thing off, you're much more enthusiastic than when you get to the middle. If you're running a race, you shoot out like Jesse Owens reborn. Playing ball? That enthusiasm might make you think you're Joe Montana.[4] Then after a couple of interceptions the thrill is gone. This happens in almost every activity in the world.

---

2. *Etymology* means "the history of a word."
3. *Claves* are a two-bar syncopated pattern of music.
4. *Jesse Owens* was an Olympic gold medalist in track. *Joe Montana* is a former professional football player.

Wynton Marsalis, 1999. New York City.

So when you play, don't get carried away or burned out by the importance of your own effort. Start good. Finish good. Sound good. No more complicated than that. And when I say sound good, I mean sounding good enough to get a job. Because when you sound good, people will hire you; when you sound good, people will be calling.

Of course, sounding good also goes beyond the marketplace; it goes right to the heart of your personal objectives—our third base of playing. Although objectives vary, depending on the individual, there exists a central, common point: What do you want to give to people? Let me lay this on you.

Once I asked Sweets Edison,[5] "Why is it that you always sound good, from the first note that you play?"

"There's only one way to play, baby boy," Sweets answered. "There ain't but one way to do it."

Sweets means that you project your way with the ultimate feeling all the time, whether you're playing in a sad band, a great band, for elementary school students, at someone's birthday party at their house, or 'cause someone fixed a meal for you. When you pull your horn out, you should play as if that's the most important moment in your life. If it's not, make it be.

Remember when you were a kid and you really, really wanted something? It could have been the most trivial thing. Remember the way you begged and pleaded for it? Imagine playing with that passion, that desire, as if this was the most needed thing in your life. When we get older, we learn how to temper our wanting, our desire. Well, tap back into that childhood fervor and freedom of expression. That's what you have to have when you play. That thing you wanted the most and the way you were willing to sacrifice any speck of pride or dignity to obtain it. Remember how you wanted it; remember how you cried when you didn't get it? What about the girl who couldn't stand you? Or who liked you until Amos came around? Play with *that* passion.

Realize that the fundamentals of jazz help you develop your individuality, help you find that passion. Don't say, "I'm not going to really play blues," or "I'm not going to address swing." Don't run from you. Running carries a cost. Have you ever noticed that when you hear a contemporary Latin band play and juxtapose it with

5. *Sweets Edison* is the late jazz trumpeter Harry "Sweets" Edison.

a jazz band, the Latin music almost always sounds better? You wonder why that's the case? Just look at the bandstand. You'll see that the Latin musicians appear invested and involved; they believe in the integrity of their groove. Now look at the jazz band: not accepting the swing, trying to find some quasi-funk groove or, even worse, that sad jazz quasi-Latin groove. You can practically hear them muttering to themselves—"Swing is dead; let's try something else." They take detours to avoid sounding bad and run right into what they flee. The fourth and perhaps most important facet of playing jazz, *swing* and swinging.

You may hear about "quintessentially American" things. Well, what makes a thing quintessential is that it reflects the values of the thing it is supposed to be quintessentially about. In the case of an art form, it not only reflects the values, it embodies them, it ennobles them, and it emboldens them. That's why people study art forms with such intensity, because the artist channels the spirit of the nation. In the case of the swing, no one person created it; democracy is a collective experience. And swing is a democratic and *quintessentially* American concept.

Swing is supreme coordination under the duress of time. Swing is democracy made manifest; it makes you constantly adjust. At any given time, what's going to go on musically may not be to your liking. You have to know how to maintain your equilibrium and your balance, even if things are changing rapidly. Swing is designed for you to do that. Why? Each musician has a different concept of time. Sometimes I tell my students, "I want you all to stand up when a minute is over." And some people get up after twenty seconds. Some get up after a minute and a half. That shows the variance between individual concepts of time. As a player you

have to, of your own volition, come to a conclusion about how you approach time.

But swing has a hierarchy, like a government. The president of the swing is the drummer. The drummer has the loudest instrument and the cymbal is in the highest register. In African music it's called the bell rhythm. It's always the high rhythm, because you can hear that rhythm. In jazz, the bell rhythm is on the cymbal. You follow the bell rhythm.

But, like a government, swing also has checks and balances, because if the drummer rushes, the bass player might bring the time back. Sometimes the president of the swing is whoever has the best time. When Charlie Parker played, his time was so good that the bell rhythm would follow him. So you have that possibility. This is also a democratic proposition. If you have a weak president, man, you might need a strong legislative branch, or a stronger judiciary—checks and balances.

Swing ties in with the heart of the American experience: You make your way; you invent your way. In jazz, that means you challenge the time, and you determine the degree of difficulty of the rhythms you choose to play. You could play quarter notes, which are difficult to play in time. Or any type of impossible, fun syncopations. Or you could just play strings of eighth notes. You try to maintain your equilibrium with style, and work within the flow. That's what the swing offers. ✎

> **Discussion Starter**
>
> What is the author's purpose in writing this letter? Why does he discuss learning about different types of music? Why does he want the boy to understand the "democracy" of swing? Discuss your opinions in a small group.

Wrap-Up: Comparing Literature

Across Genres

- **Dream Boogie** and **Motto** by Langston Hughes

- **Dizzy Gillespie, Explorer of New Sounds** from **Giants of Jazz** by Studs Terkel

- **Playing Jazz** by Wynton Marsalis

COMPARE THE Big Idea Issues of Identity

Writing Many musicians have found their identities in jazz. Think about the texts you have just read. Write a paragraph in which you compare these writers in terms of the subjects they discuss. Are the writers alike in some ways? What makes each writer unique? How has music, specifically jazz, affected each writer?

Jump Up, 2000. Margie Livingston Campbell. Watercolor.

COMPARE Theme

Partner Activity Themes are often influenced by events in the authors' worlds. With a partner, discuss the questions below and make inferences and draw conclusions about the themes of these three texts. Consider any differences in the cultural, historical, or contemporary contexts of the works. Cite evidence from the texts to support your inferences and conclusions.

1. What are two major themes in these texts?

2. How are these themes similar? How are they different?

3. Consider how race relations have changed since the time Hughes was writing in the 1930s, to when Terkel was writing in the 1950s, to recent years when Marsalis was writing. How do you think the time periods in which these authors wrote influenced the similarities and differences in their themes?

COMPARE Author's Perspective

Speaking and Listening Langston Hughes, Studs Terkel, and Wynton Marsalis each have a different perspective on the subject of jazz. Draw conclusions about each author's perspective on the following topics:

- the role of improvisation and experimentation in jazz
- the place of tradition in jazz
- the importance of creating a personal style

Present your conclusions to the class in an oral report. Be sure to support your conclusions with evidence from the texts.

LOG ON **Literature** Online

Selection Resources For Selection Quizzes, eFlashcards, and Reading-Writing Connection activities, go to glencoe.com and enter QuickPass code GL57805u3.

TEKS

For pages 606–613

10.15.C.i-iii Write an interpretative response to an expository or a literary text (e.g., essay or review) that extends beyond a summary and literal analysis; addresses the writing skills for an analytical essay and provides evidence from the text using embedded quotations; and analyzes the aesthetic effects of an author's use of stylistic and rhetorical devices.

Planning Checklist

Your essay should include the following traits:

☑ an effective introduction to share your thoughts about the poem with the reader

☑ a clear thesis to state the goal of the essay

☑ a solid organizing structure to guide the reader

☑ embedded quotations to support the thesis

☑ a strong conclusion to resolve the goal introduced by the thesis

 Scoring Rubric

Check the Expository Texts **Scoring Rubric** on page R29 for more guidance on crafting your best essay.

 # Writing Workshop

Interpretive Response Essay

Literature Connection: The poets you have studied in this unit use many devices to create meaning, including imagery, figurative language, rhyme and rhythm, repetition, and symbolism. Poets also evoke meaning in their selection of poetic form. By using poetic devices and making stylistic choices, poets create texts with meaning that goes beyond the literal level.

Purpose: Your purpose for writing this interpretive response essay is to analyze how a poet uses one or more of these devices to enhance the overall meaning of his or her poem.

Audience: You will be submitting your essay to a Literary Journal, which you will create and design as a class. A copy of your class's Literary Journal will be shared with other English classes in your school to showcase your insights and expertise in poetry.

Choose Your Topic

Option A: Choose a prompt.

1. In "Ode to My Socks," how does Pablo Neruda use figurative language to make a profound statement about ordinary objects?

2. In "Shall I Compare Thee to a Summer's Day?" how does William Shakespeare use imagery to immortalize the beauty of his subject?

Option B: Write a prompt.

In the poem_____, how does the poet use _____ (device or devices) to show _____ (your interpretation of the poem's overall meaning)?

Sample Prompt:

In "miss rosie," how does Lucille Clifton use poetic devices to show what has happened to Miss Rosie?

Analyze a Professional Model

Read for Guidance Read the following excerpt from an essay by Professor Ted Humphrey analyzing Lucille Clifton's poem "miss rosie." The notes in the side column point out writing traits that make this essay interesting and effective.

from *"Miss Rosie: Criticism"* by Ted Humphrey, PhD

Lucille Clifton has said, "I am interested in trying to render big ideas in a simple way." Reading the poems in the volume *Good Woman: Poems and a Memoir 1969–1980*, which contains "Miss Rosie," one is immediately struck by Clifton's success in reaching her goal. Her ideas are big: love, respect, race relations, sacrifice, religion, loss, and childhood, to name a few. These ideas and more are present in her short poems, which are characterized by their short lines, their unambiguous syntax, and a tone—tough sometimes, tender others— that is always under control. . . .

   Does Clifton's poetry, and in particular "Miss Rosie," have a political agenda? Is it possible that this apparently simple poem describing a "bag lady," a "homeless person," a "derelict" might have a moral and political purpose behind its surface simplicity? Consider the shift in focus created by the repetition of the refrain "when I watch you." Consider how necessary it is to see a problem before one may see a solution. Consider how necessary it is for one person to have such a vision before a "political" solution can be dreamed, articulated, shared, and enacted. What is the solution to the "problem" of the homeless, the derelicts, the abandoned, the "brown bag" of this particular woman and the thousands like her? Clifton suggests that the solution is, first, to see her, to acknowledge her, and then to "stand up / through your destruction" as the speaker emphatically does in the last line.

Introduction

The writer uses an interesting quotation to pique the reader's interest in the topic.

Voice

Repetition and parallel structure are used to challenge the reader to think more deeply about the poem.

Embedded Quotations

Quoted words from the poem are seamlessly embedded into the writer's own sentence.

PLAN Your Essay

Key Trait Ideas When you are asked to write about a piece of literature, your most interesting ideas will come from the literature. So the first step in planning your interpretive essay is to start with the text.

▶ Step 1: Reread the Text

Reread the text and write a list of your favorite quotations. Explain what each quotation means to you and identify any poetic devices.

quotations	what it means
"when i watch you / wrapped up like garbage" (simile)	the speaker sees her a lot; she's disgusted by her
"wet brown bag of a woman/ used to be the best looking" (alliteration)	the speaker's known her for a long time
"i stand up / through your destruction" (no poetic devices)	the speaker is inspired by her

▶ Step 2: Freewrite to Discover Ideas

Next, freewrite to come up with ideas.

The speaker must be someone close to Miss Rosie who sees her often. Why is the speaker "i" always lowercased? I don't understand why the speaker would "stand up" for herself and not "stand up" for Miss Rosie. Unless maybe Miss Rosie is really the speaker. Maybe both the "i" and the "you" are Miss Rosie, the inner and outer parts of her. Maybe her inner self is strong, but her outer self has suffered the "destruction" of being poor and alone.

▶ Step 3: Develop a Thesis

Write a thesis statement based on the discoveries you make in your freewriting. Remember that your classmates will be reading your essay when it appears in the Literary Journal. Make sure your thesis clearly states your interpretation of the poem.

Thesis: Clifton uses similes and alliteration to show that Miss Rosie and the speaker are two sides of the same person, a person who is struggling between her inner self and outer self.

SOAPS

If you experience difficulty asking a question about your poem, try using **SOAPS** to develop your ideas. Ask yourself these questions.

Subject: What is the poem about?

Occasion: When and where was it written?

Audience: Who was the poem written for?

Purpose: Why was it written?

Speaker: Who is the speaker?

Answering these questions will help you find a deeper meaning to the poem you selected to interpret.

Literature Online

Writing and Research For planning, drafting, and revising tools, go to glencoe.com and enter QuickPass code GL57805u3.

DRAFT Your Essay

Key Traits Ideas and Organization Now that you have explored your ideas about the poem, prepare to write your first draft by organizing your ideas and developing the details of your interpretation.

▶ Step 1: Organize Your Ideas

Choose an organizational plan that will help the reader follow your thinking. Your thesis often suggests an organizational plan.

> Clifton uses *similes and alliteration* to show that Miss Rosie and the speaker are two sides of the same person, a person who is struggling between her inner self and outer self.

Two natural subtopics for your essay are the poetic devices you selected. Organize ideas in an outline by focusing one paragraph on similes and one paragraph on alliterations.

> I. Introduce the idea that people may not be what they seem
>
> II. Show how similes are used to make comparisons
>
> III. Show how alliteration emphasizes the speaker's attitude
>
> IV. Remind people to be strong in difficult times

▶ Step 2: Develop Your Interpretation

To interpret, you must explain your textual evidence. Keep the poem and your prompt in front of you as you begin drafting. Here are three steps to follow:

1. Embed a quotation in your own sentence.

> The speaker uses alliteration when she calls Rosie a "wet brown bag of a woman."

2. Restate what the quotation means in your own words.

> The repetition of the "b" and "w" words makes the line sound as if the speaker is disgusted by Rosie, almost spitting the words at her.

3. Explain how the quotation supports your thesis statement.

> The use of alliteration emphasizes the comparison of Miss Rosie to garbage. The sentence is so harsh that it is hard to imagine that someone would say this to a helpless and homeless woman.

Drafting Checklist

Your essay should include the following traits:

- ☑ Focus—all the ideas relate to the thesis
- ☑ Organization—ideas appear in a logical order
- ☑ Development—ideas are thoughtful and have depth

Poor Miss Rosie

Introduction

The opening sentence appeals to the real world interests of the audience.

Introduce Author and Title

After stating the author's full name in the introduction, you can refer to her by last name only.

Thesis

The thesis states the interpretation that the writer wants to share with the audience.

Embedded Quotation

Incorporate quotations from the text into your own writing. Carefully explain your interpretation of each quotation.

Our outward appearances do not always represent how we feel inside. Being homeless and wearing torn, stinky clothes, but still trying to feel like yourself on the inside, could be frustrating. Lucille Clifton shows this frustration in her poem "miss rosie." The speaker in the poem has a sense of anger and disgust toward Miss Rosie, who used to be beautiful but is now falling apart. The speaker, who represents the inner self of Miss Rosie, is trying to understand what she has become on the outside. She feels separate from her outer self that she calls "you" and it makes her feel angry. Clifton uses similes and alliteration to show that Miss Rosie and the speaker are two sides of the same person, a person who is struggling between her inner self and her outer self.

It is obvious that the speaker, who represents Miss Rosie's inner self, despises the outward appearance of Miss Rosie today. Most of Clifton's descriptions compare Miss Rosie to trash, something that is useless and should be thrown out. In the simile, "i watch you / wrapped up like garbage," she is saying that there is a wrapping or a cover over Miss Rosie, making her appear to be useless trash. This shows that there are two sides to Miss Rosie.

Similarly, Clifton uses alliteration to create the effect of conflict between inner and outer selves. The speaker calls Rosie a "wet brown bag of a woman." The repetition of the "b" and "w" words makes the line sound as if the speaker is disgusted by Rosie, almost spitting the words at her. As a result, the use of alliteration emphasizes this second comparison Clifton makes between Rosie and trash. The "wet brown bag" is also something that holds garbage. The sentence is so harsh that it is hard to imagine that someone would say this to a helpless and homeless woman.

It is difficult to imagine that someone who knows Miss Rosie so well could feel so angry toward her and judge her so harshly just by looking at her outer self. The speaker says she will "stand up" through Miss Rosie's destruction at the end. I think it is as if she is trapped inside a rotting garbage bag and is going to break out. Through poetic devices, Clifton creates a powerful poem that shows that no matter how difficult life becomes, we have to use our inner strength to keep fighting.

Transition

Clear transitions emphasize the organizational structure of your essay.

Explanation of Evidence

Be sure to explain how your quotations relate to your thesis statement or topic sentence.

Conclusion

The conclusion returns to the real world connection between the poem and the reader.

Your Turn

Using your thesis, outline, and interpreted quotations, write the first draft of your essay. Be sure your introduction draws the reader into the essay and your conclusion amplifies the importance of what you have found.

REVISE Your Essay

Key Traits Word Choice and Sentence Fluency Revising your first draft can involve everything from rearranging the order of your ideas to making changes in word choice. How you revise each essay depends on the strengths and weaknesses of your first draft and how effectively the draft meets the purpose of your essay. Reread your essay using the Revising Checklist and these steps.

Revising Checklist

Before you start your revision, ask yourself these questions:

- ☑ Does my essay have a clear purpose? Does it accomplish what I intended to do?

- ☑ Will my audience understand my interpretation of the poem? Do all the paragraphs relate to my interpretation?

- ☑ Does my word choice and sentence structure seem appropriate for my audience?

- ☑ Do I include the traits in the Planning Checklist (on page 606) and the Drafting Checklist (on page 609)?

▶ Step 1: Focus Your Draft

Do you sustain your focus from paragraph to paragraph? Check by analyzing the relationship between the first sentences of every paragraph.

The first three paragraphs all opened with "outward appearances" or "outer selves." I revised the last paragraph to keep the pattern.

It is difficult to imagine that someone who knows Miss Rosie so well could feel so angry toward her and judge her so harshly just by looking at her outer self.

▶ Step 2: Use Transitions

Have you shown the progress of your ideas by using transitions? Choose two sentences from the middle of any paragraph. Does the second sentence build on, clarify, or draw a conclusion about the information in the first sentence? Choose transitional words and phrases such as *additionally, for example,* or *as a result,* to make relationships clear.

The repetition of the "b" and "w" words makes the line sound as if the speaker is disgusted by Rosie, almost spitting at her. As a result, the use of alliteration emphasizes this second comparison Clifton makes between Rosie and trash.

▶ Step 3: Improve Word Choice

Will the words you have chosen be interesting and meaningful to your audience? Check your essay for places where your word choice can be improved.

Original:

It is obvious that the speaker, who is Miss Rosie's inner self, does not like the outward appearance of Miss Rosie today.

Revision:

It is obvious that the speaker, who represents Miss Rosie's inner self, despises the outward appearance of Miss Rosie today.

EDIT Your Essay

Key Trait Conventions Edit by correcting any errors in spelling, grammar, and mechanics. Review the grammar tips and workshops in the unit to identify areas in your writing that you would like to strengthen.

> ## ▶ Grammar Tip
>
> **Avoid Run-On Sentences** Run-on sentences appear when two or more complete sentences are combined without proper punctuation. Correcting run-on sentences provides an opportunity for revising. Here is a run-on sentence from the first draft:
>
> *The speaker represents the inner self of Miss Rosie, she is trying to understand what she has become on the outside.*
>
> **Here are three ways to correct the run-on sentence:**
>
> **1.** Create two sentences.
>
> *The speaker represents the inner self of Miss Rosie. She is trying to understand what she has become on the outside.*
>
> **2.** Use a coordinating conjunction (*and, but, or, nor, for, yet, so*).
>
> *The speaker represents the inner self of Miss Rosie, and she is trying to understand what she has become on the outside.*
>
> **3.** Change the first independent clause into a subordinate clause by adding *who*.
>
> *The speaker, who represents the inner self of Miss Rosie, is trying to understand what she has become on the outside.*

PUBLISH Your Essay

Key Trait Presentation Literary journals are magazines that publish original works of fiction and poetry, book reviews, and essays analyzing already published works. As a class, you will produce a Literary Journal, featuring all the essays from students in your class. The final journal can be a printed magazine, a Web site, or a blog.

As a class, you should select a title for the magazine or Web site and design an attractive cover or homepage. Decide how the essays in the journal will be organized. By poem? By time period? By students' last names?

Ask a parent or friend to read your essay to check for errors. Read through your essay carefully one more time before publishing it in the Literary Journal. Add a design or an image that relates to the thesis statement.

Editing Checklist

For your final revision, check the following:

- ☑ Have I misspelled any words? If you are unsure of the spelling of a word, check an online or print dictionary or use your computer's spell checker.

- ☑ Have I made any errors in mechanics or grammar? Have I followed the rules of Standard American English? Use the Language Handbook on pages R48–R71 to correct common grammar and mechanics errors.

- ☑ Is my writing legible? Be sure your handwriting is neat or that you have followed your teacher's guidelines for word-processing.

 LOG ON ▶ **Literature** Online

Writing and Research For editing and publishing tools, go to glencoe.com and enter QuickPass code GL57805u3.

TEKS

For pages 614–615

10.24.C Evaluate how the style and structure of a speech support or undermine its purpose or meaning.

Speaking, Listening, and Viewing Workshop

Oral Response to Literature

Literature Connection From ancient bards retelling Homer's *Odyssey* to poetry slammers today, the spoken word has always been the most exciting way to get to know a poem and appreciate its rhyme, rhythm, repetition, and other devices. In this workshop, you will learn to present your response-to-literature essay as an oral response to literature, which will include quotations from your poem.

> **Assignment** **Plan and present an oral response to literature.**

Plan Your Presentation

Review these requirements for an effective oral response to literature.

- State a thesis or make a judgment that shows your understanding of the poem.
- Support your thesis and argument with accurate and detailed references to the poem, including quotations.
- If you use sources other than the poem, make sure they are reliable.
- Present your evidence in a way that makes sense.
- Show your appreciation for the author's style and explain how it affects your understanding. Discuss shades of meaning, subtle details, and complex ideas in the poem.

To turn your essay into an effective oral presentation, follow these guidelines.

- Select your thesis and the best evidence for presentation. How can you adjust the language to fit your purpose?
- Think of ways to make your introduction and conclusion more exciting or memorable for your listeners, perhaps by starting with a quotation or telling a brief story.
- Make note cards or cue cards to help you recall the main ideas and details of your presentation. Jot down your thesis, main ideas, and well-chosen details, as well as your best quoted evidence from the poem.

Select Lines

To support your oral response to literature, choose lines from the poem to illustrate the points you want to make. Be sure the lines accurately represent the context in which they appear. To capture your audience's attention, look for dramatic quotations with vivid images that your listeners can relate to.

Listen Responsively

When you are listening to the presentation,

☑ use comprehension skills to listen attentively

☑ take notes that summarize, synthesize, or highlight the speaker's ideas

☑ ask questions related to the content for clarification and elaboration

Remember to wait until the speaker has finished presenting before asking any questions.

Communicate Your Ideas

When you give a presentation with quotes from a poem, use your voice to communicate the meaning of the lines. Speak like an actor: the examples and quotations you use to support your thesis will capture your listeners' attention if you present them expressively rather than in a monotone. Try to memorize your quotations so you can make eye contact with your audience while speaking.

Consider the following two quotations from "miss rosie," by Lucille Clifton. How would you say each line in order to show the contrast between their tones?

▶"sitting, surrounded by the smell / of too old potato peels" (lines 3–4)

▶"i stand up / through your destruction / i stand up." (lines 16–18)

Rehearse

Practice delivering your oral response with a partner to strengthen your speaking and listening skills. Talk about the mood you want to create and how to do so. Discuss the audience and the occasion. Who will be listening? Where will they be sitting in relation to you? Your partner can help you identify any flaws that you missed. How formal or informal, theatrical or informative, will they expect or want you to be?

Also discuss how you might use each of the following verbal and nonverbal techniques to achieve your purpose.

Techniques for Presenting an Oral Response to Literature

Verbal Techniques	Nonverbal Techniques
☑ **Rate** Speak at a normal pace, using pauses for effect.	☑ **Visibility** Be sure that everyone can see your presentation.
☑ **Language** Use the conventions of language (correct grammar) to communicate ideas effectively.	☑ **Eye Contact** Make eye contact with people in the audience.
☑ **Enunciation** Speak clearly and to the point.	☑ **Posture** Avoid leaning or slouching.
☑ **Volume** Speak loudly enough that everyone can hear you.	☑ **Gestures** Use purposeful gestures to emphasize important ideas.

Presentation Tips

Use the following checklist to evaluate your oral response to literature.

☑ Did you present and support a clear thesis?

☑ Did you support your thesis with quotations and other references to the poem?

☑ Did you use verbal and nonverbal techniques to create the right mood and tone?

Evaluate the Presentation

As you listen to the presentation, ask yourself these questions:

☑ What is the presentation's purpose?

☑ What is the style of the presentation: formal or informal, straightforward or creative? Does it support the purpose?

☑ How is the presentation structured? Does it follow chronological order? Show cause and effect? List ideas in order of importance? Does the structure support the purpose and meaning?

LOG ON ▶ **Literature** Online

Speaking, Listening, and Viewing For project ideas, templates, and presentation tips, go to glencoe.com and enter QuickPass code GL57805u3.

Independent Reading

Poetry and Novels

POETRY IS THE MOST CONCENTRATED, ABBREVIATED GENRE. IN RELATIVELY few words, a poet may present the same themes that a novelist explores over hundreds of pages. As you have seen in this unit, poetry ranges from momentary glimpses of the natural world to longer, serious reflections on love and grief. For more poetry, try the two suggestions below. For novels and a play that incorporate the Big Ideas of *The Energy of the Everyday, Loves and Losses,* and *Issues of Identity,* try the titles from the Glencoe Literature Library on the next page.

Texas Author

The Space Between Our Footsteps: Poems and Paintings from the Middle East

selected by Naomi Shihab Nye

This collection of works from more than one hundred poets and artists from nineteen Middle Eastern countries explores themes about family, childhood, journeys, war, peace, and joy. Texan and award-winning poet and anthologist Naomi Shihab Nye pairs poems with full-color art from the countries represented. Nye's respect for and appreciation of Middle Eastern culture is apparent throughout the book. Yet, the overall effect of the anthology is one that emphasizes the similarities between people.

A Haiku Menagerie: Living Creatures in Poems and Prints

Stephen Addiss with Fumiko and Akira Yamamoto

Showing how fascinating the smallest animal or insect can be, this collection of more than one hundred Japanese haiku features master poets' insights into the natural world. More than 48 woodblock prints illustrate the creatures described in the poems. The poems are presented both in English translations and the original Japanese.

Nothing But the Truth: A Documentary Novel

Avi

A simple action gives new meaning to the energy of the everyday and leads to a national scandal.

Cyrano de Bergerac

Edmond Rostand

A poetic play about loves and losses features love, deception, and heartbreak.

Picture Bride

Yoshiko Uchida

In this novel about issues of identity, a woman leaves Japan to marry a stranger in San Francisco.

CRITICS' CORNER

"Mary Oliver would probably never admit to anything so grandiose as an effort to connect the conscious mind and the heart (that's what she says poetry can do), but that is exactly what she accomplishes in this stunning little handbook, ostensibly written 'to empower the beginning writer. . . .' Oliver gives us tools for 'the listening mind,' tools we need to write poetry."

—Susan Salter Reynolds, the *Los Angeles Times Book Review*

A Poetry Handbook

Mary Oliver

In this highly readable handbook, Oliver reminds aspiring poets about sound, line, and diction. Citing works from other poets, Oliver reveals that writing good poetry is a craft. She urges would-be poets to take care of the special place within them that "houses the possibility of poems."

 Write a Response

Read one of the books shown and write a response to it for your classmates. Select a genre for your response that will best express the message you wish to communicate to your audience about the book. For example, you can write a personal narrative that describes the effect the book had on you, a persuasive essay to convince others to read it, or a series of poems to express your thoughts about the book.

Assessment

English Language Arts

Reading: Poetry and Fiction

Read the following passages and answer the questions that follow them.

"Daybreak in Alabama" by Langston Hughes

When I get to be a composer
I'm gonna write me some music about
Daybreak in Alabama
And I'm gonna put the purtiest songs in it
5   Rising out of the ground like a swamp mist
And falling out of heaven like soft dew.
I'm gonna put some tall tall trees in it
And the scent of pine needles
And the smell of red clay after rain
10   And long red necks
And poppy colored faces
And big brown arms
And the field daisy eyes
Of black and white black white black people
15   And I'm gonna put white hands
And black hands and brown and yellow hands
And red clay earth hands in it
Touching everybody with kind fingers
And touching each other natural as dew
20   In that dawn of music when I
Get to be a composer
And write about daybreak
In Alabama.

from *"Red Velvet Dress"* by Naomi Shihab Nye

1   In the next neighborhood over from their neighborhood lived the Collins boys and the Parker boys that Lena knew from their jobs together working on the berry-picking farm and the Emerson girls who spent every Saturday morning at the library like Lena did and sometimes they all traded favorite books and the big grandmother with the high hair that Lena's mother stared at once in the grocery checkout

line. "I should have been her," she whispered to Lena, which Lena found very strange. How could anybody be anyone else? But Lena would never go to their houses and ask to see the Africans.

2   Because once you knew Ricky Collins, you knew about his lizard collection and his turquoise stone that he kept in a pouch inside an egg carton with old pennies worth ten dollars each and the rusted key he dug out of the ground one day while they were plucking the berries. You knew his voice and shirts. You did not think A Group of Different People, when you were thinking of friends.

3   Maybe the Robitailles weren't even like any other French-Canadians at all. Maybe Annie's grandfather who snapped his suspenders and brought them a fancy cold dessert called Tiramisu which he carried on ice cubes in his green car was just himself more than An Italian. In those days not many people talked about being half-and-half, but years later Lena would know it was one of the richest kinds of milk.

4   So her father burned the dry leaves and a bat flew over him. Lena called out, "Bat! Daddy! Look, it's not a bird!" and he looked up. "Ahlan wa sahlan," he called out, which meant "Welcome" in his own first language of Arabic, and she laughed as the bat dipped and rose in graceful arcs. He did not say, Get away. He did not say, I wish you were something else. He said "Welcome" and the bat seemed to understand by circling close above his head.

5   Then she took a deep breath and called out to him. "Daddy, some children came to the door. They wanted to see the Arab and I said we didn't have one. I never saw them on this street before. I never saw them at school either. But they might be from school. Are you mad at me?"

6   And her father came and sat beside her and took her hand in his own hand. . . .

7   Her father said, "The world asks us all a lot of questions, doesn't it," and stared off into a strip of pink sky. . . .

8   Then there was the clatter-bang muffler sound of Peter's father turning into his driveway next door.

9   Lena thought his feelings might be hurt. She said, "I'm sorry," and her daddy laughed so loudly he startled her. . . .

10   "You could have said Yes, but you were also right in saying No! All the questions have more than one good answer, don't you think? . . .

11   I could have put on my headdress for them! You could have pretended I didn't speak English. Maybe they'll come back and we can make them happy."

Questions 1–6 apply to "Daybreak in Alabama."

1   What literary device is used in the poem's first six lines?
  A   Repetition
  B   Enjambment
  C   Juxtaposition
  D   Personification

2   The similes in lines 5 and 6 suggest that the speaker's music will be —
  F   unpleasant
  G   gentle and natural
  H   sudden and unexpected
  J   made up of only low notes and high notes

3   Lines 14–18 in the poem suggest that the speaker's music will be —
  A   loud
  B   complex
  C   inclusive
  D   energizing

4   What literary element is found throughout the entire poem?
  F   Imagery
  G   Symbolism
  H   Sound devices
  J   Figurative language

5   For which of the characteristics of music does the speaker of this poem express the strongest desire?
  A   Rhythm
  B   Melody
  C   Structure
  D   Harmony

6   The tone of the poem could best be described as —
  F   critical
  G   regretful
  H   hopeful
  J   humorous

Questions 7–9 apply to "Red Velvet Dress.""

7   How does Lena's father react to the visitors' question?
  A   With bitter anger
  B   With sad resignation
  C   With humorous acceptance
  D   With energetic determination

8   Lena's father suggests that they might have deceived the visiting children in order to show the children —
  F   how foolish they were
  G   what they had hoped to see
  H   that their question had no answer
  J   that Lena's father could take a joke

9   What is the theme of this excerpt?
  A   Neighbors should stick together.
  B   America is a great melting pot.
  C   All people are essentially the same.
  D   Labeling people is senseless and ignorant.

Question 10 applies to both selections.

10   **Open-Ended Item**   What is one characteristic shared by the speaker of "Daybreak in Alabama" and Lena's father in "Red Velvet Dress"? Support your answer with evidence from the selections.

Vocabulary Skills: Sentence Completion

For each item, choose the word that best completes the sentence.

1 "Please, stop whining!" the father begged his _____ child.
   A hoary
   B meticulous
   C querulous
   D embroidered

2 The _____ heat made it difficult for us to enjoy our summer vacation.
   F russet
   G sacred
   H searing
   J mature

3 Erin would no longer tolerate her employee's _____ tardiness.
   A chronic
   B primal
   C disgruntled
   D ceremonious

4 Walter could not _____ precisely when he had learned to read.
   F lag
   G tread
   H marvel
   J recollect

5 Although many in the crowd were quite _____ to the game's outcome, they cheered anyway.
   A austere
   B melancholy
   C indifferent
   D serpentine

6 As the days passed into years, his memories of the farm faded into _____.
   F stupor
   G oblivion
   H essence
   J conflagration

7 The applause was enthusiastic and, at its _____, deafening.
   A crest
   B gorge
   C bough
   D glyph

8 The _____ amount of water in the cup was only enough for one sip.
   F hapless
   G decrepit
   H translucent
   J minuscule

9 A feeling of _____ led me to apologize for my rude and inconsiderate behavior.
   A chaos
   B remorse
   C scythe
   D affirmation

10 When Aileen visited her parents, she became _____ about her childhood.
   F immense
   G meticulous
   H nostalgic
   J ceremonious

LOG ON ▶ **Literature** Online

Standards Practice For more standards practice, go to glencoe.com and enter QuickPass code GL57805u3.

Revising and Editing

Read the following draft of part of a student's essay and answer the questions that follow it.

(1) Walt Whitman's poem "When I Heard the Learn'd Astronomer" contrasts two distinctly different ways of looking at the world. (2) The astronomer gives a lecture that shows a scientific approach to life. (3) In contrast, the speaker prefers to simply appreciate the world and, unlike the astronomer cares little about "charts and diagrams." (4) The speaker seems bored by the scientific understanding that is so important to the astronomer. (5) Each man has their own way of looking at nature—a fact the speaker seems to recognize. (6) While the astronomer tries to understand and classify information, the speaker wants only to appreciate what seems "mystical" to him.

(7) Because the poem begins with the speaker's description of the astronomer's lecture, his attitude--one that many people share--is clear. (8) The speaker becomes "tired and sick" in the lecture hall, he isn't sure why. (9) He seems to believe that his view of nature is the better one to have. (10) Why this would be the case is not explained. (11) If the speaker was an astronomer himself, instead of not being "learn'd," would he be unable to see beauty in the night sky?

1 What change, if any, should be made in sentence 3?
   A Delete the comma after *contrast*
   B Delete the comma after *and*
   C Insert a comma after *astronomer*
   D Make no change

2 In sentence 4, the word *understanding* is used as a —
   F verb
   G noun
   H adverb
   J adjective

3 What revision, if any, is needed in sentence 5?
   A Each man has his own way of looking at nature—a fact the speaker seems to recognize.
   B Each man has his own way of looking at nature,—a fact the speaker seems to recognize.
   C Each man has their own way of looking at nature, a fact the speaker seems to recognize.
   D No revision is needed.

4 What error appears in sentence 7?

F Run-on sentence

G Unclear pronoun referent

H Incorrect use of dashes

J Lack of pronoun/antecedent agreement

5 What revision, if any, is needed in sentence 8?

A The speaker becomes "tired and sick" in the lecture hall. He isn't sure why.

B The speaker becomes "tired and sick" in the lecture hall, the speaker isn't sure why.

C The speaker becomes "tired and sick" in the lecture hall but he isn't sure why.

D No revision is needed.

6 What change, if any, should be made in sentence 11?

F Change *was* to **were**

G Delete the comma after *himself*

H Delete the comma after *"learn'd"*

J Make no change

Written Composition

Read the instructions below in order to write a short essay.

Reread "Daybreak in Alabama," paying attention to the use of sensory imagery in the poem and how this imagery affects your interpretation of the poem. Then write a short essay, interpreting the meaning of the poem.

REMEMBER—YOU SHOULD

❑ provide a thesis that states the goal of your essay

❑ use a clear organizing structure

❑ focus on sensory imagery in the poem

❑ explain how the imagery affects your interpretation

❑ give examples from the selection as evidence to support your interpretation

❑ correct errors in spelling, capitalization, punctuation, grammar, and sentence structure

Chorus Members, also called the *Extras,* 1877. Edgar Degas. Pastel on monotype. Louvre, Paris.

View the Art Edgar Degas (dā gä´) was a French Impressionist painter known for his images of dancers and other figures in motion. What type of drama is probably being depicted in this painting? How can you tell?

DRAMA

Looking Ahead

A drama, or play, is a story told mainly through the words and actions of characters. The story might unfold on a stage or on a movie or television screen. Readers of plays imagine actors speaking the dialogue and envision the setting, lighting, and actions described in the stage directions. Drama allows readers to see the story unfold before their very eyes.

Each part in Unit Four focuses on a Big Idea that can help you connect the literary works to your life.

PREVIEW	Big Ideas	Literary Focus
PART 1	Loyalty and Betrayal	Tragedy
PART 2	Portraits of Real Life	Comedy and Modern Drama

TEKS

For pages 626–630

10.4 Understand, make inferences and draw conclusions about the structure and elements of drama and provide evidence from text to support understanding.

GENRE FOCUS

How does drama differ from other genres of literature?

Playwright August Wilson said of his purpose, "I'm trying to take culture and put it onstage, demonstrate it is capable of sustaining you. There is no idea that can't be contained by life: Asian life, European life, certainly black life. My plays are about love, honor, duty, betrayal—things humans have written about since the beginning of time." Drama contains ideas in live action. Its characters, costumes, sets, and lighting combine to communicate the message, or theme, of the work.

Elements of Drama

Acts and Scenes

In plays, **acts** and **scenes** are the major divisions, similar to chapters in a book or stanzas in a poem. Plays usually have between one and five acts. Acts are further divided into scenes. Scene changes often indicate a change in location or the passage of time. One-act plays are usually not divided into scenes.

Stage Directions

Stage directions can describe the setting of a play. They may also tell actors how they should appear and actions they should take onstage. They might describe sets, props, sound effects, or lighting. Stage directions are usually set off from the dialogue with parentheses or brackets and are written in italics.

Dialogue

Plays consist mostly of **dialogue,** or conversation, between the characters. Through dialogue, the characters reveal themselves and the plot of the play moves forward. In the script, the name of the character comes before the dialogue he or she speaks.

SCENE: *Before the palace of Creon, King of Thebes. A central double door, and two lateral doors. A platform extends the length of the façade, and from this platform three steps lead down into the "orchestra," or chorus-ground.*

—Sophocles, **from** *Antigone*, **Scene 1**

SCENE: *Chubukov's mansion—the living room [LOMOV enters, formally dressed in evening jacket, white gloves, top hat. He is nervous from the start.]*

CHUBUKOV. [*Rising.*] Well, look who's here!

—Anton Chekhov, **from** *A Marriage Proposal*

MARICA. I'll never marry again.

RAQUEL. You're only twenty. You'll think differently when you're twenty-eight, or nine, or thirty.

—Josefina Niggli, **from** *The Ring of General Macias*

Tragedy

Tragic Plots

In tragedy, the main character is often a **tragic hero**—someone who has a **tragic flaw,** such as hubris (excessive pride), that leads to the character's downfall. The tragic hero is usually a man of high status and has qualities superior to those of his kinsmen. Tragic plots are driven by the hero's tragic flaw, which can be the result of either fate or choice. During the rising action of the play, the audience is often aware of the flaw, which the hero cannot perceive. Tension mounts as the hero takes the inevitable action that seals his or her fate. Then, in a frequently violent climax, the tragic finale plays out.

> **CAESAR.** Nor heaven nor earth have been at peace tonight.
> Thrice hath Calphurnia in her sleep cried out, "Help, ho! they murther Caesar!" Who's within?
>
> —William Shakespeare, **from *The Tragedy of Julius Caesar*, Act 2, Scene 2**

Comedy and Modern Drama

Comedy

Many modern dramas are a type of comedy. **Comedy** is drama that deals with light and amusing subjects or with serious subjects in a light, familiar, or satirical manner. A **satire** is a kind of comedy that ridicules people, practices, or institutions in order to reveal their failings. A **farce** is a kind of comedy that places flat, one-dimensional characters in ridiculous situations.

> **NATALIA.** I'm dying. Get him!
> **CHUBUKOV.** All right, all right, right away! Only don't yell!
> [*He runs out.*]
> **NATALIA.** What are they doing to me? Get him! Bring him back! Bring him back!
>
> —Anton Chekhov, **from *A Marriage Proposal***

LOG ON ▶ **Literature** Online

Literature and Reading For more selections in this genre, go to glencoe.com and enter QuickPass code GL57805u4.

LITERARY ANALYSIS MODEL

How do dramatists use literary elements?

August Wilson (1945–2005), a two-time Pulitzer prize winning dramatist, chronicled the African American experience in an epic series of ten plays.

The Janitor, one of Wilson's earlier plays, may have been informed by growing up with a mother he admired who worked as a cleaning lady.

APPLYING
Literary Elements

Characters

SAM and MR. COLLINS are the characters in *The Janitor*.

Setting

The story unfolds in the ballroom of a hotel.

Stage Directions

The italic text in parentheses tells the actor what to do when he first comes onto the stage.

Dialogue

The words that come after the character's name are spoken by the actor on the stage. The ellipses suggest the manner in which the words should be spoken.

Monologue

A long speech by a character spoken either to others or as if alone is a monologue.

The Janitor
by August Wilson

CHARACTERS

SAM

MR. COLLINS

SETTING: A hotel ballroom

5 (*SAM enters pushing a broom near the lectern. He stops and reads the sign hanging across the ballroom.*)

SAM. National . . . Conference . . . on . . . Youth.

(*He nods his approval and continues sweeping. He gets an idea, stops, and approaches the lectern. He clears his throat and begins to speak. His*
10 *speech is delivered with the literacy of a janitor. He chooses his ideas carefully. He is a man who has approached life honestly, with both eyes open.*)

SAM. I want to thank you all for inviting me here to speak about youth. See . . . I's fifty-six years old and I knows something about youth. The first thing I knows . . . is that youth is sweet
15 before flight . . . its odor is rife with speculation and its resilience . . . that's its bounce back . . . is remarkable. But it's that sweetness that we victims of. All of us. Its sweetness . . . and its flight. One of them fellows in that Shakespeare stuff said, "I am not what I am." See. He wasn't like Popeye. This fellow
20 had a different understanding. "I am not what I am." Well, neither are you. You are just what you have been . . . whatever you are now. But what you are now ain't what you gonna become . . . even though it is with you now . . . it's inside you now this instant. Time . . . see, this how you get to this . . .

25　Time ain't changed. It's just moved. Or maybe it
ain't moved . . . maybe it just changed. It don't
matter. We are all victims of the sweetness of
youth and the time of its flight. See . . . just like
you I forgot who I am. I forgot what happened
30　first. But I know the river I step into now . . . is
not the same river I stepped into twenty years
ago. See. I know that much. But I have forgotten
the name of the river . . . I have forgotten the
names of the gods . . . and like everybody else I
35　have tried to fool them with my dancing . . . and
guess at their faces. It's the same with everybody.
We don't have to mention no names. Ain't
nobody innocent. We are all victims of ourselves.
We have all had our hand in the soup . . . and
40　made the music play just so. See, now . . . this
what I call wrestling with Jacob's angel. You lay
down at night and that angel come to wrestle
with you. When you wrestling with that angel
you bargaining for you future. See. And what
45　you need to bargain with is that sweetness of
youth. So . . . to the youth of the United States I
says . . . don't spend that sweetness too fast! 'Cause you gonna
need it. See. I's fifty-six years old and I done found that out.
But it's all the same. It all comes back on you . . . just like reap-
50　ing and sowing. Down and out ain't nothing but being caught
up in the balance of what you put down. If you down and out
and things ain't going right for you . . . you can bet you done
put a down payment on your troubles. Now you got to pay
up on the balance. That's as true as I'm standing here.
55　Sometimes you can't see it like that. The last note on Gabriel's
horn always gets lost when you get to realizing you done
heard the first. See, it's just like. . . .

MR. COLLINS. *(Entering.)* Come on, Sam . . . let's quit wasting
time and get this floor swept. There's going to be a big
60　important meeting here this afternoon.

SAM. Yessuh, Mr. Collins. Yessuh.
(SAM goes back to sweeping as the lights go down to—)

BLACK

August Wilson.

Plot

The emotional high
point, or climax, occurs
when we experience the
gap between Sam's wis-
dom and the way Mr.
Collins treats him.

Reading Check

Analyze Why might Wilson have set the play in a
hotel ballroom?

Wrap-Up

Guide to Reading Drama

- Like fiction, drama has plot, setting, characters, and theme.

- As you read drama, you may imagine the actors on a stage performing, or you may imagine the characters as real people.

- Preview the characters before you read.

- Read the stage directions as well as the dialogue.

- Pay special attention to what happens to the main character.

Elements of Drama

- **Drama** is written to be performed by actors in front of an audience.

- Most plays are divided into **acts** and **scenes**.

- Written drama consists mostly of **dialogue** and **stage directions.**

- In a **tragedy,** the **tragic hero** suffers a downfall.

- **Comedy** is drama that deals with light and amusing subjects or with serious subjects in a light or humorous way.

LOG ON ▶ **Literature** Online

Unit Resources For additional skills practice, go to glencoe.com and enter QuickPass code GL57805u4.

Activities ➤

Use what you have learned about reading and analyzing drama to do one of these activities.

1. Write and Evaluate How well does August Wilson employ the elements of drama in *The Janitor*? What inferences can you make about Sam based on his monologue? How might your perception of Sam change if there were more dialogue between him and another character? Support your inferences in a written paragraph. Provide evidence from the text to support your response.

2. Speaking and Listening Act out some of the lines from *The Janitor* in front of the class. Then, as a class, discuss how the lines express the message of the play.

3. Take Notes Try using this study organizer to explore your personal responses to the plays you read in this unit.

 FOLDABLES Study Organizer   **BOUND BOOK**

Reader-Response Journal

Loyalty and Betrayal

Brutus and Portia, c. 1500–1550. Michelle da Verona (attr. to). Oil on canvas. Czartoryaski Museum, Poland.

View the Art The painting depicts an encounter between Brutus and his wife Portia, who are two important characters in *Julius Caesar.* What do you think is happening in this scene? Consider the facial expressions and body language of the subjects.

BIG IDEA

It can be hard to know whom to trust. When people pursue wealth or power, they accumulate what other people are bound to desire. Even the most loyal ally can betray someone who possesses what his or her heart longs for. The literary works in Part 1 deal with issues of loyalty and betrayal that have life-and-death consequences. As you read, ask yourself, What do I want most in the world, and what would I do or not do to get it?

TEKS

For pages 632–633

10.4 Understand, make inferences and draw conclusions about the structure and elements of drama and provide evidence from text to support understanding.

LITERARY FOCUS

Tragedy

What are the elements that define a tragedy?

If you are interested in movie reviews, you might have noticed that comedies rarely receive more than two stars. The majority of "four star" movies are dramas that deal with serious themes and issues. Maybe you have asked yourself how it is possible that people enjoy being entertained by pain, loss, disappointment, and death. However, there is more to it than that. The human heart likes to be moved, and seeing how others deal with the pain and difficulties of the human experience can give a viewer insight into his or her own problems.

from *Julius Caesar*, Act 3, Scene 2

by William Shakespeare

BRUTUS. Had you rather Caesar were living, and die all slaves, than that Caesar were dead, to live all free men? As Caesar lov'd me, I weep for him; as he was fortunate, I rejoice at it; as he was valiant, I honor him; but, as he was ambitious, I slew him. There is tears for his love; joy for his fortune; honor for his valor; and death for his ambition.

Who is here so base that would be a bondman? If any, speak, for him have I offended. Who is here so rude, that would not be a Roman? If any, speak, for him have I offended. Who is here so vile that will not love his country? If any, speak, for him have I offended. I pause for a reply.

The Death of Caesar. Guillaume Lethiere (1760–1832). Oil on paper. 47.5 x 71.5 cm. Private collection.

Literature Online

Literature and Reading For more about literary elements, go to glencoe.com and enter QuickPass code GL57805u4.

Tragedy

A **tragedy** is a play in which the main character suffers a downfall. Heroes of tragedies are often royalty. In that way, they have a lot to lose. Sometimes the character's downfall is the result of outside forces. Other times, the character is undone by him- or herself.

Tragic Hero

The **hero** is the main character of a literary work. He or she is usually someone with admirable traits or someone who performs noble deeds. The hero of a tragedy is often called a **tragic hero.**

A tragic hero evokes both pity and fear in the audience. Often, the audience is aware of the hero's tragic flaw before the hero is. The audience may realize that the hero has made an irreversible mistake that will lead to a terrible fall from grace or even death.

Tragic Flaw The **tragic flaw** is the part of the hero's character that leads to his or her ruin or sorrow. The art of creating a tragic character is to create a tragic flaw that does not prevent the audience from admiring the hero. The tragic flaw is not always a character defect. For example, Antigone suffers a downfall because of her staunch loyalty to the laws of the gods.

CREON. [*To Antigone.*] Tell me, tell me briefly: Had you heard my proclamation touching this matter?
ANTIGONE. It was public. Could I help hearing it?
CREON. And yet you dared defy the law.
ANTIGONE.   I dared.
It was not God's proclamation. That final Justice
That rules the world below makes no such laws.
Your edict, King, was strong,
But all your strength is weakness itself against
The immortal unrecorded laws of God.

—Sophocles, **from** *Antigone*, **Scene 2**

Dramatic Devices

Playwrights cannot comment directly on how a character is thinking or feeling, so they rely on dramatic devices. In a **monologue,** a character speaks directly to another character or to himself or herself. For example, in Act 3, Scene 2 of *Julius Caesar,* Antony delivers a famous monologue to the people of Rome that begins, "Friends, Romans, coutrymen, lend me your ears!" In a **soliloquy,** a character speaks his or her innermost thoughts when no other characters are on stage. In an **aside,** a character says something to the audience that the other characters are not supposed to hear. In addition to these devices, some tragedies also have a **chorus,** or group of performers whose function is to comment on the action in a drama and serve as a bridge between the actors and the audience. The chorus is an important part of Sophocles' *Antigone.*

Quickwrite

Evaluate a Character Characters are an important literary element in drama. Choose a character from Part 1 of this unit. As you read the play, complete a graphic organizer like the one below to list the character's attributes. What does the character have to lose? What are the character's positive qualities? Does the character have a tragic flaw? If so, what is it? When your chart is complete, ask yourself, What inferences can I make about this character? Is this character a tragic hero? Provide evidence from the text to support your response.

character's name:

↓

position or assets present at the opening that the character could lose:

↓

positive qualities:

↓

tragic flaw:

TEKS

For pages 634–635

10.4 Understand, make inferences and draw conclusions about the structure and elements of drama and provide evidence from text to support understanding.

Literary History

Classical Greek Drama

THEATER WAS FAR MORE THAN ENTERTAINMENT FOR THE people of ancient Greece. It was part of their religion, a way of displaying loyalty to their city-state, and a method of honoring local heroes. It was also a major social event, a thrilling competition, and a place where important philosophical issues could be aired.

> *"In every dramatic hero there is the idea of the Greek people, their fate, their will, and their destiny."*
>
> —Arthur Miller, from "On Social Plays"

Two statuettes of elderly comic actors. c. 375–350 B.C., Attica.

In ancient Greece, plays grew out of religion and myths. From the sixth century B.C., religious festivals featured a chorus, or group of actors, that danced and sang hymns to Dionysos, the god of wine. In about 534 B.C., the lyric poet Thespis introduced the use of a single actor separate from the chorus. The chorus voiced the attitudes of the community while the actor delivered speeches, answered the chorus, and performed the story. In the early fifth century, the great dramatist Aeschylus (525–456 B.C.) added a second actor to the stage; within a few years, his rival Sophocles (496–406 B.C.) responded by adding a third. With these changes, drama (from the Greek word for *doing,* rather than *telling*) was born, and actors today are still called thespians.

At the Theater

What would you have seen from the benches of an ancient Greek theater? As many as 15,000 spectators could watch performances in the Theater of Dionysos in Athens. Perched in the upper rows of seats, a spectator was more than 55 yards from the action below. The actors' gestures had to be exaggerated and dramatic, for no one in the back row could have perceived slight movements.

Only men were allowed to perform. All the actors wore masks made of wool, linen, wood, or plaster. In the mid-fifth century, the time of Sophocles, masks were fairly realistic representations of human faces. In later centuries, masks grew in size and became less realistic, featuring deep eye sockets and wide, gaping mouths, making actors appear larger against the background. Typically, tragic actors wore striking, richly decorated robes that set them apart from the audience. Chorus members wore more conventional costumes, which identified the roles they were playing: soldiers, priests, mourners, or even—in the case of comedies—frogs, birds, or wasps.

Ancient Greek theaters were open-air, so the lighting was natural. There were very few props. A hunter might carry a bow; an old man, a stick; a soldier, a sword and shield. These props served more as symbols to identify the character's role in the play than to provide an imitation of life. The violence—murder, suicide, and battles—almost always occurred offstage. Typically, a messenger would appear after the event and describe in gory detail what had just happened.

Relief in honor of Euripides. Late Hellenistic period. Height: 60 cm. Archaeological Museum, Istanbul, Turkey.

The Golden Age

During the fifth century B.C., known as the golden age of Greek drama, drama grew to be a vital part of life in Athens. The festival of Dionysos, the most important Greek religious festival, introduced a drama competition. The four greatest Greek dramatists—Aeschylus, Sophocles, Euripides (480–406 B.C.), and Aristophanes (448–385 B.C.)—presented their plays at these festivals.

These dramatists—all from Athens—wrote plays in verse, based on themes familiar to their audiences. They retold myths, rewrote history, and ridiculed politicians. Aristophanes, the sole comic writer among the four Athenian masters, boldly and uproariously satirized society, politics, and even the gods, landing himself in legal trouble for doing so. However,

his three great contemporaries were all tragic poets, whose plays captured humankind's timeless struggle to find the purpose of life and to achieve self-understanding.

Central to the tragedy is the fall of a great man (or woman, though her part would have been acted by a man). According to the Greek philosopher Aristotle, who wrote the first study of tragedy, the tragic hero should be neither very good nor very bad. The hero's fate is brought about by a flaw within his or her own character. In this way, the downfall of the tragic hero would encourage audiences to examine their own lives, to define their beliefs, and to cleanse their emotions of pity and terror through compassion for the character.

LOG ON ▶ **Literature** Online

Literary History For more about classical Greek drama, go to glencoe.com and enter QuickPass code GL57805u4.

Respond and Think Critically

1. **Compare and Contrast Details** In your opinion, what is the most significant difference between ancient Greek theater and modern American theater?

2. **Analyze Details** How did the purposes of Greek comedy and tragedy differ?

3. **Make Inferences About Genre** Suppose a tragic hero in a tragedy were especially bad. What can you infer about how this might change the impact of a tragedy? Use evidence from the text to support your inference.

Before You Read

Antigone

Meet **Sophocles**

(C. 496 B.C.–406 B.C.)

T he year is 468 B.C. Athenians of all stripes expect the upcoming festival to be thrilling. The streets are abuzz with talk about a newcomer to the competition. This young man is going to give the old champion a run for his money, people are saying. The authorities in charge know it too. They have appointed ten well-known generals to serve on the jury that declares the winner. It turns out that the event lives up to all expectations. The winner and new champion is the 28-year-old Sophocles, whose plays—the first he has produced—are judged the best at the festival. For more than fifty years after this victory, Sophocles will be the reigning champion of Greek drama. To this day, he is revered as one of the greatest dramatists of all time.

> "The honor of life lies not in words but in deeds."
>
> —Sophocles

Born to Succeed Sophocles was born to a wealthy family from Colonus, a village near Athens. Handsome, athletic, and skilled in music, the young man was groomed for stardom. At sixteen he was chosen to lead a chorus in honor of Greece's victory at the Battle of Salamis. He studied music under Lamprus, the most acclaimed musician of his time, and tragedy, musical composition, and choreography under Aeschylus, the great writer of tragedy. Sophocles would later dethrone Aeschylus in the 468 B.C. drama competition.

This period is called the Golden Age of Greece, and Sophocles was the golden superstar of the Greek stage. He acted and played the lyre (an instrument like the harp) in dramatic productions, retiring only when his voice became too weak to fill the enormous, open theaters of the day.

A Dramatist for the Ages As a writer, Sophocles was tireless, continuing to produce plays until the very end of his ninety-year life. He brought new possibilities to drama by adding a third actor to the stage, and he is said to have introduced the art of "scene painting" to the theater. In all, he wrote 123 dramas, won 24 of 30 competitions, and never finished lower than second place. Only seven of his plays have survived in their entirety, but they are still studied and performed throughout the world.

LOG ON **Literature** Online

Author Search For more about Sophocles, go to glencoe.com and enter QuickPass code GL57805u4.

Literature and Reading Preview

Connect to the Play

When have you had a hard time deciding to do what was right? Discuss this question with a partner.

Build Background

This play takes place in ancient Greece, in the city of Thebes, about thirty miles northwest of Athens. The Greeks of Sophocles' day believed that if a corpse was not buried or cremated according to a strict ritual, its soul would be forced to wander the earth, bringing shame upon relatives and angering the gods.

Set Purposes for Reading

Big Idea Loyalty and Betrayal

Although we assume that loyalty is a good thing, loyalty to an unworthy cause may be even worse than betrayal. As you read *Antigone,* ask yourself, What are the complexities in the relationship between loyalty and betrayal?

Literary Element Protagonist and Antagonist

The **conflict** in a work of literature is a struggle between opposing forces. The **protagonist** is the central character and the one whom the reader is generally meant to sympathize with. The **antagonist** is the person or force that opposes the protagonist. As you read, ask yourself, Who is the antagonist, who is the protagonist, and what is their conflict?

Reading Strategy Interpret Imagery

Imagery, descriptive language that appeals to the senses, brings the written word to life. As you read, make inferences about how the author's language creates imagery and ask yourself, What feelings or meanings do the images suggest?

....

Tip: Take Notes Use a chart like the one below to help you infer how the author creates images. Use the blue highlighted passages and questions to help you get started.

Image	Inference
"But his body must lie in the fields, a sweet treasure / For carrion birds to find as they search for food."	This disgusting image shows how cruel Creon's edict is and how much Antigone hates it.

TEKS

For pages 636–658

10.4 Understand, make inferences and draw conclusions about the structure and elements of drama and provide evidence from text to support understanding.

Vocabulary

repulse (ri puls´) *n.* an act of beating back or driving away, as with force; p. 639 *A day of celebration followed the repulse of the invading army.*

famished (fam´isht) *adj.* intensely hungry; ravenous; p. 643 *Exhausted and famished, the missing hikers finally struggled out of the wilderness.*

comprehensive (kom´pri hen´siv) *adj.* including nearly everything; large in scope; complete; p. 646 *A comprehensive review of our safety procedures revealed many areas that are in need of improvement.*

pious (pī´əs) *adj.* devoutly religious; p. 648 *The streets of the holy city were crowded with pious pilgrims.*

arrogance (ar´ə gəns) *n.* overbearing pride; p. 657 *Her confidence seemed like arrogance to the judge.*

....

Tip: Context Clues Context clues often immediately precede or follow an unfamiliar word. Use context clues to infer an unfamiliar word's meaning.

ANTIGONE

Sophocles

Translated by
Dudley Fitts and
Robert Fitzgerald

Mask of Dionysos, 2nd to 1st century B.C. Artist unknown. Terra-cotta from Myrina. Louvre, Paris.

CHARACTERS

ANTIGONE: daughter of Oedipus

ISMENE: daughter of Oedipus

EURYDICE: wife of Creon

CREON: King of Thebes, uncle of Antigone and Ismene

HAIMON: son of Creon

TEIRESIAS: a blind prophet

A SENTRY

A MESSENGER

CHORUS: elders of Thebes

CHORAGOS: leader of the Chorus

SCENE: *Before the palace of Creon, King of Thebes. A central double door, and two lateral doors. A platform extends the length of the façade, and from this platform three steps lead down into the "orchestra," or chorus-ground.* **TIME:** *Dawn of the day after the* **repulse** *of the Argive army from the assault on Thebes.*

Antigone—Chorus. Artist unknown. Collection van Branteghem, Brussels. Reproduced in *Le Theatre,* 1899.

ANTIGONE

Prologue

[*ANTIGONE and ISMENE enter from the central door of the Palace.*]

ANTIGONE. Ismene,° dear sister,
   You would think that we had already suffered enough
   For the curse on Oedipus:°
   I cannot imagine any grief
5 That you and I have not gone through. And now—
   Have they told you of the new decree of our King Creon?

ISMENE. I have heard nothing: I know
   That two sisters lost two brothers, a double death
   In a single hour; and I know that the Argive army°
10 Fled in the night; but beyond this, nothing.

ANTIGONE. I thought so. And that is why I wanted you
   To come out here with me. There is something we must do.

ISMENE. Why do you speak so strangely?

ANTIGONE. Listen, Ismene:
15 Creon buried our brother Eteocles
   With military honors, gave him a soldier's funeral,
   And it was right that he should; but Polyneices,
   Who fought as bravely and died as miserably,—
   They say that Creon has sworn
20 No one shall bury him, no one mourn for him,
   But his body must lie in the fields, a sweet treasure
   For carrion birds to find as they search for food.
   That is what they say, and our good Creon is coming here
   To announce it publicly; and the penalty—
25 Stoning to death in the public square!
                                        There it is,
   And now you can prove what you are:
   A true sister, or a traitor to your family.

ISMENE. Antigone, you are mad! What could I possibly do?

ANTIGONE. You must decide whether you will help me or not.

30 ISMENE. I do not understand you. Help you in what?

ANTIGONE. Ismene, I am going to bury him. Will you come?

ISMENE. Bury him! You have just said the new law forbids it.

ANTIGONE. He is my brother. And he is your brother, too.

ISMENE. But think of the danger! Think what Creon will do!

---

1 Antigone: (an tig′ ə nē). **Ismene:** (is mē′ nē).

3 Oedipus: (ed′ ə pəs).

8–9 two sisters . . . Argive army: After the death of Oedipus, King of Thebes (thēbz), his sons, Eteocles (ē tē′ ə klēz′) and Polyneices (pä′ lə nī′ sēz), struggled to gain the throne. Argos, a rival city-state, sent its army in support of Polyneices. Before the Argive (ar′ jīv) army was driven back, both Eteocles and Polyneices were killed in battle. Creon (krē′ on), their uncle and Oedipus's brother-in-law, became king.

Protagonist and Antagonist *From what you have read so far, what conflict do you think may develop?*

35   **ANTIGONE.** Creon is not strong enough to stand in my way.

     ISMENE. Ah sister!
     Oedipus died, everyone hating him
     For what his own search brought to light, his eyes
     Ripped out by his own hand; and Jocasta died,
40   His mother and wife at once: she twisted the cords
     That strangled her life;° and our two brothers died,
     Each killed by the other's sword. And we are left:
     But oh, Antigone,
     Think how much more terrible than these
45   Our own death would be if we should go against Creon
     And do what he has forbidden! We are only women,
     We cannot fight with men, Antigone!
     The law is strong, we must give in to the law
     In this thing, and in worse. I beg the Dead
50   To forgive me, but I am helpless: I must yield
     To those in authority. And I think it is dangerous business
     To be always meddling.

    ANTIGONE.   If that is what you think,
     I should not want you, even if you asked to come.
     You have made your choice, you can be what you
        want to be.
55   But I will bury him; and if I must die,
     I say that this crime is holy: I shall lie down
     With him in death, and I shall be as dear
     To him as he to me.

                    It is the dead,
     Not the living, who make the longest demands:
60   We die for ever . . .

                   You may do as you like,
     Since apparently the laws of the gods mean nothing to you.

    ISMENE. They mean a great deal to me; but I have no strength
     To break laws that were made for the public good.

    ANTIGONE. That must be your excuse, I suppose. But as for me,
65   I will bury the brother I love.

    ISMENE.   Antigone,
     I am so afraid for you!

    ANTIGONE.   You need not be:
     You have yourself to consider, after all.

37–41 Oedipus died . . . her life: Oedipus had killed Laïos (lī′ əs), the king of Thebes at the time, and married the queen, Jocasta (jō kas′ tə). Together, they had four children—Antigone, Ismene, and two sons. When it was revealed that Oedipus had, without realizing it, killed his own father and married his own mother, he blinded himself, was banished from Thebes, and died, and Jocasta hanged herself.

Running or fleeing maiden, 5th century B.C. Artist unknown. Greek sculpture. Archaeological Museum, Eleusis, Greece.

Loyalty and Betrayal *What is Antigone suggesting about her sister in lines 64–65?*

Antigone. Marie Spartali Stillman. Oil on Canvas. Simon Carter Gallery, Woodbridge, Suffolk, England.

View the Art Marie Spartali Stillman's paintings are known for their focus on heroic women in history. What characters are portrayed here? What do the women's looks and gestures convey?

ISMENE. But no one must hear of this, you must tell no one!
    I will keep it a secret, I promise!

ANTIGONE.   Oh tell it! Tell everyone!
70   Think how they'll hate you when it all comes out
    If they learn that you knew about it all the time!

ISMENE. So fiery! You should be cold with fear.

ANTIGONE. Perhaps. But I am only doing what I must.

ISMENE. But can you do it? I say that you cannot.

75 ANTIGONE. Very well: when my strength gives out, I shall
      do no more.

ISMENE. Impossible things should not be tried at all.

ANTIGONE. Go away, Ismene:
    I shall be hating you soon, and the dead will too,
    For your words are hateful. Leave me my foolish plan:

80   I am not afraid of the danger; if it means death,
    It will not be the worst of deaths—death without honor.

  ISMENE. Go then, if you feel that you must.
    You are unwise,
    But a loyal friend indeed to those who love you.

[*Exit into the Palace.* ANTIGONE *goes off, L. Enter the* CHORUS.]

Parodos°

  CHORUS. Now the long blade of the sun, lying
    Level east to west, touches with glory
    Thebes of the Seven Gates. Open, unlidded
    Eye of golden day! O marching light
5   Across the eddy and rush of Dirce's stream,°
    Striking the white shields of the enemy
    Thrown headlong backward from the blaze of morning!

  CHORAGOS. Polyneices their commander
    Roused them with windy phrases,
10   He the wild eagle screaming
    Insults above our land,
    His wings their shields of snow,
    His crest their marshalled helms.

  CHORUS. Against our seven gates in a yawning ring
15   The **famished** spears came onward in the night;
    But before his jaws were sated with our blood,
    Or pinefire took the garland of our towers,
    He was thrown back; and as he turned, great Thebes—
    No tender victim for his noisy power—
20   Rose like a dragon behind him, shouting war.

  CHORAGOS. For God° hates utterly
    The bray of bragging tongues;
    And when he beheld their smiling,
    Their swagger of golden helms,
25   The frown of his thunder blasted
    Their first man from our walls.

  CHORUS. We heard his shout of triumph high in the air
    Turn to a scream; far out in a flaming arc

Parodos (păr′ ə dos): the first "song" of the Chorus.

5 Dirce's stream: This stream, which flows past Thebes, was named after a murdered queen.

21 God: Here, "God" refers to Zeus (zo͞os), the king of the gods, who used thunderbolts to strike down the invading Argives.

Protagonist and Antagonist *Reread lines 82–84. At this point, do you think Antigone is a protagonist or an antagonist? Explain.*

Interpret Imagery *What is being described in the opening stanza of the Parodos?*

Vocabulary

famished (fam′isht) *adj.* intensely hungry; ravenous

He fell with his windy torch, and the earth struck him.
30　And others storming in fury no less than his
Found shock of death in the dusty joy of battle.

CHORAGOS. Seven captains at seven gates
Yielded their clanging arms to the god
That bends the battle-line and breaks it.°
35　These two only, brothers in blood,
Face to face in matchless rage,
Mirroring each the other's death,
Clashed in long combat.

CHORUS. But now in the beautiful morning of victory
40　Let Thebes of the many chariots sing for joy!
With hearts for dancing we'll take leave of war:
Our temples shall be sweet with hymns of praise,
And the long night shall echo with our chorus.

SCENE 1

CHORAGOS. But now at last our new King is coming:
Creon of Thebes, Menoikeus'° son.
In this auspicious° dawn of his reign
What are the new complexities
5　That shifting Fate° has woven for him?
What is his counsel? Why has he summoned
The old men to hear him?

[*Enter* CREON *from the Palace, C. He addresses the* CHORUS *from the top step.*]

CREON. Gentlemen: I have the honor to inform you that our
Ship of State, which recent storms have threatened to
10　destroy, has come safely to harbor at last,° guided by the
merciful wisdom of Heaven. I have summoned you here this
morning because I know that I can depend upon you: your
devotion to King Laïos was absolute; you never hesitated in
your duty to our late ruler Oedipus; and when Oedipus
15　died, your loyalty was transferred to his children.
Unfortunately, as you know, his two sons, the princes
Eteocles and Polyneices, have killed each other in battle; and
I, as the next in blood, have succeeded to the full power of
the throne. I am aware, of course, that no Ruler can

32–34 Seven captains . . . breaks it: The Thebans offered the captains' armor (arms) as a sacrifice to Ares (ā´ rēz), the god of war.

2 Menoikeus (me noi´ kē əs)

3 auspicious: favorable, indicating good fortune.

5 Fate: The ancient Greeks believed that three sisters, called the Fates, controlled human destiny. The first sister was said to spin the thread of human life, the second decided its length, and the third cut it.

8–10 Gentlemen . . . at last: The expression "Ship of State" likens a nation to a ship under sail. In reassuring the citizens of Thebes that the "storms" are over, Creon is referring to the Argive invasion and the many troubles in the house of Oedipus.

Interpret Imagery *What does the image in lines 35–36 suggest about the two brothers?*

20 expect complete loyalty from his subjects until he has been tested in office. Nevertheless, I say to you at the very outset that I have nothing but contempt for the kind of Governor who is afraid, for whatever reason, to follow the course that he knows is best for the State; and as for the man

25 who sets private friendship above the public welfare,—I have no use for him, either. I call God to witness that if I saw my country headed for ruin, I should not be afraid to speak out plainly; and I need hardly remind you that I would never have any dealings with an enemy of the

30 people. No one values friendship more highly than I; but we must remember that friends made at the risk of wrecking our Ship are not real friends at all.

These are my principles, at any rate, and that is why I have made the following decision concerning the sons of Oedipus:

35 Eteocles, who died as a man should die, fighting for his country, is to be buried with full military honors, with all the ceremony that is usual when the greatest heroes die; but his brother Polyneices, who broke his exile to come back with fire and sword against his native city and the

40 shrines of his fathers' gods, whose one idea was to spill the blood of his blood and sell his own people into slavery— Polyneices, I say, is to have no burial: no man is to touch him or say the least prayer for him; he shall lie on the plain, unburied; and the birds and the scavenging dogs can do

45 with him whatever they like.

This is my command, and you can see the wisdom behind it. As long as I am King, no traitor is going to be honored with the loyal man. But whoever shows by word and deed that he is on the side of the State,—he shall have my

50 respect while he is living, and my reverence when he is dead.

CHORAGOS. If that is your will, Creon son of Menoikeus, You have the right to enforce it: we are yours.

CREON. That is my will. Take care that you do your part.

CHORAGOS. We are old men: let the younger ones carry it out.

55 CREON. I do not mean that: the sentries have been appointed.

CHORAGOS. Then what is it that you would have us do?

CREON. You will give no support to whoever breaks this law.

Horseman and foot soldier fighting, 4th century B.C. Artist unknown. Relief. National Archaeological Museum, Athens.

Protagonist and Antagonist *From his speech up to line 32, how would you characterize Creon?*

Loyalty and Betrayal *What does loyalty mean to Creon?*

ANTIGONE

CHORAGOS. Only a crazy man is in love with death!

CREON. And death it is; yet money talks, and the wisest
60   Have sometimes been known to count a few coins too many.

[*Enter* SENTRY *from L.*]

SENTRY. I'll not say that I'm out of breath from running, King,
because every time I stopped to think about what I have to
tell you, I felt like going back. And all the time a voice kept
saying, "You fool, don't you know you're walking straight
65   into trouble?"; and then another voice: "Yes, but if you let
somebody else get the news to Creon first, it will be even
worse than that for you!" But good sense won out, at least
I hope it was good sense, and here I am with a story that
makes no sense at all; but I'll tell it anyhow, because, as
70   they say, what's going to happen's going to happen, and—

CREON. Come to the point. What have you to say?

SENTRY. I did not do it. I did not see who did it. You must not
punish me for what someone else has done.

CREON. A **comprehensive** defense! More effective, perhaps,
75   If I knew its purpose. Come: what is it?

SENTRY. A dreadful thing . . . I don't know how to put it—

CREON. Out with it!

SENTRY.   Well, then;
   The dead man—

                    Polyneices—

[*Pause. The* SENTRY *is overcome, fumbles for words.*
CREON *waits impassively.*]

                    out there—

                              someone,—

   New dust on the slimy flesh!

[*Pause. No sign from* CREON.]

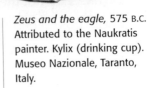

Zeus and the eagle, 575 B.C.
Attributed to the Naukratis
painter. Kylix (drinking cup).
Museo Nazionale, Taranto,
Italy.

Protagonist and Antagonist *From what you have read up to line 70, what stand
does the sentry take in the conflict? Explain.*

Vocabulary

comprehensive (kom′pri hen′ siv) *adj.* including nearly everything; large in
scope; complete

80   Someone has given it burial that way, and
      Gone . . .

[*Long pause.* CREON *finally speaks with deadly control.*]

      CREON.   And the man who dared do this?

      SENTRY.   I swear I
      Do not know! You must believe me!
                                        Listen:
      The ground was dry, not a sign of digging, no,
85   Not a wheeltrack in the dust, no trace of anyone.
      It was when they relieved us this morning: and one of them,
      The corporal, pointed to it.
                              There it was,
      The strangest—
                    Look:
      The body, just mounded over with light dust: you see?
90   Not buried really, but as if they'd covered it
      Just enough for the ghost's peace. And no sign
      Of dogs or any wild animal that had been there.

      And then what a scene there was! Every man of us
      Accusing the other: we all proved the other man did it,
95   We all had proof that we could not have done it.
      We were ready to take hot iron in our hands,
      Walk through fire, swear by all the gods,
      It was not I!
      I do not know who it was, but it was not I!

[CREON's *rage has been mounting steadily, but the* SENTRY *is too intent upon his story to notice it.*]

100   And then, when this came to nothing, someone said
      A thing that silenced us and made us stare
      Down at the ground: you had to be told the news,
      And one of us had to do it! We threw the dice,
      And the bad luck fell to me.° So here I am,
105   No happier to be here than you are to have me:
      Nobody likes the man who brings bad news.

      CHORAGOS.   I have been wondering, King: can it be that the
      gods have done this?

      CREON.   [*Furiously.*] Stop!

103–104 We threw . . . to me: Like tossing a coin, throwing dice is a way to determine something randomly. In this case, it is who must do what no one wants to do.

Loyalty and Betrayal *Why might the sentries be so willing to betray each other?*

Protagonist and Antagonist *Reread lines 107–108. What new role has the choragos begun to assume in this conflict?*

110 Must you doddering wrecks
Go out of your heads entirely? "The gods!"
Intolerable!
The gods favor this corpse? Why? How had he served them?
Tried to loot their temples, burn their images,
115 Yes, and the whole State, and its laws with it!
Is it your senile opinion that the gods love to honor bad
men?
A **pious** thought!—
No, from the very beginning
There have been those who have whispered together,
Stiff-necked anarchists, putting their heads together,
120 Scheming against me in alleys.° These are the men,
And they have bribed my own guard to do this thing.
[*Sententiously.*] Money!
There's nothing in the world so demoralizing as money.
Down go your cities,
125 Homes gone, men gone, honest hearts corrupted,
Crookedness of all kinds, and all for money!
[*To* SENTRY.] But you—!
I swear by God and by the throne of God,
The man who has done this thing shall pay for it!
Find that man, bring him here to me, or your death
130 Will be the least of your problems: I'll string you up
Alive, and there will be certain ways to make you
Discover your employer before you die;
And the process may teach you a lesson you seem to
have missed:
The dearest profit is sometimes all too dear:
135 That depends on the source. Do you understand me?
A fortune won is often misfortune.

SENTRY. King, may I speak?

CREON. Your very voice distresses me.

SENTRY. Are you sure that it is my voice, and not your
conscience?

CREON. By God, he wants to analyze me now!

117–120 A pious . . . in alleys:
Anarchy is a state of disorder and confusion or lawlessness, often due to the absence of governmental authority. Anarchists believe that all forms of government are unjust and should be resisted. Here, Creon calls those who oppose him anarchists.

Loyalty and Betrayal *How does Creon ensure the loyalty of his people?*

Vocabulary

pious (pī′əs) *adj.* devoutly religious

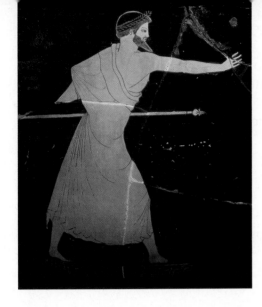

Zeus, 500 B.C. *(detail),* Attributed to the Berlin painter. Red-figure krater. Musée du Louvre, Paris.

View the Art Ancient Greeks believed that Zeus was deeply committed to morals, law, and civic justice. How do Antigone and Creon differ in their interpretations of Zeus's will?

140   SENTRY.   It is not what I say, but what has been done, that
         hurts you.

      CREON.   You talk too much.

      SENTRY.   Maybe; but I've done nothing.

      CREON.   Sold your soul for some silver: that's all you've done.

      SENTRY.   How dreadful it is when the right judge judges wrong!

      CREON.   Your figures of speech
145   May entertain you now; but unless you bring me the man,
      You will get little profit from them in the end.

      [*Exit* CREON *into the Palace.*]

      SENTRY.   "Bring me the man"—!
      I'd like nothing better than bringing him the man!
      But bring him or not, you have seen the last of me here.
150   At any rate, I am safe!

      [*Exit* SENTRY.]

ODE° 1

Ode: a song chanted by the Chorus.

      CHORUS.   Numberless are the world's wonders, but none
      More wonderful than man; the stormgray sea
      Yields to his prows,° the huge crests bear him high;
      Earth, holy and inexhaustible, is graven°
5   With shining furrows where his plows have gone
      Year after year, the timeless labor of stallions.

3 prows: ships.
4 graven: formed or shaped with a chisel; sculpted.

Protagonist and Antagonist *What insight about Creon does the sentry express in line 143?*

The lightboned birds and beasts that cling to cover,
The lithe° fish lighting their reaches of dim water,
All are taken, tamed in the net of his mind;
10 The lion on the hill, the wild horse windy-maned,
Resign to him; and his blunt yoke has broken
The sultry shoulders of the mountain bull.

Words also, and thought as rapid as air,
He fashions to his good use; statecraft is his,
15 And his the skill that deflects the arrows of snow,
The spears of winter rain: from every wind
He has made himself secure—from all but one:
In the late wind of death he cannot stand.

O clear intelligence, force beyond all measure!
20 O fate of man, working both good and evil!
When the laws are kept, how proudly his city stands!
When the laws are broken, what of his city then?
Never may the anarchic man find rest at my hearth,
Never be it said that my thoughts are his thoughts.

8 **lithe:** easily bent; flexible.

SCENE 2

[*Re-enter* SENTRY *leading* ANTIGONE.]

CHORAGOS. What does this mean? Surely this captive woman
Is the Princess, Antigone? Why should she be taken?

SENTRY. Here is the one who did it! We caught her
In the very act of burying him.—Where is Creon?

5 CHORAGOS. Just coming from the house.

[*Enter* CREON, C.]

CREON.   What has happened?
Why have you come back so soon?

SENTRY. [*Expansively.*]   O King,
A man should never be too sure of anything:
I would have sworn
That you'd not see me here again: your anger

Interpret Imagery *Why does the author refer to snow and rain in terms of "arrows" and "spears" in lines 15–16?*

10 Frightened me so, and the things you threatened me with;
But how could I tell then
That I'd be able to solve the case so soon?

No dice-throwing this time: I was only too glad to come!

Here is this woman. She is the guilty one:
15 We found her trying to bury him.
Take her, then; question her; judge her as you will.
I am through with the whole thing now, and glad of it.

CREON. But this is Antigone! Why have you brought her here?

SENTRY. She was burying him, I tell you!

CREON. [*Severely.*]   Is this the truth?

20 SENTRY. I saw her with my own eyes. Can I say more?

CREON. The details: come, tell me quickly!

SENTRY.   It was like this:
After those terrible threats of yours, King,
We went back and brushed the dust away from the body.
The flesh was soft by now, and stinking,
25 So we sat on a hill to windward and kept guard.
No napping this time! We kept each other awake.
But nothing happened until the white round sun
Whirled in the center of the round sky over us:
Then, suddenly,
30 A storm of dust roared up from the earth, and the sky
Went out, the plain vanished with all its trees
In the stinging dark. We closed our eyes and endured it.
The whirlwind lasted a long time, but it passed;
And then we looked, and there was Antigone!
35 I have seen
A mother bird come back to a stripped nest, heard
Her crying bitterly a broken note or two
For the young ones stolen. Just so, when this girl
Found the bare corpse, and all her love's work wasted,
40 She wept, and cried on heaven to damn the hands
That had done this thing.
                                    And then she brought more dust
And sprinkled wine three times for her brother's ghost.

Loyalty and Betrayal *Why is Creon surprised that Antigone has been arrested?*

Interpret Imagery *What are some of the senses to which the images in the sentry's speech appeal up to line 34?*

ANTIGONE

We ran and took her at once. She was not afraid,
Not even when we charged her with what she had done.
45   She denied nothing.
                     And this was a comfort to me,
And some uneasiness: for it is a good thing
To escape from death, but it is no great pleasure
To bring death to a friend.
                 Yet I always say
There is nothing so comfortable as your own safe skin!

50   CREON. [*Slowly, dangerously.*] And you, Antigone,
    You with your head hanging,—do you confess this thing?

ANTIGONE. I do. I deny nothing.

CREON. [*To SENTRY.*]   You may go.

[*Exit SENTRY.*]

    [*To ANTIGONE.*] Tell me, tell me briefly:
    Had you heard my proclamation touching this matter?

55   ANTIGONE. It was public. Could I help hearing it?

CREON. And yet you dared defy the law.

ANTIGONE.   I dared.
    It was not God's proclamation. That final Justice
    That rules the world below makes no such laws.

    Your edict,° King, was strong,
60   But all your strength is weakness itself against
    The immortal unrecorded laws of God.
    They are not merely now: they were, and shall be,
    Operative for ever, beyond man utterly.

    I knew I must die, even without your decree:
65   I am only mortal. And if I must die
    Now, before it is my time to die,
    Surely this is no hardship: can anyone
    Living, as I live, with evil all about me,
    Think Death less than a friend? This death of mine

Creon in Antigone. Artist unknown. Musée Jatta-Ruro. Reproduced in Le Theatre, 1899.

59 edict: an official order or decree issued by a person in authority.

Loyalty and Betrayal *Explain the sentry's philosophy about loyalty.*

Loyalty and Betrayal *What is Antigone saying about betrayal in lines 60–61? Who does she suggest is betraying whom? Explain.*

70   Is of no importance; but if I had left my brother
      Lying in death unburied, I should have suffered.
      Now I do not.
                     You smile at me. Ah, Creon,
      Think me a fool, if you like; but it may well be
      That a fool convicts me of folly.

75   CHORAGOS. Like father, like daughter: both headstrong, deaf
          to reason!
      She has never learned to yield.

      CREON.   She has much to learn.
      The inflexible heart breaks first, the toughest iron
      Cracks first, and the wildest horses bend their necks
      At the pull of the smallest curb.
                                Pride? In a slave?
80   This girl is guilty of a double insolence,
      Breaking the given laws and boasting of it.
      Who is the man here,
      She or I, if this crime goes unpunished?
      Sister's child, or more than sister's child,
85   Or closer yet in blood—she and her sister
      Win bitter death for this!
      [*To* SERVANTS.]   Go, some of you,
      Arrest Ismene. I accuse her equally.
      Bring her: you will find her sniffling in the house there.

      Her mind's a traitor: crimes kept in the dark
90   Cry for light, and the guardian brain shudders;
      But how much worse than this
      Is brazen boasting of barefaced anarchy!

      ANTIGONE. Creon, what more do you want than my death?

      CREON.   Nothing.
      That gives me everything.

      ANTIGONE.   Then I beg you: kill me.
95   This talking is a great weariness: your words
      Are distasteful to me, and I am sure that mine
      Seem so to you. And yet they should not seem so:
      I should have praise and honor for what I have done.
      All these men here would praise me
100   Were their lips not frozen shut with fear of you.
      [*Bitterly.*] Ah the good fortune of kings,

Paestan Red figured bell-krater,
c. 330 B.C. Python. Clay.

Protagonist and Antagonist *In lines 82–83, what other conflict does Creon suggest
may exist between him and Antigone?*

Licensed to say and do whatever they please!

CREON. You are alone here in that opinion.

ANTIGONE. No, they are with me. But they keep their tongues
in leash.

105 CREON. Maybe. But you are guilty, and they are not.

ANTIGONE. There is no guilt in reverence for the dead.

CREON. But Eteocles—was he not your brother too?

ANTIGONE. My brother too.

CREON.　　　　　　　And you insult his memory?

ANTIGONE. [*Softly.*] The dead man would not say that I insult it.

110 CREON. He would: for you honor a traitor as much as him.

ANTIGONE. His own brother, traitor or not, and equal in blood.

CREON. He made war on his country. Eteocles defended it.

ANTIGONE. Nevertheless, there are honors due all the dead.

CREON. But not the same for the wicked as for the just.

115 ANTIGONE. Ah Creon, Creon,
　　　Which of us can say what the gods hold wicked?°

CREON. An enemy is an enemy, even dead.

ANTIGONE. It is my nature to join in love, not hate.

CREON. [*Finally, losing patience.*] Go join them, then; if you
　　　must have your love,

120 Find it in hell!

CHORAGOS. But see, Ismene comes:

[*Enter ISMENE, guarded.*]

　　　Those tears are sisterly, the cloud
　　　That shadows her eyes rains down gentle sorrow.

CREON. You too, Ismene,

125 Snake in my ordered house, sucking my blood
　　　Stealthily—and all the time I never knew
　　　That these two sisters were aiming at my throne!
　　　　　　　　　　　　　　　　　　Ismene,

116 Which . . . wicked: Note Antigone's belief that people cannot understand the thinking of the gods.

Loyalty and Betrayal *What is Antigone suggesting about the loyalty of the chorus in line 104?*

Protagonist and Antagonist *How is Creon trying to strengthen his position in this debate?*

Interpret Imagery *How does Creon use imagery to make Ismene seem guilty in lines 125–126?*

Do you confess your share in this crime, or deny it?
Answer me.

130 ISMENE. Yes, if she will let me say so. I am guilty.

ANTIGONE. [*Coldly.*] No, Ismene. You have no right to say so.
You would not help me, and I will not have you help me.

ISMENE. But now I know what you meant; and I am here
To join you, to take my share of punishment.

135 ANTIGONE. The dead man and the gods who rule the dead
Know whose act this was. Words are not friends.

ISMENE. Do you refuse me, Antigone? I want to die with you:
I too have a duty that I must discharge to the dead.

ANTIGONE. You shall not lessen my death by sharing it.

140 ISMENE. What do I care for life when you are dead?

ANTIGONE. Ask Creon. You're always hanging on his opinions.

ISMENE. You are laughing at me. Why, Antigone?

ANTIGONE. It's a joyless laughter, Ismene.

ISMENE.   But can I do nothing?

ANTIGONE. Yes. Save yourself. I shall not envy you.
145   There are those who will praise you; I shall have honor, too.

ISMENE. But we are equally guilty!

ANTIGONE.   No more, Ismene.
You are alive, but I belong to Death.

CREON. [*To the CHORUS.*] Gentlemen, I beg you to observe
these girls:
One has just now lost her mind; the other,
150   It seems, has never had a mind at all.

ISMENE. Grief teaches the steadiest minds to waver, King.

CREON. Yours certainly did, when you assumed guilt with
the guilty!

ISMENE. But how could I go on living without her?

CREON.   You are.
She is already dead.

ISMENE.   But your own son's bride!

Protagonist and Antagonist *The word* antagonize *has the same root as* antagonist
*and means "to provoke dislike or hostility." How is Antigone antagonizing Ismene in
line 141?*

The Sisters, 2004. Chris Gollon. Mixed media on canvas, 91.4 x 61 cm. Private collection.

View the Art How do the sisters in this painting reflect the sisters in Sophocles' drama?

155   CREON. There are places enough for him to push his plow.
    I want no wicked women for my sons!°

  ISMENE. O dearest Haimon, how your father wrongs you!

  CREON. I've had enough of your childish talk of marriage!

  CHORAGOS. Do you really intend to steal this girl from
    your son?

160   CREON. No; Death will do that for me.

  CHORAGOS.   Then she must die?

  CREON. [*Ironically.*] You dazzle me.
               —But enough of this talk!
  [*To GUARDS.*] You, there, take them away and guard
    them well:
  For they are but women, and even brave men run
  When they see Death coming.

  [*Exit ISMENE, ANTIGONE, and GUARDS.*]

154–156 She is . . . sons: Here is a new complication: Antigone is engaged to marry Creon's son, Haimon. Thus, punishing her means punishing him, a fact that doesn't appear to bother Creon greatly.

ODE 2

CHORUS. Fortunate is the man who has never tasted God's
     vengeance!
    Where once the anger of heaven has struck, that house is
     shaken
    For ever: damnation rises behind each child
    Like a wave cresting out of the black northeast,
5   When the long darkness under sea roars up
    And bursts drumming death upon the windwhipped sand.
    I have seen this gathering sorrow from time long past
    Loom upon Oedipus' children: generation from generation
    Takes the compulsive rage of the enemy god.
10   So lately this last flower of Oedipus' line
    Drank the sunlight! but now a passionate word
    And a handful of dust have closed up all its beauty.

      What mortal **arrogance**
      Transcends° the wrath of Zeus?
15   Sleep cannot lull him, nor the effortless long months
    Of the timeless gods: but he is young for ever,
    And his house is the shining day of high Olympos.°
       All that is and shall be,
       And all the past, is his.
20   No pride on earth is free of the curse of heaven.

      The straying dreams of men
      May bring them ghosts of joy:
    But as they drowse, the waking embers burn them;
    Or they walk with fixed eyes, as blind men walk.
25   But the ancient wisdom speaks for our own time:
      Fate works most for woe
      With Folly's fairest show.
    Man's little pleasure is the spring of sorrow.

14 Transcends: is greater or better than.

17 Olympos: Zeus and the other gods and goddesses were believed to live on Mount Olympus.

Zeus (detail), Greek Art. Archeological Museum, Athens.

Interpret Imagery *In lines 1–9, to what does the chorus compare the rage of the gods against Oedipus's children?*

Loyalty and Betrayal *According to the chorus, what does Zeus consider to be the ultimate sin?*

Vocabulary

arrogance (ar´ ə gəns) *n.* overbearing pride

After You Read

Respond and Think Critically

1. **Connect to Personal Experience** What would you say to Antigone? To Creon?

2. **Compare and Contrast Beliefs** Why is Antigone brought to Creon? Compare and contrast what Antigone believes to be important with what Creon values.

3. **Analyze Character** How is the sentry different from the other characters? What does he add to your appreciation of the play? Explain.

4. **Analyze Character** What role does the chorus play in the drama? How does its participation affect your understanding of the play?

5. **Compare and Contrast Characters** How are Antigone and Creon different? How are they alike? Did you think it was still possible for them to resolve their differences at any point before the end of Scene 2? Give evidence from the play to support your answer.

6. **Big Idea** **Draw Conclusions About Theme** How does Sophocles demonstrate that the concepts of loyalty and betrayal are not as simple as they may seem? Include examples from the play in your answer.

Literary Element Protagonist and Antagonist

The **protagonist** in a work of literature may be in conflict with several **antagonists**.

7. **Make Inferences About Conflict** What type of internal conflict might Creon be experiencing in Scenes 1 and 2?

8. **Draw Conclusions About Characters** Based on the events of Scenes 1 and 2, what conclusion can you draw about which character is the protagonist and which character is the main antagonist? Use evidence from the text to support your conclusion.

Reading Strategy Interpret Imagery

Look back at the chart you created on page 637 to make inferences based on imagery.

9. Look at Ode 1 on pages 649–650. What images does the author create in the second stanza?

10. In line 12 of Ode 2 on page 657, the chorus speaks of "a handful of dust." What does this image refer to?

Vocabulary Practice

Practice with Context Clues Identify the context clues that help you determine the meaning of each boldfaced vocabulary word.

1. After the **repulse**, the enemy was so badly hurt that it never attacked again.

2. If you do not eat all day, you will be **famished**.

3. Our report was **comprehensive**, unlike yours, which contained little information.

4. The **pious** woman prayed every day.

5. Hannah, known for her **arrogance**, thought she was the smartest in the room.

Writing

Write an Advice Column Imagine you are an advice columnist and Ismene has written you asking for help. Write a response in which you explain how understanding the conflict between the protagonist and the antagonist might help her find a solution.

LOG ON ▶ **Literature** Online

Selection Resources For Selection Quizzes, eFlashcards, and Reading-Writing Connection activities, go to glencoe.com and enter QuickPass code GL57805u4.

Before You Read

Antigone, Scenes 3, 4, and 5

Build Background

The ancient Greeks believed in the underworld, where the dead went after life. There, the unfortunate were condemned to Tartarus, sometimes described as the deepest of hells, and would be tortured by hideous women known as Furies.

Set Purposes for Reading

Literary Element **Tragic Flaw**

According to the Greek philosopher Aristotle (384–322 B.C.), the hero of a tragedy is a person of great ability who comes to grief because of a **tragic flaw:** a fault within his or her character. Pride, ambition, jealousy, self-doubt, and anger are among those human weaknesses that can defeat the tragic hero. A tragic flaw can be an excess of virtue, such as the love of honor or the pursuit of duty. *Antigone* is one of the tragedies from which Aristotle derived his definition of a tragic flaw. A tragic hero with a tragic flaw is now what's called a character **archetype,** or a character type that recurs throughout literature across cultures. As you read, take notes on how internal forces determine the fate of the characters.

Reading Strategy **Recognize Author's Purpose**

Authors usually write fiction or drama with a **purpose:** to entertain, to inform or teach a lesson, to tell a story, or to persuade readers to accept an idea. As you read the conclusion of *Antigone,* ask yourself, Why did the author choose to tell this story in this particular manner?

Tip: Record Thoughts Use a chart like the one below to record your responses to events and the author's purpose for including them. Use the blue highlighted passages and questions to help you.

Event	My Thoughts	Author's Purpose
The choragos's opinions slowly shift during the play.	He is feeling sorry for Antigone and begins to question Creon.	Sophocles is creating sympathy for Antigone.

TEKS

For pages 659–681

10.2.B Analyze archetypes (e.g., tragic flaw) in mythic, traditional, and classical literature.

Vocabulary

deference (def′ər əns) *n.* respect and honor due to another; p. 660 *My grandmother complains that kids today do not show any deference.*

perverse (pər vurs′) *adj.* determined to go against what is reasonable, expected, or desired; contrary; p. 664 *My dad tells me I am perverse when I say that I want to go winter camping.*

absolve (ab zolv′) *v.* to free from blame; p. 665 *The DNA results will absolve the suspect.*

prevail (pri vāl′) *v.* to be superior in power or influence; to succeed; p. 668 *Cunning will often prevail over brute force.*

defile (di fīl′) *v.* to spoil the purity of; to make dirty or unclean; p. 672 *His horrible crime defiled his reputation forever.*

SCENE 3

CHORAGOS. But here is Haimon, King, the last of all your
    sons.
    Is it grief for Antigone that brings him here,
    And bitterness at being robbed of his bride?

[*Enter HAIMON.*]

CREON. We shall soon see, and no need of diviners.°

                             —Son,

5   You have heard my final judgment on that girl:
    Have you come here hating me, or have you come
    With **deference** and with love, whatever I do?

HAIMON. I am your son, father. You are my guide.
    You make things clear for me, and I obey you.
10   No marriage means more to me than your continuing
    wisdom.

CREON. Good. That is the way to behave: subordinate
    Everything else, my son, to your father's will.
    This is what a man prays for, that he may get
    Sons attentive and dutiful in his house,
15   Each one hating his father's enemies,
    Honoring his father's friends. But if his sons
    Fail him, if they turn out unprofitably,
    What has he fathered but trouble for himself
    And amusement for the malicious?

                      So you are right
20   Not to lose your head over this woman.
    Your pleasure with her would soon grow cold, Haimon,
    And then you'd have a hellcat in bed and elsewhere.
    Let her find her husband in Hell!
    Of all the people in this city, only she
25   Has had contempt for my law and broken it.

    Do you want me to show myself weak before the people?
    Or to break my sworn word? No, and I will not.

4 diviners: people who predict the future.

Recognize Author's Purpose *Why do you think Sophocles makes Haimon appear so calm and reasonable in lines 8–10?*

Tragic Flaw *What character archetype does Creon's tragic flaw suggest?*

Vocabulary

deference (def′ ər əns) *n.* respect and honor due to another

Aegeus, King of Athens, Consulting the Delphic Oracle, 6th–5th centuries B.C. Red-Figured Kylix. Staatliche Museen zu Berlin, Germany.

The woman dies.
I suppose she'll plead "family ties." Well, let her.
30   If I permit my own family to rebel,
How shall I earn the world's obedience?
Show me the man who keeps his house in hand,
He's fit for public authority.
                                         I'll have no dealings
With law-breakers, critics of the government:
35   Whoever is chosen to govern should be obeyed—
Must be obeyed, in all things, great and small,
Just and unjust! O Haimon,
The man who knows how to obey, and that man only,
Knows how to give commands when the time comes.
40   You can depend on him, no matter how fast
The spears come: he's a good soldier, he'll stick it out.

Anarchy, anarchy! Show me a greater evil!
This is why cities tumble and the great houses rain down,
This is what scatters armies!

45   No, no: good lives are made so by discipline.
We keep the laws then, and the lawmakers,
And no woman shall seduce us. If we must lose,
Let's lose to a man, at least! Is a woman stronger than we?

CHORAGOS. Unless time has rusted my wits,
50   What you say, King, is said with point and dignity.

HAIMON. [*Boyishly earnest.*] Father:
Reason is God's crowning gift to man, and you are right
To warn me against losing mine. I cannot say—
I hope that I shall never want to say!—that you
55   Have reasoned badly. Yet there are other men
Who can reason, too; and their opinions might be helpful.
You are not in a position to know everything
That people say or do, or what they feel:
Your temper terrifies them—everyone
60   Will tell you only what you like to hear.
But I, at any rate, can listen; and I have heard them
Muttering and whispering in the dark about this girl.

Loyalty and Betrayal *According to Creon, why is loyalty such an important trait?*

The Kauffmann Head, Head of
Aphrodite, copy of the Aphrodite
of Cnidus by Praxiteles, c. 150 B.C.
Marble Louvre, Paris.

They say no woman has ever, so unreasonably,
Died so shameful a death for a generous act:
65 "She covered her brother's body. Is this indecent?
She kept him from dogs and vultures. Is this a crime?
Death?—She should have all the honor that we can give
    her!"

This is the way they talk out there in the city.

You must believe me:
70 Nothing is closer to me than your happiness.
What could be closer? Must not any son
Value his father's fortune as his father does his?
I beg you, do not be unchangeable:
Do not believe that you alone can be right.
75 The man who thinks that,
The man who maintains that only he has the power
To reason correctly, the gift to speak, the soul—
A man like that, when you know him, turns out empty.

Tragic Flaw *How does Haimon manage to suggest that his father is flawed without
directly criticizing him?*

It is not reason never to yield to reason!

80 In flood time you can see how some trees bend,
And because they bend, even their twigs are safe,
While stubborn trees are torn up, roots and all.
And the same thing happens in sailing:
Make your sheet fast, never slacken,—and over you go,
85 Head over heels and under: and there's your voyage.
Forget you are angry! Let yourself be moved!
I know I am young; but please let me say this:
The ideal condition
Would be, I admit, that men should be right by instinct;
90 But since we are all too likely to go astray,
The reasonable thing is to learn from those who can teach.

CHORAGOS. You will do well to listen to him, King,
If what he says is sensible. And you, Haimon,
Must listen to your father.—Both speak well.

95 CREON. You consider it right for a man of my years and
    experience
    To go to school to a boy?

HAIMON.   It is not right
    If I am wrong. But if I am young, and right,
    What does my age matter?

CREON. You think it right to stand up for an anarchist?

100 HAIMON. Not at all. I pay no respect to criminals.

CREON. Then she is not a criminal?

HAIMON. The City would deny it, to a man.

CREON. And the City proposes to teach me how to rule?

HAIMON. Ah. Who is it that's talking like a boy now?

105 CREON. My voice is the one voice giving orders in this City!

HAIMON. It is no City if it takes orders from one voice.

CREON. The State is the King!

HAIMON.   Yes, if the State is a desert.

[Pause.]

CREON. This boy, it seems, has sold out to a woman.

HAIMON. If you are a woman: my concern is only for you.

Parthenon, Porch of Caryatiids
at Erechteion, Athens.

Tragic Flaw *What character fault does Haimon seem to think that his father has, and does it fit with Creon's character archetype? Explain.*

Recognize Author's Purpose *What point does Sophocles make in lines 92–94? How do you think Creon will react to this observation by the choragos?*

110   **CREON.** So? Your "concern"! In a public brawl with your father!

   HAIMON. How about you, in a public brawl with justice?

   CREON. With justice, when all that I do is within my rights?

   HAIMON. You have no right to trample on God's right.

   CREON. [*Completely out of control.*] Fool, adolescent fool!
     Taken in by a woman!

115   **HAIMON.** You'll never see me taken in by anything vile.

   CREON. Every word you say is for her!

   HAIMON. [*Quietly, darkly.*]   And for you.
     And for me. And for the gods under the earth.

   CREON. You'll never marry her while she lives.

   HAIMON. Then she must die.—But her death will cause another.

120   **CREON.** Another?
     Have you lost your senses? Is this an open threat?

   HAIMON. There is no threat in speaking to emptiness.

   CREON. I swear you'll regret this superior tone of yours!
     You are the empty one!

   HAIMON.   If you were not my father,
125   I'd say you were **perverse.**

   CREON. You girlstruck fool, don't play at words with me!

   HAIMON. I am sorry. You prefer silence.

   CREON.   Now, by God—!
     I swear, by all the gods in heaven above us,
     You'll watch it, I swear you shall!
     [*To the* SERVANTS.]   Bring her out!
130   Bring the woman out! Let her die before his eyes!
     Here, this instant, with her bridegroom beside her!

Loyalty and Betrayal *How has Haimon turned the argument to question his father's loyalty?*

Tragic Flaw *What character fault besides inflexibility does Creon exhibit in his dialogue with Haimon?*

Tragic Flaw *What new aspect of Creon's character is hinted at in lines 129–131?*

Vocabulary

perverse (pər vurs´) *adj.* determined to go against what is reasonable, expected, or desired; contrary

HAIMON. Not here, no; she will not die here, King.
    And you will never see my face again.
    Go on raving as long as you've a friend to endure you.

[*Exit* HAIMON.]

135   CHORAGOS. Gone, gone.
    Creon, a young man in a rage is dangerous!

CREON. Let him do, or dream to do, more than a man can.
    He shall not save these girls from death.

CHORAGOS.   These girls?
    You have sentenced them both?

CREON.   No, you are right.
140   I will not kill the one whose hands are clean.

CHORAGOS. But Antigone?

CREON. [*Somberly.*]   I will carry her far away
    Out there in the wilderness, and lock her
    Living in a vault of stone. She shall have food,
    As the custom is, to **absolve** the State of her death.
145   And there let her pray to the gods of hell:
    They are her only gods:
    Perhaps they will show her an escape from death,
    Or she may learn,
                though late,
    That piety shown the dead is pity in vain.

[*Exit* CREON.]

ODE 3

CHORUS. Love, unconquerable
    Waster of rich men, keeper
    Of warm lights and all-night vigil
    In the soft face of a girl:
5   Sea-wanderer, forest-visitor!
    Even the pure Immortals cannot escape you,
    And mortal man, in his one day's dusk,
    Trembles before your glory.

Recognize Author's Purpose *What happens in lines 139–140 for the first time? Are you surprised by this? Explain.*

Vocabulary

absolve (ab zolv´) *v.* to free from blame

Surely you swerve upon ruin
10   The just man's consenting heart,
As here you have made bright anger
Strike between father and son—
And none has conquered but Love!
A girl's glance working the will of heaven:
15   Pleasure to her alone who mocks us,
Merciless Aphrodite.°

16 **Aphrodite** (af´ rə dī´ tē): the goddess of love and beauty.

SCENE 4

CHORAGOS. [*As ANTIGONE enters guarded.*] But I can no longer
stand in awe of this,
Nor, seeing what I see, keep back my tears.
Here is Antigone, passing to that chamber
Where all find sleep at last.

5   ANTIGONE. Look upon me, friends, and pity me
Turning back at the night's edge to say
Good-by to the sun that shines for me no longer;
Now sleepy Death
Summons me down to Acheron,° that cold shore:
10   There is no bridesong there, nor any music.

9 **Acheron** (ak´ ə ron): The Greeks believed that the souls of the dead inhabited an underworld bordered by the river Acheron.

CHORUS. Yet not unpraised, not without a kind of honor,
You walk at last into the underworld;
Untouched by sickness, broken by no sword.
What woman has ever found your way to death?

15   ANTIGONE. How often I have heard the story of Niobe,
Tantalos' wretched daughter, how the stone
Clung fast about her, ivy-close: and they say
The rain falls endlessly
And sifting soft snow; her tears are never done.
20   I feel the loneliness of her death in mine.°

15–20 **How often . . . mine:** Niobe (nī´ ō bē´), a former queen of Thebes, was punished by the gods for excessive pride. After all of her children were killed, she was turned to stone, but she continued to shed tears.

CHORUS. But she was born of heaven, and you
Are woman, woman-born. If her death is yours,
A mortal woman's, is this not for you
Glory in our world and in the world beyond?

Recognize Author's Purpose *What is the topic of Ode 3? Why might the author have included this idea?*

Recognize Author's Purpose *Why might Sophocles have opened Scene 4 with the observation by the choragos in lines 1–2?*

25 ANTIGONE. You laugh at me. Ah, friends, friends,
Can you not wait until I am dead? O Thebes,
O men many-charioted, in love with Fortune,
Dear springs of Dirce, sacred Theban grove,
Be witnesses for me, denied all pity,
30 Unjustly judged! and think a word of love
For her whose path turns
Under dark earth, where there are no more tears.

CHORUS. You have passed beyond human daring and come
   at last
Into a place of stone where Justice sits.
35 I cannot tell
What shape of your father's guilt appears in this.

ANTIGONE. You have touched it at last: that bridal bed
Unspeakable, horror of son and mother mingling:
Their crime, infection of all our family!
40 O Oedipus, father and brother!
Your marriage strikes from the grave to murder mine.

Statue of Chrysippus, the Greek philosopher, 3rd century B.C. Marble. Musée du Louvre, Paris.

View the Art Western philosophy—a field of study devoted to the pursuit of knowledge—originated in ancient Greece. What emotions does this sculpture convey? How might these emotions compare with what Creon experiences in this play?

I have been a stranger here in my own land:
All my life
The blasphemy of my birth has followed me.°

45 CHORUS. Reverence is a virtue, but strength
Lives in established law: that must **prevail.**
You have made your choice,
Your death is the doing of your conscious hand.

ANTIGONE. Then let me go, since all your words are bitter,
50 And the very light of the sun is cold to me.
Lead me to my vigil, where I must have
Neither love nor lamentation;° no song, but silence.

[CREON *interrupts impatiently.*]

CREON. If dirges and planned lamentations could put off death,
Men would be singing for ever.
[*To the* SERVANTS.]   Take her, go!
55 You know your orders: take her to the vault
And leave her alone there. And if she lives or dies,
That's her affair, not ours: our hands are clean.

ANTIGONE. O tomb, vaulted bride-bed in eternal rock,
Soon I shall be with my own again
60 Where Persephone° welcomes the thin ghosts underground:
And I shall see my father again, and you, mother,
And dearest Polyneices—
                              dearest indeed
To me, since it was my hand
That washed him clean and poured the ritual wine:
65 And my reward is death before my time!

And yet, as men's hearts know, I have done no wrong,
I have not sinned before God. Or if I have,
I shall know the truth in death. But if the guilt
Lies upon Creon who judged me, then, I pray,

35–44 I cannot . . . followed me: Incest, or sexual relations between siblings or between parents and children, was a sin against the gods. Oedipus and Jocasta did not know, at the time, that they were committing incest, but their marriage was cursed nonetheless, and that curse now plagues their daughter, Antigone.

52 lamentation: mournful outcry of sorrow or grief.

60 Persephone (pər sef´ ə nē): Persephone is the queen of the underworld of the dead.

Tragic Flaw *Do you think Antigone's statement in lines 42–44 suggests that her flaws are inherent or beyond her control? Explain.*

Loyalty and Betrayal *Has the chorus changed its attitude about the struggle between Creon and Antigone in lines 45–48? Explain.*

Tragic Flaw *Why does Creon say what he does in lines 56–57?*

Vocabulary

prevail (pri vāl´) *v.* to be superior in power or influence; to succeed

70 May his punishment equal my own.

CHORAGOS.   O passionate heart,
 Unyielding, tormented still by the same winds!

CREON. Her guards shall have good cause to regret their
 delaying.

ANTIGONE. Ah! That voice is like the voice of death!

CREON. I can give you no reason to think you are mistaken.

75 ANTIGONE. Thebes, and you my fathers' gods,
 And rulers of Thebes, you see me now, the last
 Unhappy daughter of a line of kings,
 Your kings, led away to death. You will remember
 What things I suffer, and at what men's hands,
80 Because I would not transgress° the laws of heaven.
 [To the GUARDS, simply.] Come: let us wait no longer.

[Exit ANTIGONE, L., guarded.]

80 **transgress:** break or violate.

ODE 4

CHORUS. All Danäe's beauty was locked away
 In a brazen cell where the sunlight could not come:
 A small room, still as any grave, enclosed her.
 Yet she was a princess too,
5 And Zeus in a rain of gold poured love upon her.
 O child, child,
 No power in wealth or war
 Or tough sea-blackened ships
 Can prevail against untiring Destiny!°

10 And Dryas' son also, that furious king,
 Bore the god's prisoning anger for his pride:
 Sealed up by Dionysos in deaf stone,
 His madness died among echoes.
 So at the last he learned what dreadful power
15 His tongue had mocked:
 For he had profaned the revels,
 And fired the wrath of the nine
 Implacable Sisters that love the sound of the flute.°

1–9 All Danäe's . . . Destiny: The Chorus briefly relates three Greek legends. Danäe (dɑn′ āē′) was imprisoned by her father when it was foretold that she would bear a child who would kill him. After Zeus visited Danäe, she gave birth to Zeus's son, who did eventually kill his grandfather.

10–18 And Dryas' . . . flute: Dionysos (dī′ ə nī′səs) is the god of wine and fertility, and the Implacable Sisters (also called the Muses) are the goddesses of the arts and sciences. After Dryas's son (King Lycurgus) objected to the worship of Dionysos, the Sisters imprisoned him and drove him mad.

Tragic Flaw *Antigone explains that she is being punished because she "would not transgress the laws of heaven." Might there be other reasons for her misfortune? Explain.*

And old men tell a half-remembered tale
20   Of horror done where a dark ledge splits the sea
And a double surf beats on the gray shores:
How a king's new woman, sick
With hatred for the queen he had imprisoned,
Ripped out his two sons' eyes with her bloody hands
25   While grinning Ares watched the shuttle plunge
Four times: four blind wounds crying for revenge,

Crying, tears and blood mingled.—Piteously born,
Those sons whose mother was of heavenly birth!
Her father was the god of the North Wind
30   And she was cradled by gales,
She raced with young colts on the glittering hills
And walked untrammeled in the open light:
But in her marriage deathless Fate found means
To build a tomb like yours for all her joy.°

Venus de Milo, detail of the back of the head, 100 B.C. Greek artist. Marble. Musée du Louvre, Paris.

19–34 And old men . . . all her joy: It was King Phineus who imprisoned his first wife (the queen) and allowed his jealous new wife to blind the queen's sons. This horrible act was done under the gleeful gaze of Ares, the war god.

SCENE 5

[*Enter blind* TEIRESIAS, *led by a boy. The opening speeches of* TEIRESIAS *should be in singsong contrast to the realistic lines of* CREON.]

TEIRESIAS. This is the way the blind man comes, Princes,
    Princes, Lock-step, two heads lit by the eyes of one.

CREON. What new thing have you to tell us, old Teiresias?

TEIRESIAS. I have much to tell you: listen to the prophet, Creon.

5   CREON. I am not aware that I have ever failed to listen.

TEIRESIAS. Then you have done wisely, King, and ruled well.

CREON. I admit my debt to you. But what have you to say?

TEIRESIAS. This, Creon: you stand once more on the edge of
    fate.°

CREON. What do you mean? Your words are a kind of dread.

10   TEIRESIAS. Listen, Creon:
    I was sitting in my chair of augury, at the place
    Where birds gather about me. They were all a-chatter,

1–8 This is . . . of fate: The blind prophet serves as the gods' agent, or go-between, in their dealings with people.

Recognize Author's Purpose *How do the legends in Ode 4 relate to Antigone's situation? What moral is the chorus communicating here?*

Recognize Author's Purpose *Reread line 8. How does Sophocles prepare us for the importance of Teiresias's prediction?*

As is their habit, when suddenly I heard
A strange note in their jangling, a scream, a
15 Whirring fury; I knew that they were fighting,
Tearing each other, dying
In a whirlwind of wings clashing. And I was afraid.°
I began the rites of burnt-offering at the altar,
But Hephaistos failed me: instead of bright flame,
20 There was only the sputtering slime of the fat thighflesh
Melting: the entrails dissolved in gray smoke,
The bare bone burst from the welter. And no blaze!
This was a sign from heaven. My boy described it,
Seeing for me as I see for others.

25 I tell you, Creon, you yourself have brought
This new calamity upon us. Our hearths and altars
Are stained with the corruption of dogs and carrion birds
That glut themselves on the corpse of Oedipus' son.
The gods are deaf when we pray to them, their fire
30 Recoils from our offering, their birds of omen
Have no cry of comfort, for they are gorged
With the thick blood of the dead.°
                                                    O my son,
These are no trifles! Think: all men make mistakes,
But a good man yields when he knows his course is wrong,
35 And repairs the evil. The only crime is pride.

Give in to the dead man, then: do not fight with a corpse—
What glory is it to kill a man who is dead?
Think, I beg you:
It is for your own good that I speak as I do.
40 You should be able to yield for your own good.

CREON. It seems that prophets have made me their especial
        province.
All my life long
I have been a kind of butt for the dull arrows
Of doddering fortune-tellers!
                                              No, Teiresias:
45 If your birds—if the great eagles of God himself
Should carry him stinking bit by bit to heaven,
I would not yield. I am not afraid of pollution:

11–17 I was sitting . . . afraid:
Teiresias sits in his chair of augury to listen to the birds, whose sounds he interprets as messages from the gods, allowing him to foretell, or augur, the future. The birds' fighting is a very bad sign.

18–32 I began . . . of the dead:
Another bad sign: Hephaistos (hi fes′təs), the god of fire, is withholding fire. Teiresias says that the gods are rejecting the Thebans' sacrificial offerings because the animals have fed on Polyneices's corpse.

Tragic Flaw *If Creon stays true to archetype, will he follow Teiresias's advice in lines 33–34? Explain. How might his decision affect the plot?*

No man can **defile** the gods.

                              Do what you will,
Go into business, make money, speculate
50   In India gold or that synthetic gold from Sardis,°
Get rich otherwise than by my consent to bury him.
Teiresias, it is a sorry thing when a wise man
Sells his wisdom, lets out his words for hire!

TEIRESIAS. Ah Creon! Is there no man left in the world—

55   CREON. To do what?—Come, let's have the aphorism!°

TEIRESIAS. No man who knows that wisdom outweighs any
     wealth?

CREON. As surely as bribes are baser than any baseness.

TEIRESIAS. You are sick, Creon! You are deathly sick!

CREON. As you say: it is not my place to challenge a prophet.

60   TEIRESIAS. Yet you have said my prophecy is for sale.

CREON. This generation of prophets has always loved gold.

TEIRESIAS. The generation of kings has always loved brass.

CREON. You forget yourself! You are speaking to your King.

TEIRESIAS. I know it. You are a king because of me.°

65   CREON. You have a certain skill; but you have sold out.

TEIRESIAS. King, you will drive me to words that—

CREON.   Say them, say them!
Only remember: I will not pay you for them.

TEIRESIAS. No, you will find them too costly.

CREON.   No doubt. Speak:
Whatever you say, you will not change my will.

70   TEIRESIAS. Then take this, and take it to heart!
The time is not far off when you shall pay back
Corpse for corpse, flesh of your own flesh.

Loyalty and Betrayal *How does Creon question Teiresias's loyalty in lines 52–53?*

Tragic Flaw *What is Teiresias accusing Creon of in line 62?*

Recognize Author's Purpose *Why might Sophocles have Creon say lines 68–69?*

Vocabulary

defile (di fīl′) *v.* to spoil the purity of; to make dirty or unclean

---

50 synthetic gold from Sardis: The people of Sardis, the capital of ancient Lydia (in modern-day Turkey), invented metallic coinage, the "synthetic gold" that Creon speaks of.

55 aphorism: a concise statement of a general truth.

64 I know . . . me: It was Teiresias who revealed the truth of Oedipus's relationship to Jocasta and thus set off the chain of events that led to Creon's becoming king.

Pallas Athena, or *Armoured Figure,* 1664–1665. Rembrandt Harmensz van Rijn. Oil on canvas, 118 x 81.1 cm. Museu Calouste Gulbenkian, Lisbon, Portugal.

You have thrust the child of this world into living night,
You have kept from the gods below the child that is theirs:
75 The one in a grave before her death, the other,
Dead, denied the grave. This is your crime:
And the Furies° and the dark gods of Hell
Are swift with terrible punishment for you.

Do you want to buy me now, Creon?

Not many days,
80 And your house will be full of men and women weeping,
And curses will be hurled at you from far
Cities grieving for sons unburied, left to rot
Before the walls of Thebes.

These are my arrows, Creon: they are all for you.

85 [*To* BOY.] But come, child: lead me home.
Let him waste his fine anger upon younger men.
Maybe he will learn at last
To control a wiser tongue in a better head.

[*Exit* TEIRESIAS.]

CHORAGOS. The old man has gone, King, but his words
90 Remain to plague us. I am old, too,
But I cannot remember that he was ever false.

CREON. That is true. . . . It troubles me.
Oh it is hard to give in! but it is worse
To risk everything for stubborn pride.

95 CHORAGOS. Creon: take my advice.

CREON. What shall I do?

CHORAGOS. Go quickly: free Antigone from her vault
And build a tomb for the body of Polyneices.

CREON. You would have me do this?

CHORAGOS. Creon, yes!
And it must be done at once: God moves
100 Swiftly to cancel the folly of stubborn men.

CREON. It is hard to deny the heart! But I
Will do it: I will not fight with destiny.

CHORAGOS. You must go yourself, you cannot leave it to
others.

Tragic Flaw *Given what you know of Creon's character, is the change of heart he mentions in lines 101–102 likely? Explain.*

ANTIGONE

CREON.   I will go.

           —Bring axes, servants:
105   Come with me to the tomb. I buried her, I
Will set her free.

          Oh quickly!

My mind misgives—
The laws of the gods are mighty, and a man
    must serve them
To the last day of his life!

[*Exit* CREON.]

Paean°

CHORAGOS.   God of many names

CHORUS.   O Iacchos°

                    son

of Kadmeian Semele

            O born of the Thunder!

Guardian of the West

            Regent

of Eleusis' plain

          O Prince of maenad Thebes

5   and the Dragon Field by rippling Ismenos:°

CHORAGOS.   God of many names

CHORUS.   the flame of torches
flares on our hills

          the nymphs of Iacchos

dance at the spring of Castalia:

from the vine-close mountain

             come ah come in ivy:°

10   *Evohé*° *evohé!* sings through the streets of Thebes

CHORAGOS.   God of many names

CHORUS.   Iacchos of Thebes
  heavenly Child

        of Semele bride of the Thunderer!

Paean (pē´ən): a song of praise, joy, or thanksgiving. Here, the Chorus praises Dionysos.

1 Iacchos (yä´kəs): considered Thebes' special protector because his mother had been a Theban princess. The Chorus begs Dionysos to come to Thebes and drive out evil.

1–5 God of . . . Ismenos: The names of Dionysos refer to people and places associated with him. His mother, **Kadmeian Semele** (sem´ə lē), was the daughter of Kadmos, a king of Thebes. His father was Zeus, who controlled thunder. This plain was the site of religious ceremonies performed in honor of Dionysos, and the river **Ismenos** ran near Thebes. The **maenads** (mē´nadz) were Dionysos's devoted priestesses.

7–9 the nymphs . . . come in ivy: Dionysos was raised by **nymphs,** long-lived women who were associated with trees and other parts of nature. The **spring of Castalia** is on Parnasos, a holy mountain. The grape **vine** and ivy were symbols of Dionysos.
10 Evohé: "Hallelujah."

Recognize Author's Purpose *How does Sophocles build up suspense in lines 104–107?*

Loyalty and Betrayal *How does Creon's statement in lines 108–109 represent a significant change in his attitude?*

The shadow of plague is upon us:
                                        come
    with clement° feet
                            oh come from Parnasos
15   down the long slopes
                                across the lamenting water

    CHORAGOS. Io Fire! Chorister of the throbbing stars!
        O purest among the voices of the night!
        Thou son of God, blaze for us!

    CHORUS. Come with choric rapture of circling Maenads
20   Who cry *Io Iacche!*
                    God of many names!

Exodos°

[*Enter MESSENGER, L.*]

    MESSENGER. Men of the line of Kadmos, you who live
        Near Amphion's citadel:°
                                    I cannot say
    Of any condition of human life "This is fixed,
    This is clearly good, or bad." Fate raises up,
5   And Fate casts down the happy and unhappy alike:
    No man can foretell his Fate.
                            Take the case of Creon:
    Creon was happy once, as I count happiness:
    Victorious in battle, sole governor of the land,
    Fortunate father of children nobly born.
10   And now it has all gone from him! Who can say
    That a man is still alive when his life's joy fails?
    He is a walking dead man. Grant him rich,
    Let him live like a king in his great house:
    If his pleasure is gone, I would not give
15   So much as the shadow of smoke for all he owns.

    CHORAGOS. Your words hint at sorrow: what is your news
        for us?

    MESSENGER. They are dead. The living are guilty of their death.

    CHORAGOS. Who is guilty? Who is dead? Speak!

    MESSENGER.   Haimon.
        Haimon is dead; and the hand that killed him

14 **clement:** forgiving; merciful.

Exodos: the last part of the play.

2 **Amphion's citadel:** the wall around Thebes, which Amphion built by charming stones into place with music.

Head of Zeus. Artist unknown. Bronze. National Archaeological Museum, Athens.

Recognize Author's Purpose *What is the effect of lines 19–20 and of the Paean as a whole?*

Recognize Author's Purpose *What point is the Messenger making in lines 14–15?*

Antigone

20   Is his own hand.

CHORAGOS.   His father's? or his own?

MESSENGER. His own, driven mad by the murder his father
        had done.

CHORAGOS. Teiresias, Teiresias, how clearly you saw it all!

MESSENGER. This is my news: you must draw what
        conclusions you can from it.

CHORAGOS. But look: Eurydice, our Queen:
25   Has she overheard us?

[Enter EURYDICE from the Palace, C.]

EURYDICE. I have heard something, friends:
        As I was unlocking the gate of Pallas'° shrine,
        For I needed her help today, I heard a voice
        Telling of some new sorrow. And I fainted
30   There at the temple with all my maidens about me.
        But speak again: whatever it is, I can bear it:
        Grief and I are no strangers.°

MESSENGER.   Dearest Lady,
        I will tell you plainly all that I have seen.
        I shall not try to comfort you: what is the use,
35   Since comfort could lie only in what is not true?
        The truth is always best.

                          I went with Creon
        To the outer plain where Polyneices was lying,
        No friend to pity him, his body shredded by dogs.
        We made our prayer in that place to Hecate°
40   And Pluto,° that they would be merciful. And we bathed
        The corpse with holy water, and we brought
        Fresh-broken branches to burn what was left of it,
        And upon the urn we heaped up a towering barrow
        Of the earth of his own land.

                          When we were done, we ran
45   To the vault where Antigone lay on her couch of stone.
        One of the servants had gone ahead,
        And while he was yet far off he heard a voice
        Grieving within the chamber, and he came back
        And told Creon. And as the King went closer,

27 Pallas: the goddess of wisdom; also known as Athena.

32 Grief and I . . . strangers: Eurydice (yoo rid´ i sē) is referring to the death of Megareus (me gär´ ā o͞os), her older son, who died in the battle for Thebes.

39 Hecate (hek´ ə tē): another name for Persephone, the goddess of the underworld.
40 Pluto: another name for Hades, the god of the underworld.

Recognize Author's Purpose *Why might Sophocles introduce Creon's wife at this late point in the play?*

Loyalty and Betrayal *What does the order in which Creon and the messenger do their business tell you about Creon's new priorities?*

50　The air was full of wailing, the words lost,
　　And he begged us to make all haste. "Am I a prophet?"
　　He said, weeping, "And must I walk this road,
　　The saddest of all that I have gone before?
　　My son's voice calls me on. Oh quickly,
　　　　quickly!
55　Look through the crevice there, and tell me
　　If it is Haimon, or some deception of the gods!"

　　We obeyed; and in the cavern's farthest corner
　　We saw her lying:
　　She had made a noose of her fine linen veil
60　And hanged herself. Haimon lay beside her,
　　His arms about her waist, lamenting her,
　　His love lost under ground, crying out
　　That his father had stolen her away from him.

Dionysos and his mother Semele, 6th century B.C. Artist unknown. Black-figured cup. Staatliche Antikensammlung, Munich.

　　When Creon saw him the tears rushed to his eyes
65　And he called to him: "What have you done, child? Speak
　　　　to me.
　　What are you thinking that makes your eyes so strange?
　　O my son, my son, I come to you on my knees!"
　　But Haimon spat in his face. He said not a word,
　　Staring—
　　　　　　And suddenly drew his sword
70　And lunged. Creon shrank back, the blade missed; and
　　　　the boy,
　　Desperate against himself, drove it half its length
　　Into his own side, and fell. And as he died
　　He gathered Antigone close in his arms again,
　　Choking, his blood bright red on her white cheek.
75　And now he lies dead with the dead, and she is his
　　At last, his bride in the houses of the dead.

　[*Exit* EURYDICE *into the Palace.*]

　CHORAGOS. She has left us without a word. What can this
　　　　mean?

　MESSENGER. It troubles me, too; yet she knows what is best,
　　Her grief is too great for public lamentation,
80　And doubtless she has gone to her chamber to weep
　　For her dead son, leading her maidens in his dirge.

Recognize Author's Purpose *Why might Sophocles have included the description in lines 72–74?*

Recognize Author's Purpose *Do you think Sophocles expected his audience to accept the messenger's assumption that Eurydice has left to grieve privately? Explain.*

ANTIGONE

CHORAGOS. It may be so: but I fear this deep silence

[*Pause.*]

MESSENGER. I will see what she is doing. I will go in.

[*Exit* MESSENGER *into the Palace.*]

[*Enter* CREON *with attendants, bearing* HAIMON's *body.*]

CHORAGOS. But here is the King himself: oh look at him,
85   Bearing his own damnation in his arms.

CREON. Nothing you say can touch me any more.
    My own blind heart has brought me
    From darkness to final darkness. Here you see
    The father murdering, the murdered son—
90   And all my civic wisdom!

    Haimon my son, so young, so young to die,
    I was the fool, not you; and you died for me.

CHORAGOS. That is the truth; but you were late in learning it.

CREON. This truth is hard to bear. Surely a god
95   Has crushed me beneath the hugest weight of heaven,
    And driven me headlong a barbaric way
    To trample out the thing I held most dear.

    The pains that men will take to come to pain!

[*Enter* MESSENGER *from the Palace.*]

MESSENGER. The burden you carry in your hands is heavy,
100   But it is not all: you will find more in your house.

CREON. What burden worse than this shall I find there?

MESSENGER. The Queen is dead.

CREON. O port of death, deaf world,
    Is there no pity for me? And you, Angel of evil,
105   I was dead, and your words are death again.
    Is it true, boy? Can it be true?
    Is my wife dead? Has death bred death?

MESSENGER. You can see for yourself.

[*The doors are opened, and the body of* EURYDICE *is disclosed within.*]

CREON. Oh pity!
110   All true, all true, and more than I can bear!
    O my wife, my son!

Funerary Mask, c. 1600 B.C. Mycenaean.

Tragic Flaw *Why was Creon unable to realize the truth earlier?*

MESSENGER. She stood before the altar, and her heart
　　Welcomed the knife her own hand guided,
　　And a great cry burst from her lips for Megareus dead,
115　And for Haimon dead, her sons; and her last breath
　　Was a curse for their father, the murderer of her sons.°
　　And she fell, and the dark flowed in through her closing
　　　eyes.
CREON. O God, I am sick with fear.
　　Are there no swords here? Has no one a blow for me?

120　MESSENGER. Her curse is upon you for the deaths of both.
CREON. It is right that it should be. I alone am guilty.
　　I know it, and I say it. Lead me in,
　　Quickly, friends.
　　I have neither life nor substance. Lead me in.

125　CHORAGOS. You are right, if there can be right in so much
　　　wrong.
　　The briefest way is best in a world of sorrow.
CREON. Let it come,
　　Let death come quickly, and be kind to me.
　　I would not ever see the sun again.

130　CHORAGOS. All that will come when it will; but we,
　　　meanwhile,
　　Have much to do. Leave the future to itself.
CREON. All my heart was in that prayer!
CHORAGOS. Then do not pray any more: the sky is deaf.
CREON. Lead me away. I have been rash and foolish.
135　I have killed my son and my wife.
　　I look for comfort; my comfort lies here dead.
　　Whatever my hands have touched has come to nothing.
　　Fate has brought all my pride to a thought of dust.

[As CREON is being led into the house, the CHORAGOS advances and
speaks directly to the audience.]

　　CHORAGOS. There is no happiness where there is no wisdom;
140　No wisdom but in submission to the gods.
　　Big words are always punished,
　　And proud men in old age learn to be wise.

---

116 Was a curse . . . sons: Note that even though Haimon stabbed himself and Megareus died in battle, Eurydice blames Creon for their deaths.

Tragic Flaw *Has your attitude toward Creon changed over the course of the play? Explain.*

Recognize Author's Purpose *Why do you think Sophocles allows Creon's character to live on after those around him die?*

Loyalty and Betrayal *What is the play's final position on the issue of loyalty?*

After You Read

Respond and Think Critically

1. **Connect to Personal Experience** Rank the main characters in order of how sympathetic you feel toward them. Explain your rankings.

2. **Explain Conflict** Why does Haimon come to see his father? How does their exchange of ideas evolve into a bitter argument?

3. **Analyze Character** What does Teiresias tell Creon? In your opinion, why does Creon change his mind? Do you think he is motivated by compassion or by self-interest? Explain.

4. **Summarize Events** Summarize the events that occur after Teiresias leaves Creon. What message, or lesson, does the audience take from these events? Support your response. OER

5. **Evaluate Character** Compare Antigone's demeanor in Scene 4 with her attitude in previous scenes. How has she changed? Does her transformation seem believable to you? Why or why not? Provide evidence from the play in your response.

6. **Evaluate Allusions** Explain how the house of Oedipus plays a role in *Antigone*. Do these allusions affect your appreciation of the play? Explain.

7. **Big Idea** **Draw Conclusions About Theme** For Creon, what constitutes betrayal? Are his expectations about loyalty reasonable? Support your answer with evidence from the play.

Visual Literacy

Determine Loyalty and Popularity

Much of the struggle in *Antigone* revolves around where the characters' loyalties lie. With a group, review the words and actions of the main characters to determine how loyal each one is in terms of religious law, the king's law, and family bonds. Then rank each character's position on line graphs with ten meaning "very much" and zero meaning "not at all." Share your results with the the class and discuss any differences. Then answer the questions.

1. Is one type of loyalty more important or valuable than the others? Do you think Sophocles believed that one type of loyalty was the most noble? Explain.

2. What effect does a character's loyalty have on his or her popularity? Explain.

Religious Law

King's Law

Family Bonds

Tragic Flaw

Today we label people as heroes to acknowledge their bravery or hard work. To the writer of classical tragedies, however, a hero was a more complex character. The tragic hero **archetype** is a strong, often admirable character who failed to live up to his or her promise because of a **tragic flaw.** This might be a negative trait or a positive one that is inflexible or taken to excess.

8. **Make Inferences About Character** Reread Teiresias's warning to Creon in lines 33–35 of Scene 5. What flaw does the prophet specifically identify in the king's character? Do you believe this weakness is sufficient to cause the tragedy that results? Explain.

9. **Analyze Archetypes** How would you describe Antigone's personality? Does she have a trait that might qualify as a tragic flaw? Does she fit the tragic hero archetype, or is she just an innocent victim of Creon? Explain.

Review: Characterization

As you learned on page 124, **characterization** refers to the methods an author uses to develop a character. In drama we often learn about characters through **indirect characterization,** particularly through their words and actions.

10. **Partner Activity** With a partner, create a graphic organizer like the one below. In the left-hand box write Creon's exact words. In the right-hand box describe things he does. Write your conclusion about Creon—based on these examples—in the bottom box. Then choose another character and create another graphic profile.

Reading Strategy Recognize Author's Purpose

 Texas Test Practice (10.4)

1. Sophocles wrote *Antigone* with the primary purpose of

   (A) encouraging citizens to commit acts of civil disobedience

   (B) describing the traditional burial practices of ancient Greek culture

   (C) entertaining audiences at the Greek festivals

   (D) teaching the history of a famous family from Thebes

   (E) urging old and young to live and work together in harmony

Vocabulary Practice

Practice with Word Parts For each bold-faced word in the left column, identify the related word with a shared root in the right column. Write each word and underline the part they have in common. Use a dictionary to find the meaning of the related word. Then explain how it is related to the vocabulary word.

1.	absolve	solvent
2.	deference	confer
3.	prevail	ambivalent
4.	perverse	aversion
5.	defile	defilement

EXAMPLE:

<u>biblio</u>graphy, <u>biblio</u>phile

A bibliography is a list of books and other sources. A bibliophile is a book lover.

LOG ON ▶ **Literature** Online

Selection Resources For Selection Quizzes, eFlashcards, and Reading-Writing Connection activities, go to glencoe.com and enter QuickPass code GL57805u4.

Respond Through Writing

Persuasive Essay

TEKS

10.16.A,C,D,F Write persuasive texts to influence the attitudes or actions of a specific audience on specific issues. Write an argumentative essay to the appropriate audience that includes a clear thesis or position; counter-arguments; an organizing structure; and a range of appropriate appeals.

Argue a Position Would Antigone's fate have been different if she had been a man? Use details you have drawn from the play, as well as appeals to logic and emotion, to write a persuasive essay addressing this question.

Purpose and Audience Your purpose is to write a persuasive essay using **appeals to logic** (any reference to reason, facts, or statistics to support a claim or an opinion) and **appeals to emotion** (any use of words or information to arouse the reader's emotions in order to persuade). Your audience is other students who have read the play.

Plan Make a two-column chart. In the left column, list statements from the play that reveal characters' attitudes toward women and their role in Theban society. In the right column, reflect on whether these statements support the idea of gender as the determiner of Antigone's fate. Then list statements that seem to show that Antigone acts beyond the constraints of gender. When you are done, decide which side of the question you can argue most effectively, and formulate a thesis supported by logical reasons.

Draft As you draft, strengthen your argument through the use of persuasive techniques such as appeals to logic and emotion. Save your most persuasive reason for last. Create a clear structure by transitioning with phrases such as *more important* or *most important*.

Revise Exchange papers with a partner. Identify and evaluate each other's appeals to logic and emotion. Evaluate the use of evidence in the paper for its relevance and precision. Identify at least one way in which your partner might refute a counterclaim, using a frame like this one:

> It is true that ___, but ___.

As needed, also suggest ways for explaining evidence and relating it to your thesis by using frames such as these:

> Based on this evidence, it is clear that ___.
> If ___, then ___.

Revise based on your classmate's feedback.

Edit Edit your essay, correcting any errors in spelling, grammar, and punctuation. Use the Grammar Tip in the side column to help you use infinitives and infinitive phrases.

> **Grammar Tip**
>
> **Verbals**
>
> An **infinitive** is a verb form that can be used as a noun or modifier. It usually contains the word *to*.
>
> *Antigone needs **to act.** [noun]*
> *She is a woman **to admire.** [modifier]*
>
> Infinitives and infinitive phrases fall into a broad category called verbals. **Verbals** are all formed from verbs, but they act as nouns, adjectives, or adverbs in sentences. Other verbals are gerunds and participles.
>
> **Participles**, which end in *-ed* or *-ing,* function as adjectives.
>
> ***Determined,*** *Antigone acts against the law.*
>
> **Gerunds**, which end in *-ing,* function as nouns.
>
> ***Dying*** *does not frighten Antigone.*

Vocabulary Workshop

Denotation and Connotation

TEKS

10.1.B Analyze textual context (within a sentence and in larger sections of text) to distinguish between the denotative and connotative meanings of words.

Literature Connection A word's **denotation** is its literal, or dictionary, meaning. Its **connotation** is its implied, or cultural, meaning, which often evokes a positive or negative response depending on the context of the word. In the passage below from *Antigone*, Sophocles uses words that have negative connotations—*damnation, darkness,* and *death*—to describe the vengefulness of the gods. Such **loaded words** can make speech and writing persuasive.

> *For ever: damnation rises behind each child*
> *Like a wave cresting out of the black northeast,*
> *When the long darkness under sea roars up*
> *And bursts drumming death upon the windwhipped sand.*

Here are three types of loaded words:

- **Bias**—language that expresses an author's prejudice
  Antigone <u>bravely</u> wants to give her brother a proper burial.

With the word *bravely,* the writer shows positive bias toward Antigone. A writer with a negative bias might have chosen *recklessly* instead.

- **Hyperbole**—exaggerated language used to make a point
  <u>The entire world</u> was against Antigone.

This broad overstatement by the writer expresses extreme disapproval.

- **Propaganda**—language that often includes bias and hyperbole and may distort the truth to influence the public
  Anyone who does not agree with the logic of Creon <u>must be an anarchist.</u>

This exaggerated and distorted statement reveals the writer's positive bias toward Creon and an attempt to influence people to think similarly.

Loaded Words

Loaded words express strong opinions or emotions. You can read between the lines and identify a writer's opinion when you look for bias, hyperbole, and propaganda.

Tip

To identify loaded language in a reading passage, consider the context and ask yourself, "Why did the writer write this? What is his or her point of view?" Then look for words or phrases that have strong connotations to support that stance.

Practice Fill in each blank with the loaded word or phrase below that best expresses the view of a writer who sides with Antigone.

Antigone is a woman who **1.** _____ stands up for the **2.** _____ principles she believes in. Being a **3.** _____ man, Creon **4.** _____ wants his nephew unburied. The situation puts Antigone in **5.** _____.

1. a. determinedly	**b.** stubbornly	**c.** obstinately
2. a. traditional	**b.** simple	**c.** noble
3. a. respectable	**b.** vengeful	**c.** honorable
4. a. strangely	**b.** generously	**c.** selfishly
5. a. a stalemate	**b.** a moral dilemma	**c.** a cipher

Literature Online

Vocabulary For more vocabulary practice, go to glencoe.com and enter QuickPass code GL57805u4.

TEKS

For pages 684–687

10.9 Analyze, make inferences and draw conclusions about expository text and provide evidence from text to support understanding.

Set a Purpose for Reading

Read to analyze expository text and learn about the history of Cleopatra VII, her legend, and how she is celebrated.

Preview the Article

1. From the title, do you think the writer is biased about her subject, Cleopatra VII? Explain.

2. Read the *deck,* or the sentence that appears in purple type underneath the title, and the subheads. What do you think will be the article's main focus?

Reading Strategy

Evaluate Evidence

When you **evaluate evidence,** you make a judgment or form an opinion about the evidence a writer uses to make a point or support an argument. Evaluating evidence also involves distinguishing between fact and opinion. As you read, use a chart like the one below to help evaluate the writer's evidence. In the first column, summarize statements from the article. In the second column, infer whether each statement is fact or opinion.

Statement	
exhibit had artifacts from some 30 sources	

TIME

EVER ALLURING

Cleopatra could draw the crowds in ancient Rome. Now she's turning on her seductive charm in London.

By MARYANN BIRD

SHE IS ONE OF THE MOST FAMOUS FIGURES OF ancient history, a name synonymous with beauty, yet no one knows what she really looked like. A Macedonian Greek, she ruled Egypt and was known for her relationships—political and romantic—with the two great Roman leaders of her time, Julius Caesar and Mark Antony. Her legend—wrapped in intrigue, conflict, and romance—lives on to this day. As Shakespeare wrote of Cleopatra in his play *Antony* and *Cleopatra:* "Age cannot wither her nor custom stale her infinite variety."

Although she has been dead since 30 B.C., Cleopatra VII, the last of the Ptolemaic rulers, still wields considerable power. The magic of her name drew big crowds to a 2001 exhibition called "Cleopatra of Egypt: From History to Myth" at the British Museum in London. For the show, which included new finds and interpretations, the museum attracted loans of many Cleopatra-related artifacts. Among them were sculptures, coins, paintings, ceramics, and jewelry from some 30 museums, libraries, and private collections around the world.

The Many Sides of Cleopatra

"Cleopatra's name is more evocative than any image of her," said co-curator Peter Higgs in an interview at the time of the exhibition's opening. He described the show as a "biographical study" that presented many different sides of Cleopatra, all of which contributed to the legend that she began building during her lifetime. Higgs acknowledged that not all classical scholars would concur with the museum's view of Cleopatra. "We know that not everyone is going to agree with us," he said. "We're not saying we're right about everything. This is our interpretation."

On the coins on display, Cleopatra appeared masculine and powerful. In the sculptures, some of which portrayed her as the goddess Isis, the divine mother whose cult she followed, she looked slim and serene. The show also featured Renaissance paintings that portrayed her as a sensual and tragic figure. Modern representations of her came straight from Hollywood, embodied most famously by Elizabeth Taylor in the 1963 film *Cleopatra*. Taylor's famous off-screen affair with the film's Mark Antony, co-star Richard Burton, recalled the 14th century writer Giovanni Boccaccio's description of Cleopatra as a woman "who became an object of gossip for the whole world."

The star of the museum's exhibition, though, was a 40-inch black basalt statue on loan from the Hermitage Museum in St. Petersburg, Russia. One of the best-preserved representations of a Ptolemaic queen, it has been identified as Cleopatra VII. The striking figure holds a double horn of plenty and wears a headdress decorated with three cobras—symbols associated only with her.

A Bad Reputation

Not all the images in the exhibition were as flattering. Cleopatra's reputation in Rome declined after Octavian (later to become the emperor Augustus) defeated her and Antony at the Battle of Actium in 31 B.C. "Everything we know about Cleopatra comes from later Roman writers," explained Higgs, "and it's nearly all negative." He added that it was not surprising that "prudish and snobbish" Romans would have a low opinion of Egypt's queen, given that "she had taken away from them both Julius Caesar and Mark Antony." Still, said Higgs, even Cleopatra's critics acknowledged that she had some admirable qualities. Apart from her beauty, she is said to have been a humorous and charming conversationalist. Intelligent and savvy, she was a skilled diplomat who spoke several languages—and was clearly loved by Caesar and Antony, the fathers of her four children.

Like the pharaohs who came before her in the three centuries following Alexander the Great's conquest of Egypt in 332 B.C., Cleopatra had to appeal to both Greeks and Egyptians. She had to be seen as both a Greek monarch and an Egyptian pharaoh. She also needed to present herself as a powerful figure amid all the violence and chaos in the Mediterranean region at the time. Indeed, Cleopatra must have been ruthless in order to even gain the throne, given the blood-baths that long characterized her family line.

Following Octavian's conquest of Egypt and Antony's death—he killed himself by falling on his sword—Cleopatra committed suicide, possibly with the help of a poisonous snake such as an asp or cobra. The new emperor then ordered that all statues of Cleopatra be

Love and Power

Basantite bust of Caesar

destroyed. Most of the images of her that survived depict an attractive figure with a strong face, masculine in its features, emphasizing power. Old coins bearing her image, particularly rare Greek ones, have helped to identify Cleopatra in marble and limestone sculptures. So, too, did the tiniest item displayed at the museum—a half-inch piece of etched blue glass bearing Cleopatra's profile in a more realistic Greek style.

Cleopatra's Children

On public view for the first time was a 30-inch granite head believed to represent Ptolemy XV Caesar, Cleopatra's son by Julius Caesar. Also known as Caesarion, he co-ruled Egypt with his mother from 44 B.C. to 30 B.C. The sculpture was found in the harbor at Alexandria, Cleopatra's capital, by French archaeologists in 1997. The exhibition also included rare images of Cleopatra's other children. A marble statue of Cleopatra Selene—her daughter by Mark Antony—was lent by the Archaeological Museum in Cherchel, Algeria, where it was found. (Cherchel was the capital of the ancient kingdom of Mauretania, where Cleopatra Selene lived.) The statue had never been outside Algeria before. Another marble rendering of Cleopatra Selene, found near her husband's palace, showed her as a more mature woman, with a heavier face and "snail-shell" curls around her forehead.

Also on display was a bronze statuette which historians believe depicts Cleopatra's second son, Alexander Helios, as Prince of Armenia. According to the writings of the ancient Greek historian Plutarch, Mark Antony gave his sons by Cleopatra the title of kings, as well as many lands to rule. He gave Armenia, Media, and the Parthian Empire to Alexander. He gave Phoenicia, Syria, and Cilicia to Alexander's younger brother, Ptolemy Philadelphus. After Mark Anthony and Cleopatra died, though, their children were made to live out their lives in obscurity. Their half-brother Caesarion was not so fortunate. He was executed by Octavian.

> **"Everything we know about Cleopatra comes from later Roman writers, and it's nearly all negative."**
>
> —Peter Higgs,
> co-curator
> British Museum in London

Queen of the Silver Screen

Cleopatra's amazing life and dramatic death made Egypt's exotic queen an icon—to many, the first female superstar. For several hundred years after her death, Cleopatra and all things Egyptian intrigued even those Romans who demonized her. Her influence on Roman style, customs, and culture continued for a long time. By the early Renaissance in Europe, with its revival of interest in classical traditions, Cleopatra again became a subject of art, literature, and fashion. Many of the most famous events in her life—the luxurious banquet she held for Mark Antony, his death, her grief at his tomb, and her own death—were represented in paintings and sketches at the exhibition, as well as on other objects such as watches, fans, and vases. The Renaissance portrayal of the tough and tragic seductress—as derived from the early Romans—has trickled down to the current day.

Cleopatra found her way onto the silver screen even before movies had sound. In 1917, Theda Bara starred in a silent-film version of Cleopatra. Seventeen years later, Claudette Colbert played the Egyptian queen, and Hollywood waged

Cleopatra Dropping the Pearl into the Wine, c 1715. William Kent after Carlo Maratta. Red chalk drawing, 36.4 x 25.7 cm. The British Museum, London.

an all-out publicity campaign to encourage female movie-goers to adopt the "Cleopatra look." Many copied Colbert's dark bangs after hearing the speech in which she described her feelings about Mark Antony: "I've seen a god come to life. I'm no longer a queen. I'm a woman."

A woman she was, and one for all time. With so much, yet so little, known about this queen without a face, this figure of history and myth, Cleopatra lives on in the "infinite variety" cited by Shakespeare. And like so many intrigued observers through the ages, visitors to the British Museum exhibition could draw their own picture of her.

—from TIME

Respond and Think Critically

1. **Summarize Main Ideas** Write a brief summary of the main ideas in this article before you answer the following questions. For help on writing a summary, see page 389.

2. **Make Inferences About Historical Context** Do historians know what Cleopatra looked like? Explain. Why do you think there have been so many interpretations of her appearance? Support your response with text evidence.

3. **Analyze Description** What words does the writer use to describe Cleopatra's image and character? Do you think the writer's conclusions are based on facts or opinions? Explain.

4. **Evaluate Details** What are some of the artifacts from Cleopatra's time on exhibit at the British Museum? How accurate a representation of history do you think can be derived from such artifacts? Explain.

5. **Draw Conclusions About Expository Text** Does the writer provide sufficient background information about Cleopatra? Explain.

6. **Analyze Evidence** The writer calls Cleopatra "the first female superstar." What evidence does she offer to substantiate this opinion?

7. **Synthesize Ideas** How are ancient writers' characterizations of Antigone and Cleopatra similar and different?

TEKS

For pages 688–689

10.4 Understand, make inferences and draw conclusions about the structure and elements of drama and provide evidence from text to support understanding.

Literary History

Shakespearean Drama

IN THE LATE 1500S, WHEN SHAKESPEARE BEGAN HIS CAREER, ENGLISH theater was going through major changes. For hundreds of years before this time, traveling actors, called "players," had toured the countryside, performing for audiences in towns and villages. They set up makeshift stages in public halls, marketplaces, and the courtyards of inns. Local officials, many of whom believed that "play-acting" violated biblical commandments, typically greeted acting companies with hostility.

> "Every day at two o'clock in the afternoon in the city of London two or sometimes three comedies are performed…"
>
> —Thomas Platter, diary entry from 1599

The Globe Theatre, 1616. Cornelius de Visscher. Engraving. British Library, London.

Distrust of theater was so great that in 1574 the Common Council of London issued an order banishing players from London. To get around the order, actor James Burbage and his company of players built a playhouse in nearby Shorebridge. Completed in 1576, the building resembled the courtyard of an inn. Burbage's playhouse became the first public theater in England and was an immediate success, leading to the construction of other public theaters over the next few years.

Shakespeare's Globe

Shakespeare's theater company, the Lord Chamberlain's Men, performed at Burbage's theater until 1599, when they built their own playhouse, the Globe. Shakespeare referred to the Globe as "this wooden O," a term that has led historians to believe that it was a roughly circular building. The theater had three levels of galleries, covered by thatched roofs, overlooking an open courtyard. Projecting out into the yard was a platform stage about forty feet wide, with trapdoors for the entrance and exit of actors who played ghosts or other supernatural characters. At the back of the main stage was a small curtained inner stage used for indoor scenes. Above this stood a two-tiered gallery. The first tier was used to stage balcony and bedroom scenes; the second, to house musicians. Sound effects, such as the booming of thunder, were produced in a hut on top of the stage roof.

The Globe could hold about three thousand spectators. Members of the middle class and nobility typically sat in the galleries after paying a twopence admission. For sixpence (what a skilled laborer earned in a day), wealthier members of the audience could sit in the "lords' room" directly over the stage. Less well-to-do-spectators, called "groundlings," could stand and watch from the courtyard for only a penny. Their close proximity to the stage created a noisy theatrical experience. Accounts of the time suggest that the groundlings did

not hesitate to shout comments to the actors onstage. As theater became more profitable, its reputation improved. Eventually, Shakespeare's company received the support of Queen Elizabeth and her successor, King James.

Elizabethan Stagecraft

Because there was no artificial lighting, all performances at the Globe took place in the afternoon. There were few props and no movable scenery. Shakespeare made up for the lack of scenery by inviting audiences to visualize the scenes based on descriptive passages spoken by the characters. For example, a character's description of a raging storm would help Elizabethan audiences picture the fury of the weather.

What the Elizabethan stage lacked in scenery, it made up for in costumes. Shakespeare's audiences considered clothing an important indication of social rank, so they demanded extravagant yet realistic costuming. An elaborate wardrobe was an Elizabethan theater company's biggest expense and most important asset.

In Shakespeare's time, audiences thought it immoral for women to appear on the stage, so boys performed the female roles. Very popular with Elizabethan theatergoers, these boy actors must have been highly skilled performers, who created convincing and moving portrayals of Shakespeare's great female roles, from Lady Macbeth and Cleopatra to Rosalind and Juliet.

The New Globe, London, interior.

LOG ON ▶ **Literature** Online

Literary History For more about Elizabethan drama, go to glencoe.com and enter QuickPass code GL57805u4.

Respond and Think Critically

1. **Make Inferences About Historical Context** What feature of Elizabethan stagecraft do you think a modern audience would have the most difficulty accepting? Explain.

2. **Make Inferences About Genre** What elements of Shakespearean drama might have been different if players had had access to more props and moveable scenery? Support your inference.

Before You Read

The Tragedy of Julius Caesar

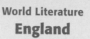
Meet **William Shakespeare**
(1564–1616)

When the question "Who is the greatest writer that ever lived?" is asked, one frequent response is "William Shakespeare." Shakespeare's writings are more widely read and more often quoted than any other literary work, aside from the Bible. Unfortunately, there are no biographies of Shakespeare from his own time. The information we have comes from public records and comments by his rivals and admirers, such as the playwright Ben Jonson. "He was not of an age, but for all time," proclaimed Jonson shortly after Shakespeare's death.

> "*It seems to me most strange that men should fear, Seeing that death, a necessary end, Will come when it will come.*"
>
> —William Shakespeare, from *Julius Caesar*

The Family Man Shakespeare was born in Stratford-upon-Avon, where his father was elected bailiff (the equivalent of a mayor). William was the third of at least eight children. He was the first boy and the first child to survive past childhood. Most likely, he attended the local grammar school, where he would have studied Latin and classical literature. At age eighteen, Shakespeare married 26-year-old Anne Hathaway. The couple had three children: Susanna and twins Judith and Hamnet. Hamnet, their only son, died when he was eleven.

Success in the City Shakespeare moved to London sometime between 1585 and the early 1590s and worked as an actor and a playwright. He was celebrated for his comedies and historical plays. In 1599 he and his company of players built the Globe theater. Writers at that time received no royalties and most plays were never printed, but Shakespeare grew wealthy from his share in his theater company's profits.

An Artist for All Time Shakespeare's tragic masterpieces include *Hamlet, Romeo and Juliet, Othello, Macbeth,* and *King Lear.* His comedies are also classics. Modern audiences still respond to the antics and wordplay of *A Midsummer Night's Dream, Twelfth Night,* and *Much Ado About Nothing* as Shakespeare's own audiences did four centuries ago.

Seven years after Shakespeare's death, a group of friends brought out a collection of his works known as the *First Folio.* This volume played a crucial role in preserving his plays for future generations and—very possibly—"for all time."

LOG ON ▶ **Literature** Online

Author Search For more about William Shakespeare, go to glencoe.com and enter QuickPass code GL57805u4.

Literature and Reading Preview

Connect to the Play

Who is the best leader you have ever known? Discuss this question with a small group. Consider what makes a leader exceptional.

Build Background

Born in 100 B.C., Julius Caesar was an immensely gifted military leader and politician. Although he could be charming, Caesar's arrogance and ambition created enemies in the senate, and a group of conspirators assassinated him in 44 B.C.

Set Purposes for Reading

Big Idea Loyalty and Betrayal

History is full of people who have turned against a cause or a person they once respected. As you read *Julius Caesar,* ask yourself, How does Shakespeare depict this change in his characters?

Literary Element Blank Verse

Much of *Julius Caesar* is written in a form of unrhymed poetry known as **blank verse.** Each line has a basic pattern of five iambic feet, or units of rhythm, with each foot made up of an unstressed syllable followed by a stressed syllable.

⏑ ´ ⏑ ´ ⏑ ´ ⏑ ´ ⏑ ´

   He had a fever when he was in Spain . . .

As you read, ask yourself, Which characters in Act 1 speak in blank verse?

Reading Strategy Make Inferences About Characters

When you **make inferences about characters,** you use reason and knowledge of a situation or historical circumstances in order to understand a character's reason for acting in a certain way. As you read, ask yourself, What can I infer about a character in order to discover what the author is not telling?

Tip: Examine the Evidence Use a graphic organizer like the one below to record details you are sure of. Then write the inferences you make based on those details.

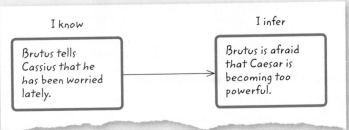

I know	I infer
Brutus tells Cassius that he has been worried lately.	Brutus is afraid that Caesar is becoming too powerful.

TEKS

For pages 690–712

10.4 Understand, make inferences and draw conclusions about the structure and elements of drama and provide evidence from text to support understanding.

Vocabulary

servile (sur´vil) *adj.* lacking self-respect; behaving as if other people are superior; p. 696 *The emperor's servile advisors bowed deeply in his presence.*

entreat (en trēt´) *v.* to ask earnestly; to beg; p. 701 *The charity will entreat the public to help the many flood victims.*

enterprise (en´tər prīz´) *n.* an important project or undertaking; p. 705 *Sending human beings to Mars is an expensive and dangerous enterprise.*

incense (in sens´) *v.* to make very angry; p. 707 *Learning that three of his players have been suspended will incense the coach.*

THE TRAGEDY OF

JULIUS

CAESAR

William Shakespeare

The Triumph of Julius Caesar. Paolo Uccello. Tempera on panel.
Musee des Arts Decoratifs, Paris.

CHARACTERS

JULIUS CAESAR: ambitious military leader and politician; the most powerful man in Rome

CALPHURNIA: wife of Caesar

MARCUS BRUTUS: friend of Caesar, appointed by him to high office in the Roman government; a believer in the republic and member of the conspiracy against Caesar

PORTIA: wife of Brutus and daughter of a Roman patriot

CAIUS CASSIUS: brother-in-law of Brutus and member of the conspiracy against Caesar

MARK ANTONY: friend of Caesar, senator, and eloquent orator; member of the triumvirate, the three-man governing body that ruled Rome after Caesar's death

OCTAVIUS CAESAR: Caesar's great-nephew and official heir; member of the triumvirate

M. AEMILIUS LEPIDUS: military leader and member of the triumvirate

Conspirators Against Caesar

CASCA	METELLUS CIMBER	TREBONIUS
CINNA	DECIUS BRUTUS	CAIUS LIGARIUS

Senators

CICERO	PUBLIUS	POPILIUS LENA

Tribunes *(Public Officials)*

FLAVIUS	MURELLUS

Officers in the Armies of Brutus and Cassius

LUCILIUS	MESSALA	VOLUMNIUS
TITINIUS	YOUNG CATO	FLAVIUS

Servants of Brutus

LUCIUS	CLITUS	STRATO
VARRUS	CLAUDIO	DARDANIUS

Others

A SOOTHSAYER (one who predicts the future)

ARTEMIDORUS OF CNIDOS: teacher of rhetoric

CINNA: a poet

PINDARUS: servant of Cassius

ANOTHER POET

SERVANTS TO CAESAR, ANTONY, AND OCTAVIUS; CITIZENS, GUARDS, SOLDIERS

ACT 1

SCENE 1. Rome. A street.

[*Enter FLAVIUS, MURELLUS, and certain COMMONERS over the stage.*]

FLAVIUS. Hence! Home, you idle creatures, get you home!
Is this a holiday? What, know you not,
Being mechanical,° you ought not walk
Upon a laboring day without the sign
5   Of your profession? Speak, what trade art thou?°

CARPENTER. Why, sir, a carpenter.

MURELLUS. Where is thy leather apron and thy rule?
What dost thou with thy best apparel on?
You, sir, what trade are you?

10 **COBBLER.** Truly, sir, in respect of° a fine workman, I am but,
as you would say, a cobbler.°

MURELLUS. But what trade art thou? Answer me directly.

COBBLER. A trade, sir, that, I hope, I may use° with a safe
conscience, which is indeed, sir, a mender of bad soles.

15 **FLAVIUS.** What trade, thou knave? Thou naughty knave,
what trade?

COBBLER. Nay, I beseech you, sir, be not out° with me; yet, if
you be out,° sir, I can mend you.

MURELLUS. What mean'st thou by that? Mend me, thou saucy
fellow?

20 **COBBLER.** Why, sir, cobble you.

FLAVIUS. Thou art a cobbler, art thou?

COBBLER. Truly, sir, all that I live by is with the awl;° I meddle
with no tradesman's matters, nor women's matters; but
withal, I am indeed, sir, a surgeon to old shoes; when they

2–5 Is this a . . . art thou: Flavius and Murellus, public officials, remind the laborers that they should be dressed in their work outfits rather than their best clothes.
3 mechanical: manual laborers.

10 in respect of: in comparison with.
11 cobbler: "clumsy worker" or "shoemaker." The cobbler plays on the word's double meaning. Murellus and Flavius fail to understand his pun at first and keep pressing him to reveal a trade he has already identified.
13 use: practice.

16 out: angry.
16–17 if you be out: if your shoes are worn out.

22 awl: a tool for making holes in leather. The Cobbler puns on the words *all, awl,* and *withal,* which means "nevertheless."

Blank Verse *Is the cobbler speaking in blank verse? Are Flavius, Murellus, or the carpenter speaking blank verse? What inference can you make about the structure or organization of this play based on this? Use evidence from the text to support your answer.*

Make Inferences About Characters *What attitude do Flavius and Murellus have toward commoners, such as the carpenter and the cobbler?*

25   are in great danger, I recover them. As proper men as ever
       trod upon neat's leather° have gone upon my handiwork.

       FLAVIUS.   But wherefore art not in thy shop today?
       Why dost thou lead these men about the streets?

       COBBLER.   Truly, sir, to wear out their shoes, to get myself into
30   more work. But indeed, sir, we make holiday to see Caesar
       and to rejoice in his triumph.°

       MURELLUS.   Wherefore rejoice? What conquest brings he home?
       What tributaries° follow him to Rome,
       To grace in captive bonds° his chariot wheels?
35   You blocks, you stones, you worse than senseless things!
       O you hard hearts, you cruel men of Rome,
       Knew you not Pompey? Many a time and oft
       Have you climb'd up to walls and battlements,
       To tow'rs and windows, yea, to chimney tops,
40   Your infants in your arms, and there have sate
       The livelong day, with patient expectation,
       To see great Pompey pass the streets of Rome;
       And when you saw his chariot but° appear,
       Have you not made an universal shout,
45   That Tiber° trembled underneath her banks
       To hear the replication° of your sounds
       Made in her concave shores?
       And do you now put on your best attire?
       And do you now cull out a holiday?°
50   And do you now strew flowers in his way,
       That comes in triumph over Pompey's blood?°
       Be gone!
       Run to your houses, fall upon your knees,
       Pray to the gods to intermit° the plague
55   That needs must light on this ingratitude.

       FLAVIUS.   Go, go, good countrymen, and, for this fault,
       Assemble all the poor men of your sort;
       Draw them to Tiber banks and weep your tears
       Into the channel, till the lowest stream
60   Do kiss the most exalted shores of all.°

   [Exit all the COMMONERS.]

       See, whe'er their basest mettle be not mov'd;°
       They vanish tongue-tied in their guiltiness.

Loyalty and Betrayal *Why is Murellus so angry with the commoners?*

---

**Side notes:**

26 neat's leather: cowhide. The Cobbler claims that his shoes have been worn by as fine men as ever walked in shoes.

31 triumph: triumphal celebration. (The triumph was held to celebrate Julius Caesar's defeat of two sons of Pompey the Great, his former rival. Caesar gained control over Rome upon defeating Pompey in 48 B.C.)
33 tributaries: captured enemies who pay tribute, or ransom money, for their release.
34 captive bonds: the chains of prisoners.

43 but: only.

45 Tiber: a river running through Rome.
46 replication: echo.

49 cull out a holiday: pick out this day as a holiday.

51 Pompey's blood: Pompey's sons.

54 intermit: hold back.

58–60 Draw them to . . . of all: Flavius wants the commoners to weep into the Tiber until the river's lowest water reaches its highest banks.
61 whe'er . . . mov'd: whether their humble spirits have not been touched.

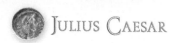

Go you down that way towards the Capitol,
This way will I. Disrobe the images,
65   If you do find them deck'd with ceremonies.°

MURELLUS. May we do so?
You know it is the feast of Lupercal.°

FLAVIUS. It is no matter, let no images
Be hung with Caesar's trophies.° I'll about,
70   And drive away the vulgar° from the streets;
So do you too, where you perceive them thick.
These growing feathers pluck'd from Caesar's wing
Will make him fly an ordinary pitch,°
Who else would soar above the view of men
75   And keep us all in **servile** fearfulness.

[*They exit.*]

SCENE 2. Rome. A public place.

[*Enter* CAESAR, ANTONY *for the course,* CALPHURNIA,
PORTIA, DECIUS, CICERO, BRUTUS, CASSIUS, CASCA, CITIZENS,
and a SOOTHSAYER; *after them* MURELLUS *and* FLAVIUS.]

CAESAR. Calphurnia!

CASCA.   Peace, ho, Caesar speaks.

[*All fall silent as* CAESAR *calls for his wife.*]

CAESAR.   Calphurnia!

CALPHURNIA. Here, my lord.

CAESAR. Stand you directly in Antonio's way
When he doth run his course. Antonio!

5   ANTONY. Caesar, my lord?

CAESAR. Forget not in your speed, Antonio,
To touch Calphurnia; for our elders say,
The barren, touched in this holy chase,
Shake off their sterile curse.°

ANTONY.   I shall remember;
10   When Caesar says, "Do this," it is perform'd.

Make Inferences About Characters *How would you describe the relationship between Caesar and Antony based on Antony's comment in lines 9–10?*

Vocabulary

servile (sur′vil) *adj.* lacking self-respect; behaving as if other people are superior

---

64–65 Disrobe the images . . . ceremonies: Flavius directs Murellus to remove any decorations from the statues.

67 feast of Lupercal: religious festival for a god worshiped by shepherds as a protector of flocks

69 trophies: decorations honoring Caesar.

70 vulgar: common people.

72–73 These growing . . . pitch: Plucking feathers from a bird's wings prevents it from flying. Flavius uses this metaphor for his plan to keep Caesar's power at an ordinary **pitch,** or height.

Head of a woman, sometimes identified as Marciana, 1st quarter of the 2nd century A.D. Roman. Bronze. Louvre Museum, Paris.

<u>View the Art</u> Describe the woman portrayed here. How might she reflect Calphurnia's feelings at this point in the drama?

6–9 Forget not . . . curse: Caesar, who has no children, refers to a traditional belief that barren women could become fertile if they were struck by leather thongs carried by runners who passed through Rome on the feast of Lupercal.

CAESAR. Set on, and leave no ceremony out. [*Flourish.*]

SOOTHSAYER. Caesar!

CAESAR. Ha! Who calls?

CASCA. Bid every noise be still; peace yet again!

15 **CAESAR.** Who is it in the press° that calls on me?
    I hear a tongue shriller than all the music,
    Cry "Caesar!" Speak, Caesar is turn'd to hear.°

SOOTHSAYER. Beware the ides of March.°

CAESAR.   What man is that?

BRUTUS. A soothsayer bids you beware the ides of March.

20 **CAESAR.** Set him before me, let me see his face.

CASSIUS. Fellow, come from the throng, look upon Caesar.

CAESAR. What say'st thou to me now? Speak once again.

SOOTHSAYER. Beware the ides of March.

CAESAR. He is a dreamer, let us leave him. Pass.

[*They exit. BRUTUS and CASSIUS remain.*]

25 **CASSIUS.** Will you go see the order of the course?°

BRUTUS. Not I.

CASSIUS. I pray you do.

BRUTUS. I am not gamesome;° I do lack some part
    Of that quick spirit that is in Antony.
30   Let me not hinder, Cassius, your desires;
    I'll leave you.

CASSIUS. Brutus, I do observe you now of late;°
    I have not from your eyes that gentleness
    And show of love as I was wont to° have.
35   You bear too stubborn and too strange a hand
    Over your friend that loves you.°

BRUTUS.   Cassius,
    Be not deceiv'd: if I have veil'd my look,

---

15 press: crowd.

17 turn'd to hear: Caesar turns his good ear to the Soothsayer (he was deaf in one ear).

18 ides of March: March 15. In the Roman calendar, a day in the middle of every month was called the ides.

25 order . . . course: progress of the race.

28 gamesome: fond of games and sports.

32 of late: lately.

34 was wont to: used to.

35–36 You bear . . . loves you: Cassius uses the metaphor of a rider holding a tight rein on an unfamiliar horse to suggest Brutus's unfriendly behavior toward him.

Blank Verse *Reread line 18. How does Shakespeare maintain the rhythm of blank verse during dialogue?*

Make Inferences About Characters *What does Caesar's behavior toward the soothsayer suggest about his character?*

I turn the trouble of my countenance
Merely upon myself.° Vexed I am
40 Of late with passions of some difference,°
Conceptions only proper to myself,
Which give some soil, perhaps, to my behaviors;°
But let not therefore my good friends be griev'd
(Among which number, Cassius, be you one),
45 Nor construe any further° my neglect,
Than that poor Brutus, with himself at war,
Forgets the shows of love to other men.

CASSIUS. Then, Brutus, I have much mistook your passion,°
By means whereof this breast of mine hath buried
50 Thoughts of great value, worthy cogitations.°
Tell me, good Brutus, can you see your face?

BRUTUS. No, Cassius; for the eye sees not itself
But by reflection, by some other things.

CASSIUS. 'Tis just,
55 And it is very much lamented, Brutus,
That you have no such mirrors as will turn
Your hidden worthiness into your eye,
That you might see your shadow.° I have heard
Where many of the best respect in Rome
60 (Except immortal Caesar), speaking of Brutus
And groaning underneath this age's yoke,
Have wish'd that noble Brutus had his eyes.°

BRUTUS. Into what dangers would you lead me, Cassius,
That you would have me seek into myself
65 For that which is not in me?

CASSIUS. Therefore, good Brutus, be prepar'd to hear;
And since you know you cannot see yourself
So well as by reflection, I, your glass
Will modestly discover to yourself
70 That of yourself which you yet know not of.°
And be not jealous on° me, gentle Brutus;
Were I a common laughter, or did use
To stale with ordinary oaths my love
To every new protester; if you know

37–39 Be not . . . upon myself: If I have seemed withdrawn, my displeased looks have been turned only on myself.
40 passions of some difference: conflicting emotions.
42 Which give . . . behaviors: Which might blemish my conduct.
45 Nor . . . further: Nor should you think any more of.

48 mistook your passion: misunderstood your feelings.

49–50 By means . . . cogitations: Because of this I have kept important thoughts to myself.

58 shadow: reflection.

58–62 I have heard . . . eyes: Cassius claims that many highly respected Roman citizens, groaning under the oppression of Caesar's rule, wished that Brutus would recognize his own worth.

68–70 I, your . . . not of: I, your mirror, will reveal without exaggeration what you do not yet know about yourself.
71 jealous on: suspicious of.

Make Inferences About Characters *What do Brutus's words in lines 46–47 suggest about his personality and inner state?*

Loyalty and Betrayal *What does Cassius reveal about his feelings in line 60?*

75   That I do fawn on men and hug them hard,
    And after scandal them; or if you know
    That I profess myself in banqueting
    To all the rout, then hold me dangerous.°

[*Flourish and shout.*]

  BRUTUS. What means this shouting? I do fear the people
80   Choose Caesar for their king.

  CASSIUS.   Ay, do you fear it?
    Then must I think you would not have it so.

  BRUTUS. I would not, Cassius, yet I love him well.
    But wherefore° do you hold me here so long?
    What is it that you would impart to me?
85   If it be aught toward the general good,
    Set honor in one eye and death i' th' other,
    And I will look on both indifferently;°
    For let the gods so speed° me, as I love
    The name of honor more than I fear death.

90   CASSIUS. I know that virtue to be in you, Brutus,
    As well as I do know your outward favor.°
    Well, honor is the subject of my story:
    I cannot tell what you and other men
    Think of this life; but for my single self,
95   I had as lief not be as live to be
    In awe of such a thing as I myself.°
    I was born free as Caesar; so were you;
    We both have fed as well, and we can both
    Endure the winter's cold as well as he;
100   For once, upon a raw and gusty day,
    The troubled Tiber chafing with her shores,°
    Caesar said to me, "Dar'st thou,° Cassius, now
    Leap in with me into this angry flood,
    And swim to yonder point?" Upon the word,
105   Accoutred° as I was, I plunged in,
    And bade him follow; so indeed he did.
    The torrent roar'd, and we did buffet it
    With lusty sinews,° throwing it aside
    And stemming it with hearts of controversy;°
110   But ere we could arrive the point propos'd,
    Caesar cried, "Help me, Cassius, or I sink!"

72–78 Were I . . . dangerous: If I were a laughingstock or used to cheaply offering my affection to anyone, or if you know me to slander men after fawning on them, or if you know me to proclaim friendship to the common crowd while drinking, then consider me dangerous.

83 wherefore: why.

85–87 If it be aught . . . indifferently: If it is anything that concerns the public welfare, I will face honor and death impartially.
88 speed: favor.

91 favor: appearance.

94–96 for my single . . . myself: Personally, I would rather not live than live in awe of another human being.

101 chafing with her shores: dashing into the shores (as if angry with them for their restraint).
102 Dar'st thou: Do you dare?

105 Accoutred: dressed in armor.

108 sinews: muscles.
109 stemming . . . controversy: making headway against the river's flow in a spirit of rivalry.

Make Inferences About Characters *How would you describe Cassius's attitude toward Brutus? Why might Cassius behave in this manner?*

The Flight of Aeneas from Troy. Carle van Loo. 1705–1765. Painting. Louvre, Paris.

View the Art What comparison does Cassius make between himself and Aeneas, as pictured here?

I, as Aeneas,° our great ancestor,
Did from the flames of Troy upon his shoulder
The old Anchises bear, so from the waves of Tiber
115 Did I the tired Caesar. And this man
Is now become a god, and Cassius is
A wretched creature, and must bend his body°
If Caesar carelessly but nod on him.
He had a fever when he was in Spain,
120 And when the fit was on him, I did mark
How he did shake—'tis true, this god did shake;
His coward lips did from their color fly,
And that same eye whose bend° doth awe the world
Did lose his° luster; I did hear him groan;
125 Ay, and that tongue of his that bade the Romans
Mark him, and write his speeches in their books,
Alas, it cried, "Give me some drink, Titinius,"
As a sick girl. Ye gods, it doth amaze me
A man of such a feeble temper should
130 So get the start of the majestic world,
And bear the palm alone.°

[*Shout. Flourish.*]

112 Aeneas (i nē′ əs): the legendary founder of Rome, who carried his father, Anchises, on his back as he fled the burning city of Troy after it was conquered by the Greeks.

117 bend his body: bow.

123 bend: glance, look.
124 his: its.

130–131 So get the . . . alone: get ahead of all others and carry the victor's prize himself.

Make Inferences About Characters *What is Cassius's attitude toward the idea that Caesar is a god?*

Blank Verse *Review lines 125–131. How many of these lines are in regular iambic pentameter, and how many vary the pattern?*

BRUTUS. Another general shout?
I do believe that these applauses are
For some new honors that are heap'd on Caesar.

135 **CASSIUS.** Why, man, he doth bestride the narrow world
Like a Colossus,° and we petty men
Walk under his huge legs, and peep about
To find ourselves dishonorable graves.
Men at some time are masters of their fates;
140 The fault, dear Brutus, is not in our stars,°
But in ourselves, that we are underlings.
Brutus and Caesar; what should be in that "Caesar"?
Why should that name be sounded more than yours?
Write them together, yours is as fair a name;
145 Sound them,° it doth become the mouth as well;
Weigh them, it is as heavy; conjure° with 'em,
"Brutus" will start a spirit as soon as "Caesar."
Now, in the names of all the gods at once,
Upon what meat doth this our Caesar feed,
150 That he is grown so great? Age,° thou art sham'd!
Rome, thou hast lost the breed of noble bloods!
When went there by an age, since the great flood°
But it was fam'd with more than with one man?°
When could they say, till now, that talk'd of Rome,
155 That her wide walks encompass'd but one man?
Now is it Rome indeed and room enough,°
When there is in it but one only man.
O! you and I have heard our fathers say
There was a Brutus once that would have brook'd
160 Th' eternal devil to keep his state in Rome
As easily as a king.°

BRUTUS. That you do love me, I am nothing jealous;°
What you would work me to, I have some aim.°
How I have thought of this, and of these times,
165 I shall recount hereafter. For this present,
I would not (so with love I might **entreat** you)
Be any further mov'd.° What you have said
I will consider; what you have to say
I will with patience hear, and find a time
170 Both meet° to hear and answer such high things.

136 Colossus: The Colossus of Rhodes, a gigantic statue of the Greek god Apollo in the harbor of Rhodes, was said to be so tall that ships could sail through its legs.

140 stars: fate (believed to be determined by the position of the stars and planets at someone's birth).

145 Sound them: say them.
146 conjure: call up spirits.

150 Age: the present era.

152 great flood: a time, according to Roman mythology, when a god let loose a flood that drowned all but two people.
153 But it was . . . man: That was not celebrated for more than one great man.
156 Now is it . . . enough: Cassius makes a pun on the words *Rome* and *room*, which were sometimes pronounced alike in Shakespeare's time.
159–161 There was . . . king: There once was a Brutus who would have accepted the devil ruling in Rome as easily as a king. (Cassius refers to Lucius Junius Brutus, who expelled the king and made Rome a republic in 509 B.C. Brutus claimed this hero as his ancestor.)
162 am nothing jealous: have no doubt.
163 have some aim: can guess.
167 mov'd: urged.
170 meet: suitable.

Loyalty and Betrayal *What angers Cassius about Caesar's leadership? Explain.*

Vocabulary

entreat (en trēt´) *v.* to ask earnestly; to beg

Gaius Julius Caesar; Roman statesman and general—"Caesar dictates his commentaries"—Painting (detail), 1812. Pelagio Palagi. Oil on canvas. Rome Palazzo del Quirinale.

View the Art What qualities of Caesar does this painting depict? Do you think they are accurate? Why or why not?

Till then, my noble friend, chew° upon this;
Brutus had rather be a villager
Than to repute himself a son of Rome
Under these hard conditions as this time
175   Is like to lay upon us.

CASSIUS. I am glad that my weak words
    Have struck but thus much show of fire from Brutus.

[*Enter* CAESAR *and his* TRAIN.]

BRUTUS. The games are done, and Caesar is returning.

CASSIUS. As they pass by, pluck Casca by the sleeve,
180   And he will (after his sour fashion) tell you
What hath proceeded worthy note today.°

BRUTUS. I will do so. But look you, Cassius,
The angry spot doth glow on Caesar's brow,
And all the rest look like a chidden train;°
185   Calphurnia's cheek is pale, and Cicero°
Looks with such ferret° and such fiery eyes
As we have seen him in the Capitol,
Being cross'd in conference by some senators.

CASSIUS. Casca will tell us what the matter is.

190 CAESAR. Antonio!

ANTONY. Caesar?

CAESAR. Let me have men about me that are fat,

171 chew: ponder.

181 What hath . . . today: what noteworthy things have occurred today.

184 chidden train: scolded band of followers.
185 Cicero: a Roman senator famous for his oratory.
186 ferret: a weasel-like animal with red eyes.

Make Inferences About Characters *To what extent has Cassius succeeded in winning Brutus over to his side? Explain.*

Sleek-headed men, and such as sleep a-nights.
Yond Cassius has a lean and hungry look,
195   He thinks too much; such men are dangerous.

    ANTONY. Fear him not, Caesar, he's not dangerous,
      He is a noble Roman, and well given.°

    CAESAR. Would he were fatter! But I fear him not.
      Yet if my name were liable to fear,°
200   I do not know the man I should avoid
      So soon as that spare Cassius. He reads much,
      He is a great observer, and he looks
      Quite through the deeds of men.° He loves no plays,
      As thou dost, Antony; he hears no music;
205   Seldom he smiles, and smiles in such a sort
      As if he mock'd himself, and scorn'd his spirit
      That could be mov'd to smile at any thing.°
      Such men as he be never at heart's ease
      Whiles they behold a greater than themselves,
210   And therefore are they very dangerous.
      I rather tell thee what is to be fear'd
      Than what I fear; for always I am Caesar.
      Come on my right hand, for this ear is deaf,
      And tell me truly what thou think'st of him.

    [CAESAR *and his* TRAIN *exit.* CASCA *stays.*]

215   CASCA. You pull'd me by the cloak, would you speak with me?

    BRUTUS. Ay, Casca; tell us what hath chanc'd° today,
      That Caesar looks so sad.°

    CASCA. Why, you were with him, were you not?

    BRUTUS. I should not then ask Casca what had chanc'd.

220   CASCA. Why, there was a crown offer'd him; and being offer'd
      him, he put it by° with the back of his hand, thus, and then
      the people fell a-shouting.

    BRUTUS. What was the second noise for?

    CASCA. Why, for that too.

225   CASSIUS. They shouted thrice; what was the last cry for?

    CASCA. Why, for that too.

    BRUTUS. Was the crown offer'd him thrice?

197 well given: favorably disposed (toward Caesar).

199 if my name . . . fear: if it were possible for me to fear anyone.

202–203 looks . . . of men: sees people's true motives in their actions.

206–207 scorn'd . . . any thing: scorned anyone who ever smiles.

216 chanc'd: happened.
217 sad: serious.

221 put it by: pushed it aside.

Loyalty and Betrayal *Why does Caesar think that Cassius is to be avoided?*

Blank Verse *What difference do you notice between Casca's way of speaking and that of Caesar in this scene?*

CASCA. Ay, marry, was't,° and he put it by thrice, every time
gentler than other; and at every putting-by mine honest
230   neighbors° shouted.

CASSIUS. Who offer'd him the crown?

CASCA. Why, Antony.

BRUTUS. Tell us the manner of it, gentle Casca.

CASCA. I can as well be hang'd as tell the manner of it; it was
235   mere foolery, I did not mark° it. I saw Mark Antony offer
him a crown—yet 'twas not a crown neither, 'twas one of
these coronets°—and as I told you, he put it by once; but
for all that, to my thinking, he would fain° have had it.
Then he offer'd it to him again; then he put it by again; but
240   to my thinking, he was very loath to lay his fingers off it.
And then he offer'd it the third time; he put it the third
time by; and still as he refus'd it, the rabblement hooted,
and clapp'd their chopp'd° hands, and threw up their
sweaty nightcaps, and utter'd such a deal of stinking
245   breath because Caesar refus'd the crown, that it had,
almost, chok'd Caesar; for he swounded,° and fell down at
it; and for mine own part, I durst not laugh, for fear of
opening my lips and receiving the bad air.

CASSIUS. But, soft,° I pray you; what, did Caesar swound?

250 CASCA. He fell down in the market place, and foam'd at
mouth, and was speechless.

BRUTUS. 'Tis very like, he hath the falling sickness.°

CASSIUS. No, Caesar hath it not; but you, and I,
And honest Casca, we have the falling sickness.

255 CASCA. I know not what you mean by that, but I am sure
Caesar fell down. If the tag-rag people° did not clap him
and hiss him, according as he pleas'd and displeas'd them,
as they use to do the players in the theater, I am no true man.

BRUTUS. What said he when he came unto himself?

260 CASCA. Marry, before he fell down, when he perceiv'd the
common herd was glad he refus'd the crown, he pluck'd
me ope his doublet,° and offer'd them his throat to cut.
And I had been a man of any occupation,° if I would not
have taken him at a word,° I would I might go to hell
265   among the rogues. And so he fell. When he came to

Make Inferences About Characters   *Why does Caesar refuse the crown?*

228 marry, was't: indeed it was.

229–230 mine honest neighbors:
Casca refers ironically to his "honest
neighbors," for whom he has
contempt.

235 mark: pay attention to.

237 coronets: small crowns.
238 fain: rather.

243 chopp'd: chapped.

246 swounded: fainted.

249 soft: wait a minute.

252 'Tis very . . . falling sickness:
It's very likely that he has epilepsy.

256 tag-rag people: ragged mob.

261–262 pluck'd . . . doublet:
ripped open his short jacket.
263 And I . . . occupation:
If I had been "a man of action"
(or "a laborer").
264 a word: his word.

himself again, he said, if he had done or said anything amiss, he desir'd their worships to think it was his infirmity. Three or four wenches, where I stood, cried, "Alas, good soul!" and forgave him with all their hearts.
270   But there's no heed to be taken of them; if Caesar had stabb'd their mothers, they would have done no less.

BRUTUS. And after that, he came thus sad away?

CASCA. Ay.

CASSIUS. Did Cicero say anything?

275   CASCA. Ay, he spoke Greek.

CASSIUS. To what effect?

CASCA. Nay, and I tell you that, I'll ne'er look you i' th' face again. But those that understood him smil'd at one another, and shook their heads; but for mine own part, it was Greek
280   to me.° I could tell you more news too; Murellus and Flavius, for pulling scarfs off Caesar's images, are put to silence.° Fare you well. There was more foolery yet, if I could remember it.

CASSIUS. Will you sup with me tonight, Casca?

CASCA. No, I am promis'd forth.

285   CASSIUS. Will you dine with me tomorrow?

CASCA. Ay, if I be alive, and your mind hold,° and your dinner worth the eating.

CASSIUS. Good, I will expect you.

CASCA. Do so. Farewell, both. [Exit.]

290   BRUTUS. What a blunt fellow is this grown to be!
        He was quick mettle° when he went to school.

CASSIUS. So is he now in execution
        Of any bold or noble **enterprise**,
        However he puts on this tardy form.°
295   This rudeness is a sauce to his good wit,
        Which gives men stomach to disgest° his words
        With better appetite.

279–280 it was Greek to me: I couldn't understand a word of it.
281 put to silence: barred from speaking in public (or perhaps exiled or executed).

286 your mind hold: you don't change your mind.

291 quick mettle: lively, clever.

294 However . . . form: Although he puts on this dull manner.

296 disgest: digest.

Make Inferences About Characters *What does Casca mean by his remark in line 271? What is his attitude toward the people in the crowd?*

Loyalty and Betrayal *What does the punishment of Murellus and Flavius indicate about Caesar and his rule?*

Vocabulary

enterprise (en′tər prīz′) *n.* an important project or undertaking

BRUTUS. And so it is. For this time I will leave you.
Tomorrow, if you please to speak with me,
300   I will come home to you, or, if you will,
Come home to me, and I will wait for you.

CASSIUS. I will do so. Till then, think of the world.°

[*Exit* BRUTUS.]

Well, Brutus, thou art noble; yet I see
Thy honorable mettle may be wrought
305   From that it is dispos'd;° therefore it is meet°
That noble minds keep ever with their likes;
For who so firm that cannot be seduc'd?
Caesar doth bear me hard,° but he loves Brutus.
If I were Brutus now and he were Cassius,
310   He should not humor° me. I will this night,
In several hands, in at his windows throw,
As if they came from several citizens,
Writings, all tending to the great opinion
That Rome holds of his name; wherein obscurely
315   Caesar's ambition shall be glanced at.°
And after this, let Caesar seat him sure,°
For we will shake him, or worse days endure. [*Exit.*]

SCENE 3. A Roman street. One month later.

[*Thunder and lightning. Enter (from opposite sides)* CASCA *(with his sword drawn) and* CICERO.]

CICERO. Good even,° Casca; brought you Caesar home?
Why are you breathless? And why stare you so?

CASCA. Are not you mov'd, when all the sway° of earth
Shakes like a thing unfirm? O Cicero,
5   I have seen tempests, when the scolding winds
Have riv'd° the knotty oaks, and I have seen
Th' ambitious ocean swell and rage and foam,
To be exalted with° the threat'ning clouds;
But never till tonight, never till now,
10   Did I go through a tempest dropping fire.
Either there is a civil strife in heaven,
Or else the world, too saucy° with the gods,

---

302 the world: the present state of affairs.

304–305 Thy honorable . . . dispos'd: Your honorable nature can be manipulated to go against its normal inclinations.
305 meet: appropriate.
308 doth bear me hard: dislikes me.

310 humor: influence.

310–315 I will . . . glanced at: Tonight I will throw letters in different handwriting, as if they came from several citizens, into Brutus's windows. The letters will relate that Brutus is highly regarded in Rome and will subtly hint at Caesar's ambition.
316 seat him sure: seat himself securely.

1 even: evening.

3 sway: realm.

6 riv'd: split.

8 exalted with: raised as high as.

12 saucy: insolent.

Make Inferences About Characters *What aspect of Cassius's character becomes clear in line 307? What are his true feelings about Brutus?*

Blank Verse *In what way are lines 316–317 not blank verse? Why might Shakespeare have written them this way?*

Incenses them to send destruction.

CICERO. Why, saw you any thing more wonderful?

15 CASCA. A common slave—you know him well by sight—
　　　　Held up his left hand, which did flame and burn
　　　　Like twenty torches join'd; and yet his hand,
　　　　Not sensible of° fire, remain'd unscorch'd.
　　　　Besides—I ha' not since put up my sword—
20　　　　Against the Capitol I met a lion,
　　　　Who glaz'd° upon me and went surly by,
　　　　Without annoying me. And there were drawn
　　　　Upon a heap° a hundred ghastly women,
　　　　Transformed with their fear, who swore they saw
25　　　　Men, all in fire, walk up and down the streets.
　　　　And yesterday the bird of night° did sit
　　　　Even at noonday upon the marketplace,
　　　　Hooting and shrieking. When these prodigies°
　　　　Do so conjointly meet,° let not men say,
30　　　　"These are their reasons, they are natural";
　　　　For I believe they are portentous things
　　　　Unto the climate that they point upon.°

CICERO. Indeed, it is a strange-disposed time;
　　　　But men may construe things after their fashion,
35　　　　Clean from the purpose of the things themselves.°
　　　　Comes Caesar to the Capitol tomorrow?

CASCA. He doth; for he did bid Antonio
　　　　Send word to you he would be there tomorrow.

CICERO. Good night then, Casca; this disturbed sky
40　　　　Is not to walk in.

CASCA.　　　　　　　　Farewell, Cicero.　　　　[*Exit* CICERO.]

[*Enter* CASSIUS.]

CASSIUS. Who's there?

CASCA.　　　　　　　A Roman.

CASSIUS.　　　　　　　　　　　Casca, by your voice.

18 **sensible of:** sensitive to.

21 **glaz'd:** stared.

22–23 **drawn . . . heap:** huddled together.

26 **bird of night:** screech owl.

28 **prodigies:** bizarre events.
29 **conjointly meet:** coincide.

31–32 **portentous . . . point upon:** bad omens for the place where they occur.

34–35 **But men may . . . themselves:** But people may interpret things in their own way, regardless of the real meaning of the things.

Owl, 20th century. Graham Sutherland. Oil on canvas. Private collection.

<u>View the Art</u> Can you infer a symbolic meaning from the presence of the "bird of night"? Explain. How does this detail affect the mood?

Loyalty and Betrayal *What connection might there be between the unnatural events described by Casca and the events of previous scenes? How might Caesar's rule be a betrayal?*

Blank Verse *The five syllables in the last line on this page make up the end of a line of blank verse. Which syllables make up the beginning of the line?*

Vocabulary

incense (in sens´) *v.* to make very angry

CASCA. Your ear is good. Cassius, what night is this!°

CASSIUS. A very pleasing night to honest men.

CASCA. Who ever knew the heavens menace so?

45 CASSIUS. Those that have known the earth so full of faults.
For my part, I have walk'd about the streets,
Submitting me° unto the perilous night;
And thus unbraced,° Casca, as you see,
Have bar'd my bosom to the thunder-stone;°
50 And when the cross blue lightning seem'd to open
The breast of heaven, I did present myself
Even in the aim° and very flash of it.

CASCA. But wherefore did you so much tempt the heavens?
It is the part of men to fear and tremble
55 When the most mighty gods by tokens° send
Such dreadful heralds to astonish° us.

CASSIUS. You are dull,° Casca; and those sparks of life
That should be in a Roman you do want,°
Or else you use not. You look pale, and gaze,
60 And put on fear, and cast yourself in wonder,
To see the strange impatience of the heavens;
But if you would consider the true cause
Why all these fires, why all these gliding ghosts,
Why birds and beasts from quality and kind,°
65 Why old men, fools, and children calculate,°
Why all these things change from their ordinance,
Their natures and preformed faculties,
To monstrous quality—why, you shall find
That heaven hath infus'd them with these spirits,
70 To make them instruments of fear and warning
Unto some monstrous state.°
Now could I, Casca, name to thee a man
Most like this dreadful night,
That thunders, lightens, opens graves, and roars
75 As doth the lion in the Capitol—
A man no mightier than thyself, or me,
In personal action, yet prodigious grown
And fearful,° as these strange eruptions are.

CASCA. 'Tis Caesar that you mean; is it not, Cassius?

42 what night is this: what a night this is!

47 Submitting me: exposing myself.
48 unbraced: with jacket open.
49 thunder-stone: thunderbolt.

52 in the aim: at the point where it was directed.

55 tokens: ominous signs.
56 astonish: stun with fear.

57 dull: stupid.
58 want: lack.

64 from quality and kind: act contrary to nature.
65 calculate: make prophecies.

66–71 Why all these . . . state: Cassius argues that things have changed from their normal behavior as a heavenly warning of some unnatural state of affairs.

77–78 yet prodigious . . . fearful: yet has become ominous and threatening.

Loyalty and Betrayal *Cassius has been making an argument about Roman politics. Which side of the argument does he believe nature is taking?*

80　CASSIUS.　Let it be who it is; for Romans now
　　　　Have thews° and limbs like to their ancestors;
　　　　But, woe the while,° our fathers' minds are dead,
　　　　And we are govern'd with our mothers' spirits;
　　　　Our yoke and sufferance° show us womanish.

85　CASCA.　Indeed, they say, the senators tomorrow
　　　　Mean to establish Caesar as a king;
　　　　And he shall wear his crown by sea and land,
　　　　In every place, save here in Italy.

　　CASSIUS.　I know where I will wear this dagger then;
90　　　Cassius from bondage will deliver Cassius.°
　　　　Therein,° ye gods, you make the weak most strong;
　　　　Therein, ye gods, you tyrants do defeat;
　　　　Nor stony tower, nor walls of beaten brass,
　　　　Nor airless dungeon, nor strong links of iron,
95　　　Can be retentive to the strength of spirit;
　　　　But life, being weary of these worldly bars,
　　　　Never lacks power to dismiss itself.
　　　　If I know this, know all the world besides,
　　　　That part of tyranny that I do bear
100　　I can shake off at pleasure.

　　[Thunder still.]

　　CASCA.　　　　　　　　　　　　　So can I;
　　　　So every bondman in his own hand bears
　　　　The power to cancel his captivity.

　　CASSIUS.　And why should Caesar be a tyrant then?
　　　　Poor man, I know he would not be a wolf,
105　　But that he sees the Romans are but sheep;
　　　　He were no lion, were not Romans hinds.°
　　　　Those that with haste will make a mighty fire
　　　　Begin it with weak straws. What trash° is Rome?
　　　　What rubbish and what offal?° when it serves
110　　For the base matter° to illuminate
　　　　So vile a thing as Caesar! But, O grief,
　　　　Where hast thou led me? I, perhaps, speak this
　　　　Before a willing bondman; then I know
　　　　My answer must be made.° But I am arm'd,
115　　And dangers are to me indifferent.

　　CASCA.　You speak to Casca, and to such a man
　　　　That is no fleering° tell-tale. Hold, my hand.

81　thews: muscles.
82　woe the while: alas for these times.
84　yoke and sufferance: servitude and patient submission.

89–90　I know . . . deliver Cassius: Cassius says that he would rather kill himself than submit to Caesar.
91　Therein: in that way (referring to suicide).

106　hinds: deer.

108　trash: twigs or garbage.
109　offal: chips of wood or garbage.
110　base matter: kindling.

112–114　I, perhaps . . . be made: Perhaps I am speaking to one who accepts his slavery; if so, I shall have to answer for my words (suggesting that Casca might inform on him).

117　fleering: sneering.

Make Inferences About Characters　*Why might Cassius not want to name Caesar directly in line 80?*

Augustus and lictors, detail from the south frieze of the Ara Pacis Augustae, 13–9 B.C. Roman. Museum of the Ara Pacis, Rome.

<u>View the Art</u> One of the duties of Roman officers called *lictors* was to accompany officials such as Caesar in public appearances. What does this image suggest to you about the government of Rome in Caesar's time?

Be factious for redress of all these griefs,°
And I will set this foot of mine as far
120   As who goes farthest.
   CASSIUS.   There's a bargain made.
Now know you, Casca, I have mov'd° already
Some certain of the noblest-minded Romans
To undergo with me an enterprise
Of honorable-dangerous consequence;
125   And I do know, by this they stay for me
In Pompey's Porch;° for now, this fearful night,
There is no stir or walking in the streets;
And the complexion of the element
[In] favor's like the work we have in hand,°
130   Most bloody, fiery, and most terrible.
  [*Enter* CINNA.]
   CASCA. Stand close awhile, for here comes one in haste.
   CASSIUS. 'Tis Cinna, I do know him by his gait,
He is a friend. Cinna, where haste you so?
   CINNA. To find out you. Who's that? Metellus Cimber?

118 Be factious . . . griefs: Form a group to straighten out all these problems.

121 mov'd: persuaded.

125–126 by this . . . Porch: By this time they wait for me in the entrance to the theater built by Pompey.

128–129 the complexion . . . in hand: The condition of the sky appears similar to the work we have to do.

Loyalty and Betrayal *What bargain has been made? How are Cassius and Casca now bound by loyalty and by betrayal?*

| 135 | CASSIUS. No, it is Casca, one incorporate° | 135 **incorporate:** joined. |

CASSIUS. No, it is Casca, one incorporate°
　　To our attempts. Am I not stay'd for, Cinna?

CINNA. I am glad on't. What a fearful night is this!
　　There's two or three of us have seen strange sights.

CASSIUS. Am I not stay'd for? tell me.

CINNA.　　　　　　　　　　　　　Yes, you are.
140　O Cassius, if you could
　　But win the noble Brutus to our party—

CASSIUS. Be you content. Good Cinna, take this paper,
　　And look you lay it in the praetor's chair,
　　Where Brutus may but find it; and throw this
145　In at his window; set this up with wax
　　Upon old Brutus' statue.° All this done,
　　Repair° to Pompey's Porch, where you shall find us.
　　Is Decius Brutus and Trebonius there?

CINNA. All but Metellus Cimber, and he's gone
150　To seek you at your house. Well, I will hie,°
　　And so bestow these papers as you bade me.

CASSIUS. That done, repair to Pompey's theater.

[*Exit* CINNA.]

　　Come, Casca, you and I will yet ere day
　　See Brutus at his house. Three parts of him
155　Is ours already, and the man entire
　　Upon the next encounter yields him ours.°

CASCA. O, he sits high in all the people's hearts;
　　And that which would appear offense in us,
　　His countenance, like richest alchemy,
160　Will change to virtue and to worthiness.°

CASSIUS. Him, and his worth, and our great need of him,
　　You have right well conceited.° Let us go,
　　For it is after midnight, and ere day
　　We will awake him and be sure of him.

[*They exit.*]

142–146 **Good Cinna . . . statue:** Marcus Brutus held the office of praetor, a high-ranking judge who settled disputes brought before him. Cassius directs Cinna to leave one letter on Brutus's chair, throw a second into his window, and fasten a third onto the statue of the hero Lucius Junius Brutus.
147 **Repair:** go.
150 **hie:** hurry.

155–156 **the man . . . ours:** When we next meet him, he will be entirely in our hands.

159–160 **His countenance . . . worthiness:** Alchemy was the "science" of trying to turn base metals into gold. Casca says that Brutus's noble reputation will change the public's attitude toward their plot from condemnation to admiration.
162 **conceited:** understood.

Loyalty and Betrayal *Why is it so important for the conspirators to have Brutus on their side?*

After You Read

Respond and Think Critically

1. **Connect to Personal Experience** Which character in Act 1 made the strongest impression on you? Why?

2. **Explain Events** After seeing the public celebrating Caesar's triumph, what do Flavius and Murellus do? Why do they respond this way?

3. **Examine Dialogue** What stories about Caesar does Cassius tell Brutus? What concerns Cassius the most?

4. **Analyze Theme** What themes do you see emerging during Act I of the play? Provide evidence from the text to support your answer.

5. **Evaluate Characterization** Do you think Shakespeare's portrayal of the commoners in Act 1 is realistic? Explain.

6. **Big Idea** **Draw Conclusions About Motivation** From what you have read so far, do you think the conspirators are traitors or patriots? What motivates them? Support your response with text evidence.

7. **Draw Conclusions About Historical Context** In what way does the choice facing Roman politicians between loyalty and betrayal remind you of present-day conflicts?

Literary Element Blank Verse

Review the pink highlighted passages and questions to help you answer the following questions.

8. **Draw Conclusions About Character** Review Casca's lines throughout Act 1. Does he speak in blank verse? What conclusion can you draw about him based on this?

9. **Make Inferences About Structure** Based on what you know about Shakespeare's use of blank verse in Act 1, what inferences can you make about characters in subsequent acts based on whether they speak in blank verse? Use evidence from Act 1 in your response.

Reading Strategy Make Inferences About Characters

Review the graphic you made on page 691. Then read the sentences below and identify at least two reasons why each character behaved as he did.

10. Cassius wants Caesar out of power.

11. Caesar refuses to accept the crown.

Literature Online

Selection Resources For Selection Quizzes, eFlashcards, and Reading-Writing Connection activities, go to glencoe.com and enter QuickPass code GL57805u4.

Vocabulary Practice

Practice with Synonyms A synonym is a word that has nearly the same meaning as another word. With a partner, brainstorm three synonyms for each boldfaced vocabulary word below. Then discuss the different shades of meaning that each synonym carries.

1. servile
2. entreat
3. enterprise
4. incense

EXAMPLE:

serviceable

Synonyms: *helpful, practical, usable*

Sample explanation: *Helpful* means "giving support"; *practical* means "serving a useful purpose"; and *useful* means "able to be used."

Writing

Write an Editorial Imagine you are a journalist who has heard rumors about a plot to overthrow Caesar. Write an editorial in which you explain whether or not you think Caesar should be deposed. Use details from the play to support your opinion.

Before You Read

The Tragedy of Julius Caesar, Act 2

Build Background

Ancient Romans believed that observing the natural world could inform them about the future. Great storms and unusual behavior by animals were indications that not all was well.

Set Purposes for Reading

Literary Element Monologues, Soliloquies, and Asides

In drama, a **monologue** is a long speech by one character. A **soliloquy** is a monologue delivered while a character is alone onstage. An **aside** is a character's comment that is directed to the audience or another character but is not heard by any other characters on stage. As you read, ask yourself, What do you learn about the characters through these devices?

Reading Strategy Analyze Theme

A **theme** is the message about life in a work of literature. A play may have multiple themes that are revealed through its plot, characters, dialogue, setting, and **motifs**—significant words, phrases, images, descriptions, or ideas that are repeated throughout the play. For example, the motif of omens—events or signs that supposedly foretell the future—recurs throughout *Julius Caesar* and connects to the larger idea of betrayal. As you read Act 2, ask yourself, What themes are expressed through motifs? How does the motif of omens foreshadow plot events?

···

Tip: Take Notes As you read, fill in a chart like the one shown below to identify motifs in Act 2 and analyze how they relate to theme. Use the blue highlighted passages and questions to help you get started.

Motif	Example	Theme
prophetic dreams	Calphurnia calls out in her sleep that "they murther Caesar!"	People may sense or intuit when danger is coming to their loved ones.

TEKS

For pages 713–733

10.4 Analyze how archetypes and motifs in drama affect the plot of plays.

Vocabulary

interim (in´tər im) *n.* the space of time that exists between events; p. 716 *We enjoyed the wedding and the reception, but there was nothing to do in the interim.*

commend (kə mend´) *v.* to speak highly of; to praise; p. 719 *The president's speech will commend the senator's service to the country.*

disperse (dis purs´) *v.* to break up and send in different directions; to scatter; p. 721 *It was hard for the mother dog to watch the vet disperse her litter.*

···

Tip: Word Usage You should select words to suit the situation and your particular audience. For example, in a conversation you might use the word *praise;* in a formal speech, you might use the word *commend.*

ACT 2

SCENE 1. BRUTUS's garden. The ides of March.

[*Enter BRUTUS in his orchard.*]

BRUTUS. What, Lucius, ho!
I cannot, by the progress° of the stars,
Give guess how near to day. Lucius, I say!
I would it were my fault° to sleep so soundly.
5   When, Lucius, when? Awake, I say! What, Lucius!

[*Enter LUCIUS.*]

LUCIUS. Call'd you, my lord?

BRUTUS. Get me a taper° in my study, Lucius.
When it is lighted, come and call me here.

LUCIUS. I will, my lord.

[*Exit LUCIUS.*]

10   BRUTUS. It must be by his death;° and for my part,
I know no personal cause to spurn° at him,
But for the general.° He would be crown'd:
How that might change his nature, there's the question.
It is the bright day that brings forth the adder,°
15   And that craves° wary walking. Crown him that,°
And then I grant we put a sting in him
That at his will he may do danger with.
Th' abuse of greatness is when it disjoins
Remorse from power;° and, to speak truth of Caesar,
20   I have not known when his affections° sway'd
More than his reason. But 'tis a common proof°
That lowliness° is young ambition's ladder,
Whereto the climber-upward turns his face;
But when he once attains the upmost round,°
25   He then unto the ladder turns his back,
Looks in the clouds, scorning the base degrees
By which he did ascend. So Caesar may;

2 **progress:** position.

4 **I would . . . fault:** I wish it were my weakness.

7 **taper:** candle.

10 **his death:** Caesar's death.
11 **spurn:** strike out.
12 **the general:** the public good.

14 **adder:** poisonous snake.
15 **craves:** demands. **Crown him that:** If we crown him.

18–19 **Th' abuse . . . power:** Greatness is misused when it separates mercy from power.
20 **affections:** feelings; desires.
21 **a common proof:** a common occurrence.
22 **lowliness:** humility.
24 **upmost round:** top rung.

Monologues, Soliloquies, and Asides *What type of speech begins here? How do you know?*

Loyalty and Betrayal *What prediction is Brutus making?*

Two serpents (detail), 1st century A.D. Artist unknown. Fresco painting.
Museo Archeologico Nazionale, Naples, Italy.

View the Art What qualities are generally associated with serpents?
Which characters in the play display such qualities? Explain.

Then lest he may, prevent.° And since the quarrel
Will bear no color for the thing he is,
30   Fashion it thus: that what he is, augmented,
Would run to these and these extremities;°
And therefore think him as a serpent's egg,
Which hatch'd, would as his kind grow mischievous,
And kill him in the shell.

[*Enter LUCIUS.*]

35   LUCIUS. The taper burneth in your closet,° sir.
Searching the window for a flint, I found
This paper thus seal'd up, and I am sure
It did not lie there when I went to bed.

[*Gives him the letter.*]

BRUTUS. Get you to bed again, it is not day.
40   Is not tomorrow, boy, the [ides] of March?

LUCIUS. I know not, sir.

BRUTUS. Look in the calendar, and bring me word.

LUCIUS. I will, sir. [*Exit.*]

BRUTUS. The exhalations° whizzing in the air
45   Give so much light that I may read by them.

28 Then lest . . . prevent: Let us
act in advance to prevent it.

**28–31 since the quarrel . . .
extremities:** Since our complaints
are not supported by Caesar's
present behavior, we will have to put
our case the following way: if given
more power, Caesar's nature would
lead him to such and such extremes.

35 closet: small private room.

44 exhalations: meteors.

[*Opens the letter and reads.*]

"Brutus, thou sleep'st; awake, and see thyself!
Shall Rome, etc. Speak, strike, redress!"°
"Brutus, thou sleep'st; awake."
Such instigations° have been often dropp'd

50   Where I have took them up.
"Shall Rome, etc." Thus must I piece it out:°
Shall Rome stand under one man's awe? What, Rome?
My ancestors did from the streets of Rome
The Tarquin° drive when he was call'd a king.

55   "Speak, strike, redress!" Am I entreated
To speak and strike? O Rome, I make thee promise,
If the redress will follow, thou receivest
Thy full petition at the hand of Brutus!°

[*Enter LUCIUS.*]

LUCIUS. Sir, March is wasted fifteen days.

[*Knock within.*]

60   BRUTUS. 'Tis good. Go to the gate, somebody knocks.

[*Exit LUCIUS.*]

Since Cassius first did whet° me against Caesar,
I have not slept.
Between the acting of a dreadful thing
And the first motion,° all the **interim** is

65   Like a phantasma,° or a hideous dream.
The Genius and the mortal instruments°
Are then in council, and the state of a man,
Like to a little kingdom, suffers then
The nature of an insurrection.°

[*Enter LUCIUS.*]

70   LUCIUS. Sir, 'tis your brother° Cassius at the door,
Who doth desire to see you.

BRUTUS.   Is he alone?

LUCIUS. No, sir, there are moe° with him.

47 redress: correct a wrong.

49 instigations: letters urging action.

51 piece it out: fill in the gaps in meaning.

54 Tarquin (tär′ kwin): the last king of Rome, driven out by Lucius Junius Brutus.

55–58 Speak, strike . . . Brutus: Brutus vows that Rome's petition for redress will be granted if it can be done through his words and actions.

61 whet: incite.

64 motion: prompting.
65 phantasma: nightmare.
66 Genius . . . instruments: the mental and physical powers that allow someone to take action.

67–69 the state . . . insurrection: Brutus compares his conflicted state of mind to a kingdom paralyzed by civil unrest.
70 brother: brother-in-law. (Cassius is married to Brutus's sister, Junia.)

72 moe: more.

Loyalty and Betrayal *What does the audience know about the origin of these notes?*

Analyze Theme *To whom does Brutus ally himself? Why? How does this connect to a larger theme of the play?*

Vocabulary

interim (in′ tər im) *n.* the space of time that exists between events

BRUTUS. Do you know them?

LUCIUS. No, sir; their hats are pluck'd about their ears,
And half their faces buried in their cloaks,
75 That by no means I may discover° them
By any mark of favor.°

75 discover: identify.
76 favor: appearance.

BRUTUS. Let 'em enter.

[*Exit LUCIUS.*]

They are the faction. O Conspiracy,
Sham'st thou° to show thy dang'rous brow by night,
When evils are most free? O then, by day
80 Where wilt thou find a cavern dark enough
To mask thy monstrous visage? Seek none, Conspiracy;
Hide it in smiles and affability;
For if thou path, thy native semblance° on,
Not Erebus° itself were dim enough
85 To hide thee from prevention.°

78 Sham'st thou: Are you
ashamed?

83 path . . . semblance: go about
undisguised.
84 Erebus (er′ ə bəs): in classical
mythology, the dark place through
which the dead pass on their way to
Hades, the underworld.
85 prevention: discovery.
86 too bold upon: intruding upon.
87 morrow: morning.

[*Enter the CONSPIRATORS, CASSIUS, CASCA, DECIUS, CINNA, METELLUS,
and TREBONIUS.*]

CASSIUS. I think we are too bold upon° your rest.
Good morrow,° Brutus, do we trouble you?

BRUTUS. I have been up this hour, awake all night.
Know I these men that come along with you?

90 **CASSIUS.** Yes, every man of them; and no man here
But honors you; and every one doth wish
You had but that opinion of yourself
Which every noble Roman bears of you.
This is Trebonius.

BRUTUS. He is welcome hither.

95 **CASSIUS.** This, Decius Brutus.

BRUTUS. He is welcome too.

CASSIUS. This, Casca; this, Cinna; and this, Metellus Cimber.

BRUTUS. They are all welcome.
What watchful cares do interpose themselves
Betwixt your eyes and night?°

100 **CASSIUS.** Shall I entreat a word?

[*They whisper.*]

DECIUS. Here lies the east; doth not the day break here?

Night. Simeon Solomon.
Watercolour, ink and bodycolour
on paper. Royal Albert Memorial
Museum, Exeter, Devon, UK.

View the Art What mood or
emotional quality does this
painting express?

98–99 What watchful . . . night:
What cares keep you awake?

CASCA. No.

CINNA. O, pardon, sir, it doth; and yon gray lines
　　That fret° the clouds are messengers of day.

105 CASCA. You shall confess that you are both deceiv'd.
　　Here, as I point my sword, the sun arises,
　　Which is a great way growing on the south,
　　Weighing the youthful season of the year.
　　Some two months hence, up higher toward the north
110 He first presents his fire, and the high east
　　Stands, as the Capitol, directly here.°

BRUTUS. Give me your hands all over,° one by one.

CASSIUS. And let us swear our resolution.

BRUTUS. No, not an oath. If not the face of men,
115 The sufferance of our souls, the time's abuse—
　　If these be motives weak, break off betimes,°
　　And every man hence to his idle bed.
　　So let high-sighted° tyranny range on
　　Till each man drop by lottery.° But if these
120 (As I am sure they do) bear fire° enough
　　To kindle cowards and to steel with valor
　　The melting spirits of women, then, countrymen,
　　What need we any spur but our own cause
　　To prick° us to redress? What other bond
125 Than secret Romans that have spoke the word
　　And will not palter?° and what other oath
　　Than honesty to honesty engag'd
　　That this shall be, or we will fall for it?°
　　Swear priests and cowards and men cautelous,°
130 Old feeble carrions,° and such suffering souls
　　That welcome wrongs; unto bad causes swear
　　Such creatures as men doubt; but do not stain
　　The even virtue of our enterprise,
　　Nor th' insuppressive mettle of our spirits,
135 To think that or our cause or our performance

104 fret: interlace.

106–111 Here, as I . . . directly here: Casca insists that in the early spring the sun rises south of the spot pointed out by Decius and Cinna; it will rise farther north in about two months.
112 all over: all of you.

114–116 If not . . . betimes: The sadness in people's faces, the suffering of our souls, the corruption of our age—if these are weak motives, let's give up at once.
118 high-sighted: arrogant.
119 drop by lottery: die by chance (at Caesar's whim).
120 bear fire: are spirited.

124 prick: spur.

126 palter: waver; deceive.

126–128 what other oath . . . for it: What other oath is needed than that of honest men who have pledged to each other that they will prevail or die trying?
129 cautelous: wary; crafty.
130 carrions: men no better than corpses.

Analyze Theme *Why do you think Shakespeare included this exchange between Decius, Casca, and Cinna? What theme might be emerging here?*

Monologues, Soliloquies, and Asides *What argument does Brutus make against swearing an oath?*

Loyalty and Betrayal *What does Brutus think is virtuous about their enterprise?*

Did need an oath;° when every drop of blood
That every Roman bears, and nobly bears,
Is guilty of a several bastardy,°
If he do break the smallest particle
140   Of any promise that hath pass'd from him.°

CASSIUS. But what of Cicero? Shall we sound him?°
    I think he will stand very strong with us.

CASCA. Let us not leave him out.

CINNA.   No, by no means.

METELLUS. O, let us have him, for his silver hairs
145   Will purchase us a good opinion,
    And buy men's voices to **commend** our deeds.
    It shall be said his judgment rul'd our hands;
    Our youths and wildness shall no whit° appear,
    But all be buried in his gravity.°

150 BRUTUS. O, name him not! Let us not break with him,°
    For he will never follow anything
    That other men begin.

CASSIUS.   Then leave him out.

CASCA. Indeed, he is not fit.

DECIUS. Shall no man else be touch'd but only Caesar?

155 CASSIUS. Decius, well urg'd. I think it is not meet
    Mark Antony, so well belov'd of Caesar,
    Should outlive Caesar; we shall find of him
    A shrewd contriver; and you know, his means,°
    If he improve them,° may well stretch so far
160   As to annoy us all; which to prevent,
    Let Antony and Caesar fall together.

BRUTUS. Our course will seem too bloody, Caius Cassius,
    To cut the head off and then hack the limbs—
    Like wrath in death and envy afterwards;°
165   For Antony is but a limb of Caesar.
    Let's be sacrificers, but not butchers, Caius.
    We all stand up against the spirit of Caesar,°
    And in the spirit of men there is no blood.
    O that we then could come by° Caesar's spirit,

Analyze Theme *What does Brutus mean by this? How might this sentiment relate to one of the play's themes Explain.*

Vocabulary

commend (kə mend′) *v.* to speak highly of; to praise

132–136 do not stain . . . oath: Do not insult the steadfast virtue of our undertaking or the indomitable courage of our spirits to think that either our cause or our actions require an oath.
138 Is guilty . . . bastardy: is illegitimate.
136–140 every drop . . . from him: Brutus claims that no one of true Roman blood would break a promise.
141 sound him: find out his feelings.

148 no whit: not in the least.
149 gravity: dignity.
150 break with him: reveal our plot to him.

158 means: abilities.
159 improve them: uses them fully.

164 Like wrath . . . afterwards: as if the killings were motivated by anger and malice.

167 the spirit of Caesar: what Caesar represents.

169 come by: get possession of.

170   And not dismember Caesar! But, alas,
    Caesar must bleed for it. And, gentle friends,
    Let's kill him boldly, but not wrathfully;
    Let's carve him as a dish fit for the gods,
    Not hew him as a carcass fit for hounds;
175   And let our hearts, as subtle masters do,
    Stir up their servants° to an act of rage,
    And after seem to chide 'em. This shall make
    Our purpose necessary, and not envious;
    Which so appearing to the common eyes,
180   We shall be call'd purgers, not murderers.
    And for Mark Antony, think not of him;
    For he can do no more than Caesar's arm
    When Caesar's head is off.

CASSIUS.   Yet I fear him,
    For in the ingrafted° love he bears to Caesar—

185 BRUTUS.   Alas, good Cassius, do not think of him.
    If he love Caesar, all that he can do
    Is to himself—take thought and die° for Caesar.
    And that were much he should,° for he is given
    To sports, to wildness, and much company.

190 TREBONIUS.   There is no fear in him;° let him not die,
    For he will live and laugh at this hereafter.

  [*Clock strikes.*]

  BRUTUS.   Peace, count the clock.

  CASSIUS.   The clock hath stricken three.

  TREBONIUS.   'Tis time to part.

  CASSIUS.   But it is doubtful yet
    Whether Caesar will come forth today or no;
195   For he is superstitious grown of late,
    Quite from the main opinion° he held once
    Of fantasy, of dreams, and ceremonies.°
    It may be these apparent prodigies,
    The unaccustom'd terror of this night,
200   And the persuasion of his augurers°
    May hold him from the Capitol today.

  DECIUS.   Never fear that. If he be so resolv'd,
    I can o'ersway him; for he loves to hear

176 servants: hands.

184 ingrafted: deep-rooted.

187 take thought and die: die from grief.
188 that were much he should: It is unlikely that he would do such a thing.

190 no fear in him: nothing to fear from him.

196 Quite from the main opinion: contrary to the strong opinion.
197 ceremonies: omens.

200 augurers: religious officials who interpreted omens to predict future events.

Loyalty and Betrayal *What does Brutus mean in distinguishing between "purgers" and "murderers"? What do you think of this distinction? Explain.*

205 That unicorns may be betray'd with trees,
And bears with glasses, elephants with holes,
Lions with toils, and men with flatterers;°
But when I tell him he hates flatterers
He says he does, being then most flattered.
Let me work;
210 For I can give his humor the true bent,°
And I will bring him to the Capitol.

CASSIUS. Nay, we will all of us be there to fetch him.

BRUTUS. By the eight hour; is that the uttermost?°

CINNA. Be that the uttermost, and fail not then.

215 METELLUS. Caius Ligarius doth bear Caesar hard,°
Who rated° him for speaking well of Pompey.
I wonder none of you have thought of him.

BRUTUS. Now, good Metellus, go along by him.
He loves me well, and I have given him reasons;
220 Send him but hither, and I'll fashion° him.

CASSIUS. The morning comes upon 's; we'll leave you, Brutus.
And, friends, **disperse** yourselves; but all remember
What you have said, and show yourselves true Romans.

BRUTUS. Good gentlemen, look fresh and merrily;
225 Let not our looks put on our purposes,
But bear it as our Roman actors do,
With untir'd spirits and formal constancy.°
And so good morrow to you every one.

[*They exit. BRUTUS remains.*]

Boy! Lucius! Fast asleep? It is no matter,
230 Enjoy the honey-heavy dew of slumber.
Thou hast no figures nor no fantasies,
Which busy care draws in the brains of men;
Therefore thou sleep'st so sound.

[*Enter PORTIA.*]

PORTIA.   Brutus, my lord!

BRUTUS. Portia! what mean you? wherefore rise you now?
235 It is not for your health thus to commit
Your weak condition to the raw cold morning.

203–206 for he loves . . . flatterers: Decius refers to legends that the mythical unicorn could be tricked into charging a tree and getting its horn stuck, and that bears can be lured by mirrors. He also refers to trapping elephants in pits and using nets to catch lions, and tricking men with flattery.
210 give his . . . bent: put him in the right mood.
213 uttermost: latest.

215 bear Caesar hard: strongly resents Caesar.
216 rated: rebuked.

220 fashion: persuade.

224–227 look fresh . . . constancy: Brutus warns the others not to let their serious expressions show their intentions; they should carry out their plot appearing at ease and dignified.

Loyalty and Betrayal *What do these lines suggest about the type of loyalty Caesar expects from his fellow Romans? Explain.*

Vocabulary

disperse (dis purs´) *v.* to break up and send in different directions; to scatter

PORTIA. Nor for yours neither. Y'have ungently,° Brutus,
    Stole from my bed; and yesternight at supper
    You suddenly arose and walk'd about,
240   Musing and sighing, with your arms across;°
    And when I ask'd you what the matter was,
    You star'd upon me with ungentle looks.
    I urg'd you further; then you scratch'd your head,
    And too impatiently stamp'd with your foot.
245   Yet I insisted, yet you answer'd not,
    But with an angry wafter° of your hand
    Gave sign for me to leave you. So I did,
    Fearing to strengthen that impatience
    Which seem'd too much enkindled, and withal°
250   Hoping it was but an effect of humor,°
    Which sometimes hath his° hour with every man.
    It will not let you eat, nor talk, nor sleep,
    And could it work so much upon your shape
    As it hath much prevail'd on your condition,
255   I should not know you Brutus.° Dear my lord,
    Make me acquainted with your cause of grief.

BRUTUS. I am not well in health, and that is all.

PORTIA. Brutus is wise and, were he not in health,
    He would embrace the means to come by it.

260 BRUTUS. Why, so I do. Good Portia, go to bed.

PORTIA. Is Brutus sick, and is it physical°
    To walk unbraced and suck up the humors
    Of the dank morning?° What, is Brutus sick,
    And will he steal out of his wholesome bed,
265   To dare the vile contagion of the night,
    And tempt the rheumy and unpurged air°
    To add unto his sickness? No, my Brutus;
    You have some sick offense° within your mind,
    Which by the right and virtue of my place,°
270   I ought to know of; and upon my knees
    I charm you, by my once commended beauty,
    By all your vows of love, and that great vow
    Which did incorporate and make us one,
    That you unfold to me, yourself, your half,

237 ungently: discourteously.

240 across: folded.

246 wafter: waving.

249 withal: also.
250 but an . . . humor: only a passing mood.
251 his: its.

253–255 And could . . . Brutus: And if it could change your appearance as much as it has changed your state of mind, I would not recognize you as Brutus.

261 physical: healthy.

262–263 humors . . . morning: damp morning mist.
266 tempt the . . . air: risk the damp and impure air. (It was believed that the night air was dangerous to breathe because it wasn't purified by the sun's rays.)
268 sick offense: harmful disorder.

269 by the right . . . place: as your wife.

Loyalty and Betrayal *What effect is thinking about the conspiracy having on Brutus?*

Analyze Theme *Is Portia correct here? Why or why not? How does this relate to a theme of the play?*

Statue of Julius Caesar.
Artist unknown. Museo Laternanense, Vatican Museums, Vatican State.

View the Art What words would you use to describe Caesar in this depiction? Explain.

275 Why you are heavy, and what men tonight
Have had resort to you; for here have been
Some six or seven, who did hide their faces
Even from darkness.

BRUTUS.   Kneel not, gentle
Portia.

PORTIA. I should not need, if you were gentle Brutus.
280 Within the bond of marriage, tell me, Brutus,
Is it excepted I should know no secrets
That appertain to you? Am I your self
But, as it were, in sort or limitation,°
To keep with you at meals, comfort your bed,
285 And talk to you sometimes? Dwell I but in the
    suburbs°
Of your good pleasure? If it be no more,
Portia is Brutus' harlot, not his wife.

BRUTUS. You are my true and honorable wife,
As dear to me as are the ruddy drops
290 That visit my sad heart.

PORTIA. If this were true, then should I know this
    secret.
I grant I am a woman; but withal
A woman that Lord Brutus took to wife.
I grant I am a woman; but withal
295 A woman well reputed, Cato's daughter.°
Think you I am no stronger than my sex,
Being so father'd and so husbanded?
Tell me your counsels, I will not disclose 'em.
I have made strong proof of my constancy,
300 Giving myself a voluntary wound
Here, in the thigh;° can I bear that with patience,
And not my husband's secrets?

BRUTUS.   O ye gods!
Render me worthy of this noble wife! [*Knock.*]

283 in sort or limitation: after a fashion or within limits.

285 suburbs: outskirts.

295 Cato's daughter: Portia's father, Marcus Porcius Cato, killed himself rather than submit to Caesar's rule after Pompey was defeated.

299–301 I have made . . . thigh: Portia reveals that she intentionally cut her thigh before approaching Brutus to show her strong determination.

Monologues, Soliloquies, and Asides *To whom does Brutus make this remark?*

Hark, hark, one knocks. Portia, go in a while,
305   And by and by thy bosom shall partake
The secrets of my heart.
All my engagements I will construe° to thee,
All the charactery of my sad brows.°
Leave me with haste.

[Exit PORTIA.]

                Lucius, who's that knocks?

[Enter LUCIUS and CAIUS LIGARIUS.]

310   LUCIUS. Here is a sick man that would speak with you.

BRUTUS. Caius Ligarius, that Metellus spake of.
    Boy, stand aside. *[Exit LUCIUS.]* Caius Ligarius, how?°

CAIUS. Vouchsafe° good morrow from a feeble tongue.

BRUTUS. O, what a time have you chose out, brave Caius,
315   To wear a kerchief!° Would you were not sick!

CAIUS. I am not sick, if Brutus have in hand
    Any exploit worthy the name of honor.

BRUTUS. Such an exploit have I in hand, Ligarius,
    Had you a healthful ear to hear of it.

320   CAIUS. By all the gods that Romans bow before,
    I here discard my sickness!
                    Soul of Rome!
    Brave son, deriv'd from honorable loins!
    Thou, like an exorcist,° hast conjur'd up
    My mortified° spirit. Now bid me run,
325   And I will strive with things impossible,
    Yea, get the better of them. What's to do?

BRUTUS. A piece of work that will make sick men whole.

CAIUS. But are not some whole that we must make sick?

BRUTUS. That must we also. What it is, my Caius,
330   I shall unfold to thee, as we are going
    To whom it must be done.°

CAIUS.   Set on your foot.°
    And with a heart new-fir'd I follow you,
    To do I know not what; but it sufficeth
    That Brutus leads me on.

Analyze Theme *How has the motif of the sick man reappeared throughout this scene? What impact has this had on the plot and on the theme? Provide evidence from the text to support your answer.*

---

307 **construe:** explain.

308 **charactery of . . . brows:** what is written in my sad brows (the reasons I am sad).

312 **how:** how are you?

313 **Vouchsafe:** Please accept.

315 **kerchief:** a scarf (wrapped around an ill person's head to protect against drafts).

323 **exorcist:** one who summons up spirits.
324 **mortified:** deadened.

330–331 **I shall . . . done:** They are going to Caesar's house to escort him to the Capitol.
331 **Set on your foot:** Go ahead.

[*Thunder.*]

BRUTUS.   Follow me, then. [*They exit.*]

SCENE 2. CAESAR's house. A few hours later.

[*Thunder and lightning. Enter JULIUS CAESAR in his nightgown.*]

CAESAR. Nor heaven nor° earth have been at peace tonight.
Thrice hath Calphurnia in her sleep cried out,
"Help, ho! they murther° Caesar!" Who's within?

[*Enter a SERVANT.*]

SERVANT. My lord?

5   CAESAR. Go bid the priests do present sacrifice,
And bring me their opinions of success.°

SERVANT. I will, my lord. [*Exit.*]

[*Enter CALPHURNIA.*]

CALPHURNIA. What mean you, Caesar? Think you to walk
forth?
You shall not stir out of your house today.

10   CAESAR. Caesar shall forth; the things that threaten'd me
Ne'er look'd but on my back; when they shall see
The face of Caesar, they are vanished.

CALPHURNIA. Caesar, I never stood on ceremonies,°
Yet now they fright me. There is one within,
15   Besides the things that we have heard and seen,
Recounts most horrid sights seen by the watch.°
A lioness hath whelped° in the streets,
And graves have yawn'd,° and yielded up their dead;
Fierce fiery warriors fight upon the clouds
20   In ranks and squadrons and right form of war,°
Which drizzled blood upon the Capitol;
The noise of battle hurtled in the air;
Horses did neigh, and dying men did groan,
And ghosts did shriek and squeal about the streets.
25   O Caesar, these things are beyond all use,°
And I do fear them.

CAESAR.   What can be avoided
Whose end is purpos'd by the mighty gods?

1 Nor . . . nor: neither . . . nor.

3 murther: murder.

5–6 Go bid . . . success: Tell the priests to make a sacrifice immediately, and bring me their interpretations of the results.

13 stood on ceremonies: believed in omens.

16 watch: night watchmen.

17 whelped: given birth.

18 yawn'd: opened.

20 right form of war: proper military formation.

25 use: normal experience.

Analyze Theme *Describe some images in Calphurnia's lines. How are these part of a larger motif? How do they relate to the play's theme? Use evidence from the text to support your answer.*

Yet Caesar shall go forth; for these predictions
Are to the world in general as to Caesar.°

30   CALPHURNIA.   When beggars die, there are no comets seen;
The heavens themselves blaze forth the death of princes.

CAESAR.   Cowards die many times before their deaths,
The valiant never taste of death but once.
Of all the wonders that I yet have heard,
35   It seems to me most strange that men should fear,
Seeing that death, a necessary end,
Will come when it will come.

[*Enter a* SERVANT.]

                                 What say the augurers?

SERVANT.   They would not have you to stir forth today.
Plucking the entrails of an offering forth,
40   They could not find a heart within the beast.°

CAESAR.   The gods do this in shame of° cowardice;
Caesar should be a beast without a heart
If he should stay at home today for fear.
No, Caesar shall not; Danger knows full well
45   That Caesar is more dangerous than he.
We [are] two lions litter'd in one day,°
And I the elder and more terrible;
And Caesar shall go forth.

CALPHURNIA.   Alas, my lord,
Your wisdom is consum'd in confidence.
50   Do not go forth today; call it my fear
That keeps you in the house and not your own.
We'll send Mark Antony to the Senate House,
And he shall say you are not well today.
Let me, upon my knee, prevail in this.

55   CAESAR.   Mark Antony shall say I am not well,

---

29 **Are to the . . . Caesar:** apply to everyone as well as to me.

39–40 **Plucking the . . . beast:** Augurers would examine the inner organs of a sacrificed animal to predict the future. The absence of a heart would be a strange and unfavorable omen.
41 **in shame of:** to shame.

44–46 **Danger knows . . . day:** Caesar uses two figures of speech, first personifying danger and then using the metaphor that he and danger are lions born on the same day.

Analyze Theme *What motif appears in these lines? Analyze how it impacts the plot and theme. Provide evidence from the text to support your response.*

Caesar and his wife Calpurnia, 1703–1767. Fabio Canal. Palazzo Mangilli-Guion, Venice.

View the Art Is this artwork effective at portraying Calphurnia's character and emotions? Explain.

Electrotype copies of two lions from Rosenborg Castle, 17th century. Elkington & Co.
Electroplated copper, silvered, 98 x 165 x 64 cm and 98 x 165 x 60 cm. Victoria and Albert Museum, London.

And for thy humor,° I will stay at home.

[*Enter* DECIUS.]

Here's Decius Brutus, he shall tell them so.

DECIUS. Caesar, all hail! good morrow, worthy Caesar,
I come to fetch you to the Senate House.

60 CAESAR. And you are come in very happy time°
To bear my greeting to the senators,
And tell them that I will not come today.
Cannot, is false; and that I dare not, falser;
I will not come today. Tell them so, Decius.

65 CALPHURNIA. Say he is sick.

CAESAR.   Shall Caesar send a lie?
Have I in conquest stretch'd mine arm so far
To be afeard to tell graybeards the truth?°
Decius, go tell them Caesar will not come.

DECIUS. Most mighty Caesar, let me know some cause,
70 Lest I be laugh'd at when I tell them so.

CAESAR. The cause is in my will, I will not come:
That is enough to satisfy the Senate.
But for your private satisfaction,
Because I love you, I will let you know.
75 Calphurnia here, my wife, stays° me at home:
She dreamt tonight° she saw my statue,
Which, like a fountain with an hundred spouts,

56 **humor:** whim.

60 **in very happy time:** at the right moment.

66–67 **Have I . . . truth:** Have I made such conquests to be afraid to tell old men the truth?

75 **stays:** keeps.
76 **tonight:** last night.

Loyalty and Betrayal *Does Decius seem sincere to you? Why or why not?*

Did run pure blood, and many lusty Romans
Came smiling and did bathe their hands in it.

80   And these does she apply for° warnings and portents
And evils imminent, and on her knee
Hath begg'd that I will stay at home today.

DECIUS. This dream is all amiss interpreted,
It was a vision fair and fortunate.

85   Your statue spouting blood in many pipes,
In which so many smiling Romans bath'd,
Signifies that from you great Rome shall suck
Reviving blood, and that great men shall press
For tinctures, stains, relics, and cognizance.°

90   This by Calphurnia's dream is signified.

CAESAR. And this way have you well expounded it.

DECIUS. I have, when you have heard what I can say;
And know it now: the Senate have concluded
To give this day a crown to mighty Caesar.

95   If you shall send them word you will not come,
Their minds may change. Besides, it were a mock
Apt to be render'd,° for someone to say,
"Break up the Senate till another time,
When Caesar's wife shall meet with better dreams."

100   If Caesar hide himself, shall they not whisper,
"Lo, Caesar is afraid"?

80 apply for: interpret as.

**85–89 Your statue . . .
cognizance: Tinctures** are features
added to a coat of arms; **relics** are
the remains of saints; **cognizance** is
a mark identifying one as a lord's
follower. Decius interprets
Calphurnia's dream as a sign of
Caesar's prestige, with great men
coming to him to show their political
loyalty and reverence.

96–97 it were a . . . render'd: it
would be a joke likely to be made.

Loyalty and Betrayal *What does Decius's response here suggest
about how the conspirators will behave as the plot unfolds?*

*Grave relief of an Athenian
married couple,* 330 A.D.
Artist unknown. Marble attic
relief. Antikensammlung,
Staatliche Museen zu Berlin.

View the Art How would
you describe the scene
featured in this relief?
Which characters in *Julius
Caesar* would best fit in
your description? Why?

Pardon me, Caesar, for my dear dear love
To your proceeding° bids me tell you this;
And reason to my love is liable.°

105 CAESAR. How foolish do your fears seem now, Calphurnia!
I am ashamed I did yield to them.
Give me my robe, for I will go.

[Enter BRUTUS, LIGARIUS, METELLUS CIMBER, CASCA, TREBONIUS,
CINNA, and PUBLIUS.]

And look where Publius is come to fetch me.

PUBLIUS. Good morrow, Caesar.

CAESAR.   Welcome, Publius.
110   What, Brutus, are you stirr'd so early too?
Good morrow, Casca. Caius Ligarius,
Caesar was ne'er so much your enemy°
As that same ague° which hath made you lean.
What is't o'clock?

BRUTUS.   Caesar, 'tis strucken eight.

115 CAESAR. I thank you for your pains and courtesy.

[Enter ANTONY.]

See, Antony, that revels long a-nights,°
Is notwithstanding up. Good morrow, Antony.

ANTONY. So to most noble Caesar.

CAESAR.   Bid them prepare within;
I am to blame to be thus waited for.
120   Now, Cinna; now, Metellus; what, Trebonius,
I have an hour's talk in store for you;
Remember that you call on me today;
Be near me, that I may remember you.

TREBONIUS. Caesar, I will [Aside.] and so near will I be,
125   That your best friends shall wish I had been further.

CAESAR. Good friends, go in, and taste some wine with me,
And we, like friends, will straightway go together.

BRUTUS. [Aside.] That every like is not the same, O Caesar,
The heart of Brutus earns to think upon.°

[They exit.]

Analyze Theme *Does Caesar seem easily persuaded? Why or why not? How does this relate to a theme of the play?*

Monologues, Soliloquies, and Asides *What attitude toward the plot to murder Caesar does Brutus reveal here?*

102–103 my dear . . .
proceeding: my very deep desire for your advancement.
104 liable: subservient. Decius says that his love for Caesar forces him to say this, even though he may be overstepping himself.

112 your enemy: Caesar had recently pardoned Ligarius for his support of Pompey during the civil war.
113 ague: sickness.

116 that revels long a-nights: who carouses late into the night.

128–129 That every . . . upon: Brutus grieves to think that not everyone who appears to be a friend is a real friend.

SCENE 3. A street near the Capitol. Shortly afterward.

[*Enter* ARTEMIDORUS *(reading a paper).*]

ARTEMIDORUS. "Caesar, beware of Brutus; take heed of Cassius;
come not near Casca; have an eye to Cinna; trust not
Trebonius; mark well Metellus Cimber; Decius Brutus loves
thee not; thou hast wrong'd Caius Ligarius. There is but
5 one mind in all these men, and it is bent against Caesar. If
thou beest not immortal, look about you; security gives
way to conspiracy.° The mighty gods defend thee!
    Thy lover,° Artemidorus."
Here will I stand till Caesar pass along,
10 And as a suitor° will I give him this.
My heart laments that virtue cannot live
Out of the teeth of emulation.°
If thou read this, O Caesar, thou mayest live;
If not, the Fates with traitors do contrive.° [*Exit.*]

6–7 security gives . . . conspiracy: overconfidence opens the way for enemy plots.
8 lover: devoted friend.
10 suitor: person presenting a special request to a ruler.
12 Out of . . . emulation: beyond the reach of envy.
14 contrive: conspire.

SCENE 4. Another Roman street. Immediately after.

[*Enter* PORTIA *and* LUCIUS.]

PORTIA. I prithee, boy, run to the Senate House;
Stay not to answer me, but get thee gone.
Why dost thou stay?

LUCIUS.   To know my errand, madam.

PORTIA. I would have had thee there and here again
5 Ere I can tell thee what thou shouldst do there—°
O constancy,° be strong upon my side;
Set a huge mountain 'tween my heart and tongue!
I have a man's mind, but a woman's might.
How hard it is for women to keep counsel!—°
10 Art thou here yet?

LUCIUS.   Madam, what should I do?
Run to the Capitol, and nothing else?
And so return to you, and nothing else?

PORTIA. Yes, bring me word, boy, if thy lord look well,
For he went sickly forth; and take good note
15 What Caesar doth, what suitors press to him.
Hark, boy, what noise is that?

LUCIUS. I hear none, madam.

PORTIA.   Prithee, listen well.

4–5 I would . . . do there: You could go there and return here before I could explain what you should do there.
6 constancy: firmness.
9 counsel: a secret.

Analyze Theme *How well does this line articulate one theme of the play? Explain.*

I heard a bustling rumor, like a fray,°
And the wind brings it from the Capitol.

20 LUCIUS. Sooth,° madam, I hear nothing.

[*Enter the* SOOTHSAYER.]

PORTIA. Come hither, fellow; which way hast thou been?

SOOTHSAYER. At mine own house, good lady.

PORTIA. What is't a'clock?

SOOTHSAYER.   About the ninth hour, lady.

PORTIA. Is Caesar yet gone to the Capitol?

25 SOOTHSAYER. Madam, not yet; I go to take my stand,
To see him pass on to the Capitol.

PORTIA. Thou hast some suit to Caesar, hast thou not?

SOOTHSAYER. That I have, lady, if it will please Caesar
To be so good to Caesar as to hear me:
30   I shall beseech him to befriend himself.

PORTIA. Why, know'st thou any harm's intended towards him?

SOOTHSAYER. None that I know will be, much that I fear
may chance.
Good morrow to you. Here the street is narrow;
The throng that follows Caesar at the heels,
35   Of senators, of praetors, common suitors,
Will crowd a feeble man almost to death.
I'll get me to a place more void,° and there
Speak to great Caesar as he comes along.

[*Exit.*]

PORTIA. I must go in. Ay me! How weak a thing
40   The heart of woman is! O Brutus,
The heavens speed thee in thine enterprise!
Sure, the boy heard me—Brutus hath a suit
That Caesar will not grant.—°O, I grow faint.—
Run, Lucius, and commend me to my lord,°
45   Say I am merry. Come to me again,
And bring me word what he doth say to thee.

[*They exit separately.*]

18 bustling . . . fray: noise of some activity such as a fight.

20 Sooth: truly.

37 void: empty.
42–43 Brutus hath . . . grant: Portia makes up this excuse about Brutus's petition to explain her nervousness to Lucius.
44 commend me to my lord: send my regards to my husband.

Portrait of a woman in encaustic on limewood with added gold leaf,
c. 160–170 A.D., Roman period, Egypt. 44.3 x 20.4 cm. The British Museum, London.

View the Art What qualities do you think this woman possesses? Which of these qualities do you think Portia or Calphurnia shares? Explain.

After You Read

Respond and Think Critically

1. **Connect to Personal Experience** Which character are you most sympathetic toward? Why?

2. **Explain Motivation** Why does Brutus want to spare Antony's life? What opinion does Brutus seem to have of Antony? Explain. ⟵OER

3. **Make Inferences About Characters** According to Brutus, why must Caesar be killed? What can you infer about Cassius, Casca, and Brutus as they make their plans?

4. **Analyze Character** Why does Portia send her servant to the Capitol? What impression do you have of Portia and her relationship with Brutus? Support your response with text evidence.

5. **Evaluate Mood** Suspense is the feeling of anticipation, even dread, which you experience as you read. Does Shakespeare succeed in creating a suspenseful mood in Act 2? Explain. Provide evidence from the text to support your answer.

6. **Big Idea** **Draw Conclusions About Motivation** How do Brutus's intentions relate to the ideas of loyalty and betrayal? Do you accept Brutus's justification for killing Caesar? Why or why not? Support your response with text evidence.

Literary Element Monologues, Soliloquies, and Asides

A **soliloquy** is a monologue delivered while a character is alone onstage. An **aside** is a comment heard only by the audience.

7. **Summarize Soliloquy** What does Brutus reveal in his soliloquy at the beginning of Act 2?

8. **Interpret Asides** What does Trebonius mean in Scene 2, lines 124–125? Why are these lines written as asides?

Reading Strategy Analyze Theme

Review your chart on page 713 and answer the following questions.

9. Choose one motif from your chart. What does it mean? How does it affect the plot and theme of Act 2? Support your answer.

10. What do you think is the main theme in Act 2? Do you think this theme will carry throughout the rest of the play? Explain.

LOG ON ▶ **Literature** Online

Selection Resources For Selection Quizzes, eFlashcards, and Reading-Writing Connection activities, go to glencoe.com and enter QuickPass code GL57805u4.

Vocabulary Practice

Practice with Usage Respond to these statements to help you explore the meanings of the boldfaced vocabulary words from the play.

1. Identify an **interim** that you have experienced.

2. Name two things for which you might **commend** a parent.

3. Tell what happens when people **disperse** after a gathering.

Writing

Write a Summary Write a summary of the plot of Act 2. Your summary should include the main events and important exchanges between the characters. Use transition words to highlight cause-and-effect relationships. For help with summarizing, see page 35.

Before You Read

The Tragedy of Julius Caesar, Act 3

Build Background

The Greek historian Plutarch recorded that Caesar attempted to defend himself against the assassins, "but when he saw Brutus with his sword drawn in his hand, then he pulled his gown over his head, and made no more resistance. . . ."

Set Purposes for Reading

Literary Element Plot

Plot is the sequence of events in a work. Conflicts, characters, and setting are introduced in the **exposition. Rising action** builds suspense and leads to the **climax,** or turning point. The **falling action** and **resolution** reveal the results of the climax. As you read, ask yourself, What stages of the plot can I identify?

Reading Strategy Analyze Figurative Language

Figurative language uses **figures of speech,** or language that is not literally true but that expresses some truth beyond the literal level. A **simile** compares two seemingly unlike things using the words *like* or *as*. A **metaphor** also compares two things, but without using *like* or *as*. **Personification** gives human characteristics to a nonhuman thing. **Hyperbole** uses exaggeration to express a strong emotion. Figurative language can be specific to the historical and cultural setting of a work. For example, a character in a modern work might compare a swift runner to a speeding train, but a character in *Julius Caesar* would compare the runner to the swift Roman god Mercury. As you read, ask yourself, What figures of speech can I identify?

Tip: Chart Memorable Language Use a chart to record striking figures of speech and your ideas about how they relate to the cultural or historical setting.

Figurative Language	Type of Figures of Speech	How It Relates to Setting
"But I am constant as the northern star" p. 737	simile	People at the time thought that the North star was stationary and that the other stars moved around it.

TEKS

For pages 734–756

10.2.C Relate the figurative language of a literary work to its historical and cultural setting.

Vocabulary

thrive (thrīv) *v.* to be successful; to grow well; p. 735 *My sister will thrive at college.*

misgiving (mis giv′ing) *n.* a feeling of doubt; apprehension; p. 740 *My mom had one minor misgiving about the camping trip, but she let me go anyway.*

malice (mal′is) *n.* a desire to hurt another person; p. 741 *My cousin sometimes acts with malice.*

vanquish (vang′kwish) *v.* to defeat; to overcome; p. 751 *The Greeks planned to vanquish the Trojans through a surprise attack on their city.*

orator (ôr′ə tər) *n.* a person skilled in public speaking; p. 752 *Martin Luther King Jr. was a famous and admired orator.*

ACT 3

SCENE 1.   The Capitol in Rome. The ides of March.

[*Flourish. Enter* CAESAR, BRUTUS, CASSIUS, CASCA, DECIUS, METELLUS, TREBONIUS, CINNA, ANTONY, PUBLIUS, POPILIUS, LEPIDUS, ARTEMIDORUS, *and the* SOOTHSAYER.]

 CAESAR. The ides of March are come.

 SOOTHSAYER. Ay, Caesar, but not gone.

 ARTEMIDORUS. Hail, Caesar! Read this schedule.°

 DECIUS. Trebonius doth desire you to o'er-read,
5 (At your best leisure) this his humble suit.

 ARTEMIDORUS. O Caesar, read mine first; for mine's a suit
  That touches Caesar nearer. Read it, great Caesar.

 CAESAR. What touches us ourself shall be last serv'd.

 ARTEMIDORUS. Delay not, Caesar, read it instantly.

10 CAESAR. What, is the fellow mad?

 PUBLIUS.   Sirrah,° give place.

 CASSIUS. What, urge you your petitions in the street?
  Come to the Capitol.

[CAESAR *enters the Capitol, the rest following.*]

 POPILIUS. I wish your enterprise today may **thrive**.

 CASSIUS. What enterprise, Popilius?

 POPILIUS.   Fare you well. [*Leaves*
   him and joins CAESAR.]

15 BRUTUS. What said Popilius Lena?

 CASSIUS. He wish'd today our enterprise might thrive.
  I fear our purpose is discovered.

3 schedule: document.

10 Sirrah: an insulting form of address to an inferior.

Loyalty and Betrayal *From this remark, what can you infer about Caesar's character?*

Plot *What might happen if the plotters are discovered?*

Vocabulary

thrive (thrīv) *v.* to be successful; to grow well

BRUTUS. Look how he makes° to Caesar; mark him.

CASSIUS. Casca, be sudden, for we fear prevention.°

20   Brutus, what shall be done? If this be known,
Cassius or Caesar never shall turn back,°
For I will slay myself.

BRUTUS.   Cassius, be constant;°
Popilius Lena speaks not of our purposes,
For look he smiles, and Caesar doth not change.

25   **CASSIUS.** Trebonius knows his time; for look you, Brutus,
He draws Mark Antony out of the way.

[*ANTONY and TREBONIUS exit.*]

DECIUS. Where is Metellus Cimber? Let him go
And presently prefer° his suit to Caesar.

BRUTUS. He is address'd;° press near and second him.

30   **CINNA.** Casca, you are the first that rears your hand.

CAESAR. Are we all ready? What is now amiss
That Caesar and his Senate must redress?

METELLUS. Most high, most mighty, and most puissant° Caesar,
Metellus Cimber throws before thy seat

35   An humble heart. [*Kneeling.*]

CAESAR.   I must prevent thee, Cimber.
These couchings and these lowly courtesies
Might fire the blood of ordinary men,
And turn preordinance and first decree
Into the [law] of children. Be not fond

40   To think that Caesar bears such rebel blood
That will be thaw'd from the true quality
With that which melteth fools—I mean sweet words,
Low-crooked curtsies, and base spaniel fawning.°
Thy brother by decree is banished;

45   If thou dost bend, and pray, and fawn for him,
I spurn thee like a cur° out of my way.
Know, Caesar doth not wrong, nor without cause
Will he be satisfied.°

METELLUS. Is there no voice more worthy than my own,

50   To sound more sweetly in great Caesar's ear
For the repealing of my banish'd brother?

18 makes: makes his way.

19 be sudden . . . prevention: be quick, for we fear that we will be stopped.

21 turn back: return alive.

22 constant: calm.

28 presently prefer: immediately present.

29 address'd: ready.

33 puissant: powerful.

36–43 These couchings . . . fawning: This kneeling and humble behavior might influence ordinary men and turn laws and decisions that have been firmly established into the whims of children. But don't be foolish enough to think that Caesar's emotions are so out of control that he will be swayed from the proper course with compliments, bowing, and fawning like a dog.

46 spurn thee . . . cur: kick you like a dog.

47–48 Know . . . satisfied: Caesar is not unjust, nor will he grant a pardon without good reason.

Analyze Figurative Language *What does Caesar mean when he says that Metellus's compliments are "base spaniel fawning"?*

The Death of Julius Caesar, 1793. Vincenzo Camuccini. Galleria d'Arte Moderna, Rome.

View the Art What emotions do you see expressed in this painting? Do you think the same emotions are expressed in this scene in the play? Explain.

BRUTUS. I kiss thy hand, but not in flattery, Caesar;
    Desiring thee that Publius Cimber may
    Have an immediate freedom of repeal.°

55 CAESAR. What, Brutus?

CASSIUS.   Pardon, Caesar! Caesar,
    pardon!
    As low as to thy foot doth Cassius fall,
    To beg enfranchisement° for Publius Cimber.

CAESAR. I could be well mov'd, if I were as you;
    If I could pray to move, prayers would move me;
60   But I am constant as the northern star,
    Of whose true-fix'd and resting quality
    There is no fellow in the firmament.°
    The skies are painted with unnumb'red sparks,
    They are all fire and every one doth shine;
65   But there's but one in all doth hold his place.
    So in the world: 'tis furnish'd well with men,
    And men are flesh and blood, and apprehensive;°
    Yet in the number I do know but one
    That unassailable holds on his rank,

54 freedom of repeal: permission to be recalled from exile.

57 enfranchisement: restoration of his rights as a citizen.

62 no fellow in the firmament: no equal in the heavens. (Because the North Star appears directly above the North Pole, it seems to be stationary; the other stars seem to change position as the earth rotates.)

67 apprehensive: capable of reason.

Loyalty and Betrayal *In your opinion, why is Cassius behaving this way?*

Analyze Figurative Language *What is Caesar suggesting by comparing himself to the North Star?*

70   Unshak'd of motion; and that I am he,
      Let me a little show it, even in this—
      That I was constant° Cimber should be banish'd,
      And constant do remain to keep him so.

CINNA.   O Caesar—

CAESAR.   Hence! Wilt thou lift up Olympus?°

75   DECIUS.   Great Caesar—

CAESAR.   Doth not Brutus bootless° kneel?

CASCA.   Speak hands for me!

[*They stab CAESAR.*]

CAESAR.   Et tu, Brute?°—Then fall Caesar. [*Dies.*]

CINNA.   Liberty! Freedom! Tyranny is dead!
      Run hence, proclaim, cry it about the streets.

80   CASSIUS.   Some to the common pulpits,° and cry out
      "Liberty, freedom, and enfranchisement!"

BRUTUS.   People, and senators, be not affrighted.
      Fly not; stand still; ambition's debt is paid.°

CASCA.   Go to the pulpit, Brutus.

DECIUS.   And Cassius too.

85   BRUTUS.   Where's Publius?

CINNA.   Here, quite confounded with this mutiny.°

METELLUS.   Stand fast together, lest some friend of Caesar's
      Should chance—

BRUTUS.   Talk not of standing. Publius, good cheer,
90   There is no harm intended to your person,
      Nor to no Roman else. So tell them, Publius.

CASSIUS.   And leave us, Publius, lest that the people,
      Rushing on us should do your age some mischief.

BRUTUS.   Do so; and let no man abide° this deed,
95   But we the doers.

[*All but the CONSPIRATORS exit. Enter TREBONIUS.*]

CASSIUS.   Where is Antony?

TREBONIUS.   Fled to his house amaz'd.°

---

72 constant: determined.

74 lift up Olympus: try to do the impossible. (Olympus is a mountain in Greece; in classical mythology, it was the home of the gods.)
75 bootless: in vain.

77 *Et tu, Brute?:* Latin for, "And you, Brutus?" (He is shocked that even Brutus would betray him.)

80 pulpits: platforms for public speaking.

83 ambition's debt is paid: Ambition received what was due to it.

86 confounded with this mutiny: confused by this uproar.

94 abide: pay the penalty for.

96 amaz'd: stunned.

Loyalty and Betrayal *What do Caesar's dying words reveal?*

Men, wives, and children stare, cry out and run,
As° it were doomsday.

BRUTUS.   Fates,° we will know your pleasures.
That we shall die, we know, 'tis but the time,
100   And drawing days out, that men stand upon.°

CASCA. Why, he that cuts off twenty years of life
Cuts off so many years of fearing death.

BRUTUS. Grant that, and then is death a benefit.
So are we Caesar's friends, that have abridg'd
105   His time of fearing death. Stoop, Romans, stoop,
And let us bathe our hands in Caesar's blood
Up to the elbows, and besmear our swords.
Then walk we forth, even to the marketplace,
And waving our red weapons o'er our heads,
110   Let's all cry "Peace, freedom, and liberty!"

CASSIUS. Stoop then, and wash. How many ages hence
Shall this our lofty scene be acted over
In states unborn and accents yet unknown!

BRUTUS. How many times shall Caesar bleed in sport,°
115   That now on Pompey's basis° [lies] along
No worthier than the dust!

CASSIUS.   So oft as that shall be,
So often shall the knot of us be call'd
The men that gave their country liberty.

DECIUS. What, shall we forth?

CASSIUS.   Ay, every man away.
120   Brutus shall lead, and we will grace his heels
With the most boldest and best hearts of Rome.

[Enter a SERVANT.]

BRUTUS. Soft, who comes here? A friend of Antony's.

SERVANT. Thus, Brutus, did my master bid me kneel;
Thus did Mark Antony bid me fall down;
125   And, being prostrate, thus he bade me say;
Brutus is noble, wise, valiant, and honest;°
Caesar was mighty, bold, royal, and loving.
Say, I love Brutus, and I honor him;
Say, I fear'd Caesar, honor'd him, and lov'd him.

The Three Fates, detail from the Month of March (upper portion).
Francesco del Cossa (1435–1478). Fresco painting. Palazzo Schifanoia, Ferrara, Italy.

98 As: as if.
98 Fates: in classical mythology, three goddesses who determined human destiny.
99–100 'tis but . . . upon: It is only the time of death and prolonging of life that men care about.
114 in sport: for entertainment. (These prophecies—of reenacting Caesar's assassination in countries not yet founded and in languages not yet known—are fulfilled by the performance of Shakespeare's play.)
115 Pompey's basis: the base of Pompey's statue.

126 honest: honorable.

Plot *What inference can you make about what plot stage has been reached? Provide evidence from the text to support your inference.*

Loyalty and Betrayal *What does this remark suggest about how Brutus is feeling about his betrayal?*

130   If Brutus will vouchsafe° that Antony
      May safely come to him, and be resolv'd°
      How Caesar hath deserv'd to lie in death,
      Mark Antony shall not love Caesar dead
      So well as Brutus living; but will follow
135   The fortunes and affairs of noble Brutus
      Thorough the hazards of this untrod state°
      With all true faith. So says my master Antony.

     BRUTUS.   Thy master is a wise and valiant Roman;
      I never thought him worse.
140   Tell him, so please him come unto this place,
      He shall be satisfied and, by my honor,
      Depart untouch'd.

     SERVANT.   I'll fetch him presently.° [*Exit* SERVANT.]

     BRUTUS.   I know that we shall have him well to friend.°

     CASSIUS.   I wish we may; but yet have I a mind
145   That fears him much; and my **misgiving** still
      Falls shrewdly to the purpose.°

   [*Enter* ANTONY.]

     BRUTUS.   But here comes Antony. Welcome, Mark Antony.

     ANTONY.   O mighty Caesar! dost thou lie so low?
      Are all thy conquests, glories, triumphs, spoils,
150   Shrunk to this little measure? Fare thee well.
      I know not, gentlemen, what you intend,
      Who else must be let blood,° who else is rank.°
      If I myself, there is no hour so fit
      As Caesar's death's hour, nor no instrument
155   Of half that worth as those your swords, made rich
      With the most noble blood of all this world.
      I do beseech ye, if you bear me hard,°
      Now, whilst your purpled° hands do reek and smoke,
      Fulfill your pleasure. Live a thousand years,
160   I shall not find myself so apt° to die;

---

130 vouchsafe: allow.
131 be resolv'd: receive a satisfactory explanation.

136 Thorough . . . state: through all the dangers of this new and uncertain state of affairs.

142 presently: immediately.
143 well to friend: as a good friend.

145–146 my misgiving . . . purpose: My suspicions always turn out to be close to the truth.

152 let blood: killed. **rank:** swollen with disease. In Antony's metaphor, political corruption is like a disease that must be treated by drawing blood from the patient.

157 bear me hard: have a grudge against me.
158 purpled: blood-stained.

160 apt: ready.

Plot *What position does Mark Antony take with regard to the killing of Caesar? Will this be important to the plot? Explain.*

Analyze Figurative Language *What does Mark Antony mean when he says he would not find himself so apt to die if he "lived a thousand years"? What type of figurative language is this? Explain.*

Vocabulary

misgiving (mis giv´ing) *n.* a feeling of doubt; apprehension

No place will please me so, no mean of death,°
As here by Caesar, and by you cut off,
The choice and master spirits of this age.

BRUTUS. O Antony! beg not your death of us.
165   Though now we must appear bloody and cruel,
As by our hands and this our present act
You see we do, yet see you but our hands
And this the bleeding business they have done.
Our hearts you see not, they are pitiful;°
170   And pity to the general wrong of Rome—
As fire drives out fire, so pity pity—
Hath done this deed on Caesar.° For your part,
To you our swords have leaden° points, Mark Antony;
Our arms in strength of **malice**,° and our hearts
175   Of brothers' temper, do receive you in
With all kind love, good thoughts, and reverence.

CASSIUS. Your voice shall be as strong as any man's
In the disposing of new dignities.°

BRUTUS. Only be patient till we have appeas'd
180   The multitude, beside themselves with fear,
And then we will deliver you the cause°
Why I, that did love Caesar when I struck him,
Have thus proceeded.

ANTONY.   I doubt not of your wisdom.
Let each man render me his bloody hand.
185   First, Marcus Brutus, will I shake with you;
Next, Caius Cassius, do I take your hand;
Now, Decius Brutus, yours; now yours, Metellus;
Yours, Cinna; and, my valiant Casca, yours;
Though last, not least in love, yours, good Trebonius.
190   Gentlemen all—alas, what shall I say?
My credit° now stands on such slippery ground
That one of two bad ways you must conceit° me,
Either a coward or a flatterer.
That I did love thee, Caesar, O, 'tis true;
195   If then thy spirit look upon us now,
Shall it not grieve thee dearer than thy death,
To see thy Antony making his peace,

161 **mean of death:** way of dying.

169 **pitiful:** full of pity.
170–172 **And pity . . . Caesar:**
Brutus says that just as one fire can extinguish another, their pity for Rome overcame their pity for Caesar.
173 **leaden:** blunt.
174 **Our arms . . . malice:** our arms seemingly full of malice (because still blood-stained).

177–178 **Your voice . . . dignities:** You will have equal say in deciding who will hold political office.

181 **deliver you the cause:** explain.

191 **credit:** reputation (because he was Caesar's friend).
192 **conceit:** judge; consider.

Loyalty and Betrayal *Why is Brutus so eager to reassure Antony?*

Vocabulary

malice (mal´is) *n.* a desire to hurt another person

Shaking the bloody fingers of thy foes,
Most noble, in the presence of thy corse?°
200 Had I as many eyes as thou hast wounds,
Weeping as fast as they stream forth thy blood,
It would become me better than to close°
In terms of friendship with thine enemies.
Pardon me, Julius! Here wast thou bay'd,° brave hart,°
205 Here didst thou fall, and here thy hunters stand,
Sign'd in thy spoil,° and crimson'd in thy lethe.°
O world! thou wast the forest to this hart,

199 corse: corpse.

202 close: come to an agreement.

204 bay'd: cornered like a hunted animal. **hart:** male deer. Antony plays on the words *hart* and *heart* later in this speech.
206 Sign'd in thy spoil: marked with your slaughter. **lethe:** bloodstream. (In classical mythology, Lethe was a river in Hades, the underworld.)

Bedroom From the Villa of P. Fannius Sinistor (detail of west wall). 1st century B.C., Roman. Fresco on lime plaster, height: (average) 8 ft. The Metropolitan Museum of Art, New York. Rogers Fund, 1903.

View the Art Do the details in this fresco reinforce or alter the images you have developed of Brutus's and Caesar's homes? Explain.

And this indeed, O world, the heart of thee.
How like a deer, strooken by many princes,
210 Dost thou here lie!

CASSIUS. Mark Antony—

ANTONY.   Pardon me, Caius Cassius!
The enemies of Caesar shall say this:
Then, in a friend, it is cold modesty.°

CASSIUS. I blame you not for praising Caesar so,
215 But what compact mean you to have with us?
Will you be prick'd° in number of our friends,
Or shall we on,° and not depend on you?

ANTONY. Therefore I took your hands, but was indeed
Sway'd from the point by looking down on Caesar.
220 Friends am I with you all, and love you all,
Upon this hope, that you shall give me reasons
Why, and wherein,° Caesar was dangerous.

BRUTUS. Or else were this a savage spectacle.
Our reasons are so full of good regard°
225 That were you, Antony, the son of Caesar,
You should be satisfied.

ANTONY.   That's all I seek;
And am moreover suitor° that I may
Produce° his body to the marketplace,
And in the pulpit, as becomes a friend,
230 Speak in the order° of his funeral.

BRUTUS. You shall, Mark Antony.

CASSIUS.   Brutus, a word with you.
[Aside to BRUTUS.] You know not what you
    do. Do not consent
That Antony speak in his funeral.
Know you how much the people maybe mov'd
235 By that which he will utter?

BRUTUS.   By your pardon—
I will myself into the pulpit first,
And show the reason of our Caesar's death.
What Antony shall speak, I will protest°

---

213 modesty: restraint.

216 prick'd: marked down; counted.
217 on: proceed.

222 wherein: in what way.

224 good regard: sound considerations.

227 am moreover suitor: furthermore I ask.
228 Produce: bring forth.

230 order: ceremony.

238 protest: declare.

Analyze Figurative Language *To what things does Antony compare Caesar? How do these comparisons help to characterize Caesar's death?*

Plot *What is Cassius's objection to Antony's speaking at Caesar's funeral?*

He speaks by leave and by permission;
240 And that we are contented Caesar shall
Have all true rites and lawful ceremonies.
It shall advantage° more than do us wrong.

CASSIUS. I know not what may fall,° I like it not.

BRUTUS. Mark Antony, here, take you Caesar's body.
245 You shall not in your funeral speech blame us,
But speak all good you can devise of Caesar,
And say you do't by our permission;
Else shall you not have any hand at all
About his funeral. And you shall speak
250 In the same pulpit whereto I am going,
After my speech is ended.

ANTONY.   Be it so;
I do desire no more.

BRUTUS. Prepare the body then, and follow us.

[*They exit.* ANTONY *remains.*]

ANTONY. O pardon me, thou bleeding piece of earth,
255 That I am meek and gentle with these butchers!
Thou art the ruins of the noblest man
That ever lived in the tide of times.°
Woe to the hand that shed this costly blood!
Over thy wounds now do I prophesy
260 (Which like dumb mouths do ope their ruby lips
To beg the voice and utterance of my tongue)
A curse shall light° upon the limbs of men;
Domestic fury and fierce civil strife
Shall cumber° all the parts of Italy;
265 Blood and destruction shall be so in use,°
And dreadful objects so familiar,
That mothers shall but smile when they behold
Their infants quartered° with the hands of war;
All pity chok'd with custom of fell deeds;°
270 And Caesar's spirit, ranging° for revenge,
With Ate° by his side come hot from hell,
Shall in these confines with a monarch's voice
Cry "Havoc!"° and let slip the dogs of war,

The Fatal Hour: Fantastic Subject II, 19th century.
Alexandre Evariste Fragonard. Oil on canvas, 56 x
45.7 cm. Private collection.

View the Art What mood does this painting
express? Does it correspond to the mood in the play
at this point? Explain.

242 **advantage:** benefit.
243 **fall:** happen.
257 **the tide of times:** all of
history.

262 **light:** fall.

264 **cumber:** burden; harass.
265 **in use:** common.

268 **quartered:** cut to pieces.
269 **custom of fell deeds:**
familiarity with cruel deeds.
270 **ranging:** roving (like an animal
in search of prey).
271 **Ate:** goddess of vengeance
and strife.
273 **Havoc:** a battle cry to kill
without mercy. (Only a king could
give this order.)

Loyalty and Betrayal *What do these words reveal about Antony's true feelings
regarding the conspirators?*

Analyze Figurative Language *How does this figurative language relate to the play's
historical and cultural setting? Explain. Use evidence from the text in your response.*

That this foul deed shall smell above the earth

275 With carrion° men, groaning for burial.

[*Enter Octavius's* SERVANT.]

You serve Octavius Caesar, do you not?

SERVANT. I do, Mark Antony.

ANTONY. Caesar did write for him to come to Rome.

SERVANT. He did receive his letters and is coming,

280 And bid me say to you by word of mouth—
[*Seeing the body.*] O Caesar!—

ANTONY. Thy heart is big;° get thee apart and weep.
Passion, I see, is catching, [for] mine eyes,
Seeing those beads of sorrow stand in thine,

285 Began to water. Is thy master coming?

SERVANT. He lies tonight within seven leagues° of Rome.

ANTONY. Post° back with speed, and tell him what hath
chanc'd.
Here is a mourning Rome, a dangerous Rome,
No Rome of safety for Octavius yet;

290 Hie hence,° and tell him so. Yet stay awhile,
Thou shalt not back till I have borne this corse
Into the marketplace. There shall I try,°
In my oration, how the people take
The cruel issue° of these bloody men,

295 According to the which thou shalt discourse
To young Octavius of the state of things.
Lend me your hand.

[*They exit (with* CAESAR's *body).*]

SCENE 2. The Roman Forum, the city's great public square. A few days later.

[*Enter* BRUTUS *and* CASSIUS *with the* PLEBEIANS.]

PLEBEIANS. We will be satisfied!° Let us be satisfied!

BRUTUS. Then follow me, and give me audience, friends.
Cassius, go you into the other street,
And part the numbers.°

5 Those that will hear me speak, let 'em stay here;
Those that will follow Cassius, go with him;
And public reasons shall be rendered°
Of Caesar's death.

275 **carrion:** dead and rotting.

282 **big:** swollen with grief.

286 **seven leagues:** twenty-one miles.
287 **Post:** ride back quickly.

290 **Hie hence:** Go quickly from here.

292 **try:** test.

294 **cruel issue:** outcome of cruelty.

1 **satisfied:** The common people (plebeians) demand a full explanation of the assassination.

4 **part the numbers:** divide the crowd.

7 **rendered:** presented.

Plot *What are the plebeians demanding? Is this important to the plot? Explain.*

FIRST PLEBEIAN. I will hear Brutus speak.

SECOND PLEBEIAN. I will hear Cassius, and compare their reasons,

10 When severally° we hear them rendered.

[*Exit* CASSIUS *with some of the* PLEBEIANS. BRUTUS *goes into the pulpit.*]

THIRD PLEBEIAN. The noble Brutus is ascended; silence!

BRUTUS. Be patient till the last.°
Romans, countrymen, and lovers,° hear me for my cause, and be silent, that you may hear. Believe me for mine
15 honor, and have respect to mine honor,° that you may believe. Censure° me in your wisdom, and awake your senses,° that you may the better judge. If there be any in this assembly, any dear friend of Caesar's, to him I say, that Brutus' love to Caesar was no less than his. If then
20 that friend demand why Brutus rose against Caesar, this is my answer; Not that I lov'd Caesar less, but that I lov'd Rome more. Had you rather Caesar were living, and die all slaves, than that Caesar were dead, to live all free men? As Caesar lov'd me, I weep for him; as he was fortunate, I
25 rejoice at it; as he was valiant, I honor him; but, as he was ambitious, I slew him. There is tears for his love; joy for his fortune; honor for his valor; and death for his ambition. Who is here so base that would be a bondman?° If any, speak, for him have I offended. Who is here so rude,° that
30 would not be a Roman? If any, speak, for him have I offended. Who is here so vile that will not love his country? If any, speak, for him have I offended. I pause for a reply.

ALL. None, Brutus, none.

BRUTUS. Then none have I offended. I have done no more to
35 Caesar than you shall do to Brutus. The question of his death is enroll'd in the Capitol;° his glory not extenuated,° wherein he was worthy; nor his offenses enforc'd,° for which he suffer'd death.

[*Enter* MARK ANTONY *(and others) with* CAESAR'S *body.*]

Here comes his body, mourn'd by Mark Antony, who,
40 though he had no hand in his death, shall receive the benefit of his dying, a place in the commonwealth,° as which of you shall not? With this I depart, that, as I slew my best lover for the good of Rome, I have the same dagger for

10 **severally:** separately.

12 **last:** end of the speech.
13 **lovers:** dear friends.

15 **have respect . . . honor:** remember that I am honorable.
16 **Censure:** judge.
17 **senses:** reason.

28 **bondman:** slave.
29 **rude:** uncivilized.

35–36 **The question . . . Capitol:** The reasons for his death are recorded in the public archives of the Capitol.
37 **extenuated:** diminished.
38 **enforc'd:** exaggerated.

41 **a place in the commonwealth:** citizenship in a free republic.

Loyalty and Betrayal *What is Brutus implying here? Is this a valid conclusion? Explain.*

The Roman Forum, 19th century. Francis Vyvyan Jago Arundale. Watercolour on paper, 64.5 x 100 cm. Private collection.

View the Art What events in the play might this painting depict? Explain.

myself, when it shall please my country to need my death.

45   ALL. Live, Brutus, live, live!

FIRST PLEBEIAN. Bring him with triumph home unto his house.

SECOND PLEBEIAN. Give him a statue with his ancestors.

THIRD PLEBEIAN. Let him be Caesar.

FOURTH PLEBEIAN.   Caesar's better parts°
  Shall be crown'd in Brutus.

FIRST PLEBEIAN.   We'll bring him to his house

50   With shouts and clamors.

BRUTUS.   My countrymen—

SECOND PLEBEIAN. Peace, silence! Brutus speaks.

FIRST PLEBEIAN. Peace, ho!

BRUTUS. Good countrymen, let me depart alone,
  And, for my sake, stay here with Antony.

55   Do grace to Caesar's corpse, and grace his speech

48 parts: qualities.

Plot *How do the people react to Brutus's speech? Why do they react in this way?*

Tending to Caesar's glories,° which Mark Antony
(By our permission) is allow'd to make.
I do entreat you, not a man depart,
Save I alone, till Antony have spoke.

FIRST PLEBEIAN. Stay, ho, and let us hear Mark Antony.

THIRD PLEBEIAN. Let him go up into the public chair;°
We'll hear him. Noble Antony, go up.

ANTONY. For Brutus' sake, I am beholding° to you.

[*Goes into the pulpit.*]

FOURTH PLEBEIAN. What does he say of Brutus?

THIRD PLEBEIAN.   He says, for Brutus' sake,
He finds himself beholding to us all.

FOURTH PLEBEIAN. 'Twere best he speak no harm of Brutus
here!

FIRST PLEBEIAN. This Caesar was a tyrant.

THIRD PLEBEIAN.   Nay, that's certain.
We are blest that Rome is rid of him.

SECOND PLEBEIAN. Peace, let us hear what Antony can say.

70 **ANTONY.** You gentle Romans—

[*The noise continues.*]

ALL.   Peace, ho, let us hear him.

ANTONY. Friends, Romans, countrymen, lend me your ears!
I come to bury Caesar, not to praise him.
The evil that men do lives after them,
The good is oft interred° with their bones;
75 So let it be with Caesar. The noble Brutus
Hath told you Caesar was ambitious;
If it were so, it was a grievous fault,
And grievously hath Caesar answer'd° it.
Here, under leave° of Brutus and the rest
80 (For Brutus is an honorable man,
So are they all, all honorable men),
Come I to speak in Caesar's funeral.
He was my friend, faithful and just to me;
But Brutus says he was ambitious,
85 And Brutus is an honorable man.
He hath brought many captives home to Rome,
Whose ransoms did the general coffers° fill;

55–56 Do grace . . . glories: Pay respect to Caesar's body and listen respectfully to Antony's speech dealing with Caesar's glories.

61 public chair: pulpit.

63 beholding: indebted.

74 interred: buried.

78 answer'd: paid the penalty for.
79 leave: permission.

87 general coffers: public treasury.

Plot *What does the plebeian mean by this remark?*

Did this in Caesar seem ambitious?
When that the poor have cried, Caesar hath wept;
90 Ambition should be made of sterner stuff:
Yet Brutus says he was ambitious;
And Brutus is an honorable man.
You all did see that on the Lupercal°
I thrice presented him a kingly crown,
95 Which he did thrice refuse.° Was this ambition?
Yet Brutus says he was ambitious;
And sure he is an honorable man.
I speak not to disprove what Brutus spoke,
But here I am to speak what I do know.
100 You all did love him once, not without cause;
What cause withholds you then to mourn for him?
O judgment, thou art fled to brutish beasts,
And men have lost their reason. Bear with me,
My heart is in the coffin there with Caesar,
105 And I must pause till it come back to me.

FIRST PLEBEIAN. Methinks there is much reason in
his sayings.

SECOND PLEBEIAN. If thou consider rightly of the matter,
Caesar has had great wrong.

THIRD PLEBEIAN.   Has he, masters?
I fear there will a worse come in his place.

110 FOURTH PLEBEIAN. Mark'd ye° his words? He would not take
the crown,
Therefore, 'tis certain he was not ambitious.

FIRST PLEBEIAN. If it be found so, some will dear abide it.°

SECOND PLEBEIAN. Poor soul, his eyes are red as fire with
weeping.

THIRD PLEBEIAN. There's not a nobler man in Rome than
Antony.

115 FOURTH PLEBEIAN. Now mark him, he begins again to speak.

ANTONY. But yesterday the word of Caesar might
Have stood against the world; now lies he there,
And none so poor to do him reverence.°
O masters! if I were dispos'd to stir

Marcus Antonius (Mark Antony) as Triumvirate. Artist unknown. Roman portrait bust. Vatican Museums, Vatican State.

93 Lupercal: See Act 1, Scene 1, line 67.

95 Which he . . . refuse: the incident described by Casca in Act 1, Scene 2, lines 234–242.

110 Mark'd ye: Did you listen to?

112 dear abide it: pay dearly for it.

118 none . . . reverence: No one is humble enough to honor him.

Analyze Figurative Language *In what way is this an example of figurative language? What mood, or feeling, does Antony's language help to create?*

Loyalty and Betrayal *Why do the plebeians call Antony noble?*

120 Your hearts and minds to mutiny and rage,
 I should do Brutus wrong and Cassius wrong,
 Who (you all know) are honorable men.
 I will not do them wrong; I rather choose
 To wrong the dead, to wrong myself and you,
125 Than I will wrong such honorable men.
 But here's a parchment with the seal of Caesar;
 I found it in his closet, 'tis his will.
 Let but the commons° hear this testament—
 Which, pardon me, I do not mean to read—
130 And they would go and kiss dead Caesar's wounds,
 And dip their napkins° in his sacred blood;
 Yea, beg a hair of him for memory,
 And dying, mention it within their wills,
 Bequeathing it as a rich legacy
135 Unto their issue.°

FOURTH PLEBEIAN. We'll hear the will; read it, Mark Antony.

ALL. The will, the will! we will hear Caesar's will!

ANTONY. Have patience, gentle friends, I must not read it.
 It is not meet° you know how Caesar lov'd you:
140 You are not wood, you are not stones, but men;
 And being men, hearing the will of Caesar,
 It will inflame you, it will make you mad.
 'Tis good you know not that you are his heirs,
 For if you should, O, what would come of it?

145 **FOURTH PLEBEIAN.** Read the will, we'll hear it, Antony.
 You shall read us the will, Caesar's will.

ANTONY. Will you be patient? Will you stay awhile?
 I have o'ershot myself° to tell you of it.
 I fear I wrong the honorable men
150 Whose daggers have stabb'd Caesar; I do fear it.

FOURTH PLEBEIAN. They were traitors; honorable men!

ALL. The will! the testament!

SECOND PLEBEIAN. They were villains, murderers. The will,
 read the will!

ANTONY. You will compel me then to read the will?

---

128 commons: common people.

131 napkins: handkerchiefs. (Antony refers to the custom of dipping cloths in the blood of martyrs.)

135 issue: children.

139 meet: proper.

148 o'ershot myself: gone further than I intended.

Loyalty and Betrayal *Why does Antony flatter the plebeians?*

Plot *How would you characterize the tension in this scene? What plot complications are developing?*

155 Then make a ring about the corpse of Caesar,
And let me show you him that made the will.
Shall I descend? And will you give me leave?

ALL. Come down.

SECOND PLEBEIAN. Descend.

160 THIRD PLEBEIAN. You shall have leave.

[*ANTONY comes down from the pulpit.*]

FOURTH PLEBEIAN. A ring, stand round.

FIRST PLEBEIAN. Stand from the hearse, stand from the body.

SECOND PLEBEIAN. Room for Antony, most noble Antony.

ANTONY. Nay, press not so upon me; stand far° off.

165 ALL. Stand back; room, bear back.

ANTONY. If you have tears, prepare to shed them now.
You all do know this mantle.° I remember
The first time ever Caesar put it on;
'Twas on a summer's evening, in his tent,
170 That day he overcame the Nervii.°
Look, in this place ran Cassius' dagger through;
See what a rent° the envious Casca made;
Through this the well-beloved Brutus stabb'd,
And as he pluck'd his cursed steel away,
175 Mark how the blood of Caesar followed it,
As rushing out of doors, to be resolv'd
If Brutus so unkindly knock'd or no;°
For Brutus, as you know, was Caesar's angel.°
Judge, O you gods, how dearly Caesar lov'd him!
180 This was the most unkindest cut of all;
For when the noble Caesar saw him stab,
Ingratitude, more strong than traitors' arms,
Quite **vanquish'd** him. Then burst his mighty heart,
And, in his mantle muffling up his face,
185 Even at the base of Pompey's statue
(Which all the while ran blood) great Caesar fell.
O, what a fall was there, my countrymen!
Then I, and you, and all of us fell down,

164 far: farther.
167 mantle: cloak, toga.

170 Nervii: a fierce Gallic tribe defeated by Caesar in 57 B.C.

172 rent: rip.

176–177 As rushing . . . no: as if rushing outside to learn for certain whether or not Brutus so cruelly and unnaturally "knocked."
178 angel: favorite.

Analyze Figurative Language *Where in these lines do you see an example of personification? How does Antony's use of this figurative language help to create sympathy for Caesar?*

Vocabulary

vanquish (vang′kwish) *v.* to defeat; to overcome

Whilst bloody treason flourish'd° over us.

190 O now you weep, and I perceive you feel
The dint° of pity. These are gracious drops.
Kind souls, what weep you when you but behold
Our Caesar's vesture wounded? Look you here, [*Lifting
   CAESAR's mantle.*]
Here is himself, marr'd as you see with traitors.°

195 **FIRST PLEBEIAN.** O piteous spectacle!

SECOND PLEBEIAN. O noble Caesar!

THIRD PLEBEIAN. O woeful day!

FOURTH PLEBEIAN. O traitors, villains!

FIRST PLEBEIAN. O most bloody sight!

200 **SECOND PLEBEIAN.** We will be reveng'd.

ALL. Revenge! About! Seek! Burn! Fire! Kill! Slay!
Let not a traitor live!

ANTONY. Stay, countrymen.

FIRST PLEBEIAN. Peace there, hear the noble Antony.

205 **SECOND PLEBEIAN.** We'll hear him, we'll follow him, we'll die
   with him.

ANTONY. Good friends, sweet friends, let me not stir you up
To such a sudden flood of mutiny.
They that have done this deed are honorable.
What private griefs° they have, alas, I know not,
210 That made them do it. They are wise and honorable,
And will, no doubt, with reasons answer you.
I come not, friends, to steal away your hearts.
I am no **orator**, as Brutus is;
But (as you know me all) a plain blunt man
215 That love my friend, and that they know full well
That gave me public leave to speak of him.
For I have neither wit, nor words, nor worth,
Action, nor utterance, nor the power of speech
To stir men's blood;° I only speak right on.
220 I tell you that which you yourselves do know,

189 flourish'd: swaggered.

191 dint: force; blow.

192–194 Kind souls . . . traitors: In a dramatic gesture, Antony uncovers Caesar's mutilated body after remarking how much the commoners weep when they gaze merely upon Caesar's mutilated clothing.

209 private griefs: personal grievances. Antony suggests that the conspirators killed Caesar not for the public reasons Brutus has declared but rather for personal, and therefore less worthy, motives.

217–219 For I have . . . blood: Antony claims that he does not have the cleverness (**wit**), fluency (**words**), high personal standing or reputation (**worth**), gestures (**action**), and manner of speaking (**utterance**) of a skilled orator.

Loyalty and Betrayal *Antony emphasizes that he is not trying to turn the crowd against Brutus and the other plotters. Is he sincere? Explain.*

Vocabulary

orator (ôr´ ə tər) *n.* a person skilled in public speaking

William Shakespeare: Julius Caesar—Forum—Stage design, 1914. Ludwig Sievert.

<u>View the Art</u> What feelings does this design evoke? Do you think it is a good representation of the play? Explain.

Show you sweet Caesar's wounds, poor, poor, dumb mouths,
And bid them speak for me. But were I Brutus,
And Brutus Antony, there were an Antony
Would ruffle up° your spirits, and put a tongue
225 In every wound of Caesar, that should move
The stones of Rome to rise and mutiny.

ALL. We'll mutiny.

FIRST PLEBEIAN. We'll burn the house of Brutus.

THIRD PLEBEIAN. Away then, come, seek the conspirators.

ANTONY. Yet hear me, countrymen, yet hear me speak.

230 ALL. Peace, ho, hear Antony, most noble Antony!

ANTONY. Why, friends, you go to do you know not what.
Wherein hath Caesar thus deserv'd your loves?
Alas, you know not! I must tell you then;
You have forgot the will I told you of.

235 ALL. Most true. The will! Let's stay and hear the will.

ANTONY. Here is the will, and under Caesar's seal:
To every Roman citizen he gives,
To every several° man, seventy-five drachmas.°

SECOND PLEBEIAN. Most noble Caesar! we'll revenge his death!

240 THIRD PLEBEIAN. O royal° Caesar!

ANTONY. Hear me with patience.

224 ruffle up: enrage.

238 several: individual. **drachmas:** silver coins.

240 royal: most generous.

Analyze Figurative Language *Why does Antony again make this comparison?*

ALL. Peace, ho!

ANTONY. Moreover, he hath left you all his walks,
His private arbors and new-planted orchards,°
245 On this side Tiber; he hath left them you,
And to your heirs forever—common pleasures,°
To walk abroad and recreate yourselves.
Here was a Caesar! when comes such another?

FIRST PLEBEIAN. Never, never! Come, away, away!
250 We'll burn his body in the holy place,°
And with the brands° fire the traitors' houses.
Take up the body.

SECOND PLEBEIAN. Go fetch fire.

THIRD PLEBEIAN. Pluck down benches.

255 **FOURTH PLEBEIAN.** Pluck down forms,° windows,° anything.

[*Exit PLEBEIANS with the body.*]

ANTONY. Now let it work. Mischief, thou art afoot,
Take thou what course thou wilt!

[*Enter SERVANT.*]

How now, fellow?

SERVANT. Sir, Octavius is already come to Rome.

ANTONY. Where is he?

260 **SERVANT.** He and Lepidus° are at Caesar's house.

ANTONY. And thither will I straight to visit him;°
He comes upon a wish.° Fortune is merry,
And in this mood will give us anything.

SERVANT. I heard him say, Brutus and Cassius
265 Are rid° like madmen through the gates of Rome.

ANTONY. Belike° they had some notice of the people,
How I had mov'd them. Bring me to Octavius.

[*They exit.*]

SCENE 3. Shortly afterward. A street near the Forum.

[*Enter CINNA the poet, and after him the PLEBEIANS.*]

Loyalty and Betrayal *What does this remark reveal about Antony?*

Analyze Figurative Language *What does Antony mean by this?*

Plot *How would you characterize the tension at this point in the act? What conclusion can you draw about which plot stage has been entered? Provide evidence from the text to support your answer.*

244 **orchards:** gardens.

246 **common pleasures:** public recreation areas.

250 **the holy place:** the site of the most sacred Roman temples.
251 **brands:** pieces of burning wood.

255 **forms:** benches. **windows:** shutters.

260 **Lepidus:** one of Caesar's generals.
261 **thither will . . . him:** I will go there immediately to visit him.
262 **upon a wish:** just as I had wished.

265 **Are rid:** have ridden.

266 **Belike:** probably.

CINNA.° I dreamt tonight° that I did feast with Caesar,
And things unluckily charge my fantasy.°
I have no will to wander forth of doors,
Yet something leads me forth.

5   FIRST PLEBEIAN. What is your name?

SECOND PLEBEIAN. Whither are you going?

THIRD PLEBEIAN. Where do you dwell?

FOURTH PLEBEIAN. Are you a married man or a bachelor?

SECOND PLEBEIAN. Answer every man directly.

10   FIRST PLEBEIAN. Ay, and briefly.

FOURTH PLEBEIAN. Ay, and wisely.

THIRD PLEBEIAN. Ay, and truly, you were best.°

CINNA. What is my name? Whither am I going? Where do I
dwell? Am I a married man or a bachelor? Then, to answer
15   every man directly and briefly, wisely and truly: wisely I
say, I am a bachelor.

SECOND PLEBEIAN. That's as much as to say, they are fools that
marry. You'll bear me a bang° for that, I fear. Proceed
directly.

20   CINNA. Directly, I am going to Caesar's funeral.

FIRST PLEBEIAN. As a friend or an enemy?

CINNA. As a friend.

SECOND PLEBEIAN. That matter is answer'd directly.

FOURTH PLEBEIAN. For your dwelling—briefly.

25   CINNA. Briefly, I dwell by the Capitol.

THIRD PLEBEIAN. Your name, sir, truly.

CINNA. Truly, my name is Cinna.

FIRST PLEBEIAN. Tear him to pieces, he's a conspirator.

CINNA. I am Cinna the poet, I am Cinna the poet.

30   FOURTH PLEBEIAN. Tear him for his bad verses, tear him for his
bad verses.

CINNA. I am not Cinna the conspirator.

FOURTH PLEBEIAN. It is no matter, his name's Cinna. Pluck but
his name out of his heart, and turn him going.

35   THIRD PLEBEIAN. Tear him, tear him!
Come, brands, ho, firebrands! To Brutus', to Cassius'; burn
all! Some to Decius' house, and some to Casca's; some to
Ligarius'. Away, go!

[*All the* PLEBEIANS *exit (dragging off* CINNA).]

Loyalty and Betrayal *Why is the crowd behaving this way?*

After You Read

Respond and Think Critically

1. **Connect to Personal Experience** What was your reaction to Caesar's murder?

2. **Interpret Events** What most surprises Caesar when he is attacked? What might Caesar have been thinking as he died? Explain.

3. **Summarize Events** Summarize the crowd's reactions to Brutus's and Antony's funeral speeches. Why do they react this way?

4. **Make Inferences About Motivation** What can you infer about why Antony responds as he does to the conspirators immediately after Caesar's murder?

5. **Analyze Character** Analyze Caesar's behavior outside the Capitol just before he dies. Did it change your overall opinion of him? Explain.

6. **Evaluate Events** Why might Shakespeare have chosen to include the incident of the attack on Cinna the poet? Was it effective? Provide evidence from the text to support your response.

7. **Big Idea** **Draw Conclusions About Character** As a friend to others, does Antony display loyalty, disloyalty, or both qualities? Support your answer with text evidence.

Literary Element Plot

Review the pink highlighted text and questions to help you answer the following questions.

8. **Identify Plot Elements** Identify Act 3's exposition and rising action, including details that contribute to the tension.

9. **Draw Conclusions About Plot** Identify two events in Act 3 that might be identified as its climax. Which do you think is the actual climax? Support your response with text evidence.

Reading Strategy Analyze Figurative Language

Review your chart on page 734.

10. What figure of speech does Casca use when he stabs Caesar? Explain its meaning.

11. Identify and explain how one example of figurative language in Act 3 is specific to the cultural or historical setting of the play. Use text evidence to support your response.

LOG ON ▶ **Literature** Online

Selection Resources For Selection Quizzes, eFlashcards, and Reading-Writing Connection activities, go to glencoe.com and enter QuickPass code GL57805u4.

Vocabulary Practice

Practice with Context Clues Identify the context clues that help you determine the meaning of each boldfaced vocabulary word below.

1. The plants are **thriving** as a result of good light, fertilization, and correct watering.

2. His expression was full of **malice;** his friend also gave me a hateful look.

3. The **orator** stepped onto the podium to begin his speech.

4. Although the troops fought hard, they could not **vanquish** their determined opponents.

5. The plan appealed to the rest of the team, so Sofia did not state her **misgivings** about how it could go wrong.

Writing

Write a Memo Reread the servant's speech (Scene 1, lines 123–137) and then rewrite it as an e-mail memo from Antony to Brutus. See page R25 for the format to use for such a message. Your e-mail should include organized and accurately conveyed information, anticipate any questions the reader (in this case, Brutus) might have, and be properly formatted.

Before You Read

The Tragedy of Julius Caesar, Act 4

Build Background

When Antony took charge of the city, he was joined by eighteen-year-old Gaius Octavius, Caesar's great-nephew and adopted son. Octavius was intelligent, handsome, and skilled at oratory. Together with a governor named Lepidus, Octavius and Antony created a ruling group of three—a triumvirate.

Set Purposes for Reading

Literary Element Foil

A **foil** is a character who provides a strong contrast with another character, usually a main character. A foil helps readers perceive strengths and weaknesses of another character. As you read, ask yourself, Which characters are foils?

Reading Strategy Make and Verify Predictions

When you **make predictions** as you read, you make reasoned guesses about what will happen based on clues the author provides along with your own understanding of characters and events. Then, as you continue reading, you **verify** the accuracy of the predictions and modify your thinking. As you read, ask yourself, What predictions can I make about the outcome of events in Act 4?

Tip: Chart Predictions Use a chart like the one below to make and verify predictions as you read. Use the blue highlighted passages and questions to help you get started.

Prediction	My Reason	Outcome
Brutus and Cassius are going to argue and end their alliance.	They are very different. Brutus is thoughtful and honest. Cassius is emotional and cunning.	They fight but reconcile and resolve their differences.

TEKS

For pages 757–773

10.4 Understand, make inferences and draw conclusions about the structure and elements of drama and provide evidence from text to support understanding.

Vocabulary

barren (bar′ ən) *adj.* empty and dreary; without life; desolate; p. 760 *No one lives in the area surrounding the town; the land is barren.*

covert (kō′ vərt) *adj.* secret; hidden; p. 760 *The reporter discovered a covert plan to escape.*

deceitful (di sēt′ fəl) *adj.* untruthful and cunning; false; p. 761 *Some advertisements are honest; others are deceitful.*

rash (rash) *adj.* marked by haste and lack of caution or consideration; p. 766 *Meena's decision to end their friendship seemed rash to Laura.*

Tip: Denotation and Connotation A word's **denotation** is its dictionary meaning; its **connotations** are the emotional associations it evokes. To infer whether a word has positive or negative connotations, identify the images, ideas, and other words it brings to mind. For example, in the sentence *Meena's decision to end their friendship seemed rash to Laura,* the word *rash* has a negative connotation and suggests foolishness.

ACT 4

SCENE 1. ANTONY's **house in Rome. A year and a half after** CAESAR's **death.**

[*Enter ANTONY, OCTAVIUS, and LEPIDUS.*]

> ANTONY.   These many then shall die, their names are
>   prick'd.°
>
> OCTAVIUS.   Your brother too must die, consent you,
>   Lepidus?°
>
> LEPIDUS.   I do consent—

1 **prick'd:** marked down on a list.

2 **Your brother . . . Lepidus:** Lepidus's brother was a prominent politician who sided with the conspirators after Caesar's assassination.

Ancient Romans. Artist unknown. Mosaic. Currier Gallery of Art, Manchester, NH.

View the Art What impressions of people in ancient Rome do you get from this mosaic? How do those impressions relate to characters in the play?

OCTAVIUS. Prick him down, Antony.

LEPIDUS. Upon condition Publius shall not live,
5   Who is your sister's son, Mark Antony.

ANTONY. He shall not live; look, with a spot I damn him.
    But, Lepidus, go you to Caesar's house;
    Fetch the will hither, and we shall determine
    How to cut off some charge in legacies.°

10   **LEPIDUS.** What? shall I find you here?

OCTAVIUS. Or here or at the Capitol.

[*Exit LEPIDUS.*]

ANTONY. This is a slight unmeritable man,
    Meet° to be sent on errands; is it fit,
    The threefold world° divided, he should stand
15   One of the three to share it?

OCTAVIUS.   So you thought him,
    And took his voice who should be prick'd to die
    In our black sentence and proscription.°

ANTONY. Octavius, I have seen more days than you,
    And though we lay these honors on this man
20   To ease ourselves of divers sland'rous loads,°
    He shall but bear them as the ass bears gold,
    To groan and sweat under the business,
    Either led or driven, as we point the way;
    And having brought our treasure where we will,
25   Then take we down his load, and turn him off
    (Like to the empty ass) to shake his ears
    And graze in commons.°

OCTAVIUS.   You may do your will;
    But he's a tried and valiant soldier.

ANTONY. So is my horse, Octavius, and for that
30   I do appoint him store of provender.°
    It is a creature that I teach to fight,
    To wind,° to stop, to run directly on,
    His corporal° motion govern'd by my spirit;
    And in some taste° is Lepidus but so.
35   He must be taught, and train'd, and bid go forth;

---

9 cut off . . . legacies: reduce the amount of money left to the people in Caesar's will.

13 Meet: fit.

14 threefold world: three parts of the Roman world. (In the autumn of 43 B.C., Antony, Octavius Caesar, and Lepidus formed a triumvirate—a committee of three—to rule Rome. They divided up among themselves territory that the Romans had conquered.)

15–17 So you . . . proscription: Octavius wonders why Antony asked Lepidus to name people who should be sentenced to death if he had so poor an opinion of him.

20 divers sland'rous loads: the burden of accusations for our various actions.

24–27 And having . . . commons: When Lepidus has brought our treasure where we want it, we will send him off to shake his ears and graze on public land like an unburdened donkey.

30 appoint . . . provender: allot him a supply of food.

32 wind: turn.

33 corporal: bodily.

34 taste: degree.

Loyalty and Betrayal *What does Antony's statement here suggest about him?*

Foil *What does Octavius's statement indicate about the difference between Octavius and Antony?*

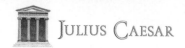

A **barren**-spirited fellow; one that feeds
On objects, arts, and imitations,
Which, out of use and stal'd by other men,
Begin his fashion.° Do not talk of him

40   But as a property.° And now, Octavius,
Listen great things. Brutus and Cassius
Are levying powers; we must straight make head;
Therefore let our alliance be combin'd,
Our best friends made, our means stretch'd;

45   And let us presently go sit in council,
How **covert** matters may be best disclos'd,
And open perils surest answered.°

OCTAVIUS. Let us do so; for we are at the stake,
And bay'd about with many enemies,°

50   And some that smile have in their hearts, I fear,
Millions of mischiefs. [*They exit.*]

SCENE 2. A military camp near Sardis in Asia Minor. Several months later.

[*Drum. Enter* BRUTUS, LUCILIUS, LUCIUS, *and the army.* TITINIUS *and* PINDARUS *meet them.*]

BRUTUS. Stand ho!

LUCILIUS. Give the word ho! and stand.°

BRUTUS. What now, Lucilius, is Cassius near?

LUCILIUS. He is at hand, and Pindarus is come

5   To do you salutation from his master.

BRUTUS. He greets me well. Your master, Pindarus,
In his own change, or by ill officers,
Hath given me some worthy cause to wish
Things done undone,° but if he be at hand,

10   I shall be satisfied.°

PINDARUS.   I do not doubt
But that my noble master will appear
Such as he is, full of regard and honor.

36–39 A barren-spirited . . . fashion: a man with no originality, one who indulges in curiosities, tricks, and fashions, which he takes up only after they have become outmoded.
40 a property: a mere tool.

41–47 Listen great . . . answered: Listen to important matters. Brutus and Cassius are raising armies; we must press forward immediately. Therefore let us become united, choose our allies, and make the most of our resources. And let us decide at once how hidden threats may be uncovered and open dangers most safely confronted.
48–49 we are . . . enemies: Octavius's metaphor refers to bear-baiting, a popular entertainment during Shakespeare's time in which bears were tied to stakes and surrounded by vicious dogs.

2 Give the . . . stand: Lucilius, one of Brutus's officers, tells his sub-ordinates to pass on Brutus's command for the army to halt (**stand**). He has returned from Cassius's camp with Titinius, one of Cassius's officers, and Pindarus, Cassius's servant.

6–9 Your master . . . undone: Either a change in Cassius or the misconduct of his officers has given me good reason to wish I could undo what I have done. (Brutus is having some misgivings about having participated in the conspiracy because of incidents that have occurred in Cassius's army.)
10 be satisfied: receive an explanation.

Make and Verify Predictions *Who do you predict will emerge victorious, the conspirators or Rome's new rulers? Explain.*

Vocabulary

barren (bar´ən) *adj.* empty and dreary; without life; desolate
covert (kō´vərt) *adj.* secret; hidden

BRUTUS. He is not doubted. A word, Lucilius.
How he receiv'd you; let me be resolv'd.°

14 **resolv'd:** informed.

15 **LUCILIUS.** With courtesy and with respect enough,
But not with such familiar instances,°
Nor with such free and friendly conference,°
As he hath us'd of old.

16 **familiar instances:** signs of friendship.
17 **conference:** conversation.

BRUTUS.   Thou hast describ'd
A hot friend cooling. Ever note, Lucilius,
20 When love begins to sicken and decay
It useth an enforced ceremony.°
There are no tricks in plain and simple faith;
But hollow men, like horses hot at hand,
Make gallant show and promise of their mettle;

21 **enforced ceremony:** strained formality.
23–27 **But hollow . . . trial:** Brutus compares insincere men to horses that are spirited at the start but drop their proud necks as soon as they feel the spur, failing like nags (**jades**) when put to the test.
29 **horse in general:** main part of the cavalry.

[*Low march within.*]

25 But when they should endure the bloody spur,
They fall their crests, and like **deceitful** jades
Sink in the trial.° Comes his army on?

LUCILIUS. They mean this night in Sardis to be quarter'd.
The greater part, the horse in general,°
30 Are come with Cassius.

[*Enter CASSIUS and his POWERS.*]

BRUTUS.   Hark! He is arriv'd.
March gently on to meet him.

CASSIUS. Stand ho!

BRUTUS. Stand ho! Speak the word along.

FIRST SOLDIER. Stand!

35 **SECOND SOLDIER.** Stand!

THIRD SOLDIER. Stand!

CASSIUS. Most noble brother, you have done me wrong.

BRUTUS. Judge me, you gods! wrong I mine enemies?
And if not so, how should I wrong a brother.

40 **CASSIUS.** Brutus, this sober form° of yours hides wrongs,
And when you do them—

A group of soldiers of the Praetorian guard, possibly from the Forum of Emperor Trajan, 1st–3rd century A.D. Artist unknown. Marble relief. Louvre, Paris.

40 **sober form:** dignified manner.

Loyalty and Betrayal *What attitude toward Cassius is Brutus expressing?*

Make and Verify Predictions *What do you predict will happen when Brutus and Cassius meet?*

Vocabulary

deceitful (di sēt′fəl) *adj.* untruthful and cunning; false

BRUTUS. Cassius, be content.
Speak your griefs softly; I do know you well.
Before the eyes of both our armies here
45 (Which should perceive nothing but love from us)
Let us not wrangle. Bid them move away;
Then in my tent, Cassius, enlarge your griefs,
And I will give you audience.°

CASSIUS. Pindarus,
Bid our commanders lead their charges off
50 A little from this ground.

BRUTUS. Lucius, do you the like, and let no man
Come to our tent till we have done our conference.
Let Lucilius and Titinius guard our door.

[*They exit.* BRUTUS *and* CASSIUS *remain and withdraw into* BRUTUS'S
tent, while LUCILIUS *and* TITINIUS *mount guard without.*]

SCENE 3. BRUTUS'S **tent. A few minutes later.**

CASSIUS. That you wrong'd me doth appear in this;
You have condemn'd and noted Lucius Pella
For taking bribes here of the Sardians;
Wherein my letters, praying on his side,
5 Because I knew the man, was slighted off.°

BRUTUS. You wrong'd yourself to write in such a case.

CASSIUS. In such a time as this it is not meet
That every nice offense should bear his comment.°

BRUTUS. Let me tell you, Cassius, you yourself
10 Are much condemn'd to have an itching palm,°
To sell and mart° your offices for gold
To undeservers.

CASSIUS. I, an itching palm?
You know that you are Brutus that speaks this,
Or, by the gods, this speech were else your last.

15 **BRUTUS.** The name of Cassius honors this corruption,
And chastisement doth therefore hide his head.°

CASSIUS. Chastisement?

47–48 enlarge . . . audience:
Explain your grievances, and I will
listen.

1–5 That you . . . off: Cassius
complains that Brutus publicly
disgraced (**noted**) a man for taking
bribes, ignoring Cassius's request for
leniency.

7–8 not meet . . . comment: not
fitting that each minor offense
should be criticized.
10 condemn'd to . . . palm:
blamed for being greedy.
11 mart: trade.

15–16 The name . . . head:
Because you have become
associated with this corruption, the
bribe-takers go unpunished.

Foil *What contrast between Cassius and Brutus does this passage suggest?*

BRUTUS.   Remember March, the ides of March remember:
Did not great Julius bleed for justice' sake?
20   What villain touch'd his body, that did stab
And not for justice? What? shall one of us,
That struck the foremost man of all this world
But for supporting robbers,° shall we now
Contaminate our fingers with base bribes?
25   And sell the mighty space of our large honors
For so much trash as may be grasped thus?
I had rather be a dog, and bay the moon,
Than such a Roman.

CASSIUS.   Brutus, bait° not me,
I'll not endure it. You forget yourself
30   To hedge me in.° I am a soldier, I,
Older in practice, abler than yourself
To make conditions.°

BRUTUS.   Go to; you are not, Cassius.

CASSIUS.   I am.

BRUTUS.   I say you are not.

35   CASSIUS.   Urge me no more, I shall forget myself;
Have mind upon your health; tempt me no farther.

BRUTUS.   Away, slight man!

CASSIUS.   Is't possible?

BRUTUS.   Hear me, for I will speak.
Must I give way and room to your rash choler?°
40   Shall I be frighted when a madman stares?

CASSIUS.   O ye gods, ye gods, must I endure all this?

BRUTUS.   All this? ay, more. Fret till your proud heart break.
Go show your slaves how choleric you are,
And make your bondmen tremble. Must I budge?°
45   Must I observe you?° Must I stand and crouch
Under your testy humor?° By the gods,
You shall digest the venom of your spleen
Though it do split you;° for, from his day forth,
I'll use you for my mirth, yea, for my laughter,
50   When you are waspish.

CASSIUS.   Is it come to this?

23 **supporting robbers:** Brutus now suggests that one of Caesar's offenses was to protect corrupt officials.

28 **bait:** provoke.

30 **hedge me in:** limit my freedom.

32 **conditions:** regulations.

39 **rash choler:** quick temper.

44 **budge:** flinch.
45 **observe you:** defer to you.
46 **testy humor:** irritable mood.

47–48 **digest . . . split you:** swallow the poison of your own anger, even if it makes you burst. (The spleen was thought to be the source of anger.)

Loyalty and Betrayal *What point does Brutus make in lines 18–28?*

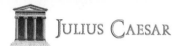
BRUTUS. You say you are a better soldier;
    Let it appear so; make your vaunting° true,
    And it shall please me well. For mine own part,
    I shall be glad to learn of noble men.°

55 **CASSIUS.** You wrong me every way; you wrong me, Brutus;
    I said, an elder soldier, not a better.
    Did I say "better"?

BRUTUS.   If you did, I care not.

CASSIUS. When Caesar liv'd, he durst° not thus have
    mov'd° me.

BRUTUS. Peace, peace, you durst not so have tempted him.

60 **CASSIUS.** I durst not?

BRUTUS. No.

CASSIUS. What? durst not tempt him?

BRUTUS.   For your life you
    durst not.

CASSIUS. Do not presume too much upon my love,
    I may do that° I shall be sorry for.

65 **BRUTUS.** You have done that you should be sorry for.
    There is no terror, Cassius, in your threats;
    For I am arm'd so strong in honesty
    That they pass by me as the idle wind,
    Which I respect not. I did send to you

70   For certain sums of gold, which you denied me;
    For I can raise no money by vile means.
    By heaven, I had rather coin my heart
    And drop my blood for drachmas than to wring
    From the hard hands of peasants their vile trash°

75   By any indirection.° I did send
    To you for gold to pay my legions,
    Which you denied me. Was that done like Cassius?
    Should I have answer'd Caius Cassius so?
    When Marcus Brutus grows so covetous

80   To lock such rascal counters° from his friends,
    Be ready, gods, with all your thunderbolts,

52 vaunting: boasting.

54 learn of noble men: "learn from noble men" or "find out that you are noble."

58 durst: dared. **mov'd:** provoked.

64 that: something that.
74 vile trash: small sums of money.
75 indirection: dishonest means.
80 rascal counters: grubby coins.

Jupiter Hurling a Flash of Lightning at the Titan, 17th century. Alessandro Algardi. Bronze sculpture. Louvre, Paris.

Make and Verify Predictions *What do you predict will happen next?*

Foil *What distinction does Brutus draw between himself and Cassius?*

Dash him to pieces!

CASSIUS.   I denied you not.

BRUTUS. You did.

CASSIUS. I did not. He was but a fool that brought
85 My answer back. Brutus hath riv'd° my heart.
  A friend should bear his friend's infirmities;°
  But Brutus makes mine greater than they are.

BRUTUS. I do not, till you practice them on me.

CASSIUS. You love me not.

BRUTUS.   I do not like your faults.

90 CASSIUS. A friendly eye could never see such faults.

BRUTUS. A flatterer's would not, though they do appear
  As huge as high Olympus.

CASSIUS. Come, Antony, and young Octavius, come,
  Revenge yourselves alone on Cassius,
95 For Cassius is aweary of the world;
  Hated by one he loves, brav'd° by his brother,
  Check'd like a bondman,° all his faults observ'd,
  Set in a notebook, learn'd and conn'd by rote,°
  To cast into my teeth. O, I could weep
100 My spirit from mine eyes! There is my dagger,
  And here my naked breast; within, a heart
  Dearer than Pluto's mine,° richer than gold:
  If that thou be'st a Roman, take it forth.
  I, that denied thee gold, will give my heart:
105 Strike as thou didst at Caesar; for I know,
  When thou didst hate him worst, thou lovedst him better
  Than ever thou lovedst Cassius.

BRUTUS.   Sheathe your dagger.
  Be angry when you will, it shall have scope;
  Do what you will, dishonor shall be humor.°
110 O Cassius, you are yoked° with a lamb
  That carries anger as the flint bears fire,
  Who, much enforced,° shows a hasty spark,
  And straight° is cold again.

CASSIUS.   Hath Cassius liv'd

---

85 riv'd: broken.
86 bear . . . infirmities: accept his friend's faults.

96 brav'd: challenged.
97 Check'd like a bondman: scolded like a slave.
98 conn'd by rote: memorized.

102 Pluto's mine: all the riches in the earth. (Pluto, the Roman god of the underworld, was often confused with Plutus, the god of wealth.)

108–109 Be angry . . . humor: Brutus says that he will give Cassius's anger free play (**scope**) and will consider his insults merely the result of a bad mood.
110 yoked: allied.
112 enforced: struck hard; irritated.
113 straight: immediately.

Loyalty and Betrayal *What different ideas about loyalty and friendship are expressed here? With whose ideas do you agree? Explain.*

To be but mirth and laughter to his Brutus
115   When grief and blood ill-temper'd° vexeth him?

BRUTUS. When I spoke that, I was ill-temper'd too.

CASSIUS. Do you confess so much? Give me your hand.

BRUTUS. And my heart too.

CASSIUS.   O Brutus!

BRUTUS.   What's the matter?

CASSIUS. Have you not love enough to bear with me,
120   When that **rash** humor which my mother gave me
Makes me forgetful?°

BRUTUS.   Yes, Cassius, and from henceforth,
When you are over-earnest with your Brutus,
He'll think your mother chides, and leave you so.°

[*Enter a* POET (*to* LUCILIUS *and* TITINIUS *as they stand on guard*).]

POET. Let me go in to see the generals;
125   There is some grudge between 'em; 'tis not meet
They be alone.

LUCILIUS. You shall not come to them.

POET. Nothing but death shall stay me.

[*BRUTUS and* CASSIUS *step out of the tent.*]

CASSIUS. How now. What's the matter?

130   POET. For shame, you generals! what do you mean?
Love, and be friends, as two such men should be,
For I have seen more years, I'm sure, than ye.

CASSIUS. Ha, ha! how vilely doth this cynic° rhyme!

BRUTUS. Get you hence, sirrah! saucy fellow, hence!

135   CASSIUS. Bear with him, Brutus, 'tis his fashion.

BRUTUS. I'll know his humor when he knows his time.°
What should the wars do with these jigging° fools?
Companion,° hence!

Statuette of Jupiter Dolichenus (standing on a bull) detail of the god, from a shrine, 200–250 B.C. Bronze, height 32 cm. Kunsthistorisches Museum, Vienna, Austria.

115 blood ill-temper'd: moodiness.
121 forgetful: forget myself.
122–123 When you . . . so: When you are too difficult with me, I will attribute it to the quick temper you inherited from your mother, and leave it at that.

133 cynic: rude fellow.

136 I'll know . . . time: I'll accept his quirks when he learns the proper time for them.
137 jigging: rhyming.
138 Companion: fellow (used here as a term of contempt).

Make and Verify Predictions *Is this how you predicted the argument would end? Explain. What will likely happen next?*

Foil *How might the poet be a foil to Brutus and Cassius?*

Vocabulary

rash (rash) *adj.* marked by haste and lack of caution or consideration

CASSIUS.   Away, away, be gone! [*Exit* POET.]

BRUTUS. Lucilius and Titinius, bid the commanders
140   Prepare to lodge their companies tonight.

CASSIUS. And come yourselves, and bring Messala with you
Immediately to us.

[LUCILIUS *and* TITINIUS *exit.*]

BRUTUS. [*To* LUCIUS *within.*] Lucius, a bowl of wine!

[BRUTUS *and* CASSIUS *return into the tent.*]

CASSIUS. I did not think you could have been so angry.

BRUTUS. O Cassius, I am sick of many griefs.

145 **CASSIUS.** Of your philosophy you make no use,
If you give place to accidental evils.°

BRUTUS. No man bears sorrow better. Portia is dead.

CASSIUS. Ha? Portia?

BRUTUS. She is dead.

150 **CASSIUS.** How scap'd I killing° when I cross'd you so?
O insupportable and touching° loss!
Upon what sickness?

BRUTUS.   Impatient of° my absence,
And grief that young Octavius with Mark Antony
Have made themselves so strong—for with her death
155   That tidings came.° With this she fell distract,°
And (her attendants absent) swallow'd fire.°

CASSIUS. And died so?

BRUTUS.   Even so.

CASSIUS.   O ye immortal gods!

[*Enter Boy* (LUCIUS) *with wine and tapers.*]

BRUTUS. Speak no more of her. Give me a bowl of wine.
In this I bury all unkindness, Cassius. [*Drinks.*]

160 **CASSIUS.** My heart is thirsty for that noble pledge.
Fill, Lucius, till the wine o'erswell the cup;
I cannot drink too much of Brutus' love.

[*Drinks. Exit* LUCIUS.]

BRUTUS. Come in, Titinius. [*Enter* TITINIUS *and* MESSALA.]
Welcome, good Messala.
Now sit we close about this taper here,

Brutus, c. 1539–1540.
Michelangelo Buonarroti. Marble,
height: 29⅛, in. Museo Nazionale
del Bargello, Florence, Italy.

View the Art What traits of Brutus
are depicted in this statue? How do
they compare with the character
you have read about?

145–146 Of your . . . evils:
According to the philosophy Brutus
studied, people should not accept
chance misfortunes.
150 How scap'd I killing: How did
I escape being killed?
151 touching: painful.
152 Impatient of: unable to
endure.
154–155: with her death . . . came:
I received news of her death and of
their strength at the same time.
155 distract: insane.
156 fire: burning coals.

Loyalty and Betrayal *How would you characterize Portia's loyalty to Brutus? Explain.*

165   And call in question our necessities.°

    CASSIUS. Portia, art thou gone?

    BRUTUS.   No more, I pray you.
       Messala, I have here received letters
       That young Octavius and Mark Antony
       Come down upon us with a mighty power,°
170   Bending their expedition toward Philippi.°

    MESSALA. Myself have letters of the selfsame tenure.°

    BRUTUS. With what addition?

    MESSALA. That by proscription° and bills of outlawry
       Octavius, Antony, and Lepidus
175   Have put to death an hundred senators.

    BRUTUS. Therein our letters do not well agree;
       Mine speak of seventy senators that died
       By their proscriptions, Cicero being one.

    CASSIUS. Cicero one?

    MESSALA.   Cicero is dead,
180   And by that order of proscription.
       Had you your letters from your wife, my lord?

    BRUTUS. No, Messala.

    MESSALA. Nor nothing in your letters writ of her?

    BRUTUS. Nothing, Messala.

    MESSALA.   That methinks is strange.

185   BRUTUS. Why ask you? Hear you aught of her in yours?

    MESSALA. No, my lord.

    BRUTUS. Now as you are a Roman, tell me true.

    MESSALA. Then like a Roman bear the truth I tell,
       For certain she is dead, and by strange manner.

190   BRUTUS. Why, farewell, Portia. We must die, Messala.
       With meditating that she must die once,°
       I have the patience to endure it now.

    MESSALA. Even so great men great losses should endure.

    CASSIUS. I have as much of this in art as you,
195   But yet my nature could not bear it so.°

    BRUTUS. Well, to our work alive.° What do you think

---

165 call . . . necessities: discuss what we must do.

169 power: army.

170 Bending . . . Philippi: Directing their march toward Philippi (an ancient town in northern Greece).
171 tenure: basic meaning.
173 proscription: condemning to death.

191 once: at some time.
181–195 Had you your . . . bear it so: This passage contradicts lines **147–158**, where Brutus tells Cassius of Portia's death. Many scholars believe that the second passage was mistakenly printed in a revised version of the play. According to this theory, Shakespeare originally emphasized Brutus's philosophical composure, but in rewriting the play, he decided to offer a warmer view of Brutus grieving for his wife.
194–195 I have as . . . so: Cassius says that although he shares Brutus's ideal of philosophical self-control, he could not practice it as Brutus does.
196 alive: "at hand" or "of the living."

Foil *Compared to Cassius, how does Brutus react to Portia's death?*

Make and Verify Predictions *Considering this news, what do you predict might happen? Why?*

Of marching to Philippi presently?

CASSIUS.   I do not think it good.

BRUTUS.   Your reason?

CASSIUS.   This it is;
  'Tis better that the enemy seek us;
200   So shall he waste his means,° weary his soldiers,
  Doing himself offense,° whilst we, lying still,
  Are full of rest, defense, and nimbleness.

BRUTUS.   Good reasons must of force give place to better:
  The people 'twixt Philippi and this ground
205   Do stand but in a forc'd affection;°
  For they have grudg'd us contribution.
  The enemy, marching along by them,
  By them shall make a fuller number up,
  Come on refresh'd, new-added° and encourag'd;
210   From which advantage shall we cut him off
  If at Philippi we do face him there,
  These people at our back.

CASSIUS.   Here me, good brother.

BRUTUS.   Under your pardon.° You must note beside
  That we have tried the utmost of our friends,°
215   Our legions are brimful,° our cause is ripe:
  The enemy increaseth every day;
  We, at the height, are ready to decline.
  There is a tide in the affairs of men,
  Which, taken at the flood, leads on to fortune;
220   Omitted, all the voyage of their life
  Is bound in shallows and in miseries.°
  On such a full sea are we now afloat,
  And we must take the current when it serves,
  Or lose our ventures.

CASSIUS.   Then with your will° go on;
225   We'll along ourselves, and meet them at Philippi.

BRUTUS.   The deep of night is crept upon our talk,
  And nature must obey necessity,
  Which we will niggard with a little rest.°
  There is no more to say?

---

200 waste his means: use up his supplies.
201 Doing himself offense: harming himself.

205 Do stand . . . affection: Are friendly toward us only because they have no choice.

209 new-added: reinforced.

213 Under your pardon: I beg your pardon (let me continue).
214 tried . . . friends: demanded from our allies all that they can give.
215 brimful: at full strength.

218–221 There is a . . . miseries: Brutus says that if men fail to act when the tide of fortune is flowing, they may never get another opportunity.

224 with your will: as you wish.

227–228 nature must . . . rest: Human nature has its needs, which we will grudgingly satisfy (**niggard**) by resting briefly.

Make and Verify Predictions *How are the plans proposed by Brutus and Cassius different? What is the likely outcome of their disagreement?*

Make and Verify Predictions *Whose ideas about strategy do you think will ultimately be proven correct, those of Cassius or those of Brutus? Explain.*

CASSIUS.   No more. Good night.
230   Early tomorrow will we rise, and hence.

BRUTUS. Lucius. [*Enter LUCIUS.*] My gown. [*Exit LUCIUS.*]
                    Farewell, good Messala.
         Good night, Titinius. Noble, noble Cassius,
         Good night, and good repose.

CASSIUS.   O my dear brother!
         This was an ill beginning of the night.
235   Never come such division 'tween our souls!
         Let it not, Brutus.

[*Enter LUCIUS with the gown.*]

BRUTUS.   Everything is well.

CASSIUS. Good night, my lord.

BRUTUS.   Good night, good brother.

TITINIUS AND MESSALA. Good night, Lord Brutus.

BRUTUS.   Farewell
         every one.

[*Exit (all but BRUTUS and LUCIUS).*]

         Give me the gown. Where is thy instrument?

240 **LUCIUS.** Here in the tent.

BRUTUS.   What, thou speak'st drowsily?
         Poor knave,° I blame thee not; thou art o'erwatch'd.°
         Call Claudius and some other of my men,
         I'll have them sleep on cushions in my tent.

LUCIUS. Varrus and Claudio!

[*Enter VARRUS and CLAUDIO.*]

245 **VARRUS.** Calls my lord?

BRUTUS. I pray you, sirs, lie in my tent and sleep;
         It may be I shall raise° you by and by
         On business to my brother Cassius.

VARRUS. So please you, we will stand and watch your
         pleasure.°

250 **BRUTUS.** I will not have it so. Lie down, good sirs,
         It may be I shall otherwise bethink me.°

[*VARRUS and CLAUDIO lie down.*]

         Look, Lucius, here's the book I sought for so;

---

241 knave: lad. **o'erwatch'd:** tired from staying awake too long.

247 raise: awaken.

249 stand . . . pleasure: stay awake and be ready to serve you.

251 It may be . . . me: I might change my mind.

Loyalty and Betrayal *Why does Cassius make this request? What does it tell you about Cassius's character?*

I put it in the pocket of my gown.

LUCIUS. I was sure your lordship did not give it me.

255 BRUTUS. Bear with me, good boy, I am much forgetful.
Canst thou hold up thy heavy eyes awhile,
And touch thy instrument a strain or two?°

LUCIUS. Ay, my lord, an't° please you.

BRUTUS.   It does, my boy.
I trouble thee too much, but thou are willing.

260 LUCIUS. It is my duty, sir.

BRUTUS. I should not urge thy duty past thy might;
I know young bloods look for a time of rest.

LUCIUS. I have slept, my lord, already.

BRUTUS. It was well done, and thou shalt sleep again;
265 I will not hold thee long. If I do live,
I will be good to thee.

[*Music, and a song.*]

This is a sleepy tune. O murd'rous slumber!
Layest thou thy leaden mace° upon my boy,
That plays thee music? Gentle knave, good night;
270 I will not do thee so much wrong to wake thee.
If thou dost nod, thou break'st thy instrument;
I'll take it from thee; and, good boy, good night.
Let me see, let me see; is not the leaf turn'd down
Where I left reading? Here it is, I think.

[*Enter the GHOST OF CAESAR.*]

275 How ill this taper burns!° Ha! who comes here?
I think it is the weakness of mine eyes
That shapes this monstrous apparition.
It comes upon me. Art thou anything?
Art thou some god, some angel, or some devil,
280 That mak'st my blood cold, and my hair to stare?°
Speak to me what thou art.

GHOST. Thy evil spirit, Brutus.

BRUTUS.   Why com'st thou?

GHOST. To tell thee thou shalt see me at Philippi.

BRUTUS. Well; then I shall see thee again?

285 GHOST. Ay, at Philippi.

257 touch thy . . . two: play a song or two. (Lucius probably plays the lute, a stringed instrument.)
258 an't: if it.

267–268 O murd'rous . . . mace: Officers used to touch a rod (mace) to a person's shoulder as a sign of arrest. Brutus calls the mace of deathlike (murd'rous) sleep "leaden" because of its heaviness.
275 How ill . . . burns: It was believed that candles burn dimly when a ghost appears.
280 stare: stand on end.

Julius Caesar, Act IV, Scene III, Brutus & The Ghost, 1906. Edwin Austin Abbey. Illustration created for *Harper's Monthly.*

Loyalty and Betrayal *What character traits does Brutus demonstrate in this scene?*

BRUTUS. Why, I will see thee at Philippi then.

[*Exit GHOST.*]

Now I have taken heart thou vanishest.
Ill spirit, I would hold more talk with thee.
Boy! Lucius! Varrus! Claudio! Sirs, awake!
290   Claudio!

LUCIUS. The strings, my lord, are false.°

BRUTUS. He thinks he still is at his instrument.
Lucius, awake!

LUCIUS. My lord?

295 **BRUTUS.** Didst thou dream, Lucius, that thou so criedst out?

LUCIUS. My lord, I do not know that I did cry.

BRUTUS. Yes, that thou didst. Didst thou see anything?

LUCIUS. Nothing, my lord.

BRUTUS. Sleep again, Lucius. Sirrah Claudio!
300   [*To CLAUDIO and then VARRUS.*] Fellow thou, awake!

VARRUS. My lord?

CLAUDIO. My lord?

BRUTUS. Why did you so cry out, sirs, in your sleep?

BOTH. Did we, my lord?

BRUTUS.   Ay. Saw you anything?

305 **VARRUS.** No, my lord, I saw nothing.

CLAUDIO.   Nor I, my lord.

BRUTUS. Go and commend me° to my brother Cassius;
Bid him set on his pow'rs betimes before,°
And we will follow.

BOTH.   It shall be done, my lord.

[*They exit.*]

---

291 false: out of tune.

306 commend me: send my regards.
307 set on . . . before: start his troops moving early, at the lead.

Make and Verify Predictions *What does the ghost's visit suggest to you? What do you think will happen at Philippi?*

After You Read

Respond and Think Critically

1. **Connect to Personal Experience** What do you think about the relationship between Brutus and Cassius?

2. **Examine Theme** What point does Shakespeare make in Scene 1 about the effect of political power on those who hold it? Explain.

3. **Explain Motivation** What battle plan does Cassius propose? Why does he agree to march to Philippi?

4. **Analyze Character** What is your impression of Antony in Act 4? Do his actions surprise you? Explain. Support your response.

5. **Make Inferences About Author's Purpose** Why do you think Shakespeare included the conflict between Cassius and Brutus?

6. **Evaluate Mood** How does the introduction of the ghost in Scene 3 change the play's mood? In your opinion, is this a positive or negative change? Explain.

7. **Big Idea** **Draw Conclusions About Characters** What examples of loyalty do you see in the characters' actions in this act of the play? Support your response with evidence.

Literary Element Foil

One character's personality traits are sharper when a character with contrasting traits, a **foil**, is on stage.

8. **Draw Conclusions About Characters** Based on the dialogue in Scene 1, draw a conclusion about which character serves as a foil to Antony. How does this character differ from Antony? Support your response with text evidence.

9. **Compare and Contrast Characters** What differences do you see between Cassius and Brutus? Explain.

Reading Strategy Make and Verify Predictions

Review the chart you made on page 757 and then answer the following questions.

10. What have you predicted correctly in the play so far? What has surprised you? Explain.

11. What do you predict will happen at Philippi? Why?

Vocabulary Practice

Practice with Denotation and Connotation
Denotation is the literal, or dictionary, meaning of a word. **Connotation** is the implied, or cultural, meaning of a word. For example, the words *feeble* and *weak* have a similar denotation, "lack of strength or vigor," but *feeble* has a more negative connotation.

Each of the vocabulary words below is listed with a word that has a similar denotation. Choose the word that has a more negative connotation.

1. barren   empty
2. covert   sneaky
3. deceitful   false
4. rash   careless

Writing

Write a Journal Entry In your journal, describe a quarrel you had with a close friend. What caused the disagreement? How did you try to settle it? Were you able to remain friends afterward? Compare your conflict with that between Cassius and Brutus.

Before You Read

The Tragedy of Julius Caesar, Act 5

Build Background

Julius Caesar portrays Rome's transition from a republic to an empire. The republic was governed by citizen assemblies. The defeat of the republicans who assassinated Caesar ended Rome's republican form of rule.

Set Purposes for Reading

Literary Element Tragic Hero

A tragedy is a drama that ends in the downfall of its main character, or **tragic hero.** The tragic hero is an example of a **character archetype,** or a type of universal character who appears in oral or written literature across many cultures. The tragic hero is usually a high-ranking or respected person who has a fatal weakness, or tragic flaw that causes his or her downfall. This flaw may be a good quality or virtue that is carried to excess. As you read, ask yourself, Which character or characters might be the tragic hero?

Reading Strategy Evaluate Characters

When you **evaluate characters,** you make judgments about their attitudes, actions, words, and ethics. Understanding why a character behaves in a certain way can improve your understanding of the character and the work as a whole. As you read, ask yourself, What details can help me evaluate each character?

....

Tip: Track Details Use a chart like the one below to track your evaluations of the characters' actions and motivations.

Character	Detail	Significance of Detail
Octavius	Says "I was not born to die on Brutus' sword."	Octavius is determined. He will be a formidable opponent.

TEKS

For pages 774–789

10.4 Analyze how archetypes and motifs in drama affect the plot of plays.

Vocabulary

peevish (pē´vish) *adj.* irritable; bad-tempered; p. 777 *My mood was peevish due to lack of sleep.*

peril (per´əl) *n.* exposure to harm or danger; p. 778 *A mother elephant will always protect her offspring from peril.*

disconsolate (dis kon´sə lit) *adj.* dejected; mournful; unable to be comforted; p. 781 *Maria was disconsolate after missing a penalty shot in the playoffs.*

misconstrue (mis´kən strōō´) *v.* to misinterpret; to misunderstand; p. 782 *Diplomats choose their words carefully so they are not misconstrued.*

attain (ə tān´) *v.* to accomplish; to arrive at; p. 786 *If we work hard, we will attain our goal of graduating from high school.*

....

Tip: Analogies To complete an analogy, decide on the relationship represented by the first pair of words. Then apply that relationship to the second pair of words.

ACT 5

SCENE 1. The Plains of Philippi in Greece. A few weeks later.

[*Enter OCTAVIUS, ANTONY, and their ARMY.*]

OCTAVIUS. Now, Antony, our hopes are answered.
You said the enemy would not come down,
But keep the hills and upper regions.
It proves not so: their battles° are at hand;
5   They mean to warn° us at Philippi here,
Answering before we do demand of them.°

ANTONY. Tut, I am in their bosoms,° and I know
Wherefore they do it. They could be content
To visit other places, and come down
10   With fearful° bravery, thinking by this face
To fasten in our thoughts that they have courage;°
But 'tis not so.

[*Enter a MESSENGER.*]

MESSENGER.   Prepare you, generals,
The enemy comes on in gallant show;
Their bloody sign° of battle is hung out,
15   And something to be done immediately.

ANTONY. Octavius, lead your battle softly° on
Upon the left hand of the even° field.

OCTAVIUS. Upon the right hand I, keep thou the left.

ANTONY. Why do you cross me in this exigent?°

20   OCTAVIUS. I do not cross you; but I will do so.° [*March.*]

[*Drum. Enter BRUTUS, CASSIUS, and their ARMY; LUCILIUS, TITINIUS, MESSALA, and others.*]

BRUTUS. They stand, and would have parley.°

CASSIUS. Stand fast, Titinius; we must out and talk.

OCTAVIUS. Mark Antony, shall we give sign of battle?

ANTONY. No, Caesar, we will answer on their charge.°
25   Make forth, the generals would have some words.

---

4 battles: armies.

5 warn: defy.

6 Answering before . . . them: responding hostilely before we even challenge them to fight.
7 am in their bosoms: know what is in their hearts.

10 fearful: frightening; full of fear.

8–11 They could . . . courage: Antony dismisses his enemy's bravery as a false show (**face**), saying that they would really prefer to be somewhere else.

14 bloody sign: A red flag was flown from a Roman general's tent to signal the start of battle.
16 softly: slowly.
17 even: level.

19 cross me in this exigent: oppose me at this moment of crisis.
20 I will do so: I will do as I said. (Octavius insists on attacking from the right, which is usually the position of the most experienced general.)
21 would have parley: request a conference.

24 answer on their charge: respond when they attack.

Evaluate Characters *In your opinion, what quality or qualities does Octavius display here? Explain.*

OCTAVIUS. Stir not until the signal.

BRUTUS. Words before blows; is it so, countrymen?

OCTAVIUS. Not that we love words better, as you do.

BRUTUS. Good words are better than bad strokes, Octavius.

30 **ANTONY.** In your bad strokes, Brutus, you give good words;
Witness the hole you made in Caesar's heart,
Crying, "Long live! hail, Caesar!"

CASSIUS.   Antony,
The posture of your blows are yet unknown;°
But for your words, they rob the Hybla° bees,
35 And leave them honeyless.

ANTONY.   Not stingless too?

BRUTUS. O, yes, and soundless too;
For you have stol'n their buzzing, Antony,
And very wisely threat before you sting.

ANTONY. Villains! you did not so, when your vile daggers
40 Hack'd one another in the sides of Caesar.
You show'd your [teeth]° like apes, and fawn'd like hounds,
And bow'd like bondmen, kissing Caesar's feet;
Whilst damned Casca, like a cur, behind
Struck Caesar on the neck, O you flatterers!

45 **CASSIUS.** Flatterers? Now, Brutus, thank yourself;
This tongue had not offended so today,
If Cassius might have rul'd.°

OCTAVIUS. Come, come, the cause.° If arguing make us sweat,
The proof of it° will turn to redder drops.
50 Look,
I draw a sword against conspirators;
When think you that the sword goes up again?°
Never, till Caesar's three and thirty wounds
Be well aveng'd; or till another Caesar
55 Have added slaughter to the sword of traitors.°

BRUTUS. Caesar, thou canst not die by traitors' hands,
Unless thou bring'st them with thee.°

OCTAVIUS.   So I hope;
I was not born to die on Brutus' sword.

---

33 The posture . . . unknown: We don't know what kind of blows you will strike.
34 Hybla: an area in Sicily noted for its honey. (Cassius is reminding Antony of his "sweet" words to the conspirators after the assassination.)

41 show'd your [teeth]: grinned.

47 If Cassius . . . rul'd: if Cassius had had his way (when he argued that Antony should be killed).
48 cause: business at hand.
49 The proof of it: deciding the argument in battle.

52 goes up again: goes back into its sheath.

54–55 till another . . . traitors: until the conspirators have killed another Caesar (that is, Octavius himself).
56–57 Caesar . . . thee: Brutus suggests that all the traitors are on the side of Octavius and Antony.

Loyalty and Betrayal *What flaws does Antony accuse Brutus and Cassius of having?*

Tragic Hero *What earlier error on Brutus's part does Cassius allude to here?*

BRUTUS. O, if thou wert the noblest of thy strain,°

60   Young man, thou couldst not die more honorable.

CASSIUS. A **peevish** schoolboy,° worthless of such honor,
Join'd with a masker and a reveler!°

ANTONY. Old Cassius still!

OCTAVIUS.   Come, Antony; away!
Defiance, traitors, hurl we in your teeth.

65   If you dare fight today, come to the field;
If not, when you have stomachs.°

[*Exit OCTAVIUS, ANTONY, and ARMY.*]

CASSIUS. Why, now blow wind, swell billow, and swim bark!
The storm is up, and all is on the hazard.°

BRUTUS. Ho, Lucilius, hark, a word with you.

[*LUCILIUS and (then) MESSALA stand forth.*]

LUCILIUS.   My lord?

[*BRUTUS and LUCILIUS converse apart.*]

70   **CASSIUS.** Messala!

MESSALA.   What says my general?

CASSIUS.   Messala,
This is my birthday; as this very day
Was Cassius born. Give me thy hand, Messala;
Be thou my witness that against my will
(As Pompey was)° am I compell'd to set

75   Upon one battle all our liberties.
You know that I held Epicurus strong,°
And his opinion; now I change my mind,
And partly credit things that do presage.°
Coming from Sardis, on our former ensign°

80   Two mighty eagles fell, and there they perch'd,
Gorging and feeding from our soldiers' hands,
Who to Philippi here consorted° us.
This morning are they fled away and gone,
And in their steads do ravens, crows, and kites°

85   Fly o'er our heads, and downward look on us
As° we were sickly prey. Their shadows seem
A canopy most fatal, under which

Evaluate Characters *What is Cassius's judgment of Antony? Do you agree? Explain.*

---

Side notes:

59 **strain:** family.

61 **schoolboy:** Octavius was 21 at the time of the battle.
62 **a masker and a reveler:** one who indulges in lavish entertainment and drunken feasts.

66 **stomachs:** appetite for battle.

68 **all is . . . hazard:** Everything is at stake.

74 **As Pompey was:** Pompey was persuaded against his better judgment to fight at Pharsalus, where he was defeated by Caesar.
76 **held Epicurus strong:** have been a firm believer of Epicurus (a Greek philosopher whose followers did not believe in omens).
78 **presage:** foretell the future.
79 **former ensign:** foremost banner.
82 **consorted:** accompanied.

84 **kites:** hawks. (All three birds are omens of death.)

86 **As:** As if.

Our army lies, ready to give up the ghost.

MESSALA. Believe not so.

CASSIUS.   I but believe it partly,
90 For I am fresh of spirit, and resolv'd
    To meet all **perils** very constantly.°

BRUTUS. Even so, Lucilius.°

CASSIUS.   Now, most noble Brutus,
    The gods today stand friendly, that we may,
    Lovers in peace, lead on our days to age!°
95 But since the affairs of men rests still incertain,
    Let's reason with the worst that may befall.°
    If we do lose this battle, then is this
    The very last time we shall speak together:
    What are you then determined to do?

100 BRUTUS. Even by the rule of that philosophy
    By which I did blame Cato for the death
    Which he did give himself—I know not how,
    But I do find it cowardly and vile,
    For fear of what might fall, so to prevent
105 The time of life—arming myself with patience
    To stay the providence of some high powers
    That govern us below.°

CASSIUS.   Then, if we lose this battle,
    You are contented to be led in triumph
    Thorough the streets of Rome?

110 BRUTUS. No, Cassius, no. Think not, thou noble Roman,
    That ever Brutus will go bound to Rome;
    He bears too great a mind.° But this same day
    Must end that work the ides of March begun.
    And whether we shall meet again I know not;
115 Therefore our everlasting farewell take:
    Forever, and forever, farewell, Cassius!
    If we do meet again, why, we shall smile;
    If not, why then this parting was well made.

91 constantly: resolutely.

92 Even so, Lucilius: Brutus finishes his discussion with Lucilius.

93–94 The gods . . . age: May the gods remain friendly today, so that we, dear friends in peace with each other, may live to see old age.
96 Let's reason . . . befall: Let's consider the worst that can happen.

100–107 Even by the . . . below: Brutus says that according to his beliefs, suicide is cowardly (he refers to his father-in-law, Cato, who killed himself after Caesar's defeat of Pompey). He would endure his fate rather than cut short (**prevent**) his life because of what might happen.

110–112 Think not . . . mind: Brutus is suggesting that even though he rejects suicide, his pride would force him to commit such an act rather than allow himself to be paraded through the streets of Rome.

Tragic Hero *What are Brutus's beliefs concerning honor?*

Evaluate Characters *How would you describe Brutus's good-bye to Cassius? What does it suggest about him as a character?*

Vocabulary

peril (per′əl) *n.* exposure to harm or danger

Warrior on his death bed surrounded by mourners, 2nd century A.D. Artist unknown. Relief on a funeral stele. Museo Ostiense, Ostia, Italy.

CASSIUS. Forever, and forever, farewell, Brutus!
120   If we do meet again, we'll smile indeed;
        If not 'tis true this parting was well made.

BRUTUS. Why then, lead on. O, that a man
            might know
        The end of this day's business ere it come!
        But it sufficeth that the day will end,
125   And then the end is known. Come, ho, away!

[*BRUTUS, CASSIUS, and their ARMY withdraw to begin the battle.*]

SCENE 2. The field of battle. Shortly afterward.

[*Alarm. Enter BRUTUS and MESSALA.*]

BRUTUS. Ride, ride, Messala, ride, and give these bills°
        Unto the legions on the other side.°

[*Loud alarm.*]

        Let them set on at once; for I perceive
        But cold demeanor° in Octavio's wing,
5   And sudden push gives them the overthrow.
        Ride, ride, Messala, let them all come down.

[*They exit.*]

SCENE 3. Another part of the battlefield. Several hours later.

[*Alarms. Enter CASSIUS and TITINIUS.*]

CASSIUS. O, look, Titinius, look, the villains° fly!
        Myself have to mine own turn'd enemy.°
        This ensign° here of mine was turning back;
        I slew the coward, and did take it° from him.

5   TITINIUS. O Cassius, Brutus gave the word too early,
        Who, having some advantage on Octavius,
        Took it too eagerly. His soldiers fell to spoil,°
        Whilst we by Antony are all enclos'd.

[*Enter PINDARUS.*]

PINDARUS. Fly further off, my lord, fly further off;
10   Mark Antony is in your tents,° my lord;
        Fly, therefore, noble Cassius, fly far off.

CASSIUS. This hill is far enough. Look, look, Titinius!
        Are those my tents where I perceive the fire?

TITINIUS. They are, my lord.

Loyalty and Betrayal *Who has betrayed Cassius's army? What has Cassius done about it?*

---

1 bills: written orders.

2 legions on . . . side: other wing of troops (led by Cassius).

4 cold demeanor: lack of spirit.

1 villains: Cassius's own troops (who are retreating).
2 Myself have . . . enemy: I have turned to fighting my own men.
3 ensign: standard bearer.
4 it: the standard, or army flag.

7 spoil: looting.

10 tents: camp.

CASSIUS.   Titinius, if thou lovest me,
15   Mount thou my horse, and hide° thy spurs in him
        Till he have brought thee up to yonder troops.
        And here again, that I may rest assur'd
        Whether yond troops are friend or enemy.

        TITINIUS. I will be here again, even with a thought.°

[*Exit.*]

20   CASSIUS. Go, Pindarus, get higher on that hill;
        My sight was ever thick;° regard Titinius,
        And tell me what thou not'st about the field.

[*PINDARUS goes up.*]

        This day I breathed first: time is come round,
        And where I did begin, there shall I end;
25   My life is run his compass.° Sirrah, what news?

        PINDARUS. [*Above.*] O my lord!

        CASSIUS. What news?

        PINDARUS. Titinius is enclosed round about
        With horsemen, that make to him on the spur,°
30   Yet he spurs on. Now they are almost on him.
        Now, Titinius! Now some light.° O, he lights too!
        He's ta'en!° [*Shout.*] And, hark, they shout for joy.

        CASSIUS. Come down; behold no more.
        O, coward that I am, to live so long,
35   To see my best friend ta'en before my face!

[*PINDARUS descends.*]

        Come hither, sirrah.
        In Parthia did I take thee prisoner,
        And then I swore thee, saving of thy life,°
        That whatsoever I did bid thee do,
40   Thou shouldst attempt it. Come now, keep thine oath;
        Now be a freeman, and with this good sword,
        That ran through Caesar's bowels, search° this bosom.
        Stand not° to answer; here, take thou the hilts,°
        And when my face is cover'd, as 'tis now,

15 hide: dig.	
19 even with a thought: as quick as a thought.	
21 My sight . . . thick: I have always been nearsighted.	
25 is run his compass: has come full circle.	
29 make to . . . spur: ride quickly toward him.	
31 some light: some of them dismount.	
32 ta'en: taken prisoner.	
38 swore thee . . . life: made you swear when I saved your life.	
42 search: penetrate.	
43 Stand not: don't wait. **hilts:** sword handles.	

Tragic Hero *From the reports of Titinius and Pindarus, what does Cassius believe is happening?*

Evaluate Characters *In your opinion, what does this remark indicate about the character of Cassius?*

45   Guide thou the sword. [*PINDARUS stabs him.*] Caesar, thou
       art reveng'd,
    Even with the sword that kill'd thee. [*Dies.*]

PINDARUS. So, I am free; yet would not so have been,
    Durst I have done my will. O Cassius,
    Far from this country Pindarus shall run,
50   Where never Roman shall take note of him. [*Exit.*]

[*Enter TITINIUS and MESSALA.*]

MESSALA. It is but change,° Titinius; for Octavius
    Is overthrown by noble Brutus' power,
    As Cassius' legions are by Antony.

TITINIUS. These tidings will well comfort Cassius.

55 MESSALA. Where did you leave him?

TITINIUS.   All **disconsolate**,
    With Pindarus his bondman, on this hill.

MESSALA. Is not that he that lies upon the ground?

TITINIUS. He lies not like the living. O my heart!

MESSALA. Is not that he?

TITINIUS.   No, this was he, Messala,
60   But Cassius is no more. O setting sun,
    As in thy red rays thou dost sink tonight,
    So in his red blood Cassius' day is set!
    The sun of Rome is set. Our day is gone,
    Clouds, dews,° and dangers come; our deeds are done!
65   Mistrust of my success° hath done this deed.

MESSALA. Mistrust of good success° hath done this deed.
    O hateful error, melancholy's child,°
    Why dost thou show to the apt° thoughts of men
    The things that are not? O error, soon conceiv'd,
70   Thou never com'st unto a happy birth,
    But kill'st the mother that engend'red thee!°

TITINIUS. What, Pindarus? Where art thou, Pindarus?

MESSALA. Seek him, Titinius, whilst I go to meet
    The noble Brutus, thrusting this report

51 but change: only an exchange of fortune. (Pindarus was mistaken when he reported Titinius's capture—he had in fact come upon Brutus's troops.)

64 dews: Dews were considered unhealthy.
65 Mistrust of my success: Fear of my mission's outcome.
66 Mistrust of good success: Fear of how the battle would turn out.
67 O hateful . . . child: Messala suggests that Cassius's melancholy temperament caused him to misperceive events.
68 apt: ready (to be deceived).

71 the mother . . . thee: the mind that conceived the error.

Loyalty and Betrayal *What Roman ideas about loyalty and destiny does this passage suggest?*

Vocabulary

disconsolate (dis kon′sə lit) *adj.* dejected; mournful; unable to be comforted

75   Into his ears; I may say "thrusting" it;
For piercing steel and darts° envenomed

76 **darts:** arrows.

    Shall be as welcome to the ears of Brutus
    As tidings of this sight.

TITINIUS.   Hie you, Messala,
    And I will seek for Pindarus the while.

[*Exit* MESSALA.]

80   Why didst thou send me forth, brave Cassius?
    Did I not meet thy friends? and did not they
    Put on my brows this wreath of victory,
    And bid me give it thee? Didst thou not hear their shouts?
    Alas, thou hast **misconstrued** everything.

85   But hold thee, take this garland on thy brow;
    Thy Brutus bid me give it thee, and I
    Will do his bidding. Brutus, come apace,°

87 **apace:** quickly.

    And see how I regarded° Caius Cassius.

88 **regarded:** honored.

    By your leave, gods!—this is a Roman's part;°

89 **By your . . . part:** Titinius asks the gods to pardon him because he is cutting his life short to fulfill a Roman's duty **(part)**.

90   Come, Cassius' sword, and find Titinius' heart. [*Dies.*]

[*Alarm. Enter* BRUTUS, MESSALA, LUCILIUS, VOLUMNIUS, YOUNG CATO, *and* STRATO.]

BRUTUS. Where, where, Messala, doth his body lie?

MESSALA. Lo, yonder, and Titinius mourning it.

BRUTUS. Titinius' face is upward.

CATO.°   He is slain.

93 **Cato:** Brutus's brother-in-law, the son of Marcus Cato.

BRUTUS. O Julius Caesar, thou art mighty yet!
95   Thy spirit walks abroad, and turns our swords
    In our own proper° entrails. [*Low alarms.*]

96 **our own proper:** our very own.

CATO.   Brave Titinius!
    Look, whe'er he have not crown'd° dead Cassius!

97 **Look . . . crown'd:** see how he has crowned.

BRUTUS. Are yet two Romans living such as these?
    The last of all the Romans, fare thee well!
100   It is impossible that ever Rome
    Should breed thy fellow.° Friends, I owe moe° tears

101 **fellow:** equal. **moe:** more.

Evaluate Characters *What do you learn of Cassius's character from the reactions of Messala and Titinius to his death?*

Loyalty and Betrayal *Why does Brutus invoke the name of Julius Caesar?*

Vocabulary

misconstrue (mis´kən stroo´) *v.* to misinterpret; to misunderstand

Base of the Column of
Antoninus Pius, A.D. 138–161,
Roman. Vatican State.

View the Art How does this
scene add to your under-
standing of the battles in this
play?

To this dead man than you shall see me pay.
I shall find time, Cassius; I shall find time.
Come, therefore, and to Thasos° send his body;
105   His funerals shall not be in our camp,
Lest it discomfort° us. Lucilius, come,
And come, young Cato; let us to the field.
Labio and Flavio set our battles on.
'Tis three a'clock; and, Romans, yet ere night
110   We shall try fortune in a second fight.

[*They exit.*]

104 Thasos: an island near
Philippi.

106 discomfort: dishearten.

SCENE 4. Another part of the battlefield. Shortly later.

[*Alarm. Enter* BRUTUS, MESSALA, *(young)* CATO, LUCILIUS, *and* FLAVIUS.]

BRUTUS. Yet, countrymen, O, yet hold up your heads!°
      [*They exit.*]

CATO. What bastard doth not?° Who will go with me?
      I will proclaim my name about the field.
      I am the son of Marcus Cato,° ho!
5   A foe to tyrants, and my country's friend.
      I am the son of Marcus Cato, ho!

[*Enter* SOLDIERS *and fight.*]

1 Yet . . . heads: Brutus urges his
troops to keep fighting.

2 What bastard doth not: Who
among us was born so low that he
doesn't?
4 Marcus Cato: Portia's father.

Tragic Hero *What admirable qualities does Brutus display in this scene?*

LUCILIUS. And I am Brutus, Marcus Brutus, I;
 Brutus, my country's friend; know me for Brutus!°

[YOUNG CATO is slain.]

 O young and noble Cato, art thou down?
10 Why, now thou diest as bravely as Titinius,
 And mayst be honor'd, being Cato's son.

FIRST SOLDIER. Yield, or thou diest.

LUCILIUS.   Only I yield to die;
 There is so much that thou wilt kill me straight:°
 Kill Brutus, and be honor'd in his death.

15 FIRST SOLDIER. We must not. A noble prisoner!

[Enter ANTONY.]

 SECOND SOLDIER. Room, ho! Tell Antony, Brutus is ta'en.

 FIRST SOLDIER. I'll tell the news. Here comes the general.
 Brutus is ta'en. Brutus is ta'en, my lord.

 ANTONY. Where is he?

20 LUCILIUS. Safe, Antony, Brutus is safe enough.
 I dare assure thee that no enemy
 Shall ever take alive the noble Brutus;
 The gods defend him from so great a shame!
 When you do find him, or alive or° dead,
25 He will be found like Brutus, like himself.°

 ANTONY. This is not Brutus, friend, but, I assure you,
 A prize no less in worth. Keep this man safe,
 Give him all kindness; I had rather have
 Such men my friends than enemies. Go on,
30 And see whe'er Brutus be alive or dead,
 And bring us word unto Octavius' tent
 How everything is chanc'd.

[They exit.]

SCENE 5. Another part of the field. Late in the day.

[Enter BRUTUS, CLITUS, DARDANIUS, VOLUMNIUS, and STRATO.]

 BRUTUS. Come, poor remains of friends, rest on this rock.

7–8 And I am . . . Brutus: Lucilius impersonates his leader to divert the enemy's attention from the real Brutus.

13 There is . . . straight: You have good reason to kill me immediately.

24 or . . . or: either . . . or.
25 like himself: behaving like his noble self.

Evaluate Characters *What character traits does Shakespeare give the officers in the army of Cassius and Brutus?*

Evaluate Characters *What traits does Antony show in his response to Lucilius's admission that he is not actually Brutus?*

CLITUS. Statilius show'd the torchlight,° but, my lord,
　　He came not back. He is or ta'en or slain.

BRUTUS. Sit thee down, Clitus; slaying is the word,
5　　It is a deed in fashion.° Hark thee, Clitus. [*Whispering.*]

CLITUS. What, I, my lord? No, not for all the world.

BRUTUS. Peace then, no words.

CLITUS. 　　　　　　　　　　I'll rather kill myself.

BRUTUS. Hark thee, Dardanius. [*Whispering.*]

DARDANIUS. 　　　　　　　　Shall I do such a deed?

CLITUS. O Dardanius!

10　DARDANIUS. O Clitus!

CLITUS. What ill request did Brutus make to thee?

DARDANIUS. To kill him, Clitus. Look, he meditates.

CLITUS. Now is that noble vessel full of grief,
　　That it runs over even at his eyes.

15　BRUTUS. Come hither, good Volumnius; list° a word.

VOLUMNIUS. What says my lord?

BRUTUS. 　　　　　　　　　　Why, this, Volumnius;
　　The ghost of Caesar hath appear'd to me
　　Two several° times by night; at Sardis once,
　　And this last night, here in Philippi fields.
20　　I know my hour is come.

VOLUMNIUS. 　　　　　　　　Not so, my lord.

BRUTUS. Nay, I am sure it is, Volumnius.
　　Thou seest the world, Volumnius, how it goes;°
　　Our enemies have beat us to the pit.°

[*Low alarms.*]

　　It is more worthy to leap in ourselves
25　　Than tarry till they push us. Good Volumnius,
　　Thou know'st that we two went to school together;
　　Even for that our love of old, I prithee
　　Hold thou my sword-hilts, whilst I run on it.

VOLUMNIUS. That's not an office° for a friend, my lord.

[*Alarm still.*]

30　CLITUS. Fly, fly, my lord, there is no tarrying here.

BRUTUS. Farewell to you, and you, and you, Volumnius.
　　Strato, thou hast been all this while asleep;

Tragic Hero *What does Clitus think of Brutus?*

2 **show'd the torchlight:** signaled with a torch. (Statilius was sent out to see whether their camp was occupied by the enemy.)

5 **It is . . . fashion:** So many are being killed.

15 **list:** hear.

18 **several:** separate.

22 **Thou seest . . . goes:** You see how things are going.
23 **pit:** a hole into which hunted animals are driven (also, a grave).

29 **office:** job.

Farewell to thee too, Strato. Countrymen,
    My heart doth joy° that yet in all my life
35   I found no man but he was true to me.°
    I shall have glory by this losing day
    More than Octavius and Mark Antony
    By this vile conquest shall **attain** unto.°
    So fare you well at once, for Brutus' tongue
40   Hath almost ended his life's history.
    Night hangs upon mine eyes; my bones would rest,
    That have but labor'd to attain this hour.

[*Alarm. Cry within, "Fly, fly, fly!"*]

CLITUS. Fly, my lord, fly!

BRUTUS.   Hence! I will follow.

[*CLITUS, DARDANIUS, and VOLUMNIUS exit.*]

    I prithee, Strato, stay thou by thy lord,
45   Thou art a fellow of a good respect;°
    Thy life hath had some smatch° of honor in it.
    Hold then my sword, and turn away thy face,
    While I do run upon it. Wilt thou, Strato?

STRATO. Give me your hand first. Fare you well, my lord.

50 BRUTUS. Farewell, good Strato. [*Runs on his sword.*] Caesar,
    now be still,
    I kill'd not thee with half so good a will.

[*Dies.*]

[*Alarm. Retreat. Enter* ANTONY, OCTAVIUS, MESSALA, LUCILIUS, *and
the* ARMY.]

OCTAVIUS. What man is that?

MESSALA. My master's man. Strato, where is thy master?

STRATO. Free from the bondage you are in, Messala;
55   The conquerors can but make a fire of him;
    For Brutus only overcame himself,°
    And no man else hath honor by his death.

LUCILIUS. So Brutus should be found. I thank thee, Brutus,
    That thou hast prov'd Lucilius' saying true.

---

34 joy: rejoice.

35 no man . . . me: no man to be unfaithful to me.

36–38 I shall . . . unto: I shall have more glory from this defeat than Octavius and Antony will achieve from their ignoble victory.

45 respect: reputation.
46 smatch: taste.

56 Brutus . . . himself: only Brutus conquered himself.

Evaluate Characters *What judgments of Brutus might you form based on his request?*

Vocabulary

attain (ə tān´) *v.* to accomplish; to arrive at

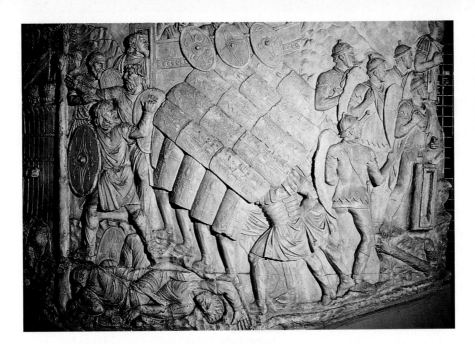

60 OCTAVIUS. All that serv'd Brutus, I will entertain them.°
      Fellow, wilt thou bestow thy time with me?

STRATO. Ay, if Messala will prefer° me to you.

OCTAVIUS. Do so, good Messala.

MESSALA. How died my master, Strato?

65 STRATO. I held the sword, and he did run on it.

MESSALA. Octavius, then take him to follow thee,
      That did the latest° service to my master.

ANTONY. This was the noblest Roman of them all;
      All the conspirators, save only he,
70   Did that they did in envy of great Caesar;
      He, only in a general honest thought
      And common good to all, made one of them.°
      His life was gentle,° and the elements
      So mix'd in him that Nature might stand up
75   And say to all the world, "This was a man!"°

OCTAVIUS. According to his virtue let us use° him,
      With all respect and rites of burial.
      Within my tent his bones tonight shall lie,
      Most like a soldier, ordered honorably.°
80   So call the field to rest, and let's away,
      To part° the glories of this happy day.
      [*All exit.*]

60 entertain them: take them into my service.

62 prefer: recommend.

67 latest: last.

71–72 He, only . . . them: He joined them only with honorable intentions for the public good.
73 gentle: noble.
73–75 His life . . . man: The Elizabethans believed that four elements (earth, water, air, and fire) in the body determined a person's temperament. Antony says that in Brutus the elements were perfectly balanced.
76 use: treat.
79 ordered honorably: with all due honor.
81 part: divide.

Tragic Hero *How does Antony claim that Brutus was different from the other conspirators? Do you agree with him? Explain.*

After You Read

Respond and Think Critically

1. **Connect to Personal Experience** What went through your mind as you finished reading this play? Explain.

2. **Explain Events** What does Brutus say about Caesar's spirit at Philippi? How does Brutus think Caesar is affecting the events on the battlefield? Support your answer with evidence from Act 5.

3. **Analyze Dialogue** Compare Antony's speech at the end of the play with his remarks about Brutus at Caesar's funeral. How does his dialogue show that his views of Brutus have changed? Why have they changed?

4. **Make Inferences About Theme** What actions does Octavius take at the end of the play? What message about leadership do his actions suggest? Support your response. **OER**

5. **Analyze Motivation** Are Antony and Octavius motivated more by the desire for power or the wish to avenge Caesar's death? Explain and include evidence from the text in your response.

6. **Draw Conclusions About Events** What do you consider the most significant mistake committed at Philippi? Explain.

7. **Big Idea Draw Conclusions About Characters** What loyalties would you say are strongest in this play? What betrayals seem the most damaging? Support your response.

Primary Visual Artifact

Statues of Caesar

In the days before photography, how was the memory of a person's appearance kept alive? If you were a wealthy Roman, you likely commissioned an artist to paint or sculpt the face of the person you wanted to remember. Artists also created busts, or sculpted representations of the upper part of the human figure. One figure of Caesar stood in a Roman temple with the inscription, "To the undefeated god." To celebrate the circus games, Romans carried an ivory likeness of Caesar through the streets. Many antique busts of Caesar still survive.

Group Activity Discuss the following questions with your classmates.

1. What aspects of Caesar's character does this bust reveal?

2. Do you think a piece of sculpture, such as this one, can convey certain human qualities better than a photograph can? Explain.

Contemporary bust of Gaius Julius Caesar, c. 60–44 B.C. Capitoline Palace, Rome.

Tragic Hero

More than one character in *Julius Caesar* may fit the **tragic hero** archetype. Caesar is the title character, and his death is the central event in the play. However, the play focuses more on Brutus and ends with his death rather than Caesar's death. Review the pink highlighted passages and questions to help you answer the following questions.

8. **Analyze Archetypes** What is Caesar's tragic flaw? What is Brutus's? How does the presence of these two archetypal tragic heroes affect the plot of this play? Explain. Use evidence from the text in your response.

9. **Evaluate Events** In your opinion, which character's fate is more tragic? Who do you think is the true tragic hero? Support your response.

Review: Theme

As you learned on page 275, the **theme** of a piece of literature is its central idea about life. Works of literature from different time periods can have similar themes.

10. **Partner Activity** With a classmate, identify one important theme of *Julius Caesar* and the evidence that supports it. Together create a web diagram like the one below.

Then compare and contrast this theme with a theme in *Antigone.* How are they similar and different? Support your response with text evidence.

Evaluate Characters

When you **evaluate a character,** you make judgments about his or her abilities and qualities.

11. Which aspects of Caesar's character do you consider admirable? Which aspects of his character are you critical of? Explain.

12. In the first half of the play, what judgments did you form about Cassius? Did these judgments change as the play progressed? Explain.

13. Do you agree with Antony that all the conspirators, except Brutus, are motivated by envy? Support your opinion with examples from the play.

Vocabulary Practice

Practice with Analogies Choose the word that best completes each analogy.

1. peevish : pleasant :: brief :
   a. sad   **b.** abbreviated   **c.** lengthy

2. danger : peril :: fear :
   a. terror   **b.** confidence   **c.** enjoyment

3. joyous : victory :: disconsolate :
   a. loss   **b.** sadness   **c.** consolation

4. bolster : undermine :: misconstrue :
   a. confuse   **b.** understand   **c.** steal

5. improve : practice :: attain :
   a. mistake   **b.** fail   **c.** strive

Foreign Words in English

Brutus's dramatic death at the end of Julius Caesar *can be considered a* **coup de grace.**

Coup de grace is a foreign phrase that is commonly used in English. Using an online or a print dictionary, determine the relationship between the original source language and original meaning of this phrase. Then write the modern definition of *coup de grace.* Finally, demonstrate your knowledge of the phrase by using it in a sentence of your own creation.

Respond Through Writing

Script

TEKS

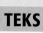

10.14.C Write a script with an explicit or implicit theme and details that contribute to a definite mood or tone.

Apply Theme In *Julius Caesar*, Shakespeare dramatizes a tragic story of loyalty and betrayal in ancient Rome. Write a script for a one-act play in which you tell a modern story of a character who is forced to decide between carrying out an act of loyalty and committing an act of betrayal. Include a main character who must make a decision and a foil who complicates the life of the main character. Convey either an explicit or implicit theme about loyalty and betrayal through the characters' actions.

Purpose and Audience The purpose for writing this play is to explore how Shakespeare's themes apply to our world today. You will also share your observations of human nature while you entertain your audience, people who have read or seen a performance of *Julius Caesar*.

Plan Interview several people about times when they have been affected by acts of either loyalty or betrayal. Observe or ask about the emotions involved in their stories. After hearing several stories, create a situation with which the people you interviewed could easily identify.

Draft To create a short but complete play, use the following outline.

I. Introduce the main character, setting, and situation. Be sure to establish a clear mood and tone.
II. Introduce the foil who changes the situation and forces the main character to make a choice.
III. Show the main character's struggle to decide.
IV. Add a complication before the character is able to decide.
V. End with the character choosing an act of loyalty or of betrayal.

Use both stage directions and dialogue to dramatize your story. Stage directions can describe the actions of the characters, establish the tone of their dialogue, or create a mood with lighting or scenery. Dialogue moves the story forward and communicates the thoughts of the characters.

Revise Give each character a distinct way of speaking that emphasizes the most important differences between them. For example, characters could speak in either short or long sentences which may suggest that one character is impulsive and the other is thoughtful.

Edit Edit your script, correcting any errors in grammar, spelling, and punctuation. Use the Grammar Tip in the side column to help you use commas with appositives. If you are writing your script by hand, be sure it is legible.

> **Grammar Tip**
>
> **Commas with Appositives**
>
> An **appositive** is a noun or pronoun, with or without modifiers, placed next to another noun or pronoun to identify it or give additional information about it. Use commas to set off an appositive if it is nonrestrictive and not essential to the meaning of the sentence.
>
> *Caesar, a **military leader**, is the most powerful man in Rome.*
>
> Do not set off an appositive with commas if it gives necessary information about the noun.
>
> *Caesar is wary of the conspirator **Cassius**.*
>
> Since there was more than one conspirator, the name *Cassius* is necessary, not merely additional, information.

Media Workshop

Plays On Film

TEKS

For pages 791–796

10.12.B Analyze how messages in media are conveyed through visual and sound techniques (e.g., editing, reaction shots, sequencing, background music).

Literature Connection Since the movie industry began, William Shakespeare's plays have provided filmmakers with rich, dramatic narratives. There have been hundreds of film adaptations of the Bard's timeless tales. *Julius Caesar* has been portrayed on film more than twenty times, including an early silent version filmed in 1908. The historic nature of the play, as well as its strong characters and compelling story line, translates well from the page to the screen.

From Page to Screen

Adapting a play to the film medium poses a number of problems for filmmakers. Creating a screenplay requires the writer and director to make decisions about what dialogue to keep (or omit) from the original play and how to portray the world of the play on screen.

With a source like Shakespeare, the screenplay writer is working with exceptional dialogue that has come to be regarded as some of the best in the English language. Most adaptations of Shakespeare's plays maintain the original dialogue, sometimes cutting away sections of scenes in order to make the movie shorter. Some filmmakers have chosen to update Shakespeare's dialogue. Though there have been some notable successes with this approach, most attempts at updating Shakespeare's dialogue have fallen flat.

Creating the world of Shakespeare's plays for movies allows filmmakers great freedom and creativity. The visual nature of film demands that the filmmakers imagine and construct a fully realized world for the action to occur. Costumes, landscapes, interiors of rooms—the director has to plan and decide on every visual detail in order to create a convincing environment for the story. He or she can maintain the integrity of the narrative even while setting the story in very different locations.

One great advantage film has in bringing Shakespeare's tales to life is the intimacy and vision of the movie camera. The camera limits what the audience can see at any given time during a scene, so if the director wants you to see only how one character reacts to action in the story, the director can use a close-up shot of only that character. Shakespeare often includes asides in his plays, where characters reveal their thoughts to the audience or speak secretly to another character. In film, the director can use the camera to isolate the aside and make sure the audience hears what is being said without distraction. Camera work and techniques are at the heart of filmmaking.

Visual and Sound Techniques

How filmmakers choose to present their stories can tell us much about the messages they hope their films convey. Refer to the chart to help you analyze film techniques.

Strategies for Evaluating Film Techniques

Strategy		Definition		Questions to Ask Yourself
composition	☑	Directors must determine the light, camera angle, movement, and placement of the actors in a frame.	☑	Does the composition provide any information about the characters? Does the lighting emphasize anything?
camera angle	☑	In a **low angle** shot, the camera is placed below eye level and looks up at the subject. For a **high angle** shot, the camera is placed above the subject and looks down.	☑	Is the director trying to make us feel a certain way about a character by using a low angle shot? What do high angle shots suggest about a character?
reaction shot	☑	A reaction shot shows one character's response to something he or she has just heard or seen.	☑	What do we learn about a character in a reaction shot? How does a reaction inform our understanding of a scene?
close-up shot	☑	A close-up is a tightly framed shot of one character's face.	☑	Does the close-up reveal anything about the character?
editing	☑	Editing is the process of arranging and selecting shots to form a scene.	☑	Does the editing of a scene affect the way we view the scene?
shot sequence	☑	A shot sequence is the order of shots put together to create a scene.	☑	Why did the filmmakers choose to link this series of shots in this order?
sound	☑	Some sound is intended as background sound or music; other sounds are effects used to elicit a specific reaction from the audience.	☑	What effect does the background music have on the scene? Does the director use any sound clues to identify characters or plot points?

Activity

Analyze Film Techniques

Choose one image from movie versions of *Julius Caesar* in this workshop. Identify at least one technique the filmmaker used from this chart. In a paragraph, explain why you think the filmmaker chose to use that technique.

Media Impact: **Movie Poster**

Build Background The 1953 movie version of *Julius Caesar* featured three of the film world's most celebrated actors: John Gielgud, James Mason, and Marlon Brando. Gielgud was a classically trained Shakespearean actor who had appeared in many stage and screen adaptations of Shakespeare's work. Mason was a respected actor trained on the British stage who became much sought after in both American and British films. Brando was the odd man out: the Nebraska native made his early reputation as an actor as a raw, fiery force of energy who played very rough-hewn characters. The same year Brando played Marc Antony in *Julius Caesar,* he played a delinquent motorcycle rebel in search of trouble in *The Wild One.* Brando's Marc Antony is unlike any other portrayal of the role.

Activity
Listening and Speaking

Meet in small groups to discuss the following questions.

1. Why might the poster designer have chosen the individual character poses depicted?

2. Consider the placement of the characters in the poster. What message is being conveyed about the characters?

3. Based on what you see in the poster, what kind of music might you expect to hear in the movie?

Close-up

The three characters huddled together conspiratorially are captured in close-up. Notice the way they appear to be looking across the poster toward Caesar.

Angle

Julius Caesar is separated from the other characters and is drawn from a low angle, which gives him the appearance of dominance or superiority.

Composition

The gold band on the bottom provides information on the actors and their roles. The colorful drawn image highlights the different starring actors in a variety of poses.

Media Impact: **Film**

Build Background Shakespeare's *Julius Caesar* is filled with intrigue, conspiracy, and prophecies. Though the plot is dramatic and full of twists and turns, Shakespeare was exploring questions of how one handles extreme power and how the powerful rule over their subjects. Of the many *Julius Caesar* film adaptations that have been produced, the 1953 version stands out for its superb performances and powerful storytelling. Director Joseph Mankiewicz expertly balances both the grandeur of the plot and setting with the larger questions of power that Shakespeare explored in his play.

Reaction Shot

The director frames this close-up so you can see both Caesar speaking and Brutus reacting to him. Notice how the actors' faces are in focus but most of the frame surrounding them is not.

Caesar appeals to his friend Brutus for help.

Marc Antony urges the crowd to remain calm after Caesar's death.

Camera Angle

This scene uses a high angle shot. By placing the camera above the action, the director provides a "bird's eye view" of the action, showing spatial relationships between characters or commenting on the scene and its subjects.

Composition

Notice how Marc Antony is placed in this frame: holding back the angry mob, he is boxed in by the people of Rome and the white marble steps of the palace.

Activity
Listening and Speaking

Meet in small groups to discuss the following questions.

1. In the reaction shot of Caesar and Brutus, what do the filmmakers want us to understand about Brutus and his relationship with Caesar?

2. When Antony speaks to the crowd outside the palace, what message is the director trying to convey through the composition of the shot?

3. Based on your reading of the play, how effectively did the filmmakers capture Antony's interaction with the crowd? Explain.

4. If you were directing this film, describe the sequence of shots you might use to depict Antony's speech to the crowd. Use the chart on page 792 for help.

Media Impact: **Storyboards**

Activity

Listening and Speaking

1. Take another look at the storyboard you created. Are there places where you might edit shots differently to change the pacing of your scene? Describe the changes you would make.

2. What did you find to be most important in planning your scene—the composition of the shots or the sequence of the shots? Explain your answer.

3. Exchange your storyboard with a fellow student and direct the scene your own way. Reread the section of the play your partner storyboarded, and then create storyboards for the same scene the way you would do it if you were directing that scene. Then you and your partner can compare and discuss how you both chose to interpret the scene.

Build Background Filmmakers use storyboards to plan out each shot in a movie. Each individual camera shot is sketched out in small boxes to represent the sequence of shots in a scene. This allows everyone to know what the director wants each scene and shot to look like.

How to Storyboard You will create a storyboard for a scene from *Julius Caesar*. You'll need to provide a sketch of how you want the scene to look, as well as notes on any music or sound effects you want included in the scene. You also need to make dialogue notes for each storyboard square. Refer to the chart on page 792 for help in designing your storyboard. As you create your storyboard, consider the following points.

- How should I compose each shot? What do I want the audience to see?
- What camera angles would best convey the scene? Do I need close-up or reaction shots?
- How will the shots flow together in sequence? Do I want the scene to be jarring or flow smoothly?
- How will these shots be edited together to create the scene?
- What kind of sound do I want in the scene? Background sounds? Special effects sounds? Dramatic music?

Use the sample below as a guide for creating your storyboard.

1. High angle shot

Sound:
•angry crowd noise

Brutus: Then follow me, and give me audience, friends...

2. Reaction shot

Sound:
•angry crowd noise

Citizens: We will be satisfied; let us be satisfied!

3. High angle, close-up

Sound:
•angry crowd noise

First Citizen: I will hear Brutus speak.

4. Close-up, reaction shot

Sound:
•angry crowd noise

Second Citizen: I will hear Cassius, and compare their reasons.

Portraits of Real Life

Marian Anderson, Singer, 1944. Laura Wheeler Waring. Oil on canvas. National Portrait Gallery, Smithsonian Institution, Washington, DC.

View the Art Marian Anderson began her singing career in a church as a young girl. In 1955, she became the first African American to sing with the New York Metropolitan Opera. How would you describe this painting? What does it suggest about the plays you will read in this part of the unit?

BIG IDEA

When reading a comedy, sometimes it is hard to know whether to laugh or cry. People find humor in the mistakes and misfortunes that comic characters experience. Maybe we laugh because we know that, in real life, we could be in their situations. Part 2 includes plays set in realistic situations. As you read, ask yourself, What is most interesting about realistic plays? Do they mirror life as it really is?

TEKS

For pages 798–799

10.4 Understand, make inferences and draw conclusions about the structure and elements of drama and provide evidence from text to support understanding.

LITERARY FOCUS

Comedy and Modern Drama

What are the elements of comedy and modern drama?

Modern drama often deals with everyday people. Characters in modern plays can be average people involved in personal, even petty conflicts.

Drama can be used as a synonym for *play.* Drama is traditionally separated into sub-categories of comedy and tragedy. Dramas can include acts (large divisions) and scenes (smaller divisions within acts).

Comedy

In the broadest sense, a **comedy** is a play that is humorous and often has a happy ending. Comedies typically poke fun at people's faults and limitations in order to teach a lesson about human nature. There are different styles of comedy. **Farce** places flat characters in ridiculous situations. **Satire** exposes and ridicules vice or folly in individuals or societies. In this scene from Anton Chekhov's *A Marriage Proposal,* after fighting bitterly with Lomov, Natalia becomes hysterical upon learning that Lomov meant to propose to her.

NATALIA. He's a monster! First he tries to steal our land, and then he has the nerve to yell at you.
CHUBUKOV. Yes, and that turnip, that stupid rooster, has the gall to make a proposal. Some proposal!
NATALIA. What proposal?
CHUBUKOV. Why, he came to propose to you.
NATALIA. To propose? To me? Why didn't you tell me before?
CHUBUKOV. So he gets all dressed up in his formal clothes. That stuffed sausage, that dried up cabbage!
NATALIA. To propose to me? Ohhhh! [*Falls into a chair and starts wailing.*] Bring him back! Back! Go get him! Bring him back! Ohhhh!

Modern Drama

While satire and farce use deliberately unrealistic situations and characters, many modern plays find their humor and sadness in everyday life. Such plays can be either comedy or tragedy, but they often do not follow the traditional elements of these forms.

In *That's Your Trouble,* for example, Harold Pinter uses everyday language to create a dialogue between two characters in a park. A conflict arises when they argue about whether a stranger will get a headache from wearing a sandwich board. Though comic on the surface, the play suggests an underlying message about the nature of human interactions, a hallmark of the Absurdist movement of the 1950s and 1960s.

Elements of Drama

Dialogue **Dialogue** is the conversation characters have in a play. In each line of dialogue below, the name of the character is followed by what he or she says.

NATALIA. I hate to interrupt you, my dear Ivan Vassilevitch, but you said: "my Oxen Meadows." Do you really think they're yours?
LOMOV. Why of course they're mine.
NATALIA. What do you mean?
The Oxen Meadows are ours, not yours!

—Anton Chekhov, **from** *A Marriage Proposal*

Stage Directions Stage directions are indications to the director, actors, and reader about the movement and appearance of characters as well as details about sets, props, costumes, sound effects, and lighting. Stage directions also guide specific actions, such as entrances and exits of characters, as well as the delivery of lines—which characters are being addressed and how.

In the excerpt below, the stage directions appear in italics within brackets. Notice the references to actions and props.

MARICA. [*Trying to hide the bottle behind her.*] Raquel! What are you doing here?
RAQUEL. What did you have hidden behind the books, Marica?
MARICA. [*Attempting a forced laugh.*] I? Nothing. Why do you think I have anything?
RAQUEL. [*Taking a step toward her.*] Give it to me.
MARICA. [*Backing away from her.*] No. No, I won't.

—Josefina Niggli, **from** *The Ring of General Macías*

Props Short for the word *properties*, **props** are the objects and small physical elements of a stage play or movie set. Props are often mentioned in stage directions.

RAQUEL. Good night, little one.
[*MARICA goes out through the house door Left, taking her candle with her. RAQUEL stares down at the bottle of poison in her hand, then puts it away in one of the small drawers of the desk.*]

—Josefina Niggli, **from** *The Ring of General Macías*

Quickwrite

Draw Conclusions Reread the excerpts from *A Marriage Proposal* on the previous page and *The Ring of General Macías* on this page. What can you conclude about why the two authors use stage directions and props as they do? Write a paragraph that addresses this question. Explain how your understanding of the excerpts would change if the excerpts only contained dialogue and no other elements.

 Literature Online

Literature and Reading For more about literary elements, go to glencoe.com and enter QuickPass code GL57805u4.

A Marriage Proposal

Meet **Anton Chekhov**

(1860 –1904)

Anton Chekhov was an unlikely genius. Who would suspect that a provincial Russian doctor and the son of a grocer would revolutionize literature? As a doctor, Chekhov was trained to observe and analyze without judging his patients; in his writing, he applied the same principles to his characters. Chekhov's stories and plays focused on everyday life, illuminating the human flaws and the failures all people experience. His new approach helped popularize the Realist school of writing.

Humble Beginnings At age sixteen, Chekhov lived alone and supported himself. His father had gone bankrupt and rushed the rest of the family to Moscow to avoid debtor's prison. Chekhov remained at home to complete his studies while supporting himself as a tutor. Three years later, in 1879, Chekhov joined his family to study medicine on scholarship at the University of Moscow. He was deeply affected by his family's financial failure, and he would frequently turn to similar topics and situations in his plays and short stories.

> "The dramatist is not meant to be a judge of his characters and what they say; his only job is to be an impartial witness."
>
> —Anton Chekhov

While he was studying medicine, Chekhov began selling anecdotes and articles to comic magazines as a way of supporting his family. In these humorous pieces, critics see the revolutionary techniques that flourished in his later works.

A "Real" Writer By 1885 Chekhov had begun submitting his stories to more serious literary journals and magazines. In 1888 he won Russia's coveted Pushkin Prize for his short story collection *In the Twilight*.

In 1895 Chekhov decided to focus on playwriting. Following the successful second run of *The Seagull* in 1898, Chekhov continued to write plays for the Moscow Art Theatre. He described his plays, including *Uncle Vanya*, *Three Sisters*, and *The Cherry Orchard*, as light social comedies. He was annoyed by productions that staged the plays as melodramas.

Just as he began to experience great success on the stage, Chekhov's career was cut short. Untreated tuberculosis had weakened his heart and he died of a heart attack at the age of 44. His style of narrative realism would later influence nearly every major playwright of the twentieth century, including George Bernard Shaw, Samuel Beckett, Eugene O'Neill, and Tom Stoppard.

Literature Online

Author Search For more about Anton Chekhov, go to glencoe.com and enter QuickPass code GL57805u4.

Literature and Reading Preview

Connect to the Play

Have you ever made plans that someone or something later interfered with? Write a journal entry describing this experience.

Build Background

In the late 1800s, Russian serfs had been freed, yet aristocratic farmers still depended on landless peasants to work on their estates. Chekhov's plays give a sense that the "old" Russia was dying.

Set Purposes for Reading

Big Idea Portraits of Real Life

As you read this play, ask yourself, How do Chekhov's characters' speech and actions mimic those in real life?

Literary Element Farce

A **farce** is a type of comedy with stereotyped characters in ridiculous situations. Stereotypes are one kind of **character archetype**—familiar personalities that recur in the stories of different cultures and eras, such as the reluctant hero, the clumsy sidekick, or the absent-minded old man. In a farce, authors place these exaggerated characters in humorous situations that often involve physical antics, improbable events, and surprises. Farce is a way to make fun of human traits and customs. As you read, ask yourself, Which traits and customs is Chekhov highlighting?

Reading Strategy Recognize Author's Purpose

Authors often write for a particular purpose: to entertain, to inform or to teach a lesson, to tell a story, to try to persuade readers to accept an idea, or for a variety of other purposes. As you read, ask yourself, What is Chekhov's purpose?

Tip: Note Details Use a chart like the one below to help you track details and draw conclusions about them that relate to Chekhov's purpose.

Details	Conclusions
Chubukov repeats the phrase "and so forth" often.	Chekhov uses this trait to show that Chubukov speaks without purpose, repeating a phrase with no real meaning.

TEKS

For pages 800–815

10.4 Analyze how archetypes and motifs in drama affect the plot of plays.

Vocabulary

impudence (im′pyə dəns) *n.* speech or behavior that is aggressively forward or rude; p. 806 *Arnie showed his impudence when he cut in front of those who had been standing in the lunch line.*

oblivious (ə bliv′ē əs) *adj.* unmindful or unaware; not noticing; p. 813 *Ana and Maria were oblivious to their teacher's desire to start class.*

Tip: Word Origins Word origins are the history and development of words. Also called **etymologies**, they are often included in dictionary entries.

A Marriage Proposal

Anton Chekhov
Translated by Theodore Hoffman

Return from the Fair, 1883. Illarion Mikhailovich Pryanishnikov. Oil on canvas, 48.5 x 71.5 cm.
State Russian Museum, St. Petersburg.

View the Art Nineteenth-century rural life in Russia was hard for the peasant class. How do the details in this image affect your understanding of the play's background?

CHARACTERS

STEPAN STEPANOVITCH CHUBUKOV
(ste pän′ ste pä′nô vich choo boo′ kôf):
a landowner; elderly, pompous, but
affable

IVAN VASSILEVITCH LOMOV
(i vän′ vä sil′ē vich lô′môf):
a landowner and Chubukov's neighbor;
healthy, but a hypochondriac; nervous,
suspicious

NATALIA STEPANOVNA (nä täl′yə ste pä nôv′ nə):
Chubukov's daughter; twenty-five but
still unmarried

SCENE: Chubukov's mansion—the living
room

[*LOMOV enters, formally dressed in evening
jacket, white gloves, top hat. He is nervous
from the start.*]

CHUBUKOV. [*Rising.*] Well, look who's here!
Ivan Vassilevitch! [*Shakes his hand warmly.*]
What a surprise, old man! How are you?

LOMOV. Oh, not too bad. And you?

CHUBUKOV. Oh, we manage, we manage.
Do sit down, please. You know, you've
been neglecting your neighbors, my dear
fellow. It's been ages. Say, why the formal
dress? Tails, gloves, and so forth. Where's
the funeral, my boy? Where are you
headed?

LOMOV. Oh, nowhere. I mean, here; just to
see you, my dear Stepan Stepanovitch.

CHUBUKOV. Then why the full dress, old
boy? It's not New Year's, and so forth.

LOMOV. Well, you see, it's like this. I have
come here, my dear Stepan Stepanovitch,
to bother you with a request. More than
once, or twice, or more than that, it has
been my privilege to apply to you for
assistance in things, and you've always,
well, responded. I mean, well, you have.
Yes. Excuse me, I'm getting all mixed up.
May I have a glass of water, my dear
Stepan Stepanovitch? [*Drinks.*]

CHUBUKOV. [*Aside.*] Wants to borrow some
money. Not a chance! [*Aloud.*] What can I
do for you my dear friend?

LOMOV. Well, you see, my dear Stepanitch.
. . . Excuse me, I mean Stepan my
Dearovitch. . . . No, I mean, I get all confused, as you can see. To make a long story
short, you're the only one who can help
me. Of course, I don't deserve it, and
there's no reason why I should expect you
to, and all that.

CHUBUKOV. Stop beating around the bush!
Out with it!

LOMOV. In just a minute. I mean, now, right
now. The truth is, I have come to ask the
hand. . . . I mean, your daughter, Natalia
Stepanovna, I, I want to marry her!

CHUBUKOV. [*Overjoyed.*] Great heavens! Ivan
Vassilevitch! Say it again!

LOMOV. I have come humbly to ask for the
hand. . . .

CHUBUKOV. [*Interrupting.*] You're a prince!
I'm overwhelmed, delighted, and so forth.
Yes, indeed, and all that! [*Hugs and kisses
LOMOV.*] This is just what I've been hoping
for. It's my fondest dream come true.
[*Sheds a tear.*] And, you know, I've always
looked upon you, my boy, as if you were
my own son. May God grant to both of
you His Mercy and His Love, and so forth.
Oh, I have been wishing for this. . . . But

Portraits of Real Life *How would you describe Lomov's
manner here?*

Recognize Author's Purpose *Why does Chekhov have
Chubukov respond in this way?*

why am I being so idiotic? It's just that I'm off my rocker with joy, my boy! Completely off my rocker! Oh, with all my soul I'm. . . . I'll go get Natalia, and so forth.

LOMOV. [*Deeply moved.*] Dear Stepan Stepanovitch, do you think she'll agree?

CHUBUKOV. Why, of course, old friend. Great heavens! As if she wouldn't! Why she's crazy for you! Good God! Like a love-sick cat, and so forth. Be right back. [*Leaves.*]

LOMOV. It's cold. I'm gooseflesh all over, as if I had to take a test. But the main thing is, to make up my mind, and keep it that way. I mean, if I take time out to think, or if I hesitate, or talk about it, or have ideals, or wait for real love, well, I'll just never get married! Brrrr, it's cold! Natalia Stepanovna is an excellent housekeeper. She's not too bad looking. She's had a good education. What more could I ask? Nothing. I'm so nervous, my ears are buzzing. [*Drinks.*] Besides, I've just got to get married. I'm thirty-five already. It's sort of a critical age. I've got to settle down and lead a regular life. I mean, I'm always getting palpitations,[1] and I'm nervous, and I get upset so easy. Look, my lips are quivering, and my eyebrow's twitching. The worst thing is the night. Sleeping. I get into bed, doze off, and, suddenly, something inside me jumps. First my head snaps, and then my shoulder blade, and I roll out of bed like a lunatic and try to walk it off. Then I try to go back to sleep, but, as soon as I do, something jumps again! Twenty times a night, sometimes. . . .

---

1. If Lomov does in fact get *palpitations,* he experiences rapid, irregular heartbeats, which are often caused by stress or nervousness.

> **Farce** *What makes Chubukov's reaction to Lomov's request an example of farce?*

> **Recognize Author's Purpose** *How do you think Chekhov wants the audience to feel about Lomov?*

[*NATALIA STEPANOVNA enters.*]

NATALIA. Oh, it's only you. All Papa said was: "Go inside, there's a merchant come to collect his goods." How do you do, Ivan Vassilevitch?

LOMOV. How do you do, dear Natalia Stepanovna?

NATALIA. Excuse my apron, and not being dressed. We're shelling peas. You haven't been around lately. Oh, do sit down. [*They do.*] Would you like some lunch?

LOMOV. No thanks, I had some.

NATALIA. Well, then smoke if you want. [*He doesn't.*] The weather's nice today . . . but yesterday, it was so wet the workmen couldn't get a thing done. Have you got much hay in? I felt so greedy I had a whole field done, but now I'm not sure I was right. With the rain it could rot, couldn't it? I should have waited. But why are you so dressed up? Is there a dance or something? Of course, I must say you look splendid, but. . . . Well, tell me, why are you so dressed up?

LOMOV. [*Excited.*] Well, you see, my dear Natalia Stepanovna, the truth is, I made up my mind to ask you to . . . well, to, listen to me. Of course, it'll probably surprise you and even maybe make you angry, but. . . . [*Aside.*] It's so cold in here!

NATALIA. Why, what do you mean? [*A pause.*] Well?

LOMOV. I'll try to get it over with. I mean, you know, my dear Natalia Stepanovna that I've known, since childhood, even, known, and had the privilege of knowing, your family. My late aunt, and her husband, who, as you know, left me my estate, they always had the greatest respect for your father, and your late mother. The Lomovs and the Chubukovs have always been very friendly,

> **Portraits of Real Life** *Why do you suppose it is taking so long for Lomov to ask Natalia his question?*

you might even say affectionate. And, of course, you know, our land borders on each other's. My Oxen Meadows touch your birch grove. . . .

NATALIA. I hate to interrupt you, my dear Ivan Vassilevitch, but you said: "my Oxen Meadows." Do you really think they're yours?

LOMOV. Why of course they're mine.

NATALIA. What do you mean? The Oxen Meadows are ours, not yours!

LOMOV. Oh, no, my dear Natalia Stepanovna, they're mine.

NATALIA. Well, this is the first I've heard about it! Where did you get that idea?

LOMOV. Where? Why, I mean the Oxen Meadows that are wedged between your birches and the marsh.

NATALIA. Yes, of course, they're ours.

LOMOV. Oh, no, you're wrong, my dear Natalia Stepanovna, they're mine.

NATALIA. Now, come, Ivan Vassilevitch! How long have they been yours?

LOMOV. How long! Why, as long as I can remember!

NATALIA. Well, really, you can't expect me to believe that!

LOMOV. But, you can see for yourself in the deed, my dear Natalia Stepanovna. Of course, there was once a dispute about them, but everyone knows they're mine now. There's nothing to argue about. There was a time when my aunt's grandmother let your father's grandfather's peasants use the land, but they were supposed to bake bricks for her in return. Naturally, after a few years they began to act as if they owned it, but the real truth is. . . .

NATALIA. That has nothing to do with the case! Both my grandfather and my great-grandfather said that their land went as far as the marsh, which means that

the Meadows are ours! There's nothing whatever to argue about. It's foolish.

LOMOV. But I can show you the deed, Natalia Stepanovna.

NATALIA. You're just making fun of me. . . . Great Heavens! Here we have the land for hundreds of years, and suddenly you try to tell us it isn't ours. What's wrong with you, Ivan Vassilevitch? Those meadows aren't even fifteen acres, and they're not worth three hundred rubles, but I just can't stand unfairness! I just can't stand unfairness!

LOMOV. But, you must listen to me. Your father's grandfather's peasants, as I've already tried to tell you, they were supposed to bake bricks for my aunt's grandmother. And my aunt's grandmother, why, she wanted to be nice to them. . . .

NATALIA. It's just nonsense, this whole business about aunts and grandfathers and grandmothers. The Meadows are ours! That's all there is to it!

LOMOV. They're mine!

NATALIA. Ours! You can go on talking for two days, and you can put on fifteen evening coats and twenty pairs of gloves, but I tell you they're ours, ours, ours!

LOMOV. Natalia Stepanovna, I don't want the Meadows! I'm just acting on principle. If you want, I'll give them to you.

NATALIA. I'll give them to *you!* Because they're ours! And that's all there is to it! And if I may say so, your behavior, my dear Ivan Vassilevitch, is very strange. Until now, we've always considered you a

---

Portraits of Real Life *What does Natalia and Lomov's conversation tell you about the life of the Russian aristocracy in the nineteenth century?*

good neighbor, even a friend. After all, last year we lent you our threshing machine, even though it meant putting off our own threshing until November. And here you are treating us like a pack of gypsies. Giving me my own land, indeed! Really! Why that's not being a good neighbor. It's sheer **impudence,** that's what it is. . . .

LOMOV. Oh, so you think I'm just a land-grabber? My dear lady, I've never grabbed anybody's land in my whole life, and no one's going to accuse me of doing it now! [*Quickly walks over to the pitcher and drinks some more water.*] The Oxen Meadows are mine!

NATALIA. That's a lie. They're ours!

LOMOV. Mine!

NATALIA. A lie! I'll prove it. I'll send my mowers out there today!

LOMOV. What?

NATALIA. My mowers will mow it today!

LOMOV. I'll kick them out!

NATALIA. You just dare!

LOMOV. [*Clutching his heart.*] The Oxen Meadows are mine! Do you understand? Mine!

NATALIA. Please don't shout! You can shout all you want in your own house, but here I must ask you to control yourself.

LOMOV. If my heart wasn't palpitating the way it is, if my insides weren't jumping like mad, I wouldn't talk to you so calmly. [*Yelling.*] The Oxen Meadows are mine!

NATALIA. Ours!

LOMOV. Mine!

Farce *How does Chekhov make Lomov's behavior farcical here?*

Vocabulary

impudence (im´pyə dəns) *n.* speech or behavior that is aggressively forward or rude

NATALIA. Ours!

LOMOV. Mine!

[*Enter CHUBUKOV.*]

CHUBUKOV. What's going on? Why all the shouting?

NATALIA. Papa, will you please inform this gentleman who owns the Oxen Meadows, he or we?

CHUBUKOV. [*To LOMOV.*] Why, they're ours, old fellow.

LOMOV. But how can they be yours, my dear Stepan Stepanovitch? Be fair. Perhaps my aunt's grandmother did let your grand-father's peasants work the land, and maybe they did get so used to it that they acted as if it was their own, but. . . .

CHUBUKOV. Oh, no, no . . . my dear boy. You forget something. The reason the peasants didn't pay your aunt's grandmother, and so forth, was that the land was disputed, even then. Since then it's been settled. Why, everyone knows it's ours.

LOMOV. I can prove it's mine.

CHUBUKOV. You can't prove a thing, old boy.

LOMOV. Yes, I can!

CHUBUKOV. My dear lad, why yell like that? Yelling doesn't prove a thing. Look, I'm not after anything of yours, just as I don't intend to give up anything of mine. Why should I? Besides, if you're going to keep arguing about it, I'd just as soon give the land to the peasants, so there!

LOMOV. There nothing! Where do you get the right to give away someone else's property?

CHUBUKOV. I certainly ought to know if I have the right or not. And you had better

---

Farce *What makes Chubukov's statement here ridiculous?*

Agnus. Peter Harrap. Oil on canvas. Private collection.

realize it, because, my dear young man, I am not used to being spoken to in that tone of voice, and so forth. Besides which, my dear young man, I am twice as old as you are, and I ask you to speak to me without getting yourself into such a tizzy, and so forth!

LOMOV. Do you think I'm a fool? First you call my property yours, and then you expect me to keep calm and polite! Good neighbors don't act like that, my dear Stepan Stepanovitch. You're no neighbor, you're a land grabber!

CHUBUKOV. What was that? What did you say?

NATALIA. Papa, send the mowers out to the meadows at once!

CHUBUKOV. What did you say, sir?

NATALIA. The Oxen Meadows are ours, and we'll never give them up, never, never, never, never!

LOMOV. We'll see about that. I'll go to court. I'll show you!

CHUBUKOV. Go to court? Well, go to court, and so forth! I know you, just waiting for a chance to go to court, and so forth. You pettifogging[2] cheater, you! All of your family is like that. The whole bunch of them!

LOMOV. You leave my family out of this! The Lomovs have always been honorable, upstanding people, and not a one of them was ever tried for embezzlement,[3] like your grandfather was.

CHUBUKOV. The Lomovs are a pack of lunatics, the whole bunch of them!

---

2. A *pettifogging* person squabbles over unimportant matters or uses mean, tricky methods.
3. *Embezzlement* is the act of stealing money entrusted to one's care; a bank official, for example, might embezzle funds from customers' accounts.

Recognize Author's Purpose *What do you think is Chekhov's purpose in including this detail?*

NATALIA. The whole bunch!

CHUBUKOV. Your grandfather was a drunkard, and what about your other aunt, the one who ran away with the architect? And so forth.

NATALIA. And so forth!

LOMOV. Your mother limped! [*Clutches at his heart.*] Oh, I've got a stitch in my side. . . . My head's whirling. . . . Help! Water!

CHUBUKOV. Your father was a gambler.

NATALIA. And your aunt was queen of the scandalmongers![4]

LOMOV. My left foot's paralyzed. You're a plotter. . . . Oh, my heart. It's an open secret that in the last elections you brib. . . . I'm seeing stars! Where's my hat?

NATALIA. It's a low-mean, spiteful. . . .

CHUBUKOV. And you're a two-faced, malicious schemer!

LOMOV. Here's my hat. . . . Oh, my heart. . . . Where's the door? How do I get out of here? . . . Oh, I think I'm going to die. . . . My foot's numb. [*Goes.*]

CHUBUKOV. [*Following him.*] And don't you ever set foot in my house again!

NATALIA. Go to court, indeed! We'll see about that!

[*LOMOV staggers out.*]

CHUBUKOV. The devil with him! [*Gets a drink, walks back and forth excited.*]

NATALIA. What a rascal! How can you trust your neighbors after an incident like that?

CHUBUKOV. The villain! The scarecrow!

NATALIA. He's a monster! First he tries to steal our land, and then he has the nerve to yell at you.

---

4. People who spread vicious gossip are *scandalmongers.*

Farce *How does Lomov's hypochondria contribute to the farcical aspects of the play?*

CHUBUKOV. Yes, and that turnip, that stupid rooster, has the gall[5] to make a proposal. Some proposal!

NATALIA. What proposal?

CHUBUKOV. Why, he came to propose to you.

NATALIA. To propose? To me? Why didn't you tell me before?

CHUBUKOV. So he gets all dressed up in his formal clothes. That stuffed sausage, that dried up cabbage!

NATALIA. To propose to me? Ohhhh! [*Falls into a chair and starts wailing.*] Bring him back! Back! Go get him! Bring him back! Ohhhh!

CHUBUKOV. Bring who back?

NATALIA. Hurry up, hurry up! I'm sick. Get him! [*Complete hysterics.*]

CHUBUKOV. What for? [*To her.*] What's the matter with you? [*Clutches his head.*] Oh, what a fool I am! I'll shoot myself! I'll hang myself! I ruined her chances!

NATALIA. I'm dying. Get him!

CHUBUKOV. All right, all right, right away! Only don't yell!

[*He runs out.*]

NATALIA. What are they doing to me? Get him! Bring him back! Bring him back!

[*A pause. CHUBUKOV runs in.*]

CHUBUKOV. He's coming, and so forth, the snake. Oof! You talk to him. I'm not in the mood.

NATALIA. [*Wailing.*] Bring him back! Bring him back!

To propose to me? Ohhhh!

CHUBUKOV. [*Yelling.*] I told you, he's coming! What agony to be the father of a grown-up daughter. I'll cut my throat some day, I swear I will. [*To her.*] We cursed him, we insulted him, abused him, kicked him out, and now . . . because you, you. . . .

NATALIA. Me? It was all your fault!

CHUBUKOV. My fault? What do you mean my fau . . . ? [*LOMOV appears in the doorway.*] Talk to him yourself! [*Goes out. LOMOV enters, exhausted.*]

LOMOV. What palpitations! My heart! And my foot's absolutely asleep. Something keeps giving me a stitch in the side. . . .

NATALIA. You must forgive us, Ivan Vassilevitch. We all got too excited. I remember now. The Oxen Meadows are yours.

LOMOV. My heart's beating something awful. My Meadows. My eyebrows, they're both twitching!

NATALIA. Yes, the Meadows are all yours, yes, yours. Do sit down. [*They sit.*] We were wrong, of course.

LOMOV. I argued on principle. My land isn't worth so much to me, but the principle. . . .

NATALIA. Oh, yes, of course, the principle, that's what counts. But let's change the subject.

LOMOV. Besides, I have evidence. You see, my aunt's grandmother let your father's grandfather's peasants use the land. . . .

NATALIA. Yes, yes, yes, but forget all that. [*Aside.*] I wish I knew how to get him going. [*Aloud.*] Are you going to start hunting soon?

---

5. *Gall,* a synonym for *impudence,* means "shocking boldness; scornful disrespect."

Farce *What makes Natalia's reaction here farcical?*

Recognize Author's Purpose *What is the author saying here about his characters' convictions?*

LOMOV. After the harvest I'll try for grouse.[6] But oh, my dear Natalia Stepanovna, have you heard about the bad luck I've had? You know my dog, Guess? He's gone lame.

NATALIA. What a pity. Why?

LOMOV. I don't know. He must have twisted his leg, or got in a fight, or something. [*Sighs.*] My best dog, to say nothing of the cost. I paid Mironov 125 rubles for him.

NATALIA. That was too high, Ivan Vassilevitch.

LOMOV. I think it was quite cheap. He's a first class dog.

NATALIA. Why Papa only paid 85 rubles for Squeezer, and he's much better than Guess.

LOMOV. Squeezer better than Guess! What an idea! [*Laughs.*] Squeezer better than Guess!

NATALIA. Of course he's better. He may still be too young but on points[7] and pedigree,[8] he's a better dog even than any Volchanetsky owns.

LOMOV. Excuse me, Natalia Stepanovna, but you're forgetting he's overshot, and overshot dogs are bad hunters.

NATALIA. Oh, so he's overshot, is he? Well, this is the first time I've heard about it.

LOMOV. Believe me, his lower jaw is shorter than his upper.

NATALIA. You've measured them?

LOMOV. Yes. He's all right for pointing, but if you want him to retrieve. . . .

NATALIA. In the first place, our Squeezer is a thoroughbred, the son of Harness and Chisel, while your mutt doesn't even have a pedigree. He's as old and worn out as a peddler's horse.

LOMOV. He may be old, but I wouldn't take five Squeezers for him. How can you argue? Guess is a dog, Squeezer's a laugh. Anyone you can name has a dog like Squeezer hanging around somewhere. They're under every bush. If he only cost twenty-five rubles you got cheated.

NATALIA. The devil is in you today, Ivan Vassilevitch! You want to contradict everything. First you pretend the Oxen Meadows are yours, and now you say Guess is better than Squeezer. People should say what they really mean, and you know Squeezer is a hundred times better than Guess. Why say he isn't?

LOMOV. So, you think I'm a fool or a blind man, Natalia Stepanovna! Once and for all, Squeezer is overshot!

NATALIA. He is not!

LOMOV. He is so!

NATALIA. He is not!

LOMOV. Why shout, my dear lady?

NATALIA. Why talk such nonsense? It's terrible. Your Guess is old enough to be buried, and you compare him with Squeezer!

LOMOV. I'm sorry, I can't go on. My heart . . . it's palpitating!

NATALIA. I've always noticed that the hunters who argue most don't know a thing.

LOMOV. Please! Be quiet a moment. My heart's falling apart. . . . [*Shouts.*] Shut up!

---

6. A fowl-like bird, the *grouse* is often hunted for game or food.
7. Natalia is referring to her dog's physical characteristics and ancestry. In dog shows today, a dog is judged on specific characteristics, or *points*. Each breed has point standards that cover everything from skull shape and tail length to eye color and hair texture.
8. A dog's ancestry, or *pedigree*, is proof that a dog is purebred.

Farce *How does the argument over the dogs increase the farcical element of the play?*

Golden Autumn in the Village, 1889. Isaak Ilyich Levitan. Oil on canvas, 43 x 67.2 cm. State Russian Museum, St. Petersburg.

NATALIA. I'm not going to shut up until you admit that Squeezer's a hundred times better than Guess.

LOMOV. A hundred times worse! His head. . . . My eyes . . . shoulder . . .

NATALIA. Guess is half-dead already!

LOMOV. [*Weeping.*] Shut up! My heart's exploding!

NATALIA. I won't shut up!

[*CHUBUKOV comes in.*]

CHUBUKOV. What's the trouble now?

NATALIA. Papa, will you please tell us which is the better dog, his Guess or our Squeezer?

LOMOV. Stepan Stepanovitch, I implore you to tell me just one thing: Is your Squeezer overshot or not? Yes or no?

CHUBUKOV. Well what if he is? He's still the best dog in the neighborhood, and so forth.

LOMOV. Oh, but isn't my dog, Guess, better? Really?

CHUBUKOV. Don't get yourself so fraught up,[9] old man. Of course, your dog has his

---

9. The expression *fraught up* means "excited; charged up."

good points—thoroughbred, firm on his feet, well sprung ribs, and so forth. But, my dear fellow, you've got to admit he has two defects; he's old and he's short in the muzzle.

LOMOV. Short in the muzzle? Oh, my heart! Let's look at the facts! On the Marusinsky hunt my dog ran neck and neck with the Count's, while Squeezer was a mile behind them. . . .

CHUBUKOV. That's because the Count's groom hit him with a whip.

LOMOV. And he was right, too! We were fox hunting; what was your dog chasing sheep for?

CHUBUKOV. That's a lie! Look, I'm going to lose my temper . . . [*Controlling himself.*] my dear friend, so let's stop arguing, for that reason alone. You're only arguing because we're all jealous of somebody else's dog. Who can help it? As soon as you realize some dog is better than yours, in this case our dog, you start in with this and that, and the next thing you know—pure jealousy! I remember the whole business.

LOMOV. I remember too!

Ha! You only go hunting to get in good with the count, and to plot, and intrigue, and scheme. . . .

CHUBUKOV. [*Mimicking.*] "I remember too!" What do you remember?

LOMOV. My heart . . . my foot's asleep . . . I can't . . .

NATALIA. [*Mimicking.*] "My heart . . . my foot's asleep." What kind of a hunter are you? You should be hunting cockroaches in the kitchen, not foxes. "My heart!"

CHUBUKOV. Yes, what kind of a hunter are you anyway? You should be sitting at home with your palpitations, not tracking down animals. You don't hunt anyhow. You just go out to argue with people and interfere with their dogs, and so forth. For God's sake, let's change the subject before I lose my temper. Anyway, you're just not a hunter.

LOMOV. But you, you're a hunter? Ha! You only go hunting to get in good with the count, and to plot, and intrigue, and scheme. . . . Oh, my heart! You're a schemer, that's what!

CHUBUKOV. What's that? Me a schemer? [*Shouting.*] Shut up!

LOMOV. A schemer!

CHUBUKOV. You infant! You puppy!

LOMOV. You old rat!

CHUBUKOV. You shut up, or I'll shoot you down like a partridge! You fool!

LOMOV. Everyone knows that—oh, my heart—that your wife used to beat you. . . . Oh, my feet . . . my head . . . I'm seeing

---

Farce *How does Chekhov make Chubukov's insight here seem humorous?*

stars . . . I'm going to faint! [*He drops into an armchair.*] Quick, a doctor! [*Faints.*]

CHUBUKOV. [*Going on, oblivious.*] Baby! Weakling! Fool! I'm getting sick. [*Drinks water.*] Me! I'm sick!

NATALIA. What kind of a hunter are you? You can't even sit on a horse! [*To her father.*] Papa, what's the matter with him? Look, papa! [*Screaming.*] Ivan Vassilevitch! He's dead.

CHUBUKOV. I'm choking, I can't breathe. . . . Give me air.

NATALIA. He's dead! [*Pulling LOMOV's sleeve.*] Ivan Vassilevitch! Ivan Vassilevitch! What have you done to me? He's dead! [*She falls into an armchair. Screaming hysterically.*] A doctor! A doctor! A doctor!

CHUBUKOV. Ohhhh. . . . What's the matter? What happened?

NATALIA. [*Wailing.*] He's dead! He's dead!

CHUBUKOV. Who's dead? [*Looks at LOMOV.*] My God, he is! Quick! Water! A doctor! [*Puts glass to LOMOV's lips.*] Here, drink this! Can't drink it—he must be dead, and so forth. . . . Oh what a miserable life! Why don't I shoot myself! I should have cut my throat long ago! What am I waiting for? Give me a knife! Give me a pistol! [*LOMOV stirs.*] Look, he's coming to. Here, drink some water. That's it.

Portraits of Real Life *What do you think audiences in Russia would have thought of this argument when this play was first produced?*

Farce *Do you think Lomov is actually dead? Why or why not?*

Vocabulary

oblivious (ə blivʹē əs) *adj.* unmindful or unaware; not noticing

LOMOV. I'm seeing stars . . . misty . . . Where am I?

CHUBUKOV. Just you hurry up and get married, and then the devil with you! She accepts. [*Puts LOMOV's hand in NATALIA's.*] She accepts and so forth! I give you my blessing, and so forth! Only leave me in peace!

LOMOV. [*Getting up.*] Huh? What? Who?

CHUBUKOV. She accepts! Well? Kiss her!

NATALIA. He's alive! Yes, yes, I accept.

CHUBUKOV. Kiss each other!

LOMOV. Huh? Kiss? Kiss who? [*They kiss.*] That's nice. I mean, excuse me, what happened? Oh, now I get it . . . my heart . . . those stars . . . I'm very happy, Natalia Stepanovna. [*Kisses her hand.*] My foot's asleep.

NATALIA. I . . . I'm happy too.

CHUBUKOV. What a load off my shoulders! Whew!

NATALIA. Well, now maybe you'll admit that Squeezer is better than Guess?

LOMOV. Worse!

NATALIA. Better!

CHUBUKOV. What a way to enter matrimonial bliss! Let's have some champagne!

LOMOV. He's worse!

NATALIA. Better! Better, better, better, better!

CHUBUKOV. [*Trying to shout her down.*] Champagne! Bring some champagne! Champagne! Champagne!

CURTAIN

Farce *What makes this dialogue humorous?*

After You Read

Respond and Think Critically

1. **Connect to Personal Experience** Did you like the ending of the play? Explain why or why not.

2. **Explain Character Traits** Why has Lomov come to Chubukov's house? What does his behavior tell you about his personality?

3. **Interpret Conflict** What is the cause of both arguments? Why, in your opinion, do the arguments start so easily?

4. **Compare and Contrast Conflicts** Compare and contrast the bickering between characters in the play with similar interactions you have witnessed between people in real life. How is it similar? How is it different?

5. **Draw Conclusions About Characters** In your opinion, are Lomov and Natalia a good match for each other? Explain. Do you think they should marry? Why or why not?

6. **Evaluate Dialogue** Does the **dialogue**, or speech, in Chekhov's play seem realistic to you? Explain and support your response.

7. **Big Idea** **Draw Conclusions About Setting** Chekhov's characters seem to be in their own little world; they have no interaction with people outside their province. What can you conclude about how realistic this detail is for Chekhov's time and place? For yours? Explain, using text evidence to support your response.

Literary Element Farce

Many authors use **farce** to ridicule societal norms and make their audiences laugh. In *A Marriage Proposal*, Chekhov has Lomov continually complain about physical ailments in order to mock him.

8. **Analyze Archetypes and Plot** Look at the pink highlighted passages on pages 804 and 812. What familiar character archetype does Chekhov depict with Chubukov's lines? How does this archetype affect the plot of the play?

9. **Analyze Farce** Identify three points in this play that you found particularly funny. Why are they humorous? What techniques of farce does Chekhov use to create each situation?

Review: Irony

As you learned on page 137, **irony** is a contrast between expectation and reality. In **situational irony**, the outcome of a situation is the opposite of what is expected. In **dramatic irony**, the audience knows something that the characters do not know.

10. **Partner Activity** Find one example of situational irony and one example of dramatic irony in the play and record them in a chart like the one below. Share your findings with your class.

Example	Type of Irony
When Natalia enters on p. 804, she does not know that Lomov intends to propose.	Dramatic irony— the audience knows Lomov's intent.

Literature Online

Selection Resources For Selection Quizzes, eFlashcards, and Reading-Writing Connection activities, go to glencoe.com and enter QuickPass code GL57805u4.

1. One of Chekhov's reasons for writing *A Marriage Proposal* was probably to

   (A) mock the landowning class

   (B) satirize a society in which land owner-ship evoked more passion than marriage

   (C) point out how foolish it is to want to be married at any cost

   (D) suggest that most squabbles arise over property rights

   (E) make fun of hypochondriacs

Vocabulary Practice

Practice with Word Origins Studying the etymology, or origin and history, of a word helps you understand and explore its meaning. Create a word map, like the one below, for each of these vocabulary words from the play.

impudence   oblivious

EXAMPLE:

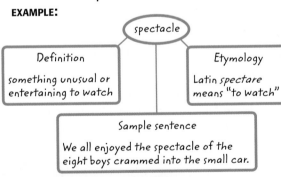

Academic Vocabulary

A reader can only wonder what married life will be like for the **couple** *in* A Marriage Proposal.

Couple is a multiple-meaning word. In casual conversation, a person might mention a **couple** of days. Using context clues, figure out the meaning of the word in the sentence about the play above. Check your guess in a dictionary.

For more on academic vocabulary, see pages 36–37 and R92–R94.

Write with Style

 Apply Irony

Assignment A twist ending is a type of situational irony. Write a script of at least 750 words that includes dialogue, an implicit or explicit theme, and a twist ending.

Get Ideas Look through newspapers, magazines, or blogs for accounts of events with unexpected outcomes. Choose an event and recount the story as a dramatic exchange between two or more characters. Feel free to change or add to the story. Be sure to focus on the twist ending.

Give It Structure Make two timelines to list major story events. On the first, record the events that lead to an expected outcome. On the second, plot the events in your script that lead to the twist ending. As you write, draw on the first timeline for plot structure and background information, but use the second timeline to create rising action and deliver the surprise ending.

Look at Language In your script, consider creating a suspenseful mood and a tone that will keep the reader guessing. You may want to deliberately mislead the reader by having characters emphasize the wrong events. As you revise, try to ensure that your twist ending is truly a surprise.

TEKS

10.18.B.i Use correct punctuation marks including comma placement in nonrestrictive phrases, clauses, and contrasting expressions.

Grammar Workshop

Commas with Interjections and Parenthetical Expressions

Literature Connection In the quotation below from *A Marriage Proposal,* Chekhov introduces the sentences with the expressions *of course* and *well.*

> "Of course, I must say you look splendid, but . . . Well, tell me, why are you so dressed up?"

Of course is a **parenthetical expression,** which adds explanatory information to the sentence. Other common parenthetical expressions include *in fact, on the other hand, for example, by the way,* and *nevertheless.* The word *well* is an **interjection,** a word that expresses emotion. *Alas, good grief, oh, uh-oh, hey,* and *wow* are other common interjections. Because interjections and parenthetical expressions are **nonrestrictive elements**—they are not essential to the meaning of the sentence—they should be set off with commas.

Interjections These usually occur at the beginning of a sentence. Interjections that express strong emotion may be followed by an exclamation point.

> Sorry, we weren't expecting you.
> Good heavens, he was wearing a suit and top hat!

Parenthetical expressions These may appear at the beginning, at the end, or in the middle of a sentence and are set off by one or two commas.

> In fact, Lomov had come to Natalia with the intention of proposing.
> Lomov had come to Natalia, in fact, with the intention of proposing.
> Lomov had come to Natalia, with the intention of proposing, in fact.

Interjections and Parenthetical Expressions

Interjections and **parenthetical expressions** act as interrupters that express emotion or add explanatory information. They are **nonrestrictive elements,** however, so should be set off with commas.

Test-Taking Tip

Overuse of interjections and parenthetical expressions can make writing appear over-casual and informal, so use them sparingly when writing for a test.

Language Handbook

For more about interjections and parenthetical expressions, see the Language Handbook, p. R66.

Revise Rewrite these sentences to correct any comma mistakes.

1. Well if you check the background information, you can see that the story was written in the year 1888.
2. Oh I see that Chekhov earned a degree in medicine.
3. Chekhov unfortunately was poor and had to support himself by writing hundreds of articles for comic magazines.
4. These writings on the other hand showed the revolutionary literary style and promise of the masterpieces he was soon to create.
5. One masterpiece is of course the one-act play *A Marriage Proposal.*

LOG ON **Literature** Online

Grammar For more grammar practice, go to glencoe.com and enter QuickPass code GL57805u4.

That's Your Trouble

Meet **Harold Pinter**
(1930–2008)

After a performance of his play *The Collection*, Harold Pinter gave an unusual bit of feedback to one of the actors. "Michael, I wrote dot, dot, dot," Pinter told the actor, "and you're giving me dot, dot."

The comment was more than just critical nit-picking. As one of the twentieth century's top playwrights, Pinter reinvented the language of drama. Using small talk and long silences, he suggests deeper layers of meaning and conflict beneath the surface of daily life. In a style that has often been called "the comedy of menace," Pinter dramatizes tense, antagonistic relationships that break down into brutal power struggles. As a tribute to his unique style, critics have added a word to the *New Shorter Oxford English Dictionary*: "Pinteresque."

> *"There are no hard distinctions between what is real and what is unreal."*
>
> —Harold Pinter

Art and Danger As a child in England, Pinter experienced both beauty and violence. Pinter's father was a working-class tailor, but his family loved art and culture. In contrast, Pinter's mother came from a hardscrabble family whose behavior, including that of her bare-knuckle boxer brother, sometimes verged on criminal.

The young Pinter also faced the terrors of World War II. Threatened by Nazi bombings, Pinter was twice evacuated from London with other children.

Stage and Screen In 1956 Pinter began writing his own plays. Influenced by Samuel Beckett, he also wrote Absurdist plays. One of his early plays, *The Birthday Party*, initially flopped, but it later won acclaim. Later successes included *The Caretaker* (1960) and *The Homecoming* (1965).

In *Betrayal* (1978), Pinter used material inspired by his life and wrote dialogue that was less stylized than in his earlier plays. But the play was still revolutionary: Pinter shows how a marriage falls apart, but he presents the scenes in reverse chronological order.

Pinter continued to act and direct, both in his own plays and in those by other playwrights. He also had a career as a screenwriter. Some of his screenplays include *The French Lieutenant's Woman* (1981), *The Handmaid's Tale* (1990), and *Sleuth* (2007).

In 2005 Pinter was awarded the Nobel Prize in Literature. The Nobel presenter described Pinter as "the foremost representative of British drama in the second half of the twentieth century."

LOG ON ▶ **Literature** Online

Author Search For more about Harold Pinter, go to glencoe.com and enter QuickPass code GL57805u4.

Literature and Reading Preview

Connect to the Play

How can everyday language mask or hide how a person really feels about something? Write a list of words or phrases you use regularly that might hide your true feelings.

Build Background

Theater of the Absurd, or Absurdism, is a dramatic style marked by plays lacking traditional plots but composed, instead, of scenes in which characters talk and act to little or no purpose. Absurdist plays are comic on the surface but can express underlying feelings of dread or uncertainty.

Set Purposes for Reading

Big Idea Portraits of Real Life

As you read, ask yourself, How do the characters communicate, or miscommunicate, with each other?

Literary Element Structure

Structure is the order or pattern a writer uses to present ideas. In conventional dramas, like those of Shakespeare, the **plot** forms the structure, with events generally unfolding in a chronological order. Because Absurdist works lack traditional plots, they may take their structure from devices such as cycles, repetition, or patterns in the dialogue. As you read, ask yourself, How does Pinter establish the structure of this short play?

Reading Strategy Analyze Mood

When you **analyze mood,** you examine the emotional quality of a literary work. A writer's choice of language, subject matter, setting, and tone, as well as sound devices such as repetition and rhythm, contribute to mood. As you read, ask yourself, How do the setting and stage directions of the play contribute to the overall mood?

....

Tip: Ask Questions When trying to determine mood, ask yourself questions and record these questions and your answers in a chart like the one below. Use the blue highlighted question to help you get started.

Question	Answer
At what point does a character dramatically change the mood?	

TEKS

For pages 817–821

10.4 Understand, make inferences and draw conclusions about the structure and elements of drama and provide evidence from text to support understanding.

That's Your Trouble

Harold Pinter

Sandwich Man in Trafalgar Square, 1898. William Nicholson. Stapleton Collection, London.

Two men in a park. One on the grass, reading.
The other making cricket° strokes with umbrella.

1. A.: *(stopping in mid-stroke)*: Eh, look at that bloke°, what's he got on his back, he's got a sandwich board° on his back.
2. B.: What about it?
3. A.: He wants to take it off, he'll get a headache.
4. B.: Rubbish.°
5. A.: What do you mean?
6. B.: He won't get a headache.
7. A.: I bet he will.
8. B.: The neck! It affects his neck! He'll get a neckache.
9. A.: The strain goes up.
10. B.: Have you ever carried a sandwich board?
11. A.: Never.
12. B.: Then how do you know which way the strain *goes*? (*Pause.*)

Cricket is a game played with a ball and bat.
1 bloke: British slang for "man" or "guy." **sandwich board:** two hinged boards that hang front and back from the shoulders of a person. It typically is used as a display advertisement.
4 Rubbish: British term for "garbage," "lies," or "nonsense."

Analyze Mood *Describe the mood that the setting creates.*

Structure *Do the pauses in B's dialogue serve to heighten or reduce the tension in the scene? Explain.*

It goes down! The strain goes down, it starts with the neck and it goes down. He'll get a neckache and a backache.

13. A.: He'll get a headache in the end.

14. B.: There's no end.

15. A.: That's where the brain is.

16. B.: That's where the *what* is?

17. A.: The brain.

18. B.: It's nothing to do with the brain.

19. A.: Oh, isn't it?

20. B.: It won't go anywhere *near* his brain.

21. A.: That's where you're wrong.

22. B.: I'm not wrong. I'm right. *(Pause.)* You happen to be talking to a man who knows what he's talking about. *(Pause.)* His brain doesn't come into it. If you've got a strain, it goes down. It's not like heat.

23. A.: What do you mean?

24. B.: (*ferociously*): If you've got a strain it goes down! Heat goes up! *(Pause.)*

25. A.: You mean sound.

26. B.: I what?

27. A.: Sound goes up.

28. B.: Sound goes anywhere it likes! It all depends where you happen to be standing, it's a matter of physics, that's something you're just completely **ignorant** of, but you just try carrying a sandwich board and you'll find out soon enough. First the neck, then the shoulders, then the back, then it worms° into the buttocks, that's where it worms. The buttocks. Either the right or the left, it depends how you carry your weight. Then right down the thighs—a straight drop to his feet and he'll collapse.

29. A.: He hasn't collapsed yet.

30. B.: He will. Give him a chance. A headache! How can he get a headache? He hasn't got anything on his head! I'm the one who's got the headache. *(Pause.)* You just don't know how to listen to what other people tell you, that's your trouble.

31. A.: I know what my trouble is.

32. B.: You don't know what your trouble is, my friend. That's your trouble. 〰

28 worms: moves down into; makes its way.

Portraits of Real Life *Does the dialogue between A and B seem realistic? Why or why not?*

> **Vocabulary**

ferociously (fə rō′shəs lē) *adv.* cruelly; savagely

ignorant (ig′nər ənt) *adj.* lacking knowledge or experience; uninformed

After You Read

Respond and Think Critically

1. **Connect to Personal Experience** What was your first reaction to this short play? What is your opinion of the dialogue in *That's Your Trouble*?

2. **Explain Conflict** After reading the dialogue, what does the conflict appear to be about? What is the underlying conflict between these two men?

3. **Analyze Irony** What is ironic about B's accusation that his companion is ignorant? What purpose does irony serve in this dialogue? **OER**

4. **Make Inferences About Characters** Do you think the two men are friends? Explain, using text evidence to support your response. How do these characters change or complicate your definition of friendship?

5. **Big Idea** **Draw Conclusions About Author's Perspective** What larger comments about human interaction does Pinter make through his characters? Support your response.

Literary Element Structure

In a conventional drama's plot, action steadily progresses toward a climax and resolution. Modern dramas, however, may be little more than a conversation between characters. In these works, the **structure**—the order or pattern the author uses to present ideas—may be seen within the subtle use of repeated phrases or patterns in the dialogue.

6. **Make Inferences About Structure** If this sketch were one scene within a traditional drama, what stage of the plot might it represent? Explain.

7. **Analyze Dialogue** What general pattern can you see in the dialogue between A and B? Support your answer with text evidence.

Reading Strategy Analyze Mood

Mood is the emotional quality of a literary work. Refer to your chart on page 818 and then answer the following questions

8. What is the overall mood of this dramatic sketch? Support your response with text evidence.

9. How does the mood contribute to the playwright's tone?

LOG ON ▶ **Literature** Online

Selection Resources For Selection Quizzes, eFlashcards, and Reading-Writing Connection activities, go to glencoe.com and enter QuickPass code GL57805u4.

Vocabulary Practice

Practice with Connotation and Denotation
Denotation is the literal, or dictionary, meaning of a word. **Connotation** is the implied, or cultural, meaning of a word. For example, the words *incapable* and *helpless* have a similar denotation, "unable to act or accomplish something," but they have different connotations:

Negative	More Negative
incapable	helpless

Each boldfaced vocabulary word is listed below with a word that has a similar denotation. Choose the word that has a more negative connotation.

1. ferociously   cruelly

2. ignorant   uninformed

Writing

Write a List Harold Pinter is noted for his use of pauses in dialogue to signal conflicts within and between characters. Reread the play and note each instance of the stage direction "Pause." Make a list in which you explain, in one sentence for each entry, why you think Pinter has his character pause at that particular moment.

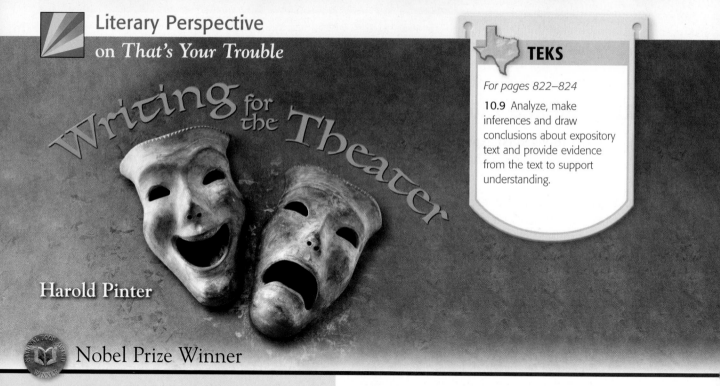

Writing for the Theater

Harold Pinter

Nobel Prize Winner

TEKS

For pages 822–824

10.9 Analyze, make inferences and draw conclusions about expository text and provide evidence from the text to support understanding.

Set a Purpose for Reading

Read to discover the author's opinion and how he supports it.

Build Background

Harold Pinter, a British playwright, was the recipient of the Nobel Prize in Literature in 2005. In "Writing for the Theater," Pinter discusses how he creates roles and chooses the language he uses in plays.

Reading Strategy

Evaluate Argument

Evaluating an argument in an expository or persuasive text requires that you analyze the text and make a judgment or form an opinion about what you have read. Consider whether the author clearly states a position and supports it with reasons and examples. Also, decide if you agree with the author's opinion. As you read, use a chart to keep track of Pinter's opinions and how he supports them. Then, think of an opposing viewpoint for each opinion.

Pinter's Opinion	Support	Opposing Viewpoint
What he writes only has obligations to itself	Responsibility is to the play, not the audience	Playwrights need to consider their audiences

The theater is a large, energetic, public activity. Writing is, for me, a completely private activity, a poem or a play, no difference. These facts are not easy to reconcile. The professional theater, whatever the virtues it undoubtedly possesses, is a world of false climaxes, calculated tensions, some hysteria, and a good deal of inefficiency. And the alarms of this world which I suppose I work in become steadily more widespread and intrusive. But basically my position has remained the same. What I write has no obligation to anything other than to itself. My responsibility is not to audiences, critics, producers, directors, actors or to my fellow men in general, but to the play in hand, simply. I warned you about definitive statements but it looks as though I've just made one.

I have usually begun a play in quite a simple manner; found a couple of characters in a particular context, thrown them together and listened to what they said, keeping my nose to the ground. The context has always been, for me, concrete and particular, and the characters concrete also. I've never started a play from any kind of abstract idea or theory

. . . Apart from any other consideration, we are faced with the immense difficulty, if not the impossibility, of verifying the past. I don't mean merely years ago, but yesterday, this morning. What took place, what was the nature of what took place, what happened? If one can speak of the difficulty of knowing what in fact took place yesterday, one can I think treat the present in the same way. What's happening now? We won't know until tomorrow or in six months' time, and we won't know then, we'll have forgotten, or our imagination will have attributed quite false characteristics to today. A moment is sucked away and distorted, often even at the time of its birth. We will all interpret a common experience quite differently, though we prefer to subscribe to the view that there's a shared common ground, a known ground. I think there's a shared common ground all right, but that it's more like a quicksand. Because "reality" is quite a strong firm word we tend to think, or to hope, that the state to which it refers is equally firm, settled and unequivocal.[1] It doesn't seem to be, and in my opinion, it's no worse or better for that.

. . . There is a considerable body of people just now who are asking for some kind of clear and sensible engagement to be evidently disclosed in contemporary plays. They want the playwright to be a prophet. There is certainly a good deal of prophecy indulged in by playwrights these days, in their plays and out of them. Warnings, sermons, admonitions,[2] ideological exhortations,[3] moral judgments, defined problems with built-in solutions; all can camp under the banner of prophecy. The attitude behind this sort of thing might be summed up in one phrase: *"I'm telling you!"*

It takes all sorts of playwrights to make a world, and as far as I'm concerned "X"

can follow any course he chooses without my acting as his censor. To propagate[4] a phoney war between hypothetical schools of playwrights doesn't seem to me a very productive pastime and it certainly isn't my intention. But I can't but feel that we have a marked tendency to stress, so glibly, our empty preferences. The preference for "Life" with a capital *L,* which is held up to be very different to life with a small *l,* I mean the life we in fact live. The preference for goodwill, for charity, for benevolence, how facile they've become, these deliverances.

If I were to state any moral precept[5] it might be: beware of the writer who puts forward his concern for you to embrace, who leaves you in no doubt of his worthiness, his usefulness, his altruism,[6] who declares that his heart is in the right place, and ensures that it can be seen in full view, a pulsating mass where his characters ought to be. What is presented, so much of the time, as a body of active and positive thought is in fact a body lost in a prison of empty definition and cliché.

This kind of writer clearly trusts words absolutely. I have mixed feelings about words myself. Moving among them, sorting them out, watching them appear on the page, from this I derive a considerable pleasure. But at the same time I have another strong feeling about words which amounts to nothing less than nausea. Such a weight of words confronts us day in, day out, words spoken in a context such as this, words written by me and by others, the bulk of it a stale dead terminology; ideas endlessly repeated and permutated,[7] become platitudinous,[8] trite, meaningless. Given this nausea, it's very easy to be overcome by it and step back into paralysis. I

---

1. *Unequivocal* means "clear" or "without doubt."
2. *Admonitions* are "cautionary advice."
3. *Exhortations* are "appeals" or "arguments."

4. Here, *propagate* means "publicize."
5. *Precept* means "standard."
6. *Altruism* means "unselfish behavior" or "attention to the welfare of others."
7. *Permutated* means "transformed entirely."
8. *Platitudinous* means "unoriginal" or "banal."

imagine most writers know something of this kind of paralysis. But if it is possible to confront this nausea, to follow it to its hilt, to move through it and out of it, then it is possible to say that something has occurred, that something has even been achieved.

Language, under these conditions, is a highly ambiguous business. So often, below the word spoken, is the thing known and unspoken. My characters tell me so much and no more, with reference to their experience, their aspirations, their motives, their history. Between my lack of biographical data about them and the ambiguity of what they say lies a territory which is not only worthy of exploration but which it is compulsory to explore. You and I, the characters which grow on a page, most of the time we're inexpressive, giving little away, unreliable, elusive,[9] evasive,[10] obstructive, unwilling. But it's out of these attributes that a language arises. A language, I repeat, where under what is said, another thing is being said. ꙮ

Musee Grevin Poster, 1900. Jules Cheret.

9. *Elusive* means "not able to be defined or described."
10. *Evasive* means "intentionally vague."

Respond and Think Critically

1. **Summarize Main Ideas** Write a brief summary of the main ideas in this text before you answer the following questions. For help on writing a summary, see page 389. As you write, be sure to distinguish between a summary and a critique. Remember that a critique includes critical analysis and evaluation of a text and a summary does not.

2. **Analyze Author's Purpose** Does Pinter write plays to convey a certain ideology or make a moral judgment? Explain. What does this say about how readers and audiences interpret theatrical works?

3. **Make Inferences About Main Idea** What does Pinter say language offers other than the actual "words spoken"? What do you think actors must do to convey the meaning of Pinter's language?

4. **Evaluate Argument** What is Pinter's opinion about the responsibility of the playwright? How well does his position relate to the idea of theater being a collaborative art form? Support your answer with evidence from the text.

5. **Draw Conclusions About Drama** Konstantin Stanislavsky was a Russian actor and theorist who developed an acting technique known as The Method. He asked students to consider the subtext of characters, or the meaning that underlies the written text. How does Pinter's writing serve Stanislavsky's approach to acting?

6. **Synthesize Ideas** How do Pinter's ideas about characterization apply to *That's Your Trouble*?

Comparing Literature

Across Genres

TEKS

For pages 825–853

10.2 Analyze, make inferences and draw conclusions about theme and genre in different cultural, historical, and contemporary contexts and provide evidence from the text to support understanding.

Compare Literature About Loyalty

Expectations for women have varied tremendously across countries, cultures, and time periods. In most places today, women can expect to have choices when it comes to education, employment, and marriage. A century or more ago, expectations for women were very different. The three works compared here—by Josefina Niggli, Carmen Tafolla, and Isak Dinesen—explore cultural expectations, especially those relating to women, and how the characters in their works face the challenges that result from those expectations.

COMPARE THE Big Idea **Portraits of Real Life**

Capturing life in literature is a task that requires an author to incorporate realistic characters, events, and details into a literary work. Josefina Niggli, Carmen Tafolla, and Isak Dinesen attempt to portray real life with their writing. As you read, ask yourself, While each author focuses on a different time and place, how do they develop their characters in such a way that allows the reader to form a personal connection with them?

COMPARE Theme

The **theme** is the central message of a work of literature. The theme provides some insight or lesson with which readers can connect. The cultural and historical context of a work, as well as a work's genre, can all influence the theme. As you read, ask yourself, How do Niggli, Tafolla, and Dinesen each explore themes related to loyalty and its impact on the lives of women in different cultural and historical contexts?

COMPARE Cultures

Culture is an important consideration for the authors of the following literary works. All of the authors draw heavily on their surroundings and heritages for the inspiration and content of their works. As you read, ask yourself, How do these writers use their cultural backgrounds to draw the reader into their literary worlds?

In the Trenches (En la trinchea). Diego Rivera. Banco de Mexico Trust. Mural, 2.03 x 3.98 m. Secretaria de Educacion Publica, Mexico City, Mexico.

LOG ON ▶ **Literature** Online

Author Search For more about the authors, go to glencoe.com and enter QuickPass code GL57805u4.

Before You Read

The Ring of General Macías

Meet **Josefina Niggli**
(1910–1983)

Although Josefina Niggli was the child of European American parents, she most strongly identified with the Mexican culture into which she was born and raised. Her willingness to tackle subjects such as the oppression of women in Mexican culture and the Mexican Revolution inspired a new generation of Mexican American authors.

Between Borders Niggli came of age during the Mexican Revolution. In 1913, the assassination of President Francisco Madero led the Niggli family to flee Mexico, which had descended into political turmoil. The family lived in various places in the Southwestern United States but never settled down. In 1925, Niggli was sent to school in San Antonio, Texas. There, Niggli's talent was recognized and encouraged by a teacher—a nun who locked Niggli in her room until she emerged with a finished short story to enter in a magazine competition. Her entry won second place.

> "Once you have experienced the emotion of having a play produced, you are forever lost to the ordinary world."
>
> —Josefina Niggli, from *Pointers on Playwriting*

After college, Niggli left San Antonio for North Carolina, where she joined the Carolina Playmakers, a graduate program at the University of North Carolina at Chapel Hill.

During this time, she wrote several plays that focused on the Mexican Revolution.

Critical Acclaim Niggli's first novel, *Mexican Village*, portrays the experiences of an obstinate Mexican American who gradually learns to appreciate Mexican village culture and traditions. Critic Raymond Paredes writes that *Mexican Village* "pointed forward to an emerging school of realism, confronting such issues as racism, the oppression of women, and the failure of the Mexican Revolution." The novel remains her most famous work. Like much of Niggli's writing, *Mexican Village* reflects both alienation from and loyalty to the two cultures in which she was raised.

Niggli won a number of awards and fellowships for her writing, and spent time as a Hollywood screenwriter in the 1950s. Eventually, she returned to North Carolina, where she taught playwriting at Western Carolina University for many years.

Literature and Reading Preview

Connect to the Play

What qualities or things are you proud of? List several things you are proud of and explain their significance in your life.

Build Background

The Mexican Revolution had its roots in the dictatorship of President Porfirio Díaz, under whose rule the majority of citizens suffered hardship and repression. In 1910 armed resistance to Díaz's rule began. The revolution helped define Mexican identity.

Set Purposes for Reading

Big Idea Portraits of Real Life

Notice how Niggli describes the women in the play. As you read, ask yourself, How do these women represent women in real life?

Literary Element Characterization

The methods a writer uses to develop a character are called **characterization**. A character's personality might be revealed indirectly through the character's own words, thoughts, or actions or through what other characters think and say about the character. As you read, ask yourself, How is the author showing me what I need to know about the characters?

Reading Strategy Analyze Plot and Setting

The **plot,** or sequence of events in a narrative work, reveals the events and conflicts that keep a story moving forward. The **setting** is the time and place in which a story takes place. By **analyzing the plot and the setting** of a play or other literary work, you can learn about the author's purpose for the work. As you read, ask yourself, What is the significance of the sequence of events and the setting in the play?

Tip: Note Sequence of Events Use a graphic organizer like the one below to record the sequence of events that forms the plot. Use the blue highlighted questions to help you get started.

Sequence of Events

In the play, the problem begins when	After this,	Next,

Vocabulary

regally (rē′gəl lē) *adv.* in a grand, dignified manner befitting a king or a queen; p. 833 *The homecoming queen waved regally at the crowd.*

ostentatiously (os′tən tā′shəs lē) *adv.* in a way intended to attract attention or impress others; p. 833 *Their home was decorated ostentatiously.*

notorious (nō tôr′ē əs) *adj.* widely and unfavorably known; p. 838 *The students' antics were notorious among the substitute teachers.*

repressed (ri prest′) *adj.* held back or kept under control; restrained; p. 839 *The two normally exuberant boys repressed their behavior.*

impertinent (im purt′ən ənt) *adj.* inappropriately bold or forward; p. 841 *The girl's brash behavior toward her teacher was impertinent.*

Tip: **Word Parts** Word meanings are changed by adding suffixes, prefixes, or both, to root words.

THE RING OF
★ ★ ★ ★ ★ ★ ★ ★ ★ ★
General Macias

Josefina Niggli

In the Trenches (En la trinchea). Diego Rivera. Banco de Mexico Trust. Mural, 2.03 x 3.98 m. Secretaria de Educacion Publica, Mexico City, Mexico.

CHARACTERS

MARICA (mär ē′kə): the sister of General Macías

RAQUEL (rə kel′): the wife of General Macías

ANDRÉS DE LA O (än′dräs dā lə ō): a captain in the Revolutionary Army

CLETO (klä′tō): a private in the Revolutionary Army

BASILIO FLORES (bə sēl′yō flô′räs): a captain in the Federal Army

PLACE: *Just outside Mexico City.*

TIME: *A night in April 1912.*

[*The living room of General Macías's[1] home is luxuriously furnished in the gold and ornate style of Louis XVI.[2] In the Right wall are French windows leading into the patio. Flanking these windows are low bookcases. In the Back wall is, Right, a closet door; and, Center, a table holding a wine decanter[3] and glasses. The Left wall has a door Upstage, and Downstage a writing desk with a straight chair in front of it. Near the desk is an armchair. Down Right is a small sofa with a table holding a lamp at the Upstage end of it. There are pictures on the walls. The room looks rather stuffy and unlived in.*

When the curtains part, the stage is in darkness save for the moonlight that comes through the French windows. Then the house door opens and a young girl in negligee enters stealthily. She is carrying a lighted candle. She stands at the door a moment listening for possible pur-

suit, then moves quickly across to the bookcase Down Right. She puts the candle on top of the bookcase and begins searching behind the books. She finally finds what she wants: a small bottle. While she is searching, the house door opens silently and a woman, also in negligee, enters. (These negligees are in the latest Parisian style.) She moves silently across the room to the table by the sofa, and as the girl turns with the bottle, the woman switches on the light. The girl gives a half-scream and draws back, frightened. The light reveals her to be quite young—no more than twenty—a timid, dovelike creature. The woman has a queenly air, and whether she is actually beautiful or not, people think she is. She is about thirty-two.*]

MARICA. [*Trying to hide the bottle behind her.*] Raquel! What are you doing here?

RAQUEL. What did you have hidden behind the books, Marica?

MARICA. [*Attempting a forced laugh.*] I? Nothing. Why do you think I have anything?

RAQUEL. [*Taking a step toward her.*] Give it to me.

MARICA. [*Backing away from her.*] No. No, I won't.

RAQUEL. [*Stretching out her hand.*] I demand that you give it to me.

MARICA. You have no right to order me about. I'm a married woman. I . . . I . . . [*She begins to sob and flings herself down on the sofa.*]

RAQUEL. [*Much gentler.*] You shouldn't be up. The doctor told you to stay in bed. [*She bends over MARICA and gently takes the bottle out of the girl's hand.*] It was poison. I thought so.

1. Macías (mä sē′əs)
2. France's King *Louis XVI* lived a life of luxury and elegance until he was beheaded in 1793 during the French Revolution.
3. A *decanter* is a decorative bottle with a stopper.

Analyze Plot and Setting *What might you infer about the house and its occupants from the setting?*

Characterization *What can you infer about Raquel from the description of her?*

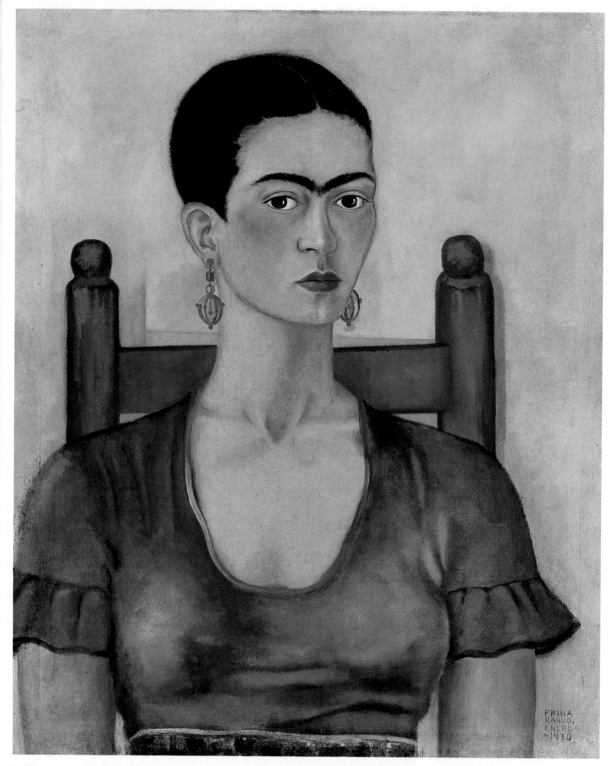

Self-Portrait, 1930. Frida Kahlo. Oil on canvas, 25½ x 21⅛ in. Museum of Fine Arts, Boston. Anonymous loan.

View the Art Frida Kahlo, a Mexican painter, is known for her vibrant and dramatic self-portraits. Is the woman portrayed here closer to the image you have developed of Marica or of Raquel? Explain.

MARICA. [*Frightened.*] You won't tell the priest, will you?

RAQUEL. Suicide is a sin, Marica. A sin against God.

MARICA. I know. I . . . [*She catches* RAQUEL'S *hand.*] Oh, Raquel, why do we have to have wars? Why do men have to go to war and be killed?

RAQUEL. Men must fight for what they believe is right. It is an honorable thing to die for your country as a soldier.

MARICA. How can you say that with Domingo[4] out there fighting, too? And fighting what? Men who aren't even men. Peasants. Ranch slaves. Men who shouldn't be allowed to fight.

RAQUEL. Peasants are men, Marica. Not animals.

MARICA. Men. It's always men. But how about the women? What becomes of us?

RAQUEL. We can pray.

MARICA. [*Bitterly.*] Yes, we can pray. And then comes the terrible news, and it's no use praying any more. All the reason for our praying is dead. Why should I go on living with Tomás[5] dead?

RAQUEL. Living is a duty.

MARICA. How can you be so cold, so hard? You are a cold and hard woman, Raquel. My brother worships you. He has never even looked at another woman since the first day he saw you. Does he know how cold and hard you are?

RAQUEL. Domingo is my—honored husband.

MARICA. You've been married for ten years. And I've been married for three months. If Domingo is killed, it won't be the same for you. You've had ten years. [*She is crying wildly.*] I haven't anything . . . anything at all.

RAQUEL. You've had three months—three months of laughter. And now you have tears. How lucky you are. You have tears. Perhaps five months of tears. Not more. You're only twenty. And in five months Tomás will become just a lovely memory.

MARICA. I'll remember Tomás all my life.

RAQUEL. Of course. But he'll be distant and far away. But you're young . . . and the young need laughter. The young can't live on tears. And one day in Paris, or Rome, or even Mexico City, you'll meet another man. You'll marry again. There will be children in your house. How lucky you are.

MARICA. I'll never marry again.

RAQUEL. You're only twenty. You'll think differently when you're twenty-eight, or nine, or thirty.

MARICA. What will you do if Domingo is killed?

RAQUEL. I shall be very proud that he died in all his courage . . . in all the greatness of a hero.

MARICA. But you'd not weep, would you? Not you! I don't think there are any tears in you.

RAQUEL. No, I'd not weep. I'd sit here in this empty house and wait.

MARICA. Wait for what?

RAQUEL. For the jingle of his spurs as he walks across the tiled hall. For the sound of his laughter in the patio. For the echo of

4. Domingo (də ming′gō)
5. Tomás (tō mäs′)

Analyze Plot and Setting *What do Marica's lines about the fighting tell you about the culture in which the play takes place?*

Characterization *How does Niggli characterize Marica?*

his voice as he shouts to the groom to put away his horse. For the feel of his hand . . .

MARICA. [*Screams.*] Stop it!

RAQUEL. I'm sorry.

MARICA. You do love him, don't you?

RAQUEL. I don't think even he knows how much.

MARICA. I thought that after ten years people slid away from love. But you and Domingo—why, you're all he thinks about. When he's away from you he talks about you all the time. I heard him say once that when you were out of his sight he was like a man without eyes or ears or hands.

RAQUEL. I know. I, too, know that feeling.

MARICA. Then how could you let him go to war? Perhaps to be killed? How could you?

RAQUEL. [*Sharply.*] Marica, you are of the family Macías. Your family is a family of great warriors. A Macías man was with Ferdinand when the Moors were driven out of Spain. A Macías man was with Cortés when the Aztecans surrendered. Your grandfather fought in the War of Independence. Your own father was executed not twenty miles from this house by the French.[6] Shall his son be any less brave because he loves a woman?

MARICA. But Domingo loved you enough to forget that. If you had asked him, he wouldn't have gone to war. He would have stayed here with you.

---

6. In 1492 *Ferdinand* of Aragon defeated the *Moors*, a Muslim people from northwest Africa who had controlled most of Spain since the 700s. Through the *War of Independence*, Mexico won freedom from Spain in 1821. The *French* invaded and occupied Mexico City in 1863.

> Characterization *What do Raquel's lines at the end of this column tell you about her attitude toward men going to war?*

RAQUEL. No, he would not have stayed. Your brother is a man of honor, not a whining, creeping coward.

MARICA. [*Beginning to cry again.*] I begged Tomás not to go. I begged him.

RAQUEL. Would you have loved him if he had stayed?

MARICA. I don't know. I don't know.

RAQUEL. There is your answer. You'd have despised him. Loved and despised him. Now come, Marica, it's time for you to go to bed.

MARICA. You won't tell the priest—about the poison, I mean?

RAQUEL. No. I won't tell him.

MARICA. Thank you, Raquel. How good you are. How kind and good.

RAQUEL. A moment ago I was hard and cruel. What a baby you are. Now, off to bed with you.

MARICA. Aren't you coming upstairs, too?

RAQUEL. No . . . I haven't been sleeping very well lately. I think I'll read for a little while.

MARICA. Good night, Raquel. And thank you.

RAQUEL. Good night, little one.

[*MARICA goes out through the house door Left, taking her candle with her. RAQUEL stares down at the bottle of poison in her hand, then puts it away in one of the small drawers of the desk. She next selects a book from the Downstage case and sits on the sofa to read it, but feeling chilly, she rises and goes to the closet, Back Right, and takes out an afghan.[7] Coming back to the sofa, she makes herself comfortable, with the afghan across her knees. Suddenly she hears a noise in the patio. She listens, then convinced it is*

---

7. An *afghan* is a knitted or crocheted wool blanket.

nothing, returns to her reading. But she hears the noise again. She goes to the patio door and peers out.]

RAQUEL. [*Calling softly.*] Who's there? Who's out there? Oh! [*She gasps and backs into the room. Two men—or rather a man and a young boy—dressed in the white pajama suits of the Mexican peasants, with their sombreros tipped low over their faces, come into the room. RAQUEL draws herself up **regally**. Her voice is cold and commanding.*] Who are you, and what do you want here?

ANDRÉS. We are hunting for the wife of General Macías.

RAQUEL. I am Raquel Rivera de Macías.

ANDRÉS. Cleto, stand guard in the patio. If you hear any suspicious noise, warn me at once.

CLETO. Yes, my captain. [*The boy returns to the patio.*]

[*The man, hooking his thumbs in his belt, strolls around the room, looking it over. When he reaches the table at the back he sees the wine. With a small bow to RAQUEL he pours himself a glass of wine and drains it. He wipes his mouth with the back of his hand.*]

RAQUEL. How very interesting.

ANDRÉS. [*Startled.*] What?

RAQUEL. To be able to drink wine with that hat on.

ANDRÉS. The hat? Oh, forgive me, señora. [*He flicks the brim with his fingers so that it drops off his head and dangles down his back*

from the neck cord.*] In a military camp one forgets one's polite manners. Would you care to join me in another glass?

RAQUEL. [*Sitting on the sofa.*] Why not? It's my wine.

ANDRÉS. And very excellent wine. [*He pours two glasses and gives her one while he is talking.*] I would say Amontillado[8] of the vintage of '87.

RAQUEL. Did you learn that in a military camp?

ANDRÉS. I used to sell wines . . . among other things.

RAQUEL. [***Ostentatiously** hiding a yawn.*] I am devastated.

ANDRÉS. [*Pulls over the armchair and makes himself comfortable in it.*] You don't mind, do you?

RAQUEL. Would it make any difference if I did?

ANDRÉS. No. The Federals are searching the streets for us, and we have to stay somewhere. But women of your class seem to expect that senseless sort of question.

RAQUEL. Of course I suppose I could scream.

ANDRÉS. Naturally.

RAQUEL. My sister-in-law is upstairs asleep. And there are several servants in the back of the house. Mostly men servants. Very big men.

ANDRÉS. Very interesting. [*He is drinking the wine in small sips with much enjoyment.*]

RAQUEL. What would you do if I screamed?

Characterization *What do the remarks that Raquel makes to Andrés reveal about her?*

Vocabulary

regally (rē′gəl lē) *adv.* in a grand, dignified manner befitting a king or a queen

---

8. *Amontillado* (ə môn′til ä dō) is a kind of sherry, which is a strong wine.

Vocabulary

ostentatiously (os′tən tā′shəs lē) *adv.* in a way intended to attract attention or impress others

JOSEFINA NIGGLI   **833**

ANDRÉS. [*Considering the request as though it were another glass of wine.*] Nothing.

RAQUEL. I am afraid you are lying to me.

ANDRÉS. Women of your class seem to expect polite little lies.

RAQUEL. Stop calling me "woman of your class."

ANDRÉS. Forgive me.

RAQUEL. You are one of the fighting peasants, aren't you?

ANDRÉS. I am a captain in the Revolutionary Army.

RAQUEL. This house is completely loyal to the Federal government.

ANDRÉS. I know. That's why I'm here.

RAQUEL. And now that you are here, just what do you expect me to do?

ANDRÉS. I expect you to offer sanctuary to myself and to Cleto.

RAQUEL. Cleto? [*She looks toward the patio and adds sarcastically.*] Oh, your army.

CLETO. [*Appearing in the doorway.*] I'm sorry, my captain. I just heard a noise. [*RAQUEL stands. ANDRÉS moves quickly to her and puts his hands on her arms from the back. CLETO has turned and is peering into the patio. Then the boy relaxes.*] We are still safe, my captain. It was only a rabbit. [*He goes back into the patio. RAQUEL pulls away from ANDRÉS and goes to the desk.*]

RAQUEL. What a magnificent army you have. So clever. I'm sure you must win many victories.

ANDRÉS. We do. And we will win the greatest victory, remember that.

RAQUEL. This farce has gone on long enough. Will you please take your army and climb over the patio wall with it?

ANDRÉS. I told you that we came here so that you could give us sanctuary.

RAQUEL. My dear captain—captain without a name . . .

ANDRÉS. Andrés de la O, your servant. [*He makes a bow.*]

RAQUEL. [*Startled.*] Andrés de la O!

ANDRÉS. I am flattered. You have heard of me.

RAQUEL. Naturally. Everyone in the city has heard of you. You have a reputation for politeness—especially to women.

ANDRÉS. I see that the tales about me have lost nothing in the telling.

RAQUEL. I can't say. I'm not interested in gossip about your type of soldier.

ANDRÉS. Then let me give you something to heighten your interest. [*He suddenly takes her in his arms and kisses her. She stiffens for a moment, then remains perfectly still. He steps away from her.*]

RAQUEL. [*Rage forcing her to whisper.*] Get out of here—at once!

ANDRÉS. [*Staring at her in admiration.*] I can understand why Macías loves you. I couldn't before, but now I can understand it.

RAQUEL. Get out of my house.

ANDRÉS. [*Sits on the sofa and pulls a small leather pouch out of his shirt. He pours its contents into his hand.*] So cruel, señora, and I with a present for you? Here is a holy medal. My mother gave me this medal. She died when I was ten. She was a street beg-

---

Analyze Plot and Setting *What does Andrés's second comment in this column imply about wealthy women at the time the play is set?*

Portraits of Real Life *Is Raquel's abrupt change in behavior toward Andrés realistic? Explain.*

gar. She died of starvation. But I wasn't there. I was in jail. I had been sentenced to five years in prison for stealing five oranges. The judge thought it a great joke. One year for each orange. He laughed. He had a very loud laugh. [*Pause.*] I killed him two months ago. I hanged him to the telephone pole in front of his house. And I laughed. [*Pause.*] I also have a very loud laugh. [*RAQUEL abruptly turns her back on him.*] I told that story to a girl the other night and she thought it very funny. But of course she was a peasant girl—a girl who could neither read nor write. She hadn't been born in a great house in Tabasco.[9] She didn't have an English governess.[10] She didn't go to school to the nuns in Paris. She didn't marry one of the richest young men in the Republic. But she thought my story very funny. Of course she could understand it. Her brother had been whipped to death because he had run away from the plantation that owned him. [*He pauses and looks at her. She does not move.*] Are you still angry with me? Even though I have brought you a present? [*He holds out his hand.*] A very nice present—from your husband.

RAQUEL. [*Turns and stares at him in amazement.*] A present! From Domingo?

ANDRÉS. I don't know him that well. I call him the General Macías.

RAQUEL. [*Excitedly.*] Is he well? How does he look? [*With horrified comprehension.*] He's a prisoner . . . your prisoner!

---

9. On the southern coast of the Gulf of Mexico, *Tabasco* is one of Mexico's 35 states.
10. A *governess* is a woman employed to teach children in a private household.

Characterization *Why do you think Andrés describes what the young woman did not have or do?*

ANDRÉS. Naturally. That's why I know so much about you. He talks about you constantly.

RAQUEL. You know nothing about him. You're lying to me.

[*CLETO comes to the window.*]

ANDRÉS. I assure you, señora . . .

CLETO. [*Interrupting.*] My captain . . .

ANDRÉS. What is it, Cleto? Another rabbit?

CLETO. No, my captain. There are soldiers at the end of the street. They are searching all the houses. They will be here soon.

ANDRÉS. Don't worry. We are quite safe here. Stay in the patio until I call you.

CLETO. Yes, my captain. [*He returns to the patio.*]

RAQUEL. You are not safe here. When those soldiers come I shall turn you over to them.

ANDRÉS. I think not.

RAQUEL. You can't escape from them. And they are not kind to you peasant prisoners. They have good reason not to be.

ANDRÉS. Look at this ring. [*He holds his hand out, with the ring on his palm.*]

RAQUEL. Why, it's—a wedding ring.

ANDRÉS. Read the inscription inside of it. [*As she hesitates, he adds sharply.*] Read it!

RAQUEL. [*Slowly takes the ring. While she is reading her voice fades to a whisper.*] "D. M.—R. R.—June 2, 1902." Where did you get this?

ANDRÉS. General Macías gave it to me.

RAQUEL. [*Firmly and clearly.*] Not this ring. He'd never give you this ring. [*With dawning horror.*] He's dead. You stole it from his dead finger. He's dead.

ANDRÉS. Not yet. But he will be dead if I don't return to camp safely by sunset tomorrow.

RAQUEL. I don't believe you. I don't believe you. You're lying to me.

ANDRÉS. This house is famous for its loyalty to the Federal government. You will hide me until those soldiers get out of this district. When it is safe enough Cleto and I will leave. But if you betray me to them, your husband will be shot tomorrow evening at sunset. Do you understand? [*He shakes her arm. RAQUEL looks dazedly at him. CLETO comes to the window.*]

CLETO. The soldiers are coming closer, my captain. They are at the next house.

ANDRÉS. [*To RAQUEL.*] Where shall we hide? [*Raquel is still dazed. He gives her another little shake.*] Think, woman! If you love your husband at all—think!

RAQUEL. I don't know. Marica upstairs—the servants in the rest of the house—I don't know.

ANDRÉS. The General has bragged to us about you. He says you are braver than most men. He says you are very clever. This is a time to be both brave and clever.

CLETO. [*Pointing to the closet.*] What door is that?

RAQUEL. It's a closet . . . a storage closet.

ANDRÉS. We'll hide in there.

RAQUEL. It's very small. It's not big enough for both of you.

Analyze Plot and Setting *How does Andrés's demand that Raquel hide him contribute to the plot development?*

Characterization *Is the General's description of his wife consistent with the characterization of her thus far? Explain.*

ANDRÉS. Cleto, hide yourself in there.

CLETO. But, my captain . . .

ANDRÉS. That's an order! Hide yourself.

CLETO. Yes, Sir. [*He steps inside the closet.*]

ANDRÉS. And now, señora, where are you going to hide me?

RAQUEL. How did you persuade my husband to give you his ring?

ANDRÉS. That's a very long story, señora, for which we have no time just now. [*He puts the ring and medal back in the pouch and thrusts it inside his shirt.*] Later I will be glad to give you all the details. But at present it is only necessary for you to remember that his life depends upon mine.

RAQUEL. Yes—yes, of course. [*She loses her dazed expression and seems to grow more queenly as she takes command of the situation.*] Give me your hat. [*ANDRÉS shrugs and passes it over to her. She takes it to the closet and hands it to CLETO.*] There is a smoking jacket hanging up in there. Hand it to me. [*CLETO hands her a man's velvet smoking jacket. She brings it to ANDRÉS.*] Put this on.

ANDRÉS. [*Puts it on and looks down at himself.*] Such a pity my shoes are not comfortable slippers.

RAQUEL. Sit in that chair. [*She points to the armchair.*]

ANDRÉS. My dear lady . . .

RAQUEL. If I must save your life, allow me to do it in my own way. Sit down. [*ANDRÉS sits. She picks up the afghan from the couch and throws it over his feet and legs, carefully tucking it in so that his body is covered to the waist.*] If anyone speaks to you, don't answer. Don't turn your head. As far as you are concerned, there is no one in this room—not even me. Just look straight ahead of you and . . .

ANDRÉS. [*As she pauses.*] And what?

Triumph of the Revolution—Distribution of Food (Trionfo de la revolucion, reparto de los alimentos), 1926-1927. Diego Rivera. Banco de Mexico Trust. Fresco, 3.54 x 3.67 m. Chapel, Universidad Autonoma, Chapingo, Mexico.

View the Art Diego Rivera, a world famous Mexican muralist, believed art should have a political message. The heroes in his paintings are ordinary hard-working Mexicans. What insight does this scene give you about social conditions in Mexico at the time of this play?

RAQUEL. I started to say "and pray," but since you're a member of the Revolutionary Army I don't suppose you believe in God and prayer.

ANDRÉS. My mother left me a holy medal.

RAQUEL. Oh, yes, I remember. A very amusing story. [*There is the sound of men's voices in the patio.*] The Federal soldiers are here. If you can pray, ask God to keep Marica upstairs. She is very young and very stupid. She'll betray you before I can shut her mouth.

ANDRÉS. I'll . . .

RAQUEL. Silence! Stare straight ahead of you and pray. [*She goes to the French window and speaks loudly to the soldiers.*] Really! What is the meaning of this uproar?

FLORES. [*Off.*] Do not alarm yourself, señora. [*He comes into the room. He wears the uniform of a Federal officer.*] I am Captain Basilio Flores, at your service, señora.

RAQUEL. What do you mean, invading my house and making so much noise at this hour of the night?

FLORES. We are hunting for two spies. One of them is the **notorious** Andrés de la O. You may have heard of him, señora.

RAQUEL. [*Looking at* ANDRÉS.] Considering what he did to my cousin—yes, I've heard of him.

FLORES. Your cousin, señora?

RAQUEL. [*Comes to* ANDRÉS *and puts her hand on his shoulder. He stares woodenly in front of him.*] Felipe[11] was his prisoner before the poor boy managed to escape.

---

11. *Felipe* (fə lē pā)

Vocabulary

notorious (nō tôr ´ ē əs) *adj.* widely and unfavorably known

FLORES. Is it possible? [*He crosses to* ANDRÉS.] Captain Basilio Flores, at your service. [*He salutes.*]

RAQUEL. Felipe doesn't hear you. He doesn't even know you are in the room.

FLORES. Eh, it is a sad thing.

RAQUEL. Must your men make so much noise?

FLORES. The hunt must be thorough, señora. And now if some of my men can go through here to the rest of the house . . .

RAQUEL. Why?

FLORES. But I told you, señora. We are hunting for two spies . . .

RAQUEL. [*Speaking quickly from controlled nervousness.*] And do you think I have them hidden someplace, and I the wife of General Macías?

FLORES. General Macías! But I didn't know . . .

RAQUEL. Now that you do know, I suggest you remove your men and their noise at once.

FLORES. But, señora, I regret—I still have to search this house.

RAQUEL. I can assure you, captain, that I have been sitting here all evening, and no peasant spy has passed me and gone into the rest of the house.

FLORES. Several rooms open off the patio, señora. They needn't have come through here.

RAQUEL. So . . . you do think I conceal spies in this house. Then search it by all means. Look under the sofa . . . under the table. In the drawers of the desk. And don't miss

---

Characterization *What do Raquel's lines at the end of this column tell you about her?*

that closet, captain. Inside that closet is hidden a very fierce and wicked spy.

FLORES. Please, señora . . .

RAQUEL. [*Goes to the closet door.*] Or do you prefer me to open it for you?

FLORES. I am only doing my duty, señora. You are making it very difficult.

RAQUEL. [*Relaxing against the door.*] I'm sorry. My sister-in-law is upstairs. She has just received word that her husband has been killed. They were married three months ago. She's only twenty. I didn't want . . .

MARICA. [*Calling off.*] Raquel, what is all that noise downstairs?

RAQUEL. [*Goes to the house door and calls.*] It is nothing. Go back to bed.

MARICA. But I can hear men's voices in the patio.

RAQUEL. It is only some Federal soldiers hunting for two peasant spies. [*She turns and speaks rapidly to FLORES.*] If she comes down here, she must not see my cousin. Felipe escaped, but her husband was killed. The doctor thinks the sight of my poor cousin might affect her mind. You understand?

FLORES. Certainly, señora. What a sad thing.

MARICA. [*Still off.*] Raquel, I'm afraid! [*She tries to push past RAQUEL into the room. RAQUEL and FLORES stand between her and ANDRÉS.*] Spies! In this house. Oh, Raquel!

RAQUEL. The doctor will be very angry if you don't return to bed at once.

MARICA. But those terrible men will kill us. What is the matter with you two? Why are you standing there like that? [*She tries to see past them, but they both move so that she can't see ANDRÉS.*]

FLORES. It is better that you go back to your room, señora.

MARICA. But why? Upstairs I am alone. Those terrible men will kill me. I know they will.

FLORES. Don't be afraid, señora. There are no spies in this house.

MARICA. Are you sure?

RAQUEL. Captain Flores means that no spy would dare to take refuge in the house of General Macías. Isn't that right, captain?

FLORES. [*Laughing.*] Of course. All the world knows of the brave General Macías.

RAQUEL. Now go back to bed, Marica. Please, for my sake.

MARICA. You are both acting very strangely. I think you have something hidden in this room you don't want me to see.

RAQUEL. [*Sharply.*] You are quite right. Captain Flores has captured one of the spies. He is sitting in the chair behind me. He is dead. Now will you please go upstairs!

MARICA. [*Gives a stifled sob.*] Oh! That such a terrible thing could happen in this house. [*She runs out of the room, still sobbing.*]

FLORES. [*Worried.*] Was it wise to tell her such a story, señora?

RAQUEL. [*Tense with **repressed** relief.*] Better that than the truth. Good night, captain, and thank you.

Portraits of Real Life *How is Raquel handling the search? Is her behavior realistic? Explain.*

Vocabulary

repressed (ri prest´) *adj.* held back or kept under control; restrained

Wall with a Door and Tree (Muro con puerta y arbol). Pablo Burchard.

View the Art This painting draws the viewer's eye to the brightness visible just beyond the partially opened door. What is the mood of this painting? How does it compare with the mood in the play?

FLORES. Good night, señora. And don't worry. Those spies won't bother you. If they were anywhere in this district, my men would have found them.

RAQUEL. I'm sure of it.

[*The Captain salutes her, looks toward* ANDRÉS *and salutes him, then goes into the patio. He can be heard calling his men. Neither* ANDRÉS *nor* RAQUEL *moves until the voices outside die away. Then Raquel staggers and nearly falls, but Andrés catches her in time.*]

ANDRÉS. [*Calling softly.*] They've gone, Cleto. [ANDRÉS *carries Raquel to the sofa as Cleto comes out of the closet.*] Bring a glass of wine. Quickly.

CLETO. [*As he gets the wine.*] What happened?

ANDRÉS. It's nothing. Just a faint. [*He holds the wine to her lips.*]

CLETO. She's a great lady, that one. When she wanted to open the closet door my knees were trembling, I can tell you.

ANDRÉS. My own bones were playing a pretty tune.

CLETO. Why do you think she married Macías?

ANDRÉS. Love is a peculiar thing, Cleto.

CLETO. I don't understand it.

RAQUEL. [*Moans and sits up.*] Are they—are they gone?

ANDRÉS. Yes, they're gone. [*He kisses her hand.*] I've never known a braver lady.

RAQUEL. [*Pulling her hand away.*] Will you go now, please?

ANDRÉS. We'll have to wait until the district is free of them—but if you'd like to write a letter to your husband while we're waiting . . .

RAQUEL. [*Surprised at his kindness.*] You'd take it to him? You'd really give it to him?

ANDRÉS. Of course.

RAQUEL. Thank you. [*She goes to the writing desk and sits down.*]

ANDRÉS. [*To* CLETO, *who has been staring steadily at* RAQUEL *all the while.*] You stay here with the señora. I'm going to find out how much of the district has been cleared.

CLETO. [*Still staring at* RAQUEL.] Yes, my captain.

[ANDRÉS *leaves by the French windows.* CLETO *keeps on staring at* RAQUEL *as she starts to write. After a moment she turns to him.*]

RAQUEL. [*Irritated.*] Why do you keep staring at me?

CLETO. Why did you marry a man like that one, señora?

RAQUEL. You're very **impertinent.**

CLETO. [*Shyly.*] I'm sorry, señora.

RAQUEL. [*After a brief pause.*] What do you mean: "a man like that one"?

CLETO. Well, you're very brave, señora.

RAQUEL. [*Lightly.*] And don't you think the general is very brave?

CLETO. No, señora. Not very.

RAQUEL. [*Staring at him with bewilderment.*] What are you trying to tell me?

CLETO. Nothing, señora. It is none of my affair.

RAQUEL. Come here. [*He comes slowly up to her.*] Tell me what is in your mind.

Portraits of Real Life *If this were a true story, would you expect this behavior from a revolutionary toward his enemy? Why or why not?*

Vocabulary

impertinent (im purt´ ən ənt) *adj.* inappropriately bold or forward

JOSEFINA NIGGLI **841**

CLETO. I don't know, señora. I don't understand it. The captain says love is a peculiar thing, but I don't understand it.

RAQUEL. Cleto, did the general willingly give that ring to your captain?

CLETO. Yes, señora.

RAQUEL. Why?

CLETO. The general wanted to save his own life. He said he loved you and he wanted to save his life.

RAQUEL. How would giving that ring to your captain save the general's life?

CLETO. The general's supposed to be shot tomorrow afternoon. But he's talked about you a lot, and when my captain knew we had to come into the city, he thought perhaps we might take refuge here if the Federals got on our trail. So he went to the general and said that if he fixed it so we'd be safe here, my captain would save him from the firing squad.

RAQUEL. Was your trip to the city very important—to your cause, I mean?

CLETO. Indeed yes, señora. The captain got a lot of fine information. It means we'll win the next big battle. My captain is a very clever man, señora.

RAQUEL. Did the general know about this information when he gave his ring to your captain?

CLETO. I don't see how he could help knowing it, señora. He heard us talking about it enough.

RAQUEL. Who knows about that bargain to save the general's life beside you and your captain?

CLETO. No one, señora. The captain isn't one to talk, and I didn't have time to.

RAQUEL. [While the boy has been talking, the life seems to have drained completely out of her.] How old are you, Cleto?

CLETO. I don't know, señora. I think I'm twenty, but I don't know.

RAQUEL. [Speaking more to herself than to him.] Tomás was twenty.

CLETO. Who is Tomás?

RAQUEL. He was married to my sister-in-law. Cleto, you think my husband is a coward, don't you?

CLETO. [With embarrassment.] Yes, señora.

RAQUEL. You don't think any woman is worth it, do you? Worth the price of a great battle, I mean?

CLETO. No, señora. But as the captain says, love is a very peculiar thing.

RAQUEL. If your captain loved a woman as much as the general loves me, would he have given an enemy his ring?

CLETO. Ah, but the captain is a great man, señora.

RAQUEL. And so is my husband a great man. He is of the family Macías. All of that family have been great men. All of them—brave and honorable men. They have always held their honor to be greater than their lives. That is a tradition of their family.

CLETO. Perhaps none of them loved a woman like you, señora.

RAQUEL. How strange you are. I saved you from the Federals because I want to save my husband's life. You call me brave, and yet you call him a coward.

Analyze Plot and Setting *How might the fact that no one else knows about the bargain affect the plot?*

There is no difference in what we have done.

CLETO. But you are a woman, señora.

RAQUEL. Has a woman less honor than a man, then?

CLETO. No, señora. Please, I don't know how to say it. The general is a soldier. He has a duty to his own cause. You are a woman. You have a duty to your husband. It is right that you should try to save him. It is not right that he should try to save himself.

RAQUEL. [Dully.] Yes, of course. It is right that I should save him. [Becoming practical again.] Your captain has been gone some time, Cleto. You'd better find out if he is still safe.

CLETO. Yes, señora. [As he reaches the French windows she stops him.]

RAQUEL. Wait, Cleto. Have you a mother—or a wife, perhaps?

CLETO. Oh, no, señora. I haven't anyone but the captain.

RAQUEL. But the captain is a soldier. What would you do if he should be killed?

CLETO. It is very simple, señora. I should be killed, too.

RAQUEL. You speak about death so calmly. Aren't you afraid of it, Cleto?

CLETO. No, señora. It's like the captain says . . . dying for what you believe in—that's the finest death of all.

RAQUEL. And you believe in the Revolutionary cause?

CLETO. Yes, señora. I am a poor peasant, that's true. But still I have a right to live like a man, with my own ground, and my own family, and my own future. [He stops speaking abruptly.] I'm sorry, señora. You are a fine lady. You don't understand these things. I must go and find my captain. [He goes out.]

RAQUEL. [Rests her face against her hand.] He's so young. But Tomás was no older. And he's not afraid. He said so. Oh, Domingo—Domingo! [She straightens abruptly, takes the bottle of poison from the desk drawer and stares at it. Then she crosses to the decanter and laces the wine with the poison. She hurries back to the desk and is busy writing when ANDRÉS and CLETO return.]

ANDRÉS. You'll have to hurry that letter. The district is clear now.

RAQUEL. I'll be through in just a moment. You might as well finish the wine while you're waiting.

ANDRÉS. Thank you. A most excellent idea. [He pours himself a glass of wine. As he lifts it to his lips she speaks.]

RAQUEL. Why don't you give some to—Cleto?

ANDRÉS. This is too fine a wine to waste on that boy.

RAQUEL. He'll probably never have another chance to taste such wine.

ANDRÉS. Very well. Pour yourself a glass, Cleto.

CLETO. Thank you. [He pours it.] Your health, my captain.

RAQUEL. [Quickly.] Drink it outside, Cleto. I want to speak to your captain. [The boy looks at Andrés, who jerks his head toward the patio. CLETO nods and goes out.] I want you to give my husband a message for me. I

Portraits of Real Life *What does Cleto's statement tell you about the culture in which he lives?*

Characterization *Based on Raquel's actions and words, how does she feel about Cleto?*

can't write it. You'll have to remember it. But first, give me a glass of wine, too.

ANDRÉS. [*Pouring the wine.*] It might be easier for him if you wrote it.

RAQUEL. I think not. [*She takes the glass.*] I want you to tell him that I never knew how much I loved him until tonight.

ANDRÉS. Is that all?

RAQUEL. Yes. Tell me, captain, do you think it possible to love a person too much?

ANDRÉS. Yes, señora. I do.

RAQUEL. So do I. Let us drink a toast, captain—to honor. To bright and shining honor.

ANDRÉS. [*Raises his glass.*] To honor. [*He drains his glass. She lifts hers almost to her lips and then puts it down. From the patio comes a faint cry.*]

CLETO. [*Calling faintly in a cry that fades into silence.*] Captain. Captain.

[*ANDRÉS sways, his hand trying to brush across his face as though trying to brush sense into his head. When he hears CLETO he tries to stagger toward the window but stumbles and can't quite make it. Hanging on to the table by the sofa he looks accusingly at her. She shrinks back against her chair.*]

ANDRÉS. [*His voice weak from the poison.*] Why?

RAQUEL. Because I love him. Can you understand that?

ANDRÉS. We'll win. The Revolution will win. You can't stop that.

RAQUEL. Yes, you'll win. I know that now.

ANDRÉS. That girl—she thought my story was funny—about the hanging. But you didn't . . .

RAQUEL. I'm glad you hanged him. I'm glad.

[*ANDRÉS looks at her and tries to smile. He manages to pull the pouch from his shirt and extend it to her. But it drops from his hand.*]

RAQUEL. [*Runs to French window and calls.*] Cleto. Cleto! [*She buries her face in her hands for a moment, then comes back to ANDRÉS. She kneels beside him and picks up the leather pouch. She opens it and, taking the ring, puts it on her finger. Then she sees the medal. She rises and, pulling out the chain from her own throat, she slides the medal on to the chain. Then she walks to the sofa and sinks down on it.*]

MARICA. [*Calling off.*] Raquel! Raquel! [*RAQUEL snaps off the lamp, leaving the room in darkness. MARICA opens the house door. She is carrying a candle which she shades with her hand. The light is too dim to reveal the dead ANDRÉS.*] What are you doing down here in the dark? Why don't you come to bed?

RAQUEL. [*Making an effort to speak.*] I'll come in just a moment.

MARICA. But what are you doing, Raquel?

RAQUEL. Nothing. Just listening . . . listening to an empty house.

QUICK CURTAIN

Portraits of Real Life *Why do you think Raquel agrees that the Revolution will win? Is her response realistic? Explain.*

After You Read

Respond and Think Critically

1. **Connect to Personal Experience** What aspect of the play did you find most surprising? Explain.

2. **Make Inferences About Historical Context** How does this play help an audience understand the Mexican Revolution?

3. **Analyze Symbols** What do the ring of General Macías and the medal of Andrés symbolize to their owners? What do they represent to Raquel?

4. **Make Inferences About Conflict** What conflicting thoughts and emotions does Raquel experience near the end of the play? Why do you think she does what she does? Support your response with evidence from the text.

5. **Big Idea Draw Conclusions About Theme** Explain how this play speaks to both loyalty and betrayal. What connections can you make between loyalty and betrayal in the play and loyalty and betrayal in real life?

6. **Analyze Cultural Context** Niggli's works show a concern for social issues, particularly those related to women. How does this play demonstrate Raquel's oppression as well as her strength?

Literary Element Characterization

Characterization might be revealed to the reader through the character's own words. Sometimes authors will have characters present a long speech, or **monologue**, that tells the reader something about the character's personality.

7. **Interpret Monologue** Which character in the play delivers a monologue? What does the reader learn about that character as a result?

8. **Make Inferences About Description** How does Andrés's description of the peasant girl on page 835 aid Niggli in characterizing Raquel?

Reading Strategy Analyze Plot and Setting

A reader needs to understand the basic chain of events that make up the story (**plot**) and the time and place in which the story takes place (**setting**).

9. How does the description of the setting help you understand the characters and their actions?

10. What is the **climax**, or highest emotional point, in *The Ring of General Macías*? Explain.

LOG ON ▶ **Literature** Online

Selection Resources For Selection Quizzes, eFlashcards, and Reading-Writing Connection activities, go to glencoe.com and enter QuickPass code GL57805u4.

Vocabulary Practice

Practice with Word Parts Use a dictionary to find the meaning of each boldfaced vocabulary word's root. Look for definitions of any prefixes or suffixes in the word. Then use the word correctly in a sentence.

regally   ostentatiously   notorious
        repressed   impertinent

EXAMPLE: <u>Disdainful</u>; <u>Prefix:</u> dis-, apart, away, reversal; <u>Root:</u> dignare, "to deign"; <u>Suffix:</u> -ful, "full of" <u>Sentence:</u> Disdainful of the simple food, Rick refused to touch it.

Writing

Write an Interior Monologue What is going through Raquel's mind as she sits "listening to an empty house" at the end of the play? Write an interior monologue—an account of her thoughts, as if she were speaking them to herself—that conveys her situation, feelings, and outlook on the future. Include details that contribute to a definite mood and tone and try to convey an explicit or implicit theme related to loyalty.

Build Background

Carmen Tafolla uses the word *m'ija* (mē′hə), a contraction of the Spanish words *mi* ("my") and *hija* ("daughter"). By calling the reader "m'ija," Tafolla follows the Mexican American tradition of addressing readers as if they were her own children and makes the poem a message to them. Tafolla grew up in San Antonio, Texas and went to college and graduate school in Austin.

Marked

Carmen Tafolla

Never write with pencil,
m'ija
It is for those
who would
5   erase.
Make your mark proud
      and open,
Brave,
        beauty folded into
10   its imperfection,
Like a piece of turquoise
      marked.

Never write
with pencil,
15 m'ija.
Write with ink
     or mud,
or berries grown in
gardens never owned,
20 or, sometimes,
    if necessary,
      blood.

Collage Series II, No. 3, 1993. Katherine S. Nemanich.
Oil pastel on paper and board, 12 x 9 in. Private collection.

💬 Discussion Starter

How is Carmen Tafolla's advice about making a mark in the world useful? With a small group, discuss the question. Refer to the poem's words and discuss situations where her advice might be most beneficial.

Build Background

"The Ring" is about a life-changing encounter in the Danish countryside around 1800. At that time, most people in Denmark lived on farms.

The Ring

Isak Dinesen

On a summer morning a hundred and fifty years ago a young Danish squire and his wife went out for a walk on their land. They had been married a week. It had not been easy for them to get married, for the wife's family was higher in rank and wealthier than the husband's. But the two young people, now twenty-four and nineteen years old, had been set on their purpose for ten years; and in the end her haughty parents had had to give in to them.

They were wonderfully happy. The stolen meetings and secret, tearful love letters were now things of the past. To God and man they were one; they could walk arm in arm in broad daylight and drive in the same carriage, and they would walk and drive so till the end of their days. Their distant paradise had descended to earth and had proved, surprisingly, to be filled with the things of everyday life: with jesting and railleries,[1] with breakfasts and suppers, with dogs, haymaking and sheep. Sigismund, the young husband, had promised himself that from now there should be no stone in his bride's path, nor should any shadow fall across it. Lovisa, the wife, felt that now, every day and for the first time in her young life, she moved and breathed in perfect freedom because she could never have any secret from her husband.

To Lovisa—whom her husband called Lise—the rustic atmosphere of her new life was a matter of wonder and delight. Her husband's fear that the existence he could offer her might not be good enough for her filled her heart with laughter. It was not a long time since she had played with dolls; as now she dressed her own hair, looked over her linen press and arranged her flowers she again lived through an enchanting and cherished experience: one was doing everything gravely and solicitously, and all the time one knew one was playing.

It was a lovely July morning. Little woolly clouds drifted high up in the sky, the air was

---

1. *Railleries* are instances of good-natured ridicule or teasing.

full of sweet scents. Lise had on a white muslin frock and a large Italian straw hat. She and her husband took a path through the park; it wound on across the meadows, between small groves and groups of trees, to the sheep field. Sigismund was going to show his wife his sheep. For this reason she had not brought her small white dog, Bijou, with her, for he would yap at the lambs and frighten them, or he would annoy the sheep dogs. Sigismund prided himself on his sheep; he had studied sheep-breeding in Mecklenburg[2] and England, and had brought back with him Cotswold rams by which to improve his Danish stock. While they walked he explained to Lise the great

possibilities and difficulties of the plan.

She thought: "How clever he is, what a lot of things he knows!" and at the same time: "What an absurd person he is, with his sheep! What a baby he is! I am a hundred years older than he."

But when they arrived at the sheep-fold the old sheep-master Mathias met them with the sad news that one of the English lambs was dead and two were sick. Lise saw that her

Visual Vocabulary
Cotswold is a breed of sheep with long, coarse hair, originally bred in the Cotswold Hills of southwestern England.

---

2. *Mecklenburg* is a farming region in northeastern Germany.

Gentle Spring, 1889. Edward Wilkins Waite. Oil on canvas, 51 x 76 cm. Private collection.

<u>View the Art</u> This painting depicts a landscape with animals. What is the mood of this painting? At what point in "The Ring" does the story reflect this mood?

husband was grieved by the tidings; while he questioned Mathias on the matter she kept silent and only gently pressed his arm. A couple of boys were sent off to fetch the sick lambs, while the master and servant went into the details of the case. It took some time.

Lise began to gaze about her and to think of other things. Twice her own thoughts made her blush deeply and happily, like a red rose, then slowly her blush died away, and the two men were still talking about sheep. A little while after their conversation caught her attention. It had turned to a sheep thief.

This thief during the last months had broken into the sheepfolds of the neighborhood like a wolf, had killed and dragged away his prey like a wolf and like a wolf had left no trace after him. Three nights ago the shepherd and his son on an estate ten miles away had caught him in the act. The thief had killed the man and knocked the boy senseless, and had managed to escape. There were men sent out to all sides to catch him, but nobody had seen him.

Lise wanted to hear more about the horrible event, and for her benefit old Mathias went through it once more. There had been a long fight in the sheep house, in many places the earthen floor was soaked with blood. In the fight the thief's left arm was broken; all the same, he had climbed a tall fence with a lamb on his back. Mathias added that he would like to string up the murderer with these two hands of his, and Lise nodded her head at him gravely in approval. She remembered Red Riding-hood's wolf, and felt a pleasant little thrill running down her spine.

Sigismund had his own lambs in his mind, but he was too happy in himself to wish anything in the universe ill. After a minute he said: "Poor devil."

Lise said: "How can you pity such a terrible man? Indeed Grandmamma was right when she said that you were a revolutionary and a danger to society!" The thought of Grandmamma, and of the tears of past days, again turned her mind away from the gruesome tale she had just heard.

The boys brought the sick lambs and the men began to examine them carefully, lifting them up and trying to set them on their legs; they squeezed them here and there and made the little creatures whimper. Lise shrank from the show and her husband noticed her distress.

"You go home, my darling," he said, "this will take some time. But just walk ahead slowly, and I shall catch up with you."

So she was turned away by an impatient husband to whom his sheep meant more than his wife. If any experience could be sweeter than to be dragged out by him to look at those same sheep, it would be this. She dropped her large summer hat with its blue ribbons on the grass and told him to carry it back for her, for she wanted to feel the summer air on her forehead and in her hair. She walked on very slowly, as he had told her to do, for she wished to obey him in everything. As she walked she felt a great new happiness in being altogether alone, even without Bijou. She could not remember that she had ever before in all her life been altogether alone. The landscape around her was still, as if full of promise, and it was hers. Even the swallows cruising in the air were hers, for they belonged to him, and he was hers.

She followed the curving edge of the grove and after a minute or two found that she was out of sight to the men by the sheep house. What could now, she wondered, be sweeter than to walk along the path in the long flowering meadow grass, slowly, slowly, and to let her husband overtake her there? It would be sweeter still, she reflected, to steal into the grove and to be gone, to have vanished from the surface of the earth from him when, tired of the sheep and longing for her company, he should turn the bend of the path to catch up with her.

An idea struck her; she stood still to think it over.

A few days ago her husband had gone for a ride and she had not wanted to go with him, but had strolled about with Bijou in order to explore her domain. Bijou then, gamboling, had led her straight into the grove. As she had followed him, gently forcing her way into the shrubbery, she had suddenly come upon a glade in the midst of it, a narrow space like a small alcove with hangings of thick green and golden brocade, big enough to hold two or three people in it. She had felt at that moment that she had come into the very heart of her new home. If today she could find the spot again she would stand perfectly still there, hidden from all the world. Sigismund would look for her in all directions; he would be unable to understand what had become of her and for a minute, for a short minute—or, perhaps, if she was firm and cruel enough, for five—he would realize what a void, what an unendurably sad and horrible place the universe would be when she was no longer in it. She gravely scrutinized the grove to find the right entrance to her hiding-place, then went in.

She took great care to make no noise at all, therefore advanced exceedingly slowly. When a twig caught the flounces of her ample skirt she loosened it softly from the muslin, so as not to crack it. Once a branch took hold of one of her long golden curls; she stood still, with her arms lifted, to free it. A little way into the grove the soil became moist; her light steps no longer made any sound upon it. With one hand she held her small handkerchief to her lips, as if to emphasize the secretness of her course. She found the spot she sought and bent down to divide the foliage and make a door to her sylvan[3] closet. At this the hem of her dress caught her foot and she stopped to loosen it. As she rose she looked into the face of a man who was already in the shelter.

He stood up erect, two steps off. He must have watched her as she made her way straight toward him.

She took him in in one single glance. His face was bruised and scratched, his hands and wrists stained with dark filth. He was dressed in rags, barefooted, with tatters wound round his naked ankles. His arms hung down to his sides, his right hand clasped the hilt of a knife. He was about her own age. The man and the woman looked at each other.

This meeting in the wood from beginning to end passed without a word; what happened could only be rendered by pantomime. To the two actors in the pantomime it was timeless; according to a clock it lasted four minutes.

She had never in her life been exposed to danger. It did not occur to her to sum up her position, or to work out the length of time it would take to call her husband or Mathias, whom at this moment she could hear shouting to his dogs. She beheld the man before her as she would have beheld a forest ghost: the apparition itself, not the sequels[4] of it, changes the world to the human who faces it.

Although she did not take her eyes off the face before her she sensed that the alcove

---

3. *Sylvan* means "in or among woods" or "formed by trees."
4. Here, *sequels* means "results or consequences."

Weary but Watchful, late 19th Century. John Sargent Noble.

View the Art In the story, the husband and wife have very different feelings about Sigismund's flock of sheep. How might each react to this image?

had been turned into a covert.[5] On the ground a couple of sacks formed a couch; there were some gnawed bones by it. A fire must have been made here in the night, for there were cinders strewn on the forest floor.

After a while she realized that he was observing her just as she was observing him. He was no longer just run to earth and crouching for a spring, but he was wondering, trying to know. At that she seemed to see herself with the eyes of the wild animal at bay[6] in his dark hiding-place; her silently approaching white figure, which might mean death.

He moved his right arm till it hung down straight before him between his legs. Without lifting the hand he bent the wrist and slowly raised the point of the knife till it pointed at her throat. The gesture was mad, unbelievable. He did not smile as he made it, but his nostrils dis-

tended,[7] the corners of his mouth quivered a little. Then slowly he put the knife back in the sheath by his belt.

She had no object of value about her, only the wedding ring which her husband had set on her finger in church, a week ago. She drew it off, and in this movement dropped her handkerchief. She reached out her hand with the ring toward him. She did not bargain for her life. She was fearless by nature, and the horror with which he inspired her was not fear of what he might do to her. She commanded him, she besought[8] him to vanish as he had come, to take a dreadful figure out of her life, so that it should never have been there. In the dumb[9] movement her young form had the grave authoritativeness of a priestess conjuring down some monstrous being by a sacred sign.

He slowly reached out his hand to hers, his finger touched hers, and her hand was steady at the touch. But he did not take the ring. As she let it go it dropped to the ground as her handkerchief had done.

For a second the eyes of both followed it. It rolled a few inches toward him and stopped before his bare foot. In a hardly perceivable movement he kicked it away and again looked into her face. They remained like that, she knew not how long, but she felt that during that time something happened, things were changed.

He bent down and picked up her handkerchief. All the time gazing at her, he again

---

5. As a noun, *covert* means "a hiding place." More often, you will see the word used as an adjective to mean "secret, hidden, or concealed."
6. *At bay* refers to the position of a cornered animal that is forced to turn and confront its pursuers.
7. *Distended* means "enlarged or expanded."
8. *Besought* is the past tense of *beseech* and means "begged or asked earnestly."
9. Here, *dumb* means "silent" and "without words."

ISAK DINESEN **851**

drew his knife and wrapped the tiny bit of cambric[10] round the blade. This was difficult for him to do because his left arm was broken. While he did it his face under the dirt and sun-tan slowly grew whiter till it was almost phosphorescent.[11] Fumbling with both hands, he once more stuck the knife into the sheath. Either the sheath was too big and had never fitted the knife, or the blade was much worn—it went in. For two or three more seconds his gaze rested on her face; then he lifted his own face a little, the strange radiance still upon it, and closed his eyes.

The movement was definitive and unconditional. In this one motion he did what she had begged him to do: he vanished and was gone. She was free.

She took a step backward, the immovable, blind face before her, then bent as she had done to enter the hiding-place, and glided away as noiselessly as she had come. Once outside the grove she stood still and looked round for the meadow path, found it, and began to walk home.

Her husband had not yet rounded the edge of the grove. Now he saw her and helloed to her gaily; he came up quickly and joined her.

The path here was so narrow that he kept half behind her and did not touch her. He began to explain to her what had been the matter with the lambs. She walked a step before him and thought: All is over.

After a while he noticed her silence, came up beside her to look at her face and asked, "What is the matter?"

She searched her mind for something to say, and at last said: "I have lost my ring."

"What ring?" he asked her.

She answered, "My wedding ring."

As she heard her own voice pronounce the words she conceived their meaning.

Her wedding ring. "With this ring"—dropped by one and kicked away by another—"with this ring I thee wed." With this lost ring she had wedded herself to something. To what? To poverty, persecution, total loneliness. To the sorrows and the sinfulness of this earth. "And what therefore God has joined together let man not put asunder."[12]

"I will find you another ring," her husband said. "You and I are the same as we were on our wedding day; it will do as well. We are husband and wife today too, as much as yesterday, I suppose."

Her face was so still that he did not know if she had heard what he said. It touched him that she should take the loss of his ring so to heart. He took her hand and kissed it. It was cold, not quite the same hand as he had last kissed. He stopped to make her stop with him.

"Do you remember where you had the ring on last?" he asked.

"No," she answered.

"Have you any idea," he asked, "where you may have lost it?"

"No," she answered. "I have no idea at all." ∾

---

12. *Asunder* (ə sun′dər) means "in separate parts." This biblical quotation (Matthew 19:6) is often repeated at the end of a traditional Christian marriage ceremony.

---

10. *Cambric* is the soft, lightweight linen of which Lise's handkerchief is made.

11. Here, *phosphorescent* (fos′fə res′ənt) means "glowing."

Quickwrite

Reread the story to identify passages that reveal the personalities of Sigismund, Lise, and the thief. Then refer to these passages and write an analysis of how Dinesen uses characterization to reveal the characters' personalities. Write at least one paragraph for each character.

Wrap-Up: Comparing Literature

Across Genres

- ***The Ring of General Macías*** by Josefina Niggli

- ***Marked*** by Carmen Tafolla

- ***The Ring*** by Isak Dinesen

COMPARE THE **Big Idea** Portraits of Real Life

Writing Are the concerns portrayed in these works still relevant to all women today or only to certain groups of women? Might these concerns apply to men as well? Consider contemporary issues and how they affect the lives of women today. Then write a brief essay in which you discuss your thoughts about these issues in relation to the texts.

COMPARE Theme

Group Activity A **genre** is a category, or type, of literature. Each of the texts compared here represents a different genre—drama, poetry, and short story—while conveying a theme, or message, about loyalty. With a small group, discuss the following questions, citing specific examples from the texts in your responses:

1. How do the main characters in these texts differ in what they express about the idea of loyalty? Consider the historical and cultural context of each text.

2. How do the different genres affect the way the theme is communicated to the reader in each of these three works?

Collage Series II, No. 3, 1993. Katherine S. Nemanich. Oil pastel on paper and board, 12 x 9 in. Private collection.

COMPARE Cultures

Speaking and Listening Josefina Niggli and Carmen Tafolla both weave Latino culture into their literary works. Niggli was raised in Mexico by Anglo parents, while Tafolla was raised in the United States by Mexican American parents. Do these different cultural and historical contexts have an effect on the writers' attitudes and beliefs? Make inferences about each author's beliefs regarding the following:

1. the role of women and girls in society

2. the importance of culture in people's lives

3. the effect of history—especially family history—upon future generations

Support your inferences with details from the texts. Then share your insights by presenting an oral report to the class.

Literature Online

Selection Resources For Selection Quizzes, eFlashcards, and Reading-Writing Connection activities, go to glencoe.com and enter QuickPass code GL57805u4.

TEKS

For pages 854–861

10.16.A–F Write an argumentative essay to the appropriate audience that includes a clear thesis or position; consideration of the whole range of information and views on the topic; counter-arguments; an organizing structure; an analysis of the relative value of specific data, facts, and ideas; and a range of appropriate appeals.

Planning Checklist

Your speech should include the following traits:

☑ a clear thesis statement supported by evidence

☑ counterarguments to anticipate and address objections

☑ a solid organizing structure appropriate to purpose, audience, and context

☑ appropriate appeals, such as descriptions, anecdotes, case studies, and illustrations

☑ persuasive techniques, such as appeals to authority and emotion, repetition, and word choice

🚀 Scoring Rubric

Check the Persuasive Texts **Scoring Rubric** on page R30 for more guidance on crafting your best persuasive speech.

🚀 Writing Workshop

Persuasive Speech

Literature Connection: After Brutus kills Caesar in William Shakespeare's *The Tragedy of Julius Caesar,* he must convince his audience that his reasons for killing Caesar were both noble and just.

> *"If [you] demand why Brutus rose against Caesar, this is my answer: Not that I lov'd Caesar less, but that I lov'd Rome more."*

Purpose: Your purpose for writing a persuasive speech is to take a position on an issue you feel strongly about and then convince your audience that your position is right by using persuasive appeals, supporting evidence, and persuasive language.

Audience: You will be delivering your speech to your classmates. Select an issue and use persuasive techniques that will appeal to that audience.

Choose Your Topic

Option A: Choose a Prompt

1. Write a speech in which you present convincing arguments that Brutus was right to kill Caesar.

2. Write a speech in which you argue that the voting age should be lowered.

Option B: Write a Prompt

Write a speech in which you argue _____.

Sample Prompt:

Write a speech in which you argue for a change in some policy at your school.

Analyze a Professional Model

Read for Guidance In this short speech, notice how Dirksen presents a clear opinion, uses logic, and addresses counterarguments.

Why Marigolds Should Be the National Flower
by Senator Everett Dirksen, Republican, Illinois

Mr. President: On January 8, 1965, I introduced Senate Joint Resolution 19, to designate the American marigold—*Tagetes erecta*—as the national floral emblem of the United States. Today I am introducing the same resolution with the suggestion that it again be referred to the Committee on the Judiciary.

The American flag is not a mere assembly of colors, stripes and stars but, in fact, symbolizes our origin, development, and growth.

The American eagle, king of the skies, is so truly representative of our might and power.

A national floral emblem should represent the virtues of our land and be national in character.

The marigold is a native of North America and can in truth and in fact be called an American flower.

It is national in character, for it grows and thrives in every one of the fifty states of this nation. It conquers the extremes of temperature. It well withstands the summer sun and the evening chill.

It is as sprightly as the daffodil, as colorful as the rose, as resolute as the zinnia, as delicate as the carnation, as haughty as the chrysanthemum, as aggressive as the petunia, as ubiquitous as the violet, and as stately as the snapdragon.

Thesis
The thesis statement is clear and to the point.

Persuasive Techniques
The emotional appeal to national symbols and the analogy "king of the skies" arouse feelings of pride and appeal to the audience's emotions and logic.

Support
These facts about the marigold bolster the senator's argument that it is a fitting national symbol.

Counterarguments
This series of similes argues that the marigold is as fit to be the national flower as any flower its detractors might nominate.

PLAN Your Speech

Key Trait Ideas An effective persuasive speech always starts with an issue that is important to the speaker, one that he or she is passionate about. Don't be afraid to show your passion for your topic.

▶ Step 1: Brainstorm

In small groups, brainstorm possible issues to write about. You might be surprised to hear a suggestion from a member of the group that you hadn't been thinking of but that really interests you. Write down the most interesting suggestions in your own words.

> the need for more computer stations to better serve the growing student population
>
> the school board's desire to institute a strict new dress code
>
> the cafeteria's newly-announced plan to introduce a more healthful lunch menu

▶ Step 2: Evaluate the Issues

It is important that the issue you choose to write about has two clear sides. You can test this out by making a pro-con chart.

New School Dress Code

Pro	Con
prepares students for the "real" world	business world is much more casual today
builds students' self-esteem	self-esteem is not based on clothing
will encourage respect for teachers and students	why? based on what evidence?
dress-code clothes will look nicer	dress-code clothes will be more expensive

▶ Step 3: Develop a Thesis

Your thesis statement can be based on your pro-con chart. You can revise it during the drafting or revising stages to make it sharper, clearer, or more accurate.

Working Thesis: The new dress code is bad and we can't allow it to happen.

Prepare to Organize

Review your pro-con chart when considering your organizational pattern. Speeches need to have a solid and clear structure to guide audience members through your argument. Two basic patterns would be to go column-by-column or row-by-row through your pro-con chart. Do you want to fully explain each position? Or present the issues point-by-point?

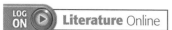
Literature Online

Writing and Research For planning, drafting, and revising tools, go to glencoe.com and enter QuickPass code GL57805u4.

DRAFT Your Speech

Key Traits Organization Organizing your ideas effectively can dramatically impact the success of your speech. Think about how your audience will respond to the information you present.

▶ Step 1: Assemble Your Arguments

Use Your pro-con chart to develop a list of arguments in favor of your position and likely counterarguments. Consider the whole range of information and views that pertain to your issue. Edit the list so that only the strongest arguments appear in your speech. Assign a number to each argument to show the order in which you will present it.

Arguments

- *Casual clothes are comfortable, wear well, and are easy to maintain.* 1
- *"Dress" clothes cost more to buy and maintain.* 2
- ~~*Dress codes discriminate against students.*~~
- *The business world is more casual today than in the past.* 3

Likely Counterarguments

- *Well-dressed students will behave more like adults.* 1
- *Dress codes enhance self-respect and respect for others.* 3
- ~~*Dress codes promote discipline.*~~
- *Well-dressed students will learn more and get better grades.* 2

▶ Step 2: Develop Your Speech

As you draft your speech, use effective persuasive techniques and rhetorical devices to strengthen your arguments.

1. Parallelism and repetition are effective ways to drive home a point.

Imagine never again being permitted to wear jeans, sneakers, or baseball caps to school. Imagine being told that most jewelry is now off-limits. Imagine discovering that the way you wear your hair is "inappropriate."

2. Logical appeals address the audience's common sense.

Jeans are comfortable, wear well, and are machine-washable. Sneakers are more comfortable than dress shoes, provide better support, and their rubber soles prevent skids on slick tile floors.

3. Emotional appeals stir the audience's feelings.

Also, casual clothes are more affordable. Many families in our community live on limited budgets. Having to outfit their children in dress clothes would be prohibitively expensive . . . .

Drafting Checklist

Your speech should include the following traits:

- ☑ Thesis—a clear position statement on the issue
- ☑ Arguments—based on solid evidence and convincing reasoning
- ☑ Counterarguments—opposing arguments effectively addressed
- ☑ Persuasion—use of successful persuasive techniques, such as emotional appeals, explanations, and persuasive language

The Case Against Dress Codes

Imagine never again being permitted to wear jeans, sneakers, or baseball caps to school. Imagine being told that most jewelry is now off-limits. Imagine discovering that the way you wear your hair is "inappropriate." Well if the school board has its way, that is what will happen at Jefferson High. We must not allow this unrealistic and impractical dress code to become reality.

The board has offered two principal reasons for their proposal. First, they claim that the new code will prepare students for the real world. According to the board, well-dressed students will behave better, learn more, and get better grades. Second, the board stresses that the new code will build students' self-esteem because they will take pride in their appearance. In turn, this will translate into more respect for teachers and other students.

These arguments have no basis in fact. First, there is no evidence that well-dressed students learn more or get better grades. Second, self-esteem is not based on the clothes you wear or the way you comb your hair. Self-esteem grows from your accomplishments at school, your contributions to your community, and your commitment to success. The proposed dress code shows a lack of respect for students' maturity and common sense.

Let's examine the case against the board's proposal. Many students wear jeans and sneakers to school. Why?

Jeans are comfortable, wear well, and are machine-washable. Sneakers are more comfortable than dress shoes, provide better support, and their rubber soles prevent skids on slick tile floors.

Also, casual clothes are more affordable. Many families in our community live on limited budgets. Having to outfit their children in dress clothes would be prohibitively expensive, especially when you consider that dress clothes wear out more quickly than jeans and sneakers.

Finally, in today's business world, people dress much more casually than in decades past. In fact, many businesses designate one day a week for casual dress. What is more, many workers now telecommute, working from home. These people can work in jeans, wearing sweats, or in pajamas if they want to.

It is admirable for the school board to look for ways to improve the environment at Jefferson High and enhance students' prospects for a good education. Unfortunately, dictating to students what they can and cannot wear to school is not the way to achieve those goals.

Persuasive Techniques

The writer offers logical reasons for the position he has taken.

Emotional Appeal

The phrases "more affordable," "live on limited budgets," and "prohibitively expensive" appeal to the audience's concern for low-income families.

Transitions

The writer introduces his last argument with an appropriate transitional word.

Conclusion

In his conclusion, the writer acknowledges the board's good intentions but then firmly restates his opposition to their plan.

Your Turn

Use your arguments and evidence to begin writing the first draft of your speech. Be sure your introductory paragraph grabs the audience's attention.

REVISE Your Speech

Key Traits Ideas and Voice You can make your draft more effective by sharpening your thesis statement, elaborating on ideas with explanations, and adding punch to your conclusion.

▶ Step 1: Sharpen Your Thesis Statement

Does your thesis statement guide and focus your speech? Make sure it's as clear and to the point as possible.

Working Thesis:

> The new dress code is bad and we can't allow it to happen.

Revised Thesis:

> We must not allow this unrealistic and impractical dress code to become reality.

▶ Step 2: Elaborate with Explanations

Do you effectively explain your ideas? Strengthen your persuasive message by explaining exactly what you mean.

Original:

> These arguments have no basis in fact. First, there is no evidence that well-dressed students learn more or get better grades. Second, self-esteem is not based on the clothes you wear or the way you comb your hair.

Revised:

> These arguments have no basis in fact. First, there is no evidence that well-dressed students learn more or get better grades. Second, self-esteem is not based on the clothes you wear or the way you comb your hair. Self-esteem grows from your accomplishments at school, your contributions to your community, and your commitment to success.

▶ Step 3: Add Punch to Your Conclusion

Does your conclusion drive home your point? Make it forceful.

Original:

> I know the board wants to improve Jefferson High. But this dress code isn't it.

Revised:

> It is admirable for the school board to look for ways to improve the environment at Jefferson High and enhance students' prospects for a good education. Unfortunately, dictating to students what they can and cannot wear to school is not the way to achieve those goals.

Revising Checklist

Before you start your revision, ask yourself these questions:

- ☑ Is my position on the issue clear?
- ☑ Have I crafted my arguments specifically for my audience?
- ☑ Have I used persuasive techniques, such as explanations, emotional and logical appeals, and persuasive language effectively?
- ☑ Have I analyzed any relevant data, facts, and ideas?
- ☑ Does my conclusion forcefully restate my position?

EDIT Your Speech

Key Trait Conventions Edit by correcting any errors in spelling, grammar, and mechanics and making sure you have used the conventions of academic language. Revise your draft to improve style, word choice and sentence variety after rethinking how well you have addressed your purpose and audience.

▶ Grammar Tip

Parallel Construction

Parts of a sentence joined by *and* or another coordinating conjunction must be parallel. This means that these parts must all be nouns, verbs, or the same type of phrases or clauses.

Problem:

> These people can work in jeans, wearing sweats, or in pajamas if they want to.

Three items—*jeans, wearing sweats,* and *in pajamas*—joined by a coordinating conjunction are not parallel: *jeans* is a noun, *wearing sweats* is a participial phrase, and *in pajamas* is a prepositional phrase.

Solution A: Make all of the items noun objects of prepositions.

> These people can work in jeans, sweats, or pajamas if they want to.

Solution B: Make all of the items participial phrases.

> These people can work dressed in jeans, clothed in sweats, or clad in pajamas if they want to.

Solution C: Make all of the items prepositional phrases.

> These people can work in jeans, in sweats, or in pajamas if they want to.

PUBLISH Your Speech

Key Trait Presentation Now that you've written your speech, you'll want to deliver it in front of an audience. Think of a group in your community that might be interested in what you have to say. Contact the group to see if they'd be interested.

Another option is to videotape yourself giving your speech. If your school has video production facilities, you might be able to record your speech there. For tips on preparing and giving a speech, see the Speaking, Listening, and Viewing Workshop on pages 862–863.

Editing Checklist

For your final revision, check the following:

☑ Have I misspelled any words? If you are unsure of the spelling of a word, check an online or print dictionary or use your word processor's spell checker.

☑ Have I made any errors in mechanics or grammar? Have I followed the rules of Standard American English? Use the Language Handbook on pages R48–R71 to correct common grammar and mechanical errors.

☑ Is my writing legible? Be sure your handwriting is neat or that you have followed your teacher's guidelines for word-processing.

Literature Online

Writing and Research For editing and publishing tools, go to glencoe.com and enter QuickPass code GL57805u4.

For pages 862–863

10.25 Advance a coherent argument that incorporates a clear thesis and a logical progression of valid evidence from reliable sources and that employs eye contact, speaking rate (e.g., pauses for effect), volume, enunciation, purposeful gestures, and conventions of language to communicate ideas effectively.

Argument and Evidence

As you prepare your speech, check that you have included the following elements:

☑ a coherent argument

☑ a clear thesis

☑ a logical progression of evidence

☑ reliable sources

Speaking, Listening, and Viewing Workshop

Persuasive Speech

Literature Connection When Brutus presented his speech after Caesar's assassination, persuading his audience was a matter of life or death. Brutus could not afford to mumble, speak too softly, shuffle his feet, or forget an important point. Instead, he had to master all of his rhetorical skills to make his message convincing. In this workshop, you will learn how to deliver an effective, powerful, and persuasive speech to a real audience.

▶ **Assignment**   **Deliver a persuasive speech to an audience.**

Plan Your Delivery

A speech *may* be read aloud. It is far more effective, however, when the written word, which readers can study and review, is transformed into the spoken word, which listeners must understand as it is delivered. Follow these steps to turn your persuasive writing into persuasive speaking:

- Start by reading your speech aloud to a partner. Find out what your listener notices immediately and what he or she misses. Most important, ask your partner whether he or she can identify your thesis, or opinion statement, and a logical progression of evidence. Then ask to what extent your speech was persuasive.
- Use your partner's comments to help you make your thesis clearer or more definite. Also brainstorm with your partner to devise ways to make your speech more dramatic, forceful, interesting, and persuasive.
- Make note cards that list the main ideas and details of your speech. Number the cards and refer to them only if needed.

School Board's Position
Dress codes prepare students for the professional world
Increase effort to improve learning and grades...

Rehearse

Practice your speech several times before you deliver it in class. Set a goal of learning your speech so well that you need no more than a glance at your note cards. Rehearse by yourself in front of a mirror. Try different gestures and tones of voice. Then, when you are confident that you are almost ready, ask a classmate or family member to listen. Work with that person to iron out any remaining wrinkles in your delivery.

Evaluate a Speech

Use these techniques to evaluate the content of your own speech or a partner's speech.

- Identify the thesis and the evidence that supports it.
- Analyze the types of arguments the speaker uses, such as appeals to emotion, logic, or authority, or the use of an analogy, anecdotes, or a case study.
- Study how well the speech anticipates and answers the listener's counterarguments.

Use the chart below to help you evaluate the delivery of your own speech or a partner's speech.

Techniques for Delivering a Persuasive Speech

Verbal Techniques	Nonverbal Techniques
☑ **Language** Use the conventions of language to communicate ideas effectively.	☑ **Audience Feedback** Watch people's faces for hints that you are speaking too quickly, too slowly, too loudly, or too softly.
☑ **Volume** Speak loudly enough so that everyone can hear you.	☑ **Eye Contact** Look directly at your audience except to refer briefly to note cards.
☑ **Tone** Be sure that your tone of voice suits the seriousness of your subject.	☑ **Body Language** Show interest by standing tall and comfortably.
☑ **Rate** Speak at a normal pace, using pauses for effect.	☑ **Facial Expressions** Make sure your facial expressions suit the content of your speech.
☑ **Enunciation** Speak clearly and to the point.	☑ **Gestures** Use purposeful gestures to emphasize ideas.

Presentation Tips

Use the following checklist to evaluate your speech.

☑ Did you organize your ideas effectively?

☑ Did you identify the thesis and the evidence that supports it?

☑ Did you use effective verbal and nonverbal techniques?

Evaluate the Presentation

As you listen to the presentation, ask yourself these questions:

- What is the speaker trying to communicate? What evidence is presented?

- What is the style of the presentation? How well does it support the purpose of the speech?

- How is the presentation structured? Does it follow chronological order? Show cause and effect? List ideas in order of importance? How well does the structure of the speech support its purpose?

Speaking, Listening, and Viewing For project ideas, templates, and presentation tips, go to glencoe.com and enter QuickPass code GL57805u4.

Independent Reading

Drama and Novels

D RAMA RELIES ALMOST ENTIRELY ON TWO THINGS: DIALOGUE AND STAGE direction. Most dramas tell a story, present a theme, and move, shock, or entertain their viewers by means of conversations between characters as well as movements on a stage. Readers who wish to get the most out of a play have to hear those conversations and visualize those movements. For more drama on a range of themes, try the two suggestions below. For novels that incorporate the Big Ideas of *Loyalty and Betrayal* and *Portraits of Real Life,* try the titles from the Glencoe Literature Library on the next page.

Seven Against Thebes

Aeschylus

A prophecy was made about the two sons of Oedipus, Eteocles and Polyneices: they would divide their inheritance with a sword in order to obtain equal shares. As *Seven Against Thebes* opens, Thebes is under siege by an Argive army led by Polyneices, the son of Oedipus and brother of Eteocles. Eteocles pledges to save Thebes and fiercely defend its seven gates against the Argive army's seven armored chiefs and their warriors. Trying to avoid disaster, the Theban women warn Eteocles to stay away from the seventh gate. A battle ensues, and the prophecy proves true.

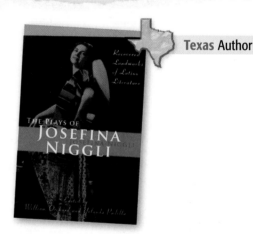

Texas Author

The Plays of Josefina Niggli

Josefina Niggli

In 1913 Josefina Niggli's family fled the violence of the Mexican Revolution for the safety of Texas. Although Niggli lived most of her life in Texas and North Carolina, the series of poems and six short plays in this collection depict life in her native Mexico. Whether she is writing about famous revolutionaries, young families, or abandoned wives, she brings questions of culture, gender, and identity to life with her vivid characters. The collection also includes valuable critical perspectives on Niggli's work.

Wuthering Heights

Emily Brontë

This brooding romance tells of loyalty and betrayal through the story of the thwarted relationship between a privileged woman and the penniless servant who loves her.

A House for Mr Biswas

V. S. Naipaul

In this portrait of real life in Trinidad in 1961, a man struggles to break the bonds of dependence on the domineering family he married into as he tries to buy a house of his own.

CRITICS' CORNER

"[Antony and Cleopatra] may be world leaders but they are also, after all, only human beings—flawed and aging ones at that. We as human beings share their mortality; many of us recognize their strong feelings of jealousy, love, shame, and insecurity. Despite their historical grandeur and thanks to Shakespeare's sensitive portrayal of them, Antony and Cleoptara are no more—and no less—extraordinary than we are."

—Kathy D. Darrow and Ira Mark Milne,
Shakespeare for Students Review

Antony and Cleopatra

William Shakespeare

The married Roman leader Mark Antony, who is living in Alexandria, Egypt, falls in love with Cleopatra, the Queen of Egypt. In this thrilling tale, both Antony and Cleopatra face the harsh reality of their ill-fated love.

 Write a Review

Read one of the books listed on this page and write a review of it for your classmates. Be sure to explain why other students might enjoy the book, or offer suggestions on how they might overcome difficulties in reading the book. Present your review to the class.

Assessment

English Language Arts

Reading: Drama

Read the following passage and answer the questions that follow it.

from *Oedipus the King* by Sophocles

TIME AND SCENE: *Many years have passed since Laius, the former king of Thebes, was killed and the current king, Oedipus, ascended the throne and married the queen, Jocasta. Oedipus is unaware that the man he killed long ago was, in fact, Laius. Now, a plague has struck the city. A Chorus (which represents the citizens of Thebes), Oedipus, and Jocasta are on stage.*

Chorus.   My king
     I've said it once, I'll say it time and again—
     I'd be insane, you know it,
     senseless, ever to turn my back on you.
5   You who set our beloved land—storm-tossed, shattered—
     straight on course. Now again, good helmsman,
     steer us through the storm!
[*The Chorus draws away, leaving* Oedipus *and* Jocasta *side by side.*]
Jocasta.   For the love of god,
     Oedipus, tell me too, what is it?
     Why this rage? You're so unbending.
10   **Oedipus.** I will tell you. I respect you, Jocasta,
     much more than these men here . . . [*Glancing at the Chorus.*]
     Creon's to blame. Creon schemes against me.
Jocasta. Tell me clearly, how did the quarrel start?
Oedipus. He says I murdered Laius—I am guilty.
15   **Jocasta.** How does he know? Some secret knowledge
     or simply hearsay?
Oedipus.   Oh, he sent his prophet in
     to do his dirty work. You know Creon,
     Creon keeps his own lips clean.
Jocasta.   A prophet?
     Well then, free yourself of every charge!
20   Listen to me and learn some peace of mind:
     no skill in the world,
     nothing human can penetrate the future.
     Here is proof, quick and to the point.

An oracle came to Laius one fine day
25 (I won't say from Apollo himself
but his underlings, his priests) and it said
that doom would strike him down at the hands of a son,
our son, to be born of our own flesh and blood. But Laius,
so the report goes at least, was killed by strangers,
30 thieves, at a place where three roads meet . . . my son—
he wasn't three days old and the boy's father
fastened his ankles, had a henchman fling him away
on a barren, trackless mountain. There, you see?
Apollo brought neither thing to pass. My baby
35 no more murdered his father than Laius suffered—
his wildest fear—death at his own son's hands.
That's how the seers and their revelations
mapped out the future. Brush them from your mind.
Whatever the god needs and seeks
40 he'll bring to light himself, with ease.

Oedipus.   Strange,
hearing you just now . . . my mind wandered,
my thoughts racing back and forth.

Jocasta. What do you mean? Why so anxious, startled?

Oedipus. I thought I heard you say that Laius
45 was cut down at a place where three roads meet.

Jocasta. That was the story. It hasn't died out yet.

Oedipus. Where did this thing happen? Be precise.

Jocasta. A place called Phocis, where two branching roads,
one from Daulia, one from Delphi,
50 come together—a crossroads.

Oedipus. When? How long ago?

Jocasta. The heralds no sooner reported Laius dead
than you appeared and they hailed you king of Thebes.

Oedipus. My god, my god—what have you planned to do to me?

55 **Jocasta.** What, Oedipus? What haunts you so?

Oedipus.   Not yet.
Laius—how did he look? Describe him.
Had he reached his prime?

Jocasta.   He was swarthy,
and the gray had just begun to streak his temples,
and his build . . . wasn't far from yours.

Oedipus.   Oh no no,
60 I think I've just called down a dreadful curse
upon myself—I simply didn't know!

1   The metaphor used in lines 6 and 7 suggests that the citizens of Thebes view Oedipus with —
    A   respect
    B   hatred
    C   suspicion
    D   affection

2   What is Oedipus' main reaction to being accused by Creon of being a murderer?
    F   Fear
    G   Anger
    H   Confusion
    J   Amusement

3   Why does Jocasta say that Oedipus need not worry about a prophecy?
    A   She thinks that people simply invent prophecies.
    B   She believes an earlier prophecy was not fulfilled.
    C   She is aware that people misunderstand prophecies.
    D   She considers Oedipus to be more powerful than the gods.

4   What does Oedipus mean by saying, in line 18, "Creon keeps his own lips clean"?
    F   Creon is careful to tell the truth.
    G   Creon cares only about himself.
    H   Creon refuses to offend anyone.
    J   Creon uses others to spread rumors.

5   The details of Jocasta's long speech suggest that a *seer* (line 37) is a —
    A   servant
    B   prophet
    C   murderer
    D   terrible fate

6   Why does Oedipus insist on knowing the details of Laius' death?
    F   He hopes to capture the murderer.
    G   He is afraid that Jocasta was involved in the murder.
    H   He is desperate to find out the truth of what happened.
    J   He wants to be able to defend himself against accusations.

7   What is the overall mood of this excerpt?
    A   Calm
    B   Vengeful
    C   Troubled
    D   Confident

8   Throughout this excerpt, what does Jocasta seem to be most interested in doing?
    F   Protecting Creon
    G   Soothing Oedipus
    H   Defending her actions
    J   Discovering and facing the truth

9   Oedipus' reaction at the end of this excerpt suggests that he —
    A   is angry with Jocasta
    B   is trying to protect Jocasta
    C   will do anything to remain king
    D   now understands his role in Laius' death

10 **Open-Ended Item** What do you think the theme of this excerpt is? Explain your answer and support it with details from the selection.

Vocabulary Skills: Sentence Completion

For each item, choose the word that best completes the sentence.

1 My opponent was positive he would win, and I found such _____ annoying.
   A misgiving
   B deceit
   C arrogance
   D ignorance

2 The old woman's illness had left her with a serious _____ that required care.
   F enterprise
   G infirmity
   H peril
   J orator

3 Many athletes _____ in a competitive atmosphere.
   A thrive
   B vanquish
   C commend
   D disperse

4 Listen carefully and ask questions if you don't understand; it would be a disaster for you to _____ the instructions.
   F absolve
   G repulse
   H prevail
   J misconstrue

5 The hermit lived high in the mountains, _____ to what was happening in the world below.
   A perverse
   B oblivious
   C peevish
   D ferocious

6 The gang of bandits was _____ in the territory.
   F ostentatious
   G notorious
   H impertinent
   J repressed

7 She worked for many years to _____ success.
   A disperse
   B commend
   C thrive
   D attain

8 Her sudden and _____ decision to quit school limited her job opportunities.
   F rash
   G imminent
   H servile
   J comprehensive

9 The spy's missions into enemy territory involved _____ actions.
   A pious
   B disconsolate
   C covert
   D barren

10 When I looked down and saw how high up we were, I had a sudden _____ about crossing such a rickety bridge.
   F malice
   G interim
   H misgiving
   J deference

LOG ON **Literature** Online

Standards Practice For more standards practice, go to glencoe.com and enter QuickPass code GL57805u4.

Revising and Editing

Read the following passage from the first draft of a student's essay. Then answer the questions that follow it.

(1) *Oedipus the King*, Sophocles' most famous play, is based on a Greek legend that was in fact familiar to nearly everyone at that time. (2) Oedipus does not control what happens to him; instead, destined for tragedy, he is a victim of powers outside himself. (3) Of course, Oedipus' problems are difficult, uncontrollable, and tragic, but his story is so complicated that his fate unlike that of other tragic heroes sometimes seems ridiculous.

(4) Sophocles presents Oedipus as a capable leader. (5) He also shows the king as wise and compassionate. (6) Nevertheless the gods of Mt. Olympus, those pitiless beings, have made prophecies involving him and his wife, Jocasta. (7) Sophocles is saying that Oedipus' tragic misfortune is the intentional work of the gods.

(8) Sophocles wrote during the Golden Age of Athens. (9) This was a time of thought, science, inventing things, and philosophy. (10) The Greeks of the time were impressed with the power of reason, and human potential seemed to them to be less limited than had previously been thought. (11) Perhaps they were asking themselves if they still believed in their gods. (12) If, indeed, the Greeks questioned this credo, or belief system, they must also have wondered about the individual's ability to affect his or her future and been questioning the concept of fate.

1 What revision, if any, is needed in sentence 1?
  A Oedipus the King Sophocles' most famous play, is based on a Greek legend that was in fact familiar to nearly everyone at that time.
  B Oedipus the King, Sophocles' most famous play is based on a Greek legend that was, in fact, familiar to nearly everyone at that time.
  C Oedipus the King, Sophocles' most famous play, is based on a Greek legend that was, in fact, familiar to nearly everyone at that time.
  D No revision is needed.

2 Which word in sentence 2 is a verbal?
  F *does*
  G *control*
  H *happens*
  J *destined*

3 What change, if any, should be made in sentence 3?
  A Delete the comma after *Of course*
  B Change *uncontrollable* to **can't be controlled**
  C Insert commas after *fate* and *heroes*
  D Make no change

4 What change, if any, should be made in sentence 6?

   F Insert a comma after *Nevertheless*

   G Delete the commas after *Olympus* and *beings*

   H Delete the comma after *wife*

   J Make no change

5 What revision, if any, is needed in sentence 9?

   A This was a time of thought, science, invention, and philosophy.

   B This was a time of thinking, science, inventing things, and philosophy.

   C This was a time of thought, of science, of inventing things, and of philosophy.

   D No revision is needed.

6 What change, if any, should be made in sentence 12?

   F Delete the commas after *If* and *indeed*

   G Delete the commas after *credo* and *system*

   H Change *been questioning* to **questioned**

   J Make no change

Written Composition

Read the instructions below in order to write a short essay.

Think about the concept of fate. Are we controlled by forces outside ourselves? Has what will happen to us already been determined? Can we affect what happens in our lives? Consider these questions, and then write a persuasive speech that supports your views about how much control people have over their own destinies.

> REMEMBER—YOU SHOULD
>
> ❑ focus on the topic
>
> ❑ support your thesis with relevant evidence
>
> ❑ present your ideas clearly
>
> ❑ use arguments that appeal to logic
>
> ❑ use arguments that appeal to emotion
>
> ❑ correct errors in spelling, capitalization, punctuation, grammar, and sentence structure

Theseus and the Minotaur, from the Story of Theseus (detail), c. 1510. Master of the Campana Cassoni.
Oil on panel, Musée du Petit Palais, Avignon, France.

<u>View the Art</u> According to legend, Theseus, a great Greek hero, conquered the Minotaur, a fearsome creature that lived in a labyrinth and was half man and half bull. Based on the depiction of Theseus in this painting, what are some of the characteristics of heroes in legends and myths?

Legends and Myths

Looking Ahead

Legends and myths are stories that usually have long histories. Often, they have been written and rewritten, or told and retold, for countless generations. Both legends and myths come from **oral tradition**—that is, literature passed by word of mouth from generation to generation. Legends are usually based on historical figures such as saints or kings, and they generally involve less of the supernatural than myths do. Myths may reflect the values, beliefs, and deepest truths of the cultures they spring from.

Each part in Unit Five focuses on a Big Idea that can help you connect the texts to your life.

PREVIEW	Big Ideas	Literary Focus
PART 1	Acts of Courage	The Hero
PART 2	Rescuing and Conquering	Oral Tradition and Myth

TEKS

For pages 874–878

10.2.B Analyze archetypes in mythic, traditional, and classical literature.

Genre Focus

What is unique about legends and myths?

The role models, beliefs, and values of a culture are often preserved in their legends and myths. According to Thomas Bulfinch, one of America's first collectors of world myths and legends, "if that which tends to make us happier and better can be called useful, then we claim that epithet for our subject. For Mythology is the handmaid of literature; and literature is one of the best allies of virtue and promoters of happiness." Here, happiness and the deepest truths go hand in hand.

The Hero

Legends and Epics

Legends are traditional stories handed down from generation to generation. Legends are usually based on actual events that have been exaggerated over time. Many legends describe the deeds of kings and noble heroes. An **epic** is a long narrative poem that recounts the actions, adventures, and travels of a heroic figure called the epic hero. Some modern versions of traditional epics are written in prose form.

Hero

A **hero** is the main character in a literary work. **Legendary heroes** are idealized figures, sometimes based on real people, who embody qualities admired by the cultural group to which they belong. **Epic heroes** are typically strong, courageous, noble, and confident men who embark on a journey to save their nation or its people.

> Sir Launcelot took another spear, and unhorsed sixteen more of the King of North Galys' knights, and with his next, unhorsed another twelve; and in each case with such violence that none of the knights ever fully recovered.
>
> —Sir Thomas Malory, **from *Le Morte d'Arthur***

> In order to defeat Soumaoro it was necessary first of all to destroy his magical power. At Sibi, Sundiata decided to consult the soothsayers, of whom the most famous in Mali were there.
>
> —D. T. Niane, **from *Sundiata***

 Literature Online

Literature and Reading For more selections in the genre, go to glencoe.com and enter QuickPass code GL57805u5.

Oral Tradition and Myth

Oral Tradition

A culture's **oral tradition** includes myths and folktales that were originally passed down orally from one generation to the next. **Folktales** are traditional stories that include legends, tall tales, and fairy tales. Most stories from the oral tradition include **archetypes**—images, characters, plot patterns, and themes that recur across time and place.

Myth

A **myth** is an ancient story whose author is unknown, or anonymous. Myths tell of gods and goddesses, their interventions in the lives of heroes, and supernatural events. Many myths attempt to account for a belief, a custom, or a force of nature. Myths often include archetypes such as the dangerous quest or battles with powerful enemies.

Gilgamesh, the Sumerian King of Uruk, Slays the Bull of Ishtar Helped by Ea-bani, ca. 20th century. E. Wallcousins.

The Minotaur was a monster, half bull, half human, the offspring of Minos' wife Pasiphaë and a wonderfully beautiful bull. Poseidon had given this bull to Minos in order that he should sacrifice it to him, but Minos could not bear to slay it and kept it for himself. To punish him, Poseidon had made Pasiphaë fall madly in love with it.

—Edith Hamilton, *from* **"Theseus"**

When I hear the old men
Telling of heroes,
Telling of great deeds
Of ancient days,
When I hear that telling
Then I think within me
I, too, am one of these.

—Chippewa Traditional, *from* **"A Song of Greatness"**

Literary Analysis Model
How is *The Journey of Gilgamesh* an epic?

Gilgamesh may be the oldest story known to have been written down. The character of Gilgamesh is based on a historical Babylonian king.

Epic Hero

Gilgamesh has great self-confidence typical of an **epic hero.**

Epic Hero

Gilgamesh embarks on a quest and demonstrates strength and courage, two heroic traits.

from *The Journey of Gilgamesh*
(Sumerian epic)

retold by Joan C. Verniero and Robin Fitzsimmons

"Gilgamesh, although you come from the gods, part of you is still mortal. You cannot know and experience everything. One day you will die, as all mortals die."

When Gilgamesh heard what his mother had told him, he
5 flew into a rage.

"I do not wish to die!" he exclaimed angrily. "My great friend Enkidu died. I miss him terribly, and I do not wish to follow him into the land of the dead. I will learn the secret of living forever."

Gilgamesh's mother tried to comfort her son.

10 "I only know of one person who has managed to escape death. His name is Uta-Napishtim, or Uta-Napishtim, the Remote. He survived a mighty ordeal and was granted everlasting life. He lives beyond Mount Mashu, which is very far away."

Gilgamesh made up his mind to find Uta-Napishtim, the
15 Remote. He traveled toward Mount Mashu. It was a long journey filled with many perils. He was pursued by the fierce lions of the forest. The Scorpion Men, who hid behind the boulders of the mountains, jumped out at him and tried to frighten him.

Gilgamesh continued on his way. Sometimes it was so dark
20 he could barely see in front of himself. Finally, in the distance, Gilgamesh saw a great, glowing light. He had reached the home of Uta-Napishtim.

The old man greeted Gilgamesh and asked him why he had come so far from his home.

25 "Tell me how you have earned the right to live forever, Uta-Napishtim," Gilgamesh asked him. "This is what I wish to learn."

Uta-Napishtim invited Gilgamesh to sit beside him on the ground.

"Here is my story. I lived in Shurippak, the city of the sun.
30 One day the god Ea came to me and told me that the gods were

displeased with humans and wished to destroy the earth. They were going to send a great flood to cover the world.

"Ea instructed me to build a very large ship and to prepare for the deluge. Then he told me to bring my family into the ship, as 35 well as many animals, and to wait for the rains to fall. I did this. A great storm came and the skies were filled with black clouds. Thunder shook the ground and bolts of lightning raced through the heavens with hot, white light. For many days it rained and rained without stopping. We almost forgot what it was like to see the sun 40 or to walk on dry land.

"We were very afraid, but I trusted that Ea had told me the truth, and that I would be saved. After a long while, the rains stopped falling and I sent a bird out from my ship to seek land. The bird returned to me, exhausted after failing to find a place to land. 45 In time I sent another bird, a raven, to fly from the ship. I was overjoyed when the raven did not return to me, for it had found a dry patch of earth on which to live. This was a very good sign.

"Eventually the great flood waters receded and our ship rested upon a cliff. We left the ship with all of the creatures we had carried 50 with us, and gave thanks to Ea and Ishtar, the goddess of heaven."

"But how did you come to be immortal?" Gilgamesh asked.

"The gods saw that I obeyed Ea, and as a reward they granted me immortality."

Gilgamesh jumped to his feet. "That does not help me, Uta-
55 Napishtim, for I have not been tested as you have. Is there no way I can live forever?"

"Everything in this world lives and dies, Gilgamesh," Uta-Napishtim told him. "Yet, there may be a way for you to get your wish. Here is a special plant. Take this plant with you, 60 back to your home. When you are there, you may eat it, and perhaps it will give you eternal youth."

Gilgamesh did as he was told and began the long journey home again. On the way he stopped to rest near a clear pool of water. He was so thirsty that he put the magic plant on the 65 ground, and stepped into the pool to drink from it. Gilgamesh did not notice the snake that crawled in the grass, not far from the water. The snake saw the plant and ate it.

Gilgamesh had lost his chance for immortality. Finally he realized that even though he was a rich and powerful man, he 70 could not escape death.

Legend tells us that the snake, after eating the plant intended for Gilgamesh, was able to shed his skin and regain his youth. Therefore, all snakes have kept this unique ability to this very day.

Humbaba, demon genie and guardian of the cedar forests of the Lebanon-range. Period of the Amorite dynasties, ca. 20th-16th BC. Terracotta. Iraq Museum, Baghdad, Iraq. In the Gilgamesh epic, Gilgamesh and his friend Enkidu cut off the demon's head.

Epic
The story encourages its audience to learn along with Gilgamesh to accept their mortality.

Epic
This story explains an aspect of the natural world.

Reading Check

Analyze How is this epic similar to and different from a myth? Explain.

Wrap-Up

Guide to Reading Legends and Myths

- Consider the purpose of the work. Was it written to inspire, instruct, or motivate?

- Be aware of the cultural origin of the story.

- If you are reading a legend, be aware of historical elements in the text.

- If you are reading a myth, look for hints about the values of the culture that created it.

- Look for archetypes in myths and legends.

Elements of Legends and Myths

- **Legends** are ancient stories with elements of history and elements of fantasy.

- **Legendary heroes** are admirable and noble. They perform great deeds, often with the help of gods.

- **Myths** tell stories of gods, heroes, and supernatural interventions.

- **Folktales** tell stories of common people.

- **Oral tradition** is the myths and folktales of a culture that are passed orally from generation to generation.

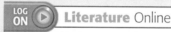

LOG ON ▶ **Literature** Online

Unit Resources For additional skills practice, go to glencoe.com and enter QuickPass code GL57805u5.

Activities ▶

Use what you have learned about reading and analyzing legends, myths, and folktales to complete one of the following activities.

1. Speaking and Listening Analyze and compare the use of language in several literary works in this unit from a variety of cultures. Share your findings with the class in an oral presentation.

2. Visual Literacy Design and present a visual display analyzing the influence of myths and folktales from a variety of world cultures on later literature and film.

3. Take Notes Try using this study organizer to identify archetypes in legends, myths, and folktales. For each literary work, analyze how the archetypes contribute to the overall meaning of the work.

 FOLDABLES Study Organizer **THREE-TAB BOOK**

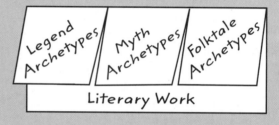

See page R20 for folding instructions.

Acts of Courage

A Joust Between Two Knights, late 15th century. Artist unknown. The British Library, London.

View the Art Jousting, which is depicted in this painting, was a popular form of entertainment in the Middle Ages. Two knights wearing heavy armor would gallop toward each other and with their lances attempt to knock their opponent off his horse. What qualities do the jousters display? What does this painting suggest about legendary heroes?

Courage comes in many forms. An audition, a first date, a speech—all kinds of everyday situations can require acts of courage. The legends in Part 1 tell of acts of courage that made people heroes to entire cultures. As you read the texts, ask yourself, Who are some modern heroes? What makes them heroic?

TEKS

For pages 880–881

10.2.B Analyze archetypes in mythic, traditional, and classical literature.

LITERARY FOCUS

The Hero

What qualities make a hero?

The word *legend* originates from the Latin word *legenda,* an adjective that means "for reading" or "to be read." Initially, *legenda* was used only when referring to written stories, not the stories that made up the oral tradition. Beginning in the fifteenth century, *legend* began to be used to refer to traditional stories as well. Legends communicated the heroic acts of knights and the greatness of kings and queens. Eventually the term *legend* acquired its current meaning—a person or an act worthy of inspiring a story.

The secret of Arthur's birth was known only to a few of the nobles surviving from the days of King Uther. The Archbishop urged them to make Arthur's cause their own; but their support proved ineffective. The tournament was repeated at Candlemas and at Easter, and with the same outcome as before.

Finally at Pentecost, when once more Arthur alone had been able to remove the sword, the commoners arose with a tumultuous cry and demanded that Arthur should at once be made king. The nobles, knowing in their hearts that the commoners were right, all knelt before Arthur and begged forgiveness for having delayed his succession for so long. Arthur forgave them, and then, offering his sword at the high altar, was dubbed first knight of the realm. The coronation took place a few days later, when Arthur swore to rule justly, and the nobles swore him their allegiance.

—Thomas Malory, **from** *Le Morte d'Arthur*

An illustration from *A History of the Development and Customs of Chivalry* by Dr. Franz Kottenkamp, published in 1842. Friedrich Martin von Reibisch.

Hero

The **hero** is the main character, generally one the reader admires, in a literary work. His or her good deeds and noble character allow the hero to defeat all enemies. The hero often sets out on a journey or quest to save his or her nation or family. A test or a series of tests during the quest reveals the hero's true worth.

An **epic hero** is the main character in an epic and is usually a man of high social status who embodies the ideals of his people. **Legendary heroes** are idealized figures, sometimes based on real people, who embody qualities admired by the cultural group to which they belong. King Arthur is an example of a well-known legendary hero.

The hero figure and the hero's journey appear in various forms in the stories, legends, and oral traditions of cultures across the world. Such recurring, familiar characters and plot patterns are called **archetypes.**

Legend

A **legend** is a traditional story handed down from one generation to the next, originally by word of mouth. Legends are believed to be based on true events and a historical hero. Over the years, legends have gained elements of fantasy and magic. Because legends are the stories of the people, they often express the values or character of a nation. In the following passage, King Arthur becomes king of Britain by pulling a sword from a stone.

"Why," said Arthur, "do you both kneel before me?" "My lord," Sir Ector replied, "there is only one man living who can draw the sword from the stone, and he is the true-born King of Britain."

—Thomas Malory, **from** *Le Morte d'Arthur*

LOG ON ▶ **Literature** Online

Literature and Reading For more about literary elements, go to glencoe.com and enter QuickPass code GL57805u5.

Epic

A long poem that tells the story of a hero and his or her adventures is called an **epic.** Like legends, epics have extraordinary heroes. One of the supernatural elements that often appears in epics is the intervention of gods and goddesses in the lives of humans. Such supernatural happenings are less common in legends.

Shield of the duchy of Krain, 1463. Gilded and painted wood. Wien Museum Karlsplatz, Vienna, Austria.

Quickwrite

Analyze Achetypes These days, we use the word *legend* more loosely than it was used in the fourteenth century. We speak of music legends and sports legends; anyone whose fame is likely to last might be called a legend. Many modern legends embody archetypes found in traditional literature, however. Choose a modern legend from the list below or think of your own. Write a paragraph analyzing how the life of your legend embodies certain archetypes such as journeys, battles of good versus evil, or the underdog succeeding against great odds.

Rosa Parks
Tiger Woods
Eleanor Roosevelt
Abraham Lincoln
Martin Luther King Jr.

Before You Read

from *Le Morte d'Arthur*

Meet **Sir Thomas Malory**
(c. 1405–1471)

Who wrote one of the most famous works in literary history, *Le Morte d'Arthur*? For years, scholars have argued about the answer to this question. Considered by some to be the first novel and largely based on French poems of Arthurian legends, *Le Morte d'Arthur* is said to exist in two versions. One is the printed version that William Caxton published in 1485, of which one complete, original copy exists. The other is a mysterious manuscript discovered at Winchester College in 1934. Known as the Winchester text, its relationship to the Caxton manuscript is not clear.

> *"There is only one man living who can draw the sword from the stone…."*
>
> —Sir Thomas Malory,
> from *Le Morte d'Arthur*

The Knight Prisoner Because a "syr Thomas Maleore knight" is named in the colophon, or inscription, of the 1485 version, Sir Thomas Malory is often identified as the author. Malory spent the first part of his life as a soldier and then as a country gentleman. He inherited estates from his father, married, fathered a son, and in 1445 became a member of Parliament. Thereafter, however, his life seemed to spiral out of control. Malory was cited in a multitude of lawsuits from the period; he was charged with murder, robbery, and an attack on a religious institution, the Abbey of Coombe. In one incident, he was accused of stealing 7 cows, 2 calves, 335 sheep, and a farmer's cart. During the last twenty years of his life, Malory served

at least four prison sentences for his crimes. In fact, he likely completed *Le Morte d'Arthur* while in prison during 1469 and 1470. At the end of his retelling of the epic tale, Malory describes himself as a "knight prisoner" and urges his readers to pray for his safe release.

A Lasting Work of Art Malory's version of the legend has had the most influence and longevity; the book has remained in print since its first publication, more than five hundred years ago. According to scholar Edmund Reiss, "Many writers had worked on the French Arthurian prose romances between the thirteenth and fifteenth centuries; there had been adaptations of it in Spain and Germany. All this is now dead and buried, and Malory alone stands as a rock, defying all changes of taste and style and morals; not as a grand paradox of nature, but as a lasting work of art."

 Literature Online

Author Search For more about Sir Thomas Malory, go to glencoe.com and enter QuickPass code GL57805u5.

Literature and Reading Preview

Connect to the Legend

Who is your hero? What makes that person a hero to you? Freewrite for a few minutes about these questions.

Build Background

In late-medieval Europe (the twelfth to fifteenth centuries A.D.), knights and noblemen tried to behave according to a strict code of chivalry. *Chivalry* is derived from the French word *chevalier*, meaning "horseman." A chivalrous knight, however, was more than a skilled rider. He also strove to be generous to the weak and courteous to women.

Set Purposes for Reading

Big Idea Acts of Courage

As you read this legend, ask yourself, How does Malory provide evidence that Arthur is a courageous hero?

Literary Element Dialogue

Dialogue is conversation between characters in a literary work. Dialogue can contribute to characterization, create mood, advance the plot, and develop theme. As you read, ask yourself, How is dialogue used in this legend?

Reading Strategy Analyze Plot

When you **analyze plot**, you critically examine the sequence of events in a narrative work. Most plots develop around a conflict, or a struggle between opposing forces. A legend's plot often consists of a series of conflicts that together form a **plot pattern archetype**—a story that occurs in many cultures. The journey of a hero, completion of a seemingly impossible task, or outwitting a formidable enemy are all archetypal plots. As you read, ask yourself, Which aspects of this plot do I recognize?

Tip: Compare and Contrast Compare and contrast the archetypal plot of *Le Morte d'Arthur* with that of another story you have read. Take notes in a Venn diagram like the one below. Use the blue highlighted passages and questions to get started.

LE MORTE D'ARTHUR — [SHORT STORY TITLE]

series of conflicts / characters, conflict / one main conflict

TEKS

For pages 882–903

10.2.B Analyze archetypes (e.g., journey of a hero) in mythic, traditional, and classical literature.

Vocabulary

abashed (ə basht´) *adj.* self-conscious; embarrassed or ashamed; p. 886 *Mike was abashed about his too-short haircut.*

inscribe (in skrīb´) *v.* to write, carve, or mark on a surface; p. 888 *The wedding band was inscribed with the couple's initials.*

ignoble (ig nō´ bəl) *adj.* of low birth or position; without honor or worth; p. 889 *They were shocked to discover that the charming young man had such ignoble beginnings.*

tumultuous (too mul´ choo əs) *adj.* wildly excited, confused, or agitated; p. 889 *The horse galloped away, taking the girl on a tumultuous ride.*

prowess (prou´ is) *n.* great ability or skill; p. 890 *Her prowess on the violin was evident as she played the solo.*

MAGNUS ARTURUS REX POTENTISSIMUS ANGLIAE

DOMINUS LAUNCELOT DU LAC EQUES INVICTUS

King Arthur and Sir Lancelot, 1862. William Morris. Stained glass. Bradford Art Galleries and Museums, West Yorkshire, UK.

from

Le Morte d'Arthur
The Tale of King Arthur

Sir Thomas Malory
Retold by Keith Baines

king Uther[1] Pendragon,[2] ruler of all Britain, had been at war for many years with the Duke of Tintagil in Cornwall when he was told of the beauty of Lady Igraine,[3] the duke's wife. Thereupon he called a truce and invited the duke and Igraine to his court, where he prepared a feast for them, and where, as soon as they arrived, he was formally reconciled to the duke through the good offices of his courtiers.

In the course of the feast, King Uther grew passionately desirous of Igraine and, when it was over, begged her to become his paramour.[4] Igraine, however, being as naturally loyal as she was beautiful, refused him.

"I suppose," said Igraine to her husband, the duke, when this had happened, "that the king arranged this truce only because he wanted to make me his mistress. I suggest that we leave at once, without warning, and ride overnight to our castle." The duke agreed with her, and they left the court secretly.

The king was enraged by Igraine's flight and summoned his privy council.[5] They advised him to command the fugitives' return under threat of renewing the war; but when this was done, the duke and Igraine defied his summons. He then warned them that they could expect to be dragged from their castle within six weeks.

The duke manned and provisioned[6] his two strongest castles: Tintagil for Igraine,

Merlin the Magician, c.1352 Ms. Add. Meladius, 12228, fol. 202v. British Library, London.

View the Art Merlin was a wise and trusted advisor to the king and could perform powerful acts of magic. How does this image suggest Merlin's power?

and Terrabyl, which was useful for its many sally ports, for himself. Soon King Uther arrived with a huge army and laid siege to Terrabyl; but despite the ferocity of the fighting, and the numerous casualties suffered by both sides, neither was able to gain a decisive victory.

Visual Vocabulary
Sally ports are gates or openings in castle walls through which a ruler's troops could make sudden attacks.

Still enraged, and now despairing, King Uther fell sick. His friend Sir Ulfius came to him and asked what the trouble was. "Igraine has broken my heart," the king

---

1. *Uther* (o͞o′ thər)
2. In ancient Britain, *Pendragon,* meaning "supreme leader," was a title attached after a ruler's name.
3. *Igraine* (ē grān′)
4. A *paramour* is an illicit lover.
5. A *privy council* is a group of a ruler's closest advisors.
6. The duke supplied (*provisioned*) the castles with food and goods.

Dialogue *How does this dialogue help characterize Igraine?*

replied, "and unless I can win her, I shall never recover."

"Sire," said Sir Ulfius, "surely Merlin the Prophet could find some means to help you? I will go in search of him."

Sir Ulfius had not ridden far when he was accosted by a hideous beggar. "For whom are you searching?" asked the beggar; but Sir Ulfius ignored him.

"Very well," said the beggar, "I will tell you: You are searching for Merlin, and you need look no further, for I am he. Now go to King Uther and tell him that I will make Igraine his if he will reward me as I ask; and even that will be more to his benefit than to mine."

"I am sure," said Sir Ulfius, "that the king will refuse you nothing reasonable."

"Then go, and I shall follow you," said Merlin.

Well pleased, Sir Ulfius galloped back to the king and delivered Merlin's message, which he had hardly completed when Merlin himself appeared at the entrance to the pavilion. The king bade him welcome.

"Sire," said Merlin, "I know that you are in love with Igraine; will you swear, as an anointed[7] king, to give into my care the child that she bears you, if I make her yours?"

The king swore on the gospel that he would do so, and Merlin continued: "Tonight you shall appear before Igraine at Tintagil in the likeness of her husband, the duke. Sir Ulfius and I will appear as two of the duke's knights: Sir Brastius and Sir Jordanus. Do not question either Igraine or her men, but say that you are sick and retire to bed. I will fetch you early in the morning, and do not rise until I come; fortunately Tintagil is only ten miles from here."

The plan succeeded: Igraine was completely deceived by the king's impersonation of the duke, and gave herself to him, and conceived Arthur. The king left her at dawn as soon as Merlin appeared, after giving her a farewell kiss. But the duke had seen King Uther ride out from the siege on the previous night and, in the course of making a surprise attack on the king's army, had been killed. When Igraine realized that the duke had died three hours before he had appeared to her, she was greatly disturbed in mind; however, she confided in no one.

Once it was known that the duke was dead, the king's nobles urged him to be reconciled to Igraine, and this task the king gladly entrusted to Sir Ulfius, by whose eloquence[8] it was soon accomplished. "And now," said Sir Ulfius to his fellow nobles, "why should not the king marry the beautiful Igraine? Surely it would be as well for us all."

The marriage of King Uther and Igraine was celebrated joyously thirteen days later; and then, at the king's request, Igraine's sisters were also married: Margawse, who later bore Sir Gawain, to King Lot of Lowthean and Orkney; Elayne, to King Nentres of Garlot. Igraine's daughter, Morgan le Fay, was put to school in a nunnery; in after years she was to become a witch, and to be married to King Uryens of Gore, and give birth to Sir Uwayne of the Fair Hands.

A few months later it was seen that Igraine was with child, and one night, as she lay in bed with King Uther, he asked her who the father might be. Igraine was greatly **abashed.**

---

7. An *anointed* king was believed to have been chosen by God to be king.

Analyze Plot *How do you think this event will advance the plot?*

8. Here, *eloquence* is speech or writing that is expressive, stirring, and effective.

Vocabulary

abashed (ə basht´) *adj.* self-conscious; embarrassed or ashamed

"Do not look so dismayed," said the king, "but tell me the truth and I swear I shall love you the better for it."

"The truth is," said Igraine, "that the night the duke died, about three hours after his death, a man appeared in my castle—the exact image of the duke. With him came two others who appeared to be Sir Brastius and Sir Jordanus. Naturally I gave myself to this man as I would have to the duke, and that night, I swear, this child was conceived."

"Well spoken," said the king; "it was I who impersonated the duke, so the child is mine." He then told Igraine the story of how Merlin had arranged it, and Igraine was overjoyed to discover that the father of her child was now her husband.

Sometime later, Merlin appeared before the king. "Sire," he said, "you know that you must provide for the upbringing of your child?"

"I will do as you advise," the king replied.

"That is good," said Merlin, "because it is my reward for having arranged your impersonation of the duke. Your child is destined for glory, and I want him brought to me for his baptism. I shall then give him into the care of foster parents who can be trusted not to reveal his identity before the proper time. Sir Ector would be suitable: he is extremely loyal, owns good estates, and his wife has just borne him a child. She could give her child into the care of another woman, and herself look after yours."

Sir Ector was summoned, and gladly agreed to the king's request, who then rewarded him handsomely. When the child was born he was at once wrapped in a gold cloth and taken by two knights and two ladies to Merlin, who stood waiting at the rear entrance to the castle in his beg-

Lancelot witnessed by King Arthur draws the sword out of the rock, 1470. French illumination.

__View the Art__ What does the king's expression seem to suggest? Why do you think so?

gar's disguise. Merlin took the child to a priest, who baptized him with the name of Arthur, and thence to Sir Ector, whose wife fed him at her breast.

Two years later King Uther fell sick, and his enemies once more overran his kingdom, inflicting heavy losses on him as they advanced. Merlin prophesied that they could be checked only by the presence of the king himself on the battlefield, and suggested that he should be conveyed there on a horse litter.[9] King Uther's army met the invader on the plain at St. Albans, and the king duly appeared on the horse litter. Inspired by his presence, and by the lively leadership of Sir Brastius and Sir Jordanus, his army quickly defeated the enemy and

---

Acts of Courage *Read to the end of the next paragraph. What is courageous about the king's statement?*

---

9. The king was to be carried *(conveyed)* on a stretcher *(litter)* pulled by a horse.

the battle finished in a rout.[10] The king returned to London to celebrate the victory.

But his sickness grew worse, and after he had lain speechless for three days and three nights Merlin summoned the nobles to attend the king in his chamber on the following morning. "By the grace of God," he said, "I hope to make him speak."

In the morning, when all the nobles were assembled, Merlin addressed the king: "Sire, is it your will that Arthur shall succeed to the throne, together with all its prerogatives?"[11]

The king stirred in his bed, and then spoke so that all could hear: "I bestow on Arthur God's blessing and my own, and Arthur shall succeed to the throne on pain of forfeiting my blessing."[12] Then King Uther gave up the ghost. He was buried and mourned the next day, as befitted his rank, by Igraine and the nobility of Britain.

During the years that followed the death of King Uther, while Arthur was still a child, the ambitious barons fought one another for the throne, and the whole of Britain stood in jeopardy. Finally the day came when the Archbishop of Canterbury, on the advice of Merlin, summoned the nobility to London for Christmas morning. In his message the Archbishop promised that the true succession to the British throne would be miraculously revealed. Many of the nobles purified themselves during their journey, in the hope that it would be to them that the succession would fall.

The Archbishop held his service in the city's greatest church (St. Paul's), and when matins[13] were done the congregation filed out to the yard. They were confronted by a marble block into which had been thrust a beautiful sword. The block was four feet square, and the sword passed through a steel anvil which had been struck in the stone, and which projected a foot from it. The anvil had been **inscribed** with letters of gold:

WHOSO PULLETH OUTE THIS SWERD
OF THIS STONE AND ANVLYD IS RIGHTWYS
KYNGE BORNE OF ALL BRYTAYGNE

The congregation was awed by this miraculous sight, but the Archbishop forbade anyone to touch the sword before mass had been heard. After mass, many of the nobles tried to pull the sword out of the stone, but none was able to, so a watch of ten knights was set over the sword, and a tournament proclaimed for New Year's Day, to provide men of noble blood with the opportunity of proving their right to the succession.

Sir Ector, who had been living on an estate near London, rode to the tournament with Arthur and his own son Sir Kay, who had been recently knighted. When they arrived at the tournament, Sir Kay found to his annoyance that his sword was missing from its sheath, so he begged Arthur to ride back and fetch it from their lodging.

Arthur found the door of the lodging locked and bolted, the landlord and his wife having left for the tournament. In order not to disappoint his brother, he rode on to St. Paul's, determined to get for him the sword which was lodged in the stone. The yard was empty, the guard also having slipped

---

10. A *rout* is an overwhelming defeat.
11. *Prerogatives* (pri rog´ ə tivz) are the rights and privileges belonging solely to a particular person (such as a king) or group.
12. *Forfeiting my blessing* means that Uther is withholding his blessing if Arthur does not eventually become king.

Analyze Plot *What purpose have the events in this story served up until this point?*

13. *Matins* (mat´ inz) are morning prayers.

Vocabulary

inscribe (in skrī b´) *v.* to write, carve, or mark on a surface off to see the tournament, so Arthur strode up to the sword, and, without troubling to read the inscription, tugged it free. He then rode straight back to Sir Kay and presented him with it.

Sir Kay recognized the sword, and taking it to Sir Ector, said, "Father, the succession falls to me, for I have here the sword that was lodged in the stone." But Sir Ector insisted that they should all ride to the churchyard, and once there bound Sir Kay by oath to tell how he had come by the sword. Sir Kay then admitted that Arthur had given it to him. Sir Ector turned to Arthur and said, "Was the sword not guarded?"

"It was not," Arthur replied.

"Would you please thrust it into the stone again?" said Sir Ector. Arthur did so, and first Sir Ector and then Sir Kay tried to remove it, but both were unable to. Then Arthur, for the second time, pulled it out. Sir Ector and Sir Kay both knelt before him.

"Why," said Arthur, "do you both kneel before me?"

"My lord," Sir Ector replied, "there is only one man living who can draw the sword from the stone, and he is the true-born King of Britain." Sir Ector then told Arthur the story of his birth and upbringing.

"My dear father," said Arthur, "for so I shall always think of you—if, as you say, I am to be king, please know that any request you have to make is already granted."

Sir Ector asked that Sir Kay should be made Royal Seneschal,[14] and Arthur declared that while they both lived it should be so. Then the three of them visited the Archbishop and told him what had taken place.

All those dukes and barons with ambitions to rule were present at the tournament on New Year's Day. But when all of them had failed, and Arthur alone had succeeded in drawing the sword from the stone, they protested against one so young, and of **ignoble** blood, succeeding to the throne.

The secret of Arthur's birth was known only to a few of the nobles surviving from the days of King Uther. The Archbishop urged them to make Arthur's cause their own; but their support proved ineffective. The tournament was repeated at Candlemas and at Easter,[15] and with the same outcome as before.

Finally at Pentecost,[16] when once more Arthur alone had been able to remove the sword, the commoners arose with a **tumultuous** cry and demanded that Arthur should at once be made king. The nobles, knowing in their hearts that the commoners were right, all knelt before Arthur and begged forgiveness for having delayed his succession for so long. Arthur forgave them, and then, offering his sword at the high altar, was dubbed first knight of the realm. The coronation took place a few days later, when Arthur swore to rule justly, and the nobles swore him their allegiance. ⌒

---

14. In medieval times, the *Royal Seneschal* (sen′ ə shəl) managed the king's estate, ran his household, and sometimes also had official state or military duties.

Analyze Plot *How does this episode illustrate an archetype?*

Dialogue *What does this statement reveal about Arthur?*

15. *Candlemas* and *Easter* are Christian festivals; *Candlemas* is celebrated on February 2 and *Easter* in early spring.

16. *Pentecost* is a Christian feast observed on the seventh Sunday after Easter.

Vocabulary

ignoble (ig nō′ bəl) *adj.* of low birth or position; without honor or worth

tumultuous (too mul′ choo əs) *adj.* wildly excited, confused, or agitated

The Tale of Sir Launcelot du Lake

When King Arthur returned from Rome he settled his court at Camelot, and there gathered about him his knights of the Round Table, who diverted[17] themselves with jousting and tournaments. Of all his knights one was supreme, both in **prowess** at arms and in nobility of bearing, and this was Sir Launcelot, who was also the favorite of Queen Gwynevere, to whom he had sworn oaths of fidelity.[18]

One day Sir Launcelot, feeling weary of his life at the court, and of only playing at arms, decided to set forth in search of adventure. He asked his nephew Sir Lyonel to accompany him, and when both were suitably armed and mounted, they rode off together through the forest.

Head of King Arthur, from the *Beautiful Fountain,* 14th century. Artist unknown. Statue. Germanisches Nationalmuseum, Nuremberg, Germany.

At noon they started across a plain, but the intensity of the sun made Sir Launcelot feel sleepy, so Sir Lyonel suggested that they should rest beneath the shade of an apple tree that grew by a hedge not far from the road. They dismounted, tethered their horses, and settled down.

"Not for seven years have I felt so sleepy," said Sir Launcelot, and with that fell fast asleep, while Sir Lyonel watched over him.

Soon three knights came galloping past, and Sir Lyonel noticed that they were being pursued by a fourth knight, who was one of the most powerful he had yet seen. The pursuing knight overtook each of the others in turn, and as he did so, knocked each off his horse with a thrust of his spear. When all three lay stunned he dismounted, bound them securely to their horses with the reins, and led them away.

Without waking Sir Launcelot, Sir Lyonel mounted his horse and rode after

---

17. Here, *diverted* means "amused" or "entertained."
18. Launcelot swore his loyalty and devotion *(fidelity)* to Gwynevere.

Dialogue *What atmosphere does this statement establish?*

the knight, and as soon as he had drawn close enough, shouted his challenge. The knight turned about and they charged at each other, with the result that Sir Lyonel was likewise flung from his horse, bound, and led away a prisoner.

The victorious knight, whose name was Sir Tarquine, led his prisoners to his castle, and there threw them on the ground, stripped them naked, and beat them with thorn twigs. After that he locked them in a dungeon where many other prisoners, who had received like treatment, were complaining dismally.

Meanwhile, Sir Ector de Marys, who liked to accompany Sir Launcelot on his adventures, and finding him gone, decided to ride after him. Before long he came upon a forester.

"My good fellow, if you know the forest hereabouts, could you tell me in which direction I am most likely to meet with adventure?"

"Sir, I can tell you: Less than a mile from here stands a well-moated castle. On the left of the entrance you will find a ford where you can water your horse, and across from the ford a large tree from which hang the shields of many famous knights. Below the shields hangs a caldron, of copper and brass: strike it three times with your spear, and then surely you will meet with adventure—such, indeed, that if you survive it, you will prove yourself the foremost knight in these parts for many years."

"May God reward you!" Sir Ector replied.

The castle was exactly as the forester had described it, and among the shields Sir Ector recognized several as belonging to knights of the Round Table. After watering his horse, he knocked on the caldron and Sir Tarquine, whose castle it was, appeared.

They jousted, and at the first encounter Sir Ector sent his opponent's horse spinning twice about before he could recover.

"That was a fine stroke; now let us try again," said Sir Tarquine.

This time Sir Tarquine caught Sir Ector just below the right arm and, having impaled him on his spear, lifted him clean out of the saddle, and rode with him into the castle, where he threw him on the ground.

"Sir," said Sir Tarquine, "you have fought better than any knight I have encountered in the last twelve years; therefore, if you wish, I will demand no more of you than your parole[19] as my prisoner."

"Sir, that I will never give."

"Then I am sorry for you," said Sir Tarquine, and with that he stripped and beat him and locked him in the dungeon with the other prisoners. There Sir Ector saw Sir Lyonel.

"Alas, Sir Lyonel, we are in a sorry plight. But tell me, what has happened to Sir Launcelot? for he surely is the one knight who could save us."

"I left him sleeping beneath an apple tree, and what has befallen him since I do not know," Sir Lyonel replied; and then all the unhappy prisoners once more bewailed their lot.

While Sir Launcelot still slept beneath the apple tree, four queens started across the plain. They were riding white mules and accompanied by four knights who held above them, at the tips of their spears, a green silk canopy, to protect them from the sun. The party was startled by the neighing of Sir Launcelot's horse and, changing direction, rode up to the apple tree, where they discovered the sleeping knight. And as each of the queens gazed at the handsome Sir Launcelot, so each wanted him for her own.

---

19. A knight's *parole* was his pledge to fulfill certain conditions in exchange for full or partial freedom.

Analyze Plot *How does this statement help to advance the plot?*

King Arthur and Queen Guinevere, 14th century. Artist unknown. British Library, London.

"Let us not quarrel," said Morgan le Fay. "Instead, I will cast a spell over him so that he remains asleep while we take him to my castle and make him our prisoner. We can then oblige him to choose one of us for his paramour."

Sir Launcelot was laid on his shield and borne by two of the knights to the Castle Charyot, which was Morgan le Fay's stronghold. He awoke to find himself in a cold cell, where a young noblewoman was serving him supper.

"What cheer?"[20] she asked.

---

20. *What cheer?* meant the same as asking "How are you?"

"My lady, I hardly know, except that I must have been brought here by means of an enchantment."

"Sir, if you are the knight you appear to be, you will learn your fate at dawn tomorrow." And with that the young noblewoman left him. Sir Launcelot spent an uncomfortable night but at dawn the four queens presented themselves and Morgan le Fay spoke to him:

"Sir Launcelot, I know that Queen Gwynevere loves you, and you her. But now you are my prisoner, and you will have to choose: either to take one of us for your paramour, or to die miserably in this cell—just as you please. Now I will tell you who we are: I am Morgan le Fay, Queen of Gore; my companions are the Queens of North Galys, of Estelonde, and of the Outer Isles. So make your choice."

"A hard choice! Understand that I choose none of you, lewd sorceresses[21] that you are; rather will I die in this cell. But were I free, I would take pleasure in proving it against any who would champion[22] you that Queen Gwynevere is the finest lady of this land."

"So, you refuse us?" asked Morgan le Fay.

"On my life, I do," Sir Launcelot said finally, and so the queens departed.

Sometime later, the young noblewoman who had served Sir Launcelot's supper reappeared.

"What news?" she asked.

"It is the end," Sir Launcelot replied.

"Sir Launcelot, I know that you have refused the four queens, and that they wish to kill you out of spite. But if you will be ruled by me, I can save you. I ask that you

---

21. Launcelot accuses the women of being unchaste *(lewd)* witches *(sorceresses).*

22. As a verb, *champion* means "to defend a person or cause."

Acts of Courage *From this statement, what do you think Sir Launcelot values?*

will champion my father at a tournament next Tuesday, when he has to combat the King of North Galys, and three knights of the Round Table, who last Tuesday defeated him ignominiously."[23]

"My lady, pray tell me, what is your father's name?"

"King Bagdemagus."[24]

"Excellent, my lady, I know him for a good king and a true knight, so I shall be happy to serve him."

"May God reward you! And tomorrow at dawn I will release you, and direct you to an abbey which is ten miles from here, and where the good monks will care for you while I fetch my father."

"I am at your service, my lady."

As promised, the young noblewoman released Sir Launcelot at dawn. When she had led him through the twelve doors to the castle entrance, she gave him his horse and armor, and directions for finding the abbey.

"God bless you, my lady; and when the time comes I promise I shall not fail you."

Sir Launcelot rode through the forest in search of the abbey, but at dusk had still failed to find it, and coming upon a red silk pavilion, apparently unoccupied, decided to rest there overnight, and continue his search in the morning. . . .

As soon as it was daylight, Sir Launcelot armed, mounted, and rode away in search of the abbey, which he found in less than two hours. King Bagdemagus' daughter was waiting for him, and as soon as she heard his horse's footsteps in the yard, ran to the window, and, seeing that it was Sir Launcelot, herself ordered the servants to stable his horse. She then led him to her chamber, disarmed him, and gave him a long gown to wear, welcoming him warmly as she did so.

King Bagdemagus' castle was twelve miles away, and his daughter sent for him as soon as she had settled Sir Launcelot. The king arrived with his retinue[25] and embraced Sir Launcelot, who then described his recent enchantment, and the great obligation he was under to his daughter for releasing him.

"Sir, you will fight for me on Tuesday next?"

"Sire, I shall not fail you; but please tell me the names of the three Round Table knights whom I shall be fighting."

"Sir Modred, Sir Madore de la Porte, and Sir Gahalantyne. I must admit that last Tuesday they defeated me and my knights completely."

"Sire, I hear that the tournament is to be fought within three miles of the abbey. Could you send me three of your most trustworthy knights, clad in plain armor, and with no device,[26] and a fourth suit of armor which I myself shall wear? We will take up our position just outside the tournament field and watch while you and the King of North Galys enter into combat with your followers; and then, as soon as you are in difficulties, we will come to your rescue, and show your opponents what kind of knights you command."

This was arranged on Sunday, and on the following Tuesday Sir Launcelot and the three knights of King Bagdemagus waited in a copse,[27] not far from the pavilion which had been erected for the lords

---

23. The woman's father was defeated shamefully or dishonorably (*ignominiously*).
24. *Bagdemagus* (bag′ də mag′ əs)

Dialogue *What does this dialogue reveal about Sir Launcelot?*

---

25. The king's *retinue* is the group of people who accompany and serve him.
26. Armor with no *device* has no ornamental design.
27. A *copse* is a thicket of trees.

Analyze Plot *Why does Sir Launcelot make the requests in this paragraph? How do they advance the plot?*

and ladies who were to judge the tournament and award the prizes.

The King of North Galys was the first on the field, with a company of ninescore knights; he was followed by King Bagdemagus with fourscore[28] knights, and then by the three knights of the Round Table, who remained apart from both companies. At the first encounter King Bagdemagus lost twelve knights, all killed, and the King of North Galys six.

With that, Sir Launcelot galloped on to the field, and with his first spear unhorsed five of the King of North Galys' knights, breaking the backs of four of them. With his next spear he charged the king, and wounded him deeply in the thigh.

"That was a shrewd blow," commented Sir Madore, and galloped onto the field to challenge Sir Launcelot. But he too was tumbled from his horse, and with such violence that his shoulder was broken.

Sir Modred was the next to challenge Sir Launcelot, and he was sent spinning over his horse's tail. He landed head first, his helmet became buried in the soil, and he nearly broke his neck, and for a long time lay stunned.

Finally Sir Gahalantyne tried; at the first encounter both he and Sir Launcelot broke their spears, so both drew their swords and hacked vehemently at each other. But Sir Launcelot, with mounting wrath, soon struck his opponent a blow on the helmet which brought the blood streaming from eyes, ears, and mouth. Sir Gahalantyne slumped forward in the saddle, his horse panicked, and he was thrown to the ground, useless for further combat.

Sir Launcelot took another spear, and unhorsed sixteen more of the King of North Galys' knights, and with his next, unhorsed another twelve; and in each case

with such violence that none of the knights ever fully recovered. The King of North Galys was forced to admit defeat, and the prize was awarded to King Bagdemagus.

That night Sir Launcelot was entertained as the guest of honor by King Bagdemagus and his daughter at their castle, and before leaving was loaded with gifts.

"My lady, please, if ever again you should need my services, remember that I shall not fail you."

The next day Sir Launcelot rode once more through the forest, and by chance came to the apple tree where he had previously slept. This time he met a young noblewoman riding a white :palfrey:

Visual Vocabulary
A *palfrey* is a gentle saddle horse, especially one trained for a woman rider.

"My lady, I am riding in search of adventure; pray tell me if you know of any I might find hereabouts."

"Sir, there are adventures hereabouts if you believe that you are equal to them; but please tell me, what is your name?"

"Sir Launcelot du Lake."

"Very well, Sir Launcelot, you appear to be a sturdy enough knight, so I will tell you. Not far away stands the castle of Sir Tarquine, a knight who in fair combat has overcome more than sixty opponents whom he now holds prisoner. Many are from the court of King Arthur, and if you can rescue them, I will then ask you to deliver me and my companions from a knight who distresses us daily, either by robbery or by other kinds of outrage."

"My lady, please first lead me to Sir Tarquine, then I will most happily challenge this miscreant[29] knight of yours."

---

28. One *score* is twenty, so more than 260 knights have gathered.

29. A *miscreant* knight is an evil, villainous one.

Miniature Painting Depicting the Knights of the Round Table, 15th century. Artist unknown. Archivo Iconográfico, S.A.

View the Art During the Middle Ages, most tables were rectangular or square, and round tables were highly unusual. Why do Arthur and his knights sit at a round table? What might a round table symbolize?

Gaheris, Sir Gawain's brother and a knight of the Round Table.

"Good knight," said Sir Launcelot, "it is known to me that you have put to shame many of the knights of the Round Table. Pray allow your prisoner, who I see is wounded, to recover, while I vindicate[30] the honor of the knights whom you have defeated."

"I defy you, and all your fellowship of the Round Table," Sir Tarquine replied.

"You boast!" said Sir Launcelot.

At the first charge the backs of the horses were broken and both knights stunned. But they soon recovered and set to with their swords, and both struck so lustily that neither shield nor armor could resist, and within two hours they were cutting each other's flesh, from which the blood flowed liberally. Finally they paused for a moment, resting on their shields.

"Worthy knight," said Sir Tarquine, "pray hold your hand for a while, and if you will, answer my question."

"Sir, speak on."

"You are the most powerful knight I have fought yet, but I fear you may be the one whom in the whole world I most hate. If you are not, for the love of you I will release all my prisoners and swear eternal friendship."

When they arrived at the castle, Sir Launcelot watered his horse at the ford, and then beat the caldron until the bottom fell out. However, none came to answer the challenge, so they waited by the castle gate for half an hour or so. Then Sir Tarquine appeared, riding toward the castle with a wounded prisoner slung over his horse, whom Sir Launcelot recognized as Sir

---

30. Launcelot wishes to defend against opposition, or *vindicate*, the honor of Tarquine's prisoners.

Roman de Tristan: Scenes from the Legend of King Arthur, 15th century. Artist unknown. Archivo Iconográfico, S.A.

tell you: I am Sir Launcelot du Lake, son of King Ban of Benwick, of Arthur's court, and a knight of the Round Table. So defend yourself!"

"Ah! this is most welcome."

Now the two knights hurled themselves at each other like two wild bulls; swords and shields clashed together, and often their swords drove into the flesh. Then sometimes one, sometimes the other, would stagger and fall, only to recover immediately and resume the contest. At last, however, Sir Tarquine grew faint, and unwittingly lowered his shield. Sir Launcelot was swift to follow up his advantage, and dragging the other down to his knees, unlaced his helmet and beheaded him.

Sir Launcelot then strode over to the young noblewoman: "My lady, now I am at your service, but first I must find a horse."

Then the wounded Sir Gaheris spoke up: "Sir, please take my horse. Today you have overcome the most formidable knight, excepting only yourself, and by so doing have saved us all. But before leaving, please tell me your name."

"Sir Launcelot du Lake. Today I have fought to vindicate the honor of the knights of the Round Table, and I know that among Sir Tarquine's prisoners are two of my brethren, Sir Lyonel and Sir Ector, also your own brother, Sir Gawain. According to the

"What is the name of the knight you hate above all others?"

"Sir Launcelot du Lake; for it was he who slew my brother, Sir Carados of the Dolorous Tower, and it is because of him that I have killed a hundred knights, and maimed[31] as many more, apart from the sixty-four I still hold prisoner. And so, if you are Sir Launcelot, speak up, for we must then fight to the death."

"Sir, I see now that I might go in peace and good fellowship, or otherwise fight to the death; but being the knight I am, I must

---

31. To *maim* is to injure seriously or horribly.

Acts of Courage *Why do you think Launcelot reveals himself, exposing himself to further danger?*

shields there are also: Sir Brandiles, Sir Galyhuddis, Sir Kay, Sir Alydukis, Sir Marhaus, and many others. Please release the prisoners and ask them to help themselves to the castle treasure. Give them all my greetings and say I will see them at the next Pentecost. And please request Sir Ector and Sir Lyonel to go straight to the court and await me there."

When Sir Launcelot had ridden away with the young noblewoman, Sir Gaheris entered the castle, and finding the porter in the hall, threw him on the ground and took the castle keys. He then released the prisoners, who, seeing his wounds, thanked him for their deliverance.

"Do not thank me for this work, but Sir Launcelot. He sends his greetings to you all, and asks you to help yourselves to the castle treasure. He has ridden away on another quest, but said that he will see you at the next Pentecost. Meanwhile, he requests Sir Lyonel and Sir Ector to return to the court and await him there."

"Certainly we shall not ride back to the court, but rather we shall follow Sir Launcelot wherever he goes," said Sir Ector.

"And I too shall follow him," said Sir Kay.

The prisoners searched the castle for their armor and horses and the castle treasure; and then a forester arrived with supplies of venison, so they feasted merrily and settled down for the night in the castle chambers—all but Sir Ector, Sir Lyonel, and Sir Kay, who set off immediately after supper in search of Sir Launcelot.

Sir Launcelot and the young noblewoman were riding down a broad highway when the young noblewoman said they were within sight of the spot where the knight generally attacked her.

"For shame that a knight should so degrade his high calling," Sir Launcelot replied. "Certainly we will teach him a much-needed lesson. Now, my lady, I suggest that you ride on ahead, and as soon as he molests you, I will come to the rescue."

Sir Launcelot halted and the young noblewoman rode gently forward. Soon the knight appeared with his page, and seized the young noblewoman from her horse; she cried out at once, and Sir Launcelot galloped up to them.

"Scoundrel! What sort of knight do you think you are, to attack defenseless women?"

In answer the other knight drew his sword. Sir Launcelot did likewise, and they rushed together. With his first stroke Sir Launcelot split open the knight's head, down to the throat.

"Let that be your payment, though long overdue," said Sir Launcelot.

"Even so; he certainly deserved to die. His name was Sir Percy of the Forest Sauvage."

"My lady, do you require anything more of me?"

"No, good Sir Launcelot; and may the sweet Lord Jesu[32] protect you, for certainly you are the bravest and gentlest knight I have known. But pray tell me one thing: why is it you do not take to yourself a wife? Many good ladies, both high born and low born, grieve that so fine a knight as yourself should remain single. It is whispered, of course, that Queen Gwynevere has cast a spell over you so that you shall love no other."

"As for that, people must believe what they will about Queen Gwynevere and me. But married I will not be, for then I should

---

32. *Jesu* (jē′ zoō) is a form of *Jesus*.

Dialogue *How do the other characters' responses to Launcelot help characterize them?*

Acts of Courage *The noblewoman tells Launcelot that he is the "bravest and gentlest" knight she has known. What is the significance of these two adjectives?*

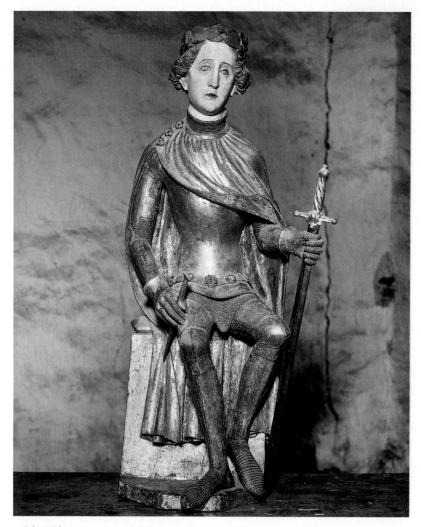

Knight with Armor. Artist unknown. Archivo Iconografico. S. A.

Sir Launcelot then took his leave of the young noblewoman, and for two days wandered alone through the forest, resting at night at the most meager of lodgings. On the third day, as he was crossing a bridge, he was accosted by a churlish porter,[34] who, after striking his horse on the nose so that it turned about, demanded to know by what right Sir Launcelot was riding that way.

"And what right do I need to cross this bridge? Surely, I cannot ride beside it," said Sir Launcelot.

"That is not for you to decide," said the porter, and with that he lashed at Sir Launcelot with his club. Sir Launcelot drew his sword, and after deflecting the blow, struck the porter on the head and split it open.

At the end of the bridge was a prosperous-looking village, overtopped by a fine castle. As Sir Launcelot advanced he heard someone cry: "Good knight, beware! You have done yourself no good by killing the chief porter of the castle."

Sir Launcelot rode on regardless, through the village and into the castle court, which was richly grassed. Thinking to himself that this would be a good place for combat, Sir Launcelot tied his horse to a

have to attend my lady instead of entering for tournaments and wars, or riding in search of adventure. And I will not take a paramour, both for the fear of God and in the belief that those who do so are always unfortunate when they meet a knight who is purer of heart; for whether they are defeated or victorious in such an encounter, either result must be equally distressing and shameful. I believe that a true knight is neither adulterous nor lecherous."[33]

---

33. A true knight is pure. He does not commit adultery (*adulterous*), nor is he preoccupied with indecent thoughts and desires (*lecherous*).

34. Here, the gatekeeper (*porter*) is bad-tempered and very rude (*churlish*).

ring in the wall and started across the lawn. Meanwhile people were peering at him from every door and window, and again he heard the warning: "Good knight, you come here at your peril!"

Before long two giants appeared, fully armed except for their heads, and brandishing huge clubs. Together they rushed at Sir Launcelot, who raised his shield to defend himself, and then struck at one of the giants and beheaded him. Thereupon the second giant roared with dismay and fled into the forest, where Sir Launcelot pursued him. In a few minutes, Sir Launcelot drew abreast of the giant and struck him on the shoulder with a blow that carried through to the navel, and the giant dropped dead.

When Sir Launcelot returned to the castle, he was greeted by threescore ladies, who all knelt before him.

"Brave knight! we thank you for delivering us. Many of us have been prisoners for seven years now, and although we are all high born, we have had to work like servants for our keep, doing silk embroidery. Pray tell us your name, so that our friends can know who has saved us."

"My ladies, I am called Sir Launcelot du Lake."

"Welcome, Sir Launcelot! It was you alone whom the giants feared, and you alone who could have overcome them. How often have we prayed for your coming!"

"My ladies, please greet your friends for me; and when I pass through this country again, grant me what hospitality you may feel is my due. Please recompense[35] yourselves from the castle treasure, and then insure that the castle is restored to the rightful owner."

"Sir Launcelot, this is the castle of Tintagil, and belonged formerly to the duke of that name. But after his death, Igraine, who had been his wife, was made queen by King Uther Pendragon, to whom she bore Arthur, our present king."

"And so, after all, I know the owner of this castle. My ladies, I bless you, and farewell."

Always in quest of adventure, Sir Launcelot rode through many different countries, through wild valleys and forests, and across strange rivers; and at night he slept where he could, often in the roughest of lodgings. Then one day he came to a well-kept house where the lady offered him the best of hospitality. After supper he was taken to his chamber, which overlooked the front door, and there Sir Launcelot disarmed and fell comfortably asleep.

He was awakened a short time later by a tremendous knocking at the door below, and looking through the window recognized Sir Kay in the moonlight, and three knights galloping toward him with drawn swords. The moment they got to the house, they dismounted and set upon Sir Kay, who turned about and drew his sword to defend himself. Sir Launcelot hastily armed, saying to himself: "If they kill Sir Kay I shall be a party to his death, for three against one is unjust."

He let himself down from the window by means of his sheet, and then challenged the three attackers, whispering to Sir Kay to stand by while he dealt with them. Sir Kay did as he was advised, and then Sir Launcelot, with seven tremendous blows, brought all three knights to their knees and begging for mercy.

"Your lives will be spared if you yield to Sir Kay," said Sir Launcelot.

"Sir, it is surely you to whom we should yield, since we could easily have overcome Sir Kay."

---

35. Launcelot invites the ladies to *recompense* themselves, or divide the treasure among themselves, as a way to make up for their treatment by the giants.

Analyze Plot *Why do you think Malory has Sir Launcelot return to Tintagil?*

"If you wish to be spared, you will go as prisoners of Sir Kay, and yield to Queen Gwynevere."

Each of the knights then swore on his sword to abide by the conditions of his surrender, and Sir Launcelot knocked once more at the door of the house.

"Why, I thought you were safely in bed," said the landlady, recognizing Sir Launcelot as she opened the door.

"Madam, I was, but then I had to jump out of the window and rescue this comrade of mine."

As they came into the light, Sir Kay recognized Sir Launcelot and thanked him humbly for twice saving his life.

"It was no more than I should have done, but come up to my chamber; you must be tired and hungry."

When Sir Kay had eaten, he lay on Sir Launcelot's bed, and they slept together until dawn. Sir Launcelot woke first, and rising quietly, clad himself in Sir Kay's armor, and then, mounting Sir Kay's horse, rode away from the house.

When Sir Kay awoke, he was astonished to find that Sir Launcelot had exchanged armor with him, but then he realized he had done it so that he should ride home unmolested, while Sir Launcelot encountered his opponents. And when Sir Kay had taken his leave of the landlady he rode back to the court without further incident.

For several days Sir Launcelot rode through the forest, and then he came to a countryside of low meadows and broad streams. At the foot of a bridge he saw three pavilions, and a knight standing at the entrance to each, with a white shield hanging above, and a spear thrust into the ground at one side. Sir Launcelot recognized the three knights, who were from Arthur's court, as Sir Gawtere, Sir Raynolde, and Sir Gylmere. However, he rode straight past them, looking neither to right nor to left, and without saluting them.

"Why, there rides Sir Kay, the most overbearing[36] knight of all, in spite of his many defeats. I think I will challenge him and see if I cannot shake his pride a little," said Sir Gawtere.

He then galloped up to Sir Launcelot and challenged him. They jousted, and Sir Gawtere was flung violently from the saddle.

"That is certainly not Sir Kay," said Sir Raynolde. "For one thing, he is very much bigger."

"Probably it is some knight who has killed Sir Kay and is riding in his armor," Sir Gylmere replied.

"Well, since he has overcome our brother we shall have to challenge him. But I think it must be either Sir Launcelot, Sir Tristram, or Sir Pelleas; and we may not come well out of this."

Sir Gylmere challenged Sir Launcelot next, and was also overthrown. Then Sir Raynolde rode up to him.

"Sir, I would prefer not to challenge a knight so powerful as you, but since you have probably killed my brothers, I am obliged to; so defend yourself!"

They jousted; both broke their spears and they continued the combat with swords. Sir Gawtere and Sir Gylmere recovered, and attempted to rescue their brother, but Sir Launcelot saw them in time, and using more strength than hitherto, struck each off his horse again. At this, Sir Raynolde, badly wounded as he was, and with blood streaming from his

---

36. An *overbearing* person is excessively proud and superior in attitude and behavior.

Dialogue *What does this statement reveal about the code of behavior followed by the knights?*

head, picked himself up and once more rushed at Sir Launcelot.

"Sir, I should let things be," said Sir Launcelot. "I was not far away when you were knighted, and I know you to be worthy: therefore do not oblige me to kill you."

"May God reward you!" Sir Raynolde replied. "But speaking both for myself and my brothers, I would prefer to know your name before yielding to you, because we know very well that you are not Sir Kay, whom any one of us could have overcome."

"That is as may be; but I still require that you yield to Queen Gwynevere at the next Pentecost, and say that Sir Kay sent you."

The three brothers took their oath, and Sir Launcelot left them. He had not ridden much further when, coming to a glade, he found four more knights of the Round Table: Sir Gawain, Sir Ector, Sir Uwayne, and Sir Sagramour le Desyrus.

"Look!" said Sir Sagramour, "there rides Sir Kay. I will challenge him."

Sir Sagramour first, then each of the other knights in turn, challenged Sir Launcelot, and was flung from his horse. Sir Launcelot left them gasping on the ground, and said to himself as he rode away: "Blessed be the maker of this spear; with it I have tumbled four knights off their horses." Meanwhile the four knights were picking themselves up and consoling each other.

"To the devil with him! He is indeed powerful," said one.

"I believe that it must be Sir Launcelot," said another.

"Anyhow, let him go now; we shall discover when we return to Camelot," said a third, and so on. . . .

Sir Launcelot returned to Camelot two days before the feast of Pentecost, and at the court was acclaimed[37] by many of the knights he had met on his adventures.

Sir Gawain, Sir Uwayne, Sir Ector, and Sir Sagramour all laughed when they saw him in Sir Kay's armor, but without the helmet, and readily forgave his joke at their expense.

Sir Gaheris described to the court the terrible battle Sir Launcelot had fought with Sir Tarquine, and how sixty-four prisoners had been freed as a result of his victory.

Sir Kay related how Sir Launcelot had twice saved his life, and then exchanged armor with him, so that he should ride unchallenged.

Sir Gawtere, Sir Gylmere, and Sir Raynolde described how he had defeated them at the bridge, and forced them to yield as prisoners of Sir Kay; and they were overjoyed to discover that it had been Sir Launcelot nevertheless.

Sir Modred, Sir Mador, and Sir Gahalantyne described his tremendous feats in the battle against the King of North Galys; and Sir Launcelot himself described his enchantment by the four queens, and his rescue at the hands of the daughter of King Bagdemagus. . . .

And thus it was, at this time, that Sir Launcelot became the most famous knight at King Arthur's court. ❧

---

37. Launcelot was *acclaimed*, or greeted with loud, enthusiastic praise.

Acts of Courage *Why does Sir Launcelot refrain from describing his acts of courage?*

After You Read

Respond and Think Critically

1. **Connect to Personal Experience** What is your reaction to the world of King Arthur and his knights? If you could be transported there for a day, would you go? Why or why not?

2. **Summarize Events** In your own words, summarize the events that lead Arthur to pull the sword from the stone. What does Arthur's behavior immediately after pulling the sword free tell you about him?

3. **Make Inferences About Motivation** Why is Sir Tarquine so determined to kill Sir Launcelot? Why do you think Sir Launcelot reveals his identity, knowing that the ensuing fight will lead to death? **OER**

4. **Analyze Foreshadowing** What do you learn about Sir Kay's character in "The Tale of King Arthur" that foreshadows what his fellow knights think of him in "The Tale of Sir Launcelot du Lake"?

5. **Evaluate Character** Do the characters of King Uther Pendragon and Igraine seem realistic? Why or why not? Support your response.

6. **Big Idea** **Draw Conclusions About Archetypes** Why would Sir Launcelot be described as courageous? What can you conclude about his fulfillment of the hero archetype? Support your response.

7. **Draw Conclusions About Motivation** In "The Tale of Sir Launcelot du Lake," Sir Launcelot repeatedly risks his own life to protect and defend others. Who are the people who take those risks in the modern world? What might be their motivation?

Literary Element Dialogue

Le Morte d'Arthur uses **dialogue**, the written conversation between characters. Dialogue can reveal a character's personality and feelings. For example, the reader learns about King Uther's feelings when he says, "Igraine has broken my heart, and unless I can win her, I shall never recover."

8. **Draw Conclusions About Historical Context** Reread the section that ends with the pink highlighted passage on page 893. Which part of the dialogue shows the seriousness of a knight's obligations during the medieval period?

9. **Analyze Characterization** Dialogue doesn't always reflect the way people actually speak. Identify one passage where Malory uses dialogue more to characterize a figure than to accurately represent real conversation. What effect does this type of dialogue have on the text?

Review: Hero

As you learned on page 881, a **hero** is the main character in a literary work and typically has qualities that arouse the admiration of the reader.

10. **Partner Activity** Critic Jeffrey Helterman observes that "Arthur institutes a code of behavior which stresses always succoring [aiding] ladies . . . and never taking up battles for a wrongful cause." With a partner, find examples from "The Tale of Sir Launcelot du Lake" of knights following this code of behavior. Use a chart like the one below. What can you infer from the code about the values held by this society?

Example	Inference
When a knight attacks a noblewoman, Sir Launcelot fights and defeats him.	Protecting women and their honor is valued in his society.

Reading Strategy — Analyze Plot

Episodes in a legend's plot are often **archetypal**—in their plot patterns, the characters and images they involve, or the themes they reveal. Refer to your diagram from page 883.

11. Arthur's life is filled with archetypes associated with the journey of a hero, such as completing an "impossible" task (pulling the sword from the stone). What aspects of his early life do you recognize from other stories?

12. Why might Malory have included Launcelot's killing of Sir Tarquine as part of the plot?

Vocabulary Practice

Practice with Word Origins Studying the etymology, or origin and history, of a word can help you better understand its meaning. Create a word map for each vocabulary word below.

abashed   inscribe   ignoble   tumultuous prowess

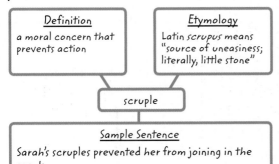

Definition
a moral concern that prevents action

Etymology
Latin *scrupus* means "source of uneasiness; literally, little stone"

scruple

Sample Sentence
Sarah's scruples prevented her from joining in the prank.

Academic Vocabulary

The Knights of the Round Table formed a **semicircle** *around Arthur.*

Semicircle is a discipline-specific word that derives from Latin. The prefix *semi-* means "half." Using your knowledge and context clues, determine the meaning of *semicircle* in the model sentence above. Check your response by consulting a dictionary. Finally, demonstrate your understanding by using each of these related words in a sentence.

a. semitropical   **b.** semitranslucent   **c.** semiweekly

Write with Style

 Apply Dialogue

Assignment Write a short dialogue that reveals the personality traits of two characters of your own invention.

Get Ideas How a writer uses dialogue reveals part of his or her personal style. Recall how the dialogue in *Le Morte d'Arthur* and in the Literary Analysis Model "The Journey of Gilgamesh" on pages 876–877 helps reveal the characters. Then think of two contrasting traits, such as aggressiveness and reluctance, confidence and uncertainty, or cruelty and sympathy. List words and phrases that might be spoken by characters with those traits.

Responsible	Irresponsible
I'll do it.	Who says I have to do that?
This is my job, and I won't let you down.	It's not my job!
No matter what it takes, I'm going to come through for you.	If you care so much about it, do it yourself!

Give It Structure Think of an issue that might pit two characters with contrasting personality traits against each other. Then write a dialogue in which the issue comes to light. Use speaker tags to convey the tone of what each character says. Embrace your personal style and make your dialogue realistic by using everyday speech and by allowing characters to interrupt each other or trail off.

Look at Language Use a thesaurus to replace weak verbs, such as *said,* in your speaker tags with more specific verbs, such as *insisted, demanded,* or *jested.*

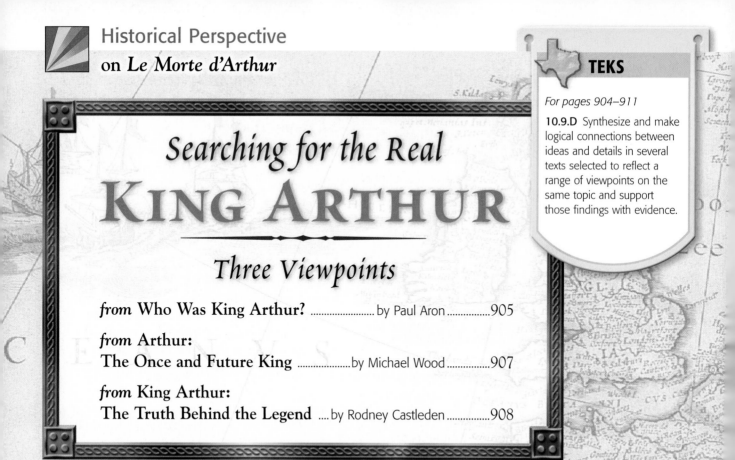

Searching for the Real
KING ARTHUR

Three Viewpoints

TEKS

For pages 904–911

10.9.D Synthesize and make logical connections between ideas and details in several texts selected to reflect a range of viewpoints on the same topic and support those findings with evidence.

Set a Purpose for Reading

Read to synthesize and make connections between ideas and details in several texts that reflect a range of viewpoints on a topic.

Build Background

The debate over whether King Arthur was real or merely an enduring legend has raged for centuries. The legend as we know it today, and as related by Malory, largely originated with Geoffrey of Monmouth's greatly fictionalized *History of the Kings of Britain.* Written in 1138, it tells the story of a king who was conceived under magical circumstances and rose to power during a turbulent time in British history.

Welsh writings recorded long before Geoffrey's *History* seem to suggest that someone like Arthur did exist. Several of these sources mention the key sixth-century Battle of Badon, where a fearless king led the Britons to victory over Saxon invaders. Scholars have debated where exactly the battle occurred and whether it was in fact Arthur who led the British victory. The following three texts present different viewpoints on these questions.

Reading Strategy Synthesize

When you **synthesize**, you combine ideas and details from several texts to reach a new understanding. As you read the following texts, think about the ideas you learn and ask yourself, Do these ideas add up to more than what is in each text? Can I come to a new understanding based on what I now know? Take notes on a timeline like the one below, putting historical people and events above the line and ideas and details below the line.

Battle of Badon	Gildas	Nennius	Geoffrey of Monmouth
Britons beat Saxons; location unknown	describes Briton victory	describes "Arthur" slaying 960 Saxons	

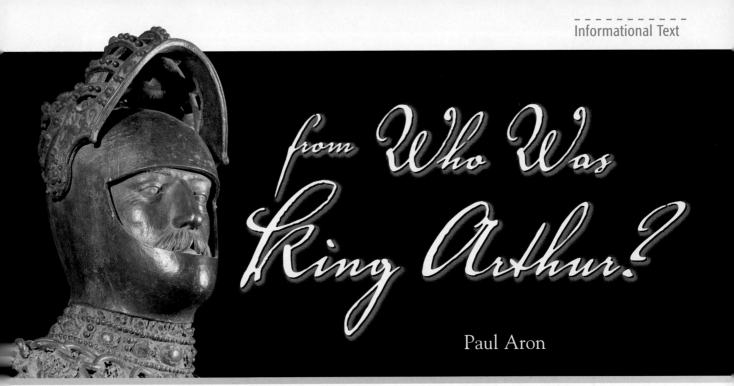

from Who Was King Arthur?

Paul Aron

Even in Geoffrey of Monmouth's own lifetime, it was clear that his History was anything but. In about 1197, William of Newburgh called Geoffrey's work a "laughable web of fiction" and calculated that there weren't as many kingdoms in the world as Geoffrey had Arthur conquering.

Since then, historians following in William's footsteps have attempted to sift from the legend the "historical" Arthur—if, indeed, he really existed.

Above all, that meant turning to the (very few) sources that preceded Geoffrey of Monmouth and were thus both closer to Arthur's time and less likely to have been corrupted by later mythologizing. These were mostly Welsh writings, since it was the Welsh who were descendants of the ancient Britons.[1]

These Britons came to power after the fall of the Roman Empire, early in the fifth century.[2] They had wielded considerable power under the empire, so it seemed natural (to them) that they take over after the Roman legions left. That was unlike other areas of the former empire, where the invaders who drove out the Romans seized power. Independent Britain was therefore still in many ways Roman; the Britons, or at least their upper class, saw themselves as the heirs to the imperial culture and civilization.

Unfortunately for them, they also inherited the Roman enemies. The Britons immediately found themselves under attack from groups they thought of as barbarians: the Irish from the west, the Picts from the north, and the Anglo-Saxons from across the North Sea. The invaders saw no reason to withdraw just because the Britons had replaced the Romans.

The situation the Welsh bards described was desperate—every bit as much as that faced by the British in Geoffrey of Monmouth's account. But if we can believe a Welsh monk named Gildas, in about the year 500 the Britons won a great victory at a spot called Mount Badon. In The Ruin of Britain, written only about fifty years after

---

1. The *Britons* were the people who lived in England prior to the Anglo-Saxon invasion in the ninth century.
2. In A.D. 43 the Romans conquered the Britons and ruled until the collapse of the Roman Empire.

Antique map of the British Isles. John Speed.

that, Gildas described the battle and the two generations of relative peace and prosperity that followed.

Was this interregnum[3] of Gildas the brief, shining moment of Camelot? Perhaps. But, as skeptics have been quick to point out, nowhere does Gildas mention the name of Arthur. Frustratingly, Gildas never says who commanded the Britons.

That was left to Nennius, another Welsh cleric. In the History of the Britons, which Nennius compiled sometime early in the ninth century, there's no doubt about the identity of the hero: it is "the warrior Arthur." According to Nennius, Arthur defeated the Saxons in twelve battles, at one point slaying 960 of the enemy in a single charge.

But can Nennius be trusted? Such obviously impossible deeds as single-handedly killing 960 of the enemy clearly belong to the traditions of epic poetry, not history. His notoriously disorganized material didn't help, either; the cleric himself described his approach as "making one heap" of all he found. Some historians found comfort in that, arguing that someone unable to organize anything probably also couldn't invent anything, but others just found it frustrating.

Welsh writers who followed Nennius also credited Arthur with the victory at Mount Badon. But, like Nennius, they were all writing at least three hundred years after the actual events. It was impossible to tell whether the oral tradition they recounted was the actual history of fifth-century Britain. ∾

Reading Check

Analyze Does the author believe that Arthur existed? Explain. What evidence does he use to support his claims?

---

3. An *interregnum* is a period without the usual ruling power or authority.

from ARTHUR:
THE ONCE AND FUTURE KING

Michael Wood

Frustratingly, no one has yet been able to locate Badon with certainty. Nennius identifies it with Bath, but surely mistakenly (Badon is a Celtic name, Bath is the Anglo-Saxon name for the Roman town of Aquae Sulis). However, the fact that the battle was a siege of a hill strongly suggests that, like other battles of the time, it took place at a hill-fort. We don't know the name of Liddington Castle in the late Roman period, but in Anglo-Saxon times it bore the name Baddeburi, which could derive from the *burh*, or fort, of Badon. Nearby too is Baydon, an ancient village surrounded by Celtic and Romano-British fields. If anywhere, one would think, the battle was fought here. It was a great victory for the Britons, which is why it was remembered by later bards and chroniclers, who claimed that Arthur had been the leader. And, as it happens, there is a near-contemporary source for the battle, one of the most important narratives in British history. The book was written by a Welsh cleric called Gildas and it is called *On the Ruin of Britain*.

Though the British commander at the battle of Badon is not specifically named by Gildas, their chief leader in the war against the Saxons is not Arthur but Ambrosius. . . .

According to Gildas, though, writing only forty-four years after the battle of Badon, it is Ambrosius who is the key historical figure in the wars of the mid to late fifth century. And it is therefore significant that in early Welsh tradition it is Ambrosius and Vortigern who are at the center of the myths surrounding these events; Arthur only comes later. . . .

But if Ambrosius was the leader in the war, where does that leave Arthur? If Arthur won twelve battles which climaxed at Badon Hill; if he bore the cross on his back, and killed hordes of pagan Saxons, then it is strange that he is not mentioned in Gildas's account of the battle. Arguments from silence are never entirely satisfactory, of course, but on the face of it, no source before the ninth century mentions Arthur as a war leader against the Saxons, and none in a form or context that can safely be taken as historical. The twelve battles of Arthur look like later poetic conflation. Our one contemporary source from the sixth century, Gildas, does not mention him and tells us that the British leader in these battles was called Ambrosius. The case for a fifth- or sixth-century Arthur fighting Anglo-Saxons in southern Britain looks decidedly flimsy. He is simply not there. . . . ∾

Reading Check

Interpret Who was Ambrosius? How does his existence cast doubt on Arthur's role at the battle of Badon?

Arthur, 14th century. Anonymous artist. Ann Ronan Picture Library, London.

from KING ARTHUR: The Truth Behind the Legend

Rodney Castleden

In 516, came the great Battle of Badon, in which the British were victorious over the Saxons. Ambrosius the Younger was by now dead and the command had passed to Arthur. Gildas, writing not long after the event, does not say who the commander was at Badon. Much has been made of this by opponents of the historical Arthur. Oliver Padel[1] argues that Gildas implies Ambrosius was still in command. The passage in question reads, "Wretched people fled to them from all directions . . . their leader was Ambrosius Aurelianus . . . This lasted right up till the year of the siege of Mount Badon." Modern editions invariably separate the sentence about Badon from the preceding sentence, but the oldest surviving copy of Gildas, a tenth-century manuscript, has no paragraph division here. Padel argues from this that Ambrosius was still commander in 516, but the passage implies a series of battles between the mention of Ambrosius' leadership and Badon, so it is possible for the leadership to have changed hands and for the successor to have commanded at Badon. Other documents, such as the *Welsh Annals*, specifically identify Arthur as commander at Badon, so it is more natural and consistent to suppose that Arthur had succeeded as commander by 516.

So decisive was Badon that it held the Saxons back for several decades, and it is largely to his exploits during this single action that Arthur owes his reputation as a great warrior. There has been much discussion about the site of the battle, and many candidates have been offered. Gildas was close enough to Badon—according to one reading he claimed to have been born in the same year as the battle, but this is disputed—to have correct details about it. Yet the name "Mons Badonicus" must be a Latinization of the real place-name, which may subsequently have been anglicized[2] to an extent that it is no longer easy to identify.

A second candidate for the battle site is Baydon, a village 3 miles to the south-east of Liddington Castle, also on the Roman road to Silchester. It is likely that most battles took place on or near major roads, as these would have been the obvious medium for moving large numbers of troops from one region to another, whether on foot or horse. Baydon is at the highest point reached by the road.

---

1. *Oliver Padel* is a prominent scholar who does not believe a historical Arthur existed.

2. When a word is *anglicized,* it is adopted into English from a foreign language and may undergo changes in pronunciation, form, or meaning.

Set high between deep valleys to north and south, it does justice to Gildas' use of the word *mons*. There is nevertheless no sign of any earthwork at Baydon, which makes it an unlikely site for a siege lasting a number of days.

It has nevertheless been very convincingly argued that Bath was Badon, and there are unmistakable early references to Bath, specifically mentioning its hot and cold springs, in which the place-name is spelled *Badon*. The location makes sense in terms of general situation. . . .

It is, in effect, in the no-man's-land or buffer zone between two sixth-century cultural provinces and must for some time have been on or very close to the political frontier, however defined, separating Celt from Saxon.

Another location has been suggested, at Baden Hill east of Thornbury. Although it too is in the likely conflict zone and its name has the right sort of sound, its claim is not as strong as that of Bath.

All in all, Bath makes excellent sense as a location for a decisive frontier battle in the year 516, Liddington and Baydon less so because there were well-established Anglo-Saxon settlements close at hand to the east, north, south, north-west and south-west: that area was already a lost cause.

Tellingly, the spellings Bathe, Baderan and Badan were the same as far as thirteenth-century scribes in England and Wales were concerned. Even Nennius seems to be using the spelling "Badon" to mean "Bath." In *The Wonders of Britain* he refers to "the hot lake" "in quo balnea sunt Badonis," "the hot lake where the baths of Badon are." Nennius mentions that Badon is in the country of the Hwicce; Osric of the Hwicce granted land to Bath Abbey in 675, so Badon/Bath was in the hands of the Hwicce in the years up to 650 and it had hot baths. There really cannot be much doubt that when Nennius referred to the Battle of Badon he knew what he meant by

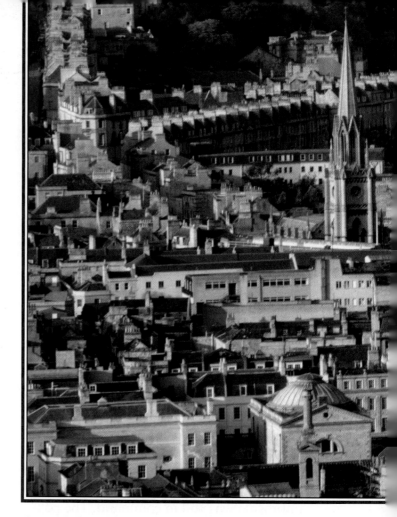

the name Badon, nor can there be any real doubt that he meant Bath.

In the seventeenth century one of the hills round Bath was known by two names— Lansdown Hill and Mons Badonica. The Latinized form is suspicious, of course, because it implies that an antiquarian had looked at Gildas and maybe Nennius too, and worked out that this was the right place to be Mount Badon; I am doubtful whether this is a piece of locally preserved folk memory of the great battle. The idea that Bath was Badon is certainly not a new discovery; as early as 1848 Todd noted that "no doubt can exist of Badon being Bath."

Reading Check

Interpret Where does the author believe the battle of Badon took place? Why does he believe this?

Aerial View of
Bath, England.

Respond and Think Critically

1. **Summarize Main Ideas** Write a brief summary of the main ideas in these three texts before you answer the following questions. For help on writing a summary, see page 389.

2. **Make Logical Connections** Nennius was the first commentator to mention Arthur by name, and he also wrote that Arthur killed 960 Saxons in a single charge. Why do some modern historians question the accuracy of his account?

3. **Synthesize Ideas** According to these three texts, how clear is our picture of the real King Arthur? Can historians confidently say that he was the leader of the Britons at one time? Why or why not? Support your response with evidence from the texts.

4. **Evaluate Evidence** Michael Wood and Rodney Castleden present opposing views on the location of the Battle of Badon. What evidence does each author present to support his conclusion? How convincing is each author's evidence? Explain.

5. **Evaluate Viewpoints** Based on the information in the texts, where do you think the Battle of Badon most likely took place? Support your choice with evidence from the texts.

6. **Draw Conclusions About Legends** Sir Thomas Malory's 15th-century King Arthur walks through castles that resemble those of Malory's own time, and his knights use armor and weapons that hadn't even been imagined in the sixth century. If the Arthur legend were placed in the modern world, how would it differ from Malory's version?

TEKS

10.18.B.i Use correct punctuation marks, including comma placement in nonrestrictive phrases, clauses, and contrasting expressions.

Grammar Workshop

Main and Subordinate Clauses

Literature Connection In *Le Morte d'Arthur,* Keith Baines uses sentences that include both main (or independent) and subordinate (or dependent) clauses.

> *"In the course of the feast, King Uther grew passionately desirous of Igraine and, when it was over, begged her to become his paramour."*

Both main and subordinate clauses contain subjects and predicates. A **main clause**, however, expresses a complete thought, so it can stand alone as a sentence. A **subordinate clause** is dependent for its meaning on the main clause. In the quotation above, the main clause is *In the course of the feast, King Uther grew passionately desirous of Igraine and begged her to become his paramour.* The subordinate clause, *when it was over,* cannot stand alone.

Here is how to identify main and subordinate clauses and turn subordinate clauses into complete sentences.

Main clause *The story was written by Malory and retold by Baines*

Explanation Because the clause has a subject (*story*) and a compound predicate (*was written* and *retold*) and expresses a complete thought, it can stand alone as a complete sentence. To create a sentence, add a period to the main clause.

The story was written by Malory and retold by Baines.

Subordinate clause *Because the story was interesting*

Problem The clause has a subject (*story*) and a predicate (*was*) but does not express a complete thought.

Solution To create a sentence, combine subordinate and main clauses.

Because the story was interesting, I wanted to read more of it.

Clauses

A **main clause** has a subject and a predicate, expresses a complete thought, and can stand alone as a sentence. A **subordinate clause** has a subject and a predicate, does not express a complete thought, and cannot stand alone as a sentence.

Tip

A subordinate clause that isn't essential to the meaning of a sentence is called a **nonrestrictive clause.** Use commas to set off these clauses. In the example quotation from *Le Morte d'Arthur,* the appositive "when it was over" doesn't change the meaning of the sentence, so it is set off with commas.

Language Handbook

For more on main and subordinate clauses, and the punctuation of nonessential elements, see the Language Handbook, p. R66.

Grammar For more grammar practice, go to glencoe.com and enter QuickPass code GL57805u5.

Revise Rewrite the subordinate clauses to make complete sentences. Write "correct" if the clause is a sentence.

1. Since the boy was able to pull the sword out easily, unlike the others who tried.

2. While it was clear that he was the new king.

3. Sir Ector and the other men were amazed by the feat.

4. After Arthur pulled the sword.

Set a Purpose for Reading

Read to discover contrasting ideas about heroes.

Preview the Article

1. What answers can you give to the question in the article's title?

2. Analyze the use of text features such as subheads and captions. Compare how they are used here with how they are used in other articles you have read.

Reading Strategy Analyze Text Structure

When you **analyze text structure,** you make and defend inferences and draw conclusions about the pattern a writer uses to organize ideas and how it affects meaning. Analyzing the structure can help you focus your attention on the important ideas and underlying logic of a text. As you read, ask yourself, How are the ideas in this text organized, and how does this structure affect meaning? Take notes in a chart like this one.

Structure	Inference/Conclusion

TIME

What Makes A HERO?

Some heroes act boldly on the world stage. Others make a difference outside the public eye by identifying problems, finding solutions, and inspiring the rest of us.

By AMANDA RIPLEY

WAR BREEDS HEROES—AND A DEEP NEED TO ANOINT them. The soldier who sacrifices himself for his comrades, the civilian who walks more than six miles to get help for a wounded prisoner of war, the medic who makes no distinction between a bleeding ally and a bleeding enemy, the aid worker who passes through a combat zone to bring water to a crippled city—all are called heroes, and all deserve to be. But the word *hero* is also used as a way to excuse senseless deaths, a way to support the fiction that courage and bravery will be enough to carry men and women through the valley of death. The truth is more complicated and sad. Sometimes heroic virtue means the difference between life and death and sometimes it does not. Sometimes a hero is not born until the moment he or she recognizes that heroism may not solve anything—and yet behaves heroically anyway.

In the 1980s, Xavier Emmanuelli, cofounder of the medical humanitarian organization Doctors Without Borders, was working on the border between Cambodia and Thailand. With bombs falling uncomfortably nearby, Emmanuelli and another doctor attended to wounded refugees. The first victim was a young woman. She was alive but critically wounded, her body nearly sliced in two by a bomb fragment. Emmanuelli made a quick diagnosis. "I thought there was nothing to be done and went on to another victim," he remembers.

But when he looked back, the other doctor, a young man named Daniel Pavard, had not moved on. He was cradling the woman's head and caressing her hair. "He was helping her die," says Emmanuelli. "He did it very naturally. There was no public, no cameras, no one looking. The bombing continued, and he did this as if he was all alone in his humanity."

In his 35-year career, Emmanuelli has witnessed most of the tragedies of our era, from Saigon to Sierra Leone, locations where warfare has resulted in thousands of deaths—places where heroes are made if ever there are heroes. But he has never found heroes in the obvious spots—behind podiums, say, or on armored personnel carriers. Sometimes he has not even recognized them until later, reflecting on what he has seen them do. "It is in gestures," he says, "that you know a person's true nature—gestures that almost escape detection."

Today, the newspapers are full of hero nominees, some more convincing than others. The British papers gushed over Lieut. Colonel Tim Collins, who became a national hero in England for giving a speech to his troops before they marched into war in Iraq: "We go to liberate, not to conquer,"

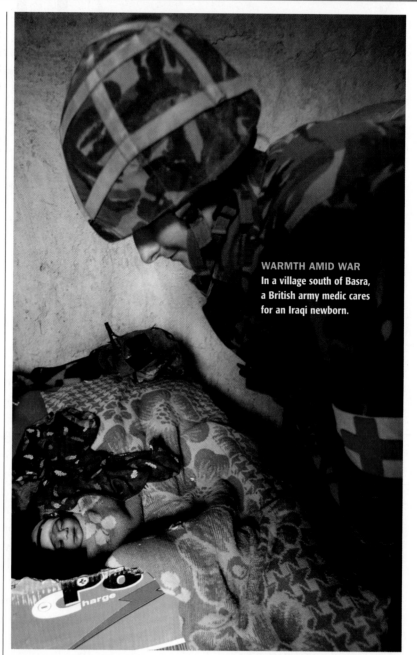

WARMTH AMID WAR
In a village south of Basra, a British army medic cares for an Iraqi newborn.

he said. "If you are ferocious in battle, remember to be magnanimous [noble and fair-minded] in victory."

News reporters have been called heroic for doing their jobs, and bombing victims have been called courageous for surviving. There have been grainy black-and-white portraits of U.S. General Tommy Franks and sad images of France's President Jacques Chirac, the "white knight of peace," as the French newspaper *Le Figaro* called him. Still, many people find it hard to believe in any of the major leaders for more than half an hour. A hero, by most definitions, must be both brave and generous, a rare combination.

American and European Heroes

For some, the very idea of a "European hero" is problematic. It is Americans, after all—whom the Irish-born writer Oscar Wilde mockingly called "hero worshippers"—who put all their faith in a romantic notion of the individual. Europeans like to put their faith in the group; they believe that they know better than to overestimate the lone actor. Is it not unrealistic to think that a single, flawed human can change the world? Have we not learned by now that history is a mix of complicated circumstances, not a totem pole of individual men—heroic as they may be?

"In the U.S., it is more likely that the rugged individualist will be admired more," says Oxford University philosopher Roger Crisp. "It's kind of old-fashioned. There's a sense [in Europe] that we've already been through that." Billionaire businessmen are not embraced as society's saviors. That is what the state is for. When TIME asked Italian novelist Umberto Eco who his hero was, he responded with a quotation from German playwright Bertolt Brecht: "Unhappy the land that needs heroes."

And yet, for all of Europe's worldly skepticism, there is no

LIBERATION
Lech Walesa, founder of Poland's Solidarity movement (top), and Charles de Gaulle. Both helped to free their nations from tyrannical rule.

doubt that heroes live there—and not all of them went to the war zone. People still crave heroes, still rely on individuals—if not to solve problems single-handedly, then at least to identify them, to point the way toward a solution and, not least, to inspire the rest of us.

"People do need heroes in Europe," insists Sister Emmanuelle, the Belgian-born nun who spent 22 years living among the garbage pickers of Cairo, Egypt, forcing the rest of the world to acknowledge their existence. "Currently there is a real search for grandness, in a different way than wealth. I can see how people need this when they cry as I tell them about the love and deep commonality that saves people. That touches them deep in their hearts," says Emmanuelle. She is living proof that for the European hero, the good of the

group and individual accomplishment can exist together.

Heroes Past and Present

In ancient Greece, heroes inhabited a space between gods and men. "Their heroes were very often flawed," says Crisp. "[The ancient Greek warrior] Achilles was sulky and arrogant, but admired because he was big and tough." The same might be said of some European heroes today. In a 2003 survey of six European nations, people were asked to name a famous figure from European history with whom they would like to pass an hour. The study, sponsored by three European associations, was meant to identify the "great men" who inhabit an overall European memory.

In the end, despite the fact that they have spent decades throwing politicians out of office, people chose their country's current leaders. The Germans wanted an hour with Foreign Minister Joschka Fischer. The British picked their prime minister, Tony Blair. The Spanish, President José María Aznar. The French . . . well, the French picked Charles de Gaulle, of course. The greatly admired general and statesman became the symbol of France during its battle against Nazi occupation and later as its president. But the second most popular choice in France was the current president, Chirac.

Even as we disparage our leaders, we still want to believe in them. In late 2002, the BBC television channel caused hours of dinner-table bickering when it invited the public to vote for the greatest Briton of all time. Beatle John Lennon and Princess Diana made the short list. But the winner was Winston Churchill, who led the country through the dark and difficult days of the Second World War.

Everyday Heroes

If you asked a thousand people for a definition of heroism, you would get a thousand different answers. The French celebrity philosopher Bernard-Henri Levy defines a hero narrowly, as someone who tells the truth when it means risking his or her life. Others are so uncomfortable with the word that they prefer to use different, subtle labels like "role model" or "uncommon man."

Many people take a broader view and define heroes as people who have stood without flinching in the face of very bad odds. Some say people who put themselves in mortal danger are heroes. Others define heroes as activists, in the old-fashioned sense, stubbornly beating a drum to remind us of problems we would prefer to ignore. Some believe that heroes are able to turn grief that would have destroyed most of us into defiant hope. Still others say that heroes live comfortably while inspiring millions to hope for better things.

Most heroes are walking contradictions. A hero has to be, on the one hand, a dreamer—to believe against overwhelming odds that something can change. But a hero is also a realist who does something useful; giving up is not an option.

And so in France, a businessman has begun collecting résumés in the decaying housing projects of the Parisian suburbs so he can help young

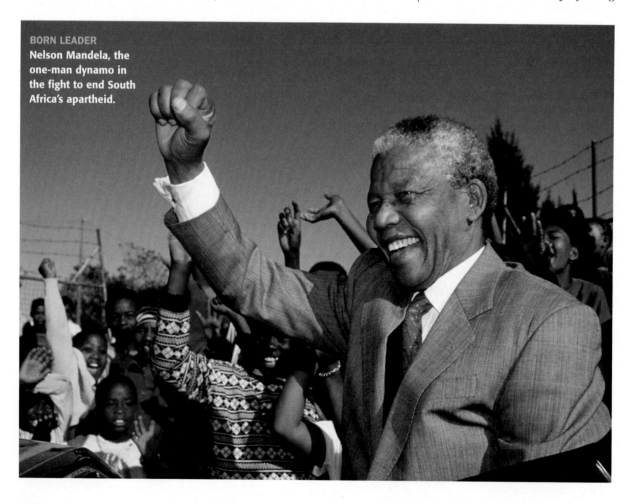

BORN LEADER
Nelson Mandela, the one-man dynamo in the fight to end South Africa's apartheid.

immigrants find jobs. In Iceland, a former engineer convinced people to save the whales not because they are pretty, but because the whale-watching industry could make more money than the whale-killing industry. And in the West Bank, a Palestinian surgeon endures a six-hour round-trip commute through armed checkpoints to save lives—both Arab and Jewish—in the operating room of an Israeli hospital. After decades of assuming the state would look after the collective good, Europeans—and Americans—have been forced to acknowl-edge that the government cannot manage the job alone. Individuals must fill the gaps.

True heroes, adds Emmanuelli, never know that they are heroes. They just find themselves in a situation for which they have been pre-paring, unwittingly, all their lives. Then they do the right thing. "A hero understands that he is a tool," he says.

In every case, if heroism requires courage and generos-ity, the last ingredient is circumstance. Novelist Jean-Christophe Rufin, winner of France's top literary award, and president of *Action Contre la Faim* (Action Against Hunger), a private humanitar-ian organization, says his model of a hero was his grand-father. Until he was sent to a Nazi prison camp for hiding people in his garage, he raised Rufin himself. "Physically, he was absolutely not a hero. He was short, thin and weak, though he resisted many things that would have killed me 10 times," Rufin says. "All the choices he made were kind of obvious things. It was the circum-stances that made him a hero."

—from TIME

Respond and Think Critically

1. **Summarize Main Ideas** Write a brief summary of the main ideas in this article before you answer the following questions. For help on writ-ing a summary, see page 389.

2. **Clarify Details** Why did Xavier Emmanuelli, cofounder of Doctors Without Borders, think that his colleague, Daniel Pavard, was a hero? How does this challenge the traditional definition of a hero?

3. **Evaluate Ideas** According to Oxford University philospher Roger Crisp, how do people in the United States define heroes? Do you agree with him? Why or why not?

4. **Make Inferences About Ideas** According to the writer, what are two qualities that a hero must have? Based on the comparisons and con-trasts in the text, what do you think other quali-ties of a hero might be? Defend your response.

5. **Evaluate Conclusion** How does the writer con-clude the article? Do you think it is an effective conclusion? Why or why not?

6. **Draw Conclusions About Structure** The article compares and contrasts many visions of the idea of heroism. Does this organizational pattern lead you to think that people can recognize true hero-ism wherever they're from, or are ideas about heroism just too diverse? Defend your conclusion with evidence from the text.

7. **Compare and Contrast Subjects** Compare and contrast the heroes of Sir Thomas Malory's *Le Morte d'Arthur* and those described in this article. How are they alike and how are they different? Support your response with text evidence.

Before You Read

from *Sundiata*

Meet **D. T. Niane and the Storytellers of Mali**

The *Sundiata* (so͞on dyä′tə) is the national epic of the Mandingo people, who live in present-day Mali and parts of the coastal region of West Africa. It celebrates the founding of the ancient Mali empire, which occurred around 1235. A king named Sundiata played an important role in establishing Mali as a powerful state. Stories and legends about Sundiata are told to this day.

The Griot All over the world, storytellers have helped to pass down history and tradition from generation to generation in times and places where literacy was not widespread. In Africa one name for the storyteller—a name which may come from French or Portuguese—is *griot* (grē′o). A Mende (Mandingo) word for griot is *jali* (also spelled *jeli* or *djali*). Griots are steeped in oral tradition from childhood onward.

During Sundiata's time, griots were employed by kings and other leaders to recite their country's legendary history. In West African society prior to colonization, griots held a high place in social hierarchies. They were valued for

recording the history and traditions of their societies. Since they did not work from a written text, they could alter their stories to suit occasions and audiences. This process led to the development of many different versions of the *Sundiata*. The episode you will read comes from a version told by storyteller Mamadou Kouyaté (ma′mä do͞o ko͞oyä′ tä) to historian and professor D. T. Niane, who adapted it into prose.

> "We are repositories which harbor secrets centuries old. . . ."
>
> —Mamadou Kouyaté

From the Storytellers to Us Today, the *Sundiata* is recited by Mandingo griots. Their performances, which can last several hours, are enlivened by musical accompaniment, dramatic gestures, and frequent interjections from the audience, suggesting agreement and enthusiasm.

When D. T. Niane, a specialist in the Mandingo world, met griots in Mali, he felt that his eyes had "been opened [to the] mysteries of eternal Africa." In his introduction to the *Sundiata*, he wrote, "May this book open the eyes of more than one African and induce him to come and sit humbly beside the ancients and hear the words of the griots who teach wisdom and history."

SAHARA

Mali Niger River AFRICA

ATLANTIC OCEAN

LOG ON ▶ **Literature** Online

Author Search For more about D. T. Niane and the storytellers, go to glencoe.com and enter QuickPass code GL57805u5.

Literature and Reading Preview

Connect to the Epic

Why do people enjoy listening to stories about heroes? Discuss this question with a partner.

Build Background

Sundiata came to power around 1235, when he freed Mali from the control of a neighboring kingdom. Mali was known as a safe and orderly place. "Neither traveler nor inhabitant in it has anything to fear from robbers or men of violence," wrote an early Arab visitor.

Set Purposes for Reading

Big Idea **Acts of Courage**

As you read, ask yourself, How do the characters in the *Sundiata* display their courage?

Literary Element **Dialogue**

Dialogue is the conversation between characters in a literary work. Through dialogue, an author reveals the feelings, thoughts, and intentions of characters, develops conflicts, and moves the plot forward. As you read, ask yourself, How does the dialogue reveal characters and advance the plot?

Reading Strategy **Identify Genre**

A **genre** is a category of literary work characterized by a particular form or style. One genre is the **epic**, a long narrative poem about a larger-than-life hero who embodies the values of his or her culture and people. Some epics, like this one, have been adapted into prose form. As you read, ask yourself, What elements of this story indicate that it is an epic?

Tip: Focus on Details Record details of the *Sundiata* that help you identify it as an epic. Consider the historical and cultural context of the story. Use the blue highlighted questions to help you.

Epic element	Form in the *Sundiata*
Details that reveal customs, beliefs, and values	Sundiata has great charm and the strength of ten men. Charm and strength are valued.

TEKS

For pages 918–926

10.2 Analyze, make inferences and draw conclusions about theme and genre in different historical and contemporary contexts and provide evidence from the text to support understanding.

Vocabulary

scrupulous (skrōō′pyə ləs) *adj.* thoroughly attentive to even the smallest details; precise; p. 921 *Ana's knitting was scrupulous.*

elude (i lōōd′) *v.* to avoid or escape, especially through cleverness or quickness; p. 921 *As one child gave chase, the other child tried to elude her.*

confidante (kon′ fə dant′) *n.* a person who is entrusted with secrets or private affairs; p. 922 *Only Eric's confidante knew about his secret plans.*

perpetuate (pər pech′ōō āt′) *v.* to cause to continue to be remembered; p. 923 *Gossip can perpetuate hurtful and untrue rumors.*

Sahelian Landscape, Mali, 1991. Tilly Willis. Oil on canvas. Private collection.

from SUNDIATA

Retold by D. T. Niane
Translated by G. D. Pickett

$\mathcal{E}$*ven before he was born, Sundiata was destined for greatness. Acting on the instructions of a soothsayer,[1] his father, the king of Mali, had married a hideous, hunchbacked woman named Sogolon. As foretold, the couple had a son. It seemed, however, that the boy was unlikely to become a great leader as had been predicted. The young Sundiata could not even walk. He and his ugly mother became the object of cruel jokes and jealous abuse by the old king's first wife. At the age of seven, Sundiata suddenly reacted to an insult by standing up and tearing a tree from the ground. He instantly became the center of attention, a boy with great charm and the strength of ten men. Among his constant companions were the princes Fran Kamara and Kamandjan.[2] Even more important to him was his griot, Balla Fasséké,[3] who taught*

---

1. A *soothsayer* is someone who claims to be able to foretell the future.

2. *Kamara* (kä´mä rä); *Kamandjan* (kä´män jän)
3. *Balla Fasséké* (bä´lä fä sä´kä)

him the history of his people and of the world beyond.

Still fearing persecution from the jealous queen, Sogolon escaped with Sundiata to neighboring Ghana. There the amazing boy grew up. In his absence, Mali was taken over by the king of Sosso, a cruel sorcerer named Soumaoro,[4] whose secret chamber was tapestried with human skins and adorned with the skulls of his enemies. Soumaoro captured Balla Fasséké and Sundiata's half-sister, Nana Triban.[5] Enraged by Soumaoro's barbarism, Sundiata raised an army and prepared to restore his country to its rightful people. Although he succeeded in defeating Soumaoro in a great battle, he could not capture or kill the man himself, for the magician had the power to appear and disappear at will. While Sundiata rested in the town of Sibi,[6] Soumaoro once again raised a powerful army. The two prepared to meet in a final battle.

Sundiata and his mighty army stopped at Sibi for a few days. The road into Mali lay open, but Soumaoro was not yet vanquished. The king of Sosso had mustered a powerful army and his sofas were numbered by the thousand. He had raised contingents[7] in all the lands over which he held sway and got ready to pounce again on Mali.

With **scrupulous** care, Sundiata had made his preparations at Sibi. Now he had sufficient sofas to meet Soumaoro in the open field, but it was not a question of having a lot of troops. In order to defeat Soumaoro it was

necessary first of all to destroy his magical power. At Sibi, Sundiata decided to consult the soothsayers, of whom the most famous in Mali were there.

On their advice Djata[8] had to sacrifice a hundred white bulls, a hundred white rams and a hundred white cocks. It was in the middle of this slaughter that it was announced to Sundiata that his sister Nana Triban and Balla Fasséké, having been able to escape from Sosso, had now arrived. Then Sundiata said to Tabon Wana, "If my sister and Balla have been able to escape from Sosso, Soumaoro has lost the battle."

Leaving the site of the sacrifices, Sundiata returned to Sibi and met his sister and his griot.

"Hail, my brother," said Nana Triban.

"Greetings, sister."

"Hail Sundiata," said Balla Fasséké.

"Greetings, my griot."

After numerous salutations, Sundiata asked the fugitives to relate how they had been able to **elude** the vigilance of a king such as Soumaoro. But Triban was weeping for joy. Since the time of their childhood she had shown much sympathy towards the crippled child that Sundiata had been. Never had she shared the hate of her mother, Sassouma Bérété.

"You know, Djata," she said, weeping, "for my part I did not want you to leave the country. It was my mother who did all that. Now Niani is destroyed, its inhabitants scattered, and there are many whom Soumaoro has carried off into captivity in Sosso."

---

4. *Soumaoro* (sōō´mər ō)
5. *Nana Triban* (nä´na tri´ban)
6. *Sibi* (si´bē)
7. The *sofas* are soldiers or warriors, and *contingents* are additional troops.

Identify Genre *Which items in the summary paragraphs indicate that the epic will include exaggerated elements?*

Vocabulary

scrupulous (skrōō´pyə ləs) *adj.* thoroughly attentive to even the smallest details; precise

---

8. *Djata* (dyä´ tə) is a shortened form of Sundiata.

Dialogue *What does Nana Triban wish to convey to her half-brother in the last paragraph on this page?*

Vocabulary

elude (i lōōd´) *v.* to avoid or escape, especially through cleverness or quickness

Archer Figure. Inland Delta Region, Mali. Ceramic. Height 61.9 cm. National Museum of African Art, Smithsonian Institution.

She cried worse than ever. Djata was sympathetic to all this, but he was in a hurry to know something about Sosso. Balla Fasséké understood and said, "Triban, wipe away your tears and tell your story, speak to your brother. You know that he has never thought ill of you, and besides, all that was in his destiny."

Nana Triban wiped her tears away and spoke.

"When you left Mali, my brother sent me by force to Sosso to be the wife of Soumaoro, whom he greatly feared. I wept a great deal at the beginning but when I saw that perhaps all was not lost I resigned[9] myself for the time being. I was nice to Soumaoro and was the chosen one among his numerous wives. I had my chamber in the great tower where he himself lived. I knew how to flatter him and make him jealous. Soon I became his **confidante** and I pretended to hate you, to share the hate which my mother bore you. It was said that you would come back one day, but I swore to him that you would never have the presumption[10] to claim a kingdom you had never possessed, and that you had left never to see Mali again. However, I was in constant touch with Balla Fasséké, each of us wanting to pierce the mystery of Soumaoro's magic power. One night I took the bull by the horns and said to Soumaoro: 'Tell me, oh you whom kings mention with trembling, tell me Soumaoro, are you a man like others or are you the same as the jinn[11] who protects

9. When Nana *resigned* herself, she gave in without resistance or complaint.
10. Here, *presumption* means "excessive boldness."
11. In Islamic mythology, a *jinn*, or genie, is an angel-like spirit that has magical powers and can take on other forms.

Vocabulary

confidante (kon´fə dant´) *n.* a person who is entrusted with secrets or private affairs humans? No one can bear the glare of your eyes, your arm has the strength of ten arms. Tell me, king of kings, tell me what jinn protects you so that I can worship him also.' These words filled him with pride and he himself boasted to me of the might of his Tana. That very night he took me into his magic chamber and told me all.

"Then I redoubled my zeal to show myself faithful to his cause, I seemed more overwhelmed than him. It was even he who went to the extent of telling me to take courage, that nothing was yet lost. During all this time, in complicity[12] with Balla Fasséké, I was preparing for the inevitable flight. Nobody watched over me any more in the royal enclosure, of which I knew the smallest twists and turns. And one night when Soumaoro was away, I left that fearsome tower. Balla Fasséké was waiting for me at the gate to which I had the key. It was thus, brother, that we left Sosso."

Balla Fasséké took up the story.

"We hastened to you. The news of the victory of Tabon made me realize that the lion had burst his chains. Oh son of Sogolon, I am the word and you are the deed, now your destiny begins."

Sundiata was very happy to recover his sister and his griot. He now had the singer who would **perpetuate** his memory by his words. There would not be any heroes if

deeds were condemned to man's forget-fulness, for we ply our trade to excite the admiration of the living, and to evoke the veneration[13] of those who are to come.

Djata was informed that Soumaoro was advancing along the river and was trying to block his route to Mali. The preparations were complete, but before leaving Sibi, Sundiata arranged a great military review in the camp so that Balla Fasséké, by his words, should strengthen the hearts of his sofas. In the middle of a great circle formed by the sofas, Balla Fasséké extolled[14] the heroes of Mali. To the king of Tabon he said: "You whose iron arm can split ten skulls at a time, you, Tabon Wana, king of the Sinikimbon and the Djallonké,[15] can you show me what you are capable of before the great battle is joined?"

The griot's words made Fran Kamara leap up. Sword in hand and mounted on his swift steed he came and stood before Sundiata and said, "Maghan Sundiata, I renew my oath to you in the sight of all the Mandingoes gath-ered together. I pledge myself to conquer or to die by your side. Mali will be free or the smiths[16] of Tabon will be dead."

The tribes of Tabon shouted their approval, brandishing their weapons, and Fran Kamara, stirred by the shouts of the sofas, spurred his charger and charged forward. The warriors opened their ranks and he bore down on a great mahogany tree. With one stroke of his sword he split the giant tree just as one splits a paw-paw.[17] The flabbergasted army shouted, "Wassa Wassa . . . Ayé . . . "

Then, coming back to Sundiata, his sword held aloft, the king of Tabon said, "Thus on

---

12. People acting *in complicity* are involved together, as accomplices in a crime or, as here, in secret activities.

Acts of Courage *What risks does Nana Triban take while staying with Soumaoro? What does the epic imply about how one should act in times of danger?*

Dialogue *What do you think Balla Fasséké means by his remark beginning "I am the word"?*

13. To *evoke veneration* is to call up feelings of deep respect.
14. Balla highly praised (*extolled*) the heroes.
15. *Sinikimbon* (si′ nē kim′ bōn); *Djallonké* (jä lôn′ kā)
16. The *Mandingoes* were various peoples who inhabited the upper and middle Niger River valley. *Smiths* make or repair metal objects, such as swords, but Fran Kamara is speaking figuratively, referring to his sword-bearing troops.
17. *Paw-paw* is a banana-like fruit.

Seated Figure, 13th century. Terracotta, height: 10 in. Purchase, Buckeye Trust and Mr. and Mrs. Milton Rosenthal Gifts, Joseph Pulitzer Bequest and Harris Brisbane Dick and Rogers Funds, 1981. The Metropolitan Museum of Art, New York, NY.

the Niger plain will the smiths of Tabon cleave those of Sosso in twain."[18] And the hero came and fell in beside Sundiata.

Turning towards Kamandjan, the king of Sibi and cousin of the king of Tabon, Balla Fasséké said, "Where are you, Kamandjan, where is Fama Djan? Where is the king of the Dalikimbon Kamaras? Kamandjan of Sibi, I salute you. But what will I have to relate of you to future generations?"

Before Balla had finished speaking, the king of Sibi, shouting his war cry, started his fiery charger off at full gallop. The sofas, stupefied, watched the extraordinary horseman head for the mountain that dominates[19] Sibi. . . . Suddenly a tremendous din filled the sky, the earth trembled under the feet of the sofas and a cloud of red dust covered the mountain. Was this the end of the world? . . . But slowly the dust cleared and the sofas saw Kamandjan coming back holding a fragment of a sword. The mountain of Sibi, pierced through and through, disclosed a wide tunnel!

Admiration was at its highest pitch. The army stood speechless and the king of Sibi, without saying a word, came and fell in beside Sundiata.

Balla Fasséké mentioned all the chiefs by name and they all performed great feats; then the army, confident in its leadership, left Sibi. ❧

---

18. To *cleave in twain* is to split in two.
19. The mountain *dominates* Sibi because it towers over it.

Dialogue *Why does Balla Fasséké ask the question, "But what will I have to relate of you to future generations?"?*

Identify Genre *What characteristic of epics can you identify in this column?*

After You Read

Respond and Think Critically

1. **Connect to Personal Experience** Which aspect of the story seemed most realistic to you? Why?

2. **Summarize Events** In your own words, summarize what Sundiata first plans to do in order to defeat Soumaoro. Later, what does he do before leaving Sibi? What do his methods suggest about him as a leader?

3. **Make Inferences About Characters** What knowledge of human nature does Balla Fasséké reveal through his speeches?

4. **Draw Conclusions About Character** Why do you think Sundiata has such a strong desire to be remembered by future generations? Support your conclusion with evidence from the text.

5. **Big Idea** **Draw Conclusions About Ideas** At one point, the narrator of the story says, "There would not be any heroes if deeds were condemned to man's forgetfulness." What does this statement say about the relationship between heroes and memory? Support your response with text evidence.

6. **Draw Conclusions About Contemporary Context** Does our society today have any methods comparable to Balla Fasséké's for making people famous? Explain.

Literary Element Dialogue

In this epic, **dialogue** helps to advance the plot and to develop the characters. Dialogue brings characters to life by showing what they are thinking and feeling as they react to other characters.

7. **Clarify Dialogue** What astonishing deeds do Fran Kamara and Kamandjan perform at the urging of Balla Fasséké? Why do Balla Fasséké's words cause the warriors to react as they do?

8. **Make Inferences About Characterization** Why do you think Nana Triban mentions that she "knew how to flatter [Soumaoro] and make him jealous"? From her words, what impressions do you have of Nana Triban? Explain.

9. **Analyze Figurative Language** What does the king of Tabon mean when he says, "Thus on the Niger plain will the smiths of Tabon cleave those of Sosso in twain"? Explain.

Review: Epic

As you learned on page 881, **epics** have extraordinary heroes. Epics blend myths, legends, and history, reflecting the values of the cultural and historical context in which they originate. Although a king named Sundiata played an important role in establishing Mali as a powerful state, the *Sundiata* is not a historical account of his rule. Instead, Sundiata functions as the **epic hero**, someone of high social standing whose fate affects the destiny of his people. Epic plots typically involve supernatural events, long periods of time, distant journeys, and life-and-death struggles between good and evil. Many epics, such as the *Sundiata*, have uncertain authorship and arise, usually through oral storytelling, from the collective experiences of a people.

10. **Partner Activity** Work with a partner to answer the following questions. Listen actively and effectively to your partner's ideas.

- What extraordinary qualities make Sundiata an epic hero?

- Why do you think epics are important in many cultural and historical contexts?

Identify Genre

Kings and other leaders in Mali employed griots, or oral poets, to recite the *Sundiata,* their nation's epic. Review the chart you made on page 919 and answer the following questions.

11. Identify three exaggerated or fantastic details in this epic. Which detail did you consider most entertaining or inspiring? Explain.

12. From the cultural and historical context of this epic, what traits or qualities would you say the Mandingo people valued in a person?

Vocabulary Practice

Practice with Connotation and Denotation
A word's **denotation** is its dictionary meaning; its **connotations** are the emotional associations it evokes. For example, the words *delighted* and *euphoric* have a similar denotation, "a positive emotional feeling," but *euphoric* has a stronger connotation.

Work with a partner to complete a graphic organizer like the one below for each bold-faced vocabulary word. Include the vocabulary word in one box and a word that has a similar denotation in another. Then explain which of the two words has the stronger connotation.

scrupulous   elude   confidante   perpetuate

EXAMPLE:

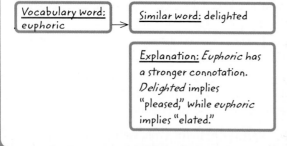

Vocabulary word: euphoric

Similar word: delighted

Explanation: *Euphoric* has a stronger connotation. *Delighted* implies "pleased," while *euphoric* implies "elated."

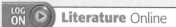
LOG ON ▶ **Literature** Online

Selection Resources For Selection Quizzes, eFlashcards, and Reading-Writing Connection activities, go to glencoe.com and enter QuickPass code GL57805u5.

Enrich and Extend

 Speaking and Listening

Debate The *Sundiata* tells the story of an epic hero and his larger-than-life deeds. Do you think that Sundiata as a leader of the people is more heroic than leaders from the recent past or the present day, such as Dr. Martin Luther King Jr. or Nelson Mandela? Divide into two teams to conduct a debate on this question. Use evidence from the text and real life examples to support your argument.

Teamwork To participate productively in your group, listen to others, build on their ideas, and contribute relevant information. You can avoid conflict by setting up ground rules up front for making decisions and building consensus.

Prepare Work with your group to create a list of arguments that support your side of the issue. Organize your arguments and evidence in a chart like the one shown to make sure you include all the important points.

Argument	Evidence
Sundiata inspires his warriors to perform superhuman feats.	Fran Kamara splits a giant tree; Kamandjan carves out a tunnel through a mountain.

Debate During the debate, use comprehension skills to listen attentively, effectively, and critically to your team members' points so you can build on them when it is your turn to speak. Interpret each speaker's message and identify the position taken and the evidence presented in support of that position. Also listen to the opposing team's arguments so you can challenge them with counterarguments and evidence. When you speak, use effective and interesting language and appropriate eye contact, body movements, and vocal tones.

Evaluate Write one paragraph evaluating your team's performance and that of your opponents. Consider the preparation and delivery of the arguments.

Visual Perspective
on *Sundiata*

THE LION OF MALI

FROM *SUNDIATA: A LEGEND OF AFRICA*
retold by Will Eisner

National Book Award Winner

TEKS

For pages 927–930

10.5 Understand, make inferences and draw conclusions about the structure and elements of fiction and provide evidence from text to support understanding.

Set a Purpose for Reading

Read to discover similarities and differences between the graphic-novel and traditional prose versions of the tale of Sundiata.

Build Background

The tale of Sundiata is based on the real monarch who established the West African empire of Mali. According to oral tradition, he had eleven brothers, all of whom were killed by Sumanguru. Sundiata, who was ill and weak, was spared. Will Eisner, an acclaimed comic and graphic-novel artist, depicts the beginning of Sundiata's tale in this graphic-novel version of "The Lion of Mali."

Reading Strategy

Compare and Contrast Versions of a Story

There are many different versions of the tale of Sundiata. When you **compare and contrast versions,** you identify similarities and differences between them. When the same story is presented in varying genres, the structure of the text can affect how the story is conveyed. The graphic novel has many structural elements that are not part of traditional prose, such as the arrangement of panels to show time passing, speech bubbles for dialogue and narration, and the ability to show visual aspects of the story through illustration. As you read, think about how literary elements such as plot, setting, and characters are conveyed in each excerpt, and ask yourself how they are affected by the structure of each text. Use a Venn diagram like the one below to help you keep track of similarities and differences.

Prose Version — Similarities — Graphic Novel

WHAT CAN WE DO NOW? WE ARE OUT-NUMBERED!

SO AS SUMANGURU'S WARRIORS ENTERED THE VALLEY THEY WERE MET BY ONLY HALF OF THE MALI.

...WHO PRETENDED TO FLEE WHILE SUMANGURU'S MEN PURSUED THEM INTO THE VALLEY...

WHERE THEY WERE ATTACKED FROM ABOVE.

THEY WERE TRAPPED

SUMANGURU'S BEST FIGHTERS TURNED AND FLED

OH, LOOK, SUMANGURU! THE MEN OF MALI ARE WINNING THE BATTLE!

Respond and Think Critically

1. **Summarize Plot Events** Write a brief summary of the story told in this graphic novel before you answer the following questions. For help on writing a summary, see page 35.

2. **Indetify Genre** What characteristics of legends are demonstrated in this retelling of the tale of Sundiata?

3. **Analyze Simile** What are two examples of simile in this excerpt? How do the illustrations reinforce the meaning of the similes?

4. **Make Inferences About Characterization** In a graphic novel, characterization occurs in part through the drawings of the characters. Based on his illustrations, what feeling might Eisner intend the reader to have toward Sumanguru? Explain.

5. **Draw Conclusions About Structure** Refer to the Venn diagram you made on page 927. What are the similarities and differences between the two versions of *Sundiata*? What are the pros and cons of using a graphic novel structure to retell a legend? Support your conclusion.

PART 2

Rescuing and Conquering

The Life Line, 1884. Homer, Winslow. Oil on canvas, 28.62 x 44.75 in. Philadelphia Museum of Art, PA.

View the Art Some of Homer's paintings depict scenes from the English fishing village of Cullercoats on the North Sea. He created images of the sea and humans' attempts to deal with the uncontrollable elements of nature. What does Homer's painting suggest about rescuing and conquering?

BIG IDEA

Leaders and warriors may use their strength to rescue allies and conquer enemies. But often strength is not enough. The tales in Part 2 tell of heroes who use their brains and bravery in rescues and conquests—and sometimes outwit themselves. As you read these myths and folktales, ask yourself, How do the heroes' intelligence and other personal qualities contribute to these rescues and conquests?

TEKS

For pages 932–933

10.2.B Analyze archetypes in mythic, traditional and classical literature.

LITERARY FOCUS

Oral Tradition and Myth

What are the elements of folktales and myths?

Joseph Campbell devoted his career to the study and teaching of world myths and oral traditions. He once said: "Read myths. They teach you that you can turn inward, and you begin to get the message of the symbols." In the passage from a myth below, the king of the giants has stolen Thor's hammer, which is Thor's protector. The Norse gods meet in council to plan how to get the hammer back.

from *The Stealing of Thor's Hammer*

by Brian Branston

Such a serious situation had to be made known to Odin. At once, he called a council meeting of all the Æsir and without delay they sat in deliberation upon their judgement stools. "Who's the first with any ideas?" asked Odin.

Tyr suggested an armed invasion of Jotunheim. Niord agreed, saying it should be an attack by sea and land and air with the Valkyries on their flying horses spear-heading the aerial battalions.

Loki said, "I can tell you this: a direct attack will be useless. Let me remind you of the magic spells employed by the giant king to frustrate Thor in the past. Even if an attack was successful, the hammer would still lie hidden. There is only one way to get it back and that is to trick King Loki of Outgard into producing it."

Thor's Fight with the Giants, 1872. Marten Eskil Winge. Oil on canvas, 484 x 333 cm. National Museum, Stockholm, Sweden.

Archetypes

Archetypes are characters, images, plot patterns, or themes that are common to human experience across cultures and throughout time. Archetypes originated in the oral tradition, but now appear in many written works of literature, including myths and folktales. A **character archetype** is a familiar individual, such as the trickster or the damsel in distress. An **image archetype** is an object or a place that has universal symbolism. For example, a cup often represents one's lot in life. **Plot pattern archetypes** are basic, familiar story outlines that recur across time and place, such as the hero's quest. **Theme archetypes** are universal ideas, such as *good can overcome evil*.

Oral Tradition

A culture's **oral tradition** includes stories and other oral transmissions that preserve the culture's history, ancestry, and literature. Although writing allows a story to be remembered unchanged, oral transmission allows a story to evolve for the benefit of each generation of listeners. Oral tradition includes myths and folktales.

Folktale

A **folktale** is a traditional story that has been passed down orally long before being written down. Animal stories, trickster stories, fairy tales, myths, and legends are all included in the larger category of folktales. A **tall tale** is a kind of folktale in which the fantastic adventures and amazing feats of folk heroes are wildly exaggerated, but the realistic local settings and tone suggest that the exaggerations are true.

John Henry told his Captain,
Man ain't nothing but a man,
And 'fore I'll let that steam drill beat me down
I'll die with this hammer in my hand,
Die with this hammer in my hand.

—Zora Neale Hurston, *from "John Henry"*

Myth

Myths are traditional stories that deal with gods, heroes, and supernatural forces. They may offer role models, try to explain the natural world, or suggest the beliefs, customs, or ideals of a society.

He [Theseus] steadfastly refused, therefore, the ship his mother and grandfather urged on him, telling them that to sail on it would be a contemptible flight from danger, and he set forth to go to Athens by land. The journey was long and very hazardous because of the bandits that beset the road. He killed them all, however; he left not one alive to trouble future travelers. His idea of dealing justice was simple, but effective: what each had done to others, Theseus did to him.

—Edith Hamilton, *from "Theseus"*

Quickwrite

Analyze Archetypes In a few sentences, explain how each of the quoted text examples on pages 932–933 illustrates an archetype. Compile your findings in a chart like the one below. Then, as you read the full text of these works in this part, analyze the effects these archetypes have on the texts.

Text	Archetype
"The Stealing of Thor's Hammer"	
"John Henry"	
"Theseus"	

Before You Read

The Stealing of Thor's Hammer

Meet **Brian Branston**
(born 1914)

How many writers do you know who have visited the most remote, inaccessible corners of the world, including Iceland, Greenland, and the Great Barrier Reef? How many writers have ridden the Great Rapids of the Orinoco River in South America—in a hovercraft? British writer Brian Branston, author of "The Stealing of Thor's Hammer," has done these things and more, including traveling in a dugout canoe in search of the Yanamamo Indians in Brazil. Branston, working in the Travel and Exploration unit for the British Broadcasting Corporation (BBC), traveled to remote locations all over the world to capture them on film.

For 25 years, Branston also wrote many books on mythology. In *Gods & Heroes from Viking Mythology* (1978), he brings Viking myths to life with vivid descriptions.

> "*Our forefathers of fifteen hundred years ago . . . were not creatures apart, different from the birds, plants, or animals.*"
>
> —Brian Branston

Seafaring Warriors Viking mythology (also called Norse or Scandinavian mythology) encompasses stories from four countries: Iceland, Norway, Sweden, and Denmark. The Vikings are most familiar to modern readers as seafaring warriors.

The Vikings were not merely fearsome, unimaginative brutes, however. The long, dark

Thor with a hammer. Bronze. National Museum of Iceland, Reykjavik.

Scandinavian winters were conducive to storytelling. Viking storytellers tried to make sense of their world with its dark forests and forbidding mountains. Their mythology makes use of natural elements familiar in that northern landscape, such as volcanoes and bears.

Viking mythology is based on several gods: Odin (the One-Eyed Allfather, also known as Woden or Wotan), Thor (god of thunder), Tyr (god of war and treaties), and Frey and Freya (god and goddess of fertility). On a plain called Ida, these gods built the city of Asgard, which had twelve realms the highest being Valhalla, where the heroic went after death.

Influences of Mythology Traces of Viking mythology are still found in the English language, music, and literature today. For example, the Viking gods gave their names to the days of the week: Tuesday (Tyr), Wednesday (Woden), Thursday (Thor), and Friday (Frey). J. R. R. Tolkien drew heavily from these stories to create his *Lord of the Rings* trilogy. Composer Richard Wagner used the myths in his "Rings of the Nibelung" opera cycle. The archetypal plots and characters of these stories give them lasting appeal.

Literature Online

Author Search For more about Brian Branston, go to glencoe.com and enter QuickPass code GL57805u5.

Literature and Reading Preview

Connect to the Myth

Which is more important in resolving a conflict: physical strength or cunning? In a small group, discuss the pros and cons of mental and physical strength.

Build Background

In Viking mythology, the Norse god Thor is known as the strongest of the gods but not the smartest. Armed with the hammer Mjollnir, he defends the gods against their enemies. When Thor throws his hammer, it creates lightning.

Set Purposes for Reading

Big Idea Rescuing and Conquering

As you read, ask yourself, Why is it so important for the characters to retrieve Thor's hammer?

Literary Element Plot Pattern Archetype

Plot pattern archetypes are story elements and themes common to a wide variety of cultures and stories. An example of a plot pattern archetype is characters fooling dangerous and powerful enemies. As you read, ask yourself, What are some possible plot pattern archetypes in the story?

Reading Strategy Make Inferences About Characters

When you **make inferences about characters,** you make assumptions about characters based on your reason and experience and on how they act and on how the author describes them. As you read, ask yourself, How does the author use description, narration, and dialogue to reveal information about the characters?

....

Tip: Create a Web Use a web like the one below to record the inferences you draw about one of the main characters in this myth. Use the blue highlighted passages and questions to help you.

TEKS

For pages 934–942

10.2.B Analyze archetypes (e.g., journey of a hero) in mythic, traditional and classical literature.

Vocabulary

disdainful (dis dān′fəl) *adj.* scornful; mocking; p. 936 *The senator held a disdainful view of the opposing candidate.*

aggrieved (ə grēvd′) *adj.* disturbed; upset; p. 936 *The aggrieved customer got a refund.*

guile (gīl) *n.* cunning; p. 937 *The spy used guile to outsmart the guards.*

deliberation (di lib′ə rā′shən) *n.* an official meeting or consultation; p. 939 *The town leaders decided that deliberation was necessary.*

jubilantly (jōō′bə lənt lē) *adv.* joyfully or happily; p. 940 *The bride and groom walked jubilantly down the aisle together.*

....

Tip: Word Usage Always select words carefully, keeping their specific usage in mind. For example, you might not use the word *jubilantly* if you are merely pleased.

The Stealing of Thor's Hammer

Brian Branston

Thor, 1911. Arthur Rackham. In Wagner's 'The Reingold & the Valkyrie.'

T he god Thor always resented the **disdainful** way he had been treated by King Loki of Outgard.[1] He was quite determined that one day he would get his own back. Then a dreadful thing happened which made him fear that revenge might prove impossible: his hammer was stolen!

One evening he had retired as usual after a hearty supper in his palace of Bilskirnir and in an unusually tidy mood he placed his shoes together neatly, folded his clothes and laid his hammer on the table next to his pillow before getting into bed beside Sif.[2]

Daylight was squeezing through the gaps in the shutters and the dawn chorus of birdsong was pealing in from the countryside when Thor awoke from a disturbing dream. He fancied in his sleep that a thief had crept into the bedroom and had stolen the one sure protection the gods had against the giants— his hammer. Half awake, he fumbled a hand out of the sheets and felt along the top of the bedside table. It was empty.

He sat up in bed with such a jolt that his wife Sif was shot out onto the floor. Before she could open her mouth to protest, Thor was yelling, "My hammer! My hammer's been stolen! Æsir![3] Elves! Quick! Wait! No! Yes! Who's stolen my hammer? LOKI! LOKEE … !" and his red hair and beard tossed about in all directions as he wrathfully dragged on his clothes. He absent-mindedly picked the **aggrieved**

---

1. *King Loki* (lō′kē) is the king of the giants in Norse mythology. *Outgard* is the name of his home. *King Loki* is not to be confused with *Loki*, the fire god.
2. *Sif* (sif) is the wife of Thor and the Norse goddess of fertility and crops.
3. *Æsir* (a′zir) is another name for the group made up of the principal Norse gods.

Sif off the floor and put her back into bed, by which time Loki[4] had come running up panting.

"You had anything to do with this, Loki?" bellowed Thor.

"What, what … ?" gasped Loki as Thor gripped him by the scruff.

"My hammer—have you stolen it?"

"No, no, no," stammered Loki. "Only one lot dare do that, and you don't need me to tell you who they are. The giants!"

"Come on then!" cried Thor, "My chariot—you are coming with me to Jotunheim[5] to get it back!" and he started to drag Loki downstairs to the stables.

"Stop!" shouted Loki. "Do have the sense to stop! Can't you see that's just what the giants want? Without your hammer you'd be killed. We need stealth here. We need **guile**."

"Well, you're the one for that," replied Thor, simmering down, "What do you suggest?"

The upshot was that Loki volunteered to borrow Freya's[6] feather coat and fly as a hawk into Jotunheim to find out if possible what had happened to Thor's hammer. He winged his way swiftly over the ocean to the shores of Jotunheim and across the tops of the towering forest trees towards the mountains and the stronghold of King Loki.

From a distance he saw the king sitting on the gravemound of his ancestors just outside the city walls. There was a rune-carved stone commemorating the dead giants who were sitting upright in their high seats below in the mound waiting for the Ragnarok.[7] Loki flew to the top of the tall stone and perched there. King Loki of Outgard was amusing himself plaiting[8] gold leashes for his hunting dogs and trimming the manes of his horses. He glanced up.

"It's Loki, isn't it?" he asked.

"Yes," replied the hawk, "you are quite right, of course."

"How goes it with the Æsir, and how with the elves? Very well, I trust?"

"The elves are upset and the Æsir worse. Someone has stolen Thor's hammer."

"And who's the culprit?" asked King Loki of Outgard.

"You are, your gigantic majesty," answered the Mischief Maker at which the giant let out such an exploding guffaw of cruel laughter that his horses shied in fear and his hounds cringed in terror.

"There's no use pretending with a clever fellow like you," he said. "You are quite right. I *have* stolen Thor's hammer; and the Thundering Nuisance will only get it back on conditions."

"What conditions?"

"Don't think the hammer can be regained by force. It can't. I have buried it deep in the earth, seven leagues[9] down. Only one thing will redeem it. You must bring me the goddess Freya to be my wife!"

---

4. Here, *Loki* refers to the god of fire and mischief, not to be confused with King Loki.

5. *Jotunheim* (yo'toon ham') is one of the nine worlds in Norse mythology and the realm of the giants. *Jotun* is another word for *giant*.

6. *Freya* (frā'ə) is the Norse goddess of fertility and love.

Make Inferences About Characters *From what you have read so far, what can you infer about Thor's personality?*

Vocabulary

guile (gīl) *n.* cunning

---

7. *Ragnarok* is the climactic final battle between the gods in Norse mythology.

8. *Plaiting* (plāt'ing) means "braiding."

9. One *league* (lēg) is equal to about three miles.

Make Inferences About Characters *What qualities does King Loki possess? Which quality might allow him to be tricked?*

Donar-Thor (detail), School wall Chart. Colour print after a painting by Max Koch. No. 4 of Series, 1905. Sagenbilder, Leipzig.

View the Art This print shows a powerful Thor brandishing his hammer while riding in a chariot. How does this image compare with Branston's description of Thor?

Thor was dragging him to Freya's palace, bursting into it without any politeness or ceremony.

"Here's your feather coat, dear Freya," said Thor, "thanks for the loan of it. Now hurry up please and find yourself a bride's veil."

"A bride's veil?" asked Freya, surprised.

"Who's getting married?"

"You are," said Thor.

"I?" exclaimed Freya beginning to get angry, "to whom, pray? Or is it a secret?"

"It's no secret," said the simple Thor, "to Loki of Outgard, of course."

Freya's lovely breasts rose with such fury that her famous necklace Brisingamen snapped apart and the precious jewels scattered across the marble floor. She picked up the nearest weapon to hand, a distaff,[11] and started to belabor[12] Loki, shouting, "I shan't, I shan't, I shan't!" It was no use trying to reason with her. She flatly refused to marry any giant even though he was a king.

Such a serious situation had to be made known to Odin.[13] At once, he called a council meeting of all the Æsir and without

Loki made no reply but flew straight back to Asgard[10] and before he could alight Thor was asking him for news.

"Tell me at once, before you perch," he cried, "have you found out where my hammer is?"

The Mischief Maker explained precisely all he knew and told the terms necessary for retrieving the hammer. He had scarcely taken off the feather coat when

---

10. *Asgard* (as′gärd′) is another of the nine worlds and the realm where the gods live.

11. A *distaff* (dis′taf) is a pole used to hold wool for spinning.
12. To *belabor* (bi la′bər) is to strike or hit.
13. *Odin* is a Norse god of war. He is also the god of poets.

Plot Pattern Archetypes *What universal plot elements do you recognize so far in this story?*

delay they sat in **deliberation** upon their judgement stools. "Who's first with any ideas?" asked Odin.

Tyr suggested an armed invasion of Jotunheim. Niord[14] agreed, saying it should be an attack by sea and land and air with the Valkyries[15] on their flying horses spear-heading the aerial battalions.

Loki said, "I can tell you this: a direct attack will be useless. Let me remind you of the magic spells employed by the giant king to frustrate Thor in the past. Even if an attack was successful, the hammer would still lie hidden. There is only one way to get it back and that is to trick King Loki of Outgard into producing it."

Heimdall,[16] the whitest and sometimes the wisest of the gods, said he had an idea.

"If we were to dress Thor himself up as a bride and send Loki disguised as a handmaid to do the talking, then once the hammer is brought out Thor can snatch it up and—hey presto!—heads will roll!"

"Jumping Jormungander!"[17] shouted Thor, foaming at the mouth. "Vexatious Vergelmir![18] Nobody dresses me up as a woman!"

But it was no use Thor's continuing to protest. Heimdall's suggestion was voted best in the end and the Thunderer had to submit to being clothed in petticoats to hide his hairy legs and a long-sleeved blouse stuffed out a bit in the appropriate places, topped by an embroidered tunic. Brooches were pinned onto his false bust and a set of housewife's keys was set to dangle from his girdle.[19] To show he really was 'Freya', he had to wear the goddess's famous necklace, now repaired, Brisingamen. And to complete the disguise he was draped to the waist in a white bride's veil. Loki in turn was dressed up as a woman, a rather saucy[20] lady's maid.

Thor's goats[21] were led from the stable and harnessed to the chariot. "Come on there, Toothgnasher! Gee up, Toothgrinder!" he shouted and cracked his whip while the smile vanished from Loki's lips as he nearly slipped out of the back. In a flash of lightning they were halfway across the sky.

In Jotunheim King Loki of Outgard heard the thunder of the chariot wheels and he called out to his servants to strew the carved wooden settles with cushions and goat skins to make them comfortable, to broach the sparkling, foamy ale, to set up the trestle tables and prepare the wedding feast for him and his new bride the lovely, the delectable, the incomparable Freya. He rubbed his gigantic hands with satisfaction as he thought of all his possessions, of the gold-horned oxen with jet black hides thronging his paddocks, of his horses and hounds, his hunting hawks, of the gold and jewels in his iron-bound

---

14. *Niord* is the Norse god of the sea.
15. *Valkyries* (val kēr′ēs) are Odin's twelve handmaidens, who ride onto the battlefield on winged horses to take souls of the brave to Valhalla, one of the nine realms.
16. *Heimdall* (hīm dəl) is the watchman of the gods; he possesses keen eyesight and hearing, as well as the ability to see the future.
17. The *Jormungander* is Loki's son, a mighty serpent that encircles the Earth.
18. *Vexatious* (vek sā′shēs) means "troublesome." *Vergelmir* is a spring in Norse mythology that was instrumental in forming the first giants.

Rescuing and Conquering *Why might the gods decide against attacking King Loki directly?*

Vocabulary

deliberation (di lib′ə rā′shən) *n.* an official meeting or consultation

19. Thor's female costume includes *petticoats* (pet′ē kōts′), which are decorative feminine undergarments; a *tunic* (tōō′nik), which is a long, loose shirt; and a *girdle* (gurd′əl), which here means "a wide belt." He is also wearing a set of *housewife's keys*. Women in Scandinavian cultures ruled the household and, therefore, held the keys to the house.
20. *Saucy* (sô′sē) means "spirited."
21. Thor drove a chariot pulled by two *goats*.

coffers;[22] he seemed to need only one thing to complete his happiness—the goddess Freya.

By the time the 'bride' and her 'lady's maid' had arrived it was early evening and the banquet was ready.

The bride was placed on King Loki's right hand and the maid on his left. The giant was very surprised when, during the feasting, the bride had no difficulty in despatching a whole ox, eight fine salmon and all the dainties intended for the lady giants. He was even more astonished to see this mountain of food washed down with three firkins of mead—and a firkin holds nine gallons! "I don't think I ever saw a giant maiden with such a thirst or such an appetite," he said. "It *is* unusual," said the cunning lady's maid, "but you have to remember that when Freya knew she was going to marry you . . . " and here Loki was forced to gulp as he thought of the thumping lie he was about to tell, "she was so excited, your majesty, that she couldn't eat for a week. Not a morsel passed her lovely lips. When we arrived here she was ravenous."[23]

"You can say that again," muttered King Loki. He was getting impatient and wanted to steal a kiss from the bride so he lifted a corner of her veil.

> ## And the giant king's hair almost stood on end at the sight of the flashing eyes he saw there in the lacy shadows.

Loki was petrified. And the giant king's hair almost stood on end at the sight of the flashing eyes he saw there in the lacy shadows. Handmaid Loki hastened to tell him not to worry, Freya's eyes were rather red because she had not been able to sleep for a week before coming to Outgard.

At last King Loki of Outgard called for the marriage to be solemnized[24] in the traditional way by the bride and groom swearing their vows on Thor's hammer. The hammer was fetched from its hiding-place and laid on the bride's lap while the happy pair placed their hands on it and swore to be true to each other.

Thor's hand was underneath and when he felt Mullicrusher[25] within his grasp once more all his confidence returned. He did not bother to throw off his veil. With one great lunge he felled his old enemy the giant king.

Then the pair of imposters strode out of the hall, mounted the chariot and rattled **jubilantly** back to Asgard again. ❧

---

22. *Settles* (set′əls) are large wooden benches or seats. Here, to *broach* (brōch) means "to open." *Paddocks* (pad′əks) are fields where horses graze, and *coffers* (kô′fərs) are chests or boxes used to store valuables.
23. *Ravenous* (rav′ə nəs) means "very hungry."

Plot Pattern Archetypes *Based on stories you have read or heard before, what might happen next between the fake bride and the eager groom?*

---

24. When a marriage is *solemnized* (sol′ əm nīzd ′), it is formally established.
25. *Mullicrusher* (mə lē′ crə shər) is the nickname the author uses for Thor's hammer.

Rescuing and Conquering *Why do you think Thor's confidence returns when he grasps his hammer?*

Vocabulary

jubilantly (joo′bə lənt lē) *adv.* joyfully or happily

After You Read

Respond and Think Critically

1. **Connect to Personal Experience** What is your view of Norse heroes and villains after reading this myth? How did the events of the story influence your view?

2. **Make Inferences About Characters** Who does Thor initially suspect of stealing his hammer? What does this suspicion indicate about their relationship?

3. **Interpret Events** What course of action do Tyr and Niord suggest? If their suggestions had been followed, how would this story have changed?

4. **Examine Characters** How would you describe the role of females in this story? How does this role pertain to Thor dressing up as a bride? Support your response with text evidence.

5. **Make Inferences About Cultural Context** Explain Loki's role in this story. What does the prominence of such a character in a heroic myth suggest about the values of the Norse people?

6. **Big Idea** **Draw Conclusions About Genre** Thor went to extreme and comic measures to retrieve his hammer. Why does this myth cast the thunder god in such a role? What does Thor's story suggest about the gods' personalities and about the importance placed on recovering stolen items? Support your response with text evidence.

Literary Element Plot Pattern Archetype

The plot of a story that seems familiar may incorporate **plot pattern archetypes.**

The archetype of a stolen item being recovered through trickery is central to "The Stealing of Thor's Hammer."

7. **Summarize Plot Patterns** List the major plot points from this myth. What other stories have a similar plot pattern?

8. **Make Inferences About Archetypes** Why do you think the archetype of stolen artifacts being recovered is used so often?

Thor's hammer amulet. Bronze. National Museum, Reykjavik, Iceland.

Review: Myth

As you learned on page 933, a **myth** is a type of literature, or genre, that reflects different cultural and historical contexts and uses gods and supernatural forces to explain a belief, a custom, a force of nature, or some aspect of human behavior. The gods in myths have established roles and use tools that help them perform their symbolic duties.

9. **Partner Activity** Pair up with a classmate and create a chart like the one below showing how the characteristics of "The Stealing of Thor's Hammer" define it as a myth. After you have completed your chart, discuss the cultural and historical context of this myth with your partner. What can you conclude about the Viking culture based on the myth? Listen actively and effectively to your partner's ideas.

Characteristics of Myth	Examples
Explains a force of nature	Thor's hammer creates lightning.

Texas Test Practice (RC-10.B)

1. A reader can infer that Thor has an impulsive and vengeful nature when he:

   I. discovers that his hammer is missing.

   II. masquerades as Freya at the feast.

   III. asks Loki how to get his hammer back.

     A. I and II only

     B. I and III only

     C. II and III only

     D. I, II, and III

Vocabulary Practice

Practice with Usage Respond to these statements to help you explore the meanings of the boldfaced vocabulary words from the myth.

1. Name something you are **disdainful** of and explain why.

2. Describe an action or a situation that might cause you to feel **aggrieved.**

3. Identify a circumstance in which the use of **guile** might be a good idea.

4. Name two decisions that would require **deliberation** on your part.

5. Identify two things that you might say or shout **jubilantly.**

Academic Vocabulary

The oral tradition enabled the **transfer** *of many myths and folktales from one area of a country to another.*

Transfer is an academic word that derives from Latin. The prefix *trans-* means "across; through; over," or "so as to change completely." Using your knowledge and context clues, determine the meaning of *transfer* in the model sentence above. Check your response by consulting a dictionary. Finally, demonstrate your understanding by using each of these related words in a sentence.

a. transpire   **b.** translate   **c.** transgress

Enrich and Extend

 Speaking and Listening

Performance With a group of classmates, plan and present a multimedia theatrical production of the scene in which the Æsir sit in council to decide how to recover Thor's hammer.

Prepare Together, assign a character to each group member. Then plan how to present the scene in a way that will appeal to the rest of your class. Discuss staging (how and where actors move on the stage), any necessary props, sound effects, graphics, or images. Agree on how best to convey the humor of the scene, and what additional dialogue to add beyond that supplied by the text. Then write the dialogue for your assigned character. Make sure it conveys the character's distinctive voice. Rehearse your performance, making eye contact and using appropriate body language and tone.

Perform Present your performance to your class. Be sure that your chosen body language and tone of voice match your character, contribute to the comic effect, and grab the attention of your audience. Use props, graphics, and images.

Evaluate After the performance, get together with your group and discuss how successful your performance was and how it might have been better. Use a chart like the one below to record your group's ideas.

What worked well	What needed improvement
We got the humor across. (Audience laughed.)	At times actors were playing to the audience rather than staying "in the scene."

Vocabulary Workshop

Norse Word Origins

TEKS

10.1.A Determine the meaning of grade-level technical academic English words in multiple content areas (e.g., science, social studies) derived from Latin, Greek, or other linguistic roots and affixes.

Literature Connection The angry, noisy Thor was the Norse god of thunder. The English word *Thursday* ("Thor's day") comes from his name combined with the root *daeg* ("day").

> *"The god Thor always resented the disdainful way he had been treated by King Loki of Outgard."*
>
> —Brian Branston, from "The Stealing of Thor's Hammer"

Tracing the **word origins,** or etymology, of this word explains how this Norse name entered our language. Modern English has its roots in the language of the Anglo-Saxons who lived in England in the early Middle Ages. Viking peoples from Denmark and other Scandinavian countries later invaded and settled in England. Terms from the Vikings' Old Norse language and mythology, like *Thor*, were assimilated into English.

"The Stealing of Thor's Hammer" offers other examples of terms from Norse myths that have entered the English language and pertain to multiple content areas such as science and social studies.

This chart shows the Old Norse origins of some English words through their roots and affixes.

English Word	Old Norse Word
bylaw *n.* law regulating the internal affairs of a government body, corporation, or organization	**bylog** *n.* village law
Friday *n.* sixth day of the week	**Frigga** *n.* wife of Odin, + **daeg** *n.* day (Frigga's Day)
geyser *n.* a spring that produces jets of water	**geysa** *v.* to gush; to rush forward
Wednesday *n.* fourth day of the week	**Odin** *n.* king of the Norse gods, + **daeg** *n.* day (Odin's Day)

Word Origins

Word origins, or etymology, is the history and development of words.

Tip

To determine the meaning of an unfamiliar word in a reading passage, break the word into its parts—root, prefix, and suffix. If you recognize the root, you can probably figure out what the word means.

Practice A. Use a dictionary (printed or electronic) to match the English words below with their Old Norse roots.

1. bloom
2. law
3. reindeer

   a. log
   b. blōm
   c. hreinn + deer

B. Many Old Norse words begin with *sk, kn,* or *th* or end with *sk* or *ft.* Use a dictionary to find the origin and definition of each of the following words.

   1. loft   **2.** thrift   **3.** skirl

 Literature Online

Vocabulary For more vocabulary practice, go to glencoe.com and enter QuickPass code GL57805u5.

Before You Read

from *Theseus*

Meet **Edith Hamilton**
(1867–1963)

Throughout her life, Edith Hamilton was committed to education. As headmistress at Bryn Mawr School in Baltimore (a preparatory school for girls), she touched the lives of hundreds of students. Later in life, Hamilton brought the ancient world to life for a new generation of readers by providing the modern world with engaging editions of Greek and Roman literature.

Early Education Hamilton was born in Dresden, Germany, to an intellectual family. For most of her childhood, she was educated at her home in Fort Wayne, Indiana. From an early age, Hamilton was fascinated with Greek and Roman literature, and she began studying Latin with her father when she was only seven years old. She also studied French, German, and Greek.

> "To be able to be caught up into the world of thought—that is educated."
>
> —Edith Hamilton

Scholar and Teacher Hamilton left home to attend a girls' finishing school at age sixteen. She next attended Bryn Mawr College and received her master's degree in classics in 1894. After graduation, Hamilton and her younger sister, Alice, studied in Germany. Together, they were the first women to attend courses at the university in Munich.

After returning to the United States, Hamilton accepted an offer to serve as the first headmis-

tress of Bryn Mawr School. Hamilton was a success as a teacher and an administrator. Students enjoyed her classes (especially her senior class on the Roman poet Virgil) and admired her high standards.

A Second Career Hamilton retired from Bryn Mawr in 1922 with the intention of writing about the classics. Her friends, enthusiastic about her teachings of Greek tragedies, encouraged her to publish her works. Hamilton wrote various articles about Greek drama, which were so successful that she was encouraged to rework them as a book. As a result, she published *The Greek Way* in 1930. Hamilton went on to write numerous books and translations, including *The Roman Way* (1932), *Mythology* (1943), and *Echo of Greece* (1957).

Hamilton almost single-handedly popularized the study of the ancient world. When Hamilton died at age 95, she left behind fans worldwide who treasured her as a teacher and a writer.

 Literature Online

Author Search For more about Edith Hamilton, go to glencoe.com and enter QuickPass code GL57805u5.

Literature and Reading Preview

Connect to the Myth

How do you handle difficult choices? Write a journal entry in which you describe how you deal with challenging decisions.

Build Background

The body of stories that tell of the gods, heroes, and ceremonies of the ancient Greeks is known as Greek mythology. This mythology is a source of inspiration for contemporary writers.

Set Purposes for Reading

Big Idea Rescuing and Conquering

As you read, ask yourself, How do the opposing ideas of rescuing and conquering emerge, often side by side?

Literary Element Image Archetype

Image archetypes, or images that recur throughout literature across cultures, often have universal meaning. The stone in Greek mythology, for example, represents an obstacle in life. A cup represents one's fate or destiny. As you read, ask yourself, What archetypal images can I find?

Reading Strategy Identify Sequence

Identifying sequence in a story means recognizing the logical order of events or ideas. Events in fiction often occur in chronological order, or the order in which they happen in time. As you read, ask yourself, Where are signal words such as *first*, *there*, *following*, *during*, and *before*?

....

Tip: Annotate When you read, annotate (or take note of) time and place sequences. Watch for transitional and signal words. Write critical notes that comment on the sequences.

Signal Word	Type of Sequence	Annotation
"Aegeus went back to Athens <u>before</u> the child was born, but <u>first</u> he placed in a hollow a sword. . . ."	time and place	The words "before" and "first" signal time sequences linking key events.

TEKS

For pages 944–954

10.2.B Analyze archetypes (e.g., journey of a hero) in mythic, traditional and classical literature.

Vocabulary

contemptible (kən temp´tə bəl) *adj.* worthy of contempt; loathsome; p. 947 *The bank robbery was a contemptible act that endangered lives.*

endear (en dēr´) *v.* to cause to adore or admire; p. 948 *Writing a letter to show gratitude would endear the child to his parents' friend.*

confinement (kən fīn´mənt) *n.* the state of being restricted or confined; p. 948 *Confinement was the most dreaded punishment for the teenager.*

....

Tip: Word Parts You can find the meanings of common roots online. Choose sites associated with reputable print dictionaries or sites sponsored by respected institutions.

The Passions of Pasiphae, wife of King Minos of Crete, from the *Story of Theseus,* c.1510.
Master of the Campana Cassoni. Oil on panel, 69 x 182 cm. Musée du Petit Palais, Avignon, France.

From

THESEUS

Retold by Edith Hamilton

The great Athenian hero was Theseus. He had so many adventures and took part in so many great enterprises[1] that there grew up a saying in Athens, "Nothing without Theseus."

He was the son of the Athenian King, Aegeus. He spent his youth, however, in his mother's home, a city in southern Greece. Aegeus went back to Athens before the child was born, but first he placed in a hollow a sword and a pair of shoes and covered them with a great stone. He did this with the knowledge of his wife and told her that whenever the boy—if it was a boy—grew strong enough to roll away the stone and get the things beneath it, she could send him to Athens to claim him as his father. The child was a boy and he grew up strong far beyond others, so that when his mother finally took him to the stone he lifted it with no trouble at all. She told him then that the time had come for him to seek his father, and a ship was placed at his disposal[2] by his grandfather. But Theseus refused to go by water, because the voyage was safe and easy. His idea was to become a great hero as quickly as possible, and easy safety was certainly not the way to do that. Hercules, who was the most magnificent of all the heroes of Greece, was always in his mind, and the determination to be just as magnificent himself. This was quite natural since the two were cousins.

---

1. Here, *enterprises* are undertakings or projects of great difficulty, risk, or complication.

2. Here, *disposal* means "to use as one chooses."

Image Archetype *What might lifting a great stone typically represent?*

Theseus Discovering His Father's Sword. Reynaud Levieux. Oil on canvas.
The Cummerland Museum of Art and Gardens, Jacksonville, FL.

View the Art Theseus easily moved the large stone to discover his father's sword and shoes.
Is this how you picture the scene Hamilton describes? Why or why not?

He steadfastly refused, therefore, the ship his mother and grandfather urged on him, telling them that to sail on it would be a **contemptible** flight from danger, and he set forth to go to Athens by land. The journey was long and very hazardous because of the bandits that beset[3] the road. He killed them all, however; he left not one alive to trouble future travelers. His idea of dealing justice was simple, but effective: what each had done to others, Theseus did to him. Sciron, for instance, who had made those he captured kneel to wash his feet and then kicked them down into the sea, Theseus hurled over a precipice.[4] Sinis, who killed people by fastening them to two pine trees bent down to the ground and letting the trees go, died in that way himself. Procrustes was placed upon the iron bed which he used for his victims, tying them to it and then making them the right length for it by stretching

---

3. *Beset* means "to trouble or badger."

Vocabulary

contemptible (kən temp′tə bəl) *adj.* worthy of contempt; loathsome

---

4. A *precipice* is an extremely steep place.

Rescuing and Conquering *How does Theseus's method of justice show the ideas of rescuing and conquering?*

those who were too short and cutting off as much as was necessary from those who were too long. The story does not say which of the two methods was used in his case, but there was not much to choose between them and in one way or the other Procrustes' career ended.

It can be imagined how Greece rang with the praises of the young man who had cleared the land of these banes[5] to travelers. When he reached Athens he was an acknowledged hero and he was invited to a banquet by the King, who of course was unaware that Theseus was his son. In fact he was afraid of the young man's great popularity, thinking that he might win the people over to make him king, and he invited him with the idea of poisoning him. The plan was not his, but Medea's, the heroine of the Quest of the Golden Fleece[6] who knew through her sorcery who Theseus was. She had fled to Athens when she left Corinth in her winged car, and she had acquired great influence over Aegeus, which she did not want disturbed by the appearance of a son. But as she handed him the poisoned cup Theseus, wishing to make himself known at once to his father, drew his sword. The King instantly recognized it and dashed the cup to the ground. Medea escaped as she always did and got safely away to Asia.

Aegeus then proclaimed to the country that Theseus was his son and heir. The new heir apparent soon had an opportunity to **endear** himself to the Athenians.

Years before his arrival in Athens, a terrible misfortune had happened to the city. Minos, the powerful ruler of Crete, had lost his only son, Androgeus, while the young man was visiting the Athenian King. King Aegeus had done what no host should do, he had sent his guest on an expedition full of peril—to kill a dangerous bull. Instead, the bull had killed the youth. Minos invaded the country, captured Athens and declared that he would raze it to the ground unless every nine years the people sent him a tribute of seven maidens and seven youths. A horrible fate awaited these young creatures. When they reached Crete they were given to the Minotaur to devour.

The Minotaur was a monster, half bull, half human, the offspring of Minos' wife Pasiphaë and a wonderfully beautiful bull. Poseidon had given this bull to Minos in order that he should sacrifice it to him, but Minos could not bear to slay it and kept it for himself. To punish him, Poseidon had made Pasiphaë fall madly in love with it.

When the minotaur was born Minos did not kill him. He had Daedalus, a great architect and inventor, construct a place of **confinement** for him from which escape was impossible. Daedalus built the Labyrinth, famous throughout the world. Once inside, one would go endlessly along its twisting paths without ever finding the exit. To this place the young Athenians were each time taken and left to the Minotaur. There was no possible way to escape. In whatever direction they ran they might be running straight to the monster; if

---

5. *Banes* refers to harmful or poisonous things.
6. In Greek mythology, Jason and the Argonauts went on the *Quest of the Golden Fleece* to secure Theseus the throne.

Image Archetype *A sword in Greek mythology often represents legacy. Why is it important that Theseus establishes his legacy at this point in the story?*

Identify Sequence *What does the signal word "then" indicate at the bottom of this column?*

Vocabulary

endear (en dēr′) *v.* to cause to adore or admire
confinement (kən fīn′mənt) *n.* the state of being restricted or confined

Theseus Fighting the Minotaur. Antoine-Louis Barye, 1795–1875.
Bronze Sculpture. Mohammed Khalil Museum, Cairo.

View the Art This sculpture depicts Theseus dominating the Minotaur. What aspects of the sculpture show Theseus's strength?

told his father, however, and promised him that if he succeeded, he would have the black sail which the ship with its cargo of misery always carried changed to a white one, so that Aegeus could know long before it came to land that his son was safe.

When the young victims arrived in Crete they were paraded before the inhabitants on their way to the Labyrinth. Minos' daughter Ariadne was among the spectators and she fell in love with Theseus at first sight as he marched past her. She sent for Daedalus and told him he must show her a way to get out of the Labyrinth, and she sent for Theseus and told him she would bring about his escape if he would promise to take her back to Athens and marry her. As may be imagined, he made no difficulty about that, and she gave him the clue she had got from Daedalus, a ball of thread which he was to fasten at one end to the inside of the door and unwind as he went on. This he did and, certain that he could retrace his steps whenever he chose, he walked boldly into the maze looking for the Minotaur. He came upon him asleep and fell upon him, pinning him to the ground; and with his fists—he had no other weapon—he battered the monster to death.

they stood still he might at any moment emerge from the maze. Such was the doom which awaited fourteen youths and maidens a few days after Theseus reached Athens. The time had come for the next installment of the tribute.

At once Theseus came forward and offered to be one of the victims. All loved him for his goodness and admired him for his nobility, but they had no idea that he intended to try to kill the Minotaur. He

---

Rescuing and Conquering *How does the ball of thread reflect the idea of rescuing and conquering?*

Theseus with Ariadne and Phaedra, the Daughters of Minos, 1702.
Benedetto Gennari.

<u>View the Art</u> Hamilton claims that women often fell in love with Theseus at first sight. What artistic choices did Gennari make that allowed him to successfully depict Theseus's allure?

On the way there they put in at the island of Naxos and what happened then is differently reported. One story says that Theseus deserted Ariadne. She was asleep and he sailed away without her, but Dionysus found her and comforted her. The other story is much more favorable to Theseus. She was extremely seasick, and he set her ashore to recover while he returned to the ship to do some necessary work. A violent wind carried him out to sea and kept him there a long time. On his return he found that Ariadne had died, and he was deeply afflicted.

Both stories agree that when they drew near to Athens he forgot to hoist the white sail. Either his joy at the success of his voyage put every other thought out of his head, or his grief for Ariadne. The black sail was seen by his father, King Aegeus, from the Acropolis, where for days he had watched the sea with straining eyes. It was to him the sign of his son's death and he threw himself down from a rocky height into the sea, and was killed. The sea into which he fell was called the Aegean ever after.

So Theseus became King of Athens, a most wise and disinterested king. He declared to the people that he did not wish to rule over them; he wanted a people's government where all would be equal. He resigned his royal power and organized a commonwealth,[7] building a

As an oak tree falls on the hillside
Crushing all that lies beneath,
So Theseus. He presses out the life,
The brute's savage life,
and now it lies dead.
Only the head sways
slowly, but the horns are
useless now.

When Theseus lifted himself up from that terrific struggle, the ball of thread lay where he had dropped it. With it in his hands, the way out was clear. The others followed and taking Ariadne with them they fled to the ship and over the sea toward Athens.

7. A *commonwealth* is a political unit that gives supreme power to the common man.

Identify Sequence *How does the first sentence in this column help you understand the sequence of events?*

Theseus's Arrival in Crete, 1990. Peter Connolly. Watercolor.

council hall where the citizens should gather and vote. The only office he kept for himself was that of Commander in Chief. Thus Athens became, of all earth's cities, the happiest and most prosperous, the only true home of liberty, the one place in the world where the people governed themselves. It was for this reason that in the great War of the Seven against Thebes, when the victorious Thebans refused burial to those of the enemy who had died, the vanquished[8] turned to Theseus and Athens for help, believing that free men under such a leader would never consent to having the helpless dead wronged. They did not turn in vain. Theseus led his army against Thebes, conquered her and forced her to allow them to be buried. But when he was victor he did not return evil to the Thebans for the evil they had done. He showed himself the perfect knight. He refused to let his army enter and loot the city. He had come not to harm Thebes, but to bury the Argive dead, and that duty done he led his soldiers back to Athens.

In many other stories he shows the same qualities. He received the aged Oedipus whom everyone else had cast out. He was with him when he died, sustaining and comforting him. He protected his two helpless daughters and sent them safely home after their father's death. When Hercules in his madness killed his wife and children and upon his return to sanity determined to kill himself, Theseus alone stood by him. Hercules' other friends fled, fearing to be polluted by the presence of one who had done so horrible a deed, but Theseus gave him his hand, roused his courage, told him to die would be a coward's act, and took him to Athens. ∾

---

8. Here, *vanquished* is used as a noun and means "those overcome through battle."

Rescuing and Conquering *Explain how Theseus's actions employ both rescuing and conquering.*

After You Read

Respond and Think Critically

1. **Connect to Personal Experience** From this retelling, what are your impressions of Theseus's character?

2. **Make Inferences About Character** According to Hamilton, why did the saying "Nothing without Theseus" develop? What does this saying reflect about the main character?

3. **Explain Events** Why does Theseus refuse to seek his father by water? How does this decision affect the myth's plot?

4. **Analyze Character** How has Theseus changed by the story's conclusion? What events have led to this change, and why are they significant? **OER**

5. **Evaluate Tone** How does the author's tone reveal a lack of certainty in the myth's legacy? Does this uncertainty diminish the myth's credibility? Explain.

6. **Big Idea** **Draw Conclusions About Events** Greek mythology encompasses many acts of rescuing and conquering. Which do you think is more prevalent in "Theseus"—rescuing or conquering? Support your opinion.

7. **Analyze Influences** How has Greek mythology influenced contemporary literature and film? Support your response with examples.

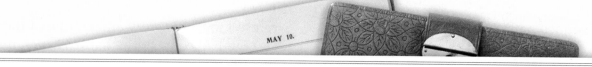

Daily Life & Culture

Pleasing the Gods

Greeks, in their daily lives, had to consider the happiness of countless gods. Pleasing the gods through daily rituals was more important than knowing exactly how many gods there were. In fact, some special altars were created specifically for worshipping potential unknown gods. The contentment of the gods was assured not through correct beliefs, but through proper action. Greek people worshipped their gods diligently and made appropriate sacrifices to them to lessen the chances of retribution.

Group Activity Discuss the following questions with your classmates.

1. The ancient Greeks were expected to keep the gods happy. How might everyday activities be affected by this responsibility? Explain.

2. In Greek mythology, what action might take place if a human displeased a god?

Jupiter. Benvenuto Cellini (1500–1571). Bronze Sculpture. Museo Nazionale del Bargello, Florence.

The use of **image archetypes** in works of mythology can help an author communicate with his or her readers. Since the meanings and importance of a work's images have already been established, the author does not have to work to make readers understand the significance of the images.

8. **Interpret Archetypes** Which image archetypes stand out most in "Theseus"? Select one that you think is true to life. Explain your choice. Use the pink highlighted questions to help you.

9. **Analyze Archetypes** How does Aegeus intend to kill Theseus? What image archetype does this represent? Explain why this archetype might have the significance it does.

10. **Evaluate Archetypes** Does the use of image archetypes in "Theseus" strengthen or weaken the plot? Explain, using text evidence to support your response.

Review: Plot Pattern Archetype

As you learned on page 935, **plot pattern archetypes** are recurring plot arrangements found across cultures in literary works.

11. **Partner Activity** Meet with a classmate to discuss the plot pattern archetypes of "Theseus." Work with your partner to create a two-column chart like the one below. Fill in the left-hand column with examples of plot pattern archetypes. Use the right-hand column to list examples of each archetype from "Theseus."

Plot Pattern Archetype	Example from Text
secret birth	Theseus is born and lives his childhood without any knowledge of who his father is.
journey of a hero	
revelation as favored heir	

Reading Strategy Identify Sequence

 Texas Test Practice (10.5)

1. Minos's son, Androgeus, is killed by a bull:

   A. a few days before Theseus first arrives in Athens.

   B. a few days after fourteen young people go to meet their doom.

   C. at about the time Theseus lifts the stone and discovers his father's sword.

   D. long before Theseus meets his father.

Vocabulary Practice

Practice with Word Parts For each boldfaced vocabulary word, use a dictionary to find the meaning of the word's root. Also look for definitions of any prefixes or suffixes in the word. List the meanings in a diagram like the one shown. Then use the word correctly in a sentence.

contemptible   endear   confinement

EXAMPLE:

objection →

Prefix:
ob-, "against, opposite"

Root:
jacere, "to throw"

Suffix:
-ion, "act of"
Sentence: My parents raised an objection to my going to the party.

Respond Through Writing

Expository Essay

Analyze Cause and Effect Hamilton retells a series of heroic episodes from the life of Theseus in a unified narrative. Choose one critical point in the life of Theseus and analyze the causes, or the causal chain of events, that lead up to it. Also explain how the effects of those events stretch beyond the life of the hero.

Purpose and Audience Your purpose is to analyze the causes that lead up to one significant point in Theseus's life and the effects that result. Your audience is your teacher and other students.

Plan Review the sequence chart you made as you read. Jot down two or more events that interest you. Then develop a cause-and-effect chain like the one below for one of those events, adding as many boxes as you need to explain the event and its results.

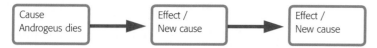

Cause
Androgeus dies → Effect /
New cause → Effect /
New cause

Draft Use a clear organizing structure for your paper that begins with an introduction to spark the reader's interest about Theseus. Present a thesis that provides an overview of the cause-and-effect relationships you will analyze. In your body paragraphs, discuss the causal chain of events in chronological order, drawing the best evidence from the text to support your claims about causes, a critical or crisis point, and effects. In your conclusion, use a graphic to summarize your points or include a restatement of your thesis.

Revise Trade papers with a partner. Ask your partner to make sure your style, word choice, sentence variety, and subtlety of meaning are appropriate for your purpose and audience. Have your partner underline any examples of figurative language or rhetorical devices you used that are unclear and recommend improvements. Your partner should make sure that any information and evidence you have included is relevant and that your inferences are valid. Revise by substituting stronger evidence or by making clearer connections between your claims and evidence.

Edit Edit your paper for proper voice, syntax, tense, and other standard English conventions. Correct any errors in grammar, spelling, and punctuation. Use the Grammar Tip in the side column to help you use transitional expressions. If you wrote your paper by hand, make sure your writing is legible.

 TEKS

10.15.A.i–v Write an analytical essay of sufficient length that includes effective introductory and concluding paragraphs and a variety of sentence structures; rhetorical devices, and transitions between paragraphs; a thesis; an organizing structure; and relevant evidence and well-chosen details.

> **Grammar Tip**

Transitional Expressions

Make your writing clearer and more coherent by using cause-and-effect transitional words and phrases.

Because Theseus failed to change the sail, Aegeus leapt into the sea. **Therefore,** the bull killed the youth, and Minos invaded the country.

Other transitional words and phrases that show cause-and-effect relationships include:

as a result	consequently
and so	then
led to	since
for	so that

You might use the following sentence frames in your essay to incorporate transitional expressions.

- As a result, _____.

- Hamilton shows how a chain of events beginning with _____ eventually led to _____.

Vocabulary Workshop

Greek and Latin Word Origins

TEKS

10.1.A Determine the meaning of grade-level technical academic English words in multiple content areas (e.g., science, social studies, the arts) derived from Latin, Greek, or other linguistic roots and affixes.

Literature Connection In the passage below from "Theseus," Edith Hamilton mentions the Labyrinth built by Daedalus, the famed mythological architect and sculptor.

> *"Daedalus built the Labyrinth, famous throughout the world. Once inside, one would go endlessly along its twisting paths without ever finding the exit."*

The term *labyrinth* initially referred only to Daedalus's creation, which was used to house the Minotaur. However, over time the term's meaning has come to refer to any kind of maze, or complex structure or idea. Greek and Latin roots and affixes are the source of many English words from multiple content areas, including science, social studies, and the arts. Becoming familiar with Greek and Latin word origins can increase your vocabulary.

This chart shows the Greek and Latin origins of some English words.

Word	Definition	Prefix, Root, or Suffix	Discipline
anarchy	disorder; lack of government	Greek prefix *an-*, "not" or "without"	social studies
biology	science dealing with the study of living things	Greek prefix *bio-*, "life"	science
capitalism	a kind of economic system	Latin suffix *-ism*, "system"	social studies
omnivore	something that eats both meat and plants	Latin roots *vor*, "eat greedily" and *omni*, "all"	science
philharmonic	pertaining to a musical organization, such as an orchestra	Greek root *phil*, "loving"	arts
physician	doctor	Latin suffix *-cian*, "possessing a specific skill"	science
transcontinental	extending across a continent	Latin prefix *trans-*, "across"	social studies

Word Origins

Word origins, or etymologies, are the histories of words. Word origins generally include the other languages or earlier forms of English that words came from.

Tip

Learning to recognize Greek and Latin roots and affixes, such as those in the chart, can help you determine the meanings of unfamiliar words on a test. Use a printed or electronic dictionary when possible to confirm the etymologies of words.

Practice Using a dictionary and the chart above, identify and define the Latin or Greek prefix, root, or suffix in each of the following words. Then find each word's definition.

1. macroeconomics
2. herbicide
3. bibliophile
4. molecule
5. transatlantic
6. monarchy
7. geopolitics
8. cirumnavigate
9. corpus
10. dystopia
11. tonsillectomy
12. flexor

LOG ON ▶ **Literature** Online

Vocabulary For more vocabulary practice, go to glencoe.com and enter QuickPass code GL57805u5.

Comparing Literature

Across Time and Place

TEKS

For pages 956–967

10.2.B Analyze archetypes in mythic, traditional and classical literature.

Compare Literature About Heroism

Heroes come in many forms and show up in the most unexpected places. In times of war, some heroes fall and new heroes rise. Faced with the possibility of becoming obsolete, heroes will fight to prove themselves. And, with history to inspire and guide them, heroism is born in the hearts and minds of children. The three works compared here explore timeless themes of heroism: self-sacrifice, courage, and the strength of the human spirit.

COMPARE THE Big Idea Rescuing and Conquering

Every culture tells heroic stories of rescue and victory. The Native American and African American cultures depicted in these literary works experienced the horror of conquest at the hands of white settlers. As you read, ask yourself, How do these works turn the bleak history of conquest into a celebration of the strength of the human spirit?

COMPARE Archetypes of Traditional Literature

Archetypes are themes, characters, plot patterns, or images that are common to human experience across cultures and throughout time. Many archetypes originated in the oral tradition, but now appear in the written versions of traditional literature. Traditional literature is a genre of literature that includes myths, legends, and folktales, all of which are shaped by their cultural and historical context. Some common archetypes that appear in traditional literature include the underdog as a hero, helpful tools, and the family or social network that supports individuals. As you read, ask yourself, What archetypes do I notice?

COMPARE Cultural Beliefs

Although these literary works come from different cultures—Cheyenne, African American, and Chippewa—they all center on the theme of the individual's power to change the world. As you read, ask yourself, How does this theme reveal the common humanity inherent in all cultures?

Dress. 19th century, Southern Cheyenne. Buckskin, elk teeth, glass beads, tin cones, and yellow and red pigments, length: 48 in., width: 35 in. Smithsonian Institution, Washington, DC.

Author Search For more about the authors, go to glencoe.com and enter QuickPass code GL57805u5.

Before You Read

Where the Girl Rescued Her Brother

Meet **Joseph Bruchac**
(born 1942)

Meet **Gayle Ross**
(born 1951)

Joseph Bruchac and Gayle Ross share a common interest—they both draw from their Native American heritage for their literary inspiration. Bruchac is a writer of Abenaki descent who has published books of poetry, essays, and novels that weave together Native American history and myth. Ross is a direct descendant of John Ross, Principal Chief of the Cherokee during the Trail of Tears. As a child, she learned traditional Cherokee stories and songs from her grandmother.

Native American Mythology Native American mythology is a rich collection of legends and folklore. Different tribal groups each developed their own stories about the creation of the world and why things are the way they are. These stories have been passed down by word of mouth. Many traditional myths are sacred and are narrated through movement, song, and dance using symbols and imagination. They begin and end in a certain way each time they are told. According to Ross, she and Bruchac have been taught "that stories are living spirits and that the role of the storyteller is to care for the tales in [his or her] keeping."

Native American myths consist of hero stories, trickster stories, stories that impart a moral lesson or give warnings to children, and stories that celebrate family and community. For example, the myth of Apotamkin, a hairy human figure with long fangs, was used to instill fear into children to prevent them from wandering away from parental supervision.

> *"In a sense, you could say the stories know more than we do, and so we have a great responsibility to tell them well."*
>
> —Joseph Bruchac

Native American mythology often draws upon living things or natural objects regarded as sacred representations of their beliefs and values. In many tribal creation stories, animals are considered equals of humans and the creators of the universe. In some myths, animals have the ability to speak, think, and behave like humans.

Native Americans do not share a unified body of mythology. Hundreds of different tribes have their own languages, as well as a variety of unique rituals and traditions. By studying their myths, we can learn how Native Americans view themselves and the world and discover similarities between the different tribes that lived many years ago and those that thrive today.

LOG ON ▶ **Literature** Online

Author Search For more about Joseph Bruchac and Gayle Ross, go to glencoe.com and enter QuickPass code GL57805u5.

Literature and Reading Preview

Connect to the Legend

Have you heard about a person who responded heroically in a crisis? Freewrite about what made this person a hero.

Build Background

After a series of unprovoked attacks on his people, Sitting Bull (chief of the Sioux nation) summoned the Sioux, Cheyenne, and Arapaho to Montana. Soon after, this confederation surprised General George Crook's troops at Rosebud Creek in southern Montana, and a battle took place there on June 17, 1876. Buffalo Calf Road Woman was a real Cheyenne woman whose heroic actions during the battle have never been forgotten.

Set Purposes for Reading

Big Idea Rescuing and Conquering

As you read this story, ask yourself, How do Bruchac and Ross explore women's roles in rescuing and conquering?

Literary Element Suspense

Suspense is a feeling of curiosity, uncertainty, or even dread about what is going to happen next in a story. Suspense can heighten your interest in a story's outcome. As you read, ask yourself, How do Bruchac and Ross create and build suspense?

Reading Strategy Synthesize

To **synthesize** is to build an understanding of a literary work by combining your knowledge of different subjects and applying it to your reading. As you read, ask yourself, How does my knowledge of legend, Native American culture, gender roles, and U.S. history help me to synthesize ideas?

Tip: Make a Checklist What elements are common to acts of heroism? Create a checklist that identifies heroic acts. As you read, fill in the checklist with heroic elements and examples of these elements from the text.

Heroic Elements	Examples
courage	

Vocabulary

confront (kən frunt´) v. to come face-to-face with; to oppose; p. 960 *James had to confront his fear of flying when his employer made him travel to New York.*

vault (vôlt) v. to jump; to spring; p. 961 *Maria vaulted over the puddle to keep her shoes dry.*

strategic (strə tē´ jik) adj. highly important to an intended goal; p. 962 *The president knew the most strategic way to advertise the product.*

Tip: Synonyms Some dictionary entries list synonyms. Look for them at the end of the entry.

Where the Girl Rescued Her Brother

A Cheyenne Brave, 1901. Frederic Remington. Color lithograph. Private collection.

Retold by Joseph Bruchac and Gayle Ross

It was the moon when the chokecherries were ripe. A young woman rode out of a Cheyenne camp with her husband and her brother. The young woman's name was Buffalo Calf Road Woman. Her husband, Black Coyote, was one of the chiefs of the Cheyenne, the people of the plains who call themselves Tsis-tsis-tas, meaning simply "The People." Buffalo Calf Road Woman's brother, Comes-in-Sight, was also one of the Cheyenne chiefs, and it was well-known how close he was to his sister.

Like many of the other young women of the Cheyenne, Buffalo Calf Road Woman was respected for her honorable nature. Although it was the men who most often went to war to defend the people—as they were doing on this day—women would accompany their husbands when they went to battle. If a man held an important position among the Cheyenne, such as the keeper of the Sacred Arrows, then his wife, too, would have to be of the highest moral character, for she shared the weight of his responsibility.

Buffalo Calf Road Woman was well aware of this, and as she rode by her husband she did so with pride. She knew that today they were on their way to meet their old allies, the Lakota.[1] They were going out to try to drive back the *veho,* the spider people who were trying to claim all the lands of the Native peoples.

The Cheyenne had been worried about the *veho,* the white people, for a long time. They had given them that name because, like the black widow spider, they were

---

1. The *Lakota* were the largest group of the Sioux (sōō) people. Their traditional hunting grounds were in the western Dakotas and Nebraska.

very beautiful but it was dangerous to get close to them. And unlike the Cheyenne, they seemed to follow a practice of making promises and not keeping them. Although their soldier chief Custer had promised to be friendly with the Cheyenne, now he and the others had come into their lands to make war upon them.

Buffalo Calf Road Woman wore a robe embroidered with porcupine quills. The clothing of her brother and her husband, Black Coyote, was also beautifully decorated with those quills, which had been flattened, dyed in different colors, folded, and sewed on in patterns. Buffalo Calf Road Woman was proud that she belonged to the Society of Quilters. As with the men's societies, only a few women—those of the best character—could join. Like the men, the women had to be strong, honorable, and brave. Buffalo Calf Road Woman had grown up hearing stories of how Cheyenne women would defend their families when the men were away. The women of the Cheyenne were brave, and those in the Society of Quilters were the bravest of all.

Buffalo Calf Road Woman smiled as she remembered one day when the women of the Society of Quilters showed such bravery. It was during the Moon of Falling Leaves. A big hunt had been planned. The men who acted as scouts had gone out and located the great buffalo herd. They had seen, too, that there were no human enemies anywhere near their camp. So almost none of the men remained behind.

On that day, when all the men were away, a great grizzly bear came into the camp. Such things seldom happened, but this bear was one that had been wounded in the leg by a white fur-trapper's bullet. It could no

longer hunt as it had before, and hunger brought it to the Cheyenne camp, where it smelled food cooking.

When the huge bear came walking into the camp, almost everyone scattered. Some women grabbed their little children. Old people shut the door flaps of their tepees, and the boys ran to find their bows and arrows. Only a group of seven women who had been working on the embroidery of an elk-skin robe did not run. They were members of the Society of Quilters, and Buffalo Calf Road Woman was among them. The seven women put down their work, picked up the weapons they had close to hand, and stood to face the grizzly bear.

Now of all of the animals of the plains, the only one fierce enough and powerful enough to attack a human was the grizzly. But **confronted** by that determined group of women, the grizzly bear stopped in its tracks. It had come to steal food, not fight. The head of the Society of Quilters stepped forward a pace and spoke to the bear.

"Grandfather," she said, her voice low and firm, "we do not wish to harm you, but we will protect our camp. Go back to your own home."

The grizzly shook its head and then turned and walked out of the camp. The women stood and watched it as it went down through the cottonwoods and was lost from sight along the bend of the stream.

Buffalo Calf Road Woman turned her mind away from her memories. They were

Rescuing and Conquering *How is the grizzly bear similar to and different from other threats confronting the Cheyenne?*

Vocabulary

confront (kən frunt′) *v.* to come face-to-face with; to oppose close to Rosebud Creek. The scouts had told them that a great number of the *veho* soldiers would be there and that the Gray Fox, General George Crook, was in command. The Cheyenne had joined up now with the Oglala,[2] led by Crazy Horse. The Lakota people were always friends to the Cheyenne, but this man, Crazy Horse, was the best friend of all. Some even said that he was one of their chiefs, too, as well as being a war leader of his Oglala.

There were Crow and Shoshone[3] scouts with Crook, and the *veho* had many cannons. The Lakota and the Cheyenne were outnumbered by the two thousand men in Crook's command. But they were prepared to fight. They had put on their finest clothes, for no man should risk his life without being dressed well enough so that if he died, the enemy would know a great warrior had fallen. Some of the men raised their headdresses three times, calling out their names and the deeds they had done. Those headdresses of eagle feathers were thought to give magical protection to a warrior. Other men busied themselves painting designs on their war ponies.

Now they could hear Crook's army approaching. The rumble of the horses' hooves echoed down the valley, and

Cheyenne war shirt.

View the Art Cheyenne warriors earned the right to wear decorated garments like the one above through acts of bravery in battle. What types of status symbols do people from your own or other societies receive when they show great bravery?

there was the sound of trumpets. War ponies reared up and stomped their feet. Many of the Cheyenne men found it hard to put on the last of their paint as their hands shook from the excitement of the coming battle.

Crazy Horse **vaulted** onto his horse and held up one arm. *"Hoka Hey,"* he cried. "It is a good day to die."

Buffalo Calf Road Woman watched from a hill as the two lines of men—the blue soldiers to one side, and the Lakota and Cheyenne to the other—raced toward each other. The battle began. It was not a quick fight or an easy one. There were brave men on both sides. Two Moons, Little Hawk, Yellow Eagle, Sitting Bull, and Crazy Horse

Suspense *To which senses do the images in the paragraph at the top of this column appeal in order to create suspense?*

Vocabulary

vault (vôlt) *v.* to jump; to spring

---

2. Also a Sioux people, the *Oglala* (ōglä′lə) lived in what is now South Dakota.
3. The *Crow* and *Shoshone* (shə shō′nē) peoples lived primarily in the Rocky Mountains.

were only a few of the great warriors who fought for the Cheyenne and the Lakota. And Crook, the Gray Fox general of the whites, was known to be a tough fighter and a worthy enemy.

Buffalo Calf Road Woman's husband, Black Coyote, and her brother, Comes-in-Sight, were in the thick of the fight. The odds in the battle were almost even. Although the whites had more soldiers and guns, the Lakota and the Cheyenne were better shots and better horsemen. Had it not been for the Crow and Shoshone scouts helping Crook, the white soldiers might have broken quickly from the ferocity of the attack.

From one side to the other, groups of men attacked and retreated as the guns cracked, cannons boomed, and smoke filled the air. The war shouts of the Lakota and the Cheyenne were almost as loud as the rumble of the guns. The sun moved across the sky as the fight went on, hour after hour, while the confusion of battle swirled below.

Then Buffalo Calf Road Woman saw something that horrified her. Her brother had been drawn off to one side, sur-rounded by Crow scouts. He tried to ride free of them, but his pony went down, struck by a rifle bullet and killed. Now he was on foot, still fighting. The Crow warriors were trying to get close, to count coup[4] on him. It was more of an honor to touch a living enemy, so they were not firing their rifles at him. And he was able to keep them away with his bow and arrows. But it was clear that soon he would be out of ammunition and would fall to the enemy.

Buffalo Calf Road Woman waited no longer. She dug her heels into her pony's sides and galloped down the hill. Her head low, her braids streaming behind her, she rode into the heart of the fight. Some men moved aside as they saw her coming, for there was a determined look in her eyes. She made the long howling cry that Cheyenne women used to urge on the warriors. This time, however, she was the one going into the fight. Her voice was as strong as an eagle's. Her horse scattered the ponies of the Crow scouts who were closing in on her brother, Comes-in-Sight. She held out a hand; her brother grabbed it and vaulted onto the pony behind her. Then she wheeled, ducking the arrows of the Crow scouts, and heading back up the hill.

That was when it happened. For a moment, it seemed as if all the shooting stopped. The Cheyenne and the Lakota, and even the *veho* soldiers, lowered their guns to watch this act of great brav-ery. A shout went up, not from one side but from both, as Buffalo Calf Road Woman reached the safety of the hilltop again, her brother safe behind her on her horse. White men and Indians cheered her.

So it was that Buffalo Calf Road Woman performed the act for which the people would always remember her. Inspired by her courage, the Cheyenne and Lakota drove back the Gray Fox—Crook made a **strategic** withdrawal.

"Even the *veho* general was impressed," said the Cheyenne people. "He saw that if our women were that brave, he would stand no chance against us in battle."

So it is that to this day, the Cheyenne and the Lakota people do not refer to the fight as the Battle of the Rosebud. Instead, they honor Buffalo Calf Road Woman by calling the fight Where the Girl Rescued Her Brother. ∾

---

4. Among some Native Americans, to *count coup* (ko͞o) was to touch a living enemy and get away safely—an act requiring both skill and courage.

Vocabulary

strategic (strə tē′ jik) *adj.* highly important to an intended goal

After You Read

Respond and Think Critically

1. **Connect to Personal Experience** Were you surprised by the response of those who witnessed Buffalo Calf Road Woman's actions at Rosebud Creek? Explain.

2. **Interpret Symbols** What does Buffalo Calf Road Woman's clothing represent? Support your response with text evidence. **OER**

3. **Make Inferences About Attitudes** What can you infer from the battle preparations about these Native Americans' attitude toward battle?

4. **Analyze Historical Context** How do the Cheyenne people seem to view the role of women in their society? Do you think their views are typical for other people in the United States during that time period? Explain.

5. **Make Inferences About Author's Purpose** Why might the authors have included the bear story in their tale?

6. **Big Idea** **Draw Conclusions About Character** What can you conclude about Buffalo Calf Road Woman's character based on her actions?

Literary Element Suspense

Writers build **suspense** through characters' actions and words and by providing sensory details.

7. **Summarize Images** What images, or sensory details, in the battle scene describe the ferocity of the battle?

8. **Make Inferences About Suspense** How do these sensory details, combined with your prior knowledge, build suspense?

Reading Strategy Synthesize

Review your checklist from page 958 and the blue highlighted question on page 960 before you answer the following questions.

9. Based on what you know about past relations between Native Americans and whites, why are the Cheyenne worried about the *veho*? Is their concern justified? Explain.

10. At what points in the story does legend become more important than history? Explain.

LOG ON ▶ **Literature** Online

Selection Resources For Selection Quizzes, eFlashcards, and Reading-Writing Connection activities, go to glencoe.com and enter QuickPass code GL57805u5.

Vocabulary Practice

Practice with Synonyms A synonym is a word that has the same or nearly the same meaning as another word. With a partner, match each boldfaced vocabulary word below with its synonym. You will not use all the answer choices. Use a dictionary or the glossary on pages R76–R91 to check your answers.

1. confront
2. vault
3. strategic

a. oppose
b. crucial
c. languish
d. jump
e. diminish

Writing

Write a Blurb If you worked in the marketing department of a publishing company, how would you describe this story on its book jacket in a way that would make a reader want to buy the book? Write a brief account of the story that builds interest and suspense without giving away the ending.

Build Background

"John Henry" is a **tall tale**, a type of folktale associated with the U.S. frontier. Zora Neale Hurston retells the tall tale of John Henry, a worker who died during his successful, superhuman attempt to out-hammer a steam drill. The story is told in the form of a **ballad**, a narrative song or poem.

John Henry

Zora Neale Hurston

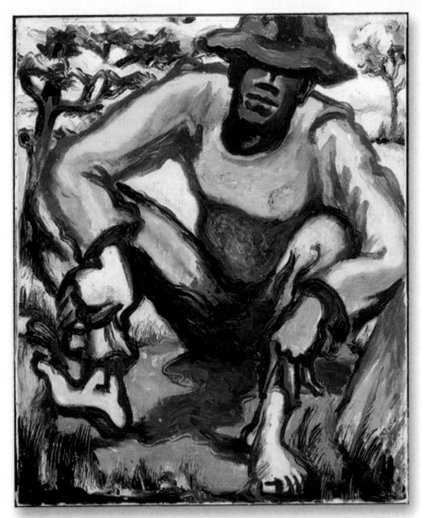

Resting, 1944. Claude Clark.
Smithsonian American Art Museum, Washington, DC.

1   John Henry driving on the right
        hand side,
    Steam drill[1] driving on the left,
    Says, 'fore I'll let your steam drill
        beat me down
    I'll hammer my fool self to death,
    Hammer my fool self to death.

2   John Henry told his Captain,[2]
    When you go to town
    Please bring me back a nine
        pound hammer
    And I'll drive your steel on down,
    And I'll drive your steel on down.

3   John Henry told his Captain,
    Man ain't nothing but a man,
    And 'fore I'll let that steam drill beat
        me down
    I'll die with this hammer in my
        hand,
    Die with this hammer in my hand.

4   Captain ast John Henry,
    What is that storm I hear?
    He says Cap'n that ain't no storm,
    'Tain't nothing but my hammer in
        the air,
    Nothing but my hammer in the air.

5   John Henry told his Captain,
    Bury me under the sills of the floor,
    So when they get to playing good
        old Georgy skin,[3]
    Bet 'em fifty to a dollar more,
    Fifty to a dollar more.

6   John Henry had a little woman,
    The dress she wore was red,
    Says I'm going down the track,
    And she never looked back.
    I'm going where John Henry fell dead,
    Going where John Henry fell dead.

7   Who's going to shoe your pretty li'l'
        feet?
    And who's going to glove your hand?
    Who's going to kiss your dimpled
        cheek?
    And who's going to be your man?
    Who's going to be your man?

8   My father's going to shoe my pretty
        li'l' feet;
    My brother's going to glove my hand;
    My sister's going to kiss my dimpled
        cheek;
    John Henry's going to be my man,
    John Henry's going to be my man.

9   Where did you get your pretty li'l'
        dress?
    The shoes you wear so fine?
    I got my shoes from a railroad man,
    My dress from a man in the mine,
    My dress from a man in the mine. ✆

---

1. A *steam drill* is a steam-powered machine used to drill
   through rock. The human workers hammer the rock by
   hand.
2. Here, the *Captain* is the boss of the railroad workers.
3. *Georgy skin* is slang for Georgia Skin, a card game.

Quickwrite

Write a two- or three-paragraph response to the
following questions: Why do you think Henry
competes with the steam drill? What heroic traits
does Henry possess? What flaw(s) does Henry
possess? Why do you think "John Henry" is
considered an important tall tale?

Build Background

The Chippewa (chip′ə wä′), or Ojibwa (ō jib′wā′), is a Native American group that lives in Canada and on reservations in the northern United States. From the seventeenth until the nineteenth centuries, the Chippewa were involved in a number of conflicts. After the War of 1812, they enacted a treaty with the United States.

A SONG OF GREATNESS

Chippewa

Fireside. Eanger Irving Couse (1866–1936).

When I hear the old men
Telling of heroes,
Telling of great deeds
Of ancient days–
5   When I hear that telling,
Then I think within me
I, too, am one of these.

When I hear the people
Praising great ones,
10   Then I know that I too–
Shall be esteemed;
I, too, when my time comes
Shall do mightily.

💬 Discussion Starter

Meet with a small group to discuss the roles of history and heritage in the life of a hero. How old is the speaker in the poem? Why does the speaker believe he/she will "do mightily"? How is the oral tradition important to this poem? Participate actively and listen effectively when others speak.

Wrap-Up: Comparing Literature

Across Genres

- ***Where the Girl Rescued Her Brother*** retold by Joseph Bruchac and Gayle Ross

- ***John Henry*** by Zora Neale Hurston

- ***A Song of Greatness*** Chippewa Traditional

COMPARE THE `Big Idea` Rescuing and Conquering

Writing "Where the Girl Rescued Her Brother," "John Henry," and "A Song of Greatness" explore the ideas of rescuing and conquering—ideas that appear in stories from a variety of world cultures. Write a brief essay analyzing how legends such as these that involve rescuing and conquering have influenced later literature and film about rescuing and conquering.

COMPARE Archetypes of Traditional Literature

Partner Activity Archetypes can fall into several categories: **character archetypes** include familiar individuals such as the wise leader or the rebel; **image archetypes** include objects or places that have a universal symbolism, such as water, a tree, or a snake; **plot pattern archetypes** are universal stories, such as the hero's quest; **theme archetypes** are ideas common to literature across time and place, including the idea that good can overcome evil. With a partner, answer the questions below.

Great Plains Indian hunting Bufflao with bow and arrow. c1890–c1927.

1. What character archetype do all three texts share? Why might this particular archetype exist in different cultural and historical contexts?

2. Consider the purpose of Buffalo Calf Road Woman's horse and John Henry's hammer. How might these things function as archetypes?

3. How does the genre of each text help the author convey his or her theme? What similarities and differences do you see in the theme archetypes of the three texts?

COMPARE Cultural Beliefs

Speaking and Listening "Where the Girl Rescued Her Brother" comes from the Cheyenne people, "John Henry" from the African American culture, and "A Song of Greatness" from the Chippewa tradition. Make inferences about each culture's beliefs, the role of women in society, and the importance of history, heritage, and courage. Support your inferences with details from the texts. Then present your findings in an oral report to the class.

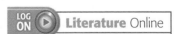

LOG ON ▶ **Literature** Online

Selection Resources For Selection Quizzes, eFlashcards, and Reading-Writing Connection activities, go to glencoe.com and enter QuickPass code GL57805u5.

TEKS

For pages 968–977

10.23.A–E Organize and present ideas and information according to the purpose of the research and audience. Synthesize the research into a written or an oral presentation.

 # Writing Workshop

Research Report

Literature Connection: In *Le Morte d'Arthur,* Sir Thomas Malory presents a fiction that is often confused with fact.

> *"Whoso pulleth oute this swerd of this stone and anvyld is rightwys kynge borne of all brytaygne"*

Legends, do, however, contain hints of events that may have actually happened. In a research report, a writer may explore the possibility of historical truth in such events as well as other questions related to the work.

Purpose: Your purpose for writing a research report is to research a topic and present your conclusions supported by evidence.

Audience: Your audience is, literally, the world. You will place your research report online so others can enjoy and learn from your work.

Choose Your Topic

Planning Checklist

Your research report should include the following traits:

- ☑ a clear thesis statement

- ☑ an engaging introduction that presents the thesis, an informative body that supports the thesis with relevant evidence, and a satisfying conclusion that restates the thesis

- ☑ a logical organizational structure

- ☑ supporting details from a variety of reliable sources

- ☑ properly cited sources both within the report and on the "Works Cited" page

---

Option A: Choose a Prompt

1. Write a research report in which you document the origins of tall tales like "John Henry" in the early years of the United States.

2. Write a research report in which you discuss the similarities and differences between the African epic *Sundiata* and the *Iliad,* an epic from ancient Greece.

Option B: Write a Prompt

Write a research report in which _____.

Sample Prompt:

Write a research report in which you investigate whether the legend of King Arthur is based on historical fact.

🖋 Scoring Rubric

Check the Research Reports **Scoring Rubric** on page R31 for more guidance on crafting your best research paper.

PLAN Your Research Report

Key Traits Ideas Research reports have many purposes. They may answer questions, document events, or explore literature.

▶ Step 1: Choose a Topic

In small groups, brainstorm ideas that you can research. Focus on topics that interest you and your classmates.

> urban legends
> Navaho myths
> the legend of King Arthur
> courage in Aesop's Fables

▶ Step 2: Ask Questions

Once you've settled on a topic, ask yourself what you'd like to know about it. Write out a series of questions to guide your research.

> Is there any evidence of a man named Arthur living at that time?
>
> Have archeologists found any artifacts from Camelot?
>
> Was the Holy Grail ever found?

Look for answers to your questions on reliable Web sites and in encyclopedias, books, and magazines. Where appropriate, use such primary sources as letters, diaries, audio recordings, and interviews.

▶ Step 3: Develop a Working Bibliography

As you conduct your research, create a bibliography card for every source. Give each card a number. To create cards for a variety of sources, see the Writing Handbook, page R36.

⑤	← Source number
Lacey, Norris J., ed.	← Author
The New Arthurian Encyclopedia	← Title
New York: Garland Pub.	← City of publication/publisher
1991	← Date of publication
University of Chicago Library	← Location of source
DA152.6A7N480	← Library call number

Audience and Purpose

Most research reports are formal writing exercises. Remember that your purpose is to inform and not to entertain. Usually teachers will ask you to use the third person and to avoid using *I*. Maintain a serious tone and avoid slang and contractions.

Narrow Your Topic

Think about the length of your report. If your topic is too broad, you won't be able to discuss it in full. If your topic is too narrow, you likely won't be able to find enough information about it.

too broad:

> the legends of King Arthur

too narrow:

> King Arthur's sword

appropriately narrowed:

> fact in the legend of King Arthur

Literature Online

Writing and Research For planning, drafting, and revising tools, go to glencoe.com and enter QuickPass code GL57805u5.

PLAN Your Research Report

▶ Step 4: Take Notes

As you read through your source materials, make notes about important ideas and facts and copy direct quotations word-for-word. You can do this on note cards, in a notebook, or in a computer file. When you're not quoting directly from a source, write relevant information as either a paraphrase or a summary. To learn more about note cards, see the Writing Handbook, page R37.

▶ **Direct Quotation Note Card**

Arthur's Tomb   Source number ⟶ ⑤

many historians "dismissed the ⟵ Main idea group
grave as a fabrication and a
publicity stunt."

▶ Step 5: Write a Working Thesis Statement

When you've done enough research, evaluate and synthesize your notes, and write a working thesis statement. As you develop and revise your report, you may want to rewrite the thesis statement.

Working Thesis Statement:

The legend of King Arthur is all fiction.

▶ Step 6: Organize Your Research

The last step before drafting your research report is to develop an organizational plan. This plan serves two purposes. First, it helps you to see whether all your main ideas relate to your thesis statement. Second, it enables you to decide on a logical progression in which to present those ideas.

Working Thesis: The legend of King Arthur is all fiction.

Main Idea: Stories exist about a historical figure named Artorius, but he was not a king.

Main Idea: The person named Artorius did not live and fight where Arthur is supposed to have lived and fought.

Main Idea: There is much doubt about the "body" of King Arthur and the site of his tomb.

Main Idea: The "Round Table" found at Winchester is a fake.

DRAFT Your Research Report

Key Traits Ideas As you draft, remember that all of the information you provide should support, or further explain, your thesis.

▶ Step 1: Draft an Engaging Introduction

There are many ways to ensure that your introduction will grab the reader's interest. You might start with an intriguing anecdote, a startling fact, a surprising statistic, or a thought-provoking question.

> *Did Merlin exist? Was there once a place called Camelot? Did Sirs Lancelot, Gawain, Galahad, and other knights ever sit around a round table? The answer to all of these questions is no.*

▶ Step 2: Incorporate Quotations

Directly quoting a reliable source is a powerful way to support and develop your thesis. Embedding quotations in sentences offers you the opportunity to combine your voice with that of the writer you're quoting.

> *Historian William of Newburgh, who wrote between 1196 and 1198, said that Geoffrey of Monmouth "weaves the most ridiculous figments of imagination." He also said that Geoffrey "cloaked" his fables about Arthur with the "honorable name of history" (Echard).*

▶ Step 3: Cite Sources Correctly

When you write a research report, you must give credit to the authors whose ideas and words you use. You must do this both in the report itself and on a separate Works Cited page. Use the style guide your teacher prefers—either the *MLA Guide for Writers of Research Papers,* published by the Modern Language Association, or the *Chicago Manual of Style,* published by the University of Chicago Press. Following are some examples of correct citations using the MLA guide. Note that in handwritten text italics are indicated by underlining. For more information on citing sources, see the Writing Handbook, pages R41–R43.

In-text Citation:

> *Others cite a hero called Arth Fawr, a Welsh term meaning "great bear," which sounds very much like Arthur (Barber 37).*

Works Cited Citation:

> *Barber, Chris, and David Pykitt. <u>Journey to Avalon: The Final Discovery of King Arthur.</u> York Beach: Weiser, 1997. Print.*

Avoid Plagiarism

Plagiarism is using other people's exact words or their ideas as if they are one's own. One good way to avoid plagiarism is to use several sources. Doing this will help you develop a broader view of your topic. What is common knowledge—that is, what almost all the sources say—will become clear, and so will what is unique and must therefore be acknowledged in your paper.

Drafting Checklist

Your research report should include the following traits:

- ☑ Thesis—a clearly written statement of your controlling idea
- ☑ Unity—all of the details support and expand on the thesis
- ☑ Organization—information is presented in a logical sequence
- ☑ Quotations—quotations are word-for-word from the source and are correctly cited
- ☑ Citations—sources are cited following the designated style guide

The Legend of King Arthur: The Facts of the Matter

Did Merlin exist? Was there once a place called Camelot? Did Sirs Lancelot, Gawain, Galahad, and other knights ever sit around a round table? The answer to all of these questions is no. The legend of King Arthur is powerful, enduring, and important to many people, but it is not true. There is nothing about the legend of King Arthur that is definitely based on fact.

Nevertheless, there most certainly were knights like the ones named above, and people want to believe in a factual basis for the King Arthur legend. Their most important argument is that there really was a man named Arthur who has come down in legend as King Arthur. Some think that they find Arthur in an actual historical figure called Artorius, which may be a Roman name for Arthur. Others cite a hero called Arth Fawr, a Welsh term meaning "great bear," which sounds very much like Arthur (Barber 37). If the existing records can be believed, Artorius or Arth Fawr lived in the late fifth and early sixth centuries A.D. (Lacey 18). This was a terrible time in the history of Great Britain, which had been part of the Roman Empire. As the Empire declined in the fourth and fifth centuries, killing, looting, and burning began. Many Britons (people living on the island that now forms part of Great Britain) were killed, and

Thesis Statement

The thesis statement makes it clear that this report will contend there is no evidence that King Arthur was an actual historical figure.

Main Idea

These sentences state the main idea of this paragraph.

Supporting Details

These details support the main idea of the paragraph.

Audience

The parenthetical information explains to readers who the Britons were.

many lived in fear. After about A.D. 450, the whole eastern part of the land fell to two groups of invaders: the Angles and the Saxons. The "West Country" remained free (Day 29).

About the year 500, a man appeared who won a series of twelve battles against the invaders (Byrd). A sixth-century document, *The Ruin and Conquest of Britain* by Gildas describes these battles, including the final battle known as the Battle of Badon Hill. This was the decisive battle that brought peace to the people of the West Country for perhaps forty years. This account also includes an unidentified fierce fighter whose name may—or may not—have been some form of Arthur (Alexander). The fighter's name is never mentioned in this account, but people have assumed the warrior has to be Arthur. An early ninth-century source by Nennius is the first text that mentions Arthur's name. Nennius's account also associates Arthur (or in this case, Artorius) with the Battle of Badon and eleven other victories. It does not refer to Artorius as king, however. Instead, it records Arthur's title as *Dux Bellorum,* or "leader of battles" (Echard). Neither source proves that the leader is Arthur.

Once a hero story is started, it is easy to see how it can grow. If Artorius really was a fierce fighter, the stories about him probably kept getting bigger. In *The Search for King Arthur,* David Day comments on Arthur's growing fame.

> The deeds of the Dux Bellorum [who brought peace after so much war] were forever remembered by proud Britons. Arthur was not only the saviour of a people on the brink of extinction, but he gave them the glory of a dozen victories. The deeds of other heroes . . . soon became associated with his name (15).

Paraphrase

These sentences offer information in the writer's own words from a source. The source is properly cited at the end of the paraphrase.

Multiple Sources

This paragraph weaves together information from three sources to make an important point.

Long Quotations

If a quotation is more than four lines long, set it off from the paragraph by indenting it. Use ellipsis to show where something has been left out and brackets to enclose information you have added and that is not part of the original quotation.

This quotation explains why Arthur—or Arth Fawr, or Artorius—became so famous. It does not, however, prove that the stories about this figure were true.

There are also geographical problems with the story of Arthur and his battles. One proposed site of Arthur's supposed last great battle is Badon Hill, which is thought to be located in southwest England (Echard). The historical *Dux Bellorum* did not live there, however. Instead, Day says, "[T]here is little doubt" that he lived and fought north of where the English border is today, in an area we now call southern Scotland (18). It is unlikely that Arthur lived and fought in two places that were so far away from each other.

In about 1124, the medieval historian William of Malmesbury called the stories of Arthur "deceitful fables." Historian William of Newburgh, who wrote between 1196 and 1198, said that Geoffrey of Monmouth "weaves the most ridiculous figments of imagination." He also said that Geoffrey "cloaked" his fables about Arthur with the "honorable name of history" (Echard). In so many words, then, real historians called these stories about Arthur lies.

Even though the facts of invention are so clear and so well-known, no one seems to stop looking for proof that Arthur existed. In 1191 monks claimed to have "discovered" the tomb of Arthur and Guinevere at Glastonbury in southern England, a place some call Avalon. As Caroline Alexander notes, however, the monks certainly had their motives. The abbey had burned to the ground in 1184, but the "discovery" brought a rich tourist industry that helped the monks rebuild. Also, no one could really disprove or prove the claim. After all, there was no DNA testing then, and the tomb conveniently disappeared in 1589, so there is

Multiple Sources

The writer presents information from two sources to show that even scholars cannot agree where Arthur may have lived and fought.

no DNA testing now, either. The article on Glastonbury in *The New Arthurian Encyclopedia* notes that many historians "dismissed the grave as a fabrication and a publicity stunt" (200). Nevertheless, to this day, a sign proudly marks the spot as "Site of King Arthur's Tomb," and tourists remain eager to visit—and to believe.

The truest thing that can be said is that there is a history of trying to turn the legend of King Arthur into fact. If a great battle leader named Arthur existed, he was not a king, and he could not have lived in both the North and the Southwest at once. Those who love the story of King Arthur may want desperately to believe that some part of the legend really took place, but that seems as likely as pulling a sword from a stone.

Works Cited

Alexander, Caroline. "A Pilgrim's Search for Relics of the Once and Future King." *Smithsonian* Feb. 1996. Web. 25 Mar. 2008. <http://www.gale.cengage.com/>

Barber, Chris, and David Pykitt. *Journey to Avalon: The Final Discovery of King Arthur.* York Beach: Weiser, 1997. Print.

Byrd, Laura. "A Place of Legends." *World and I* 16.11 (2001). 3 Oct. 2008. Print.

Day, David. The Search for King Arthur. New York: Facts on File, 1995. Print.

Echard, Siân. "King Arthur in History: Texts." Web. <http://faculty.arts.ubc.ca/sechard/344art.htm>.

Lacey, Norris J., ed. *The New Arthurian Encyclopedia.* New York: Garland, 1996. Print.

"The Tomb of King Arthur: Gerald of Wales on the Finding of King Arthur's Tomb." Trans. John William Sutton. *The Camelot Project at the University of Rochester.* 2008 Oct. 20. University of Rochester Libraries. 30 Oct. 2008. Web. <http://www.library.rochester.edu/camelot/gerald.htm#bib>.

Embedded Quotations

Inserting a quotation as part of the running text of a sentence offers support for the point you're trying to make.

Conclusion

The writer ends the report by restating the thesis using different language, including a clever simile at the end of the last sentence.

Variety of Sources

Use a variety of sources. What different kinds of sources are shown here?

Reliable Sources

A quick Google search attests to David Day's reliability as a source.

Encyclopedias

An encyclopedia devoted to just one subject will usually offer a wealth of reliable information and other sources to consult.

Your Turn

Using your research and your organizational plan, write the first draft of your research report. Remember to cite all the sources that you use as you draft.

REVISE Your Research Report

Key Traits Ideas and Organization As you revise, look for ways to strengthen your focus, organization, unity, coherence, and word choice.

▶ Step 1: Refine Your Thesis Statement

Does your thesis statement encapsulate your first draft? Now that your draft is complete, you have a better sense of the focus of your report than you did at the start. Check to see if your working thesis statement still accurately reflects the focus of your report.

Working Thesis Statement:

> The legend of King Arthur is all fiction.

Refined Thesis Statement:

> The legend of King Arthur is powerful, enduring, and important to many people, but it is not true. There is nothing about the legend of King Arthur that is definitely based on fact.

▶ Step 2: Develop Coherence

Do all the parts flow together smoothly and logically? Because a research report is lengthy, it is especially important that it be coherent. One way to achieve coherence is through the use of transitions.

> Also, no one could really disprove the claim. After all, there was no DNA testing then, and the tomb conveniently disappeared in 1589, so there is no DNA testing now either. The article on Glastonbury in *The New Arthurian Encyclopedia* notes that many historians "dismissed the grave as a fabrication and a publicity stunt" (200). Nevertheless, to this day, a sign proudly marks the spot as "Site of King Arthur's Tomb," and tourists remain eager to visit—and to believe.

▶ Step 3: Enlist the Aid of a Peer Reviewer

A fresh set of eyes may discover deficiencies in your draft that you can't see. Ask a classmate, friend, or family member to read your draft, keeping these questions in mind. Use their observations to further revise your draft.

- What grabbed your attention in my introduction?
- Which details supported my thesis and which did not?
- Where does my report seem to lose focus?
- What did you learn from my report?
- Where in my conclusion do I restate my thesis?

Revising Checklist

Before you start your revision, ask yourself these questions:

- ☑ Is the focus of my report clearly stated?
- ☑ Is my topic and writing style appropriate for my audience?
- ☑ Have I strengthened the coherence of my report?
- ☑ Did I include the traits in the Planning and Drafting Checklists?

EDIT Your Research Report

Key Trait Conventions Edit by correcting any errors in spelling, grammar, and mechanics and making sure you are using conventions of academic language.

> ## ▶ Grammar Tip
>
> ### Use Commas with Nonessential Transitions
>
> Generally, commas are used to set off contrasting expressions and transitions—such as *not, unlike, first, as a result, consequently, on the other hand*—whether they are introductory elements (at the beginning of sentences) or interrupters (in the middle of a sentence).
>
> **Original:** In this sentence, *nevertheless* is an introductory transition word.
>
> > *Nevertheless people want to believe in a factual basis for the King Arthur legend.*
>
> **Improved:** Add a comma after the introductory transition word.
>
> > *Nevertheless, people want to believe in a factual basis for the King Arthur legend.*
>
> **Original:** In this sentence, the transitional word *however* interrupts the sentence to show contrast.
>
> > *It does not however prove that the stories about this figure were true.*
>
> **Improved:** Use commas before and after the transition.
>
> > *It does not, however, prove that the stories about this figure were true.*

PUBLISH Your Research Report

Key Trait Presentation You've done a lot of work researching and writing your report. Now it's time to share that work with a larger audience. Build a Web site using design software. Web design software offers you the capability to post audio and video clips as well as still images. Including one or more of these will add pizzazz to your report. Many informative Web sites include a "Comments" section where visitors can respond to what's been posted on the site. Such a feature would be a great way to get feedback on your work.

Editing Checklist

For your final revision, check the following:

- ☑ Have I misspelled any words? If you are unsure of the spelling of a word, check an online or print dictionary or use your word processor's spell checker.

- ☑ Have I made any errors in mechanics or grammar? Have I followed the rules of Standard American English? Use the Language Handbook on pages R48–R71 to correct common grammar and mechanical errors.

- ☑ Is my writing legible? Be sure your handwriting is neat or that you have followed your teacher's guidelines for word-processing.

 LOG ON ▶ **Literature** Online

Writing and Research For editing and publishing tools, go to glencoe.com and enter QuickPass code GL57805u5.

TEKS

For pages 978–981

10.15.D Produce a multimedia presentation with graphics, images, and sound that conveys a distinctive point of view and appeals to a specific audience.

Workshop Model

In this workshop, note the examples used from a multimedia presentation titled "King Arthur: The Facts of the Matter." You might try out some of the techniques shown in the multimedia presentation that you create.

Real-World Connection

History museums often present multimedia exhibits. Before delivering your presentation, visit a gallery for inspiration and ideas. If you cannot visit a museum, use the Internet to find multimedia images. Evaluate how the messages in your multimedia presentation reflect social and cultural views in ways different from traditional texts, such as books, and consider how these added perspectives can contribute to your presentation.

Speaking, Listening, and Viewing Workshop

Multimedia Presentation

Literature Connection When Malory wrote *Le Morte d'Arthur,* he probably had many sounds and images in mind. Options for presenting them, however, were limited by the technology of the time. Today the story of Arthur can be told in many ways, ranging from stage and film productions to Web sites and Web casts. In this workshop, you will learn how to transform your research report into a multimedia presentation.

> ### Assignment
>
> Plan and deliver a multimedia presentation of your research report. As you develop your presentation, keep your audience and purpose in mind.
>
> **Audience:** classmates and teacher
> **Purpose:** to inform and describe; to engage

Plan Your Presentation

A **multimedia presentation** combines text, sound, graphics, and images (art, photos, video clips, animation, and print). Multimedia presentations include narrated slide or transparency presentations, Web sites, and Web casts.

Begin by thinking about the type of multimedia presentation that you will create. Consider your access to equipment. Check with your school media or IT (information technology) person to find out which of the following resources might be available for your use:

- digital cameras
- sound and video recording equipment
- projection equipment
- software programs, including photo, graphics, animation, and multimedia authorship programs

Keep in mind that a librarian or media specialist can also point out available databases or free programs for downloadable audio and video clips. The chart on the next page shows some options for a multimedia presentation.

Ways to Create a Multimedia Presentation		
	Equipment	**Application**
Low-tech ↓ **High-tech**	Camera, slide or overhead projector, and tape recorder	Use 35-mm slides or overhead transparencies for the visuals—images or text, or images with text.
	Computer with speakers, monitor, and microphone	Use presentation software to create a computer-based slide show combining text, graphics, images, and sound.
	Computer with speakers, monitor, microphone, digital camera, video camera, and scanner	Use a hypertext program to combine text, graphics, images, and sounds to create a series of "cards" containing hyperlinks that make different sequences possible.

Choose Your Media

After you have decided on a type of presentation, examine your research report for ideas you might portray using sound and images. Notice how the writer has annotated this sentence outline with ideas for sounds and images.

1. Introduction; Thesis: The legend of King Arthur is pure fiction.
Images: Show different images of Camelot, Arthur, Guinevere, Lancelot
Sound: Soundtrack from the movie King Arthur or Camelot?
Sound: Dramatic reading of introduction to my report
2. Stories of a historical Artorious, but he was not a king.
Image: map of West Country?
Image: page/text from Ruin and Conquest of Great Britain?
Image: Write out/ explain term/find or create image of Dux Bellorum
Sound: Dramatic reading of quotation from David Day
3. Artorius did not live or fight where Arthur is supposed to have lived and fought.
Image: map of Wales, northern and southern England today
4. The "body" of the King and his tomb are highly questionable
Image: Glastonbury
Image: sign
5. The "Round Table" found at Winchester is a fake.
Image: Winchester Castle
Image: fake Round Table
6. Conclusion
Sound: Return to soundtrack from the movie King Arthur or Camelot?
Image: Fine art image of Arthur or the sword in the stone

Use a search engine and databases to find sounds and images, or locate recordings using your school and public library.

Select Appropriate Media

When you wrote your research report, you made sure that your sources were objective, reliable, and valid. Before you select media, evaluate them too. Identify the author or sponsoring institution of any site or source from which you draw. Ask yourself whether the writer or sponsor is an authority, why the work was created, and how the work might have been checked or edited before publication or release.

Edit the Media

Select only parts of the media you find, being sure that what you choose either explains or supports your thesis or proposition—or engages your audience. Use your narration to help your audience understand what the images and sounds convey and to make meaningful links between the different parts of your presentation.

Develop Your Presentation

Avoid Plagiarism

Correctly credit each image, video clip, and sound, along with all your print sources, in your Works Cited list. (See pages R40–R43 for standardized citation styles.)

Evaluate Tone

Make sure that the tone and the formality of your language are appropriate for your audience and purpose. During script development and after rehearsal, ask yourself or a partner to answer these questions about your presentation.

- ☑ What is the tone of the presentation?
- ☑ Is the tone appropriate for the audience and purpose?
- ☑ Were there any shifts in tone or formality?
- ☑ Were those shifts purposeful or distracting?

- **Focus on your purpose.** Your main purpose is to inform. Above all, be accurate and clear as you explain and present ideas. Synthesize your research and draw conclusions. Advance a coherent argument that incorporates a clear thesis and a logical progression of valid evidence from reliable sources. Consider displaying title pages or print examples of information on the topic, so that your listeners can focus on the information as you explain how your sources treated different ideas.
- **Remember the audience and occasion.** Your main proposition, claim, or thesis is the most important idea you will present. Your audience could miss it if you only read it once, so take care to display and repeat it. Think about other potential problems your audience might have in understanding or following your presentation. Be sure to explain any unfamiliar or technical terms; to use maps, graphs, or charts to display unfamiliar concepts; and to address biases your audience may have. Keep in mind that you can use various software programs, as well as drawing tools within some word-processing programs, to create precise and professional looking charts, spreadsheets, graphs, and other visual displays.
- **Add narration.** Carefully consider what you need to explain and how and where you will convey information from your sources to complement and link the sounds and images.

Organize Your Presentation

Create a storyboard like the one below. Make a frame for each slide, card, or transparency you will use. Begin with a title and author frame. End with a Works Cited frame for listing, in standardized form, all your research sources, as well as all your visual and sound sources. In all the remaining frames of your storyboard, note which images, sounds, and text you will use.

• title • fine art of the Round Table "Camelot" music	• thesis bring music down • read my introduction	• map—West Country • explain Dux Bellorum • read source quotation	• source title page • explain how sources vary
• map—England today • recall thesis • point out different places	• photo—Glastonbury • text—varying beliefs monks chanting (low volume)	• photo—Winchester • photo—Round Table sound effect: clash of armor • narration	• thesis • Works Cited "Camelot" music

Note these two examples of slides based on ideas mapped out in the model storyboard.

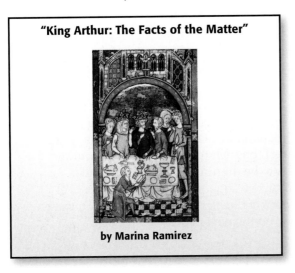

"King Arthur: The Facts of the Matter"

by Marina Ramirez

Map of England
- Setting of King Arthur legends

Rehearse and Deliver Your Presentation

Practice the entire presentation until you have the timing down. Then rehearse the presentation in front of a small audience of classmates or family members. Ask them to interpret your message and identify your position and your supporting evidence. You may need to adjust your pace, volume, images, and narration.

As you rehearse and deliver your presentation, keep the presentation techniques below in mind. When you are an audience member, keep the listening and viewing techniques in mind.

Techniques for a Multimedia Presentation

Presentation Techniques	Listening and Viewing Techniques
☑ **Pace** Give your audience enough time to view and hear each segment.	☑ **Body Language** Show respect for the presenter by sitting upright.
☑ **Volume** Make your words and sounds loud enough so that your entire audience can hear them, but do not blast them.	☑ **Movement and Facial Expression** Show that you are listening and understanding. Nod occasionally. Keep an interested look on your face.
☑ **Eye Contact** Look at your images as you direct audience attention to them.	☑ **Focus** Look only at the presenter or the images.

Evaluate the Presentation

☑ What is the speaker trying to communicate?

☑ What is the style of the presentation? Is it formal, informal, straightforward, creative?

☑ How is the presentation structured?

☑ Does it follow chronological order? Show cause and effect? List ideas in order of importance?

☑ How well do the style and structure support the purpose or meaning?

☑ How well do the words, images, graphics, and sounds work together to impact meaning?

LOG ON ▶ **Literature** Online

Speaking, Listening, and Viewing For project ideas, templates, and presentation tips, go to glencoe.com and enter QuickPass code GL57805u5.

Independent Reading

Legends and Myths

LEGENDS, MYTHS, AND FOLKTALES ARE ALL TRADITIONAL STORIES THAT VARY in their forms and content. Legends generally glorify historical figures, giving them fictional traits and describing them in a sentimental tone. Folktales often focus on justice and may have a serious, humorous, or sentimental tone. Myths often explain natural phenomena or human relationships; their tone tends to be dignified. For more legends, myths, and folktales on a range of themes, try the first two suggestions below. For a novel and an epic poem that incorporate the Big Ideas of *Acts of Courage* and *Rescuing and Conquering*, try the titles from the Glencoe Literature Library on the next page.

The Light Beyond The Forest

Rosemary Sutcliff

In this retelling of part of the legend of King Arthur, the Knights of the Round Table set out in search of a relic known as the Holy Grail. This is a tale of heroism and adventure, but it also has tender, human moments, such as when the brave Lancelot first meets up with his son Galahad. Sir Lancelot, Sir Galahad, Sir Bors, and Sir Percival encounter many adventures but always triumph over the forces of evil that threaten them physically and spiritually. This book is the second in a trilogy.

Cut from the Same Cloth: American Women of Myth, Legend, and Tall Tale

Robert D. San Souci

Discover the United States' unheralded heroines who are as strong-willed and clever as their male counterparts. San Souci retells fifteen folktales, ballads, and stories about legendary women, presenting three tales from each of five regions of the United States: the Northeast, South, Midwest, Southwest, and West. The heroines, who range from Molly Cottontail to Pale-Faced Lightning, represent African Americans, Anglo Americans, Native Americans (including the Inuit and Hawaiians), and Mexican Americans.

Apache Gold and Yaqui Silver

J. Frank Dobie

Folklorist Dobie collects some two dozen tales of lost mines and legendary treasures as passed down in the oral tradition of Texas and the Southwest.

GLENCOE LITERATURE LIBRARY

The Red Badge of Courage

Stephen Crane

Facing his own fears, Henry Fleming performs acts of courage and returns to fight in the Civil War.

Beowulf

translated by Burton Raffel

A great warrior leads his people and slays a dragon in this tale of adventure and rescuing and conquering.

CRITICS' CORNER

"[The] quick, plainly told fables [in The Girl Who Married a Lion and Other Tales from Africa] feature places where people and animals live in close proximity and somebody has to walk miles to a river everyday just to collect water. The personalities of Africa's animals—the wiliness of the hare, the gullibility of the lion, the laziness of the baboon—take shape as the book proceeds. And there are clear moral lessons here. . . ."

—Maggie Galehouse, the *New York Times Book Review*

The Girl Who Married a Lion and Other Tales from Africa

Alexander McCall Smith

The values and traditions of Zimbabwe and Botswana come alive in this collection of short tales collected and edited by fiction writer Alexander McCall Smith. Like other tales from around the world, these stories involve ambition, jealousy, and love; they value community; they show greed being punished and loyalty rewarded; and they reflect a sense of humor.

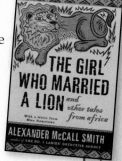

Write a Review

Read one of the books listed on these pages and write a review of it for your classmates. Be sure to explain the typical characteristics of the book's fictional genre and discuss how the author uses that genre to convey the book's theme. Present your review to the class.

Assessment

English Language Arts

Reading: Legends

Read the following passage and answer the questions that follow.

from "King Arthur" by Donna Rosenberg

based on *History of the Kings of Britain* by Geoffrey of Monmouth

King Arthur is one of the most familiar legendary heroes of all time. He is often accompanied by one or more of his loyal knights, but in the following excerpt, he has gone ahead of his companions to fight a brutal giant and has only his sword, Excalibur, and a shield to assist him.

1   The horrible appearance of the fiend was matched only by the terrible nature of his deeds. His face was darkly splotched like the skin of a frog. His eyebrows hung low over his eyes, which burned with fire. His ears were enormous, and his nose was hooked like a hawk's beak. His mouth was as flat as a flounder's, and his fat, loose, fleshy lips spread apart to display his swollen gums. His bristly black beard fell over his chest, concealing part of his fat body. He had the broad neck and shoulders of a bull. His arms and legs stretched out like the limbs of a mighty oak tree. From the top of his head to the tip of his shovel-shaped feet, he was thirty feet tall.

2   The giant wore a tunic made from human hair, fringed with the beards of men. He carried the corpses of twelve peasants tied together on his back. In his hand, he carried a club so mighty that the two strongest farmers in the land could not have lifted it off the ground.

3   The giant dropped the corpses by the fire and approached Arthur with broad strides. As Arthur fingered Excalibur, he saw that the giant's mouth was still smeared with the clotted blood and scraps of flesh from his last meal. Even his beard and his hair were strewn with gore.

4   Arthur said to him, "May great God in heaven, who rules the world, give you a short life and a shameful death! Surely you are the most foul fiend that was ever formed! Guard yourself, you dog, and prepare to die, for this day my hands will kill you!"

5   The giant responded by raising his fearsome club. He grinned like a ferocious boar, confident of its menacing tusks. Then he growled, and foam spilled from his gaping mouth.

6   King Arthur raised his shield and prayed to God that it would protect him against the fiend's mighty club. The giant's first blow fell upon Arthur's shield, making the cliffs clang like an anvil and shattering his source of protection. The shock of the impact almost knocked Arthur to the ground, but he quickly recovered.

7   The blow ignited King Arthur's rage, and he furiously struck the giant on the forehead with his sword. Blood gushed into the giant's eyes and down his cheeks, blinding him.

8   Just as an enraged boar, its flesh torn from the attacks of hunting hounds, turns and charges upon a hunter, so the giant, maddened with the pain of his wound, rushed with a roar upon King Arthur.

(Continued)

Groping blindly with his hands, the giant grabbed the king by the shoulders and clasped him to his chest, trying to crush Arthur's ribs and burst his heart. King Arthur summoned all of his strength and twisted his body out from under the giant's grasp.

9   "Peace to you, my lord!" the giant exclaimed. "Who are you that fights so skillfully with me? Only Arthur, the most noble of all kings, could defeat me in combat!"

10   "I am that Arthur of whom you speak," the king replied. Then, quick as lightning, Arthur struck the giant repeatedly with his sword. Unable to see through the blood in his eyes, the giant never knew where the next blow would fall. Arthur's sword thrusts rained upon him relentlessly until one finally entered his ear and plunged into his skull.

11   The giant gave a dreadful roar and crashed to the ground like a mighty oak tree torn up by a furious wind storm. Arthur gazed upon his fallen prey and laughed with relief.

---

1 The imagery and figurative language in paragraph 1 serve to emphasize —
- **A** how much scorn the giant has faced
- **B** how much damage the giant has done
- **C** how hideous and powerful the giant is
- **D** how eager the giant is to destroy his enemies

2 This excerpt strongly suggests that the giant has been killing people in order to —
- **F** eat them
- **G** steal from them
- **H** protect himself
- **J** rule the kingdom

3 Arthur's dialogue in this excerpt serves to emphasize —
- **A** how powerful the giant is
- **B** how determined Arthur is
- **C** how skillful and strong Arthur is
- **D** where the battle is taking place

4 The giant's first response to Arthur is one of —
- **F** rage
- **G** anxiety
- **H** respect
- **J** self-assurance

5 Which quotation from the excerpt contains an example of onomatopoeia?
- **A** *His face was darkly splotched*
- **B** *making the cliffs clang like an anvil*
- **C** *trying to crush Arthur's ribs and burst his heart*
- **D** *Arthur's sword thrusts rained upon him relentlessly*

6 The imagery in paragraph 8 appeals mainly to the sense of —
- **F** sight
- **G** smell
- **H** touch
- **J** hearing

7 Which quotation from the excerpt makes it clear that Arthur has been searching for the giant rather than having run into him accidentally?
- **A** *King Arthur raised his club and prayed to God*
- **B** *The blow ignited King Arthur's rage*
- **C** *"I am that Arthur of whom you speak"*
- **D** *Arthur gazed upon his fallen prey*

8 At what point does the giant indicate that he wishes to stop fighting?

  F When Arthur threatens him
  G When Arthur escapes his grasp
  H When he is first struck by Arthur's sword
  J When he is unable to knock Arthur down with his club

9 The word *combat*, used in paragraph 9, contains a prefix meaning "together" and a root. Which of the following words is most likely to come from the same root as *combat*?

  A Batch
  B Battle
  C Rebate
  D Probation

10 What is emphasized by the use of the simile in paragraph 11?

  F How huge and heavy the giant is
  G How difficult the battle has been
  H How surprising Arthur's victory is
  J How painful the giant's final injury was

11 Which of these sentences from the excerpt shows that Arthur is widely acknowledged as a hero?

  A *The giant dropped the corpses by the fire and approached Arthur with broad strides.*
  B *"Guard yourself, you dog, and prepare to die, for this day my hands will kill you!"*
  C *King Arthur raised his shield and prayed to God that it would protect him against the fiend's mighty club.*
  D *"Only Arthur, the most noble of all kings, could defeat me in combat!"*

12 The antagonist in this excerpt is —

  F Arthur
  G Arthur's shield
  H the giant
  J the giant's club

13 Which of the following plot-pattern archetypes is illustrated by this excerpt?

  A Secret birth
  B Revelation as favored heir
  C Using trickery to fool an enemy
  D Facing a seemingly impossible task

14 **Open-Ended Item** What qualities does Arthur demonstrate in this excerpt that support the idea that he is a hero? Explain your answer and support it with evidence from the excerpt.

Vocabulary Skills: Sentence Completion

For each item, choose the word from the word list that best completes the sentence. Do not use the same word more than once.

abashed	contemptible	guile	prowess
aggrieved	deliberation	ignoble	scrupulous
confidante	disdainful	inscribe	strategic
confinement	elude	jubilantly	tumultuous
confront	endear	perpetuate	vault

1 When the knight tripped over his sword and fell in the mud, the _____ look on his face revealed how foolish he felt.

2 As Arthur's trusted companion and _____, Sir Launcelot is aware of many of Arthur's deepest feelings.

3 A gigantic fiend has been terrorizing the countryside, and the peasants are justifiably _____ about the situation.

4 There is no doubt that only a man with great courage would deliberately _____ the huge and horrible giant.

5 The giant has never dealt with anyone who presented any threat to him, so he is _____ of Arthur when they begin to fight.

6 Striking the giant in the forehead is a _____ move that makes all of Arthur's later thrusts more likely to hit their target.

7 Although Arthur is clever enough to succeed by using _____, he defeats the giant purely by the use of determination, courage, and fighting skill.

8 His enemy's _____ in combat suggests to the giant that his foe may be "Arthur, the most noble of all kings."

9 When the giant is blinded by blood pouring down his face, he becomes unable to _____ the thrusts Arthur makes with his sword.

10 It is certainly likely that the peasants who have lived in fear of the giant will respond _____ to the news of his death.

11 Arthur's protective feelings toward the people of his kingdom is sure to _____ him to his subjects.

12 New versions of the old tales of King Arthur, both stories and movies, have served to _____ his fame.

Literature Online

Assessment For additional test practice, go to glencoe.com and enter QuickPass code GL57805u5.

Revising and Editing

Read the following draft of student's essay and answer the questions that follow it.

(1) Because King Arthur was not a real person. (2) The tales of his adventures are legends, not biographical writing. (3) Arthur may however have been based on a real person who, near the beginning of the 6th century, led battles against the Saxons. (4) There is some evidence to support the idea that such a man, a leader of the Celts, existed. (5) First, there was a period of peace that lasted for a generation around the time Arthur supposedly lived; second Saxon expansion was halted during this period. (6) If the Celts did, indeed, have a powerful and inspirational leader at this time. (7) This man may have been the person we think of as King Arthur.

(8) The real Arthur, if there was one, was probably quite unlike the Arthur of legend. (9) Nonetheless, very few readers let this interfere with their enjoyment of the tales, even if those stories are fictional. (10) Whether King Arthur was real or is merely an invented hero who symbolizes all that is admirable.

(11) The stories are filled with brave knights, beautiful ladies, and stirring struggles of good versus evil. (12) Therefore, people who like stories of romance and adventure will always find something that appeals to them in the legends of King Arthur and his Knights of the Round Table.

1 Why is sentence 1 unable to stand alone as a complete sentence?
   A It lacks only a subject.
   B It lacks only a verb.
   C It lacks both a subject and a verb.
   D It does not express a complete thought.

2 What change, if any, should be made in sentence 3?
   F Insert commas after *may* and *however*
   G Delete the comma after *who*
   H Delete the comma after *century*
   J Make no change

3 What change, if any, should be made in sentence 5?
   A Delete the comma after *First*
   B Insert commas after *lasted* and *generation*
   C Insert a comma after *second*
   D Make no change

4 What is the best way to correct the error in sentence 6?
   F Delete the commas around *indeed*
   G Insert a comma after *powerful*
   H Identify the time to which the sentence refers
   J Combine sentences 6 and 7 with a comma

5 What change, if any, should be made in sentence 9?

A Delete the comma after *Nonetheless*

B Insert a comma after *few*

C Delete the comma after *tales*

D Make no change

6 What error, if any, appears in sentence 10?

F It does not express a complete thought.

G It contains a nonrestrictive clause not preceded by a comma.

H It contains a nonessential transition not followed by a comma.

J The sentence contains no errors.

Written Composition

Read the information and instructions below in order to write a short personal narrative.

We are all familiar, to one extent or another, with the concept of the "hero" as he or she is depicted in legends, stories, movies, and plays. However, we also run into heroes in our everyday life.

Write a short, true story about an event that made an ordinary person seem heroic to you. The hero in your story should be someone who meets your own personal ideas about what a hero is.

REMEMBER—YOU SHOULD

❏ write a nonfiction story

❏ use first-person narration

❏ organize your story so that it has a beginning, middle, and end

❏ use dialogue if and where it is appropriate

❏ include sensory details that add descriptive clarity to your story

❏ correct errors in spelling, capitalization, punctuation, grammar, and sentence structure

The Homecoming, 1996. Peter Szumowski. Oil on canvas, 91.4 x 152.4 cm. Private collection.

<u>View the Art</u> This painting depicts a scene that might come from a science fiction story. How does this image relate to the Big Idea of The Extraordinary and Fantastic in Unit 6?

Genre Fiction

Looking Ahead

Genre fiction is a term used to group works of fiction that have similar characters, plots, or settings. Bookstores and libraries often shelve some of their fiction by genre categories—for example, romance, mystery, science fiction, and fantasy. Different from myths and folktales, genre fiction does not emerge from the oral traditions of cultures, nor is it usually rooted in history. Mysteries are often set in the present, fantasies in an indeterminate past or a distorted present, and science fiction in a distant future. This unit includes genres that reveal the unlimited potential of the human imagination.

Each literary work in Unit 6 focuses on a Big Idea that can help you make connections to your life.

PREVIEW	Big Idea	Literary Focus
	The Extraordinary and Fantastic	Description and Style

TEKS

For pages 992–996

10.2 Analyze, make inferences and draw conclusions about theme and genre in different cultural, historical, and contemporary contexts and provide evidence from the text to support understanding.

Genre Focus

What are science fiction, fantasy, modern fables, and mystery?

This unit addresses four kinds of genre fiction: science fiction, fantasy, modern fable, and mystery. Writers of these kinds of fiction use all of the techniques of good storytelling. The writers create unusual settings and characters, develop intriguing plot patterns, and use vivid descriptions to draw readers into imagined worlds or investigations. Writers of science fiction, fantasy, and mystery often create characters who appear in subsequent works, where the story develops further. In this way, genre fiction writers create series.

Types of Genre Fiction

Science Fiction

Science fiction is fiction that deals with the impact of science and technology—real or imagined—on society and individuals. Sometimes occurring in the future, science fiction commonly portrays space travel, exploration of the planets, future societies, and scientific and technological advances.

> She was suddenly aware, with some shock, that the Old Woman had an electron gun in the pocket of her smock. Dr. Calvin had come prepared for just that.
>
> "We'll see," said Calvin. "The robot may prove too valuable to dismantle."
>
> "But how can it dream?"
>
> —Isaac Asimov, *from* **"Robot Dreams"**

Fantasy

Fantasy is a highly imaginative type of fiction, usually set in an unfamiliar world or a distant, heroic past. Fantasy stories may include people, but they often include gnomes, elves, or other fantastical beings or supernatural forces. The use of magic is common in fantasy stories.

> I walked for I don't know how long before I came up to a big body of water. I wanted to get across it but I couldn't swim. I wanted to get across it but it would take me years to build a boat. I wanted to get across it but it would take me I didn't know how long to build a bridge. Years passed and then one day, feeling like it, I got into my boat and rowed across.
>
> —Jamaica Kincaid, *from* **"What I Have Been Doing Lately"**

Fable

A **fable** is a brief, usually simple story intended to teach a lesson about human behavior or to give advice about how to behave. Themes in fables are often stated directly. **Modern fables** also focus on themes relating to human behavior, with little development of individual characters.

> "Here's what you must do. Look for a happy man, a man who's happy through and through, and exchange your son's shirt for his."
>
> —Italo Calvino, *from* **"The Happy Man's Shirt"**

Mystery

The genre of **mystery** includes a variety of types, all of which follow a standard plot pattern. Spy stories are often mysteries, as are tales of danger or adventure. A **detective story** usually follows a standard plot pattern—a crime is committed and a detective searches for clues that lead him or her to the criminal. Any story that relies on the unknown or the terrifying can be considered a mystery.

> "Who, then, in your opinion, murdered Miss French?"
>
> "Why, a burglar, of course, as was thought at first. The window was forced, you remember. She was killed with a heavy blow from a crowbar, and the crowbar was found lying on the floor beside the body."
>
> —Agatha Christie, *from* **"The Witness for the Prosecution"**

Style and Description

Style and Tone

The expressive qualities that distinguish an author's work, including diction (word choice), sentence structure, and figures of speech, contribute to **style. Voice,** an author's distinctive use of language to convey the author's or narrator's personality to the reader, is determined by elements of style. **Tone** is the writer's attitude toward his or her subject and is conveyed through elements of style.

Description and Imagery

Description is writing that seeks to convey the impression of a setting, a person, an animal, an object, or an event by appealing to the senses. Descriptive writing usually includes **imagery,** or language that appeals to one or more of the five senses. Imagery may contain **figurative language**— expressions that are not literally true, but express some truth beyond the literal level.

> Mr. Mayherne adjusted his pince-nez and cleared his throat with a little dry-as-dust cough that was wholly typical of him. Then he looked again at the man opposite him, the man charged with willful murder.
>
> —Agatha Christie, *from* **"The Witness for the Prosecution"**

LOG ON **Literature** Online

Literature and Reading For more selections in this genre, go to glencoe.com and enter QuickPass code GL57805u6.

Literary Analysis Model

How do literary elements impact genre fiction?

Italo Calvino (1923–1985) is one of the most important Italian fiction writers of the twentieth century. "The Happy Man's Shirt" is Calvino's retelling of a traditional Italian fable, one of two hundred he collected for his 1956 book, *Italian Folktales*.

The Happy Man's Shirt

retold by Italo Calvino
translated by George Martin

APPLYING Literary Elements

Tone

The tone is objective, which makes the narrator sound reliable.

Style

Paragraph length is a stylistic choice. This paragraph is just one sentence long.

Imagery

The "word picture" Calvino creates of the prince's face causes the reader to feel pity for the prince.

A king had an only son that he thought the world of. But this prince was always unhappy. He would spend days on end at his window staring into space.

"What on earth do you lack?" asked the king. "What's wrong
5 with you?"

"I don't even know myself, Father."

"Are you in love? If there's a particular girl you fancy, tell me, and I'll arrange for you to marry her, no matter whether she's the daughter of the most powerful king on earth or the
10 poorest peasant girl alive!"

"No, Father, I'm not in love."

The king tried in every way imaginable to cheer him up, but theaters, balls, concerts, and singing were all useless, and day by day the rosy hue drained from the prince's face.

15 The king issued a decree, and from every corner of the earth came the most learned philosophers, doctors, and professors. The king showed them the prince and asked for their advice. The wise men withdrew to think, then returned to the king. "Majesty, we have given the matter close thought and we have
20 studied the stars. Here's what you must do. Look for a happy man, a man who's happy through and through, and exchange your son's shirt for his."

That same day the king sent ambassadors to all parts of the world in search of the happy man.

25 A priest was taken to the king. "Are you happy?" asked the king.

"Yes, indeed, Majesty."

"Fine. How would you like to be my bishop?"

"Oh, Majesty, if only it were so!"

30 "Away with you! Get out of my sight! I'm seeking a man who's happy just as he is, not one who's trying to better his lot."

Thus the search resumed, and before long the king was told about a neighboring king, who everybody said was a truly happy man. He had a wife as good as she was beautiful and a
35 whole slew of children. He had conquered all his enemies, and his country was at peace. Again hopeful, the king immediately sent ambassadors to him to ask for his shirt.

The neighboring king received the ambassadors and said, "Yes, indeed, I have everything anybody could possibly want.
40 But at the same time I worry because I'll have to die one day and leave it all. I can't sleep at night for worrying about that!" The ambassadors thought it wiser to go home without this man's shirt.

At his wit's end, the king went hunting. He fired at a hare
45 but only wounded it, and the hare scampered away on three legs. The king pursued it, leaving the hunting party far behind him. Out in the open field he heard a man singing a refrain. The king stopped in his tracks. "Whoever sings like that is bound to be happy!" The song led him into a vineyard, where
50 he found a young man singing and pruning the vines.

"Good day, Majesty," said the youth. "So early and already out in the country?"

"Bless you! Would you like me to take you to the capital? You will be my friend."

55 "Much obliged, Majesty, but I wouldn't even consider it. I wouldn't even change places with the Pope."

"Why not? Such a fine young man like you . . ."

"No, no, I tell you. I'm content with just what I have and want nothing more."

60 "A happy man at last!" thought the king. "Listen, young man. Do me a favor."

"With all my heart, Majesty, if I can."

"Wait just a minute," said the king, who, unable to contain his joy any longer, ran to get his retinue. "Come with me! My
65 son is saved! My son is saved!" And he took them to the young man. "My dear lad," he began, "I'll give you whatever you want! But give me. . . give me . . ."

"What, Majesty?"

"My son is dying! Only you can save him. Come here!"
70 The king grabbed him and started unbuttoning the youth's jacket. All of a sudden he stopped, and his arms fell to his sides.

The happy man wore no shirt.

Diyon

The choice of the word *slew* is informal.

Voice

Medium-length sentences contribute to the narrator's straightforward reporter-like voice.

Imagery

The vivid physical description appeals to the sense of touch.

Reading Check

Evaluate Would you say that Calvino's stylistic choices were successful in "The Happy Man's Shirt"? Explain your answer.

Wrap-Up

Guide to Reading Genre Fiction

- Identify the genre category.

- Monitor your enjoyment as you read.

- Pay attention to characters, settings, plot development, and themes, as you do with other genres of fiction.

- Evaluate the consistency with which the author creates the imaginary world.

- Notice elements of the author's style.

Elements of Genre Fiction

- **Style** refers to all the choices the author makes and includes voice, diction, and tone.

- **Diction** refers to the words the author chooses.

- **Voice** tells the reader about the author's or narrator's personality.

- **Tone** communicates the author's attitude toward the audience or the subject matter.

- **Description** is a detailed portrayal of a person, a place, an object, or an event.

- **Imagery** is descriptive language that appeals to one or more of the five senses.

LOG ON ▶ **Literature** Online

Unit Resources For additional skills practice, go to glencoe.com and enter QuickPass code GL57805u6.

Activities ➤

Use what you have learned about reading and analyzing genre fiction to do one of these activities.

1. Visual Literacy Create an illustration for one part of "The Happy Man's Shirt" and share it with your class. Discuss which details of the story support the illustration.

2. Speaking and Listening "The Happy Man's Shirt" was translated from Italian. In a small group, discuss the likely effects of translation on style, diction, tone, and voice. Then compare the use of language in this work with that in another translated work you have read in this book. Prepare a statement summing up the writing techniques that help make a translation good.

3. Take Notes Try using this study organizer to make inferences about genre in different cultural, historical, and contemporary contexts as you read the works in this unit. Use your notes to help you infer the themes of the texts. Use text evidence to support your inferences.

 FOLDABLES Study Organizer   **BOUND BOOK**

Reader-Response Journal

The Extraordinary and Fantastic

Classic Domed Disk with Windows and Four-Piece Landing Gear Hovers over Country Home near Helena, Montana, USA, ca. 20th century. Artist Unknown.

View the Art This painting appears to depict the moments just before the residents of the home encounter the spaceship. Based on your knowledge of the science fiction genre in literature and movies, what would you expect to happen in this scene?

BIG IDEA

Imagine a world where extraordinary things happen. Imagine traveling to distant galaxies or living in a world where dreams become real. The science fiction, fable, and mystery in Unit 6 will expand your imagination. As you read these tales, ask yourself, What makes these stories so appealing?

TEKS

For pages 998–999

10.7 Understand, make inferences and draw conclusions about how an author's sensory language creates imagery in literary text and provide evidence from text to support understanding.

LITERARY FOCUS

Description and Style

How do writers of genre fiction use description and style?

Description is writing that seeks to convey the impression of a setting, a person, an animal, an object, or an event by appealing to the senses. **Style** is the distinctive way that a writer uses language. In the following description of a child's room, notice the specific images and vivid words that make an everyday place extraordinary and that characterize Ray Bradbury's style.

Four-thirty.
The nursery walls glowed.
Animals took shape: yellow giraffes, blue lions, pink antelopes, lilac panthers cavorting in crystal substance. The walls were glass. They looked out upon color and fantasy. Hidden films docked through well-oiled sprockets, and the walls lived. The nursery floor was woven to resemble a crisp, cereal meadow.

—Ray Bradbury, *from* **"There Will Come Soft Rains"**

Description

Good descriptive writing often includes figurative language and imagery.

Figurative Language **Figurative language** uses expressions that are not literally true but express truths that go beyond the literal level. Three types of figurative language are simile, metaphor, and personification.

Simile and **metaphor** are figures of speech that compare two seemingly unlike things in order to suggest their underlying similarities. A simile uses *like* or *as*, whereas a metaphor makes a direct comparison. Notice how the following simile conveys the futuristic quality of the robotic mice in Bradbury's story.

Then, like mysterious invaders, they popped into their burrows. Their pink electric eyes faded.

—Ray Bradbury, *from* **"There Will Come Soft Rains"**

Personification is a figure of speech that attributes human qualities to an animal, an object, a force of nature, or an idea. Notice how the personification of the fluorescent light in Levertov's poem creates a vivid image.

The fluorescent light flickers sullenly, a
pause. But you command. It grabs
each face and holds it up
by the hair for you, mask after mask.

—Denise Levertov, *from* **"People at Night"**

Imagery Good descriptive writing uses
imagery—language that appeals to one or
more of the five senses: sight, sound, touch,
taste, and smell. Imagery helps to create an
emotional response in the reader.

Style

The expressive qualities that distinguish an
author's work are his or her **style.** An important
element of an author's style is **diction,** a writer's
choice of words. Good writers choose their words
carefully to convey a particular meaning or feeling. Notice how Stephen Vincent Benét's word
choice and short sentences create suspense in the
passage below.

I was in darkness—I found stairs and climbed. There
were many stairs, turning around till my head was
dizzy. At the top was another door—I found the
knob and opened it.

—Stephen Vincent Benét, *from* **"By the Waters of Babylon"**

LOG ON ▶ **Literature** Online

Literature and Reading For more about literary
elements, go to glencoe.com and enter QuickPass code
GL57805u6.

Tone

Tone is a writer's attitude toward his or her
subject matter. Tone is conveyed through elements such as diction, punctuation, sentence
structure, and figurative language. A writer's
tone may be sympathetic, objective, serious,
ironic, sad, bitter, or humorous, among other
things.

Imagine a prison. There is something you know
that you have not yet told. Those in control of the
prison know that you know.

—Margaret Atwood, *from* **"Bread"**

Quickwrite

Make Inferences About Imagery Select an
image from one of the excerpts on these
pages. What sensory details does the author
use to create the image? Use a graphic organizer like the one below to record your ideas.
In the center oval, write the image you have
selected. In the outer ovals, record the sensory
details the author uses to create that image.

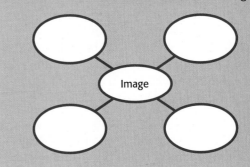

Before You Read

There Will Come Soft Rains

Meet **Ray Bradbury**

(Born 1920)

From the time he began reading at age four, Ray Bradbury loved stories containing fantasy plots, such as *The Wizard of Oz* and *Tarzan.* Bradbury was also a fan of the *Buck Rogers* comic strip, one of the first series in a genre people were calling "science fiction."

At the age of twelve, his dream of writing his own stories came closer to reality when his parents gave him a toy typewriter for Christmas. Bradbury wrote, "I stormed it with words. Anytime I liked I could turn a faucet on each finger and let the miracles out, yes, into machines and onto paper where I might freeze and control them forever. I haven't stopped writing since."

> "*The act of writing is, for me, like a fever—something I must do.*"
> —Ray Bradbury

Storming the World with Words Bradbury, who had no formal education beyond high school, did not follow any formulas for writing success. He has described his writing process as "[My stories] run up and bite me on the leg—I respond by writing down everything that goes on during the bite. When I finish, the idea lets go and runs off." He published his first science fiction stories in pulp magazines, and later in the *New Yorker* and the *Saturday Evening Post.*

"There Will Come Soft Rains" was part of his book *The Martian Chronicles,* published in 1950. The collection of stories describing the colonization of Mars was a major breakthrough in Bradbury's career. It included many of Bradbury's signature topics, such as his longing for a simpler world and the fear of nuclear war.

Fantasy or Science Fiction? Bradbury's novel *Fahrenheit 451* is often hailed as his greatest work. Published in 1953, it is set in a future world where firefighters are considered heroes for burning books. Other novels include *The Illustrated Man,* and *Something Wicked This Way Comes.* Bradbury also wrote scripts for television series, including *Alfred Hitchcock Presents* and *The Twilight Zone.*

Although many of his stories contained futuristic elements that could only be imagined in the 1950s, Bradbury claims that *Fahrenheit 451* was his only science fiction work. He describes all his other works as fantasy. Bradbury defines fantasy as being about things that cannot happen. Science fiction, he explains, is about things that can happen. Bradbury's more than five hundred published works have played a large role in changing the way people think about their world.

Author Search For more about Ray Bradbury, go to glencoe.com and enter QuickPass code GL57805u6.

Literature and Reading Preview

Connect to the Story

What would it be like to live in a house that does everything for you? Freewrite about what it might be like to live in a world that is totally run by computers and robots.

Build Background

Ray Bradbury wrote "There Will Come Soft Rains" in 1951 when people were still recovering from World War II. People had seen that one atomic bomb can destroy an entire city and were concerned about nuclear war destroying everything on Earth.

Set Purposes for Reading

Big Idea The Extraordinary and Fantastic

As you read, ask yourself, How does Bradbury use extraordinary or fantastic elements to develop his message?

Literary Element Diction

Diction is a writer's choice of words. Skilled writers choose their words carefully to convey a particular meaning or feeling. Writers must consider a word's connotations, or implied or suggested meanings. As you read, ask yourself, What is Bradbury suggesting through his word choices?

Reading Strategy Identify Genre

A **genre** is a category or type of literature, such as fiction or poetry. Each genre can be subdivided into more specific categories. When you **identify a genre,** you use the style, content, and historical and cultural context of the text and your own understanding to figure out the category into which a literary work falls. As you read, ask yourself, What clues can help me determine the genre of this story?

Tip: Analyze Clues As you read, use a chart like the one below to note clues in the text that can help you infer the genre attention to the historical, cultural, and contemporary co the story. Use the blue highlighted questions to help yo

Clue	Inference About Genre
voice from the ceiling stated the day's schedule	This seems like a futuristic setting.

TEKS

For pages 1000–1011

10.2 Analyze, make inferences and draw conclusions about theme and genre in different cultural, historical, and contemporary contexts and provide evidence from the text to support understanding.

Vocabulary

paranoia (par´ ə noi´ ə) *n.* the mental state of being very afraid or suspicious of others; p. 1004 *John's paranoia caused him to check the locks on all the doors and windows each night.*

frenzy (fren´ zē) *n.* a state of wild, intense emotion, as of excitement; p. 1004 *Anna raced around in a frenzy trying to complete her science project before the deadline.*

sublime (sə blīm´) *adj.* noble; exalted; above all others; p. 1009 *The photograph captured the sublime beauty of the sunset.*

Tip: Analogies An **analogy** is a stated or implied comparison that shows a relationship between two things. For example, *paranoia : suspicion* has a synonymous relationship.

There Will Come Soft Rains

Ray Bradbury

*I*n the living room the voice-clock sang, *Tick-tock, seven o'clock, time to get up, time to get up, seven o'clock!* as if it were afraid that nobody would. The morning house lay empty. The clock ticked on, repeating and repeating its sounds into the emptiness. *Seven-nine, breakfast time, seven-nine!*

In the kitchen the breakfast stove gave a hissing sigh and ejected from its warm interior eight pieces of perfectly browned toast, eight eggs sunnyside up, sixteen slices of bacon, two coffees, and two cool glasses of milk.

"Today is August 4, 2026," said a second voice from the kitchen ceiling, "in the city of Allendale, California." It repeated the date three times for memory's sake. "Today is Mr. Featherstone's birthday. Today is the anniversary of Tilita's marriage. Insurance is payable, as are the water, gas, and light bills."

Somewhere in the walls, relays clicked, memory tapes glided under electric eyes.

Eight-one, tick-tock, eight-one o'clock, off to school, off to work, run, run, eight-one! But no doors slammed, no carpets took the soft tread of rubber heels. It was raining outside. The weather box on the front door sang quietly: "Rain, rain, go away; rubbers, raincoats for today . . ." And the rain tapped on the empty house, echoing.

Outside, the garage chimed and lifted its door to reveal the waiting car. After a long wait the door swung down again.

At eight-thirty the eggs were shriveled and the toast was like stone. An aluminum wedge scraped them into the sink, where hot water whirled them down a metal throat which digested and flushed them away to the distant sea. The dirty dishes were dropped into a hot washer and emerged twinkling dry.

Nine-fifteen, sang the clock, *time to clean*.

Out of warrens[1] in the wall, tiny robot mice darted. The rooms were acrawl with the small cleaning animals, all rubber and metal. They thudded against chairs, whirling their mustached runners, kneading the rug nap, sucking gently at hidden dust. Then, like mysterious invaders, they popped into their burrows. Their pink electric eyes faded. The house was clean.

Ten o'clock. The sun came out from behind the rain. The house stood alone in a city of rubble and ashes. This was the one house left standing. At night the ruined city gave off a radioactive glow which could be seen for miles.

Ten-fifteen. The garden sprinklers whirled up in golden founts, filling the soft morning air with scatterings of brightness. The water pelted windowpanes, running down the charred west side where the house had been burned evenly free of its white paint. The entire west face of the house was black, save for five places. Here the silhouette in paint of a man mowing a lawn. Here, as in a photograph, a woman bent to pick flowers. Still farther over, their images burned on wood in one titanic instant, a small boy, hands flung into the air; higher up, the image of a thrown ball, and opposite him a girl, hands raised to catch a ball which never came down.

The five spots of paint—the man, the woman, the children, the ball—remained. The rest was a thin charcoaled layer.

The gentle sprinkler rain filled the garden with falling light.

Until this day, how well the house had kept its peace. How carefully it had

---

Diction *What attitude or feelings do the words hissing and ejected suggest in this passage?*

Identify Genre *From what you've read so far, what elements help you infer the genre of this story?*

1. *Warrens* are the burrows, or little holes, that animals such as mice dig out and live in.

The Extraordinary and Fantastic *What is Bradbury suggesting happened to the city?*

RAY BRADBURY **1003**

inquired, "Who goes there? What's the pass-word?" and, getting no answer from lonely foxes and whining cats, it had shut up its windows and drawn shades in an old-maid-enly preoccupation with self-protection which bordered on a mechanical **paranoia.**

It quivered at each sound, the house did. If a sparrow brushed a window, the shade snapped up. The bird, startled, flew off! No, not even a bird must touch the house!

The house was an altar with ten thou-sand attendants, big, small, servicing, attending, in choirs. But the gods had gone away, and the ritual of the religion contin-ued senselessly, uselessly.

Twelve noon.

A dog whined, shivering, on the front porch.

The front door recognized the dog voice and opened. The dog, once huge and fleshy, but now gone to bone and covered with sores, moved in and through the house, tracking mud. Behind it whirred angry mice, angry at having to pick up mud, angry at inconvenience.

For not a leaf fragment blew under the door but what the wall panels flipped open and the copper scrap rats flashed swiftly out. The offending dust, hair, or paper, seized in miniature steel jaws, was raced back to the burrows. There, down tubes which fed into the cellar, it was dropped into the sighing vent of an incinerator[2] which sat like evil Baal[3] in a dark corner.

The dog ran upstairs, hysterically yelp-ing to each door, at last realizing, as the house realized, that only silence was here.

It sniffed the air and scratched the kitchen door. Behind the door, the stove was making pancakes which filled the house with a rich baked odor and the scent of maple syrup.

The dog frothed at the mouth, lying at the door, sniffing, its eyes turned to fire. It ran wildly in circles, biting at its tail, spun in a **frenzy,** and died. It lay in the parlor for an hour.

Two o'clock, sang a voice.

Delicately sensing decay at last, the regi-ments[4] of mice hummed out as softly as blown gray leaves in an electrical wind.

Two-fifteen.

The dog was gone.

In the cellar, the incinerator glowed sud-denly and a whirl of sparks leaped up the chimney.

Two thirty-five.

Bridge tables sprouted from patio walls. Playing cards fluttered onto pads in a shower of pips.[5] Martinis manifested on an oaken bench with egg-salad sandwiches. Music played.

But the tables were silent and the cards untouched.

At four o'clock the tables folded like great butterflies back through the paneled walls.

---

4. *Regiments* are groups of soldiers.
5. *Pips* are the small printed symbols that show a playing card's value.

Diction *What do the words in this paragraph tell you about the dog?*

Identify Genre *What might Bradbury be suggesting about the significance of life and death in the way the house responds to the death of the dog?*

---

2. An *incinerator* is a kind of furnace for burning trash.
3. *Baal* was a god worshipped in ancient times.

Diction *What does Bradbury suggest about the house with this description?*

Vocabulary

paranoia (par´ ə noi´ ə) *n.* the mental state of being very afraid or suspicious of others

Vocabulary

frenzy (fren´ zē) *n.* a state of wild, intense emotion as of excitement

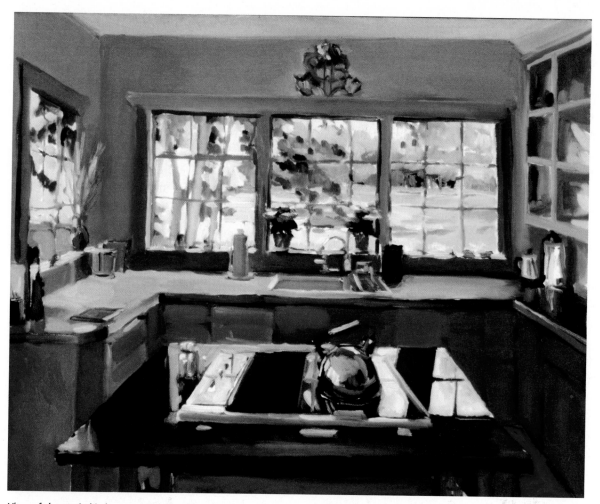

View of domestic kitchen. Connie Hayes.

Four-thirty.

The nursery walls glowed.

Animals took shape: yellow giraffes, blue lions, pink antelopes, lilac panthers cavorting[6] in crystal substance. The walls were glass. They looked out upon color and fantasy. Hidden films clocked through well-oiled sprockets, and the walls lived. The nursery floor was woven to resemble a crisp, cereal[7] meadow. Over this ran aluminum roaches and iron crickets, and in the hot still air butterflies of delicate red tissue wavered among the sharp aromas of animal spoors![8] There was the sound like a great matted yellow hive of bees within a dark bellows, the lazy bumble of a purring lion. And there was the patter of okapi[9] feet and the murmur of a fresh jungle rain, like other hoofs, falling upon the summer-starched grass. Now the walls dissolved into distances of parched weed, mile on mile, and warm endless sky. The animals drew away into thorn brakes and water holes.

6. When the animals are *cavorting*, they are running and playing.
7. A *cereal* meadow is a grassy field.
8. *Spoors* are animal droppings.

9. An *okapi* is an African mammal with zebralike black and white stripes on the upper legs and hindquarters.

Diction *How does the description of the nursery contrast with the earlier description of the world outside the house? Why do you think Bradbury includes this description of the nursery?*

It was the children's hour.

Five o'clock. The bath filled with clear hot water.

Six, seven, eight o'clock. The dinner dishes manipulated[10] like magic tricks, and in the study a *click.* In the metal stand opposite the hearth where a fire now blazed up warmly, a cigar popped out, half an inch of soft gray ash on it, smoking, waiting.

Nine o'clock. The beds warmed their hidden circuits, for nights were cool here.

Nine-five. A voice spoke from the study ceiling:

"Mrs. McClellan, which poem would you like this evening?"

The house was silent.

The voice said at last, "Since you express no preference, I shall select a poem at random." Quiet music rose to back the voice. "Sara Teasdale.[11] As I recall, your favorite. . . .

*There will come soft rains and the smell of
the ground,
And swallows circling with their shimmering sound;*

*And frogs in the pools singing at night,
And wild plum trees in tremulous white;[12]*

*Robins will wear their feathery fire,
Whistling their whims on a low fence-wire;*

*And not one will know of the war, not one
Will care at last when it is done.*

*Not one would mind, neither bird nor tree,
If mankind perished utterly;*

*And Spring herself, when she woke at dawn
Would scarcely know that we were gone.*

The fire burned on the stone hearth and the cigar fell away into a mound of quiet ash on its tray. The empty chairs faced each other between the silent walls, and the music played.

At ten o'clock the house began to die.

The wind blew. A falling tree bough crashed through the kitchen window. Cleaning solvent,[13] bottled, shattered over the stove. The room was ablaze in an instant!

"Fire!" screamed a voice. The house lights flashed, water pumps shot water from the ceilings. But the solvent spread on the linoleum, licking, eating, under the kitchen door, while the voices took it up in chorus: "Fire, fire, fire!"

The house tried to save itself. Doors sprang tightly shut, but the windows were broken by the heat and the wind blew and sucked upon the fire.

The house gave ground as the fire in ten billion angry sparks moved with flaming ease from room to room and then up the stairs. While scurrying water rats squeaked from the walls, pistoled their water, and ran for more. And the wall sprays let down showers of mechanical rain.

But too late. Somewhere, sighing, a pump shrugged to a stop. The quenching rain ceased. The reserve water supply which had filled baths and washed dishes for many quiet days was gone.

---

10. Here, *manipulated* means "moved around."
11. *Sara Teasdale,* a twentieth-century American poet, often wrote about the beauty of nature.
12. *In tremulous white* means that the plum trees, full of white blossoms, are shaking.

13. A *cleaning solvent* is a liquid chemical that burns easily.

Identify Genre *How does the detail about the voice picking out a poem contribute to the futuristic setting of the story?*

Diction Bradbury chooses the word die *instead of a synonym such as* perish *or* expire. *What effect does his word choice have?*

Legato, 1983. Jeremy Annett. Oil on hardboard. Private collection.

__View the Art__ How does the mood of this painting compare with the mood of the story? Explain.

House with Electrical Symbols. Chris Spollen.

The fire crackled up the stairs. It fed upon Picassos and Matisses[14] in the upper halls, like delicacies, baking off the oily flesh, tenderly crisping the canvases into black shavings.

Now the fire lay in beds, stood in windows, changed the colors of drapes!

And then, reinforcements.

From attic trapdoors, blind robot faces peered down with faucet mouths gushing green chemical.

The fire backed off, as even an elephant must at the sight of a dead snake. Now there were twenty snakes whipping over the floor, killing the fire with a clear cold venom of green froth.

---

14. *Picassos* and *Matisses* are valuable paintings by twentieth-century artists Pablo Picasso and Henri Matisse. The narration suggests that the burning paintings are delicacies, or delicious things for the fire to eat.

Diction *How do the author's word choices in describing the fire personify the house and the fire?*

But the fire was clever. It had sent flame outside the house, up through the attic to the pumps there. An explosion! The attic brain which directed the pumps was shattered into bronze shrapnel on the beams.

The fire rushed back into every closet and felt of the clothes hung there.

The house shuddered, oak bone on bone, its bared skeleton cringing from the heat, its wire, its nerves revealed as if a surgeon had torn the skin off to let the red veins and capillaries quiver in the scalded air. Help, help! Fire! Run, run! Heat snapped mirrors like the first brittle winter ice. And the voices wailed, Fire, fire, run, run, like a tragic nursery rhyme, a dozen voices, high, low, like children dying in a forest, alone, alone. And the voices fading as the wires popped their sheathings like hot chestnuts. One, two, three, four, five voices died.

In the nursery the jungle burned. Blue lions roared, purple giraffes bounded off. The panthers ran in circles, changing color, and ten million animals, running before the fire, vanished off toward a distant steaming river. . . .

Ten more voices died. In the last instant under the fire avalanche, other choruses, oblivious, could be heard announcing the time, playing music, cutting the lawn by remote-control mower, or setting an umbrella frantically out and in, the slamming and opening front door, a thousand things happening, like a clock shop when each clock strikes the hour insanely before or after the other, a scene of maniac confusion yet unity; singing, screaming, a few last cleaning mice darting bravely out to carry the horrid ashes away! And one voice, with **sublime** disregard for the situation, read poetry aloud in the fiery study, until all the film spools burned, until all the wires withered and the circuits cracked.

The fire burst the house and let it slam flat down, puffing out skirts of spark and smoke.

In the kitchen, an instant before the rain of fire and timber, the stove could be seen making breakfasts at a psychopathic rate, ten dozen eggs, six loaves of toast, twenty dozen bacon strips, which, eaten by fire, started the stove working again, hysterically hissing!

The crash. The attic smashing into kitchen and parlor. The parlor into cellar, cellar into sub-cellar. Deep freeze, armchair, film tapes, circuits, beds, and all like skeletons thrown in a cluttered mound deep under.

Smoke and silence. A great quantity of smoke.

Dawn showed faintly in the east. Among the ruins, one wall stood alone. Within the wall, a last voice said, over and over again and again, even as the sun rose to shine upon the heaped rubble and steam:

"Today is August 5, 2026, today is August 5, 2026, today is . . ." ∾

The Extraordinary and Fantastic *Consider what happens to the animals in the nursery. What might this event symbolize?*

Identify Genre *What might Bradbury wish to convey by ending the story this way?*

Vocabulary

sublime (sə blīm´) *adj.* noble; exalted; above all others

After You Read

Respond and Think Critically

1. **Connect to Personal Experience** Did the story cause you to think differently about the future or the role of machines in society? Explain.

2. **Make Inferences About Characters** What can you infer about the people who lived in the house? Who were they? What was their lifestyle like? Use details from the story to support your answer.

3. **Analyze Characterization** Who or what is the main character in this story? How does Bradbury use literary devices to characterize this character? Support your response with examples from the story.

4. **Analyze Historical Context** What historical event might have motivated Bradbury to write "There Will Come Soft Rains?" What part of the story mirrors that event? How might this event relate to Bradbury's overall theme?

5. **Draw Conclusions About Meaning** What is the significance of the Sara Teasdale poem in this story? Support your response with text evidence. **OER**

6. **Evaluate Setting** Which technology in the house do you find most believable? Which technology do you think could not exist? Are there any parts of the setting that seem out of place for the year 2026? Explain.

7. **Big Idea** **Draw Conclusions About Theme** What theme does Bradbury convey in the story through his use of extraordinary and fantastic elements? Support your response with text evidence.

Literary Element | Diction

The author's **diction,** or word choice, helps establish a mood and helps the reader visualize events. **Denotation** (a word's dictionary definition) and **connotation** (a word's implied meaning) are closely related to diction.

8. **Analyze Denotation and Connotation** Bradbury describes the cleaning robots as "mysterious invaders." What is the denotation of the word *invaders*? What connotation does the word have in the story?

9. **Draw Conclusions About Theme** Bradbury uses words such as *regiments, reinforcements,* and *shrapnel* in the story. How would you characterize these words? How do these word choices reflect the theme of the story?

Review: Personification

As you learned on page 513, **personification** is a figure of speech in which an animal, an object, a force of nature, or an idea is given human form or characteristics.

10. **Partner Activity** With a partner, skim the story and find at least five examples of personification. Discuss how each example makes the house and its mechanized parts seem human. Compile your findings in a chart like the one below.

Personification	Effect
"In the living room the voice-clock sang . . ."	The singing clock makes the house seem inviting.

Some subgenres of fiction include adventure, fantasy, mystery, romance, and science fiction.

11. What subgenre does "There Will Come Soft Rains" fall into? What clues in the historical and cultural context helped you to identify this subgenre?

12. In the author biography on page 1000, Bradbury differentiates between fantasy and science fiction. Do you agree with him that this story is fantasy because it could never happen? Explain.

Vocabulary Practice

Practice with Analogies For each item below, decide what the relationship is between the first pair of words. Then apply that relationship to the second pair.

1. worry : concern :: paranoia :
  a. excitement   **c.** suspicion
  b. mind   **d.** delight

2. oak : tree :: frenzy :
  a. emotion   **c.** chaotic
  b. rapid   **d.** calm

3. attractive : unattractive :: sublime :
  a. haughty   **c.** beneath
  b. magnificent   **d.** ordinary

Academic Vocabulary

The destruction of the world outside the house leads one to form the **deduction** *that an atomic bomb has gone off.*

Deduction is an academic word that describes a form of reasoning. If you know that atomic bombs cause great destruction, you can *deduce* that the damage was caused by such a bomb. To further explore the meaning of this word, answer the following question: From the overall mood and theme of the story, what **deduction** can you make about Bradbury's attitude toward the interaction between humans and machines?

For more on academic vocabulary, see pages 36–37 and R92–R94.

Write with Style

 Apply Figurative Language

Assignment Write an engaging science fiction story with a well-developed conflict and resolution, interesting and believable characters, and figurative language that helps define the mood and tone.

Get Ideas Think about a serious or humorous event that might take place in a futuristic or alien world. Review how Bradbury uses figurative language, such as simile, metaphor, and personification, to enhance the tone, mood, and meaning of his story.

EXAMPLES:
"Rain, rain, go away; rubbers, raincoats for today" uses both rhyme and alliteration to create a light-hearted tone.

"But the gods had gone away, and the ritual of the religion continued senselessly, uselessly" is part of a metaphor that creates a darker mood.

Create a chart like the one below in which you list examples of figurative language you might use to create the desired mood in your story.

	Setting	Characters	Actions
Figurative language			

Give It Structure Use suspense to enhance the plot and conflict. Bring your characters to life by using realistic and interesting dialogue. Try to convey a particular theme in your story that fits well with the science fiction genre.

Look at Language Focus on the use of figurative language in your story. You can use sound devices such as alliteration or onomatopoeia to enhance the mood. Metaphors help the reader visualize an entire scene through a few words. However, don't overdo devices to the point that they distract from the content of your story.

Before You Read

By the Waters of Babylon

Meet **Stephen Vincent Benét**
(1898–1943)

Themes of history and war march through the works of Stephen Vincent Benét, who was born in Bethlehem, Pennsylvania, into a military family.

Benét spent his childhood on army posts in California and attended school at a military academy. Benét's first book of poems, *Five Men and Pompey*, was published in 1915 when he was just seventeen years old and a student at Yale University. His studies were interrupted by a year of government service during World War I, when he worked as a code clerk in the same department as writer James Thurber. After returning to school, Benét submitted a volume of poems entitled *Heavens and Earth* his master's degree thesis.

> "*Books are not men and yet they stay alive.*"
>
> —Stephen Vincent Benét

A Literary Career Benét then turned to fiction, publishing the autobiographical novel *The Beginning of Wisdom* in 1921. He moved to France to continue his studies at the Sorbonne, where he met his wife, writer Rosemary Carr.

While living in France, Benét wrote the epic Civil War poem *John Brown's Body*. The poem achieved immediate critical and popular acclaim, and Benét won the Pulitzer Prize for the book in 1929. That same year, he was elected to the National Institute of Arts and Letters.

Benét also was interested in horror, mystery, and science fiction. In 1937 he published a one-act play entitled *The Headless Horseman*, based on the Washington Irving story "The Legend of Sleepy Hollow." That same year, Benét published the short story collection *Thirteen O'Clock*, which included his famous story "The Devil and Daniel Webster." Based on the German legend of Faust, it features a man who sells his soul to the devil. The story was adapted as a play, an opera, and two movies.

During the 1940s, Benét worked in radio and as a screenwriter in Hollywood. Throughout his life, he suffered from poor vision and other illnesses but continued to publish and earn honors as a writer, receiving the O. Henry Story Prize and the Roosevelt Medal. Benét was awarded a second Pulitzer Prize posthumously for his epic poem *Western Star*.

LOG ON ▶ **Literature** Online

Author Search For more about Stephen Vincent Benét, go to glencoe.com and enter QuickPass code GL57805u6.

Literature and Reading Preview

Connect to the Story

How do you know when you become an adult? Discuss this question with a partner.

Build Background

Many readers and critics have interpreted this story as an allegory about the aftermath of a nuclear holocaust. Although this story was written in 1937, years before the first atomic weapons were developed, our knowledge of the devastation caused by nuclear bombings makes the scenes depicted in Benét's tale all the more affecting.

Set Purposes for Reading

Big Idea The Extraordinary and Fantastic

As you read, ask yourself, How is the narrator awed and amazed by the places he visits?

Literary Element Narrator

The **narrator** is the person who tells the story. The narrator may be outside of the story, or a character in the story. Narrators may be reliable or unreliable. **Unreliable narrators** sometimes intentionally mislead readers or fail to understand the true meaning of the events they describe. As you read, ask yourself, Is the narrator of this story reliable?

Reading Strategy Visualize

Visualizing, or creating sensory images, means using an author's words to form a mental picture of what is being described. Visualizing allows you to enter a story's world and better understand the action taking place. As you read, ask yourself, What do I see in each scene?

· ·

Tip: Note Descriptive Words Practice creating sensory images to reflect on your understanding and monitor comprehension. Use a chart like the one below to record what you visualize in each paragraph.

Paragraph	Visualization
"Yet, after a while, my eyes were opened and I saw."	I picture the ruins of road bridges crossing over a river.

TEKS

For pages 1012–1028

10.5.C Evaluate the connection between forms of narration (e.g., unreliable) and tone in works of fiction.

Vocabulary

bade (bād) *v.* past tense of bid; commanded, ordered, or asked; p. 1015 *The babysitter bade the two naughty children to stop running in the house.*

anteroom (an′ tē rōom′) *n.* a small room serving as a waiting area or an entrance to a larger, main room; p. 1021 *My grandmother always greeted her guests in the anteroom.*

perplexed (pər plekst′) *adj.* troubled with doubt or uncertainty; puzzled; p. 1024 *I felt perplexed by the complicated math formula.*

· ·

Tip: Word Usage Reserve formal usage, such as the word *bade*, for formal occasions, such as a speech or paper; reserve informal usage, such as *asked*, for conversation or friendly e-mail.

A Pyramid of Skulls, 1898–1900. Paul Cézanne. Oil on canvas. Private collection.

By the Waters of Babylon

Stephen Vincent Benét

The north and the west and the south are good hunting ground, but it is forbidden to go east. It is forbidden to go to any of the Dead Places except to search for metal and then he who touches the metal must be a priest or the son of a priest. Afterwards, both the man and the metal must be purified.[1] These are the rules and the laws; they are well made. It is forbidden to cross the great river and look upon the place that was the Place of the Gods—this is most strictly forbidden. We do not even say its name though we know its name. It is there that spirits live, and demons—it is there that there are the ashes of the Great Burning. These things are forbidden—they have been forbidden since the beginning of time.

My father is a priest; I am the son of a priest. I have been in the Dead Places near us, with my father—at first, I was afraid.

---

1. *Purification* refers to the process of cleansing one's body to rid it of impurities. Here, the word has the additional meaning of detoxifying or removing any harmful contaminants from the metal.

Narrator *What have you learned about the identity of the narrator? Is the narrator inside or outside the story?*

When my father went into the house to search for the metal, I stood by the door and my heart felt small and weak. It was a dead man's house, a spirit house. It did not have the smell of man, though there were old bones in a corner. But it is not fitting that a priest's son should show fear. I looked at the bones in the shadow and kept my voice still.

Then my father came out with the metal—a good, strong piece. He looked at me with both eyes but I had not run away. He gave me the metal to hold—I took it and did not die. So he knew that I was truly his son and would be a priest in my time. That was when I was very young—nevertheless, my brothers would not have done it, though they are good hunters. After that, they gave me the good piece of meat and the warm corner by the fire. My father watched over me—he was glad that I should be a priest. But when I boasted or wept without a reason, he punished me more strictly than my brothers. That was right.

After a time, I myself was allowed to go into the dead houses and search for metal. So I learned the ways of those houses—and if I saw bones, I was no longer afraid. The bones are light and old—sometimes they will fall into dust if you touch them. But that is a great sin.

I was taught the chants and the spells— I was taught how to stop the running of blood from a wound and many secrets. A priest must know many secrets—that was what my father said. If the hunters think we do all things by chants and spells, they may believe so—it does not hurt them. I was taught how to read in the old books and how to make the old writings—that was hard and took a long time. My knowledge made me happy—it was like a fire in my heart. Most of all, I liked to hear of the Old Days and the stories of the gods. I asked myself many questions that I could not answer, but it was good to ask them. At night, I would lie awake and listen to the wind—it seemed to me that it was the voice of the gods as they flew through the air.

We are not ignorant like the Forest People—our women spin wool on the wheel, our priests wear a white robe. We do not eat grubs from the tree, we have not forgotten the old writings, although they are hard to understand. Nevertheless, my knowledge and my lack of knowledge burned in me—I wished to know more. When I was a man at last, I came to my father and said, "It is time for me to go on my journey. Give me your leave."

He looked at me for a long time, stroking his beard, then he said at last, "Yes. It is time." That night, in the house of the priesthood, I asked for and received purification. My body hurt but my spirit was a cool stone. It was my father himself who questioned me about my dreams.

He **bade** me look into the smoke of the fire and see—I saw and told what I saw. It was what I have always seen—a river, and, beyond it, a great Dead Place and in it the gods walking. I have always thought about that. His eyes were stern when I told him—he was no longer my father but a priest. He said, "This is a strong dream."

"It is mine," I said, while the smoke waved and my head felt light. They were

Visual Vocabulary
A *grub* is the soft, wormlike larva of an insect, especially of a beetle.

Visualize *What image of the narrator does the metaphor "my spirit was a cool stone" create?*

Vocabulary

bade (bād) *v.* past tense of bid; commanded, ordered, or asked

Where Eagles Dare! James Noel Smith.

singing the Star song in the outer chamber and it was like the buzzing of bees in my head.

He asked me how the gods were dressed and I told him how they were dressed. We know how they were dressed from the book, but I saw them as if they were before me. When I had finished, he threw the sticks three times and studied them as they fell.

"This is a very strong dream," he said. "It may eat you up."

"I am not afraid," I said and looked at him with both eyes. My voice sounded thin in my ears but that was because of the smoke.

He touched me on the breast and the forehead. He gave me the bow and the three arrows.

"Take them," he said. "It is forbidden to travel east. It is forbidden to cross the river. It is forbidden to go to the Place of the Gods. All these things are forbidden."

"All these things are forbidden," I said, but it was my voice that spoke and not my spirit. He looked at me again.

"My son," he said. "Once I had young dreams. If your dreams do not eat you up, you may be a great priest. If they eat

---

The Extraordinary and Fantastic *What does John's father mean when he says the dream "may eat you up"?*

Narrator *Do you think the narrator believes that all things are forbidden? How might this lead to a conflict?*

you, you are still my son. Now go on your journey."

I went fasting,[2] as is the law. My body hurt but not my heart. When the dawn came, I was out of sight of the village. I prayed and purified myself, waiting for a sign. The sign was an eagle. It flew east.

Sometimes signs are sent by bad spirits. I waited again on the flat rock, fasting, taking no food. I was very still—I could feel the sky above me and the earth beneath. I waited till the sun was beginning to sink. Then three deer passed in the valley, going east—they did not wind me or see me. There was a white fawn with them—a very great sign.

I followed them, at a distance, waiting for what would happen. My heart was troubled about going east, yet I knew that I must go. My head hummed with my fasting—I did not even see the panther spring upon the white fawn. But, before I knew it, the bow was in my hand. I shouted and the panther lifted his head from the fawn. It is not easy to kill a panther with one arrow but the arrow went through his eye and into his brain. He died as he tried to spring—he rolled over, tearing at the ground. Then I knew I was meant to go east—I knew that was my journey. When the night came, I made my fire and roasted meat.

It is eight suns' journey to the east and a man passes by many Dead Places. The Forest People are afraid of them but I am not. Once I made my fire on the edge of a Dead Place at night and, next morning, in the dead house, I found a good knife, little rusted. That was small to what came afterward but it made my heart feel big. Always when I looked for game, it was in front of my arrow, and twice I passed hunt-ing parties of the Forest People without their knowing. So I knew my magic was strong and my journey clean, in spite of the law.

Toward the setting of the eighth sun, I came to the banks of the great river. It was half-a-day's journey after I had left the god-road—we do not use the god-roads now for they are falling apart into great blocks of stone, and the forest is safer going. A long way off, I had seen the water through trees but the trees were thick. At last, I came out upon an open place at the top of a cliff. There was the great river below, like a giant in the sun. It is very long, very wide. It could eat all the streams we know and still be thirsty. Its name is Ou-dis-sun, the Sacred, the Long. No man of my tribe had seen it, not even my father, the priest. It was magic and I prayed.

Then I raised my eyes and looked south. It was there, the Place of the Gods.

How can I tell what it was like—you do not know. It was there, in the red light, and they were too big to be houses. It was there with the red light upon it, mighty and ruined. I knew that in another moment the gods would see me. I covered my eyes with my hands and crept back into the forest.

Surely, that was enough to do, and live. Surely it was enough to spend the night upon the cliff. The Forest People them-selves do not come near. Yet, all through the night, I knew that I should have to cross the river and walk in the places of the gods, although the gods ate me up. My magic did not help me at all and yet there was a fire in my bowels, a fire in my mind. When the sun rose, I thought, "My journey has been clean. Now I will go home from my journey." But, even as I thought so, I knew I could not. If I went to the Place of

---

2. *Fasting* is the process of not eating, often in preparation for a religious ritual.

The Extraordinary and Fantastic *What elements of the fantastic are in the paragraph at the top of this column?*

the Gods, I would surely die, but, if I did not go, I could never be at peace with my spirit again. It is better to lose one's life than one's spirit, if one is a priest and the son of a priest.

Nevertheless, as I made the raft, the tears ran out of my eyes. The Forest People could have killed me without fight, if they had come upon me then, but they did not come. When the raft was made, I said the sayings for the dead and painted myself for death. My heart was cold as a frog and my knees like water, but the burning in my mind would not let me have peace. As I pushed the raft from the shore, I began my death song—I had the right. It was a fine song.

"I am John, son of John," I sang. "My people are the Hill People. They are the men.
I go into the Dead Places but I am not slain. I take the metal from the Dead Places but I am not blasted.
I travel upon the god-roads and am not afraid. E-yah! I have killed the panther, I have killed the fawn!
E-yah! I have come to the great river. No man has come there before.
It is forbidden to go east, but I have gone, forbidden to go on the great river, but I am there.
Open your hearts, you spirits, and hear my song.
Now I go to the Place of the Gods, I shall not return.
My body is painted for death and my limbs weak, but my heart is big as I go to the Place of the Gods!"

All the same, when I came to the Place of the Gods, I was afraid, afraid. The current of the great river is very strong—it gripped my raft with its hands. That was magic, for the river itself is wide and calm. I could feel evil spirits about me, in the bright morning; I could feel their breath on my neck as I was swept down the stream. Never have I been so much alone—I tried to think of my knowledge, but it was a squirrel's heap of winter nuts. There was no strength in my knowledge any more, and I felt small and naked as a new-hatched bird—alone upon the great river, the servant of the gods.

Yet, after a while, my eyes were opened and I saw. I saw both banks of the river—I saw that once there had been god-roads across it, though now they were broken and fallen like broken vines. Very great they were, and wonderful and broken—broken in the time of the Great Burning when the fire fell out of the sky. And always the current took me nearer to the Place of the Gods, and the huge ruins rose before my eyes.

I do not know the customs of rivers—we are the People of the Hills. I tried to guide my raft with the pole but it spun around. I thought the river meant to take me past the Place of the Gods and out into the Bitter Water of the legends. I grew angry then—my heart felt strong. I said aloud, "I am a priest and the son of a priest!" The gods heard me—they showed me how to paddle with the pole on one side of the raft. The current changed itself—I drew near to the Place of the Gods.

When I was very near, my raft struck and turned over. I can swim in our

Visualize *Explain in your own words what John describes in the second paragraph in this column.*

lakes—I swam to the shore. There was a great spike of rusted metal sticking out into the river—I hauled myself up upon it and sat there, panting. I had saved my bow and two arrows and the knife I found in the Dead Place but that was all. My raft went whirling downstream toward the Bitter Water. I looked after it, and thought if it had trod me under, at least I would be safely dead. Nevertheless, when I had dried my bowstring and restrung it, I walked forward to the Place of the Gods.

It felt like ground underfoot; it did not burn me. It is not true what some of the tales say, that the ground there burns forever, for I have been there. Here and there were the marks and stains of the Great Burning, on the ruins, that is true. But they were old marks and old stains. It is not true either, what some of our priests say, that it is an island covered with fogs and enchantments. It is not. It is a great Dead Place—greater than any Dead Place we know. Everywhere in it there are god-roads, though most are cracked and broken. Everywhere there are the ruins of the high towers of the gods.

How shall I tell what I saw? I went carefully, my strung bow in my hand, my skin ready for danger. There should have been the wailings of spirits and the shrieks of demons, but there were not. It was very silent and sunny where I had landed—the wind and the rain and the birds that drop seeds had done their work—the grass grew in the cracks of the broken stone. It is a fair island—no wonder the gods built there. If I had come there, a god, I also would have built.

How shall I tell what I saw? The towers are not all broken—here and there one still stands, like a great tree in a forest, and the birds nest high. But the towers themselves look blind, for the gods are gone. I saw a fish hawk, catching fish in the river. I saw a little dance of white butterflies over a great heap of broken stones and columns. I went there and looked about me—there was a carved stone with cut-letters, broken in half. I can read letters but I could not understand these. They said UBTREAS. There was also the shattered image of a man or a god. It had been made of white stone and he wore his hair tied back like a woman's. His name was ASHING, as I read on the cracked half of a stone. I thought it wise to pray to ASHING, though I do not know that god.

How shall I tell what I saw? There was no smell of man left, on stone or metal. Nor were there many trees in that wilderness of stone. There are many pigeons, nesting and dropping in the towers—the gods must have loved them, or, perhaps, they used them for sacrifices. There are wild cats that roam the god-roads, green-eyed, unafraid of man. At night they wail like demons but they are not demons. The wild dogs are more dangerous, for they hunt in a pack, but them I did not meet till later. Everywhere there

> *"Everywhere there are ruins of the high towers . . ."*

The Extraordinary and Fantastic *What does John think is extraordinary about this place? What do you think is extraordinary?*

Visualize *Images are descriptions that appeal to one or more of the five senses. Visualize the animals in the Dead Place. To which senses do these images appeal?*

Abismo. David Alfaro Siqueiros. Piroxyline on Masonite, 23⅝ x 27½ in. © Estate of David Alfaro Siqueiros/SOMAAP Mexico/Licensed by VAGA, NY.

View the Art What elements in this painting remind you of the setting of the story?

are the carved stones, carved with magical numbers or words.

I went north—I did not try to hide myself. When a god or a demon saw me, then I would die, but meanwhile I was no longer afraid. My hunger for knowledge burned in me—there was so much that I could not understand. After a while, I knew that my belly was hungry. I could have hunted for my meat, but I did not

hunt. It is known that the gods did not hunt as we do—they got their food from enchanted boxes and jars. Sometimes these are still found in the Dead Places— once, when I was a child and foolish, I opened such a jar and tasted it and found the food sweet. But my father found out and punished me for it strictly, for, often, that food is death. Now, though, I had long gone past what was forbidden, and I entered the likeliest towers, looking for the food of the gods.

I found it at last in the ruins of a great temple in the mid-city. A mighty temple it must have been, for the roof was painted like the sky at night with its stars—that much I could see, though the colors were faint and dim. It went down into great caves and tunnels—perhaps they kept their slaves there. But when I started to climb down, I heard the squeaking of rats, so I did not go—rats are unclean, and there must have been many tribes of them, from the squeaking. But near there, I found food, in the heart of a ruin, behind a door that still opened. I ate only the fruits from the jars—they had a very sweet taste. There was drink, too, in bottles of glass—the drink of the gods was strong and made my head swim. After I had eaten and drunk, I slept on the top of a stone, my bow at my side.

When I woke, the sun was low. Looking down from where I lay, I saw a dog sitting on his haunches. His tongue was hanging out of his mouth; he looked as if he were laughing. He was a big dog, with a gray-brown coat, as big as a wolf. I sprang up and shouted at him but he did not move—he just sat there as if he were laughing. I did not like that. When I reached for a stone to throw, he moved swiftly out of the way of the stone. He was not afraid of me; he looked at me as if I were meat. No doubt I could have killed him with an arrow, but I did not know if there were others. Moreover, night was falling.

I looked about me—not far away there was a great, broken god-road, leading north. The towers were high enough, but not so high, and while many of the

dead-houses were wrecked, there were some that stood. I went toward this god-road, keeping to the heights of the ruins, while the dog followed. When I had reached the god-road, I saw that there were others behind him. If I had slept later, they would have come upon me asleep and torn out my throat. As it was, they were sure enough of me; they did not hurry. When I went into the dead-house, they kept watch at the entrance—doubtless they thought they would have a fine hunt. But a dog cannot open a door and I knew, from the books, that the gods did not like to live on the ground but on high.

I had just found a door I could open when the dogs decided to rush. Ha! They were surprised when I shut the door in their faces—it was a good door, of strong metal. I could hear their foolish baying beyond it but I did not stop to answer them. I was in darkness—I found stairs and climbed. There were many stairs, turning around till my head was dizzy. At the top was another door—I found the knob and opened it. I was in a long small chamber—on one side of it was a bronze door that could not be opened, for it had no handle. Perhaps there was a magic word to open it but I did not have the word. I turned to the door in the opposite side of the wall. The lock of it was broken and I opened it and went in.

Within, there was a place of great riches. The god who lived there must have been a powerful god. The first room was a small **anteroom**—I waited there for some time, telling the spirits of the place that I came in peace and not as a robber. When it seemed to me that they had had time to hear me, I went on. Ah, what riches! Few, even, of the

---

The Extraordinary and Fantastic *What type of building do you think John has entered? Why does he believe it was so important to the gods?*

> **Vocabulary**
>
> **anteroom** (an′ tē roŏm′) *n.* a small room serving as a waiting area or an entrance to a larger, main room

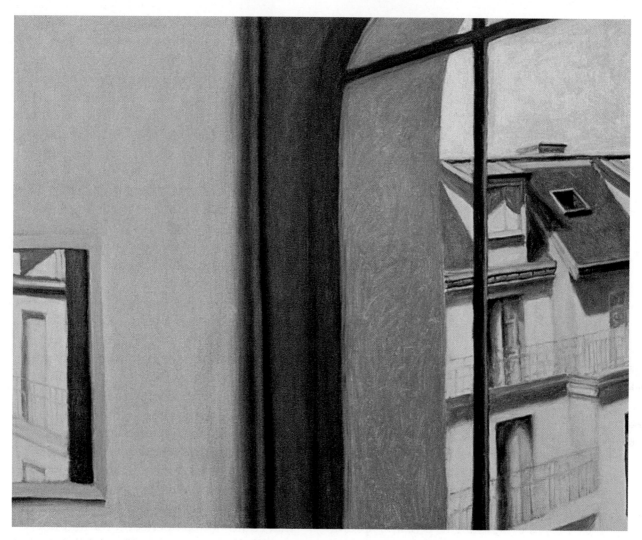

August, 1982. Avigdor Arikha. Oil on canvas, 31³/₄ x 39¹/₄ in. Marlborough Gallery, NY. Licensed by VAGA, NY.

View the Art Compare the view in this picture with what John imagines he sees when he looks out the window.

windows had been broken—it was all as it had been. The great windows that looked over the city had not been broken at all though they were dusty and streaked with many years. There were coverings on the floors, the colors not greatly faded, and the chairs were soft and deep. There were pictures upon the walls, very strange, very wonderful—I remember one of a bunch of flowers in a jar—if you came close to it, you could see nothing but bits of color, but if you stood away from it, the flowers might have been picked yesterday. It made

my heart feel strange to look at this picture—and to look at the figure of a bird, in some hard clay, on a table and see it so like our birds. Everywhere there were books and writings, many in tongues that I could not read. The god who lived there must have been a wise god and full of knowledge. I felt I had right there, as I sought knowledge also.

Visualize *What do you see when you visualize the pictures that John describes?*

Nevertheless, it was strange. There was a washing-place but no water—perhaps the gods washed in air. There was a cooking-place but no wood, and though there was a machine to cook food, there was no place to put fire in it. Nor were there candles or lamps—there were things that looked like lamps but they had neither oil nor wick. All these things were magic, but I touched them and lived—the magic had gone out of them. Let me tell one thing to show. In the washing-place, a thing said "Hot" but it was not hot to the touch—another thing said "Cold" but it was not cold. This must have been a strong magic but the magic was gone. I do not understand—they had ways—I wish that I knew.

It was close and dry and dusty in their house of the gods. I have said the magic was gone but that is not true—it had gone from the magic things but it had not gone from the place. I felt the spirits about me, weighing upon me. Nor had I ever slept in a Dead Place before—and yet, tonight, I must sleep there. When I thought of it, my tongue felt dry in my throat, in spite of my wish for knowledge. Almost I would have gone down again and faced the dogs, but I did not.

I had not gone through all the rooms when the darkness fell. When it fell, I went back to the big room looking over the city and made fire. There was a place to make fire and a box with wood in it, though I do not think they cooked there. I wrapped myself in a floor-covering and slept in front of the fire—I was very tired.

Now I tell what is very strong magic. I woke in the midst of the night. When I woke, the fire had gone out and I was cold. It seemed to me that all around me there were whisperings and voices. I

Visualize *What object does John see that says "Hot" and "Cold"?*

closed my eyes to shut them out. Some will say that I slept again, but I do not think that I slept. I could feel the spirits drawing my spirit out of my body as a fish is drawn on a line.

Why should I lie about it? I am a priest and the son of a priest. If there are spirits, as they say, in the small Dead Places near us, what spirits must there not be in that great Place of the Gods? And would not they wish to speak? After such long years? I know that I felt myself drawn as a fish is drawn on a line. I had stepped out of my body—I could see my body asleep in front of the cold fire, but it was not I. I was drawn to look out upon the city of the gods.

It should have been dark, for it was night, but it was not dark. Everywhere there were lights—lines of light—circles and blurs of light—ten thousand torches would not have been the same. The sky itself was alight—you could barely see the stars for the glow in the sky. I thought to myself "This is strong magic" and trembled. There was a roaring in my ears like the rushing of rivers. Then my eyes grew used to the light and my ears to the sound. I knew that I was seeing the city as it had been when the gods were alive.

That was a sight indeed—yes, that was a sight: I could not have seen it in the body—my body would have died. Everywhere went the gods, on foot and in chariots—there were gods beyond number and counting and their chariots blocked the streets. They had turned night to day for their pleasure—they did not sleep with the sun. The noise of their coming and going was the noise of many waters. It was magic what they could do—it was magic what they did.

I looked out of another window—the great vines of their bridges were mended and the god-roads went east and west. Restless, restless, were the gods and always in motion! They burrowed tunnels under rivers—they flew in the air. With unbelievable tools they did giant works—no part of the earth was safe from them, for, if they wished for a thing, they summoned it from the other side of the world. And always, as they labored and rested, as they feasted and made love, there was a drum in their ears—the pulse of the giant city, beating and beating like a man's heart.

Were they happy? What is happiness to the gods? They were great, they were mighty, they were wonderful and terrible.

As I looked upon them and their magic, I felt like a child—but a little more, it seemed to me, and they would pull down the moon from the sky. I saw them with wisdom beyond wisdom and knowledge beyond knowledge. And yet not all they did was well done—even I could see that—and yet their wisdom could not but grow until all was peace.

Then I saw their fate come upon them and that was terrible past speech. It came upon them as they walked the streets of their city. I have been in the fights with the Forest People—I have seen men die. But this was not like that. When gods war with gods, they use weapons we do not know. It was fire falling out of the sky and a mist that poisoned. It was the time of the Great Burning and the Destruction. They ran about like ants in the streets of their city—poor gods, poor gods! Then the towers began to fall. A few escaped—yes, a few. The legends tell

it. But, even after the city had become a Dead Place, for many years the poison was still in the ground. I saw it happen, I saw the last of them die. It was darkness over the broken city and I wept.

All this, I saw. I saw it as I have told it, though not in the body. When I woke in the morning, I was hungry, but I did not think first of my hunger for my heart was **perplexed** and confused. I knew the reason for the Dead Places but I did not see why it had happened. It seemed to me it should not have happened, with all the magic they had. I went through the house looking for an answer. There was so much in the house I could not understand—and yet I am a priest and the son of a priest. It was like being on one side of the great river, at night, with no light to show the way.

Then I saw the dead god. He was sitting in his chair, by the window, in a room I had not entered before and, for the first moment, I thought that he was alive. Then I saw the skin on the back of his hand—it was like dry leather. The room was shut, hot and dry—no doubt that had kept him as he was. At first I was afraid to approach him—then the fear left me. He was sitting looking out over the city—he was dressed in the clothes of the gods. His age was neither young nor old— I could not tell his age. But there was wisdom in his face and great sadness. You could see that he would have not run away. He had sat at his window, watching his city die—then he himself had died. But it is better to lose one's life than one's spirit—and you could see from the face that his spirit had not been lost. I knew, that, if I touched him, he would fall into dust—and yet, there was something unconquered in the face.

That is all of my story, for then I knew he was a man—I knew then that they had been men, neither gods nor demons. It is a great knowledge, hard to tell and believe. They were men—they went a dark road, but they were men. I had no fear after that—I had no fear going home, though twice I fought off the dogs and once I was hunted for two days by the Forest People. When I saw my father again, I prayed and was purified. He touched my lips and my breast, he said,

"You went away a boy. You come back a man and a priest." I said, "Father, they were men! I have been in the Place of the Gods and seen it! Now slay me, if it is the law—but still I know they were men."

He looked at me out of both eyes. He said, "The law is not always the same shape—you have done what you have done. I could not have done it in my time, but you come after me. Tell!"

I told and he listened. After that, I wished to tell all the people but he showed me otherwise. He said, "Truth is a hard deer to hunt. If you eat too much truth at once, you may die of the truth. It was not idly that our fathers

Narrator *Why is the knowledge John learns about the Gods important to him? Explain.*

Clytie, c. 1890–92. Frederic Leighton. Oil on canvas, 85.1 x 137.8 cm. Fitzwilliam Museum, University of Cambridge, UK.

View the Art What mood does this scene evoke? Is it similar to the mood evoked by this story? Explain.

forbade the Dead Places." He was right—it is better the truth should come little by little. I have learned that, being a priest. Perhaps, in the old days, they ate knowledge too fast.

Nevertheless, we make a beginning. It is not for the metal alone we go to the Dead Places now—there are the books and the writings. They are hard to learn. And the magic tools are broken—but we can look at them and wonder. At least, we make a beginning. And, when I am chief priest we shall go beyond the great river. We shall go to the Place of the Gods—the place newyork—not one man but a company. We shall look for the images of the gods and find the god ASHING and the others—the gods Lincoln and Biltmore[3] and Moses.[4] But they were men who built the city, not gods or demons. They were men. I remember the dead man's face. They were men who were here before us. We must build again. ❧

---

3. The *Biltmore* is a famous hotel in New York City.
4. Robert *Moses* (1888–1981) was a New York state public official whose name appears on many bridges and other structures built during his administration.

After You Read

Respond and Think Critically

1. **Connect to Personal Experience** Which line or passage in the story had the greatest impact on you? Why?

2. **Examine Narrator's Beliefs** Which event determines that John will one day be a priest? Does John consider his priestly calling a privilege or a burden? Explain.

3. **Identify Conflict** Where does John decide to travel? Why? What internal conflict must John overcome before choosing a direction for his journey? Support your answer with evidence from the text.

4. **Analyze Character** How does John change from the beginning to the end of the story? Explain your answer and support it with evidence from the text. ◥ OER

5. **Evaluate Behavior** Do you believe that John is being disrespectful by ignoring his father's advice and the law? Explain.

6. **Big Idea** **Draw Conclusions About Author's Perspective** While in the Place of the Gods, John has an extraordinary vision of what the world was once like, followed by a vision of its destruction. Do you think the author was making a cautionary statement about modern society through this story? Explain.

7. **Evaluate Allusion** The title "By the Waters of Babylon" alludes to Psalm 137 in the Bible, which describes the Israelites' grief over the destruction of their temple, their separation from their homeland, and their enforced captivity by the Babylonians. How does knowing the source of the title enrich your understanding of the story?

Literary Element **Narrator**

Analyzing the **narrator,** or person telling the story, can help you better understand a text. As you read, look for clues about whether the narrator is reliable—a trusted source of information—or unreliable and naive.

8. **Analyze Narrator** Is John a reliable narrator? Explain. If he is unreliable, does he intentionally mislead the reader or does he not understand the meaning of his experiences? Reread the pink highlighted question on page 1024 to help you get started.

9. **Evaluate Narrator** How might the tone of the story be affected if it were narrated by a different character or someone outside the story? In your opinion, did the author choose the best narrator for his purpose? Support your answer with evidence from the text.

Review: Archetypes

As you learned on pages 945 and 953, an **archetype** is a theme, a character, a plot pattern, or an

image that is common to human experiences across time and place. There are many archetypes in "By the Waters of Babylon" that would have been just as recognizable to the ancient Greeks as they are to readers today. The post-apocalyptic motif in the story is a common **theme archetype;** John's dangerous quest as a rite of passage is an example of a **plot pattern archetype;** the inclusion of a young idealist who breaks society's rules for the sake of knowledge is a popular **character archetype.**

10. **Partner Activity** With a classmate, discuss three categories of archetypes—theme, plot pattern, and character—as they function in "By the Waters of Babylon." Then, brainstorm a list of stories, books, movies, legends, or songs that have similar archetypes. Discuss how the items on your list compare with the archetypes in "By the Waters of Babylon."

Reading Strategy Visualize

When we read or listen, we form mental images of what the speaker or writer is describing. This mental process is called **visualizing**. Benét uses many descriptive words and phrases that encourage readers to form mental images of the setting in his story, even though we have never actually seen it with our own eyes.

11. Read the following sentence from "By the Waters of Babylon": "I saw a little dance of white butterflies over a great heap of stone." Write a few sentences describing how you imagine the scene.

12. Select another descriptive passage from the story. How do the sensory details in this image help you to understand the text? Refer to the chart you made on page 1013 to help you.

Vocabulary Practice

Practice with Usage Respond to these statements to help you explore the meanings of the boldfaced vocabulary words from the story.

1. Identify an example of something someone could have **bade** another to do.

2. Name two actions you might perform in an **anteroom.**

3. Describe the look on the face of someone who is **perplexed.**

Academic Vocabulary

*In the story, human civilization is **beset** by war; hardly anyone survives.*

Beset is an academic word that derives from Middle and Old English. The prefix *be-* means "throughout; all around; all over," or "make; cause to be." Using your knowledge and context clues, determine the meaning of *beset* in the model sentence above. Check your response by consulting a dictionary. Finally, demonstrate your understanding by using each of these related words in a sentence.

a. bestow   **b.** bequeath   **c.** behest

Enrich and Extend

Speaking and Listening

Speech Adopt the persona of John and make a speech in which you rebut your father's argument that truth is dangerous.

Prepare Reread and analyze John's inner thoughts, as well as his song, for rhetorical devices that characterize his style and voice. List examples and the devices they embody in a chart like the one below.

Example	Rhetorical Device
p. 1015, paragraph 4	• repetition ("I was taught") • dashes (used for dramatic pauses, for examples, and for amplification) • figure of speech (a fire in my heart helps make the idea memorable)
	• simple, concrete diction (stop, know, hunters, hurt, books)

Plan and develop a focused and coherent presentation that conveys a clear and distinct perspective and demonstrates solid reasoning. Create an engaging introduction and use your body paragraphs to rebut John's father's argument. Use your conclusion to present your most persuasive reason or a final, memorable thought. Link your ideas with transitions.

Deliver Speak in John's confident voice and serious tone. Maintain good posture and make frequent eye contact to reflect his confidence. Adjust your delivery, vocabulary, and length to your particular audience and purpose.

Evaluate Evaluate your speech by writing examples of and rating how well you adopted John's persona, employed his characteristic rhetorical devices, and organized your speech. Demonstrate understanding of how the style and content of your speech would vary in different contexts and influence the listener's understanding.

Grammar Workshop

Dangling Participles

TEKS

10.17.A.i Use and understand the following parts of speech in the context of reading, writing, and speaking: more complex active and passive tenses and verbals (participles).

Literature Connection In this quotation from "By the Waters of Babylon," Stephen Vincent Benét uses a **participial phrase** to add descriptive detail to the sentence and help the reader visualize the scene.

> *"He looked at me for a long time, stroking his beard, then at last he said, 'Yes. It is time.'"*

In this example, *stroking his beard* is the participial phrase. It is used to modify, or give details about, the subject, *He.*

A participial phrase must always have a **referent,** or something it modifies. If a participial phrase has no referent, it is called a **dangling participle.** Misplaced or dangling participles often cause confusion in writing; try to avoid them in your work. Below are some solutions for correcting dangling or misplaced past and present participles.

Dangling or Misplaced Participles

Problem 1 *John saw a small chamber climbing the stairs.*
Solution Place the participial phrase, *climbing the stairs,* closer to the referent.

> *Climbing the stairs, John saw a small chamber.*

Problem 2 *Coming into the room, the old man's face looked unconquered.*
Solution Change the dangling participle to a main or subordinate clause.

> *Coming into the room, John thought the old man's face looked unconquered.*

Revise Rewrite the following sentences to correct four dangling or misplaced participles.

1. Based on the title "By the Waters of Babylon," readers are reminded of a story in the Bible.
2. Taking a necessary journey, the main character is confused and alone.
3. Found intriguing, stories were written about United States history by Benét.
4. Writing, Benét's epic poem *Western Star* won the Pulitzer Prize.
5. Serving his country during World War I, Benét joined the military.

Present and Past Participles
A **participle** is a word that is usually a verb, but functions as an adjective or an adverb. **Present participles** typically end in *-ing.* For example,

*The **laughing** dog looked at John.*

Past participles are more diverse and can end in *-ed, -en, -d, -t, or -n.* For example,

*The **fallen** tower lay crumbling at his feet.*

Tip
When taking a test, check to make sure the subject your participle is modifying, the **referent,** is located close to the participle to avoid confusion.

Language Handbook
For more on participles, see the Language Handbook, pages R51–R52.

Literature Online

Grammar For more grammar practice, go to glencoe.com and enter QuickPass code GL57805u6.

Comparing Literature

Across Genres

TEKS

For pages 1030–1041

10.2 Analyze, make inferences and draw conclusions about theme and genre in different cultural, historical, and contemporary contexts and provide evidence from the text to support understanding.

Compare Literature About Dreams and Reality

Our dreams often reflect experiences in our daily lives. Our daily experiences can be as haunting as our dreams. These three literary works, which include a dream narrative, a poem about identity in the crowded darkness, and a poem about a dream, reveal fragments of both the inner and outer worlds of the narrator and speakers.

COMPARE THE Big Idea The Extraordinary and Fantastic

The relationship between the real world and the dream world is both extraordinary and fantastic. The writers featured here all explore this divide and the ways in which the two worlds are related. Jamaica Kincaid's short story integrates both the real world and two distinct dreams to show the relationship between all three. Denise Levertov's poem uses the contrasts between night and day and the individual and society to describe what is unknown and imagined. Anna Akhmatova's poem relates "unearthly dreams" and questions whether they can foretell future events. As you read, ask yourself, How does each writer use imagery to evoke the extraordinary and fantastic?

COMPARE Description

Description is writing that seeks to convey the impression of a setting, a person, an animal, an object, or an event by appealing to the senses. Each writer uses rich sensory details to re-create experiences and impressions. As you read, ask yourself, How do these details help you picture settings, events, and characters?

COMPARE Author's Culture

Each work is rooted in its author's culture: Kincaid infuses her setting with elements from her native Antigua; Levertov evokes the hectic culture of the city at night; and Akhmatova provides a glimpse into a culture of fear and loss. As you read, ask yourself, Despite their different cultural and historical contexts, do these works share any of the same themes?

LOG ON **Literature** Online

Author Search For more about the authors, go to glencoe.com and enter QuickPass code GL57805u6.

Before You Read

What I Have Been Doing Lately

Meet **Jamaica Kincaid**

(born 1949)

Troublemaker is how teachers used to describe Elaine Potter Richardson. Growing up on the tiny island of Antigua in the Caribbean was not easy. Richardson would later adopt the pen name *Jamaica Kincaid* and become famous for her poetic language, but at a young age her way with words often caused her difficulties. Precocious and rebellious, Kincaid had a rocky relationship with her mother, and she often escaped the confines of her life by stealing away to read books.

A Need to Escape As a child, Kincaid felt trapped. The sea that surrounded Antigua formed a geographic jail. Racism and conventional ways of thinking stifled her dreams. As she later commented, "In the place I'm from you don't have much room." At the age of seventeen, Kincaid left her island home to become an *au pair,* or nanny, in the United States. Within ten years of her departure, Kincaid managed to publish a few nonfiction articles in magazines. It was then that she officially changed her surname because her family disapproved of her writing. She later explained that she adopted the name *Jamaica,* subconsciously, as a way of re-creating a part of her past. Kincaid's work quickly drew the attention of William Shawn, a former editor of the *New Yorker* magazine. She wrote an article for him, and soon she was a regular contributor, which ensured that her work would reach a wide audience.

Books About Home and Family Kincaid's first book was a short story collection called *At the Bottom of the River.* It includes "What I Have Been Doing Lately" and nine other stories.

Critics immediately recognized the author's fresh, new, and compelling voice in fiction. They admired Kincaid's lyrical style, which makes use of repetition, rich details, and the narrators' suspensions between dreams and reality.

> "*For me, writing isn't a way of being public or private; it's just a way of being.*"
>
> —Jamaica Kincaid

A Writing Life Kincaid's second work of fiction, the novel *Annie John,* brought her wide popularity and ensured her literary reputation. In this work and in her second novel, *Lucy,* Kincaid explores themes about family, especially a mother-daughter relationship.

Literature and Reading Preview

Connect to the Story

Have you ever had a dream that you felt contained a message or lesson? Write a journal entry that describes a meaningful dream.

Build Background

The setting of this story is a bizarre dreamland, but it does contain some realistic elements, such as cloudless skies, monkeys, and flowering trees, that are similar to those in the author's native Antigua.

Set Purposes for Reading

Big Idea The Extraordinary and Fantastic

As you read, ask yourself, What are some of the extraordinary and fantastic places people can experience in dreams?

Literary Element Stream of Consciousness

Stream of consciousness is the literary representation of a character's free-flowing thoughts, feelings, and memories. Emotions, impressions, images, and ideas—both rational and irrational—unfold on the page as they occur in the character's mind. As you read "What I Have Been Doing Lately," ask yourself, What are the free associations that identify the narrator's thoughts as stream of consciousness?

Reading Strategy Interpret Imagery

Interpreting imagery means looking carefully at sensory details, such as those that describe things the narrator sees and hears, and determining their importance in the story. As you read, ask yourself, What is the importance of the imagery in this story?

Tip: List Images As you read, list images and interpret what they tell you about the setting, the events, or the narrator.

Image	Interpretation
p. 1033 "Either it was drizzling or there was a lot of dust in the air and the dust was damp."	• This is a world of sensation. • The narrator feels dampness but is confused about her surroundings.

Vocabulary

verandah (və ran′də) *n.* a long porch, usually with a roof, that extends along a house; p. 1034 *The man sat on the verandah and watched the rain.*

horizon (hə rī′zən) *n.* the place where the earth and sky appear to meet; p. 1034 *From the meadow, we could see the clouds on the horizon.*

dutiful (doo′ti fəl) *adj.* acting out of a sense of obligation or a sense of what is required; p. 1034 *The dutiful worker always did every task carefully.*

interlaced (in′tər lāst′) *adj.* connected by or woven together; p. 1035 *The fabric was interlaced gold threads.*

Eight Huts in Haiti. D. Roosevelt (b. 1952). Oil on canvas. Private collection.

What I Have Been Doing Lately

Jamaica Kincaid

What I have been doing lately: I was lying in bed and the doorbell rang. I ran downstairs. Quick. I opened the door. There was no one there. I stepped outside. Either it was drizzling or there was a lot of dust in the air and the dust was damp. I stuck out my tongue and the drizzle or the damp dust tasted like government school ink. I looked north. I looked south. I decided to start walking north. While walking north, I noticed that I was barefoot. While walking north, I looked up and saw the planet Venus. I said, "It must be almost morning." I saw a monkey in a tree. The tree had no leaves. I said, "Ah, a monkey. Just look at that. A monkey." I walked for I don't know how long before I came up to a big body of water. I wanted to get across it but I couldn't swim. I wanted to get across it but it would take me years to build a boat. I wanted to get across it but it would take me I didn't know how long to build a bridge. Years passed and then one day, feeling like it, I got into my boat and rowed across. When I got to the other side, it was noon and my shadow was small and fell beneath me. I set out on a path that stretched out straight ahead. I passed a house, and a dog was sitting on the **verandah** but it looked the other way when it saw me coming. I passed a boy tossing a ball in the air but the boy looked the other way when he saw me coming. I walked and I walked but I couldn't tell if I walked a long time because my feet didn't feel as if they would drop off. I turned around to see what I had left behind me but nothing was familiar. Instead of the straight path, I saw hills. Instead of the boy with his ball, I saw tall flowering trees. I looked up and the sky was without clouds and seemed near, as if it were the ceiling in my house and, if I stood on a chair, I could touch it with the tips of my fingers. I turned around and looked ahead of me again. A deep hole had opened up before me. I looked in. The hole was deep and dark and I couldn't see the bottom. I thought, What's down there?, so on purpose I fell in. I fell and I fell, over and over, as if I were an old suitcase. On the sides of the deep hole I could see things written, but perhaps it was in a foreign language because I couldn't read

them. Still I fell, for I don't know how long. As I fell I began to see that I didn't like the way falling made me feel. Falling made me feel sick and I missed all the people I had loved. I said, I don't want to fall anymore, and I reversed myself. I was standing again on the edge of the deep hole. I looked at the deep hole and I said, You can close up now, and it did. I walked some more without knowing distance. I only knew that I passed through days and nights, I only knew that I passed through rain and shine, light and darkness. I was never thirsty and I felt no pain. Looking at the **horizon**, I made a joke for myself: I said, "The earth has thin lips," and I laughed.

Looking at the horizon again, I saw a lone figure coming toward me, but I wasn't frightened because I was sure it was my mother. As I got closer to the figure, I could see that it wasn't my mother, but still I wasn't frightened because I could see that it was a woman.

When this woman got closer to me, she looked at me hard and then she threw up her hands. She must have seen me somewhere before because she said, "It's you. Just look at that. It's you. And just what have you been doing lately?"

I could have said, "I have been praying not to grow any taller."

I could have said, "I have been listening carefully to my mother's words, so as to make a good imitation of a **dutiful** daughter."

I could have said, "A pack of dogs, tired from chasing each other all over town, slept in the moonlight."

Stream of Consciousness *What is irrational or illogical about the narrator rowing across the water?*

Vocabulary

verandah (və ran′də) *n.* a long porch, usually with a roof, that extends along a house

Vocabulary

horizon (hə rī′zən) *n.* the place where the earth and sky appear to meet

dutiful (doo′ti fəl) *adj.* acting out of a sense of obligation or a sense of what is required

Instead, I said, What I have been doing lately: I was lying in bed on my back, my hands drawn up, my fingers **interlaced** lightly at the nape of my neck.[1] Someone rang the doorbell. I went downstairs and opened the door but there was no one there. I stepped outside. Either it was drizzling or there was a lot of dust in the air and the dust was damp. I stuck out my tongue and the drizzle or the damp dust tasted like government school ink. I looked north and I looked south. I started walking north. While walking north, I wanted to move fast, so I removed the shoes from my feet. While walking north, I looked up and saw the planet Venus and I said, "If the sun went out, it would be eight minutes before I would know it." I saw a monkey sitting in a tree that had no leaves and I said, "A monkey. Just look at that. A monkey." I picked up a stone and I threw it at the monkey. The monkey, seeing the stone, quickly moved out of its way. Three times I threw a stone at the monkey and three times it moved away. The fourth time I threw the stone, the monkey caught it and threw it back at me. The stone struck me on my forehead over my right eye, making a deep gash. The gash healed immediately but now the skin on my forehead felt false to me. I walked for I don't know how long before I came to a big body of water. I wanted to get across, so when the boat came I paid my fare. When I got to the other side, I saw a lot of people sitting on the beach and they were having a picnic. They were the most beautiful people I had ever seen. Everything about them was black and shiny. Their skin was black and shiny. Their shoes were black and shiny. Their hair was black and shiny. The clothes they wore were black and shiny. I could hear them laughing and chatting and I said, I would like to be with these people, so I started to walk toward them, but when I got up close to them I saw that they weren't at a picnic and they weren't beautiful and they weren't chatting and laughing. All around me was black mud and the people all looked as if they had been made up out of the black mud. I looked up and saw that the sky seemed far away and nothing I could stand on would make me able to touch it with my fingertips. I thought, If only I could get out of this, so I started to walk. I must have walked for a long time because my feet hurt and felt as if they would drop off. I thought, If only just around the bend I would see my house and inside my house I would find my bed, freshly made at that, and in the kitchen I would find my mother or anyone else that I loved making me a custard. I thought, If only it was a Sunday and I was sitting in a church and I had just heard someone sing a psalm. I felt very sad so I sat down. I felt so sad that I rested my head on my own knees and smoothed my own head. I felt so sad I couldn't imagine feeling any other way again. I said, I don't like this. I don't want to do this anymore. And I went back to lying in bed, just before the doorbell rang. ∾

---

1. The *nape of my neck* refers to the back of the neck.

Vocabulary

interlaced (in´tər lāst´) *adj.* connected by or woven together

Interpret Imagery *How would you describe the mood that the images of the picnic and the mud people evoke? Explain.*

The Extraordinary and Fantastic *In what way is this story an extraordinary and fantastic journey?*

After You Read

Respond and Think Critically

1. **Connect to Personal Experience** How might you feel if you awoke from the dream described by the narrator? Explain.

2. **Make Inferences About Narrator** Who is the narrator of this story? What can you infer about the narrator's age and family relationships? Support your inferences with details.

3. **Analyze Author's Craft** How does Kincaid's use of dialogue expand the portrayal of the subconscious mind?

4. **Make Inferences About Events** Why does the narrator go back to bed at the end of the story?

What might be the cause of the narrator's sadness and anxiety in the dream? Support your answer with evidence from the text.

5. **Evaluate Genre** Reread the definition of the fantasy genre on page 992. Do you think this story is a true example of the fantasy genre? Support your answer by listing details that match the fantasy genre and details that do not.

6. **Big Idea** **Draw Conclusions About Imagery** In what ways might the extraordinary and fantastic images of the dream world give the reader insight into the narrator's waking life?

Literary Element Stream of Consciousness

Stream of consciousness is characterized by random association of ideas, repetition, and disregard for conventional punctuation and sentence structure.

7. **Identify Style** Which stream of consciousness characteristics does the story feature?

8. **Evaluate Point of View** Is Kincaid's use of stream-of-consciousness narration and first-person point of view an effective way to tell her story? Explain. Reread the pink highlighted question on page 1034 to help you.

Reading Strategy Interpret Imagery

Refer to the chart you made on page 1032.

9. The narrator encounters obstacles: a body of water and a deep hole. What might these obstacles symbolize?

10. Name another symbolic image in the story. Discuss what it might represent.

LOG ON ▶ Literature Online

Selection Resources For Selection Quizzes, eFlashcards, and Reading-Writing Connection activities, go to glencoe.com and enter QuickPass code GL57805u6.

Vocabulary Practice

Practice with Analogies Choose the word that best completes each analogy.

1. porch : verandah :: house :
   a. car   **b.** mansion   **c.** sculptor

2. dutiful : disobedient :: plentiful :
   a. cautious   **b.** beneficial   **c.** scarce

3. sky : horizon :: color :
   a. earth   **b.** boundary   **c.** rainbow

4. interlaced : entwined :: distinct :
   a. enrobed   **b.** separate   **c.** mixed

Writing

Write an Essay Write a stream-of-consciousness essay about a day when you engaged in different activities. Include your thoughts, feelings, memories, and a few fantastical details. Capture your impressions of time passing by experimenting with sentence length, diction, imagery, and rhetorical devices.

Build Background

Denise Levertov (1923–1977) noted that "People at Night" is derived from the work of German poet Rainer Maria Rilke. Levertov's poem, like many of Rilke's poems and letters, deals with the isolation of the individual.

People at Night

Denise Levertov

Melancholy Woman.
Jose Ortega.

View the Art Ortega, originally from Ecuador, is known for his vivid murals. What mood does Ortega convey here? How does the mood suit the mood of the poem?

(Derived from Rilke)

A night that cuts between you and you
and you   and you   and you
and me : jostles us apart, a man elbowing
through a crowd.   We won't
5   look for each other, either—
wander off, each alone, not looking
in the slow crowd. Among sideshows
          under movie signs,
          pictures made of a million lights,
10   giants that move and again move
          again, above a cloud of thick smells,
          franks, roasted nutmeats—

Or going up to some apartment, yours
          or yours, finding
15   someone sitting in the dark:
who is it, really? So you switch the
light on to see: you know the name but
who is it?
     But you won't see.
20   The fluorescent light flickers sullenly, a
pause. But you command. It grabs
each face and holds it up
by the hair for you, mask after mask.
          You and you and you and I repeat
25   gestures that make do when speech
          has failed   and talk
          and talk, laughing, saying
          'I', and 'I',
meaning 'Anybody'.
30   No one.

> ### 💬 Discussion Starter
>
> In this poem, the speaker re-creates two scenes at night:
> one on the street and one in an apartment. In a small
> group, compare and contrast the speaker's experience in
> these two places. Begin by identifying the images and
> symbols in each setting, and then retell what happens in
> each place.

Build Background

In "A Dream," the speaker refers to August as "a terrible anniversary." For Anna Akhmatova, it truly was: Russia entered World War I in August 1914; her husband died in August 1921; and in August 1941, Akhmatova's friend and fellow poet Marina Tsvetaeva died.

Starry Night, 1889. Vincent van Gogh. Oil on canvas. Museum of Modern Art, New York.

View the Art Van Gogh's art is known for its intensity, both in color and in conveying impressions and emotion. How would you describe the night sky that Van Gogh depicts here? What dream-like quality does the painting convey to you?

A Dream

Anna Akhmatova
Translated by Judith Hemschemeyer

Isn't it sweet to have unearthly dreams?
A. Blok°

> **A. Blok:** Alexander Blok, one of Russia's most important poets before the communist era. Akhmatova greatly admired him.

This dream was prophetic or not prophetic . . .
Mars shone among the heavenly stars,
Becoming crimson, sparkling, sinister—
And that same night I dreamed of your arrival.

5   It was in everything . . . in the Bach Chaconne,°
And in the roses, which bloomed in vain,
And in the ringing of the village bells
Over the blackness of ploughed fields.

> **5 chaconne:** a musical form in ³⁄₄ time in which a set of variations is played over a bass line.

And in the autumn, which came close
10 And suddenly, reconsidering, concealed itself.
Oh my August, how could you give me such news
As a terrible anniversary?

How can I repay this royal gift?
Where do I go and with whom do I celebrate?
15 And now I am writing, as before, no crossing out,
My poems in the burnt notebook.°

August 14, 1956
Near Kolomna

> **16 burnt notebook:** refers to the work Akhmatova had to burn during the Stalinist era for fear of imprisonment or death. By 1956 this era had ended when Nikita Khrushchev (premier of the Soviet Union from 1958 to 1964) denounced Stalin's police.

✍ Quickwrite

In this poem, the speaker refers to "your arrival." How do you know this unidentified arrival is important to the speaker? What do you think is the "news" or "royal gift" to which the speaker refers? How does the speaker react to this news or gift? Write a paragraph in which you address these questions.

Wrap-Up: Comparing Literature

Across Genres

- **What I Have Been Doing Lately** by Jamaica Kincaid

- **People at Night** by Denise Levertov

- **A Dream** by Anna Akhmatova

COMPARE THE Big Idea The Extraordinary and Fantastic

Writing Write a brief essay in which you compare the similarities in how these three works from a variety of world cultures portray fantastic or strange people, places, or events. Consider the use of language in each work.

COMPARE Description

Group Activity Each writer uses description to transport the reader to an inner world or a dream state. With a small group, discuss the following questions. Cite evidence from the texts to support your answers.

1. How does each author use description to give the reader a sense of place?

2. How does each author use description to create atmosphere or set a mood?

3. Provide examples of imagistic or symbolic description that help you understand each work's message. Explain the examples you selected.

Man Sleeping Beneath A Nighttime Sky. Steve Kropp.

COMPARE Author's Culture

Make a Chart Each author's themes reflect her own historical and cultural context. Kincaid incorporates themes about family conflict; Levertov writes about isolation and individualism; and Akhmatova addresses the ideas of loss and grief. Using a chart like the one below, list the historical and cultural details that contribute to each work's unique themes.

Kincaid	Levertov	Akhmatova
government school ink make a good imitation of a dutiful daughter		

Literature Online

Selection Resources For Selection Quizzes, eFlashcards, and Reading-Writing Connection activities, go to glencoe.com and enter QuickPass code GL57805u6.

One Legend Found, Many Still to Go

William J. Broad

TEKS

For pages 1042–1045

10.9.C Make and defend subtle inferences and complex conclusions about the ideas in text and their organizational patterns.

Science debunks fabulous creatures, but sometimes they turn out to be more than just imaginary.

Set a Purpose for Reading

Read to analyze contrasting ideas and events.

Build Background

Often ridiculed for not being an actual science, cryptozoology is the study of animals that may or may not exist.

Reading Strategy

Analyze Text Structure

The particular order or pattern a writer uses to present ideas is called **structure**. A comparison/contrast structure is often used in expository text to show how one thing is similar to and different from another. As you read, use a Venn diagram like the one below to note the similarities and differences between the defining moments for mainstream scientists and those of cryptozoologists. Use your notes to make and defend inferences about the text's ideas and structure.

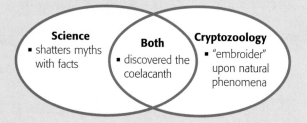

Science
- shatters myths with facts

Both
- discovered the coelacanth

Cryptozoology
- "embroider" upon natural phenomena

The human instinct to observe nature has always been mixed with a tendency to embroider upon it. So it is that, over the ages, societies have lived alongside not only real animals, but a shadow bestiary[1] of fantastic ones—mermaids, griffins,[2] unicorns and the like. None loomed larger than the giant squid, the kraken,[3] a great, malevolent devil of the deep. "One of these Sea-Monsters," Olaus Magnus[4] wrote in 1555, "will drown easily many great ships."

Science, of course, is in the business of shattering myths with facts, which it did again, last week when Japanese scientists reported that they hooked a giant squid—a relatively small one estimated at 26 feet long—some 3,000 feet down and photographed it before it tore off a tentacle to

---

1. Here, *bestiary* means "a medieval collection of symbolic tales about the traits of animals."
2. *Griffins* are mythological creatures with the body of a lion and the head of a bird.
3. *Krakens* are fabled sea monsters, based on sightings of giant squids.
4. *Olaus Magnus* (1490–1557) was a Catholic priest and an author of Scandinavian history.

escape. It was the first peek humanity has ever had of such animals in their native habitat. Almost inevitably, the creature seemed far less terrifying than its ancient image.

Scientists celebrated the find not as an end, but as the beginning of a new chapter in understanding the shy creature. "There're always more questions, more parts to the mystery than we'll ever be able to solve," said Clyde F. E. Roper, a squid expert at the National Museum of Natural History of the Smithsonian Institution.

Monster lovers take heart. Scientists argue that so much of the planet remains unexplored that new surprises are sure to show up; if not legendary beasts like the Loch Ness monster[5] or the dinosaur-like reptile said to inhabit Lake Champlain, then animals that in their own way may be even stranger.

A forthcoming book by the noted naturalist Richard Ellis, *Singing Whales, Flying Squid and Swimming Cucumbers* (Lyon Press, 2006), reinforces that notion by cataloguing recent discoveries of previously unknown whales, dolphins and other creatures, some of which are quite bizarre.

"The sea being so deep and so large, I'm sure other mysteries lurk out there, unseen and unsolved," said Mr. Ellis, also the author of *Monsters of the Sea* (Knopf, 1994). Explorers, he said, recently stumbled on an odd squid more than 20 feet long with fins like elephant ears and very skinny arms and tentacles, all of which can bend at right angles, like human elbows. "We know nothing about it," Mr. Ellis said. "But we've seen it."

Historically, many unknown creatures have come to light purely by accident. In 1938, for example, a fisherman pulled up an odd, ancient-looking fish with stubby, limblike fins. It turned out to be a coelacanth, a beast thought to have gone extinct 70 million years ago. Since then, other examples of the species have occasionally been hauled out of the sea.

Land, too, occasionally gives up a secret. About 1900, acting on tips from the local population, Sir Harry H. Johnston, an English explorer, hunted through the forests of Zaire (then the Belgian Congo) and found a giraffe-like animal known as the okapi. It was hailed as a living fossil.

In 1982, a group of animal enthusiasts founded the International Society of Cryptozoology (literally, the study of hidden creatures) and adopted the okapi as its symbol. Today, self-described cryptozoologists range from amateur unicorn hunters to distinguished scientists.

At the Web site for the group, www.internationalsocietyofcryptozoology. org, there is a list of 15 classes[6] of unresolved claims about unusual beasts, including big cats, giant crocodiles, huge snakes, large octopuses, mammoths, biped primates like the yeti in the Himalayas and long-necked creatures resembling the gigantic dinosaurs called sauropods.

Lake Champlain, on the border between Vermont and New York, is notorious as the alleged home of Champ, a beast said to be similar to a plesiosaur, an extinct marine reptile with a small head, long neck and four paddle-shaped flippers.

There, as at Loch Ness and elsewhere, myth busters and believers do constant battle. "Not only is there not a single piece of convincing evidence for Champ's existence, but there are many reasons against it," Joe Nickel, a researcher who investigates claims of paranormal[7] phenomena, argued in *Skeptical*

---

5. The *Loch Ness monster* is a fabled lake monster said to reside in Scotland's Loch Ness.

6. *Classes* are a biological classification of organism that is below the rank of phylum, above that of order.

7. *Paranormal* means "a phenomenon or an experience that is unable to be explained scientifically."

The Crew of the Alecton Attempting to Catch a Giant Squid from *L'Univers* Illustre, 1867. Artist unknown. Woodcut illustration.

Inquirer, a monthly magazine that rebuts what it considers to be scientific hokum.[8]

Then there are the blobs. For more than a century, scientists and laymen imagined that the mysterious gooey masses—some as large as a school bus—that wash ashore on beaches around the world came from great creatures with tentacles long enough to sink cruise ships. Warnings were issued. Perhaps, cryptozoologists speculated, the blobs were the remains of recently deceased living fossils more fearsome than the dinosaurs, or perhaps an entirely new sea creature unknown to science.

Then last year, a team of biologists based at the University of South Florida applied DNA analysis to the mystery. It turned out they were nothing more than old whale blubber. "To our disappointment," the scientists wrote, "we have not found any evidence that any of the blobs are the remains of gigantic octopods, or sea monsters of unknown species."

---

8. *Hokum* means "nonsense."

Psychologists say raw nature is simply a blank slate for the expression of our subconscious fears and insecurities, a Rorschach test[9] that reveals more about the viewer than the viewed.

But the giant squid is real, growing up to lengths of at least 60 feet, with eyes the size of dinner plates and a tangle of tentacles lined with long rows of sucker pads. Scientists, their appetites whetted[10] by the first observations of the creature in the wild, are now gearing up to discover its remaining secrets.

"Wouldn't it be fabulous to see a giant squid capturing its prey?" asked Dr. Roper of the Smithsonian. "Or a battle between a sperm whale and a giant? Or mating? Can you imagine that?"

"We've cracked the ice on this," he said, "but there's a lot more to do."

---

9. A *Rorschach test* is a psychological examination that evaluates personality based on interpretation of ten abstract designs.
10. Here, *whetted* means "stimulated."

Respond and Think Critically

1. **Summarize Main Ideas** Write a brief summary of the main ideas in this article before you answer the following questions. For help on writing a summary, see page 389.

2. **Make Inferences About Attitudes** What are the "blobs" that interest scientists? Why do you think people like to speculate about where the blobs originated? Explain.

3. **Make Inferences About Author's Beliefs** Do you think the author supports the belief in creatures whose existence has not been scientifically verified? Explain.

4. **Analyze Ideas** The author writes that "psychologists say raw nature is simply a blank slate for the expression of our subconscious fears and insecurities." What ideas in the text suggest that the tendency to project fears and insecurities onto nature should be combatted? Explain.

5. **Evaluate Evidence** Do you believe there is any truth to claims about the existence of creatures such as the Loch Ness monster or "Champ," the creature in Lake Champlain? Explain.

6. **Make Inferences About Structure** How does this article use comparison/contrast structure? Why do the ideas in the article lend themselves to this structure? Defend your answer with evidence from the text.

7. **Draw Conclusions About Science** Naturalist Richard Ellis explains, "The sea being so deep and so large, I'm sure other mysteries lurk out there, unseen and unsolved." What relationship does this article suggest exists between science and the extraordinary and fantastic? In what ways do the two complement each other? Support your answer.

Before You Read

Robot Dreams

Meet **Isaac Asimov**
(1920–1992)

The grandfather of present-day science fiction, Isaac Asimov exhibited a vivid imagination and dogged persistence that readied the world for the study of robotics—both fictional and real.

Born in the Soviet Union, Asimov's parents brought him to New York in 1923. A precocious youth, the four-year-old Asimov taught himself to read using Brooklyn's street signs. He skipped several grades, graduating from high school at fifteen.

Early Success Asimov earned a bachelor's degree from Columbia University in 1939 and a master's degree in 1941. That same year, Asimov's short story "Nightfall," a tale of a planet where nightfall descends once every thousand years, was published. In 1969 the Science Fiction Writers of America voted "Nightfall" the best science-fiction short story.

Asimov returned to Columbia University for a PhD in chemistry, which he earned in 1948. In 1949 he accepted a position at Boston University's School of Medicine. "By 1951 I was writing a textbook on biochemistry, and I finally realized the only thing I really wanted to be was a writer," he said in 1969.

And write Asimov did, authoring mystery novels, short stories, limericks, guides to Shakespeare and the Bible, memoirs, letters, autobiographies, children's books, and textbooks. Asimov is credited with writing nearly five hundred books at a prolific speed of ten books per year. "Writing is more fun than ever," Asimov said in a 1984 interview. "The longer I write, the easier it gets."

> "*Knowledge has its dangers, yes, but is the response to be a retreat from knowledge?*"
>
> —Isaac Asimov

The Three Laws of Robotics In 1940 Asimov formulated "The Three Laws of Robotics," rules that provide for human control over artificial intelligences. Asimov subjected all of the robots in his stories to these laws.

The influence of the Three Laws of Robotics can be seen today, from movie adaptations (*I, Robot* in 2004) to the work of real-life scientists. Joseph F. Engelberger, the pioneering engineer who built the first industrial robot in 1958 and founded the world's first robotics company in 1961, attributed his fascination with robots to his reading of *I, Robot* as a teenager. At Engelberger's request, Asimov later wrote the foreword to his robotics manual.

LOG ON ▶ **Literature** Online

Author Search For more about Isaac Asimov, go to glencoe.com and enter QuickPass code GL57805u6.

Literature and Reading Preview

Connect to the Story

Are there any technologies that frighten you? Write a journal entry about technologies that you think might have the potential to be abused or to get out of control.

Build Background

The protagonist of "Robot Dreams," Dr. Susan Calvin, appears in a number of Asimov's other robot stories. She is one of Asimov's robot experts who takes an active role in enhancing and advancing robotic intelligence. These experts track the evolution of robots from fairly mindless automatons to complex, emotional beings.

Set Purposes for Reading

Big Idea **The Extraordinary and Fantastic**

As you read, ask yourself, How does Asimov explore the conflict between humanity and technology?

Literary Element **Analogy**

An **analogy** is a comparison that shows similarities between two things that are otherwise dissimilar. Recognizing an author's use of analogies can help you better discern the meaning of or intention behind a text. As you read, ask yourself, How does Asimov use analogies?

Reading Strategy **Activate Prior Knowledge**

From *Star Trek* to *Star Wars,* machines and robots have long figured prominently in literature and film. Activating your prior knowledge about a topic can help you make relevant connections and improve your understanding of a text. As you read, ask yourself, What do I already know about technology?

....

Tip: Use Prior Knowledge Use a chart like the one below to record what you know about robots and computers, how you know it, and what you learn from the story.

What I Know About Robots	How I Know It	What I Learn from the Story
Some robots can be programmed to react with anger, happiness, or fear when they are touched in different ways.	I read about a robot called Feelix in a nonfiction book.	

TEKS

For pages 1046–1054

RC-10.A Reflect on understanding to monitor comprehension (e.g., making connections).

Vocabulary

gnarled (närld) *adj.* roughened and coarse from age or work; full of knots, as in a tree; p. 1048 *Susan found it difficult to climb the old gnarled tree.*

dismantle (dis mant′əl) *v.* to take apart; p. 1049 *The workers dismantled the broken scoreboard in the gym so they could put in a new one.*

accord (ə kôrd′) *n.* agreement; conformity; p. 1050 *The candidate acted in accord with federal law when he turned down a contribution that was too large.*

precedence (pres′ə dəns) *n.* order of importance or preference; priority; p. 1051 *Repairing the broken window takes precedence over buying baseballs.*

inert (i nurt′) *adj.* not able to move; p. 1051 *The detective examined the inert body lying on the floor.*

Robot Dreams

Isaac Asimov

"Last night I dreamed," said LVX-1, calmly. Susan Calvin said nothing, but her lined face, old with wisdom and experience, seemed to undergo a microscopic twitch.

"Did you hear that?" said Linda Rash, nervously. "It's as I told you." She was small, dark-haired, and young. Her right hand opened and closed, over and over.

Calvin nodded. She said, quietly, "Elvex, you will not move nor speak nor hear us, until I say your name again."

There was no answer. The robot sat as though it were cast out of one piece of metal, and it would stay so until it heard its name again.

Calvin said, "What is your computer entry code, Dr. Rash? Or enter it yourself if that will make you more comfortable. I want to inspect the positronic[1] brain pattern."

Linda's hands fumbled, for a moment, at the keys. She broke the process and started again. The fine pattern appeared on the screen.

Calvin said, "Your permission, please, to manipulate your computer."

Permission was granted with a speechless nod. Of course! What could Linda, a new and unproven robopsychologist, do against the Living Legend?

Slowly, Susan Calvin studied the screen, moving it across and down, then up, then suddenly throwing in a key-combination so rapidly that Linda didn't see what had been done, but the pattern displayed a new portion of itself altogether and had been enlarged. Back and forth she went, her **gnarled** fingers tripping over the keys.

---

1. *Positronic* is a fictional word often used in science fiction to refer to robotic brains. A positron is a subatomic particle equal in mass to an electron but which holds a positive charge.

Vocabulary

gnarled (närld) *adj.* roughened and coarse from age or work; full of knots, as in a tree

No change came over the old face. As though vast calculations were going through her head, she watched all the pattern shifts.

Linda wondered. It was impossible to analyze a pattern without at least a handheld computer, yet the Old Woman simply stared. Did she have a computer implanted in her skull? Or was it her brain which, for decades, had done nothing but devise, study, and analyze the positronic brain patterns? Did she grasp such a pattern the way Mozart grasped the notation of a symphony?

Finally Calvin said, "What is it you have done, Rash?"

Linda said, a little abashed, "I made use of fractal geometry."[2]

"I gathered that. But why?"

"It had never been done. I thought it would produce a brain pattern with added complexity, possibly closer to that of the human."

"Was anyone consulted? Was this all on your own?"

"I did not consult. It was on my own."

Calvin's faded eyes looked long at the young woman. "You had no right. Rash your name; rash your nature. Who are you not to ask? I myself, I, Susan Calvin, would have discussed this."

"I was afraid I would be stopped."

"You certainly would have been."

"*Am* I," her voice caught, even as she strove to hold it firm, "going to be fired?"

"Quite possibly," said Calvin. "Or you might be promoted. It depends on what I think when I am through."

"Are you going to **dismantle** El—" She had almost said the name, which would have reactivated the robot and been one more mistake. She could not afford another mistake, if it wasn't already too late to afford anything at all. "Are you going to dismantle the robot?"

She was suddenly aware, with some shock, that the Old Woman had an electron gun in the pocket of her smock. Dr. Calvin had come prepared for just that.

"We'll see," said Calvin. "The robot may prove too valuable to dismantle."

"But how can it dream?"

"You've made a positronic brain pattern remarkably like that of a human brain. Human brains must dream to reorganize, to get rid, periodically, of knots and snarls. Perhaps so must this robot, and for the same reason. Have you asked him what he has dreamed?"

"No, I sent for you as soon as he said he had dreamed. I would deal with this matter no further on my own, after that."

"Ah!" A very small smile passed over Calvin's face. "There are limits beyond which your folly will not carry you. I am glad of that. In fact, I am relieved. And now let us together see what we can find out."

She said, sharply, "Elvex."

The robot's head turned toward her smoothly. "Yes, Dr. Calvin?"

"How do you know you have dreamed?"

"It is at night, when it is dark, Dr. Calvin," said Elvex, "and there is suddenly light, although I can see no cause for the appearance of light. I see things that have no connection with what I conceive of as reality. I hear things. I react oddly. In searching my vocabulary for words to express what was happening, I came across the word 'dream.' Studying its meaning I finally came to the conclusion I was dreaming."

---

2. *Fractal geometry* is a type of mathematics that deals with irregular objects and forms.

Analogy *What does this analogy say about Susan Calvin's skill in robot science?*

Vocabulary

dismantle (dis mant′əl) *v.* to take apart

The Extraordinary and Fantastic *Why might such a humanlike robot be especially valuable?*

"How did you come to have 'dream' in your vocabulary, I wonder."

Linda said, quickly, waving the robot silent, "I gave him a human-style vocabulary. I thought—"

"You really thought," said Calvin. "I'm amazed."

"I thought he would need the verb. You know, 'I never dreamed that—' Something like that."

Calvin said, "How often have you dreamed, Elvex?"

"Every night, Dr. Calvin, since I have become aware of my existence."

"Ten nights," interposed Linda, anxiously, "but Elvex only told me of it this morning."

"Why only this morning, Elvex?"

"It was not until this morning, Dr. Calvin, that I was convinced that I was dreaming. Till then, I had thought there was a flaw in my positronic brain pattern, but I could not find one. Finally, I decided it was a dream."

"And what do you dream?"

"I dream always very much the same dream, Dr. Calvin. Little details are different but always it seems to me that I see a large panorama in which robots are working."

"Robots, Elvex? And human beings, also?"

"I see no human beings in the dream, Dr. Calvin. Not at first. Only robots."

"What are they doing, Elvex?"

"They are working, Dr. Calvin. I see some mining in the depths of the earth, and some laboring in heat and radiation. I see some in factories and some undersea."

Calvin turned to Linda. "Elvex is only ten station. How does he know of robots in such detail?"

Linda looked in the direction of a chair as though she longed to sit down, but the Old Woman was standing and that meant Linda had to stand also. She said, faintly, "It seemed to me important that he know about robotics and its place in the world. It was my thought that he would be particularly adapted to play the part of overseer[3] with his—his new brain."

"His fractal brain?"

"Yes."

Calvin nodded and turned back to the robot. "You saw all this—undersea, and underground, and aboveground—and space, too, I imagine."

"I also saw robots working in space," said Elvex. "It was that I saw all this, with the details forever changing as I glanced from place to place, that made me realize that what I saw was not in **accord** with reality and led me to the conclusion, finally, that I was dreaming."

"What else did you see, Elvex?"

"I saw that all the robots were bowed down with toil and affliction, that all were weary of responsibility and care, and I wished them to rest."

Calvin said, "But the robots are not bowed down, they are not weary, they need no rest."

"So it is in reality, Dr. Calvin. I speak of my dream, however. In my dream, it seemed to me that robots must protect their own existence."

Calvin said, "Are you quoting the Third Law of Robotics?"

"I am, Dr. Calvin."

"But you quote it in incomplete fashion. The Third Law is 'A robot must protect its own existence as long as such protection does not conflict with the First or Second Law.'"

"Yes, Dr. Calvin. That is the Third Law in reality, but in my dream, the Law ended with the word 'existence.' There was no mention of the First or Second Law."

Activate Prior Knowledge *Given what you know about how robots are generally portrayed, how significant is it that Elvex is "aware" of his existence?*

3. An *overseer* is a person who supervises or oversees.

Vocabulary

accord (ə kôrd´) *n.* agreement; conformity

Tin God, 2003. P.J. Crook. Acrylic on canvas and wood. Private collection.

First nor Second Law, but only the Third, and the Third law was 'A robot must protect its own existence.' That was the whole of the Law."

"In your dream, Elvex?"

"In my dream."

Calvin said, "Elvex, you will not move nor speak nor hear us until I say your name again." And again the robot became, to all appearances, a single **inert** piece of metal.

Calvin turned to Linda Rash and said, "Well, what do you think, Dr. Rash?"

Linda's eyes were wide, and she could feel her heart beating madly. She said, "Dr. Calvin, I am appalled. I had no idea. It would never have occurred to me that such a thing was possible."

"Yet both exist, Elvex. The Second Law, which takes **precedence** over the Third is 'A robot must obey the orders given it by human beings except where such orders would conflict with the First Law.' Because of this, robots obey orders. They do the work you see them do, and they do it readily and without trouble. They are not bowed down; they are not weary."

"So it is in reality, Dr. Calvin. I speak of my dream."

"And the First Law, Elvex, which is the most important of all, is 'A robot may not injure a human being, or, through inaction, allow a human being to come to harm.'"

"Yes, Dr. Calvin. In reality. In my dream, however, it seemed to me there was neither

"No," said Calvin, calmly. "Nor would it have occurred to me, not to anyone. You have created a robot brain capable of dreaming and by this device you have revealed a layer of thought in robotic brains that might have remained undetected, other wise, until the danger became acute."

"But that's impossible," said Linda. "You can't mean that other robots think the same."

"As we would say of a human being, not consciously. But who would have thought there was an unconscious layer beneath the obvious positronic brain paths, a layer that was not necessarily under the control of the Three Laws? What might this have

---

The Extraordinary and Fantastic *Why might this dream be dangerous for humanity?*

brought about as robotic brains grew more and more complex—had we not been warned?"

"You mean by Elvex?"

"By *you*, Dr. Rash. You have behaved improperly, but, by doing so, you have helped us to an overwhelmingly important understanding. We shall be working with fractal brains from now on, forming them in carefully controlled fashion. You will play your part in that. You will not be penalized for what you have done, but you will henceforth work in collaboration with others. Do you understand?"

"Yes, Dr. Calvin. But what of Elvex?"

"I'm still not certain."

Calvin removed the electron gun from her pocket and Linda stared at it with fascina-

Visual Vocabulary
An *ingot* is a hunk of metal.

tion. One burst of its electrons at a robotic cranium and the positronic brain paths would be neutralized and enough energy would be released to fuse the robot-brain into an inert ingot.

Linda said, "But surely Elvex is important to our research. He must not be destroyed."

"*Must* not, Dr. Rash? That will be my decision, I think. It depends entirely on how dangerous Elvex is."

She straightened up, as though determined that her own aged body was not to bow under *its* weight of responsibility. She said, "Elvex, do you hear me?"

"Yes, Dr. Calvin," said the robot.

"Did your dream continue? You said earlier that human beings did not appear *at first*. Does that mean they appeared afterward?"

Activate Prior Knowledge *What usually happens in stories and movies when robots and computers are not controlled?*

Torso, 1965. Vladimir Yankilevski. Oil, metal and wood. Private collection.

"Yes, Dr. Calvin. It seemed to me, in my dream, that eventually one man appeared."

"One man? Not a robot?"

"Yes, Dr. Calvin. And the man said, 'Let my people go!'"

"The *man* said that?"

"Yes, Dr. Calvin."

"And when he said 'Let my people go,' then by the words 'my people' he meant the robots?"

"Yes, Dr. Calvin. So it was in my dream."

"And did you know who the man was—in your dream?"

"Yes, Dr. Calvin. I knew the man."

"Who was he?"

And Elvex said, "I was the man."

And Susan Calvin at once raised her electron gun and fired, and Elvex was no more. ❧

After You Read

Respond and Think Critically

1. **Connect to Personal Experience** What was your first reaction to Elvex? Did you feel sympathy for Elvex at the end of the story? Why or why not?

2. **Make Inferences About Characters** What is Elvex's real name? Why do you think the human characters call him Elvex? Explain.

3. **Clarify Details** How did Elvex learn the word *dream*? Why do robots normally not know this word? Support your answer with details from the story.

4. **Analyze Character** How does Asimov show Linda's anxiety at the beginning of the story? How is the character of Linda developed over the course of the story? Describe Asimov's portrayal of Linda, citing details from the story. **OER**

5. **Analyze Characterization** How does Asimov convey Calvin's immense experience in robotic science? Explain.

6. **Draw Conclusions About Characters** Who is the man in Elvex's dream? Why does a man appear instead of a robot? What can you conclude about Elvex based on the dream?

7. **Big Idea** **Draw Conclusions About Events** Consider the extraordinary events of the story. Why does Susan Calvin think it necessary to destroy Elvex? Support your answer with text evidence.

Literary Element   Analogy

Writers often use an **analogy** to explain something unfamiliar by comparing it to something familiar. For example, Asimov compares brain patterns to Mozart symphonies to show that both are complex. That analogy suggests that both humans and robots use similar processes for comprehension. Asimov uses other analogies to show similarities between robots and humans throughout the story.

8. **Analyze Analogies** What other analogies does Asimov use to show how the robots are similar to humans? Use the analogies to make a Venn diagram to show the similarities and differences between robots and humans.

Robots   Both   Humans

Have brain patterns

9. **Draw Conclusions About Meaning** Why can these similarities be both beneficial and harmful to humankind? Explain.

Review: Theme Archetype

As you learned on page 933, a **theme** in a literary work is its central message about life. An **archetype** is a model or pattern that recurs throughout literature and history. One of the primary themes in "Robot Dreams" is *people must be vigilant to preserve power over machines.*

10. **Partner Activity** With a classmate, discuss the archetype of *person versus machine* as expressed in "Robot Dreams." Make a list of details from the text that exemplify the *person versus machine* archetype. Use a chart like the one below to record details. Listen actively and effectively to your partner's ideas.

Detail	How it supports the theme archetype
"In my dream, it seemed to me that robots must protect their own existence."	Elvex implies that robots have to protect their existence from humans.

Reading Strategy — Activate Prior Knowledge

Applying what you already know to your reading of a literary work can help you to put the work in perspective. Review the chart you made on page 1047 and the blue highlighted passages and questions to answer the following questions.

11. Think of a book or movie that portrays an unfriendly relationship between robots or computers and humans. Why was the relationship unfriendly? Explain.

12. Use your prior knowledge of the book or movie to make connections to "Robot Dreams." How does the robot-human relationship in the first work influence and enhance your appreciation for "Robot Dreams"? Explain.

Vocabulary Practice

Practice with Context Clues Identify the context clues in the following sentences that help you determine the meaning of each boldfaced vocabulary word.

1. The old woman's **gnarled** hands had performed decades of work in the fields.

2. The television set lay in pieces on the living room floor: Jamie had completely **dismantled** it.

3. We were in perfect **accord**: I accepted Lee's decision, and he agreed to pay me for the damage.

4. The repair to the roof takes **precedence** over the repair to the window: it's more important for us to be dry than warm!

5. Because the dog was completely **inert**, Mark thought, at first, that it was asleep.

Enrich and Extend

 Speaking and Listening

Oral Report Present an oral report in which you respond to Asimov's three laws of robotics and outline a similar set of laws for humans.

Prepare Consider whether Asimov's three laws are logical, beneficial for both humans and robots, and likely to promote civility and equality. Chart your judgments and the evidence for them:

My Judgment	Evidence/Support
laws are logically constructed—yes	the laws are hierarchical; the second law cannot contradict the first
laws benefit humans	
laws promote civility and equality	

Write your report. Then cue it for your delivery by highlighting words and statements you will emphasize, places where you will pause and make eye contact, and places where you might add gestures or incorporate movements.

Report As you report, be sure to make frequent eye contact and to use your voice and movements to call attention to key points. Include a visual in your presentation to help command your audience's attention and to help clarify your own laws or Asimov's laws. Adjust your delivery, vocabulary, and length to your audience and purpose.

Evaluate Write a paragraph evaluating your oral report for its content, especially its use of evidence and visual aids, as well as for aspects of your delivery, including your diction, movement, and eye contact.

TEKS

For pages 1055–1059

10.9.C Make and defend subtle inferences and complex conclusions about the ideas in text and their organizational patterns.

Set a Purpose for Reading

Read to learn about robots with human-like qualities and why they were invented.

Preview the Article

1. Judging from the title, what do you think this article is about?

2. Skim the article. How do the use of subheadings and other text features compare with their use in other articles you've read?

Reading Strategy Draw Conclusions About Author's Purpose

When you **draw conclusions about author's purpose,** you look for details in the text that help you understand why the author is writing. Authors may write for any and all of the following purposes: to persuade, to inform, to explain, to entertain, or to describe. As you read, draw conclusions about the writer's purpose and the structure of the text in a chart like the one below. Defend your conclusions.

Detail	Conclusion
big-eyed, babbling	author is trying to show the robot as likeable

TIME

The Machine
Nurturer

Kismet has a winning personality that draws people in. That's just what Cynthia Breazeal intended when she built her very sociable robot.

By ADAM COHEN

WALK INTO ROOM 922 OF THE ARTIFICIAL intelligence lab at the Massachusetts Institute of Technology (M.I.T.), and you may notice a robot in the corner trying desperately to get your attention. When Kismet is lonely and spots a human, it cranes its head forward. It flaps its pink paper ears and excitedly makes babylike noises. Kismet's creators call this an "attention-getting display." You would have to have a heart of stone to ignore this cute little aluminum . . . thing.

From a physical standpoint, Kismet isn't much of a robot. It can't walk and grab things, as many robots today can. It doesn't even have arms, legs, or a body. What sets Kismet apart is that it has been built with drives and equipped to interact with people. In social terms, big-eyed, babbling Kismet may be the most human robot ever built. And it may be the closest we have yet come to building the kind of robots that appear in science fiction and interact with humans in a natural way, like C-3PO from *Star Wars*.

Kismet is the creation of Cynthia Breazeal, an advanced student in the Humanoid Robotics Group at M.I.T. Breazeal has studied for years under Rodney Brooks, perhaps the leading figure in the world of robotics. Breazeal got the idea for Kismet when she was working with Cog, another robot in Brooks' lab that was built to have the physical capacities of a human infant. Cog has a head, arms, and an upper body, and it can engage in simple tasks like turning a crank or playing with a slinky. Cog is physically gifted but completely lacking in social skills.

That lack was driven home to Breazeal one day when she was interacting with Cog. Breazeal put an eraser down in front of Cog, and Cog used its arm to pick up the eraser. When the robot put the eraser down, Breazeal picked it up. Breazeal and Cog continued taking turns picking up the eraser and putting it down. To an outside observer, it might have looked like the robot was intentionally playing with Breazeal, but Cog's mind just didn't work that way. It was while taking part in this interaction that Breazeal decided to try to build a new kind of robot—one that could play the eraser game with her and mean it.

A Child of Science

Breazeal was uniquely suited to the task of building this new robot. She grew up near the technology-rich area that would become Silicon Valley. Her father was a mathematician and her mother a computer scientist, and they raised her, she says, to be "pro-technology." Breazeal became captivated by robots at age 8 when she saw Star Wars for the first time. "I just fell in love with the Droids," she says, especially R2–D2. "But I was old enough to realize those kinds of robots didn't exist." Growing up, she considered becoming a doctor and an astronaut. But she never

gave up her interest in robots. When she studied astronomy, she was particularly intrigued by lunar rovers, which are really just a specialized form of robot. After graduating from the University of California at Santa Barbara, Breazeal went to M.I.T. in the early 1990s to become part of one of the world's most innovative robotics labs.

At the time, Rodney Brooks was working on smaller, insect-like robots. Breazeal helped out and ended up with a small role in *Fast, Cheap, and Out of Control,* a documentary in which filmmaker Errol Morris profiles four people—including Brooks—who were pursuing unusual passions. When Brooks moved on to larger robots,

Breazeal became the chief architect on Cog.

Breazeal played an active role in building Kismet. Drawing on her experience helping build two prior complex robots, she worked on everything from the mechanized design for Kismet's facial features to tinkering with its body parts in the shop. Breazeal took great care with the robot's facial features, which she considered important to making it an appealing social actor. She found a special-effects expert to make human-like eyes and personally glued on false eyelashes purchased in a beauty-supply store. And she put bright red lips on its metal mouth, using surgical tubing colored in with a red pen.

Body Parts

Kismet has an array of built-in features that help it act in a human-like way. It has four color cameras that allow it to "see," and its computers are programmed to help it recognize objects and measure distances. Kismet actively seeks out colorful toys and faces. It recognizes faces by looking for flesh tones and eyes. Kismet can hear, but only when humans speak into its microphone. And Kismet has motor capabilities that allow it to shift its eyes and crane its head toward particular sights and sounds. One of the robot's best features is its ability to register expressions that correspond to its emotional state. When it is surprised, it can raise its eyebrows. When it is sad, it can frown. Kismet can also vocalize, in a sing-song babble of meaningless sounds.

Kismet was designed with motivational drives, drawn from developmental psychology. A computer attached to the robot displays bar graphs that reflect its three drives—social, stimulation, and fatigue. Kismet's desire to satisfy these drives leads it to engage in a variety of purposeful behaviors, much as a human baby would. When its social drive is high, indicating that it is lonely, the robot actively seeks out human interaction. When its stimulation drive is high, it is drawn to other forms of interaction, including playing with colorful toys. Since it has no arms, it can't pick up a toy itself. But if it stares plaintively at a toy, a nearby human will usually pick it up and bring it over. When Kismet has had enough stimulation, its fatigue drive kicks in.

Kismet is able to engage in the kind of purposeful human interactions that cousin Cog could not. Kismet calls people toward it. And when they get too close for its cameras to see them well, it protects its personal space and pulls away. When an object suddenly appears in front of it, Kismet quickly withdraws and flashes a look of bewilderment. Most winningly, the robot is able to engage in a babbling "conversation" with humans in its midst. When it "talks," it takes turns with the person with whom it is speaking; the result resembles a conversation between an adult and an infant.

By one measure, Kismet is a clear success: people love it. When visitors arrive in the lab, they are drawn to the robot. When Kismet engages them, they are invariably charmed. "It's human nature," says Breazeal. "They are very concerned about keeping it happy." Proof of its winning personality: a box of toys given to it by human friends, including a yellow teddy bear sent from Japan.

The Urge to Invent

Breazeal is attracted to inventing because it is hands-on and real-world. "I would much rather build something and interact with it than philosophize about it," she says. "Or philosophize about someone else doing it." But at the same time, she has used robotics to explore some complex intellectual issues. At M.I.T., Breazeal has studied brains and cognitive science, and her work with Kismet raises important questions about how humans think and learn.

In designing Kismet, Breazeal made a critical decision about how she wanted it to develop. There are two rival schools about ways to build robots. One holds that robotmakers should decide in advance what knowledge and skills they want their robots to have and then program them accordingly. Breazeal has a different view. She thinks robots should be designed to learn from experience and from their environment. This socially situated learning, as it is called, allows Kismet to learn much like a human baby would.

The problem is that robots have fewer opportunities than babies to learn from their environment. Humans spend a great deal of time talking to and nurturing young people. Robots do not get that kind of attention and outside stimulation. "We don't learn in impoverished educational environments, but that's what we expect the robot to do," she says. Breazeal has tried to provide Kismet with the tools to engage in this kind of socially situated learning.

Despite all the help from Breazeal, Kismet still has a lot to learn. Breazeal is working on helping the computer with some simple skills that human babies are hardwired for. She wants Kismet to be able to use the information it learns. One day, she hopes, when Kismet is told the name of a toy, it will later be able to ask for it by name. "Through more interactions, Kismet could learn, 'When I'm in this state, I can take this action that leads to a person's taking this behavior

MOOD SWINGS Kismet can use its expressive face to reflect a variety of humanlike emotions. When Kismet is startled, its expression changes from calm, left, to a widemouthed look of surprise, right.

and getting my needs satiated,'" Breazeal says. She also wants Kismet to be able to remember the people it meets, so it can distinguish old friends from people it is meeting for the first time.

Who's Teaching Whom?

Kismet's educational journey prompts an obvious question: Why? What is the purpose of building humanoid robots and then programming and training them to act like us? One view of robotics holds that being able to build a machine that acts like a human is itself a worthy goal. "There's certainly a great challenge in creating something as sophisticated as what humans do," says Breazeal. It doesn't necessarily mean engaging in the Frankensteinian mission of trying to create a human being,

she says. "Of course, we're never going to do that, but we can look for a commonality," she says. "Even though your dog is not human, it doesn't mean you can't communicate with it in a human-like way."

But Breazeal is at least as interested in using the robot to better understand humans. Thinking about how robots learn turns out to be a good way to think about human development. A case in point: In helping Kismet learn, researchers have observed that one of the hardest parts of the learning process is figuring out what to pay attention to. And watching Kismet interact with people provides insight into human social dynamics. At some point, Breazeal wants to build a second Kismet to see how the two

robots interact. "A lot of times kids compete for attention," she says. "It would be interesting to program the robot to get attention."

As a woman robotmaker, Breazeal is in a distinct minority. A major reason, she says, is that girls do not get enough support in pursuing careers in science. "Girls aren't discouraged," she says, "but they aren't encouraged either." And they don't have enough positive role models. When she was growing up, Breazeal says, she did not see many women scientists, and the ones she did encounter were mainly "difficult people" she did not want to emulate. What made the difference for her is that her mother was a scientist and encouraged her to pursue a career in the sciences.

Breazeal thinks more girls would be attracted to the hard sciences (including physics, chemistry, and biology) if they realized how creative they can be. Contrary to popular conceptions of hard science as dry and rigid, she sees it as a rich field for self-expression. "Technology is flexible enough that you can make it what you want," she says. And Breazeal is certainly doing just that. By emphasizing the social aspect of robotics, she is taking the field in a bold new direction. "I'm trying to challenge the stereotypes," she says, "[by] putting a human face on them."

It's impossible to spend time with Kismet without seeing that face. It is a long way from being a human. But it has enough human qualities that its interactions are, in some way, clearly social. And it forms bonds with people that may fall short of human bonds but are far different from the ones people form with most inanimate objects. Breazeal freely acknowledges that her little creation tugs at her own heartstrings. "I definitely have an attachment to it," she says, admitting that she missed it while on a recent trip to Australia. So what will happen if she ever has to part with Kismet? "I really don't know," she says. "The legal system doesn't have parental rights for robots."

—from TIME

Editor's note: After the publication of this article, Breazeal went on to become an associate professor at M.I.T., as well as director of the school's Robotic Life Group. She published her first book, Designing Sociable Robots, *in 2002 and continues to create robots like Kismet that work and learn in partnership with people.*

> **"Technology is flexible enough that you can make it what you want."**

Respond and Think Critically

1. **Summarize Main Ideas** Write a brief summary of the main ideas in this article before you answer the following questions. For help on writing a summary, see page 389.

2. **Make Inferences About Behavior** What is the difference between Kismet and Cog? What can their interactions reveal about human interactions?

3. **Evaluate Description** How does the author describe the characteristics of the robots and their interactions? Do the descriptions enable you to visualize the robots well? Why or why not?

4. **Make Inferences About Structure** What do you think is the author's primary purpose in writing this article? How does the structure of the article support this purpose? Use evidence from the text to defend your response.

5. **Draw Conclusions About Author's Purpose** How does the author use the subject of Cynthia Breazeal to make a point about women in science? How do you think this relates to his purpose in writing the article? Defend your response with text evidence.

6. **Synthesize Ideas** After reading about Kismet, do you think there is anything realistic about Isaac Asimov's "Robot Dreams"? Explain.

Before You Read

Bread

Meet **Margaret Atwood**

(born 1939)

Margaret Atwood has become one of Canada's most respected and popular writers, producing award-winning poems, novels, children's books, short stories, and essays. "I became a poet at the age of sixteen. I did not intend to do it. It was not my fault," Atwood has said.

Growing Up Atwood was born in Ottawa, Ontario, Canada, but her childhood was divided between a variety of Canadian cities and the forests of northwestern Quebec, where her father, a scientist, conducted research about insects. Both her parents were avid readers and encouraged her love of words.

Atwood earned a bachelor's degree from the University of Toronto in 1961 and a graduate degree from Radcliffe College a year later. For the next several years, she combined jobs waiting tables, working at a market research company, and teaching grammar, with off-and-on studies at Harvard University.

> "I began as a profoundly apolitical writer, but then I began to do what all novelists and some poets do; I began to describe the world around me."
>
> —Margaret Atwood

A Focus on Humanity In 1966 Atwood won her first major literary prize, Canada's Governor General's Award, for her second book of poems, *The Circle Game*. The publica-

tion of her first novel, *The Edible Woman*, in 1969 coincided with the growing feminist movement and helped put Atwood on the literary map. While much of her writing focuses on women, Atwood is also known for writing that explores human behavior in general.

Though critics have noted the political nature of much of Atwood's writing, Atwood says that she begins new works without a political agenda in mind. "One works by simple observation, looking into things. . . . As an artist your first loyalty is to your art. Unless this is the case, you're going to be a second-rate artist." Pressed by an interviewer to name her "discrete truth," Atwood mentioned her belief that "money should not be the measure of all things."

In recent years, Atwood has become so famous in Canada that people follow her around on the streets and in stores. She is a frequent guest on Canadian television and radio. In 2000, Atwood won the Booker Prize for her novel *The Blind Assassin*. Atwood has remarked, "I'm a serious writer and I never expected to become a popular one."

 Literature Online

Author Search For more about Margaret Atwood, go to glencoe.com and enter QuickPass code GL57805u6.

Literature and Reading Preview

Connect to the Fable

What do you think of when you hear the word *bread*? What do you associate with bread, and why do you make these associations? Respond to these questions in your journal.

Build Background

In the twentieth century, an estimated 70 million people died from famine, which is still a problem in some developing nations. Most famines are caused by climate, crop failure, disease, war, and misguided economic policies.

Set Purposes for Reading

Big Idea The Extraordinary and Fantastic

In this story, Atwood includes both realistic and fantastic details. As you read, ask yourself, What message do these details suggest about human nature?

Literary Element Point of View

Point of view refers to the perspective from which a story is told. In the second-person point of view, the word "you" establishes the reader's view of the action. As you read "Bread," ask yourself, How does Atwood's use of the second-person point of view force readers into a personal confrontation with stark realities?

Reading Strategy Recognize Author's Purpose

The **author's purpose** is the author's intent in writing a work. Authors usually write for one or more of the following purposes: to persuade, to inform, to explain, to entertain, or to describe a process. As you read, ask yourself, What does Atwood's inclusion of certain details tell you about her purpose for writing?

....

Tip: Analyze Scenes "Bread" evokes five different scenes, or contexts. As you read, record your thoughts about why Atwood included each scene.

Scene	Author's Purpose
Cutting yourself a slice of bread and eating it with honey and peanut butter	To describe how many people eat bread or take it for granted

TEKS

For pages 1060–1064

10.5 Students understand, make inferences and draw conclusions about the structure and elements of fiction and provide evidence from text to support understanding.

Vocabulary

bloated (blō′tid) *adj.* puffed up; swollen; p. 1062 *After eating too much, Rick felt bloated.*

scavenger (skav′in jər) *n.* one who searches through discarded materials for something useful; p. 1063 *A scavenger found the bicycle at the dump and began riding it.*

treacherous (trech′ ər əs) *adj.* likely to betray a trust; disloyal; p. 1063 *Her actions toward me were treacherous; I suffered as a result of them.*

dupe (do͞op) *v.* to fool; to trick; p. 1063 *The salesperson duped me into buying something I did not need.*

BREAD

Margaret Atwood

Imagine a piece of bread. You don't have to imagine it, it's right here in the kitchen, on the breadboard, in its plastic bag, lying beside the bread knife. The bread knife is an old one you picked up at an auction; it has the word BREAD carved into the wooden handle. You open the bag, pull back the wrapper, cut yourself a slice. You put butter on it, then peanut butter, then honey, and you fold it over. Some of the honey runs out onto your fingers and you lick it off. It takes you about a minute to eat the bread. This bread happens to be brown, but there is also white bread, in the refrigerator, and a heel of rye you got last week, round as a full stomach then, now going moldy. Occasionally you make bread. You think of it as something relaxing to do with your hands.

Imagine a famine. Now imagine a piece of bread. Both of these things are real but you happen to be in the same room with only one of them. Put yourself into a different room, that's what the mind is for. You are now lying on a thin mattress in a hot room. The walls are made of dried earth, and your sister, who is younger than you, is in the room with you. She is starving, her belly is **bloated**, flies land on her eyes; you brush them off with your hand. You have cloth too, filthy but damp, and you press it to her lips and forehead. The piece of bread is the bread you've been saving, for days it seems. You are as hungry as she is, but not yet as weak. How long does this take? When will someone come with more bread? You think of going out to see if you might find something that could be eaten, but outside the streets are infested with

---

Point of View *In this first scene, what mood does the point of view evoke?*

Vocabulary

bloated (blō′tid) *adj.* puffed up; swollen

scavengers and the stink of corpses is everywhere.

Should you share the bread or give the whole piece to your sister? Should you eat the piece of bread yourself? After all, you have a better chance of living, you're stronger. How long does it take to decide?

Imagine a prison. There is something you know that you have not yet told. Those in control of the prison know that you know. So do those not in control. If you tell, thirty or forty or a hundred of your friends, your comrades, will be caught and will die. If you refuse to tell, tonight will be like last night. They always choose the night. You don't think about the night, however, but about the piece of bread they offered you. How long does it take? This piece of bread was brown and fresh and reminded you of sunlight falling across a wooden floor. It reminded you of a bowl, a yellow bowl that was once in your home. It held apples and pears; it stood on a table you can also remember. It's not the hunger or the pain that is killing you but the absence of the yellow bowl. If you could only hold the bowl in your hands, right here, you could withstand anything, you tell yourself. The bread they offered you is subversive, it's **treacherous**, it does not mean life.

There were once two sisters. One was rich and had no children, the other had five children and was a widow, so poor that she no longer had any food left. She went to her sister and asked her for a mouthful of bread. "My children are dying," she said. The rich sister said, "I do not have enough for myself," and drove her away from the door. Then the husband of the rich sister came home and wanted to cut himself a piece of bread; but when he made the first cut, out flowed red blood.

Everyone knew what that meant.

This is a traditional German fairy tale.

The loaf of bread I have conjured[1] for you floats about a foot above your kitchen table. The table is normal, there are no trap doors in it. A blue tea towel[2] floats beneath the bread, and there are no strings attaching the cloth to the bread or the bread to the ceiling or the table to the cloth, you've proved it by passing your hand above and below. You didn't touch the bread though. What stopped you? You don't want to know whether the bread is real or whether it's just a hallucination I've somehow **duped** you into seeing. There's no doubt that you can see the bread, you can even smell it, it smells like yeast, and it looks old enough, solid as your own arm. But can you trust it? Can you eat it? You don't want to know, imagine that. ∞

Recognize Author's Purpose *What do the questions at the top of this column suggest about the author's purpose?*

Point of View *According to the story, you, as the prisoner, feel that the offered bread is "subversive" and "treacherous." Why might a prisoner feel this way?*

Vocabulary

scavenger (skav′in jər) *n.* one who searches through discarded materials for something useful

treacherous (trech′ ər əs) *adj.* likely to betray a trust; disloyal

---

1. *Conjured* means "caused to appear, as by magic."
2. A *tea towel* is a towel used for drying dishes.

The Extraordinary and Fantastic *What might the last story be suggesting about the reader's desire to confront reality?*

Vocabulary

dupe (do͞op) *v.* to fool; to trick

After You Read

Respond and Think Critically

1. **Connect to Personal Experience** Which scene affected you most strongly? Why?

2. **Make Inferences About Attitude** What does the narrator describe in the first paragraph? What can you infer about the narrator's attitude toward the bread from this description?

3. **Clarify Meaning** What does the author mean by "this is a traditional German fairy tale"? How does this scene's message relate to the other situations in the fable?

4. **Analyze Symbolism** What do you think happens to the prisoner in the night? What does the yellow bowl symbolize for the prisoner?

5. **Analyze Structure** How does reading the first paragraph affect your perception of the next three scenes? Explain.

6. **Big Idea** **Draw Conclusions About Ideas** How does the fable upend common ideas about what is ordinary in life and what is extraordinary? Explain.

Literary Element Point of View

Point of view is the perspective from which a story is told.

7. **Make Inferences About Point of View** What can you infer about the author's meaning through the use of second-person point of view? Support your answer with text evidence.

8. **Evaluate Point of View** How would this story be different if it had been told from the first-person point of view? Would it have been as effective? Reread the pink highlighted question on page 1062 to help you get started.

Reading Strategy Recognize Author's Purpose

Review the chart you made on page 1061 and answer the following questions.

9. Early on, the narrator says, "Put yourself into a different room, that's what the mind is for." What does this command suggest about the purpose of the fable?

10. In your opinion, what does Atwood hope to accomplish with this text? Explain.

Vocabulary Practice

Practice with Connotation and Denotation
Denotation is the literal, or dictionary, meaning of a word. **Connotation** is the implied, or cultural, meaning. For example, the words *stubborn* and *intractable* have a similar denotation, "unwilling to cooperate," but have different connotations. While *stubborn* has a negative connotation, *intractable* has a more negative connotation.

Each vocabulary word is paired with another word. For each pair, choose the word that has a more negative connotation. Explain your answer.

1. bloated   swollen
2. scavenger   searcher
3. treacherous   disloyal
4. dupe   mislead

Writing

Write a Story Write a short modern fable, similar to "Bread," in which you describe an object with symbolic meaning and teach a lesson about human behavior. Try using the second-person point of view as Atwood does.

Before You Read

The Witness for the Prosecution

Meet **Agatha Christie**
(1890–1976)

After a lifetime of writing, Agatha Christie was an expert at inventing—and solving—murder mysteries with complex plots, ingenious twists and turns, and satisfying solutions. In story after story, Christie, who was sometimes called the "Queen of Crime" and the "Duchess of Death," subtly directs the reader's attention away from the most crucial clues.

> *"There's nothing like boredom to make you write."*
>
> —Agatha Christie

Boredom Leads to Success How did this author of approximately seventy novels, more than one hundred short stories, and over a dozen plays get started? In an interview, Christie revealed that she began imagining stories as a child to combat boredom. At the age of eighteen, she was recovering from influenza when her mother suggested that she write a story. Christie's very first attempt, entitled "The House of Beauty," was published in a magazine.

By the age of 26, Christie had written her first novel, *The Mysterious Affair at Styles*, and had begun to establish her reputation.

The Christie Detectives Christie created a number of fictional detectives. Hercule Poirot is the private eye in what may be Christie's most famous work, *Murder on the Orient Express*. Jane Marple, an amateur sleuth in her seventies with a knack for solving mysteries, first appears in *The Murder at the Vicarage*. Novels featuring Poirot and Marple established Christie as the most popular mystery writer of all time.

Many Faithful Readers Only surpassed by sales of the Bible and the works of William Shakespeare, Christie's books have sold a spectacular two billion copies. Ironically, Christie once claimed, "I don't enjoy writing detective stories. I enjoy thinking of a detective story, planning it, but when the time comes to write it, it is like going to work every day, like having a job." Among the many honors she received was the New York Drama Critics Circle Award for best foreign play, *The Witness for the Prosecution*. Christie continued writing until the last year of her life, publishing her eightieth book at the age of eighty.

LOG ON ▶ **Literature** Online

Author Search For more about Agatha Christie, go to glencoe.com and enter QuickPass code GL57805u6.

Literature and Reading Preview

Connect to the Story

Do you notice habits that people perform unconsciously, such as foot tapping or nail biting? What might these habits reveal? Discuss these questions with a partner.

Build Background

"The Witness for the Prosecution" is about a man in England who is accused of "willful murder," meaning premeditated, or planned, murder. In a British court of law, the solicitor prepares the case for the defense but does not argue it at the trial. That is the job of the counsel for the defense, referred to in this story as the K.C., or King's Counsel.

Set Purposes for Reading

Big Idea The Extraordinary and Fantastic

As you read, ask yourself, What seems convincing and real, and what seems suspicious or mysterious, about the accused man, his story, and the woman who testifies against him?

Literary Element Motivation

Motivation is the stated or implied reason or cause for a character's actions. As you read, ask yourself, Which motivations do characters attribute to themselves? Which motivations do characters suggest as belonging to each other?

Reading Strategy Make Inferences About Characters

When you **make inferences about characters,** you use your reason and experience to figure out what an author is not saying directly about a character. As you read, ask yourself, What can I infer about these characters? Use the blue highlighted passages and questions for help.

....

Tip: Take Notes Use a chart like the one below to record details about the characters and your inferences.

Detail	+ My Reason or Experience	= My Inference

TEKS

For pages 1065–1086

RC-10.B Make complex inferences about text and use textual evidence to support understanding.

Vocabulary

cultivate (kul′tə vāt′) *v.* to encourage or further the development of; p. 1069 *Lauren cultivated Rachel's friendship by calling her every night.*

pretext (prē′tekst) *n.* a reason or motive offered in order to disguise real intentions; p. 1070 *Jill wanted to stay home, so she told her mother she was sick, but that was just a pretext.*

amicable (am′ə kə bəl) *adj.* friendly; p. 1073 *George and Tameka, who had an amicable relationship, talked to each other every day.*

recoil (ri koil′) *v.* to shrink back physically or emotionally; p. 1076 *Zach recoils at the thought of telling on his best friend.*

animosity (an′ə mos′ə tē) *n.* ill will or resentment; active strong dislike or hostility; p. 1082 *Jorge's animosity toward Greg showed itself in his tense posture and scowl.*

The *Witness* for the *Prosecution*

Agatha Christie

The Barrister. Thomas Davidson (1863–1908). Oil on canvas. Roy Miles Fine Paintings, London.

Visual Vocabulary
Pince-nez (pans´ nā´) are eyeglasses that are clipped to the nose rather than held on by pieces that bend around the ears.

Mr. Mayherne adjusted his pince-nez and cleared his throat with a little dry-as-dust cough that was wholly typical of him. Then he looked again at the man opposite him, the man charged with willful murder.

Mr. Mayherne was a small man, precise in manner, neatly, not to say foppishly[1] dressed, with a pair of very shrewd and piercing gray eyes, by no means a fool. Indeed, as a solicitor, Mr. Mayherne's reputation stood very high. His voice, when he spoke to his client, was dry but not unsympathetic.

"I must impress upon you again that you are in very grave danger, and that the utmost frankness is necessary."

Leonard Vole, who had been staring in a dazed fashion at the blank wall in front of him, transferred his glance to the solicitor.

"I know," he said hopelessly. "You keep telling me so. But I can't seem to realize yet that I'm charged with murder—*murder.* And such a dastardly[2] crime too."

Mr. Mayherne was practical, not emotional. He coughed again, took off his pince-nez, polished them carefully, and replaced them on his nose. Then he said:

---

1. *Foppishly* means "fashionable in a silly or vain way."

2. *Dastardly* means "mean."

Make Inferences About Characters *What can you infer about Mayherne's personality based on the details so far?*

"Yes, yes, yes. Now, my dear Mr. Vole, we're going to make a determined effort to get you off—and we shall succeed—we shall succeed. But I must have all the facts. I must know just how damaging the case against you is likely to be. Then we can fix upon the best line of defense."

Still the young man looked at him in the same dazed, hopeless fashion. To Mr. Mayherne the case had seemed black enough, and the guilt of the prisoner assured. Now, for the first time, he felt a doubt.

"You think I'm guilty," said Leonard Vole, in a low voice. "But, by God, I swear I'm not! It looks pretty black against me; I know that. I'm like a man caught in a net— the meshes of it all round me, entangling me whichever way I turn. But I didn't do it, Mr. Mayherne; I didn't do it!"

In such a position a man was bound to protest his innocence.[3] Mr. Mayherne knew that. Yet, in spite of himself, he was impressed. It might be, after all, that Leonard Vole was innocent.

"You are right, Mr. Vole," he said gravely. "The case does look very black against you. Nevertheless, I accept your assurance. Now, let us get to facts. I want you to tell me in your own words exactly how you came to make the acquaintance of Miss Emily French."

"It was one day in Oxford Street. I saw an elderly lady crossing the road. She was carrying a lot of parcels. In the middle of the street she dropped them, tried to recover them, found a bus was almost on top of her and just managed to reach the curb safely, dazed and bewildered by people having shouted at her. I recovered her parcels, wiped the mud off them as best I could, retied the string of one, and returned them to her."

"There was no question of your having saved her life?"

"Oh, dear me, no! All I did was to perform a common act of courtesy. She was extremely grateful, thanked me warmly, and said something about my manners not being those of most of the younger generation—I can't remember the exact words. Then I lifted my hat and went on. I never expected to see her again. But life is full of coincidences. That very evening I came across her at a party at a friend's house. She recognized me at once and asked that I should be introduced to her. I then found out that she was a Miss Emily French and that she lived at Cricklewood. I talked to her for some time. She was, I imagine, an old lady who took sudden and violent fancies to people. She took one to me on the strength of a perfectly simple action which anyone might have performed. On leaving, she shook me warmly by the hand, and asked me to come and see her. I replied, of course, that I should be very pleased to do so, and she then urged me to name a day. I did not want particularly to go, but it would have seemed churlish[4] to refuse, so I fixed on the following Saturday. After she had gone, I learned something about her from my friends. That she was rich, eccentric, lived alone with one maid and owned no less than eight cats."

"I see," said Mr. Mayherne. "The question of her being well off came up as early as that?"

"If you mean that I inquired—" began Leonard Vole hotly, but Mr. Mayherne stilled him with a gesture.

"I have to look at the case as it will be presented by the other side. An ordinary

---

4. Here, *churlish* means "rude" or "ill-bred."

Motivation *Why do you think Vole includes these details?*

Make Inferences About Characters *What does Vole assume is the motivation for Mayherne's question? What might Mayherne infer from Vole's anger?*

---

3. To *protest* one's *innocence* is to steadfastly declare it.

Motivation *What do you think is Mayherne's motivation for preparing the best possible defense?*

Caricature of Émile Zola, 1880. Artist unknown.

View the Art The subject of this painting, French novelist Émile Zola, wears pince-nez eyeglasses, like Mr. Mayherne in the story. What other similarities can you find between the man in the painting and the solicitor in Christie's story?

"My friend, George Harvey, at whose house the party took place."

"Is he likely to remember having done so?"

"I really don't know. Of course it is some time ago now."

"Quite so, Mr. Vole. You see, the first aim of the prosecution will be to establish that you were in low water financially—that is true, is it not?"

Leonard Vole flushed.

"Yes," he said, in a low voice. "I'd been having a run of infernal[5] bad luck just then."

"Quite so," said Mr. Mayherne again. "That being, as I say, in low water financially, you met this rich old lady and **cultivated** her acquaintance assiduously.[6] Now if we are in a position to say that you had no idea she was well off, and that you visited her out of pure kindness of heart—"

"Which is the case."

"I daresay. I am not disputing the point. I am looking at it from the outside point of view. A great deal depends on the memory of Mr. Harvey. Is he likely to remember that conversation, or is he not? Could he be confused by counsel into believing that it took place later?"

Leonard Vole reflected for some minutes. Then he said steadily enough, but with a rather paler face:

"I do not think that that line would be successful, Mr. Mayherne. Several of those present heard his remark, and one or two

observer would not have supposed Miss French to be a lady of means. She lived poorly, almost humbly. Unless you had been told the contrary, you would in all probability have considered her to be in poor circumstances—at any rate to begin with. Who was it exactly who told you that she was well off?"

---

5. *Infernal* means "hellish."
6. Here, *assiduously* means "with a great deal of effort and determination."

of them chaffed[7] me about my conquest of a rich old lady."

The solicitor endeavored to hide his disappointment with a wave of the hand.

"Unfortunate," he said. "But I congratulate you upon your plain speaking, Mr. Vole. It is to you I look to guide me. Your judgment is quite right. To persist in the line I spoke of would have been disastrous. We must leave that point. You made the acquaintance of Miss French; you called upon her; the acquaintanceship progressed. We want a clear reason for all this. Why did you, a young man of thirty-three, good-looking, fond of sport, popular with your friends, devote so much of your time to an elderly woman with whom you could hardly have anything in common?"

Leonard Vole flung out his hands in a nervous gesture.

"I can't tell you—I really can't tell you. After the first visit, she pressed me to come again, spoke of being lonely and unhappy. She made it difficult for me to refuse. She showed so plainly her fondness and affection for me that I was placed in an awkward position. You see, Mr. Mayherne, I've got a weak nature—I drift—I'm one of those people who can't say 'No.' And believe me or not, as you like, after the third or fourth visit I paid her I found myself getting genuinely fond of the old thing. My mother died when I was young, an aunt brought me up, and she too died before I was fifteen. If I told you that I genuinely enjoyed being mothered and pampered, I daresay you'd only laugh."

Mr. Mayherne did not laugh. Instead he took off his pince-nez again and polished them, a sign with him that he was thinking deeply.

"I accept your explanation, Mr. Vole," he said at last. "I believe it to be psychologically probable. Whether a jury would take that view of it is another matter. Please continue your narrative. When was it that Miss French first asked you to look into her business affairs?"

"After my third or fourth visit to her. She understood very little of money matters and was worried about some investments."

Mr. Mayherne looked up sharply.

"Be careful, Mr. Vole. The maid, Janet Mackenzie, declares that her mistress was a good woman of business and transacted all her own affairs, and this is borne out[8] by the testimony of her bankers."

"I can't help that," said Vole earnestly. "That's what she said to me."

Mr. Mayherne looked at him for a moment or two in silence. Though he had no intention of saying so, his belief in Leonard Vole's innocence was at that moment strengthened. He knew something of the mentality of elderly ladies. He saw Miss French, infatuated with the good-looking young man, hunting about for **pretexts** that would bring him to the house. What more likely than that she should plead ignorance of business and beg him to help her with her money affairs? She was enough of a woman of the world to realize that any man is slightly flattered by such an admission of his superiority. Leonard Vole had been flattered. Perhaps, too, she had not been averse[9] to letting this young man know that she was wealthy. Emily French had been a strong-willed old woman, willing to pay her price for what she wanted. All this passed rap-

---

7. *Chaffed* means "teased in a playful way."

8. *Borne out* means "verified by facts, testimony, or events."
9. Here, *averse* means "against" or "disinclined."

The Extraordinary and Fantastic *So far, what is mysterious to you about Vole's relationship with Miss French?*

idly through Mr. Mayherne's mind, but he gave no indication of it and asked instead a further question.

"And you did handle her affairs for her at her request?"

"I did."

"Mr. Vole," said the solicitor, "I am going to ask you a very serious question, and one to which it is vital I should have a truthful answer. You were in low water financially. You had the handling of an old lady's affairs—an old lady who, according to her own statement, knew little or nothing of business. Did you at any time, or in any manner, convert to your own use the securities which you handled? Did you engage in any transaction for your own pecuniary[10] advantage which will not bear the light of day?" He quelled[11] the other's response. "Wait a minute before you answer. There are two courses open to us. Either we can make a feature of your probity[12] and honesty in conducting her affairs whilst pointing out how unlikely it is that you would commit murder to obtain money which you might have obtained by such infinitely easier means. If, on the other hand, there is anything in your dealings which the prosecution will get hold of—if, to put it baldly, it can be proved that you swindled the old lady in any way—we must take the line that you had no motive for the murder, since she was already a profitable source of income to you. You perceive the distinction. Now, I beg of you, take your time before you reply."

But Leonard Vole took no time at all.

"My dealings with Miss French's affairs were all perfectly fair and aboveboard. I acted for her interests to the very best of my ability, as anyone will find who looks into the matter."

"Thank you," said Mr. Mayherne. "You relieve my mind very much. I pay you the compliment of believing that you are far too clever to lie to me over such an important matter."

"Surely," said Vole eagerly, "the strongest point in my favor is the lack of motive. Granted that I cultivated the acquaintanceship of a rich old lady in the hopes of getting money out of her—that, I gather, is the substance of what you have been saying—surely her death frustrates all my hopes?"

The solicitor looked at him steadily. Then, very deliberately, he repeated his unconscious trick with his pince-nez. It was not until they were firmly replaced on his nose that he spoke.

"Are you not aware, Mr. Vole, that Miss French left a will under which you are the principal beneficiary?"[13]

"What?" The prisoner sprang to his feet. His dismay was obvious and unforced. "My God! What are you saying? She left her money to me?"

Mr. Mayherne nodded slowly. Vole sank down again, his head in his hands.

"You pretend you know nothing of this will?"

"Pretend? There's no pretense about it. I knew nothing about it."

"What would you say if I told you that the maid, Janet Mackenzie, swears that you *did* know? That her mistress told her distinctly that she had consulted you in the matter and told you of her intentions?"

"Say? That she's lying! No, I go too fast. Janet is an elderly woman. She was a faithful watchdog to her mistress, and she didn't like me. She was jealous and suspicious. I should say that Miss French confided her intentions to Janet, and that Janet either mistook something she said or else was convinced in her own mind that I

---

10. *Pecuniary* means "relating to money" or "monetary."
11. *Quelled* means "crushed" or "quieted."
12. *Probity* is moral uprightness.

13. *A beneficiary* is a person who receives money from a will.

Bond Street, 1999. Peter Miller. Oil on canvas, 35.6 x 40.6 cm. Private collection.

View the Art Bond Street is an upscale, exclusive shopping street in London. What role does the exchange of money play in this story?

had persuaded the old lady into doing it. I daresay that she herself believes now that Miss French actually told her so."

"You don't think she dislikes you enough to lie deliberately about the matter?"

Leonard Vole looked shocked and startled.

"No, indeed! Why should she?"

"I don't know," said Mr. Mayherne thoughtfully. "But she's very bitter against you."

The wretched young man groaned again.

"I'm beginning to see," he muttered. "It's frightful. I made up to her, that's what they'll say, I got her to make a will

leaving her money to me, and then I go there that night, and there's nobody in the house—they find her the next day— oh! my God, it's awful!"

"You are wrong about there being nobody in the house," said Mr. Mayherne. "Janet, as you remember, was to go out for the evening. She went, but about half past nine she returned to fetch the pattern of a blouse sleeve which she had promised to a friend. She let herself in by the back door, went upstairs and fetched it, and went out again. She heard voices in the sitting room, though she could not distinguish what they said, but she will swear that one of them was Miss French's and one was a man's."

"At half past nine," said Leonard Vole. "At half past nine . . ." He sprang to his feet. "But then I'm saved—saved—"

Motivation *What does Vole say motivates Mackenzie? What else might motivate her?*

"What do you mean, saved?" cried Mr. Mayherne, astonished.

"By half past nine I was at home again! My wife can prove that. I left Miss French about five minutes to nine. I arrived home about twenty past nine. My wife was there waiting for me. Oh, thank God—thank God! And bless Janet Mackenzie's sleeve pattern."

In his exuberance,[14] he hardly noticed that the grave expression on the solicitor's face had not altered. But the latter's words brought him down to earth with a bump.

"Who, then, in your opinion, murdered Miss French?"

"Why, a burglar, of course, as was thought at first. The window was forced, you remember. She was killed with a heavy blow from a crowbar, and the crowbar was found lying on the floor beside the body. And several articles were missing. But for Janet's absurd suspicions and dislike of me, the police would never have swerved from the right track."

"That will hardly do, Mr. Vole," said the solicitor. "The things that were missing were mere trifles of no value, taken as a blind.[15] And the marks on the window were not at all conclusive. Besides, think for yourself. You say you were no longer in the house by half past nine. Who, then, was the man Janet heard talking to Miss French in the sitting room? She would hardly be having an **amicable** conversation with a burglar!"

"No," said Vole. "No—" He looked puzzled and discouraged. "But, anyway," he added with reviving spirit, "it lets me out. I've got an alibi. You must see Romaine—my wife—at once."

"Certainly," acquiesced[16] the lawyer. "I should already have seen Mrs. Vole but for her being absent when you were arrested. I wired to Scotland at once, and I understand that she arrives back tonight. I am going to call upon her immediately I leave here."

Vole nodded, a great expression of satisfaction settling down over his face.

"Yes, Romaine will tell you. My God! it's a lucky chance that."

"Excuse me, Mr. Vole, but you are very fond of your wife?"

"Of course."

"And she of you?"

"Romaine is devoted to me. She'd do anything in the world for me."

He spoke enthusiastically, but the solicitor's heart sank a little lower. The testimony of a devoted wife—would it gain credence?[17]

"Was there anyone else who saw you return at nine-twenty? A maid, for instance?"

"We have no maid."

"Did you meet anyone in the street on the way back?"

"Nobody I knew. I rode part of the way in a bus. The conductor might remember."

Mr. Mayherne shook his head doubtfully.

"There is no one, then, who can confirm your wife's testimony?"

"No. But it isn't necessary, surely?"

"I daresay not. I daresay not," said Mr. Mayherne hastily. "Now there's just one thing more. Did Miss French know that you were a married man?"

"Oh, yes."

"Yet you never took your wife to see her. Why was that?"

---

14. *Exuberance* means "excited enthusiasm."
15. Here, a *blind* refers to an action undertaken to throw an investigator off the track.

Make Inferences About Characters *Which details here might lead you to infer that Vole is telling the truth?*

Vocabulary

amicable (am′ə kə bəl) *adj.* friendly

16. *Acquiesced* means "agreed."
17. *Credence* is acceptance that something is true.

The Tea Party. Henry Lamb
(1885–1960). Oil on board.
The Arts Club, London.

View the Art Tea parties are a long-standing British tradition and often feature displays of hospitality and polite conversation. Who in the story could you envision joining this tea party?

For the first time, Leonard Vole's answer came halting and uncertain.

"Well—I don't know."

"Are you aware that Janet Mackenzie says her mistress believed you to be single and contemplated marrying you in the future?"

Vole laughed.

"Absurd! There was forty years' difference in age between us."

"It has been done," said the solicitor dryly. "The fact remains. Your wife never met Miss French?"

Motivation *How does this piece of information relate to Miss French leaving Vole money in her will?*

"No—" Again the constraint.[18]

"You will permit me to say," said the lawyer, "that I hardly understand your attitude in the matter."

Vole flushed, hesitated, and then spoke.

"I'll make a clean breast of it. I was hard up, as you know. I hoped that Miss French might lend me some money. She was fond of me, but she wasn't at all interested in the struggles of a young couple. Early on, I found that she had taken it for granted that my wife and I didn't get on—were living apart. Mr. Mayherne—I wanted the money—for Romaine's sake. I said nothing, and allowed

---

18. *Constraint* refers to the act of holding something back.

the old lady to think what she chose. She spoke of my being an adopted son to her. There was never any question of marriage—that must be just Janet's imagination."

"And that is all?"

"Yes—that is all."

Was there just a shade of hesitation in the words? The lawyer fancied so. He rose and held out his hand.

"Good-bye, Mr. Vole." He looked into the haggard young face and spoke with an unusual impulse. "I believe in your innocence in spite of the multitude of facts arrayed against you.[19] I hope to prove it and vindicate[20] you completely."

Vole smiled back at him.

"You'll find the alibi is all right," he said cheerfully.

Again he hardly noticed that the other did not respond.

"The whole thing hinges a good deal on the testimony of Janet Mackenzie," said Mr. Mayherne. "She hates you. That much is clear."

"She can hardly hate me," protested the young man.

The solicitor shook his head as he went out.

"Now for Mrs. Vole," he said to himself.

He was seriously disturbed by the way the thing was shaping.

The Voles lived in a small shabby house near Paddington Green. It was to this house that Mr. Mayherne went.

In answer to his ring, a big slatternly[21] woman, obviously a charwoman,[22] answered the door.

"Mrs. Vole? Has she returned yet?"

"Got back an hour ago. But I dunno if you can see her."

"If you will take my card to her," said Mr. Mayherne quietly, "I am quite sure that she will do so."

The woman looked at him doubtfully, wiped her hand on her apron and took the card. Then she closed the door in his face and left him on the step outside.

In a few minutes, however, she returned with a slightly altered manner.

"Come inside, please."

She ushered him into a tiny drawing room. Mr. Mayherne, examining a drawing on the wall, started up suddenly to face a tall, pale woman who had entered so quietly that he had not heard her.

"Mr. Mayherne? You are my husband's solicitor, are you not? You have come from him? Will you please sit down?"

Until she spoke, he had not realized that she was not English. Now, observing her more closely, he noticed the high cheekbones, the dense blue-black of the hair, and an occasional very slight movement of the hands that was distinctly foreign. A strange woman, very quiet. So quiet as to make one uneasy. From the very first Mr. Mayherne was conscious that he was up against something that he did not understand.

"Now, my dear Mrs. Vole," he began, "you must not give way—"[23]

He stopped. It was so very obvious that Romaine Vole had not the slightest intention of giving way. She was perfectly calm and composed.

"Will you please tell me about it?" she said. "I must know everything. Do not think to spare me. I want to know the worst." She hesitated, then repeated in a lower tone, with

---

19. The *multitude of facts arrayed against you* refers to the many facts that suggest Vole's guilt.

20. To *vindicate* is to free from blame or suspicion.

21. Here, *slatternly* means "disorderly in personal appearance."

22. A *charwoman* is a woman hired to clean.

Motivation *Vole just said he and his wife had no maid. What motivation might he have for not mentioning this charwoman?*

23. *Give way* suggests breaking down emotionally.

The Extraordinary and Fantastic *What about this woman is so mysterious to Mayherne?*

a curious emphasis which the lawyer did not understand: "I want to know the worst."

Mr. Mayherne went over his interview with Leonard Vole. She listened attentively, nodding her head now and then.

"I see," she said, when he had finished. "He wants me to say that he came in at twenty minutes past nine that night?"

"He did come in at that time?" said Mr. Mayherne sharply.

"That is not the point," she said coldly. "Will my saying so acquit him? Will they believe me?"

Mr. Mayherne was taken aback. She had gone so quickly to the core of the matter.

"That is what I want to know," she said. "Will it be enough? Is there anyone else who can support my evidence?"

There was a suppressed[24] eagerness in her manner that made him vaguely uneasy.

"So far there is no one else," he said reluctantly.

"I see," said Romaine Vole.

She sat for a minute or two perfectly still. A little smile played over her lips.

The lawyer's feeling of alarm grew stronger and stronger.

"Mrs. Vole—" he began. "I know what you must feel—"

"Do you?" she asked. "I wonder."

"In the circumstances—"

"In the circumstances—I intend to play a lone hand."

He looked at her in dismay.

"But, my dear Mrs. Vole—you are overwrought.[25] Being so devoted to your husband—"

"I beg your pardon?"

The sharpness of her voice made him start. He repeated in a hesitating manner:

"Being so devoted to your husband—"

Romaine Vole nodded slowly, the same strange smile on her lips.

"Did he tell you that I was devoted to him?" she asked softly. "Ah! yes, I can see he did. How stupid men are! Stupid—stupid—stupid—"

She rose suddenly to her feet. All the intense emotion that the lawyer had been conscious of in the atmosphere was now concentrated in her tone.

"I hate him, I tell you! I hate him. I hate him. I hate him! I would like to see him hanged by the neck till he is dead."

The lawyer **recoiled** before her and the smoldering passion in her eyes.

She advanced a step nearer and continued vehemently:

"Perhaps I shall see it. Supposing I tell you that he did not come in that night at twenty past nine, but at twenty past ten? You say that he tells you he knew nothing about the money coming to him. Supposing I tell you he knew all about it, and counted on it, and committed murder to get it? Supposing I tell you that he admitted to me that night when he came in what he had done? That there was blood on his coat? What then? Supposing that I stand up in court and say all these things?"

Her eyes seemed to challenge him. With an effort, he concealed his growing dismay, and endeavored to speak in a rational tone.

"You cannot be asked to give evidence against your husband—"

"He is not my husband!" The words came out so quickly that he fancied he had misunderstood her.

"I beg your pardon? I—"

---

24. Here, *suppressed* means "restrained."
25. Someone who is *overwrought* is upset or agitated.

Make Inferences About Characters *From Romaine Heilger's questions, what is Mayherne most likely to infer about what time Vole really came home?*

Vocabulary

recoil (ri koil´) *v.* to shrink back physically or emotionally

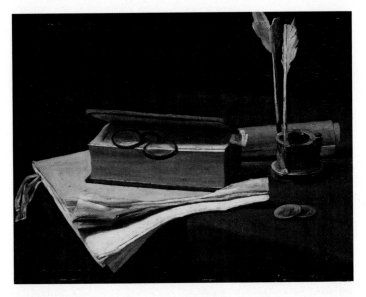

Still Life With Book, Papers, and Inkwell, 1876. François Bonvin. National Gallery, London.

View the Art The objects depicted in still life paintings in the nineteenth century often served an allegorical, or symbolic, purpose. What might the objects in this painting represent in relation to the story?

"He is not my husband." The silence was so intense that you could have heard a pin drop.

"I was an actress in Vienna. My husband is alive but in a madhouse. So we could not marry. I am glad now."

She nodded defiantly.

"I should like you to tell me one thing," said Mr. Mayherne. He contrived[26] to appear as cool and unemotional as ever. "Why are you so bitter against Leonard Vole?"

She shook her head, smiling a little.

"Yes, you would like to know. But I shall not tell you. I will keep my secret. . . ."

Mr. Mayherne gave his dry little cough and rose.

"There seems no point in prolonging this interview," he remarked. "You will hear from me again after I have communicated with my client."

She came closer to him, looking into his eyes with her own wonderful dark ones.

"Tell me," she said, "did you believe—honestly—that he was innocent when you came here today?"

"I did," said Mr. Mayherne.

"You poor little man," she laughed.

"And I believe so still," finished the lawyer. "Good evening, madam."

He went out of the room, taking with him the memory of her startled face.

"This is going to be the devil of a business," said Mr. Mayherne to himself as he strode along the street.

Extraordinary, the whole thing. An extraordinary woman. A very dangerous woman. Women were the devil when they got their knife into you.

What was to be done? That wretched young man hadn't a leg to stand upon. Of course, possibly he did commit the crime. . . .

"No," said Mr. Mayherne to himself. "No—there's almost too much evidence against him. I don't believe this woman. She was trumping up[27] the whole story. But she'll never bring it into court."

He wished he felt more conviction[28] on the point.

---

27. To *trump up* is to make up or concoct.
28. Here, *conviction* means "certainty."

Make Inferences About Characters *What can you infer about Mayherne's attitude toward Romaine Heilger based on this comment?*

---

26. Here, *contrived* means "made a great effort."

The police court proceedings[29] were brief and dramatic. The principal witnesses for the prosecution were Janet Mackenzie, maid to the dead woman, and Romaine Heilger, Austrian subject, the mistress of the prisoner.

Mr. Mayherne sat in court and listened to the damning story that the latter told. It was on the lines she had indicated to him in their interview.

The prisoner reserved his defense and was committed for trial.

Mr. Mayherne was at his wits' end. The case against Leonard Vole was black beyond words. Even the famous K.C.[30] who was engaged for the defense held out little hope.

"If we can shake that Austrian woman's testimony, we might do something," he said dubiously.[31] "But it's a bad business."

Mr. Mayherne had concentrated his energies on one single point. Assuming Leonard Vole to be speaking the truth, and to have left the murdered woman's house at nine o'clock, who was the man Janet heard talking to Miss French at half past nine?

The only ray of light was in the shape of a scapegrace[32] nephew who had in bygone days cajoled[33] and threatened his aunt out of various sums of money. Janet Mackenzie, the solicitor learned, had

Mrs. Seymour Fort, 1778. John Singleton Copley.

View the Art Painter John Singleton Copley is considered one of the most highly acclaimed portrait artists of the colonial United States. How do you imagine the personality of the woman in the painting? Which character in the story might she reflect, and why?

always been attached to this young man and had never ceased urging his claims upon her mistress. It certainly seemed possible that it was this nephew who had been with Miss French after Leonard Vole left, especially as he was not to be found in any of his old haunts.

In all other directions, the lawyer's researches had been negative in their result. No one had seen Leonard Vole entering his own house, or leaving that of Miss French. No one had seen any

---

29. *Police court proceedings* are similar to proceedings that result in an indictment in the United States: on the basis of testimony given in court, Vole is "committed for trial," or required to stand trial.
30. *K.C.* is the King's Counsel, who is referred to later in this story as Sir Charles.
31. *Dubiously* means "doubtfully."
32. A *scapegrace* is a rascal.
33. *Cajoled* means "urged in a flattering way in order to achieve one's own ends."

Motivation *What motivation might Mackenzie have for pinning the crime on Vole?*

other man enter or leave the house in Cricklewood. All inquiries drew blank.[34]

It was the eve of the trial when Mr. Mayherne received the letter which was to lead his thoughts in an entirely new direction.

It came by the six o'clock post. An illiterate scrawl, written on common paper and enclosed in a dirty envelope with the stamp stuck on crooked.

Mr. Mayherne read it through once or twice before he grasped its meaning.

"Dear Mister:
"You're the lawyer chap wot acts for the young feller. If you want that painted foreign hussy showd up for wot she is an her pack of lies you come to 16 Shaw's Rents Stepney tonight It ull cawst you 2 hundred quid Arsk for Misses Mogson."[35]

The solicitor read and reread this strange epistle. It might, of course, be a hoax,[36] but when he thought it over, he became increasingly convinced that it was genuine, and also convinced that it was the one hope for the prisoner. The evidence of Romaine Heilger damned him completely, and the line the defense meant to pursue, the line that the evidence of a woman who had admittedly lived an immoral life was not to be trusted, was at best a weak one.

Mr. Mayherne's mind was made up. It was his duty to save his client at all costs. He must go to Shaw's Rents.

He had some difficulty in finding the place, a ramshackle building in an evil-smelling slum, but at last he did so, and on inquiry for Mrs. Mogson was sent up to a room on the third floor. On this door he knocked and, getting no answer, knocked again.

At this second knock, he heard a shuffling sound inside, and presently the door was opened cautiously half an inch, and a bent figure peered out.

Suddenly the woman, for it was a woman, gave a chuckle and opened the door wider.

"So it's you, dearie," she said, in a wheezy voice. "Nobody with you, is there? No playing tricks? That's right. You can come in—you can come in."

With some reluctance the lawyer stepped across the threshold into the small dirty room, with its flickering gas jet. There was an untidy unmade bed in a corner, a plain deal table[37] and two rickety chairs. For the first time Mr. Mayherne had a full view of the tenant of this unsavory apartment. She was a woman of middle age, bent in figure, with a mass of untidy gray hair and a scarf wound tightly round her face. She saw him looking at this and laughed again, the same curious, toneless chuckle.

Visual Vocabulary
A *gas jet* is used to turn on light created by gas rather than by electricity.

"Wondering why I hide my beauty, dear? He, he, he. Afraid it may tempt you, eh? But you shall see—you shall see."

She drew aside the scarf, and the lawyer recoiled involuntarily before the almost formless blur of scarlet. She replaced the scarf again.

---

34. *Drew blank* means "were left unanswered."
35. This note is written to suggest the speech of lower-class people in London. *Wot* means "who" in the first line and "what" in the third line; *ull cawst* means "will cost"; and 200 *quid* is 200 pounds, a huge sum at the time.
36. A *hoax* is an act intended to deceive or trick.
37. A *deal table* is a simple table made of fir or pine boards, which the British call "deal."

Make Inferences About Characters *What inference might you make about this woman's condition, based on her appearance?*

The Trial of Mr Pickwick. Cecil Charles Windsor Aldin (1870–1935). Color lithograph. Dickens House Museum, London.

"So you're not wanting to kiss me, dear-ie? He, he, I don't wonder. And yet I was a pretty girl once—not so long ago as you'd think, either. Vitriol,[38] dearie, vitriol—that's what did that. Ah! but I'll be even with 'em—"

She burst into a hideous torrent of profanity which Mr. Mayherne tried vainly to quell. She fell silent at last, her hands clenching and unclenching themselves nervously.

"Enough of that," said the lawyer sternly. "I've come here because I have reason to believe you can give me information which will clear my client, Leonard Vole. Is that the case?"

Her eyes leered at him cunningly.

"What about the money, dearie?" she wheezed. "Two hundred quid, you remember."

"It is your duty to give evidence, and you can be called upon to do so."

"That won't do, dearie. I'm an old woman, and I know nothing. But you give me two hundred quid, and perhaps I can give you a hint or two. See?"

"What kind of hint?"

"What should you say to a letter? A letter from *her*. Never mind how I got hold of it. That's my business. It'll do the trick. But I want my two hundred quid."

Mr. Mayherne looked at her coldly and made up his mind.

"I'll give you ten pounds, nothing more. And only that if this letter is what you say it is."

"Ten pounds?" She screamed and raved at him.

"Twenty," said Mr. Mayherne, "and that's my last word."

---

38. *Vitriol* is a chemical substance that can burn the skin.

He rose as if to go. Then, watching her closely, he drew out a pocketbook and counted out twenty one-pound notes.

"You see," he said. "That is all I have with me. You can take it or leave it."

But already he knew that the sight of the money was too much for her. She cursed and raved impotently,[39] but at last she gave in. Going over to the bed, she drew something out from beneath the tattered mattress.

"Here you are, damn you!" she snarled. "It's the top one you want."

It was a bundle of letters that she threw to him, and Mr. Mayherne untied them and scanned them in his usual cool, methodical manner. The woman, watching him eagerly, could gain no clue from his impassive face.

He read each letter through, then returned again to the top one and read it a second time. Then he tied the whole bundle up again carefully.

They were love letters, written by Romaine Heilger, and the man they were written to was not Leonard Vole. The top letter was dated the day of the latter's arrest.

"I spoke true, dearie, didn't I?" whined the woman. "It'll do for her, that letter?"

Mr. Mayherne put the letters in his pocket, then he asked a question.

"How did you get hold of this correspondence?"

"That's telling," she said with a leer. "But I know something more. I heard in court what that hussy said. Find out where she was at twenty past ten, the time she says she was at home. Ask at the Lion Road Cinema. They'll remember—a fine upstanding girl like that—curse her!"

"Who is the man?" asked Mr. Mayherne. "There's only a Christian name here."

The other's voice grew thick and hoarse, her hands clenched and unclenched. Finally she lifted one to her face.

"He's the man that did this to me. Many years ago now. She took him away from me—a chit[40] of a girl she was then. And when I went after him—and went for him too—he threw the cursed stuff at me! And she laughed—damn her! I've had it in for her for years. Followed her, I have, spied upon her. And now I've got her! She'll suffer for this, won't she, Mr. Lawyer? She'll suffer?"

"She will probably be sentenced to a term of imprisonment for perjury,"[41] said Mr. Mayherne quietly.

"Shut away—that's what I want. You're going, are you? Where's my money? Where's that good money?"

Without a word, Mr. Mayherne put down the notes on the table. Then, drawing a deep breath, he turned and left the squalid room. Looking back, he saw the old woman crooning over the money.

He wasted no time. He found the cinema in Lion Road easily enough, and, shown a photograph of Romaine Heilger, the commissionaire[42] recognized her at once. She had arrived at the cinema with a man some time after ten o'clock on the evening in question. He had not noticed her escort particularly, but he remembered the lady who had spoken to him about the picture that was showing. They stayed until the end, about an hour later.

Mr. Mayherne was satisfied. Romaine Heilger's evidence was a tissue of lies from beginning to end. She had evolved it out of her passionate hatred. The lawyer wondered whether he would ever know what lay

---

39. Here, *impotently* means "helplessly" or "powerlessly."

The Extraordinary and Fantastic *What is extraordinary about this woman, the circumstances, and the letters?*

40. Here, *chit* refers to a rude young person.
41. *Perjury* is the act of lying under oath in a court of law.
42. *Commissionaire* is a British term for a theater attendant.

behind that hatred. What had Leonard Vole done to her? He had seemed dumbfounded when the solicitor had reported her attitude to him. He had declared earnestly that such a thing was incredible—yet it had seemed to Mr. Mayherne that after the first astonishment his protests had lacked sincerity.

He did know. Mr. Mayherne was convinced of it. He knew, but he had no intention of revealing the fact. The secret between those two remained a secret. Mr. Mayherne wondered if someday he should come to learn what it was.

The solicitor glanced at his watch. It was late, but time was everything. He hailed a taxi and gave an address.

"Sir Charles must know of this at once," he murmured to himself as he got in.

The trial of Leonard Vole for the murder of Emily French aroused widespread interest. In the first place the prisoner was young and good-looking, then he was accused of a particularly dastardly crime, and there was the further interest of Romaine Heilger, the principal witness for the prosecution. There had been pictures of her in many papers, and several fictitious stories as to her origin and history.

The proceedings opened quietly enough. Various technical evidence came first. Then Janet Mackenzie was called. She told substantially the same story as before. In cross-examination counsel for the defense succeeded in getting her to contradict herself once or twice over her account of Vole's association with Miss French; he emphasized the fact that though she had heard a man's voice in the sitting room that night, there was nothing to show that it was Vole who was there, and he managed to drive

home a feeling that jealousy and dislike of the prisoner were at the bottom of a good deal of her evidence.

Then the next witness was called.

"Your name is Romaine Heilger?"

"Yes."

"You are an Austrian subject?"

"Yes."

"For the last three years you have lived with the prisoner and passed yourself off as his wife?"

Just for a moment Romaine Heilger's eyes met those of the man in the dock. Her expression held something curious and unfathomable.[43]

"Yes." .

The questions went on. Word by word the damning facts came out. On the night in question the prisoner had taken out a crowbar with him. He had returned at twenty minutes past ten and had confessed to having killed the old lady. His cuffs had been stained with blood, and he had burned them in the kitchen stove. He had terrorized her into silence by means of threats.

As the story proceeded, the feeling of the court which had, to begin with, been slightly favorable to the prisoner, now set dead against him. He himself sat with downcast head and moody air, as though he knew he were doomed.

Yet it might have been noted that her own counsel sought to restrain Romaine's **animosity**. He would have preferred her to be more unbiased.

---

43. *Unfathomable* means "impossible to understand."

Motivation *Why would Heilger's lawyer have preferred a more unbiased testimony?*

Vocabulary

animosity (an′ ə mos′ ə tē) *n.* ill will or resentment; active strong dislike or hostility

---

The Extraordinary and Fantastic *What remains a mystery to Mayherne?*

Formidable and ponderous,[44] counsel for the defense arose.

He put it to her that her story was a malicious fabrication[45] from start to finish, that she had not even been in her own house at the time in question, that she was in love with another man and was deliberately seeking to send Vole to his death for a crime he did not commit.

Romaine denied these allegations with superb insolence.[46]

Then came the surprising denouement,[47] the production of the letter. It was read aloud in court in the midst of a breathless stillness.

Bishop Street, Coventry, 1929. Joan Murphy. Oil on canvas. Herbert Art Gallery & Museum, Coventry, UK.

"Max, beloved, the Fates have delivered him into our hands! He has been arrested for murder—but, yes, the murder of an old lady! Leonard, who would not hurt a fly! At last I shall have my revenge. The poor chicken! I shall say that he came in that night with blood upon him—that he confessed to me. I shall hang him, Max—and when he hangs he will know and realize that it was Romaine who sent him to his death. And then—happiness, Beloved! Happiness at last!"

There were experts present ready to swear that the handwriting was that of Romaine Heilger, but they were not needed. Confronted with the letter, Romaine broke down utterly and confessed everything. Leonard Vole had returned to the house at the time he said, twenty past nine. She had invented the whole story to ruin him.

With the collapse of Romaine Heilger, the case for the Crown collapsed also. Sir Charles called his few witnesses; the prisoner himself went into the box and told his

44. The phrase *formidable and ponderous* is meant to suggest the mental and emotional strength and weight of the counsel for the defense.
45. The phrase *malicious fabrication* suggests a story that has been elaborately made up for evil purposes.
46. *Insolence* is a display of an obviously contrary attitude.
47. A *denouement* (dā´nōō män´) is an action that follows a climax, or high point, of a story.

story in a manly straightforward manner, unshaken by cross-examination.

The prosecution endeavored to rally, but without great success. The judge's summing up was not wholly favorable to the prisoner, but a reaction had set in, and the jury needed little time to consider their verdict.

"We find the prisoner not guilty."

Leonard Vole was free!

Little Mr. Mayherne hurried from his seat. He must congratulate his client.

He found himself polishing his pince-nez vigorously and checked himself. His wife had told him only the night before that he was getting a habit of it. Curious things, habits. People themselves never knew they had them.

An interesting case—a very interesting case. That woman, now, Romaine Heilger.

The case was dominated for him still by the exotic figure of Romaine Heilger. She had seemed a pale, quiet woman in the house at Paddington, but in court she had flamed out against the sober background, flaunting herself like a tropical flower.

If he closed his eyes, he could see her now, tall and vehement, her exquisite body bent forward a little, her right hand clenching and unclenching itself unconsciously all the time.

Curious things, habits. That gesture of hers with the hand was her habit, he supposed. Yet he had seen someone else do it quite lately. Who was it now? Quite lately—

He drew in his breath with a gasp as it came back to him. The woman in Shaw's Rents . . .

He stood still, his head whirling. It was impossible—impossible— Yet, Romaine Heilger was an actress.

The K.C. came up behind him and clapped him on the shoulder.

"Congratulated our man yet? He's had a narrow shave, you know. Come along and see him."

But the little lawyer shook off the other's hand.

He wanted one thing only—to see Romaine Heilger face to face.

He did not see her until some time later, and the place of their meeting is not relevant.

"So you guessed," she said, when he had told her all that was in his mind. "The face? Oh! that was easy enough, and the light of that gas jet was too bad for you to see the makeup."

"But why—why—"

"Why did I play a lone hand?" She smiled a little, remembering the last time she had used the words.

"Such an elaborate comedy!"

"My friend—I had to save him. The evidence of a woman devoted to him would not have been enough—you hinted as much yourself. But I know something of the psychology of crowds. Let my evidence be wrung from me, as an admission, damning me in the eyes of the law, and a reaction in favor of the prisoner would immediately set in."

"And the bundle of letters?"

"One alone, the vital one, might have seemed like a—what do you call it?—put-up job."

"Then the man called Max?"

"Never existed, my friend."

"I still think," said little Mr. Mayherne, in an aggrieved manner, "that we could have got him off by the—er—normal procedure."

"I dared not risk it. You see, you thought he was innocent—"

"And you knew it? I see," said little Mr. Mayherne.

"My dear Mr. Mayherne," said Romaine, "you do not see at all. I knew—he was guilty!" ∽

Make Inferences About Characters *What inferences did Heilger make about both the jury and Mayherne? What does this reveal about her character?*

After You Read

Respond and Think Critically

1. **Connect to Personal Experience** Were you surprised by the ending? Explain.

2. **Summarize Plot** What crime is Leonard Vole accused of? Summarize how Vole convinces Mr. Mayherne that he did not commit the crime.

3. **Explain Resolution** What happens when Heilger testifies at the trial? How does the jury respond to Vole during the trial? Explain.

4. **Make Inferences About Plot** Why do you think Heilger's plan is so successful? Explain your answer and support it with evidence from the story. OER

5. **Analyze Author's Craft** From beginning to end, the facts are against Vole, and yet Christie convinces most readers to think of him as innocent. How does she do this? Support your answer with details from the story.

6. **Analyze Characterization** Why do you think Christie casts Vole's companion as an actress? How well does Heilger "perform" as a witness for the prosecution? Explain.

7. **Evaluate Characters** Who, in your opinion, had a better knowledge of human nature: Mayherne or Heilger? Who had a better grasp of court proceedings? Explain.

8. **Big Idea** **Draw Conclusions About Plot** What mysteries remain unanswered at the end of the story? Support your response with text evidence.

Visual Literacy

Acting on a Set

Here is a still photo from the 1957 movie version of "Witness for the Prosecution." Directed by Billy Wilder, the film features Tyrone Power as Leonard Vole and Marlene Dietrich as the witness for the prosecution. Here, Marlene Dietrich is shown in the witness box.

Group Activity Work with classmates to discuss and answer the following questions.

1. How does the woman in this picture look the same as or different from the way Christie presents Romaine Heilger in the story?

2. What visual techniques does this reaction shot use to convey a message? What message does it convey? Explain.

3. What emotions do you see in this photograph? How do they match or contradict the emotions conveyed in the parallel scene in the story?

After You Read

Literary Element | Motivation

In a mystery, the author or characters make or imply suggestions about other characters' **motivations.** Every character in this story has at least one transparent or one implied motive.

9. **Clarify Details** What motivates the jury to acquit Vole? What motivates Mayherne to visit Heilger after the acquittal? Explain.

10. **Analyze Motivation** What is Heilger's "lone hand"? What is her motivation for playing it? Is this motivation stated or implied? How does Heilger's real motivation differ from motivations that other characters assign to her? Explain.

Review: Style

As you learned on page 999, **style** is the particular way an author writes. In "The Witness for the Prosecution," Christie's **diction,** or word choice, reflects her culture, a primarily upper-middle-class British world.

11. **Partner Activity** With a partner, find several examples of Vole's polite, sophisticated speech. Write alternative, more plain-speaking, or working-class ways in which Vole might have expressed the same thoughts. Then discuss what effect Vole's diction has on Mayherne.

Example	Alternative
"I'd been having a run of infernal bad luck just then."	"I couldn't catch a break."

Reading Strategy | Make Inferences About Characters

 Texas Test Practice (RC-10.B)

1. At the end of the trial, members of the jury (and most readers) infer that Romaine Heilger is:

   I. devoted to Leonard Vole.
   II. intent on incriminating her "husband."
   III. a brilliantly successful actress.

   A. I only
   B. II only
   C. I and II only
   D. II and III only

Vocabulary Practice

Practice with Word Origins Studying the etymology, or origin and history, of a word can help you better understand and explore its meaning. Create a word map, like the one shown below for *intrigue*, for each of these boldfaced vocabulary words from the story.

cultivate pretext amicable
recoil animosity

EXAMPLE:

Definition to captivate one's interest or curiosity

Etymology Latin *intricare* means "entangle"

intrigue

Sample Sentence Christie intrigues her reader with conflicting clues.

Respond Through Writing

Expository Essay

Analyze Cause and Effect To hide the murderer in plain sight, Christie invents an ingenious chain of causes and effects. Together with both concealed and obvious motives, these causes and effects create the suspense of an entertaining plot. Analyze the cause-and-effect relationships that finally reveal the killer's identity and explain how they create suspense.

Purpose and Audience Your purpose is to write an analytical essay of sufficient length that analyzes cause-and-effect relationships and how they contribute to the story's suspense. Your audience is your teacher and your classmates.

Plan Go back and scan the story for events that lead to the revelation of the killer. Sketch a cause-and-effect chain or flowchart showing the causal relationship between the events. Study your plan to help you generate a thesis that explains how the causes and effects create suspense.

Draft After you create interest in your topic and present your thesis, create an organizing structure appropriate to your purpose, audience, and context. Use your body paragraphs to discuss the causal chain of events in chronological order and to present relevant information from and valid inferences about the story to support your statements of cause and effect. Use this frame as a guide to structuring your body paragraphs:

Sentence 1:	Statement of event or cause.
Sentence 2:	As Christie writes, [quoted evidence].
Sentence 3:	Eventually, this leads to _____.
Other Sentences:	Explanation/analysis of effects; how causes and effects create suspense.

Revise Ask a classmate to identify your evidence and tell how well it supports your main points. Decide how to make the connections between your claims and your evidence clearer or more effective. Include distinctions about the relative value of specific facts and ideas that support your thesis.

Edit Edit your essay, correcting any errors in grammar, spelling, and punctuation. Use the Grammar Tip in the side column to help you with verbs used as nouns.

 TEKS

10.15.A.iii–vi Write an analytical essay of sufficient length that includes a thesis; an organizing structure; relevant evidence; and distinctions about the relative value of specific data, facts, and ideas that support the thesis statement.

> **Grammar Tip**

Verbs Used as Nouns

A **gerund** is a verb form that ends in -*ing* and is used in the same way a noun is used.

Testifying is essential for witnesses in court cases.

An **infinitive** is a verb form that is usually preceded by the word *to* and can be used as a noun. When you use the word *to* before the base form of a verb, *to* is not a preposition but part of the infinitive form of the verb.

The old woman did not wish to testify.

Grammar Workshop

Semicolons as Connectors

Literature Connection In this quotation from "The Witness for the Prosecution," Agatha Christie uses a **semicolon,** a punctuation mark that links related ideas.

> *In cross-examination counsel for the defense succeeded in getting her to contradict herself once or twice over her account of Vole's association with Miss French; he emphasized the fact that though she had heard a man's voice in the sitting room that night, there was nothing to show that it was Vole who was there. . . .*

A semicolon may link closely related main clauses. For example, a semicolon could connect *At first she raged against the idea* and *then at last she agreed with their plan,* to create *At first she raged against the idea; then, at last, she agreed with their plan.*

Semicolons can also be used in compound sentences in place of **conjunctions,** words that connect words or groups of words of equal weight, or **conjunctive adverbs,** words that create a transition between main clauses.

Situation To accentuate a close relationship between two clauses, replace a comma and a coordinating conjunction with a semicolon.

> They were love letters, and the man they were written to was not Vole.
> They were love letters; the man they were written to was not Vole.

Situation To join two sentences, use a semicolon before a conjunctive adverb.

> His wife was to testify against him. Therefore, his chances might be doomed.
> His wife was to testify against him; therefore, his chances might be doomed.

Connectors

A **semicolon** is a punctuation mark that, among other things, can link main clauses.
A **coordinating conjunction—** such as *and, but, or,* and *yet—* connects words or groups of words of equal weight.
A **conjunctive adverb** is a word that creates a transition between main clauses.

Tip

When deciding whether to use a semicolon between main clauses, first determine whether the ideas are closely related.

Language Handbook

For more on semicolons, see the Language Handbook, p. R66.

Revise Rewrite the following sentences, using a semicolon to create a variety of correctly structured sentences.

1. Agatha Christie wrote many exciting stories and her writing was full of suspense.

2. Her story "The Witness for the Prosecution" was incredibly popular—therefore, it was made into a movie.

3. The story describes the criminal trial of Leonard Vole. He is charged with murder.

LOG ON ▶ **Literature** Online

Grammar For more grammar practice, go to glencoe.com and enter QuickPass code GL57805u6.

Vocabulary Workshop

Thesaurus Use

TEKS

10.1.E Use a dictionary, a glossary, or a thesaurus (printed or electronic) to determine or confirm the meanings of words and phrases, including their connotations and denotations, and their etymology.

Literature Connection In the quotation below from "Witness for the Prosecution," Agatha Christie uses a word that has a synonym, a word with a similar, but not usually identical, meaning and association, to describe the room.

"Then, drawing a deep breath, he turned and left the squalid room."

Christie might have described the *squalid* room as *dirty* or *filthy,* but neither term would have conveyed a sense of wretchedness.

To determine or confirm the meanings of words and phrases, you already know you can consult a dictionary or a glossary. You can also consult a **thesaurus** (printed or electronic), a source of synonyms and antonyms. They are traditionally organized in one of two ways.

Traditional Style Many thesauruses organize words by general concept. To find a synonym for the word *taste,* for example, look in the alphabetical index of categories until you find the category *senses,* which includes the subentry *taste.* The index will refer you to the page for the subentry, where you will find a list of synonyms. Probably the best-known traditional thesaurus is *Roget's Thesaurus.*

Dictionary Style This type of thesaurus presents words in alphabetical order. Each word is followed by several synonyms, which are listed by part of speech and direct the reader to related entries. In this type of thesaurus, you must look up a specific word to find its synonyms. J. I. Rodale's *The Synonym Finder* is an example of a dictionary-style thesaurus. Here is a sample entry for the word *squalid.*

Vocabulary Terms

A **thesaurus** is a specialized dictionary that lists synonyms and antonyms.

Tip

Learning the differences between the denotations (literal meanings) and the connotations (implied meanings and associations) of similar words can help you read with more understanding, write more expressively and precisely, and speak and listen more effectively. A thesaurus or a dictionary can help you evaluate differences in connotation.

squalid *adj. The unwashed, dirty dishes were piled everywhere in the squalid kitchen:* filthy, dirty, foul, nasty, fetid, unclean, neglected, seedy, sordid, low, sleazy, repulsive, immoral, dishonest, disreputable. *Ant.* clean, spotless, fresh, reputable.

— part of speech
— example sentence
— list of synonyms with the most common ones first
— list of antonyms

Practice

1. Using a thesaurus (printed or electronic), find two synonyms for each word listed below. Then find the precise meaning for each one in a dictionary.

   a. grief   **b.** honor   **c.** strange   **d.** hesitate   **e.** shining

2. Use each word and the synonyms you have found in a sentence. Be sure your sentences reflect slight differences in denotation or connotation.

LOG ON ▶ **Literature** Online

Vocabulary For more vocabulary practice, go to glencoe.com and enter QuickPass code GL57805u6.

TEKS

For pages 1090–1097

10.14.A Write an engaging story with a well-developed conflict and resolution, interesting and believable characters, a range of literary strategies (e.g., dialogue, suspense) and devices to enhance the plot, and sensory details that define the mood or tone.

Writing Workshop

Short Story

Literature Connection: To entertain the reader of "By the Waters of Babylon," Stephen Vincent Benét crafts a suspenseful plot and uses a variety of narrative techniques, including believable characters, dialogue, and sensory details.

Purpose: Your purpose for writing a short story is to entertain by including all the elements of a good short story, including setting, characters, events, exposition, conflict, rising action, resolution, falling action, and dialogue.

Audience: You and your classmates will compile your short stories in a literary anthology for the enjoyment of classmates, friends, and family.

Choose Your Topic

Planning Checklist

Your short story should include the following traits:

- ☑ a plot that has an engaging beginning, a clear conflict, and a satisfying resolution

- ☑ interesting, believable, and well-developed characters

- ☑ realistic dialogue that reveals the characters' personalities and motivations

- ☑ sensory details that set the mood or tone

Option A: Choose a Prompt

1. Write a short story in which a mystery must be solved.

2. Write a short story about the discovery of a heretofore unknown ancient civilization on Earth.

Option B: Write a Prompt

Write a short story that _____.

Sample Prompt:

Write a short story that suggests what life might be like on Earth several hundred years or more in the future.

🐺 Scoring Rubric

Check the Literary Texts **Scoring Rubric** on page R28 for more guidance on crafting your best story.

Analyze a Professional Model

Read for Guidance In the short story excerpt that follows, Isaac Asimov presents a not-so-future world in which computers are used to create conditions for, and to fight, wars.

from *"Frustration"* by Isaac Asimov

Herman Gelb turned his head to watch the departing figure. Then he said, "Wasn't that the Secretary?"

"Yes, that was the Secretary of Foreign Affairs. Old man Hargrove. Are you ready for lunch?"

"Of course. What was he doing here?"

Peter Jonsbeck didn't answer immediately. He merely stood up, and beckoned Gelb to follow. They walked down the corridor and into a room that had the steamy smell of spicy food.

"Here you are," said Jonsbeck. "The whole meal has been prepared by computer. Completely automated. Untouched by human hands. And my own programming. I promised you a treat, and here you are."

It was good. Gelb could not deny it and didn't want to. Over dessert, he said, "But what was Hargrove doing here?"

Jonsbeck smiled. "Consulting me on programming. What else am I good for?"

"But why? Or is it something you can't talk about?"

"It's something I suppose I *shouldn't* talk about, but it's a fairly open secret. There isn't a computer man in the capital who doesn't know what the poor frustrated simp is up to."

"What is he up to then?"

"He's fighting wars."

Gelb's eyes opened wide. "With whom?"

"With nobody, really. He fights them by computer analysis. He's been doing it for I don't know how long."

"But why?"

"He wants the world to be the way we are—noble, honest, decent, full of respect for human rights and so on."

"So do I. So do we all. We have to keep up the pressure on the bad guys, that's all."

Time and Place
These details set the scene—lunchtime in a cafeteria.

Sensory Details
These details appeal to the senses of smell and taste.

Dialogue
The story is told mostly through dialogue, which sounds natural and unforced.

Characterization
The phrase "poor frustrated simp" offers a window into the character of Jonesbeck, who has little respect for Hargrove.

Conflict
This dialogue introduces the conflict between Hargrove's sense of morality and that of Gelb and Jonesbeck.

"And they're keeping the pressure on us, too. They don't think we're perfect."

"I suppose we're not, but we're better than they are. You know that."

"How do you make equations for war?"

"Well, you try, old man. Men. Weapons. Surprise. Counterattack. Ships. Space stations. Computers. We mustn't forget computers. There are a hundred factors and thousands of intensities and millions of combinations. Hargrove thinks it is possible to find *some* combination of starting conditions and courses of development that will result in clear victory for us and not too much damage to the world, and he labors under constant frustration."

Plot

Gelb's comment ratchets up the tension in the story.

"But what if he gets what he wants?"

"Well, if he can find the combination—if the computer says, 'This is it,' then I suppose he thinks he can argue our government into fighting exactly the war the computer has worked out so that, barring random events that upset the indicated course, we'd have what we want."

"There'd be casualties."

"Yes, of course. But the computer will presumably compare the casualties and other damage—to the economy and ecology, for instance—to the benefits that would derive from our control of the world, and if it decides the benefits will outweigh the casualties, then it will give the go-ahead for a 'just war.'

Climax

Gelb comes to realize just how reckless and dangerous Hargrove's research is.

Gelb stared his disbelief and said, "I never knew we were sitting at the lip of a volcanic crater like that. What about the 'random events' you mentioned?"

"The computer program tries to allow for the unexpected, but you never can, of course. So I don't think the go-ahead will come. . . . And because it lacks what is most needed, the computers will always give Hargrove, and all others who hanker for war, nothing but frustration."

Resolution

Jonesbeck's final comment resolves the conflict by pointing out that Hargrove's plan assumes computers can reason like humans—only, they can't.

"What is it that a computer doesn't have, then?"

"Why, Gelb. It totally lacks a sense of self-righteousness."

PLAN Your Story

Key Traits **Ideas** Story ideas are all around you, every day. They can be found in the people you meet and the places you go.

▶ Step 1: Think About Characters

Begin with the individual elements of a short story, such as characters. Imagine different characters and use a web to explore them.

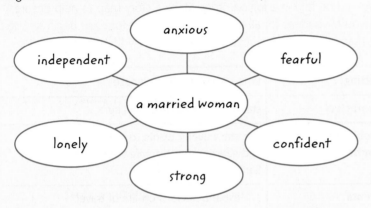

Choose one of the characteristics and explore it in more detail. What is the character anxious about? What gives her confidence?

▶ Step 2: Imagine Settings

Make a simple chart in which you create different settings. What time of day is it? What time of year? Where are you? What does it look like? Feel like?

Places	Characteristics
art museum	autumn afternoon, marble floors, white walls, echoes of footsteps, colorful paintings, quiet conversations
living room	year 3005, soft lighting, comfortable chairs, brown smog outside windows

Explore one of these places further. What might be happening there?

▶ Step 3: Create Dialogue

Take two characters you've been thinking about, put them in one of the settings, and write a conversation.

> "I'll miss you," she said.
>
> "Why don't you come with me?" he responded.
>
> "How could I? This is my home."

Where is he going? Why does she hesitate to go with him? The answers to these questions may suggest a plot for your story.

What If **Questions**

One way to think of story ideas is to ask questions that begin with *What if*, such as *What if an alien landed on the roof of my apartment building?* or *What if a child in 1858 discovered her neighbor's house was a stop on the Underground Railroad?*

Literature Online

Writing and Research For planning, drafting, and revising tools, go to glencoe.com and enter QuickPass code GL57805u6.

DRAFT Your Story

Key Traits Organization Some writers claim that their stories write themselves, and that they never know how things will turn out until they're done. Try letting your story take you where it wants to go.

▶ Step 1: Make a Story Map

Make a Story Map A story must have a conflict or a problem to solve and be told in a logical order. Make a story map to help ensure that you have ideas for all the story elements before you begin writing. The map will help you put your ideas, especially the events, in order.

Setting	time—3005; place—in space
Characters	star traveler and his wife, Laura
Problem or Conflict	The star traveler wants to visit other planets and galaxies, but his wife wants him home on Earth.
Events	1. Husband decides on life of travel. 2. Husband goes into space. 3. Husband has a crisis—is torn between star traveling and wife. 4. Husband decides on space.
Ending	the beauty and joy of star traveling

▶ Step 2: Write Realistic Dialogue

In fiction, dialogue can advance the plot, reveal character, expose conflicts, and create tension. What does this dialogue reveal about the two characters?

"You'll be gone so much. I may not see you again!" she cried.

"Come with me," I pleaded. "and work on the <u>Zodiac</u>."

▶ Step 3: Build to a Climax

As you draft, stay focused on building up to a climax, or turning point. This is the story's moment of greatest emotional intensity.

"Tonight," the captain says, breaking into my meditation, "we enter the gravitational field of Anterpodia galaxy. No further communication with the Milky Way will be possible for several years." Within hours Laura will be totally out of range.

It is not too late for me to reverse my decision. The transport room is still operative; my cozy living room is waiting for me. But then I look out at the stars and I know that I have made the right decision.

Drafting Checklist

Your short story should include the following traits:

- ☑ Characterization—characters seem real, believable
- ☑ Organization—events flow in logical order
- ☑ Dialogue—sounds natural and realistic
- ☑ Language—sensory details and figurative language are used effectively
- ☑ Climax—the story builds to an emotional turning point

Sample Student Story

"Star Traveler"

I am unwrapping my recycled Stardust Fries when my transmitter beeps. "Please come home," flashes across the screen from my wife Laura. I think of her back on Earth, just getting home from work. My thoughts are disrupted when the captain's face appears on my transmitter. He announces, "We are within sight of Paradiscus. All officers are invited on deck."

I toss my food, uneaten, into the Stardust snack-recycling bin. I remember how upset Laura was when I told her of my plan to join the crew of the *Zodiac*, a space explorer.

"You'll be gone so much. I may not see you again!" she cried.

"Come with me," I pleaded. "and work on the *Zodiac*."

She just kept shaking her head and saying, "Earth's my home." But I think, it's 3005, and the atmosphere is so toxic there. A person couldn't last thirty seconds without a suit.

After Laura had cried herself to sleep, I put on an atmosphere suit. I knew that the wide-open universe was calling me. I packed my things. In the morning, in tears, I left.

When I reach the deck, Paradiscus lies straight ahead—a marblelike mixture of blue and green in the black void of space—how Earth must have looked a thousand years ago.

"Tonight," the captain says, breaking into my meditation, "we enter the gravitational field of Anterpodia galaxy. No further communication with the Milky Way will be possible for several years." Within hours Laura will be totally out of range.

It is not too late for me to reverse my decision. The transport room is still operative; my cozy living room is waiting for me. But then I look out at the stars and I know that I have made the right decision. What drives us star travelers?

Setting

This paragraph sets the scene. The reader knows the narrator is on a spaceship.

Conflict

The writer uses interior monologue and dialogue to reveal the conflict.

Characterization

This paragraph shows that the narrator is sad to leave his wife but determined to do so.

Climax

The story builds in intensity. What will the narrator do?

Resolution

The conflict is resolved.

Your Turn

Use your story map to begin drafting your story. Be sure to include realistic dialogue, a clear conflict, and a satisfying resolution.

REVISE Your Story

Peer Review

When asked to read a class-mate's short story, read carefully and write notes as you read. Give constructive feedback. Use the following questions to get started:

- Do you get a good sense of time, place, and characters?

- Is there a series of events, a climax, and a resolution?

- Is there sensory language and other precise language?

Revising Checklist

Before you start your revision, ask yourself these questions:

☑ Does the beginning of my story set the scene or introduce the main characters?

☑ Are my characters believable?

☑ Is the dialogue realistic?

☑ Have I clearly stated the conflict?

☑ Does the ending of my story resolve the conflict satisfactorily?

☑ Have I included the traits from the Planning and Drafting Checklists?

Key Traits Ideas and Word Choice You can improve your draft by adding sensory details, using interior monologues, and clearly stating the resolution of the conflict.

▶ Step 1: Elaborate

Do you use sensory details to enable the reader to experience what the characters are experiencing? Experiment with adding key details.

Draft:

> When I reach the deck, Paradiscus lies straight ahead, looking like Earth must have looked a thousand years ago.

Revised:

> When I reach the deck, Paradiscus lies straight ahead—a marblelike mixture of blue and green in the black void of space—how Earth must have looked a thousand years ago.

▶ Step 2: Use Interior Monologues

Will your audience understand the motivation of the characters? Interior monologues record a character's emotions, memories, and opinions. Like dialogue, they can reveal character and advance the plot.

> She just kept shaking her head and saying, "Earth's my home." But I think, it's 3005, and the atmosphere is so toxic there. A person couldn't last thirty seconds without a suit.

▶ Step 3: Present a Clear Resolution

Do you leave your readers knowing exactly how the conflict is resolved? Give your audience enough clues to know the outcome of your story.

Draft:

> It is not too late for me to reverse my decision. The transport room is still operative; my cozy living room is waiting for me. What drives us star travelers?

Revision:

> It is not too late for me to reverse my decision. The transport room is still operative; my cozy living room is waiting for me. But then I look out at the stars and I know that I have made the right decision. What drives us star travelers?

EDIT Your Story

Key Trait Conventions Edit by correcting any errors in spelling, grammar, and mechanics. Revise drafts to improve style, word choice, figurative language, sentence variety, and subtlety of meaning after rethinking how well you have addressed your purpose, audience, and genre.

▶ Grammar Tip

Correct Shifts in Point of View

When stories are told from the third-person point of view, the narrator uses pronouns such as *he, she,* and *they* to tell the story. When stories are told from the first-person point of view, a character in the story uses the pronoun *I* to tell what is happening. Tell your story in third person or first person, not both. Avoid shifting to the second person. Below are examples of shifts in point of view.

Problem: The narrative shifts from the first person to the third.

> I knew that the wide-open universe was calling me. He packed his things. In the morning, in tears, he left.

Solution: Make all personal pronouns first-person pronouns.

> I knew that the wide-open universe was calling me. I packed my things. In the morning, in tears, I left.

Problem: The narrative shifts inappropriately to the second person (*you*).

> The atmosphere is so toxic there that you couldn't last thirty seconds without a suit.

Solution: Use a noun or another pronoun that makes sense in the context of the sentence.

> The atmosphere is so toxic there that a person couldn't last thirty seconds without a suit.

PUBLISH Your Story

Key Trait Presentation The word *anthology* comes from the Greek word *anthologia,* a combination of *anthos,* "flower" + *logia,* "collecting." *Anthologia* soon took on the broader meaning of a "collection," not of flowers but of literary works, such as poems or short stories.

Add your short story to the class anthology. Work with other students to design a cover and include a table of contents. To give your anthology some added flair, include an illustration that suggests something special about your story.

Editing Checklist

For your final revision, check the following:

☑ Have I misspelled any words? If you are unsure of the spelling of a word, check an online or print dictionary or use your word processor's spell checker.

☑ Have I made any errors in mechanics or grammar? Have I followed the rules of Standard American English? Use the Language Handbook on pages R48–R71 to correct common grammar and mechanical errors.

☑ Is my writing legible? Be sure your handwriting is neat or that you have followed your teacher's guidelines for word-processing.

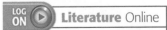

LOG ON ▶ **Literature** Online

Writing and Research For editing and publishing tools, go to glencoe.com and enter QuickPass code GL57805u6.

Speaking, Listening, and Viewing Workshop

Oral Interpretation of a Story

Literature Connection "Witness for the Prosecution" was not just a great short story. It was also very successfully adapted for both the stage and the screen. In this workshop, you will work with others to re-create your original short story or a short story from this unit as a dramatic performance.

> **Assignment**
>
> **Re-create a short story as a dramatic performance.**
> **Audience:** classmates and teacher, possibly other guests
> **Purpose:** to engage and entertain

Plan Your Presentation

- -

Follow these steps to get started:

Choose a type of performance. For example, you might present a dramatic reading of the entire story. You might act out just one scene. You might use moving images or a computer slide presentation to show all or part of the story. You might also present a radio show, a Web cast, or even a puppet show.

Consider audience and occasion. After you choose a type of performance, think about your audience and performance space. For example, consider the size of the room and the technology you may or may not have available. Consider how people might be seated and what kind of screen, stage, or other presentation size you will require for everyone to be able to see and hear easily. Think about the occasion, too. Will this be just the usual classroom scene? Or will you perform for parents or other guests?

Focus on your purpose. Your goal is to state one central message about the story through the events or scenes you portray. Your central message may be about any one or more of the following:

- the time and place
- the theme
- the characters
- the conflict and/or the resolution

Develop Your Presentation

Whatever kind of performance you present, you will want to engage your audience from beginning to end. Follow these guidelines:

- Begin boldly. Surprise, tension, conflict, and an arresting sound effect are all options. Capture your audience's attention from moment one.
- Create visual interest. If you are using computer screens, make them bold and colorful but easy to follow. For a dramatic reading or staging a scene, make a backdrop, or bring in props for visual interest. For a radio broadcast, consider projecting a series of images.
- Use language to its fullest effect. If you are presenting a story or scene from a story, use many of the author's exact words. If you are presenting your own story, add vivid language, including action verbs, and use sensory details and figurative language.
- End memorably. Think about your final words, pose, or image. Do not say, "The end." Convey the end through sound effects, well-chosen words, a fitting closing image, or another closing device.

Rehearse

Practice your dramatic presentation by performing it aloud as a group and then performing it for a small group. As you rehearse, elicit feedback from your listeners, listen to others practice their dramatic presentation, and consider the following techniques.

Techniques for Dramatic Presentations

Speaking Techniques	Listening Techniques
☑ **Use Audience Feedback** Watch the looks on your listeners' faces for clues about how to adjust your performance.	☑ **Focus** Look directly at the performers and images and concentrate on what they convey.
☑ **Volume** Adjust your volume to the size of your audience and for dramatic effect.	☑ **Respond** Show interest. If you are surprised, taken aback, amused, or momentarily startled, show it.
☑ **Entertain** Let go of the everyday you to slip into the role of performer.	☑ **Evaluate** Identify the most successful parts or aspects of the presentation.

Presentation Tips

Use the following checklist to evaluate your dramatic presentation:

- ☑ Did you entertain your audience? Where did the audience respond best?
- ☑ Did you achieve your purpose of re-creating one central idea from the story?
- ☑ Did you correctly tailor your presentation to the occasion and your performance space?

Listen Responsively

When you are listening to and watching the presentation,

- ☑ use comprehension skills to listen attentively
- ☑ take notes that summarize, synthesize, or highlight the performers' ideas
- ☑ ask questions related to the content for clarification and elaboration

Remember to wait until the performers have finished before asking any questions.

LOG ON ▶ **Literature** Online

Speaking, Listening, and Viewing For project ideas, templates, and presentation tips, go to glencoe.com and enter QuickPass code GL57805u6.

Independent Reading

Genre Fiction

SOME TYPES OF FICTION FOLLOW SUCH DISTINCT PATTERNS THAT THEY HAVE their own classification, or genre. Among these types of genre fiction are mysteries (in which characters use clues to solve a problem) and science fiction (which presents imagined events related to science or technology). Fantasy stories with invented characters, settings, and other elements are another subset of fiction. Modern fables, or stories that are usually based on a single event and use stock characters, also follow a distinct pattern. For more genre fiction on a range of themes, try the two suggestions below and the first suggestion on the next page. For novels that incorporate the Big Idea of *The Extraordinary and Fantastic*, try the titles from the Glencoe Literature Library on the next page.

The Ear, the Eye, and the Arm

Nancy Farmer

The place is Zimbabwe. The year is 2194. After sneaking into a dangerous city, three children are kidnapped and forced into a life of hard labor in a plastics mine. Many fast-paced adventures follow. The children's parents hire a trio of mutant detectives to find them, but the sensitive yet absurd rescuers are constantly just one step behind the children. This novel combines elements of science fiction, humor, and traditional African culture. Notes and a glossary help readers with the traditional African tribal language and lore.

Nightfall

Isaac Asimov and Robert Silverberg

Two of the greatest science-fiction writers of the twentieth century collaborated on this suspenseful tale, based on a 1941 short story by Asimov. *Nightfall* explores what happens when darkness slowly falls in a world that has seen nothing but sunlight for the last two thousand years. Readers experience the event through the eyes of a newspaperman, an astronomer, a psychologist, an archaeologist, and a religious person. As a terrified society verges on chaos, only a few citizens are prepared to face the truth.

Red Card: A Zeke Armstrong Mystery

by Daniel J. Hale and Matthew LaBrot

In this exciting novel, Zeke Armstrong and his teammates battle to make the soccer finals while exploring a mystery in Dallas.

GLENCOE LITERATURE LIBRARY

The Strange Case of Dr. Jekyll and Mr. Hyde

Robert Louis Stevenson

Good reigns by day and evil by night in this extraordinary and fantastic story of a man with a divided personality.

Frankenstein

Mary Shelley

Dr. Frankenstein is obsessed with bringing his own creation to life—but the results will shock him and the readers of this uncanny and fantastic gothic novel.

CRITICS' CORNER

"The pretense, disguise, play-acting, and outward show that are essential to the mystery genre are given a special intensity in Christie's work by her constant emphasis on and reference to the "theatricality" of her characters' actions. A well-known example is Murder on the Orient Express (1934), in which Hercule Poirot comes to realize that he has been an audience of one for a careful series of performances."

—Nicholas Birns and Margaret Boe Birns, from *The Cunning Craft: Original Essays on Detective Fiction and Contemporary Literary Theory*

Murder on the Orient Express

Agatha Christie

In this novel, the most well known of Agatha Christie's many mysteries, an extraordinary murder occurs on the Orient Express, a luxury train traveling from Istanbul to Paris. An American is found dead in his train compartment with the door locked from the inside.

Write a Review

Read one of the books listed on these pages and write a review of it for your classmates. Be sure to explain its strengths and why you recommend it. Present your review to the class.

Assessment

English Language Arts

Reading: Genre Fiction

Read the following passages and then answer the questions that follow them.

from *A Connecticut Yankee in King Arthur's Court* by Mark Twain

In this famous story, a 19th century American, Hank Morgan, awakens to find himself in Medieval England, which he assumes is a hospital for the insane—an asylum. Morgan, who narrates the story, has just been captured by a knight and is being forced to accompany him.

1   Presently there was a distant blare of military music; it came nearer, still nearer, and soon a noble cavalcade wound into view, glorious with plumed helmets and flashing mail and flaunting banners and . . . it took its gallant way, and in its wake we followed.

2   Followed through one winding alley and then another—and climbing, always climbing—till at last we gained the breezy height where the huge castle stood.

3   There was an exchange of bugle blasts . . . and then the great gates were flung open, the drawbridge was lowered, and the head of the cavalcade swept forward under the frowning arches; and we, following, soon found ourselves in a great paved court, with towers and turrets stretching up into the blue air on all the four sides; and all about us the dismount was going on, and much greeting and ceremony and running to and fro, and a gay display of moving and intermingling colors, and an altogether pleasant stir and noise and confusion.

4   The moment I got a chance, I slipped aside privately and touched an ancient common looking man on the shoulder and said, in an insinuating, confidential way, "Friend, do me a kindness. Do you belong to the asylum, or are you just on a visit or something like that?"

5   He looked me over stupidly, and said, "Marry, fair sir, me seemeth—"

6   "That will do," I said; "I reckon you are a patient."

7   I moved away, cogitating, and at the same time keeping an eye out for any chance passenger in his right mind that might come along and give me some light. I judged I had found one, presently; so I drew him aside and said in his ear, "If I could see the head keeper a minute—only just a minute—"

8   "Prithee do not let me."

9   "Let you *what?*"

10   "*Hinder* me, then, if the word please thee better." Then he went on to say he was an under-cook and could not stop to gossip, though he would like it another time; for it would comfort his very liver to know where I got my clothes. As he started away, he pointed and said yonder was one who was idle enough for my purpose, and was seeking me besides, no doubt. This was an airy slim boy in shrimp-colored tights that made him look like a forked carrot, the rest of his gear was blue silk and dainty laces and ruffles; and he had long yellow curls, and wore a plumed pink satin cap tilted complacently over his

(Continued)

ear. By his look, he was good-natured; by his gait, he was satisfied with himself. He was pretty enough to frame. He arrived, looked me over with a smiling and impudent curiosity; said he had come for me, and informed me that he was a page.

11 "Go 'long," I said; "you ain't more than a paragraph."

"The Fox and the Stork" by Aesop

1 There was a time when the Fox and the Stork were quite friendly, so the Fox invited the Stork to come to dinner. Amused by the idea of playing a joke on her, he served nothing but soup in a shallow bowl, which he could easily lap up but which allowed the Stork to do no more than wet the end of her long beak. After an hour of attempting to obtain some nourishment, she left the table with her stomach as empty as a dry well. She was very hungry, indeed, and more than a little angry.

2 "I am sorry," said the Fox in a pretense of regret, "that the soup is not to your liking."

3 "Pray, do not apologize," said the Stork, already planning her revenge.

4 Some weeks later, the Stork invited the Fox to dinner. That evening, the Stork presented a meal that smelled delicious but was contained in a long-necked jar. Although the Stork could easily consume this meal, the fox stood not a chance of inserting his snout and could do no more than hungrily lick the outside of the jar. The Fox then remembered his earlier actions and regretted them.

5 *Treat others as you wish to be treated.*

Use *A Connecticut Yankee in King Arthur's Court* to answer questions 1–6.

1 In paragraph 3, the main purpose of the imagery is to establish the story's —
   A plot
   B theme
   C setting
   D characters

2 The author uses a particular diction in paragraph 5 to establish that the "common looking man"—
   F is not educated
   G is a resident of an asylum
   H speaks an old form of English
   J has no interest in helping the narrator

3 Why does the "common looking man" look over the narrator in a way that the narrator interprets as "stupidly"?
   A The narrator looks odd to him.
   B The man wants to seem stupid.
   C The man is, indeed, quite stupid.
   D The man is not used to being approached.

4 Which quotation from the story uses figurative language?
   F *a distant blare of military music*
   G *much greeting and ceremony and running to and fro*
   H *yonder was one who was idle enough for my purpose*
   J *in shrimp-colored tights that made him look like a forked carrot*

5 A reader can infer that, in this excerpt, the narrator is both confused and —

A sad
B frightened
C very angry
D somewhat amused

6 In the last paragraph, the narrator's statement is his way of commenting on the page's —

F personality
G youth or size
H fancy clothing
J manner of movement

Use "The Fox and the Stork" to answer questions 7–12.

7 What type of narration is used in this story?

A first-person
B third-person, limited to the Fox
C third-person, limited to the Stork
D third-person, omniscient

8 Which type of genre fiction is this story?

F Fable
G Fantasy
H Mystery
J Science fiction

9 Which quotation from the story uses figurative language?

A *nothing but soup in a shallow bowl*
B *to do no more than wet the end of her long beak*
C *she left the table with her stomach as empty as a dry well*
D *and could do no more than hungrily lick the outside of the jar*

10 What does the story suggest was the Stork's motivation for serving dinner in a long-necked jar?

F To keep the food she served hot
G To show that she was wiser than the Fox
H To get even with the Fox for his unkindness
J To restore the two animals' friendly relationship

11 What is most likely to have been the author's main purpose in writing this story?

A To describe a process
B To teach a lesson or give advice
C To explain common animal behaviors
D To entertain the reader with an amusing story

12 **Open-Ended Item** Some versions of this story provide a different moral: "One bad deed deserves another." Which moral do you think better reflects the lesson of the story? Explain your answer and provide evidence from the story to support it.

Literature Online

Standards Practice For more standards practice, go to glencoe.com and enter QuickPass code GL57805u6.

Vocabulary Skills: Sentence Completion

For each item, choose the word from the word list that best completes the sentence. Do not use the same word more than once.

accord	cultivate	horizon	pretext
amicable	dismantle	inert	recoil
animosity	dupe	interlaced	scavenger
anteroom	dutiful	paranoia	sublime
bade	frenzy	perplexed	treacherous
bloated	gnarled	precedence	verandah

1 An unclear explanation of a difficult concept may leave the listener just as _____ as before.

2 I love dogs, but this one smelled so awful that I couldn't help but _____ when it came near me.

3 Some members of the group were cold and unsociable, so I was relieved to find myself seated next to one of the more _____ ones.

4 Was *Tyrannosaurus rex* a hunter, or was it a _____ that ate what other animals left behind?

5 When my little brother got lost, Mom was in an absolute _____ of panic and worry until he was found safe.

6 Fighting with one's enemy usually only increases the _____ the two people feel towards each other.

7 It's going to take a while to _____ the set of bunk beds in my room and take the parts down to the basement.

8 "Black ice" is a thin and almost invisible coating of clear ice on a highway, which makes it a _____ surface for driving.

9 Arthritis has swollen and twisted my grandfather's fingers, leaving them so _____ that he cannot straighten them.

10 If you need a _____ to get off the phone, set a loud timer; when it goes off, you can claim that you have to take something out of the oven.

Revising and Editing

Read the following paragraphs from the first draft of a student's autobiographical narrative and answer the questions that follow them.

(1) We all know that moving can be difficult, we all realize it can be exhausting; nonetheless, it's not supposed to be a disaster. (2) Our problems began early in the morning. (3) Filled up with gas, we started driving across the state. (4) Our car is old; its engine is small; moreover, you tend to load up a car during a move. (5) Carrying so much extra weight, Mom thought the car would break down. (6) We had to go so slowly that it took several hours longer than we expected. (7) When we arrived, the house was in worse shape than we remembered. (8) Climbing up on the porch and peeking through the window, I saw mice. (9) Once inside, we discovered that there was no electricity. (10) Finishing our breakfast the next morning, the moving men finally got there. (11) Surprise! (12) The men's truck was full of furniture and boxes, but it was all another family's possessions.

1   What change, if any, should be made in sentence 1?
    A Change the comma after *difficult* to a semicolon
    B Change the semicolon after *exhausting* to a comma
    C Delete the comma after *nonetheless*
    D Make no change

2   What revision, if any, is needed in sentence 3?
    F We started driving across the state, filled up with gas.
    G After filling the car with gas, we started driving across the state.
    H Filled up with gas, we started driving our car across the state.
    J No revision is needed.

3   What change, if any, is needed in sentence 4?
    A Change the semicolons to commas
    B Delete the comma after *moreover*
    C Change *you tend* to **one tends**
    D Make no change

4   What revision, if any, is needed in sentence 5?
    F Due to carrying so much extra weight, Mom thought the car would break down.
    G Mom thought the car would break down from carrying so much extra weight.
    H The car, Mom thought, carrying so much extra weight, would break down.
    J No revision is needed.

5 What revision, if any, is needed in sentence 8?

A Climbing up on the porch, I saw mice peeking through the window.

B I saw mice climbing up on the porch and peeking through the window.

C Climbing up on the porch and peeking through the window, mice were seen.

D No revision is needed.

6 What revision, if any, should be made in sentence 10?

F The moving men, finishing our breakfast the next morning, finally got there.

G As we were finishing our breakfast the next morning, the moving men finally got there

H Finally, the moving men got there the next morning, and we were finishing our breakfast

J No revision is needed.

Written Composition

Read the information and instructions below in order to write a short narrative.

Aesop's work is the source of many of our most common sayings, including "Necessity is the mother of invention," "Don't count your chickens before they are hatched," "Appearances can be deceiving," and "Once burned, twice shy." Each states a "general truth."

Write a short story that demonstrates the truth of one of these sayings or of another general truth that you believe is accurate.

REMEMBER—YOU SHOULD

❏ develop a plot that has a beginning, a clear conflict, and a satisfying resolution

❏ make your characters realistic through what they say and do

❏ let events flow in a logical order and build to a climax

❏ use sensory details effectively

❏ correct errors in spelling, capitalization, punctuation, grammar, and sentence structure

CONSUMER AND WORKPLACE
DOCUMENTS

TEKS

For pages 1110–1111

10.11 Understand how to glean and use information in procedural texts and documents.

FOCUS ON
FUNCTIONAL DOCUMENTS

Why Read Functional Documents?

You probably depend on functional and procedural documents every day. Functional documents do not all look the same, but they all share the same basic **purpose**: to successfully communicate information. Here are some examples of functional and procedural documents.

Examples of Functional and Procedural Documents		
product information	contracts	flyers
instructions	e-mails	written directions
cover letters	maps	memos
schedules	rules or handbooks	labels
applications	meeting agendas	warranties

Evaluating Functional Documents

What's the Plan?

Writers try to use a particular order or pattern—or **text structure**—to organize their work. By figuring out what text structure a writer uses, you can better find, follow, and understand the information you need. Here are some text structures that you'll frequently find in functional documents.

Functional Document	Text Structure
Warranty	Order of importance
Schedule or itinerary	Chronological, or time, order
Map or seating plan	Spatial order
Software installation guide	Sequence, or step-by-step order

Evaluate Credibility

Would you take a flyer for a new diet pill seriously if it claimed that the pill could cause immediate and drastic weight loss? Would you believe a promotional poster for a new CD if it stated that the CD only contained musical gems? When you read functional documents, it is important to determine the credibility of an argument or claim. Below are a few tips for evaluating credibility:

- **Examine the statements the writer makes.** Do they seem plausible based on your experiences? If, for instance, the writer of a software information document states that a certain program will allow you to create comic-book masterpieces, you might not believe him. If, on the other hand, the writer states that the program will expand your creative horizons, you might accept this statement as true.

- **Consider the evidence the writer uses to support statements.** Are there sufficient facts? Are there testimonials from users or product testers? Do they seem credible?

- **Look at the possible motivation of the writer.** Is the writer trying to sell a product? If so, you might conclude that he or she is slanting the facts so that the product sounds more appealing or more effective than it might really be.

Using Functional Documents

Publishing a Graphic Novel

In this unit, you will encounter different functional documents while you follow the progress of Devin Gregory, who is attempting to publish his graphic novel *Kosmo Fantastic Versus Mr. Meriadeck*. You will pick up on Devin's publishing adventure at the point when he is ready to enter his finished manuscript in a graphic novel contest.

As you accompany Devin through the publishing process, you will gain knowledge of a variety of functional documents. You will also learn about some of the stages involved in transforming a manuscript into a bound book.

As you read the functional documents in this unit, be sure to

- Examine text structures to understand how information is organized and how to use the information in procedural texts and documents. For more about text structure, see the Reading Handbook, page R46.

- Form opinions and make judgments about what you are reading. Use the tips above to guide you in this process.

Before You Read

Build Background

After completing what he felt was a great manuscript, Devin wanted to submit his graphic novel to a writing contest. He visited the Web site of the journal *Alamo Comics*. He then sent an **e-mail** to the journal's editor about the guidelines. Devin downloaded the **application form** that appears on page 1114 and carefully reviewed it. Next, he filled out the form as neatly as possible and checked it for grammatical, punctuation, and spelling errors. Finally, Devin composed a **cover letter** in which he demonstrated his familiarity with the journal and highlighted his qualifications that related to the contest.

Cover letters, e-mails, and **application forms** are all functional or procedural documents. The ability to understand such documents is a skill that will be helpful to you throughout your life.

TEKS

For pages 1112–1116

10.11 Understand how to glean and use information in procedural texts and documents.

Reading Preview

Make Generalizations One way to help you understand what you read is to **make generalizations.** When you form a generalization, you look at specific details or facts and try to identify patterns or trends within them. As you read each document, identify, organize, and analyze its key details and facts. Then use your analysis to make general statements about the particular topic or type of document.

Distinguish Fact and Opinion The documents in this lesson contain both **facts**—statements that can be proved—and **opinions**—statements that express personal views, attitudes, or interpretations. To help differentiate the two, use the tips below.

- Look at the author's wording. Phrases such as *I think* and *I believe* indicate opinions, as do *view, feeling,* and *always.*

- Examine the evidence. Does the author supply enough evidence and facts to support a statement?

Workplace Vocabulary

e-mail: a message sent and received electronically over a computer network

application: a form to be completed by an applicant

cover letter: a letter sent along with other documents to give additional information

Read an E-mail

Study the e-mail Devin sent to learn more about the submission process.

To: <u>mjones@alamocomics.net</u> **①**
From: <u>DGregory@dkvworld.net</u>
Date: September 7, 2010
Subject: Dragon Fire Graphic Novel Contest **②**

Dear Mr. Jones:

③ I am the author of a graphic novel, and I would like to ask you a few questions regarding the submission process for the graphic novel contest. The first question I have is, Can I submit my novel either via e-mail or via regular snail mail? I couldn't find information concerning your submissions preferences on your Web site and want to follow your guidelines correctly. My second question is, Are you open to simultaneous submissions, or do you prefer that writers submit their works to only one publication at a time? To improve my chances of being published, I would like to submit my novel simultaneously to several publishers, but I can limit myself to your contest should you disallow simultaneous submissions. **④**

Thank you in advance for your prompt response to my questions. **⑤**

Devin Gregory

① The heading identifies the recipient of the e-mail, the sender, the date, and the subject.

② The subject line tells the reader what the e-mail is about.

③ The purpose of the e-mail is stated in the first sentence.

④ The e-mail requests additional information specifically related to the submission process.

⑤ The writer expresses his thanks.

Reading Check

Distinguish Fact and Opinion Name a fact that appears in the first sentence of the e-mail. How do you know it is a fact?

Make Generalizations About Documents How is the structure of this e-mail similar to other e-mails you have seen?

Summarize Information Summarize the kinds of information Devin is asking for in the e-mail.

Read an Application

Devin downloaded this form from the Alamo Comics Web site.

Dragon Fire Graphic Novel Contest
Official Entry Form

Name of writer: ___Devin Gregory___

Name of artist: ___Devin Gregory___

Address: ___3777 N. Halsted Street, Chicago, Illinois, 60613___

Home phone: ___(773) 555-1234___ Work phone: ___none___

Cell phone: ___none___ ❶E-mail: ___DGregory@dkvworld.net___

Title of novel: ___Kosmo Fantastic Versus Mr. Meriadeck___ ❷

Story genre: ___adventure, science fiction___

Number of pages: _112 pages_ Hand drawn? _xx_ yes ___ no.

Story Synopsis: _Orphaned teenager Kosmo Fantastic must defeat the evil Mr. Meriadeck to save his planet, Bork Bersi, from destruction. Kosmo Fantastic uses his powers to defeat Meriadeck._

Have you ever had a graphic novel published? ❸___yes _xx_ no. If yes, title of work/publisher:_____

Published in a literary magazine/journal? _xx_ yes ___ no. If yes, give example: _"Stymir the Stouthearted," published in Manga Madness (Fall 2008)_ Other accomplishments? _accomplished and active musician._ **Send entry form; check for $10; 6 pages of sequential art; completed script; and a self-addressed stamped envelope to** ❹

Dragon Fire Graphic Novel Contest, Alamo Comics, 300 N. Main Avenue, San Antonio, TX 78212

❶ Contact information appears at the top of the application.

❷ The application requests information related to the book.

❸ The application is designed so that it is easy to fill out.

❹ Specific instructions for submission are given at the bottom of the application.

Reading Check

Make Generalizations About Documents How is the text in application forms typically structured?

Distinguish Fact and Opinion In which section of the application can you find opinions about the writer's experiences?

Draw Conclusions About Procedural Documents Think about the kinds of information the application is requesting. Based on this information, what do you think is the main purpose of the application?

Read a Cover Letter

Here is the letter Devin sent to inspire interest in his graphic novel.

3777 N. Halsted Street
Chicago, IL 60613
September 15, 2010

Mr. Mark Jones
Editor
Dragon Fire Graphic Novel Contest
Alamo Comics
300 N. Main Avenue
San Antonio, TX 78212

Dear Mr. Jones,

1 Enclosed is my manuscript, *Kosmo Fantastic Versus Mr. Meriadeck,* for consideration in your Dragon Fire Graphic Novel Contest. I read *Alamo Comics* and am a fan of your imaginative comics. **2**

Kosmo Fantastic Versus Mr. Meriadeck is my first novel. However, my comics have been published in literary journals, including *Manga Madness* and *American Saga: A Comic Magazine*. My comic strip *Stanley and Livingston* appeared in a local newspaper during June of 2008. **3**

Enclosed are six sample pages from my novel, a full script of the novel, a completed application form, a check for $10, and a stamped, self-addressed envelope. If you have any questions, please contact me by phone (773-555-1234) or e-mail (DGregory@dkvworld.net). **4**

I look forward to hearing from you in the near future. **5**

Sincerely, **6**

Devin Gregory

1 The main purpose of the letter is stated clearly in the first sentence.

2 The writer demonstrates familiarity with the content of the journal.

3 The writer mentions publishing credits that specifically relate to the contest.

4 The writer provides contact information.

5 The writer uses a block format. With this type of format, the text is justified left, and one line of space separates each paragraph.

6 The writer inserts four lines of space to leave adequate room for his signature.

Reading Check

Make Generalizations About Documents Why do you think the block format is the most popular format for business letters?

Distinguish Fact and Opinion Reread the second paragraph. Which sentence there is most difficult to verify? Why?

Evaluate Details Do you think the author demonstrates that he has the necessary experience to write a strong graphic novel? Explain.

After You Read

Respond and Think Critically

Directions: Read the questions about documents below and select the best answer.

1. What is the purpose of the **e-mail?**
   - **A.** to highlight Devin's publishing credits
   - **B.** to request additional information about the submissions process
   - **C.** to improve Devin's chances of having his novel accepted
   - **D.** to make the editor aware of Devin's graphic novel

2. In which section of the **application form** would you find the most information about the content of the graphic novel?
   - **A.** story synopsis
   - **B.** estimated number of pages
   - **C.** story genre
   - **D.** name of writer

3. Conventional **cover letters** have all of the following parts EXCEPT
   - **A.** a salutation
   - **B.** the recipient's inside address
   - **C.** a closing
   - **D.** the recipient's e-mail address

4. Which of the following is NOT discussed in the **cover letter?**
   - **A.** why the writer chose the Dragon Fire Graphic Novel Contest
   - **B.** which documents the writer has enclosed
   - **C.** who will enjoy reading the novel
   - **D.** what qualifications the writer has

Write a Business Letter

Assignment Many situations in life will require you to write procedural or work-related documents. Think of a situation in which writing a business letter might help you achieve a long-held goal. Perhaps you want to be chosen for an internship or receive funding for a community project. A business letter can help you in these efforts.

Once you are clear about what you want to achieve, begin drafting. Clearly state your purpose for writing and convincingly describe your qualifications in the body of the letter. Use business letter format.

Get Ideas Strive for clear, lively writing and correct spelling, punctuation, and grammar. To write an effective letter,

- Include the standard **parts** of a business letter: a return address, the date, an inside address, a salutation, the text of the letter, a complimentary close, a signature, and a printed name.

- Use either the **block format** or the **modified block format.** In the modified block style, the date and closing are centered on the page; other parts are aligned on the left.

- Use reader-friendly formatting techniques. Use only one **font** and make sure it is easy to read. Avoid fancy unreadable fonts.

- Accurately convey relevant information. Keep to the **main points** and cut out all information that is irrelevant to these points.

- Organize your information in a logical way. Arrange the information in the letter into the best **order** for getting the results you want.

Give It Structure Before you begin writing, consider your audience. Who will read your letter? Anticipate any questions your readers might have, and try to answer them. Then choose a style that your audience will find appealing and easy to understand. Strike a balance between too formal and impersonal and too casual and personal. This means using standard punctuation, spelling, and grammar and steering away from slang, jargon, or buzzwords.

Before You Read

TEKS

For pages 1117–1122

10.11 Understand how to glean and use information in procedural texts and documents.

Build Background

When Devin received an e-mail from the editor of *Alamo Comics* instructing him to submit his novel electronically, he found an online **professional article** to guide him. Devin's first step was to scan his hand-drawn cartoons into his computer. Before scanning, Devin reviewed the scanner's **schematic** to find out how it worked.

He then purchased software, reviewing its **product information description,** which appears on page 1120. Finally, Devin consulted the software **installation guide** to install the program correctly.

Schematics, product information descriptions, and installation guides are types of **consumer documents** and **procedural texts** that explain consumer products. Here are strategies to help you read these documents.

Reading Preview

Identify Sequence As you read, try to determine the order, or **sequence** that organizes a document. An effective sequence arranges content so readers understand how information is related. Here are three common types of logical sequences:

- Chronological, or time, order
- Spatial order
- Sequence, or step-by-step order

To identify the type of sequence in a document, look carefully at its features. Does the document contain numbered lists? Have words that indicate time order? Have headings that signal sequence? All of these features can provide clues about the type of order the writer uses to structure a document.

Summarize While reading, **summarize,** or briefly state, the main ideas of a passage in a logical sequence and in your own words. Ask yourself who, what, where, why, how, and when questions about the information provided.

Workplace Vocabulary

schematic: a diagram that shows the structure of something

installation guide: a manual that explains how to install or operate a product

Read a Professional Article

Here is the professional article Devin found while surfing the Internet.

Ten Tips for Creating Visually Satisfying Graphic Novels
By Maya Hering

In this article, I explain how to create a professional looking comic from your hand-drawn art. **❶**

1. Use pencil and 8 x 12 sheets of paper to create each panel. Include one action per panel; 4 to 6 panels per page. **❷**
1. Trace over your pencil lines with a black gel pen, which does not bleed.
3. Once the ink is dry, gently erase all pencil lines using a soft eraser. A scanner will capture all of the stray marks on a piece of paper.
4. Create a new folder on your computer. Name it appropriately.
5. Scan your panels into your computer. Save them in your new folder.
6. Using a comic-book software program, create a layout for each page. Create your own layouts or choose from layout templates. **❸**
7. Import your scanned drawings into the computer program; drag them into place in the layouts. Then use the Image Crop option in your program to get rid of areas of drawings that you don't want to keep.
8. Next you can edit your drawings. To get rid of bumpy lines, apply the Smoothing and Straightening options in your software program.
9. Now add color to help convey your characters' personalities. Select the blank areas inside your drawings where you want to add color and use the Color tools in your program to fill in these areas. **❹**
10. Once you've finished editing, insert captions and word balloons (i.e., the bubbles that convey characters' thoughts and spoken words) in all of the panels. First, draw ovals for the balloons and place them in the appropriate positions, and then fill the balloons with text.

❶ The purpose of the article is stated clearly and concisely.

❷ The writer makes the tips easier to follow by organizing them into a list.

❸ The writer describes when, how, and why to carry out each tip in the list.

❹ The text in each tip is brief and direct in its tone.

Reading Check

Identify Sequence In what kind of order does the writer list the tips?

Summarize Information In your own words, summarize the tips the article offers.

Draw Conclusions About Main Ideas Based on your reading of this article, what do you think are the most important things you can do to give hand-drawn artwork a professional look?

Read a Schematic

Here is the schematic that came with the scanner Devin purchased.

Kambara Super Scanner

❶ Document cover

❷ Home position

❸ Carriage and lamp

❹ Operate

❺ Scan start button

❻ USB connection

❶ The document cover must be closed for scanning to work properly.

❷ Align documents to be scanned with the top left-hand corner, or Home position.

❸ The Carriage is the surface on which documents are placed. The Lamp illuminates the documents to be scanned.

❹ The Operate button turns the scanner on and off.

❺ To start scanning, push the Scan start button.

❻ The USB connection allows the scanner to be connected to a computer.

Reading Check

Identify Sequence The information in the schematic is arranged in which type of logical sequence?

Evaluate Graphics How effective is the clarity and visual appeal of this graphic at conveying information? Explain.

Synthesize Information Based on your synthesis of the information in this schematic, what will Devin need to do to scan his cartoons?

Read Software Product Information

Here is the description for Devin's Comic Universe software program.

① The description provides a brief introduction to the software program.

② The writer uses headings that can help customers find the information they're looking for easily.

③ The clear, simple design makes the content easy to read.

④ The writer gives information that is important for readers to know.

Comic Universe

For drawing comics from scratch or manipulating scanned artwork, Comic Universe lets you create a personalized comic masterpiece in no time. **①**

Program Features

- **Layouts** Offers you more than 300 distinctive layout templates for you to turn your ideas into a professional-looking book. **②**

- **Original and Scanned Art** Allows you to draw original art or to enhance the appearance of scanned artwork.

- **Imported Art** Allows you to import photos/artwork from your own collection or from the application's extensive library of clipart.

- **Inking** Makes it possible for you to ink your drawings digitally. With the pen tool, you can trace and boldly outline drawings. **③**

- **Graphics** Includes an abundance of action-word graphics that you can position within the layout templates.

- **Text Balloons** Provides a wealth of caption boxes and text balloons or lets you easily create your own customized balloons.

- **Compatible Formats** Works with JPEG, BMP, GIF, and PNG. **④**

- **Online Sharing** Permits you to save the finished comic as a PDF or HTML file so that you can share it online with family and friends.

- **Coloring** Combines paint and erase tools so that you can create visually exciting images.

"We highly recommend this product for budding and established comic artists. It can turn their creative ideas into high-quality comics."

—Comics Galore

Reading Check

Identify Sequence Where in the document should the section "Coloring" be moved so that information is presented in a logical order?

Paraphrase Information In your own words, paraphrase the information under the heading "Imported Art."

Summarize Information Using your own words, describe the highlights of the Comic Universe software program.

Read an Installation Guide

Here is the installation guide that Devin used to install his new comic-book computer program.

Comic Universe Installation Guide ❶

1. Insert the Comic Universe installation disc into your computer's DVD-ROM drive.

2. Double-click the Comic Universe icon and follow the on-screen prompts.

3. Read the License Agreement. Click Continue. Click Agree. ❷

4. Enter your name, organization (optional), and your registration number, where appropriate. Your registration number is located inside the front cover of your user's manual. ❸
   *Please note that you must register your software in order to obtain technical support and important product updates. ❹

5. Click Register.

6. Click Install to perform the installation. If the installation doesn't proceed smoothly, refer to page 9 of the user's manual for troubleshooting information.

7. Once you have completed the installation process, click Exit.

---

❶ The title indicates the specific procedure to be explained.

❷ The writer gives direct and simple commands.

❸ The writer separates each step so that the steps are easy to follow.

❹ Additional information related to the registration process is provided.

Speaking and Listening
Following and giving instructions to perform specific tasks, answer questions, solve a problem, or complete a process related to technology is a common everyday speaking and listening task. To practice this skill, take turns with a partner to follow and give complex oral instructions about using or troubleshooting a problem with technology, such as a computer.

Reading Check

Identify Sequence The information in this Installation Guide is arranged in which type of logical sequence?

Clarify Information What is the benefit of registering the software?

Draw Conclusions About Meaning Why must readers perform the steps in the order in which they are presented?

After You Read

Respond and Think Critically

Directions: Read the questions about procedural texts and consumer documents below and select the best answer.

1. The **professional article** provides the LEAST information about
   A. preparing hand-drawn art for the scanner
   B. scanning the art
   C. enhancing the lines in the art
   D. adding color to the art

2. According to the information in the **schematic,** users must
   A. close the Document cover before scanning
   B. connect the scanner to a printer
   C. press Operate to start scanning
   D. clean the Carriage after each use

3. The **product information** description suggests that customers should purchase Comic Universe because it is
   A. unique
   B. fun to use
   C. inexpensive
   D. easy to use

4. According to the information in the **installation guide,** customers must register their software in order to
   A. obtain a refund for the cost of the software
   B. legally use the software
   C. receive updates to their program
   D. show their acceptance of the license agreement

Write Instructions

Assignment Write instructions that explain to other students how to transform information from a nondigital to a digital format. To get started, think about occasions when having a digital version of something might have made your life easier or helped you achieve a goal.

Once you have determined the content for your instructions, search on the Internet for sites related to your topic. Gather any information geared specifically toward that topic. Then use what you have learned to write organized and accurate instructions.

Get Ideas Make your instructions as useful as possible. Use the guidelines below to help you.

- **Know your audience.** When prewriting, determine your readers' level of familiarity with your topic and with the technical terms you plan to include. Anticipate any questions your readers might have. Then use what you have learned to come up with clear instructions that include easy-to-understand vocabulary and definitions for the technical terms.

- **Arrange your instructions in the right order.** Remember you can cause impatience, and even confusion, if you put your instructions in the wrong order.

- **Use a reader-friendly format.** Instructions are often presented in the form of a bulleted or numbered list, and bold type is used to emphasize key words and ideas.

Give It Structure When you are trying to explain a procedure to people, it is vital that you present information in a logical order. For example, for the creation of an online portfolio, if you told your readers to clean up and then select their best artwork, they would be thoroughly confused. If, on the other hand, you told them to choose and then clean up their best artwork, they would understand your instructions. To get the right order, try following your instructions yourself. Can you easily understand them, or do you find yourself confused in certain places? Based on what you have learned, arrange your instructions in the order that makes the most sense.

Before You Read

Build Background

Devin won the Dragon Fire Graphic Novel Contest and received a memo requesting he visit the publisher in San Antonio. He also received an envelope with **travel documents:** bus, train, and airplane **schedules** listing departure and arrival times; an **itinerary** specifying the activities that would occur; **a map** showing how to get from the airport, bus station, or train station to the publisher's office; and **walking instructions.** Devin also received a **written agenda** for each meeting.

In this lesson, you will learn how to read and interpret **travel documents** and **workplace documents,** such as these. You will also learn how to write **travel directions.** Here are strategies to help you with such documents.

Reading Preview

Review While reading, pause and summarize main points in a passage or steps in a procedure. If you want to go back and find a piece of information, **scan** the text. Look for key words or phrases and for section headings or terms in **boldfaced** type.

Visualize As you read, try to form a mental picture of what the author is describing. Turning an author's descriptions into mental images can help you better understand complex instructions, such as an involved set of directions or a complicated set of assembly instructions. In order to visualize, pay careful attention to the concrete nouns and active verbs the author uses. According to these details and your own imagination, how does one step relate to the next one in a set of instructions?

TEKS

For pages 1123–1129

10.11.B Synthesize information from multiple graphical sources to draw conclusions about the ideas presented (e.g., maps, charts).

Workplace Vocabulary

memo: a short, informal note that conveys important information

transportation schedule: a list of days and times of regular departures and arrivals

itinerary: a detailed plan for a journey or event

directions: instructions about how to get from one place to another

map: a flat representation of an area

meeting agenda: a list of things to be accomplished in a meeting

Read an Announcement Memo

Here is the memo Devin received informing him that he won the contest.

TO: Devin Gregory

FROM: Mark Jones

SUBJECT: Meetings

DATE: October 2, 2010 **❶**

Once again, I would like to send our heartfelt congratulations to you for winning the Dragon Fire Graphic Novel Contest! **❷** We are excited to be bringing your novel into print, and we look forward to meeting with you to discuss details. We have tentatively scheduled meetings for Thursday, November 3, between 2:00 and 5:30 P.M., and Friday, November 4, between 9:00 and 11:45 A.M. During the meetings, representatives from the publicity, production, and editorial departments will be on hand to discuss the schedule for the production and marketing of your novel, and to offer their advice and guidance. Our publicists will go over events related to the book's launch.

If you are unable to attend the meetings, please contact us immediately, so that we can find a date that is convenient for everyone. **❸** Next week, I will send you travel information, an itinerary, and agendas for the several meetings that will be held. If you have any questions in the meantime, you can contact me at (210) 555-1313 or send an e-mail to mjones@alamocomics.net. **❹**

❶ There is no salutation in a memo. One line space is placed between the headings and the message.

❷ All essential information is provided in the first paragraph.

❸ The second paragraph provides additional details.

❹ The contact information is succinctly summarized here.

Reading Check

Review Text Reread the first paragraph. What is the most important piece of information provided in this passage?

Make Inferences About Meaning From the clues given in the first paragraph, what inference can you draw about the publisher's plans for celebrating the release of the book?

Read a Train Schedule and Map

Once Devin confirmed his availability, Mark Jones sent him a train schedule and map to help him plan his trip to San Antonio.

Chicago–San Antonio Service

Train Name		Texas Roadrunner	Texas Cedar
Train Number		10	20
Days of Operation		Daily	Daily
	miles		
Chicago, IL	0	1:45P	6:00P
St. Louis, MO	284	7:45P	12:00A
Poplar Bluff, MO	453	11:40P	4:00A
Little Rock, AR	634	3:10A	7:30A
Texarkana, AR	774	6:00A	10:20A
Dallas, TX	991	12:00P	4:20A
Temple, TX	1150	5:15P	–
Taylor, TX	1188	6:00P	10:20P
San Antonio, TX	1306	10:30P	2:35A

Map of Train Route

- Chicago
- St. Louis
- Poplar Bluff
- Memphis
- Little Rock
- Texarkana
- Dallas
- Temple
- Taylor
- San Antonio

Reading Check

Synthesize Information Scan the train schedule and the map and synthesize the information. Based on the cities listed in each document, what can you conclude about the route that the Texas Roadrunner and the Texas Cedar take?

Make Inferences About Meaning Where will the Texas Roadrunner be at midnight of the first day of the journey from Chicago to San Antonio?

Identify Sequence In what **sequence**, or order, is the information in this schedule presented?

Read a Meeting Itinerary

Here is Devin's itinerary from Alamo Comics.

<table>
<tr><td>

① The date is set off in a separate line.

② The writer provides the timetable for each event.

③ A brief description of each event is included.

④ The writer gives the location for each event.

</td><td>

Thursday, November 3 ①

2:00–2:30 P.M.	Meet with Mark Jones, the contest judge and acquisitions editor at Alamo Comics—Suite 200
2:30–4:30 P.M.	Create a production schedule with production editor Sally Smith—Suite 200
4:30–5:00 P.M. **②**	Meet with copyeditor James Reinhart to discuss the editing style for the book—Suite 200
5:00–5:30 P.M.	Go over cover samples with designer Laura Albrecht—Suite 420
6:00 P.M.	Dinner at the Alamo Café

Friday, November 4

9:00–9:15 A.M.	Pose for a series of author photos—Building Lobby **③**
9:15–10:15 A.M.	Review the marketing schedule with publicity director Francis Adams—Suite 300
10:15–11:00 A.M.	Discuss details of book tours with publicist John Griffith—Suite 300
11:00–11:45 A.M.	Discuss details of book-release party with publicist Lisa Wrobel—Suite 300 **④**
12:00–1:00 P.M.	Lunch with staff members—Company Cafeteria

</td></tr>
</table>

Reading Check

Review Text Glance quickly over the timetables for the different activities. Has a sufficient amount of time been allotted for each activity? Explain.

Make Inferences About Meaning Who will Devin be meeting with at 10:30 Friday morning?

Identify Sequence Why does the writer list the timetable for each activity before he or she lists its location?

Read Written Directions and a Map

Because Devin will arrive in San Antonio late at night and is staying in a hotel near the Alamo, Mark Jones sent him walking directions from the Alamo to Alamo Comics. Study the walking directions and the map that Devin received.

Directions to Alamo Comics on Foot ❶

From the Alamo:

From the Alamo, walk east on E. Houston St. for about five blocks. You will pass a large hospital. When you get to N. Main Ave., turn right and walk north for another block until you reach number 300. The building is on the right side of the street. The walk should take about ten or fifteen minutes. ❷

❶ The purpose of the directions is stated clearly in the title.

❷ The information is presented in a step-by-step order.

❸ The arrows on the map show which direction Devin should walk in.

❹ Icons indicate important landmarks.

> **Speaking and Listening**
> Following and giving travel directions is a common everyday speaking and listening task. To practice this skill, take turns with a partner to follow and give complex oral directions to a certain destination, perhaps in your school, home, or even outdoors.

Reading Check

Evaluate Graphics Evaluate the map for the clarity of its graphics and its visual appeal. What could make the map clearer?

Synthesize Information Synthesize the information in the written directions with the information presented in the map. What helpful information does the map provide that the written directions do not? What helpful information do the written directions provide that the map does not? Explain.

Draw Conclusions About Information Based on the information presented in the written directions and the map, what can you conclude about the type of information that is more likely to appear in written directions?

Read a Meeting Agenda

Here is one of the meeting agendas that Mark Jones mailed to Devin.

① The purpose of the meeting is clearly stated in the title.

② The date, time, and place of the meeting follow the title.

③ The items are listed in the order in which they will be discussed.

④ A timetable is provided for each of the topics to be discussed.

Creating a production schedule for *Kosmo Fantastic Versus Mr. Meriadeck* ①

Thursday, November 3, 2010 **②**
2:30 P.M.–4:30 P.M.
Alamo Comics, 300 N. Main Avenue, Suite 200

③

Overview of the stages of book production by Sally Smith.......... 2:30 P.M.

Discussion: Establishing dates for editing steps .... 3:00 P.M.

Coffee/tea break .... 3:30 P.M.

Discussion: Establishing dates for design steps.......................... 3:45 P.M. **④**

Discussion: Creating timetable for proofreading,[1] indexing, and author book review... 4:00 P.M.

Wrap-up...4:15 P.M.

---

1. **proofreading:** reading printed materials for the purpose of identifying and correcting mistakes

Reading Check

Summarize Text Go back over the agenda. Then state, in your own words, the topics that will be covered during the meeting.

Clarify Meaning How much time does the agenda allow for a coffee/tea break?

Determine Main Idea Look carefully at the items in this agenda. Based on these items, what do you think is the main purpose of the meeting?

Speaking and Listening
Following and giving instructions to perform specific tasks, answer questions, solve a problem, or complete a process is a common everyday speaking and listening task. To practice this skill, take turns with a partner to follow and give complex oral instructions about the points you want to cover in an agenda for a meeting of your choosing (for example, a meeting to plan your sports team's Web site). Take notes during your discussion and then write up the agenda.

After You Read

Respond and Think Critically

Directions: Read the questions about workplace and procedural documents below and select the best answer.

1. Which of the following BEST describes the purpose of the **memo**?
  A. to provide information about the production schedule for the book
  B. to summarize the company's marketing plans for the book
  C. to indicate when and where important meetings will occur
  D. to congratulate the author on winning the graphic novel contest

2. Which of the following is NOT covered within the **train schedule**?
  A. the trains' point of departure
  B. the trains' names and numbers
  C. the mileage for the trip
  D. the fares for different classes

3. By synthesizing the information in the **written directions** and the **map,** what can you conclude about the advantages of written directions in general?
  A. They include travel time and landmarks.
  B. They list all the streets on the way to a destination.
  C. They include twists and turns in streets.
  D. They make visualizing compass points easier.

4. Which of the following is NOT one of the purposes served by the **meeting agenda**?
  A. to help participants prepare for the meeting
  B. to inform participants how much time is scheduled for each part of the meeting
  C. to provide an overview of the goals of the meeting
  D. to note future action items

Write Travel Directions

Assignment Imagine that a group of your friends is meeting at an unfamiliar location to plan an upcoming event, and you have been asked to write directions on how to get there from your school. To get started, locate your school and the meeting place on a map of your hometown and trace the path from one place to the other. Then write a clear set of directions that your friends could follow to get to the location from your school. Be sure to include street, route, and highway names in your directions, as well as distances between places.

Get Ideas To be effective, directions must meet the following criteria:

- The directions must contain accurate and detailed instructions. If you tell your readers, for example, to turn left when you mean right, they might not end up in the correct location.

- The directions can include comprehension aids, such as graphic elements and alternate scenarios. Arrows and U-turn, start and finish signs, for instance, can help readers follow your directions. Providing an alternative route in the event a certain highway or road is closed is also important.

Give It Structure Graphic elements can contribute to good directions, since they can help clarify the actions readers need to take. The inclusion of arrows, for example, in a set of directions can help readers quickly and easily determine when and where they need to make a turn. Before you give your directions to your friends, evaluate your text for the clarity of its graphics and its visual appeal. Check the accuracy of your directions by synthesizing what you wrote with the information on a map of the area. If you conclude that something in your directions is wrong or vague, revise accordingly.

Before You Read

Build Background

During his visit to San Antonio, Devin signed his contract and met with publicists at Alamo Comics to develop a marketing plan. They decided that a great way to generate publicity for the novel was to produce a **pamphlet** that would convince readers that the book was fresh and exciting.

Devin resolved to create a **Web site** for other emerging graphic artists that would provide them with information on imagining, creating, and publishing graphic novels. On his site, he included appropriate, appealing graphics and easy-to-read text.

Reading Preview

Here are effective strategies for reading and understanding documents such as contracts, pamphlets, and Web sites.

Determine Main Idea To increase your comprehension, identify the **main idea** of individual paragraphs and passages. First look at the major points the writer is making. Which one seems to be most important? The main idea of a paragraph is the basic point the writer is making in that paragraph.

Some writers directly state the main idea in a topic sentence. When writers imply a main idea, readers need to put examples and clues together to identify the main idea. Once you determine the main idea, you can use the **supporting details** to learn additional information about it.

Analyze Cause-and-Effect Relationships A cause-and-effect relationship exists when one event causes another to happen. If you can answer *why* something happened, you know its cause. If you can answer *what happened as a result of* something, you know the effect. Words and phrases such as *because, as a result,* and *consequently* often signal cause-and-effect relationships.

TEKS

For pages 1130–1135

10.11 Understand how to glean and use information in procedural texts and documents.

Workplace Vocabulary

pamphlet: a short printed publication that is usually stitched or stapled together

contract: an agreement between two or more parties to do or not to do something

Web site: a group of interrelated Web pages devoted to one or more topics

Read a Pamphlet

Here is the pamphlet from Alamo Comics.

New and Notable Graphic Novels

At Alamo Comics, we publish graphic novels with striking illustrations and themes that are meaningful to readers of all ages. Here are three upcoming graphic novels that we believe fit this bill. ❶

❷ **Paris: City of Light** by Emma Lyons

When Peter Jones accepts a professional opportunity in Paris, his thirteen-year-old son Jack and fourteen-year-old daughter Helen must go with him. The move from northern Michigan to the city of light disrupts everything that is important to Jack. But when he meets fifteen-year-old Jean in the Jardin du Luxembourg, this budding friendship helps Jack appreciate his new home. ❸

Kosmo Fantastic Versus Mr. Meriadeck by Devin Gregory

Orphaned teenager Kosmo Fantastic must defeat the evil Mr. Meriadeck before his planet, Bork Bersi, comes to an end. In Kosmo Fantastic's most difficult hour, he is joined by the powerful and cunning Lady in Red. ❹

The Girl Who Went Back by Ty Mooney

Award-winning cartoonist Ty Mooney tells the story of high-school student Melissa Johnson, who lives with her grandparents on the South Side of Chicago in the 1970s. Melissa discovers that her parents met after their arrest during the Montgomery Bus Boycott in 1956. As she learns more about the story of the Civil Rights Movement in the Deep South and the courage of its participants, she develops a deep pride in the parents she never knew.

❶ The topic of the pamphlet is stated clearly in the introduction.

❷ The pamphlet uses bold type to draw the reader's attention to the titles of the novels.

❸ All text is flush left.

❹ The pamphlet provides a succinct and engaging summary of each novel.

Reading Check

Determine Main Idea In the description of *Paris: City of Light,* what sentence contains the main idea?

Analyze Cause-and-Effect Relationships In the description of *Kosmo Fantastic Versus Mr. Meriadeck,* what causes Kosmo to fight Mr. Meriadeck?

Compare and Contrast Style Look carefully at the descriptions of the three novels. How are the styles of the descriptions similar and different?

Read a Contract

PUBLISHING CONTRACT

THIS AGREEMENT, made and entered into this _____5th_____ day of _____November_____, 20_10_, by and between _____Devin Gregory_____, hereinafter referred to as the Author, and Alamo Comics, hereinafter referred to as the Publisher. **❶**

Grant The Author hereby grants to the Publisher the exclusive English-language rights to publish throughout the world _Kosmo Fantastic Versus Mr. Meriadeck,_ hereinafter referred to as the Work. **❷**

Author Warranties and Representations The Author affirms that he is the sole owner of the Work, and that it is entirely original. The Author warrants that the Work does not violate any copyright or other intellectual property right or any personal right of any person or entity, and that the Work does not contain any libel[1] or obscenity. The Author agrees to indemnify[2] and hold the Publisher harmless from any liability, damage, cost, and expense in connection with any claim, action, or proceeding inconsistent with Author's warranties.

Publication and Selling Price

The Publisher shall publish the Work no later than 14 months after this contract is signed. The Publisher agrees to assign to the Work a retail price that is comparable to other works of a similar length and format.

Copyright The Author shall exclusively own the copyright of the Work. In each copy of the Work, the Publisher shall include a notice recognizing the Author as the copyright owner, per U.S. Copyright Act.

Royalty Payments The Publisher shall pay to the Author the following royalty[3] commissions. For electronic copies of the work, the Publisher shall pay the author 50% of net profits. For printed copies of the work, the Publisher shall pay the author 25% of net profits. **❸** The Publisher shall send the Author quarterly royalty statements on the following dates: September 1, December 1, March 1, and June 1. Royalties collected for the quarter shall accompany the statement. **❹**

---

❶ A space is provided for the date of the signing, and for the name of the author.

❷ Under the heading "Grant," the contract indicates that Alamo Comics will be the *only* publisher putting out the book.

❸ The contract clearly states what percentage of the sales the author will receive.

❹ The contract clearly indicates when the author will receive his share of the net profits.

---

1. **libel:** any false or malicious words or pictures that damage a person's reputation

2. **indemnify:** to compensate for expense brought on by oneself

3. **royalty:** share of the sales from a work

Termination

Either the Author or Publisher may terminate this contract with a ninety (90) day written notice, to be sent by a traceable mail service. At the time of the termination, all rights granted to the Publisher shall return to the Author and final royalty payments shall be made.

Signatures The two parties have read this contract and agree to the terms laid out herein. _____ Author

_____Publisher

5

5 Lines are provided for the signatures of the two parties.

Reading Check

Paraphrase Information Restate in your own words the information in "Author Warranties and Representations."

Analyze Cause-and-Effect Relationships What might happen if the author submitted a work that was not entirely original?

Determine Main Idea What is the main idea of the "Termination" section?

Read a Web Site

Devin reviewed these Web sites for other emerging comic artists.

How to Write a Graphic Novel This Web site will introduce you to other Web sites that contain information on imagining, creating, and publishing graphic novels.

Annotated Links

Adobe Photoshop Elements 2.0 President's Day Project

http://www.adobe.com/education/pdf/pse_tutorials/presidents_day.pdf **❶** This site takes readers through the process of creating a comic book using original hand-drawn art. It teaches how to add color to original art and how to create layout pages using Adobe Photoshop Elements.

Creating Comics **❷** http://members.shaw.ca/creatingcomics/

Creating comics provides writers and artists with various resources related to making and publishing comic books. Here you'll find links to sites that can help you with writing, illustrating, lettering, submitting, self-publishing, and publicizing.

Time Magazine http://www.time.com/time/2005/100books/0,24459,graphic_novels,00.html
A brief, engaging description for the ten best graphic novels ever written is provided on this Web site. Reading these descriptions can help you determine what makes a graphic novel exciting. **❸**

wisegeek/What are Different Types of Comic Books? http://www.wisegeek.com/what-are-different-types-of-comic-books.htm

This site provides definitions for some of the most popular comic-book genres, including superhero, alternative/esoteric, horror, humor, fantasy, action/adventure, science fiction, and manga. Look through the site to expand your ideas about suitable topics and themes for graphic novels.

❶ The writer accurately reproduces the URL (uniform resource locator) for each Web site. For more information about citing Web resources, go to pages R40–R43.

❷ The title of each Web site is included.

❸ The writer provides a concise description of each site and conveys its value or relevance.

Reading Check

Summarize Main Ideas In your own words, state the main ideas conveyed in the introductory paragraph.

Analyze Cause-and-Effect Relationships According to the description of the *Time Magazine* site, what can be an effect of reading its descriptions of great graphic novels?

Determine Main Idea What is the main idea of the description of the Wisegeek site?

After You Read

Respond and Think Critically

Directions: Read the questions about workplace and procedural documents below and select the best answer.

1. What is the main purpose of the **pamphlet**?
   - **A.** to inform readers of new titles
   - **B.** to describe the themes of new titles
   - **C.** to specify the price of new titles
   - **D.** to provide the publication dates for new titles

2. The **contract** provides the LEAST information on
   - **A.** ownership of the copyright of the novel
   - **B.** ownership of characters
   - **C.** the publication and selling price of the novel
   - **D.** the dates for royalty payments

3. Which of the following would make the **contract** easier to understand?
   - **A.** an explanation of the publisher's marketing strategy
   - **B.** the inclusion of a specific price for the novel
   - **C.** the inclusion of sample pages from the novel
   - **D.** an explanation of legal terms

4. Devin's **Web site** is an example of synthesis because it
   - **A.** includes information from only one graphical source
   - **B.** includes only information that Devin created
   - **C.** summarizes how to write a graphic novel
   - **D.** includes information based on multiple graphical sources

Write Annotations

Assignment Think about a topic that fascinates you and that will be of wide interest to other students. Then create a list of annotated links to Web sites that are related to your given topic. For each link, write a brief note summarizing the content of the site and explaining its value or significance. Refer to examples of annotated bibliographies for guidance on what exactly you should include. After writing, check to make sure that all of your links are relevant to your topic and are free of spelling, punctuation, and grammatical errors.

Get Ideas Below are a few guidelines for writing links that will help browsers find the information they're looking for easily and quickly.

- Keep your language simple and concise. Convoluted writing or complex words will confuse browsers, causing them to move on.

- Use language that conveys the central ideas, or organizing thoughts, of the site.

- Write text that is appropriate for your intended audience.

- List the links in a logical order. You may, for instance, wish to follow the style of an annotated bibliography by arranging links alphabetically.

Give It Structure When writing an explanatory note for a site, it is important to summarize the central topics that are covered. Begin by carefully reading the text on a site and writing down your findings and impressions. What is the purpose of the site? What are the most important ideas? Use your answers to these questions to write a brief summary.

After completing your summary, add a sentence explaining how the site was useful to you. You may also wish to briefly describe the site's strengths and weaknesses.

Reference Section

Literary Terms Handbook

A

Act A major unit of a drama, or *play*. A play may be subdivided into several acts. Many modern plays have one, two, or three acts. Older dramas often have five acts. Acts may be divided into one or more scenes. **(Acto)**

See page 626.

See also *DRAMA, SCENE.*

Allegory A literary work in which all or most of the characters, settings, and events stand for ideas, qualities, or figures beyond themselves. The overall purpose of an allegory is to teach a moral lesson. **(Alegoría)**

See page 58.

See also *MORAL, SYMBOL.*

Alliteration The repetition of consonant sounds at the beginnings of nonrhyming words or syllables in neighboring words, as in "towering, trembling pine-trees." Alliteration differs from *consonance,* in which consonants repeat at the ends of nonrhyming words or stressed syllables. Alliteration gives emphasis to words and is commonly used in poetry. Alliteration may occur with vowel sounds as well. **(Aliteración)**

See page 566.

See also *CONSONANCE, SOUND DEVICES.*

Allusion An indirect reference to a well-known person, character, place, event, concept, or literary work. An allusion is different from a quotation because it does not give the source of the reference; the reader is expected to know it. For example, in "I've Been to the Mountaintop," Martin Luther King Jr. refers to "Pharaoh" supporting slavery in Egypt. This allusion is to the biblical Pharaoh who enslaved the Israelites until Moses led them out of Egypt. **(Alusión)**

See page 376.

Analogy A comparison that shows similarities between two things that are otherwise dissimilar. A writer may use an analogy to explain something unfamiliar by comparing it to something familiar. In literature, most analogies are expressed in metaphors or similes. **(Analogía)**

See page 1047.

See also *METAPHOR, RHETORICAL DEVICES, SIMILE.*

Anecdote A brief story based on a single interesting event from a person's life. Anecdotes are intended to make a point. Writers and speakers often use anecdotes to support their opinions, clarify their ideas, grab the audience's attention, reveal aspects of a person's character, or entertain. **(Anécdota)**

See page 292.

Antagonist A person or a force in society or nature that opposes the *protagonist,* or central character, in a story or drama. The reader is generally not meant to sympathize with the antagonist. Mark Antony is Brutus's antagonist in Shakespeare's *Julius Caesar.* **(Antagonista)**

See page 637.

See also *CHARACTER, CONFLICT, PROTAGONIST.*

Anthropomorphism Representing animals, gods, or objects as if they had human emotions and intelligence. It is a key element in fables, in which the main characters are often animals, as well as in myths, in which gods and animals may be the main characters. **(Antropomorfismo)**

See also *FABLE, MYTH.*

Antithesis The technique of putting opposite ideas side-by-side in order to point out their differences or to draw attention to the superiority of one. Antithesis is often used in logical argument. **(Antítesis)**

See also *ARGUMENT, PERSUASION.*

Aphorism A short, pointed statement that expresses a wise or clever observation about human experience. **(Aforismo)**

Apostrophe A figure of speech in which a speaker addresses an inanimate object, an idea, or an absent person. In Emily Dickinson's poem "Heart! We Will Forget Him!," the speaker addresses her own heart. **(Apóstrofe)**

See also *PERSONIFICATION.*

Archetype Ideas, characters, stories, or images that are common to human experience across cultures and throughout the world. In their purest form, archetypes occur in oral tradition, but they also appear in written works of literature. They can be divided into categories. The *character archetype* includes familiar individuals such as the wise leader, the rebel, the damsel in distress, and the traitor. Coyote, the trickster of Native American folklore, is a character archetype. An *image archetype* is an object or a place that has universal symbolism. For example, a rose symbolizes love. A *plot pattern archetype* is a story pattern or type that occurs in many cultures. The story of a hero who embarks on a dangerous quest follows an archetypal plot. A *theme archetype* is an idea that occurs wherever people tell stories. The idea that good can overcome evil, that people can redeem themselves, or that an underworld exists are all archetypal themes. **(Arquetipo)**

See pages 935 and 945.

See also *FOLKLORE, MYTH, ORAL TRADITION, STOCK CHARACTER, SYMBOL.*

Argument In persuasion, a statement of opinion about a problem or an issue and the support for the statement. The statement is called the *proposition*, which includes a call to think about or take action on the problem or issue. The *support* includes reasons and evidence. Reasons explain why someone should accept the proposition. *Evidence* consists of examples, facts, and expert opinions. Most arguments make use of persuasive techniques such as appeals to logic (facts and logical thinking, or reasoning), emotion (shared feelings), ethics (shared values or beliefs), and authority (reliable sources). Strong arguments often include a *counterargument,* a brief argument that attempts to disprove opposing opinions about the problem or issue. **(Argumento)**

See page 392.

See also *LOGIC, PERSUASION.*

Aside In a drama, a character's comment that is directed to the audience or another character but is not heard by any other characters on the stage. The character typically turns to one side—or "aside"—away from the action onstage. Asides, which are rare in modern drama, reveal what a character is thinking or feeling. For example, Act 2, Scene 2, of Shakespeare's *Julius Caesar* includes the following exchange: **(Aparte)**

> CAESAR. Be near me, that I may remember you.
>
> TREBONIUS. Caesar, I will [*Aside.*] and so near will I be, / That your best friends shall wish I had been further.

See page 691.

See also *SOLILOQUY.*

Assonance The repetition of the same or similar vowel sounds in the stressed syllables of neighboring nonrhyming words, as in "dreaming of wheat fields." The repeated vowel sounds of each word are typically preceded and followed by different consonants than in the other words. Assonance differs from *consonance,* in which consonants repeat at the ends of nonrhyming words or stressed syllables. Assonance creates a pleasing combination of sounds and is commonly used in poetry. **(Asonancia)**

See page 573.

See also *CONSONANCE, SOUND DEVICES.*

Atmosphere The dominant emotional feeling of a literary work that contributes to the mood. Authors create atmosphere primarily through details of setting, such as time, place, and weather. The description of the rooms at the ball in Edgar Allan Poe's "The Masque of the Red Death" builds an atmosphere of suspense and foreboding. **(Atmósfera)**

See also *MOOD.*

Author's perspective The combination of experiences, values, and ideas that shape the way the author looks at the world or at a particular subject. **(Perspectiva del autor)**

See also *TONE.*

Author's purpose An author's intent in writing a literary work. Authors typically write for one or more of the following purposes: to persuade, to inform, to explain, to entertain, or to describe. **(Propósito del autor)**

See pages 801 and 1061.

See also *DICTION, STYLE, THEME, TONE.*

Autobiography The story of a person's life, written by that person. The author typically focuses on the most significant events in his or her life. Autobiographies give insights into the author's view of himself or herself and of the society in which he or she lived. **(Autobiografía)**

See page 255.

See also *BIOGRAPHY, MEMOIR, NONFICTION.*

B

Ballad A narrative poem originally meant to be sung or recited. *Folk ballads,* which usually tell of an exciting or dramatic episode, were passed on by word of mouth for generations before being written down. *Literary ballads* are written in imitation of folk ballads. **(Balada)**

See page 554.

See also *FOLKLORE, NARRATIVE POETRY, ORAL TRADITION.*

Bias A leaning toward a certain opinion or position on a topic, possibly arising from prejudice. **(Sesgo)**

Biography A nonfiction account of a person's life written by another person. Biographies can be short or book-length. They can even span several volumes. **(Biografía)**

See also *AUTOBIOGRAPHY, JOURNAL, MEMOIR.*

Blank verse Poetry or lines of dramatic verse written in unrhymed *iambic pentameter.* Each line of iambic pentameter has five units, or *feet,* with each foot made up of an unstressed syllable followed by a stressed syllable. Because it may attempt to imitate spoken language, every line need not be perfectly regular. Much of Shakespeare's work is written in blank verse.

The following line, spoken by Mark Antony in Act 3, Scene 1, of Shakespeare's *Julius Caesar,* is an example of blank verse: **(Verso blanco)**

O / pardon me / thou bleed / ing piece /

of earth . . .

See page 691.

See also *FOOT, IAMB, METER, RHYTHM*

C

Character An individual in a literary work of fiction, drama, or narrative poetry. *Main characters* are central to the story and are typically fully developed. *Minor characters* display few personality traits and are used to help develop the story. A character who shows varied and sometimes contradictory traits, such as the daughter in Amy Tan's "Two Kinds," is a *round character.* A character who reveals only one personality trait is called a *flat character.* A *stock character* is a flat character of a familiar and often-repeated type. A *dynamic character,* such as Luis in Judith Ortiz Cofer's "Catch the Moon," changes during the story. A *static character,* such as Luis's father, remains the same throughout the story. **(Personaje)**

See pages 96 and 103.

See also *ANTAGONIST, CHARACTERIZATION, FOIL, STEREOTYPE, STOCK CHARACTER, PROTAGONIST.*

Character archetype See *ARCHETYPE.*

Characterization The methods a writer uses to develop a character. In *direct characterization,* the writer makes direct statements about a character. In *indirect characterization,* the writer reveals a character's personality through that individual's words, thoughts, and actions and through what other characters think and say about that character. These techniques are frequently blended. **(Caracterización)**

See pages 124 and 827.

See also *CHARACTER.*

Climax See also *PLOT.*

Colloquialism A word or phrase used in everyday conversation but not in formal writing or speech. **(Expresión coloquial)**

See also *DIALECT, IDIOM.*

Comedy A type of drama that is humorous and often has a happy ending. **(Comedia)**

See page 798.

See also *DRAMA, FARCE, HUMOR, PARODY, SATIRE.*

Comic relief A humorous scene, an event, or a speech in a drama with a serious mood. It provides relief from emotional intensity, while at the same time highlighting the seriousness of the story. **(Alivio cómico)**

Conflict The central struggle between opposing forces in a story or drama. An *external conflict* exists when a character struggles against some outside force, such as another person, nature, society, or fate. In Doris Lessing's "Through the Tunnel," for example, when Jerry tries to swim through the tunnel, he is involved in an external conflict with nature. An *internal conflict* exists within the mind of a character who is torn between opposing feelings or goals. Jerry wrestles with an internal conflict when he tries to overcome his fear in order to swim through the tunnel. **(Conflicto)**

See page 18.

See also *ANTAGONIST, PLOT, PROTAGONIST.*

Connotation The suggested or implied meanings associated with a word beyond its dictionary definition, or *denotation.* A word can have a positive, negative, or neutral connotation. **(Connotación)**

See also *DENOTATION.*

Consonance The repetition of consonant sounds at the ends of nonrhyming words or stressed syllables, as in "morning in the barn." Consonance is different from *alliteration,* in which consonants repeat at the beginnings of words or syllables. It also differs from *assonance,* which is a repetition of vowel sounds in stressed syllables. Consonance creates a pleasing combination of sounds and is commonly used in poetry. **(Consonancia)**

See page 573.

See also *ALLITERATION, ASSONANCE, SOUND DEVICES.*

Context Anything beyond the specific words of a literary work that may be relevant to understanding the meaning. Contexts may be cultural, historical, literary, social, economic, political, and so on. The social, cultural, and political context of America during the Civil Rights Movement, for example, all have relevance for understanding the works of African American writers of that period. Context can also refer to a part of a work of literature that precedes or follows a specific word, phrase, or passage, which can be used to clarify meaning. **(Contexto)**

Couplet Two consecutive, often rhymed lines of poetry that work together as a unit to make a point or to express an idea. The last two lines of Shakespeare's "Shall I Compare Thee to a Summer's Day?" are a couplet. **(Pareado)**

See also *RHYME, SONNET, STANZA.*

Critique A critical analysis or thoughtful evaluation of a literary work. **(Crítica)**

See *LITERARY CRITICISM.*

D

Denotation The literal, or dictionary, meaning of a word. **(Denotación)**

See also *CONNOTATION.*

Denouement See *PLOT.*

Description Writing that seeks to convey the impression of a setting, a person, an animal, an object, or an event by appealing to the senses. Almost all writing, fiction and nonfiction, contains elements of description. **(Descripción)**

See pages 89 and 998.

See also *FIGURATIVE LANGUAGE, IMAGERY.*

Descriptive essay See *ESSAY.*

Dialect A variation of a language spoken within a particular region or by a particular social or ethnic group. Dialects may differ from the standard form of a language in vocabulary, expressions, pronunciation, or grammar. For example, the following lines from Langston Hughes's "Motto" make use of a dialect spoken by jazz musicians in the 1920s: **(Dialecto)**

> I play it cool
> And dig all jive

See page 49.

See also *IDIOM.*

Dialogue Conversation between characters in a literary work. Dialogue can contribute to characterization, create mood, advance the plot, and develop theme. **(Diálogo)**

See pages 883 and 919.

See also *CHARACTERIZATION.*

Diction A writer's choice of words. Diction is an important element in a writer's voice or style. Skilled writers choose their words carefully to convey a particular meaning or feeling. **(Dicción)**

See pages 520, 550, and 1001.

See also *CONNOTATION, STYLE, TONE, VOICE.*

Drama A story written to be performed by actors before an audience. Most dramas written before the mid-1800s can be divided into two basic types: tragedy and comedy. The script of a dramatic work, or *play*, includes dialogue (the words the actors speak) and often stage directions (descriptions of the action and scenery). A drama may be divided into acts, which may also be broken up into scenes, indicating changes in location or the passage of time. **(Drama)**

See page 798.

See also *ACT, COMEDY, DIALOGUE, SCENE, SCRIPT, STAGE DIRECTIONS, TRAGEDY.*

Dramatic irony See *IRONY.*

Dramatic monologue A form of dramatic poetry in which a speaker addresses a silent listener. **(Monólogo dramático)**

See also *DRAMATIC POETRY, MONOLOGUE.*

Dramatic poetry Poetry in which characters are revealed through dialogue and monologue, as well as through description. **(Poesía dramática)**

See also *DIALOGUE, DRAMATIC MONOLOGUE.*

Dynamic character See *CHARACTER.*

E

Elegy A serious poem mourning a death or a great loss. **(Elegía)**

End rhyme **(Rima consonante)** See *RHYME.*

End-stopped line A line of poetry that ends in a punctuation mark. An end-stopped line usually contains a complete thought or image. The following example from William Butler Yeats's "He Wishes for the Cloths of Heaven," contains an end-stopped line: **(Verso suspendido)**

> I have spread my dreams under your feet;
> Tread softly because you tread on my dreams.

See also *ENJAMBMENT.*

Enjambment The continuation of a sentence or phrase from one line of a poem to the next, without a pause between the lines. The following lines from Robert Hayden's "Those Winter Sundays" are an example of enjambment:

> What did I know, what did I know
> of love's austere and lonely offices.

Enjambment enables poets to create a conversational tone, breaking lines at points where people would normally pause in conversation yet still maintaining the unity of thought. **(Encabalgamiento)**

See page 460.

See also *END-STOPPED LINE.*

Epic A long narrative poem, written in a dignified style, that celebrates the adventures and achievements of one or more heroic figures of legend, history, or religion. The *epic hero* is usually a person of high social status who reflects the ideals of his or her people. Epic plots typically involve supernatural events, long time periods, distant journeys, and life-and-death struggles between good and evil. Some modern versions of traditional epics are written in prose form. **(Épica)**

See page 925.

See also *NARRATIVE POETRY, ORAL TRADITION.*

Epic hero See *EPIC, HERO.*

Essay A short work of nonfiction on a single topic. The purpose of the essay is to communicate an idea or opinion. *Descriptive essays* describe a person, place, or thing. *Narrative essays* relate true stories. *Persuasive essays* promote an opinion. *Expository essays* explain or inform, usually in an objective way. *Reflective essays* reveal an author's observations on a subject. Essays fall into two categories, according to their style. A *formal essay* is serious and impersonal, often with the purpose of instructing or persuading. Typically, the author strikes a serious tone and develops a main idea, or *thesis,* in a logical, highly organized way. An *informal,* or *personal essay,* entertains while it informs, usually in light, conversational style. **(Ensayo)**

See pages 336–337 and 339.

See also *NONFICTION, STYLE, THESIS.*

Exaggeration See *HYPERBOLE.*

Exposition See *PLOT.*

Extended metaphor A metaphor that compares two unlike things in various ways throughout a paragraph, stanza, or an entire work. William Shakespeare uses an extended metaphor in the poem "Shall I Compare Thee to a Summer's Day?" **(Metáfora extendida)**

See also *METAPHOR.*

F

Fable A short, simple tale that teaches a moral, or lesson, about human behavior. The characters in a fable are often animals who speak and act like people. The moral is usually stated outright. A *modern fable* features flat human characters and a theme about human behavior. **(Fábula)**

See also *CHARACTER, MORAL, PARABLE, THEME.*

Falling action See *PLOT.*

Fantasy A literary work, usually set in an imaginary world or a distant, heroic past. Fantasy stories may include fantastical or supernatural beings and forces as well as magic. **(Fantasía)**

See page 992.

See also *GENRE, SCIENCE FICTION.*

Farce A type of comedy with stereotyped characters in ridiculous situations. **(Farsa)**

See page 801.

See also *COMEDY, HUMOR, PARODY, SATIRE.*

Fiction A prose narrative in which situations and characters are invented by the writer. Fiction includes both short stories and novels. Some aspects of a fictional work may be based on fact or experience. **(Ficción)**

See also *DRAMA, NONFICTION, NOVEL, SHORT STORY.*

Figurative language Language used for descriptive effect, often to imply ideas indirectly. Expressions of figurative language are not literally true but express some truth beyond the literal level. For example, "Ed is tall and skinny like my brother" is not figurative; "Ed is as tall and skinny as a flagpole" is figurative. Figurative language is especially common in poetry. Types of figurative language include hyperbole, metaphor, personification, simile, and understatement. **(Lenguaje figurado)**

See page 734.

See also *ANALOGY, FIGURE OF SPEECH, HYPERBOLE, METAPHOR, OXYMORON, PERSONIFICATION, SIMILE, SYMBOL, UNDERSTATEMENT.*

Figure of speech Figurative language of a specific kind, such as metaphor, personification, or simile. **(Figura retórica)**

See *FIGURATIVE LANGUAGE.*

Flashback An interruption in the chronological order of a narrative to describe an event that happened earlier. A flashback gives readers information that may help explain the main events of the story. For example, in Leslie Marmon Silko's "Lullaby," the narrator includes a flashback to the day Ayah and Chato found out that Jimmie had died. **(Retrospectiva)**

See page 11.

See also *PLOT.*

Flat character See *CHARACTER.*

Foil A character who provides a strong contrast to another character, usually a main character. By using a foil, a writer calls attention to the strengths or weaknesses of a character. For example, the self-controlled Octavius is a foil to the excitable Mark Antony in Shakespeare's *Julius Caesar.* **(Contrapunto)**

See page 757.

See also *ANTAGONIST, CHARACTER.*

Folklore The traditional beliefs, customs, stories, songs, and dances of a culture. Folklore is based in the concerns of ordinary people and is passed down through oral tradition. **(Folclor)**

See also *BALLAD, EPIC, FOLKTALE, LEGEND, MYTH, ORAL TRADITION.*

Folktale A traditional story passed down orally long before being written down. Generally the author of a folktale is anonymous. Folktales include fables, fairy tales, myths, legends, and tall tales. **(Cuento popular)**

See also *EPIC, FABLE, FOLKLORE, LEGEND, MYTH, ORAL TRADITION, TALL TALE.*

Foot The basic unit in the measurement of a line of metrical poetry. A foot usually contains one stressed syllable (ʹ) and one or more unstressed syllables (˘). **(Pie)**

See also *METER, RHYTHM, SCANSION.*

Foreshadowing An author's use of clues or hints to prepare readers for events that will happen later in a story. **(Prefiguración)**

See page 39.

See also *PLOT, SUSPENSE.*

Form The organizing principle that shapes a work of literature. Form gives expression to the content and may refer to aspects beyond external patterns and structure, such as established criteria related to genre. Form can be categorized as *closed,* meaning formal or conventional, or *open,* meaning informal or organic. Applied to poetry, closed form is typical of genres such as the sonnet, while open form is typical of free verse. Applied to fiction, closed form is common in myths and fables, while open form is common in short stories and novels. **(Forma)**

See pages 452–453.

See also *GENRE, STRUCTURE.*

Formal essay See *ESSAY.*

Frame story A plot structure that includes the telling of a story within a story. The frame is the outer story, which usually precedes and follows the inner, more important story. Some literary works have frames that bind together many different stories. **(Metaficción)**

See also *STRUCTURE.*

Free verse Poetry that has no fixed pattern of meter, rhyme, line length, or stanza arrangement. Gwendolyn Brooks's "Horses Graze" is a poem composed in free verse. Although poets who write free verse ignore traditional rules, they use techniques such as repetition and alliteration to create musical patterns in their poems. **(Verso libre)**

See page 475.

See also *FORM, SOUND DEVICES.*

G

Genre A category or type of literature. The main literary genres are prose, poetry, and drama. Each of these is divided into smaller genres. For example, prose includes fiction (such as novels, short stories, and folktales) and nonfiction (such as biography, autobiography, and essays). The term also refers to subcategories of literature. For example, fantasy and science fiction are genres of fiction. **(Género)**

See also *PROSE, POETRY, DRAMA.*

Gothic literature A novel or short story that has a gloomy, ominous setting and contains strong elements of horror, mystery, and the supernatural. **(Literatura gótica)**

H

Haiku A traditional Japanese form of poetry that has three lines and seventeen syllables. The first and third lines have five syllables each; the second line has seven syllables. A haiku presents striking imagery. The purpose of traditional haiku is to capture a flash of insight that occurs during an observation of nature. **(Haikú)**

See page 495.
See also *IMAGERY, TANKA.*

Hero The main character in a literary work, typically a character whose qualities or deeds arouse admiration. The term can refer to either a female or male. **(Héroe)**

See also *EPIC, LEGEND, MYTH, PROTAGONIST, TRAGEDY.*

Historical fiction A narrative that sets fictional characters against the historical backdrop of a period different from the author's. The story contains many details about the period in which it is set. Some actual historical people may also be included as characters. **(Ficción histórica)**

See also *GENRE.*

Historical narrative A work of nonfiction that tells the story of important historical events or developments. **(Narrativa histórica)**

See page 257.

Humor The quality of a literary work that makes the characters and their situations seem funny, amusing, or ludicrous. Humor often points out human failings and the irony found in many situations. Humorous language includes sarcasm, exaggeration, puns, and verbal irony. Humorous writing can be equally effective in fiction and nonfiction. **(Humor)**

See page 327.
See also *COMEDY, FARCE, PARODY, PUN, SATIRE.*

Hyperbole A figure of speech that uses exaggeration to express strong emotion, make a point, or evoke humor. "You've asked me a million times" is an example of hyperbole. **(Hipérbole)**

See also *FIGURATIVE LANGUAGE, UNDERSTATEMENT.*

I

Iamb (i´amb) A two-syllable metrical foot consisting of one unaccented syllable (˘) followed by one accented syllable (´), as in the word *divide*. **(Yambo)**

Iambic pentameter A specific poetic meter in which each line has five metric units, or feet, and each foot consists of an unstressed syllable (˘) followed by a stressed syllable (´). The rhythm of a line of iambic pentameter would be indicated as shown in this example from Shakespeare's "Shall I Compare Thee to a Summer's Day?": **(Pentasílabo yámbico)**

˘   ´   ˘   ´   ˘   ´   ˘   ´
Rough winds do shake the darling
˘   ´ ˘   ´
buds of may,

See also *BLANK VERSE, METER, SCANSION.*

Idiom An expression that means something different from the literal meaning of the words that make it up. Idioms are understood by native speakers but are often puzzling to non-native speakers. Phrases such as "catch his eye," "turn the tables," "over the hill," and "keep tabs on" are idiomatic expressions in English. Idioms can add realism to dialogue in a story and contribute to characterization. **(Modismo)**

See also *COLLOQUIALISM, DIALECT.*

Image archetype See *ARCHETYPE.*

Imagery Descriptive language that appeals to one or more of the five senses: sight, hearing, touch, taste, and smell. This use of sensory detail helps create an emotional response in the reader. **(Imagen)**

See pages 495, 546, 637.

See also *FIGURATIVE LANGUAGE.*

Informal essay See *ESSAY.*

Interior monologue A technique that records a character's inner thoughts, revealing emotions, memories, and opinions. Interior monologue contributes to the stream-of-consciousness effect. **(Monólogo interior)**

See also *CHARACTERIZATION, MONOLOGUE, STREAM OF CONSCIOUSNESS.*

Internal rhyme Rhyme that occurs within a single line of poetry. Poets use internal rhyme to convey meaning, to evoke mood, or to create a musical effect. **(Rima interna)**

See also *RHYME.*

Inversion The reversal of the usual word order in a prose sentence or a line of poetry. Writers use inversion to maintain *rhyme scheme* or *meter* or to emphasize certain words or phrases. An example of inversion occurs in the final line of Shakespeare's sonnet "Shall I Compare Thee to a Summer's Day?": **(Inversión)**

> So long <u>lives this</u>, and this gives life to thee.

Irony A contrast or discrepancy between expectation and reality, or between what is expected and what actually happens. In *situational irony,* the actual outcome of a situation is the opposite of what is expected. In Shakespeare's *Julius Caesar,* for example, the suitors spare Mark Antony's life because they believe he is harmless. Instead, he turns out to be a vengeful, deadly enemy. In *verbal irony,* a person says one thing and means another. For example, in *Julius Caesar,* Mark Antony uses verbal irony when he praises Brutus and the conspirators to the crowd at Julius Caesar's funeral, while actually trying to turn the people against them. In *dramatic irony,* the audience or reader knows information that the characters do not know. For example, in *Julius Caesar,* the audience knows of the murder plot, although Caesar and his wife do not. **(Ironía)**

See page 137.

See also *HUMOR, PARADOX, SARCASM.*

J

Journal A daily record of events kept by a participant in those events or a witness to them. A journal is usually less intimate than a diary and emphasizes events rather than emotions. **(Diario)**

Juxtaposition The placement of two or more distinct things side by side in order to contrast or compare them. It is commonly used to evoke an emotional response in the reader. **(Yuxtaposición)**

See page 537.

L

Legend A traditional story handed down from past generations and believed to be based on actual people and events. Legends usually celebrate the heroic qualities of a national or cultural leader. A legend is usually exaggerated and gains elements of fantasy over time. For example, "Where the Girl Rescued Her Brother," retold by Joseph Bruchac and Gayle Ross, is a legend. **(Leyenda)**

See also *EPIC, FABLE, FANTASY, FOLKLORE, HERO, MYTH, ORAL TRADITION.*

Line The basic unit of poetry. A line consists of a word or a row of words. In metered poems, lines are measured by the number of feet they contain. **(Verso)**

See page 455.

See also *FOOT, STANZA.*

Literary criticism A type of writing in which the writer analyzes and evaluates a literary work. **(Crítica literaria)**

Literary nonfiction Nonfiction that is about literature or is regarded as having artistic value. Literary nonfiction may include autobiographies, biographies, memoirs, essays, and historically important or eloquent speeches. **(No-ficción literaria)**

See also *NONFICTION*.

Local color The fictional portrayal of a region's features or peculiarities and its inhabitants' distinctive ways of talking and behaving, usually as a way of adding a realistic flavor to a story. **(Color local)**

See also *DIALECT*.

Logic A method used to structure clear and effective arguments. The strongest arguments are based on sound reasoning, or logical thinking. An argument may be structured logically by using either inductive or deductive reasoning. *Inductive reasoning* involves drawing a general conclusion from specific facts: "The grass, sidewalk, and trees get wet every time it rains, so rain makes things outside get wet." *Deductive reasoning* involves drawing a specific conclusion from general facts and specific facts: "Rain makes things outside get wet and grass is outside, so when it rains the grass gets wet." An invalid argument is illogical and often includes logical fallacies, or errors in reasoning. Logic is only one aspect of a successful argument. Some statements cannot be logically proved or disproved. **(Lógica)**

See also *ARGUMENT, PERSUASION*.

Lyric poetry Poetry that expresses a speaker's strong personal feelings. Lyric poems are usually short and musical. Among the lyric poems in this book are Robert Hayden's "Those Winter Sundays" and Shakespeare's "Shall I Compare Thee to a Summer's Day?" **(Poesía lírica)**

See page 526.

See also *POETRY*.

M

Magical realism Fiction that combines fantasy and realism. Magical realism inserts fantastic, sometimes humorous, events and details into a believable reality. **(Realismo mágico)**

See also *GENRE*.

Memoir A type of narrative nonfiction that presents an author's personal experience of an event or period. A memoir is usually written from the first-person point of view. It often emphasizes the writer's thoughts and feelings, his or her relationships with other people, or the impact of significant historical events on his or her life. Frank McCourt's "Typhoid Fever" is an example of a memoir. **(Memoria)**

See also *AUTOBIOGRAPHY*.

Metaphor A figure of speech that compares or equates two seemingly unlike things. In contrast to a simile, a metaphor implies the comparison instead of stating it directly; hence there is no use of connectives such as *like* or *as*. **(Metáfora)**

See page 533.

See also *ANALOGY, EXTENDED METAPHOR, FIGURATIVE LANGUAGE, FIGURE OF SPEECH, SIMILE*.

Meter A regular pattern of stressed and unstressed syllables that gives a line of poetry a predictable rhythm. The unit of meter within the line is the *foot*. Each type of foot has a unique pattern of stressed (ˊ) and unstressed (˘) syllables:

> iamb (˘ˊ) as in *complete*
> trochee (ˊ˘) as in *trouble*
> anapest (˘˘ˊ) as in *intervene*
> dactyl (ˊ˘˘) as in *majesty*
> spondee (ˊˊ) as in *blue-green*

The length of a metrical line can be expressed in terms of the number of feet it contains: dimeter, two feet; trimeter, three feet; tetrameter, four feet; pentameter, five feet; hexameter, six feet; heptameter, seven feet. This line from Shakespeare's *Julius Caesar* is iambic pentameter: **(Métrica)**

> O par / don me / thou ble ed / ing pie ce / of earth

See page 465.

See also *FOOT, IAMBIC PENTAMETER, RHYTHM, SCANSION.*

Monologue A long speech by a character in a literary work, especially a drama. The burial speeches of Brutus and Antony in Act 3, Scene 2, in Shakespeare's *Julius Caesar* are monologues. **(Monólogo)**

See page 713.

See also *DRAMATIC MONOLOGUE, INTERIOR MONOLOGUE, SOLILOQUY.*

Mood The emotional quality of a literary work. A writer's choice of language, subject matter, setting, diction, and tone, as well as sound devices such as rhyme and rhythm contribute to creating mood. **(Tono)**

See pages 39 and 818.

See also *ATMOSPHERE, SETTING, TONE.*

Moral A practical lesson about right and wrong conduct. In fables, the moral is usually stated directly; in other literary forms, it is often implied. **(Moraleja)**

See also *FABLE, PARABLE, THEME.*

Motif A significant word, phrase, image, description, idea, or other element repeated throughout a literary work and related to the theme. For example, in "A Swimming Lesson," Jewelle L. Gomez repeats the word *rhythm* to convey a message about life. **(Motivo)**

See page 734.

See also *THEME.*

Motivation The stated or implied reason a character acts, thinks, or feels a certain way. Motivation may be an external circumstance, an internal moral, or an emotional impulse. **(Motivación)**

See pages 73 and 1066.

See also *CHARACTERIZATION, CONFLICT, PLOT.*

Mystery A genre of fiction that follows a standard plot pattern: a crime is committed and a detective searches for clues that lead him or her to the criminal. Any story that relies on the unknown or the terrifying can be considered a mystery. **(Misterio)**

See also *FICTION, GENRE.*

Myth A traditional story of unknown authorship, often involving goddesses, gods, heroes, and supernatural forces, that attempts to explain why or how something came to be. A myth may explain a belief, a custom, or a force of nature. Sophocles' *Antigone* draws on traditional elements of ancient Greek mythology. **(Mito)**

See pages 933, 935, and 945.

See also *EPIC, FOLKLORE, FOLKTALE, LEGEND, ORAL TRADITION.*

N

Narrative Writing or speech that tells a story. Driven by a *conflict* or problem, a narrative unfolds event by event and leads to a *resolution.* The story is narrated, or told, by a *narrator* and can take the form of a novel, an essay, a poem, or a short story. **(Narrativa)**

See also *NARRATIVE POETRY, NARRATOR, PLOT.*

Narrative essay See *ESSAY.*

Narrative nonfiction Nonfiction that reads like fiction but tells a story about real people, settings, and events rather than imaginary ones. Its purpose may be to entertain, to persuade, or describe. Narrative nonfiction includes autobiographies, biographies, memoirs, diaries, and journals. It may also include narrative or personal essays. **(Ficción no narrativa)**

See also *NARRATIVE, NONFICTION.*

Narrative poetry Verse that tells a story. Narrative poetry includes ballads and epics as well as shorter forms that are usually more selective and concentrated than are prose stories. For example, Dudley Randall's "The Ballad of Birmingham" is a narrative poem. **(Poesía en prosa)**

See page 554.

See also *BALLAD, EPIC, NARRATIVE.*

Narrator The person who tells a story. In some cases the narrator is a character in the story, as in Amy Tan's "Two Kinds," or outside the story, as in Judith Ortiz Cofer's "Catch the Moon." Narrators are not always truthful. A narrator in a work of literature may be *reliable* or *unreliable.* Some unreliable narrators intentionally mislead readers. Others fail to understand the true meaning of the events they describe. Most stories with unreliable narrators are written in the first person. **(Narrador)**

See page 1013.

See also *NARRATIVE, POINT OF VIEW, SPEAKER.*

Nonfiction Writing about real people, places, and events. Among the categories of nonfiction are biographies, autobiographies, and essays. **(No ficción)**

See also *AUTOBIOGRAPHY, BIOGRAPHY, ESSAY, FICTION, MEMOIR.*

Novel A book-length fictional prose narrative. Because of its length, the novel has greater potential to develop plot, character, setting, and theme than does a short story. A short novel is called a *novelette* or *novella.* **(Novella)**

See also *FICTION, SHORT STORY.*

O

Ode A long, complex lyric poem expressed in a dignified and serious tone and style. Some odes celebrate a person or an event; others are more private reflections. Odes are traditionally written in a formal stanza pattern and include rhyme. **(Oda)**

See also *LYRIC POETRY, RHYME, STANZA.*

Onomatopoeia The use of a word or phrase that imitates or suggests the sound of what it describes. Some examples are *mew, hiss, crack, swish, murmur,* and *buzz.* **(Onomatopeya)**

See also *SOUND DEVICES.*

Oral tradition Stories, knowledge, customs, and beliefs passed by word of mouth from one generation to the next. Oral literature, part of oral tradition, is a way of recording the past, glorifying leaders, and teaching morals and traditions to young people. **(Tradición oral)**

See also *BALLAD, EPIC, FOLKLORE, FOLKTALE, LEGEND, MYTH.*

Oxymoron A figure of speech in which opposite ideas are combined. Examples are "bright darkness," "wise fool," and "hateful love." **(Oximoron)**

See also *FIGURATIVE LANGUAGE, PARADOX.*

P

Parable A simple story pointing to a moral or religious lesson. It differs from a fable in that the characters are people instead of animals. **(Parábola)**

See also *FABLE, MORAL.*

Paradox A situation or a statement that appears to be impossible or contradictory but is actually true, either in fact or in a figurative sense. **(Paradoja)**

See also *OXYMORON.*

Parallelism The use of a series of words, phrases, or sentences that have similar grammatical form. Parallelism shows the relationship between ideas and helps emphasize thoughts. Susan B. Anthony used parallelism in "On Women's Right to Vote":

> It was we, the people; not we, the white male citizens; nor yet we the male citizens; but we, the whole people, who formed the Union.

(Paralelismo)

See page 422.

See also *REPETITION, RHETORICAL DEVICES.*

Parody A humorous imitation of a literary work that aims to point out the work's shortcomings. A parody may imitate the plot, characters, or style of another work, usually through exaggeration. **(Parodia)**

See also *COMEDY, FARCE, HUMOR, SATIRE.*

Persona The person created by the author to tell a story. Whether the story is told by an omniscient narrator or by one of the characters, the attitudes and beliefs of the persona may not be the same as those of the author. **(Persona)**

See also *NARRATOR, POINT OF VIEW.*

Personal essay See *ESSAY.*

Personification A figure of speech in which an animal, an object, a force of nature, or an idea is given human form or characteristics. William Shakespeare personifies death in this line from "Shall I Compare Thee to a Summer's Day?": **(Personificación)**

> Nor shall Death brag thou wand'rest in his shade

See page 513.

See also *APOSTROPHE, FIGURATIVE LANGUAGE, FIGURE OF SPEECH.*

Persuasion A type of speech or writing, usually nonfiction, that attempts to convince an audience to think or act in a particular way. Creators of persuasive works use appeals to logic, emotion, ethics, and authority to sway their readers. Some persuasion contains rhetorical fallacies, which are misleading and often false statements that appeal to emotion, ethics, and authority, and which often create errors in reasoning. Martin Luther King Jr.'s "I've Been to the Mountaintop" is an example of persuasion **(Persuasión)**

See also *ARGUMENT, LOGIC.*

Persuasive Essay See *ESSAY.*

Play See *DRAMA.*

Plot The sequence of events in a story, play, or narrative poem. A plot revolves around a central *conflict,* or problem, faced by the main characters. The plot usually develops in five stages. It begins with *exposition,* which introduces the story's conflict, characters, and setting. As the story progresses, *rising action* builds suspense and adds complications to the conflict, leading to the *climax,* or point of highest emo-

tional pitch. The *falling action* is the logical result of the climax. The *resolution,* sometimes called the *denouement,* presents the final outcome. In some stories the rising action includes a shift in tone or action, called a *turning point,* that helps move the story toward the climax. **(Argumento)**

See pages 8–9, 734.

See also *CONFLICT, FLASHBACK, FORESHADOWING.*

Plot pattern archetype See *ARCHETYPE.*

Poetry A form of literary expression that differs from prose in emphasizing the line, rather than the sentence, as the unit of composition. Many other traditional characteristics of poetry apply to some poems but not to others. Some of these characteristics are emotional, imaginative language; use of figures of speech; division into stanzas; and the use of rhyme and regular patterns of meter. **(Poesía)**

See also *FIGURATIVE LANGUAGE, LYRIC POETRY, METER, PROSE, RHYME, STANZA.*

Point of view The standpoint, or perspective, from which a story is told. All stories are told by a narrator, and who that narrator is affects the point of view. In a story with *first-person* point of view, the narrator is a character in the story, referred to as "I." The reader sees everything through that character's eyes. In a story told from *third-person* point of view, the narrator is someone who stands outside the story and describes the characters and action. The narrator refers to characters as "he" or "she." If the narrator describes events as only one character perceives them, the point of view is called *third-person limited. Third-person omniscient,* or all-knowing, point of view, means that the narrator knows everything about all the characters and events. **(Punto de vista)**

See pages 164, 183, and 1061.

See also *NARRATOR, SPEAKER.*

Prologue An introductory section of a play, speech, or other literary work. Sophocles' play *Antigone* contains a prologue. **(Prólogo)**

Propaganda Written or spoken material designed to influence ideas or opinions through the use of emotionally charged words, name-calling, misleading or false information, or other techniques. **(Propaganda)**

Props A theater term (short for *properties*) for the objects and elements of the scenery used in a stage play, movie, or television show. **(Utilería)**

See also *STAGE DIRECTIONS.*

Prose Writing that is similar to everyday speech and language, as opposed to poetry. Its form is based on sentences and paragraphs rather than lines and stanzas. Essays, short stories, magazine articles, and most plays are examples of prose. **(Prosa)**

See also *POETRY.*

Prose poem Short prose composition that uses rhythm, imagery, and other poetic devices to express an idea or emotion. Prose poetry does not have line breaks; instead, the sentences appear in standard paragraph form. **(Poema en prosa)**

See page 483.

See also *POETRY, PROSE.*

Protagonist The central character in a narrative literary work around whom the main conflict revolves. Generally, the reader or audience is meant to sympathize with the protagonist, who usually changes after the climax of the plot. **(Protagonista)**

See page 637.

See also *ANTAGONIST, CHARACTER, CONFLICT, HERO, PLOT.*

Pun A humorous use of words that are similar in sound (*merry* and *marry*) or of a word with several meanings. In Shakespeare's *Julius Caesar,* for example, a shoemaker identifies himself by saying "all that I live by is with the *awl,*" making a pun on *all* and *awl,* a tool for punching holes in leather. **(Juego de palabras)**

See also *HUMOR.*

Q

Quatrain A four-line stanza. The quatrain is the most common stanza form in English poetry. It may be unrhymed or have a variety of rhyme schemes. **(Cuarteto)**

See also *STANZA.*

Quotation A passage by another author, used word-for-word in a literary work. A quotation is enclosed in quotation marks, or otherwise set apart, to indicate that it is not written by the person in whose work it appears. Quotations can serve to illustrate ideas and to show that other people share the author's opinions. **(Cita)**

See page 405.

R

Reflective essay See *ESSAY.*

Refrain A line or lines repeated regularly, usually in a poem or song. **(Estribillo)**

See also *REPETITION.*

Reliable narrator See *NARRATOR.*

Repetition The recurrence of sounds, words, phrases, lines, or stanzas in a speech or literary work. Writers use repetition to emphasize an important point, to expand upon an idea, to help create rhythm, and to increase the feeling of unity in a work. **(Repetición)**

See pages 422 and 541.

See also *PARALLELISM, RHETORICAL DEVICES, REFRAIN, RHYME.*

Resolution See *PLOT.*

Rhetoric The art of using language—often in public speaking—to present facts and ideas in order to persuade. **(Retórica)**

See also *RHETORICAL DEVICES.*

Rhetorical devices Persuasive techniques used by public speakers and writers of literary works, especially those written to persuade. Rhetorical devices include repetition, parallelism, analogy, logic, and the skillful use of connotation and anecdote. Effective rhetorical devices often use appeals, such as appeals to logic, emotion, ethics, or authority. **(Figuras retóricas)**

See pages 369 and 422.

See also *ANALOGY, ANECDOTE, ARGUMENT, CONNOTATION, LOGIC, PARALLELISM, PERSUASION, RHETORIC, REPETITION.*

Rhetorical question A question to which no answer is expected or the answer is obvious. **(Pregunta retórica)**

See also RHETORICAL DEVICES.

Rhyme The repetition of similar or identical sounds at the ends of words that appear close to each other, usually in a poem. *End rhyme* occurs at the ends of lines of poetry. *Internal rhyme* occurs within a single line. *Slant rhyme* occurs when words include sounds that are similar but not identical (*jackal* and *buckle*). Slant rhyme typically involves some variation of *consonance* (the repetition of similar consonant sounds) or *assonance* (the repetition of similar vowel sounds). **(Rima)**

See pages 471 and 526.

See also *ASSONANCE, CONSONANCE, RHYME SCHEME, SOUND DEVICES.*

Rhyme scheme The pattern of rhyme formed by the end rhyme in a stanza or a poem. Rhyme scheme is designated by the assignment of a different letter of the alphabet to each new rhyme. For example, one common rhyme scheme is *ababcb.* **(Estructura de la rima)**

See pages 471 and 593.

See also *RHYME.*

Rhythm The pattern of beats created by the arrangement of stressed and unstressed syllables, especially in poetry. Rhythm gives a poem a musical quality that helps to convey meaning. Rhythm can be *regular,* with a predictable pattern or meter, or *irregular.* **(Ritmo)**

See page 580.

See also *BLANK VERSE, FOOT, IAMBIC PENTAMETER, METER, SCANSION.*

Rising action See *PLOT.*

Round character See *CHARACTER.*

Run-on line See *ENJAMBMENT.*

S

Sarcasm The use of bitter, mocking, or caustic language to point out shortcomings or flaws. **(Sarcasmo)**

See also *HUMOR, IRONY, SATIRE.*

Satire Writing that uses humor or wit to ridicule the vices or follies of people or societies. The purpose of satire may be to bring about change or improvement or to entertain. Satire uses devices such as hyperbole, understatement, and irony. Luisa Valenzuela's short story "The Censors" is a satire of repressive government. **(Sátira)**

See also *COMEDY, FARCE, HUMOR, PARODY, SARCASM.*

Scansion The analysis of the meter of a line of verse. To scan a line of poetry means to note the stressed (ˊ) and unstressed syllables (˘) and to divide the line into its *feet,* or rhythmical units. **(Escansión)**

See also *FOOT, METER, RHYTHM.*

Scene A subdivision of an act in a play. Each scene usually takes place in a specific setting and time. **(Escena)**

See also *ACT, DRAMA.*

Science fiction Fiction that deals with the impact of real or imaginary science and technology on individuals and societies of the past, present, or future. Common science fiction themes include aliens, man v. machine, overpopulation, utopia (ideal society) or dystopia (failing of an ideal society), time and space travel, and apocalypse (the end of the world). **(Ciencia ficción)**

See page 1047.

See also *FANTASY, GENRE.*

Screenplay The script of a film, usually containing detailed instructions about camera shots and angles in addition to dialogue and stage directions. **(Guión)**

See also *DRAMA, SCRIPT, STAGE DIRECTIONS.*

Script The text of a drama (play), film, or broadcast. **(Libreto)**

See *DRAMA, SCREENPLAY.*

Sensory details See *IMAGERY.*

Sestet A six-line poem or stanza. **(Sexteto)**

See also *SONNET.*

Setting The time and place in which the events of a literary work occur. Setting includes not only the physical surroundings, but also the ideas, customs, values, and beliefs of a particular time and place. Setting often helps create an atmosphere or mood. **(Ambiente)**

See page 827.

See also *ATMOSPHERE, MOOD.*

Short story A brief fictional narrative in prose. Elements of the short story include *plot, character, setting, point of view,* and *theme.* **(Cuento)**

See also *FICTION, NOVEL, PLOT.*

Simile A figure of speech that uses the word *like* or *as* to compare two seemingly unlike things. For example, this simile appears in Amy Tan's story "Two Kinds":

> And she also did a fancy sweep of a curtsy, so that the fluffy skirt of her white dress cascaded to the floor like the petals of a large carnation.

(Símil)

See page 533.

See also *ANALOGY, FIGURATIVE LANGUAGE, METAPHOR.*

Situational irony See *IRONY.*

Slant rhyme See *RHYME.*

Soliloquy In a drama, a long speech by a character who is alone on stage (or is under the impression of being alone). A soliloquy reveals the private thoughts and emotions of that character. **(Soliloquio)**

See page 691.

See also *ASIDE, MONOLOGUE.*

Sonnet A lyric poem of fourteen lines, typically written in *iambic pentameter* and usually following strict patterns of stanza division and rhyme. The *Shakespearean sonnet,* also called the *English sonnet,* consists of three *quatrains,* or four-line stanzas, followed by a *couplet,* or pair of rhyming lines. The rhyme scheme is typically *abab cdcd efef gg.* The rhyming couplet often presents a conclusion to the issues or questions presented in the three quatrains. In the *Petrarchan sonnet,* also called the *Italian sonnet,* fourteen lines are divided into two stanzas, the eight-line *octave* and the six-line *sestet.* The sestet usually responds to a question or situation posed by the octave. The rhyme scheme is typically *abbaabba cdecde* or *abbaabba cdcdcd.* **(Soneto)**

See also *COUPLET, LYRIC POETRY, RHYME SCHEME, STANZA.*

Sound devices Techniques used to emphasize particular sounds in writing. Writers use sound devices, such as alliteration and rhyme, to underscore the meaning of certain words, to enhance rhythm, and to add a musical quality to the work. **(Recursos sonoros)**

See pages 566–567.

See also *ALLITERATION, ASSONANCE, CONSONANCE, ONOMATOPOEIA, RHYME, RHYTHM.*

Speaker The voice speaking in a poem, similar to a narrator in a work of prose. Sometimes the speaker's voice is that of the poet, sometimes that of a fictional person or even a thing. One should never assume that the speaker and the writer are the same. For example, the speaker in Robert Hayden's poem "Those Winter Sundays" is a man thinking back to his poor childhood and remembering the sacrifices his father made while raising him. **(Hablante)**

See page 489.

See also *NARRATOR, TONE.*

Speech A public address or talk. In most speeches, the speaker tries to influence the audience's behavior, beliefs, and attitudes. Although the main purpose of a speech is usually to persuade, it can also inform and entertain. **(Parlamento)**

See also *PERSUASION, RHETORICAL DEVICES.*

Stage directions Instructions written by a playwright that describe the appearance and actions of characters, as well as the sets, props, costumes, sound effects, and lighting for a play. **(Acotaciones)**

See page 799.

See also *DRAMA, PROPS.*

Stanza A group of lines forming a unit in a poem. A stanza in a poem is similar to a paragraph in prose. Typically, stanzas are separated by a line of space. **(Estrofa)**

See page 455.

See also *FORM, STRUCTURE.*

Static character See *CHARACTER.*

Stereotype A generalization about a group of people that is made without regard for individual differences. In literature, this term is often used to describe a conventional or flat character who conforms to an expected, fixed pattern of behavior. The rebellious teenager is a stereotype. **(Estereotipo)**

See also *STOCK CHARACTER.*

Stock character A character who represents a type that is recognizable as belonging to a particular genre. For example, a cruel stepmother or charming prince is often found in fairy tales. Valiant knights and heroes are found in legends and myths. The hard-boiled detective is found in detective stories. Stock characters have conventional traits and mannerisms shared by all members of their type. **(Personaje de repertorio)**

See also *ARCHETYPE, CHARACTER, STEREOTYPE.*

Stream of consciousness The literary representation of an author's or character's free-flowing thoughts, feelings, and memories. Stream-of-consciousness writing does not always employ conventional sentence structure or other rules of grammar and usage. **(Corriente de conciencia)**

See page 1032.

See also *INTERIOR MONOLOGUE.*

Structure The particular order or pattern a writer uses to present ideas. For example, narratives commonly present a sequence of events in chronological order. The structure of persuasive or expository writing may vary. Listing detailed information, explaining steps in a process, comparing and contrasting, presenting causes and their effects, describing a scene or an object in spatial order, or describing a problem and then offering a solution are some ways a writer can structure a text. *Poetic structure* refers to the organization of words, lines, images, and ideas. **(Estructura)**

See pages 346, 460, and 818.

See also *FORM.*

Style The particular way an author writes, including the author's word choice, sentence structure, and use of imagery and figurative language. Style can reveal an author's attitude and purpose in writing. **(Estilo)**

See pages 216, 998–999, and 1066.

See also *AUTHOR'S PURPOSE, DICTION, FIGURATIVE LANGUAGE, IMAGERY, TONE, VOICE.*

Subject The topic of a literary work.

Summary A retelling of the main events or ideas of a piece of writing in a short version of the original. The events or ideas are restated in the same order, without personal opinion or comment. Nonfiction summaries are usually no more than about one-third as long as the original. A plot summary of a narrative reports the main events and explains the main characters' problems and how they are resolved. **(Resumen)**

See also *NARRATIVE, NONFICTION.*

Surprise ending An unexpected plot twist at the end of a story. The ending might surprise readers because the author provided misleading clues or withheld important information. **(Desenlace sorpresivo)**

Suspense A feeling of curiosity, uncertainty, or even dread about what is going to happen next. Writers increase the level of suspense by creating a threat to the central character and raising questions in a reader's mind about the outcome of a conflict. In Doris Lessing's "Through the Tunnel," for example, suspense builds as the reader wonders whether Jerry will be able to succeed in the physical and mental challenge he has set for himself. **(Suspenso)**

See page 958.

See also *FORESHADOWING, MOOD.*

Symbol Any object, person, place, or experience that exists on a literal level but also represents something else, usually something abstract. Swimming through the tunnel, for example, is a symbolic achievement for Jerry in Doris Lessing's "Through the Tunnel." The act means that he is growing up. **(Símbolo)**

See page 580.

See also *ALLEGORY, FIGURATIVE LANGUAGE.*

T

Tanka Unrhymed Japanese verse form consisting of five lines. The first and third lines have five syllables each; the other lines have seven syllables each. **(Tanka)**

See page 500.

See also *HAIKU.*

Teleplay A play written or adapted for television. In addition to dialogue and stage directions, a teleplay usually contains detailed instructions about camera shots and angles. **(Guión para televisión)**

See also *STAGE DIRECTIONS.*

Text elements See *TEXT FEATURES.*

Text features Visual elements of text presentation that help readers find and understand information. Common text features include titles, heads and subheads, captions, menu bars, and graphics such as photographs, tables, charts, maps, and diagrams. **(Elementos del texto)**

Text structure See *STRUCTURE.*

Theater of the Absurd Drama, primarily of the 1950s and 1960s, that does not contain a plot but instead presents a series of scenes in which the characters speak in meaningless conversations or perform actions with little purpose. The central concern of this drama is to show that people are helpless or confused in an alienating world. **(Teatro del absurdo)**

See also *DRAMA.*

Theme The central message of a work of literature, often expressed as a general statement about life. Some themes are *universal,* meaning that they are widely held ideas about life. These themes are often *recurring,* meaning that they are frequently used. Some works have a *stated theme,* which is expressed directly. More frequently works have an *implied theme,* which is revealed gradually through elements such as plot, character, setting, point of view, symbol, and irony. A literary work may have more than one theme. Themes and subjects, or topics, are different. The subject of a work might be love; the theme would be what the writer says about love, that it is painful or wonderful or both, for example. **(Tema)**

See pages 103 and 504.

See also *AUTHOR'S PURPOSE, MORAL MOTIF, SUBJECT.*

Theme archetype See *ARCHETYPE.*

Thesis The main idea of an essay or other work of persuasive or expository nonfiction. The thesis may be implied but is commonly stated directly. **(Tesis)**

See page 353.

See also *ESSAY, NONFICTION.*

Title The name given to a literary work. The title can help explain setting, provide insight into the theme, or describe the action that will take place in the work. **(Título)**

Tone An author's attitude toward his or her subject matter. Tone is conveyed through elements such as word choice, punctuation, sentence structure, and figures of speech. A writer's tone may convey a variety of attitudes, such as sympathy, seriousness, irony, sadness, bitterness, or humor. **(Tono)**

See page 392.

See also *AUTHOR'S PERSPECTIVE, AUTHOR'S PURPOSE, DICTION, STYLE, VOICE.*

Tragedy A play in which the main character suffers a downfall. That character, the tragic hero, often is a person of dignified or heroic stature. The downfall may result from outside forces or from a weakness within the character, which is known as a tragic flaw. **(Tragedia)**

See pages 632–633.

See also *DRAMA, HERO.*

Tragic hero See *TRAGEDY.*

U

Understatement Language that makes something seem less important than it really is. Understatement may be used to add humor or to focus the reader's attention on something the author wants to emphasize. **(Eufemismo)**

See also *HYPERBOLE.*

Unreliable narrator See *NARRATOR.*

V

Verbal irony See *IRONY.*

Verse paragraph A group of lines in a poem that form a unit. Unlike a stanza, which may have a fixed number of lines, a verse paragraph does not have a fixed number of lines. While poems written before the twentieth century usually contain stanzas, many contemporary poems are made up of verse paragraphs. Verse paragraphs help to organize a poem into thoughts, as paragraphs help to organize prose. Free verse poems are often structured in verse paragraphs. **(Párrafo en verso)**

See page 504.

See also *FREE VERSE, STANZA.*

Voice The distinctive use of language that conveys the author's or narrator's personality to the reader. The particular speech patterns of a character in a story or narrative poem can also create a voice for that character. Voice is determined by elements of style such as word choice and tone. **(Voz)**

See page 312.

See also *DICTION, NARRATOR, STYLE, TONE.*

W

Word choice See *DICTION.*

Reading and Thinking with Foldables®

by Dinah Zike, M.Ed., Creator of Foldables®

Using Foldables® Makes Learning Easy and Enjoyable

With paper, scissors, and a stapler or glue, it is easy and worthwhile to use Foldables in the classroom. Just follow the illustrated step-by-step directions.

 Reading Objective: to understand the ways in which one character's actions affect the other characters in a short story

Use this Foldable to keep track of what the main character does and how his or her actions affect the other characters.

 Step ❶ Place a sheet of paper in front of you so that the short side is at the top. Fold the paper in half from top to bottom.

 Step ❷ Fold the paper in half again from side to side to divide it into two columns. Unfold the paper so that the two columns show.

 Step ❸ Draw a line along the column crease. Then cut through the top layer of paper along the line you drew, forming two tabs.

 Step ❹ Label the left tab *Main Character's Actions.* Label the right tab *Effects on Others.*

Step ❺ As you read, record under the first tab the main character's actions. Under the second tab, record the effect that each of those actions has on the other characters.

 ## Short Story

Reading Objective: to analyze a short story on the basis of its literary elements

Use this Foldable to keep track of five literary elements in the short story.

 Step ❶ Stack three sheets of paper with their top edges about a half-inch apart. Be sure to keep the side edges straight.

 Step ❷ Fold up the bottom edges of the paper to form six tabs, five of which will be the same size.

 Step ❸ Crease the paper to hold the tabs in place and staple the sheets together along the crease.

Step ❹ Turn the sheets so that the stapled side is at the top. Write the title of the story on the top tab. Label the five remaining tabs *Setting, Characters, Plot, Point of View,* and *Theme.*

Step ❺ As you read, jot down on the appropriate tab notes about each of the story's literary elements.

You may adapt this simple Foldable in several ways.
- Use it with dramas, longer works of fiction, and some narrative poems—selections in which five literary elements are present.
- Change the labels to focus on a different aspect of a selection. For example, if a story or play has several settings, characters, acts, or scenes, you could devote a tab to each one.

Drama

Reading Objective: to understand conflict and plot in a drama

Use this Foldable to keep track of conflicts that arise in the drama and the ways in which those conflicts are resolved.

 Step ❶ Place a sheet of paper in front of you so that the short side is at the top. Fold the paper in half from side to side.

 Step ❷ Fold the paper again, one inch from the top as shown here.

 Step ❸ Unfold the paper and draw lines along all of the folds to create your chart.

Step ❹ At the top, label the left column *Conflicts* and the right column *Resolutions.*

Step ❺ As you read, record in the left column the various conflicts that arise in the drama. In the right column, explain the way in which each conflict was resolved.

You may adapt this simple Foldable in several ways.
- Use it with short stories, longer works of fiction, and many poems—selections in which conflicts and their resolutions are important.
- Change the labels to focus on a different aspect of a selection. For example, you could record the actions of two characters, or you could record the thoughts and feelings of a character before and after the selection's climax.

 Lyric Poem

Reading Objective: to interpret the message in a poem by analyzing the speaker's thoughts and feelings

Use this Foldable to help you distinguish between what the speaker *says* and what the poet *means.*

 Step ❶ Place a sheet of paper in front of you so that the short side is at the top. Fold the paper in half from top to bottom.

 Step ❷ Fold the paper in half again from left to right.

 Step ❸ Unfold the paper and cut through its top layer along the fold line to make two tabs.

 Step ❹ Label the left tab *Speaker's Words.* Label the right tab *Poet's Meaning.*

Step ❺ Jot down notes on your Foldable as you read the poem. Under the left tab, write key things the speaker says. Under the right tab, write what you think the poet means by having the speaker say those things.

You may adapt this simple Foldable in several ways.
- Use it to help you visualize the images in a poem. Just replace *Speaker's Words* with *Imagery* and replace *Poet's Meaning* with *What I See.*
- Replace the label *Speaker's Words* with *Speaker's Tone* and under the tab write adjectives that describe the tone of the speaker's words.
- If the poem you are reading has two stanzas, you could devote one tab to each stanza's notes.

Functional Documents

Functional documents are specialized forms of expository writing that serve specifc purposes. Functional documents are an everyday part of business, school, and even home life. They must be clear, concise, accurate, and correct in style and usage.

Letter of Application

A letter of application is a form of business writing. It can be used when applying for a job, an internship, or a scholarship. In most cases, the letter is intended to accompany a résumé or an application. Because detailed information is usually included in the accompanying form, a letter of application should provide a general overview of your qualifications and the reasons you are submitting an application. A letter of application should be concise and organized. You should clearly state which position you are applying for and then provide facts and details that prove you are qualified. The accompanying material should speak for itself.

❶ The optional subject line indicates the topic of the letter.

❷ In a business letter, the greeting is followed by a colon.

❸ The writer states her purpose directly and immediately.

❹ The writer comments briefly on her qualifications.

❺ The writer makes reference to the accompanying material.

32 South Street
Austin, Texas 78746
May 6, 2009

Melissa Reyes
City Life magazine
2301 Davis Avenue
Austin, Texas 78764

❶ Re: Internship

❷ Dear Ms. Reyes:

I am a junior at City High School and editor of the City High Herald. I am
❸ writing to apply for your summer internship at City Life magazine. As a journalism student and a longtime fan of your magazine, I feel that an internship with your magazine would provide me with valuable experience in the field of journalism. I believe that my role with the City High Herald has
❹ given me the skills necessary to be a useful contributor to your magazine this summer. In addition, my enclosed application shows that I am also a
❺ diligent worker.

I thank you for considering my application for your summer internship, and I hope to be working with you in the coming months.

Sincerely,

Anne Moris
Anne Moris

Activity

Choose a local business where you might like to work. Write a letter of application for an internship at that business. Assume that you will be submitting this letter along with a résumé or an internship application that details your experience and qualifications.

Résumé

The purpose of a résumé is to provide the employer with a comprehensive record of your background information, related experience, and qualifications. Although a résumé is intended to provide a great deal of information, the format is designed to make the résumé reader-friendly and efficient.

❶ Jane Wiley
909 West Main Street, Apt. #1
Urbana, Illinois 61802
(217) 555-0489 • jane@internet.edu

Goal
Seeking position in television news production

❷ Education
Junior standing in the College of Communications at the University of
    Illinois, Urbana-Champaign
2005 Graduate of City High School

❻

Honors
Member of National Honor Society

Activities
❸ Member, Asian American Association: 2005–Present
Environmental Committee Chairperson, Asian American Association:
    August 2006–May 2007

Work Experience
❹ Radio Reporter, WPGU, 107.1 FM, Champaign, Illinois: May 2007–Present
❺ • Rewrote and read stories for afternoon newscasts
• Served as field reporter for general assignments

Cashier, Del's Restaurant, Champaign, Illinois: May 2006–August 2006
• Responsible for taking phone orders
• Cashier for pickup orders

Assistant Secretary, Office of Dr. George Wright, Woodstock, Illinois:
May 2005–August 2005
• Answered phones
• Made appointments

❶ Header includes all important contact information.

❷ All important education background is included.

❸ Related dates are included for all listed activities.

❹ Job title is included along with the place of employment.

❺ Job responsibilities are briefly listed, with a parallel structure used in each bulleted item.

❻ Include areas of white space to help readers move through the résumé quickly.

Activity
Create an outline that lists the information that you would want to include in a résumé. Use a word processing program to help format your outline.

Job and College Applications

When applying for a job or to college, you usually need to fill out an application. When you fill out the application, read the instructions carefully. Examine the entire form before beginning to fill it out. If you fill out the form by hand, make sure that your handwriting is neat and legible. If you fill out the form online, select an appropriate font and size. Fill out the form completely, providing all information directly and honestly. If a question does not apply to you, indicate that by writing *n/a,* short for "not applicable." Keep in mind that you will have the opportunity to provide additional information in your résumé, in your letter of application, or during the interview process.

---

❶ Please type or print neatly in blue or black ink.

❷ Name: _____   **Today's date:** _____
 Address: _____
 Phone #: _____   **Birth date:** _____   **Sex:** ___   **Soc. Sec. #:** ____

* *

❸ Job History (List each job held, starting with the most recent job.)

1. Employer: _____   Phone #: _____
 Dates of employment: _____
 Position held: _____
❹ Duties: _____

2. Employer: _____   Phone #: _____
 Dates of employment: _____
 Position held: _____
 Duties: _____

* *

Education (List the most recent level of education completed.)

_____

* *

Personal References:

1. Name: _____   Phone #: _____
 Relationship: _____
2. Name: _____   Phone #: _____
 Relationship: _____

❶ The application provides specific instructions.

❷ All of the information requested should be provided in its entirety.

❸ The information should be provided legibly and succinctly.

❹ Experience should be stated accurately and without embellishment.

Activity

Pick up a job application from a local business or use the sample application shown. Complete the application thoroughly. Fill out the application as if you were actually applying for the job. Be sure to pay close attention to the guidelines mentioned above.

Activity

The Texas university system offers one online application that is accepted at every Texas public university. To complete this application, go to www.applytexas.org. There is no form to download, so follow the instructions carefully and save your work often.

Memos

A memorandum (memo) conveys precise information to another person or a group of people. A memo begins with a leading block. It is followed by the text of the message. A memo does not have a formal closing.

TO: All Employees
FROM: Jordan Tyne, Human Resources Manager
❶ SUBJECT: New Human Resources Assistant Director
DATE: November 3, 2009

❷ Please join me in congratulating Daphne Rudy on her appointment as assistant director in the Human Resources Department. Daphne comes to our company with five years of experience in the field. Daphne begins ❸ work on Monday, November 10. All future general human resource inquiries should be directed to Daphne.

Please welcome Daphne when she arrives next week.

❶ The topic of the memo is stated clearly in the subject line.

❷ The announcement is made in the first sentence.

❸ All of the important information is included briefly in the memo.

Business E-mail

E-mail is quickly becoming the most common form of business communication. While e-mail may be the least formal and most conversational method of business writing, it shouldn't be written carelessly or too casually. The conventions of business writing—clarity, attention to your audience, proper grammar, and the inclusion of relevant information—apply to e-mail. An accurate subject line should state your purpose briefly and directly. Use concise language and avoid rambling sentences.

To: LiamS@internet.com
From: LisaB@internet.com
CC: EricC@internet.com
Date: January 7, 8:13 a.m.
❶ Subject: New Product Conference Call

Liam,

❷ I just wanted to make sure that arrangements have been made for next week's conference call to discuss our new product. The East Coast sales team has already scheduled three sales meetings at the end of the month with potential buyers, so it's important that our sales team is prepared to talk about the product. Please schedule the call when the manufacturing director ❸ is available, since he will have important information for the sales team.

Lisa

❶ The subject line clearly states the topic.

❷ The purpose is stated immediately and in a conversational tone.

❸ Important details are included in a brief, direct fashion.

Activity
Write an e-mail to your coworkers. Inform them of a change in company procedure that will affect them.

Travel Directions

When planning an event or a social occasion, it is often necessary to provide people with detailed directions to the location. These directions must be clear enough that anyone who is unfamiliar with the surrounding area can easily find his or her way. Creating a map that shows the route with clearly labeled streets can also be a great help.

Directions to Darien High School's Graduation Ceremony

From I-95 North, take Exit 11. ❶

Turn Left onto Post Road (Route 1).

At the first light, turn Left onto Samuel Avenue. Travel 2.5 miles. ❷

Turn Right onto Cherry Hill Road.

Turn Left onto High School Lane. ❸

Follow signs to Visitor Parking.

❶ Begin at a point from which most people will be coming.

❷ Offer travel distances to help travelers locate streets.

❸ Give the name of each street along the route.

❶ Clearly label all streets to be traveled.

❷ Label major cross streets so the traveler can keep better track of his or her progress.

❸ Include landmarks to help identify the area.

❹ Include a legend to show scale.

❺ Include a compass rose to help orient the traveler.

Activity

Write directions and draw an accompanying map to a location in your town. Be sure to include enough details and give clear directions so that even someone who is unfamiliar with the area can synthesize the information and find the destination easily.

Technical Writing

Technical writing involves the use of very specific vocabulary and a special attention to detail. The purpose of technical writing is to describe a process clearly enough so that the reader can perform the steps and reach the intended goal, such as installing software, connecting a piece of equipment, or programming a device. The following instructions are taken from a DVD operation manual.

Instructions for Connecting DVD Player to HDTV

❶ Your DVD player can be connected to an HDTV using RCA cables or, for best picture quality, an HDMI cable.

Connecting with RCA Cables:

❷ Step 1: Insert the ends of the red, white, and yellow cables into the jacks labeled "AUDIO/VIDEO OUT." Be sure to match the colors of the cable with the color of the jack.

Step 2: Insert the other ends of the RCA cables into the jacks labeled "AUDIO/VIDEO IN" on your HDTV. These are usually located on the side or the back of the television. Again, be sure to match the colors of the cables with the colors of the jacks.

Connecting with HDMI Cable:

Step 1: Insert one end of the HDMI cable into the HDMI port located on the back of the DVD player.

Step 2: Insert the other end of the HDMI cable into the HDMI port on your HDTV.

❸ Note: Your HDTV may have more than one HDMI port. If so, be sure that you set your HDTV to the correct input when viewing.

---

❶ Use technical information in accessible language to clearly describe the process.

❷ Detail each step individually.

❸ Direct attention to possible questions the reader may have.

Activity

Choose a device that you own or have access to, such as an mp3 player or a cell phone. Write an operation manual with brief step-by-step directions on how to perform a specific function on the device, so that someone else can follow your instructions and perform the function successfully. Use formatting structures including headings and subheadings to create clear directions.

Writing Handbook

Using the Literary Text Scoring Rubric

Write a literary text to express your ideas and feelings about real or imagined people, events, and ideas. Literary texts include short stories, personal narratives, biographical narratives, and drama.

Literary Text Scoring Rubric				
Traits of Strong Writing	**4-point narratives:**	**3-point narratives:**	**2-point narratives:**	**1-point narratives:**
Ideas	• develop a strong theme • integrate story elements (character, setting, tone) • have an insightful ending • have an efficient narrator	• develop a clear theme • connect story elements • have a clear ending • use a specific point of view	• mention a theme • have disconnected story elements • have an unclear ending • have awkward shifts in point of view	• don't maintain a theme • omit story elements • have an abrupt or missing ending • include no narrator or point of view
Organization	• create an engaging story line, including: – exposition, – rising action, – climax, – falling action, and – resolution	• create a complete story line, including: – exposition, – rising action, – climax, – falling action, and – resolution	• include a clear – beginning, – middle, and – end of the story	• include some, but not all, of the story line • may confuse the progression of plot
Voice	• sustain the reader's interest • seamlessly use literary devices (figurative language, sentence variety, and word choice) to develop style and tone when appropriate	• engage the reader often • correctly use literary devices (figurative language, sentence variety, and word choice) to develop style and tone when appropriate	• engage the reader at times • make attempts to use literary devices to develop style and tone, though may have too many or too few instances to be effective	• struggle to engage the reader • make limited attempts to use literary devices
Word Choice	• use a variety of sensory details • create distinct characters through dialogue and detail	• use original sensory details • use dialogue and description to create characters	• use some sensory details • have undeveloped characters	• use limited or no details • have simple characters
Sentence Fluency	• employ a variety of sentence lengths • move at a good pace, with seamless transitions	• move the action forward through transitions	• need stronger transitions to control pacing	• contain little action or have confusing sequencing
Conventions	• have few or no errors	• have few minor errors	• have minor and major errors	• have many major errors

Activity

Voice Use the scoring rubric to develop a strong and original voice in your writing. Review the characteristics described in the scoring rubric, beginning with the 4-point essay description. Make a three-column chart, listing the terms from the descriptions in the left-hand column. In the middle column, explain what they mean. In the right-hand column, collect writing examples that meet the expectations of 4-point writing. Refer to your list for inspiration when developing your writing voice.

Using the Expository Text Scoring Rubric

Write expository texts to communicate ideas and information to specific audiences for specific purposes. Expository texts include essays, responses to literature, technical and work-related documents, articles, and reports.

Expository Text Scoring Rubric

Traits of Strong Writing	4-point essays:	3-point essays:	2-point essays:	1-point essays:
Ideas	• present accurate and in-depth understanding of topic, audience, purpose • present and develop ideas clearly with evidence from multiple sources • discriminate between relevant and irrelevant information	• address a clear topic with awareness of audience and purpose • clearly present and analyze information • fully develop most ideas with relevant evidence • discriminate between relevant and irrelevant information	• attempt to address topic with limited awareness of audience and purpose • present a confused or inaccurate understanding • present few developed ideas • may confuse opinion and fact	• demonstrate uncertainty of topic or task • do not address the topic • require more developed ideas or more relevant evidence • lack distinctions between fact and opinion
Organization	• establish and maintain a clear focus • present ideas in logical structure • use transitions to support the clear structure	• maintain a consistent focus • support a thesis with logical examples • effectively use transitions	• establish a confused or irrelevant thesis • fail to maintain a focus on the thesis • organize information poorly • have few transitions	• present no thesis or focus • lack coherence • use no transitions
Voice	• present an interesting, distinctive voice • emphasize the writer's attitude toward the topic through style	• present a professional, appropriate voice • reveal the writer's attitude toward the topic through style	• present a voice that is too formal or inappropriate for purpose/audience • need style improvements to create clear tone	• present little or no sense of the writer's voice • need style improvements to connect to reader
Word Choice	• demonstrate a clear sense of audience and purpose through precise and engaging word choice	• use language that demonstrates awareness of audience and purpose	• use language that may be inappropriate for audience or purpose	• use language that may be inappropriate to audience or purpose
Sentence Fluency	• present a variety of sentence structures • rely on transitions	• present several sentence structures • include transitions	• include a few different sentences types, some compound or complex	• have monotonous use of simple sentence structure
Conventions	• have virtually no errors • exhibit sophisticated language	• demonstrate control of conventions • may include few errors	• include several errors that may make comprehension difficult	• display serious errors that make comprehension difficult

Activity

Sentence Fluency Rubrics provide information about the differences between a good essay (a 3-point essay) and a great essay (a 4-point essay). For example, if you would like to improve the sentence fluency of your writing, you should use a variety of sentence structures, not just a couple of different types of sentences. Practice by starting and combining sentences in different ways to create variety and interest in your writing.

Using the Persuasive Text Scoring Rubric

Write persuasive texts to influence the attitudes or actions of a specific audience on specific issues. Persuasive texts include essay, speeches, reviews, or editorials.

Persuasive Text Scoring Rubric

Traits of Strong Writing	4-point essays:	3-point essays:	2-point essays:	1-point essays:
Ideas	• convey a sophisticated and mature understanding of the nuances of the argument • offer insightful and perceptive analysis of the issue or position • use logic to refute counterarguments	• convey an accurate, although somewhat basic, understanding of the topic • offer partial support for the argument or position • address counterarguments	• convey a limited or superficial understanding of the topic • offer minor support for the argument or position • have limited awareness of counterarguments	• demonstrate limited understanding of the writing task or topic • offer inappropriate explanations that fail to support the argument • make no attempt to address counterarguments
Organization	• offer a clear thesis, logical and consistent claims, powerful evidence, and complex understanding of the argument • smoothly integrate multiple sources as evidence	• establish a main thesis • make clear claims that are supported with evidence • support arguments with evidence and some analysis	• establish a basic thesis but may lose focus • need more balance in the structure of the argument and paragraphs • partly support with evidence, but lack explanation or analysis	• lack a thesis or main focus • lack supporting evidence • present no clear organization or cohesive structure to ideas
Voice	• show a sophisticated awareness of audience and purpose	• show an awareness of audience and purpose	• have an uneven or inappropriate tone for audience or purpose	• have no definable tone, no evidence of attitude toward topic
Word Choice	• use language that is clear and convincing	• use appropriate language	• use language that is unsuitable for purpose or audience	• use inappropriate language or tone
Sentence Fluency	• use transitions to guide the reader • include a range of sentence structures for interest and persuasion	• transition between paragraphs logically • include some variety of sentence structures	• use few transitions • have limited sentence variety and structure	• include no transition words or phrases • contain sentence fragments and run-on sentences that impede communication
Conventions	• are essentially error-free	• may include a few errors	• contain multiple errors that sometimes hinder comprehension	• display serious errors that make comprehension difficult

Activity

Organization Use a copy of the scoring rubric to strengthen organization. Have a partner review the rubric and read your paper. Ask him or her to indicate which box in the rubric best describes your organization. Convert all of the descriptions in that box into questions. For example, for 2-point organization ask: Do all my sentences focus on defending my thesis? Is my argument balanced? Do I explain and analyze my evidence? Once you can answer yes to each question, your paper has moved up to the next level.

Using the Research Report Scoring Rubric

Write a research report to answer questions about an interesting topic. Research-report writing requires you to determine, locate, and explore sources, evaluate information, and organize it into a written report.

Research Report Scoring Rubric

Traits of Strong Writing	4-point essays:	3-point essays:	2-point essays:	1-point essays:
Ideas	• demonstrate evidence of a clear focus, a well-chosen and explained topic, and sophisticated understanding of research subject • use multiple reputable sources • synthesize sources	• present and explain a clear research question • offer some research sources • discuss main issues related to the research question • include evidence to support main points	• present ideas that are not complex or nuanced • offer at least one research source • make an attempt to understand the subject • include details that may be irrelevant • offer little analysis or reflection on evidence	• fail to present a research topic • include no sources • exhibit no understanding of subject • include disjointed ideas and irrelevant or inaccurate details
Organization	• organize ideas into a deliberate plan • integrate sources smoothly into writing • progress effortlessly from paragraph to paragraph	• have a clear organizational plan • include sources • have structured paragraphs with main ideas and supporting sentences	• have unclear organization • fail to clearly link sources to ideas • show little attempt to structure paragraphs	• have a confusing or weak organizational plan • contain paragraphs with no discernable structure
Voice	• engage the reader • present insightful analysis and reflection • exhibit a confident and professional tone	• attempt to engage the reader • offer some analysis or reflection on the evidence	• lack attempts to engage the reader • include limited or unfocused reflection on the topic	• have an inappropriate tone for the purpose and audience • offer no analysis or reflection on evidence
Word Choice	• use precise language, well-suited for purpose and audience	• include language appropriate for audience and purpose	• use language that shows little awareness of audience or purpose	• have language that is inappropriate for audience and purpose
Sentence Fluency	• include sentences that are varied in structure and length	• include sentences that are usually varied in structure and length	• include sentences that are simplistic or poorly constructed	• contain frequent sentence fragments and run-on sentences
Conventions	• demonstrate awareness of proper use of citation methods and formatting • include few errors	• offer a list of research sources and some in-text quotations • may have a few errors	• may use an incorrect format for bibliography • have frequent errors that occasionally hinder communication	• include no bibliography or in-text references • have multiple errors that hinder communication

Activity

Ideas A research paper allows you to investigate a topic that interests you. As you gather more research, your ideas about the topic develop. Use the scoring rubric for direction on what is important when you are developing an idea. *Focused* and *sophisticated* are words that describe a 4-point score for ideas. Look for ways to show that your topic describes a clear-cut issue, with shades of meaning that make it interesting. Practice summarizing and evaluating your sources before including them in your report.

Using the Traits of Strong Writing

What are some basic terms you can use to discuss your writing with your teacher or class-mates? What should you focus on as you revise and edit your compositions? Check out the following terms, or traits, that describe the qualities of strong writing. Learn the meaning of each trait and find out how using the traits can improve your writing.

Ideas

The message or the theme and the details that develop it

Writing is clear when readers can grasp the meaning of your ideas right away. Check to see whether you're getting your message across.

- ☑ Does the title suggest the theme of the composition?

- ☑ Does the composition focus on a single topic?

- ☑ Is the thesis—the main point or central idea—clearly stated?

- ☑ Do well-chosen details elaborate your thesis?

Organization

The arrangement of main ideas and supporting details

An effective plan of organization points your readers in the right direction and guides them easily through your composition from start to finish. Find a structure, or order, that best suits your topic and writing purpose. Check to see whether you've ordered your key ideas in a way that helps your readers.

- ☑ Are the beginning, middle, and end clearly linked?

- ☑ Does the introduction capture your readers' attention?

- ☑ Do sentences and paragraphs flow from one to the next in a way that makes sense?

- ☑ Does the conclusion wrap up the composition?

Voice

A writer's unique way of using tone and style

Your writing voice comes through when your readers sense that a real person is communicating with them. Readers will respond to the **tone** (or attitude) that you express toward a topic and to the **style** (the way that you use language and shape your sentences). Read your work aloud to see whether your writing voice comes through.

- ☑ Does your writing sound interesting?

- ☑ Does your writing reveal your attitude toward your topic?

- ☑ Does your writing sound like you—or does it sound like you're imitating someone else?

Word Choice

The vocabulary a writer uses to convey meaning

Words work hard. They carry the weight of your meaning, so make sure you choose them carefully. Check to see whether the words you choose are doing their jobs well.

- ☑ Do you use lively verbs to show action?

- ☑ Do you use vivid words to create word pictures in your readers' minds?

- ☑ Do you use precise words to explain your ideas simply and clearly?

Sentence Fluency

The smooth rhythm and flow of sentences that vary in length and style

The best writing is made up of sentences that flow smoothly from one sentence to the next. Writing that is graceful also sounds musical—rhythmical rather than choppy. Check for sentence fluency by reading your writing aloud.

☑ Do your sentences vary in length and structure?

☑ Do transition words and phrases show connections between ideas and sentences?

☑ Does parallelism help balance and unify related ideas?

Conventions

Correct spelling, grammar, usage, and mechanics

A composition free of errors makes a good impression on your readers. Mistakes can be distracting, and they can blur your message. Try working with a partner to spot errors and correct them. Use this checklist to help you.

☑ Are all words spelled correctly?

☑ Are all proper nouns—as well as the first word of every sentence—capitalized?

☑ Is your composition free of sentence fragments?

☑ Is your composition free of run-on sentences?

☑ Are punctuation marks—such as apostrophes, commas, and end marks—inserted in the right places?

Presenting and Publishing

The formatting of writing for various purposes

For many writers, the writing process is not complete until they present their work to an audience. This can mean submitting your writing for publication in a school paper or a national magazine, or it can simply mean preparing your writing in a neat and presentable format. For readers to fully appreciate your writing, it is very important that you present it neatly, effectively, and according to professional standards.

☑ Have you used a standard font such as Times Roman 12 point?

☑ Have you double-spaced your work so that it is easy to read?

☑ Have you left one-inch margins on all sides of every page?

☑ Have you italicized titles and terms from other languages? You may also italicize words to add emphasis, but do this only when it is necessary to make your point clear. (If you are submitting your writing to a professional publication, underline words that should appear in italics.)

☑ Have you set the page number in the upper right-hand corner of each page? Include your last name before each page number after the first page.

☑ If you are including charts, graphs, maps, or other visual aids, have you set them on their own page? This will allow you to show the graphic at a full size that is easy to read.

Research Paper Writing

When you write a research report, you explore a topic by asking open-ended questions about it, developing a plan for answering them, and gathering facts from a wide variety of resources. You synthesize your research to develop a point of view or draw a conclusion that will be the controlling idea, or thesis, of your written or oral presentation.

Select a Topic

Because a research paper takes time to prepare and write, your choice of topic is especially important. Follow these guidelines in choosing a topic:

- If a specific topic is not assigned, brainstorm to develop a list of researchable questions about a topic you would like to explore.

- Choose one question that is neither too narrow nor too broad for the length of the paper you will write. Use that question as your topic.

- Select a topic that genuinely interests you.

- Conduct preliminary research in general resources, such as encyclopedia articles, tables of contents of books on the topic, and a computerized library catalogue that displays subheads related to general topics, to see whether sufficient information is available on your topic. If it is not, change your topic and refocus your research.

Plan Your Research

- Write a plan you will follow to do your research. Your plan should include steps for gathering research and taking notes, evaluating and documenting your sources, outlining your paper, drafting your paper, and citing your sources.

- Set deadlines for each step based on your final due date. Take into account other assignments and activities when you create your schedule.

- As you complete each step of the process, evaluate your plan. Has the focus of your research changed? If so, modify your research question or thesis statement to reflect your new direction.

Critique each step of your research. Did you do your best work on each step? If you have tried to cut corners early, you may create more work for yourself later. Be thorough at every step.

Conduct Your Research

- To find general information on your topic, look it up in an encyclopedia.

- Find specific up-to-date information in books and periodicals, on CD-ROMs and the Internet, and, if appropriate, through interviews with experts.

- To find additional information, use the library's computerized or card catalogue, the *Reader's Guide to Periodical Literature* (or an electronic equivalent), newspaper indexes, and specialized references, such as biographical encyclopedias. For help with these resources, ask the librarian.

- Read about your topic to identify its major issues and debates so that you can develop your paper's controlling idea. Although the idea may change as you do further research, your original formulation can guide your later efforts.

- Make sure each source you use relates closely to your topic and is reliable. For example, government and education Web sites (those ending in .gov and .edu) can be relied upon.

- To conduct research on the Internet, you will need to use a **search engine**—a tool that allows you to use keywords to find information on the World Wide Web. Most search engines operate the same way. Because of the huge amount of information on the Internet, you will have to visit and evaluate many sites to decide which ones have information that is most relevant and appropriate to your topic.

Activity

Use *cooking* as a keyword to conduct an Internet search. How many sites do you find? Next, narrow your search to find a recipe for your favorite dessert. Place exact phrases in quotation marks to narrow your search.

Evaluate Your Sources

Gather information from a variety of sources. Use only sources you can trust.

Primary sources are written by people who actually experienced the events they recorded.

Secondary sources are based on information gathered from primary sources and others as well.

To evaluate the credibility of your sources, consider whether they are

- authoritative—written by recognized experts on the topic. Authors who have written several books or articles about a subject for informed audiences in the field and who are frequently quoted may be considered authorities.

- accurate—able to be verified by other print or online resources.

- reliable—published in trustworthy books, periodicals, and Web sites. Use material from scholarly journals rather than from popular magazines. Be especially careful of online sources. The Web sites of well-known universities are more reliable than those of individuals.

- objective—associated with persons or organizations that are unbiased.

- up to date—based on the most current information. Use the most recent material available, particularly for subjects of current importance. Check the publication date of books and the month and the year of periodicals.

- suitable—relevant to the topic and purpose of your paper. If you are writing on a complex or controversial topic, you should include material that represents more than one point of view. Also compare publication date, point of view, coverage of the subject, and language to see whether one source is more useful than another.

Take Notes

Taking notes as you read will help you keep track of information and focus on your topic. Some people like to use notecards to make organizing information easier. You can also create documents for each source on a computer, or divide a notebook into sections. The key is to record all the information you will need the first time you read a source.

- To make organizing your notes easy later, use a new card for each piece of information.

- At the top left-hand side of each card, write a key word or phrase that identifies the subject of the information.

- Assign a number to each source of information. Write the number at the top right-hand side.

- Directly after each note, in parentheses, write the number of the page on which you found the information.

- Write only details that relate to your topic.

- Record important details in one of these ways:

Paraphrase, or use your own words, to restate specific information.

Summarize main ideas that an author presents. When you summarize several pages, be sure to note the page on which the material starts and the page on which it ends—for example, 213–221.

Quote the exact words of an author only when the actual wording is especially interesting or comes from an important source. Enclose all of the author's words in quotation marks to make it clear that the ideas belong to someone else.

See the sample note card below, which includes information about the topic from three pages.

Careers and goals	12

Many people "crave work that will spark . . . excitement and energy." (5) Sher recognizes that a career does not necessarily satisfy a person's aim in life. (24) She also offers ads on how to overcome obstacles that people experience in defining their goals. (101)

Make Source Cards

In a research report, you must document the sources of your information. To do this, write the author's name, the title, the city of publication, the publisher, the date of publication, and the location of each source on a separate index card. Give each card a number and write it in the upper right-hand corner. The cards will be useful for seeing the relationship between your sources at a glance and for preparing a bibliography. (See the last page of this handbook for instructions on how to use a database for organizing, storing, and retrieving information.)

Book

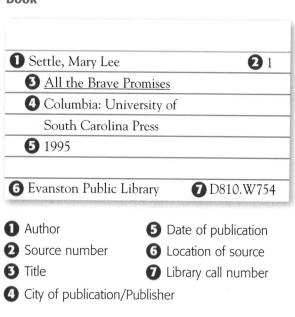

❶ Settle, Mary Lee   **❷** 1

   ❸ <u>All the Brave Promises</u>

   ❹ Columbia: University of

      South Carolina Press

❺ 1995

❻ Evanston Public Library   **❼** D810.W754

❶ Author   **❺** Date of publication

❷ Source number   **❻** Location of source

❸ Title   **❼** Library call number

❹ City of publication/Publisher

Periodicals

❶ Chelminksi, R.   **❷** 2

   ❸ "The Maginot Line"

   ❹ <u>Smithsonian,</u> June 1997, 90–99

❶ Author

❷ Source number

❸ Title

❹ Title of magazine/date/page number(s)

Online Source

❶ "Job Hunting Resources"   **❷** 3

❸ The Career Building Network

❹ CareerBuilder

❺ 14 Feb. 2002

❻ <u>http://www.careerbuilder.com</u>

❶ Title   **❹** Sponsoring organization

❷ Source number   **❺** Date of access

❸ Title of database   **❻** URL

Develop a Thesis Statement

After you have begun researching your topic, think about your audience and your purpose, the overall point you want to make. Write one sentence, your thesis statement, that says exactly what your topic is and what you intend to say about it; for example, "World War II changed the lives of African Americans and contributed to the rise of the civil rights movement."

Here are the steps:

- Start by examining your central idea.
- Refine it to reflect the information that you gathered in your research.
- Consider your approach to the topic. What is the purpose of your research? Who is your audience? Are you proving or disproving something? illustrating a cause-and-effect relationship? offering a solution to a problem? examining one aspect of the topic thoroughly? predicting an outcome?
- Revise your central idea to reflect your approach.
- Be prepared to revise your thesis statement.

Sample thesis statement

Big Bend National Park is a place where natural environments merge to create a great diversity of plants and animals.

Write an Outline

When you have finished taking notes, organize your note cards in one of many possible ways or combinations of ways so that you can develop a working outline.

- Sort the cards into piles that are related thematically.
- Put the piles together in different ways that suggest organizational patterns.
- Write down the main ideas that you want to cover and assign cards to each of those ideas.
- Do further research if you discover that you do not have enough information.

Then write your outline, putting your thesis statement at the beginning of it. Beneath your thesis statement, list the main ideas related to it, the supporting details or evidence for each of those ideas, and opinions you have about the information. Finally, use your outline as a guide in writing a summary of the information you found that supports your thesis statement. Follow the outline form below.

Sample outline

Big Bend National Park is a place where natural environments merge to create a great diversity of plants and animals.

    I.   Geology of Big Bend

        A. Rio Grande, arching linear oasis

        B. Chisos Mts., green desert island

        C. Chihuahuan Desert, arid life zone

   II. Adaptations to life in Big Bend

        A. Flora

            1. Cactus, patient seed germinator

            2. Creosote bush, toxic-leaf dropper

            3. Candelilla, waxy moisture miser

        B. Fauna

Draft Your Paper

- Write an introduction that creates interest, perhaps by beginning with a question or a controversial quotation. Include your thesis statement in the introduction. Write a paper that is of sufficient length to cover your topic thoroughly.

- Consult your working outline and your note cards as you concentrate on putting your ideas down completely and in logical order.

- Include your personal opinions that relate to the information you have found.

- Write an effective conclusion, one that restates your thesis, summarizes your main points, explains how the research points to important new questions that can be explored, and brings closure to the paper.

Document Your Information

You must document, or credit, the sources of all of the information you use in your report. There are two common ways to do this:

Footnotes In this method, in-text numerals point to documentation at the bottom of each page.

- Place a numeral at the end of the information you are documenting.
- Number the notes consecutively, beginning with 1.
- Be sure that the numerals are slightly raised and come after any punctuation.
- Place the documentation information itself, with a matching numeral, at the bottom of the page.

In-text numeral for footnote:

The Declaration of Independence was read in public for the first time on July 6, 1776.[3]

Footnote at bottom of page:

[3]John Smith, *The Declaration of Independence* (New York: DI, 2001) 221

Parenthetical Documentation In this method, in-text parenthetical citations point to a corresponding entry in your works-cited list—a list of all of your sources with their publication information that will appear as the final page of your paper.

- Place in parentheses at the end of each quotation, paraphrase, or summary of borrowed information a reference to its source and the number of the page on which it is found in the source.

- Provide just enough information for readers to be able to identify the source.

The Modern Language Association (MLA) recommends the guidelines below for crediting sources in text. You may wish to refer to the *MLA Handbook for Writers of Research Papers* by Joseph Gibaldi for more information and examples.

- Put in parentheses the author's last name and the number of the page on which you found the information.

  The declaration was first read in public by militia colonel John Nixon (Smith 222).

- If you mention the author's name in the sentence, you do not need to repeat it in the parentheses.

  According to Smith, the reading was greeted with wild applause (224).

- If your source does not identify a particular author, as in a newspaper or encyclopedia article, just give the first word or two of the piece.

  The anniversary of the reading was commemorated by a parade and fireworks ("Reading Celebrated").

Avoid Plagiarism

Plagiarism is the act of taking an author's words or ideas and presenting them as your own. In the most flagrant cases, words and ideas are lifted from an author's work exactly as the author wrote them. But in every case, you must credit a source not only for material directly quoted but also for facts or ideas obtained from it.

Consider this example:

From the original SparkNotes study guide by Melissa and Stephanie Martin

> Throughout the novel, Twain depicts the society that surrounds Huck as little more than a collection of degraded rules and precepts that defy logic. This faulty logic appears early in the novel, when the new judge in town allows Pap to keep custody of Huck.

Plagiarized usage

> Twain's depiction of society is as a collection of illogical rules and principles. A good example of this is when Pap is awarded custody of Huck.

Simply rewording the original passage is not enough. In order to legally and ethically use the words or ideas of another writer you must credit the writer of the original or rework the original into your own new idea.

Using Material Without Plagiarizing

1. **Quote the original directly and credit the author.**

   As Melissa and Stephanie Martin note in their SparkNotes study guide, Huck lives in a society that is "little more than a collection of degraded rules and precepts that defy logic." They offer the example of Pap being awarded custody of Huck.

2. **Paraphrase the original and credit the author.**

   In their SparkNotes study guide, Melissa and Stephanie Martin note that Twain's depiction of society is as a collection of illogical rules and principles. A good example of this is when Pap is awarded custody of Huck.

3. **Use the information in the original to create your own idea.**

   It is hard to blame Huck for wanting to escape from a world where he is forced to follow arbitrary rules, and where he is forced to live with an abusive father.

Crediting your source is not only fair to the writer of the original source, it is also the law. Plagiarism is a serious offense and can result in failing grades, expulsion, and even legal action.

- In addition to citing books and periodicals from which you take information, cite song lyrics, letters, and excerpts from literature.

- Also credit original ideas that are expressed graphically in tables, charts, and diagrams, as well as the sources of any visual aids you may include, such as photographs.

- You do not need to cite the source of any information that is common knowledge, such as "John F. Kennedy was assassinated in 1963 in Dallas, Texas."

Compile a List of Works Cited

At the end of your paper, list all of the sources of information that you used in preparing it. Arrange them alphabetically by the author's last name (or by the first word in the title if no author is mentioned). Title this list *Works Cited*.

- Include complete publishing information for each source.
- For magazine and newspaper articles, include the page numbers. If an article is continued on a different page, use + after the first page number.
- For online sources, include the date accessed. Many academic Internet sites and journals will provide a works cited citation for their articles. Look at the end of the article for citations you can cut and paste into your works cited.
- Cite only those sources from which you actually use information.
- Arrange entries in alphabetical order according to the author's last name. Write the last name first. If no author is given, alphabetize by title.
- For long entries, indent five spaces every line after the first.
- Double-space within and between entries.
- Center the words *Works Cited* at the top of the page.

How to Cite Sources

On the next three pages, you'll find sample style sheets that can help you prepare your list of sources—the final page of the research paper. Use the one your teacher prefers.

---

❶ Works Cited

❷ Bertram, Jeffrey. "African Bees: Fact or Myth?" Orlando Sentinel 18 Aug. 1999: D2.

❸ Gore, Rick. "Neanderthals." National Geographic. January 1996: 2–35. **❽**

❹ Gould, Stephen J. The Panda's Thumb. New York: Norton, 1982.

❺ "Governor Chiles Vetoes Anti-Everglades Bills–5/13/98." Friends of the Everglades. **❾** May 1998. 26 Aug 1998 <http://www.everglades.org/pressrel_may28.htm>.

❻ "Neanderthal man." The Columbia Encyclopedia. 5th ed. 1993.

❼ Pabst, Laura. Interview. March 11, 2008.

---

❶ Centered title
❷ Newspaper article
❸ Magazine article
❹ Book with one author
❺ On-line article
❻ Encyclopedia
❼ Interview
❽ Include page numbers for a magazine article but not for a book, unless the book is a collection of essays by different authors.
❾ Include database (underlined), publication medium (online), computer service, and date of access.

MLA Style

MLA style is most often used in English and social studies classes. Center the title *Works Cited* at the top of your list.

Source	Style
Book with one author	Isaacson, Walter. *Einstein: His Life and Universe.* New York: Simon, 2007. Print.
Book with two or three authors	Mortenson, Greg, and David Oliver Relin. *Three Cups of Tea: One Man's Mission to Promote Peace . . . One School at a Time.* New York: Penguin, 2006. Print. [If a book has more than three authors, name only the first author and then write "et al." (Latin abbreviation for "and others").]
Book with editor(s)	Lehman, David, and Heather McHugh, eds. *The Best American Poetry 2007.* New York: Scribner's, 2007. Print.
Book with an organization or a group as author or editor	Adobe Creative Team. *Adobe Photoshop CS3 Classroom in a Book.* Berkeley: Adobe, 2007. Print.
Work from an anthology	Kilmer, Joyce. "Trees." Ed. Joseph Parisi. The *Poetry Anthology, 1912–2002.* Chicago: Dec, 2004. 7. Print.
Introduction in a published book	Jackson, Peter. Introduction. *The Making of* Star Wars: *The Definitive Story Behind the Original Film.* By J. W. Rinzler. New York: Del Rey, 2007. iii. Print.
Encyclopedia article	"Jazz." *The New Encyclopaedia Britannica: Micropaedia.* 15th ed. 1998. Print.
Weekly magazine article	Sacks, Oliver. "A Bolt from the Blue." *New Yorker* 23 July 2007: 38–42. Print.
Monthly magazine article	Plotnikoff, David. "Hungry Man." *Saveur* July 2007: 35–36. Print.
Newspaper article	Long, Ray, and Jeffrey Meitrodt. "Some Budget Progress Made." *Chicago Tribune* 26 July 2007: B3. Print. [If no author is named, begin the entry with the title of the article.]
Internet	Onion, Amanda. "Americans Embracing 'Green' Cleaning." *ABC News.* ABC News Internet Ventures. 30 Jan. 2006. Web. 1 Aug. 2007. <http://abcnews.go.com/Technology/Business/story?id=1544322>. [Include a URL only when the reader cannot locate the source without it or when your teacher requires it.]
Online magazine article	Parks, Bob. "Robot Buses Pull In to San Diego's Fastest Lane." *Wired Magazine* July 2007. Web. 25 Oct. 2007. <http://www.wired.com/cars/futuretransport/magazine/15-08/st_robot>.
Radio or TV program	"Jungles." *Planet Earth.* Dir. Alastair Fothergill. Discovery Channel. 19 Nov. 2006. Television.
Videotape or DVD	*An Inconvenient Truth.* Dir. Davis Guggenheim. 2006. Paramount, 2006. DVD. [For a videotape (VHS) version, replace "DVD" with "Videocassette."]
Interview	Campeche, Tanya. E-mail interview. 25 Feb. 2004. [If an interview takes place in person, replace "E-mail" with "Personal"; if it takes place on the telephone, use "Telephone."]

CMS Style

CMS style was created by the University of Chicago Press to meet its publishing needs. This style, which is detailed in *The Chicago Manual of Style* (CMS), is used in a number of subject areas. Center the title *Bibliography* at the top of your list.

Source	Style
Book with one author	Isaacson, Walter. *Einstein: His Life and Universe.* New York: Simon & Schuster, 2007.
Book with two to ten authors	Mortenson, Greg, and David Oliver Relin. *Three Cups of Tea: One Man's Mission to Promote Peace . . . One School at a Time.* New York: Penguin Books, 2006. [If a book has more than ten authors, name only the first seven and then write "et al." (Latin abbreviation for "and others").]
Book with editor(s)	Lehman, David, and Heather McHugh, eds. *The Best American Poetry 2007.* New York: Scribner's, 2007.
Book with an organization or a group as author or editor	Adobe Creative Team. *Adobe Photoshop CS3 Classroom in a Book.* Berkeley: Adobe Press, 2007.
Work from an anthology	Kilmer, Joyce. "Trees." In *The "Poetry" Anthology, 1912–2002.* Ed. Joseph Parisi. Chicago: Ivan R. Dee, 2004.
Introduction in a published book	Jackson, Peter. Introd. to *The Making of "Star Wars": The Definitive Story behind the Original Film* by J. W. Rinzler. New York: Del Rey, 2007.
Encyclopedia article	[Credit for encyclopedia articles goes in your text, not in your bibliography.]
Weekly magazine article	Sacks, Oliver. "A Bolt from the Blue." *The New Yorker,* July 23, 2007.
Monthly magazine article	Plotnikoff, David. "Hungry Man." *Saveur* July 2007.
Newspaper article	Long, Ray, and Jeffrey Meitrodt. "Some Budget Progress Made." *Chicago Tribune,* sec. B. July 26, 2007. [Credit for unsigned newspaper articles goes in your text, not in your bibliography.]
Internet	Onion, Amanda. "Americans Embracing 'Green' Cleaning." *ABC News,* January 30, 2006. http://abcnews.go.com/Technology/Business/story?id=1544322.
Online magazine article	Parks, Bob. "Robot Buses Pull In to San Diego's Fastest Lane." *Wired Magazine,* July 2007. http://www.wired.com/cars/futuretransport/magazine/15-08/st_robot.
Radio or TV program	[Credit for radio and TV programs goes in your text, not in your bibliography.]
Videotape or DVD	Guggenheim, Davis, dir. *An Inconvenient Truth.* DVD. Hollywood, CA: Paramount Home Video, 2006. [For a videotape (VHS) version, replace "DVD" with "Videocassette."]
Interview	[Credit for interviews goes in your text, not in your bibliography.]

APA Style

The American Psychological Association (APA) style is commonly used in the sciences. Center the title *References* at the top of your list.

Source	Style
Book with one author	Isaacson, W. (2007). *Einstein: His life and universe.* New York: Simon & Schuster.
Book with two to six authors	Mortenson, G., & Relin, D. O. (2006). *Three cups of tea: One man's mission to promote peace . . . one school at a time.* New York: Penguin. [If a book has more than six authors, name only the first six and then write "et al." (Latin abbreviation for "and others").]
Book with editor(s)	Lehman, D., & McHugh, H. (Eds.). (2007). *The best American poetry 2007.* New York: Scribner's.
Book with an organization or a group as author or editor	Adobe Creative Team. (2007). *Adobe Photoshop CS3 classroom in a book.* Berkeley, CA: Adobe Press.
Work from an anthology	Kilmer, J. (2004). Trees. In J. Parisi (Ed.), *The Poetry anthology, 1912–2002* (p. 7). Chicago: Ivan R. Dee. (Reprinted from *Poetry,* August 1913, p. 25).
Introduction in a published book	[Credit for introductions goes in your text, not in your references.]
Encyclopedia article	Jazz. (1998). In *The new encyclopaedia britannica.* (Vol. 6, pp. 519–520). Chicago: Encyclopaedia Britannica.
Weekly magazine article	Sacks, O. (2007, July 23). A bolt from the blue. *The New Yorker, 83,* 38–42.
Monthly magazine article	Plotnikoff, D. (2007, July). Hungry man. *Saveur, 103,* 35–36.
Newspaper article	Long, R., & Meitrodt, J. (2007, July 26). Some budget progress made. *Chicago Tribune,* p. B3. [If no author is named, begin the entry with the title of the article.]
Internet	Onion, A. (2006, January 30). Americans embracing "green" cleaning. ABC News. Retrieved August 1, 2007, from http://abcnews.go.com/Technology/Business/story?id=1544322
Online magazine article	Parks, B. (2007, July). Robot buses pull in to San Diego's fastest lane. *Wired Magazine, 15.08.* Retrieved July 25, 2007, from http://www.wired.com/cars/futuretransport/magazine/15-08/st_robot
Radio or TV program	Fithergill, A. (Director). (2006, November 19). Jungles [Television series episode]. In S. Malone (Producer), *Planet Earth.* Silver Spring, MD: Discovery Channel.
Videotape or DVD	Bender, L. (Producer), & Guggenheim, D. (Director). (2006). *An inconvenient truth.* [Motion picture]. United States: Paramount Home Video.
Interview	[Credit for interviews goes in your text, not in your bibliography.]

Using a Computer for Writing

Use Word Processing Software A word processor is a digital tool that lets you move your words and ideas around until you find the best way to present them. Each type of word processing software is a bit different, but they all help you plan, draft, revise, edit, and present properly formatted documents.

Menus, Toolbars, and Rulers Open a word processing document. At the top of your screen, locate the menu bar, one or more toolbars, and a ruler.

Menu Bar Menus help you perform important processes. The Edit menu, for example, allows you to copy, paste, and find text within your document.

Toolbars There are two basic types of tools.
- Function tools perform some kind of computer function, such as printing a document or checking its spelling.
- Formatting tools are used to change the way a document looks—for example, changing its font (typeface) or paragraph style.

Ruler The ruler looks like a measuring stick with markers at each end. These markers control the margins of your document. Try changing the margins on your document. You can also put tabs on the ruler so that you can use the tab key on your keyboard to send your cursor to those positions.

Multimedia Presentations

You can use digital technology, such as a computer with presentation software, to create a multimedia presentation of your work. Adding pictures, video, and sound to your presentation can attract and hold your audience's attention. However, it is important that you understand the rules and laws about using other people's creations in your work.

Slides In a multimedia presentation, each screen a viewer sees is called a slide. Generally, a slide consists of text—not too much of it—and an image of some kind. Each slide should be limited to a single idea with a few supporting details. Because you want to get your point across quickly, it's important that you choose your images and words carefully. An Internet search engine can help you find downloadable images to use in your presentation. Most computer images have the file extension *.gif* or *.jpeg*.

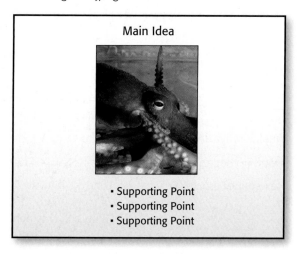

Video For some types of presentations, adding video can have a big impact. For example, if you're presenting a report on an actor, what better way to illustrate his or her style than with movie clips? You can record video clips from your TV or download them from the Internet. Most movie files have the extensions *.avi, .mov,* or *.mpeg.*

You can add your images and video clips to your presentation using the Insert menu in your presentation software. Also, most presentation software has a "wizard" or templates that will help you put together your multimedia presentation.

Activity

Working with a partner, choose a movie or television show as the basis for a complete multimedia presentation. Include in your presentation at least six slides with pictures and text and two video clips. Don't forget about media ethics, and be careful not to plagiarize as you choose media for your presentation.

Databases

An electronic database is a software program that allows you to organize, store, and retrieve information. Data are organized into a table of columns and rows. Each single piece of information is called a field.

Once the information is in your database, you can recall it in a number of ways that allow you to see the relationship between pieces of information in the fields. For example, you can arrange an address-book database to show you all the names of people who live in a certain city or zip code.

Activity

Create a database of your research materials for a current or upcoming report. Enter fields for authors, titles, types of media, and key words describing useful information you found in each. Practice organizing the database in different ways. For example, organize your database to show how many magazine articles you used in your research.

Field Columns (Categories)

Record

Name	Address	City	State	Zip
Brown, Katie	12814 South Emerald	Chicago	IL	60601
Hauser, Sam	63 Taylor	Stamford	CT	06904
Marmalard, Greg	1001 Porterhouse	Laredo	TX	78040
O'Hare, Megan	140 Blossom	Shaker Heights	OH	44118
Trumbull, Ellen	302 St. Nicolas	Darien	CT	06820

Field

Reading Handbook

Reading Handbook

Being an active reader is a crucial part of being a lifelong learner. It is also an ongoing task. Good reading skills are recursive; that is, they build on each other, providing the tools you need to understand text, to interpret ideas and themes, and to read critically.

Understanding Text Structure

To follow the logic and remember the message of a selection, analyze its **text structure**—the organization of ideas in the work. Recognizing the pattern of organization can help you discover the writer's purpose and identify the important ideas in the selection. **Look for signal words** and phrases that indicate how the author has arranged main ideas.

- **Spatial sequence**—words or phrases such as *nearby, to the left, above,* and *behind* are used to indicate the physical arrangement of people and objects in an area.
- **Order of importance**—words such as *most important* and *least necessary* are used to compare the importance of things or ideas.
- **Chronological order**—words such as *first, then, after, later,* and *finally* are used to indicate the arrangement of events according to their order of occurrence.
- **Cause-and-effect order**—words or phrases such as *so, therefore, because, subsequently,* or *as a result* indicate a chain of events.
- **Comparison-contrast order**—words or phrases such as *similarly, in contrast, likewise,* or *on the other hand* indicate similarities and differences between things.
- **Problem-solution order**—words such as *need, help, attempt,* and *obstruction* are used to present a problem and then offer one or more solutions. A problem-solution text structure may incorporate other text structures such as order of importance, chronological order, or comparison-contrast order.

Comprehension Strategies

Because understanding is the most critical reading task, lifelong learners use a wide variety of reading strategies before, during, and after reading to ensure their comprehension.

Determining the Main Idea

The **main idea** of a selection is the most important idea in the entire selection. As you read, it is helpful to determine the main idea of each paragraph. Then pause and ask yourself

- What do these details add up to?
- What is the main point of this selection?
- What is the writer trying to communicate?

Summarizing

A summary is a short restatement in logical sequence and in your own words of the main ideas and important details of a selection. Summarizing is an excellent tool for understanding and remembering a passage. Remember the following points when you summarize a selection.

- Identify the **main ideas.**
- Determine the essential **supporting details.**
- Relate all the main ideas and essential details in **logical sequence.**
- **Paraphrase,** or restate, the selection in your own words.
- Answer **who, what, where, when,** and **why** questions.

A good summary can easily be understood by someone who has not read the selection. To see whether an item is necessary to your summary, remove it. If your summary still sounds complete, the item was not needed.

Distinguishing between fact and opinion

It is always important to be able to tell whether the ideas in a selection are facts or the writer's opinions.

- **Facts** can be proven or measured; you can verify them in reference materials. Sometimes you can observe or test them yourself.

  Example: Chicago is about 800 miles from New York City.

- **Opinions** are often open to interpretation and contain phrases such as *I believe* or *from my point of view.*

  Example: As far as I'm concerned, it takes too many hours to drive from Chicago to New York.

As you read a selection, evaluate all facts as well as all opinions you find. Ask yourself

- Are the facts relevant?
- Are the facts true?
- Are the opinions well informed and based on verifiable facts? Are they persuasive?

Making inferences and supporting them

An **inference** is a supposition about a subject that you derive from your reason and experience, coupled with what a writer implies or suggests but does not state directly.

- **Drawing a conclusion** is making a statement that you have deduced from supporting details in the text.

- **Making a generalization** is inferring a general rule from particular facts or instances.

It is most important when inferring to be sure that you have based your thoughts on supporting details from the text as well as on your own knowledge.

Making a prediction

A **prediction** is an educated guess about what a text will be about, or about story events or outcomes, that is based on clues a writer provides. You can make predictions before, during, and after your reading.

- Take breaks during your reading and **ask yourself questions** about what will happen next, such as, "How will this character react to this news?"

- **Answer the questions you ask yourself** in the form of predictions, supporting your answers with evidence from the text. For example, "Sam will be jealous when he hears the news, because he is in love with Antonia."

- As you continue reading, **adjust your predictions.**

- Finally, **verify your predictions.**

Reading silently for sustained periods

When you read for long periods of time, your task is to avoid distractions. Check your comprehension regularly by summarizing what you have read so far. Use study guides or graphic organizers to help you get through difficult passages. Take breaks when you need them and vary your reading rate according to the demands of the task.

Monitoring Comprehension

Whichever strategies you choose to use while reading, it is always helpful to

- read slowly and carefully
- reread difficult passages
- take careful notes
- ask yourself questions about important ideas and story elements and answer the questions to clarify your understanding

Also, when reading difficult material, modify or change your reading strategies to include these steps if you have not understood what you read.

- Reread the passage aloud, one sentence at a time.
- Look for context clues.
- Map out the main thoughts or ideas.
- Consult other sources, including reference aids, teachers, parents, and other students.
- Write comments or questions on another piece of paper for later review or discussion.

Language Handbook

Grammar Glossary

This glossary will help you quickly locate information about parts of speech and sentence structure. Standard American English calls for observing these conventions for business and academic writing and speaking.

A

Absolute phrase. *See* Phrase.

Abstract noun. *See* Noun chart.

Action verb. *See* Verb.

Active voice. *See* Voice.

Adjectival clause. *See* Clause chart.

Adjectival phrase. A prepositional or participial phrase that functions as an adjective. *See also* Phrase.

Adjective. A word that modifies a noun or a pronoun by limiting its meaning. Adjectives appear in various positions in a sentence. **(The *gray* cat purred. The cat is *gray*.)**

A predicate adjective follows a linking verb and further identifies or describes the subject. **(The child was excited.)**

A proper adjective is formed from a proper noun and begins with a capital letter. Many proper adjectives are created by adding these suffixes: *-an, -ian, -n, -ese,* and *-ish*. **(Chinese, African)**

Many adjectives have different forms to indicate degree of comparison. **(short, shorter, shortest)**

The positive degree is the simple form of the adjective. **(easy, interesting, good)**

The comparative degree compares two persons, places, things, or ideas. **(easier, more interesting, better)**

The superlative degree compares more than two persons, places, things, or ideas. **(easiest, most interesting, best)**

Adverb. A word that modifies a verb, an adjective, or another adverb by making its meaning more specific. When modifying a verb, an adverb may appear in various positions in a sentence. **(Cats *usually* eat less than dogs. *Usually,* cats eat less than dogs.)** When modifying an adjective or another adverb, an

adverb appears directly before the modified word. **(I was *quite* pleased.)** The word *not* and the contraction *-n't* are adverbs. **(Mike *wasn't* ready for the test.)** Certain adverbs of time, place, and degree also have a negative meaning. **(He is *never* ready.)**

Some adverbs have different forms to indicate degree of comparison. **(soon, sooner, soonest)**

The comparative degree compares two actions. **(better, more quickly)**

The superlative degree compares three or more actions. **(fastest, most patiently, least rapidly)**

Adverbial clause. *See* Clause chart.

Adverbial phrase. A prepositional or participial phrase that functions as an adverb. *See also* Phrase.

Antecedent. *See* Pronoun.

Appositive. A noun or a pronoun that further identifies another noun or pronoun. **(My friend *Julie* lives next door.)** *See also* Phrase.

Appositive phrase. *See* Phrase.

Article. The adjective *a, an,* or *the.*

The indefinite article **(a *and* an)** refers to one of a general group of persons, places, or things. **(I eat *an* apple *a* day.)**

The definite article **(the)** indicates that the noun is a specific person, place, or thing. **(*The* alarm woke me up.)**

Auxiliary verb. *See* Verb.

B

Base form. *See* Verb tense.

C

Clause. A group of words that has a subject and a predicate and that is used as part of a sentence. Clauses fall into two categories: *main clauses* (also

Types of Subordinate Clauses			
Clause	**Function**	**Example**	**Begins with . . .**
Adjectival clause	Modifies a noun or a pronoun	Songs *that have a strong beat* make me want to dance.	A relative pronoun such as *which, who, whom, whose,* or *that*
Adverbial clause	Modifies a verb, an adjective, or an adverb	*Whenever Al calls me,* he asks to borrow my bike.	A subordinating conjuction such as *after, although, because, if, since, when,* or *where*
Noun clause	Serves as a subject, an object, or a predicate nominative	*What Philip did* surprised us.	Words such as *how, that, what, whatever, when, where, which, who, whom, whoever, whose,* or *why*

called *independent clauses)* and *subordinate clauses* (also called *dependent clauses).*

A main clause can stand alone as a sentence. There must be at least one main clause in every sentence. (**A cat meowed,** and **a dog barked.**)

A subordinate clause cannot stand alone as a sentence but needs a main clause to complete its meaning. Many subordinate clauses begin with subordinating conjunctions or relative pronouns. (**When Geri sang,** the audience became quiet.) The chart on this page shows the main types of subordinate clauses.

Collective noun. *See* Noun chart.

Common noun. *See* Noun chart.

Comparative degree. *See* Adjective; Adverb.

Complement. A word or phrase that completes the meaning of a verb. The four basic kinds of complements are *direct objects, indirect objects, object complements,* and *subject complements.*

A direct object answers the question *What?* or *Whom?* after an action verb. (**Kari found a dollar. Larry saw Denise.**)

An indirect object answers the question *To whom? For whom? To what?* or *For what?* after an action verb. (**Do me a favor. She gave the child a toy.**)

An object complement answers the question *What?* after a direct object. An object complement is a noun, a pronoun, or an adjective that com-

pletes the meaning of a direct object by identifying or describing it. (**The director made me understudy for the role. The girl called the dog hers.**)

A subject complement follows a subject and a linking verb. It identifies or describes a subject. The two kinds of subject complements are *predicate nominatives* and *predicate adjectives.*

A predicate nominative is a noun or a pronoun that follows a linking verb and gives information about the subject. (**The author is Poe.**)

A predicate adjective is an adjective that follows a linking verb and gives additional information about the subject. (**Ian became angry at the bully.**)

Complex sentence. *See* Sentence.

Compound preposition. *See* Preposition.

Compound sentence. *See* Sentence.

Compound-complex sentence. *See* Sentence.

Conjunction. A word that joins single words or groups of words.

A coordinating conjunction **(and, but, or, nor, for, yet, so)** joins words or groups of words that are equal in grammatical importance. (**David and Ruth are twins. I was bored, so I left.**)

Correlative conjunctions **(both . . . and, just as . . . so, not only . . . but also, either . . . or, neither . . . nor, whether . . . or)** work in pairs to join words and groups of words of equal importance. (**Choose either the muffin or the bagel.**)

A subordinating conjunction *(after, although, as if, because, before, if, since, so that, than, though, until, when, while)* joins a dependent idea or clause to a main clause. (Beth acted *as if* she felt ill.)

Conjunctive adverb. An adverb used to clarify the relationship between clauses of equal weight in a sentence. Conjunctive adverbs are used to replace *and* *(also, besides, furthermore, moreover)*, to replace *but* *(however, nevertheless, still)*, to state equality *(equally, likewise, similarly, indeed)*, or to state a result *(consequently, therefore, so, thus)*. (Ana wanted an A; *therefore,* she studied hard.)

Coordinating conjunction. *See* Conjunction.

Correlative conjunction. *See* Conjunction.

D

Declarative sentence. *See* Sentence.

Definite article. *See* Article.

Demonstrative pronoun. *See* Pronoun.

Direct object. *See* Complement.

E

Emphatic form. *See* Verb tense.

F

Future tense. *See* Verb tense.

G

Gerund. A verb form that ends in *-ing* and is used as a noun. A gerund may function as a subject, the object of a verb, or the object of a preposition. (*Smiling* uses fewer muscles than *frowning.* Marie enjoys *walking.*)

Gerund phrase. *See* Phrase.

I

Imperative mood. *See* Mood of verb.

Imperative sentence. *See* Sentence chart.

Indefinite pronoun. *See* Pronoun.

Indicative mood. *See* Mood of verb.

Indirect object. *See* Complement.

Infinitive. A verb form that begins with the word *to* and functions as a noun, an adjective, or an adverb. (No one wanted *to go.*) Note: When *to* precedes a verb, it is not a preposition but signals an infinitive.

Infinitive phrase. *See* Phrase.

Intensive pronoun. *See* Pronoun.

Interjection. A word or a phrase that expresses emotion or exclamation. An interjection has no grammatical connection to other words. Commas follow mild ones; exclamation points follow stronger ones. (*Well,* have a good day. *Wow!*)

Interrogative pronoun. *See* Pronoun.

Intransitive verb. *See* Verb.

Introductory clause. An adverbial subordinate clause that appears before the main clause in a sentence. *See also* Clause chart.

Inverted order. The transposition of subject and predicate, with the predicate coming before the subject. Some sentences are written in inverted order for variety or special emphasis. (**Up the beanstalk** *scampered Jack.*) The subject also generally follows the predicate in a sentence that begins with *here* or *there.* (*Here* was the solution to his problem.) Questions, or interrogative sentences, are often written in inverted order. In many questions an auxiliary verb precedes the subject, and the main verb follows it. (*Has* anyone *seen* Susan?) Questions that begin with *who* or *what* follow normal word order.

Irregular verb. *See* Verb tense.

L

Linking verb. *See* Verb.

M

Main clause. *See* Clause.

Mood of verb. A verb expresses one of three moods: indicative, imperative, or subjunctive.

The indicative mood is the most common. It makes a statement or asks a question. (We *are* out of bread. *Will* you *buy* it?)

The imperative mood expresses a command or makes a request. (*Stop* acting like a child! Please *return* my sweater.)

Types of Nouns		
Noun	Function	Examples
Abstract noun	Names an idea, a quality, or a characteristic	capitalism, terror
Collective noun	Names a group of things or persons	herd, troop
Common noun	Names a general type of person, place, thing, or idea	city, building
Compound noun	Is made up of two or more words	checkerboard, globe-trotter
Noun of direct addrress	Identifies the person or persons being spoken to	*Maria*, please stand.
Possessive noun	Shows possession, ownership, or the relationship between two nouns	my *sister's* room
Proper noun	Names a particular person, place, thing, or idea	Cleopatra, Italy, Christianity

The subjunctive mood is used to express, indirectly, a demand, suggestion, or statement of necessity **(I demand that he *stop* acting like a child. It's necessary that she *buy* more bread.)** The subjunctive is also used to state a condition or wish that is contrary to fact. This use of the subjunctive requires the past tense. **(If you *were* a nice person, you *would share* your candy.)**

N

Nominative pronoun. *See* Pronoun.

Nonrestrictive element. A word, phrase, or clause that is not essential to the correct understanding of a sentence and that therefore should be set off with a comma or commas.

Noun. A word that names a person, a place, a thing, or an idea. The chart on this page shows the main types of nouns.

Noun clause. *See* Clause chart.

Noun of direct address. *See* Noun chart.

Number. A noun, a pronoun, or a verb is *singular* in number if it refers to one and *plural* if it refers to more than one.

O

Object. *See* Complement..

P

Parallel construction. Similarity, in structure or grammatical form, of logically equal sentence parts.

Participle. A verb form that can function as an adjective. Present participles always end in *-ing.* **(The woman comforted the *crying* child.)** Many past participles end in *-ed.* **(We bought the beautifully *painted* chair.)** However, irregular verbs form their past participles in some other way. **(Cato was Caesar's *sworn* enemy.)**

Passive voice. *See* Voice.

Past tense. *See* Verb tense.

Perfect tense. *See* Verb tense.

Personal pronoun. *See* Pronoun; Pronoun chart.

Phrase. A group of words that acts in a sentence as a single part of speech.

An absolute phrase consists of a noun or pronoun that is modified by a participle or participial phrase but has no grammatical relation to the complete subject or predicate. **(*The roast being done,* we finally sat down to eat dinner.)**

An appositive phrase is an appositive along with any modifiers. If not restrictive, or essential to the meaning of the sentence, an appositive phrase is set off by commas. **(Jack plans to go to the jazz concert, *an important musical event.*)**

A gerund phrase includes a gerund plus its complements and modifiers. (*Knitting* is her hobby.)

An infinitive phrase contains the infinitive plus its complements and modifiers. (**It is time** *to leave for school.*)

A participial phrase contains a participle and any modifiers necessary to complete its meaning. (**The woman** *sitting over there* **is my grandmother.**)

A prepositional phrase consists of a preposition, its object, and any modifiers of the object. A prepositional phrase can function as an adjective, modifying a noun or a pronoun. (**The dog** *in the yard* **is gentle.**) A prepositional phrase may also function as an adverb when it modifies a verb, an adverb, or an adjective. (**The baby slept** *on my lap.*)

A verb phrase consists of one or more auxiliary verbs followed by a main verb. (**The job** *will have been completed* **by noon tomorrow.**)

Positive degree. *See* Adjective.

Possessive noun. *See* Noun chart.

Predicate. A verb or verb phrase (with any objects, complements, or modifiers) that expresses the essential thought about the subject of a sentence.

A simple predicate is a verb or verb phrase that tells what the subject does or is. (**We** *ran*.)

A complete predicate includes the simple predicate and any words that modify or complete it. (**We** *solved the problem in a short time.*)

A compound predicate has two or more verbs or verb phrases that are joined by a conjunction and share the same subject. (**We** *ran to the park and began to play baseball.*)

Predicate adjective. *See* Adjective; Complement.

Predicate nominative. *See* Complement.

Preposition. A word that shows the relationship of a noun or a pronoun to some other word in the sentence. Prepositions include *about, above, across, among, as, behind, below, beyond, but, by, down, during, except, for, from, into, like, near, of, on, outside, over, since, through, to, under, until, with.* (**I usually eat breakfast** *before* **school.**)

A compound preposition is made up of more than one word (*according to, ahead of, because of, as to, by means of, in addition to, on account of*). (**We played the game** *in spite of* **the snow.**)

Prepositional phrase. *See* Phrase.

Present tense. *See* Verb tense.

Progressive form. *See* Verb tense.

Pronoun. A word that takes the place of a noun, a group of words acting as a noun, or another pronoun. The word or group of words that a pronoun refers to is called its antecedent. (In the following sentence, *Mari* is the antecedent of *she:* **Mari** *likes Mexican food, but* **she** *doesn't like Italian food.*)

A demonstrative pronoun points out specific persons, places, things, or ideas. *(this, that, these, those)*

An indefinite pronoun refers to persons, places, or things in a more general way than a noun does. *(all, another, any, both, each, either, enough, everything, few, many, most, much, none, one, neither, nobody, other(s), plenty, several, some)*

An intensive pronoun adds emphasis to another noun or pronoun. If an intensive pronoun is omitted, the meaning of the sentence will be the same. (**Avra** *herself* **was the star of her play.**)

An interrogative pronoun is used to form questions. *(who? whom? whose? what? which?)*

A personal pronoun refers to a specific person or thing. Personal pronouns have three cases: nominative, possessive, and objective. The case depends upon the function of the pronoun in a sentence. The first chart on this page shows the case forms of personal pronouns.

A reflexive pronoun refers to a noun or a pronoun used earlier in the sentence, indicating a connection. (**We told** *ourselves* **to be patient.**)

A relative pronoun is used to begin a subordinate clause. *(who, whose, that, what, whom, whoever, whomever, whichever, whatever)*

Proper adjective. *See* Adjective.

Proper noun. *See* Noun chart.

R

Reflexive pronoun. *See* Pronoun.

Relative pronoun. *See* Pronoun.

Restrictive element. A word, a phrase, or a clause that is essential to the correct understanding of a sentence and that therefore should *not* be set off with a comma or commas.

S

Sentence. A group of words that expresses a complete thought. Every sentence has a subject and a predicate. Sentences can be classified by function or by structure. The second chart on this page shows the categories by function; the following subentries describe the categories by structure. *See also* Subject; Predicate; Clause.

A simple sentence has only one main clause and no subordinate clauses. *(Stephan found an old violin.)* A simple sentence may contain a compound subject or a compound predicate or both. *(Stephan and Teri found an old violin. Stephan found an old violin and tried to play it. Stephan and Teri found an old violin and tried to play it.)* The subject and the predicate can be expanded with adjectives, adverbs, prepositional phrases, appositives, and verbal phrases. As long as the sentence has only one main clause, however, it remains a simple sentence. *(Stephan, rummaging in the attic, found an old violin.)*

A compound sentence has two or more main clauses. Each main clause has its own subject and predicate, and these main clauses are usually joined by a comma and a coordinating conjunction. *(Cats meow, and dogs bark, but ducks quack.)* A semicolon may also join the main clauses in a compound sentence. *(The helicopter landed; the pilot had saved four passengers.)*

A complex sentence has one main clause and one or more subordinate clauses. *(Because the movie starts at five, we should leave home right now.)*

A compound-complex sentence has two or more main clauses and at least one subordinate clause. *(If we leave any later, we may miss the previews, and I want to see them.)*

Simple predicate. *See* Predicate.

Simple subject. *See* Subject.

Subject. The part of a sentence that tells what the sentence is about.

A simple subject is the main noun or pronoun in the subject. *(Babies crawl.)*

A complete subject includes the simple subject with any words that modify it. *(The man from New Jersey won the race.)* In some sentences, the simple subject and the complete subject are the same. *(Birds fly.)*

A compound subject has two or more simple subjects joined by a conjunction. The subjects share

Personal Pronouns			
Clause	Singular Pronouns	Plural Pronouns	Function in Sentence
Nominative	I, you, she, he, it	we, you, they	subject or predicate nominative
Objective	me, you, her, him, it	us, you, them	direct object, indirect object, or object of a preposition

Types of Sentences			
Sentence Type	Function	Ends with . . .	Examples
Declarative sentence	Makes a statement	A period	*I did not enjoy the movie.*
Exclamatory sentence	Expresses strong emotion	An exclamation point	*What a good writer Consuela is!*
Imperative sentence	Makes a request or gives a command	A period or an exclamation point	*Please come to the party. Stop!*
Interrogative sentence	Asks a question	A question mark	*Is the composition due?*

the same verb. (**Firefighters** and *police officers* protect the community.)

Subjunctive mood. *See* Mood of verb.

Subordinate clause. *See* Clause.

Subordinating conjunction. *See* Conjunction.

Superlative degree. *See* Adjective; Adverb.

T

Tense. *See* Verb tense.

Transitive verb. *See* Verb.

V

Verb. A word that expresses action or a state of being. *(cooks, seem, laughed)*

An action verb tells what someone or something does. Action verbs can express either physical or mental action. (Crystal *changed* the tire herself.)

A transitive verb is an action verb that is followed by a word or words that answer the question *What?* or *Whom?* (I *held* the baby.)

An intransitive verb is an action verb that is not followed by a word that answers the question *What?* or *Whom?* (The baby *laughed.*)

A linking verb expresses a state of being by linking the subject of a sentence with a word or an expression that identifies or describes the subject. (The lemonade *tastes* sweet. He *is* our new principal.) The most commonly used linking verb is *be* in all its forms *(am, is, are, was, were, will be, been, being).* Other linking verbs include *appear, become, feel, grow, look, remain, seem, sound, smell, stay, taste.*

An auxiliary verb, or helping verb, is a verb that accompanies the main verb to form a verb phrase. (I *have been* swimming.) The forms of *be* and *have* are the most common auxiliary verbs *(am, is, are, was, were, being, been; has, have, had, having).* Other auxiliary verbs include *can, could, do, does, did, may, might, must, shall, should, will, would.*

Verbal. A verb form that functions in a sentence as a noun, an adjective, or an adverb. The three kinds of verbals are gerunds, infinitives, and participles. *See* Gerund; Infinitive; Participle.

Verb tense. The indication of when the action or state of being occurs. All verb tenses are formed from the four principal parts of a verb: a base form *(talk),* a present participle *(talking),* a simple past form *(talked),* and a past participle *(talked).* A regular verb forms its simple past tense and past participle by adding -*ed* to the base form *(climb, climbed).* An irregular verb forms its past tense and past participle in some other way *(get, got, gotten).*

Besides present, past, and future tenses, there are perfect tenses and progressive and emphatic forms.

The present perfect tense expresses an action or a condition that occurred at some indefinite time in the past. This tense also shows an action or a condition that began in the past and continues into the present. (She *has sung* for four years.)

The past perfect tense indicates that one past action or condition began *and* ended before another past action started. (Andy *had finished* his homework before I even began mine.)

The future perfect tense indicates that one future action or condition will begin *and* end before another future event starts. Use *will have* or *shall have* with the past participle of a verb. (By tomorrow, I *will have finished* my homework too.)

The progressive form of a verb expresses a continuing action in any of the six tenses. To make the progressive forms, use the appropriate tense of the verb *be* with the present participle of the main verb. (She *is acting.* She *has been acting.*)

The emphatic form adds special force, or emphasis, to the present and past tense of a verb. For the emphatic form, use *do, does,* or *did* with the base form. (Toshi *did want* that camera.)

Verb tenses within a passage must be consistent, or compatible. Progressive and perfect forms must be in the present tense when a passage is written in the present tense and in the past when a passage is written in the past tense. (She *reads* well. She *will have been reading* six years when she *turns* ten.)

Voice The voice of a verb shows whether the subject performs the action or receives the action of the verb.

A verb is in the active voice if the subject of the sentence performs the action. (The referee *blew* the whistle.)

A verb is in the passive voice if the subject of the sentence receives the action of the verb. (The whistle *was blown*.)

Troubleshooter

The Troubleshooter will help you recognize and correct errors that you might make in your writing.

Sentence Fragment

A sentence fragment does not express a complete thought. It may lack a subject, a verb, or both parts of a complete sentence.

Problem: A fragment that lacks a subject
The grass is wet. Can't be mowed now.

Solution: Add a subject to the fragment to make it a complete sentence.
The grass is wet. It can't be mowed now.

Problem: A fragment that lacks a complete verb
We enjoyed our dinner. Beans, rice, and salad.
The storm was fierce. Blowing hard.

Solution A: Add either a complete verb or a helping verb to make the sentence complete.
We enjoyed our dinner. Beans, rice, and salad make a good meal.
The storm was fierce. The wind was blowing hard.

Solution B: Combine the fragment with another sentence.
We enjoyed our dinner of beans, rice, and salad.
The storm was fierce, with the wind blowing hard.

Problem: A fragment that is a subordinate clause
We went to the park. Where we had often gone before.
Jan won the swimming medal. Which she gave to her parents.

Solution A: Combine the fragment with another sentence.
We went to the park, where we had often gone before.
Jan won the swimming medal, which she gave to her parents.

Solution B: Rewrite the fragment as a complete sentence, eliminating the subordinating conjunction or the relative pronoun and adding a subject or other words necessary to make a complete thought.
We went to the park. We had often gone there before.
Jan won the swimming medal. She gave it to her parents.

Problem: A fragment that lacks both a subject and a verb
The birds woke us with their songs. At six in the morning.

Solution: Combine the fragment with another sentence.
The birds woke us with their songs at six in the morning.

Rule of Thumb: Sentence fragments can make writing hard to understand. Make sure that every sentence has a subject and a verb.

Note: In almost all of the writing you do, especially for school, you should avoid sentence fragments. Occasionally, however, sentence fragments can be used to create special effects, such as adding emphasis or conveying realistic dialogue.
"Not again!" she cried.
The pizza was gone. All of it!

Run-On Sentence

Problem: Comma splice—two main clauses separated only by a comma
The sky is pitch black, there is no moon.

Solution A: Replace the comma with an end mark of punctuation, such as a period or a question mark, and begin the new sentence with a capital letter.
The sky is pitch black. There is no moon.

Solution B: Insert a semicolon between the two main clauses.
The sky is pitch black; there is no moon.

Solution C: Insert a coordinating conjunction after the comma.
The sky is pitch black, and there is no moon.

Problem: Two main clauses with no punctuation between them.
We picked the apples then we made pies.

Solution A: Separate the main clauses with an end mark of punctuation, such as a period or a question mark, and begin the second sentence with a capital letter.
We picked the apples. Then we made pies.

Solution B: Separate the main clauses with a semicolon.
We picked the apples; then we made pies.

Solution C: Insert a comma and a coordinating conjunction between the main clauses.
We picked the apples, and then we made pies.

Problem: Two main clauses with no comma before the coordinating conjunction
Elephants still live in the wild but they are endangered.

Solution: Insert a comma before the coordinating conjunction to separate the two main clauses.
Elephants still live in the wild, but they are endangered.

Rule of Thumb: It often helps to have someone else read your longer sentences to see whether they are clear. When you know what the sentences are supposed to mean, you may miss the need for punctuation.

Lack of Subject-Verb Agreement

Problem: A subject that is separated from the verb by an intervening prepositional phrase
Ten pieces of the puzzle is on the floor.
The shoe department in each of our stores are closing.

Solution: Make the verb agree with the subject, which is never the object of a preposition.
Ten pieces of the puzzle are on the floor.
The shoe department in each of our stores is closing.

Rule of Thumb: When a subject and a verb are separated by a prepositional phrase, check for agreement by reading the sentence without the prepositional phrase.

Problem: A predicate nominative that differs in number from the subject
Hamburgers is tonight's dinner.
Tonight's dinner are hamburgers.

Solution: Ignore the predicate nominative and make the verb agree with the subject of the sentence.
Hamburgers are tonight's dinner.
Tonight's dinner is hamburgers.

Problem: A subject that follows the verb
On my desk is two letters from my dad.
Here is my answers to them both.

Solution: In an inverted sentence look for the subject after the verb. Then make sure that the verb agrees with the subject.

On my desk are two letters from my dad.
Here are my answers to them both.

Rule of Thumb: Reversing the order of an inverted sentence may help you decide on the verb form to use:
Two letters from my dad are on my desk.
My answers to them both are here.

Problem: A collective noun as the subject
The cross-country team are in first place.
The team gathers at the captain's house after each meet.

Solution A: If the collective noun refers to a group as a whole, use a singular verb.
The cross country team is in first place.

Solution B: If the collective noun refers to each member of a group individually, use a plural verb.
Team [members] gather at the captain's house after each meet.

Problem: A noun of amount as the subject
Five bushels are a great many tomatoes.
Three marbles is in my pocket.

Solution: Determine whether the noun of amount refers to one unit and is therefore singular or refers to a number of individual units and is therefore plural.
Five bushels is a great many tomatoes.
Three marbles are in my pocket.

Problem: A compound subject that is joined by *and*
The student and the teacher meets to discuss a project.
Spaghetti and meatballs are her favorite dinner.

Solution A: If the parts of the compound subject do not belong to one unit or if they refer to different people or things, use a plural verb.
The student and the teacher meet to discuss a project.

Solution B: If the parts of the compound subject belong to one unit or if both parts refer to the same person or thing, use a singular verb.
Spaghetti and meatballs is her favorite dinner.

Problem: A compound subject that is joined by *or* or *nor*
Neither those trees nor that shrub are healthy.

Solution: Make the verb agree with the subject that is closer to it.
Neither those trees nor that shrub is healthy.

Problem: A compound subject that is preceded by *many a, every,* or *each*
Many a dog and cat end up in an animal shelter or the pound.

Solution: When *many a, every,* or *each* precedes a compound subject, the subject is considered singular. Use a singular verb.
Many a dog and cat ends up in an animal shelter or a pound.

Problem: A subject that is separated from the verb by an intervening expression
That issue, as well as several others, are bothering me.

Solution: Certain expressions, such as those beginning with *as well as, in addition to,* and *together with,* do not change the number of the subject. Ignore an intervening expression between a subject and its verb, and make the verb agree with the subject.
That issue, along with several others, is bothering me.

Problem: An indefinite pronoun as the subject
Neither of the boys are on time.

Solution: Determine whether the indefinite pronoun is singular or plural, and make the verb agree. Some indefinite pronouns are singular—*another, anyone, everyone, one, each, either, neither, anything, everything, something,* and *somebody.* Some are plural—*both, many, few, several,* and *others.* Some can be singular or plural—*some, all, any, more, most,* and *none.* In these cases, find the noun to which the pronoun refers to determine which verb form to use.
Neither [one] of the boys is on time.

Lack of Pronoun-Antecedent Agreement

Problem: A singular antecedent that can be either male or female.
A climber must check his equipment carefully.

Solution A: Traditionally, a masculine pronoun has been used to refer to an antecedent that may be either male or female. This usage may appear to ignore or exclude the feminine gender. Reword the sentence to use *he or she, him or her,* and so on.
A climber must check his or her equipment carefully.

Solution B: Reword the sentence so that both the antecedent and the pronoun are plural.
Climbers must check their equipment carefully.

Solution C: Reword the sentence to eliminate the pronoun.
A climber must check all equipment carefully.

Rule of Thumb: Although you may see the generic masculine forms used exclusively in older literature, this construction is generally avoided in contemporary writing.

Problem: A second-person pronoun that refers to a third-person antecedent
Juan likes sitcoms that make you think as well as laugh.

Solution A: Use the appropriate third-person pronoun.
Juan likes sitcoms that make him think as well as laugh.

Solution B: Use an appropriate noun instead of a pronoun.
Juan likes sitcoms that make people think as well as laugh.

Problem: A singular indefinite pronoun as an antecedent
Each of the volumes has their own index.

Solution: *Each, every, either, neither,* and *one* are singular and therefore require singular personal pronouns even when *each* is followed by a prepositional phrase that contains a plural noun.
Each of the volumes has its own index.

Rule of Thumb: To help you remember that *each, either,* and *neither* are singular, think of *each one, either one,* and *neither one.*

Lack of Clear Pronoun Reference [Unclear Antecedent]

Problem: A pronoun reference that is weak or vague
We spent several weeks at the farm this summer, and it was exciting.
The label says to shake it before pouring a serving.

Solution A: Rewrite the sentence, adding a clear antecedent for the pronoun.
We spent our vacation at the farm this summer, and it was exciting.

Solution B: Rewrite the sentence, substituting a noun for the pronoun.
The label says to shake the bottle of salad dressing before pouring a serving.

Problem: A pronoun that could refer to more than one antecedent
Lauren and Abby wrote six songs, and she recorded them all.
Don't buy a car from that dealership: it will let you down.

Solution A: Rewrite the sentence, substituting a noun for the pronoun.
Lauren and Abby wrote six songs, and Abby recorded them all.

Solution B: Rewrite the sentence, making the antecedent of the pronoun clear.
A car from that dealership will let you down; don't buy one there.

Problem: The indefinite use of *you* or *they*
You just have to laugh at that scene in the movie.
They say the weather will be clear tomorrow.

Solution A: Rewrite the sentence, substituting a noun for the pronoun.
The audience just has to laugh at that scene in the movie.

Solution B: Rewrite the sentence, eliminating the pronoun entirely.
According to the forecast, the weather will be clear tomorrow.

Shift in Pronoun

Problem: An incorrect shift in person between two pronouns
Lynn likes the front seat, where you are most comfortable.
The Chins planted a maple on the south side of the house, where you need shade the most.

Solution A: Replace the incorrect pronoun with a pronoun that agrees with its antecedent.
Lynn likes the front seat, where she is most comfortable.

Solution B: Replace the incorrect pronoun with an appropriate noun.
The Chins plants a maple on the south side of the house, where the house needs shade the most.

Shift in Verb Tense

Problem: An unnecessary shift in tense.
The children will give their mother flowers, and they kiss her.
After the party ended, we go home.

Solution: When two or more events occur at the same time, be sure to use the same verb tense to describe each event.
The children will give their mother flowers, and they will kiss her.
After the party ended, we went home.

Problem: A lack of correct shift in tenses to show that one event precedes or follows another
By the time the concert ended, we sat for four hours.

Solution: When two past events being described have occurred at different times, shift from the past tense to the past perfect tense to indicate that one action began and ended before another past action began. Use the past perfect tense for the earlier of the two actions.
By the time the concert ended, we had sat for four hours.

Rule of Thumb: When you need to use several verb tenses in your writing, it may help to jot down first the sequence of events you are writing about. Be clear in your mind about what happened first, next, and last.

Incorrect Verb Tense or Form

Problem: An incorrect or missing verb ending
When I began taking lessons, I learn about quarter, half, and whole notes.
I had start the lessons two months before.

Solution: Add *-ed* to a regular verb to form the past tense and the past participle.
When I began taking lessons, I learned about quarter, half, and whole notes.
I had started the lessons two months before.

Problem: An improperly formed irregular verb
James brung the book back to the library.
Catherine has writed six pages on that topic.

Solution: Irregular verbs form their past tense and past participles in some way other than by adding -ed. Memorize these forms or look them up.
James brought the book back to the library.
Catherine has written six pages on that topic.

Problem: Confusion between the past form and the past participle
We have ate too many apples.
She had swam the Chesapeake last July.

Solution: Use the past participle of an irregular verb, not the past-tense form, when you use the auxiliary verb *have*.
We have eaten too many apples.
She had swum the Chesapeake last July.

Problem: Improper use of the past participle
The catcher thrown several runners out.
The DiCaprios done a fine job of rearing those children.

Solution A: The past participle of an irregular verb cannot stand alone as a verb. Add a form of the auxiliary verb *have* to the past participle to form a complete verb.
The catcher had thrown several runners out.
The DiCaprios have done a fine job of rearing those children.

Solution B: Replace the past participle with the past form of the verb.
The catcher threw several runners out.
The DiCaprios did a fine job of rearing those children.

Misplaced or Dangling Modifier

Problem: A misplaced modifier
The children were swimming in the photograph.
Swooping down on a fish, I spotted the gull.
I saw a man at the movies eating popcorn.

Solution: Modifiers that modify the wrong word or seem to modify more than one word in a sentence are called misplaced modifiers. Position the misplaced phrase as close as possible to the word or words it modifies.
The children in the photograph were swimming.
I spotted the gull swooping down on a fish.
I saw a man eating popcorn at the movies.

Problem: Incorrect placement of the adverb *only*
Tricia only has enough money to buy a pencil.

Solution: Place the adverb *only* immediately before the word or group of words it modifies.
Only Tricia has enough money to buy a pencil.
Tricia has enough money to buy only a pencil.
Tricia has only enough money to buy a pencil.

Rule of Thumb: Note that each time *only* is moved, the meaning of the sentence changes. Check to be sure that your sentence says what you mean.

Problem: A dangling modifier
Croaking loudly, I listened to the sounds of the frogs in the bog.
Stealing home, the game was won for the Pirates.

Solution: Dangling modifiers do not seem logically to modify any word in the sentence. Rewrite the sentence, adding a noun to which the dangling phrase clearly refers. Often you will have to add other words too.
I listened to the sounds of the frogs croaking loudly in the bog.
Stealing home, Layla won the game for the Pirates.

Missing or Misplaced Possessive Apostrophe

Problem: Singular nouns
The womans child liked the circuses trapeze artists.

Solution: Use an apostrophe and *s* to form the possessive case of a singular noun, even one that ends in *s*.
The woman's child liked the circus's trapeze artist.

Problem: Plural nouns ending in *s*
The hikers cars were parked at the base of the trail.

Solution: Use an apostrophe alone to form the possessive of a plural noun that ends in *s*.
The hikers' cars were parked at the base of the trail.

Problem: Plural nouns not ending in *s*
Did Brian join the mens group?

Solution: Use an apostrophe and *s* to form the possessive of a plural noun that does not end in *s*.
Did Brian join the men's group?

Problem: Pronouns
Everyones contribution helps.
These pencils are your's, and those pencils are their's.

Solution A: Use an apostrophe and *s* to form the possessive of a singular indefinite pronoun.
Everyone's contribution helps.

Solution B: Do not use an apostrophe with any of the possessive personal pronouns.
These pencils are yours, and those pencils are theirs.

Problem: Confusion between *its* and *it's*
Will you tell me when its ten o'clock?
The cat licked it's fur.

Solution: Do not use an apostrophe to form the possessive of *it.* Use an apostrophe to form the contraction of *it is.*
Will you tell me when it's ten o'clock?
The cat licked its fur.

Missing Commas with Nonessential Elements

Problem: Missing commas with nonessential participles, infinitives, and their phrases
Pounding hard on the roof the rain awakened me.
The whole set of cups chipped from many years of use was discarded.
To answer your question this software package is worth the price.

Solution: Determine whether the participle, infinitive, or phrase is essential to the meaning of the sentence. If it is not essential, set off the phrase with commas.
Pounding hard on the roof, the rain awakened me.
The whole set of cups, chipped from many years of use, was discarded.
To answer your question, this software package is worth the price.

Problem: Missing commas with nonessential adjective clauses
My mother who is a very generous woman gave us investment tips.

Solution: Determine whether the clause is essential to the meaning of the sentence. If it is not essential, set off the clause with commas.
My mother, who is a very generous woman, gave us investment tips.

Problem: Missing commas with nonessential appositives
John the lead-off batter singled on a line drive.

Solution: Determine whether the appositive is essential to the meaning of the sentence. If it is not essential, set off the appositive with commas.
John, the lead-off batter, singled on a line drive.

Rule of Thumb: To determine whether a word or phrase is essential, try reading the sentence without it.

Problem: Missing commas with interjections and parenthetical expressions
Boy what a great cat that is
On Saturdays as a rule we sleep late.

Solution: Set off the interjection or parenthetical expression with commas.
Boy, what a great cat that is!
On Saturdays, as a rule, we sleep late.

Missing Commas in a Series

Problem: Missing commas in a series of words, phrases, or clauses
Alicia Nirupam and Matt made the honor roll.
Mark made the dough kneaded it and left it to rise
The firefighter carries the child out of the apartment down the stairs and into the arms of her mother.
Joe pitched the tent Meg gathered firewood and Bud unloaded the truck.

Solution: When there are three or more elements in a series, use a comma after each element that precedes the conjunction
Alicia, Nirupam, and Matt made the honor roll.
Mark made the dough, kneaded it, and left it to rise.
The firefighter carries the child out of the apartment, down the stairs, and into the arms of her mother.
Joe pitched the tent, Meg gathered firewood, and Bud unloaded the truck.

Rule of Thumb: When you're having difficulty with a rule of usage, try rewriting the rule in your own words. Then check with your teacher to be sure you have grasped the concept.

Troublesome Words

This section will help you choose between words and expressions that are often confusing or misused.

accept, except

Accept means "to receive." *Except* means "other than."

Phillip walked proudly to the stage to **accept** *the award.*

Everything fits in my suitcase **except** *my sleeping bag.*

affect, effect

Affect is a verb meaning "to cause a change in" or "to influence." *Effect* as a verb means "to bring about or accomplish." As a noun, *effect* means "result."

Bad weather will **affect** *our plans for the weekend.*

The new medicine **effected** *an improvement in the patient's condition.*

The gloomy weather had a bad **effect** *on my mood.*

ain't

Ain't is never used in formal speaking or writing except to quote the exact words of a character or a real person. Instead of using *ain't,* say or write *am not, is not,* or *are not;* or use a contraction such as *I'm not,* or *she isn't.*

The pizza **is not** *going to arrive for another half hour.*

The pizza **isn't** *going to arrive for another half hour.*

a lot

The expression *a lot* means "much" or "many" and should always be written as two words. Some authorities discourage its use in formal writing and speaking (for business and academic purposes).

A lot *of my friends are learning Spanish.*

Many *of my friends are learning Spanish.*

all ready, already

All ready, written as two words, is a phrase that means "completely ready." *Already,* written as one word, is an adverb that means "before" or "by this time."

By the time the fireworks display was **all ready,** *we had* **already** *arrived.*

all right, alright

The expression *all right* should be written as two words. Some dictionaries do list the single word *alright* but not as a preferred spelling. Remember: *Alright* is all wrong.

Tom hurt his ankle, but he will be **all right.**

all together, altogether

All together means "in a group." *Altogether* means "completely."

The Minutemen stood **all together** *at the end of Lexington Green.*

The rebel farmers were not **altogether** *sure that they could fight the British soldiers.*

among, between

In general, use *among* for three or more people, things, or groups. Use *between* for two people, things, or groups.

Mr. Kendall divided the jobs for the car wash **among** *the team members.*

Our soccer field lies **between** *the gym and Main Street.*

Use *between* for more than two people, things, or groups only when each is considered in relation to all of the others.

The agreement between France, England, and the United States was declared binding.

amount, number

Use *amount* with nouns that cannot be counted. Use *number* with nouns that can be counted.

This recipe calls for an unusual **amount** *of pepper.*
A record **number** *of students attended last Saturday's book fair.*

bad, badly

Bad is an adjective; it modifies a noun.
Badly is an adverb; it modifies an action verb, an adjective, or another adverb.

The **badly** *burnt cookies left a* **bad** *smell in the kitchen.*
Joseph **badly** *wants to be on the track team and feels* **bad** *about missing tryouts.*

beside, besides

Beside means "next to." *Besides* means "in addition to."

The zebra is grazing **beside** *a wildebeest.*
Besides *visiting the zoo, I like to go to the aquarium.*

bring, take

Bring means "to carry from a distant place to a closer one." *Take* means "to carry from a nearby place to a more distant one."

Please **bring** *a bag lunch and subway money to school tomorrow.*
Don't forget to **take** *your art projects home this afternoon.*

can, may

Can implies the ability to do something. *May* implies permission to do something.

You **may** *take a later bus home if you* **can** *remember which bus to get on.*

Tip: Although *can* is sometimes used in place of *may* in informal speech, a distinction should be made when speaking and writing formally, for business and academic purposes.

choose, chose

Choose means "to select." *Chose*, the past tense of *choose*, means "selected."

Dad helped me **choose** *a birthday card for my grandmother.*
Dad **chose** *a card with a funny punch line inside.*

doesn't, don't

The subject of the contraction *doesn't (does not)* is the third-person singular (*he* or *she*). The subject of the contraction *don't (do not)* is *I, you, we,* or *they.*

Tanya **doesn't** *have any tickets for the concert.*
We **don't** *need tickets if we stand in the back row.*

farther, further

Farther refers to physical distance. *Further* refers to time or degree.

Our new apartment is **farther** *away from the school.*
I will not continue this argument **further***.*

fewer, less

Fewer is used to refer to things or qualities that can be counted. *Less* is used to refer to things or qualities that cannot be counted. In addition, *less* is used with figures that are regarded as single amounts.

Fewer *people were waiting after lunch than earlier.*
There is **less** *fat in this kind of peanut butter than in the other.*
Try to spend **less** *than ten dollars on a present.*
[Money is treated as a single sum, not as individual dollars.]

good, well

Good is often used as an adjective meaning "pleasing" or "able." *Well* may be used as an adverb of manner telling how ably something is done or as an adjective meaning "in good health."

That is a **good** *haircut.*
Marco writes **well***.*
Because Ms. Rodriguez had a headache, she was not **well** *enough to correct our tests.*

in, into

In means "inside." *Into* indicates a movement from outside toward the inside.

Refreshments will be sold in *the lobby of the auditorium. The doors opened, and the eager crowd rushed* into *the auditorium.*

it's, its

Use an apostrophe to form the contraction of *it is.* The possessive of the personal pronoun *it* does not take an apostrophe.

It's hard to keep up with computer technology. The computer industry seems to change its *products daily.*

lay, lie

Lay means "to place." *Lie* means "to recline."

I will lay *my beach towel here on the warm sand. Help! I don't want to* lie *next to a hill of red ants!*

learn, teach

Learn means "to gain knowledge." *Teach* means "to give knowledge."

I don't learn *very quickly. My uncle is* teaching *me how to juggle.*

leave, let

Leave means "to go away." *Let* means "to allow." With the word *alone* you may use either *let* (in the idiom meaning "besides") or *leave.*

Huang has to leave *at eight o'clock. Mr. Davio* lets *the band practice in his basement.* Leave *me alone.* Let *me alone.*

like, as

Use *like,* a preposition, to introduce a phrase of comparison. Use *as,* a subordinating conjunction, to introduce a subordinate clause, according to Standard American English.

Andy sometimes acts like *a clown. The detective looked carefully at the empty suitcase* as *she examined the room.*
Tip: *As* **can be a preposition in cases like the following:** *Jack went to the costume party as a giant pumpkin.*

loose, lose

Loose means "not firmly attached." *Lose* means "to misplace" or "to fail to win."

If you keep wiggling that loose *tooth, you may* lose *it.*

raise, rise

Raise means to "cause to move up." *Rise* means "to move upward."

Farmers in this part of Florida raise *sugarcane. The hot-air balloon began to* rise *slowly in the morning sky.*

set, sit

Set means "to place" or "to put." *Sit* means "to place oneself in a seated position."

I always set *the tips of my running shoes against the starting line. After running the fifty-yard dash, I had to* sit *down and catch my breath.*

than, then

Than introduces the second part of a comparison. *Then* means "at that time" or "after that."

I'd rather go to Disney World in the winter than *in the summer. The park is too crowded and hot* then.

their, they're

Their is the possessive form of *they*. *They're* is the contraction of *they are*.

They're *visiting Plymouth Plantation during* **their** *vacation.*

to, too, two

To means "in the direction of." *Too* means "also" or "to an excessive degree." *Two* is the number that follows *one*.

I bought **two** *tickets* **to** *the concert.*
The music was **too** *loud.*
It's my favorite group **too**.

who, whom

Who is a subject pronoun. **It can be the subject of a sentence or of a clause.** *Whom* is an object pronoun. It can be the object of a verb or of a preposition.

Who *has finished the test already?*
The students **who** *have finished may leave.*
Mr. Russo is the teacher **whom** *we most like.*
Mr. Russo is the man to **whom** *we owe our thanks.*

who's, whose

Who's is the contraction for *who is*. *Whose* is the possessive form of *who*.

Who's *going to wake me up in the morning?*
The policeman discovered **whose** *car alarm was making so much noise.*

Mechanics

This section will help you use correct capitalization, punctuation, and abbreviations in your writing.

Capitalization

This section will help you recognize and use correct capitalization in sentences.

Rule: Capitalize the first word in any sentence, including direct quotations and sentences in parentheses unless they are included in another sentence.

Example: *He said, "Come back soon" (did he mean it, though?).*
Example: *Emily Dickinson became famous only after her death. (She published only six poems during her lifetime.)*

Rule: Always capitalize the pronoun *I* no matter where it appears in a sentence.

Example: *Some of my relatives think that I should become a doctor.*

Rule: Capitalize proper nouns, including
a. names of individuals and titles used in direct address preceding a name or describing a relationship.
Example: *George Washington; Dr. Morgan; Aunt Margaret*

b. names of ethnic groups, national groups, political parties and their members, and languages.
Example: *Italian Americans; Aztec; the Republican Party; a Democrat; Spanish*

c. names of organizations, institutions, firms, monuments, bridges, buildings, and other structures.
Example: *Red Cross; Stanford University; General Electric; Lincoln Memorial; Tappan Zee Bridge; Chrysler Building; Museum of Natural History*

d. trade names and names of documents, awards, and laws.
Example: *Microsoft; Declaration of Independence; Pulitzer Prize; Sixteenth Amendment*

e. geographical terms and regions or localities.
Example: *Hudson River; Pennsylvania Avenue; Grand Canyon; Texas; the Midwest*

f. names of planets and other heavenly bodies.
Example: *Venus; Earth; the Milky Way*

g. names of ships, planes, trains, and spacecraft.
Example: *USS Constitution; Spirit of St. Louis; Apollo 11*

h. names of most historical events, eras, calendar items, and religious names and items.
Example: *World War II; Age of Enlightenment; June; Christianity; Buddhists; Bible; Easter; God*

i. titles of literary works, works of art, and musical compositions.
Example: *"Why I Live at the P.O."; The Starry Night; Rhapsody in Blue*

j. names of specific school courses.
Example: *Advanced Physics; American History*

Rule: Capitalize proper adjectives (adjectives formed from proper nouns).
Example: *Christmas tree; Hanukkah candles; Freudian psychology; American flag*

Punctuation

This section will help you use these elements of punctuation correctly.

Rule: Use a period at the end of a declarative sentence or a polite command.

Example: *I'm thirsty.*
Example: *Please bring me a glass of water.*

Rule: Use an exclamation point to show strong feeling or after a forceful command.

Example: *I can't believe my eyes!*
Example: *Watch your step!*

Rule: Use a question mark to indicate a direct question.

Example: *Who is in charge here?*

Rule: Use a colon
a. to introduce a list (especially after words such as *these, the following,* or *as follows*) and to introduce material that explains, restates, or illustrates previous material.

Example: *The following states voted for the amendment: Texas, California, Georgia, and Florida.*
Example: *The sunset was colorful: purple, orange, and red.*

b. to introduce a long or formal quotation.
Example: *It was Mark Twain who stated the following proverb: "Man is the only animal that blushes. Or needs to."*

c. in precise time measurements, biblical chapter and verse references, and business letter salutations.
Example: *3:35 P.M.*   *7:50 A.M.*
          Gen. 1:10–11   *Matt. 2:23*
          Dear Ms. Samuels: *Dear Sir:*

Rule: Use a semicolon
a. to separate main clauses that are not joined by a coordinating conjunction.
Example: *There were two speakers at Gettysburg that day; only Lincoln's speech is remembered.*

b. to separate main clauses joined by a conjunctive adverb or by *for example* or *that is.*
Example: *Because of the ice storm, most students could not get to school; consequently, the principal canceled all classes for the day.*

c. to separate the items in a series when these items contain commas.
Example: *The students at the rally came from Senn High School, in Chicago, Illinois; Niles Township High School, in Skokie, Illinois; and Evanston Township High School, in Evanston, Illinois.*

d. to separate two main clauses joined by a coordinating conjunction when such clauses already contain commas.
Example: *The designer combined the blue silk, brown linen, and beige cotton into a suit; but she decided to use the yellow chiffon, yellow silk, and white lace for an evening gown.*

Rule: Use a comma
a. between the main clauses of a compound sentence.
Example: *Ryan was late getting to study hall, and his footsteps echoed in the empty corridor.*

b. to separate three or more words, phrases, or clauses in a series.
Example: *Mel bought carrots, beans, pears, and onions.*

c. between coordinate modifiers.

Example: *That is a lyrical, moving poem.*

d. to set off parenthetical expressions, interjections, and conjunctive adverbs.
Example: *Well, we missed the bus again.*
Example: *The weather is beautiful today; however, it is supposed to rain this weekend.*

e. to set off nonrestrictive words, clauses, and phrases, such as the following:
—adverbial clauses
Example: *Since Ellen is so tall, the coach assumed that she would be a good basketball player.*
—adjectival clauses
Example: *Scott, who had been sleeping, finally woke up.*
—participles and participial phrases
Example: *Having found what he was looking for, he left.*
—multiple prepositional phrases
Example: *On Saturdays during the fall, I rake leaves.*
—infinitive phrases
Example: *To be frank, I'd like to stay a while longer.*
—appositives and appositive phrases
Example: *Ms. Kwan, a soft-spoken woman, ran into the street to hail a cab.*

f. to set off direct quotations.
Example: *"My concert," Molly replied, "is tonight."*

g. to set off an antithetical phrase.
Example: *Unlike Tom, Rob enjoys skiing.*

h. to set off a title after a person's name.
Example: *Margaret Thomas, PhD, was the guest speaker.*

i. to separate the various parts of an address, a geographical term, or a date.
Example: *My new address is 324 Indian School Road, Albuquerque, New Mexico 85350.*
          I moved on March 13, 1998, to Phoenix.

j. after the salutation of an informal letter and after the closing of all letters.
Example: *Dear Helen,   Sincerely,*

k. to set off parts of a reference that direct the reader to the exact source.
Example: *You can find the article in the* Washington Post, *April 4, 1997, pages 33–34.*

l. to set off words or names used in direct address and in tag questions.

Example: *Yuri, will you bring me my calculator?*
Shanti became a lawyer, didn't she?

Rule: Use a dash to signal a change in thought or to emphasize parenthetical material.

Example: *During the play Maureen—and she'd be the first to admit it—forgot her lines.*

Example: *Only two juniors are attending—Mike Ramos and Ron Kim.*

Rule: Use parentheses to set off supplemental material. Punctuate within parentheses only if the punctuation is part of the parenthetical expression.

Example: *If you like jazz (and I assume you do), you will like this CD. (The soloist is Miles Davis.)*
Example: *The upper Midwest (which states does that include?) was hit by terrible floods last year.*

Rule: Use brackets to enclose comments or information inserted into a quotation for clarity or to enclose a parenthetical phrase that already appears within parentheses.

Example: *"He serves his [political] party best who serves the country best."—Rutherford B. Hayes*
Example: *The staircase (which was designed by a famous architect [Frank Lloyd Wright]) was inlaid with ceramic tile.*

Rule: Use ellipsis points to indicate the omission of material from a quotation.

Example: *"Neither an individual nor a nation can commit the least act of injustice against the obscurest individual. . . . " —Henry David Thoreau*

Rule: Use quotation marks
a. to enclose a direct quotation, as follows:
Example: *"Hurry up!" shouted Lisa.*

When a quotation is interrupted, use two sets of quotation marks.

Example: *"A cynic," wrote Oscar Wilde, "is someone who knows the price of everything and the value of nothing."*

Use single quotation marks for a quotation within a quotation.

Example: *"Did you say 'turn left' or 'turn right'?" asked Leon.*

In writing dialogue, begin a new paragraph and use a new set of quotation marks every time the speaker changes.

Example: *"Do you really think the spaceship can take off?" asked the first officer.*
"Our engineer assures me that we have enough power," the captain replied.

b. to enclose titles of short works, such as stories, poems, essays, articles, chapters, and songs.
Example: *"The Lottery"* [short story]
"Provide, Provide" [poem]
"Civil Disobedience" [essay]

c. to enclose unfamiliar slang terms and unusual expressions.
Example: *The man's grandson is a "rapscallion."*

d. to enclose a definition that is stated directly.
Example: *Gauche is a French word meaning "left."*

Rule: Use italics
a. for titles of books, lengthy poems, plays, films, television series, paintings and sculptures, long musical compositions, court cases, names of newspapers and magazines, ships, trains, airplanes, and spacecraft. Italicize and capitalize an article *(a, an, the)* at the beginning of a title only when it is part of the title.
Example: E.T. *[film];* The Piano Lesson *[play]*
The Starry Night *[painting]*
the New Yorker *[magazine]*
Challenger *[spacecraft]*
The Great Gatsby *[book]*
the Chicago Tribune *[newspaper]*

b. for foreign words and expressions that are not used frequently in English.
Example: *Luciano waved good-bye, saying,* "Arrivederci."

c. for words, letters, and numerals used to represent themselves.
Example: *There is no* Q *on the telephone keypad.*
Example: *The numbers* 21 *and* 22 *appear in italics.*

Rule: Use an apostrophe

a. for a possessive form, as follows:

Add an apostrophe and *s* to all singular nouns, plural nouns not ending in *s,* singular indefinite pronouns, and compound nouns. Add an apostrophe alone to a plural noun that ends in *s.*

Example: *the tree's leaves*
the man's belt
the bus's tires
the children's pets
everyone's favorite
my mother-in-law's job
the attorney general's decision
the baseball player's error
the cats' bowls

If two or more persons possess something jointly, use the possessive form for the last person named. If they possess it individually, use the possessive form for each one's name.

Example: *Ted and Harriet's family*
Ted's and Harriet's bosses
Lewis and Clark's expedition
Lewis's and Clark's clothes

b. to express amounts of money or time that modify a noun.

Example: *two cents' worth*

Example: *three days' drive (You may use a hyphenated adjective instead: a three-day drive.)*

c. in place of omitted letters or numerals.

Example: *haven't [have not]   the winter of '95*

d. to form the plural of letters, numerals, symbols, and words used to represent themselves. Use an apostrophe and *s.*

Example: *You wrote two 5's instead of one.*

Example: *How many s's are there in Mississippi?*

Example: *Why did he use three !'s at the end of the sentence?*

Rule: Use a hyphen

a. after any prefix joined to a proper noun or proper adjective.

Example: *all-American   pre-Columbian*

b. after the prefixes *all-, cross-, ex-,* and *self-* joined to any noun or adjective, after the prefix *anti-* when it joins a word beginning with *i,* after the prefix *vice-* (some exceptions are *vice president* and *viceroy*), and to avoid confusion between words that begin with *re-* and look like another word.

Example: *ex-president*
self-important
anti-inflammatory
vice-principal
re-creation of the event
recreation time
re-pair the socks
repair the computer

c. in a compound adjective that precedes a noun.

Example: *a bitter-tasting liquid*

d. in any spelled-out cardinal or ordinal numbers up to *ninety-nine* or *ninety-ninth,* and with a fraction used as an adjective.

Example: *twenty-three   eighty-fifth*
one-half cup

e. to divide a word at the end of a line between syllables.

Example: *air-port   scis-sors*
fill-ing   fin-est

Abbreviations

Abbreviations are shortened forms of words.

Rule: Use only one period if an abbreviation occurs at the end of a sentence. If the sentence ends with a question mark or an exclamation point, use the period and the second mark of punctuation.

Example: *We didn't get home until 3:30 A.M.*
Example: *Did you get home before 4:00 A.M.?*
Example: *I can't believe you didn't get home until 3:30 A.M.!*

Rule: Capitalize abbreviations of proper nouns and abbreviations related to historical dates.

Example: *John F. Kennedy Jr.   P.O. Box 333*
800 B.C.   A.D. 456   1066 C.E.

Use all capital letters and no periods for most abbreviations of organizations and government agencies.

Example: *CBS   CIA   PIN*
CPA   IBM   NFL
MADD   GE   FBI

Spelling

The following basic rules, examples, and exceptions will help you master the spellings of many words.

Forming plurals

English words form plurals in many ways. For most nouns, simply add -s. The following chart shows other ways of forming plural nouns and some common exceptions to the pattern.

General Rules for Forming Plurals		
If the word ends in	**Rule**	**Example**
ch, s, sh, x, z	add es	glass, glasses
a consonant + y	change y to i and add -es	caddy, caddies
a vowel + y or o	add only -s	cameo, cameos monkey, monkeys
a consonant + o Latin terms and common exceptions	generally add -es but sometimes add only -s	potato, potatoes cello, cellos
f or ff common exceptions	add -s change f to v and add -es	cliff, cliffs hoof, hooves
lf	change f to v and add -es	half, halves

A few plurals are exceptions to the rules in the previous chart, but they are easy to remember. The following chart lists these plurals and some examples.

Special Rules for Forming Plurals	
Rule	**Example**
To form the plural of most proper names and one-word compound nouns, follow the general rules for plurals.	Cruz, Cruzes Mancuso, Mancusos crossroad, crossroads
To form the plural of hyphenated compound nouns or compound nouns of more than one word, make the most important word, usually the noun, plural.	sister-in-law, sisters-in-law motion picture, motion pictures
Some nouns have unusual plural forms.	goose, geese child, children
Some nouns have the same singular and plural forms.	moose scissors pants

Adding prefixes

When adding a prefix to a word, keep the original spelling of the word. Use a hyphen only when the original word is capitalized or with prefixes such as *all-*, *ex-*, and *self-* joined to a noun or adjective.

co- + operative = cooperative
inter- + change = interchange
pro- + African = pro-African
ex -+ partner = ex-partner

Suffixes and the silent *e*

Many English words end in a silent letter *e*. Sometimes the *e* is dropped when a suffix is added. When adding a suffix that begins with a consonant to a word that ends in silent *e*, keep the *e*.

like + -ness = likeness   sure + -ly = surely
COMMON EXCEPTIONS
awe + -ful = awful
judge + -ment = judgment

When adding a suffix that begins with a vowel to a word that ends in silent *e*, usually drop the *e*.

believe + -able = believable
expense + -ive = expensive
COMMON EXCEPTION
mile + -age = mileage

When adding a suffix that begins with *a* or *o* to a word that ends in *ce* or *ge*, keep the *e* so that the word will retain the soft *c* or *g* sound.

notice + -able = noticeable
courage + -ous = courageous

When adding a suffix that begins with a vowel to a word that ends in *ee* or *oe*, keep the final *e*.

see + -ing = seeing   toe + -ing = toeing

When adding a suffix that ends with an *e*, drop the final silent *e* after the letters *u* or *w*.

argue + -ment = argument
owe + -ing = owing

Keep the final silent *e* before the suffix *-ing* when it is necessary to avoid ambiguity.

singe + -ing = singeing

Suffixes and the final *y*

When adding a suffix to a word that ends in a consonant + *y*, change the *y* to *i* unless the suffix begins with *i*. Keep the *y* in a word that ends in a vowel + *y*.

try + -ed = tried
fry + -ed = fried
stay + -ing = staying
display + -ed = displayed
copy + -ing = copying
joy + -ous = joyous

Adding *ly* and *ness*

When adding *-ly* to a word that ends in a single *l*, keep the *l*, but when the word ends in a double *l*, drop one *l*. When the word ends in a consonant + *le*, drop the *le*. When adding *-ness* to a word that ends in *n*, keep the *n*.

casual + -ly = casually
practical + -ly = practically
dull + -ly = dully
probable + -ly = probably
open + -ness = openness
mean + -ness = meanness

Doubling the final consonant

Double the final consonant in words that end in a consonant preceded by a single vowel if the word is one syllable, if it has an accent on the last syllable that remains there even after the suffix is added, or if it is a word made up of a prefix and a one-syllable word.

stop + -ing = stopping
admit + -ed = admitted
replan + -ed = replanned

Do not double the final consonant if the accent is not on the last syllable, or if the accent shifts when the suffix is added. Also do not double the final consonant if the final consonant is *x* or *w*. If the word ends in a consonant and the suffix begins with a consonant, do not double the final consonant.

benefit + -ed = benefited
similar + -ly = similarly
raw + -er = rawer
box + -like = boxlike
friend + -less = friendless
rest + -ful = restful

Forming Compound Words

When joining a word that ends in a consonant to a word that begins with a consonant, keep both consonants.

> out + line = outline
> after + noon = afternoon
> post + card = postcard
> pepper + mint = peppermint

ie and *ei*

Learning this rhyme can save you many misspellings: "Write *i* before *e* except after *c* or when sounded like *a,* as in *neighbor* and *weigh.*" There are many exceptions to this rule, including *seize, seizure, leisure, weird, height, either, neither, forfeit.*

-cede, -ceed, and *-sede*

Because of the relatively few words with *sēd* sounds, these words are worth memorizing.

> These words end in *cede:* **accede, precede, secede.**
> One word ends in *sede:* **supersede.**
> Three words end in *ceed:* **exceed, proceed, succeed.**

Logic and Persuasion Handbook

Persuasion

Propositions

One of the main reasons people write and talk is to persuade each other. Persuasive writing and speaking attempts to convince someone of the truth of a **proposition,** that is, a statement or claim. There are four basic types of proposition:

- A proposition of **fact** is a claim that certain information is correct.
  Candidate Wilkins comes from Illinois.

- A proposition of **value** is a statement that a feeling or judgment is valid.
  Candidate Wilkins is a friendly woman.

- A proposition about a **problem** combines fact and judgment.
  Candidate Wilkins is not qualified to run.

- A proposition of **policy** is a claim that someone should do something.
  Everyone should vote for candidate Wilkins.

A proposition may be **true** or **false.** In evaluating persuasive speaking and writing, you need to know which type of proposition is being made so that you can decide whether it is true or false.

Argument

Persuasive writing and speaking usually includes an **argument,** a statement of opinion about a problem or an issue, and the support for the statement. The statement is the proposition (see above). The **support** includes reasons and evidence. **Reasons** explain why someone should accept the proposition. **Evidence** consists of examples, facts, and expert opinions. Strong arguments often include a **counterargument,** a brief argument that attempts to disprove opposing opinions about the problem or issue.

Everyone should vote for candidate Wilkins because she is the most qualified, with 11 years in office. Some might say she should let her opponent have a chance to serve in that office. We say she can use her experience to serve many more people than her opponent.

Appeals

Arguments are meant to appeal to certain beliefs, values, or feelings belonging to the reader or listener. Support of a proposition often makes at least one of four types of **appeal:**

- An **appeal to logic** is a claim based on fact and reason.
  Wilkins is unqualified, because she does not meet the age requirement.

- An **appeal to ethics** is a claim based on shared values or judgments.
  Wilkins is best, because she is the most honest and caring.

- An **appeal to authority** is a claim based on sources believed to be reliable.
  Wilkins is best, because the Metropolitan Bar Association supports her.

- An **appeal to emotion** is a claim based on shared feelings.
  Wilkins is best, because she has overcome hardship.

In evaluating arguments, you need to know which type of appeal is being made so that you can decide whether it is valid or invalid. Note that an argument may involve more than one type of appeal.

Exercise: Analyzing an Argument

For each statement below, identify the type of proposition and appeal.

1. If we want clean beaches, then we need to provide trash cans.

2. It is our responsibility as human beings to keep ocean ecosystems healthy.

3. According to eminent marine biologists, we have a lot to learn about deep-sea animals.

4. Restricting owners of beachfront property from building wherever they want to on their property is highly unfair.

Statement	Proposition	Appeal
1	about a problem	
2		
3		
4		to ethics or values

Logic

Logic is a method used to structure clear and effective arguments. An argument may be structured logically by using either inductive or deductive reasoning.

Inductive Reasoning

Inductive reasoning involves putting facts together to come up with a generalized statement as a conclusion.

Specific facts:

Fact 1. *Star Wars* is the second-biggest money maker of all time.

Fact 2. The number one movie at the box office in 2004 was *Shrek 2*.

Fact 3. *Spiderman* broke many box office records in 2002.

Generalization: Science fiction and fantasy films do very well at the box office.

Errors In Inductive Reasoning

To avoid errors in inductive reasoning, be sure you use a large enough sample of specific facts, and of course, make sure your facts are accurate. If you have a large enough sample of accurate facts, make sure that your generalization is logical.

For example, it would be illogical to conclude from the facts above that movies whose titles begin with the letter *S* do well at the box office.

Deductive Reasoning

Deductive reasoning is essentially the opposite of inductive reasoning. With deductive reasoning you start with a generalization to come to a conclusion about a specific case.

Generalization: Paul can only eat vegetarian food.

Specific fact: The Glory Diner offers vegetarian food.

Conclusion: Paul can eat at the Glory Diner.

Syllogisms

A syllogism is a formal statement of a deductive argument. It consists of a **major premise,** or general statement; a **minor premise,** or related fact; and a **conclusion** based on the two.

Major premise: People who travel between countries need a passport.

Minor premise: Jody is flying from the United States to Spain.

Conclusion: Jody needs a passport.

Errors In Deductive Reasoning

Errors in deductive reasoning result from faulty construction of the argument. Make sure the major premise is a universal statement, that both premises are true, and that the conclusion follows logically from the premises.

Note: A syllogism is *valid* if it follows the rules of deductive reasoning. A syllogism is *true* if the statements are factually accurate. However, a perfectly valid syllogism can be untrue. For example:

Major premise: All voters are good citizens. [There is more to good citizenship than voting.]

Minor premise: My parents are voters.

Conclusion: Therefore, my parents are good citizens.

This conclusion is valid according to the premises; however, it isn't necessarily true because the major premise is flawed.

Exercise: Analyzing Logical Reasoning

For each argument below, identify whether inductive or deductive reasoning is used. Evaluate whether the conclusion is valid or invalid and explain your evaluation.

1. An epic poem is a serious, long narrative poem centered on the life of a cultural or national hero or heroine. *El Cid* is an epic poem. In more than 30,000 lines, it celebrates the life and accomplishments of a Spanish military and political leader who lived in the eleventh century.

2. If a computer can play compact discs, the computer must have been built after 1985. This computer can play CDs. This computer must have been built after 1985.

3. Many humorists use puns. Mark Twain used puns in his writing and his speeches. Ogden Nash used puns in his poems. Woody Allen uses puns in his movies.

Exercise: Using Logical Reasoning

Write a short essay arguing a proposition. In your argument, use at least two examples each of valid inductive and deductive reasoning.

Logical and Rhetorical Fallacies

An invalid argument is illogical and often includes **logical fallacies,** errors in reasoning. Logic is only one aspect of a successful argument. Some statements cannot be logically proved or disproved. **Rhetorical fallacies** are also errors in reasoning. They result from misleading and often false statements that appeal to emotion, ethics, and authority. Fallacies often seem reasonable at face value, so they are often used, both intentionally and unintentionally. Some fallacies are so common that they have names.

To identify fallacies in the writing and speaking of others and to avoid it in your own persuasive communication, you need to be able to identify fallacies and to understand why they are illogical.

- **Ad Hominem**

  Don't listen to what Smyth says about the election; he spent time in prison.

  An ad hominem argument (literally, an argument "against the person") implies that a defect in a person's character or behavior is evidence that what he says is unreliable. Note that the ad hominem fallacy contains a hidden premise: *People who have spent time in prison cannot have valid opinions.* Because this premise is untrue, the argument about Smyth is untrue also.

- **Non Sequitur or False Causality**

  This shirt is unlucky: every time I wear it, something bad happens.

  Non sequitur literally means "it doesn't follow." Just because one event occurs after the other, it doesn't follow logically that one caused the other.

- **Circular Logic**

  She was a great basketball player because she was so good at court sports.

  Circular logic is restating the same statement in different words instead of giving supporting evidence for the original point. This argument uses circular reasoning because basketball is a court sport, so the statement is simply saying someone is good at a particlar court sport because that person is good at all court sports. It doesn't say why that person is good at the court sport of basketball.

- **Hasty Generalization**

  That public speaker created a disturbance, so all free speech must be restricted.

  A hasty generalization is drawing a conclusion based on too little evidence. It is also called "jumping to conclusions." This statement is a hasty generalization because there is no evidence or proof that if one public speaker causes a disturbance, all public speakers will do so.

- **Appeal to Commonly Held Opinion**

  Voting is a right and a privilege, so anyone who is eligible to vote and doesn't should be encouraged to do so.

  An appeal to commonly held opinion is a persuasive technique in which the evidence is based almost entirely on a widely held belief. This opinion may be common, but there is no real evidence to support it.

- **False Dilemma**

  If you don't switch to a vegetarian diet immediately, you will ruin your health.

  A false dilemma presents two choices as the only ones available, when there are actually other options. In this case, another diet might be just as healthy or more healthy than the vegetarian one.

- **Personal Attack**

  Only a coward would vote for this bill.

  A personal attack used in an argument focuses on the opponent's personality, character, or other qualities instead of on the opponent's supporting evidence. In this case, there is no reason given to vote against the bill, only an attack on the character of those who would vote for it.

- **Appeal to Pity**

  Look into the big, sad eyes of a child who doesn't know how to read. After that, you'll support an increase in funding for our local library.

  Young children depend on trusted adults to help them unlock the mysteries of reading. Increasing library funding would mean more books and more librarians for children.

  The first of these two statements is an appeal to pity, a persuasive technique that attempts to stir up compassion. If an appeal to pity is relevant to the argument for which it is used as evidence, it may not be a fallacy. The second statement, for example, is not a fallacy.

- **Glittering Generalities**

  If you love freedom, vote for Jack.

  Glittering generalities are words with overwhelmingly positive connotations, used to make it seem impossible to disagree with an idea. How can you argue against the idea of freedom? A listener's initial reaction to this statement might be, "Freedom is a good thing, so I must vote for Jack."

- **Celebrity Endorsement**
  Movie hero Jason Clay recommend Pumpidox for strong muscles.

  Companies often hire celebrities to appear in commercials for their products in the hope that audiences will respond to the likability of the famous person, even if that person has no real expert knowledge about the product.

- **The Bandwagon Effect**
  Choose America's favorite toothpaste!
  The term "jumping on the bandwagon" means doing or thinking something because everyone else is doing it or thinking it. This type of reasoning provides no evidence to support a decision or viewpoint.

Ethical Reasoning and Propaganda

Propaganda
Propaganda is the process of persuading by deliberately misleading or confusing an audience. Through the use of combinations of logical fallacies, propaganda appeals to ethics, authority, or emotion in ways that are unsupported or inappropriate.

Political propaganda
A vote for Marmelard is a vote for the enemy!
America: You're with us or against us!

Advertising
Be the best parent you can be: Serve your kids Super Goody cereal.
The most successful people shop at Blorland's Department Store.

Ethical Reasoning
Reasoning that persuades by helping its intended audience make informed decisions is called **ethical reasoning.** As a writer or speaker, you have the responsibility to use ethical reasoning and avoid propaganda. This means that you must gather complete information about a topic, check your facts for accuracy, and make sure that your reasoning includes no errors in logic or false conclusions. You should address opposing evidence with clear and accurate

argumentation. Using ethical reasoning in your persuasive writing or speeches will strengthen your positions as your audience sees that you have logically addressed all sides of an idea.

Identifying Unethical Persuasive Techniques
The following essay contains several examples of faulty reasoning. Read through the entire text once, then go back and look for logical fallacies, invalid arguments, and manipulative appeals. For each example you find, make an entry in a chart like the one shown. Then write a paragraph evaluating the essay's argument.

Passage	Type(s) of Appeals	Why Invalid
"Principal Spaly"	Appeal to logic	Ad hominem

Don't Take Away Our Freedom

The school board recently announced plans to remove all vending machines from our schools' cafeterias. They say that candy, snacks, and cola are bad for students. But is starvation good for students? Is taking away freedom to choose good for students?

Every expert on nutrition agrees that it is not healthy for kids to go for hours between meals without some sort of snack in between to tide them over. If the school board has its way, students will be passing out at their desks from hunger and dehydration. Principal Spaly claims that students are more likely to pass out from a "sugar crash." This is the same Principal Spaly who recently showed what he thought of students when he denied sophomores the right to park at the high school.

We are taught in these very schools that America is a land of liberty. It is clear that the school board has forgotten this. Any student who loves his or her school will write to the school board and let them know how we feel.

Glossary/Glosario

This glossary lists the vocabulary words found in the literary works in this book. The definition given is for the word as it is used in the text; you may wish to consult a dictionary for other meanings of these words. The key below is a guide to the pronunciation symbols used in each entry.

	Pronounciation Key				
a	at	ō	hope	ng	sing
ā	ape	ô	fork, all	th	thin
ä	father	oo	wood, put	th	this
e	end	ōō	fool	zh	treasure
ē	me	oi	oil	ə	ago, taken, pencil,
i	it	ou	out		lemon, circus
ī	ice	u	up	′	indicates primary stress
o	hot	ū	use	′	indicates secondary

English

A

abashed (ə basht′) *adj.* self-conscious; embarrassed or ashamed **p. 886**

absolve (ab zolv′) *v.* to free from blame **p. 665**

accord (ə kôrd′) *n.* agreement; conformity **p. 1050**

admonish (ad mon′ish) *v.* to warn, as against a specific action **p. 279**

advocate (ad′ və kāt′) *v.* to publicly support **p. 330**

affirmation (af ər mā′ shən) *n.* positive agreement or judgment **p. 543**

agenda (ə jen′ də) *n.* an outline of tasks to be accomplished **p. 382**

aggrieved (ə grēvd′) *adj.* disturbed; upset **p. 936**

aglow (ə glō′) *adj.* glowing **p. 547**

albeit (ôl bē′ it) *conj.* although; even if **p. 139**

Español

A

abashed/avergonzado *adj.* vergonzoso; abochornado o que siente vergüenza **p. 886**

absolve/absolver *v.* liberar de culpa **p. 665**

accord/acuerdo *s.* convenio; conformidad **p. 1050**

admonish/amonestar *v.* advertir, en oposición a una acción específica **p. 279**

advocate/abogar *v.* apoyar públicamente **p. 330**

affirmation/afirmación *s.* expresión u opinión positiva **p. 543**

agenda/agenda *s.* un esquema general de las actividades que se han de realizar **p. 382**

aggrieved/agraviado *adj.* alterado; disgustado **p. 936**

aglow/radiante *adj.* resplandeciente **p. 547**

albeit/aunque *conj.* si bien, aun cuando **p. 139**

alleviate (ə lē′vē āt′) *v.* to make easier to bear; relieve; lessen **p. 264**

amenable (ə mē′ nə bəl) *adj.* responsive; able to be controlled **p. 50**

amicable (am′ə kə bəl) *adj.* friendly **p. 1073**

animosity (an′ə mos′ə tē) *n.* ill will or resentment; active strong dislike or hostility **p. 1082**

anteroom (an′ tē rōōm′) *n.* a small room serving as a waiting area or an entrance to a larger, main room **p. 1021**

aristocracy (ar′is tok′rə sē) *n.* a type of government in which a minority of upper-class individuals rule **p. 371**

arrogance (ar′ ə gəns) *n.* overbearing pride **p. 657**

arrogant (ar′ ə gənt) *adj.* full of self-importance; haughty **p. 129**

arroyo (ə roi′ ō) *n.* a dry gully or stream bed **p. 218**

ascertaining (as′ər tan′ ing) *v.* finding out definitely **p. 104**

aspiration (as′pə rā′ shən) *n.* a desire to achieve something or the object of such a desire **p. 393**

attain (ə tān′) *v.* to accomplish; to arrive at **p. 786**

attribute (at′rə būt′) *n.* a quality or characteristic of a person or thing **p. 349**

austere (ôs tēr′) *adj.* without ornament; very simple **p. 106**

austere (ôs tēr′) *adj.* stern; severe in appearance **p. 456**

B

bade (bād) *v.* past tense of bid; commanded, ordered, or asked **p. 1015**

barren (bar′ən) *adj.* empty and dreary; without life; desolate **p. 760**

belie (bi lī′) *v.* to misrepresent; to give a false impression of **p. 304**

alleviate/aliviar *v.* hacer más fácil de soportar; atenuar; aminorar **p. 264**

amenable/dócil *adj.* receptivo; que se puede controlar **p. 50**

amicable/amigable *adj.* amistoso **p. 1073**

animosity/animosidad *s.* malevolencia o resentimiento; aversión potente u hostilidad **p. 1082**

anteroom/antesala *s.* sala pequeña que sirve de lugar de espera o entrada a una sala principal más grande **p. 1021**

aristocracy/aristocracia *s.* tipo de gobierno en el que gobierna una minoría de individuos de clase alta **p. 371**

arrogance/arrogancia *s.* orgullo dominante **p. 657**

arrogant/arrogante *adj.* engreído; altanero **p. 129**

arroyo/arroyo *s.* lecho de agua u hondonada con poco caudal **p. 218**

ascertaining/constatar *v.* averiguar en forma definitiva **p. 104**

aspiration/ambición *s.* un deseo de lograr algo o el objeto de tal deseo **p. 393**

attain/alcanzar *v.* lograr; llegar a **p. 786**

attribute/atributo *s.* calidad o característica de alguien o algo **p. 349**

austere/ austero *adj.* sin decoración, muy sencillo **p. 106**

austere/austero *adj.* riguroso; severo en apariencia **p. 456**

B

bade/pidió *v.* tiempo pasado de pedir; ordenar, requerir o solicitar **p. 1015**

barren/yermo *adj.* vacío y lúgubre; sin vida; desolado **p. 760**

belie/distorsionar *v.* tergiversar; dar una impresión falsa **p. 304**

benevolence (bə nev′ ə ləns) *n.* kindness; generosity **p. 341**

beseeching (bi sēch′ ing) *adj.* begging; asking earnestly **p. 170**

bewilderment (bi wil′ dər mənt) *n.* confusion **p. 424**

blasphemous (blas′ fə məs) *adj.* showing disrespect or scorn for God or anything sacred **p. 64**

bloated (blō′ tid) *adj.* puffed up; swollen **p. 1062**

bough (bou) *n.* a tree branch **p. 574**

bureau (byoor′ō) *n.* a chest of drawers for the bedroom **p. 461**

C

catalyst (kat′əl ist) *n.* a force that facilitates action or change **p. 395**

ceremonious (ser′ə mō′ nē əs) *adj.* carefully observant of the formal acts required by ritual, custom, or etiquette **p. 514**

chaos (kā′os) *n.* a state of disorder and confusion **p. 485**

china (chī′nə) *n.* fine, glossy pottery used for tableware **p. 547**

chronic (kron′ik) *adj.* persistent; ongoing, especially of sickness or pain **p. 456**

cipher (sī′fər) *n.* a signifying figure; a number or symbol **p. 490**

commandeer (kom′ ən dēr′) *v.* to seize for use by the military or government **p. 50**

commend (kə mend′) *v.* to speak highly of; to praise **p. 719**

commodious (kə mō′dē əs) *adj.* having or containing ample room; spacious **p. 292**

benevolence/benevolencia *s.* amabilidad; generosidad **p. 341**

beseeching/suplicante *adj.* que ruega o pide seriamente **p. 170**

bewilderment/perplejidad *s.* confusión **p. 424**

blasphemous/blasfemo *adj.* que muestra una falta de respeto o desdén por Dios o algo sagrado **p. 64**

bloated/abotagado *adj.* inflamado; hinchado **p. 1062**

bough/rama *s.* cada una de las partes que nacen del tronco del árbol **p. 574**

bureau/cómoda *s.* mueble con cajones que se usa en el dormitorio **p. 461**

C

catalyst/catalizador *s.* una fuerza que facilita la acción o el cambio **p. 395**

ceremonious/ceremonioso *adj.* que observa atentamente las formalidades requeridas por un ritual, una costumbre o el protocolo **p. 514**

chaos/caos *s.* estado de confusión y desorden **p. 485**

china/vajilla *s.* conjunto de platos, tazas y otros recipientes finos y relucientes utilizados para el servicio de mesa **p. 547**

chronic/crónico *adj.* persistente; continuo, especialmente una enfermedad o un dolor **p. 456**

cipher/cifra *s.* un guarismo significativo; un número o símbolo **p. 490**

commandeer/usurpar *v.* tomar para uso por el ejército o el gobierno **p. 50**

commend/elogiar *v.* hablar muy bien de alguien o algo; alabar **p. 719**

commodious/cómodo *adj.* que tiene espacio amplio; espacioso **p. 292**

compassionate (kəm pash′ ə nit) *adj.* having or showing sympathy for another's misfortune, combined with a desire to help **p. 383**

complexion (kəm plek′ shən) *n.* general appearance, especially of the face **p. 466**

comprehensive (kom′ pri hen′ siv) *adj.* including nearly everything; large in scope; complete **p. 646**

confidante (kon′ fə dant′) *n.* a person who is entrusted with secrets or private affairs **p. 922**

confinement (kən fīn′ mənt) *n.* the state of being restricted or confined **p. 948**

conflagration (kon′flə grā′shən) *n.* a huge fire **p. 491**

confront (kən frunt′) *v.* to come face-to-face with; to oppose **p. 960**

conscientiously (kon′ shē en′ shəs lē) *adv.* thoughtfully and carefully **p. 165**

comtemptible (kən temp′ tə bəl) *adj.* worthy of contempt; loathsome **p. 947**

contrition (kən trish′ ən) *n.* sorrow for one's sin or wrongdoing; repentance **p. 165**

convivial (kən viv′ē əl) *adj.* fond of merriment and parties with good company; sociable **p. 293**

convoluted (kon′və lo͞o′ tid) *adj.* turned in or wound up upon itself; coiled; twisted **p. 21**

coterie (kō′tə rē) *n.* a small group of people who share a particular interest and often meet socially **p. 279**

countenance (koun′ tə nəns) *n.* the face **p. 61**

covert (kō′vərt) *adj.* secret; hidden **p. 760**

credence (krēd′əns) *n.* trustworthiness, especially in the reports or statements of others **p. 283**

crest (krest) *n.* a peak, high point, or climax **p. 543**

crevice (krev′ is) *n.* a narrow crack into or through something **p. 221**

cultivate (kul′ tə vāt′) *v.* to encourage or further the development of **p. 1069**

compassionate/compasivo *adj.* que tiene o muestra compasión por el infortunio ajeno, combinado con un deseo de ayudar **p. 383**

complexion/cutis *s.* apariencia general, especialmente de la cara **p. 466**

comprehensive/exhaustivo *adj.* que incluye casi todo; amplio en alcance; completo **p. 646**

confidante/confidente *s.* persona a la que se le confían secretos o asuntos personales **p. 922**

confinement/confinamiento *s.* el estado de estar restringido o confinado **p. 948**

conflagration/conflagración *s.* un gran incendio **p. 491**

confront/confrontar *v.* enfrentar cara a cara; oponerse **p. 960**

conscientiously/concienzudamente *adv.* cuidadosamente y reflexivamente **p. 165**

contemptible/despreciable *adj.* digno de desprecio; aborrecible **p. 947**

contrition/contrición *s.* pena por los pecados o las malas acciones propias; arrepentimiento **p. 165**

convivial/convival *adj.* que le gusta la alegría y las fiestas con buena compañía; sociable **p. 293**

convoluted/retorcido *adj.* trenzado; arrollado, en espiral; enroscado **p. 21**

coterie/camarilla *s.* grupo pequeño de personas que comparten un interés particular y a menudo se reúnen socialmente **p. 279**

countenance/semblante *s.* el rostro **p. 61**

covert/encubierto *adj.* secreto; oculto **p. 760**

credence/crédito *s.* fiabilidad, especialmente en informes o declaraciones de otros **p. 283**

crest/cresta *s.* pico, punto elevado o clímax **p. 543**

crevice/hendedura *s.* una grieta angosta en o a través algo **p. 221**

cultivate/cultivar *v.* auspiciar o fomentar el desarrollo **p. 1069**

D

debasement (di bās′mənt) *n.* the state of being lowered in quality, value, or character; degradation **p. 349**

deceitful (di sēt′fəl) *adj.* untruthful and cunning; false **p. 761**

decrepit (di krep′ it) *adj.* broken down by long use or old age **p. 128**

deference (def′ər əns) *n.* respect and honor due to another **p. 660**

deferred (di furd′) *adj.* put off; postponed **p. 594**

defile (di fīl′) *v.* to spoil the purity of; to make dirty or unclean **p. 672**

deliberation (di lib′ə rā′shən) *n.* an official meeting or consultation **p. 939**

dense (dens) *adj.* thick **p. 534**

designation (dez′ig nā′shən) *n.* a distinguishing name or mark **p. 262**

disconsolate (dis kon′sə lit) *adj.* dejected; mournful; unable to be comforted **p. 781**

discordant (dis kôrd′ənt) *adj.* not in agreement or harmony **p. 78**

disdainful (dis dān′fəl) *adj.* scornful; mocking **p. 936**

disgruntled (dis grun′tld) *adj.* in a state of sulky dissatisfaction **p. 505**

dismantle (dis mant′əl) *v.* to take apart **p. 1049**

disperse (dis purs′) *v.* to break up and send in different directions; to scatter **p. 721**

dissension (di sen′shən) *n.* disagreement within a group **p. 371**

distortion (dis tôr′ shən) *n.* an appearance of being twisted or bent out of shape **p. 225**

doctrine (dok′ trin) *n.* a particular principle or position that is taught or supported, as of a religion **p. 157**

domestic (də mes′ tik) *adj.* relating to one's own country **p. 370**

D

debasement/degradación *s.* estado de ser disminuido en calidad, valor, o carácter **p. 349**

deceitful/engañoso *adj.* falso y astuto; falaz **p. 761**

decrepit/decrépito *adj.* arruinado por el uso prolongado o la edad **p. 128**

deference/deferencia *s.* respeto y honor hacia alguien **p. 660**

deferred/diferido *adj.* aplazado; pospuesto **p. 594**

defile/manchar *v.* estropear la pureza; ensuciar **p. 672**

deliberation/deliberación *s.* una reunión o consulta oficial **p. 939**

dense/denso *adj.* espeso **p. 534**

designation/designación *s.* denominación **p. 262**

disconsolate/desconsolado *adj.* afligido; acongojado; que no tiene consuelo **p. 781**

discordant/discordante *adj.* que no tiene concordancia o no está en armonía **p. 78**

disdainful/desdeñoso *adj.* despreciativo; burlón **p. 936**

disgruntled/descontento *adj.* en estado de insatisfacción **p. 505**

dismantle/desmantelar *v.* desarmar **p. 1049**

disperse/dispersar *v.* separar y repartir en distintas direcciones; desperdigar **p. 721**

dissension/disensión *s.* desacuerdo dentro de un grupo **p. 371**

distortion/distorsión *s.* apariencia de estar torcido o con otra forma **p. 225**

doctrine/doctrina *s.* un principio o una posición particular que es enseñada o mantenida, como la de una religión **p. 157**

domestic/doméstico *adj.* relacionado al país propio **p. 370**

duly (dōō′ lē) *adv.* rightfully; suitably **p. 12**

dupe (dōōp) *v.* to fool; to trick **p. 1063**

dutiful (dōō′ ti fəl) *adj.* acting out of a sense of obligation or a sense of what is required **p. 1034**

E

edifice (ed′ ə fis) *n.* a building, especially a large, important-looking one **p. 51**

elation (i lā′shən) *n.* a feeling of great joy; ecstasy **p. 347**

elude (i lōōd′) *v.* to avoid or escape, especially through cleverness or quickness **p. 921**

emancipation (i man′sə pā′shən) *n.* the process of becoming free from control or the power of another **p. 407**

embroidered (em broi′dərd) *adj.* decorated with needlework **p. 528**

endear (en dēr′) *v.* to cause to adore or admire **p. 948**

enhance (en hans′) *v.* to make greater, as in beauty or value **p. 40**

enterprise (en′ tər prīz′) *n.* an important project or undertaking **p. 705**

entreat (en trēt′) *v.* to ask earnestly; to beg **p. 701**

equanimity (ēk′ wə nim′ ə tē) *n.* the ability to remain calm and assured **p. 197**

eschew (es chōō′) *v.* to keep apart from something disliked or harmful; avoid **p. 329**

essence (es′əns) *n.* perfume **p. 574**

exultation (eg′ zul tā′ shən) *n.* joy; jubilation **p. 348**

F

famished (fam′isht) *adj.* intensely hungry; ravenous **p. 643**

ferociously (fə rō′shəs lē) *adv.* cruelly; savagely **p. 820**

duly/debidamente *adv.* justamente; apropiadamente **p. 12**

dupe/engañar *v.* embaucar; timar **p. 1063**

dutiful/cumplidor *adj.* que actúa motivado por un sentido de obligación o de lo que es necesario **p. 1034**

E

edifice/edificio *s.* una construcción, especialmente una grande o que parece importante **p. 51**

elation/elación *s.* un sentimiento de gran alegría **p. 347**

elude/eludir *v.* evitar o escapar, especialmente a través de habilidad o rapidez **p. 921**

emancipation/emancipación *s.* el proceso de liberarse del control o el poder de otro **p. 407**

embroidered/bordado *adj.* adornado con costura o bordadura **p. 528**

endear/encariñar *v.* despertar cariño o admiración **p. 948**

enhance/intensificar *v.* hacer más grande, como en la belleza o el valor **p. 40**

enterprise/empresa *s.* proyecto o emprendimiento importante **p. 705**

entreat/suplicar *v.* pedir fervientemente; rogar **p. 701**

equanimity/ecuanimidad *s.* habilidad de permanecer calmo y protegido **p. 197**

eschew/evitar *v.* separarse de algo dañoso o detestado; prevenir **p. 329**

essence/esencia *s.* perfume **p. 574**

exultation/exultación *s.* alegría; júbilo **p. 348**

F

famished/famélico *adj.* intensamente hambriento; voraz **p. 643**

ferociously/ferozmente *adv.* cruelmente; salvajemente **p. 820**

fiasco (fē as´kō) *n.* a complete or humiliating failure **p. 81**

fissure (fish´ər) *n.* a narrow crack **p. 462**

fleck (flek´) *v.* to leave spots or streaks **p. 506**

formidable (fôr´mi də bəl) *adj.* causing fear, dread, or awe by reason of size, strength, or power **p. 127**

fortitude (fôr´ tə tōōd´) *n.* firm courage or strength of mind in the face of pain or danger **p. 197**

frenzy (fren´ zē) *n.* a state of wild, intense emotion, as of excitement **p. 1004**

furtive (fur´ tiv) *adj.* secret; shifty; sly **p. 154**

G

glyph (glif) *n.* an engraved, symbolic figure **p. 490**

gnarled (närld) *adj.* roughened and coarse from age or work; full of knots, as in a tree **p. 1048**

gorge (gôrj) *n.* the passageway between two higher land areas, such as a narrow valley **p. 485**

grapple (grap´ əl) *v.* to struggle, as though wrestling; to come to terms with **p. 378**

grimace (grim´ is) *v.* to make a face expressing disgust, disapproval, or pain **p. 462**

guile (gīl) *n.* cunning **p. 937**

H

hapless (hap´ lis) *adj.* unlucky or unfortunate **p. 522**

harass (hə ras´) *v.* to bother or annoy repeatedly **p. 185**

hoary (hôr´ē) *adj.* white or gray with age; covered with frost **p. 574**

hone (hōn) *n.* whetstone or similar tool used to sharpen knives and other types of blades **p. 472**

horizon (hə rī´ zən) *n.* the place where the earth and sky appear to meet **p. 1034**

hurtle (hurt´ əl) *v.* to move rapidly, especially with much force or noise **p. 129**

fiasco/fiasco *s.* un fracaso completo o humillante **p. 81**

fissure/fisura *s.* hendidura poco profunda **p. 462**

fleck/motear *v.* dejar manchas o rayas **p. 506**

formidable/formidable *adj.* que causa miedo, temor o pavor a causa del tamaño, fuerza o poder **p. 127**

fortitude/fortaleza *s.* valor sólido o fuerza de la mente al enfrentar dolor o peligro **p. 197**

frenzy/frenesí *n.* un estado de conmoción, de emoción loca e intensa **p. 1004**

furtive/furtivo *adj.* secreto; inquieto **p. 154**

G

glyph/glifo *s.* figura simbólica grabada **p. 490**

gnarled/nudoso *adj.* áspero y grueso por la edad o el trabajo; lleno de nudos, como un árbol **p. 1048**

gorge/desfiladero *s.* pasillo entre dos zonas de tierra más altas, como un valle angosto **p. 485**

grapple/forcejear *v.* luchar, como si fuese lucha libre; enfrentarse **p. 378**

grimace/mueca *v.* hacer gestos para expresar disgusto, desaprobación o dolor **p. 462**

guile/astucia *s.* sagacidad **p. 937**

H

hapless/desventurado *adj.* desdichado o desafortunado **p. 522**

harass/atormentar *v.* molestar repetidamente **p. 185**

hoary/canoso *adj.* blanco o gris con la edad; cubierto de escarcha **p. 574**

hone/piedra de afilar *n.* herramienta que se usan para sacarle filo a cuchillos y otros tipo de hojas **p. 472**

horizon/horizonte *s.* lugar donde parecen juntarse el cielo y la tierra **p. 1034**

hurtle/lanzar *v.* moverse rápidamente, especialmente con mucha fuerza o ruido **p. 129**

I

ignoble (ig nō′ bəl) *adj.* of low birth or position; without honor or worth **p. 889**

ignorant (ig′nər ənt) *adj.* lacking knowledge or experience; uninformed **p. 820**

immense (i mens′) *adj.* immeasurable; vast; huge **p. 477**

imminent (im′ ə nənt) *adj.* likely to happen soon **p. 14**

impeccably (im pek′ə blē) *adv.* without error or flaw **p. 107**

imperative (im per′ə tiv) *adj.* expressing a command or an order **p. 407**

imperceptible (im′ pər sep′tə bəl) *adj.* slight; barely capable of being seen or sensed **p. 108**

impertinent (im purt′ən ənt) *adj.* inappropriately bold or forward **p. 841**

impetuous (im pech′ o͞o əs) *adj.* rushing head-long into things; rash **p. 41**

improvised (im′ prə vīzd′) *adj.* invented, composed, or done without preparation **p. 22**

impudence (im′pyə dəns) *n.* speech or behavior that is aggressively forward or rude **p. 806**

incantation (in′ kan tā′ shən) *n.* words spoken in casting a spell **p. 42**

incense (in sens′) *v.* to make very angry **p. 707**

incredulous (in krej′ ə ləs) *adj.* unwilling or unable to believe **p. 172**

indifferently (in dif′ər ənt lē) *adv.* not concerned about someone or something; without a preference **p. 456**

induce (in do͞os′) *v.* to lead or move by persuasion; to bring about **p. 315**

inert (i nurt′) *adj.* not able to move **p. 1051**

infirmity (in fur′mə tē) *n.* a weakness or an ailment **p. 13**

inherent (in her′ ənt) *adj.* existing naturally in someone or something **p. 418**

I

ignoble/innoble *adj.* de posición social baja; sin honor ni valor **p. 889**

ignorant/ignorante *adj.* que carece conocimiento o experiencia; sin información **p. 820**

immense/inmenso *adj.* inconmensurable; vasto; enorme **p. 477**

imminent/inminente *adj.* que está a punto de ocurrir **p. 14**

impeccably/impecablemente *adv.* sin defecto ni imperfección **p. 107**

imperative/imperativo *adj.* que expresa una orden o un comando **p. 407**

imperceptible/imperceptible *adj.* leve, apenas capaz de ser visto o sentido **p. 108**

impertinent/impertinente *adj.* atrevido o descarado de manera inapropiada **p. 841**

impetuous/impetuoso *adj.* precipitado; imprudente **p. 41**

improvised/improvisado *adj.* inventado, compuesto o hecho sin preparación de antemano **p. 22**

impudence/impudencia *s.* lenguaje o conducta que es agresivamente descarado o grosero **p. 806**

incantation/encantación *s.* palabras dichas para encantar o hechizar **p. 42**

incense/indignar *v.* enfadar mucho **p. 707**

incredulous/incrédulo *adj.* reacio o incapaz de creer **p. 172**

indifferently/indiferentemente *adv.* sin preocuparse por algo o alguien; sin una preferencia **p. 456**

induce/inducir *v.* guiar o moverse por persuasión; provocar **p. 315**

inert/inerte *adj.* que no se puede mover **p. 1051**

infirmity/padecimiento *s.* una debilidad o dolencia **p. 13**

inherent/inherente *adj.* algo que existo naturalmente en alguien o algo **p. 293**

inhibit (in hib′ it) *v.* to hold back one's natural impulses; to restrain **p. 293**

inscribe (in skrīb′) *v.* to write, carve, or mark on a surface **p. 888**

inscrutable (in skr$\overline{oo}$′ tə bəl) *adj.* mysterious **p. 94**

intact (in takt′) *adj.* entire; untouched, uninjured, and having all parts **p. 348**

interim (in′tər im) *n.* the space of time that exists between events **p. 716**

interlaced (in′ tər lāst′) *adj.* connected by or woven together **p. 1035**

interminable (in tur′ mi nə bəl) *adj.* lasting, or seeming to last, forever; endless **p. 90**

intimidation (in tim′ ə dā shən) *n.* act of making one feel afraid or discouraged **p. 113**

intuitively (in t$\overline{oo}$′ə tiv lē) *adv.* knowing, sensing, or understanding instinctively **p. 355**

invaluable (in val′ ū ə bəl) *adj.* very great in value **p. 341**

irreproachable (ir′ i prō chə bəl) *adj.* free from blame or criticism; faultless **p. 138**

J

jubilantly (j$\overline{oo}$′ bə lənt lē) *adv.* joyfully or happily **p. 940**

L

lag (lag) *v.* to fall behind **p. 515**

M

mainstream (mān′ strēm′) *adj.* representing the most widespread attitudes and values of a society or group **p. 341**

makeshift (māk′ shift′) *adj.* suitable as a temporary substitute for the proper or desired thing **p. 186**

malice (mal′is) *n.* a desire to hurt another person **p. 741**

---

inhibit/inhibir *v.* contener los impulsos naturales; refrenar **p. 293**

inscribe/inscribir *v.* escribir, labrar o señalar un superficie **p. 888**

inscrutable/inescrutable *adj.* misterioso **p. 94**

intact/intacto *adj.* entero; sin tocar, indemne y que tiene todas las partes **p. 348**

interim/ínterin *s.* intervalo de tiempo que existe entre dos hechos **p. 716**

interlaced/entrelazado *adj.* conectado por o entretejido **p. 1035**

interminable/interminable *adj.* duradero o que parece durar para siempre; infinito **p. 90**

intimidation/intimidación *s.* acto de provocar miedo o desaliento **p. 113**

intuitively/intuitivamente *adv.* con conocimiento, sensación o comprensión; instintivamente **p. 355**

invaluable/invaluable *adj.* inestimable **p. 341**

irreproachable/irreprochable *adj.* libre de culpa o crítica; sin defecto **p. 138**

J

jubilantly/alborozadamente *adv.* con gran regocijo y alegría **p. 940**

L

lag/rezagarse *v.* quedarse atrás **p. 515**

M

mainstream/predominante *adj.* que representa las actitudes y los valores más comunes de una sociedad o grupo **p. 341**

makeshift/provisional *adj.* apto como sustituto temporal de aquello adecuado o deseado **p. 186**

malice/malicia *s.* deseo de dañar a otra persona **p. 741**

malicious (mə lish′ əs) *adj.* having or showing a desire to harm another **p. 133**

marvel (mär′vəl) *v.* to become filled with wonder or astonishment **p. 551**

mature (mə choor′) *adj.* having reached a desired state **p. 534**

melancholy (mel′ən kol′ē) *adj.* depressed; dejected **p. 462**

meticulous (mi tik′yə ləs) *adj.* characterized by great or excessive concern about details **p. 291**

minuscule (min′ əs kūl′) *adj.* very, very small **p. 521**

misconstrue (mis′kən strōō′) *v.* to misinterpret; to misunderstand **p. 782**

misgiving (mis giv′ing) *n.* a feeling of doubt; apprehension **p. 740**

motto (mot′ ō) *n.* maxim or proverb that expresses a principle **p. 595**

N

negation (ni gā′ shən) *n.* act of denying; negative statement or denial p. 417

neutrality (nōō tral′ ə tē) *n.* avoidance of choosing a side **p. 424**

nostalgic (nos tal′jik) *adj.* longing for persons, things, or situations from the past **p. 551**

notorious (nō tôr′ē əs) *adj.* widely and unfavorably known **p. 838**

O

obligatory (ə blig′ə tôr′ē) *adj.* required or necessary **p. 301**

oblivion (ə bliv′ē ən) *n.* a lack of awareness or memory **p. 542**

oblivious (ə bliv′ē əs) *adj.* unmindful or unaware; not noticing **p. 813**

odious (ō′dē əs) *adj.* disgusting or offensive **p. 371**

malicious/malicioso *adj.* que muestra o que tiene un deseo de dañar a otro **p. 133**

marvel/maravillar *v.* lleno de admiración o asombro **p. 551**

mature/maduro *adj.* que ha alcanzado un estado deseado **p. 534**

melancholy/melancólico *adj.* deprimido; desanimado **p. 462**

meticulous/meticuloso *adj.* preciso; cuidadoso; preocupado por los detalles **p. 291**

minuscule/minúsculo *adj.* extremadamente pequeño **p. 521**

misconstrue/malinterpretar *v.* interpretar incorrectamente; entender mal **p. 782**

misgiving/recelo *s.* un sentimiento de duda; aprensión **p. 740**

motto/lema *n.* axioma o proverbio que expresa un principio **p. 595**

N

negation/negacion *n.* acto que niegan la veracidad de algo **p. 417**

neutrality/neutralidad *n.* estado de no alineamiento **p. 424**

nostalgic/nostálgico *adj.* que anhela a personas, cosas o situaciones del pasado **p. 551**

notorious/notorio *adj.* conocido extensa y desfavorablemente **p. 838**

O

obligatory/obligatorio *adj.* exigido o necesario **p. 301**

oblivion/inconsciencia *s.* falta de conciencia o memoria **p. 542**

oblivious/abstraído *adj.* descuidado o desprevenido; que no nota algo **p. 813**

odious/odioso *adj.* repugnante u ofensivo **p. 371**

oppress (ə pres´) v. to control or govern by the cruel and unjust use of force or authority **p. 156**

orator (ôr´ə tər) n. a person skilled in public speaking **p. 752**

ordain (ôr dān´) v. to order or establish; to appoint **p. 370**

ostentatiously (os´tən tā´shəs lē) adv. in a way intended to attract attention or impress others **p. 833**

P

pandemonium (pan´ də mō´ nē əm) n. wild disorder and uproar **p. 199**

paradox (par´ə doks´) n. something that seems contradictory and yet may be true **p. 406**

paranoia (par´ə noi´ ə) n. the mental state of being very afraid or suspicious of others **p. 1004**

paraphernalia (par´ ə fər nāl´ yə) n. things used in a particular activity; equipment **p. 42**

patriarch (pā´trē ärk´) n. the male head of a family or group **p. 261**

peevish (pē´vish) adj. irritable; bad-tempered **p. 777**

pent-up (pent´ up) adj. not expressed or released; held in **p. 26**

peril (per´əl) n. exposure to harm or danger **p. 778**

perpetuate (pər pech´ oo āt´) v. to cause to continue to be remembered **p. 923**

perplexed (pər plekst´) adj. troubled with doubt or uncertainty; puzzled **p. 1024**

peruse (pə rooz´) v. to read through or examine carefully **p. 281**

perverse (pər vurs´) adj. determined to go against what is reasonable, expected, or desired; contrary **p. 664**

pious (pī´əs) adj. devoutly religious **p. 648**

oppress/oprimir v. controlar o gobernar mediante el uso cruel o injusto de la fuerza o la autoridad **p. 156**

orator/orador s. persona especialista en hablar en público **p. 752**

ordain/decretar v. ordenar o establecer; designar **p. 370**

ostentatiously/ostentosamente adv. en una manera que intenta atraer la atención o impresionar a otros **p. 833**

P

pandemonium/pandemónium s. gran desorden y alboroto **p. 199**

paradox/paradoja s. una expresión que parece contradictoria pero que aun puede ser cierta **p. 406**

paranoia/paranoia n. el estado mental de ser muy miedoso o sospechoso de los demás **p. 1004**

paraphernalia/parafernalia s. cosas usadas en una actividad particular; equipo **p. 42**

patriarch/patriarca s. el jefe de una familia o un grupo **p. 261**

peevish/displicente adj. irritable; malhumorado **p. 777**

pent-up/contenido adj. que no se expresa o libera; reprimido **p. 26**

peril/riesgo s. exposición a daño o peligro **p. 778**

perpetuate/perpetuar v. hacer que siga siendo recordado **p. 923**

perplexed/perplejo adj. confundido; inseguro **p. 1024**

peruse/repasar v. leer o examinar con cuidado **p. 281**

perverse/obstinado adj. determinado a oponerse a lo que es razonable, previsto o deseado; contrario **p. 664**

pious/pío adj. devotamente religioso **p. 648**

piqued (pēkt) *adj.* aroused in anger or resentment; offended **p. 42**

potent (pot′ənt) *adj.* having strength or authority; powerful **p. 315**

precedence (pres′ə dəns) *n.* order of importance or preference; priority **p. 1051**

presentiment (pri zen′ tə mənt) *n.* a feeling that something is about to happen **p. 197**

pretext (prē′ tekst) *n.* a reason or motive offered in order to disguise real intentions **p. 1070**

prevail (pri vāl′) *v.* to be superior in power or influence; to succeed **p. 668**

primal (prī′məl) *adj.* a basic, original state of being **p. 485**

prodigy (prod′ə jē) *n.* an extraordinarily gifted or talented person, especially a child **p. 74**

profuse (prə fūs′) *adj.* great in amount, plentiful **p. 59**

prowess (prou′ is) *n.* great ability or skill **p. 890**

Q

querulous (kwer′ə ləs) *adj.* argumentative; uncooperative **p. 505**

R

rash (rash) *adj.* marked by haste and lack of caution or consideration **p. 766**

reaper (rē′pər) *n.* machine or person that cuts grain for harvesting **p. 472**

recoil (ri koil′) *v.* to shrink back physically or emotionally **p. 1076**

recollect (rek′ə lekt′) *v.* to remember **p. 514**

regally (rē′gəl lē) *adv.* in a grand, dignified manner befitting a king or a queen **p. 833**

relevant (rel′ ə vənt) *adj.* related to the issue at hand **p. 381**

piqued/resentido *adj.* irritado o con resentimiento; ofendido **p. 42**

potent/potente *adj.* que tiene fuerza o autoridad; poderoso **p. 315**

precedence/precedencia *s.* orden de importancia o preferencia; prioridad **p. 1051**

presentiment/presentimiento *s.* una sensación de que algo va a ocurrir **p. 197**

pretext/pretexto *s.* razón o motivo ofrecido para encubrir intenciones reales **p. 1070**

prevail/prevalecer *v.* ser superior en poder o influencia; tener éxito **p. 668**

primal/primitivo *adj.* estado de ser original y básico **p. 485**

prodigy/prodigio *s.* una persona extraordinariamente dotada o talentosa, especialmente un niño **p. 74**

profuse/profuso *adj.* grande en cantidad; abundante **p. 59**

prowess/proeza *s.* habilidad o capacidad grande **p. 890**

Q

querulous/quejumbroso *adj.* discutidor; poco dispuesto a colaborar **p. 505**

R

rash/impulsivo *adj.* marcado por la prisa y la falta de cautela o consideración **p. 766**

reaper/cosechadora *s.* persona o máquinas que sirven para cortar granos **p. 472**

recoil/retroceder *v.* encogerse física o emocionalmente **p. 1076**

recollect/recordar *v.* traer a la memoria **p. 514**

regally/regiamente *adv.* en forma majestuosa y señorial como corresponde a un rey o reina **p. 833**

relevant/pertinente *adj.* relacionado con el tema en cuestión **p. 381**

relic (rel´ik) *n.* that which is cherished for its age or sentimental associations; memento; keepsake **p. 189**

remorse (ri môrs´) *n.* distress stemming from the guilt of past wrongs **p. 478**

repressed (ri prest´) *adj.* held back or kept under control; restrained **p. 839**

reproach (ri prōch´) *n.* blame; disgrace; discredit **p. 75**

repulse (ri puls´) *n.* an act of beating back or driving away, as with force **p. 639**

retail (rē´tāl) *v.* to sell directly to consumers **p. 51**

reveling (rev´ əl ing) *adj.* taking great pleasure **p. 26**

reverie (rev´ər ē) *n.* fanciful thinking; daydream **p. 78**

russet (rus´it) *adj.* a deep reddish-brown **p. 575**

S

sacred (sā´ krid) *adj.* worthy of reverence **p. 478**

scavenger (skav´ in jər) *n.* one who searches through discarded materials for something useful **p. 1063**

scenario (si när´ ē ō´) *n.* an outline or model of an expected or imagined series of events **p. 293**

scrupulous (skrōō´ pyə ləs) *adj.* thoroughly attentive to even the smallest details; precise **p. 921**

scrutinize (skrōōt´ ən īz´) *v.* to look at closely; to inspect carefully **p. 93**

scythe (sīth) *n.* cutting implement made of a long, curved single-edged blade **p. 472**

relic/reliquia *n.* algo que se estima por su edad o por asociaciones sentimentales; recuerdo; prenda **p. 189**

remorse/remordimiento *s.* angustia que surge de la culpa de errores pasados **p. 478**

repressed/reprimido *adj.* contenido o mantenido bajo control; comedido **p. 839**

reproach/oprobio *n.* culpa, deshonra, descrédito **p. 75**

repulse/rechazo *n.* el acto de ahuyentar o alejar, con fuerza **p. 639**

retail/vender al por menor *v.* vender directamente al consumidor **p. 51**

reveling/deleitarse *adj.* producir gran placer **p. 26**

reverie/ensueño *s.* pensamientos imaginativos; fantasías **p. 78**

russet/bermejo *adj.* marrón rojizo intenso **p. 575**

S

sacred/sagrado *adj.* digno de veneración **p. 478**

scavenger/hurgador *s.* persona que busca algo útil en los materiales de desecho **p. 1063**

scenario/escenario *s.* descripción general o modelo de una serie de sucesos esperados o imaginados **p. 293**

scrupulous/escrupuloso *adj.* completamente atento hasta al más mínimo detalle; preciso **p. 921**

scrutinize/escudriñar *v.* examinar cuidadosamente; inspeccionar detenidamente **p. 93**

scythe/guadaña *s.* implemento cortantes formados por una cuchilla curva y puntiaguda, de un solo filo **p. 472**

searing (sēr′ing) *adj.* extremely hot or bright p. 485

self-possessed (self′ pə zest′) *adj.* in control of oneself; composed p. 12

serenity (sə ren′ ə tē) *n.* calmness; peacefulness p. 91

serpentine (sur′pən tēn′) *adj.* snake-like; twisting; winding p. 485

servile (sur′vil) *adj.* lacking self-respect; behaving as if other people are superior p. 696

sidle (sīd′əl) *v.* to move sideways p. 153

skeptical (skep′ ti kəl) *adj.* having or showing doubt or suspicion; questioning; disbelieving p. 94

sparse (spärs) *adj.* thinly spread or distributed p. 224

spectral (spek′ trəl) *adj.* ghostlike p. 64

squander (skwon′ dər) *v.* to waste through irresponsible behavior p. 396

stolid (stol′ id) *adj.* showing little or no emotion p. 331

strategic (strə tē′ jik) *adj.* highly important to an intended goal p. 962

stupor (stoo′pər) *n.* a state of extreme lethargy p. 514

sublime (səb līm′) *adj.* noble; exalted; above all others p. 1009

submerged (səb murjd′) *adj.* hard to see; sunken p. 461

subordinate (sə bôr′də nāt′) *v.* to cause to be, or treat as, secondary, inferior, or less important p. 270

subversive (səb vur′ siv) *adj.* seeking to weaken, destroy, or overthrow p. 140

searing/abrasador *adj.* extremadamente caliente o brillante p. 485

self-possessed/sosegado *adj.* en control de sí mismo; sereno p. 12

serenity/serenidad *s.* tranquilidad; calma p. 91

serpentine/serpentino *adj.* similar a una serpiente; serpenteante, zigzagueante p. 485

servile/servil *adj.* que carece de autoestima; que se comporta como si las otras personas fuesen superiores p. 696

sidle/andar de lado *v.* moverse hacia un lado, especialmente en una manera que no atrae atención ni provoca perturbación p. 153

skeptical/escéptico *adj.* que tiene o muestra duda o sospecha; inquisitivo; incrédulo p. 94

sparse/ralo *adj.* apenas distribuido o esparcido p. 224

spectral/espectral *adj.* fantasmal p. 64

squander/derrochar *v.* malgastar a causa de comportamiento irresponsable p. 396

stolid/impasible *adj.* que muestra poca o ninguna emoción p. 331

strategic/estratégico *adj.* de gran importancia para una meta planeada p. 962

stupor/estupor *s.* un estado de letargo extremo p. 514

sublime/sublime *adj.* noble; exaltado; por encima de todos los demás p. 1009

submerged/sumergido *adj.* difícil de ver; hundido p. 461

subordinate/subordinar *v.* hacer que esté o tratar como si fuera secundario, inferior o menos importante p. 270

subversive/subversivo *adj.* que intenta debilitar, destruir o derrocar p. 140

superfluous (soo pur´ floo əs) *adj.* not needed; unnecessary p. 341

supplication (sup´lə kā shən) *n.* an earnest and humble request p. 167

T

taboo (ta boo´) *n.* a cultural or social rule forbidding something p. 355

taut (tôt) *adj.* tense; tight p. 23

temperate (tem´pər it) *adj.* calm and free from extremes of temperature p. 466

thrive (thrīv) *v.* to be successful; to grow well p. 735

torrential (tô ren´chəl) *adj.* flowing rapidly and abundantly p. 304

transcend (tran send´) *v.* to rise above or go beyond limits p. 424

translucent (trans loo´sənt) *adj.* allowing light to pass through; almost clear; see-through p. 506

treacherous (trech´ ər əs) *adj.* likely to betray a trust; disloyal p. 1063

tread (tred) *v.* to step or walk on p. 528

tremulously (trem´ yə ləs lē) *adv.* in a trembling or vibrating way p. 329

tribulation (trib´ yə lā´ shən) *n.* great misery or distress; suffering p. 203

tumultuous (too mul´ choo əs) *adj.* wildly excited, confused, or agitated p. 889

turbulent (tur´byə lənt) *adj.* causing unrest, violent action, or disturbance p. 407

U

ulterior (ul tēr´ ē ər) *adj.* intentionally withheld or concealed p. 139

unstratified (un strat´ ə fīd) *adj.* not structured into different social classes p. 418

superfluous/superfluo *adj.* que no es necesario; innecesario p. 341

supplication/súplica *s.* un ruego serio y humilde p. 167

T

taboo/tabú *s.* regla cultural o social que prohíbe algo p. 355

taut/tirante *adj.* tenso; ajustado p. 23

temperate/templado *adj.* tranquilo y sin extremos de temperatura p. 466

thrive/prosperar *v.* tener éxito; salir adelante p. 735

torrential/torrencial *adj.* que fluye rápida y abundantemente p. 304

transcend/superar *v.* sobresalir o sobrepasar límites p. 424

translucent/translúcido *adj.* que permite que pase la luz; casi transparente p. 506

treacherous/traicionero *adj.* propenso a traicionar la confianza; desleal p. 1063

tread/pisar *v.* poner los pies sobre el suelo o andar p. 528

tremulously/trémulamente *adv.* en una manera temblorosa o vibrante p. 329

tribulation/tribulación *s.* gran miseria o dolor; sufrimiento p. 203

tumultuous/tumultuoso *adj.* excitado, confundido o agitado ferozmente p. 889

turbulent/turbulento *adj.* que causa inquietud, acción violenta o perturbación p. 407

U

ulterior/ulterior *adj.* intencionalmente retenido o disimulado p. 139

unstratified/no por estratos frase *adj.* sin capas o niveles en la sociedad p. 418

V

valor (val′ər) *n.* courageous spirit; personal bravery **p. 408**

vanquish (vang′kwish) *v.* to defeat; to overcome **p. 751**

vault (vôlt) *v.* to jump; to spring **p. 961**

vehemently (vē′ə mənt lē) *adv.* strongly; intensely; passionately **p. 285**

verandah (və ran′ də) *n.* a long porch, usually with a roof, that extends along a house **p. 1034**

vintage (vin′ tij) *adj.* characterized by enduring appeal; classic **p. 186**

vulnerable vulnerable (vul′ nər ə bəl) *adj.* easily damaged or hurt **p. 341**

W

wanton (wont′ ən) *adj.* shamelessly unrestrained; immoral **p. 62**

V

valor/valor *s.* espíritu valeroso, bravura personal **p. 408**

vanquish/subyugar *v.* derrotar o vencer **p. 751**

vault/brincar *v.* saltar; rebotar **p. 961**

vehemently/vehementemente *adv.* fuertemente; intensamente; obstinadamente **p. 285**

verandah/veranda *s.* una terraza en la parte de afuera de un edificio como una casa **p. 1034**

vintage/reliquia *adj.* caracterizado por un atractivo que perdura en el tiempo; clásico **p. 186**

vulnerable/vulnerable *adj.* que se daña o lastima con facilidad **p. 341**

W

wanton/despiadado *adj.* descaradamente desmedido; inmoral **p. 62**

Academic Word List

To succeed academically in high school and prepare for college, it is important to know academic vocabulary–special terms used in classroom discussion, assignments, and tests. These words are also used in the workplace and among friends to share information, exchange ideas, make decisions, and build relationships. Research has shown that the words listed below, compiled by Averil Coxhead in 2000, are the ones most commonly used in these ways. You will encounter many of them in the Glencoe Language Arts program. You will also focus on specific terms in connection with particular reading selections.

Note: The lists are ordered by frequency of use from most frequent to least frequent.

List One

analysis
approach
area
assessment
assume
authority
available
benefit
concept
consistent
constitutional
context
contract
create
data
definition
derived
distribution
economic
environment
established
estimate
evidence
export
factors
financial
formula
function
identified
income
indicate
individual
interpretation
involved
issues
labor
legal
legislation
major
method
occur
percent
period
policy
principle
procedure
process
required
research
response
role
section
sector
significant
similar
source
specific
structure
theory
variables

List Two

achieve
acquisition
administration
affect
appropriate
aspects
assistance
categories
chapter
commission
community
complex
computer
conclusion
conduct
consequences
construction
consumer
credit
cultural
design
distinction
elements
equation
evaluation
features
final
focus
impact
injury
institute
investment
items
journal
maintenance
normal
obtained
participation
perceived
positive
potential
previous
primary
purchase
range
region
regulations
relevant
resident
resources
restricted
security
select
site
sought
strategies
survey
text
traditional
transfer

List Three

alternative
circumstances
comments
compensation
components
consent
considerable
constant
constraints
contribution
convention
coordination
core
corporate
corresponding
criteria
deduction
demonstrate
document
dominant
emphasis
ensure
excluded
framework
funds
illustrated
immigration
implies
initial

instance
interaction
justification
layer
link
location
maximum
minorities
negative
outcomes
partnership
philosophy
physical
proportion
published
reaction
registered
reliance
removed
scheme
sequence
shift
specified
sufficient
task
technical
techniques
technology
validity
volume

List Four

access
adequate
annual
apparent
approximated
attitudes
attributed
civil
code
commitment
communication
concentration

conference
contrast
cycle
debate
despite
dimensions
domestic
emerged
error
ethnic
goals
granted
hence
hypothesis
implementation
implications
imposed
integration
internal
investigation
job
label
mechanism
obvious
occupational
option
output
overall
parallel
parameters
phase
predicted
principal
prior
professional
project
promote
regime
resolution
retained
series
statistics
status
stress

subsequent
sum
summary
undertaken

List Five

academic
adjustment
alter
amendment
aware
capacity
challenge
clause
compounds
conflict
consultation
contact
decline
discretion
draft
enable
energy
enforcement
entities
equivalent
evolution
expansion
exposure
external
facilitate
fundamental
generated
generation
image
liberal
license
logic
marginal
medical
mental
modified
monitoring
network

notion
objective
orientation
perspective
precise
prime
psychology
pursue
ratio
rejected
revenue
stability
styles
substitution
sustainable
symbolic
target
transition
trend
version
welfare
whereas

List Six

abstract
accurate
acknowledged
aggregate
allocation
assigned
attached
author
bond
brief
capable
cited
cooperative
discrimination
display
diversity
domain
edition
enhanced
estate

exceed
expert
explicit
federal
fees
flexibility
furthermore
gender
ignored
incentive
incidence
incorporated
index
inhibition
initiatives
input
instructions
intelligence
interval
lecture
migration
minimum
ministry
motivation
neutral
nevertheless
overseas
preceding
presumption
rational
recovery
revealed
scope
subsidiary
tapes
trace
transformation
transport
underlying
utility

List Seven

adaptation
adults
advocate
aid
channel
chemical
classical
comprehensive
comprise
confirmed
contrary
converted
couple
decades
definite
deny
differentiation
disposal
dynamic
eliminate
empirical
equipment
extract
file
finite
foundation
global
grade
guarantee
hierarchical
identical
ideology
inferred
innovation
insert
intervention
isolated
media
mode
paradigm
phenomenon
priority
prohibited

publication
quotation
release
reverse
simulation
solely
somewhat
submitted
successive
survive
thesis
topic
transmission
ultimately
unique
visible
voluntary

List Eight

abandon
accompanied
accumulation
ambiguous
appendix
appreciation
arbitrary
automatically
bias
chart
clarity
conformity
commodity
complement
contemporary
contradiction
crucial
currency
denote
detected
deviation
displacement
dramatic
eventually
exhibit

exploitation
fluctuations
guidelines
highlighted
implicit
induced
inevitably
infrastructure
inspection
intensity
manipulation
minimized
nuclear
offset
paragraph
plus
practitioners
predominantly
prospect
radical
random
reinforced
restore
revision
schedule
tension
termination
theme
thereby
uniform
vehicle
via
virtually
visual
widespread

List Nine

accommodation
analogous
anticipated
assurance
attained
behalf
bulk

ceases
coherence
coincide
commenced
concurrent
confined
controversy
conversely
device
devoted
diminished
distorted
duration
erosion
ethical
format
founded
incompatible
inherent
insights
integral
intermediate
manual
mature
mediation
medium
military
minimal
mutual
norms
overlap
passive
portion
preliminary
protocol
qualitative
refine
relaxed
restraints
revolution
rigid
route
scenario
sphere

subordinate
supplementary
suspended
team
temporary
trigger
unified
violation
vision

List Ten

adjacent
albeit
assembly
collapse
colleagues
compiled
conceived
convinced
depression
encountered
enormous
forthcoming
inclination
integrity
intrinsic
invoked
levy
likewise
nonetheless
notwithstanding
odd
ongoing
panel
persistent
posed
reluctant
so-called
straightforward
undergo
whereby

Index of Skills

References beginning with **R** refer to handbook pages.

Literary Concepts

Act 626, 630
Ad hominem 560
Allegory 33, 58, 67, 68
Alliteration 447, 448, 473, 566, 569, 571, 577
Allusion 66, 376, 388
Ambiguity 208
Analogy 1047, 1053
Analytical essay 426–433
Anecdotal evidence 373, 420
Anecdote 292, 296, 334
Antagonist 3, 637, 658
Appeal
   to authority 363, 374, 419
   to commonly held
      opinion 365, 366
   to emotion 252, 351, 363, 374, 419, 682, 857, 859, 860, 871
   to ethics 351, 363, 419
   to logic 351, 363, 374, 419, 682, 860, 871
   to pity 365, 367
Archetype 875, 878, 933, 956, 967, 1027, 1053
   character 659, 681, 774, 789, 801, 814, 881, 903, 933, 967, 1027
   image 933, 945, 953, 967
   plot pattern 883, 903, 933, 935, 941, 953, 967, 1027
   theme 903, 933, 967, 1027, 1053
Argument 249, 252, 362, 373, 392, 397, 822, 857, 858, 860, 871
Aside 633, 713, 733
Assonance 566, 573, 577
Author's beliefs 292, 297
Author's craft 296, 502
Author's culture 390, 403, 1030

Author's perspective 390, 403, 591, 605
Author's purpose 71, 252, 299, 308, 322, 325, 343, 359, 659, 801, 1055, 1061, 1064
Author's style 560
Autobiography 248, 251, 252, 253–254, 271
Ballad 557, 558
Bandwagon 560
Bias 321, 683
Biography 248, 251, 252, 253–254, 308
Blank verse 691, 712
Body 337
Cause-and-effect structure 350
Character 4, 6, 70, 85, 96, 135, 234, 297, 628, 630, 658, 682, 691, 712, 773, 774, 789, 935, 942, 996, 1066, 1086, 1090, 1093, 1094, 1096, 1097, 1098
   antagonist 3, 637, 658
   dynamic 70
   epic hero 874, 876, 881, 925, 926
   flat 70, 96
   foil 757, 773
   hero 633, 874
   legendary hero 874, 878, 881
   main 3
   protagonist 3, 4, 637, 658
   round 70, 96
   static 70
   tragic hero 627, 630, 633, 774, 789
Character archetype 659, 681, 774, 789, 801, 814, 881, 903, 933, 967, 1027
Characterization 71, 120, 124, 135, 681, 827, 845, 902, 1091, 1094, 1095
   direct 71, 120, 124, 135
   indirect 71, 120, 124, 135, 681

Chorus 633
Climax 2, 9, 734, 845, 1094, 1095, 1096
Comedy 627, 630, 798–799
   farce 627, 801, 814
   satire 627
Conclusion 337, 427, 431, 606, 611, 855, 859, 860
Conflict 2, 9, 34, 637, 658, 1090, 1091, 1094, 1095, 1096, 1098
   external 9, 18, 34
   internal 9, 18, 34, 73
Connotation 47, 49, 55, 299, 309, 411, 520, 524, 533, 535, 560, 683, 757, 773, 818, 821, 926, 1010, 1064, 1089
Consonance 567, 573, 577
Counterargument 321, 362, 855, 857, 858
Couplet 452
Cultural context 39, 46, 67, 586, 1030, 1041
Deductive reasoning 363
Denotation 47, 49, 55, 299, 309, 411, 520, 524, 533, 535, 683, 757, 773, 818, 821, 926, 1010, 1064, 1089
Description 2, 46, 89, 96, 548, 845, 993, 996, 998–999, 1030, 1041
Detective story 993
Dialect 49, 55
Dialogue 228, 231, 232, 235, 252, 626, 628, 630, 814, 821, 883, 902, 919, 925, 942, 1090, 1091, 1093, 1096
   realistic 1094
Diction 149, 358, 376, 388, 392, 518, 520, 524, 529, 550, 552, 995, 996, 1001, 1010, 1086
Drama 630, 624–630, 798–799, 864–865, 866–867

712, 818, 821, 913, 1110, 1042

cause-and-effect 350

chronological order 1117

problem/solution 350

spatial order 1117

step-by-step order 1117

Style 149, 216, 226, 312, 419, 432, 486, 507, 518, 993, 994, 995, 996, 998–999, 1036, 1086

Support 362. *See also* Appeal.

evidence 362, 416, 420, 560

reasons 362

Suspense 252, 958, 963

Symbol 58, 67, 580, 582

Symbolism 68, 358, 582

Syntax 376, 388

Tall tale 933

Tanka 500, 502

Tetrameter 453

Text structure 1110. *See also* Structure.

Theme 3, 5, 6, 49, 71, 89, 103, 119, 275, 289, 296, 360, 360, 497, 504, 508, 531, 591, 596, 605, 630, 713, 733, 789, 790, 825, 853, 996, 1010, 1030, 1041, 1053, 1098

implied 3, 71, 289

stated 71, 289

universal 103, 119, 591

Theme archetype 903, 933, 967, 1027, 1053

Thesis 252, 337, 353, 359, 426, 430, 432, 606, 608, 610, 854, 855, 855, 856, 858, 860, 871

Third-person point of view 3, 1097

limited 148

omniscient 148

Tone 149, 151, 161, 228, 236, 297, 388, 392, 397, 414, 455, 457, 481, 513, 517, 993, 994, 996, 999, 1090

Topic, finding 1090

Tragedy 627, 630, 631–633

Tragic flaw 627, 633, 659, 681

Tragic hero 627, 630, 633, 774, 789

Tragic plot 627

Trimeter 453

Universal theme 591

Unreliable narrator 1013

Verse paragraph 504, 507, 523

Voice 3, 4, 6, 149, 207, 289, 312, 320, 350, 432, 993, 995, 996

Reading and Critical Thinking

Activating prior knowledge 339, 344, 1047, 1054. *See also* Connecting to personal experience.

Allegory, drawing conclusions about 67

Alliteration

analyzing 473, 571

identifying 571

Allusion

evaluating 66, 680

explaining functions of 388

Analogy

evaluating 350

interpreting 492

Analyzing

alliteration 473, 571

analogy 1053

anecdote 296

archetype 681, 789, 881, 933, 953

argument 387, 392, 397

attitude 319, 410

author's beliefs 343

author's craft 296, 1036, 1085

author's motivation 252

author's perspective 582

author's purpose 322, 425, 824

biography 308

cause and effect 954

cause-and-effect relationships 137, 141, 275, 289, 1087, 1130, 1131, 1133, 1134

character 15, 55, 85, 135, 191, 226, 658, 680, 733, 756, 773, 952, 1027, 1053

characterization 902, 1010, 1053, 1085

conflict 288

connotation 1010

consonance 577

controlling idea 146

cultural context 39, 46, 96, 288, 308, 586, 590, 845

cultural influences 507

denotation 1010

description 96, 334, 497, 687

details 101, 146, 387, 397, 497, 635

dialogue 319, 788, 821

diction 486, 520, 524, 544, 552, 571

drama 629

elements of poetry 530

epic 877

events 85

evidence 146

farce 814

figurative language 457, 734, 756, 925

film technique 792

foreshadowing 45, 902

form 465, 468

genre 206

haiku 497

historical context 45, 49, 55, 308, 963, 1010

ideas 419, 1045

imagery 507, 548

influences 952

informational text 906

irony 66, 191, 206, 821

line length 457, 480

logical fallacies 365, 367, 414

lyric poetry 530

meaning 507, 590

metaphor 492, 535, 539, 571, 576, 582

meter 468, 471, 473

about setting 101, 141
about simile 535
about speaker 457, 463, 492, 497, 516, 523, 529, 535, 571, 582, 596
about structure 343, 425, 453, 460, 479, 712, 821, 1045, 1059
about suspense 963
about symbol 507
about text features 255
about theme 89, 97, 502, 504, 508, 539, 593, 596, 605, 788
about title 226
about tone 372
Inferring 37. *See also* Inferences, making.
Influences, analyzing 952
Information
  clarifying 1121
  drawing conclusions about 1127
  paraphrasing 1120, 1133
  summarizing 1118, 1120
  synthesizing 1119, 1125, 1127
Informational text
  analyzing 906
  interpreting 907, 910
Interpreting
  analogy 492
  archetype 953
  aside 733
  author's views 410
  behavior 334, 523, 590
  character 15
  comparisons 502
  conflict 814
  description 571
  dialogue 85, 96
  events 226, 756, 941
  exposition 15
  flashback 226
  imagery 58, 67, 183, 192, 195, 207, 208, 479, 495, 498, 507, 529, 569, 571, 582, 637, 658, 1032, 1036

informational text 907, 910
  meaning 516, 548, 582
  meter 468
  monologue 845
  narrator 207
  nonfiction 251
  plot 175
  speaker 457, 467
  structure 590
  symbol 358, 552, 582, 963
  title 552
Irony
  analyzing 66, 191, 206, 821
  making inferences about 557
Justifying 37
Juxtaposition, evaluating 539
Legend
  drawing conclusions about 911
Line length, analyzing 457, 480
Literary criticism, evaluating 16
Literary elements
  applying 4–5, 248–249, 250–251, 448–449, 628–629, 876–877, 994–995
  evaluating 449
Literature across genres, comparing 390–403, 591–605, 825–853, 956–967, 1030–1041
Logical connections, making 911
Logical fallacies, analyzing 365, 367, 414
Lyric poetry, analyzing 530
Main idea(s)
  determining 142, 1128, 1130, 1131, 1133, 1134
  drawing conclusions about 397, 1118
  identifying 425
  making inferences about 824
  summarizing 101, 146, 325, 397, 414, 585, 590, 687, 824, 911, 917, 1045,

1059, 1134
Making generalizations 1112
  about events 299, 309
Making inferences. *See* Inferences, making.
Making logical connections 911
Making predictions 757, 773
Meaning
  analyzing 507, 590
  clarifying 529, 539, 544, 573, 577, 1064, 1128
  drawing conclusions about 296, 346, 351, 351, 467, 492, 497, 541, 546, 548, 552, 582, 590, 596, 1010, 1121
  interpreting 516, 548, 582
  making inferences about 101, 539, 544, 573, 576, 585, 596, 1125, 1126
Media genre, comparing and contrasting 564
Memoir, drawing conclusions about 325
Message, drawing conclusions about 33
Metaphor
  analyzing 492, 535, 539, 571, 576, 582
  making inferences about 535
Meter
  analyzing 468, 471, 473
Meter, interpreting 468
Monitoring
  comprehension 151, 475, 480
Monologue, interpreting 845
Mood
  analyzing 45, 492, 502, 529, 548, 596, 818, 821
  evaluating 733, 773
Moral dilemma
  analyzing 85
  comparing and contrasting 34
  drawing conclusions about 118

Research, Test-Taking, and Study Skills

Assessment
  grammar tests 244–245, 442–443, 622–623, 870–871, 988–989, 1106–1107
  reading tests 240–242, 438–440, 618–620, 866–868, 984–986, 1102–1104
  vocabulary tests 243, 441, 621, 869, 987, 1105
  writing tests 245, 443, 623, 871, 989, 1107
Bibliography 309, 508, 969
Citing sources 97, 272, 290, 481, 508, 968, 971
  in-text 971
  works cited 971
Evaluating
  sources 97, 272, 290, 374, 428, 481, 508, 970
  web sites 97
Grammar tests 244–245, 442–443, 622–623, 870–871, 988–989, 1106–1107

Internet research 97, 272, 374, 428, 596
Note cards 272, 970
Plagiarism 971, 980
Quotations
  direct 970, 971
  embedded 971
  long 974
  punctuating 974
Quoting sources 97, 374
Reading tests 240–242, 438–440, 618–620, 866–868, 984–986, 1102–1104
Researching 16, 97, 272, 309, 428, 508, 596, 969
  organizing 969, 970
Sources 968, 980
  citing 97, 237, 272, 290, 481, 508, 968, 971
  evaluating 97, 272, 290, 374, 428, 481, 508, 970
  multiple 974
  paraphrasing 272, 508, 970, 973
  parenthetical
    references 272, 508
  primary 290, 309, 508, 970

  quoting 97, 374, 508, 970
  secondary 290, 309, 508, 970
  summarizing 272, 508, 970
  variety of 481
Test-taking tips 36, 37, 47, 122, 193
Thesis 374, 430, 432
  revising 970, 976
  statement 420, 426, 430, 970, 971, 972, 976
Vocabulary tests 243, 441, 621, 869, 987, 1105
Web sites, evaluating 97
Works cited 508, 968, 980
Writing tests 245, 443, 623, 871, 989, 1107

Interdisciplinary Activities

Art 309
Daily life and culture 118, 288, 516, 952
Social studies 508

Index of Authors and Titles

Acknowledgments

Unit 1

"Old Man at the Bridge," reprinted with permission of Scribner, an imprint of Simon & Schuster Adult Publishing Group, from *The Short Stories of Ernest Hemingway.* Copyright 1938 by Ernest Hemingway. Copyright renewed © 1966 by Mary Hemingway.

"Contents of the Dead Man's Pocket" by Jack Finney. Reprinted by permission of Don Congdon Associates. Copyright © 1956 by the Crowell Collier Publishing Company, renewed 1984 by Jack Finney.

"An Astrologer's Day" from *The Grandmother's Tale and Selected Stories* by R. K. Narayan. Copyright © 1994 by R. K. Narayan. Reprinted by permission of the Wallace Literary Agency, Inc.

"Civil Peace" from *Girls at War and Other Stories* by Chinua Achebe, copyright © 1972, 1973 by Chinua Achebe. Used by permission of Doubleday, a division of Random House, Inc. and the Emma Sweeney Agency.

"Two Kinds" by Amy Tan, copyright © 1989 by Amy Tan. First appeared in *The Joy Luck Club.* Reprinted by permission of the author and the Sandra Dijkstra Literary Agency.

"Tuesday Siesta" from *No One Writes to the Colonel and Other Stories* by Gabriel García Márquez and translated by J. S. Bernstein. Copyright © 1968 in the English translation by Harper & Row Publishers, Inc. Reprinted by permission of HarperCollins Publishers.

From *Living to Tell the Tale* by Gabriel García Márquez, translated by Edith Grossman, translation copyright © 2003 by Gabriel García Márquez. Used by permission of Alfred A. Knopf, a division of Random House, Inc.

"When Mr. Pirzada Came to Dine" from *Interpreter of Maladies* by Jhumpa Lahiri. Copyright © 1999 by Jhumpa Lahiri. Reprinted by permission of Houghton Mifflin Company. All rights reserved.

Paule Marshall, "To Da-duh, In Memoriam" from *Reena and Other Stories.* Copyright © 1983 by The Feminist Press. Reprinted with the permission of The Feminist Press at the City University of New York, www.feministpress.org.

Anderson Literary Management, LLC: "The Censors," copyright © 1988 by Luisa Valenzuela, from *Open Door: Stories* (North Point Press), copyright © 1998 by Luisa Valenzuela.

"Everyday Use" from *In Love & Trouble: Stories of Black Women,* copyright © 1973 by Alice Walker, reprinted by permission of Harcourt, Inc. and The Wendy Weil Agency.

"Through the Tunnel" from *The Habit of Loving* by Doris Lessing. Copyright © 1955 by Doris Lessing. Originally appeared in *The New Yorker.* Reprinted by permission of HarperCollins Publishers.

"The Vision Quest" from *American Indian Myths and Legends* by Richard Erdoes and Alfonso Ortiz, copyright © 1984 by Richard Erdoes and Alfonso Ortiz. Used by permission of Pantheon Books, a division of Random House, Inc.

"Catch the Moon" from *An Island Like You: Stories of the Barrio* by Judith Ortiz Cofer. Published by Scholastic Inc./ Orchard Books. Copyright © 1995 by Judith Ortiz Cofer. All rights reserved. Used by permission.

"And of Clay Are We Created" reprinted with the permission of Scribner, an imprint of Simon & Schuster Adult Publishing Group, from *The Stories of Eva Luna* by Isabel Allende. Copyright © 1989 by Isabel Allende. English translation copyright © 1991 by Macmillan Publishing Company.

Excerpt from "Volcano's Deadly Warning" from NOVA/ WGBH Educational Foundation. Copyright © 2002 WGBH/ Boston. Reprinted by permission.

By Clara Germani. Excerpted with permission from the June 6, 1986 issue of *The Christian Science Monitor.* (www. csmonitor.com) © 1986 *The Christian Science Monitor.*

"Lullaby," copyright © 1981 by Leslie Marmon Silko. Reprinted from *Storyteller* by Leslie Marmon Silko, published by Seaver Books, New York, New York.

"Suspended" by Joy Harjo. Reprinted by permission of the author.

"The Unicorn in the Garden" from *Fables for Our Time* by James Thurber. Copyright © 1939, 1940 by James Thurber. Reprinted by arrangement with the Barbara Hogenson Agency.

Unit 2

From *Zora Neale Hurston: A Literary Biography* by Robert E. Hemenway. Copyright © 1997 by the Board of Trustees of the University of Illinois. Reprinted by permission.

Unit 3

Unit 4

Unit 5

From *Le Morte d'Arthur* by Sir Thomas Malory, translated by Keith Baines, copyright © 1967 by Keith Baines. Used by permission of Clarkson Potter Publishers, a division of Random House, Inc.

From "Who Was King Arthur?" from *Unsolved Mysteries of History: An Eye-Opening Investigation Into the Most Baffling Events of All Time* by Paul Aron. Copyright © 2000 by Paul Aron. Reprinted by permission of John Wiley & Sons, Inc.

From "Arthur: The Once and Future King" from *In Search of Myths and Heroes* by Michael Wood. Copyright © 2005 by Michael Wood. Reprinted by permission of The University of California Press and Copyright Clearance Center.

From *King Arthur: The Truth Behind the Legend* by Rodney Castleden. Copyright © 2000 by Rodney Castleden. Reprinted by permission of the Taylor & Francis Group.

From *Sundiata: An Epic of Old Mali* by D. T. Niane. Copyright © 1965 by Longmans, Green & Co. Reprinted by permission of Pearson Education.

"Theseus" from *Mythology* by Edith Hamilton. Copyright © 1942 by Edith Hamilton. Copyright © renewed 1969 by Dorian Fielding Reid and Doris Fielding Reid. By permission of Little, Brown and Co., Inc.

"Where the Girl Rescued Her Brother," from *The Girl Who Married the Moon,* copyright © 1994 by Joseph Bruchac and Gayle Ross. Reprinted by permission of Barbara S. Kouts.

"John Henry" verse as taken from *Mules and Men* by Zora Neale Hurston. Copyright 1935 by Zora Neale Hurston; renewed © 1963 by John C. Hurston and Joel Hurston. Reprinted by permission of HarperCollins Publishers.

"A Song of Greatness" from *The Children Sing in the Far West* by Mary Austin. Copyright 1928 by Mary Austin, © renewed 1956 by Kenneth M. Chapman and Mary C. Wheelwright. Reprinted by permission of Houghton Mifflin Company. All rights reserved.

Unit 6

"The Happy Man's Shirt" from *Italian Folktales: Selected and Retold* by Italo Calvino, copyright © 1956 by Giulio Einaudi editore, s.p.p., English translation by George Martin copyright © 1980 by Harcourt, Inc., reprinted by permission of Harcourt, Inc.

"There Will Come Soft Rains," by Ray Bradbury. Reprinted by permission of Don Congdon Associates, Inc. Copyright © 1950 by Crowell Collier Publishing Company, 1977 by Ray Bradbury.

"By the Waters of Babylon" by Stephen Vincent Benet. Copyright © 1937 by Stephen Vincent Benet. Copyright renewed © 1965 by Thomas C. Benet, Stephanie Mahin and Rachel B. Lewis. Reprinted by permission of Brandt & Hochman Literary Agents, Inc.

"What I Have Been Doing Lately" from *At the Bottom of the River* by Jamaica Kincaid. Copyright © 1983 by Jamaica Kincaid. Reprinted by permission of Farrar, Straus & Giroux, Inc.

"People at Night" by Denise Levertov, from *Collected Earlier Poems 1940–1960,* copyright © 1957, 1958, 1959, 1960, 1961, 1979 by Denise Levertov. Reprinted by permission of New Directions Publishing Corp.

"A Dream" from *The Complete Poems of Anna Akhmatova,* translated by Judith Hemschemeyer, edited and introduced by Roberta Reeder. Copyright © 1989, 1992, 1997 by Judith Hemschemeyer. Reprinted by permission of Zephyr Press.

"One Legend Found, Many Still To Go," by William J. Broad, *The New York Times,* October 2, 2005. Copyright © 2005 by The New York Times Co. Reprinted with permission.

"Robot Dreams" by Isaac Asimov, published by permission of the Estate of Isaac Asimov c/o Ralph M. Vicinanza, Ltd.

"Bread" from *Good Bones and Simple Murders* by Margaret Atwood, copyright © 1983, 1992, 1994 by O. W. Toad Ltd. A Nan Talese Book. Used by permission of Doubleday, a division of Random House, Inc.

"Witness for the Prosecution" from *Witness for the Prosecution and Other Stories* by Agatha Christie, copyright 1924, 1926, 1929, 1943, 1947, 1948, renewed 1952, 1954 © 1957, 1971, 1975 by Agatha Christie Mallowan. Copyright 1932 by The Curtis Publishing Co. Used by permission of G.P. Putnam's Sons, a division of Penguin Group (USA) Inc.

"Frustration" by Isaac Asimov. Published by permission of The Estate of Isaac Asimov c/o Ralph M. Vicinanza, Ltd.

Reference Section

Content from The Academic Word List, developed at the School of Linguistics and Applied Language Studies at Victoria University of Wellington, New Zealand, is reprinted by permission of Averil Coxhead. http://language.massey.ac.nz/staff/awl/index.shtml.

Maps

Mapping Specialists, Inc.

Image Credits

293 Photo: Erich Lessing/Art Resource, NY ©2009 Succession H. Matisse/Artists Rights Society (ARS), NY; **295** Bridgeman Art Library; **298** Tina Fineberg/AP Images; **300** Christie's Images/CORBIS; **303** Tony Vaccaro/akg-images; **305** Bridgeman Art Library; **306** Geoffrey Clements/CORBIS ©2009 The Willem de Kooning Foundation/Artists Rights Society (ARS), NY; **311** Francine Fleischer/CORBIS; **313** Giraudon/Bridgeman Art Library; **315** Mary Evans Picture Library; **316** Erich Lessing/Art Resource, NY; **319**(t)Getty Images, (b)Bill Kaye/Paramount/Universal/The Kobal Collection; **322**(t)Francine Fleischer/CORBIS, (b)Mark Lennihan/AP Images; **324** Tore Bergsaker/Sygma/CORBIS; **326** Rollie McKenna; **328** The Andy Warhol Foundation for the Visual Arts/CORBIS; **330** Reprinted with permission of King Features Syndicate, Inc.; **332** Art Resource, NY; **335** Israel Museum, Jerusalem/Bridgeman Art Library; **336** DigitalVision/PunchStock; **337** Images.com/CORBIS; **338** Diane Sabin; **342** Private Collection/Bridgeman Art Library; **345** Bettmann/CORBIS; **347** BRAUD, DOMINIQUE/Animals Animals; **348** Wayne Lankinen/DRK Photo; **349** Photodisc/PunchStock; **352** AP Images; **354** The Art Archive/Ministry of Public Information Mexico/Dagli Orti. ©2009 Banco de Mexico, D.F./Artists Rights Society (ARS); **356** Franklin McMahon/CORBIS; **358** Getty Images; **361** Smithsonian American Art Museum, Washington, DC/Art Resource, NY; **368** Frances Benjamin Johnston/CORBIS; **370 371** Bettmann/CORBIS; **372** (tl tc)Getty Images, (b)Lake County Museum/CORBIS; **375** Flip Schulke/CORBIS; **377** Bettmann/CORBIS; **378** National Museum/akg-images; **379 382** Flip Schulke/CORBIS; **385 386** Bettmann/CORBIS; **387** (b)Steve Schapiro/CORBIS; **391** Cheron Bayna; **393** Photodisc/Alamy Images; **394-395** Jeremy Woodhouse/Getty Images; **398** Keith Brofsky/Getty Images; **400** Catherine Karnow/CORBIS; **402** Keren Su/CORBIS; **413** Library of Congress; **404** Time & Life Pictures/Getty Images; **406** North Wind/North Wind Picture Archives; **408** Chicago Historical Society, Chicago/Bridgeman Art Library; **409 415** Bettmann/CORBIS; **417** T.F. Chen Cultural Center; **421** VERNIER JEAN BERNARD/CORBIS SYGMA; **423** ASSOCIATED PRESS; **437**(t)Courtesy Vintage Publishing, (cl)Aaron Haupt Photography, (b)Aaron Haupt Photography; **444** Scala/Art Resource, NY. ©2009 Artists Rights Society (ARS), NY/ADAGP, Paris; **448** Bettmann/CORBIS; **449**(bkgd)Bettmann/CORBIS, (b)CORBIS; **451** Archivo Iconografico, S.A./CORBIS; **452** Calvin and Hobbes © 1989 Watterson. Dist. By Universal Press Syndicate. Reprinted with permission. All rights reserved.; **454** Pach/CORBIS; **456** Private Collection/Bridgeman Art Library; **459** Christopher Felver/CORBIS; **461** The Art Archive/Private Collection/Joseph Martin; **464** Bettmann/CORBIS; **466** Charles Neal/SuperStock; **467** (tl tc)Getty Images; **467** Archivo Iconografico, S.A./CORBIS; **470** Bettmann/CORBIS; **472** Ciurlionis State Art Museum, Kaunas, Lithuania/Bridgeman Art Library; **474** Getty Images; **476** SuperStock. ©2009 Successio Miro/Artists Rights Society (ARS), NY/ADAGP, Paris; **479** (t)Getty Images, Kactus Foto, Santiago, Chile/SuperStock; **482** Vyto Starinskas/Rutland Herald/CORBIS SYGMA; **484** Brenda Chrystie/CORBIS;

488 Giulio Marcocchi/Getty Images; **490** akg-images; **491** Smithsonian American Art Museum, Washington, DC/Art Resource, NY; **494** Snark/Art Resource, NY; **495** American Museum of Natural History, New York, Photo ©Boltin Picture Library/ Bridgeman Art Library; **496** Private Collection, Boltin Picture Library/Bridgeman Art Library; **499** The Art Archive/The Picture Desk; **500** Mori Sushin Tessan/British Library, London/Bridgeman Art Library.; **501** Christie's Images/CORBIS; **503** Neela Banerjee; **505** akg-images/Jean-Louis Nou; **509** Daniel Nevins/SuperStock; **510** Francis G. Mayer/CORBIS; **512** Bettmann/CORBIS; **514** Charles Neal/SuperStock; **515** akg-images/Electa; **516** Bettmann/CORBIS, (l c)Getty Images; **519** Bettmann/CORBIS; **521** Ditz/Bridgeman Art Library/Getty Images; **525** Hulton Archive/Getty Images; **527** Archivo Iconografico, S.A./CORBIS; **528** Scala/Art Resource, NY; **529** (t)Getty Images, (b)BlueMoon Stock/Alamy Images; **532** Larry Ford/CORBIS Outline; **534** Smithsonian American Art Museum, Washington, DC/Art Resource, NY; **536** The Art Archive/Culver Pictures; **538** Bridgeman-Giraudon/Art Resource, NY. ©2009 Successio Miro/Artists Rights Society (ARS), NY/ADAGP, Paris; **540** Bettmann/CORBIS; **542** Boltin Picture Library; **543** The Art Archive/Musée Guimet Paris/Gianni Dagli Orti; **545** Christopher Felver/CORBIS; **547** Images.com/CORBIS; **549** Christopher Felver/CORBIS; **551** Banque d'Images, ADAGP/Art Resource, NY. ©2009 C. Herscovici, London/Artists Rights Society (ARS), NY; **553** Reprinted by Permission of the Dudley Randall Literary Estate; **554** Julian Cifuentes/Getty Images; **556** Ben Watson III/SuperStock; **561 562** (t b)AP Photos; **564** Raymond Gehman/CORBIS; **565** Jerzy Kolacz/Getty Images; **566** Calvin and Hobbes © 1987 Watterson. Dist. By Universal Press Syndicate. Reprinted with permission. All rights reserved.; **568** Gerardo Somoza/CORBIS Outline; **570** Courtesy of the Bill Hodges Gallery. Talked to gallery Ok to re-use LM 8/9/07; **572** The Granger Collection; **574** Bourne Gallery, Reigate, Surrey, UK/Bridgeman Art Library; **576** Getty Images; **579** Gerardo Somoza/CORBIS Outline; **581** Pam Ingalls/CORBIS; **584** Ha Lam Photograhy; **586** Courtesy of Chang-Rae Lee; **588** Tara Sasrowardoyo/TIME; **589** Scott Jones/TIME; **591** Gilbert Mayers/SuperStock; **592** CORBIS; **594** Christie's Images/CORBIS; **595** Smithsonian American Art Museum, Washington, DC/Art Resource, NY; **599** Bettmann/CORBIS; **601** Maurice Faulk/SuperStock; **603** Arnold Newman/Getty Images; **605** Margie Livingston Campbell/SuperStock; **616** (r)Aaron Haupt Photography, (tl)Book provided by Little Professor Book Company. Photo by Aaron Haupt, (bl)Gerardo Somoza/CORBIS Outline; **617** (l)Book provided by Little Professor Book Company. Photo by Aaron Haupt, Haupt Photography; **624** Réunion des Musées Nationaux/Art Resource, NY; **627** Calvin and Hobbes © 1986 Watterson. Dist. By Universal Press Syndicate. Reprinted with permission. All rights reserved.; **628** Images.com/CORBIS; **629** Getty Images; **631** Michelle da Verona/Czartoryski Museum, Cracow, Poland/The Bridgeman Art Library; **632** Bridgeman Art Library; **634** Ashmolean Museum, Oxford/Bridgeman Art Library; **635** Erich Lessing/Art Resource, NY; **636** Museo Archeologico Nazionale, Naples, Italy/Bridgeman Art Library;

638 Réunion des Musées Nationaux /Art Resource, NY; **639** Mary Evans Picture Library; **641** Scala/Art Resource, NY; **642** Simon Carter Gallery/Bridgeman Art Library; **645** The Art Archive/National Archaeological Museum Athens/Dagli Orti; **646** The Art Archive/Museo Nazionale Tarant/Dagli Orti; **649** The Art Archive/Musée du Louvre Paris/Dagli Orti; **652** Mary Evans Picture Library; **653** Bridgeman Art Library/Getty Images; **656** Private Collection, Courtesy of IAP Fine Art/Bridgeman Art Library; **657** Spiros Tselentis/SuperStock; **660** The Gallery Collection/CORBIS; **662** The Bridgeman Art Library/Getty Images; **663** Grant Faint/Getty Images; **667** Bridgeman-Giraudon/Art Resource, NY; **670** Louvre, Paris, France, Peter Willi/Bridgeman Art Library; **672** Museu Calouste Gulbenkian, Lisbon, Portugal, Giraudon/Bridgeman Art Library; **675** The Art Archive/National Archaeological Museum Athens/ Dagli Orti; **677** Erich Lessing/Art Resource, NY; **678** Photo by Studio Kontos; **685 686 687** The British Museum; **688** British Library, London, Great Britain/Art Resource, NY; **689** Nigel Hawkins/Collections Picture Library; **690** The Art Archive/ Musée du Chateau de Versailles/Dagli Orti; **692** Paolo Uccello/Bridgeman Art Library/Getty Images; **694** Chase Manhattan Bank Archive; **696** (t)Historical Picture Archive/ CORBIS, (b)Louvre, Paris, France/Bridgeman Art Library; **698** Chase Manhattan Bank Archive; **700** Scala/Art Resource, NY; **702** akg-images/Pirozzi; **704 706** Chase Manhattan Bank Archive; **707** Private Collection/Bridgeman Art Library; **708** Chase Manhattan Bank Archive; **710** (t)Chase Manhattan Bank Archive, (b)Scala/Art Resource, NY; **711** Chase Manhattan Bank Archive; **714** Smithsonian Institution; **715** Erich Lessing/Art Resource, NY; **716** Smithsonian Institution; **717** Royal Albert Memorial Museum, Exeter, Devon, UK/Bridgeman Art Library; **718 720 722** Smithsonian Institution; **723** Alinari/Art Resource, NY; **724 726** Smithsonian Institution; **727** Cameraphoto Arte, Venice/Art Resource, NY; **728** Victoria & Albert Museum, London/Art Resource, NY; **729** Bildarchiv Preussischer Kulturbesitz/Art Resource, NY; **730** Smithsonian Institution; **732** (br)The Image Works, (t bl)Smithsonian Institution; **737** The Art Archive/Galleria d'Arte Moderna Rome/Dagli Orti; **739** Erich Lessing/Art Resource, NY; **742** The Metropolitan Museum of Art, Rogers Fund, 1903 (03.14.13a-g) Photograph ©1986 The Metropolitan Museum of Art; **744** Private Collection, Stair Sainty Matthiesen Gallery, New York/ Bridgeman Art Library; **747** Private Collection, Christopher Wood Gallery, London/Bridgeman Art Library; **749** Alinari/Art Resource, NY; **751** Erich Lessing/Art Resource, NY; **753** akg-images; **758** David Forbert/SuperStock; **761 764** Erich Lessing/Art Resource, NY; **766** Kunsthistorisches Museum, Vienna, Austria, Ali Meyer/Bridgeman Art Library; **767** Museo Nazionale del Bargello/Bridgeman Art Library; **771** Mary Evans Picture Library; **778** Erich Lessing/Art Resource, NY; **783** Scala/Art Resource, NY; **787** Canterbury, Kent/CM Dixon/Photo Resources; **788** Archive/Photo Researchers; **788** (tl tc)Getty Images; **793** MGM/THE KOBAL COLLECTION; **794** John Springer Collection/CORBIS; **795** MGM/THE KOBAL COLLECTION; **796** The McGraw-Hill Companies; **797** National Portrait Gallery, Smithsonian Institution/Art Resource, NY;

799 Siri Stafford/Getty Images; **800** Bettmann/CORBIS; **802** State Russia Museum/Bridgeman Art Library; **807** Private Collection/Bridgeman Art Library; **811** State Russian Museum/ Bridgeman Art Library; **817** Getty Images; **819** Stapleton Collection/CORBIS; **822** (t)CORBIS, (b)AP Images; **824** Swim Ink 2, LLC/CORBIS; **825** Schalkwijk/Art Resource, NY. ©2009 Banco de Mexico Diego Rivera Frida Kahlo Museums Trust, Mexico, D.F./Artists Rights Society (ARS), NY; **826** Courtesy of Western Carolina University; **828** Schalkwijk/Art Resource, NY. ©2009 Banco de Mexico Diego Rivera Frida Kahlo Museums Trust, Mexico, D.F./Artists Rights Society (ARS), NY; **830** Museum of Fine Arts, Boston. ©2009 Banco de Mexico Diego Rivera Frida Kahlo Museums Trust, Mexico, D.F./Artists Rights Society (ARS), NY; **837** Schalkwijk/Art Resource, NY. ©2009 Banco de Mexico Diego Rivera Frida Kahlo Museums Trust, Mexico, D.F./Artists Rights Society (ARS), NY; **840** Kactus Foto/SuperStock; **848** (t)Kelmscott Farms, (b)Edward Wilkins Waite/Private Collection/Bridgeman Art Library; **851** Christie's Images/CORBIS; **862** McGraw-Hill Companies; **864** (l)Aaron Haupt Photography, (r)Courtesy University of Wisconsin Press; **872** Master of the Campana Casson/Musee du Petit Palais, Avignon, France/Bridgeman Art Library; **875** Mary Evans Picture Library; **877** (t)Erich Lessing/Art Resource, NY; **879** The British Library/Topham-HIP/The Image Works; **880** Stapleton Collection/CORBIS; **881** Erich Lessing/Art Resource, NY; **882** Lambeth Palace Library/Bridgeman Art Library; **884** Bradford Art Galleries and Museums, West Yorkshire, UK/ Bridgeman Art Library; **885** (t)British Library, London, Great Britain/Art Resource, NY, (b)Roy Stedall-Humphryes/ Collections Picture Library; **887** akg-images; **890** Scala/Art Resource, NY; **892** HIP/Art Resource, NY; **894** Brian Shuel/ Collections Picture Library; **895 896 898** Archivo Iconografico, S.A./CORBIS; **896** Bridgeman Art Library/Getty Images; **904** Digital Vision/Getty Images; **905** Erich Lessing/Art Resource, NY; **906** Digital Vision/Getty Images; **908** HIP/Art Resource, NY; **910-911** Adam Woolfitt/CORBIS; **914** DAN CHUNG/AP Images; **915** (t)CORBIS, (b)Hulton-Deutsch Collection/CORBIS; **916** Louise Gubb/CORBIS SABA; **920** Tilly Willis Private Collection/The Bridgeman Art Library/Getty Images; **922** Archer figure; Inland Niger Delta Style, Mali; 13th -15th century; ceramic; H x W x D: 61.9 x 16.5 x 16.5 cm (24 3/8 x 6 x 6 in.) Museum purchase; 86-12-1; Photograph by Franko Khoury; National Museum of African Art, Smithsonian Institution; **924** The Metropolitan Museum of Art/Art Resource, NY; **927** (inset)Mark Lennihan/AP Images; **927-930** Excerpt from Sundiata, A Legend of Africa © 2002 Will Eisner, published by permission from NBM Publishing.; **931** The Philadelphia Museum of Art/Art Resource, NY; **932** Nationalmuseum, Stockholm, Sweden/Bridgeman Art Library; **934** National Museum of Iceland, Reykjavik, Iceland/Bridgeman Art Library; **936** MARY EVANS/ARTHUR RACKHAM; **938** akg-images; **941** Werner Forman/CORBIS; **944** Time & Life Pictures/Getty Images; **946** Musee du Petit Palais, Avignon, France, Peter Willi/Bridgeman Art Library; **947** Reynaud Levieux/Cummer Museum of Art & Gardens/ SuperStock; **949** The Art Archive/Mohammed Khalil Museum Cairo/Dagli Orti; **950** Ali Meyer/CORBIS;

951 akg-images/Peter Connolly; **952** (l c)Getty Images; **956** Catalogue No. 153048, Department of Anthropology, Smithsonian Institution.; **957** (l)Martin Benjamin/Black Star, (r)Courtesy of Gayle Ross; **959** Private Collection, Peter Newark Western Americana/Bridgeman Art Library; **961** The Art Archive/Bill Manns; **964** Smithsonian American Art Museum, Washington, DC/Art Resource, NY; **966** SuperStock; **967** Art Media/Heritage-Images/The Image Works; **981** (l)HIP/Art Resource, NY; **982** (r)Book provided by Little Professor Book Company/Aaron Haupt Photography, (l)Aaron Haupt Photography; **983** (t)Courtesy University of Texas Press, (l)Aaron Haupt Photography; **990** Peter Szumowski/Private Collection/Bridgeman Art Library; **994** Sophie Bassouls/CORBIS SYGMA; **997** Mary Evans Picture Library; **998** Stock Illustration/Getty Images; **999** Calvin and Hobbes © 1987 Watterson. Dist. By Universal Press Syndicate. Reprinted with permission. All rights reserved.; **1000** Vince Bucci/Getty Images; **1005** Connie Hayes/Stock Illustration Source/Getty Images; **1007** Private Collection/Bridgeman Art Library/Getty Images; **1008** Stock Illustration/Getty Images; **1012** Herbert Gehr/Time & Life Pictures/Getty Images; **1014** CORBIS SYGMA; **1015** David M. Schleser/Photo Researchers; **1016** James Noel Smith/Illustration Works/Getty Images; **1020** David Siqueiros/Christie's Images. ©2009 Artists Rights Society (ARS), NY/SOMAAP, Mexico City; **1022** ©Avigdor Arikha, courtesy, Marlborough Gallery, New York/Licensed by VAGA; **1025** Getty Images; **1026** Fredderic Leighton/Fitzwilliam Museum, University of Cambridge, UK/Bridgeman Art Library;

1030 Alberto Ruggieri/Stock Illustration Source/Getty Images;**1031** Jeremy Bembaron/CORBIS SYGMA; **1033** Van Hoorick/SuperStock; **1037 1038** Images.com/CORBIS; **1039** Museum of Modern Art, New York/Bridgeman Art Library; **1041** Images.com/CORBIS; **1042** age fotostock/SuperStock; **1044** Stefano Bianchetti/CORBIS; **1046** Deborah Feingold Photography; **1048** Illustration Works; **1051** Private Collection/Bridgeman Art Library; **1052** (r)Private Collection, ©DACS/Bridgeman Art Library, (l)C Squared Studios/Getty Images; **1056 1058** Jason Grow/SABA for TIME; **1060** Time Life Pictures/Getty Images; **1062** Scala/Art Resource, NY; **1065** Getty Images; **1067** (tr)Roy Miles Fine Paintings/Bridgeman Art Library; **1069** Bettmann/CORBIS; **1072** Private Collection/Bridgeman ArtLibrary; **1074** The Arts Club, London/Bridgeman Art Library; **1078** Francis G. Mayer/CORBIS; **1079** Science and Society Picture Library; **1077** National Gallery Collection; By kind permission of the Trustees of the National Gallery, London/CORBIS; **1080** Dickens House Museum, London/Bridgeman Art Library; **1083** Herbert Art Gallery & Museum, Coventry, UK/Bridgeman Art Library; **1085** akg-images; **1100** (l r)Aaron Haupt Photography; **1101** (t)Courtesy Top Publications, Ltd., (t bl)Aaron Haupt Photography; **1108** Photodisc/PunchStock; **1111** Justin Guariglia/Getty Images; **1112** DigitalVision/PunchStock; **1117** New Vision Technologies, Inc./Getty Images; **1123 1130** DigitalVision/PunchStock; **1133** Lon C. Diehl/Photo Edit.